A MARGINAL JEW

VOLUME FOUR

THE ANCHOR YALE BIBLE REFERENCE LIBRARY is a project of international and interfaith scope in which Protestant, Catholic, and Jewish scholars from many countries contribute individual volumes. The project is not sponsored by any ecclesiastical organization and is not intended to reflect any particular theological doctrine.

The series is committed to producing volumes in the tradition established half a century ago by the founders of the Anchor Bible, William Foxwell Albright and David Noel Freedman. It aims to present the best contemporary scholarship in a way that is accessible not only to scholars but also to the educated nonspecialist. It is committed to work of sound philological and historical scholarship, supplemented by insight from modern methods, such as sociological and literary criticism.

John J. Collins
GENERAL EDITOR

THE ANCHOR YALE BIBLE REFERENCE LIBRARY

A MARGINAL JEW

RETHINKING

THE HISTORICAL JESUS

VOLUME FOUR

LAW AND LOVE

JOHN P. MEIER

Yale University Press

NEW HAVEN AND LONDON

Set in Sabon type by DIX!
Printed in the United States of America.

Imprimatur—Hartford, CT, December 16, 2008—The Most Rev. Henry J. Mansell, D.D.

The Library of Congress has already cataloged earlier volumes as follows.

Meier, John P.
A marginal jew : rethinking the historical Jesus /
John P. Meier.—1st ed.
v. [1–2–3] ; maps ; 24 cm.—(The Anchor Bible
reference library)
Includes bibliographical references and index.
Contents: v. 1. The roots of the problem and the person—
v. 2. Mentor, and miracles—
v. 3. Companions and competitors.
1. Jesus Christ—Historicity.   2. Jesus Christ—Jewishness.
I. Title.   II. Series
BT303.2.M465   1991
232.9—dc20   91-10538

ISBN 978-0-300-14096-5 (v. 4)

A catalogue record for this book is available from the British Library.

This paper meets the requirements of ANSI/NISO Z39.48-1992 (Permanence
of Paper).

10   9   8   7   6   5   4   3   2   1

Contents

Acknowledgments

It is with a profound sense of sadness that I begin these acknowledgments by explaining to my faithful readers why this volume has been so long delayed. Dr. David Noel Freedman, the renowned scholar who acted as General Editor of the Anchor Bible program from its inception, died in April 2008 after a lengthy illness. A number of operations plus years of physical decline made it increasingly difficult for Dr. Freedman to carry out his many editorial projects with the speed he would have wanted—hence, the unavoidable delay in this volume's appearance. In the face of mounting obstacles, Dr. Freedman courageously continued his work until the very end, approving the final form of the manuscript of this volume just a few weeks before his death. It is only fitting that I dedicate this volume to him as well as to another mentor and friend, Msgr. Myles M. Bourke, whose lectures and writings had a formative influence on me from my days as a student at the Biblical Institute in Rome. I mourn the loss of both great guides.

On a happier note: as in Volume Three of *A Marginal Jew*, my thanks must be extended to the able doctors who have kept me healthy enough to work on the project that now comes to fruition in Volume Four. Right behind them rank my many colleagues and friends at the University of Notre Dame; their professional counsel and personal support have made this volume possible. I am especially grateful to my fellow professors in the Christianity and Judaism in Antiquity program within the Theology Department at Notre Dame. Their generosity in sharing their expertise in specific areas of research is deeply appreciated. In particular, Professors Hindy Najman (now of the University of Toronto), James C. VanderKam, Eugene C. Ulrich, Gary Anderson, Gregory E. Sterling, and Michael A. Signer have graciously given me the benefit of their vast knowledge of Second Temple Judaism, Qumran, Philo, Josephus, and rabbinic literature. Professors John C. Cavadini, Brian Daley, and Robert E. Sullivan have done the same in their fields of theology and history. Many of my former students and graduate assistants have labored tirelessly to aid my research and writing of this work. Special mention should be made of Paul Kim, Samuel Thomas, Steven Schweitzer, Jonathan Lawrence, Wes Foreman, and Eric Rowe. In the end, though, I alone must take full responsibility for all the claims made in this volume and for any errors involved in my arguments.

I have also profited greatly from various meetings and colloquia attended by some of the master scholars in the field. The opportunity to deliver a lecture during a conference honoring Dr. E. P. Sanders at Notre Dame (April 9–13, 2003) allowed me to exchange ideas both with Dr. Sanders and with many other distinguished participants. Thanks to the kind invitation of the Australian–New Zealand Society for Theological Studies (ANZSTS), I was able to deliver four lectures on Jesus and the Law during the society's annual meeting in Perth, Australia, July 4–8, 2005. The insightful suggestions of Dr. William R. G. Loader during that meeting proved to be of great help to me. Thanks likewise are due to the many members of the Catholic Biblical Association Task Force on the Historical Jesus, which I was honored to address a number of times. The kind invitation of Yale University to give the annual Shaffer lectures in October 2006 enabled me to seek the wise advice of Professors Harold W. Attridge, John J. Collins, and Adela Yarbro Collins. Likewise, an invitation to give a lecture celebrating the fiftieth anniversary of *New Testament Abstracts* (also in October 2006) allowed me to try out some of my ideas on the celebrated faculty of the Weston Jesuit School of Theology, including Professors Daniel J. Harrington and Richard J. Clifford. Under the auspices of the Historical Jesus section of the Society of Biblical Literature, I had the pleasure of delivering a lecture on Jesus' prohibition of oaths at their annual meeting in Washington, DC (November 20, 2006). The event enabled me to meet and confer with Professor Jonathan Klawans of Boston University, whose volumes on the Jewish conception of sin and purity are of immense value, and with Professor Donald A. Hagner, an outstanding commentator on the Gospel of Matthew. The annual meeting of the Notre Dame–New York University colloquium (May 29–31, 2007) allowed me to present some of my ideas on Jesus and the Law and to speak at length with two great scholars in the area of Qumran and rabbinic studies, Professors Lawrence H. Schiffman and Moshe J. Bernstein. I likewise owe a debt of gratitude to two religious communities located in Berkeley, California. Both the Jesuit community and the community of the Congregation of Holy Cross hosted me at various times during my labors in the libraries of the Graduate Theological Union and the University of California at Berkeley.

I am also happy to acknowledge the generous assistance of my former editor at Doubleday, Mr. Andrew Corbin, and my new editor at Yale University Press, Ms. Jennifer Banks, as well as her editorial assistant, Joseph Calamia.

Grateful acknowledgment is also given to the various foundations and individuals who have supported the research and writing of this volume in a most practical way. These include the Association of Theological Schools and the American Council of Learned Societies, the William Warren Family Foundation, whose chair in theology I hold at Notre Dame, and Mr. and Mrs. Robert McQuie, who have established a special fund at Notre Dame to support my work.

Grateful acknowledgment is also made to the following journals and volumes for the reprint of the substance of material originally presented in their pages. These articles and essays include: "Is There *Hălākâ* (The Noun) at Qumran?" *JBL* 122 (2003) 150–55; "The Historical Jesus and the Historical Law: Some Problems within the Problem," *CBQ* 65 (2003) 52–79; "The Historical Jesus and the Plucking of the Grain on the Sabbath," *CBQ* 66 (2004) 561–81; "Does the Son of Man Saying in Mark 2,28 Come from the Historical Jesus?" *"Il Verbo di Dio è Vivo"* (Albert Vanhoye Festschrift; AnBib 165; Rome: Biblical Institute, 2007) 71–89; "Did the Historical Jesus Prohibit All Oaths?" *Journal for the Study of the Historical Jesus* (Part I) 5 (2007) 175–204; (Part II) 6 (2008) 1–22, 47–56.

A
MARGINAL
JEW

VOLUME FOUR

THE HISTORICAL JESUS IS
THE HALAKIC JESUS

I. THE MULTIPLE DIFFICULTIES OF DEALING
WITH JESUS AND THE LAW

Now begins the hard part. As often happens in negotiations for a Mideast peace accord or a labor union contract, the most difficult issues have purposely been left till last. At the end of Volume Three of *A Marginal Jew*, I listed, with a bow to Sir Edward Elgar's *Enigma Variations*, the four final enigmas that remained to be pondered in our quest for the historical Jesus. These four questions, which seem to pose intractable problems for any quester, are the riddle of Jesus and the Law, the riddle-speech of Jesus' parables, the riddle-speech of Jesus' self-designations (or "titles"), and the ultimate riddle of Jesus' death. Having examined in the second half of Volume Three the legal positions that distinguished the Pharisees, Sadducees, and Essenes from one another and from Jesus, I think it logical to take up as the first enigma the question of Jesus and the Law. This will be the focus of Volume Four, while the other three enigmas will be treated in Volume Five.

Some scholars might immediately object that these four topics have been placed under the exegetical microscope so many times and have been analyzed to death in so many multivolume monographs that the last thing any one of them should be called is an enigma. Labels like "familiar old friends," "exegetical chestnuts," or the "not-this-again quartet" might describe them better than "enigmas." I beg to differ. Indeed, if anything, I must confess my naiveté in thinking that these four huge enigmas could be treated adequately in one volume. By itself, the question of Jesus and the Law has consumed six years of research. I remember well how, when I told a learned Jewish colleague that I was beginning to write a volume focused on the Jewish Law around the time of Jesus, the professor replied: "Don't go in there; you'll never come out." Six years later, I emerge from Moses' (not Plato's) cave,

1

perhaps wiser but certainly older. In any event, I come out convinced that, although I may not be right in my positions, every other book or article on the historical Jesus and the Law has been to a great degree wrong. This claim takes more than a little chutzpah to make, and many would object, à la Qoheleth, that there is nothing new under the sun of Jesus research. Surely I must simply be repackaging one of the systematic answers peddled in the past.

After all, as my critics would point out, in the past century almost every position imaginable has been defended in the attempt to understand Jesus' position vis-à-vis the Mosaic Law.[1] At one end of the spectrum, for instance, Jan Lambrecht declared categorically that "the historical Jesus was in reality both anti-Halachah and anti-Torah."[2] In Lambrecht's view, Jesus was consciously critical of a whole range of commandments contained in the Law. In a similar vein, Werner Georg Kümmel maintained that Jesus' declaration that nothing entering a person can defile that person (Mark 7:15) demonstrates Jesus' sovereign attitude toward the Law and his fundamental rejection of its purity commandments.[3] Pushing this view beyond the credible, Morton Smith claimed that Jesus was secretly a libertine who taught freedom from the Law to those he initiated by a nocturnal rite of baptism, while continuing to teach "legalistic material" to outsiders.[4]

Not surprisingly, other groups of scholars have found the data in the Gospels more complex, not to say confusing. Hence they have eschewed the position that Jesus, in principle if not in practice, rejected the Law. Indeed, one need only survey the stories about Jesus and the Law in the Gospels as they stand, without even trying to sift the pericopes for historical data, to see the problem with any sweeping claim that Jesus opposed the Law.[5] Most of the "dispute stories" (or *Streitgespräche*) in the Gospels present Jesus debating with other Jewish groups or individuals about the proper interpretation and practice of the Law, not about the basic obligation of faithful Israelites to obey the Law. The Law is God's gift to Israel.[6] Consequently, its overall normative force is largely taken for granted in the Gospels, although a few texts, such as the abrogation of the food laws in Mark 7:15–19, run counter to this general tendency.[7] To sweep away almost all the "legal material" in the Gospels as inauthentic or as not representing Jesus' truest intentions strikes one from the start as an unlikely, not to say a desperate, solution.

Mindful of the complexity of the Gospel data, many authors have struggled to explain Jesus' stance vis-à-vis the Law by claiming that there was some sort of dialectic or point-counterpoint inherent or implied in Jesus' teaching on the Law, whether this dialectic was consciously intended by

Jesus or not. In effect, if not in intention, Jesus, while affirming various elements of the Law or even the Law as a whole, ultimately subverted the Law as a system of "legalistic" salvation. He thus paradoxically recaptured the ultimate thrust or intent of the Law: the radical doing of God's will by loving one's neighbor.[8] In subverting, he fulfilled; in transcending, he distilled the essence.

More recently, a number of Christian scholars have rejected the idea that Jesus consciously or unconsciously, directly or dialectically, rejected the Law itself (an idea that has long been criticized by various Jewish scholars).[9] For example, in his study on *Jewish Law from Jesus to the Mishnah*, E. P. Sanders suggests that, as an experiment, we accept hypothetically that all the legal disputes in the Gospels come from the historical Jesus (a position Sanders does not really hold). Sanders maintains that, even when one accepts this hypothesis for the sake of argument, one finds nothing in Jesus' positions—apart from the question of food laws in Mark 7:15–19—that goes beyond the acceptable range of opinions held by 1st-century Jews.[10]

If I were forced to choose *either* the old-time view that Jesus (intentionally or not) abolished the Law *or* Sanders's view that practically nothing in Jesus' teaching opposes or rescinds the Law itself, I would feel much more comfortable accepting Sanders's position. Yet I do not think that even Sanders's approach does full justice to the complexity of the data. Some individual items in Jesus' teaching on the Law (e.g., the prohibition of divorce or of all oaths) and some particular commands he addresses to individual followers (e.g., "let the dead bury their dead" in Matt 8:22 par.) do not fit so neatly into Sanders's picture of a historical Jesus who never opposes the Law or issues commands contrary to it.[11]

Here we touch on the real enigma in Jesus' teaching on the Law: as will be argued at length in this volume, his approach seems to be neither total rejection of the Law, nor a dialectic that embraces yet in effect rejects the Law, nor a total affirmation of the Law that simply involves legitimate though debatable interpretations of individual practices. The real enigma is how Jesus can at one and the same time affirm the Law as the given, as the normative expression of God's will for Israel, and yet in a few individual cases or legal areas (e.g., divorce and oaths) teach and enjoin what is contrary to the Law, simply on his own authority. As so often with the historical Jesus, the different pieces of data seem, at first glance, to defy any systematization. As one struggles with this enigma—and, indeed, with the other enigmas as well— one must remain open to the possibility that not all the pieces of the puzzle fit together. At the very least, the pieces must not be forced to fit simply for the sake of satisfying the rational preferences of the modern interpreter. One begins to see, then, why Jesus and the Law is an enigma that invites further investigation but no easy solution.

Unfortunately, grappling with this enigma involves further complications. Even in "the old days," when "Jesus and the Law" often meant just confronting Gospel stories with OT precepts on the one hand and rabbinic interpretations on the other, the amount of comparative material to be canvassed was vast. Today, the Dead Sea Scrolls, notably the mass of fragmentary legal texts from Cave 4 at Qumran, have made the problem ever more complex. A treatment of Jesus and the Law that does not seriously engage the Dead Sea material is in essence flawed. Of necessity, and through no fault of the authors, this critique applies to all those treatments of the topic that were written before the Dead Sea discoveries. Moreover, if one adds to the Dead Sea legal material the revitalized study of Philo, Josephus, and what is called with distressing vagueness the OT Pseudepigrapha,[12] the problem of locating Jesus' teaching on the Law in its proper historical context looms as almost insurmountable. Any number of past studies have in effect flattened out the multidimensional context of Jesus and the Law by not taking all these different contending backgrounds or matrices into consideration.

Compounding the enigma still further is today's more cautious approach to using later rabbinic texts to re-create the legal world of Palestinian Judaism in the early decades of the 1st century A.D. This is *not* to say that no rabbinic texts may be used. As a matter of fact, I employed a number of them in my reconstruction of the Pharisees in Volume Three.[13] It *is* to say that such material must be used with the same historical-critical sensibility that is applied to other sources. After all, the whole rationale of the quest for the historical Jesus is that one may not without further ado cite a Christian Gospel written in A.D. 70 or 90 to establish what Jesus of Nazareth actually said or did in A.D. 28–30. Even though only forty years or so separate the ministry of the historical Jesus from Mark's Gospel (and perhaps from Q), the criteria of historicity must be judiciously applied to the sayings and deeds contained in Mark before one can with fair probability decide what does or does not go back to Jesus.

A fortiori, the material in the Mishna (composed ca. A.D. 200–220) and the Tosepta (redacted in the 3d century A.D.) cannot automatically be cited to illustrate legal practice at the time of Jesus. If I cannot assume, without detailed examination of the individual passage, that an introductory "Jesus said . . ." in Mark's Gospel proves that the historical Jesus actually spoke the logion so introduced, then likewise I cannot presume that an introductory "Hillel says . . ." in the Mishna guarantees that the historical Hillel made such a statement in the 1st century B.C. All claims about historicity, whether they involve the Gospels or the Mishna, must be supported by a critical investigation of the data, studied according to agreed-upon criteria of historicity. If this be true of the Mishna, then how much more is it true of the Babylonian Talmud, whose redaction takes place almost half a millennium after the time of Jesus? To be clear: this is not to rule out rabbinic parallels a priori. It is simply to require critical sifting of data and substantiation of claims. As Jacob Neusner has never tired of saying, "What you cannot show you do not know."

II. THREE VITAL DISTINCTIONS

Even after considering all these obstacles to an adequate treatment of our topic, we still have not touched on what is perhaps the greatest reason for the inadequacy of much of the past research on the historical Jesus and the Law, especially by Christian scholars. I would claim that at the root of much of the befuddlement about this topic, there is a fundamental confusion about proper categories and methods. It is vital, as we begin our trek through Jesus and the Law in Volume Four, that we make three careful distinctions about our subject matter. Actually, as we shall see, these three distinctions are simply three ways of approaching and articulating one grand underlying distinction.

(1) The first important distinction scholars often fail to make is the distinction between christology and the quest for the historical Jesus. Both are valid academic endeavors, as are the theology and history departments that major research universities support and encourage as distinct components of the overall pursuit of knowledge. As a matter of fact, at various times, I have taught courses both on christology and on the historical Jesus at a number of American universities.

Obviously, the two endeavors are related, but I always begin my courses by insisting on a clear distinction between the two subjects. Christology is a subdivision of the academic discipline called theology—in Anselm's famous phrase, *fides quaerens intellectum*, "faith seeking understanding." Christology is therefore faith seeking understanding of Jesus Christ as Lord and Savior, the object of Christian faith. Christology operates within this sphere of Christian faith, however much it may probe and challenge aspects of that faith or traditional understandings of it.

By contrast, the quest for the historical Jesus is by definition a strictly historical endeavor. Of its nature, it prescinds from or brackets Christian faith. This does not mean that it denies, rejects, or attacks such faith. The quest simply prescinds from Christian faith in the way that a world-class astronomer who happens to be a believing Christian would prescind from a theology of God the Creator when she is examining the outer reaches of a galaxy. All this is simply a matter of functional specialization, to use a phrase beloved of Bernard Lonergan.[14] To be sure, there is always the possibility of a critical correlation among various disciplines after each has done its own work according to its own proper method. But to attempt such a correlation prematurely would be to short-circuit the whole process and to violate the integrity and autonomy of each discipline.

Granted this distinction, what then do I mean by "the historical Jesus"? The historical Jesus is that Jesus whom we can recover or reconstruct by using the scientific tools of modern historical research as applied to ancient sources. Of its nature, the historical Jesus is a modern abstraction and construct. He is not coterminous with the full reality of Jesus of Nazareth, including everything Jesus of Nazareth ever said or did during the thirty-something years of his life. In other words, the historical Jesus is no more to be equated with the real Jesus than the historical Caligula is to be equated with the real Caligula—if I may cite a younger contemporary of Jesus with a somewhat different temperament.

Perhaps the common mistake of so much of the quest for the historical Jesus in the last two centuries was that it was not a truly historical quest at all. More often than not, it was an attempt at a more modern form of christology masquerading as a historical quest. At times, it might try to use the historical Jesus to overturn the "mistake called Christianity"—to quote the stated aim of one member of the American Jesus Seminar.[15] More frequently, it was used to re-articulate christology in more contemporary and scientific modes—think, for instance, of Joachim Jeremias or Ben Meyer.[16] In my opinion, there is certainly a place for a Christology that is historically informed, that seeks to absorb and integrate the quest for the historical Jesus into its understanding of the faith.[17] But such a christology, however laudable, must be carefully distinguished from the historical quest itself—something that is rarely done in a systematic fashion.

(2) This first distinction between the quest for the historical Jesus and christology naturally leads to, indeed, really embraces within itself, a second important distinction, namely, the distinction between our knowledge of a Palestinian Jew of the 1st century named Yeshua of Nazareth and our faith-knowledge of Jesus Christ, whom Christians proclaim to be their crucified and risen Lord. To be sure, believing Christians insist that these two figures are one and the same person at different stages of his existence or self-revelation. But academic historians, necessarily prescinding from faith

for the sake of their method, must insist that the precise object of their investigation, the historical Jesus, was always, solely, and entirely a 1st-century Jew, with no Christian pontifical vestments hiding underneath his Jewish cloak, with no resurrection glory reflecting backward onto the dark places of the public ministry and the cross. All a historian, precisely as a historian, can know is a particular circumcised Jewish male from Galilee who, in the early decades of the 1st century A.D., regularly went up to Jerusalem to observe the main—and even some minor—Jewish feasts in the temple as he pursued his prophetic ministry. What kind of Jew he was, where he fit on the variegated map of 1st-century Judaism, how much he may have diverged from what may be vaguely called "mainstream Judaism," are all valid questions for debate. But if there is any enduring gain from the so-called third quest, it is the one hammered home by scholars like Geza Vermes and E. P. Sanders: Jesus first, last, and only a Jew.[18]

(3) This distinction leads in turn to a third, more specific distinction, which brings us to the subject of Volume Four. This third distinction is between Christian moral theology and ethics on the one hand and Jesus' teaching about the Jewish Law on the other. Perhaps in no other area of the quest is the "Christianization" of the historical Jesus so subtle yet all-pervasive. Be it the question of divorce or the sabbath, purity rules or the taking of an oath, the unspoken thrust of most articles and books on "Jesus and the Law" is to present Jesus' teaching on Law and ethics as ultimately addressing Christian concerns or at least as amenable to a Christian viewpoint. Just as most quests for the historical Jesus have been christology in historical disguise, so too most treatments of Jesus and the Law are simply works on Christian morality and ethics wearing a yarmulke. Indeed, it could be argued that the "Christianizing" of the historical Jesus reaches its high point in the question of Jesus and the Law, where the Jewish Jesus regularly morphs into the Christian Paul, Augustine, Luther, or Barth—not to mention those anonymous Christian theologians of the Law whom we call Matthew, Mark, Luke, and John.

Here the peril of Christianizing the historical Jesus mutates into the peril of being relevant to Christians, with no hermeneutical reflection required. Many modern Christians eagerly desire either a Thomas Jefferson/ Enlightenment Jesus inculcating eternal truths or a psychobabble-counselor Jesus suggesting warm, fuzzy maybes. Still others seek moral direction from Jesus the social critic, the political activist, or the academic iconoclast. Such Jesuses are perennial crowd-pleasers. In contrast, as I can well attest from lectures I have given, Christian eyes glaze over as soon as a scholar insists on envisioning Jesus as a Jew immersed in the halakic debates of his fellow 1st-century Jews. In my opinion, the best way to treat this glazed-eye syndrome and to block any Christianizing of the historical Jesus in matters moral is *not* to sugarcoat the message. Rather, giving no quarter, one must insist on understanding this 1st-century Jew as addressing his fellow Palestinian Jews strictly within the confines of Jewish legal debates, without the slightest concern about whether any of these legal topics is of interest to Christians. In other words, to comprehend the historical Jesus precisely as a *historical* figure, we must place him firmly within the context of the Jewish Law as discussed and practiced in 1st-century Palestine. As the reader of this volume will notice, a basic insight will slowly but insistently emerge from this critical sifting of the legal material contained in the Gospels: the historical Jesus is the halakic Jesus, that is, the Jesus concerned with and arguing about the Mosaic Law and the questions of practice arising from it.

A critical investigation of the historical Jesus and the Law: a fine program, to be sure—but within this program lurks a further problem. What exactly *was* the Jewish Law in 1st-century Palestine? Early on in the so-called third quest, there was perhaps the naive assumption that all we had to do was to locate Jesus in his Jewish context, and we would have the historical Jesus. Our job would be done. What was lacking was a sufficient appreciation of how varied and fluid 1st-century Judaism was—and how that holds true especially for the Jewish Law. The more we probe, the more we awake with dismay to the realization that this problem of the relation of the *historical* Jesus to the *historical* Jewish Law may be more intractable on the Law side than on the Jesus side.

III. A ROAD MAP THROUGH VOLUME FOUR

All these distinctions and complications underline the importance of tackling this enormous problem with a methodical, step-by-step approach. The first order of business (Chapter 31) will be to grapple with the flexible and evolving concept of Law (Torah) around the time of Jesus. Once a working notion of Law is established, we will take up next those instances of Jesus' Torah-teaching that (i) treat major legal questions that had practical impact on the lives of ordinary Jews, (ii) enjoy multiple attestation of independent sources in the NT, and (iii) appear at first glance to revoke some command, permission, or social institution sanctioned by the written Mosaic Law. The two salient examples are Jesus' sweeping prohibition of divorce (Chapter 32) and his total prohibition of any and all oaths (Chapter 33).

We will then move on to a more central legal observance, one that (i) affected the lives of all Jews every week, (ii) enjoys multiple attestation in Gospel sources, but (iii) does not involve revocation of a major institution enshrined in and enjoined by the Torah. This grand topic is sabbath observance (Chapter 34), one of the most prominent identity badges of Jews in the ancient Greco-Roman world.

It is only after dealing with these *relatively* clear-cut legal domains that we dare to take up one of the most difficult, sprawling, and contentious areas of legal debate and development in ancient Judaism, namely, the purity rules (Chapter 35). Here the conflicting tendencies seen in the Gospels' treatments of Jesus and the Law appear to clash in bewildering fashion. On the one hand, Mark 7:15–19 presents us with a Jesus who, in one fell swoop and by his own authority, brushes aside all the food laws that helped maintain the boundaries that gave Jews a clear social-religious identity in a sea of Gentiles. On the other hand, various passages throughout the Gospels present a Jesus who takes for granted in his actions and sayings the purity system as well as the temple cult of Palestinian Judaism. Did the historical Jesus in effect abrogate the whole purity system by explicitly rejecting one of its key components, the food laws? Or did Jesus, in true prophetic style, simply emphasize the greater importance of inner moral purity, while not in principle rejecting ritual purity as an integral part of the Mosaic Law? Or was Jesus just indifferent to the whole system of purity, a system hotly debated and variously practiced among the diverse groups that made up Palestinian Judaism? We will struggle with these questions at length in Chapter 35.

Finally, having dealt with major individual institutions and practices commanded or regulated by the Torah, we will try to widen the scope of our inquiry by asking a broader question of meaning. Did the historical Jesus ever address the question of the Law as a whole, giving some indication of how he thought its various parts related to the totality of Torah? In other words, beyond his teachings about individual legal institutions and practices, did Jesus ever indicate his views on what are the supreme values in the Torah, or what are its guiding and governing principles, or what is the meaning of the Law as a whole? Did he in fact have any vision of the whole? To answer this question, we will sift and evaluate the various love commands attributed to Jesus in the Gospels (Chapter 36). Which—if any—of these love commands come from the historical Jesus, and what precisely are the range and meaning of each one? Do they provide a coherent system or an organizing principle for Jesus' varied pronouncements on individual parts of the Law?

As an aside, I should offer a clarification here: what I have just said about my approach to the love commands of Jesus should obviate a possible misconception—namely, that Volume Four's title, *Law and Love*, presupposes some sort of opposition or antithesis between the Mosaic Torah and the command to love. Rather, the title of Volume Four simply employs a venerable rhetorical device known as *merismus* (or, in English, *merism*).[19] Using *merismus*, a writer designates the totality of some reality or experience by naming two of its complementary parts, for example, its beginning and its end. A prime example is offered by Ps 121:8: "Yahweh will protect your going out and your coming in both now and forever." One's "going out" and "coming in" symbolize and encompass one's entire life and activity, summed up in these two actions functioning as bookends. So it is with *Law and Love*. The title is simply a convenient way of designating the whole of Volume Four by naming the first and last chapters, the alpha and omega of our investigation. As Chapter 36 will show, far from being opposed to the Law, love is for Jesus the Law's supreme value and command.[20]

Having dealt with all these questions step by step, I will conclude Volume Four with some reflections that are intended to be more than a mere laundry list of the results of various chapters. Instead of simply recapitulating the summaries at the end of each chapter, I will use the conclusion to step back, grasp a sense of the whole, and raise some larger questions about Jesus, Law, and morality.

Before we begin our long trek through the Law, I should alert the reader to some problems of terminology that will be treated at greater length in Chapter 31. There we shall see that the Hebrew word Torah (*tôrâ*) is a capacious term with a whole range of meanings. Among those meanings we may count "instruction," "teaching," "direction," "directive," or "law." When used of the Torah given by God to Moses, the term can almost be translated at times as "divine revelation." When the Jews who translated the Pentateuch into Greek chose the word *nomos* ("law") as the equivalent of *tôrâ*, they were not squeezing a Hebrew word with many meanings into a legalistic Greek straightjacket. The Greek word *nomos* likewise carried within itself a whole range of meanings. As in Hebrew, so in Greek, the precise denotation depends on the individual context. It is when we come to the standard English translation of *tôrâ* or *nomos*, namely, "law," that we encounter difficulty. In popular usage, "law" has a much more narrow semantic range than either *tôrâ* or *nomos*. Yet "law" is such an entrenched translation of the Hebrew and Greek nouns that I do not delude myself with the hope that I could decree a sudden change either in English usage or in traditional translation practice.

My short-term solution (admittedly, a practical compromise) is to alternate "Torah" and "Law" on a regular basis throughout this volume as one way of reminding the reader of the wider sense of "Law." While not perfect, this solution may be justified on the grounds that in this volume we are focusing on the legal component of the Pentateuch rather than on its narrative or poetry. To help provide some further nuance in usage, I will use "Law" with an uppercase "L" to signify the Mosaic Law as a whole, while "law" with a lowercase "l" will denote any individual command, statute, or precept, be it inside or outside the Mosaic Law.

A second point on usage flows from the first. Jesus never uses words like "morality" or "ethics" in any of his sayings. He speaks instead of doing God's will and/or keeping his commandments. In discussing these commandments, the historical Jesus never *explicitly* distinguishes between what moderns would call "moral/ethical" laws on the one hand and "ritual/ceremonial/levitical" laws on the other. Indeed, he could hardly have done so when, with the temple sacrificial system still operating, fulfilling certain moral obligations (e.g., compensating for damage done to a person or property) could involve ritual obligations (e.g., a temple sacrifice). To indicate this interweaving and overlapping of areas that we would distinguish, I will at times purposely alternate words like "moral," "ethical," and "legal." I will do this to emphasize that, far from being opposed to each other, morality and observance of the Law meshed in the mind of Jesus.

As we shall see, at times some of Jesus' sayings may *imply* a distinction between the two realms of the ethical and the ritual, but this distinction is never made explicit or thematized.[21] If anything, the friendly scribe in Mark's version of Jesus' teaching on the double command of love (Mark 12:28–34) is more explicit about such a distinction than Jesus is himself. While there is a risk that my regular alteration of the terms "Law," "Torah," "legal," and "moral" might cause confusion, I trust that my explanation in Chapter 31 will make things sufficiently clear.

IV. ONCE AGAIN, A REMINDER ABOUT THE RULES OF THE ROAD

The methodology governing *A Marginal Jew* was laid out in Part One of Volume One (pp. 1–201) and summarized at the beginning of Volume Two (pp. 4–6) and Volume Three (pp. 9–12). But even patient readers who have persevered to this fourth volume might welcome a brief refresher course on the goal of this work and the method by which we move to that goal. If, however, readers feel that they remember quite well the basic method of these volumes, they should feel free to skip ahead to Chapter 31.

To repeat what I have said above: the historical Jesus is an abstract construct created by modern scholars applying historical-critical methods to ancient sources. If scholars apply these methods to the appropriate sources with professional expertise, careful logic, and personal integrity, we have good reason to expect that their abstract construct will approach and partially coincide with the 1st-century Jew called Jesus of Nazareth. Granted the severe limitations of our sources, the match between 21st-century historical construct and 1st-century historical reality will never be perfect. At best, it will be a more or less accurate approximation.

If this historical Jesus is not the "real Jesus" (the total reality of everything Jesus said and did during his life), neither is he the "theological Jesus," the object of systematic reflection based on Christian faith.[22] To stress the need to prescind from (not deny) what a person claims to know by faith, I concocted in Volume One the fantasy of an "unpapal conclave." A Catholic, a Protestant, a Jew, a Muslim, and an agnostic—all honest historians well-versed in ancient history and ancient religious movements—are locked up in the bowels of the Harvard Divinity School library, put on a spartan diet, and not allowed to emerge until they have hammered out a consensus document on the historical Jesus of Nazareth.[23]

An essential requirement of this document would be that it is based on purely historical sources and arguments. Its conclusions would have to be open to verification by any and all sincere persons using the means of modern historical research. No doubt, such a consensus document would suffer from a narrow focus, a fragmentary vision, perhaps even some distortions. It certainly would not claim to present a complete, let alone ultimate and definitive, interpretation of Jesus, his work, and his intentions.[24] Nevertheless, at least it would provide an academically respectable common ground and starting point for dialogue among people of various faiths or no faith.

To give one concrete example of what this would involve: the unpapal conclave—or just about any quester for the historical Jesus—could agree that Jesus "was crucified under Pontius Pilate and suffered death." Although these words happen to be those of the so-called Nicene-Constantinopolitan Creed, drawn up around the time of the second ecumenical council (Constantinople I, in A.D. 381),[25] they are nevertheless, when taken in isolation, a sober statement of historical fact. They are affirmed or intimated by Josephus and Tacitus as well as by many various streams of NT traditions that are independent of one another. Thus, one does not have to be a believer to affirm this short narrative of events.

What the unpapal conclave—or any historian operating *simply as a historian*—could not affirm is a slightly longer form of the quotation from the same creed: namely, that Jesus *"for us human beings and for our salvation* . . . was crucified under Pontius Pilate *for our sake*, [and] suffered [death]." [26] The "for us human beings," "for our salvation," and "for our sake" are all expressions of Christian faith and christology, affirming the saving effect of Jesus' life and death. Unlike the plain affirmation of Jesus' crucifixion and death under Pontius Pilate, this longer statement is not open in principle to empirical investigation and verification by any and every honest observer, believer and nonbeliever alike. (Nor, for that matter, is the affirmation of the saving effect of Jesus' death open to falsification by empirical means.) Hence this affirmation is not a statement that falls under the purview of questers for the historical Jesus *in their capacity as historians—* though some questers, if they are Christians, will believe on other grounds that the statement is true. [27]

To move from definitions to sources: as Volume One showed, there are very few sources for knowledge of the historical Jesus beyond the four canonical Gospels. Paul and Josephus offer little more than tidbits. Claims that later apocryphal Gospels and the Nag Hammadi material supply independent and reliable historical information about Jesus are largely fantasy. [28] One is hardly surprised, though, that in the United States the Nag Hammadi material has generated not only sensationalistic novels but also sensationalistic monographs claiming to be scholarship. Wild claims notwithstanding, in the end serious historians are left with the difficult task of sifting through the four Gospels for historical tradition. The task is difficult indeed, primarily because these documents are all products of Christian churches in the second half of the 1st century A.D. Written some forty to seventy years after Jesus' death, they are shot through with Christian faith in Jesus as the risen Lord of the church. Hence, only a careful examination of the Gospel material in the light of the criteria of historicity (i.e., rules for judging what is historical) can hope to yield reliable results. [29]

In the quest for the historical Jesus, five criteria have proved especially useful:

(1) The criterion of *embarrassment* pinpoints Gospel material that would hardly have been invented by the early church, since such material created embarrassment or theological difficulties for the church even during the NT period—a prime example being the baptism of Jesus by John the Baptist at the beginning of the public ministry. [30] Or to take an example from the end of the public ministry: the criterion of embarrassment argues forcefully for the historicity of the public crucifixion of Jesus as a criminal by a Roman official. Crucifixion was the most shameful and degrading form of execution in the Roman world; it was largely reserved for slaves, bandits, rebels, or other persons lacking Roman citizenship and convicted of being a threat to

public order.[31] Worse still, not only was Jesus crucified, he was crucified by the supreme legal authority in Judea. There was nothing illegal or improper about his trial and execution, if one judges them simply by the rules and procedures (or lack thereof) in force at the time.[32] Hence one senses from the earliest traditions enshrined in the NT a constant struggle on the part of Christians to explain or explain away the scandalous, off-putting fact of Jesus' death by crucifixion. Besides being shocking and shameful, Jesus' crucifixion was a political event that could not help but make Christians suspect in the eyes of Roman citizens and their rulers.

Intriguingly, within the NT, the Christian response to the problem of the cross exhibits no one normative way of interpreting Jesus' death; many different strategies are employed to cope with the embarrassment. The early pre-Pauline formulas of faith, reaching back probably to the 30s of the 1st century, already interpret the crucifixion as some sort of atoning sacrifice for sins (e.g., 1 Cor 15:3–5; Rom 3:24–26; Rom 4:25; later on, this approach is developed at great length in the Epistle to the Hebrews). Paul himself stresses the paradox of God putting to shame a proud and powerful world of sinners by the shameful death of a weak Jesus on the cross (1 Cor 1:18–31). The Q document evokes the theme of the rejected and martyred prophets of the OT: Jesus, the eschatological prophet, is the last in the line of the martyred prophets as salvation history draws to its consummation. Early traditions preserved in Peter's sermons in the Acts of the Apostles (e.g., Acts 2:23–24; 3:13–15; 4:10; 5:30–31; cf. Paul's sermon at Pisidian Antioch in 13:27–30) sharply distinguish between the crucifixion (an evil act of evil men that was foreseen and permitted by God) and the resurrection (the true saving act of God, reversing the evil act of the crucifixion). Beneath the present Passion Narratives in the four Gospels, some scholars detect a primitive theology of the crucified Jesus as the suffering righteous man, a figure frequently depicted in the OT psalms of lamentation. In some passages, the mysterious figure of the suffering servant of Yahweh in Isa 52:13–53:12 seems to be evoked. The Gospel of John faces the shame of the cross head-on with a strategy of irony, paradox, and total reversal of meaning: to the eyes of faith, the cross is actually Jesus' exaltation and glorification, his condemnation of and triumph over the world that foolishly thinks it is condemning and defeating him.

In all these varied, not to say at times contradictory, strategies of apologetics, one can sense the early Christians scrambling to come up with explanations for the unexpected and shocking climax of the story of Jesus. Whatever one's expectations of a Jewish messiah or a savior of the world, a Galilean Jew crucified by a Roman prefect in Jerusalem did not fit the job description.[33] The struggle by Christian missionaries to construct an apologetic to convince or sustain converts, a struggle that permeates a good part of the NT, argues eloquently that the crucifixion of Jesus was the last thing the first Christians would have invented if left to themselves.

(2) The criterion of *discontinuity* focuses on words or deeds of Jesus that cannot be derived either from the Judaism(s) of Jesus' time or from the early church (e.g., Jesus' rejection of voluntary fasting).[34] To take a curious example from Chapter 36 of Volume Four: when asked what is the greatest commandment, Jesus replies by citing the two commandments enjoining love of God with all one's heart and love of neighbor as oneself (Mark 12:28–34). At first glance, the reader will perhaps be surprised to see that I invoke the criterion of discontinuity to establish the historicity of this anecdote. After all, the two commandments, taken by themselves, are simply citations of two precepts contained in the Pentateuch (Deut 6:4–5 and Lev 19:18b). True, but what is "discontinuous" is what Jesus does with these texts. He (i) cites each commandment word for word, (ii) joins the two of them back to back, (iii) ranks them explicitly as "first" and "second," and (iv) concludes by declaring that no other commandment is greater than these two. This fourfold configuration of a double commandment of love is found nowhere else in the OT, the literature of Second Temple Judaism, the rest of the NT, or the early patristic writings. All this constitutes a glaring discontinuity of teaching that often goes unremarked.

(3) The criterion of *multiple attestation* focuses on sayings or deeds of Jesus witnessed (i) in more than one independent literary source (e.g., Mark, Q, Paul, or John)[35] and/or (ii) in more than one literary form or genre (e.g., sayings of Jesus about the cost of discipleship plus narratives about his peremptory call of various disciples). To take a clear example from Volume Four: that Jesus forbade divorce is supported by the independent witness of Mark, Q, and Paul. The agreement of the two earliest Synoptic sources with Paul's First Letter to the Corinthians (earlier than Mark and Q from a literary point of view) is an especially strong argument. Not only do we have three independent sources, we also have three different literary genres: a dispute story within the narrative of a whole Gospel (Mark), a stray saying within a collection of logia (Q), and a letter written to a specific church about specific problems (1 Corinthians).

(4) The criterion of *coherence* is brought into play only after a certain amount of historical material has been isolated by other criteria. The criterion of coherence holds that sayings and deeds of Jesus that fit in well with the preliminary "database" established by the other criteria have a good chance of being historical. To take an example from Volume Four:

the argument for the historicity of Jesus' command, "love your enemies," is based primarily on the criterion of discontinuity. Yet this laconic command also receives a certain amount of support from the criterion of coherence. Other statements and commands of Jesus that have already been judged historical in *A Marginal Jew* display the same rhetorical strategy evinced in "love your enemies": disturbing content is articulated in brief, blunt, and shocking formulations in order to hammer home the point in memorable fashion.

(5) Instead of simply judging individual sayings or deeds of Jesus, the criterion of *Jesus' rejection and execution* looks primarily at the larger pattern of Jesus' ministry and asks what words and deeds fit in with and explain his trial and crucifixion. A Jesus whose words and deeds did not threaten or alienate people, especially powerful people, is not the historical Jesus. In a sense, then, the whole portrait of Jesus that emerges from these four volumes of *A Marginal Jew* must be evaluated in the light of this criterion. More specifically, though, certain individual sayings and deeds loom especially large in the light of Jesus' arrest and crucifixion in Jerusalem. Notable among them are the symbolic-prophetic action of Jesus' "triumphal entry" into Jerusalem, his prediction of the destruction of the Jerusalem temple, and his acting out of that prophecy in his "cleansing" of the temple.

Contrary to what some scholars have claimed, I do not think that Jesus' teachings on the Law directly led to his execution. At most, Jesus' more disturbing pronouncements and actions (e.g., his total rejection of divorce and oaths, his rejection of voluntary fasting, his apparent indifference to purity rules) would have offended not just Pharisees but also almost any devout Jew. His stance on these issues may have alienated many who might otherwise have supported or defended him when the final clash came. But, by themselves, his provocative teachings on the Law did not cause the final clash. They were, at most, an aggravating factor.

In addition to these five primary criteria of historicity, various secondary criteria may also be invoked, but usually only as "backup" or confirmation for the primary criteria. These secondary (some would say dubious) criteria include traces of the Aramaic language in the sayings of Jesus and echoes of the early 1st-century Palestinian environment in which Jesus lived. Still weaker as criteria (some would say useless) are the vivid and concrete nature of a narrative and the supposed general tendencies of the Synoptic tradition as it develops.

Given the difficulty involved in articulating and applying these criteria, it is not surprising that some scholars brush aside the whole question of method and criteria. They prefer to "muddle through." Yet every scholar engaged in the quest for the historical Jesus is de facto operating with some method and criteria, however inchoate and unexamined. The danger in "muddling through" is that one easily begins to draw from the data the conclusions one wants rather than the conclusions the data warrant. Criteria are important because, when applied methodically to the data, they can force the quester to draw conclusions he or she has not foreseen and perhaps does not desire. For instance, it was the weight of evidence rather than personal desire that constrained me to judge authentic both Jesus' double command of love and his command to love enemies. Originally, I thought a judgment of *non liquet* (not clear either way) more likely. Or, to take an opposite example: for many years, under the influence of scholars like Ernst Käsemann and Norman Perrin, I had considered Jesus' revocation of food laws (Mark 7:15) authentic on the grounds of discontinuity. It was only extended analysis of the whole text of Mark 7:1–23 and careful weighing of the complicated arguments pro and con (notice the length of Chapter 35!) that finally led me to conclude, almost against my will, that the saying was a product of the early church. In sum, my own experience throughout the writing of these four volumes has convinced me that, while methodology and criteria may be tiresome topics, they are vital in keeping the critic from seeing in the data whatever he or she has already decided to see. The rules of the road are never exciting, but they keep us moving in the right direction.

More important still, these rules of the road, as well as the whole introduction to Volume Four, are meant to reinforce a basic truth that I have stressed since the start of Volume One. In any rigorous and honest quest for the historical Jesus, we are always dealing with varying degrees of probability. Of its very nature, the quest cannot and should not try to sell the product of its hypothetical reconstruction as the new and improved version of Christian faith in Jesus Christ. That would be absurd, though it is all too often done or at least implied. Rather, as is the case with any scholarly attempt to reconstruct a lesser-known figure of ancient history, the historical-critical method, when applied to Jesus of Nazareth, exemplifies "both its importance and its limitations," as a very astute theologian has put it.[36] Indeed, paradoxically, it is only when the limitations of our historical reconstruction are fully appreciated that the proper importance of the historical Jesus can be evaluated and appropriated by further academic research, interfaith dialogue, and Christian theology.

With this sober reminder, let us turn to our first task in the attempt to grasp Jesus' relation to the Law, namely, to explore the fluid and complex meaning of the Law (Torah) around the time of Jesus.

NOTES TO THE INTRODUCTION

[1] This all-too-brief introduction to the Law question is meant both to offer a few samples of the wide range of scholarly opinions and to indicate a few of the problems connected with each major direction in research (i.e., conscious rejection of the Law, dialectical or mediating approaches to the Law, total acceptance of the Law along with "liberal," "deviant," or "controversial" teachings on individual practices). One point becomes clear very quickly. There is a single overriding challenge to be faced by each and every scholarly position on the subject, namely, how to provide a coherent explanation of Jesus' attitude toward the Law that covers all the sayings attributed to him with fair probability.

[2] Jan Lambrecht, "Jesus and the Law. An Investigation of Mk 7, 1–23," *ETL* 53 (1977) 24–79. See esp. pp. 76–79; the quotation that I cite in the main text is on p. 77. Lambrecht rejects the attempts by some exegetes to soften Jesus' opposition to the Law. At the same time, Lambrecht admits that Jesus apparently observed the Law, just like many of his fellow Jews, as a matter of course, without questioning it. Lambrecht also holds open the possibility that Jesus may not have fully realized all the consequences of his conscious attitude toward the Law.

[3] Werner Georg Kümmel, "Äussere und innere Reinheit des Menschen bei Jesus," *Das Wort und die Wörter* (Gerhard Friedrich Festschrift; ed. Horst Balz and Siegfried Schulz; Stuttgart: Kohlhammer, 1973) 35–46.

[4] See Morton Smith, *The Secret Gospel* (New York: Harper & Row, 1973) 111–14. For arguments that Smith's "Secret Gospel of Mark" is actually a forgery, see Peter Jeffery, *The Secret Gospel of Mark Unveiled* (New Haven: Yale University, 2007); Stephen C. Carlson, *The Gospel Hoax. Morton Smith's Invention of Secret Mark* (Waco, TX: Baylor University, 2005). Arguing against the idea of a forgery is Scott G. Brown, *Mark's Other Gospel* (Waterloo, Ontario: Wilfrid Laurier University, 2005).
Views about Jesus liberating people from traditional religion and law continue to be current in popular American religion, though nowadays political correctness usually keeps one from saying openly that Jesus broke with the Mosaic Law or with Judaism. Consider, for instance, what ramifications for the question of the Jewish Jesus and the Jewish Law the statement of Robert Funk (*Honest to Jesus. Jesus for a New Millennium* [San Francisco: Harper, 1996] 302) might have: "Jesus . . . may be said to have been *irreligious, irreverent,* and *impious* [emphasis in the original]. . . . because he was indifferent to the formal practice of religion, he is said to have profaned the temple, the sabbath, and breached the purity regulations of his own legacy." Not surprisingly, Funk goes on to insist that Jesus' significance should be detached from any exclusive religious context—including, I would presume, 1st-century Judaism. Ironically, various radical scholars in the past have taken almost the opposite tack from Funk to attain Funk's goal of separating the historical Jesus from traditional Christianity. In the 18th and 19th centuries,

questers for the historical Jesus who wanted to create as broad a gulf as possible between Jesus and Christianity (as Funk does) sometimes emphasized that Jesus did not wish to break with or alter the Mosaic Law, even in its ceremonial regulations; so, e.g., the supposed founder of the first quest, Hermann Samuel Reimarus in his *Fragments* (Lives of Jesus Series; ed. Charles H. Talbert; Philadelphia: Fortress, 1970; originally published in German in 1774–78) 71–72, 98–102.

[5] For a survey of Jesus' stance vis-à-vis the Law on the level of the various redactional theologies found in the NT, see the careful study of William R. G. Loader, *Jesus' Attitude towards the Law* (WUNT 2/97; Tübingen: Mohr [Siebeck], 1997); cf. his more popular presentation (which includes a brief consideration of the historical Jesus), *Jesus and the Fundamentalism of His Day* (Grand Rapids, MI/ Cambridge, UK: Eerdmans, 2001). For studies of the controversy stories, especially in their Marcan form, see Arland J. Hultgren, *Jesus and His Adversaries. The Form and Function of the Conflict Stories in the Synoptic Tradition* (Minneapolis: Augsburg, 1979); Joanna Dewey, *Markan Public Debate* (SBLDS 48; Chico, CA: Scholars, 1980); Jean-Gaspard Mudiso Mbâ Mundla, *Jesus und die Führer Israels. Studien zu den sog. Jerusalemer Streitgesprächen* (NTAbh n.s. 17; Münster: Aschendorff, 1984).

[6] Even in the highly polemical Gospel of John, the Prologue (1:17) declares that "the Law was *given* [*edothē*, namely by God (the divine passive voice)] through Moses." In Mark 7:8–13, commandments delivered by Moses in Exodus are declared to be "the commandment of God" and "the word of God." When the rich man asks Jesus what he must do to inherit eternal life, Jesus simply points him to a sampling of the commandments of the Decalogue (Mark 10:17–19).

[7] Indeed, Mark 7:15–19, in which (at least in Mark's redactional understanding) Jesus effectively revokes the food laws of the Pentateuch by declaring all foods clean, is a kind of acid test for the various authors writing on Jesus and the Law. The more authors hold that Jesus opposed or revoked the Law itself, the more Mark 7:15–19 (or at least its substance) is declared authentic and allowed to define Jesus' stance. The more authors hold that Jesus' teaching was compatible with the Law and simply expressed "liberal," "deviant," or "radical" views on debatable points of practice, the more Mark 7:15–19 is declared to be a creation of the early church as it sought to justify its so-called Law-free mission to the Gentiles.

[8] Many German authors, and many others in dependence on them, seem at times to use "dialectic" almost as a conjuring word, as though the mere presence of the word solved the problem of Jesus and the Law. Once we begin to probe beneath the surface of this widespread appeal to "dialectic," we find that different authors understand the supposed dialectic of Jesus and the Law in notably different ways. One example of the dialectical approach can be found in Walter Gutbrod, "*nomos*, etc.," *TDNT* 4 (1967) 1059–65. Gutbrod's dialectical analysis of "Jesus' Negation of the Law" and "Jesus' Affirmation of the Law" owes not a little to Pauline theology. But

at least Gutbrod tries to lay out his position in an orderly fashion. In all too many presentations of Jesus' position on the Law, "dialectic" seems to become a slogan that hides the fact that the author never really grapples with the specifics of the problem; see, e.g., Hans Conzelmann, *Jesus* (Philadelphia: Fortress, 1973) 52–54, 59–67. While Ernst Käsemann ("The Problem of the Historical Jesus," *Essays on New Testament Themes* [SBT 41; London: SCM, 1964, from an article originally published in German in 1954] 15–47) likewise speaks of Jesus' dialectical relationship to the Law, his position tends (like Lambrecht's) to the more extreme claim that Jesus in effect annulled the Law (pp. 38–39): "We can hardly say . . . that Jesus has left the law as such untouched and merely made its demands more radical. . . . Matthew obviously thought that Jesus was only attacking the rabbinate and Pharisaism with their heightening of the demands of the Torah. But the man who denies that impurity from external sources can penetrate into man's essential being is striking at the presuppositions and the plain verbal sense of the Torah and at the authority of Moses himself." Although Günther Bornkamm (*Jesus of Nazareth* [New York: Harper & Row, 1960; German original, 1956] 96–100) cites Käsemann on this point, it is noteworthy that he does not go as far as Käsemann in his own formulation of the dialectic. While insisting on Jesus' freedom and authority vis-à-vis the Law, Bornkamm also emphasizes that "Jesus does not intend to abolish the scriptures and the law, and to replace them by his own message. They are and remain the proclamation of God's will. For Jesus, however, the will of God is present in such immediate fashion that the letter of the law may be gauged by it." At the basis of the various approaches of many of these "post-Bultmannians" is the stance of Rudolf Bultmann himself; see, e.g., his summary exposition of the theme in his *Theology of the New Testament* (2 vols.; London: SCM, 1952, 1955) 1. 11–22. In heavily existentialistic fashion, he emphasizes Jesus' demand for radical obedience to the God who "claims man whole—and wholly." This proclamation of the will of God demanding the radical obedience of the whole person is seen by Bultmann as a protest against Jewish legalism and ritualism. However, Bultmann holds that Jesus did not contest the authority of the OT Law itself; rather, he opposed the interpretation of the Law common to the Jewish scribes of the time. What Jesus does with sovereign freedom is to make distinctions among the various demands of the Law. I might note at this point that, given all that has been achieved in the third quest for a truly Jewish Jesus, one can only look back in amazement at Bultmann's sweeping generalizations and denigrations of the Judaism of Jesus' day. In a sense, the fundamental problem with so many of these attempts to articulate Jesus' stance vis-à-vis the Law is a hopelessly inadequate understanding and appreciation of 1st-century Palestinian Judaism.

Similar approaches, though without the heavy existentialistic baggage, can be seen in exegetes outside the Bultmannian tradition. For example, Eduard Schweizer (*Jesus* [NT Library; London: SCM, 1971; German original, 1968] 30–34) entitles his treatment of Jesus and the Law "Jesus' Ambivalence towards the Law." He holds that Jesus, like all the Jewish parties of his day, accepted the Law "as God's great gift to Israel, transcending everything else" (p. 30). Yet Jesus inculcated radical obedience to God's will, "far transcending mere observance of the letter of the law"

(p. 31). Indeed, Jesus "goes still further: there are even places where Jesus annuls not only the Jewish interpretation but the Old Testament law itself" (p. 32). According to Schweizer, "there can be no doubt that Jesus, through his entire conduct, again and again ostentatiously transgressed the Old Testament commandment to observe the Sabbath." (p. 32). As we shall see in Chapter 34, this last claim in particular is highly questionable. More to the point, how these latter statements of Schweizer cohere with his initial claim that Jesus accepted the Law as "transcending everything else" remains unclear. A similar tack is taken by Joachim Jeremias in his *New Testament Theology. Part One. The Proclamation of Jesus* (NT Library; London: SCM, 1971) 204–8. According to Jeremias, "Jesus lived in the Old Testament," frequently citing or alluding to it, especially Isaiah, Daniel, and the Psalms (p. 205). Indeed, Jesus found in the Pentateuch the basic norms of the will of God. Yet Jesus not only radicalizes the Law; he dares to criticize and supersede the words of the written Torah. Jesus repeals or abolishes regulations in the Torah, such as divorce and the law of retaliation. At the same time, Jesus rejected "in a radical way" the "rabbinic" (*sic*) *hǎlākâ* of his day, especially concerning the sabbath (p. 208).

[9] See, e.g., the summary judgment of Joseph Klausner in his groundbreaking *Jesus of Nazareth. His Life, Times, and Teaching* (New York: Macmillan, 1925; published in Hebrew in 1922) 367: "never did Jesus think of annulling the Law (or even the ceremonial laws which it contained) and setting up a new law of his own." A similar rejection of the idea that Jesus rejected, opposed, or annulled the Law as such permeates the various works on Jesus written by Geza Vermes: *Jesus the Jew* (Philadelphia: Fortress, 1973); *Jesus and the World of Judaism* (Philadelphia: Fortress, 1983); *The Religion of Jesus the Jew* (Minneapolis: Fortress, 1993); and *The Changing Faces of Jesus* (New York: Viking, 2000). A terse summary of Vermes's view can be found in *The Religion of Jesus the Jew*, 21: "Nowhere in the Gospels is Jesus depicted as deliberately setting out to deny or substantially alter any commandment of the Torah *in itself*" [emphasis in the original]. According to Vermes, the controversies in which Jesus engages concern either conflicts between laws or the precise understanding of the extent of a precept.

[10] E. P. Sanders, "The Synoptic Jesus and the Law," *Jewish Law from Jesus to the Mishnah* (London: SCM; Philadelphia: Trinity, 1990) 1–96, esp. 1–6, 90–96.

[11] One must keep in mind the precise point at issue here: whether anything in Jesus' teaching opposes or rescinds any part of the written Law of Moses, i.e., any of its commands, prohibitions, permissions, or institutions. The query proposed in this volume is therefore broader than simply the narrow question of whether Jesus annulled an express command of the Torah. In addition, the question posed here is not whether at times other Jews might expressly and in principle rescind important elements of the Law (hence not simply by casuistry or a legal sleight of hand, as is the case, for instance, in Hillel's *Perozbol* or *Prosbul*, a legal document that circumvents the sabbatical-year cancellation of loans [see *m. Šeb.* 10:3–4]). In fact,

we know of some Jews who did such things: e.g., some Diaspora Jews who were interested in only the symbolic (or allegorical) and not the literal meaning of the Law
(see, e.g., Philo, *De migratione Abrahami* [*On the Migration of Abraham*], 89–93).
On these "extreme allegorists," see David M. Hay, "Philo's References to Other Allegorists," *Studia Philonica* 6 (1979–1980) 41–75, esp. 47–52; Peder Borgen, "Philo
of Alexandria. A Critical and Synthetical Survey of Research since World War II,"
ANRW II/21.1, 98–154, esp. 126–28. At a much later date (17th century), one finds
a very different type of antinomianism in Shabbatai Ṣevi (on whom see the classic
work by Gershom Scholem, *Sabbatai Ṣevi: The Mystical Messiah, 1626–1676* [Bol-
lingen Series 93; Princeton: Princeton University, 1973]). On pp. 802–14, Scholem
discusses the development of Nathan of Gaza's antinomian theory about a messiah who saves the world by himself transgressing the Law. On Shabbatai Ṣevi, see
also R. Hrair Dekmejian, "Charismatic Leadership in Messianic and Revolutionary Movements," *Religious Resurgence* (ed. Richard T. Antoun and Mary Elaine
Hegland; Syracuse, NY: Syracuse University, 1987) 78–107; Marcus van Loopik,
"The Messianism of Shabbatai Zevi and Jewish Mysticism," *Messianism through
History* (ed. Wim Beuken, Seán Freyne, and Anton Weiler; London: SCM; Mary-
knoll, NY: Orbis, 1993) 69–81; Moshe Idel, "Saturn and Sabbatai Tzevi: A New
Approach to Sabbateanism," *Toward the Millennium* (Studies in the History of Re-
ligion 77; ed. Peter Schäfer and Mark Cohen; Leiden: Brill, 1998) 173–202; Elliot
R. Wolfson, "The Engenderment of Messianic Politics: Symbolic Significance of
Sabbatai Ṣevi's Coronation," ibid., 203–58. In even a superficial overview of Jesus,
Philo, and Shabbatai Ṣevi, one notices immediately the very different theological,
social, and cultural contexts in which their respective teachings about the Law arose
and operated.

[12] Throughout this volume, I will use phrases like "OT Pseudepigrapha," "intertestamental literature," and "the literature of Second Temple Judaism" to refer to
nonbiblical Jewish literature around the time of Jesus, while admitting the problems
connected with each of these designations. One has to face the fact that all three
terms circulate in current usage and that there is no one satisfactory substitute for
them, despite their "fuzzy edges."

[13] *A Marginal Jew*, 3. 305–10, 313–32.

[14] Among his many works, see in particular *Method in Theology* (New York:
Herder and Herder, 1972), esp. pp. 125–45.

[15] See Paul Hollenbach, "The Historical Jesus Question in North America Today," *BTB* 19 (1989) 11–22.

[16] Jeremias, *New Testament Theology*; Ben F. Meyer, *The Aims of Jesus* (London:
SCM, 1979).

[17] I see the important work of N. T. Wright (e.g., *Jesus and the Victory of God*
[Christian Origins and the Question of God 2; Minneapolis: Fortress, 1996]) in

this light. In other words, I consider this book not an example of the quest for the historical Jesus as such, but rather a prime example of how one goes about appropriating results of the quest for a larger theological/christological project. The matter is more complicated when it comes to the fine work of James D. G. Dunn, *Jesus Remembered* [Christology in the Making 1; Grand Rapids, MI/Cambridge, UK: Eerdmans, 2003]). Much in this individual volume can stand on its own as a treatment of the historical Jesus. As the title of the series indicates, though, this volume is viewed as part of a larger christological project.

[18] I have already cited the key works of Vermes on this subject. As for E. P. Sanders, see his *Jesus and Judaism* (Philadelphia: Fortress, 1985); *Jewish Law from Jesus to the Mishnah*; *Judaism. Practice & Belief 63 BCE–66 CE* (London: SCM; Philadelphia: Trinity, 1992); *The Historical Figure of Jesus* (London: Penguin, 1993).

[19] The 1934 edition of *Webster's New International Dictionary of the English Language* defines the rhetorical term *merism* as "a form of synecdoche in which a totality is expressed by two contrasting parts."

[20] To be honest, there is also a less weighty reason for choosing *Law and Love* as the title of Volume Four: the author's abiding attraction to alliteration, as attested in *The Roots of the Problem and the Person, Mentor, Message, and Miracles*, and *Companions and Competitors*.

[21] One Gospel pericope that comes close to such a distinction is Mark 7:1–23. But, as I will show in Chapter 35, almost nothing in this pericope (except possibly for the subunit about Qorban) comes from the historical Jesus.

[22] For an understanding of the "real Jesus" that moves in the theological and christological rather than the historical realm, see Luke Timothy Johnson, *The Real Jesus* (San Francisco: Harper, 1996); cf. his *Living Jesus* (San Francisco: Harper, 1999). For example, on p. 142 of *The Real Jesus*, Johnson states that "the 'real Jesus' for Christian faith is the resurrected Jesus." I have no problem with such a definition when one is operating in the realm of faith and theology; see, e.g., *A Marginal Jew*, 1. 197. But, as I point out in that passage, there is another sense of "real," proper to modern historical investigation (cf. *A Marginal Jew*, 1. 21–24), which Johnson seems unwilling to affirm in the special case of Jesus of Nazareth.

[23] A blind spot in the constitution of my mythical "unpapal conclave" at the beginning of Volume One (p. 1) was the omission of a Muslim scholar within the group of learned historians locked up in a basement until they could hammer out a consensus document on the historical Jesus. Like the other scholars, the Muslim would be obliged, for the sake of academic dialogue, to adhere strictly to the historical-critical method and prescind from what he or she affirmed by faith.

[24] Not unlike the configuration of hard disks in computers, which allows of various levels of formatting, the writing of history and biography, while always interpre-

tive to some degree, allows of various levels of interpretation. The very gathering of data and the passing of judgment as to their historicity involve a certain "low level" of interpretation. Beyond that unavoidable low level, *A Marginal Jew* attempts as much as possible to let any overarching interpretation of Jesus and his work emerge gradually and naturally out of the convergence of the data judged historical. In particular, *A Marginal Jew* does not intend to impose on the data any predetermined interpretive grid, be it political, economic, or sociological. Such grids can be useful at a later stage of interpretation, but in the quest for the historical Jesus they neither generate data concerning Jesus nor solve the problem of the data's historicity. To be sure, *A Marginal Jew* works with presuppositions, but they are the presuppositions that are commonplace in historiography.

[25] The "Nicene-Constantinopolitan Creed" does not appear to have been officially adopted by Constantinople I, but the creed's general acceptance at a later date led to its being attributed *post factum* to this council. In popular usage, it is often referred to simply as the "Nicene Creed," though the actual creed adopted by Nicea I (A.D. 325) is notably shorter.

[26] The key phrases (including the words affirming the soteriological effect of Jesus' death) are in Greek *ton di'hēmas tous anthrōpous kai dia tēn hēmeteran sōtērian katelthonta ek tōn ouranōn . . . staurōthenta te hyper hēmōn epi Pontiou Pilatou kai pathonta* ("who for us human beings and for our salvation came down from heaven . . . and was crucified for us under Pontius Pilate and suffered"). A slightly expanded version of this creed is regularly used at Sunday Mass in Roman Catholic churches.

[27] For debates on the relation of the historical Jesus to Christian faith and christology, see the overview by William P. Loewe, "From the Humanity of Christ to the Historical Jesus," *TS* 61 (2000) 314–31.

[28] The arguments supporting this position are given in *A Marginal Jew*, 1. 112–66. On the dangers of retrojecting the theological views of later apocryphal Gospels back into the 1st century A.D., see John P. Meier, "On Retrojecting Later Questions from Later Texts: A Reply to Richard Bauckham," *CBQ* 59 (1997) 511–27.

[29] As is customary in discussions of the historical Jesus, words like "authentic" and "historical" are used in a technical sense to express the judgment that some saying or deed preserved in the Gospels does in fact go back to the historical Jesus. Gospel material that is judged not historical or not authentic in this technical sense may nevertheless be an important witness to the history of the early church or an important source of authentic Christian teaching.

[30] See *A Marginal Jew*, 2. 100–105.

[31] On this point, see Martin Hengel, *Crucifixion* (Philadelphia: Fortress, 1977).

[32] These claims will have to be examined and justified at some length when I take up the question of the trial(s) of Jesus.

[33] The off-again/on-again attempts to find a slain (or even a crucified) messiah at Qumran are documented and refuted by Joseph A. Fitzmyer, *The One Who Is to Come* (Grand Rapids, MI/Cambridge, UK: Eerdmans, 2007) 103–4, 109–15.

[34] On the prohibition of fasting, see *A Marginal Jew*, 2. 439–50. Some commentators hold that only discontinuity from early Christianity need be required; discontinuity from contemporary Judaism is asking too much of a truly Jewish Jesus. See, e.g., Tom Holmén, "Doubts about Double Dissimilarity. Restructuring the Main Criterion of Jesus-of-History Research," *Authenticating the Words of Jesus* (NTTS 28,1; ed. Bruce Chilton and Craig A. Evans; Leiden: Brill, 1999) 47–80; idem, *Jesus and Jewish Covenant Thinking* (Biblical Interpretation Series 55; Leiden: Brill, 2001) 28–32. While I agree that we should be suspicious of a historical Jesus who is strikingly discontinuous from the Judaism of his time and place, there are cases when the question of discontinuity from Jewish views of the time does arise as one sifts the Jesus tradition for a historical core. For example, when it comes to Jesus' prohibition of divorce, it is the early Christian church that preserves the tradition of Jesus' prohibition and tries to implement it, though with obvious difficulties that lead to adaptation and expansion of the core tradition. It is rather vis-à-vis most if not all of the Judaism of his time (depending on how one interprets the Qumran material) that Jesus seems discontinuous in his prohibition of divorce.

[35] As indicated throughout the first three volumes of *A Marginal Jew*, I hold that John's Gospel represents a tradition independent of the Synoptics. The treatments of the Passion tradition by C. H. Dodd *(Historical Tradition in the Fourth Gospel* [Cambridge: Cambridge University, 1963] 21–151) and at much greater length by Raymond E. Brown *(The Death of the Messiah* [ABRL; 2 vols.; New York: Doubleday, 1994; reprint New Haven: Yale University Press]) offer, in my view, convincing arguments in favor of this position, especially in regard to the Passion tradition. The view that John is basically independent of the Synoptics has been reexamined historically and defended exegetically by D. Moody Smith in the revised and updated version of his *John among the Gospels* (2d ed.; Columbia: University of South Carolina, 2001); see esp. pp. 195–241.

[36] Joseph Ratzinger (Benedict XVI), *Jesus von Nazareth. Erster Teil. Von der Taufe im Jordan bis zur Verklärung* (Freiburg/Basel/Vienna: Herder, 2007) 409. I take the German edition to be the *editio typica*. One should note that the English translation (*Jesus of Nazareth* [New York: Doubleday, 2007]) slightly alters the German text.

CHAPTER 31

JESUS AND THE LAW—BUT
WHAT IS THE LAW?

I. JESUS AND THE LAW: RECIPROCAL ILLUMINATION

Some scholars approach the problem of Jesus and the Law with the same naiveté with which they approach the problem of Jesus and the Pharisees. In each case, the presupposition is that we understand a known quantity, be it the Pharisees or the Mosaic Law. Therefore, the reasoning goes, we can use this known quantity to understand a lesser-known quantity, namely, the historical Jesus.

As we have seen to our sorrow in Volume Three of *A Marginal Jew*,[1] the quest for the historical Pharisee can at times prove more difficult than the quest for the historical Jesus. Indeed, alongside Josephus and the rabbinic literature, the NT, when critically sifted, is a major source for information about the Pharisees. Thus, as one searches for the historical Jesus by way of the historical Pharisee, a certain reciprocity or "chicken-and-egg" effect emerges. Each subject is illuminated by the other even as it illuminates the other.

The same holds true of the problem of Jesus and the Mosaic Law in 1st-century Palestine.[2] Taken simply as they stand, prior to any critical sifting, the four Gospels depict Jesus delivering teaching that, by turns, confirms, extends, internalizes, radicalizes, or even rescinds individual elements of the Law—all the while taking the Mosaic Torah for granted as the given, indeed, the divinely given. However we explain this puzzling situation, we naturally assume that understanding Jesus' stance vis-à-vis the Law will help us grasp how Jesus understood himself and his mission.[3] Yet the more we grapple with the question of the nature, extent, and meaning of the Torah in Palestinian Judaism around the turn of the era, the more we come to realize that the lens of the Law, which is supposed to help us see Jesus more clearly, may need some focusing of its own. Once again, the chicken-and-the-egg effect takes hold. On the one hand, the data in the Gospels, when correlated with the testimony of Philo, Josephus, and the Dead Sea Scrolls, may shed light on how the Law was understood or practiced around the time of Jesus. On the other hand, the Law, thus clarified and put into context, may shed more light on Jesus and his teaching. Actually, there is nothing new or surprising in this method of reciprocal illumination; scholars use it regularly in the study of ancient history. For instance, knowledge of the Roman empire's policy toward subject peoples helps us understand the confusing situation in 1st-century Judea. In turn, detailed investigation of the particular situation in Judea helps us understand the complexity and vagaries of the policy of the Roman empire toward subject peoples. This chicken-and-egg approach may raise questions in theory, but it works in practice.

II. THE MEANING(S) OF THE LAW:
THE OLD TESTAMENT AND INTERTESTAMENTAL JUDAISM

The best way to begin a study of Jesus and the Law is to realize how complex both the word and the reality "Law" are in the context of ancient Judaism. The problems reach all the way back to the correct etymology and the proper translation of the Hebrew noun *tôrâ*, from which we get the English noun Torah, commonly translated as "law."[4] Some scholars suggest that *tôrâ* comes from the Hebrew verb *yrh*, meaning "to throw," "to cast," or "to toss." The possible image implied here is either the tossing of lots to discern God's will or the "casting" of one's hand in the sense of indicating a direction (and thus giving instruction). This idea of *tôrâ* as an oracle from God is perhaps reflected in the Israelite prophets, who at times refer to the "word of Yahweh" that they proclaim to Israel as *tôrâ*.[5] Other scholars claim that there is a separate Hebrew verb, likewise made up of the letters *yrh*, that means "to teach" or "to instruct." In any case, etymology is no sure guide to later usage and meaning. When we look at the whole of the Jewish Scriptures, the sense of the noun *tôrâ* in Hebrew covers a range of meanings that include "instruction," "teaching," "direction," "directive," or "law," transmitted in either oral or written form.[6] Needless to say, not every occurrence of the word conveys the whole range of meanings;[7] but often, beyond the denotation of the noun, there are various connotations or resonances.

Human beings could and did issue *tôrâ* in contexts that were not strictly theological. For example, the wise man's instruction was called *tôrâ*; indeed, *tôrâ* occurs thirteen times in the Book of Proverbs (e.g., 3:1). This concept of the wise teacher imparting wise instruction (*tôrâ*) to his students

(Prov 13:14) is patterned on the more basic teaching of *tôrâ* that a father or a mother imparted at home (Prov 6:20; 31:26). The ideas of instruction, guidance, directions for living one's life are clear in this context of home and school. Here *tôrâ* does not mean the law as decreed and practiced by the elders or judges holding court in the city gate—a meaning found elsewhere.[8]

When, instead, teaching or direction came from Yahweh, usually through a priest or a prophet (Moses being something of both), the sense of *tôrâ* naturally became "divine instruction" or "a divine directive." Each individual directive from Yahweh qualified as a *tôrâ* in the singular (e.g., Lev 6:2), and so Yahweh could be said to issue various *tôrôt* in the plural (e.g., Exod 18:16).[9] This sense of individual *tôrôt* pronounced by Yahweh through a mediator preceded chronologically and conceptually the idea of a huge written corpus called *the* Torah.

Given the oral culture of the ancient Near East, individual *tôrôt* were originally passed down in oral form from one generation to the next by such authority figures as parents, clan and tribal leaders, and the elders or judges meeting in the gateway of the town or city. Once the Israelite monarchy arose, laws and directives from the king or his officials might be recorded in writing by court scribes and kept in royal archives.[10] Beyond the confines of the individual family or town, religious *tôrâ*[11] was proclaimed orally by priests in various sanctuaries, and later on in the central sanctuary (still later on, the only legitimate sanctuary) in Jerusalem, where priestly scribes may have kept written records. The priestly *tôrâ* could at times be an answer to a specific question asked by a worshiper about, for example, purity rules or the proper conditions for offering sacrifice (Hag 2:11). But the priestly *tôrâ* also included the basic narrative traditions and legal codes of the Israelite people (Deut 33:8–9; cf. Jer 18:18; Mal 2:7). Such traditions and codes may have been inculcated by the priests periodically when large crowds gathered for the annual harvest festivals.[12]

As various *tôrôt* from different streams of tradition (sapiential, prophetic, priestly, and judicial) came to be written down, literary collections of narratives and laws were gradually formed.[13] It was only natural to refer to such a collection as *tôrat yahweh*, the Law of Yahweh, that is, the instruction, teaching, direction, and commands that Yahweh addressed to his people Israel. Insofar as the archetypal instance of such instruction, according to the standard story of Israel's origins, was the revelation given to Moses on Mt. Sinai, the *tôrat yahweh* was also the *tôrat mōšeh*, the Law of Moses.

An important upshot of all this is that, from the beginning, *tôrâ* in its religious sense meant something more than what we usually mean by "law." Coming as it did from Yahweh, preeminently through Moses on Mt. Sinai, and comprising as it did both narratives and commandments (but also with elements of prophecy and wisdom), this religious *tôrâ* can be roughly translated as "divine revelation." [14] To be sure, this *tôrâ* included various legal corpora, intertwined with stories of Yahweh's choice and guidance of his people. These law codes were indeed key elements in the Torah, and their importance must not be minimized out of misguided apologetics. In certain contexts, especially within the law codes, *tôrâ* quite clearly means "law." [15] Still, "the Torah," used in the later comprehensive sense for what we call the Pentateuch, denotes something deeper and broader than what the English word "law" conveys. If, for the sake of convenience and brevity, I use "Law" as the customary translation of *tôrâ* in what follows, I ask the reader to understand "Law" in the profound sense just explained. As a reminder, the noun "Torah" will now and then be used interchangeably with "Law."

Talk of "the Torah of Moses" in the singular may have existed in the preexilic period, that is, before the Babylonian exile in the 6th century B.C. But it was only gradually, through the searing experience of exile, return from exile, and the struggle to formulate a new expression of the ancient Israelite religion, that "the Torah of Moses" came to designate in particular a set corpus of narrative and law that proved foundational for Judaism's future existence.

An important milestone is reached with the Book of Deuteronomy, whose composition probably spans the preexilic, exilic, and postexilic period.[16] Along with the "Deuteronomistic History" (the Books of Joshua, Judges, 1–2 Samuel, and 1–2 Kings) that it influenced, Deuteronomy shows a self-consciousness about a literary whole that it calls "the book of this Law" (Deut 28:61), and that the Deuteronomistic History identifies as "the book of the covenant" (2 Kgs 23:2; cf. 22:8), "the Law of God" (Josh 24:26), "the Law of Yahweh" (2 Kgs 10:31), and "all that is written in the book of the Law of Moses" (Josh 23:6).[17] Here the word *tôrâ* has clearly come to mean a written document that comes from God to Israel by the hands of Moses, a scroll in which the foundational stories and ordinances of Israel are woven into a literary whole that retains traits of prophetic and sapiential as well as legal *tôrâ*. In Deuteronomy, Moses is not only lawgiver but also prophet, wisdom teacher, and scribe. This idea of "the Law" as a written whole, which can be called interchangeably the Law of Yahweh or the Law of Moses, is continued and consolidated in 1–2 Chronicles and the Books of Ezra and Nehemiah.[18] In the late Persian period, perhaps in the 4th century B.C., the compilation of the Torah of Moses reached the huge compass that constitutes *the* Torah par excellence, what would come to be called at a later date the Five Books of Moses or, in Greek, *pentateuchos*, the Pentateuch.[19]

This fivefold form of the Torah was to become at a still later period the first and preeminent part of the Jewish canon of Scripture.[20] The Pentateuch's premier position—though not its canonical status as defined later on—is already reflected in the prologue to the Book of Jesus Ben Sira (Sirach). The deuterocanonical/apocryphal Book of Ben Sira was written in Palestine ca. 180 B.C., while Ben Sira's grandson translated the work into Greek and attached a prologue toward the end of the same century. In his prologue, the grandson speaks three times of "the Law and the prophets and the other books," which demonstrate Israel's "instruction and wisdom."[21] Indeed, by the 2d century B.C., Torah scrolls had become such a central part of the Jewish religion that, during the persecution unleashed by the Syrian king Antiochus Epiphanes, "books of the Law" were torn apart and burned, while Jews found to possess such scrolls were condemned to death (1 Macc 1:56–57).

Still, despite these references to the preeminence of the Mosaic Torah within the evolving corpus of Jewish Scripture, we are not to imagine that the Jewish canon (i.e., the normative and closed list) of sacred books was set in stone even at the time of Jesus.[22] The place of some books within the canon-in-process was still debated, though the position of the Five Books of Moses, the Torah par excellence, was relatively secure. This is not to say that the Mosaic Torah was a static entity in the early 1st century A.D. Four factors made the status of even the Pentateuch more fluid than we might imagine:

(1) Fragments of Torah manuscripts found among the Dead Sea Scrolls, when taken in conjunction with the Samaritan version of the Pentateuch and the standard Greek translation known as the Septuagint (which has its own variants), indicate that the Hebrew text of the Mosaic Law circulating in Palestine contained variant readings, though less so than some other books of Scripture, such as Jeremiah.[23] For example, some fragments of Deuteronomy (e.g., the divorce law of Deut 24:1–4) reflect a Septuagintal rather than a Masoretic form of the text. Indeed, some of the textual variants in the Dead Sea Scrolls may reflect conflict among competing interpretations of legal passages. For instance—to step outside the Pentateuch for a moment and to cite a case to be examined in the next chapter, we find in a fragment of the prophet Malachi a manipulation of the famous passage on divorce (Mal 2:16), with the result that the text, instead of deprecating divorce in certain circumstances, favors it—and this at Qumran! This fluctuation in text traditions within 1st-century Palestine has at least one important impact on the quest for the historical Jesus. It calls into question facile declarations that a particular citation of Scripture could not come

from the historical Jesus because the citation reflects the Septuagint rather than the Masoretic textual tradition.[24] So do some texts at Qumran.

(2) Various religious groups within Palestinian Judaism around the turn of the era obviously did not think that veneration for the Pentateuch excluded rewriting its stories and laws (e.g., in the *Book of Jubilees*)[25] to make them coincide with a group's own beliefs (e.g., a solar calendar) or with a group's expectations for a utopian future temple (e.g., the *Temple Scroll* found at Qumran). Whether these examples of the so-called rewritten Bible were meant to replace, stand alongside of, or merely provide the definitive interpretive framework for the five-book Torah of Moses is debated among scholars.[26]

(3) As is true of any law, especially law in the form of a succinct law code, the written Law of Moses could not possibly cover all conceivable contingencies. This became all the more true when this centuries-old body of law, itself a compilation of different and sometimes conflicting law codes, was applied to the greatly changed conditions of Palestine in the 1st century A.D. Hence, like any other long-lived legal corpus, the Mosaic Law required and generated a massive amount of ongoing and competing interpretations.[27] As we have seen in Volume Three, within Palestinian Judaism, competing interpretations of the Torah were one of the hallmarks of various 1st-century sects and movements (e.g., the Pharisees, the Sadducees, the Essenes, the Qumranites, the Samaritans, and the Jesus movement) as well as of subgroups within a given movement (e.g., the house of Hillel and the house of Shammai within Pharisaism, and possibly "the Hebrews" and "the Hellenists" within the Christian-Jewish movement housed in Jerusalem in the 30s).[28] Above and beyond the interpretations of specific sects and movements, there were no doubt, in rural Galilee and Judea, the traditions and customs of the individual towns and villages, handed down, interpreted, and applied by the elders. It may well be that, in specific cases that came before the elders, local customs determined judgments much more than learned debates over the proper interpretation of the written Torah.[29]

(4) A final factor is perhaps more difficult for us moderns to understand and hence requires more detailed discussion. Around the turn of the era, the Mosaic Law was open not only to competing interpretations of its text—interpretations both oral and written—but also to something more radical. After all, in itself, there was nothing terribly unheard of or surprising in the fact that, by the 1st century A.D., different legal interpretations as well as various legal practices that went beyond the Law competed for the allegiance of Palestinian Jews. We have seen, for example, how the Pharisees clearly distinguished between the written Torah of Moses and their own "tradi-

tions of the elders" (or "traditions of the fathers").[30] They held these traditions to be normative despite the fact that, by the Pharisees' own admission,
such traditions were not contained in the Mosaic Torah. For instance, the
Pharisees invented a legal fiction called the *erûb* (a "fusion" of boundaries)
to widen the space in which observant Jews could move around on the sabbath. The Pharisees vindicated their practice against the objections of the
Sadducees, but the Pharisees did not attempt to claim that the *erûb* existed
in or was sanctioned by the Mosaic Law.[31] None of this is very startling. Of
their nature, religious texts are open to different interpretations and applications by various people reading the same written document in an ongoing
community. Especially in the case of laws, oral and written supplements
become necessary as time goes on and life becomes more complex.

What *is* startling to us moderns is that, at times, knowledgeable 1st-
century Jews would claim that the written Law of Moses contained important commandments that, from our historical-critical perspective, simply
are not there in the text. A case in point is observance of the sabbath,[32] and
it is a case well worth tracing through the centuries.

Clearly, the Law of Moses, indeed, the Decalogue given on Mt. Sinai,
commands that all Israelites abstain from work on the sabbath (Exod 20:8–
11; cf. Deut 5:12–15). Resting from work, and not any organized assembly
for study and worship (the later synagogue), was from the beginning—and
remains—the essence of the biblical institution of the sabbath. The problem
inherent in the sabbath command is that neither the Pentateuch in particular nor the Jewish Scriptures in general give an exhaustive list of the kinds
of activities that qualify as work (*mĕlā'kâ*) and so violate the sabbath.[33] A
few cases are mentioned: for example, no plowing or harvesting in the fields
(Exod 34:21), no lighting a fire (Exod 35:3), no gathering or cooking food
(Exod 16:22–30, in the special case of the manna). But the Pentateuch never
supplies an extensive, let alone a complete, list of forbidden activities. So the
question would sooner or later arise: What kind of action qualifies as work
that violates the sabbath?

This question became more than an academic debating point when the
problem arose of whether, in wartime, Israelite soldiers could fight a battle on the sabbath.[34] Remarkably, the issue is never explicitly raised in the
Jewish Scriptures. In fact, the Scriptures often speak of extended military
campaigns without evincing the slightest concern about whether Israelites
stopped fighting once the sabbath began.[35] While an argument from silence
is always perilous, the most natural reading of the Jewish Scriptures' complete silence on the subject is that, at least in the preexilic period, battles
were fought by Israelite armies on the sabbath. Apparently, no qualms

were expressed because no problem was seen. That is certainly the case in 2 Kgs 11, when the high priest Jehoiada engineers an armed revolt against Queen Athaliah, distributes weapons to the temple guard, anoints the boy Joash the new king in the temple precincts, and has Athaliah killed outside the temple precincts—all on a single sabbath day in Jerusalem.

However, during the Maccabean revolt (beginning in 167 B.C.), some pious Jewish rebels began to see a contradiction between fighting to the death to defend the Mosaic Torah and violating that very Torah by fighting—and thus working—on the sabbath. Consequently, at least one stringently observant group refused to defend itself when attacked on the sabbath by the Syrian army of the persecutor Antiochus Epiphanes. The predictable result was a total slaughter (1 Macc 2:27–38). Appealing to common sense rather than to subtle legal reasoning, the Jewish forces following the rebel priest Mattathias decided that *self-defense* on the sabbath was permissible when Jews were attacked by Gentiles. The pragmatic tone is striking: "If all of us do as our brothers did and do not engage in battle with the Gentiles for our lives and our statutes, we shall speedily perish from the earth. . . . Every man who comes against us for battle on the sabbath, we shall fight against him. Let us not all die as did our brothers" (1 Macc 2:40–41). A key point here is that the zealous Jews fighting under Maccabean leadership to defend the Torah with their very lives (1) saw no problem in doing on the sabbath what some of their pious brethren considered a violation of the sabbath and (2) saw no need to justify their questionable actions by an appeal to particular Scripture passages or legal reasoning based on Scripture. A consensus based on common sense was sufficient.[36]

Apparently, though, this consensus was not universally shared. Shortly after the initial success of the Maccabean revolt, some pious Jews from among tradition-minded priests took umbrage at the upstart sons of Mattathias (the Hasmoneans), who though not of the high-priestly line of Zadok, took over control of the Jerusalem temple and its liturgy. We may hear the discontent of the pious dissenters echoed in the *Book of Jubilees*, written ca. 161–152 B.C.[37] Thus, it may not be purely by accident that *Jubilees* fiercely rejects a position that corresponds to the pragmatic legal ruling of the followers of Mattathias concerning war on the sabbath. Having stressed early on the tremendous holiness of the sabbath and the need for scrupulous observance of its rest (*Jub.* 2:17–33), the *Book of Jubilees* reaches its climax and conclusion in a list of prohibited actions on the sabbath (*Jub.* 50:7–12). Significantly, the very last of the prohibitions is against waging war on the sabbath (v 12).[38] Immediately after this prohibition comes the stern concluding threat from the Angel of the Presence, who is dictating this fuller enunciation of the Law to Moses from heavenly tablets (50:13): "Let the man who does any of these [works] on the day of the sabbath die so that the children of Israel might keep the sabbath according to the commands of the sabbaths of the land just as it was written in the tablets which he [the Lord] placed in my hands." [39]

In other words, a pragmatic decision about sabbath rest, made by non-Zadokite priests during a crisis, is here roundly condemned with the weightiest rhetoric imaginable for a Jew: such a compromise of the inviolable sanctity of the sabbath contradicts the primordial revelation preserved on heavenly tablets and revealed by the august Angel of the Presence to none other than Moses himself on Sinai. In the mind of the author of *Jubilees*, the Torah does deal directly with fighting on the sabbath, and it totally forbids it. The placing of this halakic cannon blast right at the end of the whole *Book of Jubilees* is most likely explained as a conscious rejection of the halakic decision of the followers of Mattathias—a decision that was based on common sense, not on the Torah of either Exodus or *Jubilees*.[40]

Heavenly tablets and the Angel of the Presence make for weighty warrants, and yet *Jubilees* apparently did not win the legal war, except perhaps in esoteric conventicles like Qumran. The view of Mattathias won out not because its supporters were better versed in halakic reasoning but because this view worked in practice, especially the practice of the later Hasmonean rulers. Still, even a pragmatic approach to the Law proved to have its limitations. When in 63 B.C. Pompey the Great besieged the supporters of the Hasmonean Aristobulus II, who were holed up in the Jerusalem temple, Pompey cagily filled in the ravine north of the temple on the sabbath while forbidding his soldiers to attack, since "on the sabbath they [the Jews] fight only to defend themselves" (so Josephus, *J.W.* 1.7.3 §146–47).[41] The whole story presupposes that Pompey (or probably his Jewish advisers) knew that only a direct attack by the Romans would justify fighting on the part of Aristobulus' soldiers. Hence Pompey used the sabbath rest to undertake the filling-in of the ravine, a necessary preliminary to his attack on the temple, but not, strictly speaking, part of the attack itself. Thus, a hundred years after Mattathias' practical decision, the troops of his descendants, even in a military crisis, were still following his *hălākâ*, though without the same practical result of victory.

Indeed, Josephus, in his explanation of Pompey's strategy, seems to say that "Jews" in general follow what in reality was simply Mattathias' *hălākâ*, rejected at the time by *Jubilees*.[42] Josephus himself is well aware of the origin of this *hălākâ* in the specific, pragmatic decision of Mattathias, as we see from Josephus' later retelling of 1 Macc 2:40–41 in *Ant.* 12.6.2 §276–77.

So what was originally (in the mid-2d century B.C.) a debatable practical decision, not based on or derived from the written Torah, is seen by the time of Aristobulus II (1st century B.C.) or at least of Josephus (1st century A.D.) to be a universally accepted interpretation or application of the Torah.[43]

This, however, is not the most startling point. What is truly astounding that, in Josephus' parallel narrative of Pompey's siege of the temple in his later *Jewish Antiquities*, Josephus states flatly that "the Law [*ho nomos*] permits [Jews on the sabbath] to defend themselves against those who begin a battle and attack them, but it does not allow [Jews] to fight their military opponents if the latter are doing anything else" (*Ant.* 14.4.2 §63). Since, as we see from his treatment of the Pharisees, Josephus knows full well how to distinguish between the written Law of Moses and various interpretations of it labeled "the traditions of the fathers," [44] he most likely means the written Law of Moses when he speaks here of *ho nomos*. This is all the more puzzling since, not long before this narrative (in *Ant.* 12.6.2 §276–77), Josephus has narrated in detail how this sabbath rule was created on the spot by Mattathias as a practical decision. Yet by *Ant.* 14.4.2 §63, it becomes "the Law." That its status as law was no mere scholarly opinion confined to a classroom is proven by the fact that Rome excused Jews from military service because of their obligation to avoid warfare on the sabbath—an obligation that the Romans obviously took to be a strict obligation binding on all Jews, and not just a debatable opinion of one school.[45]

Looking back at the whole history of this particular *hălākâ*, we have a paradigmatic instance of how a concrete practical decision, made to confront a pressing crisis (Mattathias in 167 B.C.), evolved over a century into a precept incumbent upon and generally observed by all Jews (the followers of Aristobulus II in 63 B.C.), only to be elevated a century later to the status of "the Law" (Josephus writing the *Jewish Antiquities* at the close of the 1st century A.D.). Yet the Jews at Qumran who read the Law through the lens of *Jubilees* read a very different Torah of Moses. We see that "the Law," even when it apparently means the written Law of Moses, is not an easy reality to define or pin down.[46]

Now, one might judge this equating of a relatively recent rule with "the Law" to be just a single and singular slip on the part of Josephus—if we did not find the same phenomenon elsewhere in Jewish or Jewish-Christian writers of the 1st century. But we do. Both Philo (*On the Creation of the World* [*De opificio mundi*] 43 §128; cf. *On Dreams* [*De somniis*] 2.18 §123–27; *On the Life of Moses* [*De vita Mosis*] 2.39 §211–16; *On the Special Laws* [*De specialibus legibus*] 2.15 §60–64) and Josephus (*Ag. Ap.* 2.17 §175; cf. *J.W.* 2.14.5 §289; *Ant.* 16.1.4 §43) affirm that Moses *commanded* in the *written* Law that Jews should study Torah (Philo: "to philosophize" in "prayer houses") and/or to attend synagogue (Josephus: "to come together") on the sabbath.[47] As a matter of fact, in the *Biblical Antiquities* 11:8, Pseudo-Philo goes so far as to include communal worship on the sabbath in his list of the Ten Commandments.[48] This making of synagogue attendance on the sabbath part of "the Law" is all the more surprising if one thinks, as some scholars do, that the synagogue as a widespread institution was of relatively recent vintage in the land of Israel.[49] As noted earlier, Josephus is quite aware of the distinction between the written Torah and "the traditions of the fathers" maintained by the Pharisees. It is therefore striking that he neither assigns synagogue attendance on the sabbath to these nonbiblical traditions nor attributes this commandment to the views of some special group like the Pharisees. Instead, he claims that the obligation to attend synagogue on the sabbath is contained in the Mosaic Law and is incumbent on all Jews.[50]

Likewise startling is the way in which the Gospel of Mark (in a dispute story), the Gospel of Matthew (in an isolated saying), and Josephus (in his *Jewish Antiquities*) cite or allude to the law on divorce in Deut 24:1–4. As we shall see in our next chapter (Chapter 32), the original intent of this particular and peculiar law was to treat the unusual case of a woman who is divorced by her first husband, then divorced by her second husband as well, and then tries to return to her first husband. Deut 24:1–4 (one long sentence) forbids such a marital (re-)union as an abomination. That is the original point of the law: the first husband may not remarry this twice-married woman. Only in passing, as part of the "setup" or protasis of the special case under consideration, does Deut 24:1 mention that the first husband gives his wife a document certifying that he has divorced her (and therefore that she is free to remarry without the danger of being accused of adultery). But this certificate of divorce, this *sēfer kĕrîtût*, is simply taken for granted and mentioned in passing. It is not the object of the Deuteronomic law expressed in the main clause (apodosis) of the sentence in v 4.

Intriguingly, a Marcan dispute story, a piece of special Matthean tradition (M), and Josephus agree in making the very act of giving the wife this certificate of divorce a distinct law within the Mosaic Torah. In Mark 10:3, Jesus asks the Pharisees, "What did Moses command [*eneteilato*] you?" The Pharisees answer (v 4), "Moses *allowed* [*epetrepsen*] [us] to write a document of divorce and to send [her] away." Jesus rejects their "dodge" of speaking of a "permission" by hammering home his point (v 5): "With a view to your hardness of heart he [i.e., Moses] *wrote* you *this commandment* [*tēn entolēn tautēn*]."[51] The giving of the document certifying the divorce is thus seen by the Marcan Jesus as a commandment of the written Torah.

The same is true of the M tradition that introduces the Q logion prohibiting divorce in Matt 5:31–32 (the so-called third antithesis in the Sermon on the Mount): "It was said: 'He who divorces his wife *must give* [*dotō*, 3d person singular imperative of the verb] her a certificate of divorce.' " It is important to note here that, in the first two antitheses, the phrase "it was said" (Matt 5:21, 27) introduces commandments from the Decalogue: "You shall not kill. . . . you shall not commit adultery." The third antithesis, likewise introduced by "it was said," continues with what was originally a subordinate clause in Deut 24:1, though the words are reformulated in Matt 5:31 as a distinct commandment.

Remarkably, Josephus likewise understands the reference to giving a certificate of divorce in Deut 24:1 as a distinct commandment of the Torah. Summarizing the prohibition of Deut 24:1–4, Josephus (*Ant.* 4.9.23 §253) makes two distinct commands out of the one command in Deuteronomy 24 that the twice-married wife not return to her first husband. For Josephus, the first command contained in Deut 24:1–4 is that the first husband, wishing to divorce his wife, must provide a firm attestation in writing that he will no longer have sexual relations with her (i.e., the certificate of divorce, mentioned in passing in Deut 24:1, that attests that she is free to marry another man). Only then does Josephus take up the main point of Deut 24:1–4, the command forbidding the twice-married woman to return to her first husband. Just as in Matt 5:31, the giving of the certificate of divorce is expressed by a 3d person singular imperative (*ischyrizesthō*, "he must provide firm attestation"), thus turning what was originally a dependent clause in Deut 24:1 into a separate command. This is all the more striking because Josephus begins his lengthy presentation of the Mosaic Law in Book 4 of the *Antiquities* with a strenuous affirmation that he is reproducing, without any addition, exactly what Moses bequeathed to the Jewish people (*Ant.* 4.8.4 §196–97).[52] Hence there is sufficient evidence to suggest that, in some Jewish and Jewish-Christian circles in the latter part of the 1st century A.D., the giving of the certificate of divorce had been elevated from a presupposed mechanism of divorce to the object of a specific command in the Torah.[53]

III. THE MEANING(S) OF THE LAW:
THE NEW TESTAMENT AND RABBINIC JUDAISM

We begin to see, then, that the complexity of treating the relation of Jesus to the Mosaic Law is not entirely on the side of the historical Jesus. The "historical Torah" at the time of the historical Jesus can be an enigmatic quantity as well. Thankfully, at least in the Synoptic Gospels, there is one constant meaning given to the Greek phrase *ho nomos*, "the Law."[54] In the Synoptic Gospels, and quite often in John's Gospel as well, "the Law" consistently refers to the written Pentateuch, which, when placed alongside the Prophets, makes up an implicit two-part "canon" of the Jewish Scriptures.[55] Reflecting the broad meaning of Torah that we saw in the Jewish Scriptures, *nomos* in the Gospels refers to the Law of Moses under a number of different aspects: the *nomos* contains laws that command (e.g., Matt 22:36–40), narratives that recount the origins of Israel (e.g., with "Moses" as a surrogate for "the Law," John 3:14; 6:31–32), and prophecies that point forward to Jesus (Matt 11:13). Although this restriction of *nomos* to the Pentateuch may seem to make its meaning in the Synoptic Gospels (and most of the time in John) relatively easy to handle, one must remember that the Synoptic Gospels use *nomos* to mean the Pentateuch as reinterpreted and sometimes rephrased by Jesus, as we have just seen in the case of the law on divorce in Deut 24:1–4.

Especially as interpreted by Jesus, "the Law" in the Gospels is never felt to be an oppressive burden or—as it is sometimes seen by Paul—a provisional and paradoxically providential instrument to occasion or multiply sin, so that God's grace in Christ might be revealed as all the more necessary and powerful (e.g., Gal 3:10–25; Rom 3:19–20; 5:12–21; 7:7–8:4). However much the Gospels may insist that the Law needs to be interpreted or fulfilled by Christ, the Gospels still basically understand *nomos* as the Jewish Scriptures: that is, as *tôrâ*, as God's revealed word to his people Israel.

That the Greek word *nomos* could so easily reflect the broad range of meanings contained in the Hebrew word *tôrâ* should be no cause for surprise. Not unlike *tôrâ*, the noun *nomos* had a breadth of meaning in ancient Greek to which our standard translation "law" does not do justice. In Greek, *nomos* was used in various and often overlapping contexts that included religion, civil society and law, philosophy, cosmology, and royal ideology.[56] Thus, we can easily understand why the Diaspora Jews who translated the Hebrew Scriptures into Greek chose *nomos* as the standard equivalent of *tôrâ*.[57] By no means did this choice betoken a narrowing of *tôrâ* that reduces it to a merely legal (let alone legalistic) entity. The noun *nomos* retains a breadth of meaning in the Gospels of the NT as it does in the Septuagint of the OT.

Similarly, far from descending to the supposed evils of legalism, the later rabbinic literature continued to reflect the many different dimensions of Torah. If anything, the meaning of Torah in the rabbis becomes still broader, even as it retains the underlying and unifying idea of the guidance and teaching that God gives to Israel by his revelation. In the rabbinic literature, Torah can still mean the Pentateuch, including its narrative as well as its legal sections.[58] More specifically, Torah can denote the heart of the legal corpus, the Decalogue. At the same time, Torah expands to mean the Jewish Scriptures as a whole; hence, the Psalms, the Book of Proverbs, and the Prophets can be cited as Torah.[59] If anything, the tendency of the rabbis is to use Torah in a holistic way for the whole corpus, while individual laws, referred to in the Scriptures as *tôrôt* ("laws"), are regularly referred to in rabbinic literature with words like *dîn* (literally, "judgment") or *hălākâ* (literally, "walking").

The broadening of Torah in a holistic direction is most famously reflected in a development we first see in the two Talmuds (4th–6th centuries A.D.). During the talmudic period, the rabbis elaborated a doctrine of the Dual Torah: alongside the written Torah of Moses stands the Oral Torah, also received by Moses on Mt. Sinai but handed down in oral rather than written form—until, of course, it is written down in the rabbinic corpus. As we saw in Volume Three of *A Marginal Jew*, this explicit doctrine of the Dual Torah (or the Two Torahs) is not witnessed in the documents of Judaism in the first centuries B.C. and A.D.[60] Hence it would be anachronistic to invoke the doctrine of the Dual Torah to interpret statements of Jesus about the Law that are found in the Gospels. Still, the emergence of this doctrine in the talmudic period underscores how the concept of Torah continued to evolve in rabbinic thought. Torah was anything but a static or ossified reality.

Another innovation that first appears in the rabbinic literature—but, in this case, as early as the Mishna (ca. A.D. 200–220)—is the use of the word *hălākâ* ("walking," "conduct," "behavior") to refer to a legal opinion or ruling concerning specific human conduct.[61] As far as we can tell from extant documents, the noun *hălākâ* in this technical legal sense was not in common use in the 1st century B.C. or A.D. Indeed, we cannot be absolutely sure that the noun even existed in Palestinian Judaism before A.D. 70. The two possible cases in the Qumran literature are complicated by problems in the texts, and, in any case, the sense of the noun, if present, would be the general one of "behavior" or "conduct."[62]

Nevertheless, even if the noun *hălākâ* was not in use prior to A.D. 70, the

rabbinic innovation in introducing it was purely semantic. The corresponding verb *hǎlak* ("to walk," "to go," "to come") is widely used in the OT to
signify human behavior in keeping with or contrary to the will of God as
expressed in his revelation to Israel. In the OT and later at Qumran, such
"walking" is brought into close connection with the Law.[63] Moreover, apart
from the narrow linguistic question and simply as a matter of fact, all sorts
of Jewish teachers, from Qumran's Teacher of Righteousness to the Pharisee
Hillel and the Nazarene called Jesus, were issuing such legal opinions and
rulings around the turn of the era. Hence it is common practice among modern scholars studying 1st-century Judaism to call such a legal opinion or
rule *hǎlākâ*, even though the technical sense of the word is not attested in a
document (the Mishna) until a century or two later. I will observe this scholarly convention in what follows. Jesus in effect taught *hǎlākâ*, whether or
not he or his contemporaries used that precise word for it. Moreover, while
he and no doubt other teachers taught *hǎlākâ* orally, it was also at times
written down, as *Jubilees* and the Qumran legal material demonstrate.
Hence *hǎlākâ* at the turn of the era should not be naively equated with the
latter rabbinic concept of the Oral Torah.[64]

IV. THE PROBLEM OF THE HISTORICAL JESUS
AND THE HISTORICAL LAW

From this rapid overview, we can begin to appreciate the difficulty of trying
to grasp Jesus' stance vis-à-vis the Mosaic Law. Both Jesus and the Law lie
on a trajectory moving (1) out of the still-fluid corpus of Jewish Scripture,
(2) through the competing views of various Jewish groups during what is
vaguely called "the intertestamental period," (3) into the still-future jelling
of Jewish traditions in the rabbinic literature. If the topic of "Jesus and the
Law" proves to be so enigmatic, it is at least partly because we are aiming at
two distinct moving targets.

To state the same difficulty from a different angle: one historical problem, the nature of the Mosaic Law at the turn of the era, is complicated
in our investigation by a second historical problem, the one that we face
constantly throughout *A Marginal Jew*—trying to identify the teaching of
the Jew named Jesus as it comes to us through the mouths and parchments
of early Christians. To make matters even more confusing, each of the four
evangelists has his own understanding of the Law, as do perhaps the different sources upon which he draws.[65] We must regularly remind ourselves
that the first and second generation of Christians selected, reformulated,

created, and probably deleted sayings of Jesus on the Law.[66] All these activities reflected the needs and problems of a group of Jews for Jesus as they both argued with other Jews and at the same time struggled to incorporate all-too-recently pagan Gentiles into their holy assembly of the last days, the church. It was this creative and somewhat chaotic matrix that gave birth to the various reinterpretations of Jesus' approach to the Law that we find in the four Gospels. Here, then, is the nub of the problem: we find in the Gospels not simply Jesus' interpretation of the Law but, first of all, the four evangelists' reinterpretation of Jesus' interpretation of the Law. Realizing this should make us more than a little wary of blithely quoting any and every pronouncement of Jesus on the Law that we find in the Gospels as though it must come from the historical Jesus, provided it sounds sufficiently Jewish.

A prime example of such a naive tendency is the way many exegetes of the past—and some still today—think that the Gordian knot of Jesus and the Law is easily cut by parroting the famous declaration of Matt 5:17: "Do not think that I have come to abolish the Law or the prophets. I have come not to abolish but to fulfill." [67] Alas, this apparently clear statement of principle is probably, at least in its present form, a creation of Matthew or his church. Matthew's redactional hand is clearly visible in both the wording and the placement of 5:17:[68]

(a) As for the wording of 5:17, the use of the verb "fulfill" (*plēroō*) to indicate Jesus' relation to the Law and the prophets is a clear indicator of Matthew's own hand.[69] It echoes Matthew's theme song of fulfillment of prophecy in the various events of Jesus' life, so well expressed in his famous formulas of introduction to citations of OT prophecy (the so-called *Reflexionszitate*): "Now all this came to pass that what was spoken by the prophet might be *fulfilled*, saying. . . ." [70] Indeed, twelve out of the sixteen occurrences of the verb in Matthew's Gospel are found in these formulas of fulfillment introducing or alluding to OT texts.[71] The other four occurrences of the verb in Matthew all have some connection with prophets, eschatological fullness, or the consummation at the end of this age (a favorite Matthean theme).[72] Using the key verb "fulfill" to summarize the whole purpose of Jesus' mission ("I have come . . .") thus fits Matthew's theology perfectly.

It also suits his christology perfectly. Notice how Jesus alone *fulfills* the Law (5:17). In contrast, in 5:19, as elsewhere in Matthew, ordinary human beings "do (*poieō*)," "keep (*tēreō*)," or "observe (*phylassō*)" the Law.[73] Interestingly, the direct statement in the active voice that Jesus *fulfills* the Law and/or the prophets is unique to Matthew within the NT; it sums up perfectly his fulfillment christology.[74] In fact, nowhere else in the NT does Jesus, speaking in the first person and the active voice, ever say that he "fulfills" anything. Other indications of Matthew's redactional hand include the introductory "Do not think that" before the main part of the christological statement, "I have come. . . ." Within the NT, only Matthew prefixes "do not think" (*mē nomisēte*) to this type of christological statement of mission (here and in 10:34).[75]

As for the placement of 5:17, Matthew carefully positions this programmatic verse to make it the introduction to and summary of the six pronouncements on the Law (the "six antitheses") that follow in vv 21–48 ("You have heard that it was said to the men of old . . . but I say to you").[76] In 5:17–48, the evangelist has created his own unique Christian catechism on Jesus and the Law as the first major part of the Sermon on the Mount (chaps. 5–7), a still larger literary structure built by the theological architect we call Matthew.[77] The glaring fact that 5:17–48, taken as a unit, is a redactional formulation of this evangelist, writing ca. A.D. 85, has not kept a long line of scholars from quoting this Christian catechism in whole or in part as though it were a tape recording of how the historical Jesus instructed his fellow Palestinian Jews on the Law somewhere around A.D. 28.

Actually, one can readily see why otherwise critically minded scholars have uncritically embraced Matt 5:17–48 as the key to understanding the historical Jesus' view of the Law. Provided not too many penetrating questions are addressed to it, Matt 5:17–48 smoothly unlocks—or so it seems—the intimidating enigma of Jesus and the Law. We may then safely move on to other questions. If instead—to change the metaphor—we start tugging critically at the loose threads hanging from Matt 5:17–48, the whole garment soon unravels into disparate strands of yarn. Some of the strands may indeed go back to the historical Jesus, but the not-quite-seamless garment of Matt 5:17–48, so prized by critics, goes back to Matthew's loom. Thus, the artistic and literary whole of 5:17–48 tells us much more about the theology of a Christian evangelist in the second half of the 1st century than it does about the teaching of a Jew named Jesus in the first half of the 1st century. The reader must pardon me if I keep harping on this point, but it never ceases to amaze me that scholars who should know better keep citing Matt 5:17–48 as the magic mantra that solves the enigma of Jesus and the Law. It doesn't. For anyone questing for the historical Jesus, Matt 5:17–48 does not offer a solution; it poses a problem.

I highlight Matt 5:17–48 because it is an extreme example of what we regularly face as we probe the Christian Gospels for material about the Jewish Jesus and the Jewish Law. The evangelists, or the traditions before them, have drawn together various sayings of Jesus on the Law, plus various sayings of early Christians that were placed on the lips of Jesus. From these meshed materials, the Gospel writers composed mini-catechisms of moral instruction. In a sense, the task of a quester for the historical Jesus is to undo what the evangelists did. We must first dissolve these complex Christian compositions into their original building blocks, the small original units of sayings that have been secondarily joined together.[78] Then we must try to discern what may have been the original wording of a saying, or at least the most primitive wording of a saying available to us.[79] Only after that can we apply the criteria of historicity to decide whether this saying, in substance if not in exact wording, goes back in all probability to the historical Jesus. Finally, we must try to understand what this teaching might have meant in the mouth of one Palestinian Jew instructing other Palestinian Jews about the Mosaic Law, as distinct from the meaning(s) the teaching might have acquired later on when it was used by one Christian to teach other Christians about Christian morality.

As long as I am insisting on distinctions to be made in any treatment of Jesus and the Law, I should also mention another type of a dichotomy or antithesis that is best avoided. All too often in the past, Christian questers for the historical Jesus have created an opposition between the "ritual," "cultic," or "legal" elements in the Law on the one hand and the "moral" or "ethical" elements on the other. One can see the problem immediately.[80] This sort of distinction usually carries with it implicit value judgments that owe more to the European Enlightenment of the 18th century and American individualism of the 21st century than to Jewish views on the Law in 1st-century Palestine. To many modern minds, as they evaluate matters religious and spiritual, what is external, ritual, ceremonial, public, legal, or institutional is of little importance, is easily dispensed with, or is downright dangerous and to be avoided. In contrast, what is internal, private, personal, spontaneous, emotional, or unstructured belongs to true religion or spirituality, and it is in this sphere that true morality is to be found.[81]

That is, to say the least, to load the dice. A modern scholar afflicted with such a typically modern moral squint can hardly hope to understand and evaluate fairly a religion like Palestinian Judaism at the turn of the era. Of its very nature, Palestinian Judaism understood itself to be a religion based on a covenant between its God and the *people* of Israel (not isolated individuals in a neo-Platonic flight of the alone to the alone), a religion that was lived and practiced by a visible community, a religion that preserved this community's identity and holiness as God's people by observing the clear boundaries of purity rules, a religion that insisted that commitment of the heart had to be embodied in commitment to right actions toward one's neighbors in the community, and a religion that embodied its people-centered consciousness by regular pilgrimages to the Jerusalem temple for communal worship.[82] Modern American monads who prefer to play off private spirituality against institutional religion should not even try to grasp Palestinian Judaism of the pre-70 period.

To be sure, great prophets and teachers from Amos and Isaiah through Jeremiah and the Psalmists to Jesus and the rabbis stressed the indispensable priority of purity of heart, sincere intention, justice, and mercy in all religion and morality. The prophets railed against endless public sacrifices and ritual observances that were an abomination to Yahweh because they were not accompanied and enlivened by an inner spirit of obedience, humility, and love as well as by exterior actions of justice and mercy. However, one must be careful here. We moderns can easily be led astray by the fiery rhetoric of the prophets who engaged in what scholars of Semitic languages call "dialectical negation."[83] For instance, the prophet Hosea uses dialectical negation when he cries out against a populace more eager for ritual sacrifices in the temple than for the sacrifice of oneself to help one's neighbor (Hos 6:6): "I desire mercy and not sacrifice."[84] A modern reader might easily take this to mean that Hosea simply rejects any and all temple sacrifice—and, by extension, any formal public worship—and reduces all religion to inner sincerity, merciful action, and social justice.

Such an interpretation misses the thrust of Hosea's dialectical negation. Since ancient Hebrew does not have the comparative forms for adjectives and adverbs, comparisons and degrees of difference must be expressed in other ways. In highly rhetorical contexts, an ancient Hebrew comparison can easily sound to modern ears like a mutually exclusive opposition. Hosea is a prime example of this. His cry, "I desire mercy and not sacrifice," is not an absolute but a relative statement, expressing priorities in a comparison. The sense is, "I prefer mercy to sacrifice," "mercy is much more important to me than sacrifice," "a sacrifice not seasoned with mercy is unacceptable to me." What is being protested by Hosea is the divorce of public worship from social and personal morality, not the very existence of public worship. Indeed, for the religious and cultural world of the ancient Near East, a private religion of personal spirituality that had no visible, public, communal, ritual expression was almost unthinkable. For the ancient Near East, human beings were not Platonic souls entombed for a while in bodies; human beings were bodies enlivened by a vital force having a mind, will, and emotions. A religion that remained locked up in the inner recesses of the psyche, a religion that had no bodily expression in visible and communal actions, was quite literally non-sense.

Even when this insight is acknowledged as applying to ancient Israelite religion in general, a tacit exception seems often to be made by scholars in the case of Jesus of Nazareth. Suddenly leaping out of his own time and place into the modern age, Jesus becomes the paragon of Enlightenment religion, the private and the interior triumphing over the public and the ritual, morality replacing rather than ensouling liturgy. Thomas Jefferson manufactured such an Enlightenment Jesus in his censored version of the Gospels, which omitted as much as possible the supernatural and the miraculous to highlight Jesus as the great teacher of universal morality.[85]

Closer to our own time, the Jesus Seminar in its heyday plucked Jesus out of his Palestinian-Jewish matrix to make of him a wandering Cynic philosopher in the Greco-Roman mold.[86] This Cynic philosopher could thus act as the surrogate of the modern critic: a nominally Jewish Jesus is depicted as opposing and subverting the Jerusalem temple, the sacrificial system, the purity rules, and all the other religious boundaries that made ancient Judaism ancient Judaism. Thus, the modern scholar could pay due deference to historical research and the social sciences while in effect de-Judaizing Jesus. Annoying little points like the fact that Cynicism was largely an urban phenomenon and that it had gone into eclipse, if not totally disappeared, from Greco-Roman cities during the time of a rural Galilean named Jesus were conveniently ignored.[87] Thus we regain our Enlightenment Jesus courtesy of ancient Cynicism, provided not too many probing questions are asked.

To sum up: an implicitly hostile opposition between the "cultic," "ritual," or "purely legal" elements of the Mosaic Law on the one hand and the "truly moral" or "ethical" elements on the other would have been alien to the mind-set of the ordinary Palestinian Jew of Jesus' day. For such a Jew, what was "moral" (if we may use that term) was to do God's will and to walk in his ways as laid out in the Torah God had given to Israel. Doing God's will applied to all areas of one's life, in and out of the temple, in and out of the marketplace, in and out of an office for paying customs on transported goods. To be sure, Jews knew which parts of the Law applied to visits to the temple, to observance of food laws in daily life, and to honest dealings with business associates. As we shall see, there is a basis for distinguishing various kinds of purity rules ("ritual," "moral," or "genealogical") within the Law. But ancient Jews saw no opposition between a type of behavior that was "purely ritual" (and hence to be considered of little value) and a type of behavior that was "purely moral" (and hence to be highly valued in the eyes of God).

As a matter of fact, not only was a clear-cut distinction between "ritual" and "moral" unintelligible to an ordinary Palestinian Jew of the 1st century, it should also be unacceptable to a 21st-century historian trying to grasp 1st-century Jewish law and practice on their own terms. In the Mosaic Torah, the elements that we label "ritual" and "moral" are often welded together in a single law or observance. For example, the supposedly "cultic" law of the sabbath rest had within itself an inherent ethical and humanistic dimension—as was noted in the OT—because it pointedly extended to servants who worked for a wealthy Jewish householder the rest that the householder himself enjoyed. Despite their lowly status, servants *had a right to share* in the householder's rest from work, not by his personal beneficence, which might be withdrawn as arbitrarily as it was given, but by the force of the Torah, which both householder and servant had to obey (Exod 20:8–11; Deut 5:12–15). The tithes paid by Jews not only supported the temple and its functionaries; they also provided a festive meal for one's extended family, including the poor and marginalized of society (Deut 14:24–27). Certain temple sacrifices were part and parcel of the process by which Israelites who had, whether consciously or inadvertently, disrupted their relationship with God and God's people, not only were brought back into a proper relationship with God but also were reintegrated into the holy community of Israel (see, e.g., Lev 4:1–6:7 [4:1–5:26 in the MT]). In particular, when one Israelite defrauded or robbed another Israelite, he had to restore to the injured party what was taken and add to it a fifth of its value in reparation *on the day* he presented his guilt offering in the temple (Lev 6:5 [5:24 in the MT]). What is striking here is how the act that does justice to one's injured neighbor is integrated into the act of confessing and atoning for one's guilt before God in the offering of a cultic sacrifice.

None of this is meant to deny that a good deal of Jesus' teaching on the Law and human behavior focuses on what we today would label as "moral" rather than "ritual" or "cultic" concerns. One might even suggest that there is an implicit dynamic in the thrust of Jesus' teaching, in the topics he chooses and the values he emphasizes, that can and did bear fruit in later religious thought—just as there is an implicit distinction in the Torah between cultic and moral purity, though such precise labels are not used. But we must constantly remind ourselves, as we examine the teaching of Jesus on the Law, that the neat modern way of distinguishing between ritual and moral instruction (with an implicit denigration of the former) was not the way a 1st-century Palestinian Jew would have spontaneously thought of such matters.

It is now time for us to turn to this instruction of Jesus, which—from our point of view—contains both ritual and ethical elements intertwined. As we have already noted when discussing Matt 5:17–48, no ordered catechism on human behavior can be traced back to the historical Jesus. Accordingly, we have no right to presuppose before examining the data that there is one organizing principle (e.g., the love commandment) that pervades all the teachings of Jesus. Hence we have no right to import such a principle a priori into the disparate, not to say scattered, sayings of Jesus on the Law. If some organizing principle emerges effortlessly along the way of our investigation, well and good. But it is safer to proceed step-by-step with individual topics or questions that Jesus treated in his teaching before we try to intuit some grand unifying principle undergirding the various units of tradition. It is not by accident that the chapter on Jesus' love commandments (Chapter 36) stands last in this volume.

Inevitably, then, the order in which we treat these units of Jesus' teaching will be somewhat arbitrary. I choose to begin with sayings (i) that treat major legal issues that had practical impact on the lives of ordinary Jews and (ii) that enjoy multiple attestation of independent sources in the NT. From this relatively firm starting point, we can move on in due course to matters that seem more isolated or have only spotty attestation. Admittedly, we cannot be certain that multiple attestation of a topic or the lack thereof in our Gospels accurately reflects the emphasis and frequency of certain types of teaching in the ministry of the historical Jesus. As in life so in the quest for the historical Jesus, we must play the hand we are dealt.

NOTES TO CHAPTER 31

[1] *A Marginal Jew*, 3. 289–388; see also John P. Meier, "The Quest for the Historical Pharisee," *CBQ* 61 (1999) 713–22.

[2] For a salutary reminder about the many difficulties that questers for the historical Jesus face when treating the relation of Jesus to the Law, see the programmatic essay of Karlheinz Müller, "Gesetz und Gesetzeserfüllung im Frühjudentum," *Das Gesetz im Neuen Testament* (QD 108; ed. Karl Kertelge; Freiburg/Basel/Vienna: Herder, 1986) 11–27. Unfortunately, within the same volume, Franz Mussner shows a lack of the critical sense that Müller seeks to inculcate; see Franz Mussner, "Das Toraleben im jüdischen Verständnis," ibid., 28–45. This lack of a critical approach is all the more regrettable since Mussner writes with the laudable desire to overcome Christian caricatures of the Law. We are reminded that good intentions do not guarantee good method or good scholarship. Fortunately, the other essays in this volume do evince a use of critical method. Most of them take the view that the historical Jesus lived as a Jew obedient to the Law and never broke with it; so, with varying emphases, Gerhard Dautzenberg, "Gesetzeskritik und Gesetzesgehorsam in der Jesustradition," ibid., 46–70; Peter Fiedler, "Die Tora bei Jesus und in der Jesusüberlieferung," ibid., 71–87; Alfons Weiser, "Zur Gesetzes- und Tempelkritik der 'Hellenisten,' " ibid., 146–68. Over against these views is that of Jan Lambrecht, "Gesetzesverständnis bei Paulus," ibid., 88–127; he holds (p. 90) that on various oc-

casions Jesus adopted positions that were not only anti- *hălākâ* but even anti-Torah. In this Lambrecht upholds the views he espoused in his earlier "Jesus and the Law," 24–79 (cited in my Introduction). For a notably different approach to the problem of Jesus and the Law, see Klaus Berger, *Die Gesetzesauslegung Jesu. Ihr historischer Hintergrund im Judentum und im Alten Testament. Teil I: Markus und Parallelen* (WMANT 40; Neukirchen-Vluyn: Neukirchener Verlag, 1972). Berger's work shows great erudition in its knowledge of a vast range of Jewish and Christian material; however, the meshing of texts that belong to different centuries and theological tendencies in order to create hypothetical streams of tradition history results in a highly speculative construct. At times the plain meaning of a text seems to be sacrificed for the sake of the grand model into which it is being inserted. For the still larger question of the Jewish Law in relation to various writings of the NT and the apocrypha (with a predominant focus on the Pauline books), see Dieter Sänger and Matthias Konradt (eds.), *Das Gesetz im frühen Judentum und im Neuen Testament* (Novum Testament et Orbis Antiquus/SUNT 57; Christoph Burchard Festschrift; Göttingen: Vandenhoeck & Ruprecht; Fribourg: Academic Press, 2006). Prescinding from critical research on the historical Jesus in favor of a synchronic comparison between Jesus (the persona presented in the Gospels, not the historical individual), Paul, and the early church on the one hand and the Talmud on the other is Chaim Saiman, "Jesus' Legal Theory—A Rabbinic Reading," *Journal of Law and Religion* 23 (2007–08) 97–130. Such an approach, while intriguing, necessarily operates on a high level of abstraction and must ignore the different portraits of Jesus in the different Gospels as well as the shifting views of Paul on the Law in his various epistles—to say nothing of conflating the views of Jesus and Paul.

³ As indicated in the Introduction, "the Law," when used absolutely and with an uppercase "L," means the Mosaic Law. This convention will save me from having to repeat "the Mosaic Law" or "the Law of Moses" every time the Law is mentioned. When "law" is used with a lowercase "l," it means a particular law or the abstract concept of law.

⁴ For general orientation and bibliography on this question and other problems relating to the concept and vocabulary of law in the OT and NT, see H. Kleinknecht and W. Gutbrod, "*nomos*, etc.," *TDNT* 4 (1967) 1022–91; S. Wagner, "*yārâ*," *TDOT* 6 (1990) 330–47; F. García López, "*tôrāh*," *TWAT* 8 (1994) cols. 597–637. Wagner distinguishes three verbs with the root *yrh*: verb I means "to throw," "to shoot [arrows]"; verb II means "to rain"; verb III means "to teach," "to instruct." If one accepts that this distinct third root existed (not all scholars do), then it is the obvious source of the noun *tôrâ*; so Wagner, "*yārâ*,"339. For general surveys on law in the ancient Near East, the OT, early Judaism, and the NT, see Samuel Greengus, Rifat Sonsino, and E. P. Sanders, "Law," *AYBD*, 4. 242–65. See also Paul Heger, "Source of Law in the Biblical and Mesopotamian Law Collections," *Bib* 86 (2005) 324–42.

⁵ See, e.g., Isa 1:10; 2:3; Jer 6:19; 26:4–5; Mic 4:2. This parallelism between Torah and the word of Yahweh is proper to the prophetic tradition of the OT. For

example, on the meaning of *tôrâ* in Isaiah, see Joseph Jensen, *The Use of* tôrâ *by Isaiah* (CBQMS 3; Washington, DC: Catholic Biblical Association of America, 1973).

[6] Taken as a single work, the Book of Psalms admirably reflects this wide range of meanings.

[7] For a critique of some simplistic approaches to the meaning of *tôrâ*, see Stephen Westerholm, "Torah, *nomos*, and law: A question of 'meaning,' " *SR* 15 (1986) 327–36.

[8] A more legal as well as theological tone seems to be present in Prov 28:4,7,9; 29:18, which may belong to the latest stratum of Proverbs; on this, see García López, "*tôrāh*," cols. 623–24.

[9] From the beginning, there is a tendency to favor the singular noun, a fact that prepares the way for the adoption of the word in the singular to designate the literary corpus that expresses the totality of God's will, *the* Torah. Of the 220 occurrences in the MT, 208 are in the singular, only twelve are in the plural.

[10] The existence and precise function of scribal schools active around the palace and/or the temple during the monarchical period are still debated among scholars; see Ben Witherington III, *Jesus the Sage. The Pilgrimage of Wisdom* (Minneapolis: Fortress, 1994) 5–6 (with the bibliography cited in the notes). For the wider question of the *Sitz im Leben* of various legal forms, see Sonsino, "Law," 253–54.

[11] As I will stress later in this chapter, religious *tôrôt* in ancient Israel encompassed what the modern mind would distinguish as either cultic or moral matters. Note the claim of Gutbrod ("*nomos*, etc.," 1045) that "the oldest literary sources . . . show that administration of the Torah was the special task of the priest." For a more nuanced view of priestly teaching of *tôrâ*, see Aelred Cody, *A History of Old Testament Priesthood* (AnBib 35; Rome: Biblical Institute, 1969) 114–19.

[12] In the Priestly strand of the Pentateuch, the emphasis (though not the entire focus) is on what we would label as the cultic, ritual character of the *tôrâ*, while Deuteronomy and those works influenced by it broaden the teaching role of priests and levites beyond the cultic. This broader idea is reflected in prophetic passages like Hos 4:4–6; Jer 2:8.

[13] The writing down of prophetic *tôrâ* is described in Isa 8:16–22; on this text, see Joseph Blenkinsopp, *Isaiah 1–39* (AYB 19; New York: Doubleday, 2000; reprint New Haven: Yale University Press) 242–45.

[14] Sanders ("Law," 254) begins his treatment of the Law in Judaism and the NT period with the flat assertion: "Most generally, 'law' meant 'divine revelation.' " This includes not just commandments but the whole story of God's gracious deliver-

ance of and dealings with his people Israel. Taking a slightly different tack, Joseph Blenkinsopp (*The Pentateuch* [AYBRL; New York: Doubleday, 1992; reprint New Haven: Yale University Press] 31) affirms that "though the basic meaning of *tôrāh* is 'instruction' or 'law,' the Pentateuch or Torah is first and foremost a narrative."

[15] See Westerholm, "*Torah*," 333–34.

[16] Blenkinsopp (*The Pentateuch*, 2) affirms that "the close association between Moses and the law" is "first clearly and consistently attested in Deuteronomy" and that it became "commonplace during the Second Temple period."

[17] These references to "the Law" may originally have referred to a more primitive form of Deuteronomy that was supposedly "discovered" by the high priest Hilkiah and given to the pious king Josiah, who, in response to the "discovery," unleashed his reform of the temple cult (2 Kgs 22:3–23:25). Be that as it may (and the historicity of the Hilkiah story is debated among exegetes), Jesus and his contemporaries in the 1st century A.D., without the historical-critical sensibility that we bring to the text today, would have understood phrases like "the book of this Law" as referring to Deuteronomy in particular and the Five Books of Moses in general.

[18] Interestingly, the use of *tôrâ* in the singular to refer to an individual rule governing cultic practice is still seen in this corpus of works, a fact that probably indicates the priestly context in which these works were written and/or redacted. The "Chronicler" (the academic label used to designate the redactor of these works) has synthesized the tendencies of both the deuteronomistic and priestly strands of thought within the Pentateuch. It may indeed be that the Chronicler knew some form of the written Pentateuch, though not necessarily the final form we have. On this, see García López, "*tôrāh*," cols. 629–30. While the priestly strand of the Pentateuch may emphasize more the cultic or liturgical elements in the Torah, one must not caricature the priestly tradition as simply "legalistic" or "ritualistic." Gutbrod ("*nomos*, etc.," 1043) rightly emphasizes that the priestly understanding of the Law "does not exclude profound joy, humble and reverent worship, or selfless self-giving. . . . In this respect it corresponds to the tenor of the Law psalms. . . . P is thus very far from what is usually called legalism or nomism."

[19] The date of the redaction of what we call the Pentateuch is still debated among scholars. Helmut Koester (*Introduction to the New Testament* [Hermeneia Foundations and Facets; 2 vols.; Berlin/New York: de Gruyter; Philadelphia: Fortress, 1982] 1. 228) reflects the view of many that "the final redaction of the Pentateuch was completed in the decades before the Hellenistic conquest" and hence in the 4th century B.C. More conservative scholars have championed a date in the 6th or 5th century B.C. In any case, as can be seen from the Dead Sea Scrolls, variations in the Hebrew text of the Pentateuch continued to exist even after its so-called final redaction. The Dead Sea Scrolls also reveal an interesting point about our somewhat anachronistic terminology: sometimes a number of the "books" of what we call the

Pentateuch were copied on a single scroll. This is a good reminder that the Palestinian Jews at the time of Jesus did not necessarily use the phrase "the Five Books of Moses" (or, obviously, "the Pentateuch," i.e., the five containers holding the five scrolls of the Law) as a fixed locution for the Torah of Moses. However, the idea that the Mosaic Torah comprised exactly five books was not unknown in the 1st century A.D., since Josephus (who spent the first part of his life in pre-70 Palestine), states flatly in his work *Against Apion* (written toward the end of the 1st century A.D.): "Of these [twenty-two books of the Jewish Scriptures], five are the [books] of Moses, which contain both the laws and the [historical] tradition from human origins down to his [Moses'] death" (*Ag. Ap.* 1.39). Slightly earlier, Philo, representing Alexandrian Judaism, affirms in his work *On the Eternity of the World*: "The Lawgiver of the Jews, Moses, said in the sacred books that the world has come into being and is incorruptible; they [the sacred books] are five, the first of which he [Moses] entitled Genesis" (*De aeternitate mundi* 19). It is legitimate, therefore, for us to use terms like "the Five Books of Moses" and "the Pentateuch," since (1) the realities they designate obviously did exist in 1st-century Palestine and (2) at least some 1st-century Jews spoke of the books of Moses as being five, even though the set phrase "the Five Books of Moses" may not have been the common formula for designating the collection in pre-70 Palestine. Even in regard to this last point, though, we cannot be absolutely certain, since in a Qumran fragment (1Q30, possibly a liturgical text), we find the Hebrew phrase *kwl . . . [s]prym ḥwmšym*. Florentino García Martínez and Eibert J. C. Tigchelaar (*The Dead Sea Scrolls Study Edition* [2 vols.; Leiden: Brill, 1997, 1998] 1. 110–11) translate this disputed phrase as "all [. . .] [. . . boo]ks, divided into five." In the original DJD edition (Dominique Barthélemy and Józef T. Milik [eds.], *Qumran Cave I* [DJD 1; Oxford: Clarendon, 1955] 132–33) Barthélemy suggests that the reference might be to the Pentateuch or more likely the Psalter. Blenkinsopp (*The Pentateuch*, 44) thinks it would be surprising to find a reference to a fivefold division of the Book of Psalms so early on. Even if the reference were to the Psalms, it would presuppose a prior fivefold division of the Mosaic Torah, which the fivefold division of the Psalter reflects and imitates. In later rabbinic Hebrew, the noun *ḥômeš* can mean one of the five books of the Torah or the Psalter, and the plural of the noun can refer to the Five Books of Moses. However, as Blenkinsopp goes on to observe, the reading of the Qumran fragment is "not entirely secure" and so "too much weight should not be placed on it." The reader will notice that, in this rapid survey of the development of the Torah of Moses, I do not enter into present-day debates concerning the existence of supposed literary sources of the Pentateuch, traditionally labeled J, E, D, and P (following Julius Wellhausen) and the successive stages of their redaction. Such ideas were, of course, completely unknown to, indeed, alien to the mind-set of Jesus and his contemporaries, who knew only the fully formed books of Moses and thought of them as one work, coming from God through Moses. Moreover, the documentary hypothesis of Wellhausen is very much under attack from various alternate schools of exegesis today; see Blenkinsopp, *The Pentateuch*, 12–28. The whole point of this brief historical sketch in Chapter 31 is to help the reader understand the development and especially the complexity of the concept and terminology of Torah, not to import our historical-critical mind-set into the minds of 1st-century Palestinian Jews. For example, it is significant for the modern exegete who accepts the traditional JEDP theory of Well-hausen that apparently in the J tradition (and in most if not all of the E tradition as well) the word *tôrâ* is lacking. Such a datum, however, is of no significance if one is investigating the understanding of the Torah among 1st-century Palestinian Jews.

[20] For an approach to the growth of the canon of Jewish Scriptures that questions the Mosaic Torah as the first and preeminent part of the canon, see Stephen B. Chapman, *The Law and the Prophets* (Forschungen zum Alten Testament 27; Tübingen: Mohr [Siebeck] 2000). While this study contains many healthy correctives to the excesses of traditional views of the growth of the canon, it is also strongly influenced by its own theological agenda as well as by the canonical criticism developed by B. S. Childs.

[21] *Prologue*, v 1 (*tou nomou kai tōn prophētōn kai tōn allōn* . . . ["the Law, and the prophets, and the other (books)"]), vv 9–10 (*tou nomou kai tōn prophētōn kai tōn allōn patriōn bibliōn* ["the Law and the prophets and the other ancestral books"]), and v 24 (*ho nomos kai hai prophēteiai kai ta loipa tōn bibliōn* ["the Law and the prophecies and the rest of the books"]). While I think these phrases, occurring three times within a short composition, argue for at least a vague notion of a three-part canon (though hardly with a clear sense of which works belong to the category of "the other ancestral books"), one should take seriously the salutary caution voiced by Eugene Ulrich, "The Non-attestation of a Tripartite Canon in 4QMMT," *CBQ* 65 (2003) 202–14, esp. 212–13. Ulrich's major concern in this article is to question the claim that a three-part canon is witnessed in a reconstructed passage in the composite text of 4QMMT. He goes on to argue (p. 214) that the references to sacred books in the *Prologue* of Ben Sira are open to "either a tripartite or a bipartite understanding" and that the bipartite interpretation is "arguably preferable." While I agree with his views on 4QMMT, I am not convinced by his reading of the *Prologue*.

In any event, the two-part canon is the standard view around the turn of the era, including almost all references in the NT. Indeed, in some of the later OT prophetic books there may already be intimations of a two-part canon of "the Law and the prophets," which is the usual way in which the Jewish Scriptures are referred to in the NT. See, e.g., Zech 7:12: "the *Law* [*hattôrâ*] and the words which Yahweh of hosts sent by his spirit through the former *prophets*." With a bit of imagination, one might also see such an intimation in Mal 3:22–24 (in English translations, Mal 4:4–6). First we hear a reference to "the Torah of Moses": "Remember the teaching of Moses [*tôrat mōšeh*] my servant, which I commanded him at Horeb for all Israel, statutes and judgments." Immediately joined to that is a reference to the eschatological prophet Elijah: "Behold I am sending you Elijah the *prophet*." Later on, with a more explicit reference to a two-part division, Judas Maccabeus exhorts his troops by appealing to "the Law and the prophets" (*tou nomou kai tōn prophētōn*) in 2 Macc 15:9. Here *nomos* can hardly mean anything other than the Pentateuch. Ulrich (ibid., 213) rightly disputes any attempt to see a reference to a tripartite canon in the rambling statement in 2 Macc 2:13–14 that mentions "the records," "the memoirs of Nehemiah," "the books concerning the kings and prophets, and the [books] of David, and epistles of kings concerning votive offerings," and "all the books that had been lost." While Luke 24:44 ("all the things written in the Law of Moses and the prophets and psalms concerning me") is often cited as an isolated example in the NT of a three-part canon, Ulrich (ibid., 214) argues that this passage as well should be understood in reference to a two-part canon, the Book of Psalms being a preeminently prophetic book for NT authors. One should note that, at the very least, Ulrich has Luke's placement of the definite articles in 24:44 on his side: *panta ta gegrammena en tō nomō Mōyseōs kai tois prophētais kai psalmois peri emou* (with definite articles before "Law of Moses" and "prophets" but none before "psalms").

[22] Whether one can even speak of the finalization of the Jewish canon of Scripture at the so-called Council of Jamnia or Yavneh (a problematic entity in itself) is increasingly questioned by scholars today; see, e.g., Jack P. Lewis, "Jamnia after Forty Years," *HUCA* 70–71 (1999–2000) 233–59; see also David E. Aune, "The Origins of the 'Council of Jamnia' Myth," *JBL* 110 (1991) 491–93.

[23] As was noted earlier, even after the pivotal event of the compilation of the Pentateuch, various forms of its text circulated in Palestine in the pre-Christian period. One form ultimately resulted in the Masoretic Text, while another form was the source of the translation into Greek that is called the Septuagint (in Alexandria in the 3d century B.C.). A third form was preserved by the Samaritans. Even in regard to the proto-Masoretic Text of the Mosaic Torah, minor changes were probably made after what scholars call "the final redaction." Small variations are visible in basically proto-Masoretic texts of the Pentateuch from Qumran, Masada, and Wadi Murabba'at; see the texts in Martin Abegg, Jr., Peter Flint, and Eugene Ulrich (eds.), *The Dead Sea Scrolls Bible* (San Francisco: Harper, 1999) 3–195. In a few manuscripts, departures from the proto-Masoretic text of the Pentateuch are notable (e.g., 4QNum[b] and 4QDeut[q]). For a good treatment of the fluidity of the biblical texts found at Qumran, see Eugene Ulrich, *The Dead Sea Scrolls and the Origins of the Bible* (Grand Rapids, MI/Cambridge, UK: Eerdmans; Leiden/Boston/Cologne: Brill, 1999); see in particular Chapter 5, "Pluriformity in the Biblical Text, Text Groups, and Questions of Canon," 79–98.

[24] That the modification of biblical texts because of theological arguments among various groups may be reflected in some of the NT citations of the OT is argued by Rick Van De Water, " 'Removing the Boundary' (Hosea 5:10) in First-Century Palestine," *CBQ* 63 (2001) 619–29.

[25] For the problem of the relation of the written Mosaic Pentateuch to the content of *Jubilees*, purportedly dictated to Moses by the Angel of the Presence, see Cana Werman, " 'The *twrh* and the *t'wdh*' Engraved on the Tablets," *Dead Sea Discoveries* 9 (2002) 75–103.

[26] The phrase "rewritten Bible" has become common in discussions about the intertestamental writings that, in one way or another, reworked, paraphrased, or added to books that later formed the canon of Scripture. However, the phrase is, technically speaking, inaccurate since no "Bible" with an agreed-upon list of all the books accepted as inspired and normative existed in the first centuries B.C.; hence there was no Bible to "rewrite." On the problem of evaluating the intent of authors of the "rewritten Bible" during the intertestamental period, see Gary A. Anderson, "Law and Lawgiving," *Encyclopedia of the Dead Sea Scrolls* (2 vols.; ed. Lawrence H. Schiffman and James C. VanderKam; Oxford: Oxford University, 2000) 1. 475–77; Florentino García Martínez, "Temple Scroll," ibid., 2. 927–33; Hindy Najman, *Seconding Sinai. The Development of Mosaic Discourse in Second Temple Judaism* (Supplements to the Journal for the Study of Judaism 77; Leiden/Boston: Brill, 2003). Especially problematic are the fragments from Cave 4 of Qumran that are given telling labels like *Reworked Pentateuch* (4Q158, 4Q364, 365, 366, 367), *Apocryphon Pentateuch A* (4Q368), *Apocryphon Pentateuch B* (4Q377), and the *Apocryphon of Moses* (4Q375, 376). To what extent these texts should be considered variant textual traditions of the Pentateuch, early targums of the Pentateuch, or attempts to replace the traditional version(s) of the Pentateuch with a new version remains unclear; the fragmentary nature of the evidence makes a final decision very difficult. On the questionable propriety of using phrases like "para-biblical," "apocryphal," "expanded biblical text," or "rewritten Bible" for these works, see Bruno Chiesa, "Biblical Texts from Qumran," *Henoch* 20 (1998) 131–51. Even the question of the proper sigla for these fragments is still debated among scholars; see, e.g., George J. Brooke, "4Q158: Reworked Pentateuch[a] or Reworked Pentateuch A?" *Dead Sea Discoveries* 8 (2001) 219–41. On the larger problem of retrieving pre-Maccabean *hălākâ* from the Dead Sea Scrolls, see Lawrence H. Schiffman, "Pre-Maccabean Halakhah in the Dead Sea Scrolls and the Biblical Tradition," *Dead Sea Discoveries* 13 (2006) 348–61.

[27] See the observations of James L. Kugel, "The Need for Interpretation," in the joint volume of James L. Kugel and Rowan A. Greer, *Early Biblical Interpretation* (Library of Early Christianity 3; Philadelphia: Westminster, 1986) 27–39.

[28] On the problem of the Hellenists in the Jerusalem church, see the standard commentaries on Acts, e.g., Joseph A. Fitzmyer, *The Acts of the Apostles* (AYB 31; New York: Doubleday, 1998; reprint New Haven: Yale University Press), 347–48; more fully, Gerhard Schneider, *Die Apostelgeschichte* (HTKNT 5; 2 vols.; Freiburg/Basel/Vienna: Herder, 1980, 1982) 1. 406–16. See also Raymond E. Brown and John P. Meier, *Antioch and Rome* (New York/Ramsey, NJ: Paulist, 1983) 5–7, 32–34, 43–44, 54–55.

[29] The importance of distinguishing what the written Torah may have enjoined in theory and what individual communities of Jews actually did in Palestine around the turn of the era is stressed by Philip R. Davies, " 'Law' in Early Judaism," *Judaism in Late Antiquity. Part Three. Where We Stand: Issues and Debates in Ancient*

Judaism (ed. Jacob Neusner and Alan J. Avery-Peck; Boston/Leiden: Brill, 2001) Section One, 3–33. It is also important to remember that ordinary observant Jews, unlike special groups and the educated elites, may not have been conscious of any distinction between the written Law and the interpretations surrounding and mediating it to pious but uneducated individuals. On this, see Sanders, "Law," 256.

[30] See *A Marginal Jew*, 3. 315–22.

[31] See *A Marginal Jew*, 3. 403. Later on in rabbinic literature (5th and 6th centuries A.D.), we find literary attestation of a "culinary *ʿerûb*" (*ʿyrwby tbšylyn*, literally, a "mixing of dishes") based on Abraham's conduct; see *Midrash Bereshit Rabba, Parsha Vayiggash*, 95:3 (ed. J. Theodor–C. Albeck; 3 vols.; Jerusalem: Wahrmann, 1965) 3. 1189, lines 4–5; *b. Yoma* 28b. But even apart from the relatively late date of documentation, the texts do not connect such a practice with the Pharisees; rather, they bolster the supposed scriptural basis of the practice by appealing to the talmudic doctrine of the two Torahs, written and oral. Moreover, *ʿerûb* is being used in these texts in a temporal rather than spatial sense. The problem addressed in these late texts is that one may not prepare food for the sabbath on a holy day that falls on the Friday preceding the sabbath. The "culinary *ʿerûb*" permits one to start preparing the sabbath food on the eve of the holy day; if the cooking continues into the holy day, it is considered simply a continuation of the weekday work.

[32] It should be emphasized that topics like sabbath rest and synagogue attendance are raised here in Chapter 31 only in passing, simply to illustrate how complex and flexible the concept of the Law of Moses, even the *written* Law of Moses, was around the time of Jesus. The question of Jesus and the sabbath will be treated at length in Chapter 34. For a full discussion of the observance of the sabbath in ancient Israel and early Judaism, see Lutz Doering, *Schabbat* (Texts and Studies in Ancient Judaism 78; Tübingen: Mohr [Siebeck], 1999).

[33] On this point, see Sanders, *Jewish Law*, 6–7.

[34] I refer here in particular to organized warfare waged by soldiers of an army or army-in-the-making.

[35] See Sanders, *Jewish Law*, 7. Sanders suggests that the incident of the massacred Jews who refused to fight on the sabbath during the Maccabean revolt may reflect "how the sabbath law had grown in force and scope during the peaceful years of the Persian period and the Hellenistic monarchies—peaceful, that is, for the Jews."

[36] This is stressed by Sanders, "Law," 257. As Müller ("Gesetz," 15–17) emphasizes in regard to the decision of the followers of Mattathias, no fixed hermeneutical rules were used at the time to deduce or defend this interpretation of the sabbath rest. The seven rules of interpretation *(middôt)* attributed to Hillel are attested in the rabbinic corpus for the first time in the Tosepta (hence, in the 3d century A.D.);

see H. L. Strack and Günter Stemberger, *Introduction to the Talmud and Midrash* (2d ed.; Minneapolis: Fortress, 1996) 16–20. Jonathan A. Goldstein (*I Maccabees* [AYB 41; New York: Doubleday, 1976; reprint New Haven: Yale University Press] 235–37) reads the whole story as Hasmonean propaganda: "the Hasmonaeans' David-like realism" is contrasted with "the foolish faith of the martyrs."

[37] On *Jubilees*, see *A Marginal Jew*, 3. 348–49 n. 14.

[38] As Doering (*Schabbat*, 107–8) notes, no distinction is made between aggressive or defensive warfare; both seem to be forbidden. Doering denies that the total prohibition first arose out of the Maccabean debate over self-defense on the sabbath. The likely dating of *Jubilees*, its apparent opposition to Hasmonean control, and the placing of the total prohibition of warfare at the very end of the entire Book of *Jubilees* incline me to think otherwise. For Doering's reading of the tradition history of this halakic question, see ibid., 537–65. A summary of different positions on the question is found on pp. 537–40; Doering gives a summary of his own position on pp. 564–65. Similar to Doering's view of the pre-Maccabean view of war on the sabbath is Yong-Eui Yang, *Jesus and the Sabbath in Matthew's Gospel* (JSNTSup 139; Sheffield: Sheffield Academic Press, 1997) 73; cf. Lohse ("*sabbaton*, etc.," 8), who speaks vaguely of "the older Halachah" that the pious Jews of 1 Macc 2:32–38 were obeying when they were slaughtered by the Syrian forces.

[39] The translation is that of O. S. Wintermute in *OTP*, 2. 142.

[40] Curiously, Sanders ("Law," 257) thinks that *Jubilees*'s prohibition of battle on the sabbath lacks "the special stress that would indicate that the point was debated." I think instead that the climactic placement of the prohibition, the solemn threat that immediately follows it, the weighty warrants that support it, and the probable dating of *Jubilees* (ca. 161–152 B.C.) a decade or two after the opposite and purely pragmatic decision by the followers of Mattathias (hence reflecting the position of the Hasmonean priests with whom *Jubilees* seems to be at odds) argue in favor of a conscious polemic.

[41] The story is also told, with a slight pagan sneer added, in Cassius Dio's *History*, 37.16.2–4; see Earnest Cary (ed.), *Dio's Roman History* (LCL; 9 vols.; Cambridge, MA: Harvard University; London: Heinemann, 1914–27) 3. 124–27.

[42] While the Greek verb *amynontai* ("defend oneself," "ward off from oneself") does not have an expressed subject, the obvious subject is the previous *Ioudaioi* ("Jews" in general), who, Josephus says, "abstain from every kind of manual labor on the sabbath because of their religion" (§146). In this explanatory aside to his audience, Josephus is clearly talking about Jews in general, not simply Aristobulus' soldiers holed up in the temple. Notice how Josephus' remark implicitly incorporates the particular and debated *hălākâ* of Mattathias' followers into the global prohibition of work contained in the written Torah of Moses.

[43] Interestingly, Josephus (*J.W.* 2.19.2 §517) narrates that, when Cestius, the governor of Syria, approached Jerusalem with his army in A.D. 66 to quell the incipient revolt, the Jews in the city, "abandoning the feast [of Sukkoth]," took up arms in disorderly fashion, "paying no attention to the rest of the seventh day (this sabbath was the one especially revered by them [namely, the sabbath that fell during the week-long festival of Sukkoth])." The way Josephus describes the disorderly crowds "abandoning" the feast of Sukkoth and "giving no thought" to the obligation of sabbath rest because "their passion shook them out of proper religious observance" (§518) makes it likely that he disapproves of their action, perhaps because they were not being attacked on the sabbath day itself and therefore, according to the *hălākâ* of Mattathias, were not justified in waging war. This is another indication that Josephus considers this *hălākâ* not a mere interpretation of the Law by some particular group but rather a precept incumbent on all Jews, even at a time of crisis.

[44] On this, see *A Marginal Jew*, 3. 314–17. It is important to remember at this juncture that the later doctrine of the Dual Torah or the Two Torahs (written and oral, both from Sinai and of equal weight) is not witnessed in Jewish documents written in the 1st century A.D; see ibid., 317–20. Sanders ("Law," 259) summarizes this point succinctly: "The term for nonbiblical rules, according to Josephus, the NT, and early rabbinic literature, was not 'oral law' but 'tradition.' " For an attempt to defend the position that Pharisaic Judaism maintained the idea of the two Torahs or at least a prohibition of writing down its own *hălākâ*, see Joseph M. Baumgarten, *Studies in Qumran Law* (SJLA 24; Leiden: Brill, 1977) 13–35, esp. 19–23; Michael Fishbane, *Biblical Interpretation in Ancient Israel* (Oxford: Clarendon, 1985) 527–28. For a more critical and detailed treatment of the problem of *hălākâ* in rabbinic sources, especially the problematic phrase "*hălākâ* [given] to Moses at Sinai," see Christine Hayes, "*Halakhah le-Moshe mi-Sinai* in Rabbinic Sources: A Methodological Case Study," *The Synoptic Problem in Rabbinic Literature* (Brown Judaic Studies 326; ed. Shaye J. D. Cohen; Providence, RI: Brown University, 2000) 61–117.

[45] On this, see *Ant.* 14.10.9–12 §217–27. Interestingly, the text of the decree of the Roman governor Dolabella does not make any distinction between self-defense and launching an attack. Perhaps the Jews thought it prudent not to introduce this halakic distinction into their general request to be excused from *all* military service. Alternately, the Roman authorities may have found the Jewish distinction both unintelligible and unworkable and therefore excused them from all military service.

[46] Sanders ("Law," 257) sums up his treatment of this development in sabbath law with the dictum: "Custom and tradition, both unconscious and conscious, could become law." As Steve Mason (*Flavius Josephus on the Pharisees* [Leiden/Boston: Brill, 1991] 97–106) points out, Josephus identifies in undifferentiated fashion as the (written) Law of Moses what we modern critics would differentiate as the written Law *plus* various customs and traditions that serve as a filter through which Josephus views the Law.

[47] The language each uses should be noted. Both Philo and Josephus speak explicitly of Moses as the author of this command. Philo states that Moses "*wrote down [anegrapsen]* the beauty" of the number seven "on the most holy tablets of the Law," "ordering" that all who were subject to him abstain from all work connected with earning a living and instead give over their time to philosophizing (i.e., studying the Law). More explicitly, in the *Hypothetica* 7.12–13, Philo claims that Moses ("the lawgiver") required Jews to come together on the seventh day and sit with one another in an orderly manner to hear the laws and receive instruction about them. Josephus states that "our lawgiver" Moses "ordered" that people come together (i.e., in synagogues) to hear the Law and to learn it accurately. The contexts clearly indicate that both Philo and Josephus are thinking of the written Law of Moses and hold that this written Law enjoins on the sabbath study of the Torah and/or synagogue attendance. This is all the more interesting because both Philo and Josephus are authors of extensive commentaries on the written Law; they are hardly ignorant of what it does or does not contain. On the statements of Philo and Josephus on sabbath and synagogue, see Doering, *Schabbat*, 350–52 (for Philo) and 488–89 (for Josephus). For the larger question of the meaning of the word "law" (*nomos*) in both Philo and Josephus, see Reinhard Weber, *Das "Gesetz" bei Philon von Alexandrien und Flavius Josephus* (Arbeiten zur Religion und Geschichte des Urchristentums 11; Frankfurt: Lang, 2001).

[48] Pseudo-Philo expands the sabbath commandment in the Decalogue with phrases taken from Ps 107:32: "You shall not do any work on it [the sabbath], you and all your help, except to praise the Lord in the assembly of the elders and to glorify the Mighty One in the council of the older men." The translation is that of Daniel J. Harrington, *OTP*, 2. 318. If one accepts Harrington's view (*OTP*, 2. 299) that the *Biblical Antiquities* comes from Palestine around the time of Jesus, we have here an indication that synagogue worship in pre-70 Palestine was seen, at least by some Jews, as commanded not only by the written Torah in general but even by the sabbath commandment of the Decalogue in particular. But not all critics accept the pre-70 date; see Doering, *Schabbat*, 18.

[49] The origin, extent, and function of the synagogue in pre-70 Palestine remain a matter of intense debate. For overviews and extensive bibliography, see Anders Runesson, *The Origins of the Synagogue: A Socio-Historical Study* (ConBNT 37; Stockholm: Almqvist & Wiksell, 2002); Lee Levine, *The Ancient Synagogue. The First Thousand Years* (New Haven: Yale University, 2000); the various essays in Howard Clark Kee and Lynn H. Cohick (eds.), *Evolution of the Synagogue. Problems and Progress* (Harrisburg, PA: Trinity, 1999); and the various essays in Section Four, "The Special Problem of the Synagogue," in *Judaism in Late Antiquity. Part Three. Where We Stand: Issues and Debates in Ancient Judaism* (ed. Jacob Neusner and Alan J. Avery-Peck; Boston/Leiden: Brill, 2001).

[50] Other examples of interpretations and expansions of the Law that are presented as the Law itself are listed by Sanders, "Law," 257–58. For example, Philo (*On the*

Special Laws [*De specialibus legibus*] 3.9 §51; cf. *On Joseph* [*De Josepho*] 9.43) claims that the Mosaic Law forbids prostitution and commands that the prostitute be put to death—something that goes far beyond what the prohibition of Deut 23:17–18 (vv 18–19 in the MT) stipulates.

[51] Unlike many commentators on Mark at this point, Robert H. Gundry (*Mark* [Grand Rapids, MI: Eerdmans, 1993] 529–30, 537–38) rightly emphasizes the difference between Jesus' insistence on what is *commanded* and the Pharisees' attempt to speak of what is *permitted*.

[52] Obviously, this is not true from our modern historical-critical perspective. Josephus does add to, omit, and modify the laws as contained in the Mosaic Torah. How he understands his claim of complete fidelity is debated among scholars: (1) Josephus is simply issuing a general reassurance to his readers concerning his reliability; (2) Josephus is quite aware of his modifications but presumes that his mostly non-Jewish readers do not know the biblical text and would not check his claims against a Greek translation of the Jewish Scriptures (if such a translation were available to them); (3) Josephus thinks of the biblical text and the interpretative tradition surrounding and mediating it as an undivided whole (though one must be careful here not to import the later rabbinic distinction between the Written Torah and the Oral Torah back into Josephus' mind-set); (4) in some cases, Josephus may be using a different biblical text from the one we find in either the MT or the standard version of the LXX. These various explanations do not necessarily exclude one another.

[53] No doubt the attentive reader has already noticed that certain documents prove to be of much more use in discussing the historical Jesus vis-à-vis the historical Torah than others. Those documents that are chronologically prior to or simultaneous with the historical Jesus, that are reflective of the interpretive traditions of Palestinian Judaism, and that deal with the topic of the Law are obviously primary sources. Hence this chapter stresses works like *Jubilees*, the Qumran documents and allied material, 1 Maccabees, Pseudo-Philo's *Biblical Antiquities*, and Josephus. The vast apocalyptic library we call *1 Enoch*, while largely qualifying by time and place (though the *Similitudes of Enoch* is probably from the post-70 period), has little to say by way of commentary on particular statutes of the Mosaic Torah. The few precise legal questions that are brought up mostly concern defense of the sectarian solar calendar, censure of priests for taking foreign wives, and complaints about impure food offered on the altar. Granted the strange mix of cosmological speculation, esoteric lore about angels, wisdom traditions, and apocalyptic expectation of imminent judgment of the wicked and vindication of the righteous, one should not be surprised that detailed discussions of specifically Mosaic *hălākôt* are absent from *1 Enoch*.

Philo's various commentaries on the Law, while suffused with the allegorical hermeneutic reflective of the Middle Platonism of his Alexandrian milieu, are useful when they expound the literal or plain sense of the text with a view to actual observance—something Philo never rejected. At least Philo enjoys the unique status of being a famous Jewish writer who lived at the same time as Jesus and who wrote extensive commentaries on the Mosaic Law. While most of Philo's allegorical interpretation of the Law hardly reflects the major tendencies we see in Palestinian traditions at the turn of the era, some of Philo's comments on specific laws do find parallels either in Josephus or in later rabbinic statements. Hence he is not to be dismissed out of hand; on this, see Jacques E. Ménard, "Les rapports de Philon avec le judaïsme palestinien et Josèphe," *DBSup*, 7. 1299–1304. On Philo's understanding of the Law and Scripture, see R. Arnaldez, "Philon et les 'disciples de Moïse,' " *DBSup*, 7. 1305–6; idem, "Moïse et la Loi," ibid., 1306–12; André Myre, "La loi dans l'ordre moral selon Philon d'Alexandrie," *ScEs* 24 (1972) 93–113; idem, "La loi dans l'ordre cosmique et politique selon Philon d'Alexandrie," *ScEs* 24 (1972) 217–47; idem, "La loi et le Pentateuque selon Philon d'Alexandrie," *ScEs* 25 (1973) 209–25; idem, "Les caractéristiques de la loi mosaïque selon Philon d'Alexandrie," *ScEs* 27 (1975) 35–69; idem, "La loi de la nature et la loi mosaïque selon Philon d'Alexandrie," *ScEs* 28 (1976) 163–81; Helmut Burkhardt, *Die Inspiration heiliger Schriften bei Philo von Alexandrien* (Giessen/Basel: Brunnen, 1988) 73–146. On Philo's approach to the Law and its commandments, see Yehoshua Amir, *Die hellenistische Gestalt des Judentums bei Philon von Alexandrien* (Forschungen zum jüdisch-christlichen Dialog 5; Neukirchen-Vluyn: Neukirchener Verlag, 1983) 37–51, 67–106; Adele Reinhartz, "The Meaning of *nomos* in Philo's *Exposition of the Law*," *SR* 15 (1986) 337–45; Peder Borgen, "Philo of Alexandria," *AYBD*, 5. 333–42.

Josephus, while writing in Rome in the post-70 period, no doubt knows and reflects some legal interpretations and practices of his pre-70 Palestinian provenance. Besides paralleling at times the opinions of Philo or the later rabbis, Josephus' legal interpretations sometimes echo what we find in various Qumran documents; on this, see Louis H. Feldman, "Josephus," *AYBD*, 3. 981–98, esp. 992–94. For various scholarly interpretations of Josephus' views on *hălākâ*, see the works discussed by Louis H. Feldman in his *Josephus and Modern Scholarship (1937–1980)* (Berlin/New York: de Gruyter, 1984) 492–527; cf. David Goldenberg, "The Halakha in Josephus and in Tannaitic Literature," *JQR* 67 (1976) 30–43 (the article argues for a basic agreement between Josephus and "contemporary" rabbinic literature, which, for Goldenberg, includes various parts of the Mishna, Tosepta, Palestinian Talmud, and Babylonian Talmud); Geza Vermes, "A Summary of the Law by Flavius Josephus," *NovT* 24 (1982) 289–303. Josephus had intended to write a full, detailed treatise on the Torah, to be entitled "On Customs and Causes" (see *Ant.* 4.8.4 §198; cf. 1.1.4 §25; 20.12.1 §268); but his plan, perhaps already mapped out in his mind, never came to fruition. We are left with two partial treatments of the Mosaic Law in Josephus: the first in Books 3 and 4 of the *Antiquities* (*Ant.* 3.5.5–12.3 §91–286; 4.8.4–43 §196–301), the other in *Against Apion* (taken broadly, 2.14–30 §145–219). Fortunately, Josephus' overall view of the Five Books of Moses is basically the same in both the *Antiquities* and the *Against Apion*—a statement that perhaps does not apply to the way Josephus' two works handle the historical books, the prophets, and the later writings that come to constitute the Jewish Bible; on this, see Peter Höffken, "Zum Kanonsbewusstsein des Josephus Flavius in *Contra Apionem* und in den *Antiquitates*," *JSJ* 32 (2001) 159–77.

Once one moves away from Palestinian provenance into the wider range of Jewish Diaspora literature, nuggets of information relevant to our particular quest are few and far between. Much of the Diaspora literature, while concerned with general or specific moral exhortation, does not base its ethical views explicitly on specific commandments of the Mosaic Torah. In varying degrees, this is the case in such diverse works as the *Testament of Job*, *Testaments of the Twelve Patriarchs*, and *Joseph and Aseneth*. For example, while the *Testaments of the Twelve Patriarchs* inculcates obedience to the Law (alias fear of the Lord, integrity, conscience, and love of God and neighbor), the Law is for the most part a matter of universal moral values—in other words, the natural law as understood by Stoicism. It is symptomatic that, in the *Testaments*, the sabbath laws are never mentioned, circumcision is mentioned only in the context of the story of the slaughter of the Shechemites by the sons of Jacob (*T. Levi* 6:3,6), and food laws are mentioned briefly only as a metaphor for moral purity (*T. Asher* 2:9; 4:5). Levi is said to know "the Law of God" and to give instructions concerning justice and sacrifice for Israel (*T. Reuben* 6:8), but we are never told in detail what these instructions are (cf. the passing reference to various types of sacrifice in *T. Levi* 9:7 and to offering the harvest and the firstborn to God through the priest in *T. Issachar* 3:6). (In all this, we must remember that we have the *Testaments* in a form redacted by Christians; the problem of the amount of Christian content in the *Testaments* will loom large in subsequent chapters, especially Chapter 36 on the love commandments.) While the *Letter of Aristeas* does discuss various foods laws contained in the Torah and obviously wishes them to be observed by Jews of the Diaspora, *Aristeas* reflects the common Diaspora apologetic of interpreting these laws in a rationalizing manner: they are ways by which God keeps his holy people from immorality and points them symbolically toward righteousness. By contrast, in the legal traditions that most likely come from the historical Jesus, one does not detect a need to defend the Mosaic Torah by apologetic arguments or to interpret its laws allegorically in order to make sense of them. The Mosaic Law is taken for granted as the given; the proper way to observe its laws literally (not by allegorical sublimation) is what is at stake. On the whole question of the proper sources to be used for understanding the Law at the time of Jesus, see Müller, "Das Gesetz," 21–22.

[54] Actually, the word *nomos* does not occur in Mark. Instead, "Moses" is used to refer to the Mosaic Law in Mark 1:44; 7:10; 10:3–4; 12:19,26. The same usage occurs in Matt 8:4; 19:7–8; 22:24; Luke 5:14; 16:29,31; 20:28,37; 24:27. Interestingly, in John's Gospel, where *nomos* refers to the Psalms in John 10:34 and 15:25, all the passages that use "Moses" as a symbol of the Scriptures refer directly (e.g., 1:45) or indirectly (e.g., 3:14) to the Pentateuch.

[55] See John P. Meier, *Law and History in Matthew's Gospel* (AnBib 71; Rome: Biblical Institute, 1976) 70–71. In the NT, the two-part division of the Law and the prophets occurs ten times: four times in Matt (5:17; 7:12; 11:13; 22:40), once in Luke 16:16 (= Matt 11:13; therefore the phrase existed already in Q), once in John (1:45, but not in perfect coordination), three times in Acts (13:15; 24:14; 28:23),

and once in Paul (Rom 3:21). In addition, Luke's Gospel uses "Moses and the prophets" (16:29; 16:31; 24:27) three times. This implicit idea of a two-part canon may already be intimated in CD 7:15–17, which speaks of the books of the Law as distinct from the books of the prophets. Among the evangelists, Luke alone speaks in his Gospel (24:44: the Law of Moses, the Prophets, *and the Psalms*; cf. the two-part division in 24:27) in terms of a three-part division reminiscent of the prologue to Sirach and foreshadowing the later normative division of the Jewish canon into Law, Prophets, and Writings (in Hebrew, *tôrâ*, *něbî'îm*, and *kětûbîm*—hence the acronym *TaNaK* for the Jewish Scriptures).

[56] Kleinknecht, "*nomos*," 1023–35.

[57] Laurent Monsengwo Pasinya, *La notion de* nomos *dans le Pentateuque grec* (AnBib 52; Rome: Biblical Institute, 1973); see in particular pp. 53–54, 60–61, 99–100, 139–40, 158–59, 201–5. Of 220 occurrences of *tôrâ* in the MT of the Jewish Scriptures, some 200 passages are translated as *nomos* in the LXX. In agreement with Monsengwo Pasinya is Sanders, "Law," 255. The opposite view, that the translation of *tôrâ* by *nomos* was misleading, is maintained by Berger, *Gesetzesauslegung*, 32. Westerholm ("*Torah*," 334) notes that the translators of the LXX were not the first Jews to decide to translate *tôrâ* with a word that meant, among other things, "law." The Aramaic parts of the MT do the same thing. The Aramaic word *dāt* ("law," "decree") in Ezra 7:12–26 reflects the Hebrew *tôrâ* (7:12,21: Ezra is "a scribe of the law [*dāt*] of the God of heaven; 7:14: the law of God that is in your hand; 7:25: all those who know the law of your God; 7:26: the law of your God and the law of the king), as the surrounding Hebrew context shows (Ezra is called "a scribe skilled in the law [*tôrat*] of Moses" in Ezra 7:6; in v 10, Ezra "has prepared his heart to search the law [*tôrat*] of Yahweh"; cf. the secular meaning in Dan 6:9,13,16).

[58] See, e.g., Baruch J. Schwartz, "Torah," *The Oxford Dictionary of the Jewish Religion* (ed. R. J. Zwi Werblowsky and Geoffrey Wigoder; New York/Oxford: Oxford University, 1997) 696–98. One may also consult, with due caution regarding the theological polemic typical of all too many of the *TDNT* statements about rabbinic Judaism, Gutbrod, "*nomos*, etc." 1054–59.

[59] In this, the rabbinic literature is closer to Paul than to the Synoptic Gospels; notice, for instance, how a catena of citations from the Psalms, Isaiah, and the wisdom literature in Rom 3:10–18 can be summed up in v 19 as "the Law" (*ho nomos*). Indeed, in 1 Cor 14:21, a reworked form of Isa 28:11–12 is introduced by Paul with "in the Law it is written that. . . ." This wider use of *nomos* is not found in the Synoptic Gospels. While in general this is also true of John's Gospel, there are exceptions in John 10:34 (= LXX Ps 81:6); 15:25 (= LXX Ps 34:19; or LXX 68:5). John 12:34 may be a vague, global reference to the whole of the Jewish Scriptures, especially to the Psalms and the Prophets.

[60] *A Marginal Jew*, 3. 317–20.

[61] The word also came to be used for Jewish law in general, but here I am focusing on the aspect of an individual opinion or ruling in a legal matter.

[62] At times, scholars state flatly that the noun *hălākâ* "appears nowhere in the Qumranian corpus" (so Martin S. Jaffee, *Torah in the Mouth. Writing and Oral Tradition in Palestinian Judaism 200 BCE–400 CE* [Oxford: Oxford University, 2001] 43). However, the *Dictionary of Classical Hebrew* (ed. David J. A. Clines; Sheffield: Academic Press, 1993–) lists *sub voce* (vol. 2, p. 559) two occurrences of the noun *hălākâ*, both from the *Rule of the Community* (1QS); the noun never occurs in the canon of Jewish Scriptures or in the deuterocanonical/apocryphal book of Ben Sira. As the *Dictionary* properly indicates, there are problems with both supposed occurrences at Qumran. In 1QS 1:25, the dictionary entry first presents the form *hlktnw* as the noun *hălākâ* plus the 1st person plural suffix *-nû* ("our"). Hence it translates the phrase *hrš'nw . . . hlktnw* as: "We have made our conduct wicked." However, the entry goes on to note that the Hebrew letter *hê* at the beginning of the word is not clear (as a matter of fact, this is due to a scribe's attempt to erase the *hê*); hence the *Dictionary* lists the alternate reading *blktnw*, "in our going" (the preposition *bě* with the qal infinitive of the verb *hālak* [*leket*] plus the 1st person plural suffix). The sense of the whole statement would then have to be: "We have acted wickedly in our conduct." What is curious in the *Dictionary*'s first reading is that the letter *bêt*, which is clearly visible in the photographs of the manuscript, is not represented, while the *hê*, which is obscured in the text by a scribal erasure (more about this below), is represented. For photographs of 1QS, see Millar Burrows (ed.), *The Dead Sea Scrolls of St. Mark's Monastery. Volume II. Fascicle 2: Plates and Transcription of the Manual of Discipline* (New Haven: The American Schools of Oriental Research, 1951) (where a space with a dot is placed to signify the lacuna: *b.lktnw*); and Frank M. Cross and John C. Trever (eds.), *Scrolls from Qumran Cave 1* (Jerusalem: The Albright Institute of Archaeological Research and the Shrine of the Book, 1972). Quite rightly, therefore, in their editions of the Qumran texts, both James H. Charlesworth and Elisha Qimron (*The Dead Sea Scrolls. Volume 1. Rule of the Communty and Related Documents* [Princeton Theological Seminary Dead Sea Scrolls Project; Tübingen: Mohr (Siebeck); Louisville: Westminster/John Knox, 1994] 8) and Florentino García Martínez and Eibert J. C. Tigchelaar (*The Dead Sea Scrolls Study Edition* [2 vols.; Leiden: Brill, 1997, 1998] 70) print the Hebrew text with the letter *bêt* without parentheses or brackets and then the letter *hê* in parentheses or brackets. Charlesworth–Qimron translate the disputed word as "by our walking"; García Martínez–Tigchelaar translate it as "inasmuch as we walk." At least the latter translation seems to take the disputed form to be the qal infinitive construct of the verb. Indeed, in his vocalized text, Eduard Lohse (*Die Texte aus Qumran* [2d ed.; Munich: Kösel, 1971]) simply reads 1QS 1:25 as *bělektēnû* (the preposition *bě* plus the qal infinitive construct of the verb plus the 1st personal plural suffix); he does not even consider the possibility of reading a form of *hălākâ* in this passage. In the end, the state of the manuscript leaves one uncertain. One possibility entertained by scholars like Preben Wernberg-Møller (*The Manual of Discipline* [STDJ 1; Grand Rapids, MI: Eerdmans, 1957] 40) is that *bhlktnw* was the original reading and that it was subsequently corrected

to read *blktnw*. This may well be, but it leaves unanswered the more basic question of whether the supposed original *bhlktnw* was a scribal error or an intelligible and intended form. Jacob Licht (*mgylt hsrkym. The Rule Scroll* [Jerusalem: Bialik Institute, 1965] 68) suggests that the scribe who wrote 1QS first wrote either *bklktnw* or *bhlktnw* (only the top of the second consonant is visible in the manuscript) and then erased the second consonant (be it a *hê* or a *kāp*). Presumably, the second consonant was from the beginning a scribal error that the original scribe caught and corrected. If one should accept this hypothesis, then 1QS 1:25 would drop out of consideration as a text attesting the use of the noun *hălākâ* at Qumran.

The second occurrence, in 1QS 3:9, would seem, at first glance, to provide solid attestation of the noun. Both the Charlesworth–Qimron edition and the García Martínez–Tigchelaar edition read the key words as *lhlkt tmym*; this would seem to be the preposition *lě* ("to," "for") plus the noun *hălākâ* in the construct state (*hilkat*, "walking," i.e., "conduct," "behavior") plus *tāmîm* ("perfect," "perfectly," "in perfection"). Charlesworth–Qimron (p. 15) render this "for walking perfectly," while García Martínez–Tigchelaar render it "in order to walk with perfection." A problem arises, however, when one compares 1QS 3:9 with what appears to be fragments of the *Rule of the Community* from Cave 4, specifically 4QS[a] 2:5 (alias 4QpapS[a], alias 4Q255, also identified by Charlesworth–Qimron as 4QS MS A, but in any case identified by both editions as coming from the *Rule of the Community*). Though badly damaged, fragment 2 of this Cave 4 manuscript clearly corresponds to 1QS 3:7–13 (although with some differences in wording), with line 5 of fragment 2 corresponding to the end of 1QS 3:9 and the beginning of 3:10 (almost word for word). However, instead of *lhlkt tmym*, found in 1QS 3:9, 4QS[a] 2:5 reads *lhlk tmym*, which, as *The Dictionary of Classical Hebrew* suggests, might be read as the preposition *lě* with the piel infinitive construct of the verb (*hallēk*), a verb form that does not occur in the MT. Alternately, one could read *hlk* as the qal infinitive construct form *hālōk*, which is rare in Biblical Hebrew (seven times in the MT). Interestingly, in the DJD edition of fragment 2 of 4QS[a] (Philip S. Alexander and Geza Vermes [eds.], *Qumran Cave 4 XIX: Serekh ha-Yahad and Two Related Texts* [DJD 26; Oxford: Clarendon, 1998] 33–36), the editors (on p. 35) reject a suggestion made by some of the early commentators on 1QS, namely, that *lhlkt* in 1QS 3:9 should be read as the verbal noun *hălîkâ* ("going," "procession," "advance," "caravan"). They state that, while *hălîkâ* is found rarely in Biblical Hebrew (a point that is perfectly true), it never occurs in Qumran Hebrew. Actually, the latter claim does not seem to be true, for *hălîkâ* is probably found in 4Q223–24, fragment 2, col. 1, line 50, although the initial *hê* must be supplied. In any event, the word in 4Q223–24 is clearly spelled with a *yôd* ([h]lykt), which is not present in the *lhlkt* of 1QS 3:9; Alexander–Vermes are thus probably correct in refusing to read *lhlkt* as a form of *hălîkâ*. Likewise correct, in my opinion, is the suggestion of Alexander–Vermes that *lhlkt* in 1QS 3:9 represents either (1) a scribal error caused by the dittography of the *taw* in the following *tmym* or (2) an imperfect correction by a scribe who tried, without complete success, to change the less common form of *lě* + qal infinitive construct, namely, *lahălōk* (a combination found five times in Biblical Hebrew) to the frequent biblical form *lāleket*. Both forms of the infinitive construct, *lhlk* and *llkt*, occur in

Qumran Hebrew, but the latter predominates. However, Alexander–Vermes also allow that *lhlk* could be pointed in fragment 2 as the piel infinitive construct, a suggestion, as we have seen, that is also made by the *Dictionary of Classical Hebrew*. For our purposes, what is perhaps most striking is that, in their whole treatment, Alexander–Vermes never consider the possibility that the form in 1QS 3:9 might be the noun *hălākâ*. The suggestion of Alexander–Vermes that *lhlkt* in 1QS 3:9 might represent an imperfect scribal correction in the direction of the common infinitive construct *lāleket* conjures up a further hypothesis, one that might explain both 1QS 1:25 and 1QS 3:9 in basically the same way. Both problematic forms might reflect the use of the letter *hê* as a *mater lectionis* for the vowel *ā*: *bhlktnw* (i.e., *bālektēnû*) in 1QS 1:25 and *lhlkt* (i.e., *lāleket*) in 1QS 3:9. In this hypothesis, the scribe erased the superfluous *hê* in the first case but not in the second. In sum, granted the textual problems connected with both passages from 1QS, and granted the alternate readings suggested by various scholars, the attestation of the noun *hălākâ* in the pre-Mishnaic Hebrew of Qumran is not as clear as some might think. In my view, 1QS 3:9 is the best candidate for such attestation, but the parallel from Cave 4 and the possibility of *hê* used as a *mater lectionis* create doubts.

In any event, even if both texts from 1QS did contain the noun, it would have the general sense of "walking," "conduct," "behavior" (though certainly in a context dealing with behavior in accordance with or contrary to the Law), not the later rabbinic sense of a legal opinion or ruling on the proper way to act in a particular situation. Granted, it remains possible that this more specific rabbinic sense of *hălākâ* was already in use in the early 1st century A.D. and that it is purely by accident that no written attestation of it has survived. Moreover, the decipherment of all the puzzles connected with the Dead Sea Scrolls is hardly completed. All that can be said at the moment is that (1) we have no textual evidence for the existence of this rabbinic sense of *hălākâ* in the 1st century B.C. or A.D. and (2) even the manuscript evidence for the existence of the noun *hălākâ* at Qumran is at best debatable, at worst nonexistent. Needless to say, unless we engage in a strange form of nominalism, the absence of the noun in no way affects the presence of the reality. Still, it is wise to be aware of when we use labels anachronistically.

As a further aside, I should note that this clarification of the status of the noun *hălākâ* at Qumran may also make a slight contribution to the debate over the meaning of the cryptic phrase "the seekers after smooth things" (*dôrĕšê (ha)hǎlāqôt*), found in 1QH 2 (or, in the alternate enumeration of columns, 10):15,32; 4QpNah fragments 3 + 4, 1:2,7; 2:2,4; 3:3,6–7; 4Q163 (4Q Isaiah Pesher[c]) fragment 23, 2:10; cf. CD 1:18. While some critics, like Anthony J. Saldarini ("Pharisees," *AYBD*, 5. 289–303, esp. 301), think that the phrase refers to a broad coalition opposing Alexander Jannaeus (which included, but was not identical with, the Pharisees), many other distinguished scholars (e.g., Lawrence H. Schiffman, "New Light on the Pharisees," *Understanding the Dead Sea Scrolls* [ed. Hershel Shanks; New York: Random House, 1992] 217–24, esp. 220–21; similarly, Stephen Goranson, "Others and Intra-Jewish Polemic as Reflected in Qumran Texts," *The Dead Sea Scrolls after Fifty Years* [ed. Peter W. Flint and James C. VanderKam; 2 vols.; Leiden: Brill, 1998, 1999] 2. 534–51, esp. 542–44; Jaffee [*Torah in the Mouth*, 41], who maintains that "the common identification of the Expounders [of Smooth Things] as Pharisees seems nearly incontrovertible") hold that the phrase refers disparagingly to the Pharisees. Indeed, Goranson (ibid., 543–44) claims that "the identification of Essenes, Pharisees, and Sadducees in the pesharim, especially 4QpNah, is one of the most assured results of Qumran historical research, though a few scholars of late neglect this result." One reason sometimes put forward for the identification of the seekers with the Pharisees is the supposed play on words between *ḥălāqôt* and the *hălākôt* of the Pharisees, with obvious mocking intent (so, e.g., Goranson, ibid., 542–43).

There are a number of problems with this reasoning: (1) A play on words, especially one with polemical force, must be understood by a reader if it is to have its intended effect. Therefore, claiming such a play on words in *dôrĕšê (ha)hălāqôt* presupposes a relatively early and widespread knowledge and use of the noun *hălākâ*. The previous observations call this presupposition into question. (2) The play on words seems to demand that the noun *hălākâ* was especially associated with the Pharisees; otherwise, why would a reader make the intended connection? Yet the only two possible cases of the noun in the Dead Sea Scrolls occur in the document most directly connected with the Qumran community's own identity, the *Rule of the Community*. 1QS 1:25 refers to the conduct of candidates seeking membership in Qumran; the candidates confess the sinfulness of their former lives, a sinfulness that is attributed to "the sons of Israel" (line 23: *bĕnê yiśrāēl*) in general and not to any specific group within Israel. 1QS 3:9 refers in positive fashion to the person joining the community; he must walk "perfectly in all God's ways" (lines 3–10: [if we accept Lohse's correction] *lāleket tāmîm bĕkôl darkê ʾēl*), where *llkt* (or *lhlkt*) reflects the favorable light in which Qumran sees the conduct of its own members. There is no evidence in the scrolls (or anywhere else in the pre-70 period) for the use of the noun in connection with any other special group within Judaism. (3) In any event, our observations above highlight the fact that, if the noun *hălākâ* does occur at Qumran (and then only twice), the meaning of the noun is the general one of "walking," "conduct," "behavior," not the later technical rabbinic sense. Hence it is difficult to see how there could be a mocking reference to the *hălākôt* of the Pharisees, since such a veiled reference would seem to demand taking *hălākôt* in the later rabbinic sense—a usage not witnessed in any documents in the pre-70 period. Notice also that the claim that there is a play on words between *ḥălāqôt* and *hălākôt* demands as a presupposition that the noun *hălākâ* had already been used regularly in the plural—an idea for which there is absolutely no documentation in the pre-70 period. In sum, as we have seen throughout *A Marginal Jew*, examining our presuppositions makes us more modest in our claims.

[63] Examples of the verb *hālak* ("to walk," "to go") used with the preposition *bĕ* ("with," "in," "according to") and various "legal" nouns include, e.g., Exod 16:4; 2 Kgs 10:31; Jer 9:12; 26:4; 32:23; 44:10,23; Ps 78:10; 119:1; Dan 9:10; Neh 10:30; 2 Chr 6:16 (all with *tôrâ*, "law"); Lev 18:3–4; 20:23; 26:3; 1 Kgs 3:3; 6:12; 8:61; 2 Kgs 17:8,19; Jer 44:10,23; Ezek 5:6–7; 11:12,20; 18:9,17; 20:13,16,19,21; 33:15 (all with *ḥuqqâ*, "statute"); Ezek 11:12; 36:27 (all with *ḥōq*, "statute"); 1 Kgs 6:12;

2 Chr 17:4 (all with *miṣwâ*, "commandment"); Ezek 37:24; Ps 89:31; Job 34:23 (all with *mišpāṭ*, "judgment," "ordinance"); and Jer 44:23 (with *'adût*, "testimony"). Qumran examples include 11QT 59:16 (with *ḥōq,*, "statute") and 1QS 8:20 (with *mišpāṭ*, "judgment," "ordinance").

[64] On *hălākâ* in rabbinic usage, see Jaffee, *Torah in the Mouth*, 73–83, 187–89.

[65] On this question, see Loader's *Jesus' Attitude towards the Law*.

[66] We must take seriously the possibility that early Christians, when they missionized Gentiles, simply dropped certain parts of Jesus' halakic teaching because these parts were considered unintelligible or irrelevant to the Gentile audience. A further possibility is that some of Jesus' teaching entered into the general moral exhortations we hear in the NT epistles without the authors of the epistles or their sources specifying (or perhaps even knowing) that the teaching came from Jesus; see John Piper, *"Love Your Enemies." Jesus' Love Command in the Synoptic Gospels and the Early Christian Paraenesis* (SNTSMS 38; Cambridge: Cambridge University, 1979); contrast Jürgen Sauer, "Traditionsgeschichtliche Erwägungen zu den synoptischen und paulinischen Aussagen über Feindesliebe und Wiedervergeltungsverzicht," *ZNW* 76 (1985) 1–28. Commentators often point out intriguing similarities between sections of the Epistle of James and Matthew's Sermon on the Mount. See, e.g., Peter H. Davids, "James and Jesus," *Gospel Perspectives. The Jesus Tradition Outside the Gospels. Volume 5* (ed. David Wenham; Sheffield: JSOT, 1985) 63–84; for a fuller consideration of possible parallels between the sayings of Jesus and the Epistle of James, see D. B. Deppe, *The Sayings of Jesus in the Epistle of James* (Chelsea, MI: Brookcrafters, 1989); Patrick J. Hartin, *James and the 'Q' Sayings of Jesus* (JSNTSup 47; Sheffield: JSOT, 1991). In *Gospel Perspectives. The Jesus Tradition Outside the Gospels. Volume 5*, see also David Wenham, "Paul's Use of the Jesus Tradition: Three Samples," 7–37; and Peter Richardson and Peter Gooch, "Logia of Jesus in 1 Corinthians," 39–62. For Paul in particular, see Dale C. Allison, Jr., "The Pauline Epistles and the Synoptic Gospels. The Patterns of the Parallels," *NTS* 28 (1982) 1–32; Nikolaus Walter, "Paulus und die urchristliche Tradition," *NTS* 31 (1985) 298–522; Frans Neirynck, "Paul and the Sayings of Jesus," *L'Apôtre Paul* (BETL 73; ed. A. Vanhoye; Leuven: Leuven University/Peeters, 1986) 265–321. On 1 Peter, see Ernest Best, "I Peter and the Gospel Tradition," *NTS* 16 (1969–70) 95–113; Gerhard Maier, "Jesustradition im 1. Petrusbrief?" *Gospel Perspectives. The Jesus Tradition Outside the Gospels. Volume 5*, 85–128; further discussion and bibliography can be found in Paul J. Achtemeier, *1 Peter* (Hermeneia; Minneapolis: Fortress, 1996) 9–12; John H. Elliott, *1 Peter* (AYB 37B; New York: Doubleday, 2000; reprint New Haven: Yale University Press) 20–30. See also Helmut Koester, *Ancient Christian Gospels* (London: SCM; Philadelphia: Trinity, 1990) 49–75. For the time being, I simply note this problem in general. We will have to return to specific instances of possible allusions to Jesus' moral teaching in the epistles in later chapters, especially Chapter 33 on oaths and Chapter 36 on the love commandments.

[67] The point of the remarks that follow is not to present an exegesis of Matt 5:17–20 or of the antitheses in 5:21–48; various topics mentioned in the antitheses will be treated in subsequent chapters of this volume (specifically, divorce in Chapter 32, oaths in Chapter 33, and love of enemies in Chapter 36). The point here is simply to emphasize from the start that it is illegitimate to treat Matt 5:17–20 as a programmatic statement of the Law uttered by the historical Jesus. A prime example of the old German "liberal lives" of Jesus that did just that is Adolf von Harnack's "Hat Jesus das alttestamentliche Gesetz abgeschafft?" *Aus Wissenschaft und Leben* (2 vols.; Giessen: Töpelmann, 1911) 2. 227–36. A somewhat more critical approach that still takes Matt 5:17 as a statement of the stance of the historical Jesus is Werner Georg Kümmel, "Jesus und die jüdische Traditionsgedanke," *ZNW* 33 (1934) 105–30; see also Hans Joachim Schoeps, "Jésus et la loi juive," *RHPR* 33 (1953) 1–20. Closer to our own day, Robert Banks (*Jesus and the Law in the Synoptic Tradition* [SNTSMS 28; Cambridge: Cambridge University, 1975] 204–13) defended the substantial authenticity of Matt 5:17. Robert A. Guelich (*The Sermon on the Mount* [Waco, TX: Word, 1982] 162–64) also defended the basic authenticity of 5:17, while allowing for some Matthean redaction. Davies and Allison (*The Gospel According to Saint Matthew* [ICC; 3 vols.; Edinburgh: Clark, 1988, 1991, 1997] 1. 482) leave open a slight possibility of the verse coming from Jesus. More recently, in his summary style that avoids particular questions about particular verses, Wright (*Jesus and the Victory of God*, 288–89) affirms that Jesus "would have said things like" 5:17–20. Without any concern for the critical problems involved, Bruce Chilton (*Rabbi Jesus. An Intimate Biography* [New York: Doubleday, 2000]140) cites 5:17 to show that "the old Galilean loyalty to the Torah was in his [i.e., Jesus'] bones."

[68] For various views on the degree of Matthean redaction in 5:17, see Meier, *Law and History*, 65–89, 120–24 (Matthew has heavily redacted a traditional saying); H. Stephenson Brooks, *Matthew's Community. The Evidence of His Special Sayings Material* (JSNTSup 16; Sheffield: JSOT, 1987) 26–27 (5:17 is a Matthean redactional creation). In a larger sense, the whole of 5:17–20, carefully crafted and positioned by Matthew, acts as the grand introduction to the six antitheses in 5:21–48; cf. Roland Deines, *Die Gerechtigkeit der Tora im Reich des Messias. Mt 5,13–20 als Schlüsseltext der mattäischen Theologie* (WUNT 177; Tübingen: Mohr [Siebeck], 2004) 95–434; Matthias Konradt, "Die vollkommene Erfüllung der Tora und der Konflikt mit den Pharisäern im Matthäusevangelium," *Das Gesetz im frühen Judentum und im Neuen Testament* (Novum Testamentum et Orbis Antiquus/SUNT 57; Christoph Burchard Festschrift; ed. Dieter Sänger and Matthias Konradt; Göttingen: Vandenhoeck & Ruprecht; Fribourg: Academic Press, 2006) 129–52. Matt 5:20 in particular is a prime candidate for being a pure Matthean creation; on this, see Rudolf Bultmann, *Die Geschichte der synoptischen Tradition* (FRLANT 29; 8th ed. with *Ergänzungsheft* by Gerd Theissen; Göttingen: Vandenhoeck & Ruprecht, 1970, originally 1921) 143, 147, 161; Albert Descamps, "Essai d'interprétation de Mt 7, 17–48. Formgeschichte ou Redaktionsgeschichte?" *SE I*, 156–73 (in which Descamps changes his earlier view that 5:20 goes back to the historical Jesus; this earlier view can be found in his *Les justes et la justice*

dans les évangiles et le christianisme primitif hormis la doctrine proprement pauli-nienne [Gembloux: Duculot, 1950] 120–21, 181–83); Herbert Braun, *Spätjüdisch-häretischer und frühchristlicher Radikalismus: Jesus von Nazareth und die essenische Qumransekte* (BHT 24; 2 vols.; Tübingen: Mohr [Siebeck], 1957) 2. 10 and n. 1; Meier, *Law and History*, 116–19. Not unlike Descamps, Jacques Dupont earlier (in vol. 1 of *Les béatitudes*) thought that 5:20 was traditional; by the time he wrote vol. 3, he had come to favor the view that it was a Matthean creation. See his *Les béatitudes* (3 vols.; 2d ed.; Paris: Gabalda, 1969 [vols. 1 and 2], 1973 [vol. 3]); cf. in particular 1. 133 and 3. 251 n. 2. On the general question of Matthew and the Law, see also Wolfgang Reinbold, "Das Matthäusevangelium, die Pharisäer und die Tora," *BZ* 50 (2006) 51–73; idem, "Matthäus und das Gesetz," *BZ* 50 (2006) 244–50.

[69] For the full argument in favor of Matthew's heavy redaction, if not creation, of 5:17, see my treatment in Meier, *Law and History*, 65–89; cf. Davies and Allison, *The Gospel According to Saint Matthew*, 1. 482–87; Donald A. Hagner, *Matthew* (Word Biblical Commentary 33A and 33B; Dallas: Word, 1993, 1995) 1. 104–6. Here I simply touch upon a few key indicators of Matthew's hand.

[70] On the formula quotations (*Reflexionszitate*) in Matthew, see Krister Stendahl, *The School of St. Matthew* (Acta Seminarii Neotestamentici Upsaliensis 20; 2d ed.; Lund: Gleerup, 1968); Robert Gundry, *The Use of the Old Testament in St. Matthew's Gospel* (NovTSup 18; Leiden: Brill, 1967); R. S. McConnell, *Law and Prophecy in Matthew's Gospel* (Theologische Dissertationen 2; Basel: F. Reinhardt Kommissionsverlag, 1969); W. Rothfuchs, *Die Erfüllungszitate des Matthäus-Evangeliums* (BWANT 88; Stuttgart: Kohlhammer, 1969); George M. Soares Prabhu, *The Formula Quotations in the Infancy Narrative of Matthew* (AnBib 63; Rome: Biblical Institute, 1976). On the larger question of the Law and the prophets in Matthew, see Alexander Sand, *Das Gesetz und die Propheten* (Biblische Untersuchungen 11; Regensburg: Pustet, 1974).

[71] The introductory formula with *plēroō* is found in full or abbreviated forms in Matt 1:22; 2:15,17,23; 4:14; 8:17; 12:17; 13:35; 21:4; 26:54 + 56 [but here as a global allusion]; 27:9); to these made be added the compound form *anaplēroō* in Matt 13:14.

[72] The other four instances of *plēroō* are Matt 3:15; 5:17; 13:48; and 23:32.

[73] For *poieō*, see Matt 5:19; 7:12,21,24; 8:9; 12:50; 19:16; 21:6,31; 23:3,23; 26:19. For *tēreō*, see 19:17; 23:3; 28:20. For *phylassō*, see 19:20.

[74] Matthew's usage is especially striking when compared to the one other context in the NT where *plēroō* and its cognates are used in reference to the Law. This is the Pauline context of the fulfillment of the Law by love of neighbor (Gal 5:14; 6:2; Rom 13:8–10; perhaps Rom 8:4 belongs here too). The intriguing point here is that

these parenetic contexts in Paul have strong thematic connections with the tradition behind Matt 22:34–40 and, to a lesser extent, 7:12 and 19:18–19. Yet it is precisely in these Matthean verses that the *plēroō* vocabulary, so widely attested elsewhere in Matthew, is missing. At the same time, Paul, while using *plēroō* in Law contexts, never uses the verb in reference to the fulfillment of prophecy. Clearly, Matthew's use of *plēroō* should not be assimilated to Paul's. Its precise philological and theological contours are unique in the NT and point to Matt 5:17 being either heavily reworked by Matthew or simply created by him. Matthew's hand can also be seen in creating an overarching theological framework in which "the Law and the prophets" are yoked together under the rubric of prophetic fulfillment. We find the same uniquely Matthean perspective in Matthew's reworking of a Q saying whose original form is seen more clearly in Luke 16:16a: "The Law and the prophets [lasted] until John" (for a fuller treatment of this text, see *A Marginal Jew*, 2. 156–63). Matthew transforms this periodization of salvation history into a statement (Matt 11:13) whose phrasing is unique in the LXX and the NT: "For all the *prophets and the Law prophesied* until John." Nowhere else in the LXX or the NT do we find the inverted order "prophets and the Law," and nowhere else in the LXX or the NT is "the Law" (*ho nomos*) the subject of the verb "prophesy" (*prophēteuō*). Thus, the same concerns about welding the Law and the prophets together under the concept of the christological fulfillment of prophecy are evinced in both 11:13 and 5:17. Not just a word here or there but the whole theological thrust of 5:17 is specifically Matthean.

[75] One can easily see the point of Matthew's redactional addition of "do not think" to the traditional formula "I have come" (in the Greek, *ēlthon*, which gives the formula its usual form-critical name: the *ēlthon*-word). In his larger redactional composition of 5:17–48, v 17 acts as an explanation and warning to the disciples hearing the Sermon on the Mount. They are about to be exposed to the radical teaching of the antitheses ("it was said to the men of old . . . but I say to you") in vv 21–48. The direct opposition between old and new, the apparent revocation of three institutions enshrined in the Mosaic Law (divorce, oaths, legal retaliation), the implicit but still daring claim that Jesus effectively stands in the place of Yahweh on Sinai—all this could conjure up the mistaken notion that moral law and sanctions were being totally rescinded. While Matthew does not represent the most extreme conservative wing of Jewish Christianity, he is intent upon inculcating right action under the rubric of *doing* the Father's will according to the commands of Jesus, which to his mind are the true interpretation and eschatological fulfillment of the Mosaic Law. Hence Matthew places 5:17 first in his programmatic statement on the Law to avoid any misconceptions about what the antitheses are saying. At the same time, 5:17 also acts as a positive explanation of what is happening in the eschatological teaching of Jesus and why (christological grounding of Christian moral teaching). In all this, we are hearing the voice of the evangelist Matthew, not that of the historical Jesus. Another indication that we are dealing here with Matthew's redactional hand is that Matt 5:17 and 10:34 are the only two cases in the Gospels of the full dialectical form of an *ēlthon*-word ("I have come" *not* to do this *but* to

do that) that repeat the key verb *ēlthon* ("I have come") in the second main clause (i.e., "do not think that I have *come*" to do such-and-such; "I have *come*" not to do this but to do that). Thus, the overall formulation of Matt 5:17 (introductory "do not think" + full dialectical form of an *ēlthon*-word + repetition of the verb *ēlthon* in the second main clause) is clearly a Matthean creation. When one adds to this Matthew's favorite verb *plēroō* and his emphasis on the Law and the prophets, one wonders if there is anything in this verse that is not a Matthean creation.

[76] On Matthew's creation and placement of the overall structure of the six antitheses, see Meier, *Law and History*, 126–35.

[77] This point is almost universally granted by critical exegetes today; for standard treatments, see W. D. Davies, *The Setting of the Sermon on the Mount* (Cambridge: Cambridge University, 1966); Robert A. Guelich, *The Sermon on the Mount* (Waco, TX: Word, 1982). The somewhat idiosyncratic views of Hans Dieter Betz on the sources and formation of the Sermon on the Mount have not received general acceptance; see his *The Sermon on the Mount* (Hermeneia; Minneapolis: Fortress, 1995). I shall return to Betz's views later in this volume, especially in Chapter 36 on the love commandments.

[78] This is not to deny a priori that some chains of sayings or longer parables might have come from Jesus himself. Indeed, such may well be the case, e.g., with some of the beatitudes, since we have examples of chains of beatitudes in Palestinian Judaism before the time of Jesus (see *A Marginal Jew*, 2. 325). The fairly secure judgment that some primitive form of the Lord's Prayer goes back to Jesus (ibid., 291–302) explodes the image of a Jesus who did nothing but spout one-line aphorisms—a strange retrojection of a common American figure, the stand-up comic. At the same time, it is a matter of fact that the careful application of critical methods usually leads us in the direction of small units of tradition, which of their nature were both striking because of their pithiness and easy to remember because of their brevity.

[79] I say this quite aware that in some cases (e.g., the prohibition of divorce, certain parables), Jesus himself may have spoken a halakic teaching or a parable a number of times in different circumstances, to different audiences, and hence in different forms. Yet this valid insight does not serve as a one-size-fits-all solution to variant forms of one basic saying. For example, among the best attested sayings of Jesus are the "eucharistic words" of Jesus over the bread and wine at the Last Supper (with four different formulations). The variations in 1 Cor 11:23–25; Mark 14:22–24; Matt 26:26–28; and Luke 22:19–20 do not stem from the fact that Jesus spoke these words a number of times on different occasions. Jesus had an opportunity to say them only once before his arrest and execution.

[80] On this distinction and its anachronistic application to Palestinian Judaism at the turn of the era, see Sanders, "Law," 256; the rejection of this distinction is also an underlying theme that runs through Sanders's essay, "The Synoptic Jesus and

the Law," *Jewish Law from Jesus to the Mishnah*, 1–96. Julius Wellhausen, one of the greatest figures in Pentateuchal criticism, was all too typical of the scholarly views of his day in maintaining that Jesus taught a "natural morality" that broke with the legal and ritual system of ancient Judaism; on this, see Blenkinsopp, *The Pentateuch*, 12. This whole topic will be treated at greater length when we examine Jewish purity rules in Chapter 35. For now, I simply lay out the essentials of my position in the main text.

[81] This privileging of the inner religious experience of the individual as set over against the external, communal, and ritual elements of religion is typical of many American philosophers and theologians, one of the greatest being William James. In an indirect way, he might be considered the grandfather, if not the father, of the modern American mantra, "spiritual but not religious."

[82] I purposely speak of "Palestinian Judaism" when making these statements, since Philo of Alexandria indicates that he knows of some extreme allegorizers in Diaspora Judaism (probably in Alexandria) who felt that they were not held to the literal observance of the Law as long as they understood and followed its symbolic sense. For all his Middle-Platonic emphasis on the invisible, spiritual world as superior to the visible world of the senses, Philo never went this far—nor, as far as we can tell, did most Diaspora Jews. Indeed, at least some Jews in the Diaspora may have striven to be all the more meticulous in their observance because of their alien and at times hostile surroundings.

[83] On dialectical negation, see Arnulf Kuschke, "Das Idiom der 'relativen Negation' im NT," *ZNW* 43 (1950–51) 263; and Heinz Kruse, "Die 'dialektische Negation' als semitisches Idiom," *VT* 4 (1954) 385–400; cf. *A Marginal Jew*, 2. 482 n. 141. We shall return to this point when we examine the purity laws in Chapter 35.

[84] Here I take the view espoused by commentators like Dennis J. McCarthy and Roland E. Murphy, "Hosea," *NJBC*, 223: "Hosea does not reject sacrifice entirely (cf. 9:4, where deprivation of sacrifice is a punishment, therefore the loss of a good thing). In Hebr[ew] fashion, he affirms now one aspect, now another, without troubling about nuances." A similar position is found in Frank I. Andersen and David Noel Freedman, *Hosea* (AYB 24; Garden City, NY: Doubleday, 1980; reprint New Haven: Yale University Press) 430: "sacrifice is not denigrated; it is simply put in second place." These critics take the pivotal Hebrew preposition *min* (literally, "from") in a comparative ("more than") rather than privative ("not") sense. For the opposite view, see A. A. Macintosh, *Hosea* (ICC; Edinburgh: Clark, 1997) 233–34.

[85] On this, see *A Marginal Jew*, 2. 617–18, 632 n. 2.

[86] For one example of this tendency, see John Dominic Crossan, *The Historical Jesus* (San Francisco: Harper, 1991) 421–22, summarizing the argument made throughout pp. 265–353.

[87] For a brief refutation of the portrait of Jesus as a Jewish type of Cynic philosopher, see Paul Rhodes Eddy, "Jesus as Diogenes? Reflections on the Cynic Jesus Thesis," *JBL* 115 (1996) 449–69. See also the thoughtful treatment of David E. Aune, "Jesus and Cynics in First-Century Palestine: Some Critical Considerations," *Hillel and Jesus* (ed. James H. Charlesworth and Loren L. Johns; Minneapolis: Fortress, 1997) 176–92.

CHAPTER 32

Jesus' Teaching on Divorce

I. INTRODUCTION: SOME PRELIMINARY CLARIFICATIONS

If we choose to start our investigation of Jesus' sayings on legal matters with those that enjoy multiple attestation, then the first candidate is naturally Jesus' sayings on divorce.[1] Appearing as they do in more than one source—Mark, Q (Matthew/Luke), and Paul (1 Corinthians)—and in more than one literary form, the sayings on divorce enjoy a remarkable abundance of attestation when compared to most other sayings on the Law. Still, one approaches the sayings on divorce with a certain trepidation, since the question of divorce leads us into a confusing morass of historical, exegetical, and theological problems. A few preliminary observations may prove helpful in clearing the ground, setting the stage, and focusing our attention on the precise question to be asked.

(1) The practice of divorce was by no means unique or specific to ancient Israel. Divorce was a widespread phenomenon throughout the ancient Near East and Mediterranean world, just as it is a widespread phenomenon throughout the modern world.[2] Then, as now, what varied from people to people were the precise rules governing divorce. But divorce was the given, and it was that given, along with the rules on how it was to be implemented by ordinary Jews living in Israel, that Jesus addressed in his teaching.

(2) Because divorce was such a universal reality, taken for granted as a necessary institution in a well-ordered society, there is no great body of divorce law in the OT. Divorce had existed in the ancient Near East long before Israel came on the scene. Israel simply adopted the institution of divorce, as it adopted many other institutions from its neighbors, with some changes here and there.[3] As throughout the ancient world, divorce in Israel was not the direct concern of the state (when the state finally came into being). As with marriage, so with divorce, there were no obligatory public ceremonies

74

or procedures imposed and registered by the state. Insofar as divorce was regulated at all, it was largely governed by immemorial custom passed down in one's tribe, clan, or family. As was true throughout the ancient Near East, divorce was mostly a matter of private, not public, law.[4] And, as one would expect in a Semitic patriarchal society, the law was controlled by the dominant males. Hence, in the land of Israel, the decision to divorce lay, with very few exceptions, within the complete control and discretion of the husband.[5] It was no one's business but his. It was with the few exceptional cases in which the husband's power was restricted that the Mosaic Law dealt. But the Law neither instituted divorce nor regulated it in great detail.

(3) As we come to treat the question of divorce within the larger project of *A Marginal Jew*, it is vital to remember what our focus is. We are asking only what a particular Palestinian Jew named Jesus taught other Palestinian Jews about divorce ca. A.D. 28. This point must be stressed because the halakic teaching of Jesus *the Jew*, addressing *other Jews*, is usually not the sole or even the major focus of most of the countless modern books and articles on "Jesus and Divorce" or "Divorce in the NT." Whether overtly or covertly, most Christian books and essays on this subject are ultimately concerned with the discipline (or lack thereof) of the Christian church(es), confronted by the modern problem of widespread divorce among people professing to be believing Christians.[6] However hard-hearted it may sound, this modern problem is not and cannot be the concern of *A Marginal Jew*. To take up this modern problem would be to reinstitute the confusion between purely historical studies on Jesus the Jew and theological claims about Jesus Christ that *A Marginal Jew* has struggled so hard to dispel.

(4) Here we run up against the uncomfortable truth that must be faced again and again by any honest quester for the historical Jesus: relevance is the enemy of history. By this I mean that a facile relevance, a rush to "what does this mean for us today?"—as though that were the only standard of truth—often hampers or distorts sober attempts to understand the past as past. To respect the past as past, as something different from our present, means to refuse to twist its arm until it yields up a desired lesson or norm for the present. To be sure, I am not against drawing lessons, ideals, values, and standards from the past to help us order our present and plan our future. But, as we engage in such a delicate dialogue with another time and place, we must constantly ask ourselves: Are we drawing our lessons from a past that really existed or a past that we prefer to make up? Are we willing to grapple intellectually with a past that is sometimes remarkably different from our present, a past that does not always share our priorities, agendas, or ways of seeing the world, a past that is therefore resistant to supplying

smooth solutions suited to our present? In brief, are we willing to be confronted, affronted, and taught by the recalcitrant other? Or is hermeneutics simply a convenient cover for retrojecting our agendas and values into the past, only to gasp in amazement as this manipulated past yields the answers we desire?

This general problem of accepting the past as past, as different, as alien, as not necessarily speaking to our concerns, is especially acute in the case of the historical Jesus. From its inception, the modern quest for the historical Jesus has all too often been pursued, explicitly or implicitly, in order to overthrow, defend, or reinterpret the Jesus proclaimed and worshiped by the church. Relatively few questers have been willing to accept a double truth that undermines this whole approach: (a) The quest for the *historical* Jesus is a valid and worthwhile *historical* endeavor within the realm of academic history, as is the quest for any other influential figure of ancient history. Apart from its relevance to some other discipline (e.g., theology or philosophy), the quest for an accurate account of the historical Jesus—like the quest for the historical Socrates or Alexander the Great—has its own inner validity. (b) Hence there can be no a priori guarantee that the results of the quest, however valid and useful for academic history, will have anything to say to Christian faith or theology. Maybe they will, maybe they won't. But a sober quest for the historical Jesus must keep the demands of theological relevance at arm's length, lest what claims to be research according to the standards of academic history be contaminated or contorted by the demands and standards of academic theology.

(5) If this is true of the quest in general, it is doubly true of the historical Jesus' teaching on divorce. Not many Christians nowadays worry about how Jesus' teaching on washing one's hands before eating or making a vow to dedicate one's property to a religious cause relates to their Christian faith and practice. Indeed, not many Christians nowadays worry about working or shopping on the Christian sabbath, to say nothing of healing the sick on that day. By contrast, Jesus' teaching on divorce has bedeviled and continues to bedevil those Catholics and Protestants who take their faith seriously. Historically, differences over whether or how to allow divorce for Christians in the face of Jesus' apparent prohibition have been a dividing line between Roman Catholics and Eastern Orthodox Christians and, later on, between Roman Catholics and Protestants (not to mention different approaches among different Protestant churches). At least among Roman Catholics, the question remains a smoldering, if not a burning, issue today.

There is therefore tremendous pressure on any Christian author writing on "Jesus and Divorce" to come up with solutions for present-day pastoral problems. With all due respect to harried pastors, such pressure must be firmly resisted by any serious quester as he or she enters the minefield of the teaching of Jesus *the Jew* on *Jewish* divorce. Decisions on how divorce was practiced by Palestinian Jews at the time of Jesus and how Jesus reacted to this practice must be made on the grounds of the historical evidence available, not on the presumed impact of such decisions on Christian marriages today. Once questers have made their historical decisions on historical grounds, Christian theologians are more than welcome to judge whether the results of this historical research do, can, or should have any impact on the present-day practice of Christians.

All this is simply one concrete reminder that the quest for the historical Jesus is, by definition, a specific area of historical research aiming at historical goals by historical means. It is not and cannot be what it all too often has been forced to be: christology masquerading as a historical quest—with the confusion then being compounded by a facile identification of the 1st-century *hălākâ* of Jesus the Jew with the later discipline of the Christian church. With this understanding of the severe limitations and narrow focus of this chapter, let us begin our quest for the historical Jesus' teaching on divorce.

II. DIVORCE IN THE PENTATEUCH

As I emphasized earlier, in ancient Israel marriage and divorce were basically private matters within a family and between families, not a state-supervised process that had to go through a court procedure. Thus, marriage had the nature of a private contract. In the Pentateuch, however, there is no indication that a *written* contract was required for a marriage. The earliest Jewish *kĕtûbôt* (contracts regulating the monetary matters involved in obtaining or dismissing a wife)[7] that have come down to us are a number of marriage contracts from an Israelite military colony on the Egyptian island of Elephantine in the Nile. These contracts, written in Aramaic, date from the 5th century B.C. and hence have great historical value. At the same time, they must be used with caution since the Elephantine community reflects a highly syncretistic, polytheistic form of the ancient Israelite religion, notably different from the mainstream Judaism of 1st-century Palestine.[8] These contracts are relevant to our major concern because they mention in passing a particular procedure for divorce, which we will examine later on in this chapter.

If we turn to the Jewish Scriptures that were revered in 1st-century Palestine, the only significant divorce law in the whole of the Pentateuch is found in Deut 24:1–4.[9] Taking divorce for granted as a private familial matter and requiring no supervision or intervention from a higher human authority, the passage seeks to regulate divorce only in a very specific case. Deut 24:1–4 has long been a puzzle for exegetes because it is one long sentence reaching from v 1 to v 4. It has the form of casuistic law:[10] *if* x is the case or is done, *then* y must follow or be done. However, it is not entirely clear where the *then* part of the law (i.e., the apodosis, the main clause) begins.[11] Most modern exegetes hold that vv 1–3 make up one long complicated *if* part (i.e., the condition, the protasis) of the law, with the *then* part (the apodosis) beginning only in v 4.[12] If that is the case, then Deut 24:1–4 might be translated literally as follows:[13]

(1) **IF** [protasis] a man takes a woman and becomes her husband,
    and [if] it happens that, if she finds no favor in his eyes
    because he finds in her a shame of a thing [= something shameful],
    he writes her a certificate of divorce
    and puts it in her hand and sends her from his house,
(2) and [if] she leaves his house and goes her way
    and becomes the wife of another [man],
(3) and [if] the second man hates her and writes her a certificate of
        divorce
    and puts it in her hand and sends her from his house
    (or if the second man who took her to be his wife dies),

(4) **THEN** [apodosis] her first husband, who sent her away,
    cannot take her again to be his wife after she was defiled,
    for this is an abomination before Yahweh,
    and you shall not bring sin upon the land
    that Yahweh your God is giving you as an inheritance.

Granted the confusing complexity of this four-verse sentence, it is not surprising that some interpreters, ancient as well as modern, have tried to begin the apodosis (the main clause) with the last part of v 1 ("he writes her a certificate of divorce"). As we saw in Chapter 31 (and as we shall see later in this chapter), Mark, Matthew, and Josephus all made a separate command out of the giving of the certificate. Later rabbinic literature was able to discover a number of laws in these four verses. Apparently, though, the real point of the original law, the precise action being regulated, lies in v 4, which is the true apodosis or conclusion of the rambling sentence stretching from v 1 to v 4.

There are many curious aspects to this law. To begin with, this law has no exact parallel to the divorce laws found elsewhere in the ancient Near East, and even in Israel it covers a relatively rare event.[14] In addition, Deut 24:1 contains a famous linguistic puzzle that centuries later was to become a bone of contention between two rabbinic schools, the House of Hillel and the House of Shammai (see *m. Git.* 9:10).[15] The puzzle revolves around the precise meaning of the phrase "shame of a thing" or "something indecent" (*'erwat dābār*, literally, "nakedness of a thing") in v 1.[16] The vagueness of the phrase strikes one as strange when one considers that this long-winded law goes on at great length to specify a precise chain of events and to use terms proper to marriage law. These include the rare biblical phrase "certificate of divorce" (*sēfer kĕrîtût*, "the scroll of cutting off") in vv 1 + 3, found again in the Jewish Scriptures only in Jer 3:8 and Isa 50:1.[17]

Perhaps "shame of a thing" is purposefully left vague in order to permit wide latitude for the husband's judgment within a patriarchal society governed by the codes of honor and shame.[18] The point of stating that the basis for divorce is "something of shame" or "something indecent" is thus, paradoxically, a refusal to specify any one precise reason, for to do that would be to narrow the husband's discretionary power. Rather, *whatever* the husband, along with the fellow males in his family, clan, or village, would find injurious to his honor or sense of propriety constitutes sufficient reason for divorcing his wife.[19] To this extent, the later interpretations of Philo, Josephus, and the House of Hillel, which emphasize the freedom of the husband to divorce his wife for any reason, probably reflect the original thrust of the text. However, we must bear in mind that, unlike the later Hillel-Shammai debate, Deut 24:1–4 is not explicitly pondering or adjudicating debates over the proper grounds for divorce. Rather, taking for granted and reflecting the almost unlimited discretion of the husband in the matter, it limits (in one very specific and presumably rare case) his power to remarry the wife he has previously divorced.

All this helps to remind us that the wife is not necessarily being divorced for moral failure. Even more to the point, personal morality (as we moderns would understand it) has nothing to do with the prohibition of the wife's return to her first husband after her second marriage. The wife is not viewed as an immoral person. Rather, the law reflects Israel's concern with purity, especially the purity of the Promised Land that is a typical concern of Deuteronomy. On the one hand, the woman could have returned to her first husband if she had not married another. (Needless to say, in a polygamous society, the fact that her husband might in the meantime have married another woman would not in itself be a barrier to the return of his first wife to him.) On the other hand, even after the second divorce, the twice-repudiated woman could marry a third man. What is prohibited is therefore a very narrow and precise type of behavior: the return of the twice-divorced wife to her first husband. To the mind of the ancient Israelite, the woman's second marriage rendered her "defiled" (we might say "taboo") in relation to her first husband, but not to other men. We are obviously in a very different world from that of the modern divorce law of the West, where concerns about such legal purity play no part.[20]

Indeed, even within the corpus of the laws of Deuteronomy, Deut 24:1–4 stands alone. Its precise subject matter as well as its mention of a step-by-step procedure in divorcing has no real parallel elsewhere in Deuteronomy. To our mind-set, the curious and relatively rare case it treats hardly qualifies it to be a major matrix of later divorce law—which was, however, to be its fate. One reason it was to meet this fate is that the law codes of the Pentateuch have precious little else to say about divorce. Significantly, the two other regulations in Deuteronomy both serve the same purpose as Deut 24:1–4: to limit the otherwise unlimited power of the husband. Like Deut 24:1–4, the two other texts treat of very specific cases. In Deut 22:13–19, a husband who falsely accuses his wife of not being a virgin at the time of their marriage is forbidden ever to divorce her. In Deut 22:28–29, a man who rapes or seduces a virgin who is not yet betrothed must marry her and may never divorce her. The only other law in the Pentateuch that touches on divorce—and then only indirectly—is Lev 21:7,13–14, which treats a very special case from a perspective quite different from that of Deuteronomy. Lev 21:7,13–14 prohibits a divorced woman (as well as a prostitute or a "defiled" woman) from marrying a priest, for such a marriage would violate his cultic holiness.[21] Thus, this law does not regulate divorce itself but rather one of the possible consequences of divorce for the divorced woman and a prospective husband.

That, remarkably, is the extent of the divorce laws in the Pentateuch. All we have are a few scattered statutes regulating a few, mostly rare, cases. Pressing questions about the support of the divorced wife and the fate of any children produced by the marriage are never addressed by these laws.[22] One can therefore appreciate how, with the lack of any detailed divorce law, the tendency over time would be to focus on the lengthy law in Deut 24:1–4, since it alone among the divorce laws mentions in passing the procedure presupposed in divorce.[23]

III. DIVORCE IN THE PROPHETS
AND WISDOM LITERATURE

The rarity of references to divorce law is not restricted to the Pentateuch. The two significant references in the major prophets (Isa 50:1; Jer 3:1–2,8) have already been mentioned; they speak of the certificate of divorce only in a metaphorical sense to describe Yahweh's less-than-smooth relations with his supposed bride, the people of Israel.[24] After the Babylonian exile, we hear of attempts by the reformer Ezra to force Jews who had married foreign wives to divorce them (Ezra 9–10). This, however, seems to have been an extraordinary policy for a critical period after the exile rather than the rule in the whole postexilic period. The most important aspect of this reform policy of Ezra is that it is one possible backdrop to a curious text in the prophet Malachi, namely, Mal 2:10–16. Regrettably, one cannot be certain about the precise thrust of this passage for two reasons. First, the exact problem the prophet is addressing is not clear. The vast majority of commentators hold that the problem has something to do with divorce, but even this interpretation is not absolutely sure.[25] Second, the Hebrew text that we have in the standard edition, the Masoretic text (MT), seems to have suffered corruption and probably does not make sense as it stands, especially at the climactic verse, 2:16.[26]

What *is* clear is that Mal 2:1–16 begins with a rebuke to Jerusalem and Judah for their faithless activity vis-à-vis Yahweh. Using a typical prophetic metaphor, Malachi likens the people's infidelity to Yahweh to marital infidelity. This image apparently slides into the allied topic of the infidelity of husbands to their wives—though the Hebrew text is far from pellucid at this point. If the general sense is a rebuke to husbands for being unfaithful to their wives, this, in itself, is a startling prophetic indictment. For, in the traditional Israelite view of marital relations, a husband could commit adultery only by having relations with another man's wife, thus violating the rights of the other husband. A man could not commit adultery against his own wife, say, by having relations with an unmarried woman, since his wife had no absolute claim on his sexual activity.[27]

It is at the climax of this remarkable prophetic indictment that the Hebrew text becomes almost unintelligible. Many standard English translations render the beginning of v 16 with phrases like "For I hate divorce, says Yahweh the God of Israel."[28] Some Christian authors wax eloquent about how this prophetic denunciation of divorce anticipates Jesus' wholesale rejection of divorce (some 500 years later). There is one slight problem: the opening Hebrew words of v 16 apparently do not make sense as they stand in the MT. In any event, they certainly do not mean "For I hate divorce." Taken literally as they appear in the MT, the initial Hebrew words of v 16 (*kî śānē' šallaḥ*) mean something like "For [or: 'if'; or: 'when'; or: 'indeed'] he hated [or possibly: 'hating'], send away! [or: 'to send away']." I purposely make this translation as confusing as possible. As one can readily see, each word has more than one possible meaning, and no combination of meanings (e.g., "for he hated to send away") really makes all that much sense in the larger context.[29] Only by changing vowel points, adding consonants, assigning words unusual meanings, or understanding words not expressed in the verse can one produce an intelligible text—but then we are reading our text, not Malachi's. Only by doing violence to the received MT can we manufacture the much beloved but textually unsupported translation "For I hate divorce."

The Greek translators were apparently as nonplussed by the unintelligible Hebrew of v 16 as their modern counterparts are. Two major approaches are seen in the Greek manuscripts of Malachi. Some manuscripts read "but if, hating [her], you send [her] away . . . , then impiety will cover your garments [or: your thoughts]." This approach seems to condemn divorce, at least when motivated purely by hatred.[30] Other manuscripts read instead "but if you hate [her], send [her] away!"[31] This approach, which takes the Hebrew verb *šallaḥ* as an imperative, actually commands (or at least counsels) divorce if the husband hates his wife. This latter interpretation was apparently already circulating among Jewish scribes in Palestine in the 2d century B.C. For, in the *Scroll of the Minor Prophets* discovered at Qumran, Mal 2:15–16 (with some lacunas) is found in a wording that differs from the MT and reflects in part the second approach of the Greek translations. The initial words of Mal 2:16 in the *Scroll* (4Q XII[a] ii. 4–7) probably mean something like "but if you hate [her], send [her] away,"[32] thus interpreting Mal 2:16 as permitting, if not actually commanding, divorce.

This interpretation, witnessed in the first centuries B.C. by both the Qumran Hebrew text of Malachi and part of the Greek tradition, becomes the dominant tradition later on, as witnessed by the translation of Mal 2:16 in the Vulgate as well as by the targum on Malachi in the *Targum Jonathan to the Prophets*, the Talmud, and later Jewish commentators.[33] What is intriguing here is that the confused text of Mal 2:16 clearly became a focal point of reflection on the rightness or wrongness of divorce quite early on. The important point for our quest is that the permissive interpretation, reflected in the Qumran *Scroll* and part of the Greek translation tradition, continues the dominant attitude of the OT and carries it forward into the intertestamental and rabbinic periods. It is this dominant view that Jesus will be addressing in his teaching on divorce.

Throughout this discussion of prophetic texts mentioning divorce, one should remember that prophetic exhortation and condemnation, however fiery, did not possess the same binding force for later Judaism as did the laws of the Pentateuch.[34] The same is true of the various observations, counsels, and condemnations in the wisdom (sapiential) literature of the OT. In a way similar to both the Pentateuch and the prophetic literature, the wisdom literature treats divorce only rarely and only in passing. Once again, we are reminded that divorce was the given; there is no hint of an idea of forbidding divorce as an institution prior to a few disputed sectarian texts at Qumran (to be discussed below). Hence the wisdom literature of the OT, written by Jewish males for Jewish males, contents itself with sage counsel aiming at moderation and balance in exercising the unquestioned male prerogative of divorce. The common thread running through the sapiential literature is simple: on the one hand, do not divorce a good wife for superficial reasons; on the other hand, divorce a bad wife, especially an adulteress.[35]

When one considers the vast sweep of the OT, both in chronology and in literary genres, one is struck by the sparseness of references to divorce. Nowhere in this vast corpus do we find texts explicitly instituting divorce, setting forth in detail the procedures to be followed in any and every divorce, discussing which grounds for divorce are valid, or questioning the basic validity and/or lawfulness of divorce. Nothing of this sort can be found in the literature emanating from Israelites living in Palestine prior to the 2d century B.C.

By a quirk of archaeology, we are better informed about the Jewish military colony that existed at Elephantine in Egypt in the 5th century B.C. Still, we must be careful in comparing the evidence this colony supplies with that of the Jewish Scriptures. As previously mentioned, the Jews at Elephantine represent a syncretistic form of Diaspora Judaism, complete with a goddess consort of Yahweh and an Egyptian temple. We should also remember that, although the Elephantine documents (in Aramaic) are often cited in discussions of Jewish divorce practices, we are not dealing with the kind of document certifying divorce that is called a *sēfer kĕrîtut* in the OT and a *gēṭ* in rabbinic literature. Rather, we are dealing at Elephantine with marriage contracts, which, however, provide for the eventuality of divorce. According to these Elephantine documents: (1) either husband or wife had the power to divorce his or her spouse,[36] (2) the divorce was apparently at the will of the divorcing partner (at least, no particular grounds for divorce are listed), (3) and apparently the divorce could be accomplished simply by a declaration in the public assembly.[37]

All this warns us not to import the practices of Elephantine into the practices of Palestinian Judaism in the last centuries B.C. or at the time of Jesus:

(1) The canonical Jewish Scriptures nowhere allow wives to divorce their husbands.[38] (2) Prior to the Book of Tobit (Tob 7:13), there is no mention in the literature of Palestinian Judaism of a written marriage contract.[39] (3) By the 1st century A.D., a written certificate of divorce is viewed not only as a mandatory part of the process but even, at least in some quarters, as a commandment of the Mosaic Torah itself. This, and not the quite different situation at Elephantine in the 5th century B.C., is the context in which Jesus addresses the issue of divorce.

IV. INTERTESTAMENTAL PERIOD:
PHILO, JOSEPHUS, AND QUMRAN

Strict chronology would demand that the Qumran materials be treated first, then Philo and Josephus. However, for strategic purposes, I place Qumran last in this section.[40] The statements of Philo and Josephus are brief and straightforward. More significantly, they simply continue the dominant view seen throughout the OT: divorce lies in the power of the husband, and he can divorce his wife for more or less any reason. When we come to the sectarian compositions found at Qumran, we are dealing with more than one document and presumably more than one author. The relevant documents do not entirely agree in their statements, and modern scholars debate whether or to what extent these documents forbid divorce. Hence the Qumran documents will demand more detailed examination than either Philo or Josephus.

A. PHILO

Philo's commentary on the key divorce law of Deut 24:1–4 is found in his treatise *On the Special Laws* (*De specialibus legibus*), more specifically in Book Three (3.5 §30–31), which covers the Decalogue commandments forbidding adultery (and other sexual sins) and murder (and other forms of violence). Philo's commentary on Deut 24:1–4 in Book Three is a parade example of why Philo should not be cavalierly dismissed in discussion of Jewish *hălākâ* at the turn of the era simply because of his allegorizing tendencies. His explanation of the divorce law is, on the whole, an accurate and sober summary of the plain meaning of the Deuteronomy text. Philo does, however, add his own rationale for the law as well as a specific sanction for breaking that law.

Philo abbreviates the complicated sentence of Deut 24:1–4 and so focuses on the main point of the law: the woman, once she has been divorced from her first husband and has likewise been deprived of her second husband by either divorce or death,[41] must not return to her first husband. Clearly compressing the complicated narrative of the two marriages and the two separations by means of one conditional clause and a series of participles, Philo highlights the main clause and the core command of the law: she *must not* go back [*mē epanitō*, 3d person imperative] to the first husband. Philo thus deftly resolves the exegetical problem of where the apodosis (main clause) in the lengthy conditional law of Deut 24:1–4 begins. Along with most modern exegetes, he plainly places the beginning of the main clause and hence the main point of the law in Deut 24:4. Unlike Mark, Matthew, and Josephus, he sees in Deut 24:1 no separate law about the writing of a certificate of divorce. Indeed, so secondary to his mind is the certificate that it is never mentioned in his summary of Deut 24:1–4.

Interestingly, Philo specifies that the divorce may happen "for any reason whatever" (*kath' hēn an tychē prophasin*), an explanation that apparently gives his interpretation of the problematic phrase "a shameful thing" (*'erwat dābār*) in Deut 24:1. As we shall see below, on this point Philo agrees with Josephus. Indeed, Philo's opinion also agrees with the broad understanding of "a shameful thing" ascribed to the House of Hillel in the latter mishnaic tractate *Giṭṭin*: any reason, even finding a woman more beautiful than one's wife (so Rabbi Aqiba), suffices to justify the divorce.[42] Still, an important difference must be noted between the "whatever reason" approach of Philo and Josephus on the one hand and the view of the House of Hillel on the other. Philo and Josephus give no indication that they are combating any other view current in mainstream Judaism concerning the sufficient reason for a divorce—for example, a view that might be more restrictive. In contrast, in *m. Giṭṭin*, the latitudinarian approach of the House of Hillel is pointedly opposed to the narrower view of the House of Shammai: the wife must have done something shameful, for example, adultery. We will return to this difference later.

Two aspects of Philo's summary of the divorce law are specific to his presentation. First, Philo feels he must give a rationalizing and moralizing reason for this curious law forbidding the return of the twice-married wife to her first husband. Hence moral blame is affixed to both parties. Philo claims that the wife, in choosing new bonds of love in preference to her old ones, has forgotten and transgressed ancient boundary lines.[43] At the same time, by accepting a renewal of his marriage to his twice-divorced wife, the first husband[44] justly acquires the reputation of an effeminate and unmanly person; losing all hatred of evil (so necessary for order in the state and the

home), he is publicly branded an adulterer and a panderer.[45] As a consequence of this heinous guilt on the part of both the thrice-married wife and
her first (and now third) husband, a further addition is made by Philo to the
biblical law: the first husband as well as the wife should be put to death.

These two additions may flow from Philo's struggle to provide a hermeneutical equivalent, intelligible to his sophisticated Hellenistic readers, of
the stern condemnation of Deut 24:4: the wife is impure vis-à-vis the first
husband and so to return to him would be an "abomination" in the sight
of Yahweh, an abomination that would bring sin upon the Promised Land.
Both the contorted explanation of why the wife and the first husband are
both morally reprehensible and the surprising decree that both parties deserve to die apparently represent Philo's attempt to translate the OT ideas of
the wife's special form of legal impurity and of the awful nature of "abomination" into concepts amenable to the rationalistic minds of his audience.
Neither the explanation nor the penalty recurs in Josephus' presentation of
the law.

B. JOSEPHUS

Where Philo does agree with Josephus (and with the opinion later ascribed
by the Mishna to the House of Hillel) is that the husband may divorce his
wife for any reason. This agreement is clear in Josephus' paraphrase of Deut
24:1–4 in *Ant.* 4.8.23 §253. Josephus begins his treatment of the law with
a clear interpretation of the ambiguous reason for divorce in Deut 24:1,
"a shameful thing." Josephus turns this into a (personally?) exculpatory
gloss:[46] "If a man, wishing to divorce his wife *for whatever reason* [*kath'
hasdēpotoun aitias*], and many such reasons may occur among human beings. . . ."

In some ways, though, Josephus' paraphrase sticks closer to the Deuteronomic law than Philo's does. For instance, Josephus focuses on the husband's actions, as does Deut 24:1–4, while Philo's paraphrase focuses on
the wife. Also, unlike Philo, Josephus includes the certificate of divorce—as
well as a parenthetical explanation of its purpose—in his paraphrase of the
law: "he [the divorcing husband] must provide firm attestation in writing
that he will no longer live with her [the wife he is divorcing], for in this way
she may receive the right to live with another [husband], for prior to this
act [of giving the certificate] it would not be permissible [for her to do so]."
Indeed, not only does Josephus refer to the giving of a written certificate,
he even makes it the object of a separate command (note the imperative
form: *grammasi . . . ischyrizesthō*, "he must provide firm attestation in writ-

ing")—an interpretive move seen also in the Gospels of Mark and Matthew as well as in the later rabbis.[47] In this exaltation of the certificate of divorce to the status of a separate law, Josephus, unlike Philo, departs from what is the most likely reading of Deut 24:1–4. As we have seen in Section II, Deut 24:1–4 is a single law that has as its purpose the prohibition of the return of the twice-divorced wife to her first husband. Having made the giving of a written certificate a separate law, Josephus then proceeds, in a separate sentence, to enunciate what is for him a second law: if the second marriage fails or the second husband dies, the wife is not permitted to return to her first husband, even if he so wishes.

C. Qumran

As I noted at the beginning of this section, the material at Qumran is much more complex than the statements of either Philo or Josephus. The major texts that may touch on divorce are found in two documents of very different genres: the *Damascus Document* (CD), which is probably a rule book for Essene communities spread throughout Palestine, and the *Temple Scroll* (11QTemple), which presents a description of the temple and temple city in a utopian future. Thus, if I may underline a key point at the risk of oversimplification, the *Damascus Document* addresses and regulates the real lives that Essenes are living or trying to live at the present moment, while the *Temple Scroll* seeks to envision and regulate an ideal future. To complicate things further, the *Damascus Document* was (in the common view of scholars today) the basic rule book of the larger Essene movement—as distinct from the *Rule of the Community* (1QS), which was the basic rule book for the community actually resident at Qumran. The *Damascus Document* may therefore be rightly called "Essene" in its very essence. In contrast, scholars still debate whether the *Temple Scroll* was composed by Essenes (or more particularly Qumranites) or whether it was a document that was originally written by some eschatological group of Jews outside of Qumran and was then brought to Qumran. It is important to keep these fundamental differences in mind as one evaluates the statements about marriage in these documents.[48] In addition, one must remember that both documents are speaking first of all about the regulation of marriage and possible multiple marriages. If divorce is discussed at all, it is discussed in reference to this larger subject within the still larger context of a sectarian present or a utopian future.

Let us begin with the writing that is clearly Essene, the *Damascus Document*. The relevant text, CD 4:19–5:9 (especially 4:20–21),[49] is polemicizing against the opponents of the Essene movement. The opponents, called cryptically "the builders of the wall," [50] are accused of having being snared by *zěnût*, which in Hebrew means first of all "prostitution," though the meaning can expand to cover other types of infidelity, be they sexual or (by way of metaphor) religious. The sense here is obviously a literal, sexual one. The opponents have been snared by *zěnût* in that they have taken two wives (*nāšîm*, literally, "women") in their lifetimes.

Now the phrase "in their lifetimes" (*běhayyêhem*) is ambiguous. [51] The possessive suffix meaning "their" has the masculine form in this text, and thus the meaning of the whole statement seems, at first glance, clear: the male opponents take two wives during their own (the males') lifetimes. Unfortunately, things are not so simple in ancient Hebrew. Especially in the later biblical books, [52] the 3d person masculine plural suffix in Hebrew (*-hem*, "their") can substitute for the feminine suffix. The difference between the two suffixes is only the final letter: *-hem* (masculine) for *-hen* (feminine). This substitution is all the more possible in the CD text we are studying because the Hebrew word for "women" (*nāšîm*) has just preceded the phrase "in their lifetimes." Curiously, in Hebrew, the plural noun *nāšîm*, although it means "women," has a masculine plural ending (*-îm*). Thus, the masculine plural form of the noun "women" might have attracted the plural suffix "their" into the masculine form. If we accept this possibility, the sense of the sentence then becomes: the male opponents take two wives during the lifetimes of the two women involved—in other words, they take a second wife while the first is still living. [53]

The possible meanings of the phrase (and therefore the object of the moral condemnation) are complicated still further by the fact that, in ancient Judaism, polygyny (i.e., the practice of one man having more than one wife at the same time) was not just a theoretical possibility but an occasional reality, though probably not the common practice of ordinary Jews. [54] Thus, the presence of polygyny in 1st-century Palestinian Judaism complicates the interpretation of CD 4:20–21 even further. For, in such a religious and social context, condemning polygyny did not necessarily mean condemning divorce, and condemning divorce did not necessarily mean condemning polygyny. In other words, a Jewish teacher (perhaps under the influence of Greek or Roman customs) might think it wrong for a man to have two wives at the same time, and yet permit the same man to marry a second wife after he divorced the first (something permitted in Deuteronomy as well as in Greek and Roman law). On the other hand, it would be theoretically possible for a radically strict Jewish moral reformer to denounce any and all divorce, but allow a man to marry a second wife as long as he kept the first (polygyny being attested in the Jewish Scriptures).

With these different possibilities in mind, which interpretation of CD 4:20–21 seems more probable? If we take the personal pronoun suffix in the phrase "in *their* lives" as feminine in meaning, the condemnation would be aimed first of all at polygyny, which, though increasingly rare among ordinary Jews, remained a viable option for the rich and the ruling classes.[55] The prohibition of a man marrying a second wife while the first wife was still living would not, strictly speaking, forbid divorce, since divorce does not, of its very nature, demand the marrying of a second wife while the first is still living. Practically speaking, a man usually divorces his first wife with the intention, proximate or remote, of marrying another woman, but this is not of the essence of divorce, which simply dissolves the first marriage. The mere act of divorcing one's wife would not fall under the censure of this text if the suffix were read with a feminine meaning. Likewise, remarrying after the death of one's first wife (divorced or not), would be permissible. Thus, if we take the suffix in the phrase "in *their* lives" to have a feminine meaning, the text directly attacks only polygyny; it would attack divorce only when the husband proceeded to marry a second wife while the first was still living.[56]

If, on the other hand, the suffix in the phrase "in *their* lives" has a masculine meaning, the man would be forbidden to enter a second marriage anytime during his life, no matter what the condition of his first marriage or first wife.[57] In this case, the prohibition would directly condemn: (1) polygyny, (2) divorce followed by a second marriage while the first wife was still living, and (3) a second marriage even if the first wife (divorced or not) had died. Under this capacious reading, a happily married man, a divorced man, and a widower would all be forbidden to marry again because they were not permitted to take two wives in *their* (masculine, the men's) lifetimes. Notice, once again, even this broad prohibition does not forbid divorce in itself. It simply forbids the divorced man ever to remarry, even if his first wife dies.[58] In contrast, a second marriage after the death of the first wife would be permissible under the feminine reading of the suffix *their*.

In sum, what is clearly condemned by CD 4:20–21 is polygyny, since this is the one action that is covered by either reading of the suffix.[59] What is not condemned in itself is the mere act of divorce. What is not clear and what scholars debate is whether the text also intends to condemn all second marriages after divorce, even when the first wife has died. That polygyny is at least the major if not the only target of the condemnation is suggested by the way the condemnation is supported by the curious concatenation of three Torah "proof texts" (CD 4:21–5:2) that at first glance seem to have little to do with each other.[60] First, Gen 1:27 (the text that Jesus also quotes in Mark 10:6 and Matt 19:4) is cited at the end of CD 4:21: "Male and female he [God] created them." To this, at the beginning of CD 5:1, is added—surprisingly, to our modern minds—Gen 7:9, which states that the animals went into Noah's ark two by two, male and female;[61] the point made by this metaphorical stretch is that the human male is to have only one female partner.

To hammer home this point, a further text is adduced as proof in CD 5:2: "He shall not multiply wives unto himself" (Deut 17:17). This text, which in its Deuteronomic context refers only to the Israelite king, seems to be applied by the author of the *Damascus Document* to all Israelite men. What is being forbidden all Israelite males seems to be, at least primarily, polygyny. That is the meaning that coheres best with the original sense of Deut 17:17, which is a polemic against any Israelite king imitating the excesses of Solomon and so creating a huge harem (including non-Israelite and therefore polytheistic wives).[62]

The possibility that at least divorce, though not necessarily remarriage, was permitted by the Essene community reflected in the *Damascus Document* finds a modicum of support in an obscure and broken text in CD 13:17. The passage refers vaguely to an individual designated by the Hebrew consonants *lmgrš* (probably the participle *lamměgārēš*, "for the one who drives out"). Some commentators have seen here a reference to divorce, since that is one of the possible meanings of the verb *gēraš* ("drive out," "expel"). At the same time, one must admit that this verb has a much wider range of meanings than just "divorce." Moreover, because of the fragmentary nature of the text, the Hebrew consonants *lmgrš* have been interpreted in strikingly different ways by different commentators.[63]

Still, the larger context of column 13 speaks of the function of the Inspector or Examiner (*měbaqqēr*) in the Essene community and of the obligation of members involved in important actions (bringing people into the community, engaging in commerce with outsiders, writing a deed of purchase or sale) to obtain the permission of the Inspector. If, as some commentators think, the end of line 16 refers to marrying a woman with the Inspector's permission, the fragmentary line 17 might well refer to the obligation of a man divorcing his wife (one of the possible meanings of the verb *gēraš*) to consult with the Inspector and obtain his permission. This would fit in with the immediately following text (again, fragmentary), which seems to speak of the Inspector's (or the divorced man's?) obligation of bringing up "their sons and their little ones." Admittedly, the incomplete state of the text prevents certitude, but at the very least a reference to the obligation of a man divorcing his wife to get the Inspector's permission fits the context better than some other suggestions.[64] In sum: granted the present state of our knowledge or nescience, CD 13:17 serves as a reminder that it is possible that the Essenes did not prohibit all divorce per se. The upshot of our survey of CD 4:20–21 may be confusing, but at a minimum it warns us not to affirm blithely and without qualification that the Essenes or the Qumranites forbade any and all divorce.[65] At least the primary target of their condemnation seems to have been polygyny.

Our second text is different from the first in a number of ways. First of all, as mentioned previously, we are not sure that the *Temple Scroll* was originally composed by the Essenes (or the Qumranites) and therefore reflects their specific views.[66] Second, instead of regulating the life of the sect in the present, it envisions a utopian future. Many of its specifications of worship and daily life in and around the temple city (presumably, Jerusalem) could not be implemented in the present state of this world.[67] Some sort of eschatological transformation is presumed by the text. That some change is assumed to have taken place is indeed intimated by the text that concerns us, 11QTemple 57:15–19. Following the thread of Deuteronomy, the text legislates the marital life of a king who will abide by the rules of this eschatological group—another reminder that we are not dealing with the real situations of the Hasmonean rulers or, a fortiori, Herod the Great in the 2d or 1st century B.C. The text of 57:15–19 is therefore speaking of an ideal future when it commands:

(15) And he [the future king] shall not take a wife from among all (16) the daughters of the nations, but instead from the house of his father he shall take to himself a wife (17) from the family of his father. And he shall not take in addition to her another wife, for (18) she alone shall be with him all the days of her life. And if she dies, he shall take (19) to himself another [wife] from the house of his father, from his family.

Yigael Yadin thought that this text helped solve the debate about the meaning of CD 4:20–21 in favor of taking the disputed suffix as feminine: men may not take two wives in their (the wives') lifetimes.[68] Taking the two texts together, Yadin held that the sect would have condemned polygyny and divorce, but not the second marriage of a widower. In his reply to Yadin, Jerome Murphy-O'Connor rightly objected that, given the uncertainty of the date of the various scrolls found at Qumran and the possibility of evolution in the sect's doctrines, we cannot presume a homogeneity of the various scrolls on this contentious point.

Complicating the whole problem is the fact that 11QTemple 57:17–19 explicitly applies its prohibition only to a future king.[69] To be sure, Joseph

Fitzmyer and other experts in Qumran literature invoke the axiom: "*Quod non licet Iovi non licet bovi*" (literally, "What is not permitted to the God Jupiter is not permitted to an ox"). In other words, if even the king is not permitted to take a second wife as long as the first is living, a fortiori this prohibition holds true of a commoner.[70] Actually, this line of reasoning is questionable. Both Lawrence H. Schiffman and David Instone Brewer note that the king in the *Temple Scroll* is often expected to follow the holiness rules binding on the high priest; moreover, a number of the Dead Sea Scrolls seem to operate with a "two-tier" approach to holiness, with greater demands made on leading figures.[71] In addition, as noted earlier, the *Temple Scroll* is legislating for a utopian future, specifically for the king who will rule in this utopian future, and more specifically still for a king who is mentioned in the corresponding law in Deut 17:17.[72]

Indeed, the larger context of 11QTemple 57 argues that the law requiring that the king have only one wife is understood to be specific to the king.[73] Seen within the whole of column 57, the special kind of consort the king has is simply the third of three special types of guardians appointed around the king to keep him from evil and sin. First, in 57:5–11, twelve thousand soldiers are to be "with him" (*'immô*) and are not to leave him "alone," lest he fall into enemy hands. Second, in 57:11–15, twelve princes, twelve priests, and twelve levites are to be "with him" (again, *'immô*) to help him interpret the law and execute judgment. Third and finally, his one wife is to be "with him [again, *'immô*] all the days of her life," presumably to keep him from sexual sin and the dangers of a harem with pagan wives. The threefold parallel structure and the bell-like repetition of "with him" argue that the sole wife, like the twelve thousand soldiers and the groups of twelve, is a special institution for the protection of the king. Granted all this, it is perilous to deduce what the sect standing behind the *Temple Scroll* thought of the ability of the ordinary Israelite to divorce and remarry in the ideal future, to say nothing of life in this present world.

Perhaps one can be even more definite on this point. There are two other passages in the *Temple Scroll* that mention divorce and take it for granted. In the first instance, columns 53 and 54 repeat with variations certain laws found in Numbers 30 that regulate vows made by women. In particular, 11QTemple 54:4–5 repeats with just a slight variation the law of Num 30:10 (30:9 in English translations): "The vow of a widow and a divorced woman (*gĕrûšâ*, literally, "a woman who has been driven out"), every [vow] by which she binds herself, shall be binding on her."[74] The existence of the divorced woman is taken for granted in this law just as much as the existence of the widow; neither status occasions comment or censure in the *Temple Scroll*.

More significantly, 11QTemple 66:8–11 repeats (with minor variations) the law of Deut 22:28–29, which commands that a man who seduces a virgin who is not yet betrothed must marry her. Both Deut 22:29 and its repetition in 11QTemple 66:11 specify that, in such a case, the husband cannot divorce this wife "all the days of his life." The point to be noted here is that this prohibition of divorce is a special penalty imposed on this particular type of husband as a punishment for having seduced a virgin. The penalty makes sense only if divorce is otherwise allowed in normal marriages.[75] That is the clear meaning of the law in Deut 22:28–29, and it is difficult to see why it should not be the clear meaning of the law in 11QTemple 66:8–11. Hence, in light of these two "divorce passages," it seems that the prohibition of divorce and remarriage, which in the *Temple Scroll* applies to the king, was not thought to extend to ordinary Israelite men. In other words, in the utopian world sketched and regulated by the *Temple Scroll*, the future king will be subject to certain special marital restrictions that will not bind commoners, who will be free to remarry after divorce.

If nothing else, our brief survey of the two key texts in the *Damascus Document* and the *Temple Scroll* shows us that sweeping statements about divorce being prohibited at Qumran should be avoided. First of all, neither the *Damascus Document* nor the *Temple Scroll* may reflect the special type of life lived at Qumran. Second, if our concern is about the *hălākâ* that actually governed the divorce practice of Palestinian Jews around the time of Jesus, the *Temple Scroll* falls out of consideration. It has its eyes fixed on a utopian future, not on Jewish society in the present moment, and it explicitly forbids divorce and remarriage only in the case of the king. Indeed, two other passages in the *Temple Scroll* imply that divorce would be a possibility for ordinary Israelites. Third, the key text of the *Damascus Document*, which seems to have governed Essene communities spread throughout Israel rather than Qumran in particular, is ambiguous. It almost certainly prohibits polygyny. Whether and to what extent it prohibits divorce is not clear. It may be that it forbids not divorce per se but rather divorce and subsequent remarriage as long as the first wife is living. Thus, it is possible that the *Damascus Document* does not prohibit divorce and later on a second marriage once the first wife has died. But, as should be clear by now, certainty is not to be had in the present state of research. On the question of divorce, the historical Essenes may be more elusive than the historical Jesus. The Essenes did forbid polygyny; their position on divorce remains a question mark.[76]

V. A GLANCE FORWARD TO THE MISHNA

The large amount of divorce legislation found in the rabbinic and post-rabbinic periods of Judaism lies beyond our narrow concern with divorce in Palestinian Judaism at the time of Jesus. It may be helpful, though, to take a quick glance forward to the earliest rabbinic corpus of *hălākâ*, the Mishna (redacted ca. A.D. 200–220). The third order (or *sēder*) of the Mishna is called *Nāšîm* ("[married] women"), and located within this order is a tractate called *Gîṭṭîn* (literally, "documents [of divorce]").[77] Most of the tractate is taken up with the proper way to draw up and deliver a document of divorce (a *gēṭ*), along with such questions as the legally authorized writers, witnesses, and intermediaries of the document, and ways in which the document can be canceled or rendered invalid. It therefore comes as something of a surprise to find, at the very end of the tractate dealing with the proper form of the document of divorce, a brief treatment of the different rabbinic opinions about the sufficient grounds for a divorce. Almost out of the blue, *m. Giṭ.* 9:10 presents the House (i.e., School) of Shammai and the House of Hillel arguing over the proper understanding of the phrase ʿerwat dābār ("the shame of a thing") from Deut 24:1. The stricter House of Shammai tries to restrict the grounds for divorce by insisting that the wife must have done something shameful, something that would injure the husband's honor within an ancient society governed by codes of honor and shame. To emphasize this key point, the House of Shammai blithely inverts the key phrase of Deut 24:1, turning "the shame of a thing" into "a thing of shame" (*dĕbar ʿerwâ*), thus stressing the element of shame. Hence, contrary to what is claimed in many treatments of the subject, the House of Shammai does not limit the grounds of divorce to adultery. Any action by the wife that would bring shame upon her husband qualifies as grounds for divorce—though improper sexual behavior would no doubt be the prime example.[78]

In this light, one can appreciate the sweeping nature of the opposing view of the House of Hillel. While the House of Shammai seized on the word ʿerwâ ("nakedness," "shame," "impropriety") to inculcate at least some restriction on the husband's power to divorce, the House of Hillel seizes on the other word in the key phrase, *dābār*, "a thing," Hence, the House of Hillel sticks to the actual order of the Deut 24:1 text: ʿerwat dābār ("the shame of a thing")—with the stress on "a thing,"understood as "anything." *Anything*, any reason whatever, is sufficient for a husband to divorce his wife. The House of Hillel gives as an example the case of a wife who spoils his husband's meal by burning it.[79] To push the point of *anything* even further, the passage adds the opinion of Rabbi Aqiba, who thinks that finding a more beautiful woman is a sufficient reason for a husband to divorce his wife. Aqiba cleverly bases his position on a different phrase in Deut 24:1: "if she [the first wife] does not find favor [*ḥēn*, which can also mean "feminine charm," "grace" or "beauty"] in his [her husband's] eyes." In reality, though, Aqiba's allowance of practically any reason, however brutally put, simply continues the mainline tradition begun in the OT and witnessed in Philo, Josephus, and the School of Hillel.[80]

The most remarkable point about this final passage in *m. Giṭṭin* is something that is often missed by commentators on the NT: only when we get to the Mishna do we have, for the first time in Palestinian Judaism, clear documentation of a scholarly dispute over what precisely constitutes sufficient grounds for divorce. As far as datable documents are concerned, this is something startlingly new in Judaism. What is found prior to this in Palestinian Judaism is (1) first of all and predominately, the near-absolute right of the husband to divorce his wife (Deuteronomy, Philo, Josephus); (2) secondarily, a sectarian attack on polygyny that may also imply (at least in the view of some scholars) an attack on divorce when it is followed by remarriage (the *Damascus Document*); and (3) finally and marginally, a total prohibition of divorce (Jesus). Nowhere in pre-70 Judaism is there any clear attestation of a detailed discussion or debate on which grounds for divorce are deemed sufficient. Therefore, despite the almost universal tendency on the part of NT exegetes to explain Jesus' prohibition of divorce against the "background" of the debate between the House of Shammai and the House of Hillel, this tendency may actually be a prime example of the anachronistic use of later texts to explain earlier ones.[81] That is, a text written down for the first time at the beginning of the 3d century A.D. (the Mishna) is called upon to elucidate a teaching of Jesus reaching back to the early part of the 1st century A.D., with written attestation in the 50s by Paul and ca. 70 by Mark. Considering the dearth of any clear attestation of the dispute over the grounds of divorce between the Houses in the pre-70 period,[82] we would do well, as least initially, to explain Jesus' teaching on divorce solely in light of what is truly prior to and contemporary with the Palestinian Judaism of the early 1st century A.D.[83]

VI. THE NEW TESTAMENT STATEMENTS ON DIVORCE

What is clear from even a cursory glance at the NT is that, in the three Synoptics Gospels and in Paul's First Letter to the Corinthians, Jesus is presented as basically forbidding divorce—though some of the relevant texts contain restrictions, expansions, or interpretations of the basic prohibition.[84] The number of witnesses to the prohibition may look promising, but almost immediately a problem arises. Of the five versions of the prohibition in the NT (two in Matthew, one in Mark, one in Luke, and one in 1 Corinthians), no two forms agree with each other word for word, with the exception of the famous "what God has joined together let no human being separate" (Mark 10:9, which is simply taken over by Matt 19:6b).[85] What, if anything, in this collection of sayings prohibiting divorce may be reasonably attributed to the historical Jesus? In addition, if we conclude that the historical Jesus did indeed prohibit divorce, can we decide which of the various versions of the prohibition contained in the NT most likely reflects Jesus' original teaching—or is this the wrong question to ask?

As we finally broach the question of the historical Jesus and divorce, a warning given at the beginning of this chapter may bear repeating. The point of our investigation is to reconstruct as best we can what a 1st-century Jewish prophet and teacher named Jesus of Nazareth said about divorce. Later interpretations of his teaching by 1st-century Christians are of interest only insofar as they are the means that help us recover the teaching of this Palestinian Jew speaking to other Palestinian Jews. A fortiori, the lengthy history of the Christian church's struggle to come to terms with this teaching of Jesus and any possible relevance of Jesus' teaching for present-day Christian practice lie beyond the scope of our quest for a marginal Jew.

Granted the number of NT texts purporting to give Jesus' teaching on divorce (the criterion of multiple attestation can already be seen peeping over the horizon), in what order should we treat them? A number of approaches are conceivable and indeed are used by various authors:

(1) The hypothetical Q form (Matt 5:32 ‖ Luke 16:18), as presumably the earliest Gospel formulation, is treated first. It is followed by the Marcan dispute story (Mark 10:2–12 ‖ Matt 19:3–9), which is often seen as a Christian expansion of the basic saying of Jesus, spun out into a whole apophthegm or *chreia* (an anecdote about a famous person that often has one of his striking sayings as its "punch line"). For all practical purposes, Matthew's version of the dispute story falls out of consideration, since it is simply a reworking of Mark's story in the light of the tradition of Matthew's church and Matthew's own theological tendencies. Paul's report in 1 Cor 7:10–11 is taken up last on the grounds that Paul does not (and does not claim to) supply a direct quotation of Jesus' saying, but gives instead only a paraphrase of it.

(2) The key passages are treated according to the chronological order of the documents in which they are preserved: 1 Corinthians, Mark, and finally Matthew and Luke.

(3) The chronological order is maintained, but the hypothetical Q source is accepted as a distinct document dating from sometime before A.D. 70. Hence, the order becomes 1 Corinthians, the Q saying (the reconstruction of which involves the treatment of the Matthean and Lucan forms of the saying), and finally Mark. Since I accept the Q hypothesis, and since this third order offers some pedagogical advantages, I will adopt it here.

A. 1 CORINTHIANS 7:10–11

The question of Jesus' teaching on divorce is remarkable because it is one of the rare cases in which Paul cites or alludes to a saying of Jesus that is also witnessed in the Gospels. One feels almost grateful to the unruly Corinthians for causing all the problems that forced Paul, contrary to his general tendency, to appeal more than once in 1 Corinthians to Jesus' teaching. Since Paul wrote 1 Corinthians ca. A.D. 54–55, this letter represents the oldest relevant document in our discussion of Jesus' teaching on divorce. Moreover, since Paul appeals to a command of Jesus, a command that he pointedly distinguishes from his own teaching on divorce, Paul is at the very least pointing to some earlier tradition, which in turn brings us back to the early 50s or the 40s, if not back to Jesus himself.

To take a quick look at the larger context: in 1 Corinthians, Paul the harried pastor is trying to solve all sorts of personal and communal problems in the Corinthian church, problems that range from basic church unity and good order in church worship to various questions of personal morality. One of the overriding problems in Corinth is that many of the enthusiastic Gentile Christians, recently converted from paganism, imagine that they are fully saved in their innermost being. Having risen spiritually from the dead, they are already leading the heavenly, angelic life of the last day ("over-realized eschatology"). Hence sin has and can have no hold over them, and nothing they do in or with their old, earthly bodies is of any relevance to their salvation, which is already achieved.

It is within this larger context that Paul approaches the problem of Christian marriage and divorce in 1 Corinthians 7. Having treated a number of disparate problems, of which he has heard by word of mouth, in chaps. 1–6, Paul begins in 1 Corinthians 7 to respond to a series of queries that the Corinthians have submitted to him by letter. A number of times, he introduces a topic with the phrase "now concerning" (*peri de* in 7:1,25; 8:1; 12:1; 16:1). Chap. 7, dealing with the first set of questions, addresses the general problem of the various states of life or social conditions in which the Corinthians find themselves. Caught between the "already" of justification by Chris-

tian faith and the "not yet" of final salvation on the last day, should the
Corinthians go on living in the old states of life that marked them prior to
their conversion? Should one remain, for example, a single person, a spouse,
a widow/widower, an uncircumcised Gentile, or a slave because that was
one's state of life before conversion, or should one seek to change one's state
to reflect the new existence one has received in Christ?

Paul's general response to the flighty, mercurial Corinthians is "stay as
you are," though he acknowledges special circumstances that can modify
this rule. In 7:1–9, Paul begins to fill in the details of this balancing act. On
the one hand, he agrees in principle with the enthusiastic Corinthians that
total abstinence from sexual activity is the ideal (v 1). The practical problem
Paul faces, though, is that even some of the married Corinthians are set
on practicing this ideal of abstinence, perhaps in imitation of Paul's own
state of life. Paul the pragmatic pastor tells these married couples instead
to continue their sexual relations. If they want to abstain from sex in order
to devote themselves completely to prayer, such abstinence should be only
temporary and by mutual consent. Paul knows only too well the unsavory
past—and, in some cases, present—sexual practices of these former pagans
(cf. 1 Cor 5:1–12; 6:9–11,15–20). He has no illusions about what the results of a program of total abstinence would probably be for most of them
(vv 2–7). Hence, as he moves on to the unmarried Corinthians (vv 8–9), he
bends his basic rule of "stay as you are." Yes, he says, it would be wonderful
for the unmarried to practice total abstinence like himself. But, in light of
the ordinary needs of ordinary individuals, chaste marriage is preferable to
unchaste celibacy.

Up until this point, Paul has been dispensing advice and argumentation
on his own authority as apostle and founder of the Corinthian church ("I
say" [v 6], "I wish" [v 7], "I say" [v 8]).[86] Suddenly, as Paul broaches the
question of divorce (vv 10–11), his basis of argumentation changes for a
brief moment to a very uncharacteristic type of support. Paul begins v 10 by
saying, "But to those who are married, I command—*not I, but the Lord*—
that a wife should not separate from [her] husband." This sudden switch is
all the more striking because, as soon as Paul closes his brief treatment of
the divorce of two married Christians and takes up the different question
of marriage between a Christian and a pagan, he returns to his ususal basis
of argumentation, namely, his own apostolic authority and insight: "But
to the rest [of the married couples], *I say, not* the Lord." [87] It would appear,
then, that Paul, contrary to his ususal manner of arguing, appeals directly to
what Jesus taught about divorce during his public ministry.

Granted, it is theoretically possible that Paul is intending instead to appeal to a saying of the risen Lord, proclaimed by an inspired prophet in the Christian community.[88] However, that seems unlikely in this case. First, the excruciatingly precise distinction Paul makes about the special authority of this command—suddenly switching from verbs of saying and desiring to the verb of command, while at the same time emphatically switching from what "I" say (v 8) to what "the Lord" commands (v 10), only to switch back again to what "I say" in v 12—is unparalleled anywhere else in Paul's letters. He may indeed appeal elsewhere to a revelation of the risen Jesus as mediated by some Christian prophet (so perhaps, e.g., in 1 Thess 4:15 and 1 Cor 15:51), and in 1 Cor 14:37 he does seem to identify his own instructions about good order in the Christian assembly as "a command of the Lord." But he never uses in such passages the careful distinction seen in 1 Cor 7:8–12 between what he says and what the Lord commands.

Second, Paul was a great apostle with a big ego. He had to fight—and did fight furiously—for acknowledgment as a full-fledged apostle of the same rank as Peter (Gal 1:11–2:14; 1 Cor 9:1–18). He is quite clear in 1 Corinthians itself about his superiority as an apostle to any prophet in the church (12:28: "first apostles, second prophets, third teachers"). In 1 Cor 7:10, Paul is seeking a higher authority than his own to undergird the hard-to-accept total prohibition of divorce that he is about to inculcate. Since Paul the apostle maintains that he has "the mind of Christ" and enjoys special revelations about heavenly things (1 Cor 2:16; 2 Cor 12:1–4; cf. 1 Cor 7:25,40), it would be odd for him to think at this critical juncture that the best way to "up the ante" is to appeal from his own authority to that of some anonymous Christian prophet speaking in Christ's name.

Third, unlike many of the other supposed cases of Paul referring to sayings of the Lord mediated through Christian prophets, in this case we have multiple attestation of Jesus' prohibition of divorce in the earliest Gospel traditions (both Mark and Q). Granted this rare coincidence of Paul appealing to a specific teaching of Jesus for which we have multiple attestation in two primitive Gospel sources, the most natural reading of Paul is that he intends to appeal to what Jesus commanded during his public ministry. Whether, historically speaking, Paul is correct in his claim is another matter. But, if the question asked is what Paul intends to do in 1 Cor 7:10, the most natural, unforced reading of the text is that he intends to appeal over his own head to the teaching of the earthly Jesus.

Fourth, this appeal to the teaching or actions of the earthly Jesus is not a one-time phenomenon in 1 Corinthians. Among Paul's letters, 1 Corinthians enjoys a remarkably high concentration of credible allusions to the words or deeds of Jesus (e.g., 9:14; 11:23–25; cf. 15:3–5). Hence, an allusion to Jesus' teaching on divorce would hardly be an alien body in this particular letter.

In light of all this, the most natural interpretation of our passage is that Paul is paraphrasing Jesus' prohibition of divorce. I purposely say "paraphrase" because (1) unlike 1 Cor 11:23–25 (the account of Jesus' words and actions over the bread and wine at the Last Supper), there is no attempt to cite Jesus' words verbatim; and (2) the Gospel texts containing Jesus' prohibition of divorce, as well as any hypothetical reconstruction of the original form of his prohibition, indicate that Paul is summarizing Jesus' teaching in his own words—words that are different from the key words contained in the various forms of Jesus' prohibition in the Synoptic Gospels.[89] Still, for all the differences in wording from the Gospel forms of the prohibition, Paul's version is similar to the Gospel texts on one point of structure: there is tendency in all the texts to express the prohibition in two parts, whatever the precise form and content of the two parts.

The two main parts of Paul's version of the prohibition are clear, as is the proviso interjected between the two:

(v 10) a *wife* should not separate from [her] *husband*
(v 11)   (but if she does separate,
            she must remain unmarried
            or be reconciled with [her] husband),
        and a *husband* should not divorce [his] *wife*

The basic parallelism in the two major parts indicates a prohibition that applies equally to both wife and husband.[90] Some commentators see an implied distinction in that a wife is ordered not to be separated or divorced (*chōrizomai*) from her husband, while a husband is ordered not to divorce (*aphiēmi*, literally, "send away") his wife. With a view to Jewish-Palestinian customs, where only the husband had the right to divorce his spouse, these commentators suggest that the verb in v 10 (*chōristhēnai*) should be taken as a true passive-voice form (instead of a passive form with an active sense): the wife has been divorced by her husband.[91] In a slightly modified form of this interpretation, the Corinthian wife is thought to have taken the initiative in separating physically from her husband, but she lacks the power to divorce him. However, this line of interpretation seems unlikely, given that the events are taking place in 1st-century Corinth. The Corinth of the 1st century A.D. was a Roman colony founded by Julius Caesar in 44 B.C. and governed by Roman law. And under Roman law in the 1st century A.D., a free woman (as distinct from a slave woman) as well as a free man had the right to divorce.[92]

That no real distinction is intended by the two verbs *chōrizomai* and *aphiēmi* is seen in the next pericope (1 Cor 7:12–16), which deals with marriages between a Christian and a non-Christian. In vv 12–13, both husband and wife are presumed to have the power to divorce (in the eyes of society); in both cases, the act of divorcing is expressed by the same verb, *aphiēmi*. Then in v 15, *chōrizomai* is used of the pagan spouse divorcing the Christian spouse; hence, the verb is being used in the active sense of "to divorce," not in the passive sense of "being divorced." [93] Obviously, both verbs signify the same thing: a true divorce (in the eyes of society); the parallelism in the two main parts of vv 10–11 underlines this fact.[94] One reason why these verbs can be used interchangeably is that in Greek, unlike Latin (*divortium/ divorto*), there was no single technical word for divorce. Various Greek verbs like *aphiēmi* and *chōrizomai* (and *apolyō* in the Synoptics) take on the technical meaning "to divorce" when used in a specific context.[95]

There are many other fascinating problems—fascinating, at least, to an exegete—in 1 Cor 7:10–11, but our concern is not with the details of this conflict between an exasperated Paul and some rambunctious Corinthians in the mid-50s. The one point that is vital to our quest is the fact that, somewhere ca. A.D. 54–55, Paul appeals to a supposed saying of Jesus forbidding divorce. Contrary to his ususal mode of arguing, Paul carefully distinguishes this teaching from his own, implicitly underlining the greater authority that adheres to a teaching coming directly from Jesus. One can safely say that this teaching is therefore already circulating among the first generation of Christians, a point that is supported by the Q and Marcan versions of Jesus' prohibition of divorce. Unlike Q and Mark, Paul, however, does not claim to be quoting Jesus' words, only paraphrasing and applying them to (presumably) Gentile Christians recently converted from paganism. Thus, as we moderns read Paul's treatment of the prohibition, we inevitably notice a hermeneutical distance that is not considered by Paul: a teaching originally addressed by a Jewish Jesus to his fellow Palestinian Jews is being applied by a Jewish-Christian apostle to the lives of Gentile Christians in Corinth.

In his application, Paul understands Jesus' prohibition to be both sweeping and stringent, at least when applied to two Christians joined in marriage. (Paul seems to be more flexible in the case of a mixed Christian-pagan marriage, treated in a somewhat ambiguous manner in 1 Cor 7:12–16.) The Christian couple, says Paul, is not to divorce. If—contrary to the command— a divorce does take place, the partners are either to remain unmarried or to be reconciled. Those are the only two options envisioned by Paul. In light of what we shall now see in Q and Mark, it is intriguing that Paul does not explicitly state what would be the moral status of or judgment upon a second marriage, if, after a divorce, one of the Christian partners proceeded to contract one. Perhaps for Paul such an action is so inconceivable for married Christians that he does not bother entertaining the possibility and its consequences. Possibly, though, his total silence on this point reflects his knowledge of how Jesus (at least according to Q and Mark) viewed such a second marriage: it is not marriage at all, but simply adultery. Such conjectures necessarily push us on to a consideration of the Q and Marcan traditions.

B. The Q Tradition (Matt 5:32 ‖ Luke 16:18)

1. *Introduction*

As we move from Paul to the Synoptic Gospels, we notice immediately that Jesus' prohibition of divorce is found in two different types of Synoptic material: (1) On the one hand, it is enshrined in a Marcan dispute story (i.e., a *Streitgespräch*, Mark 10:2–12) that is located in a block of teaching (10:1–45) delivered by Jesus as he enters Judea and leads his disciples up to Jerusalem for his passion and death. This dispute story is not present in Luke,[96] but Matthew takes it over from Mark at roughly the same point in his narrative of the public ministry (Matt 19:3–12). (2) On the other hand, the prohibition appears as a succinct logion within a larger block of sayings material in both Matthew and Luke. Matthew locates the saying (Matt 5:32) within his Sermon on the Mount (chaps. 5–7), more specifically within the third of the six antitheses ("You have heard it said . . . but I say to you") that make up Matt 5:21–48. Luke places a somewhat different version of the same logion in a small cluster of sayings on legal and moral matters (Luke 16:14–18), sandwiched between the Parable of the Dishonest Steward (16:1–13) and the Parable of the Rich Man and Lazarus (16:19–31). As is so often the case in Luke's great journey narrative (chaps. 9–19), the connection among the various sayings is loose at best. Since this succinct version of the prohibition is shared by Matthew and Luke but is absent in Mark, it is usually assigned to the Q document. We will see further reasons for this judgment below. In any event, the very different settings of Matt 5:32 and Luke 16:18 are probably both redactional creations of the two evangelists;[97] the prohibition most likely circulated in the oral tradition as an isolated unit.[98] It is this isolated unit that we seek to reconstruct.[99]

2. *Matt 5:32 and Luke 16:18 as Q Tradition*

The Matthean and Lucan forms of this brief saying on divorce evince some differences between them; yet, compared to the Marcan form of the prohibition (Mark 10:11–12), to be examined in Section C, they clearly represent the same stream of tradition, conventionally labeled Q:

Matt 5:32	*Luke 16:18*
(1) [a] Everyone who divorces his wife	Everyone who divorces his wife
pas ho apolyōn tēn gynaika autou	*pas ho apolyōn tēn gynaika autou*
except on grounds of "unchastity"	
parektos logou porneias	
	and marries another
	kai gamōn heteran
(1) [b] causes her to be involved in adultery	commits adultery
poiei autēn moicheuthēnai	*moicheuei*
(2) [a] and whoever marries a divorced woman	and the one who marries a woman divorced by [her] husband
kai hos apolelymenēn gamēsę̄	*kai ho apolelymenēn apo andros gamōn*
(2) [b] commits adultery	commits adultery
moichatai	*moicheuei*

Despite the differences between Matt 5:32 and Luke 16:18, these two verses basically agree in form and content over against the core prohibition of divorce in Mark 10:11–12. Matthew and Luke both present a single sentence with two main parts (1 and 2), each part in turn having two subdivisions [a and b]. Parts 1 and 2 both make the man the "lead agent"; not only is he the subject of all the finite verbs, he is also the person designated by all the active participles. He, and he alone, divorces; consequently he, and he alone, is responsible for the ensuing adultery. The woman, by contrast, is presented solely as the object of the action of a man (either divorcing or marrying her). In Part 1a of both Matthew and Luke, the man is designated by the exact same participial phrase, *pas ho apolyōn tēn gynaika autou* ("everyone who divorces his wife"). Part 2, for all the minor differences between Matthew and Luke, makes the same basic statement: "and whoever marries a divorced woman . . . commits adultery."

These shared traits clearly cordon off Matt 5:32 ‖ Luke 16:18 from the Marcan form of the prohibition in Mark 10:11–12. As we shall see in Section C, Mark 10:11–12 is made up of two distinct sentences. The first treats of the husband divorcing his wife, while the second, in parallel fashion, treats of the wife divorcing her husband. The first sentence (treating of the husband) begins with an indefinite relative clause ("whoever divorces his wife"), while the second (treating of the wife) begins with a conditional clause ("and if she, divorcing her husband, marries another [man]"). Thus, neither sentence begins, as does Matt 5:32 and Luke 16:18, with a participial phrase. In addition, the first Marcan sentence, treating of the husband, states surprisingly—and for the only time in any of the versions of the prohibition—that the man who divorces his wife and marries another woman "commits adultery *against her*," meaning most probably the first wife.[100] Finally, and most important from a form-critical point of view, Mark 10:11–12 provides the concluding section of a dispute story, as opposed to Matt 5:32 and Luke 16:18, which form part of a larger chain of logia in a context of discourse.

All in all, therefore, there are solid reasons for treating Matt 5:32 ∥ Luke 16:18 as one stream of the tradition on divorce (namely, the Q tradition) and Mark 10:11–12 (indeed, the whole *Streitgespräch* of Mark 10:2–12, along with its Matthean redaction in Matt 19:3–12) as another stream of the tradition. Let us turn now to the differences that exist between the Matt 5:32 and Luke 16:18 to see if we can discern what the original wording in the Q document might have been.

3. The Primitive Q Form of the Saying

Since both Matthew and Luke, for all their differences, agree word for word on the initial participial phrase ("everyone who divorces his wife"), that almost surely is the original Q wording. Immediately following this initial phrase, Matthew has his famous "exceptive clause": *parektos logou porneias*, "except on grounds of unchastity." A number of considerations argue strongly for the exceptive clause being an addition that Matthew (or his special tradition) makes to the original Q version. Among the Pauline, Marcan, Lucan, and Matthean versions of the prohibition of divorce, only Matthew has this exceptive clause. It is present in the two versions of the prohibition that Matthew has taken over from his sources and redacted for his own purposes: the Q tradition reworked in Matt 5:32 and the Marcan tradition reworked in Matt 19:9. In both Matt 5:32 and 19:9, the phrase expressing the exception overloads the clause in which it occurs, making Part 1a of the prohibition unwieldy, overlong, and not a little obscure (at least to an endless line of Christian interpreters from the patristic period onward).

Whatever the precise grounds specified by the exception (and those grounds are disputed down to the present day), the exception seems to reflect some particular pastoral problem within Matthew's church, a problem that apparently was not replicated in the same way or with the same pressing urgency in the churches of Paul, Mark, and Luke. To make the same point the other way round: if the Matthean exceptive clause had been a part of the original form of the prohibition, it is extremely difficult to understand how and why Paul, Mark, and Luke would have all come up with absolute forms of the prohibition—all the more so when Paul, a few verses later

(1 Cor 7:12–16), creates an exception for a special case on his own authority. Consequently, the vast majority of present-day exegetes assign the exceptive clause in Matt 5:32 to Matthew (or his special M tradition meshed with Q) and not to the Q document or to the earliest form of the tradition.[101]

If, on the Matthean side, we drop the exceptive clause because it overloads the wording of Part 1a, perhaps we should do the same for the participial phrase found in Luke's version of Part 1a, *kai gamōn heteran* ("and marries another [woman]"). Besides lengthening the initial description of the husband's action in Part 1a with a phrase not found in the Matthean parallel, it uses a favorite adjective of Luke (*heteros*, "another")[102] and simply makes explicit what would be taken for granted in most cases of divorce anyway: the husband divorces the wife with the intention, proximate or remote, of marrying another woman. However, the status and provenance of Luke's "and marries another" are not as clear as that of Matthew's exceptive clause. The Marcan version of the prohibition, although it stems from a different source, likewise has "and marries another" (Mark 10:11: *kai gamēsē allēn*) in its initial relative clause. Moreover, Paul, in his paraphrase of the prohibition, specifies that the woman who has divorced her husband must remain unmarried (*agamos*, 1 Cor 7:11) or be reconciled with her husband. Thus, directly or indirectly, the prohibition of a second marriage is present in the Pauline, Lucan, and Marcan versions. This multiple attestation speaks in favor of the phrase "and marries another" being original in the primitive Q form behind Luke 16:18.[103]

A further argument for keeping "and marries another" as original in Luke 16:18 stems from the basic thrust of all the Synoptic sayings on divorce, whatever the precise wording of any individual version. All the Synoptic sayings, in one way or another, reject divorce because it involves adultery. Now, even as simply a forceful metaphor, adultery would be a strange image and argument if our saying were treating only the separation of a married couple, with no further marriage contemplated within the little world of the saying. How and why is the separation of two spouses who henceforth live as celibates viewed and condemned precisely as adultery? The stigma of adultery, however rhetorical or hyperbolic it may be in this saying, makes sense only if there is a subsequent union mentioned in the saying, a union that the saying shockingly brands as adulterous.[104] Without the mention of a second marriage, the image, metaphor, or stigma of adultery does not make rhetorical sense. Hence, I incline to the view that the phrase "and marries another" in Part 1a is original to the primitive Q saying. Understandably, though, scholars remain divided on the issue, which does not admit of certitude.

Part 1b of the Q saying clearly brands the man's action in divorcing his wife as an act involving adultery, but the adultery is viewed quite differently in the Lucan and Matthean sayings. In Luke 16:18, the man's double action of divorcing his first wife and marrying a second is what is branded as adultery. This is a clear, straightforward idea, readily intelligible—if not acceptable—to modern minds. In contrast, the version in Matt 5:32 is more contorted in both grammar and thought. In an overliteral translation, Matt 5:32 (with the exceptive clause omitted) states: "Everyone who divorces his wife causes her to be adulterated"—in other words, causes her to be involved in an adulterous union by forcing her to seek the protection of a second marriage with another man.[105] This second marriage is what is branded as adulterous in Part 1b of Matt 5:32, but the responsibility for this second, adulterous union is put squarely on the shoulders of the first husband.[106] He is the one responsible for forcing his helpless wife into a second marriage by divorcing her. For all the differences between Part 1b of Matt 5:32 and Part 1b of Luke 16:18, what remains constant is that the responsibility for the ensuing adultery is ascribed to the first husband alone—something that is also true, though with different phrasing, in Mark 10:11.

The strikingly different way of viewing things in Part 1b of Matt 5:32 is deeply rooted in the social realities reflected in the Jewish Scriptures and in the Palestinian Judaism of Jesus' day. The husband, and the husband alone, had the power to initiate a divorce, and—with very few restrictions—he could do so for practically any reason that seemed good to him. If he followed the prescribed steps for a divorce, the divorce was valid, no matter how much the wife or other parties might protest. The wife was basically helpless before this raw power supported by a patriarchal society. The only way a divorced woman could hope for long-term sustenance and honor in a traditional androcentric society was to enter a second marriage, usually through the negotiations of her male relatives or patrons. Part 1b of the Matthean logion dares to brand this solution as adultery, but it lays the responsibility for the adulterous union of the woman at the feet of her first husband, who has set the chain of events in motion by initiating the divorce. The unspoken but clearly underlying presupposition of this odd version of the divorce logion is basically the same as that of all the other versions: the resulting second marriage (whether of the first husband or of his divorced wife) is adulterous because the divorce, while valid in the eyes of society, never really dissolved the first marriage, which remains valid in the eyes of God. To use later terminology, the divorce, however supported and ratified by the OT and Jewish tradition, is null and void. The bond of the first marriage remains (on the presumption, of course, that both spouses are still living), and so any second marriage by either party constitutes adultery.

So strikingly Jewish and Palestinian is the conception of marriage and divorce lying behind Part lb of Matt 5:32 that some scholars have suggested that here alone, as opposed to all the other versions of the prohibition of divorce, we have the original form not only of the Q logion but also of the saying originally spoken by Jesus to his fellow Palestinian Jews.[107] That is certainly possible, but there are a number of objections to this view. The most obvious objection arises from the isolation of Part lb of Matt 5:32 within the various sayings on divorce. For all their many differences, Luke 16:18, Mark 10:11–12, and even Matt 19:9 (Matthew's reworking of Mark 10:11) all state that the person who divorces his or her spouse and marries another is the one who commits adultery by that twofold act. Thus, multiple attestation speaks against Part 1b of Matt 5:32 being the original form of the Q logion, let alone the original form spoken by the historical Jesus. In my opinion, what we hear in Part lb of Matt 5:32 is the Jewish tradition of Matthew's church, which recast the primitive saying on divorce in a more starkly Jewish form. Granted the vagaries of the Gospel traditions, and granted in particular the possibility of a "re-Judaizing" of a saying in the Matthean stream of the tradition, it does not always follow that "the more Jewish it sounds, the more original it must be." [108]

Thus, in my view, the most probable reconstruction of Part 1 of the Q logion should read: "Everyone who divorces his wife and marries another commits adultery"—although "and marries another" must remain under a question mark. Thankfully, Part 2 of Matt 5:32 and Luke 16:18 are basically the same, apart from minor variations in the Greek wording: "And the one who [or: whoever] marries a divorced woman commits adultery." The only significant variation is that Part 2a of Luke 16:18 adds the specification that the woman has been divorced "by [her first] husband" (*apo andros*). Since this specification is found in no other version of the prohibition, and since, moreover, the noun *anēr* ("man," "husband") is a favorite word of Luke,[109] it is more likely than not that Luke has added the phrase. Perhaps Luke is underlining in his own way the point that the second marriage is adulterous precisely because, *despite* the first husband's action of divorcing his wife, the bond of the first marriage remains. He remains her husband, for his act of divorcing her has had no real effect.[110]

By way of conclusion, then: in my opinion, the most likely reconstruction of the primitive Q saying—a saying that probably circulated as an isolated logion before being taken up into Q—should read:

(Part 1a)   Everyone who divorces his wife and marries another
(Part 1b)   commits adultery,
(Part 2a)   And the one who [or: whoever] marries a divorced woman
(Part 2b)   commits adultery

The resulting two-part saying displays remarkable balance. Parts 1a and 2a are longer than Parts 1b and 2b, both of which consist of the same one-word judgment: *moicheuei* ("he commits adultery"). Moreover, Parts 1a and 2a both mention the two actions of divorcing and marrying; indeed, in the Greek text, the two actions are mentioned in that same order (divorce-marry) in Part 1a and Part 2a. In both Part 1a and Part 2a, a male is the subject who acts, a woman is the object of his actions. Nevertheless, the image of the woman who is divorced is the linchpin that connects Parts 1a and 2a: in Part 1a, she is the woman divorced by her first husband; in Part 2a, she is the already divorced woman married by her second husband. The balance, intricacy, and density of this short two-part saying on Jewish *hălākâ* are remarkable. Only later on will we consider the arguments for attributing the prohibition of divorce to the historical Jesus. But, as an aside, I might note here that this succinct and balanced rhetorical bombshell, which explodes all traditional views of divorce in the Jewish Scriptures and Palestinian Judaism, would not be unworthy of the masterful wordsmith named Jesus. Hence, it is not surprising that many commentators consider this Q version to be the most primitive form of the divorce sayings in the NT.[111]

Having seen the paraphrase of Jesus' prohibition of divorce in Paul (ca. A.D. 54–55) and one version of his saying on divorce in the primitive Q tradition (ca. A.D. 50–70), we now turn to the version of the prohibition preserved in the Gospel of Mark (composed ca. A.D. 70).

C. MARK 10:11–12

Quite often, exegetes take up the whole of the dispute story on divorce found in Mark 10:2–12 and, within that larger context, treat the final pronouncement of Jesus in vv 11–12. Given our concern about the historical Jesus rather than the theology of Mark's Gospel, I prefer to reverse the process. Since we have already examined the short prohibition of Jesus paraphrased by Paul in 1 Cor 7:10–11 and cited in the Q tradition reflected in Matt 5:32 ‖ Luke 16:18, I think it best to continue this trajectory. Hence we will first study the parallel pronouncement of Jesus at the conclusion of Mark 10:2–12, that is, the double statement prohibiting both husbands and wives to divorce their spouses in 10:11–12. After we have examined this core pronouncement in the light of the parallels already seen, and after we have applied the criteria of historicity, we can then turn back to Mark 10:2–12 as a whole.[112]

An additional reason for taking this tack is that, from the heyday of form criticism onward, it has often been held that most dispute stories in the Gospels are secondary creations of the early church, built around and enshrining some saying of Jesus (whether or not such a saying actually goes back to the historical Jesus).[113] Prescinding for the moment from the question of whether this is true of Mark 10:2–12, I think it wiser to treat 10:11–12 first, since it enjoys a direct parallel in Q and an indirect one in Paul. It will be principally on the basis of these multiple versions of the core prohibition of divorce that a decision about the teaching of the historical Jesus will be made. After that decision is reached, there will be time enough to consider the larger context of Mark 10:2–12.

Let us begin with the basic structure and content of Mark 10:11–12. Once again, not unlike the structure of the Q parallel, we find two main parts subdivided each time into two minor parts. Yet the two-part divisions are not quite the same in Mark as in Q. More clearly in Mark than in Q, we have two separate sentences. The first, Mark 10:11, deals with the husband who divorces his wife; the second, 10:12, deals in parallel fashion with the wife who divorces her husband. Each sentence has two parts: a dependent clause, stating the action of the spouse who divorces the partner and marries another, and the main clause, branding this twofold action as adultery. Even before we proceed, we cannot help noticing immediately that the structure and content of the first sentence (Mark 10:11) basically parallels Parts 1a + b of the Q logion reflected in Matt 5:32 ‖ Luke 16:18: a man who divorces his wife and marries another woman commits adultery. But before we pursue this point, let us look at the full structure and content of the two sentences in Mark 10:11–12, employing our usual divisions of Part 1 a + b and Part 2 a + b:

> *Mark 10:11*
> (1) [a] Whoever divorces his wife and marries another [woman],
>   *hos an apolysē tēn gynaika autou kai gamēsē allēn*
>   [b] commits adultery against her.
>   *moichatai ep' autēn*
>   *Mark 10:12*
> (2) [a] And if she, divorcing her husband, marries another [man],
>   *kai ean autē apolysasa ton andra autēs gamēsē allon*
>   [b] she commits adultery.
>   *moichatai*

A number of points strike one as soon as one compares this two-part Marcan structure with that of Q. The two main parts of the Q logion deal with (1) a man divorcing his wife and marrying another woman and (2) a man marrying a divorced woman; the male perspective is thus maintained in both parts. In contrast, the two main parts of the Marcan logion deal in parallel fashion with: (1) a man divorcing his wife and marrying another woman and (2) a woman divorcing her husband and marrying another man. The underlying idea common to all these parts of the Marcan and Q logia is that any combination of divorce-and-remarriage results in a judgment that this twofold act constitutes adultery.

Perhaps the most obvious difference between the Mark 10:11–12 and all the other versions of the prohibition in the Synoptics is that here alone the married woman has apparently the same right and power as her husband to divorce. Interestingly, on this point the Marcan version agrees not with any of the other Synoptic versions[114] but rather with Paul's paraphrase in 1 Cor 7:10–11, where Paul's treatment notably begins with the woman, spends more time on her, and only briefly, at the end of v 11, imposes the same obligation not to divorce on the man. Most commentators hold—rightly, in my view—that this common ground shared by Paul and Mark reflects the fact that both are writing in the context of a Greek or Roman legal system, where the wife as well as the husband could divorce the spouse.[115] This is clearly the case in 1 Corinthians, where Paul is writing to the (mostly) Gentile Christians in Corinth, a Roman colony. This scenario also fits one of the most popular and perennial candidates for the place of composition of Mark's Gospel, namely, Rome itself—though any urban area governed by a Greek or Roman legal system would do.[116]

Since, as we have already seen, ordinary Jewish women in the Palestine of Jesus' day did not have the right or power to divorce their Jewish husbands, Mark 10:12 almost automatically falls out of consideration as a saying coming from the historical Jesus.[117] In other words, if ordinary Jewish women in Palestine did not have the power to divorce their husbands, what would be the point of Jesus going out of his way to prohibit it? Moreover, even within the Marcan tradition, v 12 seems to be a secondary construction vis-à-vis 11, which is the part of the composite logion paralleled in Q. That v 12 is indeed secondary is supported not only by the lack of a parallel in any of the other Synoptic versions but also by the fact that, in both grammar and content, v 12 does not provide a precise parallel to v 11. The initial dependent clause in Mark 10:11 is an indefinite relative clause (*hos an*, "whoever" [in the masculine form]), while the corresponding dependent clause in 10:12 is the protasis of a conditional sentence (*ean autē*, "if she").[118] While the dependent clause in v 11 spells out the twofold action with two finite verbs ("Whoever divorces his wife and marries another"), the dependent clause in v 12 reduces the first action to a participle ("If she, having divorced her husband, marries another"). Moreover, v 11 alone, by way of *inclusio*, answers the initial question of the Pharisees that begins this dispute story (v 2): "Is it lawful for a man to divorce his wife?" Finally, while the end of v 11 says that the husband commits adultery "against her" (presumably, the first wife), there is no equivalent "against him" at the end of v 12. All in all, both in content and in form, v 12 seems to be an abbreviated, secondary construction providing a reverse mirror image of v 11. Hence, not only does v 12 not go back to the historical Jesus, it is also a secondary accretion in the Marcan tradition, perhaps added by Mark himself to the traditional logion he received.

As long as I have touched on the final clause in v 11, I might note here that the final words (*ep' autēn*, "against her") in v 11 likewise seem to be a later Christian addition to the primitive tradition. The idea that a husband, by having sex with a woman not his wife, commits adultery *against his wife* is not a concept found in the Jewish Scriptures, where adultery is an offense against the marriage rights of some other husband. Hence, while a straying wife commits adultery against her own husband (by violating his marriage rights), a husband commits adultery if he has sex with another man's wife because he thus violates the rights of the other husband (not the rights of his own wife). In other words, if a husband has sex with an unmarried prostitute, he does not commit adultery, since he is not violating any other husband's rights. Given this legal-moral context, the statement in 10:11 that the husband, by divorce and remarriage, commits adultery against his first wife (because the bond of the first marriage remains despite the divorce) is quite astounding. To be sure, it is not impossible that Jesus, delivering what is by any measure a radical teaching on divorce, should have included as well the radical idea that a man can commit adultery against his own wife. However, since no other version of the prohibition contains these words, and since the very concept of adultery against one's own wife might have been unintelligible to Jesus' original audience, "against her" is most likely a Christian addition (by Mark or his tradition) to a more original form of v 11.[119]

Having excluded Mark 10:12 and "against her" in v 11 as Christian additions, I suggest that the form of the prohibition that circulated in the pre-Marcan oral tradition ran as follows:

(Part 1a) Whoever divorces his wife and marries another
(Part 1b) commits adultery

As noted earlier, this form is substantially the same as Parts 1 a + b of the primitive Q form of the prohibition: "Everyone who divorces his wife and marries another commits adultery"—though there are minor difference in the Greek grammar and wording. Granted these intriguing similarities, and granted that we have now explored the three main versions of the prohibition in 1 Corinthians, Q, and Mark, it is time to ask the question that has been driving this investigation. Which, if any, of the criteria of historicity argue in favor of the claim that the prohibition of divorce, in some form or other, goes back to the historical Jesus?

D. DIVORCE AND THE CRITERIA OF HISTORICITY

The attentive reader may have already noticed that some observations made in this chapter favor the view that the prohibition of divorce is an authentic saying of Jesus. It is now time to order and tease out these observations to forge full-fledged arguments. Which criteria are applicable to the question of Jesus' prohibition of divorce?

1. *The Criterion of Multiple Attestation of Sources and Forms*

As we have seen repeatedly, Jesus' prohibition of divorce is paraphrased or cited in three independent streams of early Christian tradition, all representing first-generation Christianity: Paul in 1 Cor 7:10–11 (ca. A.D. 54–55), the Q tradition preserved in Matt 5:32 ‖ Luke 16:18 (ca. A.D. 50–70), and the Gospel of Mark (ca. A.D. 70).[120] In addition to the multiple sources, the prohibition is at the same time attested in multiple forms: the parenesis of a Pauline letter, an isolated logion in the Q sayings tradition, and a dispute story in Mark. Relatively few sayings of Jesus enjoy such a broad spread of multiple sources and forms, all stemming from the first Christian generation. On the basis of this criterion alone, I think there is sufficient reason for holding that the historical Jesus forbade divorce.[121]

2. *The Criteria of Discontinuity and Embarrassment*

As is often noted, the criteria of discontinuity and embarrassment are closely connected; indeed, some see them as simply different aspects of the same criterion. Be that as it may, discontinuity and embarrassment form an intriguing configuration, not to say alliance, when one investigates the historicity of Jesus' prohibition of divorce. The criterion of discontinuity applies more to Jesus' Jewish background and immediate context, while the criterion of embarrassment applies more to the Christian sources that have preserved his prohibition in various forms.

(a) *The criterion of discontinuity (or dissimilarity)*, in this particular case, highlights an unusual and striking teaching of Jesus that cannot be derived from or paralleled by the laws or narratives of the Jewish Scriptures before him, by the teaching and practice of mainstream Judaism contemporary with him, or indeed even by the teaching and practice of rabbinic Judaism after him. This point has been abundantly demonstrated in the earlier sections of this chapter, and the mass of data need not be repeated here. Suffice it to say that, in the writings that were to become the Jewish Scriptures and the Christian OT (including the deuterocanonical books), divorce is a social reality that is simply taken for granted. There is no real corpus of divorce law in the OT. The few laws touching on divorce restrict in small ways or extraordinary circumstances the almost unlimited power of the adult Jewish male to divorce his wife for any reason that seems good to him. That this almost unlimited power of the male to divorce his wife continued unabated in mainstream Judaism around the turn of the era is witnessed by both Philo and Josephus. There is not even an indication of a serious debate about the proper grounds for divorce in Judaism before the Mishna (ca. A.D. 200–220).

The disturbing, even shocking, nature of Jesus' total prohibition of divorce cannot be appreciated unless we understand how unthinkable such a prohibition was in a society that (like all ancient Mediterranean societies) considered divorce, however regrettable or painful in individual instances, to be the natural and necessary course of things. To be sure, the Law of Moses did not *command* divorce in the sense of commanding individual men to divorce their wives.[122] But the Law of Moses did accept and sanction divorce. It set down certain regulations to govern it, instituted a specific document to provide a legal record that a valid divorce had taken place (i.e., the certificate of divorce), and allowed the husband who divorced his wife to marry almost any other women, while forbidding a particular woman to him (i.e., his former wife who had in the meantime been married and divorced again).

By completely forbidding divorce, Jesus dares to forbid what the Law allows—and not in some minor, obscure halakic observance but in one of the most important legal institutions in society. He dares to say that a man who duly follows the Law in properly divorcing his wife and marrying another woman is in effect committing adultery. When one stops to think what this involves, Jesus' prohibition of divorce is nothing short of astounding. Jesus presumes to teach that what the Law permits and regulates is actually the sin of adultery. That is, precisely by conscientiously following the Torah's rules for divorce and remarriage, a Jewish man commits a serious sin against one of the commandments of the Decalogue, the commandment against adultery (Exod 20:14; Deut 5:18).[123] This is no small matter; it is, at least according to the Pentateuch, a capital offense. Here as perhaps nowhere else in his halakic teaching—his prohibition of oaths being the sole competitor—Jesus the Jew clashes with the Mosaic Torah as it was understood and practiced by mainstream Judaism before, during, and after his lifetime.

The reader may have noticed that, in these remarks on Jesus, divorce, and Torah, I have spoken repeatedly of "mainstream Judaism." The reason for this specification is clear from the data presented earlier in this chapter. While divorce was permitted and regulated by the Torah and was accordingly implemented in ancient Israel, in mainstream Judaism in and outside of Palestine at the turn of the era, and in subsequent stages of Judaism down to our own day, a neuralgic question about sectarian Judaism remains. Did some sectarian Jews in Palestine around the turn of the era, namely, the Qumranites in particular and the Essenes in general, also teach a total prohibition of divorce? One must be clear about the point of this question. Even if these groups did teach the same total prohibition as Jesus, that in no way lessens Jesus' sharp opposition to the way in which mainstream Judaism before, during, and after him understood and practiced the institution of divorce, which was permitted and sanctioned by the Torah. The question is rather whether Jesus, along with the disciples who accepted his teaching, stood alone against the understanding and practice of the Torah shared by all other Jews, or whether some sectarian Jews championed the same radical teaching on divorce that Jesus did.

Here one must distinguish between the Qumranites and the Essenes, just as one must distinguish among various writings found at Qumran. If we focus solely on the inhabitants of Qumran, the major document to which we must turn is their rule book or manual of discipline, the *Rule of the Community* (the *serek hayyaḥad*). Perhaps the most telling point of the *Rule of the Community* is its lack of any treatment of the question of divorce. At least the *Damascus Document*, the rule book for the Essene communities scattered throughout Israel, may touch briefly on the issue (depending on how one interprets ambiguous passages). By comparison, Qumran's *Rule of the Community* is totally silent on the issue. When one considers the many details of legal observance that are laid down in the *Rule*, this is somewhat surprising. One possible explanation is that the full-time members of the Qumran community were indeed celibate (a much disputed position) and that therefore their manual of discipline would have had no reason to treat the question of divorce in rules that governed the internal life of the community. In any case, if we ask what was the teaching on divorce held by the Qumran community, we must confess our ignorance. Whether the silence in Qumran's rule book betokens tacit consent to the divorce practices sanctioned by the Mosaic Law or instead a radical break with ordinary Jewish life, embodied in a celibate existence, is open to debate and speculation.

As we have seen earlier in this chapter, scholars who wish to draw comparisons between Jesus' prohibition of divorce and the views of sectarian groups like the Qumranites or the Essenes must turn to other documents found at Qumran. Of the two usually cited, the *Temple Scroll* (11QTemple) is the less relevant. While some commentators claim that it is a work written by the Qumran community and representing its views, other critics think that it stems from a sectarian movement outside of Qumran and perhaps even prior to Qumran's foundation. In any case, the *Temple Scroll*, unlike the *Rule of the Community*, which governed the Qumran community, and the *Damascus Document*, which governed the Essene communities throughout Israel, is not a rule book or manual of discipline regulating the practical, day-to-day life of a real Jewish group in this present world. In rewriting Deuteronomy and other parts of the Mosaic Torah, the *Temple Scroll* seeks to legislate for a utopian future and a utopian temple. To what extent any laws on divorce that it might contain would be intended to apply to Jews living in this present world remains unclear.

When, in fact, one comes to what might be taken as some sort of prohibition of divorce, the passage speaks only of a future ideal king. Reworking a similar law in Deuteronomy that sought to prevent the king from forming harems similar to those in Gentile courts, 11QTemple 57:15–19 clearly forbids polygyny and marriage with Gentile women. It might also be understood to forbid divorce and remarriage, though the future king is allowed (even commanded) to marry again if his first wife dies. Nothing indicates that this rule for the king applies to commoners in the utopian future, to say nothing of the real world of 1st-century Judaism. Indeed, the larger context of the prescriptions for the king, as well as passing references to divorce elsewhere in the *Temple Scroll*, argues just the opposite. Thus, in the search for parallels to Jesus' total prohibition of divorce, the *Temple Scroll* must drop out of consideration.

More promising is the *Damascus Document*, since it was the practical rule book governing the day-to-day life of Essenes living in Israel. Unfortunately, as we have seen, the key text, CD 4:20–21, is ambiguous. Whatever interpretation one accepts of this disputed passage, the main institution attacked by the text seems to be polygyny. Divorce with subsequent remarriage while the first wife is still alive may also be condemned, though it may be that divorce without remarriage was not included in this condemnation. In fact, other fragmentary passages in the *Damascus Document* may presume divorce.

In the end, we may have something of a comparison-and-contrast situation between the teaching on marriage (and the teaching primarily concerns marriage) contained in the *Damascus Document* and the teaching on divorce proposed by the historical Jesus. The *Damascus Document* directly and explicitly forbids polygyny; but, by that very fact, it implicitly and concomitantly forbids divorce with remarriage during the lifetime of the first wife. In contrast, Jesus directly and explicitly forbids divorce with remarriage during the lifetime of the first wife. The succinct logion preserved in Q and Mark 10:11 does not, strictly speaking, address the question of polygyny—although the argumentation ascribed to Jesus in the dispute story in Mark 10:2–9 (to be treated below) at least implicitly attacks polygyny.[124] An intriguing configuration thus arises from this comparison and contrast: the *Damascus Document* forbids polygyny explicitly and divorce with remarriage implicitly; Jesus forbids divorce with remarriage explicitly and polygyny implicitly. Yet one must admit a further point. If one restricts oneself to the question, "Is there any precise parallel in Judaism before, during, or after Jesus' lifetime to his direct, explicit, and total prohibition of divorce?" then I think the answer must be no. In this astounding opposition to a central social institution permitted and regulated by the Mosaic Law, an institution Jesus brands as adultery, the teacher from Nazareth stands alone. Even if some doubts must remain with regard to the Essenes, Jesus certainly stood alone in relation to mainstream Judaism.

(b) If the criterion of discontinuity applies to Jesus' prohibition of divorce vis-à-vis Judaism, the closely allied *criterion of embarrassment* applies to the early church.[125] From the beginning, one notices a certain "squirming," a certain desire to create "wiggle room," as the Christian church, while taking over the sweeping, absolute prohibition of divorce voiced by this Jewish eschatological prophet, struggles to find ways to apply it practically to the concrete lives of Jewish and Gentile Christians. In 1 Corinthians, it is telling that, while Paul usually teaches, argues, exhorts, and commands on the basis of his own apostolic authority, when he comes to the question of divorce and remarriage among Christians, he suddenly switches tactics. While clearly speaking in his own voice when treating other matters of marriage, sexuality, and social status in 1 Corinthians 7 ("I say," "I wish"), Paul suddenly appeals directly to Jesus' authoritative command when he comes to the question of divorce among Christians (7:10–11: "I command—not I, but the Lord"). No sooner does he finish that touchy point (no doubt a "hard sell" to recently converted Gentiles) and move on to the different question of divorce between a Christian and pagan partner, than he resumes his own voice and authority (v 12: "I say, not the Lord"). Indeed, on this question of mixed marriages (7:12–16), Paul makes Christian history by creating the first documented wiggle room in the matter of Christians and divorce. He allows divorce if the pagan spouse is unwilling to live in peace with the Christian partner; in addition, he leaves open, by a studied ambiguity in v 15, the possibility of remarriage for the Christian.[126]

All this weaving and bobbing on Paul's part unwittingly prophesies the many ways in which the church of subsequent centuries will struggle to remain faithful to Jesus' prohibition of divorce while trying to make the prohibition livable and doable for ordinary Christians. The search for wiggle room continues in the second Christian generation with Matthew, who (perhaps on the basis of a discipline already in place in his own church) famously introduces his "exceptive clause" (5:32 and 19:9: "except in the case of unchastity") into both the Q and the Marcan versions of the prohibition. Whatever the exact meaning of the exceptive clause, it speaks volumes about the difficulty Matthew and his church apparently had in making the one prohibition of Jesus fit all sizes of marriages.

By way of analogy, one is reminded of the parade example of the criterion of embarrassment applied to the life of Jesus: his baptism by John the Baptist in the Jordan. As with Jesus' baptism, so with Jesus' prohibition of divorce, the church was "stuck" with a well-known event or saying from Jesus' life that it could not in good faith deny and yet found difficult to embrace, explain, or apply. All in all, one does not get the impression from the NT church, anymore than from the later church, that, left to itself, the church would have invented out of whole cloth a rule of life that it and its members found and find so difficult to teach, enforce, or follow. Probably more than one church leader down through the ages has wished that Jesus had been more stringent in observing the sabbath and less stringent in forbidding divorce. In sum, taken together, the criteria of discontinuity and embarrassment argue that neither mainstream Judaism before, during, or after Jesus' lifetime nor the early church of the first Christian generation invented a total prohibition of divorce that was so alien to the ancient (as well as the modern) mind-set, both Jewish and Gentile.

3. Coherence

While the major arguments for the historicity of the prohibition of divorce come from multiple attestation, discontinuity, and embarrassment, the criterion of coherence supplies added support. Almost all questers for the historical Jesus describe Jesus' approach to human conduct and observance of the Mosaic Law as in some sense "radical." In light of the kingdom of God both imminent and yet somehow present already in Jesus' ministry, Jesus called his disciples to a radical doing of God's will that was complete and costly. That point has already been made in the treatment of the disciples in Volume Three of *A Marginal Jew*,[127] and we will see the same point returning any number of times as we survey other aspects of Jesus' halakic teaching. The total prohibition of divorce, perhaps resting on the belief that the end time would return to and restore the wholeness and goodness of God's original creation (so Mark 10:5–9), fits the radical thrust of Jesus' *hălākâ*.[128]

One might also suggest, though much more tentatively, that the total prohibition of divorce fits in with what seems to have been Jesus' stringent approach to sexual morality in general, an interesting point of contact (as we saw in Volume Three) with the Essene movement, if not with the desires of most modern questers.[129] More specifically, one wonders whether there is any connection between the celibate lifestyle of Jesus and his absolutist view on divorce. I remember with a smile how, after discussing the possible celibacy of Jesus during a lecture at the University of California, San Diego, the wife of my professor-host told me that the best proof that Jesus was celibate was that he totally forbade divorce—something no married man would have ever done. This may at first seem just a joke, but I invite the reader to reflect on the different approaches to divorce in the Catholic and Protestant churches and to ponder whether there is a correlation between the legal status of divorce and the marital status of the hierarchy in the discipline of each group. Celibate Catholic bishops and priests teach the Catholic laity that divorce is not permitted, while a mostly married Protestant clergy—though certainly not happy with the high divorce rate—generally do allow divorce and remarriage in their churches. Perhaps coherence applies to 21st-century churches as well as to a 1st-century Jesus.

To sum up, then: the criteria of multiple attestation of sources and forms, of discontinuity and embarrassment, and of coherence all argue in favor of the historical Jesus issuing a prohibition of divorce as part of his halakic teaching.[130] No criterion argues against historicity. Indeed, Jesus' prohibition of divorce is perhaps the single best-attested teaching in what we call his *hălākâ*. Some might object that such a severe, absolutist stance on divorce clashes with all that we know about Jesus' emphasis on compassion and forgiveness. Such an objection presupposes or implies that: (1) compassion and forgiveness are inherently incompatible with stringent moral demands, (2) compassion and forgiveness set Jesus apart as notably different from the other Jewish teachers of his time, and (3) the itinerant Jesus, preaching on different occasions in different venues to different audiences over a roughly two-year period, developed a moral-legal system that was perfectly coherent within itself. Each one of these presuppositions is questionable, especially if we are questing for a 1st-century Jewish prophet and not a 21st-century American homilist in some Catholic pulpit.

E. THE DISPUTE STORY IN MARK 10:2–12

As a strategic move, I have purposely kept the question of the dispute story in Mark 10:2–12 until last in our treatment of Jesus and divorce. The reason for this strategy is simple: a decision on the historicity of Jesus' prohibition of divorce rests to a great degree on the argument from multiple attestation, which applies to the succinct sayings cited or paraphrased in 1 Cor 7:10–11; Matt 5:32 ∥ Luke 16:18; and Mark 10:11–12. The larger unit of the dispute story of Mark 10:2–12 (the overarching context of 10:11–12) does not enjoy such multiple attestation; Matt 19:3–12 is simply Matthew's reworking of the Marcan pericope.[131] Moreover, as previously noted, many critics consider most if not all of the Synoptic dispute stories to be secondary creations of the church, providing anecdotal settings for individual sayings of Jesus that circulated in the oral tradition.[132] Now that the historicity of the prohibition has been established without using the Marcan dispute story, we can consider whether a quick overview of Mark 10:2–12 justifies the judgment that the story as a whole does not go back to Jesus.

That there are traces of Mark's redactional hand in the pericope is clear. In addition to typical Marcan vocabulary and literary style, we have in this pericope a clear example of the secrecy motif that pervades Mark's Gospel. In a number of incidents throughout the Gospel, Jesus says or does something in public that causes puzzlement or questioning; then, in private, he gives further instruction to his disciples on the puzzling point. Examples include the parable discourse (4:1–9 + 10–20), the dispute on defilement (7:14–15 + 17–23), and the healing of the possessed boy (9:14–27 + 28–29). We have the same basic pattern in 10:2–12: Jesus' public debate with the Pharisees on divorce in vv 2–9 is followed by his private instruction to the disciples in vv 10–12. Confirming and corresponding to this two-part division in 10:2–12 is the fact that each of these two parts has one type of saying on divorce. (1) The public dispute with the Pharisees (vv 2–9) culminates in a short, apodictic command (v 9): "What therefore God has joined together a human being must not separate." (2) The private instruction to the disciples (vv 10–12) enshrines the two-part prohibition of divorce on the part of either the husband or the wife (vv 11–12) that we have already investigated.

Some form critics suggest that it was Mark who joined the originally independent logion on divorce in vv 11–12 to the dispute story of vv 2–9.[133] Indeed, Mark seems to have tied the two units together by making the opening question of the Pharisees in v 2 read: "Is it lawful for a man to divorce his wife [*ei exestin andri gynaika apolysai*]?"[134] Surprisingly, after the Pharisees repeat this vocabulary of divorcing in v 4, this set of words, especially the key verb "divorce" (*apolyō*), disappears from the rest of the dispute with the Pharisees. Technically speaking, the precise question asked by the Pharisees in v 2 is never answered by Jesus with this same vocabulary anywhere in the rest of the dispute. This includes Jesus' final reply to the Pharisees in v 9, which employs different language and indeed a different perspective: God joining and a "human being" (*anthrōpos*) separating, not a husband (*anēr*) divorcing (*aplyō*) his wife (*gynē*). It is rather when Jesus retires to a house and replies to the disciples' request for further instruction that he takes up the language of the Pharisees' question ("Whosoever divorces his wife . . . if she divorces her husband"). Hence, on a first reading, Mark 10:2–12 is somewhat confusing: the precise question the Pharisees ask in v 2 is never answered in their presence (vv 2–9), but rather in the presence of the disciples (vv 10–12), who do not pose the question in the terms the Pharisees use. The answer Jesus gives the Pharisees, while relevant to the larger question of marriage and divorce, does not really address their particular question in the specific terms they use.

At the very least, Mark seems to have formulated the Pharisees' initial question, posed in public, to make it correspond, by way of *inclusio*, to the final pronouncement addressed to the disciples in private. In fact, some scholars, such as Raymond Collins, wish to go further. Collins thinks that the whole pericope is so saturated with Marcan vocabulary, style, and theology that Mark 10:2–12, as it presently lies before us, must be considered Mark's own composition. The concise saying rejecting divorce in v 9 may be an earlier creation of the Greek-speaking church, a creation that in turn called forth the dispute story with its scriptural proof as a fuller explanation of the prohibition. In the end, suggests Collins, the dispute story, including the climactic saying of v 9, is probably a Christian creation and does not go back to the historical Jesus.[135] While this is a tenable opinion, the matter is not entirely clear. Other scholars, such as Heikki Sariola, take the opposite approach: the redactional activity of Mark in vv 2–9 is slight, with the core of the story coming from pre-Marcan tradition.[136] Whether or not Sariola is right, it does seem that some elements of the story are difficult to understand if the incident is a purely Marcan creation or even a purely Christian one.

For instance, on the literary and theological level of Mark's Gospel, the initial question of the Pharisees comes out of nowhere. Unlike the Matthean

Jesus (cf. Matt 5:31–32 vis-à-vis 19:3–12), the Marcan Jesus has not addressed the issue of divorce previous to this dispute story. Moreover, on the historical level, it is hard to imagine a representative of mainstream Judaism in the 1st century questioning the basic legitimacy of divorce. Hence, whether we consider the matter on the literary or the historical level, the question posed by the Pharisees is strange in that it lacks any apparent context or matrix. To provide such a context or matrix, many commentators at this point invoke the famous dispute between the House of Shammai and the House of Hillel on the grounds for divorce.[137] But, as we have seen, there is no proof that such a dispute raged during the time of Jesus; it is first attested after A.D. 70. Consequently, if we seek a plausible historical situation behind this Marcan text, we have to suppose that the Pharisees had heard of Jesus' total rejection of divorce (a shocking position in mainstream Judaism) and wanted to query him about it.[138] Still, we must remember that in the story world of Mark's Gospel, there has been no such preparation or rationale for the question. A purely literary solution to this problem in the Marcan text is to maintain that the Pharisees' question in 10:2 is simply an artificial setup for the private instruction to the disciples in vv 10–12. In other words, the Pharisees in this dispute story are simply a convenient literary foil created by Mark to introduce Jesus' teaching on divorce.

Yet once again, the matter is not completely clear, and the suggestion that the Pharisees in v 2 are simply a Marcan literary device does not entirely solve our problem. The Pharisees' question in v 2 is absolute in the sense that it asks only about the lawfulness of divorce, not about the lawfulness of remarriage (though that may well be presupposed). This absolute question about divorce, without reference to remarriage, is the question answered by Jesus in an absolute fashion *in v 9* (no human being can separate husband and wife), *not in vv 11–12*. In vv 11–12, it is divorce and remarriage together that are branded adultery. The difference between these two types of pronouncements on divorce (v 9 versus vv 11–12) is all the more glaring because of Mark's unique addition in v 11: the husband who divorces his wife and marries another woman commits adultery *against her* (the first wife). The implication here is that the divorce by itself would not constitute adultery; it is the remarriage that does that. Thus, in substance though not in wording, Jesus' reply in v 9 corresponds to the Pharisees' initial question in a way that vv 11–12 do not. Another consideration that makes one hesitant about declaring the dispute in 10:2–9 a purely Christian invention is that, as we saw in Volume Three, the Mishna and Tosepta indicate that the Pharisees were noted for their interest in the question of divorce and the proper way of drawing up a certificate of divorce. Hence, in this particular Marcan dispute story, which focuses on divorce, the identity of the questioners as Pharisees may not be just a literary convention.

With these initial problems in mind, let us proceed to follow the thread of the story. After the Pharisees' opening question, the Marcan narrative continues in a manner typical of a dispute story. Like a good rabbi, Jesus counters the initial hostile question of the Pharisees with a counterquestion in v 3, which underlines the legal tone struck in the initial question, "Is it lawful?" Insisting that the matter at issue is nothing less than a commandment of the Torah, Jesus asks, "What did Moses *command* you?"[139] It is telling that the Pharisees seem to dodge this direct challenge by switching to the vocabulary of permission (v 4): "Moses *permitted* [the husband] to write a certificate of divorce and to divorce [his wife]."[140] The narrative thus sets up a clear opposition between Jesus and the Pharisees on the right way to interpret Deut 24:1–4 (which the Pharisees have paraphrased in their reply in v 4): commandment versus permission.

The Marcan Jesus continues to insist that the mechanism of divorce with a certificate, set up in Deut 24:1–4, is a true commandment, but he now gives his position an aggressive, negative thrust that puts the Pharisees in a bad light (v 5): "He [Moses] wrote *you*[141] this commandment with a view to *your* hardness of heart"—perhaps in the sense that Moses both knew their hardness of heart and wished to expose it by giving a commandment that would bear witness against them.[142] "Hardness of heart" refers here not to a primitive level of culture or social institutions but rather to a stubborn refusal at the core of one's being to hear and obey God's word, in this case, his will expressed in the Torah. At first glance, this seems a strange accusation, since the Pharisees have just paraphrased a passage of the Torah, Deut 24:1–4.

In vv 6–8, Jesus provides the exegetical basis for his accusation that the Pharisees, for all their claims of zeal for the Law, are actually in rebellion against God's will as revealed in the Torah. Jesus locates and defines the primordial will of God in the Torah by moving back from Deuteronomy to the creation story in Genesis 1–2. At the very beginning of the Torah, at the very beginning of creation,[143] God is said to create the human species as male and female (Gen 1:27), a duality that, according to Gen 2:24, is meant to merge into a unity that is the basis of human society.[144] "For this reason [namely, the fact that the human species is created as a duality], a man (*anthrōpos*) shall leave his father and mother and cleave to his wife,[145] and the two [implicitly, *only* two] shall become one flesh"—that is, one human reality, one human being.[146] Jesus hammers home this oneness, which he sees as indissoluble, by repeating the final phrase of Gen 2:24: "Consequently, they are no longer two but one flesh."

Jesus' rapid exegesis contains an implied hermeneutic: Genesis trumps Deuteronomy. But this is not just a question of the relative order and authority of two books within the Pentateuch. The deeper point being made is that the order of creation, revealed in Genesis 1–2, trumps the positive law of divorce in the Pentateuchal law code, promulgated in Deuteronomy.[147] From this implied hermeneutic, Jesus draws a basic conclusion—and commandment—about marriage and divorce (v 9): "What therefore God has joined together [synezeuxen, literally, yoked together][148] a human being [anthrōpos][149] must not separate [mē chōrizetō, the verb Paul uses in 1 Cor 7:10–16 for divorce]."[150] The traditional English translation, "Let not man put asunder," makes Jesus' final pronouncement sound more like a wish. But the Greek verb chōrizetō stands in the 3d person singular imperative (a form modern English does not have), and so what the Marcan Jesus utters, at least in the Greek text before us, is a concise apodictic command.[151]

Intriguingly, the thought of the dispute story has moved from the command given in Deut 24:1–4 through the primordial will of God expressed in the creation narrative of Genesis to the command issued by Jesus. God's will, inscribed in his very act of creation, is that marriage forms a permanent union between two persons. This is the foundational law built into the very structure of creation by God himself, and hence no human being can undo it—including, presumably, Moses in Deut 24:1–4. It is no wonder that the Marcan disciples find this train of thought and final command puzzling. As we have seen, their request for further instruction allows Mark to have Jesus voice his teaching in another form and with a different thrust: a two-part casuistic law that brands divorce and remarriage, be it by husband or wife, adultery (paralleling in part the Q tradition).[152] Rhetorically, the combination of the concise apodictic command in v 9 and the two-part casuistic law in vv 11–12 delivers a two-punch "knock-out" blow to divorce: divorce itself is prohibited as contrary to God's will, inscribed in the very structure of creation and marriage, and therefore anyone who divorces and remarries commits adultery.

From this brief overview of the Marcan dispute on divorce, one clearly sees that Mark 10:2–12, as it now stands in Mark's Gospel, is a literary and theological creation of Mark, welded together out of various traditions and motifs and shaped by Mark's theological agenda and literary style. However, I am less confident about the claims frequently made by critics that no historical dispute between Jesus and the Pharisees lies behind this story and in particular that Mark 10:9 must be a creation of the "Hellenistic church."

But perhaps my own view on this question can best be sketched within a summation of the major conclusions reached in this chapter.

F. CONCLUSIONS

The most important single conclusion of our investigation is that the criteria of multiple attestation, of discontinuity and embarrassment, and of coherence all argue for the historicity of Jesus' prohibition of divorce. A few further observations and tentative conclusions may now be added to this basic conclusion.

(1) The reader will have noticed that I have not offered an opinion as to what was *the* "original saying" or *the* "original form" of Jesus' prohibition of divorce. The reason for this is not hard to guess. One may reasonably suppose that this astounding and shocking teaching of Jesus called forth a great deal of debate and questioning. Jesus probably stated his prohibition a number of times, not necessarily always in the same words. Critics often suggest that Luke 16:18 (with or without the clause "and marries another"), which in their view represents the original Q logion, comes closest to Jesus' original pronouncement. It may indeed represent one form of Jesus' pronouncement. But we cannot exclude the possibility that other forms of his teaching (perhaps including a primitive form of Matt 5:32, without the exceptive clause) also come from Jesus.

(2) Our analysis of the dispute story in Mark 10:2–12 confirms the common view that this *Streitgespräch* (indeed, like every *Streitgespräch*) is, in its present form, a Christian composition. It is an "ideal scene." Yet, in this case, the ideal scene may faithfully reflect the type of debate in which the historical Jesus actually engaged when he—as he must have—answered objections to his startling and disturbing *hălākâ* on divorce. The Qumran documents (especially the *Damascus Document*'s use of Genesis) shows us that this kind of scriptural argumentation was at home in Palestinian Judaism at the turn of the era, and need not be assigned to "Hellenistic Christianity" in the Diaspora. As noted earlier, the Mishna and Tosepta indicate that the Pharisees were remembered for being especially interested in the question of divorce, especially the correct way of drawing up a certificate of divorce. All in all, while it is true that Mark 10:2–12 in its present form has been shaped by Christian rhetoric and theology, this particular dispute story may draw upon authentic memories about how the historical Jesus debated with Pharisees over what was surely his most controversial teaching on the Law.

But what of the short, sharp command of Jesus (10:9) that is the "punch line" of the Marcan dispute: "What God has joined no human must separate"? The question of the authenticity of this aphoristic imperative is difficult to decide. To be sure, unlike the prohibition attested by Paul, Q, and Mark, we lack multiple attestation of sources and forms for 10:9. However, there are some considerations that argue in favor of historicity: (a) This striking and memorable aphorism is formulated in a concise antithetical parallelism—a style that many questers consider typical of Jesus. (b) Outside of the Synoptic logia on divorce and Paul's uncharacteristic appeal to Jesus' teaching on divorce, Christian parenesis in the NT is strangely silent on the subject of divorce among Christians. Apparently, in the NT period, either one quoted Jesus on the subject or one did not talk about it. We do not get the impression from the NT that Christian teachers in the first two generations of the church developed any specific teaching on the topic apart from the sayings of Jesus (which created more than enough difficulty for the Christian teachers). (c) The aphorism of Mark 10:9 enjoys a basic coherence both with the general radical thrust of Jesus' *hălākâ* and with the prohibition of divorce (attested in Paul, Q, and Mark) that we have already judged authentic Jesus material. Taken together, these considerations incline me to accept Mark 10:9 (as well as some sort of debate with the Pharisees on the question of divorce) as more than likely going back to the historical Jesus. I readily admit, though, that this conclusion is less firmly grounded than the historicity of the prohibition attested by Paul, Q, and Mark. Hence, for strategic reasons, I have not based my main argument on it.[153]

If one accepts Mark 10:9 as authentic, this verse in turn invites further conjectures. One might, for instance, investigate its intriguing pattern of similarity-yet-difference in relation to both the prohibition attested in Luke 16:18 ‖ Mark 10:11 and the treatment of divorce in 1 Cor 7:10–11.

(a) Compared to Luke 16:18 ‖ Mark 10:11, Mark 10:9 directly prohibits (with a 3d person singular imperative) divorce and divorce alone, with no mention of remarriage. Divorce, taken by itself, is contrary to God's action in joining man and woman in marriage and must be avoided. However, in Mark 10:9, the act of divorce is not branded as in itself constituting adultery. In contrast, in a form reflecting casuistic rather than apodictic law,[154] Luke 16:18 ‖ Mark 10:11 join the two acts of divorce and remarriage and brand the twofold action as the sin of adultery.

(b) The overall pattern of these two types of Synoptic sayings on divorce (i.e., Mark 10:9 on the one hand and Luke 16:18 ‖ Mark 10:11 on the other) provides an odd and rough parallel to Paul's teaching on divorce (which appeals by way of paraphrase to Jesus' teaching) in 1 Cor 7:10–11. On the one hand, Paul, in apodictic fashion, commands (in vv 10 + 11c) that the wife not divorce her husband and the husband not divorce his wife. This concise prohibition of divorce, which does not label divorce itself as the sin of adultery, is similar in its thrust to Mark 10:9 (though the ability of both man and woman to divorce one's spouse parallels instead the double prohibition of Mark 10:11–12). Yet, in his parenthetical proviso in 1 Cor 7:11 a + b ("but if she does divorce, she must remain unmarried or be reconciled with her husband"), Paul recognizes that divorce may take place (or may have already taken place). In such a case, Paul insists that there is to be no second marriage (thus echoing the clause "and marries another" in Luke 16:18 and Mark 10:11), thus implying that the bond of the first marriage remains (and perhaps implying even further that any attempted second marriage would be adulterous).

On the basis of these observations, I would offer the intriguing surmise—and it can be nothing more than a surmise—that one reason why Paul paraphrases rather than cites Jesus' prohibition of divorce is that he is actually meshing and applying a number of various sayings on the subject that have come down to him (including perhaps a version of Mark 10:9 as well as a version of Luke 16:18). But I do not insist on this point or, for that matter, on the authenticity of Mark 10:9. The latter question remains debatable.

(3) In light of the almost universal tendency on the part of exegetes to explain Mark 10:2–12 (as well as any teaching on divorce attributed to the historical Jesus) by appealing to the debate between the House of Hillel and the House of Shammai,[155] it is important to emphasize a point made earlier in this chapter. Almost all the pre-70 Jewish texts known to us reflect a Judaism in which a man could divorce his wife for practically any reason. There is no hint of a debate over the precise grounds for divorce, let alone the specific debate over 'erwat dābār ("shame of a thing" in Deut 24:1) between the House of Hillel and the House of Shammai, as reported in the mishnaic tractate Giṭṭin. The first glimmer of a debate over grounds for divorce may (ironically) be the exceptive clause in Matt 5:32 and 19:9, though this Jewish-Christian development may not reflect the same sort of debate as that found in m. Giṭṭin.

(4) In the end, the main conclusion of this chapter, that Jesus absolutely forbade divorce and branded divorce and remarriage as the sin of adultery, raises a serious problem for our whole understanding of the Jewish Jesus and his relation to the Jewish Law. A major contention of A Marginal Jew is that Jesus arose out of and addressed mainstream Palestinian Judaism of the 1st century A.D. As stressed in the previous chapter, it is nonsense to speak of the Jewish Jesus abrogating or annulling the Mosaic Law. The Mosaic Law is the given, the sacred canopy under which Jesus and other Palestinian Jews lived and debated the precise understanding and practice of the Law.

How then are we to understand the overall position of Jesus if he embraces and affirms the Mosaic Law and yet, in one case involving a major social institution permitted and regulated by the Law, brands divorce and remarriage as the sin of adultery? How can the Law-abiding Jesus claim that a fellow Jew who dutifully follows the Law in divorcing and remarrying commits a sin against one of the commandments of the Decalogue?

For the time being, I simply note this glaring problem; we will have to return to it after we have seen other aspects of Jesus' teaching on the Law. For now, I just want to highlight two overarching contexts that we have already seen, two contexts that may contribute to understanding Jesus' apparently contradictory approach to the Law:

(a) As we can observe from the library at Qumran, various Jewish groups around the turn of the era did not think devotion to the Law of Moses prevented them from rewriting or reformulating parts of the Pentateuch—witness such works as the *Genesis Apocryphon*, the *Temple Scroll*, and the various fragments given suggestive titles like *Rewritten Pentateuch*. Not all these works were necessarily composed by the Qumran community itself. The tendency to rethink and rephrase the Mosaic Torah seems not to have been restricted to a single "monastery" in Palestine at the turn of the era.

(b) We must bear in mind the portrait of the historical Jesus that has emerged so far in *A Marginal Jew*. Far from seeing himself as just another teacher, Jesus consciously presented himself to his fellow Jews as the eschatological prophet, performing Elijah's task of beginning the regathering of Israel in the end time while also performing miracles like Elijah's. These miracles were interpreted as signs of the kingdom that was coming and yet that, in a way, was already present in Jesus' ministry. In this highly charged context of future-yet-realized eschatology, the eschatological prophet named Jesus may have inculcated as already binding certain types of behavior that pointed forward, as did his whole ministry, to the final period of Israel's total restoration as God's holy people. *Pace* Albert Schweitzer, this eschatological behavior was closer to an "already/not-yet ethic" than an "interim ethic." It was intelligible—to say nothing of being doable—only to those who accepted Jesus as the eschatological prophet who in some sense made present the kingdom of God that was soon to come.

With this hypothesis tucked away in the back of our minds, let us proceed to survey other aspects of Jesus' *hălākâ*. But what aspect should we examine next? Having started our survey with one legal institution (divorce) that Jesus presumed to prohibit, we might logically continue by asking: Can we find any other example of such troubling teaching that dares to prohibit an institution accepted and regulated by the Torah? The most likely candidate for this dubious honor is the institution of oaths.

NOTES TO CHAPTER 32

[1] A full bibliography on divorce—even if limited to Judaism and Christianity— would fill a number of volumes. In this chapter, I simply give a sample of representative works; the more scholarly books and articles among them supply more detailed bibliographies in their respective areas. The history of the interpretation of Jesus' teaching on divorce has itself generated a large amount of literature; see, e.g., V. Norskov Olsen, *The New Testament Logia on Divorce. A Study of Their Interpretation from Erasmus to Milton* (BGBE; Tübingen: Mohr [Siebeck], 1971): this work points out the great difference the view of marriage as a sacrament or as just a natural ordinance makes, and likewise the various political and juridical conflicts of the Reformation period that influenced a given thinker; Giovanni Cereti, *Divorzio, nuove nozze e penitenza nella chiesa primitiva* (Studi e ricerche 26; Bologna: Edizioni Dehoniane, 1977): this work is written with a view to rethinking the present-day practice of the Roman Catholic Church in light of the discipline of the Eastern Orthodox Churches; Alfred Niebergall, *Ehe und Eheschliessung in der Bibel und in der Geschichte der alten Kirche* (Marburger Theologische Studien 18; Marburg: Elwert, 1985); Gabriele Lachner, *Die Kirchen und die Wiederheirat Geschiedener* (Münchener Universitätsschriften; Beiträge zur Ökumenischen Theologie 21; Paderborn: Schöningh, 1991): this work is an exercise in historical and theological hermeneutics that is more concerned with the present-day ecumenical situation among Roman Catholic, Orthodox, Protestant, and Anglican churches, while also surveying the biblical data and the practice of the early church; H. J. Selderhuis, *Marriage and Divorce in the Thought of Martin Bucer* (Sixteenth Century Essays & Studies 48; Kirksville, MO: Thomas Jefferson University, 1999; Dutch original, 1994): this work carefully traces the changes in the position of this influential Reformer as he reacted to other views.

For the sake of scholars looking for a working bibliography on the subject of divorce in the Bible, I offer the following list, divided into main topics and arranged alphabetically (with the standard commentaries omitted).

ON MARRIAGE, DIVORCE, AND THE GENERAL LEGAL SITUATION IN THE ANCIENT NEAR EAST: G. Cardascia, *Les Lois Assyriennes* (Paris: Cerf, 1969); A. E. Cowley, *Aramaic Papyri of the Fifth Century BC* (Oxford: Clarendon, 1923); G. R. Driver and J. C. Miles (eds.), *The Assyrian Laws* (Oxford: Clarendon, 1939); J. Huehnergard, "Biblical Notes on Some New Akkadian Texts from Emar (Syria)," *CBQ* 47 (1985) 428–34; E. G. Kraeling, *The Brooklyn Museum Aramaic Papyri: New Documents of the Fifth Century B.C. from the Jewish Colony at Elephantine* (New Haven: Yale University, 1953); E. Lipiński, "The Wife's Right to Divorce in the Light of an Ancient Near Eastern Tradition," *Jewish Law Annual* 4 (1981) 9–27; W. Pestman, *Marriage and Matrimonial Property in Ancient Egypt* (Leiden: Brill, 1961); James B. Pritchard, *Ancient Near Eastern Texts Relating to the Old*

Testament (3d ed. with supplement; Princeton: Princeton University, 1969); Jacob J. Rabinowitz, "Marriage Contracts in Ancient Egypt in the Light of Jewish Sources," *HTR* 46 (1953) 91–97; M. Roth, *Babylonian Marriage Agreements: 7th–3rd Centuries B.C.* (AOAT 222; Kevelaer: Butzon & Bercker; Neukirchen-Vluyn: Neukirchener Verlag, 1989); idem, *Law Collections from Mesopotamia and Asia Minor* (SBL Writings from the Ancient World 6; Atlanta: Scholars, 1995); M. San Nicolò, "Vorderasiatische Rechtsgut in den ägyptischen Eheverträgen der Perserzeit," *OLZ* 30 (1927) 217–18; R. Westbrook, "Adultery in Ancient Near Eastern Law," *RB* 97 (1990) 542–80; idem, *Old Babylonian Marriage Law* (Archiv für Orientforschung 23; Horn, Austria: Berger, 1988); F. Zeman, "Le statut de la femme en Mesopotamie d'après les sources juridiques," *ScEs* 43 (1991) 69–86.

ON MARRIAGE AND DIVORCE IN THE OT IN GENERAL: W. Bäumlein, "Die exegetische Grundlage der Gesetzgebung über Ehescheidung," *TSK* 30 (1857) 329–39; Joseph Blenkinsopp, "The Family in First Temple Israel," *Families in Ancient Israel* (ed. Leo G. Perdue; Louisville: Westminster/John Knox, 1997) 48–103; Athalya Brenner, *The Israelite Woman: Social Role and Literary Type in Biblical Narrative* (Sheffield: JSOT, 1985); Michael Fishbane, *Biblical Interpretation in Ancient Israel* (Oxford: Clarendon, 1985); B. Jongeling, "*Lākēn* dans l'Ancien Testament," *Remembering All the Way* (Oudtestamentische Studien 21; Leiden: Brill, 1981); P. A. Kruger, "The Hem of the Garment in Marriage: The Meaning of the Symbolic Gesture in Ruth 3:9 and Ezek 16:9," *Journal of Northwest Semitic Languages* 12 (1984) 79–86; M. R. Lehmann, "Gen 2:24 as the Basis for Divorce in Halakhah and New Testament," *ZAW* 72 (1960) 263–67; Clemens Locher, *Die Ehre einer Frau in Israel* (OBO 70; Freiburg: Universitätsverlag; Göttingen: Vandenhoeck & Ruprecht, 1986); Jacob Milgrom, *Cult and Conscience: The Asham and the Priestly Doctrine of Repentance* (SJLA 18; Leiden: Brill, 1976); P. Mullins, "The Status of Women in Family Life: A Comparative Study of Old Testament Times," *Milltown Studies* 41 (1998) 51–81; Raphael Patai, *Sex and Family in the Bible and the Middle East* (Garden City, NY: Doubleday, 1959); Leo G. Perdue, "The Israelite and Early Jewish Family: Summary and Conclusions," *Families in Ancient Israel* (ed. Leo G. Perdue; Louisville: Westminster/John Knox, 1997) 163–222; W. Plautz, "Die Form der Eheschliessung im Alten Testament," *ZAW* 23 (1973) 349–61; J. Scharbert, "Ehe und Eheschliessung in der Rechtssprache des Pentateuch und beim Chronisten," *Studien zum Pentateuch: Walter Kornfeld zum 60. Geburtstag* (ed. G. Braulik; Vienna/Freiburg/Basel: Herder, 1977) 213–25; E. de la Serna, "La familia en la Biblia," *RevistB* 57 (1995) 93–119; J. M. Sprinkle, "Old Testament Perspectives on Divorce and Remarriage," *JETS* 40 (1997) 529–50; Lawrence E. Stager, "The Family in Ancient Israel," *BASOR* 260 (1985) 1–35; Angelo Tosato, *Il matrimonio israelitico: una theoria generale* (AnBib 100; new ed.; Rome: Biblical Institute, 2001); Roland de Vaux, *Ancient Israel* (2 vols.; New York: McGraw-Hill, 1965); G. J. Wenham, "The Restoration of Marriage Reconsidered," *JJS* 30 (1979) 36–40; idem, "Marriage and Divorce in the Old Testament," *Didaskalia* 1 (1989) 6–17; R. Yaron, "The Restoration of Marriage," *JJS* 17 (1966) 1–11; Y. Zakovitch, "The Woman's Rights in the Biblical Law of Divorce," *Jewish Law Annual* 4 (1981) 28–46.

On Deuteronomy: Calum M. Carmichael, *The Laws of Deuteronomy* (Ithaca, NY: Cornell University, 1974); D. Daube, "Repudium in Deuteronomy," *Neotestamentica et Semitica: Studies in Honour of Matthew Black* (ed. E. E. Ellis and M. Wilcox; Edinburgh: Clark, 1969) 236–39; T. R. Hobbs, "Jeremiah 3:1–5 and Deuteronomy 24:1–4," *ZAW* 86 (1974) 23–29; David Instone-Brewer, "Deuteronomy 24:1–4 and the Origin of the Jewish Divorce Certificate," *JJS* 49 (1998) 230–43; J. C. Laney, "Deut 24:1–4 and the Issue of Divorce," *BSac* 149 (1992) 3–15; R. Neudecker, "Das 'Ehescheidungsgesetz' von Dtn 24.1–4 nach altjüdischer Auslegung," *Bib* 75 (1994) 350–87; E. Otto, "Das Verbot der Wiederherstellung einer geschiedenen Ehe, Deuteronomium 24:1–4 im Kontext des israelitischen und judaischen Eherechts," *Ugarit-Forschungen* 24 (1992) 301–10; D. Volgger, "Dtn 24:1–4—Ein Verbot von Wiederverheiratung?" *BN* 92 (1998) 85–96; J. H. Walton, "The Place of the *hutqattel* within the D-stem Group and its Implications in Deuteronomy 24:4," *Hebrew Studies* 32 (1991) 7–17; A. Warren, "Did Moses Permit Divorce? Modal *weqatal* as Key to New Testament Readings of Deuteronomy 24:1–4," *TynBul* 49 (1998) 39–56; R. Westbrook, "The Prohibition on Restoration of Marriage in Deuteronomy 24:1–4," in *Studies in Bible* (ed. S. Japhet. ScrHier 31; Jerusalem: Magnes, 1986).

On Hosea: C. Barth, "Zur Bedeutung der Wustentradition," *Congress Volume* (VTSup 15; Leiden: Brill, 1966) 14–23; S. Bitter, *Die Ehe des Propheten Hosea* (Göttinger Theologische Arbeiten 3; Göttingen: Vandenhoeck & Ruprecht, 1975); H. A. Brongers, "Bemerkungen zum Gebrauch der adverbialen *we'attāh* im Alten Testament," *VT* 15 (1965) 289–99; U. Cassuto, "The Second Chapter of the Book of Hosea," *Biblical and Oriental Studies. Vol. 1* (Jerusalem: Magnes,1973) 101–40; D. J. Clines, "Hosea 2: Structure and Interpretation," *Studia Biblica 1978. I. Papers on Old Testament and Related Themes* (ed. E. A. Livingstone; JSOTSup 11; Sheffield: JSOT, 1979) 83–103; idem, "Story and Poem: The Old Testament as Literature and as Scripture," *Int* 34 (1980) 115–27; Georg Fohrer, *Die symbolischen Handlungen der Propheten* (ATANT 54; 2d ed.; Zurich: Zwingli, 1968); M. A. Friedman, "Israel's Response in Hosea 2:17b: 'You are my Husband,' " *JBL* 99 (1980) 199–204; M. J. Geller, "The Elephantine Papyri and Hosea 2,3: Evidence for the Form of the Early Jewish Divorce Writ," *JSJ* 8 (1977) 139–48; C. Gordon, "Hos 2,4–5 in the Light of New Semitic Inscriptions," *ZAW* 54 (1936) 277–80; H. Krszyna, "Literarische Struktur von Os 2,4–17," *BZ* 13 (1969) 41–59; P. A. Kruger, "Israel, the Harlot (Hos 2:4–9)," *Journal of Northwest Semitic Languages* 11 (1983) 107–116; idem, "The Marriage Metaphor in Hosea 2:4–17 against Its Ancient Near Eastern Background," *Old Testament Essays* 5 (1992) 7–25; N. Kuhl, "Neue Dokumente zum Verständnis von Hosea 2,4–15," *ZAW* 52 (1934) 102–9; J. Limburg, "The Root *ryb* and the Prophetic Lawsuit Speeches," *JBL* 88 (1969) 291–304; D. Lys, "J'ai deux amours, ou l'amant jugé: Exercise sur Osée 2,4–25," *ETR* 51 (1976) 59–77; K. Nielsen, *Yahweh as Prosecutor and Judge: An Investigation of the Prophetic Lawsuit* (JSOTSup 9; Sheffield: JSOT, 1978); J. J. Schmitt, "Yahweh's Divorce in Hosea 2—Who is that Woman?" *Scandinavian Journal of the Old Testament* 9 (1995) 119–32; J. Schreiner, "Hoseas Ehe, ein Zeichen des Gerichts," *BZ* 21 (1977) 163–83; B. Seifert, *Metaphorisches Reden von Gott im*

Hoseabuch (FRLANT 166; Göttingen: Vandenhoeck & Ruprecht, 1996); Y. Sherwood, *The Prostitute and the Prophet* (JSOTSup 212; Sheffield: Sheffield Academic Press, 1996); M.-T. Wacker, *Figurationen des Weiblichen im Hosea-Buch* (Herders Biblische Studien 8; Freiburg/Basel/Vienna: Herder, 1996); W. D. Whitt, "The Divorce of Yahweh and Asherah in Hos 2,4–7,12ff.," *Scandinavian Journal of the Old Testament* 6 (1992) 31–67.

ON MALACHI: T. Chary, *Les prophètes et le culte à partir de l'exil* (Tournai: Desclée, 1954); J. C. Collins, "The (Intelligible) Masoretic Text of Malachi 2:16 or, How does God feel about Divorce?" *Presbyterion* 20 (1994) 36–40; Russell Fuller, "Text-Critical Problems in Malachi 2:10–16," *JBL* 110 (1991) 47–57; M. J. Geller, "The Elephantine Papyri and Hosea 2,3," *JSJ* 8 (1977) 139–48; Beth Glazier-McDonald, "Intermarriage, Divorce, and the bat'-ēl nēkār: Insights into Mal 2:10–16," *JBL* 106 (1987) 603–11 [an extract from the following work]; idem, *Malachi: The Divine Messenger, A Critical Reappraisal* (SBLDS 98; Atlanta: Scholars 1987); G. P. Hugenberger, *Marriage as a Covenant: A Study of Biblical Law and Ethics Governing Marriage, Developed from the Perspective of Malachi* (VTSup 52; Leiden: Brill, 1994); D. C. Jones, "A Note on the LXX of Malachi 2:16," *JBL* 109 (1990) 683–85; idem, "Malachi on Divorce," *Presbyterion* 15 (1989) 16–22; J. Morgenstern, "Jerusalem—485 B.C.," *HUCA* 28 (1957) 15–47; K. Nielsen, *Yahweh as Prosecutor and Judge* (JSOTSup 9; Sheffield: JSOT, 1978) 34–38; M. A. Shields, "Syncretism and Divorce in Malachi 2,10–16," *ZAW* 111 (1999) 68–86; A. S. van der Woude, "Malachi's Struggle for a Pure Community. Reflections on Malachi 2:10–16," *Tradition and Re-Interpretation in Jewish and Early Christian Literature* (J. C. H. Lebram Festschrift; SPB 36; ed J. W. van Henten et al.; Leiden: Brill, 1986) 65–71.

SECOND TEMPLE JUDAISM IN GENERAL: L. J. Archer, *Her Price Is Beyond Rubies: The Jewish Woman in Graeco-Roman Palestine* (JSOTSup 60; Sheffield: JSOT, 1990); B. J. Brooten, "Konnten Frauen im alten Judentum die Scheidung betreiben? Überlegungen zu Mk 10:11–12 und 1 Kor 7:10–11," *EvT* 42 (1982) 65–80; idem, "Zur Debatte über das Scheidungsrecht der jüdischen Frau," *EvT* 43 (1983) 466–78; John J. Collins, "Marriage, Divorce, and Family in Second Temple Judaism," *Families in Ancient Israel* (ed. Leo G. Perdue; Louisville: Westminster/John Knox, 1997) 104–62; E. Eshel and A. Kloner. "An Aramaic Ostracon of an Edomite Marriage Contract from Maresha, Dated 176 BCE," *IEJ* 46 (1996) 1–22; Joseph A. Fitzmyer, "Divorce Among First-Century Palestinian Jews," *Harold L. Ginsberg Volume* (Eretz-Israel: Archaeological, Historical and Geographical Studies 14; ed. M. Haran; Jerusalem: Israel Exploration Society, 1978) 103–10; W. Gross and G. A. Hunold. "Die Ehe im Spiegel biblischer und kulturgeschichtlicher Überlieferungen," *TQ* 167 (1987) 82–95; N. Lewis, R. Katzoff, and J. C. Greenfield. "Papyrus Yadin 18," *IEJ* 37 (1987) 229–50; E. Lipiński, "Marriage and Divorce in the Judaism of the Persian Period," *Transeuphratène* 4 (1991) 63–71; E. Neufeld, "Marriage after Divorce in Early Judaism," *Didaskalia* 1 (1989) 26–33; B. Porten, "Five Fragmentary Aramaic Marriage Documents: New Collations and Restorations," *Abr-Nahrain* 27 (1989) 80–105; idem, *Archives from Elephantine: The Life of an Ancient Jewish Military Colony* (Berkeley and Los Angeles: University of California, 1968) 208–10, 261–62; O. Robleda, "Il consenso matrimoniale presso i romani," *Greg* 60 (1979) 249–84; Eduard Schweizer, "Scheidungsrecht der jüdischen Frau? Weibliche Jünger Jesu?" *EvT* 42 (1982) 294–300; Z. W. C. Trenchard, *Ben Sira's View of Women: A Literary Analysis* (Brown Judaic Studies 38; Chico, CA: Scholars 1982) 104–6; A. Wacke, "Elterliche Gewalt im Wandel der Jahrtausende: Zum Sorgerecht der geschiedenen Mutter nach römischem Recht," *Studien zur antiken Sozialgeschichte* (Friedrich Vittinghoff Festschrift; Kölner historische Abhandlungen 28; ed. W. Eck, H. Galsterer, and H. Wolff; Cologne/Vienna: Böhlau, 1980) 417–34; H. Weder, "Perspektive der Frauen?" *EvT* 43 (1983) 175–78; R. Yaron, *Introduction to the Law of the Aramaic Papyri* (Oxford: Clarendon, 1961).

DEAD SEA SCROLLS AND RELATED MATERIAL: J. M. Baumgarten, "The Laws of the *Damascus Document* in Current Research," *The Damascus Document Reconsidered* (ed. Magen Broshi; Jerusalem: Israel Exploration Society, 1992) 51–62; G. Brin, "Divorce at Qumran," *Legal Texts and Legal Issues. Proceedings of the Second Meeting of the International Organization for Qumran Studies, Cambridge, 1995* (STDJ 23; J. M. Baumgarten Festschrift; ed. M. Bernstein, F. García Martínez, and J. Kampen; Leiden/New York: Brill, 1997) 231–44; H. M. Cotton and E. Qimron, "XḤev/Se ar 13 of 134 or 135 C.E.: A Wife's Renunciation of Claims," *JJS* 49 (1998) 108–18; Joseph A. Fitzmyer, "Divorce among First-Century Palestinian Jews," *ErIsr* 14 (1978) 103*–10*; idem, "The So-Called Aramaic Divorce Text from Wadi Seiyal," *ErIsr* 26 (1999) 16*–22*; Louis Ginzberg, *An Unkown Jewish Sect* (New York: Jewish Theological Seminary, 1970; German original 1922); C. Hempel, *The Laws of the Damascus Document* (STDJ 29; Leiden: Brill, 1998); Tom Holmén, "Divorce in CD 4:20–5:2 and 11QT 57:17–18: Some Remarks on the Pertinence of the Question," *RevQ* 18 (1998) 397–408; idem, *Jesus and Jewish Covenant Thinking* (Biblical Interpretation Series 55; Leiden: Brill, 2001) 157–69; Tal Ilan, "Notes and Observations on a Newly Published Divorce Bill from the Judean Desert," *HTR* 89 (1996) 195–202; idem, *Jewish Women in Greco-Roman Palestine* (Peabody, MA: Hendrickson, 1996); idem, "How Women Differed," *BAR* 24/2 (1998) 38–39, 68; idem, "The Provocative Approach Once Again: A Response to Adiel Schremer," *HTR* 91 (1998) 203–4; idem, *Integrating Women into Second Temple History* (Peabody, MA: Hendrickson, 1999) 253–62; David Instone-Brewer, "Nomological Exegesis in Qumran 'Divorce' Texts," *RevQ* 18 (1998) 561–79; idem, "Jewish Women Divorcing Their Husbands in Early Judaism: The Background to Papyrus Ṣe'elim 13," *HTR* 92 (1999) 349–57; J. Kampen, "A Fresh Look at the Masculine Plural Suffix in CD IV, 21," *RevQ* 16 (1993) 91–97; Johann Maier, *Die Tempelrolle vom Toten Meer und das 'Neue Jerusalem'* (Uni-Taschenbücher 829; 3d ed.; Munich/Basel: Reinhardt, 1997); J. R. Mueller, "The Temple Scroll and the Gospel Divorce Texts," *RevQ* 10 (1980) 247–56; Jerome Murphy-O'Connor, "An Essene Missionary Document? CD II, 14—VI, 1," *RB* 77 (1970) 201–29; L. H. Schiffman, "Laws Pertaining to Women in the Temple Scroll," *The Dead Sea Scrolls: Forty Years of Research* (STDJ 10; ed. D. Dimant and U. Rappaport; Leiden/New York: Brill, 1992) 210–28; idem, "The Relationship of the Zadokite Fragments to the Temple Scroll," *The Damascus Document. A Centennial of Discovery* (STDJ 34; ed. J. M. Baumgarten, E. G. Chazon, and

A. Pinnick; Leiden: Brill, 2000) 133–45; Adiel Schremer, "Divorce in Papyrus Şe'elim 13 Once Again: A Reply to Tal Ilan," *HTR* 91 (1998) 193–202; idem, "Qumran Polemic on Marital Law: CD 4:20–5:11 and Its Social Background," *The Damascus Document. A Centennial of Discovery* (STDJ 34; ed. J. M. Baumgarten, E. G. Chazon, and A. Pinnick; Leiden: Brill, 2000) 147–60; Geza Vermes, "Sectarian Matrimonial Halakhah in the Damascus Rule," *JJS* 25 (1974) 197–202; P. Winter, "Şadokite Fragments IV 20, 21 and the Exegesis of Genesis 1:27 in Late Judaism," *ZAW* 68 (1956) 71–84; Yigael Yadin, "L'attitude essénienne envers la polygamie et le divorce," *RB* 79 (1972) 98–99 [with a reply by Jerome Murphy-O'Connor on pp. 99–100].

On Marriage and Divorce in Greek and Roman Societies: J. P. V. D. Balsdon, *Roman Women: Their History and Habits* (London: Bodley Head, 1962); E. Cantarella, *Pandora's Daughters: The Role and Status of Women in Greek and Roman Antiquity* (Baltimore: Johns Hopkins University, 1981); P. E. Corbett, *The Roman Law of Marriage* (Oxford: Oxford University, 1930); Willem den Boer, *Private Morality in Greece and Rome* (Leiden: Brill, 1979); R. I. Frank, "Augustus' Legislation on Marriage and Children," *California Studies in Classical Antiquity* (8 vols.; ed. R. Stroud and J. Palvel; Berkeley: University of California, 1976) 8. 41–52; J. F. Gardner, *Women in Roman Law and Society* (Bloomington: Indiana University, 1986); P. Garnsey, *Social Status and Legal Privilege in the Roman Empire* (Oxford: Clarendon, 1970); P. Garnsey and R. Saller. *The Roman Empire: Economy, Society, and Culture* (Berkeley: University of California, 1987); L. Goodwater, *Women in Antiquity: An Annotated Bibliography* (Metuchen, NJ: Scarecrow, 1975); A. A. Gratwick, "Free Or Not So Free? Wives and Daughters in the Late Roman Republic," *Marriage and Property* (ed. E. M. Craig; Aberdeen: Aberdeen University, 1984) 30–53; J. P. Hallett, *Fathers and Daughters in Roman Society: Women and the Elite Family* (Princeton: Princeton University, 1984); J. Huber, *Der Ehekonsens im römischen Recht: Studien zu seinem Begriffsgehalt in der Klassik und zur Frage seines Wandels in der Nachklassik* (Analecta Gregoriana 204; Series Facultatis Iuris Canonici, Sectio B, 38; Rome: Gregorian University, 1977); H. Jolowicz, *Historical Introduction to the Study of Roman Law* (Cambridge: Cambridge University, 1967); I. Kajanto, "On Divorce among the Common People of Rome," *Revue des Etudes Latines* 47 (1970) 99–113; N. Kampen, *Image and Status: Representations of Roman Working Women at Ostia* (Berlin: Mann, 1981); W. Kunkel, *An Introduction to Roman Legal and Constitutional History* (Oxford: Clarendon, 1966); W. K. Lacey, *The Family in Classical Greece* (London: Black, 1964); C. Leduc, "Marriage in Ancient Greece," *A History of Women in the West. Part I: From Ancient Goddesses to Christian Saints* (ed. Pauline Schmitt Pantel; Cambridge, MA: Harvard University, 1992) 235–95; M. R. Lefkowitz and M. B. Fant, *Women's Life in Greece and Rome: A Sourcebook in Translation* (Baltimore: Johns Hopkins University, 1982); R. MacMullen, *Roman Social Relations 50 B.C. to A.D. 284* (New Haven: Yale University, 1974); A. Malherbe, *Moral Exhortation: A Greco-Roman Sourcebook* (Philadelphia: Westminster, 1986); A. Mette-Dittmann, *Die Ehegesetze des Augustus: eine Untersuchung im Rahmen der Gesellschaftspolitik des Princeps* (Historia Einzelschriften 67; Stuttgart:

Steiner, 1991); R. Needham, "Remarks on the Analysis of Kinship and Marriage," *Rethinking Kinship and Marriage* (London: Tavistock, 1971); S. B. Pomeroy, *Families in Classical and Hellenistic Greece. Representations and Realities* (Oxford/New York: Clarendon,1997); idem, *Goddesses, Whores, Wives and Slaves: Women in Classical Antiquity* (New York: Schocken, 1975); B. Rawson (ed.), *Marriage, Divorce, and Children in Ancient Rome* (Canberra: Humanities Research Center; Oxford: Clarendon; New York: Oxford University, 1991); B. Rawson and P. Weaver (eds.), *The Roman Family in Italy. Status, Sentiment, Space* (Oxford/New York: Clarendon, 1997); A. Richlin, "Approaches to the Sources on Adultery at Rome," *Reflections on Woman in Antiquity* (ed. H. P. Foley; New York: Gordon and Breech, 1981) 379–404; M. Z. Rosaldo and L. Lamphere (eds.), *Women, Culture and Society* (Stanford: Stanford University, 1976); H.-A. Ruprecht, "Marriage Contract Regulations and Documentary Practice in the Greek Papyri," *Scripta Classica Israelica* 17 (1998) 60–76; J.-A. Shelton, *As the Romans Did: A Sourcebook in Roman Social History* (New York: Oxford University, 1988); S. Treggiari, "Consent to Roman Marriage: Some Aspects of Law and Reality," *Classical Views* 26 (1982) 34–44; idem, *Roman Marriage: Iusti Coniuges from the Time of Cicero to the Time of Ulpian* (Oxford: Clarendon; New York: Oxford University, 1991); C. Vatin, *Recherches sur le mariage et la condition de la femme mariée à l'époque hellénistique* (Bibliothèque des écoles françaises d'Athènes et de Rome 216; Paris: de Boccard, 1970); A. Wallace-Hadrill, "Family and Inheritance in the Augustan Marriage Laws," *Proceedings of the Cambridge Philosophical Society* 27 (1981) 50–80.

DIVORCE IN THE NT IN GENERAL: A. Alberti, *Matrimonio e divorzio nella bibbia* (Milan: Massimo, 1962); H. Baltensweiler, *Die Ehe im Neuen Testament: Exegetische Untersuchungen über Ehe, Ehelosigkeit und Ehescheidung* (ATANT 52; Zürich: Zwingli, 1967); Klaus Berger, *Die Gesetzesauslegung Jesu. Ihr historischer Hintergrund im Judentum und im Alten Testament. Teil I: Markus und Parallelen* (WMANT 40; Neukirchen-Vluyn: Neukirchener Verlag, 1972) 508–75; M.-F. Berrouard, "L'indissolubilité du mariage dans le Nouveau Testament," *Lum Vie* 4 (1952) 21–40; J. Bonsirven, *Le divorce dans le Nouveau Testament* (Paris: Desclée, 1948); K. Bornhäuser, *Die Bergpredigt* (Gütersloh: Bertelsmann, 1923) 79–84; H. Braun, *Spätjüdisch-häretischer und frühchristlicher Radikalismus. I. Das Spätjudentum. II. Die Synoptiker* (BHT 24; 2 vols. in 1; Tübingen: Mohr [Siebeck], 1957) 2. 89–113; D. R. Catchpole, "The Synoptic Divorce Material as a Traditio-Historical Problem," *BJRL* 57 (1974–75) 92–127; Raymond F. Collins, *Divorce in the New Testament* (Good News Studies 38; Collegeville, MN: Liturgical Press, 1992); John Dominic Crossan, "Divorce and Remarriage in the New Testament," *The Bond of Marriage* (ed. W. W. Bassett; Notre Dame, IN: University of Notre Dame, 1968) 1–33; Mary Rose D'Angelo, "Remarriage and the Divorce Saying Attributed to Jesus," *Divorce and Remarriage* (ed. W. P. Roberts; Kansas City: Sheed and Ward, 1990) 78–106; W. D. Davies, "The Moral Teaching of the Early Church," *The Use of the Old Testament and Other Essays* (W. F. Stinespring Festschrift; ed. J. M. Efird; Durham, NC: Duke University, 1972) 324–25; A. Descamps, "Les textes évangéliques sur le mariage," *RTL* 9 (1978) 259–86; 11

(1980) 5–50 (ET = "The New Testament Doctrine on Marriage," *Contemporary Perspectives on Christian Marriage* [ed. R. Malone and J. R. Connery; Chicago: Loyola University, 1984] 217–73, 347–63); John R. Donahue, "Divorce: New Testament Perspectives," *The Month* 242 (1981) 113–20; M. J. Down, "The Sayings of Jesus about Marriage and Divorce," *ExpTim* 95 (1984) 332–34; A. Dubarle, "Mariage et divorce dans l'évangile," *OrSyr* 9 (1964) 61–73; T. Fleming, "Christ and Divorce, *TS* 24 (1963) 107–20; Hubert Frankemölle, "Ehescheidung und Wiederverheiratung von Geschiedenen im Neuen Testament," *Geschieden, Wiederverheiratet, Abgewiesen? Antworten der Theologie* (QD 157; ed. T. Schneider; Freiburg/Basel/Vienna: Herder, 1995) 28–50; R. Gall, "Heutige Exegese des Scheidungsverbotes Jesu," *Schweizerische Kirchenzeitung* 138 (1970) 512–14, 528–31, and 549–51; H. Greeven, "Ehe nach dem Neuen Testament," *NTS* 15 (1968–69) 365–88; K. Haacker, "Ehescheidung und Wiederverheiratung im Neuen Testament," *TQ* 151 (1971) 28–37; W. Harrington, "Jesus' Attitude toward Divorce," *ITQ* 37 (1970) 199–209; A. Harvey, "Genesis versus Deuteronomy? Jesus on Marriage and Divorce," *The Gospels and the Scriptures of Israel* (JSNTSup 104; Studies in Scripture in Early Judaism and Christianity 3; ed. C. A. Evans and W. R. Stegner; Sheffield: JSOT, 1994) 55–65; P. Hoffmann, "Jesus' Saying about Divorce and Its Interpretation in the New Testament Tradition," *Concilium* 55 (1970) 51–66; Joseph Jensen, "Does *Porneia* Mean Fornication? A Critique of Bruce Malina," *NovT* 20 (1978) 161–84; John S. Kloppenborg, "Alms, Debt and Divorce: Jesus' Ethics in Their Mediterranean Context," *Toronto Journal of Theology* 6 (1990) 182–200; J. Kremer, "Jesu Wort zur Ehescheidung," *Geschieden, Wiederverheiratet, Abgewiesen? Antworten der Theolgie* (QD 157; ed. T. Schneider; Herder: Freiburg/Basel/Vienna, 1995) 51–67; Evald Lövestam, "Divorce and Remarriage in the New Testament," *The Jewish Law Annual* 11 (1981) 47–65; George W. MacRae, "New Testament Perspectives on Marriage and Divorce," *Divorce and Remarriage in the Catholic Church* (ed. L. G. Wrenn; New York: Newman, 1973) 1–15; Bruce Malina, "Does *Porneia* Mean Fornication?" *NovT* 14 (1972) 10–17; C. Marucci, *Parole di Gesù sul divorzio* (Aloisiana 16, Pubblicazioni della Pontificia Facoltà Teologica dell' Italia Meridionale, Sezione S. Luigi; Naples: Morcelliana, 1982); H. Merkel, "Jesus und die Pharisäer," *NTS* 14 (1967–68) 194–208; Francis J. Moloney, "Matthew 19, 3–12 and Celibacy: A Redactional and Form Critical Study," *JSNT* 2 (1979) 42–60; J. R. Mueller, "The Temple Scroll and the Gospel Divorce Texts," *RevQ* 10 (1979–81) 247–56; A. Myre, "Dix ans d'exégèse sur le divorce dans le Nouveau Testament," *Le divorce: L'Eglise catholique ne devrait-elle pas modifier son attitude séculaire à l'égard de l'indissolubilité du mariage?* (Montreal: Fides, 1973) 139–62; U. Nembach, "Ehescheidung nach alttestamentlichem und jüdischem Recht," *TZ* 26 (1970) 161–71; J. J. O'Rourke, "Does the New Testament Condemn Sexual Intercourse Outside Marriage?" *TS* 37 (1976) 478–97; C. Osiek, *What Are They Saying about the Social Setting of the New Testament?* (Ramsey, NJ: Paulist, 1984); C. Osiek and D. L. Balch. *Families in the New Testament World. Households and House Churches* (Louisville: Westminster/John Knox, 1997); A. Ott, *Die Auslegung der neutestamentlichen Texte über die Ehescheidung* (Münster: Aschendorff, 1911); M. Owen, "Divorce and Remarriage: Biblical and Theological Perspectives,"

Colloquium 29 (1997) 37–48; D. Parker, "The Early Traditions of Jesus' Sayings on Divorce," *Theology* 96 (1993) 372–83; Rudolf Pesch, "Die neutestamentliche Weisung für die Ehe," *BibLeb* 9 (1968) 208–21; idem, *Freie Treue: Die Christen und die Ehescheidung* (Freiburg: Herder, 1971); Quentin Quesnell, " 'Made Themselves Eunuchs for the Kingdom of Heaven' (Mt 19, 12)," *CBQ* 30 (1968) 335–58; H. J. Richards, "Christ on Divorce," *Scr* 11 (1959) 22–32; Eugen Ruckstuhl, "Hat Jesus die Unauflösigkeit der Ehe gelehrt?" *Jesus im Horizont der Evangelien* (Stuttgarter Biblische Aufsatzbände 3; Stuttgart: KBW, 1988) 49–68; E. P. Sanders, "When Is a Law a Law? The Case of Jesus and Paul," *Religion and Law: Biblical-Judaic and Islamic Perspectives* (ed. E. Firmage, B. Weiss, and J. Welch; Winona Lake, IN: Eisenbrauns, 1990, 139–58); B. Schaller, "Die Sprüche über Ehescheidung und Wiederheirat in der synoptischen Überlieferung," *Fundamenta Judaica* (SUNT 25; Göttingen: Vandenhoeck & Ruprecht, 2001) 104–24 (reprint of article originally printed in *Der Ruf Jesu und die Antwort der Gemeinde* [Joachim Jeremias Festschrift; ed. E. Lohse; Göttingen: Vandenhoeck & Ruprecht, 1970] 226–46); R. Schnackenburg, "Die Ehe nach dem Neuen Testament," *Schriften zum Neuen Testament* (Munich: Kösel, 1971) 414–34; G. Schneider, "Jesu Wort über die Ehescheidung in der Überlieferung des Neuen Testaments," *TTZ* 80 (1971) 65–87; H. J. Schoeps, "Restitutio Principii als kritisches Prinzip der Nova Lex Jesu," *Aus frühchristlicher Zeit* (Tübingen: Mohr [Siebeck], 1950) 271–85; K. Schubert, "Ehescheidung im Judentum zur Zeit Jesu," *TQ* 151 (1971) 23–27; H. Schürmann, "Neutestamentliche Marginalien zur Frage nach der Institutionalität, Unauflösbarkeit und Sakramentalität der Ehe," *Kirche und Bibel* (Eduard Schick Festschrift; ed. O. Böcher et al.; Paderborn: Schöningh, 1979) 409–30; D. W. Shaner, *A Christian View of Divorce According to the Teachings of the New Testament* (Leiden: Brill, 1969); R. N. Soulen, "Marriage and Divorce: A Problem in New Testament Interpretation," *Int* 23 (1969) 439–50; R. H. Stein, "Is It Lawful for a Man to Divorce His Wife?" *JETS* 22 (1979) 115–21; W. Stenger, "Zur Rekonstruktion eines Jesusworts anhand der synoptischen Ehescheidungslogien," *Kairos* 26 (1984) 194–205; Angelo Tosato, "The Law of Leviticus 18:18: A Reexamination," *CBQ* 46 (1984) 199–214; Bruce Vawter, "The Biblical Theology of Divorce," *Proceedings of the Catholic Theological Society of America* 22 (1967) 223–43; idem, "Divorce and the New Testament," *CBQ* 39 (1977) 528–42; D. Warden, "The Words of Jesus on Divorce," *Restoration Quarterly* 39 (1997) 141–53; P. Winter, "Genesis 1:27 and Jesus' Saying on Divorce," *ZAW* 70 (1958) 260–61; Max Zerwick, "De matrimonio et divortio in evangelio," *VD* 38 (1960) 193–212.

ON THE EXCEPTIVE CLAUSES IN MATTHEW: D. C. Allison, Jr., "Divorce, Celibacy and Joseph (Matthew 1:18–25 and 19:1–12)," *JSNT* 49 (1993) 3–10; H. Baltensweiler, "Die Ehebruchsklauseln bei Matthäus," *TZ* 15 (1959) 340–56; J. B. Bauer, "Die matthäische Ehescheidungsklausel (Mt 5, 32 und 19, 9)," *Bibel und Liturgie* 38 (1964–65) 101–6; idem, "De coniugali foedere quid edixerit Matthaeus (Mt 5, 31; 19, 3–9)," *VD* 44 (1966) 74–78; idem, "Bemerkungen zu den matthäischen Unzuchtklauseln (Mt 5,32; 19,9)," *Begegnung mit dem Wort* (H. Zimmermann Festschrift; ed. J. Zmijewski et al.; BBB 53; Bonn: Hanstein, 1980) 23–33; M. Bockmuehl, "Matthew 5:32; 19:9 in the Light of Pre-Rabbinic Halakhah," *NTS* 35

(1989) 291–95; L. Cardellino, "Il ripudio per causa di *porneia* (Mt 5,32 e 19,8–9; Mc 10,11 e Lc 16,18)," *BeO* 39 (1997) 183–90; H. G. Coiner, "Those 'Divorce and Remarriage' Passages (Matt 5:32; 19:9; 1 Cor 7:10–16), with Brief Reference to the Mark and Luke Passages," *CTM* 39 (1968) 367–84; H. Crouzel, "Le texte patristique de Matthieu V.32 et XIX.9," *NTS* 19 (1972–73) 98–119; E. Danieli, "Eccetto in caso di fornicazione (Mt 5, 32; 19, 9)," *Palestra del clero* 48 (1969) 1297–1300; W. D. Davies, *The Setting of the Sermon on the Mount* (Cambridge: Cambridge University, 1964) 388, 396–98; Jacques Dupont, *Mariage et divorce dans l'évangile: Matthieu 19,3–12 et parallèles* (Bruges: Abbaye de Saint-André; Desclée de Brouwer, 1959) 45–88, 124–53; Joseph A. Fitzmyer, "The Matthean Divorce Texts and Some New Palestinian Evidence," *To Advance the Gospel* (2d ed.; Grand Rapids, MI/Cambridge, UK: Eerdmans, 1998) 79–111; M. Geldard, "Jesus' Teaching on Divorce: Thoughts on the Meaning of *porneia* in Mt 5:32 and 19:9," *Churchman* 92 (1978) 134–43; V. Hasler, "Das Herzstück der Bergpredigt. Zum Verständnis der Antithesen in Matth. 5.21–48," *TZ* 15 (1959) 90–106; M. W. Holmes, "The Text of the Matthean Divorce Passages: A Comment on the Appeal to Harmonization in Textual Decisions," *JBL* 109 (1990) 651–64; U. Holzmeister, "Die Streitfrage über die Ehescheidungstexte bei Matthäus 5.32, 19.9," *Bib* 26 (1945) 133–46; A. Isaksson, *Marriage and Ministry in the New Testament: A Study with Special Reference to Mt. 19,3–12 and 1. Cor. 11,3–16* (ASNU 24; Lund: Gleerup, 1965); J. J. Kilgallen, "To What Are the Matthean Exception-Texts (5,32 and 19,9) an Exception?" *Bib* 61 (1980) 102–5; A. Kretzer, "Die Frage: Ehe auf Dauer und ihre mögliche Trennung nach Mt 19,3–12," *Biblische Randbemerkungen* (Rudolf Schnackenburg Festschrift; ed. H. Merklein and J. Lange; Stuttgart: Echter, 1974) 218–30; G. Lohfink, "Jesus und die Ehescheidung: zur Gattung und Sprachintention von Mt 5,32," ibid., 207–17; R. McConnell, *Law and Prophecy in Matthew's Gospel* (Basel: Fr. Reinhardt Kommissionsverlag, 1969) 51–61; A. Mahoney, "A New Look at the Divorce Clause in Mt 5,32 and 19,9," *CBQ* 30 (1968) 29–38; John P. Meier, *Law and History in Matthew's Gospel* (AnBib 71; Rome: Biblical Institute, 1976) 140–50; idem, *The Vision of Matthew* (Theological Inquiries; New York/Ramsey, NJ/Toronto: Paulist, 1979) 248–57; J. Moingt, "Le divorce 'pour motif d'impudicité' (Mt 5,32; 19,9)," *RSR* 56 (1968) 337–84; J. J. O'Rourke, "A Note on an Exception: Mt 5:32 (19:9) and 1 Cor 7:12 Compared," *HeyJ* 5 (1964) 299–302; A. Quacquarelli, "Gli incisi ellitici (5,32a e 19,9a) nella *compositio* di Matteo," *Vetera Christianorum* 6 (1969) 5–31; J. Rabinowitz, "The Sermon on the Mount and the School of Shammai," *HTR* 49 (1956) 79; L. Ramaroson, "Une nouvelle interprétation de la 'clausule' de divorce (Mt 5:32; 19:9)," *ScEs* 23 (1971) 247–51; L. Sabourin, "The Divorce Clauses (Mt. 5,32; 19,9)," *BTB* 2 (1972) 80–86; F. Salvoni, "Eccetto il caso di fornicazione," *Ricerche bibliche e religiose* 3 (1968) 138–47; Alexander Sand, "Die Unzuchtsklausel in Mt 5,31.32 und 19,3–9," *MTZ* 20 (1969) 118–29; J. Sickenberger, "Die Unzuchtsklausel im Matthäusevangelium," *Theologisch-Praktische Quartalschrift* 123 (1942) 189–206; idem, "Zwei Äusserungen zur Ehebruchklausel bei Mt," *ZNW* 42 (1949) 292–99; P. Sigal, *The Halakah of Jesus of Nazareth according to the Gospel of Matthew* (Lanham, MD: University Press of America, 1986) 83–118; D. T. Smith, "The Matthean Exception

Clauses in the Light of Matthew's Theology and Community," *Studia Biblica et Theologica* 17 (1989) 55–82; A. Stock, "Matthean Divorce Texts," *BTB* 8 (1978) 24–33; T. Stramare, "Matteo Divorzista," *Divinitas* 15 (1971) 213–35; idem, "Il 'Supplement au Dictionnaire de la Bible' e le clausole di Matteo sul divorzio," *Divinitas* 39 (1995) 269–73; A. Tafi, " 'Excepta fornicationis causa' (Mt 5:32)," *VD* 26 (1948) 18–26; A. Vaccari, "La clausola sul divorzio in Matteo 5,32; 19,9," *RivB* 3 (1955) 97–119; Bruce Vawter, "The Divorce Clauses in Matthew 5, 32 and 19, 9," *CBQ* 16 (1954) 155–67; G. J. Wenham, "Matthew and Divorce: An Old Crux Revisited [Matt 19:9]," *JSNT* 22 (1984) 95–107; P. H. Wiebe, "Jesus' Divorce Exception," *JETS* 32 (1989) 327–33; Ben Witherington, "Matthew 5:32 and 19:9—Exception or Exceptional Situation?" *NTS* 31 (1985) 571–76; H.-T. Wrege, *Die Überlieferungsgeschichte der Bergpredigt* (WUNT 9; Tübingen: Mohr [Siebeck], 1968) 66–70.

ON THE MARCAN AND LUCAN FORMS: E. Bammel, "Markus 10,11f. und das jüdische Eherecht," *ZNW* 61 (1970) 95–101; G. Delling, "Das Logion Mk x.11 (und seine Abwandlungen) im Neuen Testament," *NovT* 1 (1956) 263–74; B. Green, "Jesus' Teaching on Divorce in the Gospel of Mark," *JSNT* 38 (1990) 67–75; F. Neirynck, "The Divorce Saying in Q 16:18," *LS* 20 (1995) 201–18; H. Sariola, *Markus und das Gesetz* (Annales Academiae Scientiarum Fennicae, Dissertationes Humanarum Litterarum 56; Helsinki: Suomalainen, 1990) 121–49; J. N. M. Wijngards, "Do Jesus' Words on Divorce (Lk 16:18) Admit of No Exception?" *Jeevadhara* 6 (1975) 399–411.

ON 1 CORINTHIANS 7: D. L. Balch, "Background of I Cor vii: Sayings of the Lord in Q; Moses as an Ascetic *Theos Anēr* in II Cor. iii," *NTS* 18 (1972) 351–64; idem, "I Cor. 7.32–35 and Stoic Debate about Marriage, Anxiety and Distraction," *JBL* 102 (1983) 429–39; W. J. Bartling, "Sexuality, Marriage and Divorce in 1 Corinthians 6.12–7.16: A Practical Exercise in Hermeneutics," *CTM* 39 (1968) 355–66; G. L. Borchert, "1 Corinthians 7:15 and the Church's Historic Misunderstanding of Divorce and Remarriage," *RevExp* 96 (1999) 125–29; W. Deming, *Paul on Marriage and Celibacy: The Hellenistic Background of 1 Corinthians 7* (SNTSMS 83; Cambridge, UK/New York: Cambridge University, 1995); J. Dorcas Gordon, *Sister or Wife? 1 Corinthians 7 and Cultural Anthropology* (JSNTSup 149; Sheffield: JSOT, 1997); J. K. Elliott, "Paul's Teaching on Marriage in I Corinthians: Some Problems Considered," *NTS* 19 (1973) 219–25; J. A. Fischer, "1 Cor. 7:8–24: Marriage and Divorce," *BR* 23 (1978) 26–36; Josephine M. Ford, "Levirate Marriage in St. Paul (1 Cor. vii)," *NTS* 10 (1963–64) 361–65; Victor P. Furnish, *The Moral Teaching of Paul* (2d ed.; Nashville: Abingdon, 1985); J. Moiser, "Reassessment of Paul's View of Marriage with Reference to 1 Cor. 7," *JSNT* 18 (1983) 103–22; J. Murphy-O'Connor, "The Divorced Woman in 1 Cor 7:10–11," *JBL* 100 (1981) 601–6; R. G. Olender, "The Pauline Privilege: Inference or Exegesis?" *Faith and Mission* 16 (1998) 94–117; W. F. Orr, "Paul's Treatment of Marriage in 1 Corinthians 7," *Pittsburgh Perspective* 8 (1967) 5–22; D. Wenham, "Paul's Use of the Jesus Tradition: Three Samples," *Gospel Perspectives. The Jesus Tradition Outside the Gospels. Vol. 5* (ed. D. Wenham; Sheffield: JSOT, 1984) 7–37; H. U. Wili, "Das Privilegium Paulinum (1 Kor 7:15f.)—Pauli eigene Lebenserinnerung?" *BZ*

22 (1978) 100–108; O. L. Yarbrough, *Not Like the Gentiles: Marriage Rules in the Letters of Paul* (SBLDS 80; Atlanta: Scholars, 1985).

ON RABBINIC AND LATER JUDAISM: J. D. Bleich, "Can There Be Marriage without Marriage?" *Tradition* 33 (1999) 39–49; Robert Brody, "Evidence for Divorce by Jewish Women" *JJS* 50 (1999) 230–34; S. Y. Cohen, "The Halachic and Legal Aspects of Enforcement of Divorce in Israel," *The Jerusalem 1994 Conference Volume* (Jewish Law Association Studies 8; ed. E. A. Goldman; Atlanta: Scholars, 1996) 41–42; D. Daube, *The New Testament and Rabbinic Judaism* (London: Athlone Press, 1956); idem, "Concessions to Sinfulness in Jewish Law," *JJS* 10 (1959) 1–13; L. M. Epstein, *The Jewish Marriage Contract* (New York: Jewish Theological Seminary of America, 1927); M. A. Friedman, *Jewish Marriage in Palestine: A Cairo Geniza Study* (New York: Jewish Theological Seminary of America, 1980); P. C. Hammond, "Divorce Document from the Cairo Genizah," *JQR* 52 (1961) 131–53; Tal Ilan, "Jüdische Frauen in der Spätantike. Ein Überblick." *Kirche und Israel* 15 (2000) 7–15; idem, *Mine and Yours Are Hers. Retrieving Women's History from Rabbinic Literature* (AGJU 41; Leiden: Brill, 1997); R. Neudecker, *Frührabbinisches Ehescheidungsrecht: der Tosefta-Traktat Gittin* (BibOr 39; Rome: Biblical Institute, 1982); Jacob Neusner, *How the Rabbis Liberated Women* (South Florida Studies in the History of Judaism 191; Atlanta: Scholars, 1998); J. D. Rayner, "From Unilateralism to Reciprocity: A Short History of Jewish Divorce," *Journal of Progressive Judaism* 11 (1998) 47–68; J. Rivlin, "The Power of a Promissory Note Is Greater Than the Force of Legislation," *The Jerusalem 1994 Conference Volume* (Jewish Law Association Studies 8; ed. E. A. Goldman; Atlanta: Scholars, 1996) 155–65; B.-Z. Schereschewsky, "Divorce in Later Jewish Law," *EncJud* 6 (1971) 125–35; P. R. Weis, "Controversies of Rab and Samuel and the Tosefta," *JSS* 3 (1958) 288–97.

[2] On the near-universal phenomenon of divorce in organized societies, J. Richard Udry ("Divorce," *Encyclopedia Americana. International Edition* [30 vols.; Danbury, CT: Grolier, 1999] 9. 210) comments: "Nearly all societies provide some arrangement for divorce. Only the Incas are recorded as having no provision for dissolving marriage."

[3] See Zakovitch, "The Woman's Rights," 28–46, esp. 28.

[4] See Marucci, *Parole*, 28; on pp. 28–31, Marucci outlines the various forms of marriage that are reflected in various texts, both legal and narrative, in the OT.

[5] One is surprised to see David Instone-Brewer (*Divorce and Remarriage in the Bible* [Grand Rapids, MI/Cambridge, UK: Eerdmans, 2002] 26) claim on very slender grounds (scattered testimony to women's power of divorce in other cultures in the ancient Near East and the law concerning slave women taken as wives in Exod 21:10–11) that Israelite women had the power to divorce their husbands under certain circumstances of neglect. Instone-Brewer's claim involves more than one major leap of logic, not to say evidence. The law in Exod 21:10–11 imposes the manumis-

sion of a female slave (who has been taken as wife) if, after her husband has taken a second wife, he neglects his first wife, the slave woman. It is the law that imposes on the owner-husband the manumission (and, effectively, the divorce) of the first wife with no monetary obligations on her part. This is a far cry from free Israelite women having the power to divorce their husbands. It is difficult to know how this claim coheres with Instone-Brewer's later admission (p. 31) that the mechanism of the certificate of divorce meant that "divorce became the prerogative of the husband," thus resulting in "the enslavement of women who wished to get divorced."

[6] For some examples, both Catholic and Protestant, and both popular and scholarly, see Guy Duty, *Divorce & Remarriage* (Minneapolis: Bethany Fellowship, 1967); Donald W. Shaner, *A Christian View of Divorce According to the Teachings of the New Testament* (Leiden: Brill, 1969); Pesch, *Freie Treue*; John R. Martin, *Divorce and Remarriage* (Scottdale, PA/Kitchener, Ontario: Herald, 1974, 1976); Dwight Hervey Small, *The Right to Remarry* (Old Tappan, NJ: Revell, 1975); Myrna and Robert Kysar, *The Asundered. Biblical Teachings on Divorce and Remarriage* (Atlanta: John Knox, 1978); William A. Heth and Gordon J. Wenham, *Jesus and Divorce. The Problem with the Evangelical Consensus* (Nashville: Nelson, 1984); James M. Efird, *Marriage and Divorce. What the Bible Says* (Nashville: Abingdon, 1985); William F. Luck, *Divorce and Remarriage. Recovering the Biblical View* (San Francisco: Harper & Row, 1987); Walter Kirchenschläger, *Ehe und Ehescheidung im Neuen Testament* (Vienna: Herold, 1987); George R. Ewald, *Jesus and Divorce. A Biblical Guide for Ministry to Divorced Persons* (Waterloo, Ontario/Scottdale, PA: Herald, 1991); Craig S. Keener, *. . . And Marries Another. Divorce and Remarriage in the Teaching of the New Testament* (Peabody, MA: Hendrickson, 1991); Andrew Cornes, *Divorce & Remarriage. Biblical Principles & Pastoral Practice* (Grand Rapids, MI: Eerdmans, 1993); Marian Machinek, *Gesetze oder Weisungen? Die Frage nach der sittlichen Verbindlichkeit neutestamentlicher Aussagen über Moral, verdeutlicht am Beispiel des Scheidungsverbotes Jesu* (Moraltheologische Studien, Systematische Abteilung 21; St. Ottilien: EOS, 1995); Instone-Brewer, *Divorce and Remarriage in the Bible*. With many of these treatments, especially the popular ones, the attentive reader can readily predict after the opening comments of the author what the results of the author's study of the biblical texts will be—a classic case of modern concerns and desires controlling what is supposed to be historical-critical exegesis. The fact that many of these treatments blithely employ the opposition of Law and Gospel as well as the all-purpose condemnation of what is deemed "legalistic" in order to interpret Jesus' words demonstrates how ill-suited these treatments are to a scholarly approach to Jesus the Jew and his teaching about divorce, addressed as it is to other Jews.

[7] It is important not to equate the ancient Israelite *kĕtûbbâ* with a modern marriage license or marriage certificate issued by the state. The ancient Israelite male needed no permission or license from a state (when, around the 10th century B.C., one came into existence) to enter a marriage. What he did need was a contractual agreement with the family of the spouse-to-be about the price for obtaining the

bride, the dowry the bride might bring to the marriage, the amount of money to be returned to the bride in case of divorce (or the death of the husband), and any conditions that might excuse the husband from such payment. No doubt such agreements began as oral contracts and in due time took on a fixed written form, such as is reflected in the mishnaic tractate entitled *Ketubot*. In the view of Louis M. Epstein (*The Jewish Marriage Contract* [New York: Arno; 1973, originally 1927]), the legal mechanism of a written *kĕtûbbâ* came to Israel from Babylonia. The earliest exemplars we have of Jewish marriage contracts (and also of a certificate of divorce) written in Palestine come from the caves of Murabbaʿat in Judea; see P. Benoit, J. T. Milik, and R. de Vaux, *Les grottes de Murabbaʿat* (DJD 2; Oxford: Clarendon, 1961). The Aramaic papyri include a certificate of divorce (#19, pp. 104–9) and two marriage contracts (#20, pp. 109–14, and #21, pp. 114–17). The Greek papyri include a contract in which a Jewish man who had divorced his wife remarries her (#115, pp. 243–54) and a regular marriage contract (#116, pp. 254–56). The Aramaic papyri date from the first quarter of the 2d century A.D.; the Greek papyri are later. On this, see Marucci, *Parole*, 102–4.

[8] For a brief survey of the Elephantine papyri, see Bezalel Porten, "Elephantine Papyri," *AYBD* 2. 445–55. Three relatively intact marriage contracts (literally in the Aramaic, "documents of wifehood") have been preserved, along with four more fragmentary texts. For the Aramaic texts of the marriage contracts with commentary, see A. E. Cowley, *Aramaic Papyri of the Fifth Century* B.C. (Oxford: Clarendon, 1923; reprint Osnabrück: Otto Zeller, 1967) 44–50, 54–56, 131–32, 153; and E. G. Kraeling, *The Brooklyn Museum Aramaic Papyri* (New Haven: Yale University, 1953) 140–50, 201–22, 293–96. See also Joseph A. Fitzmyer, "A Re-Study of an Elephantine Aramaic Marriage Contract (*AP* 15)," *A Wandering Aramean. Collected Aramaic Essays* (SBLMS 25; Missoula, MT: Scholars, 1979) 243–71; Marucci, *Parole*, 100–102; John J. Collins, "Marriage," 107–9.

[9] See Raymond Collins, *Divorce in the New Testament*, 190. For a consideration of Deut 24:1–4 in relation to other laws on sex and the family contained in Deuteronomy and in the Book of the Covenant in Exodus, see Alexander Rofé, "Family and Sex Laws in Deuteronomy and the Book of the Covenant," *Henoch* 9 (1987) 131–59.

[10] On the stylistic traits in Deut 24:1–4 that link it to other laws on sex and the family in Deuteronomy and the Book of the Covenant, see Rofé, "Family and Sex Laws," 132–33. Typical of this type of casuistic law are the phrasing of the law in the third person, a lengthy protasis, introduced by *kî* ("if," "when," "in the event that"), which describes the circumstances of the case, and the apodosis, which states the legal ruling for the particular case being treated. Details of the cases, be they mentioned in the protasis or the apodosis, begin with *wĕhāyâ* ("and it shall be that"), as in Deut 24:1. Occasionally in such laws the second person (usually in the singular) is used in an address either to the people or to the judges (so Deut 24:4b). However, in these casuistic laws, "the second person is used only at the end

of the law, almost incidentally, whereas the essentials are formulated casuistically in the third person." For a detailed treatment of Deut 24:1–4, see Marucci, *Parole*, 48–67.

[11] Indeed, vv 1–3, which most probably make up the subordinate conditional clause (the protasis), contain twelve occurrences of the Hebrew conjunction *wāw* ("and"). By contrast, the long conclusion (apodosis) in v 4 contains only one *wāw*. The source of the uncertainty in locating the beginning of the apodosis lies in the fact that, in biblical Hebrew, an apodosis can begin with a *wāw*. Hence the phrase in 24:1 that most scholars translate as "and [if] he writes her a certificate of divorce" might also be translated "then he writes her a certificate of divorce," thus beginning the main part of the law. Since, for the most part, the LXX of Deut 24:1–4 follows the Hebrew closely, it is fairly clear in the LXX that the apodosis is found in v 4. A textual difference in v 2 between the MT and the LXX—a difference mirrored in fragments from Cave 4 at Qumran—does not affect our major concern. The fragment 4QDeut[k2] agrees with the MT, the Samaritan Pentateuch, the hexaplaric recension of Origen, the targums of *Onqelos*, *Neofiti I*, and *Pseudo-Jonathan*, as well as the Peshitta, in reading the longer form of 24:2, which includes the clause "and she goes forth from his house." The fragment 4QDeut[a] and the LXX (cf. the Vulgate) have the shorter form without this clause; these latter texts apparently presume (or accidentally omit by homoeoteleuton?) what is spelled out in the longer reading. For the texts, see Eugene Ulrich et al. (eds.), *Qumran Cave 4. IX. Deuteronomy, Joshua, Judges, Kings* (DJD 14; Oxford: Clarendon, 1995) 7–8, 102–3.

[12] This may be described fairly as the common view among modern critical commentaries, both the older and the more recent ones. See, e.g., C. F. Keil and F. Delitzsch, *Biblical Commentary on the Old Testament. Volume III. The Pentateuch* (Grand Rapids, MI: Eerdmans, 1956) 417: "The four verses form a period, in which vers. 1–3 are the clauses of the protasis, which describe the matter treated about; and ver. 4 contains the apodosis, with the law concerning the point in question." The same opinion can be found in S. R. Driver, *Deuteronomy* (ICC; New York: Scribner's, 1909) 269–70; Gerhard von Rad, *Das fünfte Buch Mose. Deuteronomium* (ATD 8; Göttingen: Vandenhoeck & Ruprecht, 1964) 107–8; A. D. H. Mayes, *Deuteronomy* (NCB; London: Oliphants, 1979) 322; Georg Braulik, *Deuteronomium II 16,18–34,12* (Die Neue Echter Bibel, Altes Testament 28; Würzburg: Echter, 1992) 176–77; Martin Rose, *5. Mose. Teilband 1: 5. Mose 12–25. Einführung und Gesetze* (Zürcher Bibelkommentare, Altes Testament 5; Zurich: Theologischer Verlag, 1994) 173. See also the commentary by Jeffrey H. Tigay, in which he corrects the translation of Deut 24:1–4 in *The JPS Torah Commetary. Deuteronomy* (Philadelphia/Jerusalem: Jewish Publication Society, 1996) 220–21. In what follows in the main text, I do not bother to cite these commentaries again on matters on which there is common agreement among exegetes.

[13] The Hebrew text contains various philological and exegetical problems, many of which, fortunately, do not touch directly on our major concern. For instance, to-

ward the end of v 4, the twice-married woman is said to be *huṭṭammāʾâ*, a very rare form in the OT. It is a perfect form of the root *ṭmʾ*, "become impure," "become unclean" (from a ritual point of view). The form is most likely hotpāʿal, the passive form of hitpaʿel. The literal sense would be that the woman "has been made to contaminate [or: defile] herself" (one is reminded of the awkward *poiei autēn moicheuthēnai* ["causes her to be involved in adultery"] of Matt 5:32). The verb *śānēʾ* ("hate") in v 3 occurs elsewhere both inside and outside the OT in contexts referring to a husband divorcing his wife (e.g., Prov 30:23; Sir 7:26). As is clear from Deut 24:3, however, it does not simply mean "divorce" since the whole procedure of divorce (writing the certificate, handing it over, sending the wife away) follows upon the mention of the husband's "hatred" (which can refer to all sorts of displeasure or alienation; to restrict the reference to a "groundless" divorce—"groundless" by whose standards?—is unwarranted).

[14] See Colum M. Carmichael, *The Laws of Deuteronomy* (Ithaca/London: Cornell University, 1974) 203–4; Marucci, *Parole*, 61.

[15] See Marucci, *Parole*, 137–42.

[16] Some modern commentators consider the explanation "because he finds in her a shame of a thing" in 24:1 to be a later addition to the primitive text of the law; see Marucci, *Parole*, 51; Raymond Collins, *Divorce in the New Testament*, 190. One reason why the meaning of the phrase *ʿerwat dābār* is so vague and disputed is that the phrase is also so rare. It occurs only one other time in the MT, Deut 23:15 (23:14 in English translations). Deut 23:15 commands Israelites to dig a hole when they defecate and to cover over their excrement because Yahweh is in their holy camp and must not see *ʿerwat dābār* (i.e., anything unseemly, unbecoming, or indecent, anything that would offend a sense of propriety). From this other example (close by in the deuteronomic law code), it is clear that *ʿerwat dābār* in Deut 24:1 should not be restricted to "adultery" or indeed to sexual misconduct in general. This point is clearly supported by the LXX, which interprets *ʿerwat dābār* in terms of shamefulness: *aschēmon pragma* ("a shameful thing") in Deut 24:1 and *aschēmosynē pragmatos* ("shamefulness of a thing") in Deut 23:15.

[17] Other words and phrases that are typical of marriage and divorce laws include *lāqaḥ* ("take," used of taking a woman as one's wife), *baʿal* ("husband," "owner"), *šillaḥ mibbêtô* ("send away from his house," i.e., divorce), and *śānēʾ* ("hate," as the reason for divorcing one's wife). Interestingly, both Jer 3:8 and Isa 50:1 use the phrase *sēfer kĕrîtût* metaphorically when speaking of Yahweh's divorcing (or not divorcing) his covenant-bride Israel (Jer 3:1–8 alludes to the law of Deut 24:1–4, though the Jeremiah text indicates that the legal situation is not quite parallel because of Judah's faithless and shameless behavior). Hence, within the Jewish Scriptures, only Deut 24:1 + 3 uses the phrase literally in a legal text. The Hebrew word *gēṭ*, the usual word for a divorce document in rabbinic sources (see, e.g., the mishnaic tractate *Giṭṭin* [the plural of *gēṭ*]), does not occur in the Jewish Scriptures. The

Septuagint always translates *sēfer kĕrîtût* as *biblion apostasiou*, and this Greek phrase occurs in the Septuagint only as a translation of the Hebrew phrase. In a surprising departure from this usage, Matthew uses *apostasion* by itself to designate the certificate of divorce in Matt 5:31; in contrast, he takes over the traditional *biblion apostasiou* from Mark 10:4 in Matt 19:7. These three texts contain the only occurrences of *apostasion* in the NT. Raymond Collins (*Divorce in the New Testament*, 304 n. 98) states that a similar expression, *apostasiou syggraphē*, occurs in some Hellenistic papyri, but (as far as Collins can discover), Matt 5:31 represents the earliest Greek use of *apostasion* by itself to designate the certificate of divorce.

[18] See Marucci, *Parole*, 57. The text does not state that the husband *must* divorce his wife if he finds "something shameful" in her; the very fact that this clause in Deut 24:1 serves as a further explanation of the previous clause, "If she finds no favor in his eyes," highlights how much the decision to divorce depends on the judgment or preference (not to say whim) of the husband.

[19] Carmichael (*The Laws of Deuteronomy*, 207) sums up the meaning of *'erwat dābār* as "the embarrassment caused to a husband by his wife's public behavior."

[20] On the purity concern here, see Norbert Lohfink, "Opferzentralisation, Säkularisierungsthese und mimetische Theorie," *Studien zum Deuteronomium und zur deuteronomistischen Literatur III* (Stuttgarter Biblische Afsatzbände 20; Stuttgart: KBW, 1995) 248; cf. Marucci, *Parole*, 56. Some critics consider the real grounds for the prohibition to have been economic (e.g., to prevent the first husband from profiting by receiving a dowry twice for the same bride). This is suggested by Instone-Brewer (*Divorce and Remarriage*, 7), relying on the work of Raymond Westbrook, "Prohibition of Restoration of Marriage in Deuteronomy 24.1–4," *Studies in Bible 1986* (ed. S. Japhet; ScrHier 31; Jerusalem: Magnes, 1986) 387–405. While this is possible, it demands reading a great deal into the text and between the lines. I purposely do not go into the question of purity in great detail here, since the whole of Chapter 35 will be dedicated to this vast problem.

[21] One notes a typically humanitarian thrust to Deuteronomy's laws on divorce: all three of them restrict the otherwise unrestricted power of the husband. The law in Leviticus is rather concerned with protecting the cultic purity of the priests. To the list of prohibited women, Lev 21:14 adds a widow in the case of the high priest; the law thus narrows his choice to a virgin (v 13). This last case reminds us that, in these types of laws, the divorced woman, like the widow, is marked with a certain type of "cultic stain" that is not to be equated with moral guilt or reprobation; see Marucci, *Parole*, 68.

[22] Indeed, with rare exceptions, the divorced woman (unless she is of noble rank or of independent means) is simply not a figure that is discussed for her own sake in the literature of the ancient Mediterranean world. Once divorced, she simply disappears from view.

23 Strictly speaking, Deut 24:1–4 does not state that the procedure of writing the certificate of divorce and handing it to the wife is absolutely necessary for the validity of the divorce. At a very early stage of Israelite society, especially among illiterate peasants in rural areas, the dismissal of the wife was probably done in purely oral form. The written certificate would have been introduced as civilization advanced, society became more complex, and trained scribes became more available. At any rate, the fact that Josephus, Mark, and Matthew all make the giving of a certificate of divorce a distinct commandment indicates that, by the turn of the era, a document certifying the divorce had come to be considered a necessary part of the procedure.

24 Unfortunately, the Book of Hosea, for all its concentration on Hosea's dysfunctional marriage(s), is not helpful for our quest. Apart from the many difficult questions connected with the wording, order, and tradition history of the text, a number of problems make the use of the book for our purpose extremely difficult: (1) It remains unclear whether the book is describing real events connected with a real marriage or whether it is engaging in allegorical fiction. (2) The book depicts marital relations as lived in the Northern Kingdom of Israel in the 8th century B.C.; their relevance to the legal traditions enshrined in the Pentateuch (especially Deut 24:1–4, which seems unknown or ignored) or observed in 1st-century Judea around the time of Jesus is at best problematic. One is at a loss to understand Instone-Brewer's claim (*Divorce and Remarriage*, 35) that "Hosea developed ideas inherent in the Pentateuch." Are we to think that there was a Pentateuch for Hosea to develop in the 8th-century Israel? (3) More to the point, nowhere in chaps. 1–3 is it ever said that Hosea formally divorces his wife in the course of their stormy relations—indeed, it is not entirely clear whether chaps. 1–3 are speaking of the same woman throughout or of two different women. For various scholarly views on these questions, see, e.g., Hans Walter Wolff, *Hosea* (Hermeneia; Philadelphia: Fortress, 1974; German original 1965) xxii, 12–15; James Luther Mays, *Hosea* (Old Testament Library; Philadelphia: Westminster, 1969) 3, 23, 56; Bitter, *Die Ehe* (giving a history of the interpretation of Hosea's marital relations from early Judaism and Christianity up to the 20th century); Francis I. Andersen and David Noel Freedman, *Hosea* (AYB 24; Garden City, NY: Doubleday, 1980; reprint New Haven: Yale University Press) 115–41; Sherwood, *The Prostitute and the Prophet*, 19; Seifert, *Metaphorisches Reden*, 92–138; Marvin A. Sweeney, *The Twelve Prophets. Volume One* (Berit Olam; Collegeville, MN: Liturgical Press, 2000) 38–39; Wacker, *Figurationen*, 110–14.

25 For example, the distinguished exegete A. S. van der Woude ("Malachi's Struggle," 65–71) thinks that the vast majority of commentators misunderstand the basic point of Mal 2:10–16. In van der Woude's view, the passage does not deal with divorce at all. Rather, Malachi protests against Jews who, after having married Jewish wives early on, seek higher status by marrying foreign wives as well. These husband lavish all their love and attention on their new foreign wives, while humiliating their Jewish wives. In keeping with this interpretation, van der Woude thinks that v 16 should be translated: "for he who neglects [his Jewish wife] puts forth his

hand [in hostility, understanding *yād* after *šāllaḥ*]." I mention this interpretation not because I accept it but because it shows how tenuous any theory based on the interpretation of such an ambiguous and possibly corrupt text must be.

[26] Commentators even disagree over the very problem that the prophet is addressing; for a summary of opinions, see Marucci, *Parole*, 76–84. Is Malachi simply excoriating Judah's infidelity to Yahweh, seen in its continued idolatry or syncretistic worship, by using the traditional prophetic metaphor of marital infidelity and/or divorce? Or, in addition to this, is the prophet denouncing marriages between Jewish men and Gentile wives, marriages that entail the danger of the Jewish husbands adopting the pagan worship of their wives? Or, while denouncing such marriages, is the prophet also underlining the great pain and sorrow that the necessary divorce from such pagan wives entails, thus indicating a reason why such marriages should never be contracted to begin with? Or is the prophet denouncing the practice of those Jewish males who have divorced their Jewish wives (whom they had brought back with them from the Babylonian exile) in order to marry Gentile wives who bring with themselves a dowry of Judean land? All these and other scenarios are possible. More confusing still is the state of the text in Mal 2:15–16. Critics regularly rewrite the text, supply missing (but supposedly understood) words, or understand the words and forms of the MT in unusual, not to say contorted, ways. A good summary of various opinions and options is given by Andrew W. Hill, *Malachi* (AYB 25D; New York: Doubleday, 1998; reprint New Haven: Yale University Press) 221–59. Yet one need only compare his textual and interpretative decisions with those of Marvin A. Sweeney *(The Twelve Prophets. Volume Two* [Berit Olam; Collegeville, MN: Liturgical Press, 2000] 731–39) to see how two learned commentators can arrive at very different conclusions as they ponder the obscure statements of a confused text. Hill valiantly tries to make sense of the MT as it stands (v 15: "Surely [The] One made [everything] . . . ," v 16: " 'Indeed, [The One] hates divorce!' Yahweh, the God of Israel, has said"), but the brackets in his translation as well as the questionable meanings he assigns certain words show how perilous the whole undertaking is. In contrast, Sweeney (p. 738) takes the word "one" in v 15 to refer not to God but to the man's wives (he has taken more than one wife). One readily sees the fragility of any attempt to make sense of this passage.

[27] In a letter to me (dated September 14, 2002), David Noel Freedman observes on this point: "By definition, adultery [in the OT] is not and cannot be a crime against a woman, any woman. The easiest way to describe it is as a property crime, and in this case, it is . . . the husband of the woman who is guilty of adultery, who is the offended party."

[28] So, e.g., the *NRSV*, though it then states in a footnote that the Hebrew actually means "he hates." Similar translations, some with explanatory notes and some with none, are offered by the *NAB*, the *JB*, the new *JB*, the original the *Oxford Annotated Bible*, the *New Oxford Annotated Bible*, the *Contemporary English Version* (using a paraphrase), and the *KJV* (putting the statement into indirect discourse). This

blithe ignoring of the textual facts of the case is hardly restricted to English translations or scholars. For instance, Gershon Brin ("Divorce at Qumran," 231–44), despite a learned treatment of the Qumran material, starts his essay (p. 232) with the simple affirmation that Mal 2:16 says " 'For I hate divorce,' says the Lord the God of Israel. . . ." While due cognizance is taken of the variant readings at Qumran and in the versions and commentators, his basic presupposition about what the MT of Mal 2:16 (*ky śnʾ šlḥ*) says is never examined; it is simply taken for granted. To cite another example: Angelo Tosato, in a lengthy attempt to overturn standard views about marriage and divorce in the OT period (*Il matrimonio israelitico*), simply repeats (pp. 208–9) this erroneous translation of Mal 2:16 ("Poiché: Odio il divorzio, ha detto JHWH, il Dio di Israele . . ."). Neither a detailed consideration of the context of Mal 2:16 nor an extensive consideration of the confused state of the text is offered to justify this translation. Tosato is thus free to discern a sweeping extension of the prohibition of divorce in postexilic Israel, which permitted divorce only in certain special cases (illegitimate marriages, cases of serious guilt on the part of one's spouse, cases in which the Law makes divorce obligatory). Needless to say, the clear statements of both Philo and Josephus that a Israelite man can divorce his wife for any reason whatever are never considered. For a brief list of emendations or understood words suggested by various commentators in order to make sense of Mal 2:16, see Marucci, *Parole*, 81. Even if one accepts Marucci's preference for a translation like "But if someone divorces his wife simply out of hatred [i.e., he no longer loves her, with no guilt on her part] . . . then he covers his garment with violence," the verse still does not condemn divorce in general, but only this self-centered type of divorce; cf. Instone-Brewer, *Divorce and Remarriage*, 57. As the notes that follow indicate, even this interpretation is far from certain. For modern English translations that take this tack of attributing the "hating" to the husband instead of Yahweh, see, e.g., the *NEB* and the *Revised English Bible*.

[29] The conjunction *kî* could easily mean "for" or "if" (less likely "but" or "when"); *śānēʾ*, as it stands, is the 3d person singular masculine Qal form of the verb, meaning "he hated" (or: "he hates"); if one changes the first vowel to read *śōnēʾ*, the form is the masculine singular Qal participle active, "hating." Some commentators suggest that *śānēʾ*, as it stands, can be taken as a verbal adjective equivalent to the active participle ("hating"), but such a form is otherwise unattested in the MT. The verb form *šallaḥ* is either the 2d person singular masculine of the Piel imperative, "send away!" or the Piel infinitive construct, "to send away." If one changes the first vowel, the resulting *šillaḥ* is the 3d person singular masculine of the Piel perfect, meaning "he sent away." No combination of these possibilities will supply an intelligible sentence. A fortiori, it takes no little imagination to twist the three Hebrew words into a declaration of Yahweh stating "For I hate divorce."

[30] This is the LXX text favored by Jones ("A Note on the LXX," 683–85): *alla ean misēsas exaposteilęs . . .* ("But if, hating [her], you send [her] away . . ."). Jones tends to dismiss the alternate LXX reading, *ean misēsęs exaposteilon* ("if you hate [her], send [her] away"), perhaps because he apparently did not have access to and

time to study 4Q XII[a] (see below). A slight variation on the reading favored by Jones is championed by a number of commentators today as the true sense of Mal 2:16. With some differences in wording, this variation runs thus: "For he who divorces [his wife] out of hatred . . . covers his garments with violence," or "If he hates and divorces [his wife] . . . he covers his garments with violence." In one form or another, this approach is favored by Glazier-McDonald, *Malachi*, 82–83, 109–10; Hugenberger, *Marriage As a Covenant*, 76; Shields, "Syncretism," 84–86. The drawback of this approach is that it demands some revocalization of the MT, e.g., by vocalizing the Qal perfect *śānē'* ("He hates") as the Qal active participle *śōnē'* ("hating") and by vocalizing the Piel infinitive construct *šallaḥ* as the Piel perfect *šillaḥ* (or, alternately by taking *šallaḥ* as instead the Piel infinitive absolute *šallēaḥ* with the sense of a finite verb: "He hates [and] sends away"). Needless to say, these attempts suffer from the same arbitrariness that afflicts all the other suggested emendations of the MT.

[31] For the readings of various manuscripts of the LXX tradition, see Joseph Ziegler (ed.), *Duodecim prophetae* (Vetus Testamentum Auctoritate Societatis Litterarum Gottingensis editum 13; Göttingen: Vandenhoeck & Ruprecht, 1943) 334. The reading chosen for the main text in the Göttingen Septuagint is *alla ean misēsas exaposteilēs* (with variant spellings): "But if, having hated [i.e., out of hatred], you send [her] away. . . ." This reading is supported by manuscripts B (Codex Vaticanus), Q (Codex Marchalianus), and V (Codex Venetus). An alternate reading has instead *all' ean misēsēs exaposteilon*: "But, if you hate [her], send [her] away!" This reading is witnessed by L (the Lucianic recension) and basically agrees with fragment of Malachi from Cave 4 at Qumran (4Q XII[a] ii. 4–7), as well as with the Vulgate and the targum on Malachi in the *Targum Jonathan to the Prophets*. A mixed (and perhaps mixed-up) reading, *meisēsas exaposteilon* (where *meisēsas* may simply be a scribal error for *misēsēs*) is found in W (Washington Freer Collection). On the confusing text-critical problems involved in both the LXX variants and the fragment of Malachi from Cave 4 at Qumran, see Fuller, "Text-Critical Problems," 47–57. Fuller thinks that the MT, though not the clearest text, is closest to the original, while the other witnesses may derive from various attempts to understand or consciously to change the present form of the MT.

[32] For the text of 4Q XII[a] ii. 4–7, see Eugene Ulrich et al. (eds.), *Qumran Cave 4. X. The Prophets* (DJD 15; Oxford, Clarendon, 1997) 221–32, esp. 224–25. In the Qumran fragment of Malachi from Cave 4, the opening Hebrew words at 2:16 are *ky 'm śnth šlḥ*. Brin ("Divorce at Qumran," 237) suggests that, because *ky* had lost the sense of "if" for some authors of the Qumran documents (notably the *Temple Scroll*), the original *ky* of Mal 2:16 is changed to *ky 'm* with the sense not of "rather" (as often in the MT) but instead the sense of "if." The verb *śnth* seems to be the 2d person singular Qal perfect of *śn'*, with the quiescent *ālep* lost, a phenomenon seen elsewhere in Qumran Hebrew; *šlḥ* is most likely the masculine singular imperative Piel. The meaning would thus be: "If you hate [her], send [her] away!" Shields ("Syncretism," 84) suggests that *śnth* might be taken instead as the Qal infinitive

construct with a 3d person singular feminine object suffix and *šlḥ* as a 3d person singular masculine Piel perfect form, thus supporting the reading "Whoever hates and divorces . . . covers his garments with violence"; yet Shields himself admits that this is not the most likely reading of the text. In any case, this Qumran fragment is obviously of great importance since it represents at least one form of the Hebrew text of Malachi in the 2d century B.C. (ca. 150–125 B.C.). Taken in its most likely sense, it stands relatively close to the Greek readings of L and W (as well as that of the Vulgate), although it is not completely identical with these readings.

[33] The Vulgate of Mal 2:16 is "cum odio habueris dimitte" ("when [or: since] you hate [her], send [her] away."

[34] Indeed, the changes that the text of Mal 2:16 underwent in subsequent centuries may reflect a desire to bring a prophetic text that might be read as critical of divorce into line with the written Torah (especially Deut 24:1–4) and the prevailing legal practice in mainstream Judaism.

[35] Relevant texts (many reflecting the misogyny typical of the wisdom literature of the ancient Near East) include Prov 30:21–23; 5:15–20; LXX Prov 18:22a; Qoh 7:26; 9:9; (deuterocanonical/apocryphal) Sir 7:26; 25:25–26 (plus the general essay on good and bad wives in chap. 26); on them, see Marucci, *Parole*, 84–97. Notice how, even in these passages, explicit references to divorce are few and far between.

[36] Brody ("Evidence," 230–34, esp. 231) thinks that at Elephantine either partner enjoyed the *initiative* in asking for a divorce, but that a document written by the husband was required to *effect* the divorce; here Brody may be overly influenced by later rabbinic rules. That the wife's ability to divorce her husband at Elephantine reflects not simply Egyptian circumstances but rather one strand of ancient West-Semitic legal tradition (perhaps Phoenician or Old Aramaic practice) is argued by Lipiński, "The Wife's Right," 9–27, esp. 21, 26; cf. Alfredo Mordechai Rabello, "Divorce of Jews in the Roman Empire," *Jewish Law Annual* 4 (1981) 79–102, esp. 91.

[37] One must be cautious here about an argument from silence. Since a written certificate of divorce is attested in both the OT and rabbinic literature, one might infer its existence in the divorce procedures of the Jews at Elephantine; so John J. Collins, "Marriage," 110. However, if we grant that, early on, divorce among illiterate peasants in the countryside was accomplished simply by an oral declaration, it remains possible that the quirky community at Elephantine had held on to the older custom at this point. Still, since Elephantine witnesses to written marriage contracts long before they are mentioned in the Palestinian literature of Judaism (for the first time in Tobit), one might question the idea that Elephantine Judaism lacked a written certificate of divorce.

[38] The question of whether, under at least some circumstances and in some places, Jewish women during the biblical period could divorce their husbands remains a

subject of lively debate, partly because of its relevance to present-day arguments among Orthodox Jews; see, e.g., Brody, "Evidence," 230–34. A whole issue of the *Jewish Law Annual* 4 (1981) was dedicated to the question of the right of a Jewish wife to divorce her husband (with a view to the modern problem); see the following articles: B. S. Jackson, "Introduction," 3–8 (summarizing the articles contained in the issue); Lipiński, "The Wife's Right," 9–27; Zakovitch, "The Woman's Rights in the Biblical Law of Divorce," 28–46; Lövestam, "Divorce and Remarriage in the New Testament," 47–65; Daniela Piattelli, "The Marriage Contract and Bill of Divorce in Ancient Hebrew Law," 66–78; Rabello, "Divorce of Jews in the Roman Empire," 79–102; Mordechai A. Friedman, "Divorce upon the Wife's Demand as Reflected in Manuscripts from the Cairo Geniza," 103–26. In answering the question that this issue of the *Jewish Law Annual* raises, one must carefully distinguish different contexts according to their chronological, geographical, and social dimensions. In the ancient Mediterranean world, there certainly were some places and some time periods in which Jewish women of a certain social status could divorce their husbands. (1) As we have seen, this was the case in the syncretistic Jewish military colony in Elephantine in Egypt in 5th century B.C., but this tells us nothing about Jewish-Palestinian practice at the turn of the era; see Lövestam, "Divorce and Remarriage," 47. It is perhaps significant that Philo of Alexandria, writing in the context of the Jewish Diaspora in Egypt at the turn of the era, says nothing about this right of a Jewish wife to divorce her Jewish husband within the Jewish community. (2) Two women who were royal members of the Herodian dynasty around the turn of the era divorced their husbands. Salome, the sister of Herod the Great, divorced her husband (*Ant.* 15.7.10 §259); Josephus pointedly emphasizes that this action was contrary to Jewish practice (see Marucci, *Parole*, 151). More famously, Herodias divorced her husband (a half-brother of Herod Antipas) to marry Antipas (*Ant.* 18.5.1 §109–11). The Gospel of Mark presents John the Baptist rebuking Antipas for the marriage (Mark 6:17–18), but on the grounds of his marrying his brother's wife, not on the grounds of Herodias' having initiated the divorce. (On the differences between Mark and Josephus concerning Herodias' husbands and the circumstances of the Baptist's death, see *A Marginal Jew*, 2. 19–21, 171–76. Since I judge the story of the Baptist rebuking Herod because of his second marriage not to be historically accurate, I think that attempts to understand Jesus' prohibition of divorce in light of Herod's marriage and the Baptist's condemnation of it to be misguided; cf. Raymond Collins, *Divorce in the New Testament*, 221–22.) More to the point, Herodias and her prior husband (known simply as Herod) were apparently living under Roman law at the time of the divorce; hence it is not surprising that a sophisticated Herodian princess simply took advantage of Roman law, which allowed women to divorce their husbands; on this, see Rabello, "Divorce of Jews," 92–93, 100 (although Fitzmyer ["The So-Called Aramaic Divorce Text," 20*, yet see n. 30 on p. 22*] prefers the view that Salome and Herodias simply deserted their husbands without the legal formalities of a divorce). In general, one may also observe that members of the Herodian royal family were often anything but models of Jewish ethical standards and legal observance; one need only think of Herod the Great's relationships with some of his ten wives (to say nothing of his children).

Hence, the cases of two Herodian princesses doing as they pleased (and the three daughters of Herod Agrippa I did likewise), while common in the history of royals of any period, do not tell us anything about the legal power of ordinary Jewish women in Palestine at the turn of the era. (3) As just noted, Roman law allowed both husband and wife to initiate divorce; hence it was possible for a Diaspora Jewish wife, living, e.g., in Rome and willing to take advantage of Roman law, to divorce her husband. (4) Papyrus Ṣe'elim 13 (*XḤev/Se* 13), a fragmentary and ambiguous Aramaic document from Naḥal Ḥever, dating from the Bar Kochba (Simon Ben Kosiba) revolt of A.D. 132–135 (more specifically, 135), remains a subject of debate among scholars. Ilan ("Notes and Observations," 195–202; "The Provocative Approach," 203–4; *Integrating Women*, 253–62) has argued strongly that the document testifies (either as a certificate of divorce or less likely as a waiver of claims of the wife against her ex-husband) to the power of a Jewish woman to divorce her husband. While differing on the precise nature of the document (it is not a certificate of divorce, but a receipt affirming that the ex-husband has paid all financial obligations to his ex-wife), Cotton and Qimron ("XḤev/Se ar 13," 108–18) agree that the document mentions *en passant* that the wife has given her husband a certificate of divorce. Offering still a different reading of the fragmentary Aramaic, Instone-Brewer ("Jewish Women," 349–57) thinks that the papyrus is indeed "a divorce certificate, written on behalf of the wife by a scribe." The wife is apparently using what Instone-Brewer sees as the Egyptian form of Jewish divorce, witnessed much earlier at Elephantine and (in Instone-Brewer's view) in Philo. Other scholars disagree. For instance, Schremer ("Divorce," 193–202), in his response to Ilan's initial article in the *HTR*, has argued that Ilan has misread the fragmentary and unvocalized Aramaic text. According to Schremer, the text is actually a receipt acknowledging that the ex-wife has received a certificate of divorce from her husband and that she has no outstanding financial claims against him. In a similar vein but with a different reading of the Aramaic, Brody ("Evidence," 232–33) argues from the traditional phrasing of a rabbinic *gēṭ* that the disputed text can be taken to refer to a divorce executed by the husband. Fitzmyer ("The So-Called Aramaic Divorce Text," 16*–22*), in basic agreement with Schremer, holds that the text is a receipt declaring that the ex-husband has paid all he owed his ex-wife; the Aramaic of the text, properly read, indicates that the husband, not the wife, issued the certificate of divorce. In particular, Fitzmyer thinks that Ilan has misread important pronominal suffixes that make clear that the husband has divorced his wife, not vice versa. The underlying problem in this debate is that the fragmentary and unvocalized nature of the papyrus allows of more than one interpretation. In the present state of research, no one reading can be called certain, though I think that Fitzmyer has the better part of the argument. Fortunately, this document is not directly relevant to our quest. It comes from the end of the chaotic period of the Second Jewish Revolt (A.D. 132–35), after a half-century during which Greco-Roman influence (and, Instone-Brewer would add, Egyptian influence) had already made notable inroads into Palestine after the destruction of Jerusalem in A.D. 70. Hence the relevance of this papyrus to the situation of ordinary Jewish women in Palestine in the early 1st century A.D. is at best questionable. (5) Later rabbinic literature sought to ease the

plight of a woman caught in an intolerable marital situation by allowing her to peti-
tion a Jewish court to force her husband to grant her a divorce. It is telling, though,
that even as late as the rabbinic literature, mainstream Judaism did not simply allow
women directly to divorce their husbands under certain circumstances. Rather,
even in the newly introduced concession to the wife, the husband still had to grant
the divorce, and this only under duress from an all-male court. On this, see Lipiński,
"The Wife's Right," 9–10. One can easily infer from this what the usual situation in
Jewish Palestine was before this "liberalization" was introduced. Hence, while admitting that some Jewish women at some times and in some places in the ancient
world did have the power to divorce their husbands, I think the weight of the evidence (OT, Qumran, Philo, Josephus, the earliest attainable form of Jesus' sayings
on divorce, and the nature of the later rabbinic concession to the wife caught in an
intolerable situation) favors the view that in Jewish Palestine in the early 1st century A.D., ordinary Jewish women did not have the power to divorce their husbands.
Epstein (*The Jewish Marriage Contract*, 200–201) highlights two factors embedded in ancient Near Eastern societies that tended to restrict the power to divorce to
the husband: (1) Divorce was essentially the driving out of one's spouse from one's
house on a permanent basis; since (in the domestic circumstances of ordinary Palestinian Jews) only the husband owned the house in which the couple lived, only he
could divorce his spouse by expelling her from his property. (2) An essential purpose of the act of divorce was to declare that the divorced spouse was free to marry
again without the stigma of adultery, but, in a society that practiced polygyny, the
husband was always free to marry again and needed no act of divorce to do so; only
the wife, who was not free to practice polyandry, needed the freedom granted by
divorce.

[39] On the relevant texts in Tobit, see Marucci, *Parole*, 97–99.

[40] Here I am referring to the sectarian texts either composed by or preserved at
Qumran; a fragment of the biblical Book of Malachi, discovered in Cave 4 at Qumran, was treated along with other canonical literature in the previous section.

[41] In the Greek, Philo describes the woman's loss of her second husband with the
verb form *chēreusē*, which, taken narrowly, could mean "becomes a widow" (so the
translation adopted by F. H. Colson in the LCL edition). However, Philo immediately follows this verb with the qualifying phrase "the second husband being alive
or dead," which correctly summarizes the two possibilities foreseen in Deut 24:3.
Hence the verb *chēreusē* must carry here the wider sense of "to be without," i.e., "to
become bereft of her [second] husband"—either through divorce (if he is still living)
or through his death.

[42] On this, see Epstein, *The Jewish Marriage Contract*, 194–96.

[43] The way Philo paraphrases the biblical law raises an interesting question. Deut
24:1–4 focuses on the actions of the two husbands; they are the responsible parties.

For the most part, the wife is mentioned as either the object of their actions or the one responding to their actions. The fact that, in his paraphrase of this law, Philo instead focuses from start to finish on the wife, who is the sole grammatical subject of the first sentence in §30 (which summarizes the law), suggests to some scholars that Philo is speaking here of a woman's power to divorce her husband, something seen in the Elephantine papyri of 5th-century Egypt and something that was permitted under Greek and Roman law—and Roman Egypt was directly controlled by the emperor. That Philo is indeed speaking here of a woman's power to divorce her husband is maintained by Instone-Brewer, "Jewish Women," 354. In my view, however, there are serious reasons for doubting Instone-Brewer's interpretation. To begin with, nowhere else in his extensive writings does Philo ever say that a Jewish woman, on her own authority, can divorce her Jewish husband. Granted the striking difference between what Instone-Brewer takes to be Philo's view and the reigning practice among ordinary Jews in 1st-century Palestine, one would have expected Philo to consider and explain the difference. Then, too, I do not think that Instone-Brewer takes into consideration the literary and rhetorical structure of Philo's treatment of Deut 24:1–4. The focus on the woman in Philo's first sentence flows partly from his desire to create a clear, neat summary of the rambling and ambiguous text of Deut 24:1–4. However, within Philo's first sentence, some of the verb forms that describe the woman are, in themselves, ambiguous. For instance, the verb denoting the first divorce is a 2d aorist *passive* participle (*apallageisa*). If understood as a true passive, the sense would be that the wife "was released from her husband," namely, by her husband, who divorced her. However, the passive form can also be deponent, with the intransitive meaning of "leave," "depart" (hence, "the woman, having departed from her husband"—but by whose authority and at whose behest?). More significant, in my view, is the fact that the divorce from the second husband (or his death) is denoted by the verb *chēreusē* ("be bereft of"). When a wife is "bereft of" her husband by death (one of the meanings of the verb), it is hardly by her own initiative (short of murder). Similarly, to describe a divorce in terms of the wife becoming "bereft" of her husband suggests that she is the recipient, not the initiator, of the divorce. Perhaps another reason why the first sentence in §30 focuses on the woman is the overall rhetorical structure of §30–31. §30 focuses on the wife, while §31 focuses on the first husband. The two parties are then joined together in the final sentence pronouncing the penalty of death, but in the order husband–wife. The whole of §30–31 is thus structured according to an A–B–B′–A′ pattern. In sum, neither the verb forms used of the wife nor the overall structure of Philo's treatment supplies a firm basis for claiming that Philo's paraphrase intimates that the wife has the power to divorce her husband.

[44] At this point in his explanation, Philo uses the vague phrase "if any man" (§31) for the person who marries the twice-divorced woman. But, since Philo has just said in §30 that, after her second divorce, the wife may marry any man except her first husband, the vague "if any man" in context refers to the first husband, with the vagueness reflecting the hypothetical nature of this unlikely reunion.

[45] Lying behind this moral condemnation of the first husband may be the idea that by first divorcing his wife and then receiving her back after she has been married and divorced a second time, the first husband (as well as the wife) reveals that the initial divorce was a sham from the start. Since there was no real divorce to begin with, the second marriage was actually an act of adultery connived at by the first husband and thus an act of pandering on his part. For this idea, see the comments by F. H. Colson in vol. 7 of the ten-volume edition of Philo in the LCL, pp. 492–93, note b. In his appendix on p. 633, Colson adds a suggestion from Goodenough that the death penalty may reflect Roman law on adultery (specifically, the *lex Julia de adulteriis*, which punished a man who knowingly married a woman guilty of adultery) and Greek law punishing pandering. On Philo's interpretation of Deut 24:1–4, see Marucci, *Parole*, 155–57.

[46] Louis H. Feldman (*Flavius Josephus: Translation and Commentary. Volume 3. Judean Antiquities 1–4* [ed. Steve Mason; Leiden/Boston/Cologne: Brill, 2000] 427 n. 811) suggests that Josephus may be thinking here of his own experience of divorce; see his *Life* 75 §414–15 and §426. The case of the woman mentioned in §414–15 is somewhat ambiguous. After narrating how he became a Roman prisoner at Jotapata, Josephus tells us that, at the command of Vespasian, "I took a certain virgin to myself from among the captives who were at Caesarea. . . . But she did not remain with me for any great length of time." After Josephus was freed from captivity and accompanied Vespasian to Alexandria, this woman, we are told, *apēllagē*. Once again, as in Philo's *De specialibus legibus* 3.5 §30, we confront the ambiguity of the verb *apallasō* in the 2d aorist passive form: was the woman released from captivity, released from marriage to Josephus by his divorcing her, or did she simply leave (taking the verb in its deponent, intransitive sense)? One wonders whether, in fact, there was ever a legally binding marriage and therefore the necessity of divorce. Possibly, in the chaotic situation of war and imprisonment, Vespasian had, as one sign of his benevolence toward Josephus, supplied him with a female captive to satisfy his sexual needs for the time being. Once Josephus was released from captivity, there was no need for the woman (who was likewise released from prison and ipso facto released from her relation to Josephus) to be formally divorced. However, Josephus' use of the middle voice of the verb *agō* (which he uses for what is apparently a formal marriage to another woman in §415) and his insistence on the virginity of the female captive (a fitting candidate for marriage to an aristocratic priest like Josephus) may indicate that he intends to speak of a proper marriage; cf. *Ag. Ap.* 1.7 §35. Later on, Josephus tells us that he divorced the wife he married in Alexandria; in this passage (§426), he uses the verb *apopempō* ("send away") in the middle voice for the act of divorce. The vague reason he gives for the divorce, "because I was not pleased with her *ēthesin* [habits? behavior? character?]," jibes with his interpretation of Deut 24:1 as permitting a man to divorce his wife for any reason whatever. On all this, see the comments of Steve Mason, *Flavius Josephus: Translation and Commentary. Volume 9. Life of Josephus* (ed. Steve Mason; Leiden/Boston/Cologne: Brill, 2001) 164–65 nn. 1700–1706, as well as 170 nn. 1756–57; cf. Rabello, "Divorce of Jews," 93–94.

[47] However, unlike LXX Deuteronomy 24:1, Mark, and Matthew, Josephus never uses the phrase *biblion apostasiou* (or, in Matt 5:31, the simple *apostasion*) for the certificate of divorce. In *Ant.* 15.7.10 §259, when Josephus narrates how Herod the Great's sister Salome sent her husband Costobarus a certificate of divorce, he calls the certificate a *grammateion*, a word that occurs only in this passage in Josephus. Making clear his view of the matter, Josephus emphasizes that Salome's act of divorcing her husband was illegal in Jewish eyes.

[48] Yadin ("L'attitude," 98–99) ignored this basic insight when, early on, he tried to use 11QTemple 57:15–19 to resolve the ambiguity of CD 4:20–21 without any methodological justification for using one document found at Qumran to elucidate an obscurity in the text of another document found there. In his reply (appended to Yadin's article, pp. 99–100), Murphy-O'Connor rightly protested against this approach. We have no right to presuppose that all the documents found at Qumran espouse one homogeneous doctrinal position on a given point and that (even if one grants that both of these documents come from Qumran) there was no evolution in the doctrines professed by the sect. Then, too, there is the question of the tradition and redaction of various sources that may have gone into the final composition of the two works. For a detailed source-theory of the *Temple Scroll*, see Michael Owen Wise, *A Critical Study of the Temple Scroll from Qumran Cave 11* (Studies in Ancient Oriental Civilization 49; Chicago: The Oriental Institute of the University of Chicago, 1990) 35–127. Today one might add that not all scholars hold that the *Temple Scroll* represents the theology of Qumran in particular or perhaps even of the Essene movement in general; on this, see Wise, ibid., 23–26. On the important point of the very different natures of the *Damascus Document* and the *Temple Scroll*, see Holmén, "Divorce," 397–98. In contrast, Fitzmyer ("The Matthean Divorce Texts," 91–99) basically follows the approach of Yadin in using the *Temple Scroll* to illuminate the ambiguous passage of the *Damascus Document*.

[49] A tiny fragment of CD 4:19–21 is also found in 6Q15 fragment 1, but the key words, "taking two wives in their lifetimes," have not been preserved.

[50] On the debate whether the "builders" are Pharisees in particular or ordinary Palestinian Jews in general, see Schremer, "Qumran Polemic," 147, with a bibliography in n. 1; Schremer favors the latter view (p. 160).

[51] For a brief list of the various views taken by scholars in the first part of the 20th century, see Winter, "Ṣadoqite Fragments," 75–77; an updated list and a critique of various opinions are supplied by Vermes, "Sectarian Matrimonial Halakhah," 197–99. Vermes lists as the four possible interpretations: (1) prohibition of both polygamy and remarriage after divorce (Solomon Schechter, Philip Davies, Paul Winter); (2) prohibition of polygamy alone (Louis Ginzberg, Chaim Rabin); (3) prohibition of divorce alone (R. H. Charles); (4) prohibition of any second marriage (Johannes Hempel, Jerome Murphy-O'Connor). The third opinion is practically abandoned today. The complexity of the situation is indicated by the fact that, while

Vermes himself formerly held the first position (which he considers the majority opinion), in "Sectarian Matrimonial Halakhah" he defends the second. In more recent literature, the second position has definitely gained ground. Many scholars now question whether a prohibition of divorce that is binding on ordinary Jews can be found in either the *Damascus Document* or the *Temple Scroll*.

[52] On this point, see Paul Joüon and T. Muraoka, *A Grammar of Biblical Hebrew* (Subsidia Biblica 14; 2 vols.; Rome: Biblical Institute, 1991) 2. 551 (§149b). This phenomenon is especially notable in 1–2 Chronicles, but examples are also found, e.g., in Genesis, Exodus, 1 Samuel, and Ruth. The phenomenon continues in the Dead Sea Scrolls. Some of the scholars commenting on CD 4:20–21 presume that those who argue for the feminine meaning of the pronominal suffix in *běḥayyêhem* must presuppose a scribal error that has to be emended; so, e.g., Mueller, "The Temple Scroll," 253; Instone-Brewer, "Nomological Exegesis," 571. Not only is this arbitrary, it is quite unnecessary since, as just indicated, the suffix *-hem* may easily carry a feminine sense in late biblical and Qumran Hebrew. No theory of scribal error is required. That the suffix is indeed *-hem* in the Cairo Geniza text is clear for all to see in the photographs of the MS (along with a transcription by Elisha Qimron) published in *The Damascus Document Reconsidered* (ed. Magen Broshi; Jerusalem: Israel Exploration Society, 1992) 10–49; the relevant text of CD 4:20–21 is found on pp. 16–17.

[53] Raymond Collins (*Divorce in the New Testament*, 84) thinks that the text of 11QTemple 57:17–19 tips the balance in favor of reading the disputed suffix in CD as referring to the women's lifetimes. However, as we shall see, the text of 11QTemple should not be read as a perfect parallel that speaks precisely of the same subject matter as CD 4:20–21.

[54] Scholars are not always careful about their terminology when discussing this problem. Technically speaking, the word polygamy is a broad term that simply means the practice of having more than one spouse at the same time; the multiple spouses may be either husbands or wives. The word polygyny means the practice of a husband having more than one wife at the same time. In contrast, the word polyandry refers to the practice of a wife having more than one husband at the same time. What was permitted and at times practiced in ancient Judaism was polygyny, which is sometimes loosely referred to by scholars as polygamy (being, indeed, one form of polygamy). However, polyandry was not practiced in ancient Judaism. To what extent polygyny was actually practiced at the time of Jesus is disputed among scholars. Josephus (*J.W.* 1.24.2 §477; *Ant.* 17.1.1 §14;) states that it was a revered ancestral usage (*patrion, patriōs*) for Jews to have several wives simultaneously. However, one should note that, in these two passages, Josephus is speaking specifically of the royal marriages of Herod the Great and his realtives. The governing class and the rich had the means to practice polygyny (Herod the Great had ten wives, thought not all contemporaneously), while economic constraints probably made monogamy the norm for ordinary Palestinian Jews. For a brief treatment of polygamy with

further references, see Daniel Sinclair, "Polygamy," *The Oxford Dictionary of the Jewish Religion* (ed. R. J. Zwi Werblowsky and Geoffrey Wigoder; New York/ Oxford: Oxford University, 1997) 540; cf. Marucci, *Parole*, 31–35, 124–25; Schremer, "Qumran Polemic," 156. While some Jewish teachers deprecated the practice, it remained a viable option for Ashkenazi Jews in the West until the Middle Ages, and it survived among Sephardi Jews into the modern period.

[55] For kings in particular, multiple marriages were advantageous both for sealing political alliances and guaranteeing an abundance of sons.

[56] Theoretically, one could take the suffix -*hem* to refer to both the husband and the wife at the same time; so Mueller, "The Temple Scroll," 253; Fitzmyer, "The Matthean Divorce Texts," 96; but see Marucci, *Parole*, 165. While this is grammatically possible, the resulting interpretation is somewhat convoluted, since it requires that the single word *běḥayyêhem* stipulate different legal restrictions for different people in the same breath. In the case of the man, it would be prohibiting *both* polygyny *and* divorce with remarriage while the first spouse was still living. In the case of the woman, it would be prohibiting only divorce with remarriage while the first spouse was living, since polyandry was not practiced in ancient Israel. Moreover, it would prohibit the male from executing a divorce, something that a woman could not do. At best, she could only cooperate willingly; but the man could divorce her whether or not she was willing. I tend to doubt that a legislator, lawyer, or scribe would imagine that anyone could easily understand all this from the suffix of the single word *běḥayyêhem*. We are dealing here with law, and the detailed casuistry involved in this case would require a much more differentiated statement of each partner's legal obligations. However, if one adopts this interpretation, the results for the man are the same as in the interpretation of the suffix as feminine: both polygyny and divorce with remarriage are prohibited. Developing a different line of argument first suggested by Louis Ginzberg (*An Unkown Jewish Sect* [New York: Jewish Theological Seminary, 1970; German original 1922] 19–20), Instone-Brewer (*Divorce and Remarriage*, 68–72) champions a reading of CD 4:20–21 that involves both the principle of equal application of marriage laws to both men and women, seen in some Qumran documents, and a complicated reinterpretation of Lev 18:18 by this principle. The conclusion Instone-Brewer draws from all this is that CD 4:20–21 forbids polygamy but does not take up the question of divorce and remarriage. This conclusion may well be true, but one is left wondering whether the ancient reader could be expected to have understood the convoluted hermeneutical principles and scriptural allusions supposedly underlying CD 4:20–21.

[57] This is the view espoused by Murphy-O'Connor, "An Essene Missionary Document?" 220. Johannes Hempel had already sustained this view against Paul Winter in the former's note replying to the latter's article; see *ZAW* 68 (1956) 84. A common objection to this view is that an insistence that a man be married only once in his entire lifetime is witnessed nowhere in the OT or in Palestinian Judaism around the turn of the era; see Kampen, "A Fresh Look," 93. Moreover, a fragment of

the *Damascus Document* (4Q271, alias 4QD^f) implicitly entertains (in fragment 3, lines 10–12) the possibility of a widow remarrying in that it forbids anyone to marry a widow who has had sexual relations after she has been widowed (thus apparently allowing the marriage if the widow has remained chaste). If this interpretation is correct—and it seems likely—it becomes clear that the *Damascus Document* did not on principle reject any and all second marriages. Accordingly, and not surprisingly, Murphy-O'Connor's sweeping interpretation of CD 4:20–21 is more or less abandoned in the recent literature on the subject. On all this, see Schremer, "Qumran Polemic," 157–58. Yet I would maintain that Murphy-O'Connor's methodological objection to the automatic use of the *Temple Scroll* to interpret an ambiguous passage in the *Damascus Document* still has validity. Our ignorance concerning the relative dates of the two documents, their (no doubt) lengthy tradition histories, and the provenance of the *Temple Scroll* (Qumran composition? composition by Essenes but not at Qumran? composition by Jewish sectarians who did not belong to the Essene movement? a composition representing one view in mainstream Judaism?) cautions us against a naive use of one document to interpret the other.

[58] As Holmén ("Divorce," 400) points out, even on this reading divorce and remarriage are not the direct objects of the prohibition; rather, what is directly forbidden is any second marriage under any condition whatsoever. The prohibition of divorce and remarriage is simply one corollary of this sweeping rejection of all second marriages.

[59] So, e.g., Lövestam, "Divorce and Remarriage," 50–51, esp. n. 19.

[60] Holmén ("Divorce," 401) points out that the one thing that the three proof texts have in common is that they argue against polygamy; similarly, Schremer, "Qumran Polemic," 159–60. Schremer goes on to opine that, if the author of CD 4:20–21 had intended in this passage to forbid a divorced man to remarry while the first wife was still alive, he would have included a proof text like Lev 18:18.

[61] The connection between Gen 1:27 and 7:9 would seem pellucid to the ancient Hebrew scribe: both texts speak not only of two individual beings but also pointedly describe them with the phrase "male and female" (in Hebrew, *zākār ûněqēbâ*). We have here what later rabbinic hermeneutics will call the rule of *gězērâ šāwâ* ("equal section," "equal ordinance," or "equal category"), which allows two separate passages to comment on each other by analogy when a key word or phrase is common to both. (For more on the *gězērâ šāwâ* at Qumran and in the NT, see the treatment of Jesus' double command of love in Chapter 36.) The connection between Gen 1:27 and 7:9 is all the clearer if the author of the *Damascus Document* understands the phrase "two by two" to include not just the animals but also Noah and his wife plus his three sons and their wives. If this is the case, then, as Vermes points out ("Sectarian Matrimonial Halakhah," 200), this scriptural argument makes sense only if polygamy—and polygamy alone—is the target of the author's criticism: "After all, any of the four men in question might have remarried after divorce or widowhood

and still have come to the ark 'two by two.' " Hence Vermes concludes (p. 202) that CD 4:20–21 condemns only polygamy.

[62] On all this, see John J. Collins, "Marriage," 104–62, esp. 129. Collins thinks that polygyny is the primary target of the CD text, although the text also seems to exclude divorce or at least remarriage while the first wife is alive; contrast Vermes, "Sectarian Matrimonial Halakhah," 202.

[63] For instance, the Hebrew consonants *mgrš* have been interpreted as the noun *migrāš* ("pastureland") and as the Pual participle *lamměgorāš* ("a man who has been driven out," i.e., a man who has been banished from the community; so Fitzmyer, "Divorce among First-Century Palestinian Jews," 110*). However, neither suggestion seems to make as much sense in the immediate context as the Piel active participle *měgārēš* ("a man who drives out [his wife]"). For a survey of the opinions of various scholars (Schiffman, Rabin, Davies, Fitzmyer), see Instone-Brewer, "Nomological Exegesis," 572. Holmén ("Divorce," 403) argues strongly against both "pastureland," which makes no sense in the immediate context, and "a man who has been driven out" of the group in the sense of someone who has been excommunicated from the Essene community. As for the latter suggestion, Holmén points to the likely meaning of the rest of lines 17 and 18: "and he shall bring up [or: instruct, teach, discipline, *yysr*] their children and their little ones in a spirit of humility." If this reading (reconstructed from 4Q266) is correct, the lines make more sense in a context speaking of the Inspector's duties (or possibly the duties of the divorced man) when faced with a divorce within the community.

[64] It should be noted, however, that Fitzmyer ("The Matthean Divorce Texts," 110–11 n. 104) rejects any reference to divorce in CD 13:17–19. Consequently, he interprets CD 4:20–21 as clearly prohibiting both polygamy and divorce (see p. 96). Strongly opposed to Fitzmyer's reading of the CD passages is Brin ("Divorce at Qumran," 238–39).

[65] Contrast the assertion of Raymond Collins (*Divorce in the New Testament*, 194) that "the discovery of the Dead Sea Scrolls gives evidence of the fact that at least one group within first-century Judaism, namely, the Essenes, banned divorce" with the claim of Instone-Brewer ("Nomological Exegesis," 572) that there are three references to divorce in the Qumran documents (11QTemple 54:4–5; 66:11; CD 13:17) and that none of them is critical of divorce. In Instone-Brewer's view, these texts appear to allow divorce, certainly do not condemn it, and say nothing about restrictions concerning remarriage after divorce. Indeed, Schremer, after examining all the relevant texts in the *Damascus Document*, concludes categorically ("Qumran Polemic," 159): "All these facts indicate that divorce was not forbidden by the Qumran community." A more nuanced view is taken by Schiffman, "The Relationship,"138: CD 4:19–5:2 forbids polygamy and (here Schiffman may be relying too readily on the supposed parallel in the *Temple Scroll*) apparently remarriage after a divorce as long as the first wife is alive.

⁶⁶ After surveying various views, Wise (*A Critical Study*, 23–26) concludes that the provenance of the *Temple Scroll* is still an open question; he himself (pp. 201–3) favors the theory that the *Temple Scroll* was written not by the Qumran community but by the community responsible for the *Damascus Document*, prior to the founding of Qumran. For other views, see, e.g., Hartmut Stegemann, *The Library of Qumran* (Grand Rapids, MI/Cambridge, UK: Eerdmans; Leiden: Brill, 1998) 96 (prior to the Essenes, possibly as early as 400 B.C.) and Geza Vermes, *The Complete Dead Sea Scrolls in English* (New York: Penguin, 1997) 191 (the view that the Temple Scroll is a Qumran composition "has a solid foundation"); cf. Maier (*Tempelrolle*, 47–51), who points out the difficulty of dating the *Temple Scroll*, which probably grew in stages and whose origins probably predate the foundation of Qumran. See also Instone-Brewer ("Nomological Exegesis," 566–67), who recognizes the problem of provenance but thinks that the exegete is justified in using the two texts to illuminate each other because they share many common points, including the use of Lev 18:18 as a proof text supporting monogamy. In Instone-Brewer's view, the *Temple Scroll* argues that the whole of Israel is one family under the king, and hence the king is bound by Lev 18:18 (the prohibition of marrying the sister of one's wife while one's wife is still alive) to marry no other woman as long as his first wife is still alive (every other Israelite woman being, in a sense, the first wife's sister).

⁶⁷ This is the judgment of many commentators, including Wise, *A Critical Study*, 194: "The principles governing the redactional shaping of the scroll reveal that its purpose was to serve as a law for remnant Israel during an earthly eschatological age, until God himself should usher in the 'Day of Creation.' " On the ordering of the material in the *Temple Scroll*, especially in the section that concerns us, see Mueller, "The Temple Scroll," 249.

⁶⁸ As noted above, Yadin presented his views in "L'attitude," 98–99, and Murphy-O'Connor replied on pp. 99–100. Not unlike Yadin, Mueller ("The Temple Scroll," 251–54) moves too easily from the *Temple Scroll* to the *Damascus Document*, apparently presuming that they represent the same sect and are talking basically about the same thing, although he then issues a methodological caution on p. 254.

⁶⁹ Kampen ("A Fresh Look," 96) holds that the *Temple Scroll* (recycling a prohibition found in Lev 18:18, which forbade a man to marry his wife's sister "during *her* lifetime [*běḥayyêhā*]," using the feminine singular suffix to refer to the life of the first wife) intended to limit this prohibition of polygyny and divorce to the king, who is to keep his one wife beside him "all the days of *her* life." However, says Kampen, the sectarians who received the *Temple Scroll* proceeded to extend the prohibition so that, in CD 4:20–21, the prohibition is applied to all men. Accordingly, the author of the *Damascus Document* consciously changed the feminine suffix found in Lev 18:18 (and used in the *Temple Scroll*) to the masculine plural suffix (*běḥayyêhem*) to make the point that the prohibition was not limited to the king. This whole theory (as Kampen admits) presupposes a certain history of the compo-

sition and reception of the two documents within a single community, a theory not all would hold.

[70] See Fitzmyer, "The Matthean Divorce Texts," 93; a similar view is held by Raymond Collins, *Divorce in the New Testament*, 82. If one were to pursue this position to its logical conclusion, it would follow that every Jew who accepted the teaching of the *Temple Scroll* would be bound to marry a woman only of his father's house or of his own clan, to have twelve thousands soldiers guarding him, and to have a circle of princes, priests, and levites guiding his interpretation and fulfillment of the Law. In brief, many of the laws binding the king in 11Q Temple 56:12–59:21 are not applicable to ordinary Israelites. In favor of seeing 11QTemple 57:15–19 as referring only to the king is Maier, *Die Tempelrolle*, 249; cf. Marucci, *Parole*, 164–65.

[71] Lawrence H. Schiffman, "Laws Pertaining to Women in the *Temple Scroll*," *The Dead Sea Scrolls. Forty Years of Research* (ed. Devorah Dimant and Uriel Rappaport; Leiden: Brill; Jerusalem: Magnes, 1992) 210–28, esp. 213; Instone-Brewer, "Nomological Exegesis," 567.

[72] This point is missed by commentators like Mueller ("The Temple Scroll," 251–54), who uses the very different context of the *Damascus Document* to claim that what the *Temple Scroll* says of the king in the eschatological age must be true of all Israelites even now.

[73] On this, see Holmén, "Divorce," 405–6. He suggests that the idea of three types of guardians who are constantly with the king to protect him is developed out of Deut 17:19, which states that a Torah scroll is to be "with him" (*'immô*, i.e., with the king) "all the days of his life"—a phrase that becomes "all the days of her life" as the function of protecting the king from sin is transferred to his wife.

[74] On this, see Holmén, "Divorce," 406. Unfortunately, the beginning of 11QTemple 54:4 suffers from a lacuna; the latter part of the verse reads in Hebrew *wkwl ndr 'lmnh wgrwš kwl 'šr 'srh 'l npš*. The meaning is "and every vow of a widow and a divorced woman, every [vow] by which she binds herself." The wording is almost exactly the same as that of Num 30:10.

[75] So Holmén, "Divorce," 406–7; also Brin, "Divorce at Qumran," 239. Brin stresses that the *Temple Scroll* does not simply repeat automatically any and all of the commandments of Deuteronomy. The *Temple Scroll* carefully selects which commandments it wishes to take over from Deuteronomy, orders them according to its own plan, and modifies them according to its own views. Hence one cannot plead that the *Temple Scroll* has mindlessly taken over Deut 22:28–29 without realizing what it is saying. Holmén (ibid.) claims that a similar prohibition of divorce in the case of a man who makes a false accusation against the virtue of an Israelite virgin is mentioned in 4Q159 (4QOrdinances[a]), fragments 2–4, lines 9 and 10. Brin (pp. 239–42) reads this text differently; he claims that it prescribes the expulsion

of the libelous husband from the sect. (On Brin's justification of his different reading of the Hebrew of 4Q159, see n. 14 on pp. 240–41.) The ultimate upshot of
this interpretation is the same as Holmén's, since it involves the mandatory divorce
of the libelous husband (now banished) and his wife. On either reading, then, the
fragments witness to the community's acceptance of divorce in certain cases. Brin
(pp. 424–43) also thinks that a fragmentary text in 4Q267 (= 4QD[b]), fragment 9,
column 6, lines 4 and 5, also presumes the acceptance of divorce by the community,
but the case is less clear here.

[76] Marucci (*Parole*, 165), not unlike Vermes ("Sectarian Matrimonial Halakhah,"
202), comes to the conclusion that "the community of the Dead Sea" certainly condemned polygamy, while it probably had no special teaching on the question of the
licitness of divorce.

[77] The Hebrew word *gēṭ* (*gîṭṭîn* in the plural), which does not occur in the OT but
which is found as early as a divorce document from Murabbaʿat (first quarter of the
2d century A.D.), can mean "a legal document" in general. Technically, the complete
phrase for a certificate of divorce is *gēṭ ʾiššâ* (literally, "a document of a woman [or:
wife]"); other phrases, such as "document of repudiation" or "document of driving
away [i.e., divorce]," also occur. Often, however, in rabbinic literature the specifying noun *ʾiššâ* is omitted, and *gēṭ* by itself is understood to mean "a certificate of divorce." The wider meaning of *gēṭ* helps explain why the tractate *Gîṭṭîn* also includes
scattered statements about other documents and the freeing of slaves.

[78] Within the *sēder Nāšîm* of the Mishna, some other passages also supply various
grounds for divorce: e.g., the sterility of one's wife over a ten-year period (*m. Yebam.* 6:6); transgressions by the wife of the Law of Moses (*dat mōšeh*) or Jewish
custom (*dat yĕhûdît* (*m. Ketub.* 7:6), which include giving her husband food that
has not been tithed, having sexual intercourse with him while she is menstruating,
not separating the priest's share of the dough, making a vow and not fulfilling it,
going outdoors with her hair loose, spinning in the street, conversing in loose and
indiscriminate fashion with men, cursing her husband's father or grandfather to
his face, speaking loudly to her husband in her house so that the neighbors can
hear, and having secret vows or physical defects (*m. Ketub.* 7:7). Sometimes these
grounds are not attributed to a particular rabbinic authority, and they are not said
to be opinions dividing the House of Shammai from the House of Hillel. Many of
these grounds, however, could be put under the rubric of "shame" or "indecency"
and thus may be expressions of the "Shammai approach." In any event, the Mishna
witnesses to an interest in and a development of scholarly discussion of the precise grounds required for divorce in the post-70 period. For an interpretation of
the differences between the two Houses on divorce from a modern Jewish feminist
perspective, see Tal Ilan, " 'The Daughters of Israel Are Not Licentious' (*mYeva-
mot* 13:1). Beit Shammai on the Legal Position of Women," *Integrating Women
into Second Temple History* (Peabody, MA: Hendrickson, 1999) 43–81, esp.
50–52.

[79] Some have tried to interpret the spoiling of food as a euphemism for sexual immorality, but in the social world of the ancient Near East, badly prepared meals were no minor matter; see Marucci, *Parole*, 139–41.

[80] One is astonished to read Instone-Brewer's claim (*Divorce and Remarriage in the Bible*, 110) that the House of Hillel "invented" a new type of divorce in the 1st century B.C., "called the 'any matter' divorce." Rather, the House of Hillel simply carried forward, explicated, and finally "canonized" the mainstream practice attested by the OT, Philo, and Josephus. If there was any invention, it was the failed one of the House of Shammai, which was run over by the juggernaut of history.

[81] See the caution stated by Collins, *Divorce*, 194.

[82] It is perhaps significant that, in *m. Giṭ* 9:10, the opinions on the grounds for divorce are attributed not to Shammai and Hillel themselves but rather to the two Houses, and that the only individual rabbi quoted in the discussion is Aqiba, who was active toward the end of the 1st century and in the first third of the 2d century A.D.

[83] Ironically, it may be the famous "exceptive clause" in Matt 5:32 and 19:9 ("except on grounds of *porneia*") that is the first written attestation (ca. A.D. 80–90) of a debate in a Jewish or Jewish-Christian milieu over what constitutes sufficient grounds for divorce—although in Matthew the grounds are more in the nature of the sole exception to an otherwise total prohibition. The relatively late emergence of the debate over precise grounds for divorce as well as the different opinions proposed may be reflected in the fact that the rabbinic *gēṭ*, for all the care given to its proper writing, never mentions the specific reason for which the divorce is being executed. Apparently, during the mishnaic period, a divorce executed by a husband according to the agreed-upon rules for drawing up a *gēṭ*, was always valid (cf. *Yeb.* 14:1; see Epstein, *The Jewish Marriage Contract*, 193), and not even a rabbinic tribunal could force the husband to annul the *gēṭ* and take back the wife he had divorced; see Marucci, *Parole*, 142.

[84] In what follows, the phrase "prohibition of divorce" is used broadly to include the two types of sayings attributed to Jesus: (1) a saying that reflects the form of casuistic law (with the offense expressed by an indefinite relative clause, a conditional clause, or a participial phrase) brands divorce and remarriage as the sin of adultery in the main clause; and (2) a saying that reflects the form of apodictic law commands (3d person singular imperative) that no human being separate a couple that God has joined together in marriage. Not surprisingly—as will be noted below—Paul's paraphrase of Jesus' prohibition is something of a mixture of the two forms, since his basic statement in 1 Cor 7:10 + 11c is apodictic (the Lord commands "that a wife not separate from [i.e., divorce] [her] husband . . . and a husband not send away [i.e., divorce] [his] wife"), while his parenthetic statement in v 11a + b introduces a conditional/casuistic element ("but if she does separate, she must remain

[3d person singular imperative] unmarried or be reconciled with [her] husband"). In the end, though, all these various forms and formulations are simply different ways of forbidding divorce (and remarriage) to those who accept the authority of the one issuing the teaching.

[85] On this, see Raymond Collins, *Divorce in the New Testament*, 4.

[86] On this, see Fitzmyer, "The Matthean Divorce Texts," 103 n. 13.

[87] Note that none of the 1st person singular verbs in 7:6,7,8 (*legō, thelō, legō*) carries the emphatic subject pronoun *egō* with it; hence the great emphasis of *paraggellō* ("I command"), accompanied with *ouk egō alla ho kyrios* ("not I but the Lord"). The same emphatic marker is placed when Paul switches back to himself as the authority of his teaching in v 12: *legō egō ouch ho kyrios* ("I say, not the Lord"). Likewise striking is the shift from the verbs "I say" and "I wish" (vv 6,7,8,12) to "I *command*—not I, but the Lord" in v 10; the shift in verbs matches the shift to the greater authority. This point is underlined by the choice of a verb (*paraggellō*) that occurs only two other times in the whole of the undisputed Paulines (1 Cor 11:17; 1 Thess 4:11). Hence it will not do to translate *paraggellō* at this point with the weak sense of "give directions" or "give instructions," as though Paul were merely giving wise advice or counsel. In classical and Hellenistic Greek, *paraggellō* is often employed to express the idea of giving orders, especially with a nuance of passing orders on—a nuance that would fit the present context perfectly.

[88] So, e.g., D'Angelo ("Remarriage," 78–106), who points out that Paul identifies his instructions for the Christian community at worship in 1 Cor 14:26–33 as "a commandment of the Lord" (v 37—though the presence of the noun "commandment" [*entolē*] in the original text is not entirely assured); for a reply to her argument, see Raymond Collins, *Divorce in the New Testament*, 30–31. On 1 Cor 14:37, see Gordon D. Fee, *The First Epistle to the Corinthians* (NICNT; Grand Rapids, MI: Eerdmans, 1987) 711–12.

[89] Attempts have been made to identify Paul's paraphrase with one particular version of the Synoptic logia on divorce, but in my view this is a futile endeavor. It is telling that Paul uses the same vocabulary for divorce in 7:10–11 that he uses in vv 12–15 (*aphiēmi* and *chōrizomai*), where he is speaking on his authority and in his own words. In contrast, the equivalent sayings on divorce in the Synoptics use the verb *apolyō* for the act of divorce and never mention the woman first when it comes to initiating the divorce. Paul is obviously handing on the prohibition of divorce in his own words, even though he identifies Jesus as its source. On all this, see Raymond Collins, *Divorce in the New Testament*, 32–38. I suggest below that Paul may possibly be meshing different sayings of Jesus that he knows (e.g., forms similar to Mark 10:9 and Luke 16:18 respectively). I stress, however, that this is merely a surmise; I am definitely not suggesting that Paul knew any of the written Gospels or a written text of the hypothetical Q document.

[90] The speculation of exegetes about why Paul places the case of the wife before that of the husband—a unique ordering of the spouses in the divorce sayings of the NT as well as in the immediate context of Paul's statements about husbands and wives in 1 Corinthians 7—need not detain us here, since it does not affect our concerns about the historical Jesus. It may well be that a specific case of a Corinthian Christian wife divorcing her Christian husband has occasioned Paul's treatment of the matter in 1 Cor 7:10–11. However, Paul delicately speaks in terms of a hypothetical situation by using a conditional clause (*ean*) with the subjunctive mood of the verb. Thus, if Paul is moved to speak of the problem of divorce because of a particular case, he builds on this case to articulate a general prohibition of divorce, which is binding both on Christian wives (mentioned first because of the actual case occasioning the treatment in chap. 7) and on their Christian husbands. This scenario might also explain why Paul's prohibition of the wife's separating from her husband in v 10 is expressed by the aorist infinitive (reflecting a single past act?) while the prohibition of the husband's divorcing his wife is expressed by the present infinitive (indicating a general rule that is always binding). Moreover, behind his desire to make clear that the prohibition of divorce binds husbands as well as wives may lie Paul's knowledge and experience of the legal situation in Palestinian Judaism, where the wife could not divorce her husband but the husband could divorce his wife. Paul may fear that speaking in 1 Cor 7:10–11 only of the wife's inability to divorce (a subject that is pressing because of the particular case that has moved him to treat the topic) might leave some with the impression that the husband retained the power to divorce. On this, see Raymond Collins (*Divorce in the New Testament*, 38–39), who also suggests that the mention of the husband's inability to divorce in v 11 may reflect Paul's knowledge of Jesus' prohibition, which (whatever hypothetical form we choose) always speaks of the husband divorcing his wife. Needless to say, all this is only one possible scenario among many. That the problems lying behind Paul's treatment may be understood in various ways can be readily seen by comparing the interpretations of Jerome Murphy-O'Connor (*1 Corinthians* [NT Message 10; Wilmington, DE: Glazier, 1979] 62–64: a husband influenced by the extreme asceticism of some Corinthians Christians has divorced his wife, who does not share his views) and Antoinette Clark Wire (*The Corinthian Women Prophets* [Minneapolis: Fortress, 1990] 84–85: the problem is caused by Christian wives leaving their husbands). Thankfully, our quest for the teaching of the historical Jesus does not require us to solve this problem, which belongs to a detailed exegesis of 1 Corinthians.

[91] Although Fitzmyer acknowledges the possibility of taking *chōristhēnai* in either a passive or a middle sense, he thinks that the passive sense is more likely; see "The Matthean Divorce Texts," 81, 102 n. 7.

[92] For all their differences, both Greek and Roman law around the turn of the era recognized in general the right of the (free) wife as well as the (free) husband to divorce one's spouse. On this point, see Marucci, *Parole*, 191–94 (for Greek law), 383–95 (for Roman law in general and the *lex Iulia de adulteriis coercendis* in par-

ticular). For the evolution of Roman law in regard to a woman's right to divorce her husband, see Susan Treggiari, *Roman Marriage* (Oxford: Clarendon, 1991) 443–46; cf. Percy Ellwood Corbett, *The Roman Law of Marriage* (Oxford: Clarendon, 1930) 86, 242. It seems that earlier on in Roman law, a woman did not have the right to divorce. But by the 1st century A.D., Roman law had evolved to the point that it gave a free woman who was *sui iuris* the right to divorce her husband. This meant, however, that women who were not completely free under Roman law did not enjoy such latitude. For example, the *lex Iulia et Papia* forbade a freedwoman to divorce her patron against his will. For the general socioeconomic situation in Roman Corinth, see Jerome Murphy-O'Connor, *St. Paul's Corinth. Texts and Archaeology* (Good News Studies 6; Wilmington, DE: Glazier, 1983).

[93] That the wife in vv 10–11 has both a choice in the matter and the power to divorce (and is therefore not simply the passive object of the husband's action of divorce, an interpretation favored by those who take *chōristhēnai* in v 10 as truly passive in meaning) is also seen by the fact that, in the case under consideration, it is up to the wife to decide whether she will remain unmarried or be reconciled with her husband (v 11). That the wife's action of *chōristhēnai* has effected a true divorce (in the eyes of society) is seen by the fact that Paul, in v 10, begins by addressing those who have entered marriage (*tois gegamēkosin*), turns to the case of the woman who has performed the act of *chōristhēnai* from her husband, and tells her in v 11 that her two options are to remain *unmarried* (*agamos*) or to be reconciled with her husband. Since in the past she was married to this husband, and since one of her two present options is to remain unmarried, obviously her action has produced a true divorce (in the eyes of society, if not in the eyes of Paul).

[94] Although the structure of the parallelism is somewhat obscured by the parenthetical remark about the wife remaining unmarried or being reconciled, the basic structure of vv 10–11 consists of two parallel infinitives (*chōristhēnai* and *aphienai*), both of which depend on *paraggellō* in v 10a.

[95] This can be seen from the use of these verbs in Greek authors of both the classical and Hellenistic period (as well as from koine papyri and a divorce text from Murabbaʿat Cave 2); see, e.g., Fitzmyer, "The Matthean Divorce Texts," 89–91; Raymond Collins, *Divorce in the New Testament*, 17, 38; Marucci, *Parole*, 181–83. The same absence of a distinct technical vocabulary for divorce is true of biblical Hebrew. The two commonly used Hebrew verbs (*šālaḥ* ["send away"] and *gāraš* ["drive away"]) mean "divorce" only when the context so specifies.

[96] This is probably due to Luke's general tendency to avoid doublets (i.e., repetitions that result from taking over both the Marcan and the Q tradition of some saying or event) unless such repetitions serve Luke's redactional interests; see Joseph A. Fitzmyer, *The Gospel According to Luke* (AYB 28 and 28A; Garden City, NY: Doubleday, 1981, 1985; reprint New Haven: Yale University Press) 1. 81–82. In the present case, having placed the Q version of the prohibition within the context

of the great journey up to Jerusalem, Luke sees no need to repeat the prohibition as Jesus enters Judea and begins his proximate ascent to Jerusalem (the context of the Marcan dispute story). Matthew is more open to the use of doublets; hence his Gospel, alone among the Synoptics, presents both the isolated Q logion and the Marcan dispute story, carefully placed toward the beginning and toward the end of the public ministry.

[97] It may be that the three sayings that mention or discuss the Law (Luke 16:16–18), all of which appear in different contexts in Matthew (Matt 11:12–13; 5:18; 5:32), may have stood together as a cluster in the Q document (or at least in Luke's copy of it). Since, however, the connection among the three sayings is quite tenuous (16:16 mentions the Law along with the prophets as a designation of a period of salvation history; 16:17 emphasizes the extreme difficulty of making the slightest change in the Law; 16:18 treats the legal question of divorce without using the word *nomos* ["Law"]), the cluster created by Q is clearly artificial—a point supported by the very different contexts of the prohibition in both 1 Corinthians 7 and Mark 10. On the problems of the position of Luke 16:18 within Luke's composition and its hypothetical position in the Q document, see Raymond Collins, *Divorce in the New Testament*, 175–79. Loader (*Jesus' Attitude towards the Law*, 337–39) thinks that the sayings in 16:16–18 are closely tied together in Luke's thought: "Despite the new age of the kingdom, the Torah still applies. . . . This is evident in the instance of Jesus' exposition of marriage law which Jesus applies in the strictest possible terms." I must admit I have difficulty understanding how Luke took a total prohibition of divorce to be faithful observance of the Law in the strictest way, down to "the smallest stroke of a letter" (*keraia* in v 17). In my view, it is more probable that, not unlike other passages in the great journey narrative, Luke 16:16–18 faithfully reproduces a cluster of Q material without the evangelist necessarily worrying about how to iron out all the tensions inherent in the Q collection. Interestingly, Loader also thinks that Luke is faithful to Q, since Loader (pp. 424–26) sees the same basic approach to Jesus and the Law in the Q tradition lying behind Luke 16:16–18 that he sees in 16:16–18 itself. For the various views on the coherence of 16:16–18 or the lack thereof, see the literature cited by Loader on pp. 337–39.

[98] Since the Q document is usually dated ca. A.D. 50–70, and since the prohibition of divorce most likely circulated as an isolated logion before it was taken into the Q document, the Q version of the saying is treated here before the Marcan version. A certain pedagogical concern helps determine the order as well: it is much easier to treat the short Q saying first and then proceed to the Marcan material, which includes both a parallel to Q (Mark 10:11–12) and the much longer Marcan *Streitgespräch* (10:2–9).

[99] Anyone who has worked with the divorce sayings of the Synoptic Gospels knows the many text-critical problems, large and small, that bedevil these verses. So as not to reinvent the wheel, I simply refer the interested reader to Bruce M. Metzger's explanations of the major text-critical decisions taken by the editorial committee of

the *UBSGNT* (4th rev. ed.), decisions with which I agree. His comments on the divorce passages can be found in his *TCGNT* (2d ed., 1994): p. 11 for Matt 5:32; p. 38 for Matt 19:7,9; and pp. 88–89 for Mark 10:2,6,7. Since the text-critical problems in Luke 16:18 are relatively minor, Metzger does not treat them. A more detailed treatment of the text-critical problems of all the NT divorce texts is provided by Raymond Collins as he begins his treatment of each of the logia in his *Divorce in the New Testament*.

[100] For a defense of the view that *ep'autēn* in Mark 10:11 should be translated "against her" (not, e.g., "with her") and refers to the first, not the second, wife, see Gundry, *Mark* 541–42; cf. Nolland, "The Gospel Prohibition of Divorce," 28–30.

[101] So, e.g., Fitzmyer, "The Matthean Divorce Texts," 87–89; Kremer, "Jesu Wort zur Ehescheidung," 56–57; Raymond Collins, *Divorce in the New Testament*, 186; Nolland, "The Gospel Prohibition of Divorce," 21–25. Thankfully, this exegetical decision lets us avoid a much larger exegetical problem, i.e., the exact meaning of *porneia* in the exceptive clause; for summaries of the problem, see Fitzmyer, ibid.; Collins, ibid., 199–213; Meier, *Law and History*, 140–50; Baltensweiler, "Die Ehebruchsklauseln," 340–56; idem, *Die Ehe*, esp. 88–100; Mueller, "The Temple Scroll," 255–56; and the lengthy exposition in Marucci, *Parole*, 333–95. Since the exceptive clause does not go back to the historical Jesus (indeed, it does not seem to go back to the Q document), there is no need for a historian engaged in the quest for the historical Jesus to wade through the many opinions about the nature of the Matthean exception. A fortiori, this exempts us from deciding what if anything this exceptive clause may say to Christian practice today—the hidden agenda that drives many treatments of "Jesus and divorce." This seems to be the problem underlying the attempt of Instone-Brewer (*Divorce and Remarriage in the Bible*, 134) to have it both ways by first admitting with the critical consensus that Matthew added the exceptive clause to the tradition he received and then claiming that Matthew "has correctly reinserted something that was present in the original debate." According to Instone-Brewer, the exceptive clauses could be omitted in oral and written transmission because they were so obvious and well known to the original audience. As so often with Instone-Brewer's presentation, pivotal claims are simply asserted rather than proven. His faulty reading of the larger tradition history of the OT, Philo, Josephus, and the later rabbis leads him to a faulty reading of the tradition history of Jesus' sayings on divorce. His book is a prime example of a treatment of the teaching of the historical Jesus being skewed by a desire to answer present-day problems of Christian theology and pastoral practice.

[102] Of ninety-eight occurrences in the NT, fifty are found in Luke-Acts.

[103] So Fitzmyer, "The Matthean Divorce Texts," 82–83. Nolland ("The Gospel Prohibition of Divorce," 27) suggests that the antithetical form into which Matthew has cast the prohibition of divorce in 5:31–32 may explain why he omits a specific

mention of the husband's remarriage in v 32. Matt 5:31 cites part of Deut 24:1, understood as a command: "Whoever divorces his wife must give her a certificate of divorce." The antithetical statement of Jesus in v 32 thus naturally focuses on the husband's act of divorcing his wife rather than on his action of remarrying.

104 On this, see Gundry, *Mark*, 543.

105 The odd-looking aorist passive infinitive *moicheuthēnai* is to be explained by the fact that, in the active voice, *moicheuō* is transitive; hence, e.g., in the active voice the adulterous man is the subject and the adulterous woman is the direct object of the verb. When the construction is put into the passive voice, the woman naturally becomes the subject of the verb, as is the case in Matt 5:32. While Raymond Collins (*Divorce in the New Testament*, 167) understands Matt 5:32 to refer to the husband forcing his divorced wife into an adulterous second marriage (the common view), he also mentions the possibility (p. 304 n. 100) that *poiei autēn moicheuthēnai* might mean that the husband makes his former wife resort to prostitution for economic support. Yet a direct reference to prostitution would seem to invite the use of *porneuō* rather than *moicheuō*. Even more unlikely is the suggestion of Nolland ("The Gospel Prohibition of Divorce," 30) that the passive infinitive *moicheuthēnai* indicates that the first wife is having adultery committed against her by the husband who divorces her. Nolland himself admits that this usage is not documented elsewhere in ancient Greek. Lövestam ("Divorce and Remarriage," 53), commenting on Matt 5:32, notes that some rabbinic texts point the Hebrew consonants of the Decalogue commandment against divorce as a Hiphil rather than a Qal so that "You shall not commit adultery" (Qal) becomes instead "You shall not cause adultery to be committed" (Hiphil, a form of this verb that does not occur in the MT). A prime example is *b. Šeb.* 47b, where Shimeon ben Tarphon asks rhetorically where one can find a prohibition against a panderer who obtains prostitutes for an adulterer. Replying to his own question, he states that Exod 20:14, which reads in the Qal form of the verb, "You shall not commit adultery [*lō' tin'āp*]," implies the command expressed in the Hiphil form of the verb, "You shall not cause adultery to be committed [*lō' tan'îp*]"—i.e., you shall not aid and abet an adulterer by pimping for him. While there is an intriguing similarity here, one must also notice the major difference: Matthew is speaking of a man who forces his own wife into an adulterous relationship (i.e., a second marriage) by divorcing her—a concept of divorce and remarriage as adultery that runs counter to the whole mind-set of the OT and Judaism—while the Talmud is speaking of a panderer who procures prostitutes for an adulterous man.

106 Here I differ from Fitzmyer ("The Matthean Divorce Texts," 84), who takes Matt 5:32 to mean that the husband's act of divorcing his wife, without reference to a subsequent marriage, is branded as adultery. I think instead that a subsequent marriage is mentioned (not a second marriage undertaken by the husband who divorces his wife, but rather a second marriage into which the divorced woman finds herself forced to enter), that this second marriage is branded as adulterous (because

the original marriage bond is seen as perduring), but that the responsibility for this adulterous situation is laid squarely on the shoulders of the first husband.

[107] Kremer ("Jesu Wort zur Ehescheidung," 56, 60) puts Matthew's formulation, with the idea that the husband forces his wife into adultery, at the beginning of his outline of the development of the saying's tradition history. See also Kirchenschläger, *Ehe und Ehescheidung*, 72. Likewise supportive of the view that Part 1b of Matt 5:32 is more original than Part 1b of Luke 16:18 are Marucci, *Parole*, 248; John Dominic Crossan, *In Fragments. The Aphorisms of Jesus* (San Francisco: Harper & Row, 1983) 210–12; Raymond Collins, *Divorce in the New Testament*, 183 (there is "a very strong possibility" that Matthew reflects the original form of Q). For arguments against Matthew's version being the original form of Q, see Gundry, *Mark*, 542. Against Collins's position, which leans on the supposed background of Herodias' divorce of her first husband and her marriage to her brother-in-law Herod Antipas, the following may be noted: (1) To accept such a background is to accept Mark's narrative (6:14–23) of the Baptist's rebuke of Herod and the circumstances of his subsequent death (as opposed to that of Josephus) as historically accurate; this is highly questionable (cf. Meier, *A Marginal Jew*, 2. 56–62, 171–76). (2) Josephus (*Ant.* 18. 5.1 §110) implies that Herodias divorced her first husband (who, *pace* Mark, was named Herod, not Philip), not vice versa; hence Matt 5:32a does not apply to Herodias' situation. (3) It is not entirely clear whether Antipas ever formally divorced his first wife, the daughter of the Nabatean King Aretas. We are told by Josephus that Antipas intended to divorce her. However, his first wife got wind of his plan and escaped to her father. It is not clear whether Antipas ever got to deliver the certificate of divorce to her. (4) In any case, the Baptist, in Mark's narrative, criticizes Antipas for having married *his brother's wife*, not for having married a *divorced woman*. In other words, the precise charge involves incest, not divorce. In sum, then, the attempt to make Matt 5:32 interface with Antipas' marital situation—and thus to prove that it is the primitive Q form of the divorce prohibition, perhaps even going back to the historical Jesus—fails.

[108] This point is well made (but with particular reference to Matt 19:1–9 as compared to Mark 10:2–12) by Marucci, *Parole*, 308–9.

[109] Of the 216 occurrences of *anēr* in the NT, twenty-seven are in Luke's Gospel and one hundred in Acts.

[110] So Raymond Collins, *Divorce in the New Testament*, 179.

[111] So Fitzmyer, "The Matthean Divorce Texts," 82; similarly, though without providing an exact formulation of the saying, Nolland, "The Gospel Prohibition of Divorce," 34–35. The wide acceptance of some form of Luke 16:18 as the most primitive version of the prohibition is acknowledged by Marucci (*Parole*, 325–28), who nevertheless opposes this view and, not unlike Raymond Collins, favors Matt

5:32 (without the exceptive clause). Understandably, those critics who accept some form of Luke 16:18 as the earliest attainable Q version of the saying differ on the details of their reconstructions. For example, Ivan Havener (*Q. The Sayings of Jesus* [Good News Studies 19; Wilmington, DE: Glazier, 1987] 143), who follows the reconstruction of Athanasius Polag, suggests that the Q form read: "Everyone who divorces his wife (and marries another) commits adultery, and whoever marries a divorced woman commits adultery." Havener considers the phrase in parentheses to be probably but not certainly present in the Q form. In almost identical fashion, in James M. Robinson (ed.), *The Critical Edition of Q* (Leuven: Peeters, 2000) 270–71, the hypothetical reconstruction reads *pas ho apolyōn tēn gynaika autou [[kai gamōn <allēn>]] moicheuei, kai ho apolelymenēn gamōn moich [[euei]]*. The double square brackets indicate that the phrase "and marries another" (*kai gamōn allēn*) is considered probable but uncertain; likewise uncertain is the precise form of the verb *moicheuei* (so Luke) or *moichatai* (so Matthew) at the end of the saying ("commits adultery"). The angle brackets around *allēn* ("another") indicates that this is an emendation not found in either Luke or Matthew. In this case, Matthew does not have the corresponding phrase, and Luke uses *heteran*, an adjective favored by him; the scholars reconstructing Q in this volume suggest that *allēn*, found in the Marcan parallel (Mark 10:11), may have been the original reading in Q. A similar reconstruction is found in Burton Mack, *The Lost Gospel* (San Francisco: Harper, 1993) 100; however, Mack entirely omits the disputed phrase "and marries another." Quite to the contrary, David Catchpole (*The Quest for Q* [Edinburgh: Clark, 1993] 236–37) argues cogently for the inclusion of "and marries another" in the original Q saying, a position with which I agree. The reader will have noticed by now that, unlike many critics who attempt to reconstruct of the wording of Q, I do not spend time debating the precise Greek forms of the words in Q, since my ultimate goal is a decision about whether the teaching goes back to the historical Jesus, who naturally would have spoken the prohibition in Aramaic. Hence questions about whether a particular Greek word should be restored as *moicheuei* or *moichatai*, *heteran* or *allēn*, are beside the point.

[112] Taking this approach is also justified by the fact that a very broad consensus among scholars treating this pericope maintains that Mark 10:2–12 consists of two originally isolated units (vv 2–9 and vv 11–12) and that the core of both units goes back to pre-Marcan tradition; on this, see Sariola, *Markus und das Gesetz*, 121–37.

[113] This is the view of Mark 10:2–9 taken by many NT exegetes; so, e.g., Kremer, "Jesu Wort zur Ehescheidung," 53–54.

[114] This is the only case in the Synoptic tradition when the verb *gameō* ("to marry") has a woman as the subject and a man as the object. For women as the object rather than the subject of action in the OT passages on divorce, see Zakovitch, "The Woman's Rights," 34.

[115] See, e.g., Fitzmyer, "The Matthean Divorce Texts," 85–86; Kremer, "Jesu Wort zur Ehescheidung," 53; Lövestam, "Divorce and Remarriage," 46.

[116] After reviewing arguments for the composition of Mark's Gospel in Syria (or Palestine), John R. Donahue and Daniel J. Harrington (*The Gospel of Mark* [Sacra Pagina 2; Collegeville, MN: Liturgical Press, 2002] 41–46) opt for composition in Rome. R. T. France (*The Gospel of Mark* [New International Greek Testament Commentary; Grand Rapids, MI/Cambridge, UK: Eerdmans; Carlisle, UK: Paternoster, 2002] 35–41) refuses to make a choice in the matter, but he seems to lean in the direction of Rome. In favor of a Syrian setting is Joel Marcus, "The Jewish War and the *Sitz im Leben* of Mark," *JBL* 111 (1992) 441–62. It is difficult to see how locating Mark's Gospel in Syria explains his particular form of the prohibition of divorce, which presumes the legal power of women to divorce their husbands, when this point is totally absent in the Matthean and Lucan forms of the prohibition.

[117] Unfamiliarity with source, tradition, and redaction criticism of NT documents (and perhaps also a desire for wider attestation of a Jewish woman's power to divorce in the ancient world) leads Zakovitch ("The Woman's Rights," 33) to take the highly unusual view that Mark 10:11–12, including the wife's power to initiate a divorce, is possibly the original version of Jesus' teaching, which was then changed by Matthew and Luke. For a brief summary of the chief reasons for seeing v 12 as a later addition to the prohibition, see Raymond Collins, *Divorce in the New Testament*, 101–2.

[118] While the other Synoptic versions of the prohibition use either a participial form (e.g., *ho apolyōn*, "the one divorcing") or an indefinite relative clause (e.g., *hos an apolysē*, "whoever divorces"), with Matt 5:32 moving easily from the first to the second, no Synoptic version except Mark 10:12 uses the protasis of a condition introduced by *ei* or *ean* ("if").

[119] See Fitzmyer, "The Matthean Divorce Texts," 85; Sariola, *Markus und das Gesetz*, 143–44.

[120] The number of independent sources is reduced by those critics who deny that we have a distinct Q form of the prohibition. For example, both Donald A. Hagner (*Matthew* [Word Biblical Commentary 33A and 33 B; Dallas: Word, 1993, 1995] 1. 123) and Ulrich Luz (*Matthew 1–7* [Minneapolis: Augsburg, 1989; German original 1985] 300) deny the existence of a separate Q form of the tradition. Hagner, for instance, argues that Matt 5:31–32 is Matthew's redactional reworking of the teaching contained in Mark 10:2–12. This is unlikely for a number of reasons: (1) This approach ignores the distinctively Matthean phenomenon of a frequent and willing use of doublets; see, e.g., W. D. Davies and Dale C. Allison, Jr., *The Gospel According to Saint Matthew* (ICC; 3 vols.; Edinburgh: Clark, 1988, 1991, 1997) 1. 91–92, where Matthean doublets are put under the larger rubric of Matthew's love

of repetition). In light of this phenomenon, most commentators are disposed to explain Matt 5:32 and 19:9 as overlaps of Marcan and Q traditions, both taken over by Matthew. (2) As we have seen, Matt 5:32 and Luke 16:18 agree against Mark's divorce logion in a number of significant ways: e.g., both Matthew and Luke make the first subject of the sentence a nominative singular masculine participle used with the definite article as a substantive and modified by *pas* (*pas ho apolyōn*); nothing like this form occurs in Mark 10:11–12. In addition, the whole of Mark 10:12 disappears in both Matthew and Luke. When one considers all the similarities between Matt 5:32 and Luke 16:18, it strains credulity to believe that they are all examples of coincidence: Matthew and Luke, independently of each other, just happened to rewrite Mark's prohibition of divorce in the same way. (3) Put positively: as we have seen in our treatment of the Q tradition, there are, *pace* Luz, enough agreements between Matthew and Luke to reconstruct a credible Q form of the saying. (4) Matthew's redactional tendencies supply more than sufficient reasons why some of the wording of Matt 5:32 diverges from the Q form. Besides a possible accommodation to Jewish sensibilities, Matthew may have also chosen *poiei autēn moicheuthēnai* ("he causes her to be involved in adultery") instead of Q's straightforward *moicheuei* ("he commits adultery") to give his third antithesis (5:31–32) sufficient distinctiveness over against his second antithesis (5:27–28), which has at its core the opposition between *ou moicheuseis* ("you shall not commit adultery") and *emoicheusen* ("he committed adultery"). In favor of *moicheuei* being the original main verb in the Q tradition, one may observe that it is unlikely that Luke changed an original *poiei autēn moicheuthēnai* to *moicheuei* in order to assimilate his tradition to Mark 10:11. Besides the fact that Mark 10:11 (as well as Matt 5:32 and 19:9!) has the alternate verb *moichatai*, there is no clear reason why, if Luke is assimilating his version of the prohibition to Mark's, he should omit other traits of Mark's version, such as *ep' autēn*. One might also observe that the strict parallelism of *moicheuei* in Luke 16:18 a + b is characteristic of many sayings in Q.

[121] According to many commentators, e.g., Raymond Collins, *Divorce in the New Testament*, 214.

[122] In various ways and with various formulations, a number of authors use this valid point to avoid having Jesus come into direct conflict with or contradict the written Mosaic Law; so, e.g., Raymond Collins, *Divorce in the New Testament*, 178. One sees a similar approach to the problem of Jesus, divorce, and the Mosaic Law in the works of Sanders. For example, in his *Jesus and Judaism* (Philadelphia: Fortress, 1985) 256–60, Sanders argues that, in prohibiting divorce, Jesus is not directly defying the Mosaic Law since (1) practicing the Law more stringently than the Law actually demands is not illegal and (2) Moses did not command divorce, he only permitted it. It is odd to see Sanders playing the role of the Pharisees in Mark 10:4. Still, at the end of his treatment (p. 260), Sanders is left with an unresolved tension (in Jesus' position or his own?): "Yet we do see here [in Jesus' prohibition of divorce] the view that the Mosaic dispensation is not adequate." For a similar formulation, see his *Jewish Law from Jesus to the Mishnah* (London: SCM; Phila-

delphia: Trinity, 1990) 5; it is perhaps telling that, in a book dedicated to the thesis that Jesus in the Synoptics does not seriously challenge the Law as practiced in his day (the annulling of the food laws in Mark 7:15–19 is judged an unhistorical exception), there is no detailed treatment of his prohibition of divorce.

[123] On this, see Lövestam, "Divorce and Remarriage," 53.

[124] See the comment of Gundry (*Mark*, 543) on Mark 10:11: "That a man's marrying 'another woman' after divorcing his first wife constitutes adultery (v 11) presupposes and requires monogamy; for if polygamous relationships were legitimate, nothing would be wrong with remarriage to another woman, either."

[125] I purposely make this distinction between the applicability of discontinuity and the applicability of embarrassment because, strictly speaking, in Jesus' prohibition of divorce, discontinuity does not apply to the early church's teaching or actions. We know of Jesus' prohibition of divorce only because the early Christians handed on this teaching and because early Christian leaders (as early as Paul, and presumably other leaders before him) tried to enforce it in community life. Hence I think this is a case in which Tom Holmén's claim ("Doubts about Double Dissimilarity," *Authenticating the Words of Jesus* [NTTS 28/1; ed. Bruce Chilton and Craig A. Evans; Leiden/Boston/Cologne: Brill, 1999] 47–80) that, when it comes to applying the criteria to the Jesus tradition, we should not demand discontinuity from the Judaism prior to or contemporaneous with Jesus, but only from the early church, is proven wrong. In the case of divorce, discontinuity applies precisely to Judaism, but not to the early church, while embarrassment applies to the early church, but not to Judaism. The prohibition of divorce is therefore a prime example of a case where the two closely allied criteria of discontinuity and embarrassment should be applied in tandem.

[126] See the treatment of this passage in Raymond Collins, *Divorce in the New Testament*, 40–64. While some commentators confidently affirm that Paul allows the remarriage of the Christian spouse after the dissolution of a mixed marriage, Collins (pp. 63–64) rightly emphasizes Paul's failure to speak clearly on this point. In the end, Collins judges that it is "quite likely" that Paul expected the Christian to remarry. My own view is that Paul remains silent on the subject because he is unsure in his own mind as to what the Christian caught in this difficult situation can or should do.

[127] See *A Marginal Jew*, 3. 47–73.

[128] On this, see Schoeps, "Restitutio Principii," 271–85.

[129] See *A Marginal Jew*, 3. 502–9.

[130] Some might argue that Jesus' opposition to or contradiction of the Mosaic Law's permission and regulation of divorce helps explain his trial and execution.

However, as we shall see, the precise reasons why Jesus was put to death are both complex and elusive. That any one legal position adopted by Jesus contributed in a major way to his death is, in my view, highly questionable. At most, such teaching may have been an aggravating factor within the convergence of many different causes leading to his death.

131 This is the commonly accepted view; see, e.g., the analysis of Marucci, *Parole*, 275–77.

132 The classic statement of this position is found in Rudolf Bultmann, *Die Geschichte der synoptischen Tradition* (FRLANT 29; 8th ed.; Göttingen: Vandenhoeck & Ruprecht, 1970) 39–56. However, in fairness to Bultmann it should be noted that he allows for the possibility that not only the core teaching in Mark 10:2–12 but even the scriptural argument may go back to Jesus (pp. 51–52).

133 Raymond Collins (*Divorce in the New Testament*, 71) notes that Martin Albertz, Rudolf Bultmann, Martin Dibelius, and Vincent Taylor all share this view. For Mark's editorial activity in creating a unitary composition in 10:2–12, see Collins's remarks on p. 74.

134 Because of the confused text-critical situation in Mark 10:2, some critics hold that "the Pharisees" as the subject of the verb "asked" is not original; according to this view, the 3d person plural verb was originally impersonal ("they asked," i.e., "the question was posed"). In my judgment, though, the weight of the manuscript evidence is in favor of retaining "Pharisees" as original; the only significant ancient Greek manuscript to omit "Pharisees" entirely is the quirky Codex Bezae (D). The 4th edition of the *UBSGNT* gives the presence of "Pharisees" a "B" rating (the text is "almost certain"). For the dispute among the experts, see *TCGNT* (2d ed., 1994), 88. The presence of the Pharisees in the original version of the dispute would help explain the hostile tone, seen not only in *peirazontes auton* ("testing him") in v 2 but also in Jesus' polemical references to "you" and "your hardness of heart" in vv 4–5. Without the presence of the Pharisees, the fierce thrust of "you" and "your" is rhetorically puzzling.

135 See Raymond Collins, *Divorce in the New Testament*, 73–79, 102–3. In his discussion, Collins adopts the terminology of Arland J. Hultgren (*Jesus and His Adversaries. The Form and Function of the Conflict Stories in the Synoptic Tradition* [Minneapolis: Augsburg, 1979]): Mark 10:2–12 is a conflict story of the "non-unitary" type, i.e., the adversary's question is a secondary construction. However, Collins (p. 99) holds that Jesus' command in v 9, unlike the scriptural argumentation that precedes it, stems from early tradition and is not simply a creation of Mark.

136 See his detailed treatment in Sariola, *Markus und das Gesetz*, 121–37, with a convenient summary of his views on pp. 136–37. Sariola thinks that in the first unit (vv 2–9), Marcan redaction is limited to v 2ac and v 8b.

[137] This is especially true of older commentaries on Matthew, some of which were nevertheless quite critical for their day. For example, Willoughby C. Allen (*The Gospel According to S. Matthew* [ICC; 3d ed.; Edinburgh: Clark, 1912] 201–3) connects Matthew's version of the dispute story on divorce (Matt 19:3–9) with the dispute between the Houses in *m. Giṭ* 9:10, but then uses this insight to argue that Matthew's version is secondary to Mark's and shows Matthew's accommodation of the story to "the stricter school of Jewish theologians." The older commentaries on Mark were not always so careful. For example, Ezra P. Gould (*The Gospel According to St. Mark* [ICC; Edinburgh: Clark, 1896] 182–84) interprets the Marcan version of the dispute in terms of the dispute between the Houses; quite uncritically, he claims that "there is nothing to choose between the two accounts" of Mark and Matthew. Contrast this with the emphasis on the evidence from the Dead Sea Scrolls and Murabbaʿat in the commentary of Donahue and Harrington, *The Gospel of Mark*, 292–98. In more recent commentaries, often both Qumran and the Houses are mentioned, though with the emphasis quite rightly on the Qumran material; so, e.g., Craig A. Evans, *Mark 8:27–16:20* (Word Biblical Commentary 34B; Nashville: Nelson, 2001) 76–86.

[138] This may be suggested by Mark's negative comment that the Pharisees asked Jesus the question *peirazontes auton* ("testing him"—*peirazō* always has a negative connotation in the Synoptics). Knowing Jesus' opposition to any and all divorce, they seek to draw him out on this point and perhaps accuse him of directly contradicting the Mosaic Law. While this is a conceivable scenario on the historical level, nothing in Mark prepares the reader to understand the scene in this way. Another possible scenario on the historical level is that the Pharisees knew of the rejection of divorce with remarriage by the Essenes and wanted to find out whether Jesus agreed with the Essenes on this point; so Fitzmyer, "The Matthean Divorce Texts," 97–99. But did the Essenes actually reject all possibility of divorce and remarriage? As we have seen, the answer to that question is not as clear today as it once seemed.

[139] The plural "you" (*hymin*) in v 3 means, in the world of Mark's story, the Pharisees with their (erroneous) understanding of the Law over against Jesus with his (authoritative) understanding. Loader (*Jesus' Attitude towards the Law*, 88–89) suggests that the combination of the idea of Moses giving commandments with the emphatic "you" probably implies "distance between Jesus' teaching and the instruction Moses gave," though Jesus is directly distancing himself from the Pharisees. On the level of Mark's own time and place, the opposition implied in the question may be between Judaism and first-generation Christianity.

[140] What is explicit in Matt 5:31 is implied here in Mark 10:4: the command to give the divorced wife a certificate of divorce is considered a separate command within the convoluted sentence of Deut 24:1–4. As we have seen, Josephus and the later rabbis (but not Philo) read Deut 24:1–4 in a similar way; see Marucci, *Parole*, 132–33. It should be noted that the verb that is usually translated in Mark 10:4 as "permit" (*epitrepō*) can also mean "order," "instruct." However, Walter Bauer in

his *Wörterbuch* (6th ed., 1988; likewise Frederick William Danker's revision of the 3d ed. of BAGD, 2000) assigns Mark 10:4 to the texts illustrating the meaning "permit"; in fact, Bauer lists no NT passage among his examples of the meaning "order." Similarly, Max Zerwick and Mary Grosvenor (*A Grammatical Analysis of the Greek New Testament* [5th rev. ed.; Rome: Biblical Institute, 1996] 139) give only the meaning "allow" for Mark 10:4.

141 By claiming that Moses wrote this commandment for "you" (i.e., the Pharisees) to expose "your" hardness of heart, the Marcan Jesus implicitly lumps the Pharisees together with the rebellious Israelites of the wilderness generation. The Mosaic Law they presume to cite as experts actually bears witness against them. On this, see Rudolf Pesch, *Das Markusevangelium* (HTKNT 2; 2 vols.; Freiburg/Basel/Vienna: Herder, 1976, 1977) 2. 123.

142 The Greek preposition *pros* may convey both ideas in this passage; see Loader, *Jesus' Attitude*, 89. Gundry (*Mark*, 538) prefers the idea that Moses intended to incite (rather than to expose) their hardness of heart; see also Sariola, *Markus and das Gesetz*, 139–40. On the concept of "hardness of heart," see Klaus Berger, "Hartherzigkeit und Gottes Gesetz. Die Vorgeschichte des antijüdischen Vorwurfs in Mc 10:5," *ZNW* 61 (1970) 1–47. The article is taken from a chapter of Berger's larger work, *Die Gesetzesauslegung Jesu* and enunciates one of the major theses running through the book.

143 Possibly the Greek phrase *apo de archēs ktiseōs* ("but from the beginning of creation") in Mark 10:6 alludes to the opening Hebrew words (and, in due time, the Hebrew title) of Genesis: *bĕrē'šît*, "in the beginning." It is unfortunate that some commentators (betraying a theological concern with Law within a particular Christian context) speak in too sweeping a fashion of the Marcan Jesus opposing creation to Law. In reality, the creation narrative of Genesis is the beginning of the whole Torah, the whole Law, of Moses.

144 In his argument, Jesus quietly fuses Gen 1:27, a text in which God is the subject of the sentence, with Gen 2:24, a text in which (in the original context) the narrator of Genesis is speaking of a man's natural attraction to a woman (as the narrator comments on the creation of Eve from the side of Adam—or, less likely, as Adam himself comments on the creation of Eve). By welding the two Genesis texts together, Jesus tacitly makes God the ultimate actor in the entire citation. Hence, quite logically, Jesus concludes his argument with a statement about what *God* has done as opposed to what human beings try to do but cannot do because their attempt at divorce is contrary to God's primordial will inscribed in the very structure of creation. The idea of only one male united with only one female to create a marriage of only two persons (hence a monogamous and permanent union) may already be intimated in the citation of Gen 1:27: "Male and female [understood as one each] he created them [i.e., these two and only these two persons]." As we have seen, Gen 1:27 is already cited against polygyny (and possibly divorce with remarriage) in CD

4:21. This parallel argues against taking everything in this Marcan dispute story as a creation of "the Hellenistic church" outside of Jewish Palestine.

[145] The phrase "and cleave to his wife" in Mark 10:7 is missing in a number of significant MSS (e.g., Vaticanus and Sinaiticus) and may not be original in the text. The 4th edition of the *UBSGNT* gives it a "C" rating and places it in brackets, indicating that the phrase "may be regarded as part of the text, but that in the present state of New Testament textual scholarship this cannot be taken as completely certain" (p. 2*). In the opinion of David Noel Freedman (letter addressed to me, dated September 14, 2002), the missing phrase "is just another case of patent (or probable) haplography." That is, a scribe's eye may have jumped from one phrase in the manuscript before him to a later similar phrase, accidentally omitting everything in between. Fortunately, a decision on this point does not affect our main concern about the teaching of the historical Jesus on divorce. In favor of keeping the phrase as part of the original text of Mark, see Sariola, *Markus und das Gesetz*, 123.

[146] The Greek *hoi dyo* ("the two") in v 8, while present in the LXX, is not represented in the MT. This leads many commentators to suggest that this argument could not have come from the historical Jesus and must be a formulation of the early Greek-speaking church; so, e.g., Raymond Collins, *Divorce in the New Testament*, 90. Unfortunately, we lack Qumran fragments for this verse in Genesis. However, in addition to the LXX, "the two" is found in Philo, the Samaritan Pentateuch (and its targum), the Syriac, the Vulgate, and the *Targum of Pseudo-Jonathan*. Hence there is a possibility that both the LXX and Mark 10:8 reflect an alternate Hebrew text or oral tradition current around the time of Jesus. Be that as it may, the argument as it stands in Mark's text implicitly rejects polygyny even as it explicitly rejects divorce.

[147] Here we have a typical theme of Jewish apocalyptic hope: the end time will involve a return to the holy and wholesome goodness of God's original creation (or, as the Germans put it, *Urzeit und Endzeit*: as it was in the beginning, so it shall be in the end—only better).

[148] The idea that it was God himself who joined together a husband and a wife in marriage was not foreign to early Palestinian Judaism. See, e.g., the Prayer of Tobias as he enters into marriage with his wife Sarah: "You made Adam; for him you made his wife Eve as a helper and support" (Tob 8:6). While the imagery of yoking is not common in ancient Semitic texts dealing with marriage, it is not totally absent; see Lipiński, "The Wife's Right to Divorce," 9–27, esp. p. 17.

[149] The use of *anēr* and *anthrōpos* in Mark 10:2–12 is subtle and shifting. In the opening question of the Pharisees in v 2, *anēr* means the male, the husband, who can divorce his wife (*gynē*). In v 7, in the citation of Gen 2:24, *anthrōpos* means the male who joins himself to a woman who becomes his wife. But in Jesus' concluding apodictic commandment (v 9), which flows from his exegesis of Genesis 1–2,

anthrōpos instead means "any human being" as opposed to God (at least in the present state of the Marcan text); see Marucci, *Parole*, 300. In turn, this generic use of *anthrōpos* prepares the way for the twofold casuistic prohibition in vv 11–12, where both the male (*anēr*) and the female (*gynē*) are forbidden to divorce their spouses; see Sariola, *Markus und das Gesetz*, 145. It remains hypothetically possible that, if a form of v 9 circulated independently in early Christian tradition, especially within Palestine, the word now represented by *anthrōpos* might have referred to a male, since only a male could execute a divorce in Palestinian Judaism.

[150] A number of scholars feel that the apodictic command in v 9 reflects Greek vocabulary and syntax so strongly that it cannot be attributed to the historical Jesus; so, e.g., Hultgren, *Jesus and His Adversaries*, 120–21; Raymond Collins, *Divorce in the New Testament*, 76. For the contrary view, see Gundry, *Mark*, 540–41. To be sure, the Greek verbs *sy(n)zeugnymi* ("to yoke") and *chōrizō* ("to separate") are common Hellenistic Greek verbs signifying "to marry" and "to divorce" respectively. The verb *chōrizō* ("separate"), while used for divorce in Hellenistic literature (pagan, Jewish, and Christian), is not employed in this sense in the LXX or anywhere else in the Gospels. In addition, the word order of the concise sentence in v 9, introduced by a relative pronoun in the accusative, is more typical of Greek than of Hebrew or Aramaic grammar. Nevertheless, these facts by themselves do not decide the ultimate question of the historicity of the saying in v 9 or of the incident described in Mark 10:2–12. As was pointed out in *A Marginal Jew*, 1. 178–79, "The mere fact that a particular Greek saying can be retroverted into Aramaic with ease—or, on the other hand, only with great difficulty—does not give us a sure indication that the saying existed originally in Aramaic or originally in Greek. One Aramaic saying might be translated with great skill into elegant Greek, the translator aiming at sense-equivalence rather than word-for-word rendering. Another Aramaic saying might be translated by another translator in a very literalistic, wooden fashion." In particular, while the construction of a sentence introduced by a relative pronoun in the accusative is more frequent in Greek than in Semitic languages, some examples can be found in the Hebrew text of the OT: e.g., Gen 41:55 ("Whatever he tells you, do"), Ps 69:5 ("What I did not steal, should I restore?"), and Prov 3:12 ("Whom Yahweh loves, he reproves"). In all these cases, the LXX follows the Hebrew construction word for word. Interestingly, neither the ancient Peshitta nor modern retroversions of the Gospels into Hebrew have any difficulty reproducing the grammatical construction of Mark 10:9; see, e.g., *The New Covenant Commonly Called the New Testament. Peshiṭta Aramaic Text with a Hebrew Translation* (Jerusalem: The Bible Society in Israel, 1986) 59; Franz Delitzsch, *spry hbryt hḥdš* (London: Bible Society, 1960) 81. As for the precise form of the 3d person imperative, it may represent an Aramaic imperfect used as a jussive.

[151] Raymond Collins (*Divorce in the New Testament*, 74–79) points out that the language in v 9 is different from that of the initial question in v 2. He suggests that v 9 is a logion of Jesus taken over from the tradition and supported by a scriptural proof text created ad hoc. Collins (p. 90) presupposes the common view of form

critics, namely, that Scripture in the mouth of Jesus is a secondary creation of the early church. Whether or not this is true in the specific case of Mark 10:6–8, I find it a strange presupposition that a noted Jewish teacher, preaching for over two years to his fellow Jews, would never cite or argue from the Jewish Scriptures, especially the Mosaic Torah.

[152] The theoretical difference between the two distinct prohibitions of divorce might be summarized as follows: v 9 emphasizes that divorce itself is contrary to the will of the Creator and therefore unlawful; vv 11–12 add that divorce-plus-remarriage constitutes adultery. In practice, no great difference between the two pronouncements would be felt by the ordinary Jew. In most cases, a man divorces his wife with the proximate or remote intention of remarrying.

[153] Schaller ("Die Sprüche," 104–24) takes the unusual view that the apodictic prohibition in Mark 10:9 goes back to the historical Jesus, while all the various casuistic forms of the prohibition, which equate divorce and remarriage with adultery, represent developments of the teaching in the early church. As I hope to have shown above, the criteria of historicity argue that some form of the casuistic prohibition does go back to Jesus. My own view is closer to Nolland's: after arguing for the historicity of a form of the prohibition resembling Luke 16:18, Nolland ("The General Prohibition of Divorce," 34–35) goes on to suggest that this casuistic form of the prohibition represents a particular application of Jesus' general dictum on marriage contained in Mark 10:9.

[154] In most instances of casuistic law, the first part (the protasis, some form of a subordinate conditional clause) states the case being considered or the action being prohibited; then the second part (the apodosis, the main clause) states the penalty that will be incurred if the prohibited action is performed. However, in some examples of casuistic law, the apodosis contains a statement of guilt rather than a specification of penalty. The prohibition expressed in Matt 5:32 ‖ Luke 16:18 and Mark 10:11 reflects this latter type of casuistic law; see Fitzmyer, "The Matthean Divorce Texts," 82. Raymond Collins (*Divorce in the New Testament*, 168–70) seems uncomfortable with the Matthean Jesus enunciating his prohibition of divorce in the form of casuistic law; Collins wishes to see the prohibition instead as simply the provocative language of a prophet. Yet Collins's own strategic move of relegating the Matthean exceptive clause to a later chapter (pp. 184–213) betrays the problem with this approach: one inserts a specific exception into a prohibition if one understands that prohibition to be a law commanding or forbidding particular concrete actions; one does not deal that way with prophetic exhortations. One detects a similar discomfort with Jesus' issuing of a precise command in Loader's treatment of Mark 10:9 (*Jesus' Attitude*, 89–90 n. 165). Loader insists that v 9, especially when taken in isolation, is a provocative *māšāl*, a riddle (such as we see in the dispute traditions lying behind Mark 2:1–3:6; 7:1–23), and not a prescriptive response, though he admits that the (later) introduction of the scriptural argument creates more of a prescriptive response and probably an image of Jesus "standing independently of

Moses and Judaism." Mark, says Loader, clearly understands the *māšāl* "as a statement of law by Jesus for his community." I am not sure that this does full justice to
the special character of Mark 10:9, even taken in isolation: (1) While Mark 10:9 is
indeed a short, sharp, pithy, and memorable saying—and to that extent a *māšāl*—it
contains no metaphorical comparison and so is not a *māšāl* in the fullest sense of
the word. (2) Loader's comparison with the dispute traditions lying behind Mark
2:1–3:6 and 7:1–23 is not entirely apt; nowhere in those traditions does Jesus speak
the kind of apodictic command expressed in the 3d person singular imperative that
we find in Mark 10:9. (3) When Mark 10:9 is brought into relationship with the type
of prohibition found in Luke 16:18 and Mark 10:11, the correlation with the two
basic forms of law, apodictic and casuistic, is hard to miss. In the end, one wonders
whether Christian scholars have difficulty coming to terms with a Jewish Jesus issuing normative *hălākâ* to his Jewish disciples on questions of Torah observance.

[155] So, e.g., Lövestam, "Divorce and Remarriage," 47. It is telling that Marucci
(*Parole*, 298) suggests that Mark, in his presentation of the dispute on divorce
(10:2–12), does not seem aware of the debate between the Schools of Shammai and
Hillel over the grounds for divorce found in Deut 24:1–4. Marucci does not stop to
ask whether this particular rabbinic debate existed at the time of the formulation
of the Marcan text. Mark's silence on the subject may signify something other than
ignorance.

CHAPTER 33

THE PROHIBITION OF OATHS

I. INTRODUCTION

In the previous chapter, we ran into a puzzling phenomenon. On the one hand, Jesus was a 1st-century Jew who, like any other religious Jew, lived under and embraced the value of the Mosaic Law. As we shall see in subsequent chapters, he accepted central institutions and teachings of the Law (e.g., observance of the sabbath)—although, like many of his coreligionists, he argued over the precise way one should observe the Law. On the other hand, as we saw in the last chapter, Jesus also prohibited the use of an important institution accepted and regulated by the Law: divorce. In effect, Jesus taught that a pious Jewish male who carefully observed all the requirements of Jewish law and custom in divorcing his wife sinned against the Decalogue's commandment: "You shall not commit adultery."

One suspects that his prohibition of divorce would have disturbed some of Jesus' otherwise sympathetic hearers, and for good reason. Unlike most of his other pronouncements about legal observance, Jesus' prohibition of divorce abrogated an important social institution permitted and regulated by the Torah. While such abrogation is highly unusual within Jesus' overall approach to the Law, one case of abrogation is one case too many for scholars who wish to depict a Jesus whose views on the Law were totally within the boundaries of acceptable Jewish teaching and practice of his day. The question therefore becomes pressing: Were there any other instances in which the historical Jesus abrogated an institution or practice allowed and regulated by the Law? While many authors claim that there are none, one candidate is at times suggested: Jesus' alleged prohibition of swearing, that is, taking an oath.[1] Before we take up the question of Jesus' teaching on oaths, though, it would be helpful to "clear the ground" by making some initial observations about oaths in general and more specifically about their place in Judaism before and around the time of Jesus.

II. OATHS: FROM THE JEWISH SCRIPTURES
TO THE MISHNA

A. INITIAL CLARIFICATIONS

In both the ancient and the modern world, the very word "oath" (as well as the concept it expresses) is a slippery commodity. Both Judaism and Christianity slowly developed clear definitions and classifications of oaths and vows, but such clarity is not to be presumed around the time of Jesus. After all, even today different authors make different distinctions between oaths and vows.[2] To adopt one common approach: we might define an oath as an assertion or promise that calls upon God to act as witness to the truth of what the oath-taker says, especially when the truth is uncertain or contested by others. In contrast, a vow is addressed directly to God and promises him some object or action that is supposedly pleasing to him or, alternately, promises to abstain from an object or action. In some cases, the promised action or object is offered to God by way of exclusive dedication to his temple or his service.

Even these neat, abstract definitions indicate already the possibility of confusion between oaths and vows. An oath may be either an assertion or a promise. To use later terminology not employed in the OT or intertestamental literature and only hinted at in the Mishna, an oath is either assertory or promissory.[3] An assertory oath solemnly affirms—with God as the speaker's witness—the truth about some past or present event, action, or state of affairs: for example, "I did not commit adultery" (cf. Num 5:11–31) or "I am not in possession of the stolen goods" (cf. Exod 22:6–12). A promissory oath refers instead to some future action or state of affairs: for example, "I will fulfill your commission by journeying to a foreign land and arranging a marriage for your son" (cf. Gen 24:1–9).

One can sense immediately that the promissory oath may easily overlap the legal and religious territory covered by a vow. We need not be surprised, then, that from the OT through the intertestamental literature to the Mishna and the tannaitic midrashim, the boundary lines between oaths and vows easily blur, as do the terms themselves.[4] If this is true in legal texts and sacred narratives, one can reasonably suppose that the confusion was even greater "on the ground," in the daily lives of the uneducated masses. One need only think of how, even among educated people in modern society, phrases like "swearing" and "cursing" are used vaguely and widely beyond the proper bounds of the words' technical definitions. Often any sort of vulgar, obscene, irreverent, or blasphemous speech is referred to as "swearing" or "cursing." In what follows, I will adhere to the technical sense of oaths previously outlined. More specifically, I will be concerned with oaths and swearing, but at times it will be necessary to touch on vows as well.

B. OATHS IN ANCIENT ISRAEL AND JUDAISM

In the Jewish Scriptures, as in the ancient Near East in general, oaths were taken for granted in the formal contexts of law[5] and religion as well as in the loose give-and-take of everyday life. Oaths are found in every part of the Jewish Scriptures (Law, Prophets, and the Writings), and everyone from the Deity through the king to the wife suspected of adultery is presented as swearing. The institution itself is almost never seen to be a problem. Indeed, the Mosaic Torah lists swearing by the name of Yahweh as an obligation contained within the overarching covenant obligation to fear, obey, and worship Yahweh (so, e.g., Deut 10:20).[6] Problems lie rather in the abuse of oaths: for example, affirming what one knows is not true, failing to fulfill promissory oaths, or swearing frivolously and all too frequently.

Unlike divorce, which is an option that a husband *may* employ practically at will, there are a few cases in which the Torah commands that an oath *must* be taken.[7] Especially prominent are (i) the oath taken to attest a person's innocence and therefore to absolve him of the obligation to pay damages after animals entrusted to his care have died or suffered injury (see Exod 22:9–10 [ET: 22:10–11]); and (ii) the oath administered by a priest to a wife suspected by her husband of adultery (see Num 5:11–31). As to the first instance: if, for example, a person going on journey entrusts some animals or goods to a neighbor and then the animals or goods "go missing" or suffer harm, the neighbor is to take an oath affirming that he had nothing to do with the disappearance of or harm to the animals or the goods. He is then quit of legal liability and does not have to pay damages. In the case of a husband who suspects his wife of adultery, the wife is to be brought to the sanctuary and given a mixture of holy water, dust, and ink by a priest. The priest then imposes an oath on the wife—actually, a self-curse that will cause grave harm to the wife's inner organs if she is lying in protesting her innocence. In the case of the entrusted goods, the Hebrew wording of the law gives no indication that the oath is optional for the neighbor; he is to take it.[8] Likewise, while it is up to the suspicious husband to decide whether he wishes to bring his wife to the sanctuary for the ritual of the "water of bitterness," once he does so, the wife has no option but to undergo the ritual, including the oath. Hence one sees immediately the larger problem posed by Jesus' supposed prohibition of oaths. To prohibit all oath-taking was not only to abrogate an institution permitted by the Law, as in the case of divorce. Prohibiting oaths unavoidably involved abrogating individual commandments in the Torah that enjoined oaths in specific situations. To be sure, these were commandments of casuistic rather than apodictic law. Nevertheless, they were commandments of the written Torah.

In the preexilic period in general and in the Pentateuch in particular, one does not detect any unease with the institution of oaths as such or any tendency to restrict—let alone abolish—them. Strictures are voiced only against swearing to what is not true or against failing to fulfill an oath. Similarly, in both the pre- and postexilic period, the prophets (e.g., Jer 5:2; 7:9; Zech 5:3–4; Mal 3:5) denounce false swearing, but do not criticize the institution per se. However, in the postexilic period (after 538 B.C.), especially once Hellenistic culture begins to spread in Palestine, a new attitude surfaces in some Jewish texts. Although the wisdom literature of the OT on the whole does not concern itself with oaths,[9] diffidence appears in the late wisdom literature and in some of the Dead Sea Scrolls. While Qoheleth still views oath-taking as an esteemed undertaking (Qoh 9:2),[10] Ben Sira (Sir 23:9–11) speaks bluntly against the evil of swearing too frequently or in a frivolous manner.[11] Ben Sira's critique may reflect the influence of Greek philosophy, which from early on entertained both theological and ethical reservations about oath-taking.[12]

In the Qumran manuscripts, the narrative texts speak of oaths without any indication that swearing poses a special problem. It is in the legal texts that a certain tension in the community's attitude toward oaths is detectable.[13] On the one hand, a desire to restrict oaths is visible in specific areas. For example, some texts forbid oaths using the names "God" or "Lord" (*'ēl*, *'ĕlōhîm*, or *'ădônai*) as well as oaths between two individuals in private, without any authority of the community being present (CD 15:1–4; 9:8–12). On the other hand, some texts refer to the solemn oaths that accompanied entrance into the community (1QS 1:18–2:19; CD 15:5–13). These oaths were apparently also used in other circumstances for solemn affirmations (e.g., in cases involving property crimes). The obligation of fulfilling oaths and/or vows and the power to annul them are dealt with in the *Damascus Document* (CD 16:6–12 and the parallel in 4Q271, fragment 7, column 2). The fierce emphasis in a statement like "every binding oath by which anyone imposes upon himself [the obligation] to fulfill a letter of the law, he should not annul, even at the price of death" (CD 16:7; cf. 4Q271, fragment 7, column 2, lines 8–9) hardly reflects a community that totally rejects oaths. One also finds at Qumran detailed consideration of when a vow or oath may be annulled, especially in the case of a wife or a daughter over whom a husband or father is considered to exercise authority (see, e.g., 4QInstruction[b] [4Q416], fragment 2, column 4, lines 8–9). Hence, while they were carefully regulated and their use limited, oaths were still alive and well in the Essene communities.[14] Since the Essenes in general and the Qumranites in particular were often the most radical Palestinian-Jewish groups when it came to interpreting, reinterpreting, and even rewriting the Law, the lack of a total prohibition of oaths among the Essenes may be taken as a reliable indicator that no Jewish movement in Palestine around the turn of the era absolutely forbade swearing.

The various reservations or restrictions that one sees in Ben Sira and the Essenes become much more emphatic in the great representative of Diaspora Judaism, Philo. Indeed, one can detect a noticeable tension between Philo's dislike of oaths and his loyalty to the Law of Moses.[15] On the one hand, Philo's reverence for the holy name of God and his horror at the idea that puny human beings should drag God as a witness into their legal affairs led him to urge an avoidance of oaths whenever possible. On the other hand, as an interpreter of Torah and as a cosmopolitan who knows full well the juridical and commercial necessities of the real world, Philo has to allow a place for oaths in human affairs. Philo seeks to resolve the tension he feels by stressing that swearing must be the last resort for a person who has no other legal option left. Even in such cases, swearing truthfully is still only "the second best way." [16] Nevertheless, in these cases, oaths cannot be avoided because a refusal to swear would mean that an innocent person would suffer an injustice. When faced with such extreme circumstances, one should swear—though not by God himself, but rather by some substitute formula that refers to God indirectly. Interestingly, among the substitute formulas that Philo recommends are oaths by earth or heaven[17]—a subterfuge that directly contradicts the prohibition voiced by Jesus in Matt 5:34–35. Thus, Philo is especially instructive for our purposes. Left to himself and to the inner logic of his philosophy, Philo might well have forbidden all swearing. It is precisely his identity as a Jew bound by prescriptions of the Mosaic Law that forces him to accept the institution of the oath in certain cases and with certain circumlocutions. The contrast with the Jesus of Matt 5:34–37 could not be starker.

No such tension or critique can be detected in Josephus, who, after all, is a historian rather than a philosopher.[18] Of necessity, his story of Israel from creation down to the destruction of the temple by the Romans is filled with people—as well as God—swearing oaths. Understandably, Josephus never stops to engage in detailed Philonic reflections on oaths (which he, like Philo, typically conflates with vows).[19] As a politician, military commander, turncoat supporter of the Roman emperor, and landowner, he had probably taken his fair share of oaths in his lifetime; he may have even kept some of them. His description of the Essenes, however imperfect, shows that he knew that some Jews viewed oaths as problematic.[20] But such hesitations are reported, not shared.

To complete our quick overview of oaths in ancient Judaism, let us leap forward a century or so to the Mishna, which contains the first rabbinic attempt to systematize oaths as well as to curtail the proliferation of unnecessary oaths. Significantly, the tractate on vows (*Nedarim*, "Vows") is placed in the third Seder (Division, Order) of the Mishna (i.e., *Našim*, "Women"), while the tractate on oaths (*Šebuʿot*, "Oaths") is placed in the fourth Seder (*Neziqin*, "Damages"). This separation already betrays a systematizing intention that seeks to distinguish between oaths and vows as well as to classify them. This thrust, however, is not carried through consistently. For example, while the essence of the distinction between assertory and promissory oaths can be found in *m. Šeb.* 3:1, the distinction is not applied rigorously and systematically. Moreover, a number of sayings in *Nedarim* might more properly be placed in *Šebuʿot*. The continued confusion between oaths and vows is hardly surprising since one strategy of the rabbis was to urge the use of vows to diminish the wide use of oaths. In fact, the kind of oath used by common people in everyday affairs is often referred to in talmudic literature as a *nēder* ("vow"). Nevertheless, the Mishna marks the beginning of an attempt to bring order into the messy business of swearing.

One pertinent novelty that we meet in the Mishna is the permission given to abstain from taking an otherwise obligatory oath in the case of entrusted goods that have been lost or stolen (*m. B. Meṣ* 3:1).[21] Instead of taking the oath prescribed in the Torah that he had nothing to do with the disappearance of the goods, the person entrusted with the items may choose to pay the owner of the goods compensation for the loss. A similar disinclination to take an oath is indicated in *t. Soṭa* 7:(3)4, though the precise legal situation that occasions this refusal is not specified. Possibly the reference is simply to a person who refuses to take an oath in court because he is conscious of the fact that he would be swearing falsely.[22] Be that as it may, these new mitigations of the law that make allowances for scruples about taking oaths are products of the rabbinic period, with no clear examples coming from the pre-70 era. When these mitigations do appear, they are optional ways of avoiding certain oaths, not a sweeping prohibition of all oaths. Indeed, for all the attempts of individual rabbis to restrict or even, in some cases, to suppress oath-taking, oaths were too much embedded in the legal procedures and everyday lives of Jews for swearing ever to be eradicated.[23] In sum, the major thrust of rabbinic literature is to systematize and regulate oaths, although this thrust is accompanied by an attempt to restrict or even suppress oaths where possible, especially if the oath concerns a trivial matter.[24]

III. THE PROHIBITION OF OATHS
IN THE NEW TESTAMENT

A. The Special Situation of the New Testament Sources

Granted the importance, widespread use, and yet increasingly problematic nature of oaths in ancient Judaism, the total prohibition of oaths, attributed to Jesus in Matt 5:33–37, is paradoxically both intelligible and shocking. It is intelligible in the sense that, given the common use yet growing critique of oaths in Judaism, one might readily suppose that a prominent religious teacher and ethical guide would pronounce on the subject. Moreover, granted the criticism of oaths found already in Ben Sira and magnified in Philo, and granted the stringency of Jesus' teaching on matters like divorce, one might well expect Jesus to express grave reservations about oaths and, à la Philo, command his disciples to avoid swearing whenever possible. All that would cohere perfectly with Jesus' 1st-century Jewish milieu. The shock comes when we see that Jesus—at least in Matthew's Gospel—apparently replicates his approach to divorce: the reservation and critique witnessed in some quarters of Judaism are pushed to the extreme of outright prohibition. But do we have here another radical command of the historical Jesus or an example of the idiosyncratic stream of Christian-Jewish hălākâ found in the special M tradition of Matthew's Gospel? After all, neither Paul, who swears with abandon, nor most of the other NT authors seem aware of Jesus' prohibition.[25] The question is complicated by the fact that, in the case of the prohibition of oaths, we are faced with a unique type of "Gospel parallel" that is not in a Gospel. The lone NT parallel to the prohibition in Matt 5:33–37 is found in the Epistle of James. Once we subtract the Matthean antithetical formula of 5:33–34a ("you have heard that it was said to the men of old . . . but I say to you"), Matt 5:34b–37 is identical to Jas 5:12 in its basic content and literary structure. It is to a detailed comparison and contrast of these sui generis "Gospel parallels" that we now turn.

B. An Initial Comparison of the Two Texts

Matt 5:34–37		*Jas 5:12*	
34a:	But I say to you	12a:	But above all, my brothers,
34b:	do not swear at all	12b:	do not swear
34c:	either by the heaven	12c:	either by the heaven
34d:	for it is the throne of God		
35a:	or by the earth	12d:	or by the earth
35b:	for it is the footstool of his feet		
35c:	or by Jerusalem	12e:	or by any other oath
35d:	for it is the city of the great King.		
36a:	Do not swear even by your head,		
36b:	for you cannot make one hair white or black.		
37a:	But your speech must be "yes yes, no no";	12f:	But your yes must be a yes, And [your] no [must be] a no,
37b:	anything more than these [words] is from the Evil [One].	12g:	lest you fall under judgment.

Practically no one denies that we are dealing here with two alternate forms of the same tradition.[26] (1) We have the same core content: "do not swear" + a string of (at least) three examples of formulas that are prohibited + a positive command that one's "yes" or "no" should be a straightforward and absolutely honest "yes" or "no." (2) We have the same literary structure: a negative command with *mē* ("not") that forbids any swearing, balanced antithetically with a positive command to speak simply and honestly (with the imperative of the verb "to be" plus the adversative *de* as the first two words), with a list of (at least) three examples of prohibited oath-formulas (connected by *mēti . . . mēti*, "neither . . . nor") positioned between the negative and positive commands. (3) Indeed, a good deal of the vocabulary in the Matthean and Jamesian pericopes is the same, though the precise grammatical forms often differ: for example, the verb *omnymi/omnyō* ("to swear"), preceded by the negative *mē* ("not"), a string of disjunctive particles *mēti . . . mēti* ("neither . . . nor"), *ouranos* ("heaven"), *gē* ("earth"), *hymōn* ("your"), an imperative form of the copulative verb *eimi* ("must be," "is to be"), and the emphatic repetition (in different ways) of *nai nai, ou ou* ("yes, yes," "no, no").

So striking is the shared material in Matt 5:34–37 and Jas 5:12 that the question arises whether there is a direct literary connection: that is, whether Matthew copied James or vice versa. Usually this suggestion is rejected,

and for good reason.[27] While there is a large amount of common content, structure, and vocabulary, there are also some notable differences.[28]
(1) Matthew's version of the prohibition is explicitly attributed to Jesus;
James' version is not. (2) Matthew's version of the prohibition forms the
fourth of the six antitheses (5:21–48) in his Sermon on the Mount; the antithetical formula (unique to Matt 5:21–48 in the whole of the NT) is lacking
in Jas 5:12.[29] (3) Some of the words and phrases shared by Matthew and
James are found in different grammatical forms. (4) The list of examples is
longer in Matthew (four versus the three in James), and the Matthean examples have reasons attached (the *hoti* clauses: "for . . ."). (5) The idea that the
prohibition is total is expressed clearly, but in different ways and in different
places in the two versions. Matthew expresses the totality of the prohibition at the beginning of the pericope with an adverb that is quite rare in the
NT: [*mē*] . . . *holōs* ("[not] at all").[30] James emphasizes the totality of the
prohibition not in the initial imperative but rather in the third of the three
examples, which, instead of being another specific formula, is expressed by
the generalizing phrase "or any other oath." (6) The positive imperatives of
the copulative verb ("must be") at the end of the tradition are variant forms:
Matthew uses the classical *estō*, while James has the Hellenistic popular
form *ētō*. (7) The demand for direct, simple, honest speech, inculcated in the
final command, is expressed differently. Matthew's version runs literally:
"But your speech (*logos*) must be 'yes yes, no no.' " James instead has: "But
your yes must be a yes and [your] no [must be] a no."

Some of these differences can be explained by each author's preferences
in vocabulary and style, by the redactional framework of the unit in each
author's larger composition, and finally by the overall difference in genre.
Matthew's work is a Gospel, while James' work is a parenetic composition,
that is, a work dealing with moral exhortation and admonition. Beyond
its basic parenetic character, the Epistle of James has been variously and
vaguely labeled a tractate, treatise, essay, homily, diatribe, or protreptic discourse, adorned with some of the traits of a pseudepigraphic letter (mainly
the epistolary *praescriptio* in Jas 1:1).[31] At any rate, at least some of the differences between the formulations of the prohibition in each author might
be put down to differences in genre. However, other differences do not seem
to be so easily explainable. The notably different way in which the totality
of the prohibition is expressed (Matthew's "not at all" versus James' "or by
any other oath") and the different way in which the language of "yes yes"
and "no no" is enjoined seem to argue against direct literary dependence or
a common literary source. Not surprisingly, therefore—and simply as a matter of fact—few would argue that Matthew copied from James or vice versa.

Moreover, direct literary dependence is highly unlikely if—as I think is the case—both works date from the last decades of the first century while at the same time they originate from different venues and theological contexts. As for a common literary source, the linguistic and stylistic differences listed above also make it unlikely that Matthew and James are drawing upon a single written source, such as an "M" document or the Matthean form of the Q document. In the end, all these comparisons and contrasts simply reinforce what is the common view among exegetes: Matt 5:34–37 and Jas 5:12 are two alternate literary forms (Gospel and epistolary parenesis) of a common oral tradition.[32]

C. The Earliest Available Version of the Tradition

What did the primitive oral tradition behind Matt 5:34–37 and Jas 5:12 look like?[33] Obviously, any attempt to retrieve the earliest form available to us must remain hypothetical. Still, the strong agreements between Matthew and James at key points plus notable disagreements at secondary points, along with the redactional tendencies of each author, provide us with some clues for reconstructing the primitive form of the prohibition. Since, as we have seen, neither Matthew nor James is directly dependent on the other's work, the parts of the tradition where they agree practically word for word almost certainly go back to the earlier oral source. The most secure parts of the original tradition wind up forming a two-part (negative command + positive command) formula:

Matthew	*James*
Do not swear at all	Do not swear [by any other oath]
either by the heaven or by the earth;	either by the heaven or by the earth;
but your speech must be	But your yes must be a yes
"yes yes, no no."	and your no must be a no.

As one would expect, in this pruning process the much longer Matthean version of the prohibition suffers the loss of more members than does the Jamesian version. But is this method by way of subtraction correct? To provide a check on the accuracy of our pruning, we need to engage in a closer inspection of the Matthean clauses and phrases we have omitted, with the hope that it will confirm the secondary nature of the Matthean members absent in our hypothetical "original tradition."

Almost all critics identify Matt 5:36 ("do not swear by your head . . .") as a secondary accretion to the tradition. Not only does it lack any sort of corresponding phrase in Jas 5:12, it also breaks the pattern seen in the chain of the three examples in Matt 5:34c–35d.[34] Heaven, earth, and Jerusalem are all names of places important in Israel's sacred traditions: specifically, the creation narrative and God's choice of Jerusalem for the site of his temple. Indeed, all three explanatory (*hoti*) clauses allude to Scripture texts that echo the sacral themes of creation and election (e.g., Gen 1:1; Isa 66:1; LXX Ps 10:4; LXX Ps 98:5; LXX Ps 47:3). In contrast, the reference to an oath by one's head, which is rejected on grounds of a commonsense view of life more at home in the wisdom tradition, comes from a different intellectual milieu. In other words, the explanation (*hoti* clause) for the prohibition in v 36 is entirely different from the explanations in vv 34–35. In the latter, the ultimate objection to the oath-formulas listed is that they refer indirectly to God himself and hence in the end do not avoid calling upon the all-holy, all-truthful God as witness to man's sometimes immoral, sometimes untruthful statements.[35]

The objection to the oath formula in v 36 is quite different. Swearing by one's head implies that one has control over one's life (symbolized by one's head), while in fact one cannot control even the aging process or the span of one's years (symbolized by making one's hair white or black).[36] The fact that the oath by one's head is more widely attested in the pagan Greco-Roman world than in Jewish Palestine at the turn of the era,[37] the fact that, unlike the three previous examples, the example in v 36 repeats the verb "swear" (in the aorist subjunctive) as the main verb of a separate sentence, and the fact that the rest of Matt 5:34–37 is cast in the 2d person plural while 5:36 alone is cast in the 2d person singular all reinforce the almost universal conclusion that v 36 is a secondary expansion, added either by Matthew or by the M tradition before him.[38]

Moving back to the three examples in Matt 5:34–35, we notice immediately two striking points: (1) Jas 5:12 lacks the three *hoti* clauses that explain the prohibition of the three examples. (2) The third example of a prohibited oath, that is, Jerusalem (v 35cd), finds no parallel in the third "example" in Jas 5:12. Actually, instead of a third concrete example alongside "heaven" and "earth," Jas 5:12 adds "or any other oath," which, in its meaning, really parallels the "not at all" (*mē . . . holōs*) of Matt 5:34b.[39] Furthermore, "or by Jerusalem" in Matt 5:35c sticks out from the immediate context because, unlike "heaven" and "earth," it was not regularly used in Jewish oath formulas.[40] Confirming the status of "or by Jerusalem" as a later addition to the Matthean tradition is the small stylistic point that "heaven" and "earth" are governed by the preposition *en* with the dative ("by"), while "Jerusalem" is governed by the preposition *eis* with the accusative (literally, "to" or "into"). In sum, if we drop both the *hoti* clauses and the whole example of Jerusalem in Matt 5:34d + 35, we are left with simply "do not swear (at all), either by the heaven or by the earth" as the first (negative) half of the primitive tradition.

Another clause under suspicion is the last one in both the Matthean and Jamesian versions. Apparently, those who passed on both forms of the tradition sensed a need for a concluding clause to round out the whole unit and to supply, at the same time, a final rationale for the total prohibition. The Matthean formulation in 5:37b, "but anything more than these [words] is from the Evil [One]," displays two favorite Matthean words: *perisson/perisseuō* ("to be more," "to abound," "to overflow") and *ponēros* ("evil").[41] Hence 5:37b probably stems from the creative activity of either the M tradition or Matthew himself. By the same token, the final clause in Jas 5:12 does not seem to have belonged to the primitive oral tradition. Throughout his epistle, James shows a penchant for threats of eschatological judgment, of which Jas 5:12g is a prime example. Indeed, the pericope immediately preceding 5:12 dwells on "the parousia of the Lord" (5:7), which "has drawn near" (5:8). This occasions a warning against grumbling "lest you be judged" (*hina mē krithēte*)—which in grammar, content, and even vocabulary is almost identical with the warning at the end of 5:12, "lest you fall under judgment" (*hina mē hypo krisin pesēte*).[42] In sum, both warnings, Matt 5:37b and Jas 5:12g, are probably redactional additions to supply the prohibition with a rhetorically as well as logically satisfying conclusion.[43]

Stripping away the secondary accretions, we are left with a relatively simple core:

Matthew 5	*James 5*
34b: Do not swear [at all]	12b: Do not swear
34c: either by the heaven	12c: either by the heaven
35a: or by the earth.	12d: or by the earth.
	12e: [or by any other oath]
37a: But your speech must be	12f: But your yes must be a yes
"yes yes, no no."	and [your] no [must be] a no.

The reader will notice that I have retained in brackets Matthew's "at all" (5:34b) and James' "or any other oath" (5:12e) because they are independent witnesses to the presence of some reinforcing phrase stressing that the prohibition is absolute and total. Which formulation may be the more original is impossible to say. The adverb *holōs* ("at all") is very rare in the NT; the other three occurrences are all in 1 Corinthians. At the very least, we are not dealing with a phrase typical of Matthew or his M tradition. Similarly, *horkos* ("oath") is not a very common noun in the NT (twelve times in all, distributed among eight different books), and this is its only occurrence in James. Curiously, the adjective *allos* ("other"), despite its being a very common word in the NT (159 times in all), never occurs again in James. Thus, "or any other oath" (*mēti allon tina horkon*) could hardly be called language typical of James. The likely conclusion of these observations is that the two phrases "at all" and "or any other oath" are alternate forms that the early oral tradition employed to stress the absolute nature of the prohibition.[44]

To push my hypothetical suggestions one step further: shorn of any other specific oaths ("Jerusalem" or "your head"), the phrase "either by the heaven or by the earth" may serve not as an example of specific oath-formulas but rather as another way of emphasizing the totality of the prohibition. From the first pages of Genesis (e.g., Gen 1:1) to the last pages of the Book of Revelation (Rev. 21:1), the duality (or polar opposition) of heaven and earth is a common poetic way of saying "everything," "all things." [45] Throughout the Bible, the faith that God created all things is summed up in the statement that he made heaven and earth. Matthew's version of the Lord's Prayer famously sums up the universal doing of God's will in the phrase "as in heaven so too on earth" (6:10). Hence, it is possible that in the primitive tradition of the prohibition of oaths, the phrase "either by the heaven or by the earth" did not function as a list of possible oath-formulas but rather as a rhetorical way of emphasizing "no oaths whatsoever." If this is the case, then we would have three alternate versions of the emphasis on the totality of the prohibition in the early oral tradition: "not at all" (Matthew), "or any other oath" (James), "either by the heaven or by the earth" (both traditions). Even if this interpretation of "either by the heaven or by the earth" is not correct—and some commentators prefer to drop the whole phrase in order to reconstruct a still simpler primitive tradition—the variant traditions of "not at all" and "any other oath" make it fairly certain that the primitive tradition contained some way of stressing the absolute nature of the prohibition. Simply for the sake of convenience, in what follows I will retain the Matthean "not at all," without prejudice to the Jamesian form of the tradition. In any event, the earliest form of the logion certainly contained the initial prohibition "do not swear [at all]." If one were to drop the phrase "either by the heaven or by the earth" as the earliest expansion of the tradition, one would be left with an example of the sharp antithetical parallelism seen in other sayings of Jesus: "Do not swear at all; your yes must be a yes, and your no a no."

This brings us to the positive half of the command about oaths:

Matt 5:37a	*Jas 5:12f*
But your speech must be "yes yes, no no."	But your yes must be a yes, and [your] no a no.

At first glance, these two forms seem to be simply alternate versions of the same positive command: instead of using any oath whatever, restrict yourself to direct, simple, and, above all, honest affirmations and negations. Almost all commentators agree that this is the meaning that arises naturally out of the syntax of James' formulation. Using the syntactical structure of subject + copulative verb + predicate nominative, James writes a sentence whose clear sense is: "But your yes (*hymōn to nai*) must be (*ētō*) a [simple] yes, and [your] no [must be] a [simple] no." In other words, James makes the first "yes" the subject of the verb and the second "yes" the predicate nominative.

The Matthean formulation is more problematic. Matthew makes "your speech" (*ho logos hymōn*) the subject of the copulative verb, and so the two "yes's" and the two "no's" all become predicate nominatives. The resulting sense is: "But your speech must be (*ētō*) 'yes yes, no no' (*nai nai, ou ou*)." Many commentators claim that the difference between Matthew and James at this point is stylistic rather than substantive. From Assyrian examples in the first millennium B.C. to Greco-Roman texts around the turn of the era, we have abundant evidence that duplication of a phrase, including yes and no, simply served to express emphasis, definitiveness, or certainty.[46] We would thus have in Matthew and James two alternate versions of the same primitive oral tradition, perhaps two Greek translation variants of the same Aramaic saying. Indeed, if Jesus actually spoke this prohibition, it would have created no little consternation among pious Jews. As with Jesus' prohibition of divorce, the astounding and disturbing nature of his prohibition of oaths may well have occasioned multiple repetitions of this disputed teaching, with variations in the precise wording.

Some commentators, however, offer quite a different interpretation of the positive command in Matt 5:37a; they hold that the Matthean meaning diverges notably from that of Jas 5:12. In this alternate interpretation, Matthew or the M tradition of his church has mitigated the original total prohibition of oaths by turning the logion about yes and no into a substitute oath. In this interpretation, "yes yes, no no" is not a metaphor for or an example of direct and honest speech, but rather serves as a fixed formula that the Matthean community enjoins on its members as a substitute for oaths that directly or indirectly call upon God as a witness. We would then have an example of Matthew's supposed "re-Judaizing" or "legalistic" tendency, whereby he creates a new form of Jewish-Christian *hǎlākâ* to guide the moral conduct of his coreligionists—in this case, with a new kind of substitute oath. Georg Strecker, for example, considers the Matthean "yes yes, no no" as a clever subterfuge, an "asseveration-formula" in place of the "oath-formula" forbidden by Jesus. In Strecker's view, Matthew thus adapts Jesus' absolute prohibition to the practical needs of the Christian community, although this adaptation involves a partial revocation of Jesus' radical prohibition.[47]

While this "substitute oath" or "new legalism" interpretation of Matt 5:37a is championed by some exegetes, a number of serious objections stand in its way:

(1) It is precisely the Matthean form of the saying that expresses the core of the prohibition with the absolute negation "do not swear at all (*mē omosai holōs*)!" It would be very odd for Matthew to trumpet this total prohibition at the beginning of the antithesis, proceed to include in his examples of prohibited oaths the substitute oath by one's head (which does not refer to God even indirectly, as does Jerusalem), and then climax his teaching with a different substitute oath.[48] Matthew's Gospel, like any NT book, has its share of unresolved tensions among competing traditions, but for a careful craftsman like Matthew to go out of his way via redactional additions to set up such a blatant self-contradiction in four verses strains credulity.

(2) No example of a substitute oath consisting of a double yes or a double no can be found in 1st-century Judaism. There are only two relevant Jewish parallels; both of them date from a notably later period and suffer as well from further problems of interpretation.

The first example, from 2 *Enoch* (alias *Slavonic Enoch*) labors under special difficulties.[49] The dating of the book has varied widely among experts, who have placed its composition anywhere from the 1st century B.C. to the late Middle Ages. On balance, a date in the early Middle Ages seems likely. Compounding the problem of dating is the fact that 2 *Enoch* is preserved only in Old Church Slavonic and that the twenty-odd manuscripts that contain some form of its text vary widely in dating, provenance, and readings. Indeed, no one manuscript can be said to contain 2 *Enoch*, whole and entire, without any additions. The oldest manuscript that contains extracts of 2 *Enoch* dates from the 14th century; the two main manuscripts we depend on (the longer recension labeled J and the shorter labeled A) date from the modern period. More to the point, the key passage (2 *Enoch* 49:1) that identifies yes yes or no no with swearing—but strangely, not with an oath!—is absent from the shorter recension of the work. The longer recension evinces signs of Christian redaction; in fact, some critics have even claimed that

2 *Enoch* should be considered a Christian composition. Even if we do not accept that questionable view, the relevant passage in 2 *Enoch* 49:1 shows clear signs of interpolation:[50]

> For I am swearing to you, my children—But look! I am not swearing by any oath at all, neither by heaven nor by earth nor by any other creature which the Lord created. For the Lord said, "There is no oath in me, nor any unrighteousness, but only truth." So, if there is no truth in human beings, then let them swear by means of the words "Yes, Yes!" or, if it should be the other way around, "No, No!"

Anyone reading this passage within the larger context of 2 *Enoch* is struck immediately by how this unit, missing in the shorter version of the work, disrupts the flow of thought in the longer version.[51] The unit itself suffers from internal contradiction: the seer begins to swear and then, with a sudden paroxysm of tender conscience and convoluted casuistry, explains parenthetically that his swearing does not constitute an oath, which is to be absolutely avoided. The ultimate reason for avoiding oaths is that the Lord never uses an oath—a claim that flies in the face of the abundant evidence of Scripture. This strange self-contradictory mélange probably results from the moral problem that a Christian editor sees in a holy seer swearing, an act contrary to the clear prohibition in Matthew and James. The Christian editor proceeds to insert a conflation of the Matthean and Jamesian prohibitions (traces of both forms are visible) in order to square the theological circle. The maladroit muddle that results has the seer swearing, but not by an oath. Thus, it is probably the Christian editor's attempt to resolve his self-made theological conundrum that leads him to identify the double yes and double no with a type of swearing that is not an oath.[52] In sum, the late date, poor attestation, internal contradictions, and probable Christian editing make this text useless as a parallel that supposedly sheds light on Matt 5:37a.

Similarly, the rabbinic parallels brought forward are not as probative as might first seem. In some cases, the texts adduced by commentators simply say that our direct affirmations and negations should have the strength and probity of an oath. Other texts, citing tannaitic rabbis, may exemplify the same phenomenon that we find in Matthew: a doubled expression used for emphasis.[53] For a double yes or no that counts as an oath-formula, we must wait for an Amoraic rabbi cited in the Babylonian Talmud, where a single text provides something of a parallel (*b. Šeb.*36a).[54] Rabbi Eleazar (an Amora of the second or third generation) argues that a single "yes" or "no" can constitute an oath by appealing to God's solemn promise to Noah in Gen 9:15: ". . . and the waters shall not [lô'] ever again become a flood to destroy all flesh." Raba (i.e., Raba bar Joseph Ḥama, a fourth-generation Babylonian Amora of the 4th century A.D.) counters this view with the claim that an oath is formulated only when a person says "yes" or "no" twice. He tries to prove his point by appealing to the two occurrences of "no" in God's promise to Noah in Gen 9:11.[55] It is unclear whether Raba had received this opinion about a double yes and no from earlier tradition or whether he has created it ad hoc simply to dispute Rabbi Eleazar's interpretation of Gen 9:15. Indeed, there is the larger question of whether Raba is engaged in anything more than the type of intellectual dueling often found in the Talmud. The idea that a double yes or double no, understood as an oath-formula, could function as a substitute for all other oath-formulas—all of which would now be forbidden—is not on the rabbis' mental horizon.[56] In sum, in Judaism around the time of Jesus, no Jewish text identifies a double yes or no as a (substitute) oath. The command in Matt 5:37a should therefore be read as an alternate version of the command in Jas 5:12: instead of using any oath to swear to the truth of one's assertion, one should restrict oneself to simple, direct, and always honest speech, symbolized by an emphatic "yes" or "no."[57]

D. DOES THE PROHIBITION GO BACK
TO THE HISTORICAL JESUS?

At the very least, Matt 5:34–37 and Jas 5:12 witness to an early oral tradition that existed prior to the two written documents and that enunciated a total prohibition of oaths. More precisely, if we grant (i) that both the Gospel of Matthew and the Epistle of James were written sometime in the second Christian generation (roughly A.D. 70–100); (ii) that the two works are independent of each other; and (iii) that the Matthean and Jamesian forms of the prohibition are both products of a multistage development of a primitive tradition, then this primitive tradition most likely goes back to the first Christian generation (roughly A.D. 30–70). As we have already seen, the peculiar problem that we face in dealing with the ultimate origin of this first-generation tradition is that Matthew attributes this teaching to Jesus while James does not. Is this a case of a teaching of the historical Jesus (transmitted and developed by the Matthean tradition) also being woven into the parenesis of a NT "epistle"? Or is it a case of an early Christian creation (transmitted and developed by James) being secondarily placed on the lips of Jesus (as depicted by Matthew)?[58] In my opinion, two criteria argue for origin from the historical Jesus: discontinuity and (by a circuitous route) multiple attestation.

(1) The application of the criterion of *discontinuity* should be examined first since, in the case of the prohibition of oaths, discontinuity is the clearer and stronger criterion. Happily, it can sidestep the question of the presence of Jesus tradition in the Epistle of James, a complicated problem that will be treated below. Even if the prohibition of oaths occurred only in Matthew's Gospel, the criterion of discontinuity would argue powerfully for its origin in the teaching of the historical Jesus.[59]

(a) As we have already seen, no Jewish teaching around the turn of the era and no 1st-century Christian teaching (apart from our Matthew–James parallel) ever dares to prohibit oaths entirely—or apparently even thinks of doing so. Neither the Jewish Scriptures nor most Jewish writers entertain the possibility that there might be something essentially or fundamentally wrong with the institution of oaths. Under Hellenistic influence, Ben Sira is critical of frequent swearing, and Philo recommends avoiding swearing whenever one can. But it is telling that even Philo, for all his distaste, does not dare to forbid swearing, since the Jewish Scriptures present him with clear cases of God, great persons of Jewish history, and ordinary people swearing—plus two specific cases when the Torah enjoins oaths (the cases of deposited goods and of a wife suspected of adultery). In the intertestamental and rabbinic literature, we increasingly find criticism of false swearing, frequent swearing, frivolous swearing, and unfulfilled oaths, as well as the restriction of oaths to certain formulas and occasions. None of this, however, adds up to a total prohibition of oaths. Put simply, such a prohibition appears nowhere in pre-70 Judaism. Even when attempts at prohibiting oaths begin to appear in the tannaitic literature, they are rare and isolated examples that usually reflect the desire of scrupulous persons to avoid swearing in specific cases. Even here we do not have the programmatic and total prohibition of oaths as an institution à la Matthew and James.[60]

(b) Surprisingly, discontinuity with the NT—apart from Matt 5:34–37 and Jas 5:12—is, if anything, even stronger.[61] In the first Christian generation, Paul swears on a regular basis, without giving it a second thought. His epistles are strewn with various oaths, including a passage in 2 Corinthians (1:17–23) that is sometimes cited (wrongly, in my view) as a distant parallel to Matt 5:34–37.[62] Oaths are found in other streams of the NT tradition as well. The Epistle to the Hebrews makes much of solemn oaths pronounced by God[63] and presupposes the habit of human swearing (Heb 6:16) with no hint of disapproval. In the Book of Revelation, John the seer apparently sees no difficulty in portraying an angel taking an oath by the living God who created the heaven, the earth, and the sea (Rev 10:6—note the formula's similarity to the formulas forbidden in Matt 5:34–35 ∥ Jas 5:12). Indeed, if we did not have Matt 5:34–37, we might read Jesus' excoriation of Pharisaic distinctions between binding and nonbinding oath formulas in Matt 23:16–22 as a critique that took for granted the legitimacy of oaths and simply criticized the Pharisees' casuistry.[64] Hence, given this total discontinuity with the Jewish Scriptures, pre-70 Judaism, and the whole of the NT outside of Matt 5:34–37 ∥ Jas 5:12, the criterion of discontinuity argues strongly for the prohibition of oaths going back to Jesus.

(2) The argument from the criterion of *multiple attestation* is necessarily more roundabout. Accordingly, I put it in second place, though I think that, in the end, it is valid. The special problem in this case lies in the highly unusual nature of the multiple attestation: a possible saying of the historical Jesus is attested on the one hand by the M tradition of Matthew's Gospel and on the other by an isolated piece of parenesis in the Epistle of James. The fact that James does not attribute the prohibition of oaths to Jesus seems, at first glance, to make any appeal to the criterion of multiple attestation unworkable.[65]

However, the question of whether Jesus' sayings are alluded to in NT epistolary parenesis in general and in the Epistle of James in particular is a complicated issue that has drawn a fair amount of study in recent years. Particular attention has been paid, understandably, to Paul, since, in a few cases, he does appeal directly to sayings of Jesus also recorded in the Synoptic Gospels. We have already examined in Chapter 32 Paul's appeal to Jesus' teaching on divorce (1 Cor 7:10–11 ∥ Luke 16:18 parr.). To this might be added (i) Jesus' command that the disciples sent out on mission should live off the offerings given them by their hosts (1 Cor 9:14 ∥ Luke 10:7 par.) and (ii) Jesus' words over the bread and wine at the Last Supper (1 Cor 11:23–25 ∥ Mark 14:22–24 parr.). We may reasonably suppose that if Paul could suddenly produce a relevant saying of Jesus when it was vital to his argument, he most likely knew other teachings of Jesus as well. This supposition seems verified when we comb Paul's epistles for allusions to or echoes of Jesus' moral exhortation. Prime candidates are supplied by those passages in which Paul echoes Jesus' core teachings about love, mercy, and forgiveness (e.g., Rom 12:14).[66] Thus, the use of the "Jesus tradition" by Paul is hardly monochromatic. Alongside explicit citations of Jesus' sayings are a number of cases in which Jesus' teachings are not set apart as coming from "the Lord" instead of from Paul, but rather are woven into the fabric of Paul's own parenesis.

Once we see this phenomenon in Paul's epistles, we need not be surprised that it appears elsewhere in the NT epistolary literature (broadly understood). Echoes of Jesus' teaching or of his life's story reverberate in such different works as 1 Peter and the Epistle to the Hebrews.[67] Still, when it comes to the phenomenon of Jesus' sayings being incorporated into an author's own exhortations, the Epistle of James enjoys a notable position among the non-Pauline "epistles" of the NT.[68] Many essays and whole books have investigated this phenomenon in James. For example, in a painstakingly detailed monograph, Dean B. Deppe has surveyed sixty authors, dating as far back as 1833. These authors range in their estimates of allusions to the Jesus tradition in James from a high of sixty-five to a low of four. Deppe proceeds to examine the twenty most frequently mentioned "parallels" to the Jesus tradition of the Synoptic Gospels in the Epistle of James.[69] After careful analysis, he concludes that there are eight conscious allusions to sayings of Jesus also found in the Synoptic Gospels.[70] Most of these sayings occur in the Sermon on the Mount/Sermon on the Plain found in Matthew and Luke respectively. Seen in tandem with the transmission of the Jesus tradition in Paul by both explicit citation and allusion, these data suggest that, from the start, Jesus' moral teachings were transmitted in the early church in two different ways: (i) by way of explicit attribution to Jesus, first in oral proclamation, then at times in Paul's epistles, and finally in the literary genre we call Gospels; and (ii) by way of allusive incorporation into the parenesis of a NT author writing outside of the Gospel genre. The examples in James all fall into the second category.[71]

The supposed allusions in James, however, are not all of a piece. A number of the allusions are rambling and vague, with a theme or topic in James paralleling a Synoptic saying along with a certain amount of shared vocabulary. For instance, Jas 1:5 exhorts believers to pray with confidence to God for what they need: "If any of you lacks wisdom, let him ask (*aiteitō*, 3d person singular imperative) from the God who gives to all without reserve and without reproach, and it shall be given (*dothēsetai*, future passive indicative) to him." In both Matt 7:7 and Luke 11:9, we find in a stray saying of Jesus a similar exhortation that uses the same two key verbs in similar grammatical forms, though the formulation is tighter: "Ask (*aiteite*, 2d person plural imperative), and it shall be given (*dothēsetai*) to you."[72] That this type of saying did indeed circulate in the early church as a saying of Jesus is confirmed by a variant form of the same tradition, found in the Gospel of John. At the Last Supper, Jesus promises his disciples (John 16:23–24): "Whatever you ask (*aitēsēte*) the Father in my name he will give (*dōsei*) it to you . . . ask (*aiteite*) and you shall receive (*lēmpsesthe*)." A brief exhortation to trustful prayer that receives its request, expressed by the rapid succession of the key verbs of asking (*aiteō*) and giving (*didōmi*), is thus multiply attested in Q and John, and most likely comes from the historical Jesus. That the same basic exhortation with the same key verbs, in almost the exact same grammatical forms as the Q saying, also occurs in James is a prime example of the type of incorporation of Jesus tradition into epistolary parenesis that we find in James. At times, the Jesus tradition may be vague and allusive, but the thematic and verbal connections are clear enough to reasonably suppose an origin in the sayings of Jesus. It is not that the author of James knows Q or John directly, but rather that this exhortation of Jesus has already been absorbed into the oral tradition of Christian parenesis and is taken over by James as such.[73]

Whether the author of James knew that at least some of the parenetic sayings he used (sayings that have Synoptic parallels) came in fact from Jesus is an intriguing question for which there is no clear answer. The fact that James does not explicitly cite Jesus as a source does not necessarily prove that the author did not think that some of the sayings had their origin in Jesus. Various parts of what we call the OT were known to the author as authoritative literary sources, and yet only rarely does he cite the OT explicitly.[74] Much more often he simply weaves OT allusions into his own exhortations.[75] It would hardly be surprising, then, if James employed the same basic technique in his approach to the Jesus tradition, all the more so since he probably did not know any of our written Gospels.[76] Hence, for him, the Jesus tradition was not, even in the etymological sense, "scripture." Knowing only stray oral traditions that conveyed the teaching of Jesus, he would all the more readily absorb them into his own parenesis—if, indeed, this had not already happened in some oral units of Christian parenesis prior to his writing the Epistle.

That early Christian writers would pass on sayings of Jesus without attributing them to him—even when the writers clearly knew the true origin of the sayings, since they knew at least some of the canonical Gospels!—is proved by the striking case of the *Didache*.[77] On the one hand, whatever the many different and convoluted layers of the tradition that makes up the final form of the *Didache* were,[78] the redactor of the *Didache* at times cites sayings as coming from Jesus and indeed as present "in the Gospel." For example, *Did*. 8:2 cites the Lord's Prayer in the Matthean form with the introductory words, "As the Lord commanded in his Gospel, so pray. . . ."[79] On the other hand, in the first chapter of the *Didache* (*Did*. 1:2–5), a whole series of Jesus' sayings that are found in Matthew and/or Luke are presented without being attributed to him; instead, they are woven together with other exhortations. Thus, although the final redactor of the *Didache* certainly knows the Gospel of Matthew (and possibly Luke) and therefore certainly knows that particular exhortations in 1:2–5 are identified as sayings of Jesus in Matthew and/or Luke,[80] the redactor nevertheless lets these sayings of Jesus stand "anonymous" in chap. 1, mixed in with other exhortations and with no indicator of their "dominical" origin. Moreover, almost all of Jesus' sayings in *Didache* 1 are taken from the Sermon on the Mount/Sermon on the Plain, thus giving us a further parallel with the use of the Jesus tradition in James. In sum, James' way of employing and incorporating the logia of Jesus into his parenesis is by no means unheard of, when viewed in the larger context both of other NT epistles and of early Christian works outside the canon. In fact, some of these early Christian works are notably later than James and know at least some of the written Gospels.[81]

Hence, once we grant the likelihood of James incorporating Jesus tradition into his parenesis without attribution, and once we accept certain passages of James as probable cases of this phenomenon (e.g., Jas 1:5), the appeal to Jas 5:12 both as a parallel to Matt 5:34–37 and as a legitimate part of an argument from multiple attestation is not as strange as it might first seem. More to the point, within the collection of possible parallels in the Epistle of James to the Synoptic tradition, Jas 5:12 stands out as unique in a number of ways.[82] First, no other passage in James provides so lengthy a text that parallels Synoptic material so closely in content, structure, and vocabulary. Second, the content and thrust of Jas 5:12 are so markedly different from most of the parenesis in the Epistle of James that creation by the author himself or by whatever Christian teachers served as his immediate sources is highly unlikely. One of the most striking aspects of the parenesis in James is its lack of specific, detailed rules of Jewish or Jewish-Christian *hǎlākâ*. We hear nothing about physical circumcision, rules of divorce, the sabbath rest, the food laws, the washing of hands, or any of the other concrete rules of conduct that were inculcated (and debated) as important identity badges and boundary markers for Jews (and strict Jewish Christians) living in a sea of Gentiles.

As a matter of fact, this glaring absence of any treatment of specific points of Jewish *hǎlākâ* is one reason for questioning the tradition that the Epistle of James was written by the James who was "the brother of the Lord [Jesus]" (Gal 1:19) and the later leader of the Jerusalem church (Gal 2:9; Acts 12:17; 15:13; 21:18).[83] From Paul and Acts we get a picture of the historical James as a Jew concerned about questions of circumcision and purity laws, including food laws. Nothing of the sort appears in the Epistle of James. Instead, the Epistle is replete with general moral exhortations that would be acceptable to most Jews or Christians of any stripe. Such generic parenesis pervades a good deal of Jewish-Hellenistic literature at the turn of the era. One need only dip into such works as the *Testament of Abraham*, the *Testament of Job*, or (further afield) the *Testaments of the Twelve Patriarchs* for examples.[84] Precisely because most of the exhortations in James remain quite general, one is hardly surprised to find that (apart from 5:12) no teaching in James' parenesis comes near to revoking particular rules or institutions enshrined in the Law of Moses.

It is against this background of the general parenesis of James, which is totally in accord with mainstream Jewish moral teaching, that the precise rule forbidding oaths stands out like a theological sore thumb. As we have already seen, the total prohibition of swearing has no parallel in Judaism around the time of Jesus. What we may now add is that such a revocation of an institution enshrined in and sometimes commanded by the Mosaic Torah has likewise no parallel anywhere else in James' parenesis. Revocation of particular statutes of the Law coheres neither with James' own theology nor with the theological outlook of the mass of material he has received from the various sources he employed. In the Epistle of James, revocation of a precept or institution enjoined by the Law is found only in Jas 5:12. Its literary isolation within the larger context of chap. 5—commentators cannot agree on whether it goes with what precedes or what follows in chap. 5, probably because it goes with neither—mirrors its theological isolation within the whole epistle.[85]

We can now begin to appreciate how the converging lines of our argument come together: (1) Jas 5:12 is a clear parallel to Matt 5:34–37 in content, structure, vocabulary, and most pointedly in its revocation of a particular institution and particular commandments in the Mosaic Torah. (2) There are other likely allusions to the Jesus tradition in James; but no other passage in James that allegedly parallels a saying of Jesus is so close to the Synoptic tradition in content, structure, and vocabulary as Jas 5:12 is. (3) Apart from Jas 5:12, no exhortation or command in the whole of James runs counter to or rescinds a command of the Mosaic Law. In other words, neither the author of James not his immediate sources evince such a tendency—a tendency that is found, however, in a few sayings of the Jesus tradition. Drawing all these considerations together, I think that the most reasonable conclusion is (1) that Jas 5:12 is an alternate form of the saying attributed to Jesus in Matt 5:34–37; and (2) that this Jesus tradition was transmitted in the early oral Christian tradition in two streams: the "gospel" stream that retained an attribution to Jesus and that wound up in Matthew, and the "epistolary" stream that wove sayings of Jesus into general Christian parenesis without attributing them to Jesus.

The upshot of this whole line of reasoning is that we have in Jas 5:12 ‖ Matt 5:34–37 an unusual but valid example of multiple attestation. While the major argument for origin in the teaching of the historical Jesus must remain that Matt 5:34–37 evinces discontinuity from Judaism and Christianity in the 1st century A.D., the parallel of Jas 5:12 ‖ Matt 5:34–37 does supply a secondary and supporting argument from multiple attestation. Some might also want to add an argument from coherence (the radical nature of much of Jesus' teaching on morality as well as the widely attested discussion of the proper use of oaths in Judaism at the turn of the era), but such an approach is at best confirmatory of the results achieved by other means.[86]

One final question remains. Which form of the prohibition, especially in the climactic statement about the double "yes" and the double "no" (Matt 5:37a ‖ Jas 5:12f), comes closer to the original saying of the historical Jesus?[87] There are two reasons why this question probably has no satisfactory answer.[88] (1) As with the prohibition of divorce, so with the prohibition of oaths, Jesus' shocking teaching, which presumed to revoke some institution or command of the Mosaic Law, probably evoked no little dissent and debate among his Jewish listeners. Most likely Jesus had to repeat and defend his teaching any number of times, and so the idea that there was one and only one original form of the saying may be a misconception. (2) In the debates over the original form of the prohibition of oaths, many commentators prefer the simpler formulation in Jas 5:12f ("your yes must be a yes and [your] no [must be] a no"). The wording in Matt 5:37a ("your speech must be 'yes yes,' 'no no' ") strikes many as an expanded version of the saying. However, the supposedly original form in Jas 5:12f cannot be translated word for word back into Aramaic, since the Aramaic particles for "yes" and "no" (*kēn* and *lā'*) cannot have the definite article and the possessive pronoun directly attached to them, as would be demanded by a literal translation of the Greek wording of Jas 5:12f (*hymōn to nai* = "your yes" and *to ou* = "[your] no"). Thus, the wording of Matt 5:37a and of Jas 5:12f may well represent two translation variants of the same Aramaic saying—if indeed the same Aramaic wording lies behind both Greek formulations.[89]

In any event, I conclude that the prohibition of oaths can take its place alongside the prohibition of divorce as a second example of the historical Jesus' revocation of individual institutions and/or commandments of the Mosaic Law.[90] As Ulrich Luz rightly observes, Jesus—as far as we can tell—no more considers the practical consequences of his total prohibition of oaths than he considers the practical consequences of totally forbidding divorce.[91] We probably have here another example of the eschatological prophet proclaiming the rules of conduct binding on those who already live proleptically in the kingdom of God. However, we must remember that such a rationale is our deduction from the evidence, not the reasoning explicated by Jesus himself. Jesus, as a true religious charismatic, feels no obligation to give reasons. At this point, some might begin to question our initial supposition that the Jewish Jesus affirmed—indeed, took for granted as the given—the validity of the Mosaic Torah. Are the prohibitions of divorce and oaths rare exceptions to Jesus' approach to the Law, or do we find him revoking the Law in other areas? In particular, what of his apparent revocation of observance of the sabbath (e.g., Mark 2:23–28; 3:1–6) or of foods laws (Mark 7:15–23)? To probe more deeply into this complicated question of Jesus and the Law, we must turn to the weighty and difficult questions of sabbath observance (Chapter 34) and the purity laws (Chapter 35).

NOTES TO CHAPTER 33

[1] For introduction to the question of oaths, exegesis of the two key texts (Matt 5:34–37 ‖ Jas 5:12) along with their possible sources and parallels, and further bibliography, see Rudolf Hirzel, *Der Eid. Ein Beitrag zu seiner Geschichte* (Leipzig: Hirzel, 1902; reprint: Darmstadt: Scientia Verlag Aalen, 1966); Massey H. Shepherd, Jr., "The Epistle of James and the Gospel of Matthew," *JBL* 75 (1956) 40–51; Ernst Kutsch, " 'Eure Rede aber sei ja ja, nein nein'," *EvT* 20 (1960) 206–18; Gustav Stählin, "Zum Gebrauch von Beteuerungsformeln im Neuen Testament," *NovT* 5 (1962) 115–43; Martin Dibelius, *Der Brief des Jakobus* (MeyerK 15; ed. Heinrich Greeven; Göttingen: Vandenhoeck & Ruprecht, 1964) 294–99; Franz Mussner, *Der Jakobusbrief* (HTKNT 13/1; Freiburg/Basel/Vienna: Herder, 1964) 47–53, 211–16; Hildburg Bethke, "Überhaupt nicht schwören," *Eid, Gewissen, Treuepflicht* (ed. Hildburg Bethke; Frankfurt: Stimme, 1965); Otto Bauernfeind, "Der Eid in der Sicht des Neuen Testamentes," ibid., 79–113; Arthur J. Bellinzoni, *The Sayings of Jesus in the Writings of Justin Martyr* (NovTSup 17; Leiden: Brill, 1967) 64–67; Johannes Schneider, "*horkos*, etc.," *TDNT* 5 (1968) 457–67; idem, "*omnyō*," *TDNT* 5 (1968) 176–85; E. P. Sanders, *The Tendencies of the Synoptic Tradition* (SNTSMS 9; Cambridge: Cambridge University, 1969) 57–67; idem, "The Synoptic Jesus and the Law," *Jewish Law from Jesus to the Mishnah. Five Studies* (London: SCM; Philadelphia: Trinity, 1990) 1–96, esp. 51–57; Joseph Plescia, *The Oath and Perjury in Ancient Greece* (Tallahassee: Florida State University, 1970); Paul S. Minear, "Yes or No: The Demand for Honesty in the Early Church," *NovT* 13 (1971) 1–13; Dieter Zeller, *Die weisheitlichen Mahnsprüche bei den Synoptikern* (FB 17; Würzburg: Echter, 1977); Rudolf Hoppe, *Der theologische Hintergrund des Jakobusbriefes* (FB 28; Würzburg: Echter, 1977); M. Jack Suggs, "The Antitheses as Redactional Products," *Essays on the Love Commandment* (ed. Reginald H. Fuller; Philadelphia: Fortress, 1978) 93–107; Gerhard Dautzenberg, "Ist das Schwurverbot Mt 5,33–37; Jak 5,12 ein Beispiel für die Torakritik Jesu?" *BZ* 25 (1981) 47–66; Georg Strecker, *Die Bergpredigt. Ein exegetischer*

Kommentar (2d ed.; Göttingen: Vandenhoeck & Ruprecht, 1985) 80–85 (= *The Sermon on the Mount. An Exegetical Commentary* [Nashville: Abingdon, 1988] 78–81); Ulrich Luz, *Matthew 1–7* (Minneapolis: Augsburg, 1989; German original 1985) 310–22; Davies and Allison, *The Gospel According to Saint Matthew*, 1. 532–38; Akio Ito, *Matthew's Understanding of the Law with Special Reference to the Fourth Antithesis* (Oxford: Ph.D. Thesis submitted to Westminster College, Oxford, 1989); idem, "The Question of the Authenticity of the Ban on Swearing (Matthew 5.33–37)," *JSNT* 43 (1991) 5–13; Dean B. Deppe, *The Sayings of Jesus in the Epistle of James* (Chelsea, MI: Bookcrafters, 1989) 134–49; C. M. Tuckett, "Synoptic Tradition in the Didache," *The New Testament in Early Christianity* (BETL 86; ed. Jean-Marie Sevrin; Leuven: Leuven University/Peeters, 1989) 197–230; Helmut Koester, *Ancient Christian Gospels. Their History and Development* (London: SCM; Philadelphia: Trinity, 1990) 360–63; Dennis C. Duling, "Against Oaths," *Forum* 6/2 (1990) 99–138; Patrick J. Hartin, *James and the Q Sayings of Jesus* (JSNTSup 47; Sheffield: JSOT, 1991); Daniel J. Harrington, *The Gospel of Matthew* (Sacra Pagina 1; Collegeville, MN: Liturgical Press, 1991) 88; Donald A. Hagner, *Matthew* (2 vols.; Word Biblical Commentary 33A and 33B; Dallas: Word, 1993, 1995) 1. 126–29; William R. Baker, " 'Above All Else': Contexts of the Call for Verbal Integrity in James 5.12," *JSNT* 54 (1994) 47–71; idem, *Personal Speech—Ethics in the Epistle of James* (WUNT 2/68; Tübingen: Mohr [Siebeck], 1995); Luke Timothy Johnson, *The Letter of James* (AYB 37A; New York: Doubleday, 1995; reprint New Haven: Yale University Press) 325–41; Todd C. Penner, *The Epistle of James and Eschatology. Re-reading an Ancient Christian Letter* (JSNTSup 121; Sheffield: Academic Press, 1996); Serge Ruzer, "The Technique of Composite Citation in the Sermon on the Mount (Matt 5:21–22,33–37)," *RB* 103 (1996) 65–75; Bernd Kollmann, "Das Schwurverbot Mt 5,33–37/Jak 5,12 im Spiegel antiker Eidkritik," *BZ* 40 (1996) 179–93; idem, "Erwägungen zur Reichweite des Schwurverbots Jesu (Mt 5,34)," *ZNW* 92 (2001) 20–32; Manabu Tsuji, *Glaube zwischen Vollkommenheit und Verweltlichung* (WUNT 2/93; Tübingen: Mohr [Siebeck], 1997); C. Freeman Sleeper, *James* (Abingdon NT Commentaries; Nashville: Abingdon, 1998) 137–39; Wesley Hiram Wachob and Luke Timothy Johnson, "The Sayings of Jesus in the Letter of James," *Authenticating the Words of Jesus* (NTTS 28/1; ed. Bruce Chilton and Craig A. Evans; Leiden/Boston/Cologne: Brill, 1999) 431–50; Wesley Hiram Wachob, *The Voice of Jesus in the Social Rhetoric of James* (SNTSMS 106; Cambridge: Cambridge University, 2000); Holmén, *Jesus and Jewish Covenant Thinking*, 170–87; Wiard Popkes, *Der Brief des Jakobus* (THKNT 14; Leipzig: Evangelische Verlagsanstlat, 2001) 331–37; David Hutchinson Edgar, *Has God Not Chosen the Poor? The Social Setting of the Epistle of James* (JSNTSup 206; Sheffield: Academic Press, 2001); Martin Vahrenhorst, *"Ihr sollt überhaupt nicht schwören." Matthäus im halachischen Diskurs* (WMANT 95; Neukirchen-Vluyn: Neukirchener Verlag, 2002); Leuk L. Cheung, *The Genre, Composition and Hermeneutics of the Epistle of James* (Paternoster Biblical and Theological Monographs; Carlisle, UK: Paternoster, 2003); I. Kottsieper, "*šābaʿ*," "*šĕbuʿâ*," *TDOT* 14 (2004) 311–36; Paul Foster, *Community, Law and Mission in Matthew's Gospel* (WUNT 2/177; Tübingen: Mohr [Siebeck], 2004) 113–22; Mark

E. Taylor, "Recent Scholarship on the Structure of James," *Currents in Biblical Research* 3 (2004) 86–115; Kari Syreeni, "The Sermon on the Mount and the Two Ways Teaching of the Didache," *Matthew and the Didache* (ed. Huub van de Sandt; Assen: Royal van Gorcum; Minneapolis: Fortress, 2005) 87–103; John S. Kloppenborg, "The Use of the Synoptics or Q in *Did*. 1:3b–2:1," ibid., 105–29; Joseph Verheyden, "Eschatology in the Didache and the Gospel of Matthew," ibid., 193–215; Mark E. Taylor and George H. Guthrie, "The Structure of James," *CBQ* 68 (2006) 681–705; Yael Ziegler, " 'So Shall God Do . . .': Variations of an Oath Formula and Its Literary Meaning," *JBL* 126 (2007) 59–81.

[2] It is telling that even modern reference works are wary of giving too detailed a definition of "oath" and "vow." For example, *The Oxford Dictionary of the Jewish Religion* (ed. R. J. Zwi Werblowsky and Geoffrey Wigoder; New York/Oxford: Oxford University, 1997) observes at the beginning of its article on "Vows and Oaths" (note the dual entry) on p. 716 that "the line separating oaths and vows in Jewish law is not always clearly drawn . . . particularly since swearing to do a certain thing is tantamount to a vow." Before going into detailed subdivisions of vows, the article contents itself with defining oaths as "solemn affirmations" and vows as "promises to perform, or abstain from, specific actions." The *Dictionary of Judaism in the Biblical Period* (ed. Jacob Neusner and William Scott Green; Peabody, MA: Hendrickson, 1996) is more detailed in defining an oath as "an appeal to God as a witness to the truth of one's statement" (p. 458) and a vow as "a promise either to forgo something not ordinarily forbidden, or a promise to perform some act in return for divine help or in thanksgiving for such help" (p. 661). In a similar vein, *The Westminster Dictionary of Christian Ethics* (ed. James F. Childress and John Macquarrie; Philadelphia: Westminster, 1986) defines an oath as "either a solemn affirmation of the truth or a solemn declaration of an intention to do this or that" (p. 429) and a vow as "a definite promise made to God . . . whereby a person binds himself or herself to do or not to do, or to give something by a promise to God" (p. 653). The *Catechism of the Catholic Church* (New York: Doubleday, 1997) defines an oath laconically: "Taking an oath or swearing is to take God as witness to what one affirms" (#2150). (Note that the terms "taking an oath" and "swearing" are used here synonymously, as is common in academic discussions of the question; that will be the usage observed in my own treatment of the topic.) When it comes to a vow, however, the *Catechism* (#2102) takes a slightly more detailed and juridical approach by citing the *Code of Canon Law* (canon 1191 §1): "A vow is a deliberate and free promise made to God concerning a possible and better good which must be fulfilled by reason of the virtue of religion." Interestingly, none of these definitions mentions an element that was sometimes explicitly stated but was at least always implicitly present in the OT understanding of oaths, i.e., that to take an oath was to invoke a curse upon oneself. The oath "worked" not only by calling on God as witness to the truth of one's assertion or promise but also by invoking upon oneself a curse that God would execute if the oath should be violated. On the element of self-imprecation in OT oaths, see Kottsieper, "*šābaʿ*, etc.," 313; cf. Schneider, "*horkos*, etc.," 458, 460; Sanders, "The Synoptic Jesus and the Law," 51. Bauernfeind ("Der

Eid," 106–7) goes even further in seeing a magical element in all oaths insofar as the one swearing implicitly seeks to control God as his or her witness. Another point not mentioned in the definitions cited previously is that, especially in the ancient world, not only were substitutes (e.g., heaven) used for the name of God in oaths, but at times anything dear to the person swearing (e.g., one's children) might be named as the "guarantor" or "witness" of the oath.

[3] See Vahrenhorst, *"Ihr sollt,"* 43–45. The distinction is intimated in *m. Šebu.* 3:1, but the labels "assertory" and promissory" are not used in the Mishna.

[4] One can see how easily the promissory oath and the vow become practically identical in texts like 2 Sam 3:35 and Ps 132:1–5 (cf. the two verbs *nišba'* ["swear"] and *nādar* ["vow"] in poetic parallelism in 132:2). In the *Temple Scroll* found at Qumran, 11QTemple 53:9–54:5 interweaves the vocabulary and the content of vows and oaths. In *De specialibus legibus (On the Special Laws)*, it is telling that the title of Philo's treatment of oaths and vows speaks simply of *euorkia*, the duty of keeping oaths, and that the introductory §2 uses only the vocabulary of oath and swearing (*horkos, omnymi*). In reality, in *De spec. leg.* 2.1–9 §2–38, Philo speaks of both oaths and vows (for vows, see, e.g., §24–34). Josephus (*Ag. Ap.* 1.22 §167) speaks of *korban* as an oath (*horkos*), even though, strictly speaking, it is a type of vow—a fact reflected in *Ant.* 4.4.4 §73, where Josephus treats *korban* immediately after the Nazirite vow (§72). One sees in *m. Ned.* 2:2–3 an attempt to work out a distinction between vows and oaths based on the binding force of specific formulas, but a clear distinction between oaths and vows is not maintained consistently throughout the *Mishna.* The intermingling of the vocabulary of oath and vow to designate the same reality is likewise found in the tannaitic midrashim. See, e.g., *Sipre* on Deuteronomy, chap. 27; cf. Vahrenhorst, *"Ihr sollt,"* 45 n. 11.

[5] For a brief overview of oaths in pre-Christian times, see Bauernfeind, "Der Eid," 79–83; Baker, *Personal Speech-Ethics,* 251–57 (for OT), 257–60 (for apocrypha and pseudepigrapha), 260–63 (for Qumran), 263–66 (for rabbinic literature), 267–71 (for Greco-Roman literature), and 271–74 (for Philo).

[6] Notice the language and succession of verbs in Deut 10:20: "Yahweh your God shall you fear; him shall you serve; and you shall cling to him, and by his name you shall swear." Swearing by the name of Yahweh is thus one concrete expression of the covenant loyalty to Yahweh, the one true God of Israel, that stands at the heart of the theology of Deuteronomy.

[7] On the oaths enjoined by the Torah, see Kollmann, "Erwägungen," 23–24.

[8] Vahrenhorst (*"Ihr sollt,"* 47) speaks in terms of the *possibility* the accused has of taking the oath that absolves him of paying damages. But that is to import a later rabbinic option into an OT text that speaks simply of what is to be done. The tendency throughout Vahrenhorst's treatment is to retroject later Jewish criticism

and restrictions of oaths into an earlier period in order to provide an intelligible *Sitz im Leben* for Jesus' prohibition of oaths (see pp. 263–64). For a more balanced perspective on Jewish criticism of oaths see Ito, *Matthew's Understanding*, 22–23 (arguing against the position of Dautzenberg, who denies that the prohibition of swearing goes back to the historical Jesus).

[9] Kottsieper ("*šāba'*, etc." 314) notes the almost complete absence of the root *šb'* (which occurs in the Jewish Scriptures 155 times in the niphal of the verb and 30 times each in the hiphil of the verb and in the noun derived from the verb [*šĕbû'â*, "oath"]) in the wisdom books (exceptions are Qoh 8:2 and 9:2). The vast majority of the occurrences of the root are found in the narrative literature (151 times), fewer in the prophets (43 times if we include Daniel), and still fewer in the Psalms (13 times).

[10] After listing basic dichotomies like "the good and the bad, "the pure and the impure," "the good man and sinner," Qoh 9:2 continues with "the one who swears and the one who fears [to take] an oath." The implication is that "the one who swears" belongs with the good man and the pure man; swearing is thus evaluated positively. Kottsieper ("*šāba'*, etc.," 323) points to Qoh 9:2 as a prime example of the positive view maintained in the Jewish Scriptures toward those who swear uprightly. Still, the very fact that there is such a category as the person who is afraid to take an oath may indicate that some postexilic Jews felt a diffidence toward the institution, though another explanation that fits the context is simply that liars and criminals fear to take false oaths protesting their innocence. One should also remember that the overarching context of the list in 9:2 is the lament of Qoheleth the skeptic that the good and the bad, those who swear and those who do not, all suffer the same ultimate fate. It is telling that, if any critique of oaths is to be found in Qoheleth, it is rather in the LXX translation. In LXX Qoh 8:2b, the reader is warned not to be hasty in taking an oath invoking God (*kai peri logou horkou theou mē spoudasēs*). This Greek reading does not agree with the MT of Qoh 8:2, which apparently orders the reader to obey the king's command because of one's oath. However, the MT itself is questionable, and various emendations are suggested by commentators.

[11] On Ben Sira, see Kollmann, "Erwägugen," 21–22. Vahrenhorst (*"Ihr sollt,"* 65) makes more of Ben Sira's brief statement than one should when he sees in it a warning against swearing in general. A weakness of Vahrenhorst's otherwise fine treatment of swearing is his desire to find a total prohibition of oaths in Judaism before or around the time of Jesus and thus to provide a plausible context for Jesus' total prohibition. This desire leads to a number of forced readings and/or questionable datings of texts; see, e.g., his treatment of *T. Gad* 6:4 (pp. 65–66); Jdt 8:9–31 (pp. 66–68); Pseudo-Phocylides' *Sentences* 16–17 (pp. 70–71). A total prohibition of oaths is something Vahrenhorst reads into the texts (see, e.g., his summary on p. 74), not something that is in the texts. For example, lines 16–17 of Pseudo-Phocylides' *Sentences* reads: "Do not swear a false oath [*mē d' epiorkēsēs*] either

through ignorance or by your own free will. The immortal God hates the person who swears a false oath [*pseudorkon . . . hostis omossę*]." Pascale Derron rightly interprets this teaching within the context of the great respect for oaths shown by both Greeks and Jews in antiquity. See his comments in *Pseudo-Phocylide. Sentences* (ed. Pascale Derron; Paris: Les Belles Lettres, 1986) 21; lines 16–17 are found on p. 3 of the Greek text.

[12] As early as Plato and Aristotle (as well as Socrates as reported by Plato), the use of oaths in legal proceedings is viewed as problematic. Rejection of swearing is also found in Sophocles (among trusted friends in *Oedipus at Colonus*, line 650; *Philoctetes*, lines 811–12) and Plutarch (as not befitting the Roman priest of Jupiter in *Roman Questions*, question 44 [275 C–D]), but these passages deal with special cases and do not enunciate a general or absolute prohibition. The later Greek philosophical tradition attributed a severe theological critique of oaths to Pythagoras and the neo-Pythagorean school that invoked his name. However, it is highly questionable whether we can really trace such a critique of oaths back to the historical Pythagoras (6th century B.C.), about whom little can be said with certitude. For the claim that Pythagoras taught that one should not swear by the gods, we are dependent on the testimony of Diogenes Laertius (3d century A.D.?) in his *Lives of Eminent Philosophers*, Book 8 (and, still later, on the testimony of the neo-Platonist Iamblicus). Yet even Diogenes Laertius says (8.6) that the opening words of Pythagoras' treatise *On Nature* include the following: "No, I swear by the air I breathe, by the water I drink." This is a parade example not of a total rejection of oaths but of the employment of oaths that use substitute formulas to avoid naming the gods directly. Similarly, neo-Pythagoreans criticized the use of oaths, but not all followers of the school seem to have rejected swearing entirely; on the difficulty of evaluating the evidence on the Pythagoreans, see Luz, *Matthew 1–7*, 314 n. 18. Representative of a certain "conditional absoluteness" found among philosophers of various schools are the Stoic Epictetus (late 1st century and early 2d century A.D.) and the neo-Platonist Simplicius (first half of the 6th century A.D.). Both taught that one should avoid oaths whenever possible, but conceded that sometimes they were unavoidable. For example, Epictetus, in his *Encheiridion* (33 §5) is recorded commanding: "If it is possible, refuse [or: avoid] every sort of oath; if that is impossible, [then refuse] as far as possible." Not surprisingly, one finds the same approach in Philo, a prime example of the blend of Stoicism and Middle Platonism that is often encountered around the turn of the era. Philo also reflects the solution of those Greeks who used an abbreviated or elliptical introduction to an oath such as *nē ton* ("yes, by . . .") and *ma ton* ("no, by . . ."), which avoided naming the deity by whom the oath was being taken (*De spec. leg.* 2.1 §4). We have already seen this strategy of avoiding a direct reference to God in the case of Pythagoras, as reported by Diogenes Laertius. Another example can be found in Philostratus' depiction of Apollonius of Tyana, who praises Socrates for using this kind of indirect oath; see the *Life of Apollonius of Tyana*, 6.19. Contrary to what is sometimes stated in scholarly summaries of the historical development of ancient philosophy (see, e.g., Dautzenberg, "Ist das Schwurverbot," 54; Luz, *Matthew 1–7*, 314), Greek philosophers did not

begin by criticizing the use of oaths purely on anthropological or ethical grounds, only to add theological considerations at a later date. Early and late, Greek philosophers questioned the use of oaths on grounds that at various times were theological (oaths infringe on the honor and respect owed to the gods), epistemological (oaths pretend to know with certainty what humans cannot know), and anthropological/ethical (oaths are injurious to the dignity of a free man, whose honest word should be as valid as an oath). On all this, see Kollmann, "Das Schwurverbot," 179–93, esp. 179–82; Vahrenhorst, *"Ihr sollt,"* 53–56; cf. the old but still useful book-length treatment in Hirzel, *Der Eid*, esp. 2–17.

[13] I mention the position of Qumran and the Essenes on oaths only briefly here, since I have already treated it in *A Marginal Jew*, 3. 509–10.

[14] On this point, see Baker, *Personal Speech-Ethics*, 262.

[15] For a brief summary of Philo's views, see Schneider, *"omnyō,"* 179–80; Kollmann, "Das Schwurverbot," 184–87. The major relevant passage is *De spec. leg.* 2.1–9 §2–38. In Kollmann's opinion (pp. 184–85), Philo's opposition to oaths is based primarily on anthropological/ethical reasoning; but Philo also appeals to reverence for God's name as a reason for avoiding oaths.

[16] See *De dec.* 17 §84 (i.e., Philo's treatise on the Decalogue, *De decalogo*), where the Greek phrase Philo uses (*deuteros plous*) means literally "second sailing" or "second voyage"—a standard Greek metaphor for "the next best way."

[17] See *De spec. leg.* 2.1 §5. Ito (*Matthew's Understanding*, 41) correctly observes that Philo's negative view of swearing is not as radical as Jesus' precisely because Philo recommends the use of the substitute formulas forbidden by Jesus.

[18] From Josephus and other ancient historians we hear of "loyalty oaths" imposed on the Palestinian population by civil rulers (e.g., Herod the Great, Tiberius, Caligula). In addition, the provincial census introduced by Quirinius and repeated at various intervals was probably connected with an oath given to officials for purposes of taxation. On this, see Kollmann, "Erwägungen," 24–31. For the loyalty oath(s) imposed by Herod the Great and the opposition they aroused, see *Ant.* 15.10.4 §368–72 (cf. 15. 1.1. §1–4); 17. 17.2.4 §41–44 (cf. *J.W.* 1.29.2 §571). The various accounts offered by Josephus are somewhat confused, partly because they are mixed up with narratives of court intrigues; commentators debate whether there were one or two instances of a disputed loyalty oath under Herod, who exactly opposed the oath, and why. The rejection of these oaths by some groups does not seem to have stemmed from a rejection of all oaths in principle but rather from dislike of or political resistance to particular rulers. Still, Josephus (*Ant.* 15.10.4 §371–72), in the context of narrating that Herod excused the Essenes (as well as some Pharisees) from taking the loyalty oath, does mention the similarity of the Essenes to the Pythagoreans.

[19] Josephus' definition of an oath is basically the same as Philo's: taking God as a witness (*Ant.* 6.11.8 §229–30, §276) or mediator (*Ant.* 4.6.7 §133) of the truth of agreements or promises made between human beings.

[20] From the detailed and variegated treatment of oaths in the Dead Sea Scrolls (see above), we can now appreciate that Josephus is roughly correct in his description of the Essenes' paradoxical avoidance-yet-use of oaths, though he hardly reflects all the complexities mirrored in the Scrolls. For the details of Josephus' depiction of Essene practice, see *A Marginal Jew*, 3. 509–10. Put briefly, Josephus states that anything an Essene says has more weight than an oath; hence Essenes avoid oaths as worse than perjury. Yet Josephus admits that candidates for membership in the Essenes must take frightening oaths before being admitted to full membership (see *J.W.* 2.8.6 §135; 2.8.7 §139).

[21] The permission is mentioned within the larger question of who receives restitution if the person who stole the goods is caught. Somewhat different is the case of an unpaid custodian who may stipulate that he is to be exempt from taking an oath (*m. B.Meṣ.* 7:10); here it is a question of a contract freely agreed upon beforehand.

[22] This is the interpretation of the (admittedly very laconic) text supplied by Hans Bietenhard, *Der Tosefta—Traktat Soṭa* (Bern/Frankfurt/New York: Peter Lang, 1986) 136 n. 24; the Hebrew text is found on p. 299, the German translation on p. 129.

[23] Baker (*Personal Speech-Ethics*, 266) is even of the opinion that the rabbis betray no particular concern about whether a person taking an oath should swear by one of God's names or by a legitimate substitute. Indeed, in n. 51, Baker entertains the suggestion that at least some rabbis permitted an oath by the sacred tetragrammaton (Yahweh) with all its letters pronounced.

[24] Examples of cases in which rabbis declare that oaths need not be taken include (i) a man who finds lost property and returns it to its owner, who may complain that the property has been damaged (*m. Giṭ.* 5:3); and (ii) heirs who inherit goods that the deceased had on deposit or on loan (according to the view of Rabbi Aqiba in *m. Ketub.* 9:2). Once again, Vahrenhorst (*"Ihr sollt,"* 204, 212) presses the evidence too far in order to see some sort of prohibition of oaths, at least intimated or "on the horizon," in the Mishna and Tosepta; contrast Luz, *Matthew 1–7*, 315–16. At times, commentators reviewing the Jewish material on oaths as "background" to Matt 5:34–37 include an obscure passage in an OT pseudepigraphical work, preserved in Greek, known as *The Apocalypse of Moses*; a related version of the same basic traditions is found in the Latin *Life of Adam and Eve*. For a translation (with introduction and notes) of both versions, see M. D. Johnson, "Life of Adam and Eve," in Charlesworth's *OTP*, 2. 249–95; the relevant passage, contained only in the Greek *Apocalypse of Moses* 19:1–3, is found on p. 279. In 19:1–3, Satan commands Eve to swear that she will give the forbidden fruit to her husband. Eve

replies, "I do not know by what sort of oath I should swear to you; however, that which I do know I tell you: by the throne of the Lord and the cherubim and the tree of life, I shall give (it) also to my husband to eat." When Satan receives the oath from Eve, he then climbs into the tree and sprinkles his evil poison on the fruit. After Eve eats the fruit and realizes her nakedness, she weeps "about the oath" (20:3); yet she proceeds to fulfill it, apparently thinking that even an oath to transgress God's commandment is binding. Apart from the many problems concerned with the provenance and dating of *The Apocalypse of Moses* (the traditions may range from the 1st century B.C. to the 4th century A.D.), the references to Eve's oath give no indication that oaths in principle are evil and therefore to be avoided. At most, some oaths (especially those that involve a transgression of a commandment) are seen to be problematic. On this curious text, see Ito, *Matthew's Understanding*, 47–49; Vahrenhorst, *"Ihr sollt,"* 72–73.

[25] Christian exegetes who comment on the absolute prohibition of oaths by Jesus in Matt 5:34–37 and the various oath-formulas spoken by Paul in his epistles are often guilty of apologetic harmonizing. We are assured by various authors that Paul is speaking from his unique authority as an apostle and under the charism of inspiration, or that he never misuses oaths for his own interest, or that he speaks in total awareness of making his asseverations "before God," or that, like OT prophets and Jesus himself, he speaks with immediate awareness of receiving divine revelation directly from God. For an example of such argumentation, see Stählin, "Zum Gebrauch," 138–41; Ito, *Matthew's Understanding*, 63–83. Sometimes the treatment of the NT material is focused on the question of what directives (if any) for present-day Christian practice can be extracted from the NT; see, e.g., Bauernfeind, "Der Eid," 79–113; Bethke, "Überhaupt nich schwören," 39–50. Without denigrating the sincere pastoral concerns of these authors, one must observe that much of this is Christian theology rather than a critical quest for the historical Jesus. It would be much better to admit honestly and without apologetic explanations that Paul often uses oaths and curses invoking God (the Father), Christ, or the Holy Spirit; examples include 1 Thess 2:10; 1 Cor 15:31; 2 Cor 1:23; Rom 1:9; 9:1,3; Phil 1:8. Perhaps some might argue from a historical-critical point of view that (i) Paul, who has a high sense of his authority as an apostle, thinks that the prohibition of swearing does not apply to him as an apostle; or that (ii) Paul at times falls short of the lofty Christian morality he himself inculcates (e.g., his polemical statements against the Christian adversaries mentioned in Galatians and 2 Corinthians hardly measure up to Jesus' command to love and bless one's enemies, a command echoed in Paul's epistles); or that (iii) Paul represents the phenomenon in NT Christianity of "re-Judaizing" or "legalizing" the Jesus tradition. Much more probable and much simpler is the supposition that Paul simply did not know about Jesus' prohibition of oaths, a teaching absent from the NT except for Matt 5:34–37 and Jas 5:12. Whether Paul would have modified his deeply ingrained speech patterns if he had known about Jesus' teaching is a question best left to speculative theologians.

An allied problem is whether Jesus himself ever used oaths. Once again, this problem is often presented in a theological rather than a strictly historical-critical context. In contrast, the historian questing for the historical Jesus—i.e., a historian who by definition must prescind from or bracket the insights of faith and theology for the sake of a strictly historical method—cannot exclude the possibility that the historical Jesus' words and deeds did not always perfectly match his formal teachings; the teaching and practice of Paul, mentioned above, provide an analogous case. Anyone knowledgeable of the history of religions can adduce charismatic religious leaders who explicitly claimed or implicitly seemed to think that they were not always bound by the teachings and commandments they gave to others. More to the point, though, some of the passages adduced to show that Jesus did use oaths may not be *ad rem*:

(1) A number of the passages do not meet the criteria of historicity (e.g., they do not enjoy multiple attestation); hence their use to establish the conduct of the historical Jesus remains doubtful. This is true of Mark 8:12, on which see below.

(2) Some of the examples cited ignore the insights of source and redaction criticism. For example, in Matt 26:63, the high priest is said to "adjure" [*exorkizō*] Jesus by the living to God "that you tell us whether you are the Christ, the Son of God." All too many authors fail to consider a number of problems inherent in this example: (a) Matthew is redacting a Marcan text (Mark 14:61) in which the high priest simply asks Jesus this question without "adjuring" him; in other words, Matt 26:63 reflects Matthew's redactional theology, not a historical event ca. A.D. 30. (b) We should note another Matthean redactional change: Mark has Jesus give the direct answer "I am" (14:62), while Matthew once again changes the text in order to have Jesus give an ambiguous answer, namely, "You have said it [*not* I]." That is to say, "those are your words, not mine." This hardly seems to qualify as an oath. (c) The verb Matthew uses (*exorkizō*) may mean "I place you under an oath," but it does not necessarily carry that technical legal sense. It can mean simply "I solemnly command (or urge)." (d) In my view—and in the view of many other commentators on the Passion Narratives in the Synoptic Gospels—the climactic exchange between the high priest and Jesus, drawing together the key christological titles of the Synoptic Gospels in a grand theological synthesis (Christ, Son of God, and Son of Man) is a prime example of Christian theology rather than historical reporting.

(3) Jesus' unique use of "Amen" at the beginning of a statement ("Amen, I say to you . . .") is indeed a solemn expression of religious authority, certainty, and validity, as well as a claim to special knowledge of the events of the end time. However, precisely because it is unparalleled in Jewish usage before or at the time of Jesus, and because it does the opposite of calling on God as a witness—rather, Jesus affirms the truth of what he says on his own authority ("It's so because I say it's so")—it does not qualify as a Jewish oath. Not every solemn affirmation uttered in a religious context (e.g., a prophecy uttered by the eschatological seer) is necessarily an oath. In fact, one could argue that Jesus' use of "Amen" fits in well with Matt 5:37a, since at times the Hebrew word *'amēn* is functionally equivalent to an emphatic "yes." On this, see Ito, *Matthew's Understanding*, 24. Dautzenberg ("Ist das Schwurverbot," 57–58) fails to see this point.

(4) In Mark 8:12, in the Marcan (and perhaps original) version of Jesus' refusal to give "a sign from heaven," Jesus replies in an elliptical fashion: "Amen I say to you,

if a sign shall be given to this generation. . . ." That is all he says. What we have here is an elliptical Semitic way of saying, "I tell you in no uncertain terms, a sign shall definitely not be given to this generation!" Behind this formulation is an elliptical curse formula found in the OT: "If I ever give a sign to this generation, may God do such-and-such to me as punishment"; see Joüon and Muraoka, *A Grammar of Biblical Hebrew*, 2. 618–19 (§165 a,b); BDF §372 (4). However, as a number of commentators point out, this elliptical expression had probably passed into common speech as an emphatic negation and had lost the sense of a formal curse; see Stählin, "Zum Gebrauch," 123–24; Ito, *Matthew's Understanding*, 58–59. Moreover, as Ito observes, both OT and NT texts (e.g., LXX Ps 94:11, cited in Heb 3:11) at times present God using this type of conditional formula; it is difficult to think that in such cases the element of self-imprecation (the heart of a negative oath-formula) is taken literally. Then, too, as noted above, Mark 8:12 lacks multiple attestation. In the end, firm evidence is lacking that we have here the *ipsissima verba Jesu* as opposed to another example of "Semitic interference" in Mark's style. On the whole question of whether statements of Paul or even of Jesus contradict Matt 5:34–37, see Ito, *Matthew's Understanding*, 24–28.

[26] For a summary of the arguments that, in Matt 5:34–37 and Jas 5:12, we are dealing with two forms of the same logion, see Deppe, *The Sayings of Jesus*, 141; see also Mussner, *Der Jakobusbrief*, 214–16; Wachob and Johnson, "The Sayings of Jesus," 433–44. Popkes (*Der Brief des Jakobus*, 331) makes the interesting observation that, while many words in Jas 5:12 find parallels in Matt 5:34–37, many of these same words occur either nowhere or quite rarely elsewhere in the Epistle of James; see also p. 334.

[27] One of the few exceptions is Shepherd ("The Epistle of James," 40–51), who argues from the many echoes of Q and M material in the Epistle of James to James' dependence on the Gospel of Matthew. The weakness of his argument (which involves invoking supposedly similar phenomena in the letters of Ignatius of Antioch and in the *Didache*) is that, unlike the examples in Ignatius and the *Didache*, there is no example of word-for-word correspondence between Matthew and James—and certainly no reference to "the gospel" in James—that would make literary dependence of James on Matthew the most probable explanation. Indeed, perhaps realizing the weakness of his argument, Shepherd suggests that the author of James did not have a copy of Matthew in front of him but rather remembered having heard Matthew read in church (p. 47). One is all the more puzzled when Shepherd (ibid.) also claims that Jas 5:12 "presents the strongest single case of the dependence of James upon the Gospel, despite the fact that James does not actually quote the Gospel and apparently reflects a more primitive tradition than the Gospel." If James knows and cites a more primitive version of the prohibition of swearing than the one Matthew uses, how does this prove that James knew the Gospel of Matthew? Like almost all recent commentators, Ito (*Matthew's Understanding*, 91 n. 1) rejects Shepherd's approach. Also in favor of the independence of Jas 5:12 are Davies and Allison, *Matthew*, 1. 533; Mussner, *Der Jakobusbrief*, 216; Edgar, *Has God Not Chosen the*

Poor? 68; Hartin, *James and the Q Sayings*, 188–98; Wachob and Johnson, "The Sayings of Jesus," 437–38; Tsuji, *Glaube*, 119, 122, 130; Deppe (*The Sayings of Jesus*, 149), along with the earlier commentators he cites. As I indicate in the main text, the present forms of Matthew's and James' texts are difficult to explain on the hypothesis of literary dependence.

[28] For a summary of the differences between the Matthean and Jamesian versions, see Deppe, *The Sayings of Jesus*, 140–41.

[29] Since the goal of this comparison is to isolate the core teaching that possibly goes back to the historical Jesus, I do not spend time on the redactional framework in Matthew 5 that, by the common admission of exegetes, is the product of the M tradition or of Matthew himself. For treatments of Matt 5:33–37 within the larger context of the antitheses, of chap. 5, and of the whole Sermon on the Mount, see Ingo Broer, "Die Antithesen und der Evangelist Matthäus," *BZ* 19 (1975) 50–63; Meier, *Law and History in Matthew's Gospel*, 41–161; Suggs, "The Antitheses," 93–107; Strecker, *Die Bergpredigt*, 64–98; Vahrenhorst, *"Ihr sollt,"* 217–76; Roland Deines, *Die Gerechtigkeit der Tora im Reich des Messias. Mt 5,13–20 als Schlüsseltext der matthäischen Theologie* (WUNT 177; Tübingen: Mohr [Siebeck], 2004). Ito (*Matthew's Understanding*, 93–107) reviews the various theories on the origin of the antithetical formula ("It was said to the men of old . . . but I say to you"), but fails in the end to come to a certain conclusion as to whether the fourth antithesis was formulated antithetically in the tradition before Matthew. However, on p. 149, he seems to incline in favor of Matthean redaction; similarly Suggs, "The Antitheses," 96, 103–4; Duling, "Against Oaths," 132. Suggs points out that Bultmann's classic argument that some of the Matthean antitheses (including 5:33–34) must have had the antithetical formula in the original tradition because the antithesis would be unintelligible without the thesis is clearly falsified in the case of the prohibition of oaths, where Jas 5:12 demonstrates how intelligible the prohibition is by itself; on this, see also Kollmann, "Erwägungen," 20. Whether one decides in the end that, in Matt 5:21–48, the antithetical formula is the product of the M tradition, of the Matthean form of Q, or of Matthew the redactor, the vast majority of critics today would deny that the antithetical formula as represented in Matt 5:21–48 goes back to the historical Jesus; so, e.g., Dautzenberg, "Ist das Schwurverbot," 52. The fact that this two-part antithetical formula occurs nowhere in the NT outside of Matt 5:21–48 (hence, even in Matthew's Gospel, it is isolated in a quintessentially Matthean composition), the fact that Matt 5:21–48 in structure and vocabulary displays abundant examples of Matthew's redactional style, the fact that Matthew tends throughout his Gospel to strengthen antithetical statements present in his sources or to introduce new ones, and the fact that the Q material contained in Matt 5:21–48 appears in Luke without the Matthean antithetical formula argue strongly for this conclusion. Suggs (ibid., 103) puts the point succinctly: "Dissimilarity . . . is as valid for determining genuine Matthean material as it is for determining authentic Jesus tradition." Hence I will not spend time considering the introductory antithetical statement in Matt 5:33–34a: "Again you

have heard that it was said to the men of old, 'You shall not swear falsely; but you shall fulfill your oaths to the Lord.' But I say to you. . . ." For the question of which OT texts are summarized or alluded to in Matt 5:33, see Davies and Allison, *Matthew*, 1. 533–34; Kollmann, " Das Schwurverbot," 188. If it is true that the clause "you shall render [i.e., perform, fulfill] to the Lord your oaths" is an adaptation of LXX Ps 49:14b (*kai apodos tō hypsistō tas euchas sou*, "and render to the Most High your vows"), then I agree with Davies and Allison that the more likely view is that Matthew purposely changed *euchas* ("vows") to *horkous* ("oaths") to make the entire statement refer consistently to the one topic of oaths; see also on this point Dautzenberg, "Ist das Schwurverbot," 52.

[30] The three other occurrences of *holōs* in the NT are all in 1 Corinthians: 5:1; 6:7; and 15:29. Only the last example contains the negative meaning "not at all." While Ito (*Matthew's Understanding*, 113) inclines to the view that *holōs* was present in Matthew's tradition, he considers the evidence unclear.

[31] On the literary genre of the Epistle of James, see Cheung, *The Genre*, passim.

[32] So, rightly, Schneider, "*omnyō*," 182; Vahrenhorst, "*Ihr sollt*," 256–57. Duling ("Against Oaths," 109), as he sifts all sorts of scenarios, probable and improbable, rightly rejects a direct literary relationship between Matthew and James.

[33] Ito (*Matthew's Understanding*, 86–90) distinguishes three major positions on the reconstruction of the underlying tradition: (1) Guelich: 5:33a + 34a + 37a; (2) Strecker: the core of 5:33–34a (the positive instruction in v 37 was originally unnecessary); (3) Luz: 5:34–35 without the three *hoti* clauses + 37a (in the Jamesian formulation: "let your yes be yes . . ."). Ito inclines toward Luz's position but without entirely embracing it. For Luz's reasons for his position, see his *Matthew 1–7*, 312; his position is close to the one adopted here. In a slightly different vein, Davies and Allison (*Matthew*, 1. 533) say it is "inviting" to posit 5:(33a) + 34a + 37 as the original unit. A still more comprehensive overview of opinions on the tradition history of the prohibition can be found in Duling ("Against Oaths," 110–28), who examines the positions of Minear, Guelich, Strecker, Dautzenberg, and Suggs; one should also include the hypothetical tradition history suggested by Deppe, *The Sayings of Jesus*, 144–49. One might infer that of the making of tradition histories of Matt 5:34–37 ‖ Jas 5:12 there is no end. Actually, for our purposes, reconstructing the precise order of the stages of the growth of the tradition is less important than isolating the primitive core of the tradition and testing it against the criteria of historicity. Which intermediary stages came early or late in the process is of secondary importance.

[34] Davies and Allison (*Matthew*, 1. 537) suggest that, since Matthew loves triadic structures and since 5:36 destroys the neat triadic structure of oath-formulas in 5:34–35, v 36 was probably not inserted by Matthew into the tradition. As Foster (*Community*, 119) rightly observes, the three Matthean examples of heaven, earth, and Jerusalem do not stand in tension with the absolute prohibition of v 34a.

They do not serve to limit the general principle; they simply offer some concrete examples of it. In other words, they are an illustrative, not an exhaustive, list of forbidden oaths. This seems to be the point that Luz (*Matthew 1–7*, 311) makes somewhat obscurely by insisting that *mēti* in vv 34–35 means "also not" and not "neither . . . nor."

[35] That at least by Matthew's day there existed debates among Jewish scholars on the binding character of different formulas of substitute oaths is clear from Matt 23:16–22. The debate had greatly expanded by the time of the composition of the Mishna; see, e.g., the treatment of various formulas in *m. Šebu.* 4:13 (where "by the heavens and by the earth" occurs, as in Matt 5:34–35; cf. 23:22); on this, see Davies and Allison, *Matthew*, 1. 356. While "by Jerusalem" is not mentioned among the formulas in *m. Šebu.* 4:13, the phrase "as Jerusalem" is listed among vow formulas in *m. Ned.* 1:3, and its binding force is a point of disagreements among the authorities; see Ito, *Matthew's Understanding*, 141–42. It is unclear to what extent this sort of detailed debate might go back to the time of Jesus.

[36] Granted this meaning, the fact that the use of hair dyes was well known in the ancient world is irrelevant to this saying. As Luz (*Matthew 1–7*, 317) notes, the emphasis in v 36 is on the powerlessness of human beings, the tone being that of sapiential resignation; see also Zeller, *Die weisheitlichen Mahnsprüche*, 124.

[37] For examples of the oath "by my head" in pagan Greco-Roman literature, see Ito, *Matthew's Understanding*, 115. In *m. Sanh.* 3:2, we find an oath "by the life of your head," but not simply "by my head."

[38] See Vahrenhorst, *"Ihr sollt,"* 256; Foster, *Community*, 119; Deppe, *The Sayings of Jesus*, 136.

[39] Ito (*Matthew's Understanding*, 113) is led astray by the supposed "parallel" between Matthew's "or by Jerusalem" and James' "or by any other oath." Inferring from this "parallel" that James may have found more oath-formulas in the tradition, Ito assigns "by Jerusalem" to the tradition. He thus misses the point that, in content, James' "or by any other oath" is parallel to Matthew's *holōs*; see Mussner, *Der Jakobusbrief*, 215; Johnson, *The Letter of James*, 328; Wachob and Johnson, "The Sayings of Jesus," 437.

[40] Schneider ("*omnyō*," 180 n. 46) claims that "by Jerusalem" does not appear as an oath in rabbinic texts, "though the name Jerusalem occurs in abjurations." See also Luz (*Matthew 1–7*, 311), who discusses the curious use of the preposition *eis* ("to") with "Jerusalem" in 5:35, while "heaven" and "earth" in vv 34–35 are preceded by the preposition *en* ("in," "by"). Possibly *eis* connotes orienting oneself toward Jerusalem (as at times of prayer).

[41] The neuter of the adjective *perissos* occurs in Matt 5:37 and 47 and connects by way of *inclusio* with the verb *perisseusē* in 5:20 (a verse that is most likely a redac-

tional creation of Matthew; see Meier, *Law and History*, 108–19). Apart from the doubtful case of Mark 6:51 (see Metzger, *TCGNT* [2d ed.], 79), the Matthean passages are the only occurrences of *perisson* in the Synoptic Gospels. As for the adjective *ponēros*, out of seventy-eight occurrences in the NT, Matthew has twenty-six, Mark two, Luke thirteen, and John three. Hence many commentators (e.g., Foster, *Communitiy*, 121 n. 92) favor the view that Matt 5:37b is a redactional creation of Matthew. Ito (*Matthew's Understanding*, 126–27), however, argues that we cannot be sure whether Matt 5:37b comes from the evangelist or the M tradition. In the end, though, whether the presence of these adjectives in Matt 5:37 is due to the M tradition or to the evangelist is irrelevant to our purposes. Either way, the most probable conclusion is that 5:37b does not go back to the earliest attainable tradition lying behind the Matthean and Jamesian forms of the prohibition; so Davies and Allison, *Matthew*, 1. 538. This decision also makes debates over whether *ek tou ponērou* should be translated "from evil" or "from the Evil One" moot. De facto, many commentators, appealing to the general usage of Matthew and some other NT authors, prefer "from the Evil One"; see, e.g., Stählin, "Zum Gebrauch,"121; Davies and Allison, ibid.

[42] Interestingly, the phrase *hypo krisin* ("under judgment") appears nowhere else in the LXX or the NT. Johnson (*The Letter of James*, 328–29) rightly rejects the alternate reading "lest you fall into hypocrisy (*eis hypokrisin*)," which is attested only in later Greek manuscripts; it may be an attempt by a Christian scribe to create an easier reading.

[43] Favoring the secondary nature of both the Matthean and Jamesian conclusions is Kollmann, "Das Schwurverbot," 189; Wachob and Johnson, "The Sayings of Jesus," 437; cf. Tsuji, *Glaube*, 122. Kollmann argues cogently that Matthew is not disposed to pass up a resounding concluding reference to eschatological judgment such as we find in Jas 5:12. Zeller (*Die weisheitlichen Mahnsprüche*, 125) suggests tentatively that the original prohibition of swearing may have concluded with some articulation of the reason for the prohibition similar to the negative purpose clause at the end of Jas 5:12 ("lest you fall under judgment"). Zeller's view is partially determined by his form-critical classification of the prohibition of swearing as a *Mahnsprch* (exhortation, admonition, or warning) at home in the wisdom tradition. If one instead views Jesus' prohibition as closer to a statement of apodictic law, Zeller's reasoning loses its force. Deppe (*The Sayings of Jesus*, 145–46) likewise argues in favor of keeping the conclusion of Jas 5:12, but his argument rests on a dubious parallel structure that he discerns in 5:12. On the theological difference between the ultimate source of swearing in Matt 5:37 (the Evil One) and the ultimate result of swearing in Jas 5:12 (eschatological judgment), see Bauernfeind, "Der Eid," 108.

[44] This point is missed by Kollmann ("Erwägungen," 20) and other commentators who fail to notice the functional equivalence of Matthew's "not at all" and James' "or by any other oath." However, at the end of his treatment, Kollmann (p. 32) does admit the possibility that Jesus' prohibition of oaths was absolute, but he deduces

this possibility from Jesus' overall demand for unrestricted love and truthfulness in light of the kingdom of God breaking into human history.

⁴⁵ On this interpretation of the phrase in Jas 5:12, see Baker, *Personal Speech-Ethics*, 280.

⁴⁶ While the Assyrian parallels cited by Kutsch ("Eure Rede," 206–18) are too distant in time and space (reaching back to Assarhaddon) and attest only to the use of "yes–no" as an expression of false content, there are abundant parallels in Greek literature, both classical and Koine, that witness to the use of double affirmation or negation to emphasize one's assertion. Indeed, Bauer, in his *Wörterbuch* entry on *nai* (6th ed., cols. 1078–79), lists examples of a double "yes" as far back as Archilochus of Paros in the 7th century. B.C. Vahrenhorst (*"Ihr sollt,"* 273 n. 315) gives examples of "yes yes" as an emphatic form of "yes" in such authors as Aeschylus, Sophocles, Aristophanes, and Theocritus. In the LXX, Judith uses the double "yes" in her empassioned prayer to God in Jdt 9:12: "Yes, yes, God of my father and God of the heritage of Israel" (*nai nai ho theos tou patros mou kai theos klēronomias Israēl*). Both the *NRSV* and the *NAB* translate the double *nai* as "please, please"— hardly an oath-formula. This emphasis by way of doubling a word is also found in the narrative of Judith (e.g., *sphodra, sphodra* for "very greatly" in Jdt 4:2). An emphatic double "yes" (*ita, ita*) in a pornographic scenario (not likely intended as a solemn oath) is found in Petronius' *Satyricon* 25. Vahrenhorst (ibid., 270 n. 302) likewise lists a number of passages in the tannaitic midrashim where a double "yes" (*hēn wā hēn*) is clearly just an emphatic form of a simple "yes." Other examples of doubling a phrase for emphasis in Jewish, Greek, and Roman texts can be found in Stählin, "Zum Gebrauch," 119 n. 2; Luz, *Matthew 1–7*, 317–18. A striking example in the NT itself is 2 Cor 1:17–18, where the double expression *to nai nai kai to ou ou* in v 17 is resumed in v 18 with a single *nai* and a single *ou*; see also Wachob and Johnson, "The Sayings of Jesus," 434 n. 10.

⁴⁷ Strecker, *Die Bergpredigt*, 84; against this view are Davies and Allison, *Matthew*, 1. 538. In the German text, Strecker uses the term *Beteuerungsformel* (used by many German interpreters of either the Matthean or the Jamesian form of the prohibition; see, e.g., Dibelius, *Der Brief des Jakobus*, 298); I translate the term as "asseveration formula." Strecker means that "yes yes" or "no no" functions in Matthew's eyes as a fixed formula that makes the kind of solemn declaration sometimes required in public proceedings, while avoiding what Jews or Jewish Christians would consider a technical oath-formula. Unfortunately, the word "asseveration" is open to a certain ambiguity. The word can simply mean an emphatic assertion, which a double "yes" or "no" naturally is in most languages. Emphatic speech, however, is hardly in itself an oath or a substitute oath; Dautzenberg ("Ist das Schwurverbot," 57) seems to miss this point. In discussions of Matt 5:34–37, commentators often use the language of "asseveration" in its strongest sense, to indicate a fixed formula employed as a solemn public declaration and functioning more or less like an oath, though without direct invocation of the name of God.

[48] On this argument, see Vahrenhorst, *"Ihr sollt,"* 273; also Deppe, *The Sayings of Jesus*, 138.

[49] For a general introduction to the problems surrounding the dating, provenance, and textual traditions of 2 *Enoch*, see F. I. Andersen, "2 (Slavonic Apocalypse of) Enoch," in Charlesworth's *OTP*, 1. 91–100. Because of the many problems that I mention in the main text, Vahrenhorst (*"Ihr sollt,"* 270–71) dismisses 2 *Enoch* 49:1 after only a brief discussion. In favor of composition in the 1st century A.D., prior to the destruction of the Jerusalem temple, is Andrei A. Orlov, *The Enoch–Metatron Tradition* (Texts and Studies in Ancient Judaism 107; Tübingen: Mohr [Siebeck], 2005); see, e.g., pp. 9, 148–52, 304–33. I agree with James R. Davila (Internet review of Orlov's book in the *Review of Biblical Literature* [published by the Society of Biblical Literature], December 6, 2006) that the attempt to date 2 *Enoch* before A.D. 70 is a weak point in Orlov's otherwise fine dissertation. Orlov never engages in depth (1) the problem of the late and confusing nature of the manuscripts of 2 *Enoch* or (2) the question of Christian interpolations. We are left wondering what exactly *is* the nature, extent, and wording of the text of 2 *Enoch* that supposedly predates A.D. 70. Perhaps a larger problem permeating Orlov's work is the presupposition that, within the broad stream of a given (e.g., Enochic) tradition, various theological themes, motifs, or titles develop according to a neat, evolutionary model, with various stages of development therefore being datable by their position on the evolutionary time line. One need only trace the ups and downs and sideway-movements of various christological beliefs, motifs, and titles from the NT through the early patristic period to Nicea and Chalcedon to see that this is not necessarily the case. Then, too, as Davila notes, various topics at home in pre-70 Judaism (e.g., polemics about the priesthood) continued long after the temple's destruction; one must make allowances for post-temple antiquarian and utopian interests in literature like 2 *Enoch*.

[50] The translation is (with slight modification) that of Andersen, "2 (Slavonic Apocalypse of) Enoch," *OTP*, 1. 176.

[51] See Ito, *Matthew's Understanding*, 41–42, 44–45; see also Dautzenberg, "Ist das Schwurverbot," 56; Luz, *Matthew 1–7*, 312; Deppe, *The Sayings of Jesus*, 140. A solitary voice against Christian interpolation is Penner (*The Epistle of James*, 233 n. 1), who asserts rather than argues.

[52] On the embarrassment of the Christian editor that leads to the curious casuistry of 2 *Enoch* 49:1, see Holmén, *Jesus and Jewish Covenant Thinking*, 181.

[53] On this, see Vahrenhorst, *"Ihr sollt,"* 270 n. 302.

[54] Vahrenhorst (*"Ihr sollt,"* 270) states that the argument of Raba in *b. Šeb.* 36a is the only passage in rabbinic literature where the double "yes" or "no" counts as a valid oath formula.

[55] Rabbi Eleazar cites the negative statement in Gen 9:15 to prove that one "no" can have the force of an oath: "and the waters shall not [lô'] ever again become a flood to destroy all flesh." Raba argues that two "no's" are necessary by pointing to the similar text in Gen 9:11, which has two negatives: "and all flesh shall not [lô'] be cut off ever again by the waters of the flood, and there shall not [lô'] be ever again a flood to destroy the earth." The playful tone of this battle of wits is far removed from the solemn and absolute prohibition of Matt 5:34–37.

[56] On this, see Ito, *Matthew's Understanding*, 44.

[57] So, rightly, Robert A. Guelich, *The Sermon on the Mount* (Waco, TX: Word, 1982) 216–18; Ito, *Matthew's Understanding*, 144–45; Foster, *Community*, 121. Similarly, Harrington (*The Gospel of Matthew*, 88) rightly rejects the appeal to the later rabbinic equation of the double yes or no with an oath; he states flatly that in the Matthean antithesis all oaths are prohibited. Curiously, Ito (pp. 147–48, 153–55) goes on to claim that the total prohibition of swearing is an example of a "not only . . . but also" saying—i.e., the prohibition intensifies the core demands of the Law to hallow God's name and to tell the truth, but such intensification does not involve any revocation (similarly, Harrington). Hagner (*Matthew*, 1. 126) likewise attempts to explain away the apparent abrogation of the Torah: the contradiction of the Mosaic Law "is only at the level of the letter of the text, not its spirit." One must reply that a total prohibition of swearing not only abrogates a key social and religious institution accepted and regulated by the Torah but also inevitably revokes those commandments of the Torah that impose an oath in specific circumstances.

[58] One reason that I do not belabor the arguments in favor of the prohibition of oaths coming from the historical Jesus is that relatively few authors have presented extended arguments against this generally accepted position. Interestingly, perhaps the most notable scholar to argue against the authenticity of the prohibition, Dauztenberg ("Ist das Schwurverbot," 47–66), readily admits that the authenticity of the prohibition is not doubted by most recent critics (p. 49). Holmén (*Jesus and Jewish Covenant Thinking*, 177–85) gives a point-by-point refutation of Dauztenberg's arguments. In my view, some of Dauztenberg's arguments are simply beside the point and are not worth rehashing; some of them, for instance, are directed at the questionable approach of Strecker (e.g., Strecker's rarely held view that the antithetical formulation of the prohibition in Matt 5:33–34a is part of the primitive tradition of the prohibition). Hence I spare the reader another point-by-point refutation of Dauztenberg's position. The arguments I put forward in the main text say all that need be said to refute the idea that the prohibition is an invention of the early church.

[59] In favor of the prohibition coming from Jesus is Luz, *Matthew 1–7*, 313 n. 16 and 314. He calls the argument for the authenticity of the prohibition of oaths a classic instance of the application of the criterion of dissimilarity (or discontinuity). Similarly, Wachob and Johnson ("The Sayings of Jesus," 432) state flatly that,

apart from the Matthean Jesus and James, no one else in the OT or NT categorically prohibits oaths; so also Popkes, *Der Brief des Jakobus*, 334. Wachob and Johnson go on to argue (ibid., 432 n. 7) that "if we may regard Jas 5:12 as a Jamesian performance of a saying of Jesus, then we have multiple attestation, for Matthew and James are most probably independent sources for this logion." Indeed, they also appeal to the criterion of embarrassment, "since both the Old Testament and New Testament accept and honor . . . oaths." Oddly, Duling ("Against Oaths, 133) shies away from the criterion of dissimilarity, apparently because this argument has often been connected with the antithetical formula in Matthew as a main sign of dissimilarity. Duling seems in the end to fall back on a vague argument from consistency with Jesus' other teachings.

[60] Thus, contrary to the thesis of Vahrenhorst propounded throughout *"Ihr sollt,"* I think that Holmén (*Jesus and Jewish Covenant Thinking*, 175) is correct when he claims that "there appears no regulation never to swear in Jewish literature before or after 70 A.D." In a sense, Dautzenberg ("Ist das Schwurverbot," 56) tries to have it both ways by admitting (unlike Vahrenhorst) that there is no absolute prohibition of oaths in Judaism around the time of Jesus and yet maintaining that the distance between the prohibition voiced by the Matthean Jesus and the Jewish critique of oaths around the turn of the era is "not a matter of principle and is not all that great," with the result that the criterion of discontinuity cannot be used here. *Sed contra*, the distance *is* a matter of principle and *is* immense. Criticism of an institution and total prohibition of that institution are two vastly different things.

[61] Popkes (*Der Brief des Jakobus*, 335) emphasizes the isolation of the Matthean and Jamesian prohibition of swearing within the NT.

[62] For the various interpretations of the obscure passage in 2 Cor 1:17–20, see Vahrenhorst, *"Ihr sollt,"* 271–73; Bauernfeind, "Der Eid," 105 (2 Cor 1:17 is connected by way of a convoluted exegesis to Jas 5:12); and especially the lengthy treatment in Ito, *Matthew's Understanding*, 70–83; cf. Bellinzoni, *The Sayings of Jesus*, 64 n. 2. Whatever one makes of the contorted line of thought in 2 Cor 1:17–20, the double "yes" and "no" mentioned in v 17 have clearly the same meaning as the single "yes" and "no" mentioned in vv 18,19, and 20. The doubling, as so often is the case in ancient Near Eastern and Greco-Roman texts around the turn of the era, merely expresses emphasis; there is no indication of its being an oath-formula. More to the point, *contra* Ito (ibid., 81–83), there is no reason to think that Paul is alluding to or paraphrasing Jesus' prohibition of swearing as expressed in Matt 5:34–37. On the contrary, it would be bizarre for Paul to allude to Jesus' total prohibition of oaths when he immediately proceeds in 2 Cor 1:23 to swear a formal oath: "But I call upon God as my witness at the peril of my life that it was in order to spare you that I did not come again to Corinth"; see Dautzenberg, "Ist das Schwurverbot," 63–64. Ito's assertion that Paul's oath-formulas are not oaths in the strict sense is a striking example of apologetic harmonization. In the end, Ito effectively distances himself from his own conclusion about 2 Cor 1:17–20 by arguing (p. 92 n. 1) that

this Pauline passage is too remote to employ in reconstructing the original form of Jesus' saying. This is an odd position to take, since 2 Cor 1:17–20 would represent the only form of the tradition coming from the first Christian generation. For a full exegesis of this difficult passage, see Victor Paul Furnish, *II Corinthians* (AYB 32A; Garden City, NY: Doubleday, 1984; reprint New Haven: Yale University Press) 132–53; Ralph P. Martin, *2 Corinthians* (Word Biblical Commentary 40; Waco, TX: Word, 1986) 22–35.

[63] God's oath against the wilderness generation of the Israelites ("I swore in my anger, 'Never shall they enter into my rest' ") is taken from LXX Ps 94:11 and is cited or alluded to in Heb 3:11,18; 4:3. God's oath to Abraham ("I will surely bless you and increase you") is taken from Gen 22:17 (the actual statement that God is swearing by himself is in 22:16) and is cited or alluded to in Heb 6:13–14,16–17. All of this is preliminary to the oath that is central to the argument of Hebrews, namely, the one contained in LXX Ps 109:4: "The Lord has sworn and he will not repent: 'You are a priest forever according to the order of Melchizedek.' " This LXX text is fully cited with an introductory formula specifying it as an oath in Heb 7:21, and the whole of 7:20–28 is dominated by the theological argument based on this oath (note the *inclusio* of *horkōmosias* in 7:20 + 28). The oath of LXX Ps 109:4 is also partially cited or alluded to in Heb 5:6,10; 6:20; 7:17.

[64] Sanders ("The Synoptic Jesus and the Law," 55) thinks that, in Matt 23:16–22, the Matthean Jesus, rejecting the Pharisaic attempt to distinguish between binding and nonbinding oath-formulas, holds that all the oaths listed in the passage are of equal seriousness since they are actually oaths taken in the name of God himself. Taking a different view, Vahrenhorst (*"Ihr sollt,"* 365–66) does not think that Matt 23:16–22, even taken by itself, necessarily presupposes a positive attitude toward swearing. He points out that one does not have to practice or approve of a particular religious observance to discuss or debate it. Indeed, Vahrenhorst thinks that, in the overarching redaction of Matthew, the wording of Matt 23:22 expressly takes up the wording of Matt 5:34 (heaven as the throne of God) in order to refer the reader back to Jesus' total prohibition of oaths, the only sure way of safeguarding God's holy name from the desecration of false or unfulfilled oaths. Taking a slightly different tack, Ito (*Matthew's Understanding*, 56–57) argues that, in Matt 23:16–22, Jesus' attack focuses on the fallacious distinction between valid and invalid oath-formulas made by the scribes and the Pharisees, while 5:34–37 forbids oaths in principle. Going even further, Schneider ("*omnyō*," 183) thinks that the intent of Matt 23:16–22 is "to reduce the casuistry of the scribes and Pharisees *ad absurdum*"; likewise, Deppe, *The Sayings of Jesus*, 138–39. On this point, see also Stählin, "Zum Gebrauch," 121 n. 3; Dautzenberg, "Ist das Schwurverbot," 58–59. My personal view is that we need to remember that "the M tradition" is our modern label for any and every tradition in Matthew's Gospel that is not present in Mark or Q. Examining all the sayings and events contained in "M" demonstrates that it was hardly a homogeneous stream of tradition. Most likely, it never constituted a single document. It may well be that the Matthean tradition that came to rest in Matt

5:34–37 was originally a saying of Jesus absolutely forbidding oaths, while Matt 23:16–22 represents a tradition of first-generation Christian Jews who mocked what they considered the casuistry of the Pharisees while at the same time admitted in principle the legitimacy of oaths. However, I basically agree with Vahrenhorst's holistic reading of the Matthean texts as they now stand in the Gospel. For a study of all the M sayings, see Stephenson H. Brooks, *Matthew's Community. The Evidence of His Special Sayings Material* (JSNTSup 16; Sheffield: JSOT, 1987); he discusses the tension between 5:34–37 and 23:16–22 on p. 69.

[65] For a brief survey of the arguments against Jas 5:12 reflecting a saying of Jesus, arguments that are then rejected, see Dibelius, *Der Brief des Jakobus*, 298–99.

[66] The Greek of Rom 12:14, *eulogeite tous diōkontas [hymas], eulogeite kai mē katarasthe* ("bless those who persecute [you], bless and do not curse") echoes in wording and content the Q tradition that stands behind Mat 5:43, *proseuchesthe hyper tōn diōkontōn hymas* ("pray for those who persecute you"), and Luke 6:28, *eulogeite tous katarōmenous hymas* ("bless those who curse you"). Strongly in favor of the view that Paul's parenesis in 12:14 reflects the exhortation of Jesus is Dunn, *Romans*, 2. 745. In a similar vein, Otto Michel (*Der Brief an die Römer* [MeyerK 4; 4th ed.; Göttingen: Vandenhoeck & Ruprecht, 1966] 305) describes Rom 12:14 as a "targum-like paraphrase" of Jesus' saying. With some hesitation, Cranfield (*Romans*, 2. 640) suggests that "a free reminiscence" of Jesus' teaching is "probable"; Ernst Käsemann (*An die Römer* [HNT 8a; Tübingen: Mohr (Siebeck), 1973] 331) likewise speaks of a reminiscence of a logion of Jesus; similarly, C. K. Barrett, *The Epistle to the Romans* (Black's NT Commentaries; London: Black, 1962) 241. Dunn thinks that the Epistle to the Romans supplies other examples of probable influence on early Christian parenesis from the remembered tradition of Jesus' teaching; he lists Rom 1:16; 2:1; 12:18; 13:7,9; 14:13–14,17–18; 15:1,2; 16:19. While I think Rom 12:14 is a likely candidate for a saying of Jesus being woven into Paul's parenesis, not all agree; see, e.g., Jürgen Sauer, "Traditionsgeschichtliche Erwägungen zu den synoptischen und paulinischen Aussagen über Feindesliebe und Wiedervergeltungsverzicht," *ZNW* 76 (1985) 1–28 (with extensive bibliography). For the whole question of the weaving of Jesus' sayings into Christian parenesis, see John Piper, *"Love Your Enemies." Jesus' Love Command in the Synoptic Gospels and the Early Christian Paraenesis* (SNTSMS 38; Cambridge: Cambridge University, 1979); cf. *A Marginal Jew*, 1. 47, and the bibliographical references on p. 53 n. 24. On the different ways that Paul uses the Jesus tradition, see Deppe, *The Sayings of Jesus*, 188. The question of possible echoes of Jesus' teaching in Rom 12:14 will be studied at greater length in Chapter 36.

[67] See Meier, *A Marginal Jew*, 1. 47–48. For 1 Peter, see Gerhard Maier, "Jesustradition im 1. Petrusbrief," *Gospel Perspectives. The Jesus Tradition Outside the Gospels* (ed. David Wenham; Sheffield: JSOT, 1984) 85–128. On the relation of 1 Peter to the Jesus tradition, see also Paul J. Achtemeier, *1 Peter* (Hermeneia; Minneapolis: Fortress, 1996) 9–12 (arguing against the position that reflections of say-

ings of Jesus in 1 Peter prove that the historical Simon Peter wrote the epistle); John H. Elliott, *1 Peter* (AYB 37B; New York: Doubleday, 2000; reprint New Haven: Yale University Press) 24–37. For the Epistle to the Hebrews, see Hans-Friedrich Weiss, *Der Brief an die Hebräer* (MeyerK 13; Göttingen: Vandenhoeck & Ruprecht, 1991) 89–94; Craig R. Koester, *Hebrews* (AYB 36; New York: Doubleday, 2001; reprint New Haven: Yale University Press) 106–9.

[68] On the striking nature of this phenomenon in the relatively short Epistle of James, see Edgar, *Has God Not Chosen the Poor?* 63–64; see his tabulation of the similarities between James and the Synoptic Gospels on pp. 76–94; for a simpler chart listing the correspondences between James and the Synoptic tradition, see Hartin, *James and the Q Sayings*, 141–42. Deppe, however, observes that, among the non-Pauline "epistles," James does not enjoy a preeminent position in this matter. By Deppe's count (*The Sayings of Jesus*, 221), James has eight clear allusions to the sayings of Jesus, but 1 Peter echoes twelve logia.

[69] Deppe, *The Sayings of Jesus*, 55–149; cf. Holmén, *Jesus and Jewish Covenant Thinking*, 184–85. Deppe's twenty candidates are divided up according to the contexts in which they occur: (1) in general parenesis: Jas 1:2; 1:4; 1:5; 4:2–3; 1:6; 1:19–20; 1:22–23; (2) in extended parenetic discourses: 2:5; 2:8; 2:13; 3:12; (3) in disciplinary exhortations: 3:18; 4:4; 4:9; 5:1; 4:10; 4:11–12; (4) in prophetic denunciations: 5:2–3; (5) in a primitive church order: Jas 5:10–11; 5:12. Even without detailed inspection, one notices almost immediately that the object of our concern, Jas 5:12, is the very last of all the probable examples and provides much more of a parallel in structure and wording within a single verse than do the other candidates. Interestingly, it is also a parallel that comes from the M rather than the Q tradition. For another analysis of the presence of Q, M, and L traditions in James' parenesis, see Mussner, *Der Jakobusbrief*, 47–51.

[70] The eight conscious allusions, according to Deppe (*The Sayings of Jesus*, 219–20), are Jas 1:5; 4:2c–3; 2:5; 4:9; 4:10; 5:2–3a; 5:12; and 5:1. For an alternate list of possible parallels to Synoptic logia, see Tsuji, *Glaube*, 118–19. Jas 5:12 is one of the two parallels to the Jesus tradition that Tsuji considers "almost certain."

[71] On this, see Deppe, *The Sayings of Jesus*, 188, 221–30; Hartin, *James and the Q Sayings*, 216; Tsuji, *Glaube*, 131.

[72] On the Q parallels to Jas 1:5, see Edgar, *Has God Not Chosen the Poor?* 76.

[73] Deppe (*The Sayings of Jesus*, 166) observes that, although many of the sayings of Jesus woven into James' parenesis can be found in Matthew and/or Luke, there is no one Gospel tradition that James consistently reproduces. In a catalogue of both the OT and the Jesus traditions, divided into explicit citations, allusions, and looser parallels (pp. 219–21), Deppe lists Q sayings where Matthew and Luke seem equally represented, Q sayings where James is closer to Luke, Q sayings where

James is closer to Matthew, peculiarly Lucan material, and peculiarly Matthean material (the only example being Jas 5:12). In a similar catalogue, Edgar (*Has God Not Chosen the Poor?* 66) claims that there are a number of parallels between James and Mark. One must admit, however, that many of Edgar's supposed parallels are tenuous at best.

[74] Deppe (*The Sayings of Jesus*, 33–42) identifies six explicit citations of the OT (or, in one case, possibly apocryphal material): Jas 2:8 (Lev 19:18); Jas 2:11a + b (two citations from LXX Exod 20:13 ‖ Deut 5:17 and from LXX Exod 20:15 ‖ Deut 5:18); Jas 2:23 (Gen 15:6); Jas 4:5 (possibly a midrashic adaptation of Gen 6:1–7 or Num 11:29; alternately, a citation from some apocryphal work, e.g., the *Book of Eldad and Modad*); and Jas 4:6 (Prov 3:34). Wachob and Johnson ("The Sayings of Jesus," 431) point out that not only is Lev 19:18 cited explicitly in Jas 2:8, but also that the OT text is woven allusively into a number of other passages in James. Hence, we have a clear case of a written text—known by the author as OT Scripture and cited as such—also being alluded to rather than quoted. Speaking globally, one can say that James reflects the LXX rather than the MT textual tradition.

[75] Among various possible candidates, Deppe (*The Sayings of Jesus*, 42–49) suggests Jas 1:10–11 (Isa 40:6–7; Job 14:2); 3:9 (1 Chr 29:10; Isa 3:16; Sir 23:1,4); 5:4–5 (Isa 5:9; Jer 12:3),11 (Job 1:21–22; 42:10–17),20 (Ezek 3:18–19; Prov 10:12).

[76] See Deppe, *The Sayings of Jesus*, 167.

[77] On the similarity between the Epistle of James and the *Didache* in incorporating the sayings of Jesus, see Deppe, *The Sayings of Jesus*, 187; Edgar, *Has God Not Chosen the Poor?* 64–65.

[78] Debate on the sources, stages of tradition and redaction, and the scriptural knowledge of the *Didache* continues apace. For a representative sample of the many different approaches circulating in academia, see the various essays in van de Sandt (ed.), *Matthew and the Didache*. Brief introductions to the *Didache* can be found in Robert A. Kraft, "Didache," *AYBD*, 2. 197–98; Bart D. Ehrman (ed.), *The Apostolic Fathers* (LCL; 2 vols.; Cambridge, MA/London: Harvard University, 2003) 1. 405–13; Aaron Milavec, *The Didache* (Collegeville, MN: Liturgical Press, 2003) ix–xviii; and, at greater length, Kurt Niederwimmer, *The Didache* (Hermeneia; Minneapolis: Fortress, 1998) 1–57. For the convenience of the reader, I summarize here my own views on some major topics: (1) The *Didache* has gone through a number of stages of tradition and redaction, in which various sources (a teaching on the Two Ways, a collection of dominical logia, citations from one or more written Gospels, primitive church order[s], and a final Matthew-like apocalypse) have been stitched together. (2) The opposite opinion, that the whole of the *Didache* was written at one time by one author, makes a basic methodological blunder by arguing that a modern skillful interpreter can read the *Didache* from start to finish as a meaningful whole. That is true; but the same is true of any skillful practitioner of

narrative, rhetorical, or reader-response criticism reading Matthew or Luke. That these Gospels can be read as artistic and theological wholes does not prove that they were not composed from previous (written and oral) sources such as Mark and Q. The seams, sutures, and tensions within the *Didache*, along with probable dependence on one or more written Gospels, argue for multiple stages of tradition and redaction. (3) Since sayings of Jesus contained in the *Didache* betray at times the redactional touches of Matthew (and possibly Luke), the final form of the *Didache* presupposes knowledge of Matthew and possibly of Luke. (4) Granted a number of stages of tradition and redaction and granted the *Didache*'s knowledge of Matthew and possibly Luke, I would place the final redaction of the *Didache* closer to A.D. 150 than to A.D. 100, contrary to those who would date it toward the end of the first century. (5) Where the final form of the *Didache* was composed remains uncertain; Syria or Palestine-Syria remains popular, though Egypt and Asia Minor are sometimes suggested.

[79] The Greek of the introductory words of *Did.* 8:2 echoes that of Matt 6:5 + 9. The beginning of *Did.* 8:2 commands, "Do not pray like the hypocrites, but as the Lord ordered in his Gospel, pray in this way." (*Mēde proseuchesthe hōs hoi hypokritai, all' hōs ekeleusen ho kyrios en tō euaggeliō autou, houtō proseuchesthe*). Compare Matt 6:5 + 9: "And when you pray, you shall not be like the hypocrites . . . pray therefore in this way" (*kai hotan proseuchēsthe, ouk esesthe hōs hoi hypokritai . . . houtōs oun proseuchesthe hymeis*). What follows in *Did.* 8:2 is the Matthean form of the Lord's Prayer (Matt 6:9–13), with a few minor verbal variations.

[80] Kari Syreeni ("The Sermon on the Mount and the Two Ways Teaching of the Didache," *Matthew and the Didache* [ed. Huub van de Sandt; Assen: Royal van Gorcum; Minneapolis: Fortress, 2005] 87–103) examines what he calls "the evangelical section" of the *Didache* (i.e., 1:3b–2:1) and concludes (pp. 89–90) that it is dependent on Matthew and possibly Luke. Intriguingly, Syreeni also discerns similarities between the ethos of the *Didache*'s teaching on the "Two Ways" and that of the Epistle of James: e.g., in the way Lev 19:18 (the command to love one's neighbor as oneself) is woven together with other material from the Holiness Code of Leviticus and from the Decalogue to focus on an ethical core at the heart of the Torah. Tuckett ("Synoptic Tradition in the Didache," 197–230) likewise sees evidence for the dependence of the *Didache* on Matthew's Gospel, but he begins by arguing from the "apocalyptic appendix" in *Didache* 16. Using the redactional test, Tuckett (pp. 205–8) points out that chap. 16 has links not only with Matthew's special material and with material common to Matthew and Mark in Matthew 24 (Matthew's apocalyptic discourse) but also, in at least one instance (*Did.* 16:8), with material that presupposes Matthew's redaction of Mark. This pattern of parallels between *Didache* 16 and Matthew 24 is best explained by the *Didache*'s knowledge of the finished Gospel of Matthew. Turning to *Did.* 1:3–2:1, Tuckett discerns in the dominical sayings the redactional hands of both Matthew and Luke. Joseph Verheyden ("Eschatology in the Didache and the Gospel of Matthew," *Mat-*

thew and the Didache, 193–215) also compares *Didache* 16 with Matthew 24–25 and concludes that the *Didache*'s knowledge of Matthew is "convincing." Taking a slightly different view, John S. Kloppenborg ("The Use of the Synoptics or Q in *Did.* 1:3b–2:1," *Matthew and the Didache*, 105–29) examines *Did.* 1:3b–5 in detail and concludes that the passage demonstrates a knowledge of Luke and of either Matthew or Q. It is not my purpose here to adopt the precise theory of one or another of these authors but simply to second their basic position, i.e., that the final form of the *Didache* betrays knowledge of Matthew and/or Luke. The fact that the redactor of the *Didache* could know that certain sayings came from Jesus and yet could weave them into the larger parenesis of *Didache* 1–2 without any reference to their dominical origin supplies an important parallel for understanding James' use of the sayings of Jesus.

[81] So Schneider, "*omnyō*," 182 n. 64; see also Bauernfeind, "Der Eid," 104.

[82] Indeed, Wachob and Johnson ("The Sayings of Jesus," 432) call Jas 5:12 the "surest candidate for a saying of Jesus within James." Similarly, Tsuji (*Glaube*, 118) considers Jas 5:12 one of undoubted parallels to the logia of Jesus.

[83] On this whole question, see Deppe, *The Sayings of Jesus*, 189–218. Deppe spends most of his chapter 6 arguing forcefully against composition of the Epistle by James of Jerusalem. As Deppe correctly observes, the excellent Greek style of the epistle, the "purely ethical content given to the law" (without any of the halakic concerns that exercised the historical James of Jerusalem), and the delayed acceptance of the Epistle of James into the canon of the New Testament (as contrasted, e.g., with the Epistle of Jude) all argue against composition by James of Jerusalem. It is therefore quite odd that, at the end of chapter 6, Deppe (p. 218) suddenly draws back into an acceptance of James of Jerusalem as the author simply on the grounds of "the traditional assumption of authorship" that "has stood the test of time and explains most of the exegetical givens of the text."

[84] See, e.g., the comment of E. P. Sanders on the *Testament of Abraham* in Charlesworth's *OTP*, 1. 876: "The most important observation is that the Testament of Abraham, far from presenting the particular doctrines of some Jewish sect, represents a kind of lowest-common-denominator Judaism. In some ways its most characteristic feature is its characterlessness; it lacks peculiar traits." I will treat the problem of the date, provenance, and possibly Christian nature of the *Testaments of the Twelve Patriarchs* in Chapter 36.

[85] There is a welter of literary and theological problems connected with the place of Jas 5:12 within the larger structure and thought of the epistle, problems that I do not discuss because they do not affect our quest for authentic Jesus tradition. Simply for the sake of completeness, I list my own views on a number of debated subjects: (1) It is probably a mistake either to claim that the Epistle of James has no literary structure and clear flow of thought or to claim that it is a tightly structured liter-

ary composition. The truth lies somewhere in between. Major blocks of material can be discerned along with linguistic and logical connections, but one must admit that the connections are loose. (2) Hence we are not surprised that it is difficult to decide whether 5:12 goes with the material that precedes or follows it in chap. 5. Personally, I do not think that there is a close connection either way. Attempts to see 5:12 as introducing a primitive church order or as reflecting the use of oaths to conclude literary epistles seem forced. (3) Likewise, the function of the introductory *pro pantōn de* ("but above all . . .") in 5:12 is unclear. Dibelius (*Der Brief des Jakobus*, 294–95) sees no real connection with the preceding or subsequent context; so also Hoppe, *Der theologische Hintergrund*, 14. Most commentators would agree that, at the very least, the phrase emphasizes the importance of the teaching in 5:12. Deppe (*The Sayings of Jesus*, 135–36) points out that ancient papyri supply evidence that *pro pantōn* was used for emphasis especially near the conclusion of a letter; so also, Cheung, *The Genre*, 67–68. Accordingly, Johnson (*The Letter of James*, 325) favors the view that *pro pantōn* marks a turn to the final section of the composition; he thinks that 5:12–20 forms "a unified discourse on the positive modes of speech in the community." Still, Johnson admits a connection between 5:12 and the negative commands in the preceding units (e.g., 4:11; 5:9). Edgar (*Has God Not Chosen the Poor?* 17–18, 188–89) argues for a number of parallels between the closing paragraph of the Epistle of James and the closing section of Hellenistic epistles; in such works, *pro pantōn*, followed by a health wish or an oath-formula, is characteristic of epistolary endings. In similar fashion, Jas 5:12 opens with *pro pantōn* and is followed by a prohibition of oaths and a reference to the health of the recipients (vv 13–16). Opposed to this view is Penner (*The Epistle of James*, 149–50), who connects 5:12 with 5:7–11; so also, Wachob, *The Voice of Jesus*, 188; Tsuji, *Glaube*, 93; Baker, *Personal Speech-Ethics*, 278. Maintaining that 5:12 is primarily the conclusion of 5:7–11 while not denying its function as a signal that the letter is coming to its conclusion is Popkes, *Der Brief des Jakobus*, 332. Other commentators instead see in the *pro pantōn* a sign that the author knows that he is citing a logion of Jesus, with *pro pantōn* functioning as equivalent to the *mē . . . holōs* ("not at all") of Matt 5:34. Yet, as we have seen, in Jas 5:12 the real functional equivalent of *mē . . . holōs* is "or by any other oath." In the end, it may be that *pro pantōn* is simply a rhetorical, literary equivalent of clearing one's throat. Mussner (*Der Jakobusbrief*, 211) sees it as a piece of literary rhetoric that says, effectively, "before all else, I must not forget to write you this admonition as well."

[86] While arguing that the core of the prohibition goes back to Jesus, Vahrenhorst (*"Ihr sollt,"* 259–60) rejects the argument from discontinuity and emphasizes instead the argument from coherence—an approach closely connected with his questionable view of a virtual prohibition of oaths present in some Jewish writings around the turn of the era.

[87] Critics supply many different hypothetical original forms; e.g., Zeller (*Die weisheitlichen Mahnsprüche*, 125) suggests as the "Palestinian Urform" *mē omnyete; estō de hymōn to nai nai, kai to ou ou* ("do not swear; but let you yes be yes

and your no no"). Most critical reconstructions are variations on this suggestion. In favor of James' formulation being the more original, see Dautzenberg, "Ist das Schwurverbot," 61. Tsuji (*Glaube*, 121–22) also thinks that Jas 5:12 is the more original form, but without the concluding clause. In a similar vein, Deppe (*The Sayings of Jesus*, 145–56) thinks that Jas 5:12 represents the primitive saying of Jesus, provided one removes the introductory formula "But above all, brothers," and the comprehensive oath formula "or by any other oath." Deppe's analysis of the growth of the Matt 5:34–37 (pp. 146–47) is close to the one I have adopted.

[88] From what follows, it is clear that I reject the either–or approach of Dauztenberg ("Ist das Schwurverbot," 50), who holds that only one form (either the Matthean or the Jamesian) can go back to the origin of the tradition. For him, at the origin of the tradition lies a parenetic formulation, influenced by the wisdom tradition, such as we find in Jas 5:12; the Matthean formulation is secondary.

[89] Ito (*Matthew's Understanding*, 119–25) considers all the arguments in favor of the priority of James' wording in Jas 5:12f (which he admits is probably the opinion of the majority of critics, including Strecker, Luz, and Davies), only to reject them in favor of Matthew's wording being more primitive (so also Bauernfeind and, with hesitation, Mussner). For the generally accepted counterposition that Jas 5:12f represents the primitive wording or at least an earlier form of the tradition, see Luz, *Matthew 1–7*, 312; cf. Dautzenberg, "Ist das Schwurverbot," 62–63; Holmén, *Jesus and Jewish Covenant Thinking*, 176–77; Wachob and Johnson, "The Sayings of Jesus," 438–39; Popkes, *Der Brief des Jakobus*, 334–35. Luz argues, along with many others, that the fact that Jas 5:12f ("your yes must be a yes and your no must be a no," *ētō de hymōn to nai nai kai to ou ou*) is widely attested in the citations of the prohibition of oaths by the Fathers of the Church (e.g., Justin Martyr [though with Matthew's *estō* instead of James' *ētō*], Clement of Alexandria), while the rest of the wording of their citations often follows the Matthean text, points to the Jamesian formulation as original; on this phenomenon of the mixture of Matthean and Jamesian wording in patristic citations, see also Duling, "Against Oaths," 108. I am dubious about Luz's line of argument and in general about reliance on the patristic citations as independent witnesses of the primitive logion prohibiting swearing. Much more likely, in my view, is that from Justin onwards we are dealing with catechetical digests, Gospel harmonies, or perhaps citations from memory, any of which would reflect a knowledge, however indirect, of Matthew and James. The patristic citations of the prohibition of oaths tell us a great deal about the handing on and development of the Gospel tradition in the patristic period, but I doubt that they help us as we try to move backward from Matthew and James to the historical Jesus. Hence, I do not present here a detailed investigation of the patristic parallels. For a helpful comparison of Matt 5:33–37, Jas 5:12, and patristic parallels such as Justin, the *Pseudo-Clementine Homilies*, Clement of Alexandria, Eusebius, Epiphanius, the *Apostolic Constitutions*, Gregory of Nyssa, and Cyril of Alexandria, see Duling, ibid.,103–6; also Deppe, *The Sayings of Jesus*, 147–49. Deppe, like a number of other commentators, favors the view that Justin's citation of the "dominical saying"

in *Apology* 1.16.5 represents independent oral tradition. The text of Justin's citation of the prohibition of swearing reads: *Peri de tou mē omnynai holōs, talēthē de legein aei, houtōs parekeleusato. Mē omosēte holōs. Estō de hymōn to nai nai, kai to ou ou. To de perisson toutōn ek tou ponērou* ("But concerning the [command] not to swear at all but rather to speak the truth always, thus did [Jesus] command: 'Do not swear at all; but your yes must be a yes, and your no a no; but more than these [words come] from the Evil One' "). For a full treatment of Justin's use of the sayings of Jesus, see Bellinzoni, *The Sayings of Jesus*, 64–67 for the prohibition of oaths. After exhaustive analysis, Bellinzoni (p. 140) concludes that *Apology* 1.15–17 (and hence 1.16.5) "is probably based on a primitive Christian catechism in use in Justin's school in Rome" and that this or a similar catechism was known to other early Church Fathers; this view is adopted by Koester, *Ancient Christian Gospels*, 361–63. I think that Bellinzoni's view of the source of *Apology* 1.16.5 is the most probable opinion, though the possible use of a Gospel harmony cannot be completely excluded. Whether Matt 5:34b–36 is omitted by Justin because it had already been omitted by the source he is using or whether Justin himself omits this material because he is interested only in the basic principle and not the particulars (so Sanders, *The Tendencies*, 57, 67) is difficult to decide and is not *ad rem* to our quest. I should note that, while I do not accept the view that Justin's version of the prohibition reflects independent oral tradition, I have no great quarrel with those who do, since their opinion simply strengthens my argument from multiple attestation of sources. In any event (to return to the main point), as I indicate in the main text, I consider otiose the whole debate about whether Matt 5:37a or Jas 5:12f represents more accurately the words of the historical Jesus.

[90] This is the opinion of Foster, *Community*, 115–16; see also Kollmann, "Das Schwurverbot,"191–93. Luz (*Matthew 1–7*, 317) correctly observes that Jesus' prohibition of swearing involves not simply an element of deepening the intention of the Torah but also an element of abrogation; see also Bethke, "Überhaupt nicht schwören," 39. The opposite view is taken by Sanders ("The Synoptic Jesus and the Law," 55), who claims that Jesus' prohibition of oaths is not against the biblical law, "since the person who does not swear obviously would not transgress the law which forbids swearing falsely." A similar view is held by Wachob and Johnson ("The Sayings of Jesus," 435–36), who speak of a "heightening" or "intensifying" of the Law. This position ignores two vital points: (1) In certain circumstances, the written Torah demands an oath. (2) As in the case of divorce, Jesus is abrogating an important social and legal institution that is permitted and regulated by the Torah; such a disconcerting and presumptuous act brings us beyond the safe parameters of "not only . . . but also." On this point, one notes a tension in the treatment of 5:34–37 by Davies and Allison, *Matthew*, 1. 532–38. Their word-by-word exegesis favors understanding the prohibition of the Matthean Jesus (who sometimes in Davies and Allison is conflated with the historical Jesus) as absolute, but such direct opposition to the Mosaic Torah conflicts with their overall conception of Matthew's theology of the Law. A somewhat different tension can be found in Harrington, *Matthew*, 88: Jesus' prohibition renders the Torah passages about oaths "useless"

or "superfluous," yet "this need not be taken as an abrogation or criticism of the 'old Law.' Rather it is a sharpening that Matthew understood as fulfillment." Also using the vocabulary of "superfluous," Hagner (*Matthew*, 1. 128–29) claims that Jesus' prohibition states that swearing is altogether unnecessary; since it serves no purpose, it should be avoided. One notices in all these paraphrases of Jesus' prohibition an attempt to avoid the vocabulary of abrogation or revocation. Suggs ("The Antitheses," 103–4) takes a subtle approach: in the antitheses, Matthew did not intend to present Jesus as opposed to or abrogating the Torah, but we modern readers might judge that in effect Matthew wound up doing just that. Dautzenberg ("Ist das Schwuverbot," 55) seems to miss the real point at issue by tying the question of an absolute prohibition of oaths that in effect revokes commandments in the Torah to the question of the antithetical formulation in Matthew. Dautzenberg holds that the parenetic formulation in Jas 5:12 is not an absolute prohibition, which is created only when the antithetical formulation of the Matthean tradition is created. He seems not to realize that James' "or by any other oath" is the functional equivalent of the *mē . . . holōs* ("not at all") in Matt 5:34.

[91] *Matthew 1–7*, 316. Luz goes on (p. 318) to make the interesting observation that the early Fathers of the Church took the prohibition of swearing almost always literally. The Greek Fathers kept this stringent interpretation alive for a long time; in the Latin Fathers, mitigation began early on, though Cyprian stands out as a Latin Father who consistently rejected oaths. Luz continues (p. 319): "The entire tradition of the Great Church since the early Middle Ages almost unanimously set Matt 5:33–37 aside and accepted oaths, even though often with a bad conscience." The radical tradition of a total prohibition survived in medieval fringe groups and "nonconformist" Protestants like the Catharists, Waldensians, Anabaptists, and Quakers. Luz concludes (p. 321): "It does not take much power of persuasion to demonstrate that the interpretation of the nonconformists comes closest to the text." Luz (p. 322 n. 84) cannot resist a parting shot about oaths being solidly anchored in the present Code of Canon Law. Luz has at least one point in his favor: it will not do to try to limit Jesus' absolute prohibition of oaths to oaths used in daily life or loose conversation, while oaths in courts or other formal legal situations would still be allowed. Not only does the sweeping prohibition of both the Matthean and Jamesian wording ("swear not at all"/"or any other oath") speak against such latter-day casuistry; the very rationale of the prohibition, expressed or implied in Matt 5:34–37 ‖ Jas 5:12, condemns courtroom oaths just as much as oaths in everyday life; on this, see Holmén, *Jesus and Jewish Covenant Thinking*, 182.

CHAPTER 34

JESUS AND THE SABBATH

After the problems posed by Jesus' pronouncements on divorce and oaths, the most obvious halakic question demanding our attention is Jesus' teaching on the observance of the sabbath.[1] If nothing else, Gospel traditions dealing with Jesus' attitude toward the sabbath enjoy multiple attestation of sources and forms. These traditions are found in either narratives or sayings in Mark, special Matthean material (M), special Lucan material (L), and John. Adding impetus and animus to the argument over Jesus and the sabbath is the claim by some Christian exegetes that, by violating the sabbath, Jesus was in effect, if not in intention, undermining one of the basic institutions of Judaism.[2] Hence, in addition to the criterion of multiple attestation, the criterion of discontinuity—and possibly the criterion of an adequate explanation of Jesus' death—might be invoked in order to demonstrate the historicity as well as the pivotal nature of Jesus' clashes with his fellow Jews over the sabbath.

Nevertheless, as we have often found out during our quest for the historical Jesus, first impressions from Gospel texts can be deceiving. All that glitters in the text is not historical gold. To reach an informed judgment, we need (1) to situate Jesus' actions and teaching within the context of Jewish observance of and disputes about the sabbath around the turn of the era and then (2) to apply the criteria of historicity to the Gospel material that depicts Jesus arguing over sabbath observance. This task, in turn, demands that we first inform ourselves about the origin and nature of the Jewish sabbath.

I. THE SABBATH FROM THE SCRIPTURES TO THE MISHNA

A. THE SABBATH IN THE JEWISH SCRIPTURES

Many studies of the sabbath in the OT and Judaism begin with scholarly debates over the etymology of the noun "sabbath" (*šabbāt* in the Hebrew) and the origins of this religious day of rest, observed on the seventh day of each week.[3] While such questions are important to modern scholars, they are irrelevant to the thought and practice of 1st-century Jews, who were not burdened by our historical-critical mind-set. Palestinian Jews raised in observant families first imbibed the practice of the sabbath from the rhythm of family and community life lived week after week in their towns or villages. Most Jews would learn from their parents the basic Torah commandment to observe the sabbath, which above all meant the cessation of ordinary daily work. In due time, those Jews who attended synagogues would receive more extended instruction on the meaning and application of the scriptural texts concerned with the sabbath. Needless to say, these texts were not expounded according to modern theories about sources and hypothetical datings of traditions. These texts were accepted as the Word of God addressed to Israel, as mediated through Moses or, later on, through the prophets.[4]

Foundational for any 1st-century Jew would be the sabbath command contained in the "Ten Words"—what we call the Decalogue or the Ten Commandments—found in somewhat different forms in Exodus 20 and Deuteronomy 5.[5] The form in Exod 20:8–11 harks back to the creation narrative of Gen 1:1–2:4: "Remember the day of the sabbath, to sanctify it. Six days you shall labor and do all your work. But the seventh day is a sabbath for Yahweh your God. You shall not do any work—you, your son, your daughter, your male slave, your female slave, your animals, or your resident alien who [lives] within your gates. For in six days did Yahweh make the heavens and the earth, with the sea and all that is in it. And he rested on the seventh day; therefore Yahweh blessed the seventh day and sanctified it." The corresponding command in the version of the Decalogue in Deuteronomy recalls instead Israel's enslavement in and liberation from Egypt (the exodus event) while also reflecting humanitarian concerns (Deut 5:12–15): "Observe the day of the sabbath, to sanctify it, just as Yahweh your God commanded you. Six days you shall labor and do all your work. But the seventh day is a sabbath for Yahweh your God. You shall not do any work— you, your son, your daughter, your male slave, your female slave, your ox, your donkey, any of your animals, or your resident alien who [lives] within your gates, in order that your male slave and female slave may rest as you do. And you shall remember that you were a slave in the land of Egypt and that Yahweh your God brought you out of there with a mighty hand and an outstretched arm. Therefore Yahweh your God has commanded you to keep [literally, do] the day of the sabbath."[6]

Other formulations of the sabbath command, found at various points in the Pentateuch, helped drum this basic obligation into the conscience of every pious Jew. Formulations that are probably older than those of the Decalogue (older, that is, from the modern viewpoint of tradition history) are found in Exod 34:21 (emphasizing that the cessation of labor holds true even at times of plowing and reaping) and Exod 23:12 (emphasizing the cessation of work so that the marginalized of society may "breathe freely" or "be refreshed"). Especially striking is the expansive form of the command in Exod 31:12–17: the sabbath is a perpetual sign between Israel and Yahweh the Creator. Indeed, so solemn a sign is it that anyone who profanes it or does any work on it is to be put to death. The version of the sabbath command in Exod 35:3 adds after the mention of the death penalty a specific injunction against kindling fire in anyone's dwelling on the sabbath. The death penalty is also inculcated in the story of a man caught gathering sticks (to start a fire?) on the sabbath (Num 15:32–36); the whole congregation stones him to death. In contrast to these lengthy formulations of the sabbath command, the most laconic form is found in the Holiness Code of Leviticus (Lev 19:3b): "You shall observe my sabbaths: I am Yahweh your God." Interestingly, Lev 23:3 lists the sabbath among the appointed feasts of the liturgical year and prescribes for it a "holy assembly" (held, de facto, in the Jerusalem temple, though Leviticus is speaking of the tent in the wilderness).

What is arresting in the whole range of these commands is the simple and stark nature of the essential obligation of the sabbath: every seventh day, Israelites and all belonging to their households must desist from every kind of labor. Originally, agricultural labor was the primary if not the sole object of the command. In due time, with the growth of urban centers, the prohibition of work was understood to extend to all sorts of commercial transactions as well. Intriguingly, in the Pentateuch, only a few detailed prohibitions are spelled out within the overall interdiction of work: for example, the prohibition of kindling fires in dwellings and (presumably) gathering wood for that purpose. With the exception of a few passing references to additional sabbath sacrifices and rituals to be carried out by the priests in the tent in the wilderness (symbolizing the later Jerusalem temple), no acts of worship, public or private, are enjoined on individual Israelites as part of their observance of the sabbath.[7]

Only a few further details are supplied by scattered passages in the Pentateuch, but these details were seized upon by Jews around the turn of the era as a basis for more precise directions about sabbath observance. In the story of the initial gift of the manna in the desert (Exodus 16), God provides just enough manna for each day; any excess amount that is gathered goes bad by the next morning. However, on the day before the sabbath (i.e., Friday),

God provides enough manna to last for two days (Exod 16:5,22–30). Moses accordingly commands the people to cook all necessary food on the sixth day. By a special divine dispensation, the extra food left over from the sixth day does not spoil on the sabbath, thus providing sufficient nourishment for the day of rest. This story supplies a basis for the Jewish prohibition of any food preparation, above all the cooking of food, on the sabbath. In addition, the way Moses prohibits searching for any additional manna on the sabbath (Exod 16:29: "Let each man stay where he is; let him not go forth from his place on the seventh day") provides a basis for the prohibition of journeys or any extensive movement.[8]

What this brief survey of pentateuchal references reveals is that little of the later Jewish *hălākâ* governing the details of sabbath observance finds explicit expression in the written Torah of Moses.[9] Indeed, some of the most important halakic pronouncements concerning observance of the sabbath are found not in the Mosaic Law but rather in the classical prophets—a salutary rebuke to those who would facilely play off the Spirit-led prophets against the supposed growing "casuistry" of legal interpretation. For example, in the preexilic period, it is the radical prophet Amos (8:5) who mocks the greedy grain merchants who cannot wait for the new moon and the sabbath to be over so that they can resume their (often dishonest) business.[10] Thus, it is a prophet, rather than a scribe, priest, or royal legislator, who provides us with the earliest testimony to the extension of the prohibition of agrarian labor to the bustling commerce of the northern kingdom of Israel in the 8th century B.C.[11] Likewise pivotal for the development of sabbath *hălākâ* is another "antiestablishment" prophet, Jeremiah, active in the southern kingdom of Judah in the 7th and 6th centuries B.C. Jeremiah warns both royalty and commoners not to carry burdens through the gates of Jerusalem on the sabbath or any burden out of their houses on the sabbath (Jer 17:19–27).[12] These activities are assimilated to the basic sin of "doing work" on the sabbath (17:24). We have here, then, another case in which the sabbath prohibition of work, which was originally aimed at agrarian labor, is applied to urban activity, even beyond what could strictly speaking be called commerce. So important has the sabbath command become that, according to Jeremiah, the very continuance of the reign of the house of David over the kingdom of Judah depends on its proper observance.

While Ezekiel, during the Babylonian exile, adds nothing new to the halakic development of the sabbath, he emphasizes the prophetic indictment of Israel (and especially of the priests) for having profaned the sabbath from the time Yahweh gave it to his people in the wilderness (Ezek 20:12; 22:8,26; 23:38). In the proto-apocalyptic vision of the new Jerusalem and its temple with which the Book of Ezekiel ends, one sign of the changed situation is that the priests will keep the sabbath holy (44:24).[13]

In the postexilic period after the return to Jerusalem, perhaps the greatest single contributor to later sabbath hălākâ is the anonymous prophet whom modern critics label Third Isaiah. In a single vague utterance (Isa 58:13–14), he provides abundant fodder for later halakic development.[14] The following translation conveys something of the murky nature of the text, with its confusing possibilities: (v 13) "If you hold back your foot [or: "refrain from travel"] from the sabbath [or: "on the sabbath"] so as to do [or: "from doing"] what you wish [or: "your business"] on my holy day, if you call the sabbath a delight [and] the holy [day] of Yahweh honorable, and if you honor it by not following [literally: "doing"] your ways [or: "by not traveling for business"], by not pursuing [literally: "finding"] what you wish [or: "your business"], or speaking a word [or: "making commercial agreements"; or: "engaging in idle chatter"], (v 14) then you will find delight in Yahweh." [15] It is remarkable how these two verses—precisely because they are so nebulous and open-ended—could generate so much halakic reflection in future centuries. To be sure, Jews at Jesus' time would have read this passage not as a postexilic composition but rather as part of the whole Book of Isaiah, attributed to Isaiah of Jerusalem (8th century B.C.). With great rhetorical effect, therefore, Isa 58:13–14 would be read within a grand *inclusio*, stretching from the denunciation of insincere worship in the temple on the sabbath at the beginning of the book (Isa 1:13) to the magnificent concluding prophecy (Isa 66:23), which envisions all humanity worshiping Yahweh on each sabbath in the temple.[16]

These grand prophetic exhortations and visions emphasizing the sacredness of the sabbath did not always square with the all-too-earthly reality of Jerusalem and its temple in the postexilic period. In the 5th century B.C., for example, Nehemiah had to struggle to prevent the sale of merchandise and agricultural produce, as well as the treading of wine presses, on the sabbath (Neh 10:32 [ET 10:31]; 13:15–22; cf. Neh 9:14).[17] Indeed, even by the 1st century A.D., it is not certain that all Jews in Palestine observed the ban on commerce that Nehemiah fought so vigorously to enforce.[18]

If we pause at this point to list all the sabbath prohibitions that we have just located in the Jewish Scriptures, what should strike us is that the yield is surprisingly small. In addition to the basic prohibition of agricultural work (especially sowing and reaping, but also allied activities like treading the wine press and loading beasts of burden to take the produce to market), we find prohibitions against buying and selling (and presumably other commercial activities and agreements), carrying burdens through city gates or out of houses (but what qualifies as a burden?), leaving one's "place" or under-taking a journey, lighting a fire, and preparing food, especially by cooking. That is all.

This surprise turns almost into a shock when we realize that none of these prohibitions specifically and directly applies to the controversial acts Jesus is reported to have performed on the sabbath. Most of the prohibitions—buying and selling, lighting a fire, cooking, and indeed most kinds of agri-cultural work—are completely irrelevant to the Gospel stories recounting disputes about sabbath observance. Even reaping and carrying a burden are performed not by Jesus himself but rather by his disciples (the plucking of grain on the sabbath, recounted in Mark 2:23–28 parr.) or by the paralyzed man lying by the pool of Bethesda (the healing recounted in John 5:1–9a, after which the man picks up his mat and carries it home on the sabbath). When it comes to violating the sabbath by work, the only thing that Jesus is ever directly accused of is healing—something that the Jewish Scriptures never include among the works prohibited on the sabbath. Thus, even before we come to a consideration of the Gospel stories, things begin to look a little strange.

B. The Sabbath in the Deuterocanonical (Apocryphal) Books

This strange impression is not altered by the deuterocanonical (or apocry-phal) books of the OT, included in the Septuagint. Most of the deuteroca-nonical books do not even mention the sabbath; the few that do contribute nothing to the question of Jesus' relation to the sabbath.[19] For instance, from the Book of Judith, we learn of the special ascetic practices of Judith, a pious widow who fasted throughout her widowhood except for certain holy days, including the day before the sabbath and the sabbath itself. While fasting, she lived on the roof of her house; she descended into her house only on sab-baths and feast days (Jdt 8:6; 10:2). These practices, however praiseworthy in the eyes of the author, are obviously voluntary, supererogatory works of piety. No Jewish group of the period considered them incumbent on all Israelites. The one practice that connects Judith's particular practices with those of virtually all Jews is the avoidance of fasting on the sabbath, which was supposed to be observed as a day of joy.[20] Thus, the practices of Judith have at best only an indirect connection with the Gospels. Inasmuch as Jesus forbids his disciples to practice any voluntary fasting (Mark 2:18–20 parr.), one might infer that he implicitly likens his presence and ministry to a perpetual feast day or sabbath—though the specific comparison he makes is to a wedding feast.[21]

Almost all the other references to the sabbath in the deuterocanonical literature are found in First and Second Maccabees.[22] Most of the passages have to do with the banning of sabbath observance by the pagan Syrian monarch Antiochus Epiphanes, the resulting desecration of the sabbath by some Jews, the heroic resistance, even to the point of martyrdom, by others, and the famous decision by the followers of Mattathias to fight defensive battles on the sabbath—the halakic question we have already examined in Chapter 31.[23]

A somewhat different case is presented by the narrative of 2 Macc 5:24–26: the Syrian army pretends to be visiting Jerusalem with peaceable intentions. When some Jews come out of the city on the sabbath to watch the Syrian soldiers parading under arms, the Syrians slaughter the unsuspecting Jews and then rush into the city to kill many of its inhabitants. The story presupposes that the Jews of Jerusalem saw no legal problem in leaving their city to walk some distance to the Syrian parade field. The problem of how far outside of one's own settlement one could walk on the sabbath—a problem hinted at in *Jubilees* and addressed in the Dead Sea Scrolls and the Mishna—does not seem to be on the radar screen of 2 Maccabees.

A still different type of sabbath reference is found in 1 Macc 10:34, part of a purported letter from the Syrian king Demetrius. In it, he promises the Jews that the sabbath, along with various feast days, will be a day of exemption and immunity, when no one will have authority to exact payment of duties and tolls from Jews or to force them to appear in a law court.[24] In sum, the only new sabbath practices or prescriptions mentioned in the deuterocanonical books are concerned with the rejection of fasting on the sabbath, the permissibility of waging defensive warfare, the avoidance of paying tolls and dues, and the refusal to appear in court. Clearly, none of these issues has anything to do with the sabbath disputes in the Gospels.

C. The Old Testament Pseudepigrapha and Qumran

Turning now to the intertestamental literature, including the so-called OT pseudepigrapha, we purposely restrict our attention to works composed in Palestine between the 2d century B.C. and the 1st century A.D. Within that compass, only two major sources offer a significant chance of expanding our knowledge of sabbath *hălākâ* in Palestinian Judaism during this period: the *Book of Jubilees* and the Dead Sea Scrolls (chiefly the *Damascus Document*).

(1) The *Book of Jubilees*, composed most likely within a circle of dissident Jerusalem priests ca. 161–152 B.C.,[25] is the first extant document from Jew-

ish Palestine to show an interest in gathering various prohibitions of sabbath activity into normative lists, thus pointing forward to the later list of thirty-nine forbidden actions in the Mishna's tractate *Šabbat*.[26] Parts of the lists in *Jubilees* may represent prior oral or written traditions, but certain traits suggest that the author of *Jubilees* is responsible for the present form and order of the lists.[27]

In chap. 2 of *Jubilees*, the basic commandment to abstain from all work on the sabbath is embedded in the narrative of creation itself.[28] The gift of the sabbath is first given to the angels, and then God chooses the people of Israel to share this most holy of days with the angels and himself (vv 17–24). *Jubilees* solemnly and repeatedly (four times!) insists that anyone who transgresses the holiness of the sabbath by doing any work must die (vv 25–28).[29] Verses 29–30 then detail which actions count as unlawful work, that is, work in which people, in an unseemly way, carry out their own pleasure. The forbidden actions include preparing food and drink on the sabbath rather than on the sixth day, drawing water, bringing anything in or out of one's dwelling or its "gates" (or "doors"), and carrying anything from one house to another.

Two further and more detailed lists are placed in chap. 50 as the grand conclusion of the entire book. These lists are directly connected not with the creation narrative of Gen 1:1–2:4, as was the case in chap. 2 of *Jubilees*, but rather with the giving of the Law on Mt. Sinai and specifically with the sabbath command of the Decalogue, cited in a slightly abbreviated version of Exod 20:9–10. The first list is introduced by the solemn command that anyone who works on the sabbath is to die (v 8). This introduction forms a neat if somber *inclusio* with the end of both the first and the second list of prohibitions (vv 8,13), where we are told again that anyone who does any of the specified works on the sabbath is to die.

The first list in chap. 50 (v 8) prohibits the following works on the sabbath: sexual intercourse with one's wife, discussion of work (in particular, plans to take a journey or to engage in buying or selling),[30] drawing water, lifting up any object to carry it out of one's tent or house, and preparing food or drink.[31] Verses 9–11 then exhort Israel in a positive way to sanctify the sabbath by resting from work, by blessing God for the gift of this festival, by eating and drinking, and by offering God the temple sacrifices due him. This priestly-minded document takes great care in v 11 to specify that the offering of incense and sacrifices in the Lord's sanctuary is the sole work permissible on the sabbath.

Verse 12 then supplies the second list of prohibited works contained in chap. 50. Beyond the initial global prohibition of doing work on the sabbath, the list specifically prohibits going on a journey,[32] plowing a field either at home or in another place, kindling a fire, riding an animal, traveling (or, possibly, simply being) in a boat on the sea, slaughtering or killing anything, slashing the throat of cattle or birds, snaring a beast, bird, or fish, observing a fast, or fighting a war. With the repetition of the death penalty, imposed with a view to assuring that Israel keeps the sabbath according to the commands enshrined in *Jubilees*, the book draws to a close. For our purposes, the most remarkable thing about these detailed lists is their total irrelevance to the sabbath disputes in which Jesus is directly accused of breaking the sabbath. As with the OT proscriptions, the prohibition of agricultural labor and of carrying objects touches only the disciples plucking grain (Mark 2:23–28 parr.) and the man healed of paralysis, who proceeds to carry his mat (John 5:1–9). Strange to say, even in the stringent sabbath rules inculcated by *Jubilees*, there is no prohibition of healing the sick—the only transgression with which Jesus is directly charged in the Gospels. Judged by the strict sabbath regulations of *Jubilees*, Jesus emerges absolutely blameless.

(2) A more extensive list of sabbath prohibitions is found in the *Damascus Document*. What some scholars call "the Sabbath Codex" or "Sabbath Code" comprises CD 10:14–11:18a.[33] Its basic content seems older than the *Damascus Document* taken as a literary whole. At first glance, one is surprised to see that some basic pentateuchal prohibitions are not mentioned (e.g., the kindling of fire, plowing and reaping). Their absence is a good reminder that some of the biblical prohibitions are simply presupposed by the author(s) of the *Damascus Document* and the Sabbath Codex lying behind it. The Codex does not claim to be complete compilation of all sabbath rules.[34] Rather, the prohibitions in the Sabbath Codex represent a development and expansion of certain biblical regulations in the direction of more concrete and detailed application by a sectarian group. Some prohibitions stand alone, while small groups of prohibitions that are related by content are "bundled" together.

Many prohibitions of the Sabbath Codex, while of great importance for the history of the development of sabbath *hălākâ*, have no relevance for the sabbath dispute stories in the Gospels:[35] for example, the exact time on Friday when all work must cease, the distance one may walk on the sabbath, the prohibition of wearing dirty clothing. A few, however, may be profiled, by way of comparison or contrast, with sayings about sabbath observance that are attributed to Jesus.

(a) For example, the permission to follow one's cattle to pasture outside of one's settlement for a distance of 2,000 cubits (CD 11:5b–7a) may echo the same sort of commonsense peasant practice that is also seen in Jesus' rhetorical question in Luke 13:15: "Does not each of you on the sabbath untie his ox or his donkey from the manger and lead it to drink?" While there is a thematic connection, the differences between the two texts are quite sharp: (i) The Gospel logion sees no problem with the owner walking before and leading his animal, while the Sabbath Codex permits only following one's animal as it goes to pasture. (ii) The Codex is concerned with the precise distance one is allowed to traverse while caring for one's animal; no such concern is apparent in any of Jesus' sayings about the sabbath.

(b) Some scholars see in an obscure prohibition in CD 11:9c–10a a possible context for the accusations leveled against Jesus that he broke the sabbath by healing the sick. CD 11:9c–10a reads: "Let no one carry *sammānîm* on himself [i.e., on his body], to go out or to come in, on the sabbath." Since there is no other Jewish-Palestinian text prior to Jesus that explicitly prohibits acts of healing on the sabbath, this text is sometimes seized upon as the evidence that healing was indeed forbidden by the sabbath *hălākâ* of at least some groups.[36] However, two aspects of the text make this attempt at creating a parallel highly problematic: (i) The exact meaning of the key noun *sammānîm* is disputed. Various scholars suggest the meaning of "perfume," "fragrant powder," "spices," "medicine," "healing or hurtful powder," or "poison." While the reference to medicine is possible, it is not certain.[37] (ii) In a sense, though, the precise meaning of the noun is beside the point. The context shows that the focus of the prohibition is the action of carrying objects in and out of one's house or of lifting an object (see CD 11:7b–11a). Whatever the meaning of *sammānîm*, the question is whether such an object can count as clothing, which one can certainly carry on one's body in and out of one's house, or whether it counts as some sort of "burden" that one is not allowed to transport in and out of one's house on the sabbath.[38]

(c) CD 11:13–14a provides, by way of contrast, the clearest parallel to a saying attributed to Jesus. The stringent *hălākâ* in CD 11:13–14a forbids assistance to a domestic animal in two cases: (i) no one should help an animal give birth on the sabbath; and (ii) if an animal falls into a cistern or a pit,[39] no one is to pull it up on the sabbath. The latter prohibition is strikingly contradicted by a saying of Jesus found both in the Matthean (but not the Marcan) form of the story of the healing of the man with the withered hand on the sabbath (Matt 12:9–14; cf. Mark 3:1–6) and in the Lucan story of the healing of the man with dropsy on the sabbath (Luke 14:1–6). Matt 12:11 reads: "Which man among you who has a sheep and sees it fall into a pit will not take hold of it and raise it up?" The parallel rhetorical question in Luke 14:5 reads: "Which of you, if he has a son or an ox fall into a cistern, will not immediately draw him up on the sabbath day?"[40] Interestingly, in the Qumran manuscripts, concern about this problem is not limited to the *Damascus Document*. A fragment from a like-minded document from Cave 4 of Qumran (4Q265, fragment 7, 1:6b–7a) issues a similar command: "Let no one draw up an animal that has fallen into water on the day of the sabbath."

(d) The stringent approach of the *Damascus Document* to the problem of the animal falling into a pit or into water seems slightly mitigated in the case of a human being who falls into water. CD 11:16–17a specifies: "And [as for] every living human being who falls into a place of water or into a cistern [?], let no one draw him up with a ladder or a rope or [any such] implement."[41] Despite the apparent strictness of the prohibition, the very fact that the rule specifies the tools that may *not* be used raises the possibility that a rescue attempt that dispensed with tools or instruments might be allowed. This hypothesis is supported by a like-minded fragment from Cave 4 (4Q265 fragment 7, 1:6–8). While the fragment, like the *Damascus Document*, forbids drawing up an animal that has fallen into water on the sabbath, it goes on to say: "But if a living human being is the one who has fallen into the water on the sabbath, let a man throw him his garment in order to draw him up with it, but let him not carry an implement." The overriding concern here seems to be the prohibition of carrying tools or other work instruments around in public on the sabbath. Since one is allowed to "carry" one's clothing on one's body on the sabbath, use of one's clothing is permitted in 4Q265— and probably by the group that stands behind CD 11:16–17a.[42] Despite this roundabout mitigation in order to save a human life on the sabbath, one can see that the Essenes and perhaps similar sectarian groups reflected in the Dead Sea Scrolls did not share the later rabbinic doctrine that the obligation to rescue human life that is in imminent danger of death overrode sabbath prohibitions (the principle of *piqqûaḥ nepeš*).[43]

In sum, we see that, unlike most of the sabbath *hălākôt* in *Jubilees*, some of the texts from the *Damascus Document* (along with like-minded fragments) appear strikingly relevant to a study of Jesus' attitude toward the sabbath. Intriguingly, the Qumran texts provide more contrasts than comparisons, and they bear upon the *sayings* of Jesus dealing with the sabbath rather than upon the *narratives* about Jesus' actions on the sabbath. Accordingly, we will return to these Qumran texts when we come to treat the Gospel passages dealing with sabbath disputes.

D. Jewish Diaspora Literature:
Aristobulus, Philo, and Josephus

When we search the Greek literature written by Jews of the Western Diaspora around the turn of the era but not included in the Septuagint, we are reminded of the surprising results of our search of the deuterocanonical (or apocryphal) books of the OT. Large parts of this Jewish Diaspora literature do not treat the sabbath at all. This is all the more surprising since we know from Greco-Roman pagan sources that the sabbath, along with circumcision and the food laws, was one of the most distinguishing characteristics—if not *the* most distinguishing characteristic—of Jews in the eyes of their pagan neighbors.[44]

Even when we do find references to the sabbath in the Jewish Diaspora literature, the amount of detailed halakic prescriptions is relatively thin. Indeed, in the case of Aristobulus, a Jewish philosopher and interpreter of the Law who wrote in Alexandria around the middle of the 2d century B.C., the yield is nil.[45] At least in the fragments that have come down to us, Aristobulus simply explains the meaning of "sabbath" as "rest," sees it as an expression of the sevenfold order embedded in nature, and tries to show that Greek pagan poets such as Homer and Hesiod held the seventh day holy, thus giving the sabbath a universal status. Nowhere in the preserved fragments does Aristobulus bring up any detailed prescriptions dealing with observance of the sabbath.

While Philo of Alexandria does mention a good number of sabbath prohibitions, he does not supply one compact list à la *Jubilees* or the *Damascus Document*. Rather, he takes up individual points of sabbath *hǎlākâ* as they fit into the subject he is treating at the moment. Most of them are found in his works *On the Special Laws* (*De specialibus legibus*) and *The Life of Moses* (*De vita Mosis*), though scattered references also occur in other treatises.[46] A large majority of the sabbath prohibitions Philo discusses either are directly taken from the Jewish Scriptures or are clearly developed from them. They include the prohibition of lighting a fire, gathering wood, engaging in agricultural work, carrying a burden around in an open area, engaging in judicial proceedings, demanding back deposited goods or loans, activities that make money or earn a living, and leaving one's dwelling or settlement.[47]

Thus, when compared with the sabbath disputes in the Gospels, the sabbath prohibitions found in Philo follow a now-familiar pattern. Nowhere is there any mention of prohibiting the healing of illnesses, the only action Jesus ever directly does that supposedly violates the sabbath. Once again, it is people around Jesus who break some of the prohibitions enunciated by Philo. The paralyzed man in John 5 violates the prohibition of carrying burdens in public, and the disciples' plucking of grain on the sabbath violates a very specific prohibition that Philo spells out in great detail. In a rhapsodic passage in which Philo extols the universal appeal of the sabbath, he claims that the sabbath gives rest from labor and freedom to all, not only free people but also slaves and animals (*Life of Moses*, 2. 21–22). Yes, says Philo in a splurge of poetic exuberance, the sabbath extends freedom even to all kinds of trees and plants inasmuch as no one is allowed to cut a shoot, branch, or leaf, *or to pick any sort of fruit*, or even to touch it on the sabbath. Uniquely among pre-70 Jewish writers, Philo forbids not just organized sowing and reaping as part of a larger agricultural endeavor but also any kind of cutting or plucking of any part of a tree or plant—even down to a leaf or a piece of fruit. This text supplies the closest pre-70 parallel to the dispute about plucking grain in Mark 2:23–28.

Although Philo's references to sabbath *hălākâ* may appear sparse in comparison to *Jubilees* and the *Damascus Document*, they seem almost abundant when compared to the few scattered details of sabbath practice mentioned by Josephus.[48] Despite his voluminous writings, Josephus treats questions of sabbath observance only occasionally and usually in connection with other topics. In a sense, this should not surprise us. Josephus is not a rabbi or philosopher writing tractates on legal observance. He is a Jewish-Hellenistic author writing apologetic history to defend and recommend the recently defeated Jewish people in a largely suspicious if not hostile Gentile world. Hence, when he deals with the sabbath, it is mostly as a historian (and apologist) who is writing narratives that may touch on the sabbath, not as a lawyer or rabbinic scholar who is enunciating halakic prescriptions governing the sabbath.

Josephus is clear enough about the basic obligation of Jews to abstain from work on the sabbath—which for him, as for Philo, entails the further obligation of coming together to hear and study the Law.[49] Beyond that, his descriptions of concrete sabbath prescriptions and prohibitions are few and far between.[50] The ones he does mention include (1) the prohibition of kindling fire (in connection with the prohibition of preparing food on the sabbath), (2) the prohibition of an army marching out of its camp, (3) the legal custom of eating a midday meal on the sabbath (and hence, implicitly, the prohibition of fasting that is expressed in *Jubilees* and implied in *Judith*), (4) the permissibility (at least implied in the narrative) of discussing political affairs in the sabbath assembly,[51] (5) the permissibility of fighting a defensive battle when one is attacked,[52] (6) the permissibility of certain actions

of priests in the temple, namely, offering sabbath sacrifices in addition to
the daily *tāmîd* sacrifices and replacing the old "loaves of the Presence" (or
"showbread") with twelve fresh loaves, and (7) the permissibility (at least
implied) of offering the first sheaves of barley grain and of celebrating the
Feast of Weeks even when these liturgical events fall on a sabbath.[53]

Strikingly, therefore, Josephus, unlike Philo and a number of the other
pre-70 sources we have examined, offers no material that would provide immediate background to the sabbath disputes in the Gospels. The one (negative) point on which he agrees with all the other sources we have examined
is his total silence about any prohibition of healing illnesses on the sabbath.
Hence, one remarkable upshot of our survey of Jewish *hălākâ* on sabbath
observance around the turn of the era is that the one offense of which Jesus is directly accused in the sabbath dispute stories—namely, healing the
sick—is never mentioned as a breach of sabbath law in any Jewish source
written from the 2d century B.C. to the end of the 1st century A.D. This
"disconnect" between Jewish writings around the turn of the era and the
sabbath disputes depicted in the Gospels must be kept in mind when we turn
to the Gospel stories and sayings dealing with sabbath observance.

E. A QUICK GLANCE FORWARD TO THE MISHNA

Before we turn to the Gospel texts, it would be helpful to cast a brief glance
at the first part of the rabbinic corpus, the Mishna, redacted ca. A.D. 200–
220.[54] The tendency to expand and systematize sabbath prohibitions, as
well as the tendency to create lists of prohibitions, was already evident in
Jubilees and the *Damascus Document*. This tendency blossoms into full
flower in the mishnaic tractate *Šabbat*, as well as in two allied tractates,
'*Erubin* and *Beṣa* (also called *Yom Ṭob*). Indeed, the lists in *Jubilees* and the
Damascus Document pale before the explicitly numbered list of thirty-nine
prohibited works in *m. Šabb.* 7:2: "The main works [prohibited on the Sab-
bath] are forty minus one."[55] Among the first works mentioned are the bibli-
cally prohibited activities of plowing and reaping (Exod 34:21). These two
biblical prohibitions are immediately expanded to include allied activities
such as threshing, winnowing, selecting fit produce, grinding, sifting, and
kneading. This expanded and expansive prohibition of agricultural labor
may be reflected in the objection raised against the disciples' plucking of
grain on the sabbath (Mark 2:23–28). Similarly, the prohibition of kneading may be related to Jesus' act of making clay that he then smears on the
eyes of the man born blind (John 9:6)[56]—though the subsequent dispute in
John 9 seems to focus not so much on the making of the clay as on the act

of healing on the sabbath (9:14). In fact, as the dispute proceeds (9:17), the precise means of healing fade away in favor of the central action of giving sight to a man born blind (9:18–21,25,30,32) along with its symbolic meaning (9:39–41).

Corresponding to the initial works on the Mishna's list of thirty-nine prohibited actions, the very last work mentioned in *m. Šabb.* 7:2 is likewise based on the Scriptures: carrying (literally, "bringing out") an object from one domain to another.[57] This is simply a specification of the biblical prohibition going back to the prophet Jeremiah (Jer 17:19–27). A similar but slightly different prohibition that is also based on Jer 17:19–27 is the carrying of any burden or instrument in a public area; such a prohibition is already expressed in 4Q265 fragment 7, 1:8. One or both of these prohibitions may be reflected in the objection voiced to the formerly paralyzed man in John 5:10 when he carries his mat back from the pool of Bethesda after having been cured by Jesus.[58] Yet, as in John 9 so in John 5, this specific point of sabbath *hălākâ* quickly disappears from the subsequent dispute, which focuses instead on what Jesus keeps doing (*epoiei*, John 5:16) on the sabbath: namely, performing acts of healing that, in the view of his adversaries, not only violate the sabbath but also carry the implicit claim of being equal to God (5:17–18). This typically Johannine concern with high christology, and not the halakic problem of carrying a mat on the sabbath, is the springboard for the discourse of the Johannine Jesus on the authority of the Son vis-à-vis the Father, the theme that takes up the rest of chap. 5. In the end, regardless of the judgment on their historicity, the two sabbath dispute stories in John's Gospel (and perhaps, to some degree, Mark's story of the plucking of the grain) are readily understandable from the vantage point of the Mishna's list of thirty-nine prohibited works.

The situation is not quite the same with the Synoptic stories of Jesus' healing on the sabbath. Set over against these stories, the Mishna's list of thirty-nine prohibited works is remarkable for the same reason that every other Jewish source we have examined so far is remarkable. Neither in the Jewish Scriptures, nor in the deuterocanonical books, nor in *Jubilees*, nor in the *Damascus Document*, nor in the Qumran Cave 4 fragments, nor in Philo, nor in Josephus, nor in the list of thirty-nine works in *m. Šabb.* 7:2, nor in a different list of prohibited works in *m. Beṣa* 5:2 is the mere act of healing an illness or treating a physical deformity prohibited on the sabbath.[59] To this extent, these two mishnaic lists stand in the long tradition of sabbath prohibitions reaching back to the Pentateuch. When one considers the sweep and variety of all these Jewish texts, it becomes all the more striking and puzzling that the one action of Jesus in the Gospels that is supposedly branded as a breach of the sabbath—namely, healing illnesses and physical deformities—is totally absent from these texts.

Nevertheless, while these two lists of prohibited works in the Mishna reflect the age-old tradition found in other Jewish texts, the Mishna also contains and canonizes a new approach to the question of healing. Outside of the lists of prohibited works, some passages in the tractate *Šabbat* do forbid certain acts of healing illness or relieving pain on the sabbath. Perhaps one sign of the fact that we are dealing here with the opening up of a new type of prohibition is that the prohibition is not a sweeping, blanket one. With a certain air of tentativeness, it is limited by considerations of the intention of the person performing the action and the nature of the action performed as well as the material used. In addition, the mishnaic prohibition of healing activity is accompanied by some variant or dissenting views.

For example, in the key text contained in *m. Šabb.* 14:3–4, a number of decisions about the permissibility of various measures that might have a curative effect rest on a basic principle: if one eats a type of food or uses a type of ointment that one usually takes or at least can take on the sabbath without any thought or intention of healing an illness, then one can eat this food or use this ointment on the sabbath even if, by a happy coincidence, it happens to have a curative effect. If, on the other hand, one eats a food or uses an ointment on the sabbath solely for the purpose of obtaining a cure or a relief of pain, then the action is illicit. One is reminded of the classic principle of double effect.[60]

Still, all is not clear and undisputed in this passage. For instance, in keeping with the basic principle, *m. Šabb.* 14:4 states that even on the sabbath one may relieve pain by anointing oneself with oil, since oil is an ointment used for healthy skin on any day of the week. If it just happens to have an anesthetic effect, fine.[61] However, the text adds, one may not use rose oil, since for an ordinary person that would be an extraordinary means, employed for the special purpose of healing. The text then grants that princes ("the children of kings") may use rose oil on the sabbath, since they use it as well on ordinary weekdays as an ointment. At this point in the text, Rabbi Symeon suddenly intervenes with an objection that is meant to create "wiggle room" for any and all Israelites suffering from pain: "All Israelites are princes." Hence, it is implied, all Israelites may use the special rose oil. Clearly, the prohibition of healing on the sabbath is not absolute or free of disputes.

The view that the mishnaic prohibition of curative means on the sabbath is not absolute seems confirmed by the curious provision found in *m. Šabb.* 6:2: a man is allowed to carry an amulet out of his house on the sabbath *only if* the amulet has proven curative power. An amulet without such proven ability is not permitted to be carried out of the house. The Tosepta adds that even an amulet that has not proven its effectiveness may be handled within one's house (*t. Šabb* 4:10). All this is the last thing one would expect if healing per se were an activity always, everywhere, and in all its forms forbidden on the sabbath. If that were the case, one would expect the ineffective amulet to be permitted and the effective amulet to be banned.

A related point appears in the mishnaic tractate *Yoma*, which discusses the ceremonies of Yom Kippur and the strict twenty-four-hour fast, excluding any food or drink whatsoever, that marks off this most sacred day. *M. Yoma* 8:5 specifies that, even during this absolute fast, food may be given to a sick person if a medical expert counsels it. Indeed, if such an expert is lacking, food may be given the sick person if he or she requests it. Meandering a bit from the theme of the fast of Yom Kippur, *m. Yoma* 8:6 proceeds to allow, in the case of a person with a sore throat, that medicine be dropped into the sore throat *on the sabbath* because there is a doubt as to whether the person's life is in danger. This mishna then concludes with the basic rabbinic rule—never enunciated as a distinct overarching principle in pre-70 Judaism—that the risk of loss of human life supersedes the sabbath.

The overall impression one gets from these and other rabbinic texts, when viewed in the context of the total absence of any prohibition of healing on the sabbath in the pre-70 period (notably in *Jubilees* and the *Damascus Document*), is that the post-70 rabbis had developed a new type of sabbath prohibition concerning healing, enshrined literarily for the first time in the Mishna. From the start, the newly formulated prohibition was not without its inconsistencies and disputed points, and further wiggle room continued to be created in later stages of rabbinic writings. More to the point, we should remember that all these texts represent the views of a scholarly elite, views that did not always find a ready reception among the common people. What Jewish peasants actually did in their own houses and settlements scattered throughout the Palestinian countryside when a member of their household became ill on the sabbath is a different question from what the rabbis taught to their disciples. To use a rough analogy: one would not want to take the Code of Canon Law or the Catechism of the Catholic Church as a sober historical report or sociological description of how most American Catholics actually live their daily lives or practice their faith. Not for nothing do the rabbinic texts complain at times about "the people of the land," who neither know nor practice the detailed rulings of the experts expounding *hălākâ* in their academies.[62]

Having surveyed the background and foreground of Jewish observance of the sabbath around the time of Jesus, I now turn to the Gospel texts dealing

with Jesus' actions on or sayings about the sabbath. As I have already intimated, amid the many connections with Jewish views and practices at the
time, there is a surprising "disconnect" at one vital juncture.

II. JESUS' ACTIONS ON AND SAYINGS
ABOUT THE SABBATH

The topic "Jesus and the Sabbath" is a vague, overarching rubric covering
a number of different types of stories and sayings that derive from various
sources. An orderly sifting of the material will help us sort out the texts according to form, content, sources, and possible problems contained within
them. It will also enable us to set aside from the start those passages that
are not relevant to our quest. (1) I will begin with *narratives* dealing with
miracles on the sabbath that do not qualify as sabbath dispute stories.
(2) Second, I will take up *narratives* about miracles on the sabbath that do
occasion disputes. (3) Third, I will consider Jesus' *sayings* about sabbath
observance that are embedded in the narratives in category number 2, since
some of these sayings may have circulated independently of the stories in
which they are now found. (4) Fourth, I will consider the only *narrative*
about a sabbath dispute that does not involve a miracle, that is, the plucking
of grain on the sabbath, along with (5) the various *sayings* about the sabbath
contained in it.

A. Miracles on the Sabbath That Do Not Provoke a Dispute

The Synoptic Gospels (but not John) contain a few cases of sabbath stories
dealing with miracles of Jesus that do not ignite a debate over Jesus' violation of the sabbath. Intriguingly, all these stories come from the Marcan
tradition of Jesus' miracles. With modifications, they are then taken over by
Matthew and/or Luke.

(1) In Mark, the prime example of a sabbath miracle that does not occasion a dispute is Jesus' initial miracle, an exorcism performed in the Capernaum synagogue on the sabbath (Mark 1:23–28 ‖ Luke 4:33–37).[63] Both
Jesus' teaching authority and his authority over demons arouse astonished
questions, but no dispute—and specifically no dispute about his exorcising a
demoniac on the sabbath. Hence we may put this pericope aside, all the more
so since it may well be an "ideal scene" composed by Mark or his source to
encapsulate "the sort of thing" Jesus was known to have done on the sabbath: teaching in synagogues and performing healings or exorcisms.[64]

(2) A second example in Mark follows immediately upon the first: the

healing of Peter's mother-in-law on the sabbath (1:29–31 parr.). The reasons for the absence of a dispute here are patent: the healing occurs in a private house, the people in the house are disciples of Jesus along with (presumably) their relatives or friends, and it is precisely this group of people who speak to Jesus about the afflicted woman. In addition, the pericope, taken in isolation, never explicitly states that the healing occurs on the sabbath; that is known only from Mark's overarching structure depicting the first "ideal" day in Capernaum (1:21–34).[65] Hence, this miracle story may likewise be put aside, all the more so because the judgment on its historicity in Volume Two of *A Marginal Jew* was *non liquet* (not clear one way or the other).[66]

(3) Neither the miracles mentioned by the disgruntled townspeople during Jesus' rejection at Nazareth nor the few miracles he is said to have performed at Nazareth despite the unbelief of his fellow Nazarenes are relevant (Mark 6:2,5), since Mark never specifies that any of these miracles is performed on the sabbath itself.[67] In any event, a supposed violation of the sabbath by miracle working is not the subject that occasions the townspeople's astonishment and pique. Thus, this Marcan story, like the other two listed, need not concern us further.

B. MIRACLES ON THE SABBATH THAT DO PROVOKE A DISPUTE

At first glance, disputes arising from Jesus' performance of a miracle on the sabbath seem to enjoy wide multiple attestation of sources. This narrative form is found in Mark's account of the man with the withered hand (Mark 3:1–6 parr.), in Luke's account of the woman who was bent over for eighteen years (Luke 13:10–17), in Luke's account of the man with dropsy (14:1–6), in John's account of the paralyzed man by the pool of Bethzatha or Bethesda (John 5:1–9a), and in John's account of the man born blind (9:1–7). Thus, with attestation in Mark, L, and John, the judgment that some form of a sabbath dispute occasioned by a healing goes back to the historical Jesus looks, at first, well founded.[68] But sometimes a brief inspection employing the criterion of multiple attestation can be deceiving. The material needs to be probed further. In particular, these narratives need to be divided into two groups: the Synoptic and the Johannine.

1. *The Synoptic Narratives*

Fortunately, as we come to inspect these individual narratives, we do not have to reinvent the exegetical wheel. All the miracle stories in the four canonical Gospels were studied in detail in Volume Two of *A Marginal Jew*.[69] Here we need only recall the results and correlate them with what we have learned about Jewish observance of the sabbath in this present chapter.

(a) In Volume Two, the healing of the man with the withered hand (Mark 3:1–6) received the judgment of *non liquet* (not clear).[70] The strategic positioning of this narrative at the climax of the Marcan cycle of Galilean dispute stories (2:1–3:6, with 3:1–6 corresponding in many ways to the first story in the cycle, the healing of the paralytic in 2:1–12), the clearly redactional conclusion of the dispute in 3:6 (the Pharisees consult with the Herodians on how to destroy Jesus),[71] and the function of 3:1–6 as the confirmation of Jesus' pronouncement in the previous story that the Son of Man is lord even of the sabbath (2:28) all point to Mark's redactional hand. Moreover, within the story, Jesus' basic argument in 3:4, expressed in the form of a rhetorical question ("Is it licit on the sabbath to do good or to do evil, to save a life or to kill it?"), relates not so much to the particular case being disputed as to Mark's polemical conclusion in 3:6: on the sabbath, the Pharisees and the Herodians conspire to do evil, that is, to kill Jesus, who instead does good on the sabbath.[72] In addition, the overall thrust of the pericope, seen in its larger context, is more christological than halakic. The emphasis is on the vindication of the authority of Jesus, not on detailed instructions as to what kind of action is permitted on the sabbath. Saying that one should do good rather than evil and save life rather than kill it hardly solves specific problems of sabbath observance.

Then too, on the historical rather than the redactional level, it is extremely difficult to understand how any Jew of the early 1st century could accuse Jesus, as presented in Mark 3:1–6, of breaking the sabbath by healing. Indeed, more than any other sabbath dispute story, Mark 3:1–6 is a glaring example of this difficulty. For, in the healing of the man with the withered hand, Jesus literally *does nothing*.[73] He simply issues two brief, simple commands to the afflicted man: "Stand up before the assembly . . . [and] stretch out your hand" (3:3 + 5). When the man obeys, his hand is healed. Now, in both Palestinian and Diaspora synagogues, all sorts of Jews on the sabbath discussed the Scriptures, argued vigorously about their interpretation and implementation, and urged their fellow Jews to various courses of action, without anyone accusing them of violating the sabbath rest. One need only think of the raucous political debate that took place in the "prayer house" of Tiberias on the sabbath as Josephus was trying to assert his military leadership in Galilee at the beginning of the First Jewish Revolt (*Life* 54 §276–79). Apparently, forceful speech exhorting or ordering others to undertake forceful action was not considered by any Jew present in the "prayer house" to be a violation of the sabbath rest. Why should Jesus' two short commands, which do not urge any action that would be illicit on the sabbath, constitute such a violation?[74]

Perhaps someone might reply that Jesus' speech is a breach of the sabbath because it is a special type of speech: it is speech that heals, and healing is forbidden on the sabbath. Here is where the insights that we have gained so far in this chapter come into play. As we have seen, no Jewish document prior to A.D. 70 gives the slightest indication that an act of healing was considered a violation of the sabbath rest.[75] And this is not simply a question of an argument from silence that could go in either direction. For in this case (with a nod to Cicero's *cum tacent clamant* ["when they are silent, they shout"]),[76] the silence of the sources is a metaphorical shout. The total silence in such a wide range of witnesses of different times and tendencies—the Jewish Scriptures, the deuterocanonical books, *Jubilees*, the *Damascus Document*, the Cave 4 fragments from Qumran, Philo, and Josephus—places the burden of proof on anyone who would want to claim that, prior to A.D. 70, any significant segment of Jewish opinion branded an act of healing a breach of the sabbath. This silence is especially telling in the case of *Jubilees* and the *Damascus Document*, which go out of their way to create lists of prohibited actions, many of which extend beyond what is stipulated in the Jewish Scriptures. For all the halakic stringency, not to say extremism, of the groups behind these lists, healing makes the list in neither document.[77]

All the more telling is the fact that, from a form-critical point of view, the true successor of these lists after A.D. 70 is the mishnaic list of thirty-nine prohibited actions in *m. Šabb.* 7:2. Even here, in the full flowering of lists of acts prohibited on the sabbath, healing is absent. Rather, a prohibition of healing actions on the sabbath is found for the first time in two other passages in the tractate *Šabbat* (14:3–4). In these two passages, the prohibition seems to rest on a particular principle: namely, that the forbidden act of healing involves some special action above and beyond the ordinary actions that one regularly and licitly performs on the sabbath. *That* is what makes the healing a "work" that is prohibited. Thus, even by these post-70 mishnaic standards, Jesus' healing in Mark 3:1–6 does not constitute a breach of the sabbath. For Jesus *does* nothing, he does no "work," in addition to actions regularly permitted and performed on the sabbath. He simply speaks to a person in the synagogue and asks that person to perform actions that are in themselves completely licit on the sabbath: standing up before the synagogue assembly and stretching out his hand.

Hence, when we bring together (1) our judgment of *non liquet* from Volume Two of *A Marginal Jew* and (2) the further knowledge gained in this present chapter—namely, that Jesus' mere act of speaking in Mark 3:1–6, however healing, would not have constituted a forbidden work in the view of pre-70 Palestinian Jews—the healing of the man with the withered hand "falls out of contention" in our quest for sabbath disputes that actually go back to the historical Jesus.[78] However, we should keep in mind that Matthew adds to his version of this incident a discrete saying of Jesus (12:11, actually, a rhetorical question that poses a halakic argument about proper sabbath observance) that calls for further examination. We will take up this logion when we turn to the sabbath sayings of Jesus.

(b) The special L tradition of Luke's Gospel contains two narratives involving sabbath disputes arising from Jesus' healings. In Luke 13:10–17, Jesus, while teaching in a synagogue on the sabbath, heals a woman who has been "bent over" for eighteen years. Once again, our analysis of this narrative in Volume Two yielded the verdict of *non liquet*.[79] The only significant factor that differentiates this text from Mark 3:1–6 is that Luke 13:10–17 depicts Jesus as both speaking a word of healing to the woman (v 12: "Woman, you are released from your infirmity") and laying his hands on her (v 13). Still, nothing in pre-70 Judaism brands an act of healing *via* speech and touch a violation of the sabbath. Interestingly, the two passages in *m. Šabbat* that prohibit certain acts of healing never take up a healing of this kind.[80] In brief, granted that Luke 13:10–17 has merited the judgment of *non liquet* in Volume Two and that the healing action of Jesus in this narrative would probably not have qualified as a breach of the sabbath in pre-70 Judaism, this miracle story, like that in Mark 3:1–6, falls out of consideration as a sabbath dispute going back to the historical Jesus. However, not unlike the Matthean version of the story of the man with the withered hand, Luke's narrative of the bent-over woman contains a rhetorical question of Jesus that deals with the problem of permissible actions on the sabbath (Luke 13:15). We will examine this saying below.

(c) Creating a kind of exegetical trifecta, the case of the man with dropsy (Luke 14:1–6) also merited the historical judgment of *non liquet*.[81] In this Lucan narrative, the healing action of Jesus is described more vaguely than in the case of the bent-over woman (Luke 13:10–17). In Luke 14:4, we are simply told that Jesus, "taking hold of [or: grasping] the man, healed him and let him go." The text says nothing about either a healing command or a special gesture like the laying on of hands. Thus, even less than in 13:10–17 is there any action of Jesus that would qualify in pre-70 Judaism as a "work" that would violate the sabbath rest. As in the other cases we have seen, the narrative of Luke 14:1–6 must drop out of consideration as a sabbath dispute going back to the historical Jesus. Yet, similar to Matthew's version of the healing of the man with the withered hand and to Luke's account of the healing of the bent-over woman, this story of the man with dropsy also contains a saying of Jesus—actually, as in the other cases, a rhetorical question—that poses a halakic argument about which actions are permissible on the sabbath. In fact, this saying (Luke 14:5) seems to be an alternate version of the saying preserved in Matt 12:11. Hence, along with the other two sayings, this logion will be examined below.

To sum up: the three Synoptic narratives of Jesus' healing on the sabbath pose too many problems for us to accept them as recording sabbath disputes that actually go back to the ministry of the historical Jesus. Examined simply as miracle stories, they all yield the verdict of *non liquet*. When one adds to this judgment the further difficulty that the documents of pre-70 Judaism do not witness to a prohibition of healing on the sabbath, the obstacles standing in the way of declaring any one of these narratives to be authentic seem insurmountable.[82] But what of the rhetorical questions about sabbath *hălākâ* that are embedded in these narratives? Before we turn our attention to them, we should first look at the two sabbath disputes in the Gospel of John.

2. *The Johannine Narratives*

A glance back at my treatment in Volume Two of the two Johannine narratives recounting Jesus' healing on the sabbath might at first raise hopes of a more fruitful inquiry than the Synoptic stories offered. For, in my opinion, both the healing of the paralyzed man by the pool of Bethzatha (John 5:1–9a) and the healing of the man born blind (John 9:1–7) most likely go back to events in the ministry of the historical Jesus.[83] Yet, sad to say, this positive judgment contributes nothing to our quest for the sabbath disputes of the historical Jesus. As my analysis of both John 5 and John 9 showed in Volume Two of *A Marginal Jew*, the primitive forms of these two miracles stories—and, indeed, even the miracle stories proper as they stand today in John 5:1–9a and 9:1–7—lack any reference to the sabbath.[84]

It is only after the miracle story, viewed from a form-critical point of view, has ended that the evangelist appends the further information that the healing took place on a sabbath (5:9b and 9:14).[85] In both cases, the mention of the sabbath after the miracle story proper has ended serves John's special literary and theological purposes. Indeed, the mention of the sabbath fits in perfectly with a characteristic pattern that shapes a number of large units in John's Gospel. In many of John's accounts of Jesus actions, particularly his miraculous actions or "signs," John employs a special type of progression: (1) Jesus' initial deed leads to (2) a dialogue or exchange (often an argument), which in turn leads to (3) a monologue, namely, one of Jesus' christological discourses that are so characteristic of the Fourth Gospel.

In chap. 5, for example, the mention of the sabbath (5:9b) after the miracle story proper (5:1–9a) leads to a series of exchanges (5:10–18): first between the "Jews" (i.e., the hostile authorities in Jerusalem) and the healed man (5:10–13), then between Jesus and the healed man (5:14), then again between the healed man and the "Jews" (5:15), and finally (in a summary description by the evangelist) between the "Jews" and Jesus (5:16–18). This bridge-passage of dialogue and interaction leads in turn to a complicated christological discourse on the relationship of the Son's authority to the Father's (5:19–47).

In chap. 9 (the healing of the man born blind), this basic structure of sign leading to dialogue leading in turn to monologue is even more baroque in its expanse. After the sign proper (9:1–7), we are presented with a series of dialogues between the healed man and his neighbors (9:8–12), between the healed man and the Pharisees (alias the "Jews," 9:13–17), between the Pharisees and the parents of the healed man (9:18–23), between the Pharisees and the healed man once again (9:24–34), between the healed man and Jesus (9:35–39), and finally between the Pharisees and Jesus (9:40–41). This lengthy chain (or, better, spiral) of dialogues finally leads into the grand monologue of Jesus that is usually called the Good Shepherd Discourse (John 10:1–18).

Beyond this basic pattern, chaps. 5 and 9 have another structural point in common. Just as the sabbath motif is absent in the two healing stories that introduce the two chapters, so any mention of the sabbath disappears once the two great christological monologues begin.[86] Only in the bridge-section composed of dialogue does the sabbath motif make its entrance and then speedy exit.[87] Put bluntly: the sabbath in each of the two chapters functions simply as an artificial literary and theological link, connecting what were originally short stories of healing with the lengthy Johannine discourses.

In a sense, then, we are faced with a paradox. In each of the Synoptic stories of healing on the sabbath, the sabbath motif is mentioned early on. Once introduced, it shapes the whole story, in particular what Jesus says and how his adversaries react. Unfortunately, as we have seen, none of these Synoptic narratives can be declared authentic in the sense of going back to the historical Jesus. In contrast, the healing narratives proper in John 5:1–9a and 9:1–7 most probably do go back to events in the life of Jesus. But the motif of the sabbath in both stories has been added secondarily, most likely by the evangelist for his own literary and theological purposes.[88]

In the end, the once promising batch of dispute stories involving healing on the sabbath dissolves under the glare of critical analysis. The Synoptic versions are indeed centered on the sabbath, but do not go back to Jesus, while the two Johannine narratives probably go back to Jesus, but without the later addition of the sabbath motif. Thus, despite initial appearances, we are left with a surprising and disconcerting conclusion: in all four Gospels, we have not a single narrative of a sabbath dispute occasioned by a healing that probably goes back to the historical Jesus. But what of the halakic sayings of Jesus concerning sabbath observance that we found embedded in the Synoptic stories of sabbath healing? It is time to see whether we have more promising material there.

C. SAYINGS OF JESUS ON SABBATH HĂLĀKÂ FOUND IN THE SYNOPTIC MIRACLE STORIES

When we surveyed in the preceding section the three Synoptic dispute stories about healings on the sabbath, we noticed an intriguing similarity amid all the dissimilarities. In Mark's story of the man with the withered hand (3:1–6, as well as the parallels in Matt 12:9–14 and Luke 6:6–11), in Luke's story of the bent-over woman (13:10–17), and in Luke's story of the man with dropsy (14:1–6), every version of these sabbath disputes over miracles contains some form of a rhetorical question posed by Jesus to answer the spoken or unspoken objections of his critics.

(1) In Mark 3:4, Jesus addresses a question to those who are silently and hostilely watching him to see whether he will heal on the sabbath: "Is it licit on the sabbath to do good or to do evil, to save a life or to kill [it]?"[89] His opponents (presumably, in light of v 6, the Pharisees) remain silent. With slight differences, Luke 6:9 repeats the Marcan form of this broad rhetorical question.

(2a) However, in the Matthean version of the same story, the unnamed opponents (in light of Matt 12:14, the Pharisees) make the dispute overt rather than covert by taking the offensive at the beginning of the narrative. In Matt 12:10, with the intention of accusing Jesus, they ask him: "Is it licit to heal on the sabbath?" In 12:11, Jesus replies with a rhetorical question that is much more specific than Mark 3:4 in that it takes up a concrete halakic matter disputed among Jews around the turn of the era: "Which man among you, if he has a sheep that falls into a pit on the sabbath, will not take hold of him and draw him up?"[90] In v 12a, Jesus adds a second rhetorical question, making explicit his a fortiori argument (the rabbinic *qal wāḥômer*): "How much more valuable is a human being than a sheep?" Then, in v 12b, Matthew rejoins his Marcan text. In doing so, however, Matthew not only abbreviates Mark's rhetorical question (Mark 3:4) but also turns it into the logical conclusion of his own two rhetorical questions: "Therefore it is licit to do good on the sabbath"—thus replying, by way of *inclusio*, to the initial question of the opponents in Matt 12:10.[91] One gets the definite impression that the two rhetorical questions in 12:11–12a are Matthew's redactional insertion into the Marcan story. But are these questions simply Matthew's own creation, or do they represent some traditional saying that Matthew is inserting into the Marcan text?

(2b) This rhetorical question of our own is answered by a Synoptic parallel to Matthew's rhetorical questions. Surprisingly, this parallel is found not in a Marcan or Q pericope redacted by Matthew and Luke but rather in the special Lucan (L) story of the man with dropsy (14:1–6). In 14:3, Jesus asks "the lawyers and Pharisees" a general question that, in the Lucan story, may be meant as a real rather than a rhetorical question: "Is it licit on the sabbath to cure or not?" When, in good Marcan style, his adversaries remain silent, Jesus heals the man with dropsy. Only then, in 14:5, does Jesus address to his would-be critics a rhetorical question (roughly paralleling Matt 12:11): "Which of you, if your son or ox falls into a cistern, will not immediately pull him up on the sabbath?"[92]

Whether the Matthean and Lucan versions of what is basically the same saying qualify as a Q tradition raises an interesting question of semantics. If by Q one means any and every saying or narrative that is absent in Mark but common to Matthew and Luke, this saying is by definition a Q tradition. However, if one restricts Q material to what is thought to have stood in one written document that was available independently to both Matthew and Luke, then the label Q becomes more debatable. It could be that Matt 12:11 and Luke 14:5 represent two versions of a stray oral tradition (originally in Aramaic) that came independently to Matthew and Luke in somewhat different forms.[93] Each evangelist then decided to use this stray logion by inserting it into a fitting context, which meant in practice a traditional dispute story about a healing on the sabbath. Matthew, however, chose a Marcan dispute story as the context (the man with the withered hand) while Luke selected a story unique to his own tradition (the man with dropsy).

(3) A third major form of the tradition that Jesus discussed possible exceptions to the sabbath rest by using rhetorical questions is found in the Lucan story of the bent-over woman (13:10–17). Like the dispute about healing in Luke 14:1–6, and unlike the dispute in Mark 3:1–6, Luke 13:10–17 places a specific rhetorical question about sabbath *hălākâ* after the actual healing. Unique to Luke 13:10–17 is the manner in which the critic (here, also uniquely, "the ruler of the synagogue," who is not identified as a Pharisee) begins his attack by addressing not Jesus but the crowd, criticizing it for

coming to the synagogue for healings on the sabbath when they have the six workdays on which to do that (13:14).

Surprisingly, while Jesus is said to reply to the ruler ("to him" in the singular in v 15a), his quoted words are put in the plural, apparently aimed at some presumed group of opponents (13:15): "Hypocrites! Does not each one of you on the sabbath untie his ox or donkey from the manger and lead it away to let it drink?"[94] The awkward fit (or lack of a fit) between the complaint of a single critic and the sweeping reply of Jesus addressed to a group of adversaries (in v 17a, who are hardly the same as "all the crowd" that rejoices at his miracles in v 17b) may be a sign that, like Matt 12:11–12a, Luke 13:15 is a secondary addition to an earlier form of a story about a sabbath healing. The saying itself in Luke 13:15 is reminiscent of Matt 12:11 ‖ Luke 14:5 in that it speaks of farm animals in need on the sabbath and of the permissible action taken by their owner to meet their need. The obvious difference is that while Matt 12:11 ‖ Luke 14:5 speaks of an unusual emergency situation (the animal has fallen into a well or cistern), Luke 13:15 speaks of a need that would arise on any sabbath and that would have to be met by any Jew keeping farm animals.

The Lucan story then concludes in 13:16 with Jesus invoking the generally accepted sabbath practice he has just described (13:15) to justify by analogy his sabbath healing: "As for this woman, daughter of Abraham that she is, whom Satan bound for lo these 18 years, was it not necessary that she be untied from this bond on the sabbath day?" Every analogy limps, but this one crawls. This forced connection between the halakic rule of v 15 (untying an ox or donkey from a manger to let it drink, something that would have to be done on every sabbath along with every workday) and its application in v 16 (untying a woman in the metaphorical sense of performing a singular and presumably never-to-be repeated miracle of healing her bent back) may be another indication that v 15 was originally an isolated halakic saying.[95]

The upshot of this inspection of the sayings about sabbath *hălākâ* that are embedded in miracle stories is clear: we have multiple attestation (Mark, Q [if broadly defined], and L) for the claim that Jesus used rhetorical questions to argue with his fellow Jews over the proper way to observe the sabbath rest.[96] Though it may seem a minor gain to some, this datum is of major significance. As we have already seen in his teaching on divorce and oaths, Jesus is not a vague preacher or generic prophet who provides grand visions and general moral truths while avoiding the nitty-gritty of detailed questions about observance of the Mosaic Law. Jesus, as would be expected of any 1st-century Palestinian Jew who is seriously engaged in the religious life of his people, stakes out his own halakic positions and tries to persuade others to adopt them. As this is true of divorce and oaths, so it is true of sabbath observance. Not surprisingly, a Jewish Jesus who discusses and debates with his Jewish compatriots the proper way to observe particular statutes of the Mosaic Law quickly fades away in many Christian depictions of the historical Jesus. This Christian depiction of the "historical Jesus" tends to be co-opted either for traditional Christian theology or for a radical replacement of traditional Christianity by whatever is deemed relevant in a given year or a given movement. In reality, the historical Jesus is the halakic Jesus, an important bulwark against those who would make him either the embodiment of the Epistle to the Galatians or a cipher for whatever program they are pushing at the moment.

At this point, though, someone might raise a plausible objection to my line of argument about these sayings. After all, as we saw in Section II. B, the multiple attestation of *narratives* recounting sabbath disputes that arise from healings does not, in itself, guarantee their historicity. Each narrative fell victim in turn to the dreaded verdict of *non liquet*. Why should the multiple attestation of Jesus' *sayings* about sabbath *hălākâ* guarantee the presence of such discussions in the preaching of the historical Jesus? My reply is that the case of the sabbath *narratives* and the case of the sabbath *sayings* are not the same—one reason for my insisting on distinguishing them from the start. Prior to any question of sabbath disputes, the narratives were tested in Volume Two of *A Marginal Jew* for historicity under the rubric of miracle stories. Judged like any other miracle stories, none of the narratives of sabbath healings that occasioned disputes could rise above the ambiguity of *non liquet*. Indeed, when in this present chapter we added the further consideration that acts of healing were most probably not considered violations of the sabbath by Jews in the pre-70 period, the narratives that presuppose that acts of healing would be seen as sabbath violations became even more problematic.

The same does not hold true of the sabbath *sayings* we have just inspected. None of these sayings has already suffered the verdict of *non liquet* on other grounds. None of these sayings states explicitly that some Jews hold healing to be a breach of the sabbath. More important, far from being contrary to what we know of 1st-century Palestinian Judaism, some of the sayings seem to presuppose and react to sabbath *hălākâ* that was taught by certain groups of Palestinian Jews around the turn of the era. The prime example is the Q saying that presumes the permissibility of hauling up a human being or an animal that falls into a pit or a cistern on the sabbath. As we saw in Section I. C, the *Damascus Document* explicitly forbids anyone on the sabbath to pull up an animal that falls into a cistern or a pit (CD 11:13–14a). The same stringent approach, though with a hint of mitigation, applies to a human being who falls into water or into a cistern. Such a person may not be pulled up with the help of a ladder, rope, or any other instrument (CD 11:16–17a). That some other means might be allowed is shown by a like-minded fragment from Cave 4 of Qumran. This fragment (4Q265 fragment 7, 1:6–8) does allow a would-be rescuer to throw his own garment to a person who has fallen into water on the sabbath, but no instrument may be used.

It is this sort of stringent casuistry that Jesus rejects in the rhetorical question of the Q tradition found in Matt 12:11 ‖ Luke 14:5. His use of a rhetorical question to appeal to his audience is more informative than some commentators realize. By asking "*Which man among you*, if he has a sheep that falls into a pit on the sabbath, *will not take hold* of him and draw him up?" (or alternately, "*Which of you*, if your son or ox falls into a cistern, *will not immediately pull him up* on the sabbath?"), Jesus rhetorically draws his audience to his side with the presumption that he and they will agree on these humane measures that are as obvious to them as they are to him. In effect, Jesus argues on the basis of a common view of sabbath observance that he and his audience share, as opposed to the extremely stringent views of the Essene community reflected in the *Damascus Document* and perhaps of other Jewish sectarian groups reflected in the Cave 4 fragments.[97] If, as some commentators have suggested, the strict rules of esoteric groups had a certain appeal to and influence on ordinary pious Jews who belonged to no one party or movement,[98] Jesus may be seeking to bolster among ordinary Jewish peasants a humane, commonsense approach to helping endangered humans and animals on the sabbath. While he apparently presumes this view as the generally shared opinion among ordinary Palestinian Jews, he may also be trying to confirm them in it against any encroachments from Essene influence. We may have in these sabbath sayings a rare instance of Jesus fighting a battle-at-a-distance with the Essene movement (or other sectarian groups in Palestine) for the loyalty of ordinary Jews.

If Essene *hălākâ* is a target of Jesus' rhetorical questions about the limits of sabbath rest, was Pharisaic teaching also in view? That is hard to judge because, unlike the Essenes, who were kind enough to leave us the *Damascus Document* as a witness to their legal rulings, we have no document prior to A.D. 70 that gives us a detailed description of specifically Pharisaic *hălākâ*, including sabbath observance.[99] All one can say is that in later rabbinic teaching (*t. Šabb.* 14:3), one is allowed to give fodder to an animal that has fallen into a pit or cistern on the sabbath. The fodder is meant to keep the animal alive until it can be drawn out once the sabbath is over. Implied in this slightly softened position vis-à-vis the *Damascus Document* is that the prohibition of hauling the animal out on the sabbath, clearly enunciated in CD 11:13–14a, is still accepted by the rabbis as late as the Tosepta (3d century A.D.).

Hence, while we do not have direct attestation of the Pharisees' position on the subject, the agreement of the *Damascus Document* (Essene document of the 2d century B.C.) with the Tosepta (rabbinic document of the 3d century A.D.) makes it likely that Pharisees in the early 1st century A.D. likewise prohibited drawing the animal out on the sabbath. Whether the Pharisees would have accepted the Tosepta's mitigation, which allowed the feeding of the animal to sustain its life until it could be pulled out after the sabbath, is unclear.[100] It is likely, though, that in his appeal to "what any of you would do" in Matt 12:11 ‖ Luke 14:5, Jesus is rejecting the strict practice of both the Essenes and the Pharisees on the question of the trapped animal and is siding with the commonsense approach of ordinary Jewish peasants. Such peasants, even if devout Jews, could hardly afford to sit idly by while some of their livestock perished in a pit on the sabbath.[101]

If, in addition, Jesus is consciously trying to ward off the influence of Essene or Pharisaic *hălākâ* on Jews who belonged to no particular party (some of whom might have felt the appeal and attraction of a stricter observance of the Law), one can understand why he would have clashed in particular with Pharisees, who were trying to spread their influence among the common people. It may not be just by accident or by the influence of later Christian polemic that the Pharisees rather than the Essenes or any other sectarian group are presented in the Gospels as *the* group that argues with Jesus over sabbath observance. Like Jesus, and unlike the Essenes, the Pharisees were active among the common people as they sought to spread their interpretation of the Law. The Sadducees argued with Jesus about the resurrection of the dead, a learned scribe wondered about Jesus' view on the greatest commandment, the disciples wondered what reward they would receive in God's kingdom, Caiaphas and Pilate worried about Jesus' power to stir up the Jerusalem crowds, but quite naturally it was the Pharisees who provided his debating partners on the subject of sabbath *hălākâ*.

Such, at least, was the case with the beleaguered beast in the pit. On the question of human life that becomes endangered on the sabbath, the battle lines may have shifted somewhat. As we have seen, the most that the sectarians behind the *Damascus Document* and the Cave 4 fragments would have allowed was throwing one's cloak to a person who had fallen into water (4Q265 fragment 7, 1:6–8). No tool like a ladder or a rope could be used on the sabbath, even to save human life (CD 11:16–17a). By the time we reach the Mishna, that is certainly not the view of the rabbis. In the mishnaic tractate *Yoma*, it is specifically taught that the duty to save endangered human life overrides the sabbath (the principle of *piqqûaḥ nepeš*). Indeed, even a risk of endangering human life provides a sufficient reason for overriding the sabbath (*m. Yoma* 8:6). The Tosepta is even more specific on this point. According to *t. Šabb.* 15:17, any measure or action except idolatry, illicit sexual activity, and bloodshed may be undertaken to save an endangered human life on the sabbath.

Unfortunately, we have no clear attestation of such a sweeping principle in Palestinian Judaism before the tannaitic documents of the Mishna and the Tosepta.[102] Whether the pre-70 Pharisees held to this principle or inclined instead to the rigorism of the *Damascus Document* is not clear. However, some pieces of indirect evidence may argue in favor of the Pharisees accepting danger to human life as justification for overriding the sabbath. As we saw in Chapter 31, Josephus tells us that, by the 1st century B.C. and A.D., Jews in general permitted military battles on the sabbath in cases of self-defense. This is really just one special example of saving endangered life on the sabbath. Then, too, Jesus' rhetorical question in Mark 3:4 ("Is it licit on the sabbath . . . to save life or to kill [it]?"), which meets with silence on the part of those watching him with hostile intent, suggests that Jesus and his audience share the view that one is permitted to take measures to save endangered human life on the sabbath. In Mark 3:1–6, tensions arise only when Jesus extends this principle—illegitimately, in the view of his critics— to healing a physical deformity or paralysis (a withered hand) on the sabbath when there is no immediate danger to life. Thus, while there is no certainty in the matter (only the Marcan context makes clear that Jesus' critics in this incident are Pharisees), I think it more likely than not that most, if not all, Pharisees at the time of Jesus would have allowed on the sabbath measures to save a human life that was in imminent danger of death.

If this is true, then one must differentiate the possible targets in the Lucan form of the Q saying on rescuing endangered life. Alone among the sayings we have examined, Luke 14:5 presents Jesus asking: "Which among you, if your *son* or *ox* fell into a cistern, would not immediately draw him (or it) out on the sabbath?" When it comes to the endangered ox, Jesus and ordinary Jewish peasants stand on one side of the question (of course, one would do that!) while Essenes and Pharisees stand on the other (no, you cannot directly draw the animal out yourself). When it comes to endangered human life—here Jesus shows great debating skill by speaking concretely and graphically of one's *son*—Jesus, ordinary peasants, and probably the Pharisees stand on one side (of course, you can pull your son out!) while the Essenes, perhaps with some discomfort, stand on the other (well, maybe you could throw him your cloak, but no direct use of a ladder or rope is permitted).

What Luke 13:15 has in common with Matt 12:11 ‖ Luke 14:5 is a sabbath activity that run-of-the-mill Jewish peasants would take for granted ("Which one of you does not . . . ?"). As already noted, though, the situation reflected in Luke 13:15 is different from the Q saying in that it refers to an ordinary, everyday need (untying an ox or a donkey from its manger so that it can be brought to a place where it can drink water) rather than to an extraordinary emergency (falling into a pit or into water). Moreover, unlike the problem presupposed by Matt 12:11 ‖ Luke 14:5, no documented *hălākâ* from the pre-70 period takes a position opposite to that of Luke 13:15. Indeed, CD 11:5–6 (and apparently 4Q265 fragment 7, 2:5) allows Essenes to follow their livestock as the animals graze on the sabbath up to a distance of 2,000 cubits outside their city. Unless we are to imagine that the Essenes' animals freely wandered about all the time because they were not tied to anything, this sabbath permission presupposes, without actually raising the question, that their livestock could be untied on the sabbath (and presumably, in one way or another, given to drink).[103]

Actually, in the matter of untying animals on the sabbath, the Essenes may have been more "liberal" than some of the later rabbis. Tying and untying knots are actions listed among the thirty-nine works prohibited on the sabbath in *m. Šabb.* 7:2, although the disputes among the rabbis recorded in *m. Šabb.* 15:1–2 indicate that the general prohibition was mitigated by all sorts of exceptions. Even if such opinions existed among the pre-70 Pharisees (and we have no attestation of that), we need not be surprised that these fine points debated by experts find no echo in the pragmatic custom that Jesus presupposes among his hearers in Luke 13:15.[104]

The difference in *hălākâ* between the sectarian and (later) rabbinic texts on the one hand and Luke 13:15 on the other lies in the basic focus. The sectarian and rabbinic texts demonstrate a great concern about the distance people could walk and the distance livestock could be allowed to graze on the sabbath. To this the rabbinic texts added a concern about tying and untying knots. It is telling that Luke 13:15 evinces neither concern. Distances are never brought up in any of the statements on sabbath *hălākâ* attributed to Jesus, and untying the animal to bring it to water is simply taken for granted as what anyone would do. Once again, we are dealing with the pragmatic, commonsense approach of ordinary peasants whose need to take care of their livestock crowds out the halakic niceties that might concern sectarians or scholars.

To repeat: what I am getting at in all these detailed debates about sabbath *hălākâ* is a vital point about the historical Jesus. The historical *Jewish* Jesus must be seen as a Jesus immersed in the halakic discussions, debates, and actual practice of 1st-century Palestinian Jews. In particular, Jesus was a Jew who pointedly stood over against the rigor of the Essenes, the Qumranites, and in some cases the Pharisees or even the disciples of John the Baptist (Jesus' disciples must not fast at all!). While we moderns might prefer to call Jesus' approach to sabbath observance "liberal," "broad," or "humane," his approach was first of all the commonsense approach to *hălākâ* that probably many ordinary Jewish peasants had no choice but to follow in their pinched and fragile existence. What Jesus does is to confirm that approach as the *hălākâ* that correctly reflects God's will, even as he presumes to reject what some might see as the admirable zeal and stringency of special sects and parties. It may well be that Jesus saw it as part of his teaching task to protect the common people from being attracted to sectarian rigorism.

Be that as it may, the major thrust of my observations is to show why it is reasonable to accept the historicity of the tradition of Jesus' rhetorical questions about sabbath *hălākâ* while remaining doubtful about the historicity of the narratives of disputes arising from sabbath healings. To be sure, both sayings and narratives enjoy multiple attestation of sources. The critical difference is that the dispute narratives make sense only if Jews in general at the time of Jesus held acts of healing on the sabbath to be violations of the sabbath. No such view is witnessed in any stream of Judaism by documents coming from the pre-70 period. This only aggravates the problem that, even apart from this halakic question, the miracle stories involving sabbath disputes had already succumbed to the historical verdict of *non liquet* in Volume Two.

In contrast, not only do the rhetorical questions about sabbath observance enjoy multiple attestation, they also fit perfectly into the *Sitz im Leben* of Jewish debates about sabbath *hălākâ* around the turn of the era, as seen in *Jubilees*, the *Damascus Document*, the Cave 4 fragments, Philo, Josephus, and the material from the Mishna and the Tosepta that can probably be assigned to the pre-70 period. They also fit perfectly into a credible portrait of a truly Jewish Jesus.

D. THE PLUCKING OF GRAIN ON THE SABBATH (MARK 2:23–28)

There are a number of reasons for treating separately the story of the plucking of the grain on the sabbath (Mark 2:23–28 parr.), but they all boil down to one basic impression: the oddness, not to say uniqueness, of the pericope.[105] This story stands out because its content and structure have no exact parallel anywhere else in the four Gospels. Alone among the sabbath dispute stories, Mark 2:23–28 has no connection with Jesus' miracles. Alone among the sabbath dispute stories, the controversy in Mark 2:23–28 is not ignited by something Jesus himself says or does. Alone among the sabbath dispute stories, the controversy reaches its climax not in one saying or action of Jesus but rather in a chain of three separate sayings that are at best loosely connected.[106] When one adds to all these strange traits the difficulties caused by the narrative's grammar, syntax, line of argumentation, and disputed tradition history, one can appreciate why there are almost as many opinions about this story as there are exegetes.[107]

In what follows, I will not attempt to grapple with any and every problem generated by this pericope.[108] Rather, I will (1) place 2:23–26 within its larger literary context in Mark's Gospel, (2) then examine the internal literary structure of this pericope, (3) only then raise the question of a hypothetical original form of the story, and (4) finally focus on those aspects of the narrative that may help us decide whether this story reaches back to some particular event in the ministry of the historical Jesus.

1. The Place of the Story within Mark's Cycle of Galilean Dispute Stories (Mark 2:1–3:6)

The plucking of the grain is the fourth of five dispute stories that Mark places toward the beginning of Jesus' public ministry (2:1–3:6).[109] This cycle corresponds roughly to the cycle of disputes and polemics that marks Jesus' stay in Jerusalem toward the end of his ministry (11:27–12:44). The Galilean cycle presents a complicated pattern in both its literary and theological dimensions. On the one hand, it is structured according to a *concentric* pattern; on the other, it is driven by a *thrust forward* to ever-increasing confrontation.

(a) Within the *concentric* structure, the first story (the healing of the paralytic in 2:1–12) corresponds to the fifth (the healing of the man with the withered hand in 3:1–6). In both, Jesus publicly heals a man suffering from paralysis. The healing, as well as the implicit claim to authority that the miracle involves, meets with opposition on the part of religious leaders. The second story (the call of Levi and the meal with toll collectors and sinners in 2:13–17) corresponds to the fourth story, the plucking of the grain (2:23–28). Both accounts connect the theme of eating with objections from the Pharisaic party. In the second story, Jesus' eating with toll collectors and sinners moves the scribes of the Pharisees to address a hostile question to Jesus' disciples, although it is Jesus himself, not his disciples, who answers the question. In the fourth story, the eating practices of the disciples, who are plucking grain on the sabbath, move the Pharisees to raise objections to Jesus, who defends his disciples with three distinct arguments. In the middle of this concentric pattern lies the third story (2:18–22), which continues the theme of eating by posing the question why the disciples of Jesus do not fast while the disciples of the Baptist and the disciples of the Pharisees do. Jesus replies both with the parable of the wedding feast and with the metaphors of the garment that tears and the wineskins that burst: joy at the Messiah's presence is tempered by the violent disruption it will unleash.

(b) Cutting across this concentric pattern is a *thrust forward* in the direction of increasingly open opposition and mortal enmity aimed at Jesus. Within the overarching story of the Gospel, this ever-heightened hostility toward Jesus points forward to Jesus' passion and death. In the first story, the scribes object silently in their thoughts (2:6) to Jesus' proclamation that the sins of the paralytic are forgiven. The silent but ominous charge that automatically arises in the minds of the scribes is that of blasphemy (2:7), for "Who can forgive sins except God alone?" Within Mark's narrative framework, this is a charge that already points forward to the Passion Narrative. For there, at the end of Mark's account of the Jewish trial (in which scribes will take part), Jesus will be condemned to death on the charge of blasphemy (14:64).[110] In the second story of the cycle, the scribes of the Pharisees speak aloud their objections to Jesus' actions, but they address these objections to the disciples, not to Jesus himself (2:16). In the third story, anonymous questioners address Jesus directly, challenging the lack of fasting on the part of Jesus' disciples in contrast to other religious groups. Jesus replies with a parable that culminates in the bridegroom's being taken away (2:20), another reference to Jesus' death, which will cause the disciples to fast in the future. In the fourth story, the Pharisees now directly challenge Jesus about the actions of his disciples on the sabbath (2:24). In the fifth and final story, Jesus' healing on the sabbath moves the Pharisees to take counsel with the Herodians on how they might destroy Jesus (3:6). The theme of Jesus' approaching death is thus a funeral bell that keeps tolling ever louder as we move through the five stories.

Clearly, then, this Galilean cycle of dispute stories is an intricate piece of literary art and artifice, written by a Christian theologian to advance his overall vision of Jesus as the hidden yet authoritative Messiah, Son of Man, and Son of God. As we begin to examine the fourth of the five stories, the plucking of the grain on the sabbath, the last thing we should do is treat it like a videotaped replay of a debate among various Palestinian Jews in the year A.D. 28. It is, first of all, a Christian composition promoting Christian theology. To what extent it may also preserve memories of an actual clash between the historical Jesus and Pharisees can be discerned only by analyzing the Christian text we have before us.

2. *The Structure of the Story of the Plucking of the Grain*

It is remarkable and dismaying to see how often commentators rush to a consideration of pre-Marcan tradition behind this story or even directly to the question of the story's historicity before undertaking a careful analysis of the literary structure of the Marcan pericope as it lies before us. They seem to forget that the only direct access we have is to the complicated text Mark has left us. One can get behind the text only by going through it, not by executing an end run around it.[111]

The narrative of the plucking of the grain on the sabbath belongs to the form-critical category of dispute story (*Streitgespräch*). While the form can have many particular incarnations, it basically consists of three main parts: (a) the setting of the stage, which introduces some if not all of the actors involved in the dispute and, in some cases, the action or circumstance that gives rise to the dispute; (b) the question or objection (sometimes voiced, sometimes not) that challenges the action or stance of Jesus or his disciples; (c) the response(s) of Jesus (often in the form of a counterquestion), defeating and/or silencing those posing the question or objection. In some stories, parts (a) and (b) are intertwined; in some cases, part (c) calls forth a reaction, positive or negative, from the audience.

Applying this grid to the somewhat idiosyncratic case of Mark 2:23–28, we can discern the following elaborate structure:

(a) *Setting the Stage* (here in two parts [first Jesus, then his disciples], v 23):
   (i)   And it happened that, on the sabbath, *Jesus* was passing through the standing grain [v 23a],
   (ii) and *his disciples* began to make their way, plucking the heads of grain [v 23b].
(b) *Question that Raises the Objection* (v 24):
       And the Pharisees said *to him*: "*Look*, why do *they* do on the sabbath what is not lawful?"
(c) *Jesus' Reply* (here in three parts [scriptural, anthropological, and christological], vv 25–28):
   (i)   And he says to them: "Did you never read what *David* did, when he was in need and was hungry, *he and those with him* [v 25],

how he entered the house of God when Abiathar was high priest and ate the loaves of the presence, which it is not lawful for anyone except the priests to eat, and *he* gave [the loaves] to *those with him* [v 26]?"

(ii) And he said to them: "The sabbath was made for man and not man for the sabbath [v 27].

(iii) Therefore, the Son of Man is lord also of the sabbath [v 28]."

As can be seen from this schematic outline, the three main parts of a dispute story all find a complicated expression in the narrative of the plucking of the grain.

(a) In the *setting of the stage,* two key protagonists are introduced in the two halves of v 23: Jesus, who does nothing provocative as he walks through the field of grain but who will reply to the objection raised, and his disciples, who perform the provocative act of plucking the grain but who say nothing in their own defense. As a glance forward to Jesus' first reply from Scripture shows (vv 25–26), this two-part introduction creates the pattern of distinction-yet-connection between the leader and his followers (Jesus and his disciples) that is taken up in the scriptural narrative (David and those with him).

(b) Perhaps it is this need to create the pattern of distinction-yet-connection in v 23 that explains why the mention of the people raising the *objection,* the Pharisees, is delayed until the beginning of the second major part of the story, the question that raises the objection (v 24). The two verbs of action in the question reinforce the pattern of distinction-yet-connection. The first verb (*ide,* "look," "see") is an imperative addressed to Jesus, as is made clear by the introductory clause, "and the Pharisees said *to him.* . . ." Jesus is asked to observe and explain what the second verb describes, namely, what the disciples are doing (*poiousin*) on the sabbath. The disciples are performing the objectionable action, but Jesus, as their teacher, is considered responsible for it—a common view in the ancient world, both Jewish and pagan.[112] Whether one thinks of Socrates and his disciples or the rabbis with theirs, famous teachers who were forming their followers in their doctrine and way of life were held answerable for their students' actions. The underlying pattern of distinguishing the teacher from his disciples and yet connecting him with them is thus carried forward from the setting of the scene into the question that poses the objection.

(c) This pattern of distinction-yet-connection is continued in the first of Jesus' *replies* to the Pharisees (vv 25–26), but not in the second (v 27) or third reply (v 28). In the first reply (vv 25–26), the story of David visiting the sanctuary at Nob (1 Sam 21:2–10 [ET: 1 Sam 21:1–9] is condensed and altered in such a way that both v 25 and v 26 reflect the pattern of distinction-yet-connection that has been introduced in the setting of the stage and continued in the raising of the objection. In v 25, David alone is mentioned at the beginning of the story (just as Jesus alone was mentioned at the beginning of the pericope), with all the verbs narrating the action put in the singular (what *David* did when *he* was in need and *he* felt hungry).[113] Only after this basic narrative about David is given does v 25 end somewhat awkwardly with the addition "he and those with him" (*autos kai hoi met' autou*). The pattern of distinction-yet-connection is clear. The same is true in the continuation of the story in v 26. In the first half of the verse (26a), David alone is said to enter the house of God and eat the loaves restricted to the priests. This corresponds to the mention of David alone in most of v 25. Then, in v 26b, we are told that David gave the loaves to "those with him" *as well* (notice the second *kai* in the Greek text). This corresponds to the awkward "he and those with him" at the end of v 25.

Once one realizes that all three main parts of the dispute (the setting of the stage, the question, and the first reply) are contoured according to the underlying pattern of distinction-yet-connection between leader and followers, one is struck by the sudden and total disappearance of this pattern in the second and third replies of Jesus.[114] The second reply, an axiom-like statement of a general truth about the anthropological (or humanitarian) goal of the sabbath ("the sabbath was made for man, not man for the sabbath"), mentions neither the leader (Jesus/David) nor the followers (the disciples/those with him). The third reply, a christological "trump card," mentions Jesus under the 3rd person description of Son of Man, but makes no corresponding mention of his followers. The emphasis of the final reply is clearly christological, being focused on Jesus alone: "The Son of Man is lord also of the sabbath." [115] The structural unity of 2:23–26 is also reinforced by the repetition of the key phrases "is not lawful" (*ouk exestin*) in vv 24 + 26 and "do" (*poiousin, epoiēsen*) in vv 24 + 25, phrases that are absent in vv 27 + 28.[116]

3. From Structural Analysis to a Hypothetical Original Form

The fact that the distinction-yet-connection pattern is present only in the first of Jesus' replies is all the more striking when one realizes that this formal, structuring pattern is not present in the original story of David at Nob in 1 Sam 21:2–10. In the OT story, in both the MT and the LXX (as well as the Qumran fragments from Cave 4),[117] David is desperately alone as he flees from King Saul's murderous wrath. Only David interacts with the priest at

Nob, and only he receives the loaves of the presence. As part of his lie to the priest, he mentions some young men (i.e., soldiers in Saul's army) whom he is supposed to meet somewhere. Since the following narrative never mentions these young men, David's reference to them seems to be simply part of his ruse, justifying his highly irregular request for a number of loaves of bread that are supposed to be consumed only by priests. Thus, neither in the story of David at Nob nor in the subsequent narrative of David's activity do "those with him" exist in the OT account. "Those with him" *are* present—in an awkward fashion—in the first reply of the Marcan dispute of 2:23–28, apparently for one reason only: the reply in vv 25–26 forms an organic part of the dispute story in vv 23–26, which is structured according to the distinction-yet-connection pattern.[118]

It is telling that, just as this pattern disappears as v 27 begins, the literary unity of the dispute story is disturbed by a new introductory phrase "and he [Jesus] said to them" (*kai elegen autois*). This phrase (or its equivalent) is used elsewhere in Mark to connect once isolated material into larger wholes.[119] This seems to be its function here as well. The previous two uses of the verb "to say" (*legō*) in our dispute story (v 24 + v 25) made perfect sense; they introduced and bound together the objection of the Pharisees (v 24) and the reply of Jesus (v 25). The sudden reappearance of "and he said to them" in v 27 serves no purpose within the literary structure, which it actually disrupts. This literary disruption coincides with the disruption in thought as the pattern of distinction-yet-connection, which has structured the whole pericope up until now, suddenly disappears.[120]

All this points to a likely understanding of the tradition history of Mark 2:23–28. In my opinion, the original compact form of the story consisted of the setting of the stage (v 23), the question (v 24), and Jesus' reply in vv 25–26—all three parts being bound tightly together by the pattern of distinction-yet-connection between leader and followers. The complete absence of such a pattern in the second and third replies, which lack the same structural integration into the main narrative, suggests that both v 27 (the anthropological argument) and v 28 (the explicit christological argument) were added secondarily—either at the same time or in separate stages.[121] In itself, this judgment does not decide whether these two isolated sayings ultimately come from the historical Jesus. All this judgment affirms is that these two sayings did not originally belong to the narrative of the plucking of the grain on the sabbath.

To anticipate for a moment what we shall soon see: I would further propose that the reason why these two replies in vv 27–28 were added—thus producing a dispute story overloaded with a number of discrete arguments at the end of the story—is that the original reply was increasingly felt, in the course of time, to be inadequate. One might draw a rough analogy here from text criticism. In text criticism, the reading that is judged to be the *lectio difficilior*, that is, the more difficult reading, tends to be judged the original reading of the text (though this is not the only consideration that goes into a final decision). The reason for this judgment is simple. The more difficult reading readily provokes the creation of a reading that is smoother or more easily intelligible in the larger context. If the easier reading had been the original one, it would never have provoked the creation of the more difficult reading as an improvement to the text.[122] Hence, all other things being equal, the more difficult reading is often preferred over an easily understandable reading as the original—or at least earlier—form of the text.

To press the analogy home: if vv 25–26 (the first reply) formed the original ending to the story of the plucking of the grain, one can readily understand why the more intelligible or cogent endings of vv 27–28—two replies that explicitly mention the sabbath—should be added to bolster the argument of Jesus. If, on the other hand, vv 27–28 formed the original ending to the dispute, it is difficult to see why the problematic reply of vv 25–26 (*how* problematic it is we shall soon see) should have been inserted into the middle of the story.[123] Indeed, as will be shown, the inadequacy of the first response raises some questions about the historicity of the original form of the story.

4. *The Historicity of the Original Form*

Let us suppose, then, as a working hypothesis, that the original form of the dispute about plucking grain on the sabbath consisted of Mark 2:23 (setting the scene) + 2:24 (question) + 2:25–26 (reply, a scriptural argument from 1 Sam 21:2–10). If we grant this hypothesis, what considerations argue for or against the judgment that this tradition reaches back to some incident in the public ministry of the historical Jesus? In my opinion, a number of considerations tip the scales against historicity.

First, there is the point emphasized by E. P. Sanders: having Pharisees suddenly pop up in the middle of a grain field on the sabbath to object to the disciples' activity strains credulity.[124] It almost looks like something out of a Broadway musical: "Oh what a beautiful sabbath!" Are we to imagine that Pharisees regularly patrolled grainfields on the sabbath, looking for possible violations? Or have the Pharisees sent out a special commission to spy on Jesus and his disciples in this particular grainfield? In a number of Gospel dispute stories, the Pharisees or other opponents have a strange way of suddenly appearing on the scene just when Jesus or his disciples are doing or saying something objectionable.[125] The scenario becomes even more unlikely if we accept the view of those commentators who suggest that the Pharisees did not enjoy a sizable presence in Galilee at the time of Jesus.[126] Moreover, even if the Pharisees did have an organized presence in Galilee then, we might expect them to encounter and perhaps clash with Jesus in some synagogue on the sabbath. But in a grainfield on the sabbath?

Then there is the question of how far Jesus and his disciples are from some town or settlement when this dispute occurs. If we suppose for the moment that Jesus and his disciples, like many pious Jews, observed a set limit outside of which one was not allowed to walk on the sabbath (in the Mishna, 2,000 cubits, roughly 1,000 yards), one has to ask why the disciples did not simply go into the nearby settlement to ask for food if they were hungry. If instead one conjectures that a "freewheeling" Jesus did not observe the sabbath limit that stringent students of the Law obeyed, the Pharisees could not have been present to see the plucking and object to it. Granted, all these considerations, even when taken together, do not render the account in 2:23–26 unhistorical, but they do begin to raise doubts.

These doubts are reinforced by the grave difficulty that any critical historian will detect in Jesus' reply in 2:25–26. The reply begins auspiciously enough. In a clever rhetorical flourish found in both the rabbinic and Greco-Roman philosophical tradition, Jesus parries a question with another question. But the way the counterquestion begins in v 25 signals the problems to come: "Did you never *read* what David did . . . ?" Let us remember what the supposed historical situation in Mark 2:23–26 is. Challenged by some Pharisees, who are noted for their exact and exacting study of Scripture, Jesus counterchallenges them on their home ground: exact knowledge of the written Scriptures ("Did you never *read* . . . ?"). Jesus therefore is not appealing to some stray oral tradition or his own made-up-on-the-spot version of the David story. He consciously challenges the experts in the Scriptures to recall and then properly understand a given text of Scripture, namely, 1 Sam 21:2–10.

The problem is, Jesus proceeds in the presence of these scriptural experts to mangle and distort the text of the story, whether we read the text in its Masoretic Hebrew form, the alternate form found in the Qumran fragment of 4QSam[b], the Septuagintal Greek form (which often agrees with 4QSam[b] against the MT), or the targumic Aramaic form.[127] We have seen some of the inaccuracies already. Jesus claims that David had companions with him when he came to the priest at Nob and that David gave some of the loaves of the presence "to those with him."[128] Neither the presence of David's companions nor David's act of giving bread to them is to be found anywhere in this OT text, whether the Hebrew, Greek, or Aramaic form. Indeed, when the priest at the sanctuary meets David, he asks with trepidation (1 Sam 21:2): "Why are you alone and no one is with you?" In other words, the text of 1 Sam 21:2 directly and blatantly contradicts what Jesus claims the text says. Moreover, 1 Sam 21:2–10 never states explicitly that David (let alone his nonexistent companions) is hungry and eats the loaves then and there. Such details might be inferred from David's request; but since the text never says that David eats the loaves at Nob, one might infer instead that David is providing himself with food for his subsequent journey.

A more serious problem lies in the basically irrelevant nature of the Scripture text Jesus chooses in order to defend his disciples' behavior. Nothing in the narrative of 1 Sam 21:2–10 would cause one to think that David's request for food occurs on a sabbath.[129] To be sure, the Torah specifies that the loaves of the presence are to be replaced with fresh loaves every sabbath, but the story in 1 Sam 21:2–10 in no way connects the priest's gift of the loaves to David with the regular replacement of the loaves on the sabbath. Nor is there any indication in Jewish sources prior to A.D. 70 that, at the time of Jesus, the events in 1 Sam 21:2–10 were generally understood to have taken place on the sabbath.[130] In a sense, the attempt by some modern commentators to read the sabbath into Jesus' appeal to David's action misses the point, since Jesus stresses that David's violation involved *what* David did—eating food that only priests should eat—and not *when* he ate it.[131]

Oddly, the Marcan Jesus, who freely interpolates a number of other details into the text of 1 Samuel, is careful to adhere to the written text on this pivotal point. As indicated earlier, no textual form of 1 Sam 21:2–10 gives a hint of connecting the events it narrates with the sabbath; neither, surprisingly, does the Marcan Jesus. Despite his other additions and despite his explicit reference to the sabbath in his second and third replies (vv 27 + 28), he does not venture to insert the element of the sabbath into the story of David—even though this is the one addition that would have made the story truly relevant to the objection raised by the Pharisees in Mark 2:24.[132] Without this correspondence, the case of David simply illustrates a general claim that dire human need or an emergency situation can override details of religious law—a claim that does not fit the Marcan narrative, where nothing has been said about the disciples being in dire need or facing an emergency. It is possible that, on the level of redactional theology, Mark sees Jesus' Davidic messiahship as the true link that connects the dispute about the plucking of the grain with the story of David in 1 Sam 21:2–10. But, while Mark might presuppose that such an implicit link would be understood by Christian believers, the historical Jesus could hardly suppose that such a link would be understood, let alone granted, by the historical Pharisees whom he is trying to best in scriptural argumentation.

Still more embarrassing is the error about the identity of the priest to whom David speaks at Nob. Both the Hebrew and the Greek forms of 1 Sam 21:2 make clear that the priest whom David addresses is "Ahimelech the priest"; his name is repeated in vv 3 and 9 (MT). No other individual priest is mentioned in 1 Sam 21:2–10 as being on the scene during the exchange between David and Ahimelech; in fact, no other priest is mentioned by name in the story. There is therefore no basis in the OT text of this story for the mistake the Marcan Jesus[133] makes in claiming that the "high priest" (this somewhat anachronistic title does not occur in this OT story) in charge at the time was Abiathar (Mark 2:26): "how he [David] entered the house of God when Abiathar was high priest [epi Abiathar archiereōs]." Abiathar, at least according to the most reliable OT tradition, was the son of Ahimelech, with whom the Marcan Jesus has confused him.[134]

It is amusing to see how past commentators have searched high and low for any and every exegetical escape hatch to save themselves from having to admit that Jesus, at least as Mark presents him in 2:26, makes a flagrant error about what the text of 1 Sam 21:2–10 says.[135] Alas, none of the escape hatches is convincing, unless one is determined beforehand to be convinced. The conclusion we must draw both from this error and from the other examples of Jesus' inaccurate retelling of the OT story is simple and obvious: the recounting of the David and Ahimelech incident shows both an egregious ignorance of what the OT text actually says and a striking inability to construct a convincing argument from the story.

Now one might object that all these observations fail to appreciate that Jesus, in sovereign fashion, is rewriting the OT story according to his own purposes. A simple reply to this objection is that, without the much-needed insertion of the sabbath into the David story, the purpose of Jesus' supposed rewriting remains unclear. More to the point, though, the defense that Jesus is, with sovereign freedom, rewriting the story of David at Nob does not fit the scene Mark depicts in 2:23–26, the scene that we are testing for its historicity. As we consider this scene, we need to recall the "agonistic" culture of the ancient Mediterranean world, where public debates between contending parties were a matter of honor and shame. According to Mark, Jesus has chosen to counter the Pharisees' challenge by challenging them on their knowledge of the text of 1 Sam 21:2–10 ("Did you never read . . . ?"). Jesus' challenge hopelessly falls to pieces if he immediately proceeds to document his own glaring ignorance of the written text of 1 Sam 21:2–10—which, according to Mark's account, he does.

At this point, some conservative scholars might be all too willing to deny the historicity of Mark 2:23–26, thus dodging a major theological problem by assigning the embarrassing mistakes to Mark rather than to Jesus. However, the unpapal conclave I have conjured up as a symbol of evenhanded historical-critical research does not admit theological concerns into its weighing of the arguments for and against historicity. The proper stance of a professional historian, who is obliged to weigh the evidence according to the canons of historical reasoning, is clear. If the historical Jesus made these embarrassing mistakes in his debate over who knows Scripture best, then so be it: the historical Jesus was ignorant of scripture.[136] An honest historian must let the chips fall where they may.

That said, I think that these glaring errors in Jesus' scriptural argument offer a reason for assigning the story to early Christians rather than to Jesus—but the reason is a historical, not a theological one. If there is anything certain about the ministry of the historical Jesus and its denouement, it is that Jesus was an impressive teacher and debater. Amid the fierce competition for public esteem and influence among Jews in 1st-century Palestine, he acquired a fair amount of fame and following—to the point that he was perceived to be dangerous. This basic picture of the historical Jesus seems incompatible with the Jesus Mark unwittingly portrays. This Marcan Jesus is not only ignorant but also reckless, foolishly challenging Scripture experts to a public debate about the proper reading of a specific text—only to prove immediately to both his disciples and his opponents how ignorant he is of the text that he himself has put forward for discussion.

If this scene gives us a true picture of the scriptural knowledge and teaching skill of the historical Jesus, then the natural and very effective response of the Pharisees would have been not fierce anger and concerted opposition but gleeful mockery. They would have laughed their heads off (and invited the populace to do the same) at this uneducated woodworker who insisted on making a fool of himself in public by displaying his abysmal ignorance of the very Scripture text on which he proposed to instruct the supposedly ignorant Pharisees. I dare say, if this was the actual competence of the historical Jesus in teaching and debating, his movement would not have lasted a month in 1st-century Jewish Palestine. Such a portrayal of Jesus not only fails to explain his widespread popularity, his accordingly violent end, and the impact of his ministry on subsequent history; it does not even square with one of the few significant traits of the historical Jesus that Josephus (*Ant.* 18.3.3 §63) highlights: "Jesus, a wise man, . . . was . . . a teacher of people who receive the truth with pleasure. . . . [H]e gained a following among . . . many Jews."

Consequently, I incline to the view that in Mark 2:23–26 we have a polemical composition created by Christian Jews in Palestine prior to A.D. 70 (the approximate time of the composition of Mark's Gospel). The natural objection to my suggestion is that there is no likely "setting in life" (*Sitz im Leben*) for such a story among early Christian Jews in Palestine. Are we to imagine that Christian Jews made such a habit out of plucking grain on the sabbath that it became a major point of dispute with their Jewish neighbors, thus forcing the Christians to create this anecdote by way of justification?[137] Actually, such an objection misses two important points.

First, except for the tidbits, colored by apologetics and polemics, that we get from Paul's epistles and the Acts of the Apostles, we know next to nothing about the ordinary lives of ordinary Christian Jews in pre-70 Palestine, especially in Galilee. In fact, whether there were ongoing Jewish-Christian communities in Galilee before the emperor Constantine is debated among scholars.[138] The little we do know about Christianity in pre-70 Palestine tends to focus on the Christian leaders as they wrangled with one another and at times with the priestly establishment in Jerusalem.

Second and more important, religious apologetics and polemics usually do not supply a sober description of either of the two parties engaged in argument. Despite the theoretical purpose of addressing and confuting one's adversaries *outside*, most religious apologetics and polemics are directed *inward*. Their real function is to give a sense of assurance and reinforcement to the group producing the polemics. Most apologetics and polemics are thus an attempt to shore up group solidarity and conviction within a community that feels insecure and under attack. The a priori conviction of such polemics is simple and unshakable: "We are right and they are wrong, and now we will think up some reasons to prove that they are wrong." Are we to imagine that Palestinian Pharisees actually heard and responded to such polemical traditions as Mark 2:23–26? I think rather that this dispute story, like most of the Gospel traditions, is aimed primarily inward, addressing the Christian community that is in need of support and instruction.[139]

This overall situation of a hopelessly small group of Palestinian Jews-for-Jesus, who feel beleaguered within a sea of Jews-not-for-Jesus, is the real *Sitz im Leben* of this dispute story. Speaking more to themselves than to their opponents, these Christian Jews seek to justify their less-than-stringent approach to sabbath observance by recounting how Jesus had shown that their archetypal opponents, the Pharisees, were both ignorant of Scripture and unreasonably harsh in their treatment of innocent activity on the sabbath. This is a prime example of how religious polemics generate more heat than light. Not only would the argument created in 2:23–26 not have seemed cogent to a knowledgeable Pharisee (if he had ever heard the argument), it apparently did not seem too cogent to Mark (or his source), who felt the need to add the more theologically relevant arguments of v 27 and v 28—which at least have the good sense to mention the sabbath in their replies. Hence, while certainty is not to be had in such matters, I incline to the view that the core story of the plucking of the grain on the sabbath (vv 23–26) is a not-especially-adroit polemical creation of Christian Jews in Palestine in the pre-70 period.

As previously noted, though, the judgment that v 27 and v 28 are not a part of the original story does not decide the issue of whether these two sayings go back to the historical Jesus. Indeed, paradoxically, once we judge Mark 2:23–26 to be a Christian composition, it is the very independence of v 27 and v 28 vis-à-vis the rest of the dispute story that leaves open the possibility that one or both of these sayings may go back to Jesus. It is to that question that we now turn our attention.

E. The Sabbath Sayings in Mark 2:27–28

Once one decides that vv 27–28 were added to the original dispute story at a later date in order to bolster the not-entirely-cogent argument in vv 25–26, the question arises whether vv 27–28 were appended to the narrative at the same time or separately—and, if the latter, in what order. While there can be no certainty here, I think that the very different types of argument in the two verses and their different theological "heft" suggest that v 27 ("the sabbath was made for man and not man for the sabbath") was added before v 28 ("therefore the Son of Man is lord also of the sabbath"). Just as the inadequacy of the reasoning in vv 25–26 provoked the addition of v 27, which at least mentions the sabbath and the way human beings should relate to it, the problematic nature of v 27 called forth in turn the "christological trump card" of v 28, which cuts off all dispute about the sabbath by appealing to the sovereign authority of Jesus as Son of Man.

If some Christian teacher had added the weighty christological pronouncement of v 28 immediately after vv 25–26, not only would v 28 have supplied *the* decisive argument for a Christian audience, but it would also have enjoyed at least a tenuous connection with the implicit christological comparison between David and Jesus in vv 25–26. The "therefore" (*hōste*) at the beginning of v 28 would not have lacked something to latch on to in the immediately preceding text—as in fact it does now. To have disrupted this connection between vv 25–26 and v 28 by inserting a weaker argument that lacked any christological link either backward or forward would have made no sense. Hence, it seems probable that the present order of vv 27–28 reflects the actual stages in which these two quite different verses were added to the original dispute story.

1. *Verse 27: The Sabbath Was Made for Man*

Of all the verses in this dispute story, v 27 is the one commentators most readily accept as probably coming from the historical Jesus.[140] One must admit, though, that even here the arguments for historicity are more allusive and indirect than weighty and decisive. For instance, it is often claimed by questers for the historical Jesus that Jesus characteristically taught in crisp, striking, memorable statements structured along the lines of antithetical parallelism and/or chiasm. One is justly wary of this claim if it is exalted to the status of an a priori principle or criterion of authenticity; the result would be a classic case of presupposing what is to be proved. As a matter of fact, though, this claim has been verified a posteriori in many of the sayings judged authentic throughout the volumes of *A Marginal Jew*.[141] Granted this rhetorical preference of the historical Jesus, the striking fusion of antithetical parallelism and chiasm in the short, dense logion of Mark 2:27 favors the authenticity of the saying:

the sabbath	*to sabbaton*
for man	*dia ton anthrōpon*
was made	*egeneto*
and not man	*kai ouch ho anthrōpos*
for the sabbath	*dia to sabbaton*[142]

Then, too, unlike the muddled argument of vv 25–26 and the christological trump card of v 28, the *māšāl* (proverb, axiom, aphorism, wisdom saying, or a similar striking, terse, and memorable statement) of v 27 is perfectly intelligible and plausible in the mouth of Palestinian-Jewish teacher around the turn of the era. Indeed, commentators unfailingly cite the remarkable (though partial) parallel found in the great rabbinic commentary on the Book of Exodus, the *Mekilta*. In the *Mekilta* commentary on Exod 31:13–14 (cf. *b. Yoma* 85b), Rabbi Simeon ben Menasya (ca. A.D. 180) is cited as saying, "The sabbath is handed over to you, but you are not handed over to the sabbath [*lkm šbt mswrh w'yn 'tm mswryn lšbt*]."[143] The parallel is striking, though there are a number of differences between the saying of Simeon and the saying of Jesus, at least in the present contexts of the two statements.

For one thing, Rabbi Simeon is addressing "you," who are his fellow Israelites (more specifically, in the immediate context, his fellow rabbis), not all humanity in general.[144] The rabbis stressed that the wonderful gift of the sabbath was not given indiscriminately to all human beings but only to the chosen people.[145] Rabbinic as well is Simeon's use of a pivotal verb from the rabbinic tradition: *māsar*, "to hand over," "to deliver," "to transmit." [146] For Rabbi Simeon, the sabbath is a sacred institution received from God on Mt. Sinai, an institution that has been faithfully handed on to successive generations of observant Jews. It is a life-enhancing gift of God to Israel, not a crushing burden that enslaves Israel or endangers life. In other words, the sabbath is a means to an end, not an end in itself. As with Jesus, so with Rabbi Simeon, the point of the saying is the setting of priorities; even sabbath observance has its limitations. In the immediate context, Rabbi Simeon uses this saying to teach that rescuing endangered human life takes precedence over the sabbath. Thus, far from being an "anything goes" antinomian slogan, this saying focuses on the type of emergency that permits one to ignore sabbath restrictions.

The vocabulary, thought world, and immediate context of the saying of the Marcan Jesus are somewhat different. The difference is perhaps clearest in two particular words. Instead of "you," the Marcan Jesus speaks of "man" (*anthrōpos* in the sense of "human being," "humanity"); instead of using the verb "hand over," he uses the verb "become" or "come to be" (*ginomai*). Since the OT, intertestamental literature, and the rabbis all affirm that the sabbath is God's special gift to Israel, it is at first puzzling that Jesus speaks of "man," that is, humanity in general.[147] In the Greek sentence in Mark 2:27, the explanation for this choice comes in the word that immediately follows "man": *egeneto*, "became," "came to be"—and, in this context, "was made" or "was created." The Marcan Jesus is alluding to the creation story in Genesis. In the LXX version of the creation story in Genesis 1–2, the Greek verb *egeneto* ("it was made") tolls like a bell throughout Gen 1:3–2:4.[148] In particular, the narrative of the creation of "man" (*anthrōpos*, i.e., human beings as a group) in Gen 1:26–30 ends with the set phrase *kai egeneto houtōs* ("and it was made thus," "and so it was created," or simply "and so it was"). Thus, in his teaching on proper priorities, Jesus reaches back to the story of God creating humanity, which is immediately followed in Gen 2:1–3 by the story of God resting on the seventh day, blessing and sanctifying it—an obvious pointer forward to God's gift of the sabbath to Israel when he reveals the Torah on Mt. Sinai. In effect, Jesus' argument is not so much "anthropological" or "humanitarian" as it is an expression of creation theology within the context of the end time. Both human beings and the sabbath, placed within this context, are seen in their proper perspective and in their proper relationship to each other. The temporal priority of human beings (created on the sixth day) seems to hint at their substantive priority to the sabbath (the seventh day).[149]

This harking back to the order of God's good creation before it was marred by sin is typical of Jewish apocalyptic thought and is found elsewhere in Jesus' teaching, notably in his teaching on marriage and divorce in Mark 10:2–9.[150] In a larger sense, it is part of Jesus' proclamation of the coming-yet-present kingdom of God, which will bring God's original intentions for his good creation to fulfillment. Thus, unlike Rabbi Simeon's use of his saying to support the halakic position that rescuing endangered life overrides the sabbath, Jesus' saying on sabbath and humanity reaches back to creation and the proper priorities rooted in the original order willed by God. The theological depth and force of Jesus' teaching on humanity and the sabbath may be the reason why the once isolated logion of Mark 2:27 was appended to the original dispute story in Mark 2:23–26. Mark 2:27 was added to the ending of the *Streitgespräch* to supply the sort of theologically forceful and rhetorically succinct "punch line" that would fit the form and function of a dispute story about the sabbath much better than the lengthy and less-than-cogent reworking of 1 Sam 21:2–10 in Mark 2:25–26.

At the same time, though, the cosmic sweep of Mark 2:27, which made it superior to the David story as a conclusion to the dispute, may have turned out to pose a new problem. Its sweeping nature may have been felt by some Christian Jews to be a little too sweeping. As the conclusive word on what constitutes permissible behavior on the sabbath, the saying, over the course of time, may have seemed to some to be too open to a "love God and do what you will" type of libertinism. In other words, the new ending seemed incommensurate to the original question posed. The dispute opens in 2:23–24 with a narrow focus: whether plucking grain constitutes a type of reaping forbidden on the sabbath. Far from answering only that restricted question, Jesus' final reply in 2:27 could be understood to espouse an "anything goes" approach to the sabbath. Ironically, Mark 2:27, appended to the dispute story as a solution to the problem of finding an effective argument, itself became a problem and in turn called forth the definitive christological solution of Mark 2:28. But, before we turn to 2:28, let us consider the question of whether 2:27 goes back to the historical Jesus.

The argument in favor of authenticity is not as weighty as some might imagine, but, in my opinion, a number of considerations do converge to form an adequate argument from coherence. First, as we have seen, the saying is a prime example of a terse, compact, and memorable logion marked by antithetical parallelism and chiasm—precisely the kind of axiom or aphorism that is typical of Jesus' teaching. Second, unlike the maladroit and error-plagued proof-text approach of vv 25–26, and unlike the strongly christological argument of v 28, v 27 (witness the similar-but-not-the-same pronouncement in the *Mekilta*) is intelligible as a pronouncement of a Jewish-Palestinian teacher guiding his fellow Jews on the proper way to observe the sabbath. To put the same argument slightly differently: the appeal to christology or to specific precedents supplied by Scripture texts (e.g., Mark 2:25–26; Matt 12:5–6), witnessed in verses that are generally acknowledged to be Christian creations, is notably absent in 2:27.[151] Third, the method of discerning what is correct halakic observance in the end time by harking back to God's original intent for his creation is seen elsewhere in Jesus' teaching; his *hălākâ* is eschatological *hălākâ*. Unlike some notable examples of creation theology elsewhere in the NT, there is neither implicitly nor explicitly any christological basis to the argument.[152]

Moreover, the approach to the sabbath reflected in this saying coheres with the other sayings of Jesus on the sabbath that we have already reviewed. Jesus' approach rejects a stringent observance that would place heavy burdens on ordinary people, especially those in need, but Jesus in no way rejects the sabbath itself. Rather, it is presupposed as a gift from God—a gift ultimately grounded in creation itself—whose observance must be interpreted correctly. Reflecting the self-assurance of a true charismatic, Jesus does not hesitate to tell everyone in his usual ipse-dixit style what the correct interpretation is. Hence, while I can well understand why some might prefer the judgment of *non liquet* (not clear either way), I think the evidence slightly favors the view that v 27 goes back to the historical Jesus.

Such a judgment, though, does not solve all problems of interpretation. After all, v 27 is an isolated logion. Once we detach it from its immediate (secondary) context, we have no other context that helps us understand in greater detail what exactly Jesus meant when he spoke this *māšāl* or what particular question or problem evoked his pronouncement. But then, the same is true of the saying of Rabbi Simeon in the *Mekilta*—a consideration that should keep us from playing a game of theological one-upmanship, trying to show how essentially superior Jesus's stance is to that of Rabbi Simeon's.[153] In both cases, the antithesis at the heart of the axiom must be understood as a "dialectical" or "relative" negation typical of Semitic speech. This dialectical negation emphasizes not that the sabbath is absolutely rejected for the good of humanity, but rather that the sabbath is subordinated as a means to an end—the end being the ultimate good of humanity.[154] Having understood this claim of relative importance and subordination affirmed in v 27, let us now move on to the absolute claim of v 28, which concludes the dispute story in its present form.

2. *Verse 28: The Son of Man Is Lord Even of the Sabbath*

Verse 28 involves us in an especially thorny issue that I will not be taking up directly until a later chapter: Jesus' many references to himself as the Son of Man (*ho huios tou anthrōpou*).[155] But since a full study of Mark 2:23–28 demands that v 28 be considered here, I will make—by way of a brief primer—just a few comments about the Son of Man problem, comments especially aimed at evaluating the logion in Mark 2:28.

Under the influence of Rudolf Bultmann,[156] scholars frequently divide the Son of Man sayings in the Synoptic Gospels into three main categories: (1) sayings referring to Jesus during his public ministry, (2) sayings predicting his sufferings, death, and resurrection, and (3) sayings predicting his future role as eschatological witness, judge, or savior on the last day. While this tripartite division does not do justice to the variety of content and forms found in the Son of Man sayings, I will accept it for now as a useful, though rough, tool.

That it is a rough tool is seen by the fact that each of the three categories can be subdivided according to the types of verbs expressing what the Son of Man does, is, or experiences in the present, the near future, or the absolute future of the last day. Not surprisingly, both form and content of the Son of Man sayings can change as the verbs change. Restricting ourselves for the moment to the Synoptic sayings, we notice the following divisions according to verb usage (and consequently according to content and theological affirmations):

1. In reference to Jesus' *public ministry*: the Son of Man "has" something; the Son of Man "has" done something (e.g., "has come" or "came " for some purpose); the Son of Man "is" or "shall be" someone or something; or the Son of Man is the object of hostile speech. For example, the Son of Man "has" power to forgive sins (Mark 2:10); the Son of Man "has" nowhere to lay his head (Matt 8:20 par.); the Son of Man "came" not to be served but to serve (Mark 10:45);[157] the Son of Man "came" eating and drinking (Matt 11:19; Luke's parallel, 7:34, reads "has come"); the Son of Man "came to seek out and save the lost" (Luke 19:10); someone "speaks a [hostile] word against" the Son of Man (Matt 12:32 par.); Jesus asks who do men say the Son of Man "is" (Matt 16:13); as Jonah was a sign to the Ninevites, "so shall the Son of Man be" to this generation (Luke 11:30).

2. In reference to the *suffering, death, and resurrection* of Jesus: the Son of Man "must suffer . . . and be killed . . . and rise" (Mark 8:31); the Son

of Man "is about to suffer" (Matt 17:12);[158] the Son of Man will "rise from the dead" (Mark 9:9); it is written about the Son of Man that he "will suffer many things" (Mark 9:12); the Son of Man "is being handed over" or "will be handed over" (Mark 9:31; cf. 10:33); the Son of Man "goes" [his way to death] (Mark 14:21); Judas "betrays the Son of Man with a kiss" (Luke 22:48); the Son of Man "will be in the heart of the earth" (i.e., will be buried, Matt 12:40).

3. In reference to the absolute future of the *final judgment and/or salvation*: when he comes in glory, the Son of Man "will be ashamed" of the person who was ashamed of him in this life (Mark 8:38); the Son of Man "will acknowledge" before the angels everyone who acknowledges him in this life (Luke 12:8); "they shall see the Son of Man coming on the clouds . . . and he will send out the angels and he will gather his chosen ones" (Mark 13:26–27); "you [the high priest and the sanhedrin] will see the Son of Man seated at the right hand [of God] and coming with the clouds of heaven" (Mark 14:62); the disciples will not finish preaching to the cities of Israel "before the Son of Man comes" (Matt 10:23); "the Son of Man is about to come" in the glory of his Father to render each one according to his actions (Matt 16:27); some will not taste death "until they see the Son of Man coming in his kingly power" (Matt 16:28); the Son of Man will "sit on the throne of his glory" (Matt 19:28); "the coming [*parousia*] of the Son of Man will be like lightning" (Matt 24:27); "the sign of the Son of Man will appear in heaven" (Matt 24:30); "the coming of the Son of Man will be like" the days of Noah (Matt 24:37,39); "the day on which the Son of Man is revealed" will be like the day Lot left Sodom (Luke 17:29–30); "at his coming, will the Son of Man find faith on earth?" (Luke 18:8); "the Son of Man is coming at an hour you do not expect" (Matt 24:44); "when the Son of Man comes in his glory . . . all the nations will be gathered before him" (Matt 25:31); "pray that you may be able . . . to stand before the Son of Man [on the last day]" (Luke 21:36).

A few of the Son of Man sayings, especially those that probably stem from Christian tradition rather than the historical Jesus, fall outside this neat three-part division in that they introduce the present time of the church and the Son of Man's relationship to it. For example, in his allegorical interpretation of the parable of the wheat and the weeds (Matt 13:36–43), Matthew (or his M tradition) explains that the person who sows good seed in this present world during the church's mission is the Son of Man (Matt 13:37): "The one sowing the good seed is the Son of Man." [159] Reflecting his tendency to draw together different stages of the Son of Man story, Matthew then concludes his allegorical explanation by stating that, at the last judgment, the Son of Man will send his angels to gather all evildoers out of "his" kingdom (13:41).[160] To take a different kind of example: Luke may be encompassing a number of stages of salvation history when he has Jesus tell his disciples in enigmatic fashion that "days will come when you will desire to see one of the days of the Son of Man and will not see it" (Luke 17:22).[161] Luke's focus on the present time of the church is clearly seen in his alteration of Jesus' statement at the climax of his trial before the high priest (22:69): "From now on the Son of Man will be seated at the right hand of the power of God"—carefully omitting the reference to his coming on the clouds at the last judgment.[162] This Son of Man is the risen, exalted Jesus, enthroned at God's right hand. Luke consciously echoes this present-time-of-the-church use of Son of Man at the climax of Stephen's speech in Acts 7:56: "Behold, I see the heavens opened and the Son of Man standing at the right hand of God"—a unique case of an individual other than Jesus speaking of the Son of Man.[163] This redactional tendency of Matthew and Luke to move the Son of Man into the present time of the church should be kept in mind when we come to treat Mark 2:28. But let us first turn our glance to the use of Son of Man in the Fourth Gospel.

In John's Gospel, we can likewise find Son of Man sayings that refer to Jesus' public ministry, his death and resurrection, and his glorious position as judge of the world. However, the vocabulary and time references are often quite different from those of the Synoptics because the whole Son of Man tradition has been filtered through the high christology and realized eschatology that are the hallmarks of John's theology.[164] Instead of descending from heaven on the last day, the Son of Man descends to earth in the incarnation and ascends triumphantly back to heaven by way of the cross (3:13; 6:62). Since the Jesus who speaks in John's Gospel, even during the public ministry, often sounds as though he is already the exalted one, time references are frequently hazy and shifting. For example, speaking to Nicodemus early on in his public ministry, Jesus states solemnly (3:13): "No one has ascended into heaven except the one who descended, the Son of Man." Yet practically in the next breath, Jesus speaks of his being "lifted up" on the cross as a still-future event (3:14–15; cf. 8:28;12:32–34): "The Son of Man must be lifted up in order that everyone who believes in him may have eternal life." This exaltation on the cross is the pivotal moment in the glorification of the Son of Man as he returns in triumph to his Father (12:23; 13:31).[165]

Granted this shift in the theology of the Son of Man sayings, it is not surprising that, unlike the Synoptics, John's Gospel makes the Son of Man the direct object of (Christian) faith. The prime example of this shift in the use of the Son of Man title is found at the climax of the story of the man born blind in John 9. After Jesus has given sight to the blind man, he challenges the man to receive the insight of faith as well (9:35): "Do you believe in the Son of Man?" [166] One reason why the Son of Man can be the object of faith *now* is that, in keeping with John's realized eschatology, the final judgment is *now*, in the moment of belief or unbelief in the incarnate Son (5:24–27). As the Word made flesh encounters and challenges people in the course of their ordinary daily lives, he forces these people to line up for or against him and so to pass judgment on themselves (9:39–41; cf. 3:18–21). In the evangelist's view, this encounter of judgment and salvation happens now in the time of Christian preaching just as truly as it happened during the public ministry of Jesus. Hence, every Christian believer is promised the vision of faith that Nathanael and the other first disciples are promised in 1:51: "You shall see heaven opened and the angels of God ascending and descending upon the Son of Man [who is thus the new Jacob's ladder of Gen 28:12, uniting heaven and earth]." [167] Jesus the Son of Man, the Word incarnate, embodies in his own person the union between the divine and the human, heaven and earth, that was hoped for on the last day. In John's community, this union of the divine and human in Jesus becomes for believers an ongoing experience in the eucharist, when they "eat the flesh of the Son of Man and drink his blood" (6:58; cf. v 27).[168]

This moving of the Son of Man into the present time of the church stands in striking contrast to the earliest statements about the Son of Man that we can locate in the Marcan and Q traditions.[169] In these primitive traditions, the Son of Man is always connected with Jesus' ministry, his death and resurrection, or his future coming in glory. These early traditions contain no Son of Man sayings that directly refer to the present reign and activity of Jesus as Son of Man during the ongoing time of the church. In contrast, Son of Man sayings that focus on the present time of the church are clearly visible in John's Gospel as they are in the special Matthean and Lucan traditions as well. In brief, then: as the Gospel traditions about the Son of Man move and expand through the latter part of the 1st century A.D., "Son of Man," which, from the vantage point of the earliest Christian believers, referred only to the sacred past of Jesus' life, death, and resurrection or to his future coming, now begins to refer to Christians' present experience of him in the church's faith and worship.

It is this insight that intersects with our consideration of the Son of Man saying in Mark 2:28. The problem of the authenticity of Mark 2:28, which is extremely difficult when treated in isolation or only within the context of Mark 2:23–28, becomes clearer when viewed within the broader context of the various verbal and conceptual forms of the Son of Man sayings and of their trajectory through the 1st century. What is often not noticed by commentators is that, within the full range of Son of Man sayings in all Four Gospels, Mark 2:28 stands out as unique in both form and content. Nowhere else in the Four Gospels do we have the precise grammatical pattern of "the Son of Man" (subject of the sentence) + "is" (present tense of the copulative verb) + a predicate nominative (more precisely, a noun in the nominative followed by a genitive noun with the definitive article) that describes the dignity, authority, or status of the subject of the sentence. This is exactly what we have in Mark 2:28: "The Son of Man is lord also of the sabbath." Indeed, the Greek text of Mark 2:28 makes the solemn pronouncement even more compact by moving the predicate nominative "lord" (*kyrios*) forward to the beginning of the sentence while keeping "of the sabbath" at the end, thus creating a "sandwiched" or chiastic pattern: *kyrios estin ho huios tou anthrōpou kai tou sabbatou* ("lord is the Son of Man also of the sabbath").[170]

The unique grammatical formulation of this Son of Man saying corresponds to its unique content. Tellingly, the verb accompanying "the Son of Man" in Mark 2:28 is not a verb of action, such as having, coming, suffering, or rising. Nor is "the Son of Man" the subject of an auxiliary verb like "must" (*dei*) or "is about to be" (*mellei*). Nor is the Son of Man the object of verbs like "seeing" or "speaking against." In Mark 2:28, the Son of Man is rather the subject of the present tense of the verb "to be" followed by a predicate nominative phrase expressing a quasi-title of dignity and power. Hence even the few other Son of Man sayings that use some form of the verb "to be" (*einai*) are not exact parallels. For example, when Matthew rewrites Mark 8:27 ("Who do men say that I am?") to read "Who do men say that the Son of Man is?" (Matt 16:13), the Son of Man becomes the subject of the infinitive *einai* ("to be") with *tina* (the interrogative pronoun "who?") as the predicate nominative. The Synoptic comparisons with OT figures do not supply exact parallels either. For instance, Luke 11:30 tells us that "just as Jonah became a sign to the Ninevites, so shall the Son of Man be to this generation." Even if Luke had supplied the vague "a sign" in the main clause of the comparison, it would hardly have the same weight or meaning as the solemn, quasi-titular affirmation of Mark 2:28, in which the Son of Man is uniquely and exclusively identified with a specific status or office. There can be only one "lord of the sabbath," while both Jonah and Jesus can be signs to their respective generations. Even more obviously, the use of the verb "to be" in Matt 12:40 to predict Jesus' burial ("the Son of Man will be in the heart of the earth") is no parallel; it expresses not identification but location.

Thus, in contrast to all the affirmations stating what the Son of Man does or has done to him or will be like, Mark 2:28 proclaims a direct, exclusive, and solemn identification in the present tense: Jesus the Son of Man is lord (owner, master) of the sacred Jewish institution sanctioned in the Decalogue, the sabbath. This content further underscores the uniqueness of 2:28: it is the only Son of Man saying related to a specific question of Jewish *hălākâ*. When we combine this astounding claim to unique status on the part of Jesus with the declaration's unique grammatical structure, the closest comparable pronouncements anywhere in the four Gospels are perhaps the "I am" + predicate nominative statements in John's Gospel. Indeed, if we may pass over for the moment the different order of the words in the two types of self-presentation, the parallel is perhaps even closer than might at first appear. Both Mark 2:28 and some of the Johannine self-presentations of Jesus involve a solemn subject of the sentence, referring to Jesus (*ho huios tou anthrōpous* in Mark or the emphatic *egō* in John), the verb "to be" (*estin* in Mark, *eimi* in John), and a predicate nominative followed by a genitive noun with definite article. Compare, for instance,

Mark 2:28:	The Son of Man	is	lord	of the sabbath
	ho huios tou antrōpou	*estin*	*kyrios*	*tou sabbatou*[171]
with				
John 6:35:	I	am	the bread	of life
	egō	*eimi*	*ho artos*	*tēs zōēs*

To be sure, the correlation is not perfect. The word order of Mark 2:28 differs from that of John 6:35. More important, the christology of John is much higher and more systematically developed than Mark's. Still, the parallel, however imperfect, underlines how much Mark 2:28 diverges—in both form and content—from all other Son of Man sayings in all Four Gospels and how much it approaches the self-presentation Jesus enunciates in some of the "I am" statements of the Fourth Gospel.

Having deepened our understanding of the unique form and content of Mark 2:28 by placing it within the context of all the Son of Man sayings in the Gospels, let us now return to 2:28 in its immediate context: that is, its position as the climax and conclusion of the dispute in Mark 2:23–28. The dispute over plucking grain on the sabbath progresses from a muddled and hardly apt scriptural argument (vv 25–26) through a broad (perhaps too broad) anthropological argument based on Genesis 1–2 (v 27) to the trump card of a christological argument based on Jesus' authority as the Son of Man (v 28). The problematic nature of the arguments in vv 25–26 and v 27 becomes, in a sense, moot before the decisive argument based on who Jesus is. In the present Marcan context, "the Son of Man" is the enigmatic, linguistically unusual, but characteristic way in which Jesus refers to himself solemnly in the third person. As the Son of Man, the Marcan Jesus declares not only that he *has* authority to interpret sabbath rules, not only that he *has* authority over the sabbath (other sayings tell us that the Son of Man *has* something), but that he *is* something, and that something is *lord* of the sabbath.

This solemn "titular" pronouncement indeed trumps any other argument, but only because it dares to make a claim that is almost unthinkable in the context of various Jewish-Palestinian teachers around the turn of the era quarreling over correct interpretation of the minutiae of sabbath *hălākâ*. Even if we do not give *kyrios* its full Christian weight as a title of majesty—though such a connotation would be almost unavoidable for Christian readers[172]—v 28 still solemnly identifies Jesus as the owner, master, controller of the sabbath. Such a claim is not a basis for further argument; rather, v 28 is an absolute claim that cuts off all further argument and decides the issue, period. Even as v 28 concludes what is supposedly a story about Jesus debating with his fellow Jews during the time of his public ministry, v 28 quietly breaks the bonds of time with a timeless self-presentation of Jesus. The Son of Man *is* lord of the sabbath during the whole time of the church, and hence ultimately the church need not worry about detailed halakic arguments about the sabbath, since Jesus himself is the living norm guiding believers in the proper way to observe the sabbath. Just like the Son of Man sayings in Matthew, Luke, and John that address not the sacred past of Jesus' ministry but the present time and needs of the church, so Mark 2:28 ends the dispute in 2:23–28 by moving from the sacred past of such disputes into the present time when such disputes should be moot because the Son of Man is lord—of the sabbath and everything else (hence the emphatic "even" or "also").

Here we have the basic difference, from a historical point of view, between the arguments in Mark 2:25–27 and the clinching argument in v 28. However maladroit, erroneous, vague, or overbroad the scriptural and anthropological arguments may be, they are at least conceivable in the mouth of a 1st-century Palestinian Jew (perhaps a Jew not too knowledgeable of his own Scriptures) arguing with other Jews over sabbath observance. Verse 28 is simply not conceivable in such a context. On the other hand, granted the development of Son of Man sayings toward references to the present time of the church, granted the intriguing parallel with John's "I am" sayings, and granted the mind-boggling claim made for Jesus in v 28, this verse is perfectly intelligible within the context of 1st-century Christian faith in Jesus.

As a matter of fact, it is also perfectly intelligible within the structure of the five dispute stories Mark has assembled in 2:1–3:6. Glancing backward, v 28 ("the Son of Man is lord even [or: also] of the sabbath") links up neatly with the first dispute story (2:1–12), which contains the first Son of Man saying in the whole of Mark's Gospel (2:10): "The Son of Man has authority to forgive sins on earth." Both of these Son of Man sayings conjure up a more-than-human aura around Jesus' status and power. In particular, the *kai* ("even" or "also") in v 28 consciously harks back to and connects with the claim about the Son of Man's authority in 2:10.[173] Looking forward, Mark 2:28 prepares the way for the final dispute in this Marcan cycle, which focuses on what Jesus himself (no longer his disciples) does on the sabbath.

Mark 2:28 has therefore a perfect Janus-like quality and function, acting as a clasp that reaches back to the first dispute story while stretching forward to the last. Thus, form, content, and function all argue against Mark 2:28 coming from the historical Jesus. It is a creation either of Mark himself or of a pre-Marcan redactor who first assembled the collection of dispute stories that Mark has expanded and placed within the overarching context of his Gospel, a Gospel in which "Son of Man" plays a pivotal role.[174]

As we can now see, an analysis of the growth of the dispute story in 2:23–28 yields different historical judgments for the different parts of the story. (1) The original and main part of the story, vv 23–26, arose amid disputes between Christian Jews and their fellow Jews in Palestine in the pre-70 period. The *Sitz im Leben* of the dispute was not some strange obsessive habit, rampant among Christian Jews, of plucking grain while passing through grainfields on the sabbath. Rather, the *Sitz im Leben* was the general atmosphere of religious polemic between the two groups and an attempt by the Christian Jews to crystallize their approach to sabbath observance in a paradigmatic story about Jesus. Their first attempt (vv 23–26) was hardly a smashing success. (2) The need for a more rhetorically effective ending to the dispute caused some editor, in a second stage of development, to append the originally independent axiom of v 27, which is the only verse in the pericope that has a good chance of coming from the historical Jesus. (3) In a third stage, either Mark or a pre-Marcan redactor of the cycle of dispute stories felt that even v 27 was not an entirely apt conclusion (either because it was too broad and vague or because it lacked an explicit christological reference and grounding). Accordingly, Mark or the pre-Marcan redactor made Christian history by composing a Son of Man saying that has no precise parallel in all four Gospels but that does succeed in supplying, from the viewpoint of Christian faith, the only adequate and permanent solution to the problem of sabbath *hălākâ*: the Son of Man *is lord*, even of the sabbath.

Perhaps sensing the artificial nature of the connection with v 27—or, put more bluntly, the lack of any real connection with v 27—the redactor apparently tried to make v 28 look like the natural conclusion of everything that had preceded in vv 23–27 by introducing v 28 with a bold *hōste* ("and so," "therefore," "consequently").[175] To be honest, apart from the general theme of sabbath observance, any logical link between v 28 and the preceding verses remains tenuous. There is really no direct connection with the anthropological argument in v 27,[176] and only a weak link with vv 23–26. The most one can say is that the original story in vv 23–26 presupposed the unique authority of Jesus to teach correct sabbath *hălākâ* and argued its case somewhat dubiously on an implied David-Jesus typology. Despite the *hōste*, this is a far cry from the solemn and absolute declaration that the Son of Man is lord even of the sabbath. At best, one can speak of a weak christological undertone in the first part of the story that receives an earsplitting amplification at the end of the story.

Having winnowed our way through the grainfield of all the sabbath dispute stories and sayings in the Gospels, it is high time we collected and weighed the meager results of our critical harvest.

III. CONCLUSION

Our study of Jesus and the sabbath has proved an object lesson in the dangers of applying the criterion of multiple attestation in a hasty and superficial manner. At first glance, the multiple attestation of material about Jesus and the sabbath in almost every Gospel source (Mark, M, L, and John) seemed to promise an abundance of sayings and deeds going back to the historical Jesus. Indeed, to some commentators, the issue of sabbath observance seemed to loom so large in Jesus' teaching and actions that it raised questions about his (perhaps unconscious) subversion of the Mosaic Law or at least of the sabbath.

At the end of this chapter, we realize how deceptive these first impressions were. A careful winnowing of the material has shown the need to distinguish between the narratives about Jesus and the sabbath and various isolated sayings of Jesus commenting on the sabbath. Even among the narratives, there is need for further distinctions: miracle stories versus the one story not involving a miracle, and Synoptic miracles stories versus Johannine miracle stories. With one exception, the narratives concerning the sabbath tell of miraculous healings Jesus performs on the sabbath, healings that unleash controversy over Jesus' improper activity on the sabbath. Even before the question of sabbath observance was raised in this chapter, our earlier treatment of these sabbath miracle stories in Volume Two of *A Marginal Jew* had resulted in the verdict of *non liquet* for each of the Synoptic stories. In contrast, the two Johannine miracles stories were judged to go back to actual events in the life of Jesus.

When the Synoptic stories of healing on the sabbath were reconsidered in this present chapter, their historical worth became even more questionable. Each of these stories presupposes that any act of healing violates the sabbath. Yet the Jewish Scriptures, the deuterocanonical works (Judith, 1–2 Maccabees), the *Book of Jubilees*, the *Damascus Document*, the halakic fragments from Qumran Cave 4, Aristobulus, Philo, and Josephus give no support to the idea that healing is a violation of the sabbath. The idea is completely absent in pre-70 Jewish literature. This absence is all the more telling when we notice the beginning of the tendency, first in *Jubilees* and then in the *Damascus Document*, to draw up ever-expanding as well as stringent lists of prohibited works on the sabbath. Even when we reach the full flowering of this list-tradition in the thirty-nine prohibited works in *m. Šabb.* 7:2, acts of healing are missing. In two other passages of the tractate, we find for the first time the prohibition of certain acts of healing, but even here distinctions are made among various actions. The presence of dissenting views suggests that this rabbinic innovation was not greeted with universal applause.

Aided by this insight into the growth of the Jewish tradition, we were able to appreciate more clearly why the Synoptic disputes arising from Jesus' healings on the sabbath lacked historical credibility. While it is possible that behind some of these narratives might lie historical events in which Jesus was thought to have a healed a person (perhaps on a sabbath), the stories as they now stand rest essentially on the presupposition that some, even many, Jews at the time of Jesus considered healing to be a sabbath violation. That is why they attacked Jesus for healing on the sabbath. Given the actual views of Judaism(s) contemporary with Jesus, such a presupposition is impossible to sustain. The stories as they now stand in the Gospels must be judged unhistorical. Their present form reflects Christian polemics, not the historical Jesus. To be sure, the situation is complex, as is seen from the fact that a different verdict needs to be passed on the sabbath miracles in John 5 and 9. In John, the two brief stories of healing probably do reflect events in Jesus' ministry. It is rather the motif of the healing's taking place on the sabbath that seems to be a later addition to the tradition, since this motif is present not in the miracle stories proper but rather in subsequent sections of dialogue that lead in turn to John's grand christological monologues.

A still different judgment must be made about the one sabbath dispute story in the Gospels that is not connected with a miracle: the Synoptic narrative of the plucking of grain on the sabbath. Here the motif of the sabbath is original to the narrative, but the core narrative (Mark 2:23–26) labors under too many improbabilities and outright errors to be considered historical. This core narrative is most likely a product of Christian polemics from start to finish. In the end, the once promising field of narratives about Jesus and the sabbath turns out to be a disappointing desert. Not one narrative can survive close scrutiny. Considered as they now stand, that is, as narratives about Jesus disputing with opponents about his or his disciples' activity on the sabbath, all the narratives are most likely the creations of Christian polemics and apologetics. A similar judgment, though for different reasons, must be passed on the explicitly christological norm for evaluating the sabbath that is articulated in Mark's one-of-a-kind Son of Man saying (2:28): "The Son of Man is lord also of the sabbath." Form, content, and function all point to composition by Mark or a pre-Marcan redactor of the Galilean dispute stories.

We are in a different world when we come to the other sayings of Jesus on the sabbath, many of which seem to have been incorporated secondarily into the sabbath narratives. A number of these sayings reflect halakic debates around the time of Jesus, with Jesus staking out his own ground amid competing views. For instance, the tradition found in Matt 12:11 ‖ Luke 14:5 indicates that Jesus did not disdain debating particular points of sabbath observance that would have been of vital importance to Jewish peasants in Palestine. In Matt 12:11 ‖ Luke 14:5, Jesus championed the commonsense view of rescuing both animals and humans who fall into a cistern or a pit on the sabbath. In taking this position, he is probably opposing the rigorism of the Essenes, as reflected in the *Damascus Document*, and of other Jewish sectarians, as reflected in the Cave 4 fragments. If, as some scholars suggest, pious Jewish peasants were feeling drawn to the admirable zeal of the sectarians, Jesus would be fighting to ward off these influences and confirm ordinary Jews in a more moderate and humane approach to sabbath observance.

The matter, admittedly, is complex and confusing. It may well be that dividing lines between various Jewish parties changed from one issue to another. For example, in the case of an animal fallen into a pit, Jesus may have found himself at odds with at least the more stringent wing of the Pharisees as well as with the Essenes. However, when it came to endangered human life on the sabbath, the battle lines may have shifted, with Jesus agreeing with the Pharisees against the Essenes that direct intervention to pull a human being out of danger was permissible. In contrast, the Essenes or other sectarians seem to have allowed only that a cloak might be tossed to the endangered person.

Another expression of Jesus' commonsense approach to sabbath observance is found in Luke 13:15, where Jesus addresses not an emergency situation suddenly endangering the life of a human or an animal but rather the constantly recurring need of untying an ox or donkey to lead it to drink on the sabbath. Whether or not any of the other competing Jewish groups would have objected to untying the knot of the rope holding the animal in place, many Jews would have wanted to know exactly how far one could either lead or follow one's animal on the sabbath. The fact that, as far as we know, Jesus totally ignored the problem of sabbath limits speaks volumes in itself. Far from rejecting the sabbath, Jesus wished instead to make the sabbath livable for severely pressed Jewish peasants, who could hardly afford to stand by when they were in danger of losing one of their livestock, to say nothing of their children. Jesus' espousal of a pragmatic, down-to-earth approach to these questions reflects his desire to shield ordinary pious Jews from the attraction of sectarian rigorism.[177]

Cohering perfectly with Jesus' humane, commonsense approach is the *māšāl* of Mark 2:27: "The sabbath was made for man, not man for the sabbath." While fitting in with the moderate approach to the sabbath espoused by later rabbis like Simeon ben Menasya (in the *Mekilta*), Jesus subsumes this tendency into his vision of the end time as restoring the whole and wholesome goodness of creation that God willed in the beginning. By approaching the sabbath from this eschatological vantage point, Jesus seeks to instill a proper sense of priorities. The roots of the sabbath lie in creation itself, but a creation that is meant to serve the good of a humanity created by God in the beginning and now restored by him in the last days.

Despite results that might at first seem meager and disappointing, a major insight has been gained by our grappling with sabbath *hălākâ* in the Gospels. The authentic sabbath sayings of Jesus, which engage and debate competing Jewish views of sabbath *hălākâ* around the turn of the era, reinforce the point that Jesus was neither a 1st-century Jewish hippie nor a Cynic philosopher nor a wild-eyed apocalyptic prophet who had no time for or interest in the details of *hălākâ*. Instead, in these sabbath sayings, we find a truly Jewish Jesus arguing with the halakic opinions of various Jewish groups that, like himself, were competing for the adherence of ordinary Jews attached to no one party.

Far from a Paul-disguised-as Jesus who preaches gospel versus law (which is a caricature of Paul to begin with), the historical Jesus turns out to be the halakic Jesus. If only older commentators had stopped for a moment to think about the matter from a truly historical perspective, they would have realized: How could it be otherwise? First-century Palestinian Judaism being what it was, how could a religiously oriented Jew who tried to lead a religious movement by competing to gain a following among his fellow Jews be anything else? The idea of Jesus consciously or unconsciously attacking, subverting, or annulling the sabbath—even apart from the penalty of death (at least in theory) for a serious transgression of sabbath law—is too ludicrous to be taken seriously, despite the fact that it has been taken seriously by many a critic. All questers for the historical Jesus should repeat the following mantra even in their sleep: the historical Jesus is the halakic Jesus. This is the positive gain of this chapter that we must never forget.

Nevertheless, this mantra, however vital to our understanding of Jesus and the Law, is not a magic key that opens all doors and solves all problems. All we need do is correlate the results of this chapter with the results of the last two chapters to be reminded of the enigmatic nature of Jesus' relationship to the Mosaic Law. When it comes to the sabbath, Jesus presupposes and affirms this sacred institution enshrined in the Torah, all the while arguing against sectarian rigorism and in favor of a humane, moderate approach to detailed questions of observance. Yet when it comes to divorce and oaths, two key social institutions permitted and regulated by the Torah, Jesus totally forbids both divorce and swearing—two prohibitions that, as far as we can tell, were unheard of among the various competing Jewish parties and sects of his day. In effect, Jesus presumes to tell a sincere, pious Jew who goes through the proper legal steps to divorce his first wife and marry a second that he is violating one of the commandments of the Decalogue: by divorcing and remarrying, he is committing adultery. Likewise, Jesus forbids all swearing, even though the Torah imposes oaths in certain legal circumstances. Embrace of the sabbath and rejection of divorce and oaths—how do these two apparently opposite stances cohere in the mind of the halakic teacher and charismatic prophet named Jesus? We will have to keep this underlying question in mind as we examine other aspects of Jesus' halakic teaching in the chapters to come.

NOTES TO CHAPTER 34

[1] For an extensive bibliography on the sabbath and related topics, see Lutz Doering, *Schabbat* (Texts and Studies in Ancient Judaism 78; Tübingen: Mohr [Sie-

beck], 1999) 589–639. For further bibliography on and general treatments of the sabbath, see the dictionary and encyclopedia articles of Julian Morgenstern, "Sabbath," *IDB*, 4. 135–41; Eduard Lohse, *"sabbaton*, etc.," *TDNT* 7 (1971) 1–35; Gerhard F. Hasel, "Sabbath," *AYBD*, 5. 849–56; E. Haag, *"šabbāt,"* *TWAT* vol. 7, fascicle 8 (1992) cols. 1047–57. See also Asher Eder, "The Sabbath: To Remember, to Observe, to Make," *Jewish Bible Quarterly* 34 (2006) 104–9. Relevant monographs include Niels-Erik A. Andreasen, *The Old Testament Sabbath. A Tradition-Historical Investigation* (SBLDS 7; Missoula, MT: Society of Biblical Literature, 1972); Kenneth A. Strand (ed.), *The Sabbath in Scripture and History* (Washington, DC: Review and Herald Publishing Association, 1982) 21–129; Gnana Robinson, *The Origin and Development of the Old Testament Sabbath* (BBET 21; Frankfurt: Lang, 1988); Eric Spier, *Der Sabbat* (Das Judentum 1; Berlin: Institut Kirche und Judentum, 1989); Heather A. McKay, *Sabbath and Synagogue. The Question of Sabbath Worship in Ancient Judaism* (Religions in the Graeco-Roman World 122; Leiden: Brill, 1994); Sven-Olav Back, *Jesus of Nazareth and the Sabbath Commandment* (Åbo: Åbo Akademi University, 1995); Yong-Eui Yang, *Jesus and the Sabbath in Matthew's Gospel* (JSNTSup 139; Sheffield: Sheffield Academic Press, 1997); Andrea J. Mayer-Haas, *"Geschenk aus Gottes Schatzkammer" (bSchab 10b). Jesus und der Sabbat im Spiegel der neutestamentlichen Schriften* (NTAbh 43; Münster: Aschendorff, 2003); Henry Sturcke, *Encountering the Rest of God. How Jesus Came to Personify the Sabbath* (Zurich: Theologischer Verlag, 2005).

[2] For the range of scholarly views on whether and to what degree Jesus opposed or rejected the sabbath, see the survey of research in Back, *Jesus of Nazareth*, 2–13. Opinions range from the view that there was no substantial conflict between Jesus and the Pharisees on the sabbath (so Sanders, *Jesus and Judaism*, 264–69; cf. his *Jewish Law*, 6–23) through the view that what Jesus rejected in a radical way was the Pharisaic or rabbinic *hălākâ* on the sabbath (so Jeremias, *New Testament Theology*, 208) to the view that Jesus called into question not only the "casuistic hair-splitting of the Pharisees" but also the sabbath commandment, "which enslaved human beings" (so Willy Rordorf, *Der Sonntag* [ATANT 43; Zurich: Zwingli, 1962] 63). Sometimes Christian scholars are not entirely consistent in their presentations; Back (pp. 3–4) claims that this is the case with Lohse's article on the sabbath in the *TDNT*.

[3] See, e.g., Haag, *"šabbāt,"* cols. 1047–51; Morgenstern, "Sabbath," 135–37; Hasel, "Sabbath," 849–51; Spier, *Der Sabbat*, 11–13; Lohse, *"sabbaton*, etc.," 2–3. Representing one side in a disputed question, Robinson's monograph, *The Origin and Development*, is devoted to the thesis that in the preexilic period, the practice of abstaining from work on the seventh day was not related to the sabbath, which was rather a monthly full-moon festival. For arguments against this view, see Haag, *"šabbāt,"* col. 1052; cf. Andreasen, *The Old Testament Sabbath*, 3–5, 94–121. Along with Doering (*Schabbat*, 3), we can prescind from such debatable positions since, from at least the early postexilic period onward, the sabbath was certainly identified with the day of rest observed once every seven days.

⁴ For surveys of the texts of the Jewish Scriptures (*Tanak*, i.e., the Law of Moses, the Prophets, and the Writings) that deal with the sabbath, see McKay, *Sabbath and Synagogue*, 15–42; Yang, *Jesus and the Sabbath*, 22–50; Haag, "*šabbāt*," 1051–55; Hasel, "Sabbath," 851–53; Morgenstern, "Sabbath," 137–40. A survey of the sabbath texts in the Pentateuch can be found in Andreasen, *The Old Testament Sabbath*, 62–92.

⁵ For brief surveys of scholarship on the Decalogue, with bibliography, see Raymond F. Collins, "Ten Commandments," *AYBD*, 6. 383–87; Baruch J. Schwartz, "Ten Commandments," *The Oxford Dictionary of the Jewish Religion* (ed. R. J. Zwi Werblowsky and Geoffrey Wigoder; New York/Oxford: Oxford University, 1997) 683–84. For fuller treatments, see Augustin I. Patrick, *La formation littéraire et l'origine historique du décalogue* (ALBO series 4, fascicle 15; Louvain: Publications universitaires; Bruges/Paris: Descleé de Brouwer, 1964); Johann J. Stamm, *The Ten Commandments in Recent Research* (SBT 2/2; 2d ed.; Naperville, IL: Allenson, 1967); Eduard Nielsen, *The Ten Commandments in New Perspective* (SBT 2/7; Naperville, IL: Allenson, 1968); Bo Reicke, *Die zehn Worte in Geschichte und Gegenwart* (BGBE 13; Tübingen: Mohr [Siebeck], 1973); Frank-Lothar Hossfeld, *Der Dekalog* (OBO 45; Freiburg: Universitätsverlag; Göttingen: Vandenhoeck & Ruprecht, 1982); Norbert Lohfink, "Zur Dekalogfassung von Dt 5," *Studien zum Deuteronomium und zur deuteronomistischen Literatur I* (Stuttgarter Biblische Aufstazbände 8; Stuttgart: KBW, 1990) 198–209; Ben-Zion Segal and Gershon Levi (eds.), *The Ten Commandments in History and Tradition* (Jerusalem: Magnes/Hebrew University of Jerusalem, 1990); Werner H. Schmidt, *Die zehn Gebote im Rahmen alttestamentlicher Ethik* (Erträge der Forschung 281; Darmstadt: Wissenschaftliche Buchgesellschaft, 1993); Timo Veijola, *Moses Erben* (BWANT 8/9; Stuttgart: Kohlhammer, 2000) 29–75; David Noel Freedman, *The Nine Commandments. Uncovering a Hidden Pattern of Crime and Punishment in the Hebrew Bible* (New York: Doubleday, 2000); Alex Graupner, "Die zehn Gebote im Rahmen alttestamentlicher Ethik," *Weisheit, Ethos und Gebot* (Biblisch-Theologische Studien 43; ed. Henning G. Reventlow; Neukirchen-Vluyn: Neukirchener Verlag, 2001) 61–95; Ulrich Kellermann, "Der Dekalog in den Schriften des Frühjudentums," ibid., 147–226; Innocent Himbaza, *Le Décalogue et l'histoire du texte* (OBO 207; Göttingen: Vandenhoeck & Ruprecht; Fribourg: Academic Press, 2004). Kellermann's article is valuable for its brief survey of the variant forms of the Decalogue that are found in Qumran fragments (Pentateuch manuscripts, phylacteries, and mezuzahs) as well as in the Nash papyrus. Some of the Qumran fragments may reflect a pre-Samaritan type of expansion of the Decalogue that is also found in Samaritan texts; the Nash papyrus agrees in part with the LXX. This is a healthy reminder that in the last centuries B.C. the importance of the Decalogue to Judaism did not guarantee the existence of only one standardized text. Nevertheless, the fact that the Decalogue as a distinct unit of Torah tradition was indeed important to Jews of various tendencies around the turn of the era is supported by its presence in the Nash papyrus from Egypt (an extract from Deut 5:6–6:5, dated ca. 150 B.C.), in the Qumran fragments, and (if we may believe *m. Tamid* 5:1) in the daily service

of the Jerusalem temple. (Anyone reading technical studies on the Decalogue must bear in mind that the system of assigning numbers to the various commandments takes different forms in Judaism, in the Catholic and Lutheran traditions, and in the Calvinist/Reformed and Eastern Orthodox traditions. For Catholics and Lutherans, the sabbath commandment is the third commandment; for other traditions, it is the fourth. On this, see Nielsen, *The Ten Commandments*, 10–13; Freedman, *The Nine Commandments*, 14–19.)

[6] Within rabbinic Judaism (e.g., *Bereshit Rabbah*), interplay between the sabbath command based on creation and the sabbath command based on the exodus event proved a rich matrix for the development of a whole spirituality of the sabbath, connecting God's creation of the world with his creation of the people Israel. By way of caveat, I should note from the start that this chapter's focus on Jesus' halakic teaching on the sabbath is of its nature quite narrow and in no way claims to provide an adequate treatment of the entire topic of sabbath. By the turn of the era, Judaism had developed a profound "lived theology" of the sabbath that was to receive still fuller explication in the rabbinic literature and beyond. One of the admirable qualities of Doering's *Schabbat* is that its minute analysis of sabbath *hălākâ* in Jewish literature at the turn of the era goes hand in hand with a proper appreciation of the spirituality of the sabbath in the works treated.

[7] See McKay, *Sabbath and Synagogue*, 13–14, 18–19, 24, 41–42. The distinction between sabbath *observance* (consisting essentially in abstaining from work) and sabbath *worship* (in McKay's understanding, communal prayer that is specific to the sabbath and that directly addresses God with the intention of worshiping him) lies at the heart of *Sabbath and Synagogue*; see, e.g., pp. 1–10, 247–51. McKay affirms the (abundantly witnessed) existence of the former in turn-of-the-era Judaism but questions the existence of the latter (for Qumran as a possible exception, see pp. 59–60). For briefer formulations of her basic thesis, see her "New Moon or Sabbath?" *The Sabbath in Jewish and Christian Traditions* (ed. Tamara C. Eskenazi, Daniel J. Harrington, and William H. Shea; New York: Crossroad, 1991) 19–20, 25; idem, "From Evidence to Edifice: Four Fallacies about the Sabbath," *Text as Pretext* (JSOTSup 138; Robert Davidson Festschrift; ed. Robert P. Carroll; Sheffield: JSOT, 1992) 179–99. For a critique of McKay's position that concedes its valid points but argues by way of indirect evidence for some type of sabbath worship in synagogues before A.D. 70, see Pieter W. van der Horst, "Was the Synagogue a Place of Sabbath Worship before 70 C.E.?" *Jews, Christians, and Polytheists in the Ancient Synagogue* (Baltimore Studies in the History of Judaism; ed. Steven Fine; London/New York: Routledge, 1999) 18–43. Although our concern in this chapter is basically with sabbath observance, one might note that a different (perhaps broader) definition of the concept "sabbath worship" (e.g., the communal reading and study of Scripture as acts of public worship) might yield different conclusions from those of McKay.

[8] With their holistic reading of the Torah (as opposed to our historical-critical tendency to detect various sources redacted by various hands), the later rabbis saw

in the story of the manna (narrated in Exodus 16)—which precedes the giving of the Law, including the Decalogue, on Mt. Sinai (beginning in Exodus 20)—an indication that the sabbath was the first commandment of the Torah that the people Israel experienced during its journey through the wilderness.

⁹ Of its very nature, the narrative material in the "Former Prophets" or "historical books" (Joshua, Judges, 1–2 Samuel, and 1–2 Kgs) does not aim at proposing normative sabbath *hălākâ*; at best, now and then, it reflects certain customs or presuppositions about the sabbath. For example, a passing remark indicates that at some time and in some places in the preexilic period it was the custom to visit a local sanctuary or a prophet on the sabbath (2 Kgs 4:23). More informative is the story of the revolt against Queen Athaliah in Jerusalem, narrated in 2 Kgs 11. The successful revolt was engineered by the high priest Jehoiada and was launched in the temple on the sabbath at the changing of the palace and temple guard. Thus, on a single sabbath day, the high priest supplied the guard with weapons, revealed to the people the young heir to the throne (whom he had hidden in the temple precincts), anointed him king, and had Athaliah executed. The one point of propriety that is observed, that Athaliah is dragged outside the temple before she is killed, is connected with concerns for temple purity rather than sabbath observance. One gets the definite impression that, even in the temple city, observance of the sabbath in the preexilic period was not as detailed and exacting as it would become around the turn of the era and especially in the rabbinic period.

¹⁰ On Amos 8:5 and its larger context, see Francis I. Andersen and David Noel Freedman, *Amos* (AYB 24A; New York: Doubleday, 1989; reprint New Haven: Yale University Press) 799–817; Pietro Bovati and Roland Meynet, *Le livre du prophète Amos* (Rhétorique biblique 2; Paris: Cerf, 1994) 320–26; Marvin A. Sweeney, *The Twelve Prophets. Volume One* (Berit Olam; Collegeville, MN: Liturgical Press, 2000) 251–68.

¹¹ As a guide for the modern reader, my presentation in the main text and notes refers in passing to the likely dates of various biblical books and traditions as well as to possible historical settings and lines of development. Needless to say, these modern concerns were not those of the ancient reader or audience.

¹² Scholars differ on whether the thrust if not the wording of Jer 17:19–27 reflects the thought of the historical Jeremiah. After considering the arguments in favor of a postexilic date for this passage, Jack R. Lundbom (*Jeremiah 1–20* [AYB 21A; New York: Doubleday, 1999; reprint New Haven: Yale University Press] 802–5) decides that "there is . . . no reason whatever why this passage should be denied to Jeremiah." John Bright (*Jeremiah* [AYB 21; Garden City, NY: Doubleday, 1965; reprint New Haven: Yale University Press] 120) represents a slightly more nuanced approach: Jer 17:19–27 may be a one-sided development of Jeremiah's thought by those who preserved and handed down his words, yet Jeremiah no doubt respected the sabbath as an integral part of covenant law. Hence, the text is probably based on sentiments that Jeremiah expressed. For a similar view, which defends a date no later

that the middle of the 6th century B.C., see Andreasen, *The Old Testament Sabbath*, 31–34. More common is the view that 17:19–27 is exilic or postexilic and reflects deuteronomistic redaction; see, e.g., Louis Stulman, *The Prose Sermons of the Book of Jeremiah* (SBLDS 83; Atlanta: Scholars, 1986) 70–73; William McKane, *Jeremiah* (ICC; 2 vols.; Edinburgh: Clark, 1986, 1996) 1. 414–19. Jacques Briend ("Le Sabbat en Jr 17,19–27," *Mélanges bibliques et orientaux en l'honneur de M. Mathias Delcor* (Alter Orient und Altes Testament 215; ed. A. Caquot, S. Légasse, and M. Tardieu; Neukirchen-Vluyn: Neukirchener Verlag, 1985] 23–35) takes the most radical view, assigning Jer 17:19–27 (which, in his view, is not deuteronomistic but rather priestly in its orientation) to one of the last postexilic redactions of the book, therefore at the end of the 5th or at the beginning of the 4th century B.C.

[13] On the sabbath passages in Ezekiel, see Andreasen, *The Old Testament Sabbath*, 40–48.

[14] According to Doering (*Schabbat*, 269), Isa 58:13 is the text of the Jewish Scriptures that is most frequently used in the surviving manuscripts from Qumran that deal with sabbath *hălākâ*.

[15] For the exegesis of Isa 58:13–14, see John L. McKenzie, *Second Isaiah* (AYB 20; Garden City, NY: Doubleday, 1968; reprint New Haven: Yale University Press) 162–67; Claus Westermann, *Isaiah 40–66* (OTL; Philadelphia: Westminster, 1969) 340–42; H. A. Brongers, "Einige Bemerkungen zu Jes 58:13–14," *ZAW* 87 (1975) 212–16; Brevard S. Childs, *Isaiah* (OTL; Louisville: Westminster/John Knox, 2001) 473–81; Jan L. Koole, *Isaiah. Part III, Volume 3* (Leuven: Peeters, 2001) 155–61; Joseph Blenkinsopp, *Isaiah 56–66* (AYB 19B; New York: Doubleday, 2003; reprint New Haven: Yale University Press) 174–75, 181–82. That the references in the text are to commercial activities and agreements is cogently argued by Brongers and Koole. Westermann thinks that the text reflects a time when business was conducted in Jerusalem on the sabbath, with both the sabbath laws of the Pentateuch and the threatened death penalty for breach of the laws being ignored. For a brief treatment of all the sabbath passages in Third Isaiah, see Andreasen, *The Old Testament Sabbath*, 36–40.

[16] A smaller *inclusio* is also created by the references to the sabbath in Isa 56:2 and 58:13, thus marking off chaps. 56–58 as a distinct unit. For the view that a late priestly redaction of the Book of Isaiah has highlighted the role of the sabbath, see Bernard Gosse, "Les rédactions dans le Deutéronome et dans le livre d'Esaïe," *ETR* 70 (1995) 581–85.

[17] Doering (*Schabbat*, 23–42) interprets the fragmentary evidence from the Elephantine papyri (5th century B.C.) to mean that the syncretistic Jews in Elephantine knew the sabbath as a weekly marker of time but felt free to conduct business on it—a situation not unlike the one Nehemiah denounced and tried to change in Jerusalem and its environs; on problems in the Nehemiah passages, see Andreasen,

The Old Testament Sabbath, 21–31. Interestingly, Nehemiah is the only book in the third part of the Jewish canon of Scripture (the *kĕtûbîm*, i.e., the "Writings") to pay any great attention to the sabbath as a source of halakic dispute. The sabbath is not mentioned in Job, Proverbs, Daniel, or (with the exception of the passing reference in Lam 2:6) the five *mĕgillôt* ("scrolls," i.e., Ruth, Song of Songs, Qoheleth, Lamentations, and Esther). The only reference in the Psalms is in the title or inscription placed secondarily at the beginning of Psalm 92, in what is now v 1 in the MT: "a song for the day of the sabbath." The scattered passing references in 1 and 2 Chronicles (1 Chr 9:32; 23:31; 2 Chr 2:3 [ET 2:4]; 8:13; 23:4,8; 13:3; 36:21) add nothing to our fund of information; not surprisingly, granted the theological agenda of Chronicles, all these texts except the last one refer directly or indirectly to the liturgy of the Jerusalem temple. On the sabbath passages in Chronicles, see Andreasen, *The Old Testament Sabbath*, 53–57.

[18] Doering (*Schabbat*, 386–97) argues that fragments of Jewish-Aramaic ostraca from Palestine (Ostraca Y 1, 2, and 3, dated from around the first half of the 1st century A.D.) indicate that at least some Palestinian Jews engaged in commercial activity (e.g., the delivery of merchandise) on the sabbath. While Doering's interpretation of the fragmentary texts is certainly possible, perhaps even probable, one must sympathize with the hesitation of the original editor, Ada Yardeni, over a definitive judgment; see Yardeni's article, "New Jewish Ostraca," *IEJ* 40 (1990) 130–52, with a summary expressing the author's hesitation on pp. 151–52.

[19] The word "sabbath" does not occur in Tobit, the additions to Esther, the additions to Daniel, the Wisdom of Solomon, Ben Sira, Baruch, or the Letter of Jeremiah; nor does it occur in the Prayer of Manasseh, Psalm 151, or 4 Ezra. As McKay (*Sabbath and Synagogue*, 44) points out, the absence of the word is especially striking in contexts where one might expect it, e.g., Tobit and Ben Sira. It may be, though, that McKay draws too broad a conclusion from the silence of most of the deuterocanonical (apocryphal) books of the OT: according to McKay, this silence "reinforces our earlier conclusion that different groups within Jewish society had different views of the *value* [emphasis mine] and role of the sabbath in Jewish life." That may well be, but one must remember that at times a book that later on would be declared a part of Scripture may be silent on a subject simply because the subject is not seen as disputed or problematic and is therefore taken for granted.

[20] Indeed, *Jub.* 50:12–13 forbids fasting on the sabbath under pain of death; the prohibition of fasting on the sabbath is also found possibly in the Dead Sea Scrolls and certainly in the rabbinic literature. On the sabbath joy that precludes fasting, see Doering, *Schabbat*, 105–6.

[21] See the treatment of Mark 2:18–20 in *A Marginal Jew*, 2. 439–50.

[22] See 1 Macc 1:39,43,45; 2:32,34,38,41; 9:34 (dittography of v 43), 43; 10:34; 2 Macc 5:25; 6:6; 8:26,27,28; 12:38; 15:3; for a survey of the sabbath texts in 1 and

2 Maccabees, see McKay, *Sabbath and Synagogue*, 45–50. The three references in 1 Esdras (1 Esdr 1:58 [55] [*bis*]; 5:52 [51]) simply rework verses present in the Jewish Scriptures (though a reference to sabbath that is lacking in Ezra 3:5 is inserted into 1 Esdr 5:52 [51]) and are irrelevant to our quest.

[23] Note how the pious Judas Maccabeus is presented in 2 Macc 8:24–29 as breaking off the pursuit of a defeated army because of the approaching sabbath; in this context, his fighting is not defensive and so must cease on the sabbath. On an allied theme, 2 Macc 12:38 presents Judas as ceasing to fight and leading his army to a city so that they can purify themselves for the approaching sabbath "according to the custom." Whether this sabbath purification is considered "customary" only for Jewish soldiers just finishing a battle or for all Jews is not clear from the text. As Goldstein (*II Maccabees*, 447–48) points out, neither the Jewish Scriptures nor the later rabbis know of a *law* requiring ritual purity on the sabbath; hence, the author of 2 Maccabees does well to speak of a "custom."

[24] On this text, see Goldstein, *I Maccabees*, 409.

[25] Here I accept the dating suggested in his various writings by James C. VanderKam; see *A Marginal Jew*, 3. 348–49 n. 14. While admitting the difficulty of being precise about such matters, Doering (*Schabbat*, 49) prefers a dating ca. 170–168 B.C.

[26] Scholars disagree on exactly how many kinds of work are prohibited by the lists in *Jubilees*. Some say sixteen, others twenty-two, while Yang (*Jesus and the Sabbath*, 60 n. 32) counts fourteen. A basic problem with such counts is that some of the prohibitions are repeated in slightly different form, while other prohibitions might be counted as subdivisions of more generic prohibitions.

[27] In particular, I think that the placing of the prohibition of war at the climactic end of the last list at the conclusion of the entire work is a conscious polemic against the pragmatic decision of the followers of Mattathias (defense against an enemy's aggression is permissible on the sabbath); see the treatment of this question in Chapter 31; cf. McKay, *Sabbath and Synagogue*, 58. In general, Doering (*Schabbat*, 50) sees no trace of a debate with the practices of the Hasmoneans in the traditional lists of sabbath precepts that he isolates. However, Doering (ibid., 60–62) does see traces of authorial redaction in and around the lists; for instance, he suggests that the way the author anchors the sabbath in creation itself may reflect a polemic against a cultic lunisolar calendar.

[28] In what follows, with an eye to students who may not have access to an extensive library, I use the translation of *Jubilees* by O. S. Wintermute in the widely available *OTP*, 2. 57–58, 142. However, for a critical edition, see James C. VanderKam, *The Book of Jubilees. A Critical Text* (CSCO 510–11, Scriptores Aethiopici 87–88; Louvain: Peeters, 1989).

[29] It is often claimed (so, e.g., Yang, *Jesus and the Sabbath*, 55) that in insisting on the death penalty, *Jubilees* is more severe than the *Damascus Document*, which only imposes a seven-year separation from the community under the watchful supervision of custodians (CD 12:3b–6a). But it may be that the *Damascus Document* is speaking here not of transgressions of the basic sabbath commands in the written Torah of Moses but rather of the special rules proper to the Essene communities; see the discussion of various opinions in Doering, *Schabbat*, 210–15.

[30] The construction of the sentence in Ethiopic is especially contorted at this point; see Doering, *Schabbat*, 83–87.

[31] One argument for the existence of separate lists of prohibited sabbath activities that the author of *Jubilees* is redacting is the occurrence of the actions of drawing water and carrying objects in and out of dwellings in both chap. 2 and chap. 50 (cf. 2:29–30 and 50:8); on this, see Doering, *Schabbat*, 59–60. Whether the two lists in chap. 50 are actually one traditional list separated by a redactional insertion by the author of *Jubilees* remains uncertain.

[32] The Ethiopic phrase here is quite vague ("go a way"). Scholars are divided on whether this prohibition concerns going on a journey or moving outside of one's settlement or town. Doering (*Schabbat*, 87–94) argues strongly for the latter interpretation. He sees here a position on the question of movement on the sabbath that is older and stricter than the regulations found in the *Damascus Document* or the Mishna.

[33] CD 10:14 formally introduces the Sabbath Codex with the phrase "concerning the sabbath, to keep it in accordance with its ordinance" (*'l hš[b]t lšmrh kmšpṭh*). The Codex is also framed by purity rules in the preceding (see 10:10b–13) and subsequent (see 11:18b–12:22a) context. Lohse ("*sabbaton*, etc.," 11) and Yang (*Jesus and the Sabbath*, 62–63) count twenty-eight distinct sabbath regulations in this corpus, while Doering (*Schabbat*, 133–205) counts twenty. Understandably, as with *Jubilees*, so with the Sabbath Codex, different modern authors group or subdivide regulations differently. That the Sabbath Codex itself is not a unitary piece of tradition but is rather made up of various sources is argued by Tzvee Zahavy, "The Sabbath Code of Damascus Document X, 14–XI, 18: Form Analytical and Redaction Critical Observations," *RevQ* (no. 40) 10/4 (1981) 589–91. In dialogue with the magisterial work of Lawrence H. Schiffman (*The Halakhah at Qumran* [SJLA 16; Leiden: Brill, 1975]), Zahavy suggests that a number of the laws now enshrined in the Sabbath Codex are actually purity rather than sabbath rules, while others may be rules regarding the camp of the group rather than the sabbath. Be that as it may, the final redaction of the *Damascus Document* has placed all of these various regulations within the overarching framework of the sabbath. On the Sabbath Codex and its various regulations, see also Charlotte Hempel, *The Laws of the Damascus Document. Sources, Tradition, and Redaction* (Studies on the Texts of the Desert of Judah 29; Leiden/Boston/Cologne: Brill, 1998) 187; Cana Werman, "CD XI:17:

Apart from Your Sabbaths," *The Damascus Document. A Centennial of Discovery* (Studies on the Texts of the Desert of Judah 34; ed. Joseph M. Baumgarten, Esther G. Chazon, and Avital Pinnick; Leiden/Boston/Cologne: Brill, 2000) 201–12; Joseph M. Baumgarten, "The Laws of the Damascus Document—Between Bible and Mishnah," *The Damascus Document. A Centennial of Discovery*, 17–26, esp. 21–23.

[34] See, e.g., the sabbath rules contained in 4Q264a and 4Q265, fragment 7, columns 1 and 2. For other references to the sabbath in the Qumran documents, see McKay, *Sabbath and Synagogue*, 51–56; cf. Yang, *Jesus and the Sabbath*, 62–67. One startling aspect of the Qumran material is that, while the *Damascus Document* contains a whole Sabbath Codex that lists detailed regulations about the sabbath, the *Rule of the Community* (1QS) contains no such list. Indeed, there are no detailed sabbath regulations at all in the *Rule of the Community*. This a prime example of the limitations of an argument from silence and the danger of counting up rules in a document to decide what legal topics are important to a community. Presumably, since the Qumran community governed by the *Rule of the Community* seems to have been even more radical on many halakic points than the larger Essene movement reflected in the *Damascus Document*, the Qumran community observed the sabbath very stringently. Perhaps the silence of the *Rule of the Community* concerning sabbath regulations simply indicates that this document takes for granted a whole corpus of detailed sabbath rules, both those contained in the Jewish Scriptures and those reflected in various sectarian writings. Then, too, it may well be that Qumran's halakic regulations encompassed both written and oral traditions. On the whole question, see Sanders, *Jewish Law*, 15–16.

[35] For a brief overview of the positions of the Essenes and Jesus on the sabbath, see *A Marginal Jew*, 3. 526–27. I do not bother with a separate treatment of Josephus' description of the observance of the sabbath by the Essenes (*J.W.* 2.8.9 §147). Most of what is said is simply a repetition of basic biblical injunctions that all pious Jews would keep: abstaining from work, not preparing food, not kindling a fire, and not moving a vessel from place to place on the sabbath; all of these prohibitions can be found in one form or another in the *Damascus Document* and/or the Qumran Cave 4 fragments. The one strikingly different rule mentioned by Josephus (not defecating on the sabbath) is irrelevant to our purpose.

[36] E.g., Sanders (*Jewish Law*, 13) lists CD 11:10 alongside *m. Šabb.* 14:3–4 as an example of opposition to "minor cures on the sabbath," but he neither gives the wording of CD 11:10 nor discusses its content.

[37] Joseph M. Baumgarten (*The Dead Sea Scrolls. Volume 2. Damascus Document, War Scroll, and Related Documents* [Princeton Theological Seminary Dead Sea Scrolls Project; ed. James H. Charlesworth; Tübingen: Mohr (Siebeck); Louisville: Westminster/John Knox, 1995] 48–49 and n. 168) translates *sammānîm* in CD 11:10 as "spices." Apparently he sees no reference to medicine or healing in the

text. Florentino García Martínez and Eibert J. C. Tigchelaar (*The Dead Sea Scrolls Study Edition* [2 vols.; Leiden/Boston/Cologne: Brill, 1997, 1998] 1. 568–69) translate the disputed noun as "perfumes"; again, medicine does not seem to be in view.

[38] The presence of the verb *yṣʾ* ("go out," in Hiphil "bring out"), of the verb *nśʾ* ("carry," "lift up"), and of phrases like "from one's house to outside and from outside to one's house" in the immediate context indicates that the question at hand concerns the carrying of objects from place to place rather than acts of healing. This is the view of Baumgarten (*Dead Sea Scrolls. Volume 2*, 49 n. 168), who states that "spices and perfume bottles were not considered part of the attire [by the community behind the *Damascus Document*] and were therefore subject to the prohibition of carrying in and out." As is usually the case, the *Damascus Document* is more stringent on this point than most of the later rabbis. In *m. Šabb.* 6:3, Rabbi Meir forbids a woman to go out of her house on the sabbath wearing a perfume amulet or a flask containing ointment. But the "sages" permit it, and their view in the Mishna is considered determinative. (In the Tosepta, Rabbi Eliezer permits a woman to wear a perfume box, and the "sages" also permit a balsam vial when there is perfume in it [*t. Šabb.* 4:11].) More intriguing still is the preceding mishna in *m. Šabb.* 6:2, which prohibits a man from going out of his house on the sabbath wearing an amulet (a charm thought to have curative powers) if the amulet has not been put together by an expert having the necessary skills to make an amulet that is truly curative. (For the criteria for a genuine amulet made by an expert, see *t. Šabb.* 4:9.) The interesting point here is that carrying the amulet out of one's house on the sabbath is permissible *only if* it truly has healing powers—the opposite of what one would expect if all healing active were ipso facto forbidden on the sabbath. On all this, see the section on the Mishna.

[39] Along with Doering (*Schabbat*, 1989 n. 423), I prefer the emended reading *tpwl* (Qal form with the meaning "fall") to the attested reading *tpyl* (Hiphil form with the meaning "cause to fall," "throw" [the young animal just born]). The reasons for preferring the Qal reading are cogent: (1) the Qal form of the verb is attested in the CD fragments from Cave 4 (4Q270 fragment 6 5:18a [*ypwl*] and 4Q271 fragment 5 1:8c [*tpwl*]); (2) the pronominal suffix in *yqymh* ("he shall raise *it* up") refers much more easily to the already mentioned animal than to the unmentioned offspring; and (3) the problem of dealing with an animal that has fallen into a dangerous place is attested in the similar text of 4Q265, fragment 7, 1:6b–7a (with a clear *tpwl* in Qal) as well as in the Gospel texts (Matt 12:11 ‖ Luke 14:5) that apparently deal with a similar problem.

[40] The Greek of both Gospel texts is awkward. Literally, Matt 12:11 reads: "What man shall there be among you who shall have a sheep and, if this [sheep] fall on the sabbath into a pit, will not take hold of it and raise [it]?" Luke 14:5 is likewise convoluted, literally reading: "A son or ox of which of you shall fall into a cistern, and shall he not immediately draw him up on the day of the sabbath?" The awkward syntax in both texts may point to an original Aramaic saying that circulated in the

oral tradition and in due time came to Matthew and Luke in different Greek versions.

[41] The Hebrew phrase after "a place of water" is unclear. Various scholars have attempted to emend the text. Unfortunately, the fragments from Qumran Cave 4 (4Q270 fragment 6, 5:19b–20a and 4Q 271 fragment 5, 1:10b–11a) have lacunae at this point in the text. However, it is relatively clear from the context and the script that is visible that something like a cistern, reservoir, or large basin of water is meant. On this, see Doering, *Schabbat*, 201–2.

[42] The exact relationship between the sabbath *hǎlākâ* contained in Cave 4 fragments like 4Q265 and the Sabbath Codex of the *Damascus Document* remains unclear. Doering (*Schabbat*, 224) favors the hypothesis that the 4Q fragments are, from the viewpoint of tradition history, later clarifications of outstanding problems in the Sabbath Codex. At the same time, he admits that the final redaction of the *Damascus Document* may well be later, from a literary point of view, than the 4Q fragments. Even more problematic is the precise relationship between the individual sabbath regulations of *Jubilees* and those of the *Damascus Document*. In general, the sabbath *hǎlākôt* of the *Damascus Document* are more detailed and differentiated (more "casuistic," if we may use a much-abused term without the negative connotations with which it is often burdened); in this sense, they probably represent a later stage of the tradition history of sabbath rules within Palestinian Judaism (so Doering, p. 281). Vis-à-vis the later rabbinic rules governing the sabbath in the Mishna, the *Damascus Document* and allied fragments found at Qumran are in general more stringent. Yet, in light of the short, lapidary rules of *Jubilees*, so studded with insistent repetitions of the death penalty, the *Damascus Document* may not represent the *most* stringent wing of sectarian Judaism in the 2d century B.C. In this regard, see Yang, *Jesus and the Sabbath*, 66–67; cf. Doering (*Schabbat*, 79–83) on *Jubilees*'s prohibition of sexual intercourse on the sabbath and the supposed (but unlikely) mention of such a prohibition in CD 11:4–5 and in the very fragmentary 4Q270 fragment 2, 1:18–19. Hence, Josephus' famous statement (*J.W.* 2.8.9 §147) that the Essenes were stricter than all other Jews in abstaining from work on the seventh day should not be accepted without distinctions being made about possible various streams within the larger proto-Essene and Essene movement both before and after the establishment of the settlement at Qumran.

[43] A fully enunciated doctrine of *piqqûah nepeš* (saving an endangered human life) is not found before the rabbinic literature. For the teaching that *piqqûah nepeš* supersedes the sabbath laws, see, e.g., *b. Yoma* 84b–85a.

[44] While the comments of pagans about Jewish observances, especially the sabbath, make for fascinating reading, they are not directly relevant to our quest for the historical Jesus. For detailed treatment of the pagan texts, see Chapter 4 of McKay's *Sabbath and Synagogue*, 89–131. While the chapter is somewhat rambling and loosely connected with the rest of the book (and sometimes with the topic of

sabbath), it is a useful inventory of pagan views on Jews and the sabbath around the turn of the era. Two key points that McKay seeks to prove in this chapter are that: (1) Greek and Roman pagan authors were often not as virulently hostile to Jews as some interpreters claim; and (2) the pagan references to sabbath never mention communal Jewish worship services (i.e., public liturgies that address God directly in prayer) as part of the sabbath observance. As Yang points out (*Jesus and the Sabbath*, 80–83, esp. 80), most pagan references pay attention to the sabbath's character as a day of rest (or, to hostile minds, idleness). For a briefer treatment of pagan sources, including scattered references to the sabbath in Egyptian papyri, see Doering, *Schabbat*, 285–94. Doering also considers the citation of pagan public documents and decrees in Philo and Josephus; the major Jewish concerns reflected in these documents are exemption from military service, from the obligation to post bond or surety, and from the obligation to appear in court or deal with legal matters on the sabbath (pp. 294–306).

[45] For an introduction to and translation of the fragments of Aristobulus, see Adela Yarbro Collins, "Aristobulus," *OTP*, 2. 831–42; fragment 5, which contains his treatment of the sabbath, is found on pp. 841–42. For surveys of Aristobulus, see Nikolaus Walter, *Der Thoraausleger Aristobulus* (TU 86; Berlin: Akademie, 1964); Martin Hengel, *Judaism and Hellenism* (2 vols.; Philadelphia: Fortress, 1974) 1. 163–69; John J. Collins, *Between Athens and Jerusalem* (2d ed.; Grand Rapids, MI/Cambridge, UK: Eerdmans, 2000) 186–90; Doering, *Schabbat*, 306–15.

[46] These include *On the Migration of Abraham* (*De migratione Abrahami*), *On the Sacrifices of Abel and Cain* (*De sacrificiis Abelis et Caini*), *On the Decalogue* (*De decalogo*), *On the Embassy to Gaius* (*De legatione ad Gaium*), and *On Dreams* (*De somniis*); for all the relevant texts, see Doering, *Schabbat*, 328–66. For Philo's views on the sabbath, especially in relation to his situation in the larger Greco-Roman world, see Isaak Heinemann, *Philons griechische und jüdische Bildung* (Hildesheim/New York: Olms, 1973) 110–18; Jean LaPorte, Eucharistia *in Philo* (Studies in Bible and Early Christianity 3; New York/Toronto: Mellen, 1983) 75–76; Alex Mendelson, *Philo's Jewish Identity* (Brown Judaic Studies 161; Atlanta: Scholars, 1988) 58–62.

[47] Positive injunctions, some of which are simply the reverse of the prohibitions, include allowing slaves and animals to rest from their toil, acknowledging that a military attack or a natural disaster overrides the sabbath (and thus acknowledging the obligation on the sabbath to rescue human life when endangered), affirming the obligation of priests to offer sacrifices on the sabbath in addition to the daily *tāmîd* sacrifices, affirming the permissibility of waving the ʿōmer (the first fruits of the barley harvest) on the sabbath and of observing feasts on the sabbath, and finally affirming the obligation of Jews in general to come together on the sabbath to learn the laws and receive instruction about them. Philo inculcates the death penalty for intentional breaches of sabbath law, though such a penalty was probably only a theoretical ideal in Roman Alexandria.

[48] It is only in a particular sense that Josephus can be grouped with writers like Aristobulus and Philo as authors of the Jewish Diaspora. Born ca. A.D. 37–38 in Palestine, Josephus spent most of his life there until his capture by the future emperor Vespasian during the First Jewish War. Since all of Josephus' known literary works stem from the time after his removal to Rome, and since at least part of his audience was made up of Jews in the Diaspora, he may be considered in this sense a writer of the Jewish Diaspora. For a comparison of Philo and Josephus on the sabbath in relation to the synagogue, see McKay, *Sabbath and Synagogue*, 85–88.

[49] See *Ag. Ap.* 2.17 §175 (cf. *Ant.* 16.2.4 §43) and the treatment of synagogue attendance on the sabbath as a commandment of the Mosaic Law in Chapter 31.

[50] While it is certainly true, as Yang observes (*Jesus and the Sabbath*, 69), that Josephus' works contain abundant references to the sabbath, the number of distinct sabbath regulations that Josephus discusses is quite small (so Yang, p. 74).

[51] Contrast the prohibitions against talking about work in *Jub.* 50:8 and CD 10:17–19.

[52] On the development of this halakic question from the time of the Maccabees onward and its treatment by Josephus, see Chapter 31. Yang (*Jesus and the Sabbath*, 69–71) points out the exceptional cases in which, even around the turn of the era, some Jews either took the initiative in starting a battle on the sabbath or waived any attempt to defend themselves. As Yang observes, granted the nature of Josephus' historical-narrative works, it is not surprising that many of Josephus' references to sabbath regulations deal with fighting on the sabbath.

[53] For the relevant passages in Josephus and a discussion of each text, see Doering, *Schabbat*, 492–505.

[54] For a brief discussion of which sabbath *hălākôt* in the Mishna may go back to the pre-70 Pharisees (and, by way of opposition, to the Sadducees), see Sanders, *Jewish Law*, 8–13. Most of the questions (e.g., the *'erûb*, work begun before the sabbath that continues of its own momentum on the sabbath, sacrifices on sabbaths and feast days, laying hands on sacrificial victims) are irrelevant to the question at hand, i.e., Jesus' attitude toward the sabbath.

[55] An overliteral translation of the Hebrew phrase that I render "the main works" would be "the fathers of the works" ['*ăbôt mĕlā'kôt*]. Their nature as overarching categories that can serve as sources for further sabbath *hălākôt* is reflected in the creative translation of Jacob Neusner (*A History of the Mishnaic Law of Appointed Times. Part One. Shabbat* [SJLA 34; Leiden: Brill, 1981] 81): "the generative categories of acts of labor." For a theological reflection by Neusner on the place of sabbath *hălākâ* within rabbinic thought, see his "Reading Scripture Theologically: The Sabbath Halakhah in the Context of Rabbinic Judaism's System," *Approaches to*

Ancient Judaism. New Series. Volume Fourteen (South Florida Studies in the History of Judaism; Atlanta: Scholars, 1998) 197–210; with slight modifications, this article, under the same title, can also be found in *For a Later Generation* (George W. E. Nickelsburg Festschrift; ed. Randal A. Argall, Beverly A. Bow, and Rodney A. Werline; Harrisburg: Trinity, 2000) 183–95.

[56] Doering (*Schabbat*, 475) also sees a possible connection with *m. Šabb.* 24:3 (one may put water into one's bran, but one may not knead it).

[57] The word "domain" (Hebrew: *rĕšût*) here refers to the rabbinic distinction between private and public domains. Much rabbinic thought on sabbath law revolves around the problem of whether or not one can carry a particular object from one's house (or other private domain) into a public area and vice versa.

[58] Doering (*Schabbat*, 268–69) favors the view that John 5:10 violates the prohibition of carrying a burden in a public area.

[59] The separate list in *m. Bĕṣa* 5:2 is all the more telling in that it catalogues fourteen actions that are different from the thirty-nine listed in *m. Šabb.* 7:2. That, between them, neither list includes healing is, in my view, indicative of how relatively recent the prohibition of healing was in the Jewish halakic tradition.

[60] This, at least, is the thrust of *m. Šabb.* 14:3 in its present form in the Mishna. However, if at an earlier date some of the clauses in this mishna circulated separately in the oral tradition, one may wonder whether some teachers held to the sweeping position that emerges when 14:3de is read separately, i.e., without the surrounding provisos: *kol-hā' ôkĕlîn 'ôkēl 'ādām lirĕpû' â wĕkol hammašqîn šôteh* ("A man may eat all types of food [meant] for healing and he may drink all types of liquids [meant for healing]").

[61] One sees a similar approach in the directives in *m. Šabb.* 22:6.

[62] On "the people of the land," see *A Marginal Jew*, 3. 28–29; cf. *m. 'Abot* 2:5.

[63] As with a great deal of what follows, I treat this material in summary fashion because all the miracles stories in the Four Gospels, including those involving the sabbath, have already been dealt with at length in *A Marginal Jew*, 2. 617–1038. For the most part, it will be sufficient to refer the reader back to the relevant material in that volume.

[64] See *A Marginal Jew*, 2. 648–50.

[65] The introductory phrase in 1:29, indicating that Jesus and his disciples are leaving the synagogue, might suggest a sabbath setting, but both inside and outside Palestine Jews visited synagogues during the work week for various reasons. Similarly,

the arrival of a distinguished guest in a house would naturally occasion a meal; taken in isolation, it need not be the traditional sabbath meal served around midday. That this miracle story could just as well be told without a sabbath context is demonstrated by Matthew's redaction of Mark. Matthew reorders his various sources in Matthew 8–9 to create three cycles of three miracle stories each. Peter's mother-in-law (Matt 8:14–15) joins the leper (8:1–4) and the centurion's servant (8: 5–13) to form the first cycle—without benefit of an overarching sabbath. On this, see John P. Meier, *Matthew* (NT Message 3; Wilmington, DE: Glazier, 1980) 81–86.

[66] See *A Marginal Jew*, 2. 707–8. As an aside, it may also be noted that the healings, mentioned in a summary fashion, that conclude Mark's "ideal" day in Capernaum (1:32–34) are pointedly placed after sunset and thus after the sabbath's end. Hence, they fall outside the sabbath day (from sunset to sunset) and therefore quite understandably do not occasion any sabbath dispute—which is not to be expected in a summary statement anyway.

[67] This is also true, mutatis mutandis, of Luke's version of the story (4:16–30), whether or not we consider it simply Luke's imaginative redaction of Mark's narrative; on this, see *A Marginal Jew*, 1. 269–71.

[68] Thus, for instance, Doering (*Schabbat*, 445), while cautious about the historicity of individual stories, thinks that the multiple attestation of healings on the sabbath justifies the general judgment that Jesus healed on the sabbath and that these healings occasioned controversy among his fellow Jews.

[69] See *A Marginal Jew*, 2. 646–1038. Doering's treatment of the sabbath healings is found in *Schabbat*, 441–78. It is important for the reader to remember what I mean as a historian when I speak of "the miracles" of Jesus. I do not think a historian *in his or her capacity as a historian* can decide that some past act, however astounding or apparently inexplicable, is in fact a miracle, in the sense of something done directly by God apart from and beyond all human abilities or potential. Such a judgment is in essence a *theo*-logical judgment: *God* has directly done this. It is a judgment made from the vantage point of faith (faith, first of all, that there is a God who acts directly in human history). That is not to say that such a judgment is ultimately either right or wrong; it is simply to say that it lies outside the competence of a historian *as a historian*, operating with the methods, tools, and goals and within the limits of his or her academic discipline. Hence, when I speak of the miracles of Jesus, what I mean is that certain startling events or actions narrated in the Gospels go back to some actual events or actions in the public ministry of Jesus and that Jesus and his followers believed and asserted that such events or actions were worked by divine power. More particularly, they believed that such actions belonged to Jesus' Elijah-like prophetic ministry of proclaiming and partially realizing the coming of God's kingdom. Affirming that these events and actions were actually miracles performed by Jesus lies beyond the competence of the historian as historian. What we can affirm is that some reports of Jesus' miracles and the belief that Jesus performed

miracles did not first arise in the early church but rather go back to the ministry of the historical Jesus. On all this, see *A Marginal Jew*, 2. 509–631.

[70] See *A Marginal Jew*, 2. 681–84.

[71] On the Herodians, and the dubious historicity of their presence in Mark 3:6 and 12:13, see *A Marginal Jew*, 3. 560–65.

[72] On this, see Joel Marcus, *Mark 1–8* (AYB 27; New York: Doubleday, 2000; reprint New Haven: Yale University Press) 251, 253–54. Marcus (p. 252) observes that, at least on the level of Mark's own theology, Jesus' rhetorical question makes sense. Within the apocalyptic scenario of Mark's Gospel, the eschatological battle has already begun. Granted this context, everything that one does champions the cause of either life or death. Thus, for the Marcan Jesus to withhold a cure even for a few hours would be equivalent to a deadly blow, while curing the man is equated with saving his life. While all this may be true on the level of Marcan theology, one must still agree with Sanders's observation (*Jewish Law*, 21) when one turns to the historical reality of Jewish debates over sabbath *hălākâ* in 1st-century Palestine: "The conclusion, 'lawful to do good' is too vague and might mean anything." The whole point of *hălākâ* as it develops and expands is to give precise, concrete direction for particular cases. To teach simply that on the sabbath one should do good and avoid evil both leaves the sincere inquirer perplexed and the insincere inquirer free to do anything. Doering (*Schabbat*, 450–57) argues for the authenticity of the logion in 3:4. On the whole complicated question of tradition and redaction in Mark 3:1–6, see Heikki Sariola, *Markus und das Gesetz* (Annales Academiae Scientiarum Fennicae, Dissertationes Humanarum Litterarum 56; Helsinki: Suomalainen, 1990) 87–94, 105–9.

[73] So rightly Sanders, *Jewish Law*, 21. Doering's attempt to answer this objection (*Schabbat*, 446–47) does not, in my opinion, succeed. Not only is there no proof from any document written in the 1st century A.D. that any pre-70 group within Palestinian Judaism held that healing was a sabbath violation (a point that Doering admits on p. 448); more important, when we begin to find such an opinion in the Mishna and Tosepta, the emphasis is always on some healing *action*, *activity*, or *practice* that qualifies as work and therefore is forbidden on the sabbath. Doering's conclusion (pp. 449–50) that healing on the sabbath was forbidden by Pharisees in the pre-70 period lacks convincing proof.

[74] On this, see Marcus, *Mark 1–8*, 253: Jesus heals the man "in a clever way that eludes the charge of performing work on the Sabbath"; the Pharisees wind up "bested again." Doering (*Schabbat*, 446–48) tries to explain how Jesus' command by itself could be a violation of the sabbath, but it is telling that he has to read into Mark 3:1–6 material from other dispute stories.

[75] Marcus (*Mark 1–8*, 248) claims that CD 11:9–10 teaches that diseases that are not life-threatening should not be treated on the sabbath. However, as we saw

earlier, this text deals instead with the problem of what may be carried in and out of one's house on one's person on the sabbath (see Doering, *Schabbat*, 449); moreover, it is unclear whether the Hebrew text speaks of medicine rather than perfume or spices. Marcus seems to be reading CD 11:9–10 through the Mishna.

[76] This bon mot is found in Cicero's *First Oration against Cataline*, 8.21.

[77] I emphasize this point here and elsewhere in this chapter because so many commentaries on the Gospels take for granted that at least some if not all Jewish groups in Palestine in the 1st century A.D. considered healing a sabbath violation. See, e.g., the comment by Davies and Allison, *The Gospel According to Saint Matthew*, 2. 318: "Was it in fact permitted to heal on the sabbath? Certainly the Essenes and the author of Jubilees would have answered in the negative." No specific texts are cited to support this claim. Yet the authors go on to assert that the question posed in Matt 12:10 ("Is it lawful to heal on the sabbath?") shows that the dominant opinion in the Mishna (healing is not permitted on the sabbath unless life is in immediate danger) "was held by many if not most teachers in Jesus' day."

[78] Doering (*Schabbat*, 445) thinks that, while Mark 3:1–6 is not a precise historical report of a particular individual event in Jesus' ministry, it may be considered a stylized narrative that preserves the authentic memory that the historical Jesus did heal on the sabbath, that these healings provoked conflict, and that Jesus had to defend his healings in the face of objections. The question remains, though: Which group of Palestinian Jews from the early 1st-century A.D. held that acts of healing were violations of the sabbath? Doering admits that there is not a single non-Christian source in the pre-70 period that mentions sabbath healings as a breach of the sabbath. But the Gospel dispute stories plus the prohibitions in the Mishna and the Tosepta lead Doering to suggest that, around the time of Jesus, the Pharisees or other Jews similar to the Pharisees in teaching held that healing was a sabbath violation (pp. 446–50). One wonders whether this line of argument does not involve a certain amount of circular reasoning.

[79] See *A Marginal Jew*, 2. 684–85.

[80] One must distinguish Jesus' healing touch (laying hands on the body of the sick person to cure him or her) from the laying on of hands that occasioned a dispute between the House of Shammai and the House of Hillel according to *m. Ḥag.* 2:2–3 and *m. Beṣa* 2:4; on this, see Sanders, *Jewish Law*, 10–12. In these mishnaic texts, the dispute concerns laying hands on a sacrificial victim about to be slaughtered in the Jerusalem temple. In this ritual, the laying on of hands required that the person offering the sacrifice lean on the animal with his full weight. In rabbinic thought, this leaning on the animal with one's full weight made the animal a beast of burden; consequently, one was performing a work on the sabbath. The House of Shammai forbade such laying on of hands on a feast day, when work was forbidden. The House of Hillel permitted it. Now, even if we grant, for the sake of argument, that

this dispute actually goes back to the pre-70 period, what we have here is a disagreement between two wings of the Pharisaic movement, with neither wing apparently being able to win over or force the other side to observe its practice when offering sacrifice. A fortiori, neither temple priests nor ordinary Jews who did not belong to the Pharisaic movement would feel obliged to follow the prohibition of the Shammaites. More to the point, though, Jesus' laying on of hands, in the sense of a healing touch, is hardly the same thing as solemnly leaning on a sacrificial victim with one's full weight. Doing that to the frail, bent-over woman of Luke 13:10–17 would be guaranteed to effect the opposite of healing.

[81] See *A Marginal Jew*, 2. 710–11. It is all the more interesting that the same judgment of *non liquet* was passed in Volume Two on all three stories since, in Volume Two, these stories were being approached and examined primarily from the viewpoint of miracle stories, not stories about disputes over sabbath observance. Doering (*Schabbat*, 462–63) thinks that Luke 14:1–6 does not represent a special L tradition but rather simply Luke's creation of a sabbath dispute story with Mark 3:1–6 used as a model. On Doering's reading, then, there is no point in pursuing the question of the historicity of the special Lucan narrative. As I indicate in *A Marginal Jew*, 2. 711, I think the Lucan narrative has enough distinguishing features to qualify it as a separate L tradition—although, in the end, I do not think that the question of its going back to some event in the life of Jesus can be decided one way or the other.

[82] Note in particular the strong judgment of Frans Neirynck, "Jesus and the Sabbath: Some Observations on Mark II, 27," *Jésus aux origines de la christologie* (BETL 40; 2d ed.; ed. Jacques Dupont; Leuven: Leuven University/Peeters, 1989) 227–70 (with additional bibliography and discussion on pp. 422–27), esp. 230: "There should be no doubt about the secondary character of the two healing stories in Lk XIII and XIV. In my view they are almost completely due to Lukan redaction."

[83] See *A Marginal Jew*, 2. 680–81 (the paralyzed man by the pool of Bethzatha) and 694–98 (the man born blind).

[84] On this, see Neirynck, "Jesus and the Sabbath," 229. Another reference to the sabbath occurs in the polemical dialogue material of John 7, when Jesus justifies his healing of the paralyzed man by the pool of Bethzatha on the sabbath by appealing to the obligation in the Mosaic law to circumcise every newborn Jewish male on the eighth day, even if that day falls on a sabbath (John 7:22–23). In an a fortiori argument, Jesus argues that, if the sabbath can be broken for circumcision (which "heals," as it were, one member of the body [obviously, in a religious, not a physical sense]), then the sabbath can certainly be broken to heal the whole of a man's body. Since, however, it is most likely that the transformation of the miracle story in John 5:1–9a into a story of healing on the sabbath (5:9b) is the work of the evangelist, this reference back to the healing on the sabbath is likewise redactional and cannot be attributed to the historical Jesus. On the passage, see Doering (*Schabbat*, 472–75),

who detects a possible influence on John's formulation of the argument from contemporary discussions in tannaitic Judaism.

[85] On the question of sabbath observance in John's Gospel and in chaps. 5 and 9 in particular, see Doering, *Schabbat*, 468–72, 475–76.

[86] One may detect an implied reference to the activity of God in giving life and judging (or raising) the dead even on the sabbath in John 5:19–30, but the sabbath itself is never explicitly mentioned.

[87] Notice how, in chap. 5, the explicit references to the sabbath are clustered at the beginning (vv 9b–10) and end (vv 16 + 18) of the bridge-section of dialogue, thus creating an *inclusio* that delimits the bridge-section. In the lengthy bridge-section of chap. 9, explicit references to the sabbath are limited to vv 14 + 16, in the first exchange between the healed man and the Pharisees.

[88] In his treatment of the Johannine material on sabbath (*Schabbat*, 468–76), Doering holds that the sabbath theme is not original to the healing stories in John 5 and 9.

[89] For Doering's attempt to understand this saying in context, see *Schabbat*, 450–57. One may wonder, though, whether the very general question posed by Mark 3:4 really fits the miracle story in which it is embedded or whether it functions primarily to foreshadow and condemn the evil intent of Jesus' opponents on the sabbath to kill life (i.e., Jesus' life), depicted in the redactional conclusion of v 6. The lack of Mark 3:4's relevance to the story in which it stands and the difficulty of seeing the probative force of its argument may have led Matthew to insert a much more specific halakic argument (Matt 12:11), one that reflects actual debates about sabbath *hălākâ*, into his version of the story.

[90] According to Davies and Allison (*The Gospel According to Saint Matthew*, 2. 319), the Greek form of the question in Matt 12:11, "Which man among you . . . ?" (*tis estai ex hymōn anthrōpos*), is a Semitism characteristic of Jesus; contrast the simple introduction in Luke 14:5: "Which of you . . . ?" (*tinos hymōn*).

[91] See Davies and Allison, *The Gospel According to Saint Matthew*, 2. 321.

[92] This seems to be the best reading of the Greek text of Luke 14:5; it is supported by early papyri (45 and 75) and Vaticanus. The alternate readings can be easily explained as scribal attempts to improve the *lectio difficilior* of "your son or an ox," a strange combination, to say the least. Some manuscripts, such as Sinaiticus, substitute "donkey" for "son," an easy substitution since it not only provides a more readily understandable reading (cf. Isa 1:3) but also alters the disputed Greek noun only slightly (in Greek, "son" is *huios* and "donkey" is *onos*). That the combination of ox and donkey would be natural is seen not only from Luke 13:7 but also from

m. B. Qam. 5:6 (where the ox or the donkey falls into a pit). The Codex Koridethi conflates the readings to create the unholy trinity of "donkey, son, or ox." The Codex Bezae creates a smoother reading by substituting "sheep" (possibly from Matt 12:11) for "son." We have here a prime example of how one reading (that of Vaticanus) can explain the origin of all the others as corrections, while none of the other readings can explain the origin of the remaining readings, especially that of Vaticanus. On all this, see Fitzmyer, *The Gospel According to Luke,* 2. 1042.

[93] On the various ways of understanding the source question, see Davies and Allison, *The Gospel According to Saint Matthew,* 2. 319. Doering (*Schabbat,* 458–59) takes up the suggestion, proposed, reformulated, and debated by famous Aramaic scholars like Matthew Black, Joachim Jeremias, and Joseph Fitzmyer, that behind the mention of a "sheep" falling into a "pit" (Matt 12:11) and of "a son or an ox" falling into a "cistern" (Luke 14:5) stands a wordplay in the Aramaic original; see also Eduard Lohse, "Jesu Worte über den Sabbat," *Judentum, Urchristentum, Kirche* (Joachim Jeremias Frestschrift; BZNW 26; ed. Walther Eltester; Berlin: Töpelmann, 1960) 79–89, esp. 86–87. Supposedly, the Aramaic saying originally spoke of *bĕʿîrāʾ* (a livestock animal that could be either an ox or a sheep), *bêrāʾ* (a pit or cistern), and *bĕrāʾ* (a son). Our present Greek texts would thus reflect different translation variants of the original saying. While Black and Jeremias supported versions of this theory, Fitzmyer (*The Gospel According to Luke,* 2. 1042) thinks it unlikely. Against Fitzmyer's view, Doering supports the Aramaic hypothesis, but thinks that the reference to "son" is a secondary expansion of the logion in the Aramaic. Davies and Allison (ibid., 320) explain the Matthean redactional form of the question by suggesting that (1) Matthew's desire to construct an a fortiori argument excludes the use of "son"; (2) Matthew assimilates this question to the parable of the lost sheep (18:12–14); and (3) the Greek word for "sheep" (*probaton*) is frequent in Matthew (eleven times, more than any other NT book except John's Gospel), while he never uses the Greek word for "ox" (*bous*). In the end, this whole debate, while favoring a very early date for this logion in the Palestinian Aramaic tradition of Jesus' words, does not affect the line of argument I am pursuing in the main text.

[94] Fitzmyer (*The Gospel According to Luke,* 2. 1011) thinks that, in the story as it stands, the address "Hypocrites!" must be aimed at "the crowd" (v 14), although "the epithet is evoked by the subterfuge of the leader . . . who addresses his remarks, not to Jesus, but to the crowd." I am not sure that this explanation really makes sense of the passage. Luke tells us that Jesus addressed his reply "to him" (namely, to the ruler) in v 15a, a statement that clashes hopelessly with the plural "Hypocrites!" that follows immediately in v 15b. The crowd hardly seems to be the hypocrites rebuked by Jesus since, in the typical choral conclusion to a miracle story, Luke carefully distinguishes the rejoicing crowd (*pas ho ochlos* in v 17b) from "all those who opposed him" in v 17a—as Fitzmyer himself notes (p. 1014). The tension in the text argues strongly for the bodily insertion of a separate tradition in v 15b.

[95] Luke may be consciously preparing for this connection between two types of untying or loosing (expressed by the Greek verb *lyō* in both v 15 and v 16) by narrating in v 12 that the healing word of Jesus to the woman is "Woman, you are loosed from [or: "untied from," using the compound form of the verb, *apolyō*] your infirmity." Still, a glaring non sequitur is present in the move from the obvious necessity of bringing farm animals to a source of water so that they can drink on the sabbath to the unexplained necessity (*edei* in v 16c) of healing the crippled woman precisely on the sabbath.

[96] If one prefers to categorize Matt 12:11 ‖ Luke 14:5 not as Q tradition but as M and L traditions respectively, the argument from multiple attestation might actually be strengthened. However, Q tradition is generally considered to have been formulated ca. A.D. 50–70, while at least some M and L traditions could easily have arisen in the post-70 period.

[97] On this, see Davies and Allison, *The Gospel According to Saint Matthew*, 2. 320.

[98] Doering makes this suggestion a number of times in his survey of the sabbath *hălākâ* of various Jewish groups at the turn of the era; see, e.g., *Schabbat*, 576.

[99] On the difficulty of knowing much in detail about the Pharisees and their teaching in the pre-70 period and for a sketch of what may be said with fair probability, see *A Marginal Jew*, 3. 289–388. Some critics might still want to uphold the older view that the *Psalms of Solomon* are Pharisaic compositions, but this claim is widely disputed today.

[100] Only when we get to the Talmud do we find further mitigation of the misery of the animal in the pit. In *b. Šabb.* 128b, some amoraic rabbis allow that, at least in the case where supplying fodder is not feasible, one may lay down bedspreads and cushions in the hope that the animal may be able to climb out on its own. The presumption remains that one may not directly haul the animal out by ropes or other instruments. On this point see, Doering, *Schabbat*, 195.

[101] See the remarks of Doering (*Schabbat*, 459–60), who inclines to a Galilean *Sitz im Leben*. He also suggests (p. 461) that Matthew's wording of *probaton hen* (literally, "one sheep" in 12:11) is not to be understood as an Aramaic usage equivalent to the indefinite article ("a sheep") but rather as a rhetorical emphasis on *only* one sheep, thus highlighting the poverty of the farmer whose livelihood is threatened. At the same time, Doering prefers to see the origin of Matt 12:11 ‖ Luke 14:5 not in the teaching of the historical Jesus but in the innercommunal discussions of Jewish Christians.

[102] Perhaps the closest we can come to a sweeping principle about saving human life on the sabbath in the pre-70 period is in the Egyptian Diaspora, where Philo

(*De somniis* [*On Dreams*] 2.18 §125–28) takes up the question. But even here, the text speaks only of the right to flight or the protection of oneself, family, and friends in the face of an enemy attack or a natural disaster such as flood, famine, fire, or earthquake. The passage is also problematic because Philo places these ideas in the mouth of an Egyptian official who is trying to persuade Egyptian Jews to forsake observance of the sabbath.

[103] On this point, see Doering, *Schabbat*, 465.

[104] A passage in the Babylonian Talmud (*b. 'Erub.* 20b and 21a) evinces concern about the manner in which one may give water to animals on the sabbath. According to this passage, one may not fill a bucket with water and then hold it before an animal. But one may fill a trough with water; the animal may then drink from the trough on its own. However, even though this opinion appears in a *baraita* (i.e., a talmudic text in Hebrew supposedly preserving a tannaitic tradition), to attribute such an opinion to any group in the early 1st-century A.D. involves us in a highly speculative scenario. More to the point, Luke 13:15 does not indicate the manner or circumstances in which the animal is given to drink.

[105] For studies of Mark 2:23–28 parr. and for further bibliography, see (besides the standard Marcan commentaries) I. Abrahams, "The Sabbath," *Studies in Pharisaism and the Gospels* (2 vols.; Cambridge: Cambridge University, 1917, 1924) 1. 129–35; Samuel S. Cohon, "The Place of Jesus in the Religious Life of His Day," *JBL* 48 (1929) 82–108; T. W. Manson, *The Teaching of Jesus* (Cambridge: Cambridge University, 1931) 214; idem, "Mark ii. 27f.," *Coniectanea Neotestamentica* *XI* (Anton Fridrichensen Festschrift; Lund: Gleerup, 1947) 138–46; J. W. Wenham, "Mark 2:26," *JTS* n.s. 1 (1950) 156; Alan D. Rogers, "Mark 2:26," *JTS* n.s. 2 (1951) 44–45; Jan W. Doeve, *Jewish Hermeneutics in the Synoptic Gospels and Acts* (Assen: van Gorcum, 1954) 263–67; F. W. Beare, " 'The Sabbath Was Made for Man?' " *JBL* 79 (1960) 130–36; Lohse, "Jesu Worte über den Sabbat," 79–89, esp. 81–83, 84–85; Alfred Suhl, *Die Funktion der alttestamentlichen Zitate und Anspielungen im Markusevangelium* (Gütersloh: Mohn, 1965) 82–87; H. E. Tödt, *The Son of Man in the Synoptic Tradition* (London: SCM, 1965; 2d ed. of German original, 1963) 130–33; Ernst Käsemann, "The Problem of the Historical Jesus," *Essays on New Testament Themes* (SBT 41; London: SCM, 1964) 15–47, esp. 38–39; Morna D. Hooker, *The Son of Man in Mark* (Montreal: McGill University, 1967) 93–102; Joachim Jeremias, "Das älteste Schicht der Menschensohn-Logien," *ZNW* 58 (1967) 159–72; Ernst Haenchen, *Der Weg Jesu* (2d ed.; Berlin: de Gruyter, 1968) 120–22; Lewis S. Hay, "The Son of Man in Mark 2:10 and 2:28," *JBL* 89 (1970) 69–75; Heinz-Wolfgang Kuhn, *Ältere Sammlungen im Markusevangelium* (SUNT 8; Göttingen: Vandenhoeck & Ruprecht, 1971) 72–81; Berger, *Die Gesetzesauslegung Jesu*, 1. 579–80; Arland J. Hultgren, "The Formation of the Sabbath Pericope in Mark 2:23–28," *JBL* 91 (1972) 38–43; idem, *Jesus and His Adversaries* (Minneapolis: Augsburg, 1979) 111–15; Hans Hübner, *Das Gesetz in der synoptischen Tradition* (2d ed.; Göttingen: Vandenhoeck & Ruprecht, 1973) 113–23; Rob-

ert Banks, *Jesus and the Law in the Synoptic Tradition* (SNTSMS 28; Cambridge: Cambridge University, 1975) 115–23; Hermann Aichinger, "Quellenkritische Untersuchung der Perikope vom Ährenraufen am Sabbat Mk 2,23–28 par Mt 12,1–8 par Lk 6,1–5," *Jesus in der Verkündigung der Kirche* (Studien zum Neuen Testament und seiner Umwelt A/1; ed. Albert Fuchs; Linz: Fuchs, 1976) 110–53; D. N. Cohn-Sherbok, "An Analysis of Jesus' Arguments Concerning the Plucking of Grain on the Sabbath," *JSNT* 2 (1979) 31–41; Andreas Lindemann, " 'Der Sabbat ist um des Menschen willen geworden . . . ,' " *Wort und Dienst* (1979) 79–105; C. Shannon Morgan, " 'When Abiathar Was High Priest' (Mark 2:26)," *JBL* 98 (1979) 409–10; Joanna Dewey, *Markan Public Debate* (SBLDS 48; Chico, CA: Scholars, 1980) 94–100; Christopher Tuckett, "The Present Son of Man," *JSNT* 14 (1982) 58–81; Barnabas Lindars, *Jesus Son of Man* (Grand Rapids, MI: Eerdmans, 1983) 103–6; Malcolm Lowe and David Flusser, "Evidence Corroborating a Modified Proto-Matthean Synoptic Theory," *NTS* 29 (1983) 25–47, esp. 32–33; Vernon K. Robbins, *Jesus the Teacher. A Socio-Rhetorical Interpretation of Mark* (Philadelphia: Fortress, 1984) 75–123; James D. G. Dunn, "Mark 2.1–3.6: A Bridge between Jesus and Paul on the Question of the Law," *NTS* 30 (1984) 395–415; Jarmo Kiilunen, *Die Vollmacht im Widerstreit* (Annales Academiae Scientiarum Fennicae, Dissertationes Humanarum Litterarum 40; Helsinki: Suomalainen, 1985) 196–221; Maurice Casey, "Culture and Historicity: The Plucking of the Grain (Mark 2. 23–28)," *NTS* 34 (1988) 1–23; Sariola, *Markus und das Gesetz*, 77–87, 97–105; Douglas R. A. Hare, *The Son of Man Tradition* (Minneapolis: Fortress, 1990) 190–92, 225; Menahem Kister, "Plucking on the Sabbath and Christian-Jewish Polemic," *Immanuel* 24/25 (1990) 35–51; Herold Weiss, "The Sabbath in the Synoptic Gospels," *JSNT* 38 (1990) 13–27; Rod Parrott, "Conflict and Rhetoric in Mark 2:23–28," *The Rhetoric of Pronouncement* (Semeia 64; ed. Vernon K. Robbins; Atlanta: Scholars, 1994) 117–37; Back, *Jesus of Nazareth*, 68–105; Loader, *Jesus' Attitude*, 43–53; Doering, *Schabbat*, 408–40; Mayer-Haas, *"Geschenk,"* 156–92. Neirynck's article ("Jesus and the Sabbath," 227–70, 422–27) gives a good overview of almost all the theories of tradition history and interpretation found in modern exegetical literature, especially in regard to Mark 2:27.

[106] This phenomenon, already seen in the Marcan form of the dispute, is increased by Matthew (12:1–8, especially vv 5–7) as he attempts to improve the scriptural arguments in Mark. Since I hold that the Matthean and Lucan forms of the dispute do not reflect a separate tradition but rather the redactional changes of Matthew and Luke, I do not examine their versions in detail here; cf. Neirynck, "Jesus and the Sabbath," 230–31; Doering, *Schabbat*, 432–38. For a treatment of Matthew's redaction of this pericope, see Martin Vahrenhorst, *"Ihr sollt überhaupt nicht schwören." Matthäus in halachischen Diskurs* (WMANT 95; Neukirchen-Vluyn: Neukirchener Verlag, 2002) 381–92. For the special question of the stray logion on the sabbath found in the Codex Bezae after Luke 6:4, see the treatment in Doering, *Schabbat*, 438–40. I agree with Doering's assessment that the logion, whatever its ultimate origin (Jewish-Christian tradition?), does not go back to the historical Jesus and hence need not be considered here. In my view, its isolated attestation

in the idiosyncratic Codex Bezae alone among all early Greek manuscripts makes a positive judgment on authenticity all but impossible. As far as the original text of Luke's Gospel is concerned, the *UBSGNT* (4th ed.) considers it "certain" ("A" rating) that Bezae's stray logion did not stand in Luke's text; see the comment by Metzger in his *TCGNT* (2d ed.), 117.

[107] A major focal point of dispute is the number and order of the stages of tradition and redaction in this Marcan pericope. Guelich (*Mark 1–8:26*, 119) notes four major suggestions (with useful lists of authors who support various positions): (a) 2:23–26 + 27–28; (b) 2:23–26 + 27 + 28; (c) 2:23–24, 27 + 28 + 25–26; (d) 27 + 23–24 + 25–26,28. As Guelich observes (similarly Back, *Jesus of Nazareth*, 69; Doering, *Schabbat*, 409), these four suggestions basically boil down to two: (a) either Jesus' argument from the action of David is original, with vv 27–28 being added later in one or two stages or (b) v 27 (and possibly v 28) constituted Jesus' original answer(s), with the David story being added later. (Gundry [*Mark*, 148] gives an even more detailed list of possible tradition histories, only–in his usual fashion—to reject all such hypotheses in favor of maintaining the historicity of the pericope as it stands.) As far as the formation of this pericope in the *Marcan* tradition is concerned, I shall argue that the view that 2:23–26 represents the original core tradition and that vv 27 + 28 are later additions to this core is the most probable opinion. However, this question of the tradition history of the pericope in the earliest days of the church must be carefully distinguished from the question of what, if anything, goes back to the historical Jesus. A verse that, from the viewpoint of the growth of Mark 2:23–28, may be a later addition to the story (e.g., v 27) could well turn out to go back to the historical Jesus while the rest of the pericope does not.

[108] Here I list briefly a few of the many individual exegetical questions that plague this pericope, along with the solutions I adopt:

(1) A prime example of the exegetical puzzles in this pericope is the key question: Which action of the disciples in v 23 gives rise to the dispute? In v 23, Jesus' disciples are described in the Greek thus: *ērxanto hodon poiein tillontes tous stachyas*. Some have taken this to mean that the disciples, as they walk through the field, create a path by plucking the heads of grain. Supposedly, as Jesus' escort, they are clearing a way for him through the grain, thus performing a type of work. *Pace* Marcus (*Mark 1–8*, 239–40), this does not make sense for a number of reasons. Verse 23 mentions that Jesus is passing through the standing grain before the disciples are mentioned. The picture that the verse naturally conjures up is that of Jesus preceding his disciples, who, not unlike the disciples of the later rabbis, regularly follow their master physically as well as symbolically. Moreover, merely plucking heads of grain would hardly create a path in a field of standing grain if none already existed. Then, too, since Jesus in his reply must be supposed to be discussing the type of action to which the Pharisees object, it follows that the Pharisees are objecting to some action connected with eating food. The most natural conclusion is that the Pharisees' objection to the disciples' action is aimed at their plucking grain to eat, an act that the Pharisees interpret as a work that violates the sabbath (probably on the grounds

that it is a form of reaping). That such plucking of the grain would be objectionable to various Jewish groups around the turn of the era is argued by Doering (*Schabbat*, 428–29) from the convergence of the prohibitions found in CD 10:22–23; Philo, *De vita Mosis* 2.22; and *t. Šabb.* 9:16–17 (interpreting the prohibition of reaping in *m. Šabb.* 7:2). Nothing that follows in the dispute suggests that the Pharisees' objection focuses on the alleged action of the disciples in constructing a path (still less in their violating the limits of the distance one was allowed to walk on the sabbath, a point not raised in this pericope; see Doering, *Schabbat*, 429–30). Therefore, it is best to take the disputed Greek phrase as an example of Mark's less-than-elegant Koine Greek, which intends to say that the disciples are plucking grain as they walk through the field. In this interpretation, the active verb *poiein* is equivalent to the middle form *poieisthai* (the proper form in classical Greek for the idea of going one's way); the whole phrase means "to make one's way" in the sense of "to walk along," not "to construct a path." The same construction with the same idea of journeying is found in LXX Judg 17:8: *tou poiēsai hodon autou* (a literal, though not necessarily correct, translation of the Hebrew phrase *laʿăśôt darkô*). Moreover, it is possible in Greek to express the subject's main action with a participle while the main verb indicates only an attendant or secondary action. An additional possibility is that Mark, whose Gospel contains a notable number of Latinisms, is influenced by the Latin phrase *iter facere* ("to go one's way," "to journey"). On all this, see Neirynck, "Jesus and the Sabbath," 254–59; Gundry, *Mark*, 139–40; Doering, *Schabbat*, 427–28. Casey ("Culture and Historicity," 1–2) cuts the Gordian knot by rewriting the text. He assures us that the original Aramaic story (but did the whole story ever exist in Aramaic?) read *ʿbr* ("go on one's way," "move through," "pass over," "pass by"), but the Greek translator misread the verb as *ʿbd* ("do, "make"), thus creating the difficult Greek phrase *hodon poiein*. Oddly, later on we are told that the Greek translator was not only bilingual but also "well-informed about Aramaic" (p. 20). Casey's tendency not only to rewrite the text but also to call upon much later rabbinic material to fill in Mark's perceived silences—all this being justified by an appeal to the capacious rubric of "cultural assumptions"—vitiates a good part of his argument.

(2) An allied question touches on the precise nature and/or motive of the disciples' action in plucking the grain. Commentators who wish to explain the dispute in terms of the later rabbinic doctrine of overriding the sabbath in cases of danger to human life (*piqqûaḥ nepeš*) sometimes speak of the disciples' hunger, dire need, or even a danger to their lives; this point is missed in the otherwise perceptive analysis of Sariola, *Markus und das Gesetz*, 100–101. The striking point here is that Mark never speaks of the disciples' need or hunger. This is all the more curious since he does emphasize that David was in need and hungry (v 25). In effect, Mark fails to create a connection between disputed action and scriptural justification that could easily have been supplied. It is a questionable ploy to argue that Mark simply presupposes the disciples' need and hunger in v 23. Matthew apparently felt that the point could not simply be presupposed; he added a statement that the disciples were hungry (Matt 12:1), thus supplying a reason for their action. In explaining the disciples' action, Casey ("Culture and Historicity," 1–4) takes a somewhat different tack: the "poor disciples" (though never so designated in the Marcan story) are

supposedly taking advantage of the practice of Peah (the Hebrew noun *pē'â* means "side," "edge," or "corner"). Lev 19:9 orders farmers not to reap to the very edge of their fields; they were to leave the gleanings of the harvest in the fields so that the poor and the alien could gather sustenance from what was left behind. With admirable honesty, Casey admits the "we do not have direct empirical data to tell us exactly how Peah was left at the time of Jesus" (p. 2); he then proceeds to explain the perciope in terms of the rabbinic material dealing with Peah. Apart from the fact that this approach demands reading into the text a setting at harvest time, it conveniently ignores the clear statement of Mark that Jesus and his disciples were walking *through* the fields of grain (*dia tōn sporimōn*), not searching for leavings at some corner or border of the field. To be sure, they could have been using a pathway along a border of a field that contains gleanings; but, once again, Mark does not mention the very point that is vital to Casey's interpretation.

(3) The Matthean and Lucan versions of this dispute (Matt 12:1–8 ‖ Luke 6:1–5) contain a number of intriguing "minor agreements" over against the Marcan text. A number of exegetes suggest that Matthew and Luke had access to an alternate form of the story (whether from Q, stray oral tradition, or "Deutero-Mark"), thus raising the possibility of multiple attestation of sources. See, e.g., Aichinger, "Quellenkritische Untersuchung," 110–53; Back, *Jesus of Nazareth*, 69–75. However, along with a good number of commentators, I think that the minor agreements can be explained by a mixture of similar redactional concerns on the part of Matthew and Luke (e.g., the omission of Mark's troublesome *hodon poiein*, the omission of Mark 2:27 both to highlight the christological climax in 2:28 and to avoid the problem of the logical connection between Mark 2:27 and 2:28) and a certain amount of stylistic coincidence that is to be presupposed when two Christian authors, both with better Greek styles than Mark's, undertake a revision of this pericope some twenty or so years after Mark's Gospel was published. The appeal to stylistic coincidences does not appear so arbitrary when these coincidences are put alongside the many cases where Matthew and Luke, in their revisions of Mark, go their separate ways. For a brief survey of views and arguments that ultimately rejects the solution of a second source alongside Mark, see Doering, *Schabbat*, 408–9; Sariola, *Markus und das Gesetz*, 84–86; Mayer-Haas, *"Geschenk,"* 303–8, 440–42. For Doering's refutation of David Flusser's attempt to claim priority for the special source that Luke supposedly uses, see pp. 426–27.

[109] On the Galilean cycle of dispute stories, along with the larger question of pre-Marcan collections of pericopes, see the monograph-long treatments of Kuhn, *Ältere Sammlungen*; Kiilunen, *Vollmacht*; Joanna Dewey, *Marcan Public Debate* (SBLDS 48; Chico, CA: Scholars, 1980). Against the idea of a pre-Marcan collection is Sariola, *Markus und das Gesetz*, 94–97. On the Jerusalem cycle of dispute stories, see *A Marginal Jew*, 3. 412–16, as well as Chapter 36, Section II.A.

[110] For the sake of clarity, it needs to be emphasized that this scenario is the product of Mark's theological program; it is not to be taken, without detailed examination, as a historical record of what happened after Jesus' arrest.

[111] This is the fundamental and fatal flaw in the whole approach of Casey, "Culture and Historicity," 1–23; the Marcan text is never seriously dealt with as a literary whole and on its own terms. The same can be said of the otherwise careful presentation of Doering, *Schabbat*, 409–40.

[112] On this, see David Daube, "Responsibilities of Master and Disciples in the Gospels," *NTS* 19 (1972–73) 1–15. As Doering (*Schabbat*, 412–13) points out, the presence of this motif, while not proving that the story was created by the community, does not necessarily prove that the story comes from Jesus' ministry. This well-known motif could have been employed by the community in order to invoke Jesus' authority to justify its own stance vis-à-vis the sabbath.

[113] I stress the two "he"'s in my translation, despite the fact that the Greek verbs have no pronouns preceding them (the pronouns being understood in the two verb forms, *eschen* and *epeinasen*, both 3d person *singular* aorist active). I do this because many translations, for the sake of smoothness of style, bring the phrase "he and his disciples" forward and make it the subject of the two verbs. This has the unfortunate effect of transforming the singular verbs of the Greek text into plural forms in the English translation, thus obscuring the pattern of distinction-yet-connection (so the *NRSV* as opposed to the more literal *RSV*).

[114] The attempt by Marcus (*Mark 1–8*, 243–44) to see the pattern continued in vv 27–28 by switching from the pattern of Jesus/his disciples and David/those with him to "humanity" and "the Son of Man" is strained. Notice, among other things, how this demands a reversal of the order of leader–followers to the opposite and the expansion of the idea of follower or disciple to that of humanity in general (all of humanity does not follow the Son of Man).

[115] One must remember that, at this point, we are analyzing the Greek text as it stands. Whether or not the same Aramaic phrase *bar ('ĕ)nāš(ā')* ("son of man" in the sense of "human being" or "humanity") stands behind "man" in v 27 and "Son of Man" in v 28 is worth considering, though ultimately unknowable. However, such a possibility (creating once again a relation between the group and its leader) is not present in the Greek text as it stands, where the Greek word *anthrōpos* ("man" in the sense of "human being") in v 27 is quite different from *ho huios tou anthrōpou* ("Son of Man") in v 28, where, at least in Mark's redactional theology, it is clearly a christological designation. Even if we engage in speculation about ideas of "corporate personality" or "representative figure" connected with the designation Son of Man, such connotations of the phrase are hardly the same thing as explicit references in the text to Jesus and his disciples or David and those with him.

[116] See Pesch, *Markusevangelium*, 1. 179. The different forms used to refer to the sabbath (*tois sabbasin* in vv 23 + 24, *to sabbaton* and *tou sabbatou* in vv 27 + 28) are perhaps less probative (see Gundry, *Mark*, 143), though the distinction fits the general pattern already noted. Other possible indicators of the original unity of 2:23–26, when viewed in the larger context of Mark 2:1–3:6 are that (1) 2:23–26

alone, with its theme of eating, connects backward with the pericopes dealing with Jesus' eating with toll collectors and sinners (2:13–17) and his prohibition of fasting (2:18–22), while the theme of eating is lacking in 2:27–28; (2) 2:23–26 connects structurally both with 2:13–17 (there the disciples are asked to explain the surprising action of the teacher, here the teacher is asked to explain the surprising action of the disciples) and with 2:18–22 (in both pericopes, the teacher is asked to explain the surprising action of the disciples).

[117] For a brief and easy introduction to the texts of 1–2 Samuel found in Cave 4 at Qumran (referred to as 4QSam[a], 4Q Sam[b], and 4QSam[c]), see Martin Abegg, Jr., Peter Flint, and Eugene Ulrich, *The Dead Sea Scrolls Bible* (San Francisco: Harper, 1999) 212–15; the Qumran texts, with the Qumranic peculiarities highlighted, follow on pp. 215–59. For more detailed treatment of individual questions, see, for the fragments of 4QSam[a], Eugene Ulrich, *The Qumran Text of Samuel and Josephus* (HSM 19; Missoula, MT: Scholars, 1978); idem, "Josephus's Biblical Text for the Books of Samuel," *The Dead Sea Scrolls and the Origins of the Bible* (Grand Rapids, MI/Cambridge, UK: Eerdmans; Leiden: Brill, 1999) 184–201; for 4QSam[c], see idem, "4QSamuel[c]: A Fragmentary Manuscript of 2 Samuel 14–15 from the Scribe of the *Serek Hay-yaḥad* (1QS)," *BASOR* 235 (1979) 1–25 (with plates and transcriptions). For the *editio princeps* of the three Samuel scrolls, see *Qumran Cave 4. XII. 1–2 Samuel* (DJD 17; ed. Frank Moore Cross, Donald W. Parry, Richard J. Saley, and Eugene Ulrich; Oxford: Clarendon, 2005). Fragments of 1 Sam 21:1–9 (specifically, 1 Sam 21:1–3,5–7, and 8–10) are preserved in 4QSam[b] (Qumran manuscript siglum 4Q52), which unfortunately is very poorly preserved. As for the general textual character of 4QSam[b], there are a remarkably large number of cases (ninety instances) where the readings of the manuscript agree with the Old Greek (or Septuagint [LXX]) when the latter is superior to the Masoretic Text (MT). At the same time, 4QSam[b] agrees sixty-three times with the MT against the LXX when the MT is superior. The editor of the DJD edition (p. 223) also notes some fifteen unique readings in 4QSam[b] that are superior to both the LXX and the MT. The editor comments (p. 223) that "these are marks of a remarkably pristine textual witness." For the text of 1 Sam 21:1–3,5–7 in 4QSam[b] (contained in fragments 6 and 7 of 4Q52) and a philological commentary on it, see pp. 230–39 of the DJD volume; for 1 Sam 21:8–10, contained in fragment 8 of 4Q52, see pp. 239–40. The upshot of all this for my argument is that the Qumran text of 1 Sam 21:2–10, just like the text of the LXX and the MT, supplies no support for the peculiar argument made by the Marcan Jesus. As far as we can tell, the argument of the Marcan Jesus, despite its challenge ("Did you never read . . . ?"), has no basis in any written form of the David-and-the-showbread story circulating at the turn of the era.

[118] Guelich (*Mark 1–8:26*, 122) rightly emphasizes the absence of "those with him" in the narrative of 1 Sam 21 and its striking presence in the Marcan narrative.

[119] For likely candidates, see Mark 4:13 (cf. vv 2,11),21,24,26,30; 6:10; 7:9,20; 9:1 For further examples and literature on the subject, see Neirynck, "Jesus and the

Sabbath," 264 n. 137 (continuing on p. 265). Gundry's attempt (*Mark*, 142–43) to reject various examples of this Marcan technique rests more upon his general rejection of form, tradition, and redaction criticism in his exegesis of Mark (ibid., 18–24) than upon the evidence.

[120] The difference in function of *kai elegen autois* in 2:27 vis-à-vis the verbs of saying in vv 24–25 is missed by Guelich, *Mark 1–8:26*, 124. More perceptive is Pesch, *Markusevangelium*, 1. 179, 184.

[121] Neirynck ("Jesus and the Sabbath," 231) calls this "certainly the most common opinion." For a detailed consideration of the stages of the tradition history that comes to the same basic conclusion as the one I espouse, see Sariola, *Markus und das Gesetz*, 77–87. For a contrary view, namely, that the original tradition consists of 2:23–24,25a,27bc and that vv 25b–27a and v 28 are secondary additions, see Mayer-Haas, *"Geschenk,"* 172–76. While her case is carefully argued, her literary analysis fails to exploit a vital clue to the tradition history of the pericope: i.e., the pattern of distinction-yet-connection between leader and followers that tightly ties together vv 23–26 and that is missing in both v 27 and v 28.

[122] However, the text critic must also consider the possibility that the more difficult reading is simply the product of a scribal blunder.

[123] As tradition criticism and redaction criticism frequently demonstrate, secondary material is often placed at the very beginning or the very end of a unit of tradition since these are the two easiest places to make the addition. Gundry (*Mark*, 148) raises a further objection: If the argument from an OT incident was added secondarily, why didn't the later editor choose an OT passage that at least mentioned the sabbath?

[124] See Sanders's objections in his *Jewish Law*, 20–21; he speaks of "the general improbability of the story"; similarly, Sariola, *Markus und das Gesetz*, 84; Donahue and Harrington, *The Gospel of Mark*, 112. Referring to the story as a whole, Neirynck ("Jesus and the Sabbath," 262) remarks: "In the Marcan presentation, the incident of the plucking of corn gives the impression of being much more a theoretical case than a reminiscence of an actual event in the grainfields of Galilee."

[125] On this, see Marcus, *Mark 1–8*, 240.

[126] It is hypothetically possible that the incident originally took place in Judea and that Mark or his tradition has transferred it to Galilee. In the main text, though, I am engaging in a debate with critics who almost unanimously accept (explicitly or tacitly) the Galilean setting of the incident as the basis for discussion.

[127] A brief summary of all the changes the Marcan Jesus makes to the David incident in 1 Sam 21:2–10 can be found in Donahue and Harrington, *The Gospel of Mark*, 111.

[128] Contrary to what Casey intimates ("Culture and Historicity," 8–9), the 4QSam[b] fragments do not indicate that David's men are with him when he comes to the priest at Nob. Like the MT and the LXX, 4QSam[b] has the priest ask in startled fashion why no one is with David (1 Sam 21:2). David must reply with a lie about being on a mission from King Saul; the men he supposedly has agreed to meet in a certain place are apparently part of the lie.

[129] David Daube ("Precept and Example," *The New Testament and Rabbinic Judaism* [Peabody, MA: Hendrickson, 1956] 66–71) claims that there is an even more fundamental flaw in Jesus' argument: i.e., Jesus appeals to the behavior of a noted person in a narrative section of Scripture instead of to a legal precept enshrined in the Torah. Daube points out that, while the rabbis might use such narrative (haggadic) material to illustrate or corroborate halakic decisions, it could not be the primary source of such decisions. Hence, Daube concludes that Matthew wisely introduced a halakic argument into his version of the story: i.e., what the priests are allowed to do in the temple on the sabbath (Matt 12:5; note the introductory "Or have you not read *in the Law* that . . ."). While Daube's observations are valuable for understanding the rabbinic material, it is questionable whether such carefully articulated rules of legal reasoning were widely known and accepted in early 1st-century Palestinian Judaism. This problem of anachronism is also seen in Cohn-Sherbok, "An Analysis of Jesus' Arguments," 31–41.

[130] Nothing in pre-70 Jewish literature indicates that the story in 1 Sam 21:2–10 was thought to have occurred on the sabbath. As previously noted, most of the Hebrew text of 1 Sam 21:2–10 is preserved in fragments of a manuscript of 1–2 Samuel found at Qumran (4QSam[b] [= 4Q52], fragments 3–4, dated ca. 250 B.C.). While there are minor, LXX-like variations from what we find in the MT, the sabbath is not mentioned in either the Qumran fragments or in the LXX version of the story. Indeed, it may be that this story about the sanctuary at Nob implies that, before the Jerusalem temple was built, the bread of the presence was changed every day; this is how Jacob Milgrom (*Leviticus* [AYB 3, 3A, and 3B; 3 vols.; New York: Doubleday, 1991, 2000, 2001; reprint New Haven: Yale University Press] 3. 2098–99) understands MT 1 Sam 21:7 in conjunction with Exod 25:30.

Even when we come to the Mishna, *m. Menaḥ.* 11:1–9, which deals with the loaves of the presence, simply considers whether the actions of preparing, baking, and laying out the loaves override the sabbath; no connection is made with the narrative of David's action in 1 Sam 21:2–10. The same is true of the corresponding passage in *t. Menaḥ.* 11:1–18. The commentary on Lev 24:5–9 in the halakic midrash *Sifra* (Parashat Emor, Pereq 18) has just a brief comment on the phrase "every sabbath day" (Lev 24:8): "On the sabbath one sets forth the fresh bread, and on the sabbath one burns up the old." No reference is made to David or the incident at Nob. For an analytical translation of this passage set in the larger context, see Jacob Neusner, *Sifra. An Analytical Translation* (Brown Judaic Studies 138, 139, 140; 3 vols.; Atlanta: Scholars, 1988) 3. 279. In light of all this, one is at a loss to understand Casey's claim ("Culture and Historicity," 9) that the placement of the David incident on a sabbath was "a cultural assumption" that Jesus and the Pharisees would have shared in early 1st-century Palestine. His appeal to the *Yalqut Shim'oni* to substantiate his claim only shows the weakness of his argument; the author of the *Yalqut* lived sometime around the 13th century A.D. With an airy yet breathtaking wave of his hand, Casey informs us that "Jesus' argument belongs to the same cultural environment as the Yalqut, a cultural environment which in significant respects remained unchanged for more than a millennium." Ah, the wonders of *Kultur*.

Thus, one gets the impression that the connection between David's action and the sabbath is amoraic rather than tannaitic. Since the tractate *Menaḥot* lacks a Gemara in the Jerusalem Talmud, the Babylonian Talmud is the first normative legal text to make a connection between David's eating of the loaves and the sabbath. In *b. Menaḥ* 95b–96a, Rabbi Judah and Rabbi Simeon differ on whether the loaves of the presence should be baked on a weekday or on the sabbath. The story in 1 Sam 21:2–10 is brought up to justify each one's position. In what may be a concluding observation by the final redactor of the passage, David's action is defended on the basis of saving an endangered human life. Hence, even in the Talmud, the sabbath is not so much intrinsic to the story of David as such as rather an element read into the story by the two disputing rabbis as part of their argument over when and why the loaves of the presence should be considered sanctified. Interestingly, while the translation-*cum*-paraphrase of 1 Sam 21:2–10 in the *Targum Jonathan* seems at first glance to have an echo of the talmudic debate between Rabbi Judah and Rabbi Simeon, a closer reading suggests that the targum is simply expanding upon the literal sense of the Hebrew text. In particular, the targum gives no indication that David's action occurs on a sabbath. For the Aramaic text, translation, and commentary on this passage in the *Targum Jonathan* to the Books of Samuel, see Eveline van Staalduine-Sulman, *The Targum of Samuel* (Studies in the Aramaic Interpretation of Scripture 1; Leiden/Boston/Cologne: Brill, 2002) 412–17, esp. 413–15.

[131] This is rightly emphasized by Marcus, *Mark 1–8*, 244.

[132] This glaring omission is hardly explained by Casey's observation ("Culture and Historicity," 21) that the word "sabbath" is mentioned five times in six verses; even Casey feels that he must bolster this argument with another appeal to cultural assumptions.

[133] I emphasize "the Marcan Jesus" because both Matthew and Luke, apparently independently of each other, drop the phrase "when Abiathar was high priest" when they take over Mark's version of the story. The mistake about Abiathar cannot therefore be shrugged off as a minor slip that would disturb only pedantic modern critics. It disturbed Matthew and Luke enough to make both of them cut out the phrase. This is prime example of a minor agreement of Matthew and Luke against Mark that is occasioned by something offensive, troubling, or erroneous in Mark's text that would spontaneously lead a cultured editor to omit or rewrite the problematic material.

[134] There is some confusion about the relationship between Ahimelech and Abiathar in certain OT texts, but 1 Sam 21:2–10 is not among them. See 2 Sam 8:17 in the MT and the Syriac, as well as 1 Chr 18:16 in the MT as compared with the LXX, the Syriac, and the Vulgate. On all this, see Keith W. Whitelman, "Abiathar," *AYBD*, 1. 13.

[135] Perhaps the most contorted explanation is that of Gundry (*Mark*, 141–42), who tries to explain away the mistake by claiming that we have here a conscious substitution on Jesus' part. Jesus supposedly replaces Ahimelech with Abiathar to create a link with the house of God in Jerusalem. To support this gratuitous assertion, Gundry also avails himself of a more commonly used escape hatch: i.e., the claim that *epi* + the genitive in 2:26 refers not to "time when" or "time during" but to the section of 1 Samuel in which Abiathar appears (for such a construction, see Mark 12:26). This will not do in the case of Mark 2:26 because (1) Abiathar does not appear until 1 Sam 22:20 (and is not called "high priest" in this passage); and (2) if *epi* in Mark 2:26 carried the sense of indicating a section of 1 Samuel, it would have to be placed much closer to *anegnōte* ("Did you not read?") rather than twenty-one words and a number of clauses later. Gundry tries to bolster his case by pointing out that 2:26 would be the only verse in Mark that uses *epi* with a temporal sense. Even apart from the question of the idiosyncratic Greek of Mark, this is an odd objection, since the much longer Gospels of Matthew and Luke (Matthew has roughly 18,278 words, Luke 19,404, and Mark 11,229) use *epi* + a proper noun in the genitive to indicate "time when" or "time during" only one time (Matt 1:11) and two times (Luke 3:2; 4:27) respectively. Indeed, with the exception of Acts 11:28, this precise construction (*epi* + a proper noun in the genitive to express "time when" or "time during") appears nowhere else in the NT. In fact, one might argue that Matt 1:11, not Mark 2:26, is the unparalleled usage in the NT in that it refers to an event during which something happens ("at the time of the deportation to Babylon") rather than to the reign or tenure of a king, priest, or prophet, as is the case in Mark, Luke, and Acts. Thus, the rarity of the construction in Mark proves nothing. For a better treatment of the whole problem, see Guelich, *Mark 1–8:26*, 122. By this time, we are not surprised to learn that Casey ("Culture and Historicity," 8) solves the problem by rewriting Mark when he translates the Greek text back into the supposed Aramaic original. Just to be on the safe side, though, Casey also includes the argument that Abiathar was much more important than Ahimelech; Abiathar's presence "may reasonably be deduced from the narrative in 1 Samuel." Once again, one is forced to repeat the axiom: what is gratuitously asserted may be gratuitously denied. While not engaging in apologetic damage control, Sariola (*Markus and das Gesetz*, 100) prefers the meaning of "in the presence of" for *epi* because he thinks that this sense emphasizes the transgression narrated in the story: David takes the bread in the presence of (and presumably with the help of) the priest.

[136] In light of this, one is surprised to see Haenchen (*Der Weg Jesu*, 121) claiming that someone very knowledgeable of Scripture inserted vv 25–26 before v 27.

[137] This is the objection of Haenchen, *Der Weg Jesu*, 122; this objection has been repeated by many subsequent commentators. Doering (*Schabbat*, 412–13) ably rebuts it: the story aims at justifying not a particular practice (i.e., plucking grain on the sabbath) in which the Christian community typically engaged but rather, by way of an example, the general attitude and approach of the community toward the sabbath.

[138] Franciscan archaeologists point to a supposed "house of Peter," later turned into a church, at Capernaum as evidence for an ongoing Jewish-Christian presence; see the summary and caveats of Leslie J. Hoppe, *What Are They Saying about Biblical Archaeology?* (New York/Ramsey, NJ: Paulist, 1984) 71–78. Critical of the theory of an ongoing Jewish-Christian presence in Galilee from the 1st century A.D. to the time of Constantine is Richard A. Horsley, *Archaeology, History, and Society in Galilee* (Valley Forge, PA: Trinity, 1996) 107–14. For a cautious assessment of the evidence, see Seán Freyne, *Galilee from Alexander the Great to Hadrian 323 B.C.E. to 135 C.E.* (University of Notre Dame Center for the Study of Judaism and Christianity in Antiquity 5; Wilmington, DE: Glazier; Notre Dame, IN: University of Notre Dame, 1980) 344–91. On the question of Galilean Christianity, see also L. E. Elliott-Binns, *Galilean Christianity* (SBT 16; London: SCM, 1956); Howard Clark Kee, "Early Christianity in the Galilee: Reassessing the Evidence from the Gospels," *The Galilee in Late Antiquity* (ed. Lee I. Levine; New York/Jerusalem: Jewish Theological Seminary of America, 1992) 3–22; Anthony J. Saldarini, "The Gospel of Matthew and Jewish-Christian Conflict in the Galilee," ibid., 23–38; Albert I. Baumgarten, "Literary Evidence for Jewish Christianity in the Galilee," ibid., 39–73. Given our uncertainty, the confidence with which some scholars speak of the Q community or the Jesus movement active in Galilee in the post-Easter period leaves me puzzled.

[139] Another possibility is that the story reflects a debate about sabbath practice between two groups of Christian Jews, but such speculation remains just that: speculation. Neirynck ("Jesus and the Sabbath," 269) wisely emphasizes that, "apart from the Gospel tradition evidence is lacking about the Christian practice of keeping the Sabbath as well as about conflicts with the Jews or disputes within the community."

[140] Neirynck ("Jesus and the Sabbath," 232 n. 11) notes that the authenticity of 2:27 "is generally accepted by authors who, like Lohse, consider vv. 27–28 as independent sentences appended to the pericope"; see also pp. 242–44. For a list of authors who accept the authenticity of 2:27, see Doering, *Schabbat*, 414 nn. 91, 92, 93, and 94. However, Neirynck goes on to warn (pp. 253–54) that a review of the literature shows that there is no consensus regarding the content, literary connections, or origin of 2:27.

[141] See, e.g., the eunuch statement with its three-part parallelism (Matt 19:12; cf. *A Marginal Jew*, 1. 343–45), the antithetical parallelism in the statement about

John the Baptist and the least in the kingdom (Matt 11:11 par.; cf. *A Marginal Jew*, 2. 142–44) and in the comparison of John and Jesus (Matt 11:18–19 par.; cf. ibid, 147–54), the synonymous parallelism in the Lord's Prayer (Matt 6:10 par.; cf. ibid, 295–301), the parallelism in the first three Q beatitudes (Luke 6:20–21 par.; cf. ibid, 318–23), the antithetic parallelism and chiasm in Luke 17:20b + 21b (cf. ibid, 423–30), the synonymous and antithetical parallelism in the beatitude on eye-witnesses (Luke 10:23–24 par.; cf. ibid, 434–39), the antithetical parallelism and chiasm in the various sayings on saving and losing one's life (*A Marginal Jew*, 3. 55–64), the synonymous and antithetical parallelism in Jesus' promise to James and John (Mark 10:39 par.; cf. ibid, 216–20), the chiastic structure of Jesus' argument against the Sadducees (Mark 12:18–27 parr.; cf. ibid, 411–44), antithetical parallelism in Jesus' sayings on the rich (Mark 10:25,27 parr.; cf. ibid, 515), the synonymous and antithetical parallelism in the Q exhortation against anxiety (Matt 6:25–34 par.; cf. ibid., 517) and in the mammon saying (Matt 6:24 par.; cf. ibid, 517–18), the antithetical parallelism in the saying on the coin of tribute (Mark 12:17 parr.), and the antithetical and synonymous parallelism in the various sayings on divorce (Mark 10:9 par.; Luke 16:18; cf. Chapter 32 in this volume). Since we have already seen reasons why most of these sayings may be attributed to the historical Jesus, we are not trapped in the circular reasoning of Joachim Jeremias, who begins his treatment of the historical Jesus by listing such traits as antithetic parallelism as indications of authentic material (on this, see *A Marginal Jew*, 1. 179). Rather, we have first established the authenticity of these sayings on other grounds and then noticed the frequent appearance of short, memorable sayings marked by such rhetorical characteristics as antithetical parallelism and chiasm.

[142] Throughout the volumes of *A Marginal Jew*, I try as much as possible to use inclusive language. In the case of Mark 2:27, however, I keep the traditional translation of "man" for the Greek noun *anthrōpos* (more literally, "a human being") both to maintain the terse, compact nature of the single sentence and to leave open a possible link to Jesus as the Son of Man in v 28. The fact that the almost endless literature on the Son of Man regularly translates the Greek phrase *ho huios tou anthrōpou* as "the Son of Man" militates against my employing some alternate translation (e.g., "child of humanity"), which would only serve to confuse many readers. On another point of translation: while the traditional translation of the Greek preposition *dia* is "for," it should be noted that *dia* + the accusative in Koine Greek can carry the sense of both cause and purpose; cf. Doering, *Schabbat*, 416.

[143] For the Hebrew text, English translation, and critical notes, see Jacob Z. Lauterbach, *Mekilta de-Rabbi Ishmael* (3 vols.; Philadelphia: Jewish Publication Society of America, 1933, 1961) 198 (Hebrew text on lines 27–28), which is found in the Tractate *Shabbata*, chap. 1; the Hebrew text may also be found in the edition edited by H. S. Horovitz and I. A. Rabin, *Mekîlta' deRabbi Yišma'el* (2d ed.; Jerusalem: Shalem, 1997). The saying is repeated a little further on in the discussion; see p. 199, lines 43–44 of the Hebrew text of Lauterbach's edition. Curiously, Lauterbach obscures the antithetical parallelism of the saying by using a different word for the sec-

ond occurrence of the verb *māsar* ("hand over"): "The Sabbath is given to you but you are not *surrendered* to the Sabbath" [italics mine]. For a translation of this text that is placed within an analytically structured context, see Jacob Neusner, *Mekhilta According to Rabbi Ishmael. An Analytical Translation. Volume Two* (Brown Judaic Studies 154; Atlanta: Scholars, 1988) 254. The same saying is attributed to Rabbi Jonathan ben Joseph in *b. Yoma* 85b, with a slightly different wording of the Hebrew: *hy'* [in the context, the sabbath] *mswrh bydkem wl' 'tm mswrym bydh* ("it [the sabbath] is delivered into your hand, but you are not delivered into its hand"). The variation in attribution as well as the uncertain date of the *Mekhilta*'s final redaction (hypotheses stretch all the way from the second half of the 3d century to the 8th century) should make one wary of blithe assertions that a saying like that of Rabbi Simeon would have been well known and accepted around the time of Jesus. Simply from the viewpoint of datable compositions, the Marcan Jesus is the first Jew known to have uttered a statement like this about the sabbath.

Other, more distant parallels to this terse antithetical axiom in the *Mekilta* can be found in Jewish, Christian, and pagan literature around the turn of the era, but without mention of the sabbath. For example, a chronologically earlier Jewish parallel (early 2d century A.D.) can be found in *2 Apoc. Bar.* 14:18: "Man was not created for the world, but the world for man." Here it is the theme of creation that brings this saying into close proximity to Mark 2:27, though the context in the *Syriac Apocalypse of Baruch* goes on to point out that the principle it has just enunciated is now being contradicted by the perduring existence of the world while "we" (i.e., the Jews) are perishing. Similarity in form though not necessarily in content can be found in the still earlier statement of 2 Macc 5:19: "But the Lord did not choose the people because of the Place [i.e., the Jerusalem temple], but the Place because of the people [*all' ou dia ton topon to ethnos, alla dia to ethnos ton topon ho kyrios exelexato*]." Similar in form but opposite in meaning to Mark 2:27 is the saying attributed to Pausanias, king of Sparta (408–394 B.C.): "For the laws, he said, should be lords of men, not men of laws [*tous nomous ephē tōn andrōn, ou tous andras tōn nomōn kyrious einai dei*]." This saying is cited by Plutarch, *Moralia*, 2.230F. An antithetical principle that plays with creation theology but does not refer to the sabbath is enunciated by Paul in 1 Cor 11:8–9: "For man was not [created] from woman, but woman from man. For man was not created for the sake of woman, but woman for the sake of man."

[144] Neirynck ("Jesus and the Sabbath," 250) notes that Ernst Lohmeyer was the first major exegete to stress that the rabbinic saying "the sabbath is given to *you*" refers not to mankind in general but to the people of Israel in particular. Still, Casey ("Culture and Historicity," 15) is right to caution that not too much should be made of the use of "you" rather than "man" in Rabbi Simeon's saying. At least in its redactional setting in the *Mekilta*, Simeon's saying is commenting on the text of Exod 31:13–14, which commands the keeping of the sabbath because "it is holy *to you* [*qōdeš hî' lākem*]." However, since most scholars think the Simeon's saying originally circulated in the oral tradition as an independent unit, the question of the choice of "you" cannot be explained simply by appealing to the context in the *Mekilta*.

[145] So, for instance, in a saying almost immediately following upon the famous saying of Rabbi Simeon in the *Mekilta* on Exod 31:13–14. The text of Exod 31:13 ("For this is a sign between me and you") is explained by the addition "and not between me and the nations of the world [*wl' byny wbyn 'wmwt h'wlm*]." For the Hebrew text and translation, see Lauterbach, *Mekilta*, 3. 199.

[146] This key rabbinic idea of faithfully handing on the sacred teachings of Israel is perfectly reflected in the use of the adjective "Masoretic" to describe the standardized text of the Jewish Scriptures that was edited by rabbinic scholars during the first millennium A.D. Doering (*Schabbat*, 418 n. 118) raises the possibility that the verb *māsar* ("hand over," "deliver to") is meant to allude to the revelation of the Torah at Sinai, but admits that the allusion is not certain.

[147] The supposed parallels for this usage that Casey ("Culture and Historicity," 14) cites from Philo and the rabbis are not quite apropos since the texts speak of *anthrōpōn d' hekastos* ("each of men," i.e., "every man") or *kōl ādām* ("every man").

[148] The verb form *egeneto* (aorist indicative middle of the verb *ginomai*, "to become") is used to express the event of creation in a number of slightly different ways in LXX Gen 1:3–2:4: e.g., to signify the immediate result of God's creative command, as in 1:3 (*kai egeneto phōs*, "and light was made" or "and light came to be"); to state this result more succinctly with the adverb *houtōs*, as in 1:6 (*kai egeneto houtōs*, "and it was made thus" or "thus it was"); and to indicate the passing of each of the days of creation, as in 1:5 (*kai egento hespera kai egeneto prōi*, "and there came evening and there came morning"). The verb occurs again, after the blessing of the seventh day, by way of an *inclusio*, to sum up the whole creation of heaven and earth *hote egeneto* ("when they were made"). That the verb *egeneto* does not occur in the reference to the seventh day in Gen 2:1–3 is no objection to the allusion in Mark 2:27, for the noun "sabbath" likewise does not occur in Gen 2:1–3. Since the corresponding verb in the MT of Gen 1:3–2:4 is *hāyâ* ("to be," "to happen," "to become"), the Aramaic verb lying behind the Greek text of Mark 2:27 may well be *hăwâ*, with the same meaning. This seems likely because (1) various forms of *hăwâ* are used in the Aramaic translations of Genesis 1 found in the *Targums Onqelos*, *Pseudo-Jonathan*, and *Neofiti*; and (2) at times, when an Aramaic passage in the MT uses a form of *hăwâ*, the corresponding verb form employed to translate the same text in the LXX is a middle form of *ginomai* (so, e.g., Dan 2:28–29,35 [*egeneto*]). In light of all this, Doering (*Schabbat*, 414 n. 94, continuing on p. 415) is right to reject attempts to avoid a reference to creation in the *egeneto* of Mark 2:27; cf. Pesch, *Markusevangelium*, 1. 184.

[149] This is the interpretation of Doering, *Schabbat*, 418.

[150] As we saw in the previous chapter, in its present form, the *Streitgespräch* of Mark 10:2–9 is probably a Christian composition constructed from various traditions. However, the key aphorism of 10:9 is most likely authentic, and, in my opin-

ion, Mark 10:2–9 does represent the basic thrust of Jesus' thought on marriage and divorce.

[151] On this, see Doering, *Schabbat*, 415–16.

[152] Famous NT passages that link creation theology with christology include 1 Cor 8:6; Col 1:15–20; Heb 1:2–3,10–12; Rev 22:12–13; John 1:1–5.

[153] This is correctly seen by Doering, *Schabbat*, 417. More problematic is Doering's suggestion that the original *Sitz im Leben* of Mark 2:27 may be Jesus' healing activity on the sabbath. As I have shown, the dispute stories connected with Jesus' healing on the sabbath are fraught with difficulty.

[154] On dialectical negation, see Arnulf Kuschke, "Das Idiom der 'relativen Negation' im NT," *ZNW* 43 (1950–51) 263; Heinz Kruse, "Die 'dialektische Negation' als semitisches Idiom," *VT* 4 (1954) 385–400. On the subordination of the sabbath to the larger good of humanity, see Pesch, *Markusevangelium*, 1. 185–86. While such an idea is not expressed in precisely this way in the OT, the OT certainly provides precedents: e.g., the emphasis on the sabbath rest as beneficial not only to free Israelites but even to male and female slaves (Deut 5:14–15) and as a "delight" or "joy" (Isa 58:13). This theme is taken up in rabbinic Judaism and remains an emphasis in Jewish teaching down to this day. In Moloney's view (*Mark*, 69), v 27 affirms the superiority of humanity to the sabbath, "a line of thought already present within Judaism, but never so succinctly—or perhaps universally—stated as here." Be that as it may, the biblical background and rabbinic parallel in the *Mekilta* show that Mark 2:27 is not to be understood as anti-Jewish or anti-Torah; so, rightly, Doering, *Schabbat*, 416.

[155] So as not to leave the reader completely in the dark about my views on the Son of Man question, I list the following positions that I hold on the subject. They will all have to be examined at much greater length in a subsequent chapter: (1) Widespread multiple attestation of sources and forms as well as discontinuity with Judaism before Jesus and Christianity after him argues strongly for the view that the historical Jesus did speak of himself in the third person with the enigmatic phrase "the Son of Man" (in Aramaic, *bar [ĕ]nāšā'*). (2) There is no solid proof that before or right around the time of Jesus the Aramaic phrase *bar (ĕ)nāšā'* was used by a speaker to refer to himself via a third-person circumlocution. The regular meanings of the phrase in Aramaic (and of its equivalents in Hebrew) were "human being," "humanity," "someone," "anyone," and, in a negative sentence, "no one." (3) In particular, there is no proof that, prior to the time of Jesus, *bar (ĕ)nāšā'* was used as a set title or in a quasi-titular sense with precise content or meaning (especially that of an eschatological savior figure) attached to it. (4) It is often forgotten that the famous Aramaic passage in Dan 7:13–14 does not attach to the mysterious figure "coming with the clouds of heaven" the set title of "the Son of Man." Rather, the passage speaks descriptively with metaphors and images of "one like a son of man

[kĕbar ĕnāš, i.e., someone appearing in human form, as opposed to the destructive beasts that had preceded him] coming with the clouds of heaven." To be sure, Dan 7:13–14 seems to have sparked various streams of theological reflection and development in the Judaism(s) of the following centuries, but prior to the time of Jesus one cannot speak of a single figure (certainly not a historical human individual) endowed with the fixed designation or title "the Son of Man." (5) The fact that Jesus actually used the enigmatic self-description "the Son of Man" does not guarantee that every Son of Man saying in the Four Gospels comes from the historical Jesus. Some sayings do apparently come from him (e.g., Matt 11:18–19 par., on which see *A Marginal Jew*, 2. 147–52), while others are clearly redactional creations (e.g., Matthew's rewriting of Mark 8:27, into which he inserts "the Son of Man" to create Matt 16:13). Each saying must be judged on its own merits.

156 Rudolf Bultmann, *Theology of the New Testament* (2 vols.; London: SCM, 1952, 1955) 1. 30. Even scholars who would disagree with Bultmann's assessment of the Son of Man tradition in one or another aspect often use this three-part division as a useful pedagogical tool; see, e.g., A. J. B. Higgins, *The Son of Man in the Teaching of Jesus* (SNTSMS 39; Cambridge: Cambridge University, 1980) 2; Seyoon Kim, *The Son of Man as the Son of God* (Grand Rapids, MI: Eerdmans, 1983) 7; Joseph A. Fitzmyer, *A Christological Catechism* (rev. ed.; New York/Ramsey, NJ: Paulist, 1991) 107–8; Graham Stanton, *The Gospels and Jesus* (2d ed.; Oxford: Oxford University, 2002) 248. Douglas R. A. Hare (*The Son of Man Tradition* [Minneapolis: Fortress, 1990] 7–9), besides pointing out that the origins of the three-part division reach back to scholars before Bultmann (e.g., for a slightly different type of three-part division, see F. J. Foakes Jackson and Kirsopp Lake, *The Beginnings of Christianity. Part I. The Acts of the Apostles. Vol. I. Prolegomena I* [Grand Rapids, MI: Baker, 1979, originally 1920] 375–76), warns that an uncritical acceptance of this division carries certain dangers with it.

157 This saying actually bridges Jesus' present ministry and his future death, since "not to be served but to serve" (which is true even of his earthly ministry) is then developed further by a reference to the imminent future: "and to give his life as a ransom for many."

158 The auxiliary verb *mellō* can mean "to be about to" do something; but it can also indicate the certainty of the future action or the fact that the future action is destined to happen or must happen. At times, the auxiliary verb plus infinitive simply serves as a periphrastic form of the future tense. All these possibilities need to be considered in the case of the Son of Man passion predictions.

159 That the allegorical interpretation of the parable of the wheat and the weeds is a creation either of the M tradition or of Matthew himself is a commonplace among most critical commentators on Matthew today. Davies and Allison (*Matthew*, 2. 426–27) favor creation by Matthew himself: "It is generally agreed that Mt 13.36–43 is a free Matthean composition. The word statistics are decisive. . . . [This al-

legorical interpretation] shows so many signs of Matthew's hand that the quest to discover behind it something pre-Matthean seems hopeless." In this, they agree with the judgment of Joachim Jeremias, who, in his famous *The Parables of Jesus* (rev. ed.; London: SCM, 1963), supplies a detailed study of vocabulary and style in support of his position that the allegorical interpretation is the work of Matthew (pp. 81–85). On this question, see also Harrington, *Matthew*, 208 (Matthew probably composed the allegorical interpretation); Donald A. Hagner, *Matthew* (Word Biblical Commentary 33A and 33B; 2 vols.; Dallas: Word, 1993, 1995) 1. 392 (possibly Matthew's own creation).

[160] Even though the reference in this verse is to the final judgment, with its typically Matthean separation of the good and the evil, the very fact that people are gathered "*out* of his [the Son of Man's] kingdom" indicates that the Son of Man up until the day of judgment has exercised a rule over a kingdom connected with this present world. In contrast, the kingdom in which it is promised that the righteous "will shine like the sun" is said to be "the kingdom of their Father," apparently the eternal kingdom beyond this present world.

[161] Fitzmyer (*The Gospel According to Luke*, 2. 1164–69) thinks that the "enigmatic phrase, 'one of the days of the Son of Man' (v. 22), sounds like a Lucanism." He lists a number of ways in which the phrase has been taken, but he himself stresses the general thrust of the verse: the sudden and open character of the revelation of the Son of Man at the parousia. For a similar listing of possibilities, ending in a preference for a reference to the period inaugurated by the parousia, see Marshall, *Luke*, 657–59. Whatever the precise sense of the verse, in the overall redactional theology of Luke the saying makes some sort of a connection between the present state of the suffering church and the Son of Man.

[162] Luke Timothy Johnson (*The Gospel of Luke* [Sacra Pagina 3; Collegeville, MN: Liturgical Press, 1991] 359) sees in Luke's redaction of Mark 14:62 a shift from the last day to the history of the church. By omitting the phrase "coming on the clouds of heaven," Luke makes the statement refer not to the parousia of the Son of Man but rather to Jesus' resurrection. Fitzmyer (*The Gospel According to Luke*, 2. 1467) states that the phrase "from now on," which Luke has added to Mark's version of the saying, refers to the time of Jesus' departure from this world to the Father (by way of death, resurrection, and ascension), after which the period of the church begins. Marshall (*Luke*, 850) sees here an emphasis on the present exaltation of the Son of Man and notes a possible connection with the vision Stephen has in Acts 7:56. See also Hans Conzelmann, *The Theology of St Luke* (New York: Harper & Row, 1961; German original, 1953) 116.

[163] On this, see Gerhard Schneider, *Die Apostelgeschichte* (HTKNT 5; 2 vols.; Freiburg/Basel/Vienna: Herder, 1980, 1982) 1. 473–75; Joseph A. Fitzmyer, *The Acts of the Apostles* (AYB 31; New York: Doubleday, 1998; reprint New Haven: Yale University Press) 389–93; C. K. Barrett, *The Acts of the Apostles* (ICC; 2 vols.;

Edinburgh: Clark, 1994, 1998) 1. 384–85. One should distinguish this usage from that found in Rev 1:13 (cf. 14:14), where the risen Christ is described, in a Greek solecism, as *homoion huion anthrōpou*, "one like a son of man," which points back to the "generative" text of LXX Dan 7:13 (*hōs huios anthrōpou*).

[164] For presentations of Johannine theology from a variety of viewpoints, see Bultmann, *Theology of the New Testament*, 2. 3–92; C. H. Dodd, *The Interpretation of the Fourth Gospel* (Cambridge: Cambridge University, 1953) 133–285; Rudolf Schnackenburg, *The Gospel According to St John. Volume One* (New York: Herder and Herder; London: Burns & Oates, 1968, German original 1965) 153–72; idem, "Paulinische und johanneische Christologie. Ein Vergleich," *Das Johannesevangelium. IV Teil. Ergänzende Auslegungen und Exkurse* (HTKNT 4; Freiburg/Basel/Vienna: Herder, 1984) 102–18; idem, *Jesus in the Gospels* (Louisville: Westminster/John Knox, 1995, German original 1993) 219–94, 307–8; Brown, *The Gospel According to John* 1. cv–cxxviii; John Painter, *John: Witness and Theologian* (London: SPCK, 1975); idem, *The Quest for the Messiah* (Edinburgh: Clark, 1991); Marinus de Jonge, *Jesus: Stranger from Heaven and Son of God* (SBLSBS 11; Missoula, MT: Scholars, 1977); Jacob Jervell, *Jesus in the Gospel of John* (Minneapolis: Augsburg, 1984; Norwegian original, 1978); Udo Schnelle, *Antidocetic Christology in the Gospel of John* (Minneapolis: Fortress, 1989; German original, 1987); idem, "Die Tempelreinigung und die Christologie des Johannesevangeliums," *NTS* 42 (1996) 359–73; Marianne Meye Thompson, *The Humanity of Jesus in the Fourth Gospel* (Philadelphia: Fortress, 1988); M. Theobald, *Die Fleischwerdung des Logos: Studien zum Verhältnis des Johannesprologs zum Corpus des Evangeliums und zu 1 Joh* (NTAbh ns 20; Münster: Aschendorff, 1988); Daniel J. Harrington, *John's Thought and Theology: An Introduction* (Good News Studies 33; Wilmington, DE: Glazier, 1990); A. Stimpfle, *Blinde sehen: Die Eschatologie im traditionsgeschichtlichen Prozess des Johannesevangeliums* (BZNW 57; Berlin/New York: de Gruyter, 1990); John Ashton, *Understanding the Fourth Gospel* (Oxford: Clarendon, 1991); idem, *Studying John* (Oxford: Clarendon, 1994); Martin Scott, *Sophia and the Johannine Jesus* (JSNTSup 71; Sheffield: JSOT, 1992); D. Moody Smith, *The Theology of the Gospel of John* (Cambridge: Cambridge University, 1995); C. Hoegen-Rohls, *Der nachösterliche Johannes. Die Abschiedsreden als hermeneutischer Schlüssel zum vierten Evangelium* (WUNT 2/84; Tübingen: Mohr [Siebeck], 1996); P. N. Anderson, *The Christology of the Fourth Gospel. Its Unity and Disunity in the Light of John 6* (WUNT 2/78. Tübingen: Mohr [Siebeck], 1996); P.-M. Jerumanis, *Réaliser la communion avec Dieu: Croire, vivre et demeurer dans l'Evangile selon s. Jean* (EBib ns 32; Paris: Gabalda, 1996); J. Frey, *Die Johanneische Eschatologie. Band 1, Ihre Probleme im Spiegel der Forschung* (WUNT 96; Tübingen: Mohr [Siebeck], 1997); J. J. Kanagaraj, *'Mysticism' in the Gospel of John. An Inquiry into Its Background* (JSNTSup 158.; Sheffield: JSOT, 1998); Claus Westermann, *The Gospel of John in the Light of the Old Testament* (Peabody, MA: Hendrickson, 1998); A. J. Köstenberger, *The Missions of Jesus and the Disciples According to the Fourth Gospel* (Grand Rapids: Eerdmans, 1998); M. Labahn, *Jesus als Lebensspender. Untersuchungen zu einer Geschichte der johannei-*

schen Tradition anhand ihrer Wundergeschichten (BZNW 98; Berlin/New York: de Gruyter, 1998); *Offenbarung in Zeichen und Wort* (WUNT 2/117; Tübingen: Mohr [Siebeck], 2000); S. Hamid-Kham, *Revelation and Concealment of Christ* (WUNT 2/120; Tübingen: Mohr [Siebeck], 2000); H.-C. Kammler, *Christologie und Eschatologie* (WUNT 2/126; Tübingen: Mohr [Siebeck], 2000); Adele Reinhartz, *Befriending the Beloved Disciple* (New York/London: Continuum, 2001). Useful studies on the question of the Son of Man in John include Francis J. Moloney, *The Johannine Son of Man* (Biblioteca di Scienze Religiose 14; Rome: Libreria Ateneo Salesiano, 1976); M. Pamment, "The Son of Man in the Fourth Gospel," *JTS* 36 (1985) 56–66; Delbert Burkett, *The Son of the Man in the Gospel of John* (JSNTSup 56; Sheffield: JSOT, 1991). For Moloney's more recent thoughts on Son of Man in John, see Francis J. Moloney, "Raymond Brown's New *Introduction to the Gospel of John*: A Presentation—and Some Questions," *CBQ* 65 (2003) 1–21, esp. 8–10. For a thumbnail sketch of Johannine theology (geared to a consideration of the love commandments), see Section V.A in Chapter 36.

[165] On this whole question, see Wilhelm Thüsing, *Die Erhöhung und Verherrlichung Jesu im Johannesevangelium* (NTAbh 21; 3d ed.; Münster: Aschendorff, 1979); Godfrey C. Nicholson, *Death as Departure. The Johannine Descent-Ascent Schema* (SBLDS 63; Chico, CA: Scholars, 1983).

[166] The oldest and best Greek manuscripts (papyrus 66, papyrus 75, Sinaiticus, Vaticanus, Bezae, Washingtonensis) as well as the rule of *lectio difficilior potior* (why would a Christian scribe substitute "Son of Man" for an original "Son of God" in a formal confession of faith in Jesus?) all argue convincingly for "the Son of Man" rather than "the Son of God" being the original reading in John 9:35. Bruce M. Metzger, (*TCGNT* [2d ed.], 194) considers the reading "the Son of Man" to be "virtually certain."

[167] On this interpretation of John 1:51 as well as other possible interpretations, see Brown, *The Gospel According to John*, 1. 88–91; Moloney, *The Johannine Son of Man*, 23–41; Burkett, *The Son of Man*, 112–19.

[168] This remains true whether or not the eucharistic part (John 6:51–58) of the Bread of Life discourse comes from the evangelist or the final redactor. Either way, the belief and practice of the Johannine community are reflected here in the final form of the Gospel.

[169] For convenience' sake, I use the word "church" in reference to the Johannine as well as the Matthean and Lucan communities, even though, within the Fourth Gospel and the three Johannine Epistles, the word "church" (*ekklēsia*) occurs only in 3 John (vv 6,9, and 10). On this point, see John P. Meier, "The Absence and Presence of the Church in John's Gospel," *Mid-Stream* 41/4 (2002) 27–34.

[170] The unusual (perhaps to some tastes contorted) order of Mark 2:28 is "corrected" by Matthew and Luke, who, independently of each other, both move "of the

sabbath" forward so that it follows after the verb *estin*, thus leaving the subject "the Son of Man" at the end of the sentence. This is a prime example of a "minor agreement" of Matthew and Luke against Mark arising not from some alternate source but rather from the natural, spontaneous reaction of two refined writers of Greek when faced with an unusual, and, perhaps to them, awkward construction in Mark. Mark's placement of *tou sabbatou* at the end of v 28 may have been motivated in part by an attempt to tie up the loose ends of a not especially compact and logical pericope. The words *tou sabbatou* at the end of v 28 (and hence at the end of the whole pericope) create both an *inclusio* with the beginning of the story (*en tois sabbasin* in v 23) and a parallel with v 27, which ends with the words *to sabbaton*.

[171] For the sake of lining up the Greek words with their English equivalents, I reorder the Greek text of Mark 2:28. My English translation obscures the parallel slightly because the definite article with *zōēs* ("life") in John 6:35 cannot be literally represented in English. It should also be noted that a definite article might have preceded *kyrios* in Mark 2:28 if the predicate nominative had not been thrown before the copulative verb *estin* for rhetorical emphasis. When the predicate nominative is so anticipated at the beginning of the sentence before the subject and the verb, it is necessary in Greek to make clear which noun is the predicate nominative by omitting the definite article before it, while retaining the definite article for the subject. The most famous case of this construction is John 1:1c: *kai theos ēn ho logos* ("and the Word was God"); the omission of the definite article before *theos* blocks the otherwise natural translation "and God was the Word." Thus, contrary to what many commentators claim, the omission of the definite article *ho* before *theos* in 1:1c is for grammatical, not theological, reasons—as is clear from Thomas' address to Jesus in John 20:28: *ho kyrios mou kai ho theos mou* "my Lord and my God").

[172] For *kyrios* in Mark, see Sariola, *Markus und das Gesetz*, 103–4.

[173] Commentators argue over whether the *kai* in 2:28 should be translated "even" or "also." Whatever the precise nuance, there is almost certainly a reference backward to 2:10 and hence the trace of a redactional hand. Doering (*Schabbat*, 421) objects that the reference backward is not completely certain; true (what is completely certain in NT exegesis?), but the reference backward is the most natural sense of *kai* in the present Marcan context; see Gundry, *Mark*, 144. In contrast to Doering, Sariola (*Markus und das Gesetz*, 80–81) argues strongly for a reference backward, especially to 2:10. He points out that 2:10 and 2:28 are parallel in both content and literary structure; in each verse, the first two words proclaim the basic fact of Jesus' authority ("has authority," "is lord"), the next four words state the title under which Jesus claims this authority ("the Son of Man"), and the last two or three words (the *kai* of v 28 consciously pointing back to v 10) specify the area in which this power is being exercised in each incident ("to forgive sins," "of the sabbath"):

2:10: exousian echei	*ho huios tou anthrōpou*	*aphienai hamartias*
2:28: kyrios estin	*ho huios tou anthrōpou*	*kai tou sabbatou*

Pesch's suggestion (*Markusevangelium*, 1. 185–86) that the *kai* means that humanity is lord not only of all the things created during the first six days of creation in

Genesis 1 but also of the sabbath (the seventh day mentioned in Gen 2:1–3) rests upon the dubious opinion that *ho huios tou anthrōpou* in Mark 2:28 reflects the generic *bar ʾĕnāšāʾ* ("son of man" in the sense of "humanity," "human being"). I indicate below why I think this position is unlikely.

[174] Since Sariola rejects the theory of a pre-Marcan collection, he argues strongly for the creation of 2:28 by Mark himself (*Markus und das Gesetz*, 81–82). As Tuckett points out ("The Present Son of Man," 58–81), 2:28 takes on a darker tone within the overarching context of Mark's Gospel: the Son of Man is the one who is to suffer because his rightly asserted authority is rejected.

[175] Donahue and Harrington (*The Gospel of Mark*, 112) hold that v 28 as a result clause does not follow simply from v 27 but rather "sums up the theology of the whole pericope." Doering (*Schabbat*, 422–24) tries to find a logical connection between v 27 and v 28 by suggesting that behind *ho anthrōpos* in v 27 stands the Aramaic *ʾĕnāšāʾ* ("man" in the generic sense) and behind *ho huios tou anthrōpou* in v 28 stands *bar ʾĕnāšʾā* ("man" in the individual sense, i.e., "the individual man"). To find a logical connection, though, Doering must greatly weaken the obviously strong, not to say shocking, assertion that "the individual man is lord of the sabbath." It has to be watered down to affirm simply a human being's precedence over the institution of the sabbath. Granted this weakened sense, Doering feels that he can attribute 2:27–28 to the historical Jesus.

[176] In light of my hypothesis of the three-stage growth of the dispute story in 2:23–28, I think it is a red herring to introduce a supposed link between v 27 and v 28 on the basis of a theoretical Aramaic original. In one popular version of this theory, v 27 originally stated in the Aramaic that "the sabbath was made for the son of man [i.e., human beings in general], not the son of man for the sabbath." Verse 28 then logically continued: "*Therefore* the son of man is lord even of the sabbath." Thus, in the original Aramaic, there was a linguistic and logical connection between v 27 and v 28, though the subsequent translation into Greek obscured this link by translating "son of man" as "man" in v 27. Interestingly, this supposed original link in Aramaic is understood in different ways by different commentators. Some understand "son of man" as generic in both cases: because the sabbath was made for human beings, human beings are the lords of the sabbath. Whether either Jews or Christian Jews would affirm what sounds like an invitation to do-as-you-please antinomianism is doubtful. Other commentators understand "son of man" in v 28 of Jesus as the archetypal or representative human being—or, alternately, the representative embodiment of the true Israel—with "son of man" in v 27 understood as meaning humanity in general or the faithful people of God (with a side glance at one possible interpretation of Dan 7:13–14). (Interestingly, T. W. Manson has espoused both views at different times; compare his opinion in *The Teaching of Jesus*, 214, with that in "Mark ii. 27f.," 138–46. On the various forms of these theories and their proponents, see Doering, *Schabbat*, 420–21.) There are a number of difficulties with this whole line of interpretation. (1) While Mark 3:28 supplies

an example of the use of "sons of men" (in the plural: *tois huiois tōn anthrōpōn*) to refer to human beings in general, there is no clear case anywhere in the Four Gospels where a saying of Jesus uses "the son of man" in the singular (*ho huios tou anthrōpou*) to refer to anyone but himself. (2) Another difficulty under which most of these theories labor is that they must presuppose, without any proof, that behind "man" (*anthrōpos*) in v 27 there lies not one Aramaic word meaning "man" (of which there are several: *ĕnāš, gĕbar*, and *'ădam* [cf. the use of *kwl bny 'dm*, "all the sons of Adam" or "all the sons of man" in the Aramaic text 4Q544, fragment 1, line 12]), but rather the phrase "son of man." That is something we simply cannot know. (3) Finally, if I am correct that v 28 is a creation of Mark (or a pre-Marcan redactor collecting dispute stories already extant in Greek), then the question of a hidden connection between the Aramaic forms of v 27 and v 28 is moot since v 28 was composed in Greek from the start.

[177] For a similar evaluation of the approach of the historical Jesus, see Mayer-Haas (*"Geschenk,"* 680), who speaks of Jesus' interpretation of the sabbath commandment as "liberal and determined by practical considerations," and hence not sharing in the rigorism of some of the special groups within Palestinian Judaism (e.g., the Qumranites).

CHAPTER 35

JESUS AND PURITY LAWS

After the problems of divorce, oaths, and sabbath, perhaps the most difficult question concerning Jesus and the Law is the topic of Jewish purity rules.[1] The topic is daunting because it involves not just one bundle of problems but several:

(1) The origin, meaning, and actual practice of Jewish purity rules constitute a subject of lively debate among present-day scholars, both Jewish and Christian, with the same scholar sometimes changing his or her mind over a period of time.[2]

(2) The most important Gospel text that enunciates Jesus' attitude toward purity rules is Mark 7:1–23, which combines within one sprawling pericope the disparate questions of handwashing before meals, the practice of *qorbān* (dedicating a gift to God), and the Jewish food laws (e.g., the prohibition of eating pork). The meaning of this Marcan pericope as it stands, the meaning of its various subunits in the pre-Marcan tradition, and the possible origin of any or all of these subunits in the teaching of the historical Jesus continue to be debated by NT exegetes.

(3) To round out any survey of Jesus' attitude to purity rules, one should include other scattered sayings and actions of Jesus that touch on matters of purity: (a) various woes, contained in the Q tradition, that present Jesus rebuking Pharisees and other groups for their inconsistent opinions and practices; (b) narratives in which Jesus touches a corpse or a leper or is touched by a woman with a flow of blood (Mark 5:25–34 parr.).[3]

Clearly this material is vast; these topics have taken up whole books. The danger here is that we might become so overwhelmed by data and fascinated by detail that no conclusion is ever reached. Indeed, this chapter could easily mutate into a full-scale monograph on Jewish purity laws without ever getting to the historical Jesus. Hence, we must keep a disciplined eye on the focus of this chapter: What can we know about the historical Jesus' teaching on purity rules? Everything else must be subordinated to that question.

I. PURITY LAWS IN THE PENTATEUCH AND BEYOND

What exactly comes under the rubric of "purity laws" in the Pentateuch is itself debatable. For the sake of cutting the Gordian knot, I consider purity laws those laws in the Pentateuch that qualify certain actions, states of being, persons, or things as *ṭāhôr* ("clean," "pure") or *ṭāmē᾽* ("unclean," "impure").[4] While some scholars are more restrictive in their translation of these two Hebrew words into English, I use "clean"or "pure" interchangeably to translate *ṭāhôr*; likewise, I use "unclean" or "impure" interchangeably to translate *ṭāmē᾽*.[5] In addition to these key terms, a fiercely negative judgment about certain actions or their results in the realm of purity is expressed with the vocabulary of *tô῾ēbâ* and *šeqeṣ* ("abomination").

It is extremely difficult for the modern Western mind to grasp what "impurity" or "uncleanness" meant for the ancient Israelite, especially in the area of "cultic" or "ritual" impurity. To begin with, we should note that *ṭāhôr* ("clean," "pure") and *ṭāmē᾽* ("unclean," "impure") are not generally used to designate physical cleanness or dirt as we would understand these words. Second, it would be incorrect to think of "uncleanness" or "impurity" as mere metaphors when the OT applies these terms to grave moral evil such as murder. Moral impurity in cases such as murder, incest, and idolatry was quite real and had very real effects as far as the ancient Israelite was concerned.[6]

In making this point, I have touched upon a still greater problem in dealing with impurity in the Pentateuch.[7] We moderns automatically distinguish various types of impurity in OT texts and then stick different labels on them (e.g., "ritual," "moral"). In using such labels, are we doing violence to the unity—or the purposeful vagueness—of the OT view of impurity? Admittedly, in dealing with impurity in the OT, there is a danger of imposing Cartesian "clear and distinct ideas" on realities that readily "bleed into" one another—as well as a danger of importing labels and categories that the OT never uses. Yet, as a number of present-day Jewish scholars have pointed out, the distinctions we moderns make are not entirely arbitrary. One can discern in the OT texts themselves differences in the types of impurity that are discussed. Different categories can be legitimately constructed according to the different types of action (or states of being) that create or constitute the impurity and the different ways in which the impurity is removed or dealt with. While a certain arbitrariness in both categories and labels cannot be completely avoided, in my opinion the OT texts do justify distinguishing between ritual impurity, moral impurity, and (later on) genealogical impurity, with the laws of prohibited foods constituting a special case.[8] To borrow a distinction from medieval philosophy: these categories exist formally in our modern minds, but they have a firm foundation in the reality of the ancient texts.

(1) The first type of impurity to be examined, and perhaps the one most difficult for the modern mind to understand, is what I call *ritual impurity*. One must stress from the start that ritual impurity, in itself, is neither sinful nor evil. On the contrary, ritual impurity refers to a usually temporary condition resulting from the normal cycle of human life: birth, disease, sexual activity, and death.[9] Giving birth, having sex, emitting various bodily fluids connected with sex (notably menstrual blood), and coming into contact with the body of a deceased relative in preparation for burial are all natural—yes, even necessary and unavoidable—activities or processes for any human being living in society.[10] This was all the more true in the ancient world, where modern professionals like doctors and funeral directors did not intervene in these processes in such a way as to keep spouses or close relatives at a distance.

According to the creation faith of the OT—a basically optimistic faith mirrored in Genesis 1—these physical activities and processes flowed from the creative hand of God, who made all things "very good" (Gen 1:31). There was nothing morally evil or sinful about these processes, if they were handled properly. However, these key activities of human existence involve major transitions from one human condition to another. They betoken a certain crossing of a threshold (hence the designation "liminal" experiences) and often unleash mysterious and powerful fluids connected with the conferral or diminution of life.[11]

Hence, in a symbolic universe, these energy-charged "liminal" activities need to be cordoned off from direct contact with the realm of the divine, the sacred, the holy, the "other." That is, they have to be kept separate from the realm of the life-giving God, who is himself the fullness of life, a life that does not undergo birth, change, sexual activity, diminution, or death. "Flesh" (in the Hebrew, *bāśār*, weak, limited, mortal human existence) is the opposite of "holy spirit" (*rûaḥ haqqôdeš*, the life-and-power-forever that is proper to God alone). Holiness, in all its fullness, belongs to God and no one else. In this sense, one might define holiness as the very "God-ness" of God.[12] Created beings can at best participate in God's holiness in varying degrees, depending on how closely they approach God in the ritual worship of the temple and in obedient living of the covenant.[13]

Hence, God's holiness, this essential quality of God *as* God, makes a basic demand: all that stands at the opposite end of the spectrum from God's life-and-power-forever (i.e., all that typifies the weakness and mortality of humans) must be kept separate from the divine. The processes and states that make flesh flesh—birth, sex, death—must not come into direct contact with the holy God and the realm that the holy God inhabits, most notably the holy space that is God's temple.[14] Separation is the concrete, visible expression of the inviolable holiness of God. Indeed, some scholars have maintained that the original etymology of the Hebrew verb *qādaš* ("to be holy," "to be consecrated," "to be dedicated") was "to be set apart," "to be separated," though this view is largely abandoned today. While separation is part of the complex of ideas involved in holiness, one must remember that, in temple worship and in Israelite religion in general, "to make holy" (*qiddaš*, the Piel form of the verb) meant separation *from* the ordinary world precisely in order to belong *to* God and his service. The ultimate purpose of all consecration was thus positive, though it did involve separation, spatial and/or moral, as a necessary component.

To breach this God-ordained separation between flesh in an unclean state and the holiness of God would be as dangerous to the ancient mind as mixing unstable, explosive chemicals or removing shields from around a nuclear reactor would be to a modern mind. The chemicals and the nuclear reactions are in themselves good, even useful, when properly handled—just like the processes of birth, sex, and death. But a lack of proper separation, a failure to cordon off things meant to be kept separate, could have disastrous results. It was precisely to protect his people and prevent such disasters, and not because natural biological processes are evil, that the God of Israel commanded that his realm of the holy, especially his temple, be kept separate from the realm of human birth, sexual activity, and death.[15]

It is this protective system of separate spaces that the laws of ritual purity created and maintained. In this protective system, the extreme opposites were impurity (e.g., a person directly in contact with a corpse) and the holy presence of God in his temple. The person "contaminated" ritually by a corpse had to pass through a process (a liminal experience) that would lead him from his impure state to that pure state that would allow him in turn to approach the holy, for example, to enter the temple or to handle sacred things like sacrificial food.[16] The process usually involved various combinations of immersing oneself in water, washing one's clothes, and waiting until sunset before approaching the holy. In more serious cases, sacrifices or other ritual actions were required.

This type of impurity, while not sinful or evil, was thought to be highly contagious.[17] It could easily be transmitted from one ritually impure person to another, most often by physical contact. Hence, great care was ordinarily taken to avoid touching, for example, a corpse or a person preparing a corpse for burial. Yet this very example makes clear that there were times and circumstances when incurring ritual impurity by such contact was necessary and indeed positively good (in a moral sense). A prime example was the preparation of the corpse of a close relative for burial. It would be shameful and sinful to neglect such an obligation, an obligation that was deeply felt throughout the Mediterranean world. Another obvious example would be the sexual activity of a husband and wife and the subsequent childbearing of the wife. Procreation had received the primordial blessing of God at creation (Gen 1:28). It was a duty incumbent on married couples, and to refuse to fulfill this duty would be a serious sin. Yet the very fulfillment of God's own command, "Be fertile and multiply" (Gen 1:28), involved one in temporary ritual impurity. Moral evil in such a situation would be brought about not by sex or childbirth but rather by consciously and willfully refusing to undergo the rites of purification or by entering God's temple or handling sacred things before ritual purification had been completed.

From these examples, it is clear that ritual impurity in itself had nothing to do with moral evil or, for that matter, with physical uncleanness. A person who was totally clean in a physical sense might contract ritual uncleanness by entering a room in which a corpse was laid out; such a person could regain ritual cleanness by a ritual that included immersing in a pool of water, even if such a pool happened to be unclean from our modern, hygienic point of view.[18]

(2) *Moral impurity* is quite a different matter, despite the use of the same vocabulary of "clean" (*ṭāhôr*) and "unclean" (*ṭāmēʾ*). Within the law codes of Leviticus and Deuteronomy, the vocabulary of clean and unclean is used for certain heinous sins: murder, serious sexual sins (such as incest, homosexuality, and bestiality), and idolatry. So horrendous are these actions in the eyes of Israelites that they are called "abominations" (*tôʿēbôt*).[19] The moral uncleanness arising from these actions is strikingly different from ritual uncleanness in regard to both cause and effect. In cases of moral impurity, the action that causes the impurity is by no means part of a necessary, unavoidable, or natural cycle of events in human life. Rather, moral impurity is the result of conscious sinful actions involving major breaches of the moral law—that is, willful, high-handed rebellion against God's will for his people as expressed in the Torah.

Interestingly, in cases of moral impurity, it is not just the perpetrator who contracts uncleanness.[20] In addition to his or her own personal defilement, his or her immoral action renders the land of Israel (Lev 18:25) and/or the temple of Yahweh (Lev 20:3) impure or defiled.[21] Another striking difference from ritual impurity is that the sinner, while morally impure, cannot transfer this kind of impurity to another person who happens to touch him. Moral impurity is thus not "contagious" in the way ritual impurity is.[22] Neither can moral impurity be dealt with and removed by the relatively simple mechanism of immersion-plus-sunset. Rather, the defilement of the land and/or temple, if not properly removed, will ultimately cause the people of Israel to be exiled from their land and Yahweh to forsake his temple. The only ways in which moral impurity can be properly handled are (1) for the perpetrator to be "cut off" from the people of God (whether by execution, banishment, or premature death without offspring to carry on one's line) and (2) for the impurity to be purged from the temple by the proper ritual (most notably, by the atoning sacrifices par excellence of Yom Kippur).[23] Needless to say, the best way to deal with moral impurity would be to avoid all such immoral activity from the start. Here again, we see a fundamental difference from ritual impurity, which often cannot be avoided (e.g., in matters of birth, sexual activity, menstruation, and death).[24]

(3) A third type of impurity is not enshrined in the written Torah of Moses (i.e., the Pentateuch) and so is not regulated by the laws of the Pentateuch as such. This new type of impurity, *genealogical impurity*, appeared on the Palestinian scene after the Babylonian exile (6th century B.C.), around the time of Ezra and Nehemiah (5th–4th centuries B.C.).[25] For the first time in Israel's history, intermarriage with Gentiles was forbidden (in the opinion of the stringent supporters of Ezra) not only to priests but also to all Israelites. All Israel was declared to be "holy seed" (Ezra 9:2) that was not to be defiled by admixture of Gentile seed in marriage. This innovation became a topic of hot debate among Jews throughout the intertestamental and rabbinic periods. The highly restrictive view of the Book of Ezra was carried forward by sectarian writings like *Jubilees* and the so-called Halakic Letter (4QMMT), which applied the vocabulary of profanation and defilement to intermarriage between nonpriestly Jews and Gentiles (even when the Gentiles converted to Judaism). In contrast, Philo, Josephus, and many other authors from the late Second Temple period did not extend the requirement of genealogical purity to lay Israelites.[26]

(4) An attentive reader who is acquainted with the laws of the Pentateuch will have noticed by now that one kind of purity law is not covered by the neat three-part division of ritual, moral, and genealogical purity. The "odd man out" is surprisingly *the list of prohibited foods*—or, more properly, the list of animals prohibited for use as food—found in Leviticus and Deuteronomy.[27] While these "food laws" or "dietary laws" are sometimes referred to vaguely as laws of ritual purity, they stand apart from the laws of ritual purity that treat of birth, sex, and death. All these activities are natural

experiences or conditions that any ordinary person will have to undergo or come into contact with on a regular basis during the course of his or her life. The ritual purity rules regulate how one is to act during these liminal experiences of impurity due to birth, sex, or death and how one is then to regain one's state of ritual purity.

The food laws function quite differently.[28] Rather than regulating when and how one might eat pork (to take a famous example), the food laws totally forbid such activity as an abomination (tô'ēbâ).[29] The vocabulary of "abomination" and the total prohibition of the action of eating, which involves a free choice rather than a natural, unavoidable physical process, would seem to push the dietary laws in the direction of moral impurity. In other words, instead of regulating activities that necessarily or regularly make a person ritually impure in the natural flow of human life, the food laws simply block off a type of activity as abominable—not unlike the prohibition of idolatry, murder, and incest. Hence, violations of the dietary laws may seem at first glance to belong under the rubric of moral impurity.

Yet there are differences. For example, it is never explicitly said that eating forbidden foods defiles the sanctuary. More remarkably, so unthinkable is it that an Israelite should actually eat forbidden food such as pork that the food laws never prescribe either precise punishment for such a transgression or a way of regaining one's status as a ritually or morally clean Israelite after transgressing the food laws.[30] Such a ghastly action is apparently not considered a practical possibility. The food laws presume that the prohibitions will be observed, and so no remedy (whether undergoing immersion, offering a sacrifice, or being cut off) is provided. In the end, it is perhaps better to admit that the dietary laws form a legal corpus unto themselves, floating somewhere in between ritual and moral purity. The food laws are a salutary reminder that, while the basic distinctions sketched earlier have a solid basis in the OT text, there is some overlapping.

Not surprisingly, the laws of ritual, moral, and genealogical impurity, as well as the laws of forbidden foods, have offered the social sciences fertile ground for research and hypotheses. Anthropologists, sociologists, and psychologists have all suggested theories about the origins and functions of these laws. At various times, all or some of these laws have been explained as forms of primitive hygiene, as expressions of instinctive loathing or disgust, as ways of warding off the threatening power of demons and death, as strategies for overcoming the chaos of human experience by mapping out distinct areas of life that are not to be confused or meshed, as reflections of which animals may or may not be used for sacrifice because of the practices of Israel's Gentile neighbors, as mechanisms for controlling and ordering the body politic by controlling and ordering the individual bodies of the members of a given society, as ways of disciplining human appetite, or (especially in the case of prohibited foods) as expressions of reverence for life and therefore for animals that possess life, life being the supreme gift of the gracious Creator who made all things good in the beginning.[31] One suspects that many of these theories may contain some grain of truth in regard to at least some of the purity laws. However, granted the bewildering complexity of the various types of purity in the OT, it is doubtful that any one hypothesis or model can explain the whole range of purity laws.[32]

This is not to say that one should not try. Some of the theories proposed by social scientists have provided exegetes of both the OT and the NT with intriguing starting points for their own attempts at the sociological or cross-cultural exegesis of biblical texts. Still, as with most exegetical endeavors, modesty and restraint are advisable, lest one wind up building castles on shifting sands. For example, over decades of research and writing, the distinguished anthropologist Mary Douglas significantly changed her views on the meaning and function of the foods laws in Leviticus. Exegetes who built their social-science interpretations of biblical texts on her earlier, now abandoned theories, may feel themselves left high and dry. This does not prove, of course, that such endeavors are wrongheaded or deserve to be ignored. Rather, it is simply a reminder of the difficulty that attends the project of sociological or anthropological exegesis of the Bible—in itself, a worthwhile and challenging project.

As I indicated at the beginning of Volume One of *A Marginal Jew*, the goal of my own project is quite limited and does not seek to engage in formal sociological exegesis. Keeping to a "low level" of interpretation, I attempt to establish, as best one can, what Jesus of Nazareth actually said and did during his public ministry and how his words and deeds would have been understood by his fellow Jews in 1st-century Palestine. Obviously, such Jews knew nothing of sociological models. Why did they observe the purity laws? On the simplest, commonsense level, they observed these laws because they were brought up in Jewish families and villages that observed these laws as a matter of course. From their early youth, before they could have asked any theoretical questions or undertaken any formal study (which the vast majority never had an opportunity to do), observance of the purity laws was the given reality, the meaningful ordered world in which they were reared and in which they were taught, more by example than by detailed instruction, to relate to other Israelites and to Israel's God.

(By way of comparison, one might think of an Irish-American child growing up in a staunchly Catholic neighborhood in the Boston of the 1940s.

For such a Catholic, meat on Fridays simply was not an option to be entertained, even in one's wildest imagination; meatless Fridays were the given, the natural order of the universe. The whys and wherefores of this practice might be explained to the child later on in religious education classes. But, from the psychological point of view, any explanation would be secondary to the child's primordial "lived experience" in community. In more than one sense, ritual food laws are "gut religion.")

In due time, many of Jesus' contemporaries in Jewish Palestine would have been taught by their parents or by teachers in the local synagogue that the purity laws were part of God's covenant with his chosen people. They were a concrete way in which Jews expressed their belonging to God and to his people, a concrete way of practicing imitation of the God who demanded "Be holy, for I, Yahweh, your God, am holy" (Lev 19:2).[33] The holiness, the otherness, the separateness that characterized the one true God, as opposed to all the pagan gods, had to characterize as well his people Israel, a people called to be different and separate from the Gentile nations. This "cordoning off" that the purity laws effected had become all the more important as successive Hellenistic and then Roman rulers caused their alien cultures to impinge on the traditional life of Torah-observant Israelites. It is first of all in this historical context, and not in the context of shifting sociological models, that Jews experienced the purity laws. Hence, it is in this historical context that we must seek to understand how the historical Jesus viewed and reacted to the purity laws of the Mosaic Law—if, indeed, he reacted to them at all.

By now, we have a good sense of how complicated a question "purity" in the OT is and how many pitfalls there may be when one tries to bring these categories into dialogue with the teaching of Jesus on purity issues in the Gospels. The problem becomes still more complex when one realizes that purity was not an issue frozen once and for all in some OT texts but rather remained a lively subject of debate within Palestinian Judaism around the turn of the era. Not all Palestinian Jews ca. 200 B.C.–A.D. 200 viewed ritual and moral purity in the same way.

Many authors formed by and forming Second Temple Judaism around the turn of the era basically held to the distinction between ritual and moral impurity in the Pentateuch, though some writings introduced new dimensions to the problem.[34] In the Diaspora, Philo clearly distinguished between these two types of impurity while adding a characteristic allegorical slant: ritual impurity, which is less important, helps direct our attention to moral impurity, which defiles our souls.[35] Not surprisingly, the Qumran community, which embodied a particularly rigorous brand of sectarian Judaism ca. 150 B.C.–A.D. 70, took a more radical approach. The Qumranites tended to mesh or conflate the ideas of ritual and moral impurity; hence, moral impurity was thought to defile one in the ritual sense as well.[36] This view is quite different from the approach of later rabbinic thought. From the Mishna (ca. A.D. 200–220) onward, the rabbis tended to compartmentalize ritual and moral purity in clearly separate realms of human life. In other words, the tannaitic rabbis tried to keep ritual impurity and sin "as distinct from each other as possible."[37] In practice, a large number of ritual purity rules ceased to be meaningful or practicable after the destruction of the temple in A.D. 70. Even while the temple stood, some of this compartmentalizing may have already been at work among the Pharisees or other religious groups active among the common people.[38]

Thus, around the turn of the era, there were probably contrasting and clashing tendencies within Palestinian Judaism in regard to purity.[39] Some groups seemed to be pressing for more rigorous implementation of purity rules in daily life or the extension of purity rules to new areas of life, while other groups may have sought to modify or adapt purity laws to the practical demands of daily life or even to restrict their application in a more Hellenized world—a fortiori, in the Diaspora. Those advocating an expansive thrust (i.e., extending the application of purity rules to new areas) and those favoring a restrictive approach (i.e., limiting purity obligations to what was explicitly demanded in the written Torah) may well have competed for adherents among ordinary Palestinian Jews, that is, Jews without any particular party adherence or any great education in Torah.

Moreover, the dividing lines among competing Jewish groups did not always fall where we might automatically imagine. On the one hand, Josephus recounts instances in which Jerusalem priests, caught in extraordinary situations, went to extreme means to observe their understanding of purity and food laws, even when these means went beyond anything enjoined by the Jewish Scriptures.[40] It is well to remember that, while the stringency of the Qumranites derived from priests alienated from the Jerusalem establishment, such rebel priests did not have a monopoly on rigorous observance. Apparently some priests who remained loyal to the Jerusalem establishment practiced purity rules with similar stringency. On the other hand, the Pharisees and the early rabbis sometimes differed among themselves on precise details of the food laws and yet apparently remained tolerant of the other group's views on the subject.[41] The situation was therefore a fluid one.

As we have seen so far in our study of Jesus and the Law, Jesus seems to have been capable of both great rigor (e.g., prohibiting divorce and oaths entirely) and humane leniency (e.g., on sabbath observance). Hence, one cannot decide a priori where he might have fit on the spectrum of purity observance in 1st-century Palestine. However, one thing should strike any careful reader of the Gospel immediately. The passages that treat the question of ritual impurity or the food laws are few and far between. In fact, when it comes to such questions, there is only one pericope of significant length: Mark 7:1–23, a confusing passage that begins with the question of handwashing before meals and culminates in a rejection of food laws. This long pericope has a complicated history of tradition and redaction that will demand a careful investigation. After it is examined in detail, a few short sayings of Jesus and incidents in his life may be dealt with more briefly.

II. JESUS AND PURITY IN MARK 7:1–23

The single longest pericope in the Gospels dealing with purity issues is Jesus' dispute and teaching about defilement in Mark 7:1–23.[42] In no other Gospel pericope is the issue addressed with such directness and at such length. Unfortunately, this one extended treatment of Jesus' teaching on purity is fraught with numerous problems of interpretation. One reason for this is that, at least on first reading, the focus of the discussion in Mark 7:1–23 seems to keep shifting, not to say drifting, so that the reader is left with an uneasy feeling of meandering. One senses from the start that we may be dealing with various layers of tradition that have been secondarily put together.

Another problem is that, confronted with all the confusing legal matters discussed in the pericope, the modern reader may be tempted to try an "end run" around the present form of the text (viewed as of not much value) in an attempt to move quickly to the original teaching of the historical Jesus (the real pearl of great price). Yet, as we have seen throughout the first three volumes of *A Marginal Jew*, there is no easy end run or shortcut around the present Christian text that would allow us to move swiftly and painlessly to the historical Jesus. The Gospel text is all we have; only by wrestling with it and moving through it can we hope to come to the historical Jesus who may or may not stand behind it.[43] Given our initial impression of disarray in Mark 7:1–23, perhaps the best way to begin our journey is to take a closer look at the text, to see whether Mark may in fact have composed a more orderly pericope than we first thought. Our preliminary quest for some order or structure in the text will also serve as an initial survey of the topics treated therein.

A. THE STRUCTURE OF MARK 7:1–23

Most commentators agree that Mark 7:1–23 falls naturally into two major parts: (1) 7:1–13 (a *Streitgespräch*, i.e., a debate, about unwashed hands and the tradition of the elders) and (2) 7:14–23 (a *Lehrgespräch*, i.e., Jesus' teaching about things that defile from without or from within). While I basically agree with this approach, I will argue in what follows that it is better to consider vv 14–15 (Jesus' aphorism about defilement, spoken to the crowd) as a pivot or point of transition between the two major parts. A few other commentators prefer a different sort of three-part division: vv 1–5, 6–13, and 14–23.[44] In the face of these different opinions, what justifies a preference for any particular division? To answer that question, our first step will be to try to detect signals in the text that indicate the overall structure and major divisions that the author intended. As we shall see, one significant clue is supplied by the clear change of place and the introduction of new characters or interlocutors at a key point in the text. When we find that these changes in place and interlocutors are matched by shifts in the topics treated, the resulting structural outline has a good chance of reflecting the intention of the ancient author instead of simply representing a grid that we impose on the text.

1. *Major Indicators of the Literary Structure of Mark 7:1–23*

In Mark 7:1, "the Pharisees and some of the scribes" gather around Jesus, who in the previous pericope was presented as being on something of a "healing tour" around Galilee (6:53–56). The appearance of the Pharisees and scribes at this point in Mark's story is quite sudden and unprepared. Although the scribes are said to come from Jerusalem, in a narrative sense they come out of nowhere. The same might be said of the Pharisees. Though in Mark's view the Pharisees are present and active in Galilee, they were last heard from at the end of the cycle of Galilean dispute stories (2:1–3:6, specifically in 2:16,18 [*bis*], 24; and 3:6). Indeed, at 3:6, the Pharisees conspire with the Herodians to destroy Jesus, and with that, they disappear from the narrative until 7:1. The scribes, first mentioned in passing in 1:22, likewise figured as adversaries in the Galilean dispute cycle (2:6,16). We last heard of scribes in 3:22, when a delegation of scribes came down from Jerusalem (as they do again in 7:1) and accused Jesus of performing exorcisms by the power of the prince of demons. The disappearance of both the Pharisees and the scribes from the Marcan narrative by the end of chap. 3 coincided, not surprisingly, with the disappearance of overt opposition to Jesus from organized groups.

At Mark 7:1 these two adversarial groups abruptly reappear, but now (for the first time in Mark's narrative) together—a point that signals the escalation of opposition to Jesus.[45] Clearly, Mark 7:1 indicates the beginning of a new pericope, sharply marked off by its polemical atmosphere from the triumphant and happy tone of the universally successful healing tour of Galilee in 6:53–56. As we begin 7:1–23, the "setup" (vv 1–5) of the pericope depicts the adversarial groups witnessing some of Jesus' disciples eating with defiled (i.e., unwashed) hands, a practice that supposedly violates "the tradition of the elders" to which the adversaries hold fast. In answer to their objection, Jesus issues in vv 6–13 a double reply that draws its arguments first (vv 6–8) from the Prophets, specifically Isa 29:13, and then (vv 9–13) from the Mosaic Law, specifically the Decalogue's commandment to honor one's father and mother in Exod 20:12. Jesus' first reply (vv 6–8) accuses the adversaries of being hypocrites: they neglect the commandment of God while holding fast to the tradition of the elders.[46] The second reply (vv 9–13) shores up this general charge by offering a concrete example of their hypocrisy: the adversaries allow a man to set aside certain assets as dedicated to God (qorbān), thereby depriving his parents of any support from these assets.[47]

With that, Jesus' debate with the Pharisees and scribes ends as abruptly as it began. Unlike some dispute stories, no reaction (e.g., amazement, acclamation, hostility, or fear) from the opponents or the larger audience is recorded. In fact, the Pharisees and scribes disappear from the narrative as suddenly as they appeared. In v 14, which sounds like a new beginning, Jesus summons "the crowd" (a convenient and ever-available audience in the Gospels' narrative)[48] and commands them to hear and understand. Then, in v 15, he presents the crowd with a puzzling aphorism: nothing that enters a person can defile him, but only what comes out of the person defiles him.[49] No sooner does Jesus speak this aphorism than suddenly, in v 17, he enters "a house [after departing] from the crowd." Notice: it is not said that he departs from the Pharisees and scribes, with whom he has been debating in vv 1–13. The Pharisees and scribes do not leave at the end of v 13, nor does Jesus leave them; his opponents simply vanish into thin air. Verses 14–15 thus act as a Janus-like pivot. Insofar as Jesus is still speaking in public, without any change of location, vv 14–15 belong with vv 1–13. Insofar as Jesus proposes "out of the blue" a dense, puzzling aphorism about defilement that will need to be explained throughout the rest of the pericope, vv 14–15 belong with vv 17–23. We are therefore justified in designating vv 14–15 as a transition or a pivot.

Jesus' physical movement from public to private space (a house) and the introduction of the disciples as the new questioners (as opposed to their being mere actors observed by the questioning opponents in vv 2 + 5) indicate that v 17 begins the second major half of the pericope (vv 17–23).[50] Indeed, the same verb of questioning is used with the same basic syntactical construction in both v 5 and v 17. In v 5, the Pharisees and the scribes "asked him" (*kai eperōtōsin auton*) about the disciples' eating; in v 17, the disciples "asked him" (*kai . . . epērōtōn auton*) about his aphorism.

The change in scene is matched by a change in topic. We hear nothing more of unwashed hands or the tradition of the elders, as in vv 1–13. Instead, this second major half of the pericope is totally taken up with explaining the aphorism Jesus addressed to the crowd in v 15. After an initial—and a very Marcan—rebuke to the disciples for not understanding (v 18a), Jesus explains the first half of the aphorism in vv 18b–19. Verse 18b basically repeats v 15a, while v 19 gives a "rationalistic" explanation of the inability of any food that enters a person to defile that person: the food enters not into the heart (the moral core of the person) but simply into the stomach and is then expelled into a latrine. Verse 19 ends with a weighty interpretive aside by the narrator to the reader: thus did Jesus declare all foods clean.

In v 18a, Mark introduces Jesus' explanation of the first half of his aphorism with the phrase "and he says to them" (*kai legei autois*). In similar fashion, in v 20a, Mark introduces the explanation of the second half of the aphorism with the phrase "but he said . . ." (*elegen de*). The explanation follows in the rest of vv 20–23. After repeating the substance of v 15b in v 20, Jesus proceeds in vv 21–22 to define "the things the come from within a person" in terms of evil actions (expressed by plural nouns) and evil attitudes (expressed by singular nouns). Verses 21–22 thus form a typical NT "catalogue of vices." The catalogue begins in v 21 with the overall rubric of "evil thoughts," followed by six nouns in the plural and six nouns in the singular (vv 21b–22). The entire catalogue (and, in a sense, the entire pericope) is concluded by Jesus' summary remark in v 23: "All these evil things come from within and defile a person." With that, the pericope clearly comes to a conclusion, since the next verse (7:24) depicts Jesus leaving the region of Galilee for the territory of Tyre, where he will accede to the request of an importunate Syrophoenician woman to exorcise her daughter (vv 25–30).[51]

Thus, our initial impression of Mark 7:1–23 as an overlong, meandering pericope turns out not to have done full justice to Mark's attempt to forge an ordered composition. Despite all the difficulties in interpreting the flow of thought, the major literary divisions that Mark intended are clear. To summarize what we have seen: the first major half of the pericope, vv 1–13, deals with the Pharisees and scribes' objection to the disciples' failure to

wash their hands before eating and thus their failure to observe the tradition of the elders; Jesus' double reply to this accusation argues from the
Prophets (Isaiah) and the Law (the Decalogue). The transition in vv 14–15
presents Jesus confronting the crowd with his puzzling two-part aphorism
about what really defiles. Then, in the second major half of the pericope,
vv 17–23, Jesus explains at length and in private to his disciples the two
parts of the aphorism articulated in v 15.

2. Verbal and Thematic Links

For all of Mark's skill in structuring the whole of 7:1–23, he could easily
have wound up with three juxtaposed units, two large and one small, with
no real internal connections among them. Mark has avoided this crude sort
of literary construction by making sure that a large number of key words
and phrases as well as various motifs crisscross and bind together the disparate units and subunits of the pericope, thus creating one pericope instead of
three. The more closely one examines all these major and minor connectors,
the more one becomes aware of the ever-present hand of the redactor, deftly
stitching together very different pieces of cloth.

(a) *Connectors between the two halves of the pericope.* To begin with
the most obvious connector: Jesus is the main—and very forceful—speaker
throughout the pericope. Indeed, he is almost the only speaker. Despite their
lengthy introduction in 7:1–5a, the Pharisees and scribes speak directly only
in v 5bc. Jesus' double reply takes up the rest of the first half of the pericope
(vv 6–13). Jesus likewise is the sole speaker in the transition (vv 14–15).
While we are told in v 15b that "his disciples asked him about the aphorism,"
only Jesus speaks in direct discourse in the second half of the pericope—in
fact, all the way from v 18 to v 23.

It is telling that, alongside the person of Jesus,[52] one of the very few word-
groups or motifs that span and truly unite the whole pericope is (a) the
adjective *koinos* (literally, "common," but here "unclean," "defiled," describing the disciples' hands in vv 2 + 5) and (b) the verb *koinoō* (literally,
"to make common," but here "to make unclean," "to defile," describing
what outer and inner factors can or cannot do in vv 15 [*bis*], 18, 20, and 23).
Defilement, of whatever kind, is clearly an overarching theme of the whole
pericope.

Curiously, the other key word that notably spans both halves of the
pericope is *anthrōpos* ("human being," "person," or, in the generic sense,
"man"). The noun *anthrōpos*, occurring more often in Mark 7:1–23 than
in any other whole chapter in Mark's Gospel, supplies something of a *basso
continuo* to the ever-shifting themes of the pericope. It deserves more atten-

tion than it has often received. The first two occurrences, in vv 7 + 8, carry the negative sense of "mere human beings" (and their commandments/ traditions) versus the God whose commandment is abandoned or annulled for the sake of these human traditions. The third occurrence of *anthrōpos*, the last in the first half of the pericope, is found in the dispute over the practice of *qorbān*; it has the vague sense of "if anyone. . . ." The other eight occurrences of *anthrōpos* all fall in the transitional verses (vv 14–15) and in the second half of the pericope (vv 17–23). All of them occur in the two-part aphorism defining what real defilement is and in Jesus' subsequent explanation thereof. In a nutshell (to summarize v 15), nothing outside of a "human being" can defile him by entering into him;[53] what comes out of a "human being" is the only thing that defiles a "human being."

While there is a danger of over-interpretation here, it is perhaps not entirely by accident that the word *anthrōpos* begins to appear in the text just after the words "Pharisees" and "scribes" disappear from the pericope. The first five verses of the pericope take great pains to define "Pharisees" and indeed "all the Jews" in terms of ritual purity. They are then implicitly identified in vv 7–8 as the "human beings" who annul the commandment of God with their traditions. After this restricted and polemical use of *anthrōpos* in the first half of the pericope, the second half pointedly broadens out *anthrōpos* to mean any and every human being, with no religious or ethnic restriction. It is this universal meaning that is hammered home throughout the second half as the Marcan Jesus inculcates the truth that no human being is or can be defiled by the food that enters him or her. Only the evil acts and attitudes that proceed from a human being have the power to defile that person.

The shift in the meaning of *anthrōpos* throughout the pericope thus mirrors the movement of thought from the Pharisees' purity rules, which in fact separate them from Jesus' disciples and from others who do not follow such rules, to Jesus' rule that no food has defiling power, since only evil acts and attitudes can defile an *anthrōpos*. The breaking down of ethnic/religious barriers in the definition of what defiles corresponds to the breaking down of ethnic/religious barriers in the definition of who is the *anthrōpos* that is the object of religious and ethical reflection. Obviously, in this shift, we are hearing not the words of the historical Jesus but the polemic of Mark, who speaks from the far side of a religious divide that separates him from "all the Jews" of v 3.[54]

In addition to Jesus the speaker and *anthrōpos* the concept, a few other words and motifs help tie together the two halves of Mark 7:1–23. A slight connection is supplied by "the disciples." They are mentioned as the object of the opponents' accusations in vv 2 + 5, but do not engage actively in the debate and are never mentioned again in the first half. They resurface ever so briefly in v 17b to request from Jesus the explanation of his aphorism and to receive in v 18a his typically Marcan rebuke for not understanding. Interestingly, the act of asking (*eperōtaō*, a favorite Marcan verb) also provides a minor connection between the two halves of the pericope: the Pharisees and scribes "ask" Jesus a question in v 5, and the disciples "ask" for the explanation of his aphorism in v 17. Another minor verbal link, the word "heart" (*kardia*), is found in v 6 (the citation of Isa 29:13) and in v 20 (Jesus' explanation of why foods cannot defile). In itself, the connection is tenuous, but "heart" could be seen as symbolizing the broader motif of "inner and outer" that pervades the pericope.

(b) *Connectors within units and subunits.* Other word groups and motifs serve to hold together not the pericope as a whole but rather its various units and subunits.[55] For example, the phrase "the Pharisees" (vv 1,3,5) helps bind together the somewhat disjointed first five verses (vv 1–5) of the first half (vv 1–13) of the pericope. The noun "Pharisees" then disappears, though both the Pharisees and scribes are understood to be the objects of Jesus' rebuke for the rest of the first half. Perhaps the one phrase that helps most to maintain the coherence of the entire first half of the pericope is neither "the Pharisees" nor "unwashed hands" but rather "the tradition of the elders [*hē paradosis tōn presbyterōn*]." This phrase appears as a distinguishing characteristic of the Pharisees and indeed of "all the Jews" in v 3 and forms the essence of the opponents' objection in v 5. Then, in a clever shift of phrasing, the noun "tradition" occurs *both* (a) at the end of Jesus' first reply in v 8 (where it is now "the tradition of [mere] humans," as opposed to the commandment of God), *and* (b) by way of *inclusio*, at both the beginning and end of Jesus' second reply (vv 9 + 13), where it is transformed into "*your* tradition." Thus, the movement from "the tradition of the elders" (vv 3,5) through "the tradition of [mere] humans" (v 8) to "*your* tradition" (vv 9,13) undergirds the theological polemic as well as the literary unit.[56] Contrary to many expositions of 7:1–13, the tradition of the elders is the main bone of contention, not the act of eating with unwashed hands, which is the occasion rather than the true substance of the dispute. The phrase "eat bread with unwashed hands" appears only in vv 2 + 5. In contrast, in the final subunit (vv 9–13) of the first half of the pericope, it is *qorbān*, not handwashing, that is attacked as the prime example of human tradition superseding the commandment of God.

Indeed, in addition to the word "tradition," the words *entalmata* ("commandments," i.e., of humans) in v 7 and *entolē* ("commandment," i.e., of God) in vv 8 + 9 help tie together Jesus' first and second replies to his oppo-

nents, as he contrasts divine and human commandments. In turn, "you render void [atheteite] the commandment of God" in v 9 forms an inclusio with
"annulling [akyrountes] the word of God" in v 13, thus neatly "packaging"
Jesus' second reply and rounding out the whole first half of the pericope.[57]
The two replies of Jesus are also tied together by the use of the adverb kalōs
(literally, "well," "beautifully") in vv 6 + 9. In v 6, the sense of kalōs is satirical ("how accurately did Isaiah prophesy of you hypocrites!"), while in v 9
the sense is ironic ("you make a fine art of rendering void the commandment
of God").[58] Another minor link between the two replies of Jesus is the twofold use of the verb aphiēmi (literally, "to let go" or "to send away"). In v 8
it signifies that the opponents "abandon" or "neglect" the commandment of
God," while in v 12 it means instead that the opponents, by their interpretation of qorbān, "no longer permit" (ouketi aphiete) a man to use his assets,
now dedicated to God, to support his parents. Just possibly, Mark implies
by this cross-reference that this nonpermission, arising from the practice of
qorbān, is an example of how the opponents "abandon" or "neglect" the
commandment of God. A final and slight verbal link between Jesus' first
and second reply is the verb "to honor" (timaō), which occurs both in the
Isaiah citation (honoring God with one's lips) and the Exodus citation (honoring father and mother).

Of more importance than these last-mentioned individual words is the
general motif of eating. The verb "to eat" (esthiō) occurs in vv 2,3,4,5;
hence, along with "the Pharisees," it helps tie together the first subunit of
the first half of the pericope. By the same token, though, esthiō is isolated in
this first subunit, appearing nowhere else in the pericope. More significant,
the general theme of eating, though not the verb esthiō, is taken up again in
Mark's interpretation of Jesus' aphorism in the second half of the pericope.
At least in Mark's view, all the statements about "what goes into a human
being" refer to the foods that are prohibited by the Mosaic Law but that do
not, according to Jesus, defile.

The transitional verses (vv 14–15) and the second half of the pericope
(vv 17–23) are linked by a series of key words that occur both in the two-part
aphorism of v 15 and in the two-part explanation of the aphorism's meaning that extends from v 18 to v 23. Most of the vocabulary of v 15 recurs
in various combinations throughout the second half: exōthen ("from outside"), anthrōpos ("human being," "person"), dynatai ("can"), koinoō ("to
defile"), and especially the pair eisporeuomai ("go into") and ekporeuomai
("come out of"). The typically Marcan theme of understanding/not understanding occurs in v 14 (synete, "understand!"), v 18 (asynetoi, "lacking
understanding," and ou noeite, "do you not understand?") and perhaps by

way of *inclusio* in the very last vice listed in v 22, *aphrosynē* ("foolishness," "lack of sense"). As we have already seen, the catalogue of vices at the end of the whole pericope is carefully structured to present a list of six nouns in the plural followed by six nouns in the singular, all under the general rubric of "evil thoughts"—from which, presumably, all other evil actions and attitudes proceed. Thus, a list of vices that could easily have created the impression of a pericope wandering off into vague generalities as it approaches its conclusion is instead given a clear, parallel structure that underlines the ultimately pastoral, moral, and catechetical intent of Mark in this long and curious pericope.

Long and curious it may be, but we can now appreciate that Mark 7:1–23 is not as meandering or disjointed as it may have first appeared. Mark, and perhaps pre-Marcan editors before him, have labored mightily to weld disparate traditions into a coherent whole. That very fact, however, highlights a basic insight and problem for any quester for the historical Jesus. The complex, artful, and artificial structure of Mark 7:1–23 reminds us that we are dealing with a multilayered Christian composition, not a videotaped replay of what Jesus said and did around A.D. 28. The modern quester is thus faced with the task of first dismantling the artificial framework that Mark has used to tie all this heterogeneous material together and of then sifting through the individual units to see whether the basic dispute—or at least some individual sayings within it—may go back to the historical Jesus. Fortunately, not only the literary connectors distributed throughout the text but also other traces of Mark's redactional hand (duality, explanatory asides, repeated generalizations, multiplication of verbs of saying) will aid us in our quest. First, though, it would be helpful to gather together all we have seen into an analytical, structured translation of Mark 7:1–23 that will highlight both the divisions and connections in the text.

B. A STRUCTURED TRANSLATION OF MARK 7:1–23

FIRST HALF (7:1–13): JESUS' CRITIQUE OF THE TRADITION OF THE ELDERS

First Unit (vv 1–5): The Question about Eating with Unclean Hands
[narrative setup]

1. And there gather unto him the *Pharisees* and some of the *scribes,*
          coming from Jerusalem
2. And seeing some of his disciples, that they are *EATING* the loaves
          of bread with *DEFILED* **hands,**
     —that is, [hands] not washed—   *[parenthesis]*

[explanatory parenthesis]

3. —for the *Pharisees* and all the Jews, unless they wash their **hands**
           with a fistful of water,
   do not *EAT,*
   holding to the TRADITION of the elders;
4. And [when they come in] from the marketplace, unless they
           immerse themselves,
   they do not *EAT,*
   and many other things there are that they have received [as
           traditions] to hold to,
   immersions of cups and pitchers and bronze vessels and beds—

[two-part accusation in form of two questions]

5. and the *Pharisees* and the *scribes* asked him,
   "Why do your disciples not walk according to the TRADITION
           of the elders,
   but *EAT* bread with *DEFILED* **hands**?"

*Second Unit (vv 6–13): Jesus' Two Replies, First from the Prophets,
Then from the Law*

   First Subunit (vv 6–8): Reply Quoting Isa 29:13

6. But *he said to them,*
   "Well did Isaiah prophesy about you hypocrites, as it
           stands written,   *[accusation]*
   'This people honors me with [their] lips,   *[OT quote]*
           but their **HEART** is far from me.
7.   In vain do they reverence me,
           teaching [as divine] teachings the commandments
              of **MEN**.'
8. Neglecting the commandment of God, you hold to the
           TRADITION of **MEN**."   *[accusation]*

   *Second Subunit (vv 9–13): Reply Quoting Exod 20:12 and
   Exod 21:17 (LXX 21:16)*

9. And *he said to them,*
   "Well do you render void the commandment
           of God   *[accusation]*
   in order that you may establish your TRADITION.
10. For Moses *said,*
    'Honor your father and your mother,' and   *[OT quote]*
    'The one who speaks ill of his father or mother must assuredly
           be put to death.'

11. But you **say,**
    'If a **MAN** says to [his] father or mother,
        "Whatever you might have received from me [for your support]
        [is] Qorban—that is, a gift [dedicated to God]—" '
12. you no longer permit him to do anything for [his] father or
          mother,   *[accusation]*
13. —[thus] nullifying the word of God by your **TRADITION,** which you
          have handed down.
    And you do many such things like this."   *[generalizing conclusion]*

PIVOT (7:14–15): JESUS TEACHES THE CROWD HIS APHORISM
ON DEFILEMENT

14. And summoning again the crowd,
    he said to them,
        "Hear me all [of you] and understand."
15. There is nothing outside of a **MAN** that, [by] *entering into*
          him,   *[first half of aphorism]*
    can *DEFILE* him;
    but those things that *come out* of a **MAN**   *[second half of aphorism]*
    are the things that *DEFILE* a **MAN.**"

SECOND HALF (7:17–23): JESUS EXPLAINS TO HIS DISCIPLES
HIS APHORISM ON DEFILEMENT

*First Unit (vv 17–18a): The Question of the Disciples and
Rebuking Questions of Jesus*
17. And when he entered into a house away from the
          crowd,   *[narrative setup]*
    his disciples asked him [the meaning of] the aphorism.   *[question]*
18. And *he says to them,*   *[rhetorical questions as response]*
  a.   "So are you also without understanding?
        Do you not understand that

*Second Unit (vv 18b–19): First Half of Aphorism Explained:
Nothing from Outside Defiles*
  b.   nothing from outside, [by] *entering into* a **MAN,** can *DEFILE*
          him   *[first half]*
19.   for it does not *enter* into his **HEART** but into his
          stomach   *[reason: digestion]*
    and *goes out* into the latrine"
    —[by saying this, he was] making all foods clean.   *[parenthesis]*

Third Unit (vv 20–23): Second Half of Aphorism Explained:
Things from Within Defile
20. But *he said* that
        "That which *comes out* of a **MAN**,   *[second half]*
        that *DEFILES* a **MAN**.
21. For from within, from the **HEART** of **MEN**, *come forth* evil
                thoughts,   *[reason: vices]*
        fornications, thefts, murders, [v 22a] adulteries, acts of greed,
            malicious deeds,
22b.   deceit, licentiousness, envy, slander, pride, foolishness.
23.   All these evil things *come forth* from
         within   *[generalizing conclusion]*
    and *DEFILE* a **MAN**."

C. Identifying the Hand(s) of the Christian Author(s)

Our study of the overall structure as well as of the large and small literary links holding the structure together reminds us of a basic truth of Gospel criticism. Any Gospel pericope—whether or not it ultimately goes back to the historical Jesus—is, as it stands, a Christian composition. Exegetes cannot execute a ballerina-like leap that, with breathtaking grace and ease, brings them back immediately and directly to the historical Jesus. There is no shortcut around the long, hard slog of probing and weighing the various words, phrases, and sentences of a pericope to see what elements most likely come from the Christian redactor(s) and what elements might satisfy the criteria of historicity, thus arguing for an origin in the historical Jesus.

This is all the more true of Mark 7:1–23, where one quickly detects not the single hand of one Christian redactor but the hands of several Christian authors. In this case, I prefer to speak of authors or composers rather than editors or redactors, since our analysis has confronted us with disparate material that has been skillfully woven together into a larger whole. To be sure, the seams and sutures still show, and the flow of thought is not entirely smooth. Still, considering the variety of topics treated, one has to admire the ability of the Christian authors to weld together a meaningful whole out of so many different traditions. Those who have produced the final texts are truly creative authors or composers rather than mere mechanical redactors slipping in an editorial phrase here or there.

I speak of authors in the plural because many scholars who have studied Mark 7:1–23 in detail have detected not just a Marcan redaction but also a couple of layers of Christian tradition that have reached final form via Mark's molding hands. Indeed, one of the points of lively debate among exegetes is how many different strata or different pieces of Christian tradition one can discern and how much or little Mark contributed to the final product.[59] Judgments oscillate between the view that Mark, a conservative redactor, has taken over the already existing pericope with few alterations and the view that Mark is mainly responsible for forging a unity out of disparate traditions, stamping the whole with his characteristic imprint.[60]

Fortunately, our specific goal spares us detailed debates over what should be assigned either to Mark or to the composers who preceded him. We are simply asking what, if anything, goes back to the historical Jesus. Hence, whether a particular Christian formulation or addition comes from Mark or from one of his predecessors makes no difference to our quest. In either case, any Christian contribution is to be bracketed because it is not a saying or action of the historical Jesus. For convenience' sake, in what follows I will speak simply of Mark and his additions or modifications, while tacitly granting that some redactional work may come in fact from Mark's Christian predecessors.[61] It is possible that, at times, what we consider Mark's own editorial traits were already present in his source(s) and that Mark both accepted and imitated such traits.[62] The distinction, while important for those focusing on Marcan redaction criticism, is not significant for those searching for the historical Jesus.

With this understood, our structured outline of Mark 7:1–23 highlights a number of prime candidates for the category of Marcan redaction. Three major kinds of Marcan redactional activity are especially prominent:[63]

(1) *Parenthetical Explanations.* Elsewhere in his Gospel—though not as frequently as in John's Gospel—Mark addresses explanatory asides or parenthetical remarks to his audience. These can range from mere translations of Aramaic words (e.g., *Abba* = "Father" in Mark 14:36) through awkwardly placed explanations of details in his narrative (11:13; 16:4) to knowing winks to his reader about veiled OT references (13:14). But nowhere else in his Gospel do we find a single pericope so replete with parenthetical asides and explanations, both lengthy and brief.[64] The obvious cases, marked off by various linguistic signals, include the following: (a) the phrase "that is, [hands] not washed," which acts as the explanation of "defiled hands" in v 2; (b) the lengthy explanation of various purity rituals observed by the Pharisees "and all the Jews" (a clear exaggeration) in vv 3–4 (this is an anacoluthon that disrupts the syntax between v 2 and v 5);[65] (c) the phrase "that is, a gift," explaining the meaning of the Hebrew word *qorbān* in v 11; (d) the awkwardly placed "making all foods clean," tacked on at the end

of v 19 (this phrase makes crystal-clear what, for Mark, is the meaning of Jesus' assertion in v 18 echoing in turn the first half of v 15).[66]

(2) *Generalizing or Universalizing Statements.* Scattered throughout Mark 7:1–23 are statements using the words *panta* ("all") or *polla* ("many") that suddenly broaden a particular assertion into a general or universal statement. The fact that these generalizing statements mostly occur when the opponents are being described intimates the polemical thrust of the generalizations.

(a) As the parenthesis of v 3 begins to describe the purity rituals of the Pharisees, the description is suddenly widened to include "all the Jews." On the face of it, this is strange because we know that, around the turn of the era, the Pharisees stood out precisely because of their particular views on purity. From reliable traditions in the Mishna and Tosepta, we learn that the Pharisees differed from the Sadducees on certain purity issues.[67] Moreover, documents from Qumran (the *Rule of the Community*, the *Damascus Document*, the *Temple Scroll*, and the so-called *Halakic Letter*), as well the descriptions of various Jewish sects and individuals by Josephus, inform us of Jewish groups who were stricter in their observance of purity rules than were—as far as we can tell—the Pharisees. Hence, the sudden move from "the Pharisees" to "all the Jews" in Mark 7:3 is patently false.[68]

(b) The generalizing tendency continues as the parenthesis of vv 3–4 goes on. After a reference to the Jewish practice of immersion upon returning from the marketplace, Mark 7:4 states, "And there are many other things that they have received [as traditions] to hold to."

(c) What is especially intriguing about the generalization in v 4—an aside spoken by the narrator Mark to the reader—is that the same sort of polemical generalization occurs at the end of Jesus' second reply to his opponents (vv 9–13). After accusing them (for the third time) of neglecting, rendering void, or nullifying God's commandment (or word), Jesus in v 13 concludes his indictment with a generalization in the style of v 4: "And you do many such things like this." The same sort of sweeping, polemical generalization about the Pharisees, first in the mouth of Mark and then in the mouth of Jesus, reminds us that the redactor's voice may be resonating in the words of Jesus. All this is reminiscent of the way the voice of the Fourth Evangelist blends into the voice of the Johannine Jesus. Clearly, the quester for the historical Jesus is put on guard against naively accepting the words of the Marcan Jesus in 7:1–23 as a pure and simple historical transcript of what Jesus actually said around A.D. 28.

(d) The tendency to make a sweeping statement reverts to the voice of Mark at the end of v 19, when Mark interprets the first half of Jesus' two-part aphorism on defilement to mean that Jesus was declaring and making all foods clean. Whether or not that is the natural thrust of the aphorism, the tendency of Mark, throughout this pericope, to broaden particular statements to general or universal application continues unabated. Clearly, we are dealing in Mark 7:1–23 with a controlling and pervasive redactional viewpoint, not just with occasional jottings or off-the-cuff comments.

(e) The entire pericope concludes on a final universal statement—but now the universalizing voice has moved once again from Mark to the Marcan Jesus. After Jesus has listed six vices in the plural and six in the singular that defile a person from within, he concludes in true Marcan style: "All these evil things come forth from within and defile a man." Thus, the chain of generalizations stretching from v 3 through vv 4,13,19 to v 23 functions *both* as part of the structural framework *as well as* part of the polemical drumbeat of this very Marcan pericope.

(3) Mark's redactional tendencies are not exhausted, however, by our first two points. Some of Mark's characteristic ways of structuring his narrative, seen elsewhere in his Gospel, appear in this pericope as well:

(a) *The pattern of a public pronouncement by Jesus, his withdrawal into private space, a question by the disciples, a rebuke by Jesus, and finally an explanation given by Jesus.* This pattern is part of the larger theme of mystery or secrecy that pervades Mark's Gospel. The prime example of this pattern is the parable discourse in Mark 4. In public, Jesus teaches the crowd the parable of the sower (4:2–9). Then he withdraws into private, where his disciples ask him the meaning of the parables (v 10). Jesus first rebukes his disciples with a rhetorical question, "Do you not understand this parable?" (v 13). He then explains the meaning of the parable to them (vv 15–20). The same pattern is discernible in Jesus' teaching to the crowd in 7:14–15, his withdrawal into a house in v 17a, the question of the disciples about the meaning of the parable in v 17b, Jesus' rebuke to the disciples in a rhetorical question in v 18a, and then his explanation of his teaching in vv 18b–23. Similar, though partial, examples of this pattern can be found in the teaching on divorce (10:1–12), the beginning of the eschatological discourse (13:1–8), and the curing of the demoniac boy (9:14–29).

(b) *The careful placement of dispute stories within the Gospel.* Throughout chaps. 2–3, which contain a cycle of Galilean *Streitgespräche*, Jesus is assaulted with challenges, questions, and accusations first by the scribes and then by the Pharisees. However, 7:1–5 is the first time that the Pharisees and the scribes come together to form a united front attacking Jesus. Mark's narrative plotting, which depicts an escalating tension amid gathering storm clouds, is thus clear. At the end of the public ministry in Jerusalem, Mark will bring back both the scribes (11:27; 12:35–40) and the Pharisees (12:13) as opponents of Jesus in the final *Streitgespräche* of the Gospel—though the scribes and the Pharisees will not appear in the same pericope. In this sense, Mark 7:1–23 forms a central point or pivot to all the *Streitgespräche* in the Gospel, since only here—in between the Galilean cycle (2:1–3:6) and the Jerusalem cycle (11:27–12:37)[69]—do both Pharisees and scribes appear shoulder to shoulder in the same dispute. Once again, the contouring hand of Mark is quite visible.

(c) *The tendency of Mark to string together a series of verbs of saying.* As elsewhere in Mark, the larger narrative is structured by a succession of a number of verbs of saying, with Jesus usually the speaker (see, e.g., Mark 4:2,9,11,13,21,24,26,30,33–34,35; 14:18,20,22,24,25,27,30,32,34,36,37, 39,41). In many cases, the noun "Jesus" is understood as the subject of the verb without being expressed. As in chaps. 4 and 14, so in 7:1–23, the verbs of saying act almost as punctuation marks or paragraph indentations:

v 5   and the Pharisees and the scribes asked him
v 6   but he said to them
v 9   and he said to them
v 10   for Moses said
v 11   but you say
v 14   and . . . he said to them
v 15   and his disciples asked him
v 18   and he says to them
v 20   but he said

The last two examples are especially striking, since v 20 introduces Jesus speaking again, although no other actor in the story has spoken in the meantime. Similar examples occur elsewhere in Mark (e.g., 2:25,27; 8:34; 9:1). The two verbs of speaking in 7:18 + 20 help create a neat division between the first half (vv 18–19) of the explanation of Jesus' aphorism and the second half (vv 20–22). From start to finish, Mark's structuring hand is visible.

(d) *Duality in Mark.*[70] One striking redactional trait of Mark is his tendency to say things "in two's." From individual words and phrases to whole sentences and paragraphs, Mark tends to provide us with verbal twins. This is certainly the case with Mark 7:1–23. As the structured translation shows, 7:1–23 is made up of two halves (vv 1–13 + vv 17–23) that are both joined and separated by the transitional pivot, vv 14–15.

Macro-duality is matched by micro-duality.[71] In vv 1–2, the phrase "some of the scribes" balances both "the Pharisees" before it in v 1 and "some of his disciples" after it in v 2. In v 3 we have "the Pharisees and all the Jews"; in v 5, simply "the Pharisees and the scribes." Both in v 3 and in v 4, the Pharisees are the subject of the verb *ouk esthiousin* ("they do not eat"). The opponents' question in v 5b is divided into two parts, one negative and one positive: "Why do your disciples not walk according to the tradition of the elders, but eat bread with defiled hands?"

As we have already seen, Jesus' response to this question can be divided into two subunits, vv 6–8 and vv 9–13. The two subunits are nicely joined by the mention of "the commandment of God" as well as by the repetition of the word "tradition" in both v 8 and v 9. The word "tradition" also creates an *inclusio* for the second subunit, appearing in both v 9 and v 13. Mark formulates something like a Matthean antithesis (cf. Matt 5:21–48) in vv 10 + 11: "For Moses said . . . but you say," with the Mosaic quotation actually made up of two citations from Exodus. Verse 10 contains two references to a person's father and mother, as do vv 11–12.

In the transitional pivot (vv 14–15), Jesus commands the crowd with the double imperative, "Hear . . . and understand." At the heart of the whole pericope lies the two-part aphorism of Jesus in v 15. This single verse uses the key verb "defile" twice (once in each half), and the second half of the aphorism contains two occurrences of the noun "man." The two parts of the aphorism are also balanced by the antithetical phrases "enter into" and "come out of."

The second half of the pericope (vv 17–23) has two occurrences of Jesus "saying" something to his disciples (vv 18 and v 20), corresponding to the two halves of his explanation of the aphorism (vv 18b–19 + vv 20–23). Jesus rebukes and yet answers his disciples with two rhetorical questions in v 18: "So are you also without understanding? Do you not understand that . . . ?" Verses 18b and 19a contain two occurrences of the verb "enter into," while vv 19b and 20b are joined by two occurrences of the verb "go out of," as are v 21 and v 23. Verse 20 contains two occurrences of "man" in its two halves. After the introductory rubric of "evil thoughts," the vice catalogue in vv 21–22 is made up of two lists of six vices each, the first list in the plural, the second in the singular. The pericope comes to a conclusion in v 23, which contains a double verb: "All these evil things come forth from within and defile a man." Thus, to say that Marcan duality permeates the whole of 7:1–23 is hardly an exaggeration.

By now, it is clear that the question we must struggle with in Mark 7:1–23 is not whether there are sufficient signs of a Christian author (or authors) structuring the whole pericope with his style, projecting his voice into the mouths of the speakers, and filling the pericope with his theological viewpoint. The question has instead become whether, amid all the signs of Christian composition, we can still detect any signs of material going back to the historical Jesus.[72] Granted the sprawling nature and shifting themes of 7:1–23, the best way to formulate an answer to that question is to take one unit or subunit at a time, to see whether it may contain any saying or core teaching that comes from Jesus himself.

Ordinarily, one would proceed in the order in which the units have been laid out by Mark. However, Mark 7:1–23 presents us with a special case in more ways than one. In the entire first unit (vv 1–5) of the first half of the pericope, Jesus neither speaks nor acts. The unit is entirely taken up with actions and words of the Pharisees and scribes, along with a lengthy parenthetical description of their purity rituals that comes from the Christian narrator. Jesus begins to speak only in the second unit (vv 6–13), but, from there on, the rest of the pericope is taken up almost entirely with the direct discourse of Jesus and Jesus alone. Since our quest is for the historical Jesus and not for the Christian narrator, I will begin with v 6 and move in order through all the statements of Jesus in each of the subunits of the pericope from v 6 to v 23. When that task is completed, I will return to the introductory unit in vv 1–5 and weigh its historical value in the light of what we have learned from the other parts of the pericope.

D. Searching for the Historical Jesus in the Subunits of Mark 7:6–23

1. *Verses 6–8: Jesus' First Reply, Quoting Isa 29:13*

Jesus' first reply to the question of the Pharisees and scribes is made up almost entirely of a four-line quotation from Isa 29:13 (Mark 7:6b–7), with a very brief interpretation in v 8 that applies the censure of Isaiah to the tradition of the Pharisees and scribes. Hence, it is vital to know whether (a) the historical Jesus could have cited the text of Isa 29:13 as Mark presents it and then (b) whether it is likely that Jesus would have applied the text of Isa 29:13 to the position of his interlocutors. We must begin by examining the various forms of the Isaiah text extant around the turn of the era.

What strikes one immediately is the fact that Mark presents Jesus citing not the Hebrew text of Isaiah (either in its Masoretic form or in any other Hebrew—or Aramaic—form known to us from that time) but rather the text of Isaiah as found in the Greek Septuagint (LXX). At first glance, this may not seem terribly important. After all, the LXX often varies in this or that aspect from the Hebrew text (or texts) preserved for us without creating a significant difference in meaning. However, in the case of Mark 7:6–8, the difference is significant, both in regard to the wording of Isaiah's text and in regard to the way that Jesus uses it to press his argument against his opponents.

In the Hebrew text of Isa 29:13–14, Isaiah is excoriating the people of Jerusalem for rendering the Lord an external worship in the temple that does not go hand in hand with a genuine inner commitment to the God of Israel (and, in the larger context, with the social justice such commitment demands). Using a typical form of prophetic speech called the judgment oracle, Isaiah proclaims a two-part oracle of reproach and threat in the name of the Lord.[73] In this oracle, the Lord (a) states his *reproach* or *indictment* of the people in v 13 and then (b) proclaims his corresponding *threat* or *verdict* in v 14.[74] The Masoretic text (MT) of the Hebrew reads:

v 13 And the Lord said, "*Because* this people approaches [me] with its mouth,
        and with its lips they honor me,[75]
        but its heart is far from me,
        and their fear of me is a commandment of men learned [by rote],
v 14 *therefore* I will once again act in wondrous fashion with this people,
        in a wondrous and startling way;
        and the wisdom of its wise men will perish,
        and the intelligence of its intelligent men will be hidden.

Isaiah criticizes the cultic reverence (= "fear of me") expressed in the temple liturgy because it is simply conventional and routine religion, set up and regulated by the king and the priestly aristocracy ("a commandment of men learned [by rote]"). The prescribed prayers are duly recited ("mouth," "lips"), and yet this liturgical access and nearness to God in the visible temple masks an inner, invisible distance from God in the depths of the people's religious life ("heart"). God will punish the people for this contradiction between outward appearance and inner reality by upsetting the neat religious routine and political policy created by the Jerusalem establishment (the "wise" and the "intelligent" bureaucrats in the royal palace and the temple).[76]

While there are variations from the MT in the texts of Isaiah that we have from Qumran and in the later Aramaic *Targum of Isaiah*, the grammatical structure and theological message are basically the same in all the Hebrew and Aramaic forms of the text.[77] In contrast, there is a notable shift in grammatical structure and theological meaning when we move to the LXX tradition. The situation is complicated here by the fact that the LXX text of Isa 29:13–14 is represented by two different streams of tradition: a longer one in the Codex Vaticanus (B) and a slightly shorter one in the Codices Sinaiticus (ℵ), Alexandrinus (A), and Marchalianus (Q). What follows is the longer Vaticanus form, with the shorter form found in the other three codices indicated by the bracketed words in v 13a:

v 13 And the Lord said: "This people approaches me [with its mouth,
          and] with their lips they honor me,
       but their heart is far from me.
       In vain do they reverence me,
       teaching commandments of men and teachings.
v 14 Therefore, behold, I once again will transport this people, and
          I will transport them,
       and I will destroy the wisdom of the wise,
       and I will hide the intelligence of the intelligent.

Amid all the minor variations between the LXX and the Hebrew text, we notice some major differences.[78] First of all, the basic grammatical structure of the sentence is different. In the Hebrew text (in all its forms), Isa 29:13 is a subordinate clause ("*because* this people . . ."), stating in a divine indictment the sin of the people of Jerusalem. In their temple cult, when they formally "approach" the Lord, they say all the right words of praise and observe all the proper rituals of the liturgy. But their external religious worship ("their fear [i.e., reverence] of me") is simply a mechanical ceremony learned by rote and regularly performed without any inner commitment ("its heart is far from me"). Then, *because* of this sin denounced in v 13, the Lord's verdict and punishment are announced in the main clause of v 14 ("therefore"). In contrast, in the LXX, v 13 is a separate sentence, not syntactically dependent on v 14: "This people approaches me," not "*because* this people approaches me," as in the MT.

It is this LXX form of an independent sentence that Mark (and later on, Matthew, dependent on Mark) cites in Mark 7:6–7: "This people honors me," not "*because* this people honors me." Since Isa 29:13 is treated by Mark, following the LXX, as an independent sentence, there is no need for Mark to cite Isa 29:14 as well. In Mark's mind, Isa 29:13 can stand on its own; indeed, 29:13, and not 29:14, is the theological point on which Mark wishes to focus. Already we begin to sense that not only is Mark following the LXX rather than the MT, but that he is doing so for a reason.

Mark's dependence on the LXX becomes more strikingly apparent and consequential when we examine the detailed wording and meaning of Isa 29:13 in Mark 7:6–7. In the opening words of Isa 29:13, Mark represents not simply the LXX; rather, he takes over the abbreviated form of the LXX found in Codices Sinaiticus, Alexandrinus, and Marchalianus and abbreviates it still further. Instead of the short LXX text ("This people approaches me, with their lips they honor me"), Mark gives us the still shorter "this people honors me with [their] lips."[79] Apparently, Mark is interested not so much in the first part of LXX Isa 29:13 as instead in the last clause of v 13—the clause that diverges notably in its LXX form from the Hebrew wording and thought. While the Hebrew text continues to berate "this people" for their liturgical worship "their fear of me") in the temple that is mere rote ritual ("a commandment of men learned [by rote]"), the LXX takes a very different tack. In the LXX, Isaiah states that their worship is pointless, without effect, "in vain" (matēn)[80] because—and here the theological focus shifts remarkably—they teach (didaskontes) commandments of men (i.e., mere human commandments of ritual as opposed to God's commandments) and teachings (i.e., mere human doctrines as opposed to divine revelation).[81]

Thus, with the final clause in Isa 29:13, the LXX translator has introduced a new idea into the text—something not unknown in the LXX translation of Isaiah, which tends to be free and interpretive especially in the poetic parts of the book.[82] What was in the Hebrew simply a denunciation of mechanical, routine liturgy in the Jerusalem temple now expands in the LXX into a denunciation of merely human teaching that implicitly is set over against the true teaching of God that is Torah (tôrâ meaning "teaching" or "instruction"). But, by introducing the idea of a group of people who teach (didaskontes), the LXX has also introduced a certain tension into the text. Isaiah's denunciation in LXX Isa 29:13 has as its object the whole people who honor God only with their lips; yet the participle didaskontes seems to imply a special group of teachers within the people as a whole. This implicit distinction is cleverly exploited by Mark, who has already spoken of "all the Jews" observing purity rules, but who has Jesus denounce the Pharisees and scribes in particular as hypocritical teachers.

Mark exploits this point that is specific to the LXX even further by slightly adjusting the Greek at the end of LXX Isa 29:13. Reordering the wording of the LXX's "teaching commandments of men and teachings" (didaskontes entalmata anthrōpōn kai didaskalias), Mark moves up the noun "teachings" (didaskalias), which limps along awkwardly at the end of the LXX's sentence, and drops the connecting "and" (kai), thus placing the noun "teachings" in apposition to the direct object ("the commandments of men"). In this way, Mark heightens the opposition that was implicit in the LXX's formulation, the opposition between mere human commandments and the God's own teaching. In Mark's indictment in 7:7b, the sin of the Pharisees and scribes is that they are teachers who are "teaching [as divine] teachings the commandments of [mere] men" (*didaskontes didaskalias entalmata anthrōpōn*).[83]

It is precisely this point, the point specific to the LXX text of Isa 29:13 as reworked by Mark, that the Marcan Jesus seizes upon in his application of the text to his opponents in Mark 7:8: "Neglecting [or: leaving, abandoning] the commandment of God, you hold to the tradition *of men*."[84] The Pharisees and scribes in Mark 7:5 had complained that Jesus' disciples did not observe the tradition of *the elders*, but Jesus parries their thrust by revealing that the commandments and teachings of (mere) men that are denounced by Isa 29:13 are precisely the tradition of the elders, that is, the tradition of mere men, championed by the Pharisees and scribes. This is the accuracy Jesus praises as he introduces Isaiah's prophecy in Mark 7:6 ("Well did Isaiah prophesy about you hypocrites"). In denouncing those who teach the commandments and teachings of mere men as opposed to *the* commandment of God,[85] Isaiah—in Jesus' judgment—was prophesying with pinpoint accuracy about the Pharisees and the scribes who neglect and annul God's commandment in favor of the tradition of the elders—a claim Jesus will proceed to exemplify by citing the practice of *qorbān* (7:6–13).

There is only one problem with all this prophetic denunciation and reinterpretation. Jesus' line of argument works only if Jesus has as his scriptural starting point the form of Isa 29:13 found in the LXX and slightly reordered by Mark, not the form found in the Hebrew text. The Hebrew text of Isa 29:13 contains no denunciation of people who teach mere human commandments and doctrines. It rather denounces the Jerusalem temple liturgy as mindless, mechanical cult learned and practiced by rote. Clearly, the Marcan Jesus argues from the LXX text as retooled by Mark. This creates a major problem for any scholar who wishes to claim that the argument in Mark 7:6–8 comes from the historical Jesus.[86]

This problem is only magnified when we broaden our focus and notice that Isa 29:13 is also employed by the author of the Epistle to the Colossians in his polemic against his opponents. The epistle is attacking some kind of teaching within the Christian community that propagates various purity rules or taboos.[87] In Col 2:21–22, the author complains to his audience that they foolishly submit to rules and regulations as though they were still living in the old, unredeemed world of their pagan neighbors. The rules are summed up in v 21 as "Do not handle, nor taste, nor touch!" While the precise "error" or "heresy" that Colossians is battling is endlessly debated (perhaps a syncretizing stew of pagan mysticism and Jewish purity rules, as is suggested by Col 2:16–20), the key point for us is that Colossians rejects these taboos because they are "according to the commandments and teachings of men [*kata ta entalmata kai didaskalias tōn anthrōpōn*]." This is a clear allusion, indeed, practically a quotation, of LXX Isa 29:13: "teaching commandments of men and teachings [*didaskontes entalmata anthrōpōn kai didaskalias*]."

It is telling that both Mark and the author of Colossians have slightly altered the awkward phrasing of LXX Isa 29:13, which leaves "and teachings" dangling alone at the end of the phrase, but the two Christian authors choose different paths of alteration. To adapt the citation to the larger argument in Mark 7 that pits God's commandment against the tradition of men, Mark drops the "and," thus putting "teachings" in apposition (and opposition) to "commandments of men": "teaching commandments of men [as] teachings." The error of the Pharisees, according to Mark, is that they teach mere human commandments as though they were divine teachings. This is not exactly the way Colossians uses the text. Rather, the author of Colossians moves "of men" (*anthrōpōn*) to the end of the phrase, a tactic that both makes the word order less awkward and uses the whole phrase "the commandments and teachings of men" as a summation of the regulations to which the Christians at Colossae should not submit. While in Mark these "mere human commandments" are opposed to the "commandment" or "word" of God, Colossians, with its intensely christocentric theology (cf. Col 1:15–20), simply opposes them to Christ ("if you died with Christ . . . if you were raised with Christ," Col 2:20; 3:1).[88]

This comparison between Mark and Colossians makes two points clear: (1) Colossians is not literarily dependent on Mark for its use of LXX Isa 29:13. Instead, like Mark but independently of Mark, Colossians takes over LXX Isa 29:13 with a slight alteration to serve its own polemic. (2) We may therefore infer that the LXX version of Isa 29:13—and *precisely* the LXX version—circulated among early Christians as a proof text that justified rejecting purity rules, especially those concerned with touching or eating food.[89] We need not be surprised, then, to notice that the very next verse, LXX Isa 29:14—again, with a slight variation—is cited by Paul in 1 Cor 1:19 as he rejects the "worldly wisdom" of the Corinthians. There is also a possible allusion to LXX Isa 29:14 in Matt 11:25. In Matt 11:25 (cf. Luke 10:21), Jesus addresses the Father: "you have hidden these things from the wise and intelligent men [*ekrypsas tauta apo sophōn kai synetōn*]." This most likely echoes the LXX version of Isa 29:14, with its vocabulary of *sophōn* ("wise men"), *synetōn* ("intelligent men"), and *krypsō* ("I shall hide"). In the larger context of Matthew's Gospel, the "wise and understanding" would include the Pharisees, with whom Jesus debates in the following pericope, Matt 12:1–8.

In sum, we are faced with two facts: (a) Jesus' argument in Mark 7:6–8 depends for its cogency on the LXX version of Isa 29:13 as reworked by Mark;[90] and (b) LXX Isa 29:13–14 is used by Christians elsewhere in the NT in their polemics against rival Jewish and pagan positions, including purity rules.[91] In light of these two facts, any attempt to defend Mark 7:6–8 as the authentic words of the historical Jesus incurs a heavy burden of proof. Those commentators who wish to preserve the historicity of the scene in Mark 7:6–8 usually employ one of the following defenses:

(1) One might argue that, during this debate with his opponents, the historical Jesus cited the Hebrew text of Isa 29:13 and that Mark, writing in Greek, naturally substituted the LXX version. To be sure, this approach would have to suppose that, as he was citing Isa 29:13, Jesus himself slightly edited the text, since the Hebrew text of 29:13 is a subordinate clause ("*because* this people . . ."). Cited alone, it hangs in midair. However, even if we grant some slight editing of the Hebrew text by the historical Jesus, a major problem remains. Despite claims to the contrary,[92] the Hebrew form of Isa 29:13 does not serve the precise claim Jesus is making in Mark 7:6–13. The reason why this is so is that the Hebrew form of Isa 29:13 does not contain a denunciation of teachers who teach mere human commandments and doctrines—the very point added by the LXX, the very point sharpened by Mark's redaction of the LXX, the very point that Jesus then seizes upon to accuse the Pharisees and the scribes of neglecting the commandment of God for the sake of mere human tradition. In sum, the Hebrew text of Isa 29:13 does not hand Jesus the scriptural cudgel he needs to beat his adversaries over the head; only the LXX does.

(2) One might argue that the historical Jesus knew a different Hebrew form of Isa 29:13, a form that was faithfully reproduced by the LXX translator.[93] As we have already seen, though, no such Hebrew (or Aramaic) form is attested, even in the Great Isaiah Scroll from Qumran (1QIsaᵃ), which at times does depart from the MT of Isaiah. The different thrust of LXX Isa 29:13 is apparently due to the creative theological interpretation of the LXX translator of Isaiah. It is that creative theological interpretation that the Marcan Jesus depends upon for his argument.

(3) Since the first two defenses do not work, one might argue that the historical Jesus in fact knew and quoted the LXX form of Isa 29:13. This is something of a counsel of despair. As we saw in Volume One of *A Marginal Jew*, Jesus spoke Aramaic, the ordinary, everyday language of most of his fellow Jews in 1st-century Palestine.[94] He had perhaps learned enough He-

brew to cite the Jewish Scriptures in Hebrew. But, if he knew Greek at all, it would have been the "tradesman's Greek" sufficient to write receipts and other brief notes necessary for business. It is highly unlikely that Jesus knew enough Greek to have taught at length in it; it goes beyond all likelihood that Jesus could cite the LXX from memory. That an Aramaic-speaking Jesus in 1st-century Palestine, arguing with Pharisees noted for their careful study of the (Hebrew) Scriptures, would, in the middle of a theological debate, suddenly burst into Greek with a citation of the LXX—precisely to make a point not present in the Hebrew form of Isaiah—stretches credulity beyond the breaking point.

The only probable conclusion from all that we have seen is that the scriptural debate presented by Mark in 7:6–8 is not conceivable as an event in the life of the historical Jesus. The argument Jesus lays out from Isa 29:13 demands the LXX of Isaiah, indeed, the LXX of Isaiah slightly tweaked by Mark. We must admit that, at least as far as Mark 7:6–8 is concerned, we are dealing with a Christian composition drawing upon Christian scribal activity.[95]

2. Verses 9–13: Jesus' Second Reply, Quoting Exod 20:12 and 21:17

Our decision that Jesus' first reply to his opponents (Mark 7:6–8) is a Christian composition has immediate consequences for our evaluation of the historical status of the second reply (7:9–13). In the present structure of Mark 7:1–23, vv 9–13 functions as the concrete example illustrating the general principle asserted in vv 6–8. In his first reply, Jesus denounces those teachers who place their human commandments on the level of divine teaching. Such false teachers were prophesied by Isaiah, and his prophecy has been sadly fulfilled—according to the *Marcan* Jesus—by the Pharisees and scribes who champion the tradition of the elders, even to the point of neglecting the commandment of God in favor of merely human tradition. In vv 9–13, Jesus makes his sweeping accusation specific by showing how his opponents' practice of the institution of *qorbān* supersedes the basic obligation of the Decalogue to honor one's father and mother (Exod 20:12 ‖ Deut 5:16).[96] Indeed, so serious is this obligation in the Mosaic Law that anyone who reviles or insults one's father or mother is to be put to death (Exod 21:17 [= LXX Exod 21:16]).[97] Jesus places the two quotations from Exodus side by side to emphasize that the gravity of the positive and apodictic command of the Decalogue is reinforced by the casuistic law decreeing death for those who violate the Decalogue's injunction.[98]

As we have seen in the structured translation of Mark 7:1–23, the particular example of *qorbān* has been carefully fitted by Mark into the larger flow of Jesus' argument. In v 5, the Pharisees and scribes have raised the banner of "the tradition of the elders." In vv 6–7, by citing Isa 29:13, Jesus implicitly identifies this tradition of the elders with "the commandments of [mere] men," opposed (in Mark's reworking of the LXX) to (divine) teachings. In v 8, Jesus makes this identification explicit by accusing his opponents of neglecting (or abandoning) the commandment of God and holding to the tradition of (mere) men. By borrowing the "men" (*anthrōpōn*) terminology of Isa 29:13 ("commandments of *men*"), Jesus moves from the Pharisees' terminology of "tradition of the *elders*" to "tradition of [mere] *men*."

As the Marcan Jesus begins his second reply (which illustrates his first reply with the example of *qorbān*), he reaches back to the beginning of his first reply by starting his attack once again with the ironic or satirical adverb *kalōs* ("well"). "Well [i.e., in a fine, skillful show of casuistry] do you *render void* the commandment of God, *in order that* you may establish [in place of God's commandment] *your* tradition." [99] Thus, while harking back to his first response (the repeated "well"), Jesus at the same time ratchets up his polemic by accusing his opponents of not just neglecting but actually rendering void God's commandment and of doing so with malice aforethought, with the express intention (*hina*, "in order that") of putting their tradition in the place of God's commandment. In v 9, the polemic reaches a rhetorical high point as the definition of "tradition," which began in v 5, now comes to a climax: from the tradition of the *elders* (v 5) to the commandments of *men* (v 7), to the tradition of *men* (v 8), and finally to *your* tradition (v 9), which, by definition, must mean the tradition of *you hypocrites*, since that is what Jesus called his opponents in v 6. The concrete case of *qorbān* is then neatly encased within this accusation by being framed by a rhetorical *inclusio*: the accusation of v 9 is repeated in v 13, as Jesus sums up what the Pharisees do by their practice of *qorbān*: "[thus] nullifying the word of God by *your* tradition which you have handed down." [100]

In sum, once we have decided that Jesus' first reply in vv 6–8 is a Christian composition and not an incident going back to the historical Jesus, it follows necessarily that vv 9–13, *at least in the present form and setting* of this subunit, do not go back to the historical Jesus. The whole raison d'être of vv 9–13 is to provide a concrete example of the Scripture-based accusation of vv 6–8, to which vv 9–13 are bound by rhetorical hoops of steel. Once vv 6–8 are omitted from the pericope as not coming from the historical Jesus, vv 9–13 hang in midair. One need only read vv 1–5 and then proceed immediately to vv 9–13 to realize that the latter subunit makes sense in the flow of thought only if it is preceded by Jesus' first argument in vv 6–8. Without the argument from Isa 29:13 and without Jesus' exegetical move from "tradition of the elders" through "commandments of men" and "tradition of men" to "your tradition," v 9 and the example it introduces are too abrupt and disconnected to serve as the initial, logical reply to the accusatory question in v 5.[101] Hence, Jesus' second reply, dependent as it is on his first reply, must be disqualified along with the first reply as the actual response made by the historical Jesus to the specific question raised in vv 1–5.[102]

This does not mean, however, that the argument about *qorbān*, isolated from the larger pericope of Mark 7:1–23, may not reflect some halakic teaching of the historical Jesus. In this, the core of vv 10–12 (without the framing polemic about "*your* tradition") differs notably from Jesus' first response (vv 6–8). The cogency of the first response depends on the wording of Isa 29:13 as found in the LXX and as reworked by Mark; hence, it is foreign to the precise time and place of the historical Jesus. The argument about *qorbān* presents us with a very different situation. The core of the argument fits very well into the time and place of Jesus.

As we saw in Volume Three of *A Marginal Jew*,[103] as well as in Chapter 33 of this present volume, various streams of Judaism around the turn of the era were engaged in a lively and apparently quite relevant debate over oaths and vows, including the problem of conflicting obligations arising from them. The topic finds different and sometimes contradictory treatments in the Dead Sea Scrolls, Philo, Josephus, and the later rabbis.[104]

The evidence from the Dead Sea Scrolls is intriguing yet fragmentary. The question of oaths and vows was clearly important to the Essenes, since entrance into the "new covenant" took place through a solemn ceremony involving oaths and curses.[105] Apostates from the Essene community are thus described in the *Damascus Document* as those who "rejected the covenant and the agreement that they had made in the land of Damascus, that is to say, the new covenant" (CD 20:11–12). Columns 15–16 (unfortunately fragmentary) in the *Damascus Document* stipulate in what sense or to what degree one may take oaths or vows. An Essene should avoid invoking the divine names "God" and "Lord" and instead should employ (when necessary) the oaths and curses used upon entering the covenant (CD 15:1–8). CD 16:10–12 takes up the question of annulling oaths and vows made by a member of one's family (one's wife or one's daughter), and the text (CD 16:13–14) continues with the question of what gifts may be vowed to the altar. Just as the text breaks off (CD 16:14–20), there is a tantalizing prohibition: a man is not to "sanctify the food of his mouth," for it is wrong for a person to "trap his neighbor with a ban" (line 15, citing Mic 7:2).[106] While obscure, the text is apparently condemning a particular type of religious subterfuge: namely, vowing one's food to sacred use in order to keep it from a neighbor in need.

While the word *qorbān* is not used in this context, there is an intriguing analogy to the case Jesus discusses in Mark 7:10–12, namely, employing a vow that dedicates one's possessions to sacred use in order to prevent them from being used to help another person in need (one's parents in Mark 7:10–12, a hungry neighbor in CD 16:14–15).[107] Both the Marcan Jesus and the *Damascus Document* reject this subterfuge. While CD 16:15 bases its rejection on a subtle interpretation of a text from the prophet Micah, Jesus appeals directly and bluntly to the first "social" commandment of the Decalogue: "Honor your father and your mother" (Exod 20:12). In doing this, Jesus presupposes and reinforces an important part of the original meaning of "honor" in this commandment: give not only respect and deference but also concrete aid and support to your parents, especially in their old age.[108] Jesus insists that no further refinement or specific institution of the Law can be allowed to undermine this basic obligation enshrined in the Decalogue.

There is a remarkable similarity here with Jesus' approach to divorce in Mark 10:2–12. In the case of the specific institution of divorce, Jesus appeals back to the more basic and primordial institution of the union of man and woman ordained by the Creator in Genesis 2–3. In the case of the specific institution of *qorbān* (one example of vows regulated by the Torah), Jesus appeals back to the more basic and primordial commandment of the Decalogue. Apparently Jesus operated at least implicitly with the conviction that there were certain fundamental commandments and institutions in the Mosaic Torah that overrode or annulled any secondary obligations or institutions that came into conflict with them. In the case of *qorbān*, the conflict does not seem (in this particular text) to annul the very practice of making a vow. In the case of divorce, however, the primordial will of the Creator is perceived to be in direct contradiction to the very institution of divorce, which is permitted and regulated by the Torah.

Although the word *qorbān* is not present in the key text of CD 16:14–15, we know that both the institution and the word *qorbān* were in circulation at the time of Jesus. This fact is attested by various Jewish sources beyond the Dead Sea Scrolls. A famous parallel to the words of Jesus in Mark 7:11 is found in an Aramaic inscription on an ossuary from Jebel Hallet eṭ-Ṭûri, a site located a short distance southeast of Jerusalem.[109] Dated from around the end of the 1st century B.C., the inscription contains the key word *qorbān* (*qrbn* in the unvocalized Aramaic inscription).[110] While the word *qorbān* in the OT carries only the general idea of a gift, offering, or sacrifice, the ossuary inscription is much more focused in its usage: "Everything that a

man may find to his profit in this ossuary [is] an offering (*qrbn*) to God from
the one within." [111] The very phrasing of this inscription, which speaks of
what might be to another person's profit or use and then forbids such use
because of prior dedication to God, finds an echo in Mark 7:11: "Whatever
you might have received from me [for your support] [is] Qorban—that is,
a gift [dedicated to God]." Clearly, we have here in Mark a specific Jewish
institution paralleled by a Palestinian Jewish ossuary inscription from the
same time period.

The institution and the word *qorbān* were apparently so prominent in
Judaism around the turn of the era that Josephus explains both institution
and word twice in his works, each time using the same transliteration of
the Hebrew into Greek (*korban*) and the same translation of the word into
Greek (*dōron*, "gift") that Mark 7:11 likewise uses.[112] In his *Jewish Antiquities*, while dealing with the larger question of tithes and other offerings
due priests, Josephus mentions in passing the special case of *korban* (*Ant.*
4.4.4 §73): "Those who designate themselves *korban* to God—a word that
means 'gift' [*dōron*] in Greek—if they wish to be relieved of this religious
obligation, must pay the priests a sum of money." Notice that the concern in
this passage is with how one may be released from the obligation imposed
by this particular vow called *korban*. In his *Against Apion* (*Ag. Ap.* 1.22
§167), Josephus uses *korban* of oaths (*horkoi*) instead, but once again he
interprets the word *korban* to mean "God's gift" (*dōron theou*).[113] While
Philo does not use the word *korban* in his treatment of the subject (*Hypothetica* 7.3 §358), he knows the institution. He asserts that anyone who
invokes the name of God over certain possessions and declares that they
are dedicated to God must immediately consider himself barred from using
them from then on.

The word and the practice of *qorbān* continued—but also mutated—in
later rabbinic teaching. In the Mishna's tractate *Nedarim* ("Vows"), the
word *qorbān*, along with an allied word, *qônām*, is used to mean an offering to God that therefore becomes forbidden to humans. For example,
in *m. Ned.* 1:4, *qorbān* is applied to food that is forbidden to a person—a
case similar to that of CD 16:14–15. One can see the problem of possible casuistry and subterfuge arising in the practice of *qorbān* (and similar
words of asseveration) in *m. Ned.* 2:5, where the wording of certain vows
causes a dispute as to whether the vows need to be annulled formally. In
some passages, however, the sense of dedication to God fades away, leaving simply the sense of something forbidden to another. In addition, in *m.
Ned.* 4:6, we see the development of a further meaning of *qônām*: a protestation or even a curse called down upon a person. This kind of rabbinic

development lies beyond both the thought and the time frame of Mark 7:9–13.

The question arises, though: Would the subterfuge attributed to the Pharisees in the polemic of Mark 7:10–12 have been a real possibility in Pharisaic practice in the pre-70 era? It is difficult to say, since we lack any writings coming directly from the Pharisees. It is perhaps significant, though, that the practice of *qorbān* remained a contested subject among the rabbis whose opinions are reflected in the Mishna (redacted ca. A.D. 200–220). For example, in *m. Ned.* 9:1, we encounter a variety of views concerning the grounds that would justify the annulling of a vow that a man had made to the detriment of his father and mother. The fact that assorted views on the question were allowed to stand side by side at the time of the composition of the Mishna (though the opinion of the sages is the one that prevails) suggests that earlier this question was the subject of real debate and remained unsettled. One should also note that, even in this mishnaic passage, the debate focuses on what grounds would allow a man to annul his vow; nothing is said about his having a strict obligation to annul it.

More telling still is the anecdote related in *m. Ned.* 5:6. A man had made a vow that prevented his father from receiving any food from him. To provide the father with food, the man engaged in an elaborate subterfuge *via* a legal fiction. The story presupposes that (a) vows like this were in fact made and (b) no simple way of annulling them was available.[114] A similar situation is presupposed by Philo's treatment of oaths and vows in his *Hypothetica* 7:3–5. He takes a strict view of the irrevocability of a vow, even when it works to the detriment of members of one's family. In Philo's presentation, ways of annulling the vow are quite limited, namely, refusal of the gift by the officiating priest or—expressed in vague terms by Philo—declaration by some ruler. The strictness of his view comes close to the position rejected by Jesus. It may therefore be that *m. Ned.* 5:6 represents the early state of casuistry around the time of Jesus, when the position that Jesus excoriates was actually held by some Jews or Jewish groups (possibly some Pharisees).[115] At the very least, CD 16, Philo, Mark 7:11, and *m. Ned.* 5:6 suggest that there was a lively debate around the turn of the era (a) about the vow called *qorbān*, which could deprive one's parents or neighbor of vital support, and (b) about the possibility of annulling such a vow.

What, then, can we say about the origin of the core tradition of Mark 7:10–11 (putting aside the framing *inclusio* of vv 9–13)? The witness of the *Damascus Document*, probably from the latter part of the 2d century B.C., and the various opinions on *qorbān* found in the Mishna, with various individual opinions dating from either the 1st or 2d century A.D., place Jesus' pronouncement on *qorbān* squarely within the time period when this issue was real, relevant, and debated at length among Palestinian Jews. That the core tradition in Mark 7:10–11 appears to be a discrete unit that Mark has woven into his larger composition of 7:1–23 argues for dating the core tradition some time earlier than ca. A.D. 70, the generally accepted date for the composition of Mark's Gospel. The occurrence of the Aramaic (or Hebrew) word *qorbān* in the pre-Marcan tradition, a word that Mark has to explain in Greek and a word that the supposedly Jewish Matthew drops from his retelling of the story (Matt 15:5), points to an origin within Palestinian Judaism, as does indeed the very nature of the dispute.

We are left then with two options.[116] Either the basic argument (though not necessarily the exact words) enshrined in Mark 7:11–12 goes back to the historical Jesus *or* the argument is a creation of Aramaic-speaking Christian Jews in Palestine during the first few decades of the Christian movement's existence. Either position is theoretically possible. But which is more likely?

We have no evidence from any source that the minor question of the proper practice of *qorbān* exercised any Christian Jews or their converts in the earliest days of the new Christian movement. As far as we can tell from the letters of Paul, the Acts of the Apostles, and the earliest strata of Mark and Q, the practical and theoretical problems with which Christian Jews in Palestine grappled prior to A.D. 70 included persecution from the priestly establishment in Jerusalem, the failure to attract most Palestinian Jews to the new movement, the development of and struggle over internal leadership, the apparent "delay" of the parousia, a fuller articulation of the status and work of Jesus the Messiah, sabbath observance, the observance of various forms of ritual purity, and proper relations with Gentiles who joined the Christian movement—involving eventually the thorny questions of circumcision and the food laws. As the increasingly beleaguered Christian Jews in pre-70 Palestine struggled to reply to all these problems amid the ominous loss of some of their original leaders, there is not the slightest hint that they had the time or interest to engage in an argument over the relatively obscure topic of *qorbān*, a topic that never appears anywhere in the NT apart from Mark 7:10–12 ‖ Matt 15:4–6. Hence, while complete certainty is not possible, I think it more probable, by the criterion of discontinuity (from early Christianity), that the small unit of tradition preserved fossil-like in Mark 7:10–12 goes back to the historical Jesus.[117]

In itself, this does not tell us very much, since we lack the original context of Jesus' remarks about *qorbān* and since his remarks seem to be part of an ad hominem retort rather than a detailed disquisition on the question of vows. His debating partners might have been a group of Pharisees (not *all* Pharisees)[118] who took a very strict approach to the institution and who therefore refused any annulment of the vow, no matter what the consequences, perhaps for fear of opening the door to the type of casuistry seen at times in the mishnaic tractate *Nedarim*. Yet we must admit that this is mere conjecture; the original interlocutors are lost to us. What can be deduced from this brief tradition does, however, confirm what we have seen already in the previous chapters of Volume Four—and, to that extent, the criterion of coherence supports historicity as well. Far from being merely a one-line aphorist or spinner of enigmatic parables, Jesus the Jew, as an intensely engaged and deeply religious teacher in 1st-century Jewish Palestine, put forth his views on the Law and *hălăkâ* while debating Jews with opposing views. This was true of major questions like divorce and sabbath; but it was also true of minor questions like *qorbān*.

In addition, this slight tradition about *qorbān* reminds us that, as a Palestinian Jew debating major and minor matters involving observance of the Mosaic Law, Jesus would at times have inevitably quoted the Jewish Scriptures to prove his point. The idea, so entrenched in form and tradition criticism from the time of Rudolf Bultmann onward, that any citation of the OT in the Gospels is a sure sign of Christian composition is not only a priori unlikely but also a posteriori refuted by units like the *qorbān* debate in Mark 7:10–12. Not only did the historical Jesus cite Scripture for his purpose, he was quite capable of stringing together Scripture texts (as in Mark 7:10) or of playing one text off against another (if we may suppose that the basic argument about divorce in Mark 10:2–9 goes back to the historical Jesus). To be sure, this does not mean that every Scripture citation in the Gospels must come from the historical Jesus. As we have seen, that is not the case in Jesus' first reply in Mark 7:6–7. But the juxtaposition of the citation of Isaiah in Jesus' first reply (a Christian product) and the citation of Exodus in Jesus' second reply (probably authentic tradition from Jesus) reminds us that judgments must be made on the merits of the individual case. A magic wand from form criticism will not automatically decide every instance.

At the very least, the *qorbān* tradition reminds us that a Jesus who never cited the Jewish Scriptures, which were at the heart of his religious tradition, which provided the basis and models for his own message and mission, and which were the object of fierce debate among his Jewish contemporaries, is practically a contradiction in terms. Certainly, such a Jesus would have been the strangest Jewish teacher on the 1st-century Palestinian scene, a teacher who would not have been taken seriously, and a teacher who would have wound up with no audience. For this small reminder of who Jesus was as a Jewish teacher and how he would have taught his fellow Jews, we can be grateful to the *qorbān* tradition of Mark 7:10–12.

3. *Verses 14–23: Jesus' Aphorism on Defilement and His Explanation*

In this section, I treat together the pivot (vv 14–15) of the pericope and the entire second half (vv 17–23) for two reasons:

(1) As we saw in our initial survey of the structure of 7:1–23, vv 14–15 + vv 17–23 reflect the literary style and theological concerns of Mark to a striking degree. Jesus first enunciates a puzzling teaching in public and then withdraws into a private space where (a) his disciples question him (v 17), (b) he rebukes them for not understanding (v 18a), and (c) he explains to them alone the meaning of his obscure public teaching, with the two-part explanation (vv 18b–19 + vv 20–23) paralleling the two parts of the aphorism in v 15.[119]

(2) Granted this Marcan composition, when it comes to a quest for the historical Jesus, everything hangs upon the authenticity of v 15. If the two-part aphorism of v 15 comes from the historical Jesus, then there is a fair probability that the two-part explanation (vv 18b–23), which repeats and expands upon the language of v 15, likewise comes from him, at least in part, if not in total. If, however, v 15, the font from which the whole second half of the pericope springs, is not authentic, it becomes extremely difficult to defend the authenticity of vv 18b–23. We focus therefore on the pivotal verses, 14–15.

(a) *The pivot of vv 14–15*

(i) Most commentators readily admit that v 14 is an introduction formulated by Mark.[120] The reason for this judgment is simple: it echoes in many ways the structure and vocabulary of other redactional verses in Mark. The participial phrase beginning v 14, "and summoning again the crowd" (*kai proskalesamenos palin ton ochlon*), is suffused with Marcan vocabulary. In addition to Mark's beloved *kai* ("and") used to introduce a clause, the verb "to summon," "to call to oneself" (*proskaleomai*) is a Marcan favorite among the Four Gospels (Matthew 4x, Mark 9x, Luke 4x, John 0).[121] We find the Marcan Jesus calling to himself the disciples, the Twelve, or the crowds in 3:13,29; 6:7; 7:4; 8:1,34; 10:42; and 12:43. In many of these passages, the purpose of Jesus' summons is to deliver some new and striking teaching. This is certainly the case in the precise parallel found in Mark 8:34, "and summoning the crowd" (*kai proskalesamenos ton ochlon*), where Jesus announces the necessity for any disciple to take up his cross and follow him on the way to his passion. Among the Synoptic Gospels, the adverb "again" (*palin*) is likewise a favorite Marcan word for beginning pericopes or subsections thereof (Matthew 17x, Mark 28x, Luke 3x). As for "he said to them," we saw earlier, in our analysis of the structure of 7:1–23 (C.3.c.), how Mark uses verbs of saying to structure the various sub-units of this whole pericope. The emphatic command, "hear me all [of you] and understand," echoes both the calls of the Marcan Jesus to hear and his complaints—as well as Mark's—that neither the crowd nor his disciples in the end understand or believe (e.g., 4:3,9,12,23,40; 6:52; 8:14–21). When, in addition, we consider the larger structural as well as the particular verbal similarities to Mark's composition of the parable discourse (4:1–34),[122] we may safely consign v 14 to Mark's redaction. He has created it to introduce the pivot of the whole pericope, 7:15.

(ii) A brief initial examination of 7:15 suggests arguments both for and against its authenticity. On the positive side, v 15 is a disturbing, subversive aphorism cast in two-part antithetical parallelism:

There is nothing outside a man that, by entering into him, can defile him; but those things that come out of a man are the things that defile him.

Thus, both discontinuity from the Judaism of Jesus' day (which, almost without exception, inculcated the food laws of the Pentateuch)[123] and a style coherent with those sayings of Jesus that are generally considered authentic argue for historicity.

On the negative side, after all that we have seen so far in the four volumes of *A Marginal Jew*, it hardly seems credible that the popular Palestinian Jewish teacher named Jesus should have rejected or annulled in a single logion all the laws on prohibited foods enshrined in Leviticus and Deuteronomy. To have done so would have meant tearing down one of the major boundaries and barriers that defined 1st-century Jews over against the Gentile world that regularly threatened to engulf them. Are we to imagine that this 1st-century Jewish prophet taught such a shocking revocation of a key element in the Mosaic Law, a revocation that could endanger the very existence of the Jewish people as a distinct religious and ethnic group? If Jesus did actually annul the food laws, how did he remain so popular and influential among the common people, to the extent that the Jerusalem authorities considered him a threat to their power? Coherence with Jesus' own sense of being a prophet sent to his people Israel—and not to the Gentiles—as well as coherence with 1st-century Palestinian Judaism (however varied and sectarian it was) would seem to argue against the authenticity of 7:15. In addition, and perhaps even more to the point, how could such a revolutionary overturning of Jewish food laws be so quickly forgotten by Jesus' own disciples? As we see in Paul's epistles and the Acts of the Apostles, the church of the first Christian generation was embroiled in a bitter argument over whether the laws of prohibited foods applied to *Gentile* converts (to say nothing of Jewish Christians), with no appeal being made by any side in the argument to Jesus' supposed teaching on the subject. I will be unpacking these arguments below.

These clashing arguments for and against the historicity of 7:15 have generated an interesting history of interpretation. To focus on the last half-century: back in the days of the "Second Quest for the Historical Jesus" (1950s and 1960s), scholars like Ernst Käsemann and Norman Perrin, following the lead of Rudolf Bultmann, favored the authenticity of the saying on the ground of discontinuity from the Judaism of Jesus' day.[124] With the Third Quest's emphasis on the Jewishness of Jesus, many recent scholars have rejected the logion as being incompatible with a 1st-century Palestinian Jewish teacher addressing his fellow Jews.[125]

Still others have sought a mediating position: in their view, Mark 7:15 is conceivable in the mouth of the Jewish Jesus if we detach it from the Christian theology within which the redactor Mark has encased and modified the saying. In other words, reading this Jewish saying through the lens of the decades-long disputes over food laws, Mark has given the logion a radical twist that was not original to the saying. Interpreters from this school base their approach on various combinations of three basic arguments:

(1) One must appreciate the phenomenon of "dialectical negation" in ancient Semitic speech, all the more so in the fiery rhetoric of OT prophets.[126] Many a prophetic declaration may seem to be saying "not x, but y," when actually it is inculcating in a dramatic way that "y is more important than x," without meaning to reject x entirely. A famous example is Yahweh's insistence in Hos 6:6, "I desire mercy and not sacrifice." What Hosea means is that, in the worship of Yahweh, mercy toward one's neighbor is much more important than cultic sacrifice, though the latter is not totally rejected.[127] Mark likewise supplies examples of such dialectical negation. Jesus' declaration in Mark 9:37, "Whoever receives me receives not me but the One who sent me," hardly intends to deny that a person accepting Jesus either physically (into one's house) or in faith (into one's heart) is actually receiving Jesus.[128] The point is one of emphasis: in receiving Jesus, one is receiving, more important, the God who sent Jesus. Granted the rhetoric of dialectical negation, the original point of Mark 7:15 might well have been that Jesus wished to emphasize the importance of avoiding the *moral* impurity that humans generate within themselves and then unleash on the world. Such

moral impurity must be one's major concern, without, however, totally ignoring *ritual* impurity.

(2) According to Joachim Jeremias, many of the sayings of Jesus cast in antithetical parallelism exemplify the rhetorical pattern of "end stress," that is, the emphasis in the saying falls on the second half of the statement (so, e.g., Mark 6:10–11; 8:12,35; 10:18,27,31; 11:17; 12:44; 13:20,31; 14:7).[129] According to this opinion, in 7:15, the major emphasis falls on v 15b, which denounces the moral impurity that comes forth from within the human heart.

(3) To bolster this "mild" interpretation of Jesus' logion on defilement, some authors argue that the original form of Jesus' saying is found not in Mark 7:15, but rather in Matt 15:11, which some judge to be an independent tradition: "Not what enters into the mouth defiles a man, but what comes out of the mouth, this defiles a man." That this Matthean version is the earlier form of Jesus' saying is supported, according to these critics, by the criterion of multiple attestation. For, in the opinion of these critics, the Coptic *Gospel of Thomas* preserves an independent form of this saying (at the end of logion 14) that is very close ot Matt 15:11: "For what goes into your mouth will not defile you, but what comes out of your mouth, that is what will defile you." In the opinion of some commentators, this milder form of Matt 15:11 (without the Mark's emphatic "there is *nothing* outside a man that . . . *can* defile him") is perfectly intelligible in the mouth of the Jewish Jesus, who, like the prophets before him, stressed interior moral purity over exterior ritual purity without totally rejecting the latter. Matt 15:11 is emphasizing not rejection but priorities—a good description of much of Jesus' moral exhortation.

While these three arguments seem cogent at first glance, closer examination makes them less so.

(1) It is possible to understand Mark 7:15 in terms of dialectical negation, but this interpretation is not necessary. In the Bible, there are many statements of antithetical parallelism that mean precisely what they say in an exclusive sense: "not x, but y." This exclusive opposition is most clearly seen in the OT when the text inculcates worship of Yahweh alone (Deut 5:6): "I am the Lord your God . . . you shall have no other God before me." Absolute opposition is also expressed in rules of behavior (Deut 5:13): "Six days you shall labor and do all your work . . . but [on] the seventh day . . . you shall not do any work." The same absolute opposition is found in some NT statements of antithetical parallelism, including sayings attributed to Jesus: for example, Mark 2:17: "It is not the healthy who need a doctor but the sick"; Mark 2:27: "The sabbath was made for man, and not man for the sabbath";

and Mark 10:45: "The Son of Man came not to be served but to serve." [130] In brief, the form of antithetical parallelism, by itself, does not tell us whether the statement should be understood in a relative or absolute sense. Only an inspection of content and context can tell us that.

(2) The appeal to the supposed rule of "end stress" in Jesus' sayings misses an important point about the slightly unbalanced nature of the antithetical parallelism in Mark 7:15.[131] The first half of the verse makes a sweeping, emphatic statement about the *impossibility* of an event; this emphasis is not paralleled with the same stress in the second half of the saying:

> There is *nothing* [*ouden*] outside a man that, by entering into him, *can*
> [*dynatai*] defile him;
> but those things that come out of a man are the things that defile him.

The forceful assertion of absolute impossibility ("there is *nothing* . . . that *can* defile him") is not replicated in the second half, which is rhetorically bland by comparison ("those things . . . defile a man"). This does not mean that the second half of the statement is unimportant for Mark. It certainly is, as the lengthy exposition in vv 21–23 (employing a list of vices) makes clear.[132] But, rhetorically, the stress plainly lies on the first half of the saying; the absence of a corresponding *dynatai* ("can") in the second half is telling. This is all the more so because the presence of *dynatai* would make the claim of the second half more precise. After all, is it true without qualification that "those things that come out of a man" are the things that defile him? [133] All sorts of good words and deeds come forth from a man without defiling him (to say nothing of physical excretions). Hence, the restriction that the verb "can" would bring to the statement in v 15b would actually clarify the sense. The absence of "can" in the second half of v 15, when it could easily be there, serves all the more to place the accent on the first half of the verse. Granted this, the sweeping nature of the assertion that "there is nothing . . . that can defile" is more naturally understood as an absolute rather than a relative statement. Indeed, in my opinion, to take this forceful, not to say shocking, affirmation as a case of relative dialectic goes against the obvious thrust of the logion.[134] What is being asserted is wholesale impossibility, not relative importance.[135]

(3) One might still escape the obvious consequences of this observation if one could establish that Matt 15:11 (along with *G. Thom.* 14) was an independent form, in fact the original form, of Jesus' statement, which is also reflected in Mark 7:15. The first half of Matt 15:11 pointedly lacks the emphatic formulation of Mark ("there is nothing . . . that can defile"). Instead,

lacking any auxiliary *dynatai* ("can"), Matt 15:11 displays greater balance (and blandness) in its antithetical parallelism:

Not what enters into the mouth defiles a man,
but what comes out of the mouth, this defiles a man.

The lack of the emphatic negation and of the assertion of impossibility makes Matt 15:11 more amenable to a relative interpretation: that is, what comes out of the mouth is much more defiling than what goes in. However, absolute negation remains a possible interpretation of Matt 15:11; the saying is ambiguous in a way that Mark 7:15 is not.

What, then, can be said of the view that Matt 15:11 represents an independent and more primitive version of the logion? In my view, not much. The whole pericope of Matt 15:1–20 displays Matthew's typical redactional tendencies in rewriting Mark. It is a shame that recent—and in itself legitimate—emphasis on the ongoing influence of oral tradition in the 1st-century church has led some exegetes to forget or ignore the valuable insights gained by redaction criticism, especially the work done on Matthew's redaction of Mark in the 1950s and 1960s.[136] For example, Gerhard Barth's masterful essay on the Law in Matthew—however debatable individual points may be—shows how Matt 15:1–20 is a striking example of Matthew's redaction of Mark—and of Mark 7:1–23 in particular—according to the theological and literary preferences of Matthew.[137]

To give some examples: in his redaction of Mark, Matthew regularly abbreviates or tightens up Mark's sprawling narratives. This often involves omitting Mark's errors of fact, shortening his wordy and sometimes superfluous expositions, reordering the parts of the pericope for a more logical presentation, softening statements that could be offensive to observant Jewish Christians, and improving the quality of the Greek style and vocabulary.

All these tendencies can be seen in Matthew's redaction of Mark 7:1–23. The Marcan material is shortened by omitting Mark's intrusive, meandering, erroneous, and (for pious Jewish Christians) offensive parenthesis in Mark 7:2–4. Matthew, ever concerned about "the Law and the prophets," inverts Jesus' two responses in Mark 7:6–8 and 7:9–13 to create his favored order of Law (honoring father and mother, from the Pentateuch) and prophets (the Isaiah citation). At the same time, he omits Mark's vague and generalizing polemic, "and you do many such things like this" (Mark 7:13b; cf. the omission of "all the Jews" [v 3] and "many other things" [v 4]). Also characteristic of Matthew is his willingness at certain junctures to en-

large the narrative framework that he has inherited from Mark in order
(a) to create or expand a place for Peter (Matt 15:15; cf. Matt 14:28–31;
16:17–19; 17:24–27; 18:21), or (b) to heighten the polemic against Pharisees (Matt 15:12–14)—but, at this point in his story, not against Jews in
general. Indeed, as elsewhere, Matthew takes pains to soften or eliminate,
when possible, statements about the Law that could scandalize pious Jewish
Christians. He omits Mark's editorial comment that Jesus, by his teaching
on inside and outside, was making all foods clean (Mark 7:19). In a final
deft touch (15:20b), Matthew concludes his pericope with the redactional
addition, "but eating with unwashed hands does not defile a man"—thus,
in one fell stroke, creating an *inclusio* with the beginning of the pericope
(15:2), tightening up the meandering focus of Mark 7:1–23, and deflecting
attention away from the problematic statement that prohibited foods do not
defile (preserved in a mild form in 15:11) and back to the less central and
more debatable problem of eating with unwashed hands.

Granted this heavy and purposeful redaction that pervades Matthew's
reworking of Mark 7:1–23, it is difficult to maintain that the differences
in Matt 15:11 vis-à-vis Mark 7:15 are due not to Matthew's editorial hand
but rather to a stray independent logion that suddenly pops up in the midst
of a pericope that is otherwise simply and solely the product of Matthew's
recasting of Mark. This is all the more the case when we notice that Matt
15:11 exemplifies the same softening tone (i.e., avoiding as much as possible
direct conflict with the heart of the Law) that we see elsewhere in Matthew
and indeed in this pericope (e.g., the omission of Mark 7:19c). Within 15:11
itself, Matthew's redactional hand is seen both in the introduction of the
characteristically Matthean word "mouth" (*stoma*) and in the abbreviation
of the Marcan logion in a way that creates greater balance between the
two halves.[138] Unless we are to forget suddenly all that redaction criticism
has taught us about Matthew's consistent redaction of Mark throughout
his Gospel, the simplest and most natural explanation of Matthew 15:11 is
that, like the rest of Matt 15:1–20, it is the theologically motivated rewriting
of Mark 7:15 by Matthew.

This conclusion carries an important corollary. If Matt 15:11 is nothing
more than Matthew's redactional rewriting of Mark 7:15—with the typically Matthean word "mouth" inserted into the saying—then G. *Thom.* 14
must be judged not an independent tradition but rather a slightly redacted
version of Matt 15:11: "For what goes *into your mouth* will not defile you,
but what comes *out of your mouth*, that is what will defile you." The use of
"into [your] mouth" and "out of your mouth" in the two halves of the aphorism, the resumptive "this" (or: "that") in the second half, and the carefully

balanced parallelism all reveal Matthew's fingerprints on logion 14 of the *Gospel of Thomas*.[139] Once again, the academic dogma of *Thomas*' independence of the Synoptics and its possession of a more primitive tradition does not hold up to close scrutiny.[140]

The results of this comparison of Mark, Matthew, and the *Gospel of Thomas* suggest the following conclusions about the authenticity of Mark 7:15: (1) Mark 7:15 represents the earliest available form of this saying. Matt 15:11 is simply Matthew's reworked version of the logion, echoed by *G. Thom.* 14. (2) Mark 7:15, the earliest form, is the only form containing the emphatic and uncompromising wording *ouden . . . dynatai*, which Matthew felt a need to soften. (3) Hence, the earliest available form of this logion, Mark 7:15, presents Jesus as emphatically declaring that no food that enters a man can defile him.[141]

These conclusions, in turn, confront us with a basic question. Is Mark 7:15 credible in the mouth of the historical Jesus? The fact that it in effect revokes key purity laws of the Pentateuch, laws that had become major identity badges of Jews vis-à-vis Gentiles, may give us pause; but this fact, in itself, does not prove that Jesus could not have spoken this aphorism. As we have seen, the historical Jesus forbade both divorce and oath-taking, institutions sanctioned and regulated by the Pentateuch and considered by almost everyone, Jew and Gentile alike, to be necessary for the smooth functioning of society. If Jesus could revoke two practices enshrined in the Pentateuch, he could revoke another.

While this is true, there are notable differences between the divorce and oath-taking on the one hand and food laws on the other. To begin with, divorce as an institution is never directly set up or commanded by the Pentateuch. It is rather presupposed as a common social institution, known and used by all surrounding populations. The Pentateuch simply regulates divorce in a few extraordinary cases. Moreover, although Jesus' total prohibition of divorce would be shocking and disturbing to his fellow Jews, in practice it would affect the actions of only some Jewish males at some times in their lives, not every Jew every day of his or her life. And while oath-taking was indeed commanded in two very precise situations (goods entrusted to another that then were lost and the wife suspected of adultery), these two cases hardly occurred everyday in the lives of most Jews. By contrast, the laws governing permitted and forbidden foods are laid out at great length and are strictly enjoined on all Israelites by Leviticus and Deuteronomy. Unlike divorce and oath-taking, the detailed dietary provisions stood out all the more because, in some cases, the OT rules contradicted common eating practices among Israel's neighbors, thus creating an identity badge

for Israelites. Thus, wiping out the distinction between clean and unclean
foods would mean both altering the habits of all Jews every day of their lives
and destroying one of the major socioreligious boundaries between Jews
and Gentiles. Hence, while the revocation of food laws may be similar in
some ways to the revocation of divorce and oath-taking—all three imply a
remarkable claim to authority on Jesus' part—the revocation of food laws
constitutes a far more radical blow to the authority of the Mosaic Law and
the separate identity of Jews in a Gentile world.

Once one grasps this key difference, one begins to notice other differences
between the revocation of divorce and oath-taking on the one hand and the
revocation of the food laws as presented in the Gospels on the other. These
further differences call into question the authenticity of Mark 7:15—and let
us remember that the entire question of the historical Jesus revoking food
laws basically hangs by the single thread of 7:15.

(1) One of the main arguments for the historicity of Jesus' prohibition of
divorce is the multiple attestation of sources and forms: Mark, Q, and Paul.
Multiple attestation is not as strong an argument in the case of oath-taking,
but Jas 5:12 probably does join Matt 5:34–37 to supply multiple attestation.
In contrast, Jesus' revocation of food laws enjoys no such multiple attestation. As we have seen, Matt 15:11 (cf. *G. Thom.* 14) is Matthew's reworking
of Mark 7:15, and everything in Mark 7:17–23 is simply an extended explanation of Mark 7:15. Take away 7:15 along with its subsequent explanation
in vv 17–23, and there is no primitive logion in the Gospels (indeed, anywhere in the NT) that states that Jesus during his public ministry revoked
the food laws. The claim that this teaching goes back to the historical Jesus
thus rises or falls on the authenticity of 7:15, which lacks multiple attestation.[142]

(2) Jesus' prohibition of divorce would have had no immediate and necessary impact on his own behavior (presuming that he was unmarried) or
probably on the behavior of his disciples (some of whom were married and
traveling away from home, but none of whom is said to have divorced his
spouse before or after his call to discipleship).[143] Neither would the prohibition of oath-taking, at least in the two cases when oath-taking was commanded by the Torah, have impinged all that much on the daily life of Jesus
and his disciples. This lack of immediate impact on the teacher and his disciples in the case of divorce and oath-taking contrasts sharply with the one
teaching of Jesus on food that is generally considered authentic, that is, his
prohibition of fasting (Mark 2:18–20 parr.).[144] The question of fasting arises
and an explanation of the practice of not fasting is offered by Jesus because
his disciples are observed by others as not practicing voluntary fasting, in

contrast to pious Jewish groups like the Pharisees and the disciples of the Baptist. What Jesus taught about fasting, his disciples publicly practiced. It is difficult to believe that the disciples would have acted in this way if Jesus himself had acted otherwise. It is precisely this publicly observed practice of not fasting voluntarily that calls forth both the question and Jesus' response.

The case of Mark 7:15 is just the opposite. We have in Mark 7:15 a saying of Jesus revoking the food laws, and yet nowhere in any Gospel is it claimed that Jesus and/or his disciples ever ate forbidden food. Indeed, granted the volatile nature of legal disputes among various Jewish groups in 1st-century Palestine, one can well imagine the unavoidable uproar if Jesus' disciples had regularly eaten forbidden food. Such public flouting of key provisions of the Pentateuch could easily have called forth violent protest. Yet nowhere in any of the Gospels is there the slightest hint or trace of such a provocative act by the disciples or of any corresponding reaction on the part of a Jewish party or the populace in general. In the Gospels, much of Jesus' teaching in parables and controversies and much of his activity in miracle working and table fellowship with toll collectors and sinners call forth puzzlement, questions, admiration, or fierce objections. By contrast, the truly shocking revocation in Mark 7:15 calls forth no response whatever from the crowd, the disciples, or the opponents. Indeed, one of the most striking contradictions at the heart of Mark 7:1–23 is the fact that the relatively minor question of eating bread with unwashed hands (minor, at least, in the early 1st century A.D.) evokes a sharp objection from the Pharisees and scribes, while no one—Pharisees, scribes, disciples, or the crowd—objects vociferously to Jesus' shattering statement on food laws in 7:15. In true Marcan fashion, the disciples ask in private for a further explanation (7:17). Yet, when the Marcan Jesus makes absolutely clear that he is making all foods clean (see Mark's comment in 7:19c), we hear not a peep from the disciples.

This lack of reverberation anywhere in the Gospel tradition raises serious questions about the authenticity of Mark 7:15. If the historical Jesus had actually revoked the food laws of the Pentateuch, and if (as happened with the rejection of fasting) his disciples had proceeded to put their master's teaching into practice, the resulting firestorm would have engulfed the Nazarene and his followers in a major battle with observant Palestinian Jews of any and every stripe. Instead, nothing further is heard of this teaching during the public ministry, and no echo of it resounds in the various accusations made against Jesus in the Passion Narratives.[145] No sooner is Mark 7:15–23 spoken than it disappears from Jesus' public ministry. This is hardly credible.

(3) This silence in the Gospels (apart from Mark 7:15–23 par.) concerning Jesus' revocation of the food laws corresponds to an intriguing silence noticeable in the early church's response to the crisis over the observance of food laws.[146] Both Paul in his epistles (especially Galatians and Romans) and Luke in his Acts of the Apostles struggle with the question of why Gentile converts to Christianity need not follow the food laws—or, in Luke's case, *all* the food laws—of Leviticus and Deuteronomy.[147] To be sure, Paul and Luke differ in their approaches and rationales. Paul proclaims that the death-resurrection of Jesus and the gift of the Spirit received by faith have liberated his Gentile converts from such Mosaic observances (Gal 2:15–4:7; Rom 2:1–8:39). In Acts, Luke instead appeals (a) to a special revelation given to Peter (Acts 10:9–16; cf. 11:5–17; 15:7–11,14) within the larger context of the conversion of the centurion Cornelius (Acts 10:1–48) and (b) to the Spirit-led decision of the so-called Council of Jerusalem (Acts 15:1–29). Now, for all the twists and turns in the arguments of Galatians, Romans, and Acts 10–15, what is striking is that neither Paul nor the disputing parties in Luke's narrative ever think of appealing to the teaching of Jesus on the subject, be it the logion of Mark 7:15 or some other saying. Indeed, for all their differences, Paul and Acts agree in conveying the general impression that the obligatory nature of the food laws for Gentile converts was a new problem that had suddenly burst upon the scene. From both authors one gathers that this was a problem that the early church had to grapple with and think through either (a) on the basis of the new situation created by Jesus' death-resurrection and the sending of the Spirit (so Paul) or (b) on the basis of a new revelation given to Peter (Acts 10:9–16) and then confirmed by James' eschatological interpretation of Amos 9:11–12 during the Council of Jerusalem (Acts 15:13–21), along with his pragmatic compromise enshrined in the so-called Apostolic Decree (in the letter of Acts 15:23–29).

Hence, precisely because of their vast differences in theological outlook, ecclesial situation, and chosen literary genre, the silence of both Paul and Luke about Jesus' supposed teaching is impressive. Between the two of them, Paul and Luke, in their activities, journeys, sources, writings, and followers (as well as the problems and opponents they faced), spanned almost all of the regions in which Christianity existed in the 1st century A.D. That neither they nor their colleagues nor their opponents within the church should ever have brought up Mark 7:15 as relevant to the fierce debate over prohibited foods in first-generation Christianity speaks volumes.[148] The silence on all sides is deafening.

The objection that Paul was simply ignorant of this particular teaching of Jesus and hence did not invoke it is not as cogent as might at first seem. In the first place, Paul's supposed blanket ignorance of the teachings of Jesus is hardly confirmed by his epistles.[149] When Paul has to argue with his Christian audience over such specific issues of practice as divorce (1 Cor 7:10–11), the economic support of the apostles (9:14), or the proper observance of the Lord's Supper (11:23–26), he is quite capable of citing or paraphrasing sayings that most likely go back to the historical Jesus.[150] This seems to be his tactic especially when he fears that his usual theological arguments, put forward on his own authority and on the basis of his understanding of what the crucified and risen Christ means for believers, may not carry the day with his audience. It strains credulity to think that on one of the most pivotal questions that rocked the early church, one that could have threatened his whole Gentile mission, Paul would not have inquired after and cited any relevant saying of Jesus that was circulating in the early church.[151]

This claim may seem at first just general surmise, but it has a concrete point of connection in one of Paul's own pronouncements on disputes over food.[152] Addressing conflicts over dietary observance that have arisen between "the strong" and "the weak" in the Christian community in Rome, Paul states solemnly (Rom 14:14): "I know and I am convinced in the Lord Jesus that nothing is common [koinon][153] in itself; but if someone thinks something is common, then it is common for that person." While some critics have taken the phrase "I know . . . in the Lord Jesus" to mean that Paul is appealing to Jesus' teaching enshrined in Mark 7:15,[154] Paul's phrasing elsewhere and the whole thrust of his argument in Romans 14 indicate that he is proposing, on the basis of his apostolic authority, the correct view of Christian life that flows from the death and resurrection of Christ (see Rom 14:7–9).[155] This is clearly the case in v 14, since Paul grounds his argument in v 15 with the exhortation, "Do not by the food you eat destroy that [brother] for whom Christ died."

Rom 14:14 thus sheds an intriguing light on the question of the origin of Mark 7:15. Somewhere around the year A.D. 58, Paul explains to the Roman community that no food is intrinsically "common" or "unclean" (koinon). He does so on the basis of the new eschatological situation that the death and resurrection of Jesus has created for believers, not on the basis of any special teaching proclaimed by Jesus during his ministry (contrast 1 Cor 7:10–11). Then, somewhere around the year A.D. 70, Mark the evangelist writes a Gospel, most likely for the church in Rome. This Gospel, for the only time in the NT (as far as independent sayings are concerned) presents Jesus, during his ministry, revoking the OT food laws (Mark 7:15). Like Rom 14:14, Mark 7:1–23 also uses the vocabulary of koinon ("common") to deal with the question of what is "unclean" in matters of eating. If one had to draw a line of influence from point A to point B, the more likely direction of the line would be from Paul's pronouncement in Rom 14:14, based on his understanding of the new situation created by Jesus' death-resurrection, to the pronouncement of the Marcan Jesus in 7:15.[156] While one cannot prove that the line of influence moved in this direction—and I am not claiming that Mark knew the Epistle to the Romans as such—I think that this view is more likely than the opposite theory: namely, that the saying of Mark 7:15, after being spoken by the historical Jesus, went mysteriously underground, remained unknown to Paul and apparently anyone else involved in the food controversy in first-generation Christianity, only to resurface mysteriously in Mark's Gospel and never to be heard from again in the NT, apart from the weak echo in the Matthean parallel (Matt 15:11).

The position that Mark 7:15 is an authentic word of Jesus that mysteriously disappears during the first Christian generation becomes all the more shaky when we place Luke's treatment of the food controversy alongside that of Paul. Luke, who omits Mark's treatment of clean and unclean in Mark 7:1–23,[157] is intent in his Acts of the Apostles on emphasizing peace and unity in the first-generation church. Yet Luke cannot conceal the apparently well-known fact that disputes over observance of the Mosaic Law arose in and outside Palestine in the late 40s and early 50s and that these disputes were serious enough to engage the most prominent leaders of the church. According to Luke, the matter is finally resolved by a high-level meeting in Jerusalem, where, on the basis of Peter's revelation and his experience of converting Cornelius, "the apostles and the presbyters" of the church decide that Gentile converts need not be circumcised and need not observe the Mosaic Law in its entirety. Still, as a practical compromise to spare the sensitivities of Jews and Jewish Christians,[158] the Gentile Christians living in the same community with Jewish Christians are told to avoid meat sacrificed to idols, foods made with or mixed with blood, meat from animals that have been strangled (i.e., not slaughtered in the proper kosher manner, with the blood being drained from the meat), and illicit sexual unions.[159] Neither in the initial debate nor in this final solution of the controversy is there any indication that anyone in the early church knew of some teaching of the earthly Jesus that would have been helpful in solving the problem.

For all the differences in narrative and theology, there is an interesting connection here between Acts 10–15 and Paul's account of the debate over dietary laws in Galatians 2:11–14.[160] According to Galatians, the clash over food laws (as distinct from the question of circumcision of Gentile converts) *first* broke out at Antioch not between Peter and Paul (according to

Gal 2:12, Peter had been happily eating with Gentiles in Antioch), but between Peter and "certain men from James." Upon their arrival at Antioch, these "men from James," who belonged to "the circumcision party," proceeded to pressure Peter and other Christian Jews into withdrawing from table fellowship with Gentile Christians. If, then, this conflict involved at its origin Peter, Barnabas, and certain prominent Christian Jews connected with James, why could not or would not Peter or some other follower of Jesus during the public ministry cite Jesus' teaching as presented in Mark 7:15 and thus resolve the debate? If Peter or any other early follower of Jesus did not know, remember, or cite the radical pronouncement of Mark 7:15, supposedly delivered by Jesus in the presence of his disciples, then who in the first Christian generation would have known or remembered it? If—on the supposition that Mark 7:15 is authentic—Peter, the Twelve, or other early disciples of Jesus did not act as tradition-bearers of this saying during the first Christian generation, then who did or could have? This pivotal question of the early tradition history of Mark 7:15 is often overlooked by commentators.[161]

In sum, the most telling objection to the authenticity of Mark 7:15 is its lack of any impact on or repetition by the disciples of Jesus in the period of A.D. 30 to 70—precisely the critical period when the logion would have been most relevant. When we take full cognizance of the fact that this radical saying first appears in what is form-critically an isolated unit in Mark 7:15–23 and that this teaching has no effect or echo even in the rest of Mark's Gospel, to say nothing of the rest of the NT outside of the Matthean parallel, we cannot avoid two probable conclusions: (1) The debate over food laws in the early church was conducted on other grounds than this pronouncement of Jesus in Mark 7:15, a pronouncement that would have been extremely relevant to the debate had it been known by any party involved in the dispute. (2) Hence, Mark 7:15 is most likely a Christian formulation created in order to give the settled teaching and practice of the church ca. A.D. 70 a basis in the teaching of the earthly Jesus. Perhaps, secondarily, Mark 7:15 was also aimed at pockets of resistance remaining within Jewish-Christian circles.[162]

(b) *Verses 17–23*

The decision that Mark 7:15 does not come from the historical Jesus has an immediate impact on the way we view all that follows in Mark 7:17–23. As I have already indicated, 7:17–23 is simply an extended explanation and application of v 15. If v 15 is judged authentic, then the possibility arises that at least the substance of vv 17–23 likewise comes from Jesus. If, however—as we have decided—v 15 is a creation of the early church, then vv 17–23 are almost certainly not authentic.[163] One might end the discussion right there.

Nevertheless, it is wise to seek confirmation of this global assessment by a quick inspection of vv 17–23. As I have shown at length earlier in this chapter (especially in Section II.A), vv 17–23 clearly display Marcan traits in their vocabulary, structure, and theology. The basic pattern is clearly Marcan: after a puzzling public pronouncement (v 15), Jesus withdraws into a private place (sometimes, as here, a house), where the befuddled disciples query him about the meaning of his public teaching (v 17). The disciples are rebuked for their lack of understanding (v 18a), and then Jesus proceeds to explain his teaching to them (vv 18b–23).[164]

The explanation falls into two parts (vv 18b–19 + vv 20–23), corresponding to the two halves of the aphorism in v 15. The division and correspondence are clear both (a) because Mark introduces the two halves of the explanation with the same verb of saying (legō), which he has used as a structural element throughout the whole pericope, and (b) because v 18b (what enters a man) and v 20 (what comes out of a man) repeat the wording of v 15a (what enters a man) and v 15b (what comes out of a man) with only slight variations. Obviously, then, if v 15 does not come from Jesus, neither do v 18b and v 20.

Verse 19 simply gives a graphic physiological—or, as some critics say, a "rationalistic"—reason why food cannot defile: the food passes through the stomach, not through the heart (the true seat of clean and unclean), and is ejected into the latrine.[165] To hammer the point home, Mark adds editorially at the end of v 19 the observation that, in saying this, Jesus "was declaring [and making] all foods clean." [166] Being nothing but a nature-centered, quasi-philosophical rationale for v 18b (indeed, a rationale that would be at home in Greco-Roman thought but would hardly convince an observant Palestinian Jew), v 19 has no chance of being authentic if v 18b is not authentic—and it is not.

The expansive explanation of v 20 in vv 21–23 seems to come from a different theological universe. Verses 21–22 constitute a distinct literary genre known as a "vice catalogue" or a "vice list." While examples abound in both Greco-Roman philosophy and in the NT epistles, the list in Mark 7:21–22 ‖ Matt 15:19 is unique within the Four Gospels. Nowhere else in the Gospels is Jesus presented as rattling off such a catalogue of bad attitudes and habits. To be sure, similar (thought not exactly the same) lists can be found in Jubilees, 1 Enoch, the Dead Sea Scrolls, and later rabbinic literature. One cannot therefore declare a priori that the historical Jesus would never have uttered Mark 7:21–22. Yet, granted that (a) vv 21–22 is the explanation of the inauthentic v 20, (b) the vice list of Mark 7:21–22 ‖ Matt 15:19 finds no parallel anywhere else in the sayings of Jesus in all Four Gospels, (c) and all but two Greek words (or their cognates) in Mark's catalogue are also found in the vice lists of the NT epistles, derivation of vv 21–22 from the historical Jesus is highly unlikely.[167]

The concluding v 23 is almost certainly a product of Mark's redaction. It simply repeats v 18b and v 20 in a lightly altered form, with the addition of Mark's generalizing or universalizing tendency ("*all* these evil things," cf. 7:3–4,13,19). In sum, our inspection of the individual parts of vv 17–23 confirms our initial suspicion. Just as v 15 is a creation of the early church, so are all the verses that follow and explain it.

E. Verses 1–5: The Question about Eating with Unwashed Hands

At long last, we return to the first unit (vv 1–5) of the pericope, which contains the opening salvo of the Pharisees and scribes objecting to the disciples' practice of eating bread with "common" (i.e., unwashed) hands. When I began the unit-by-unit examination of 7:1–23, I adopted what must have seemed to some readers an odd strategy: I postponed consideration of the "presenting problem" in the first unit until the rest of 7:1–23 had been probed in detail. My original rationale was based on the idiosyncratic nature of the "setup" of this dispute story, which differs notably from the structure of many other dispute stories. In the whole opening unit of vv 1–5, Jesus neither says nor does anything. Indeed, his presence is not even mentioned until the final verse of the unit (v 5), and even then he is referred to only by personal pronouns ("him," "your") and not by name. Only the Pharisees and scribes observe and speak in this first unit, and the object of their observation and protest is a particular group of disciples, not Jesus himself (vv 1–2). A good part of the unit (vv 3–4) is taken up by the narrator's lengthy parenthetical—and hardly accurate—explanation of Jewish purity practices. As a result, only in v 5 do the Pharisees and scribes actually voice their objection.

Accordingly, it is only in the second unit (vv 6–13) of the pericope that Jesus speaks; and it is only in the pivot (vv 14–15) and the second half (vv 17–23) of the pericope that he does anything (namely, calling the crowd in v 14 and entering a house in v 17). Granted the strange configuration of this dispute story and granted the object of our question (the historical Jesus), it made sense first to examine the units where Jesus—and almost no one else—speaks (vv 6–23) and then to return to the opening unit where Jesus says and does nothing.

The pragmatic "payoff" of this strategy of postponement should now be clear. Our detailed examination of vv 6–23 has shown that, with the possible exception of the stray tradition about *qorbān* in vv 10–12, the whole of vv 6–23 is the product of Christian tradition and Marcan redaction. Different exegetes have laid out different scenarios detailing the growth and convergence of the various subunits in vv 6–23, and the exact amount of Mark's contribution to the whole continues to be debated.[168] However, whatever the precise theory of tradition and redaction one adopts, the overall result of our analysis is clear: the substance of vv 6–23, with the possible exception of vv 10–12, does not go back to the historical Jesus.[169] In particular, Jesus never used the reworked Septuagintal form of Isa 29:13 as an ad hominem reply to an objection about eating with unwashed hands. Nor did he speak the two-part aphorism annulling the food laws in v 15. Nor, a fortiori, did he deliver the two-part explanation of the aphorism that follows in vv 17–23. As for the *qorbān* tradition in vv 10–12 (vv 9 + 13 being the *inclusio* that connects the *qorbān* tradition to the previous subunit that cites Isa 29:13), it may indeed come from the historical Jesus. But, shorn of the redactional verses around it, it has nothing to do with the protest against eating with unwashed hands in vv 1–5. Only the modern redactional activity of an imaginative exegete, replacing the ancient redactional activity of an imaginative Mark, could forge a direct connection between vv 1–5 and vv 10–12.

The full wisdom of postponing a consideration of vv 1–5 now becomes apparent. As they stand in chap. 7 of Mark, vv 1–5 exist and have meaning only as an introduction to the dispute story that continues in vv 6–23. If vv 6–9 + 13–23 do not come from the historical Jesus, and if vv 10–12 have no connection with the problem raised in vv 1–5, then there is no historical Jesus tradition for which vv 1–5 can serve as the introduction. Put another way: vv 1–5 are a gateway, a setup; their only function is to lead into a dispute between Jesus and his opponents. If almost all the Jesus material in vv 6–23 that might possibly supply an answer to the initial objection in vv 1–5 proves to be inauthentic, then the initial objection in vv 1–5 must be judged inauthentic as well. Hence, there is no need to probe vv 1–5 in great detail. However interesting the verses may be for a study of early Christian polemic or Marcan redaction, they are of no value in a quest for the historical Jesus.[170]

Thus, the primary reason for judging vv 1–5 inauthentic is the very nature of the material that the verses introduce, that is, the inauthentic nature of the bulk of vv 6–23. Still, I think that one can add further arguments to this primary argument. In my opinion, the dubious historical character of the first unit, viewed by itself, lends additional support to the primary reason for judging the verses inauthentic.

(1) To begin with the obvious, it is simply not true that "all the Jews" of the early 1st century A.D. observed all the purity rituals listed by Mark in vv 3–4. Indeed, the claim verges on self-contradiction, since "holding to the tradition of the elders" (v 3), on top of the obligations imposed by Scripture, was a defining characteristic of the Pharisees, a characteristic that distinguished them from Jews in general and from other Jewish parties and sects in particular.

(2) Although many commentators quickly dismiss the inaccuracy of vv 3–4 with the label of "hyperbole" or "exaggeration," the question remains whether all the purity practices in vv 3–4 were observed by all 1st-century Pharisees, to say nothing of all Jews.[171] None of the purity laws in the Pentateuch obliges laypeople to wash their hands before eating,[172] nor is such an obligation imposed anywhere else in the OT.[173] Despite the fact that we have abundant information about various purity rules from *Jubilees*, the Dead Sea Scrolls (including the *Rule of the Congregation*, the *Damascus Document*, 4QMMT, the *Temple Scroll*, and various scraps of purity regulations from Cave 4, some of which may stem from groups other than Qumran), Philo, Josephus, the *Letter of Aristeas*, and passages in the *Sibylline Oracles*, there is no clear evidence that any Palestinian or Diaspora group of Jews in the pre-70 period taught that handwashing by laypeople before eating meals was obligatory.[174] In the Qumran literature, total immersion of the body, not handwashing, is the proper preparation for communal meals. In the Diaspora literature, when washing (either of hands or of the whole body) by laypersons is mentioned, it is usually connected with prayer, not meals.

(3) The first indisputable attestation of obligatory handwashing by Jewish laypeople before meals is found in the Mishna (specifically, the tractate *Yadayim*), and—not unlike the prohibition of healing on the sabbath—the mention of this obligation is accompanied by some countervailing opinions. For example, in *m. ʿEd.* 5:6–7, Eleazar ben Enoch (or, in some manuscripts, Eleazar ben Ha-Ner) is excommunicated by the sages (a generic title for the rabbinic scholars representing the normative majority opinion) because he contests the validity of the sages' teaching concerning purity of hands.[175] Thus, even at the time of the Mishna's composition, the obligation of handwashing seems to be relatively new. Scattered opinions that handwashing before meals is not obligatory are found later on in the Tosepta and the Jerusalem Talmud, and still later in the rabbinic midrash on Numbers, *Numbers Rabbah* (*Bemidbar Rabbah*).[176] In *t. Ber.* 5:27, we find a rabbinic teaching that "handwashing does not apply to profane food" [*ḥûllîn*]. A Hebrew text (a *baraita*) in the Babylonian Talmud (*b. Ber.* 52b) represents the House of

Hillel frankly telling the House of Shammai that the rule enjoining hand-washing for unconsecrated food does not come from the Torah—thus admitting in effect that it is an invention of the rabbis.[177] In fact, it is possible (though hardly provable) that the practice of handwashing before meals, along with certain other purity practices, first arose in the Diaspora, perhaps as a compensatory or substitutive observance for Jews who would not have had ready access to the Jerusalem temple and its purificatory rituals for lengthy periods. Since it is likely that Mark and Matthew composed their Gospels outside Palestine in the post-70 period, their portraits of Judaism may well have been influenced by Diaspora practices with which they were acquainted.[178]

(4) My doubts about the historicity of Mark 7:1–5 are only reinforced by the attempts made by scholars to formulate a plausible *Sitz im Leben* for the dispute of 7:1–23 within the ministry of the historical Jesus. A prime example of serious erudition put in service of salvaging the historicity of the dispute is supplied by Roger P. Booth in his monograph *Jesus and the Laws of Purity*. It is telling that, in order to create a probable historical setting for the dispute, Booth must introduce a number of important factors not mentioned in or indicated by the Marcan text:

(a) To make the issue of handwashing raised in Mark 7:1–5 more plausible in a pre-70 Palestinian context, Booth elaborates on the exact nature of the purity rules that are supposedly at issue in vv 1–5. To do this, Booth collects various rabbinic debates and rulings scattered throughout the Mishna, Tosepta, Jerusalem Talmud, and Babylonian Talmud to substantiate his claim that Hillel and Shammai decreed the susceptibility of hands to ritual impurity no later than A.D. 10. (One must remember that in the Jewish Scriptures, it is the whole body of a person, not just the hands, that becomes ritually unclean.[179]) This decree of Hillel and Shammai was then supposedly reinforced by eighteen rules promulgated ca. A.D. 51. Anyone acquainted with present-day critical scholarship on rabbinic literature will immediately sense a problem with Booth's whole approach. Claims made by rabbinic works written from the 2d to the 6th century A.D. are taken at face value by Booth as historical proof for what actually happened in Jewish Palestine in the pre-70 period, without any corroborating Jewish evidence from that period.[180] The fact that the individual rabbinic texts that Booth adduces are themselves often subject to various interpretations only weakens his argument further. Still more difficulty is created by Booth retrojecting into the pre-70 period the distinctions between first-degree, second-degree, and third-degree impurity that is not attested before the rabbinic literature.

In the end, all of this leads nowhere, since Booth must admit that, since the itinerant disciples of Jesus probably were ritually unclean in their whole bodies (e.g., from regular sexual emission and possibly from corpse contamination), merely washing their hands would not remove their bodily impurity. Such bodily impurity, in Booth's interpretation, would be transmitted to the bread the disciples were eating because their hands were presumed to have had contact with moisture. Faced with this dead end, Booth takes a sudden turn in his argument.

(b) It was not Jews in general, says Booth, or even Pharisees in general, who held to the necessity of handwashing before meals.[181] Rather, the opponents insisting on handwashing in the Marcan story are a special group known from later rabbinic literature, the ḥăbûrâ, that is, an especially observant fellowship or association of Pharisees who banded together to keep food and tithing rules with the rigor of priests.[182] Their members, called ḥăbērîm ("fellows," "associates"), took upon themselves the supererogatory practice of handwashing before meals and tried to persuade other Jews to do the same. But is this importation of the ḥăbērîm into Mark 7:1–5 historically justifiable?

(c) The major objection to Booth's reading of the ḥăbērîm into Mark 7:1–5 reflects the basic problem that plagues Booth's whole project: neither the NT writings nor any pre-70 Jewish documents mention a set institution or sectarian group called the ḥăbûrâ with members labeled ḥăbērîm. In the technical sectarian sense, both terms surface for the first time in the Mishna and go on to enjoy a long life in subsequent rabbinic literature.[183] Not unlike the obligation of handwashing before meals and the prohibition of healing on the sabbath, the ḥăbûrâ does not appear on the religious radar screen before the Mishna. Even then, it is not entirely clear whether the ḥăbērîm are coterminous with the Pharisees, are a subset of the Pharisees, partially overlap with the Pharisees, or are simply another intensely observant group alongside the Pharisees. To transform the pre-70 Pharisees—indeed, "all the Jews" (v 3)—into the ḥăbûrôt of the Mishna involves an arbitrary alteration of what Mark says. Even if we were to accept the transformation of "the Pharisees and some of the scribes" of Mark 7:1 into ḥăbērîm, understood by Booth as a stringent subset of the Pharisees, a number of problems would remain. Handwashing before meals is considered by Mark 7:1–5 to be an example of "the tradition of the elders" that characterizes the Pharisees in general (indeed, in Mark's inaccurate statement, "all the Jews"). Yet for Booth's historical reconstruction of the Marcan scene to work, handwashing must instead be a supererogatory custom adopted by the stringent ḥăbērîm, not by the Pharisees in general (and certainly not Mark's "the Pharisees and some of the scribes").[184] Then, too, there is the commonsense question: Why don't the *ḥăbērîm* try to convert their fellow Pharisees to their special custom instead of journeying to Galilee to focus on a most unlikely candidate, the relatively freewheeling Jesus and his disciples? In any scholarly construct, there is a point at which so many fragile hypotheses have to be piled on so many other fragile hypotheses that the whole theory collapses of its own weight. Such, in my opinion, is the case with Booth's scholarly endeavor—and with many others like it.

(5) It is often claimed that the aphorism in 7:15, with or without the material that follows, is the original answer that the historical Jesus gave to the objection voiced in vv 1–5.[185] Even if we put aside for the moment the reasons that have led us to judge that v 15 is inauthentic and is therefore disqualified from being an answer given by the historical Jesus on any occasion, there is another reason to doubt the original coupling of vv 1–5 and v 15 as question and answer. The reason lies in our study of the purity laws of the Pentateuch, presented in section I of this chapter.

In Section I, we saw that there are two notably different forms of impurity regulated by Leviticus and Deuteronomy: ritual impurity and moral impurity. This distinction, which arises from the different causes and effects of these two types of impurity, is present in the pentateuchal texts and is not simply the product of some ingenious modern commentator. As we saw, the Book of Ezra added a third type of impurity, genealogical impurity, though this category was not accepted or interpreted in the same way by all Jews.

What was especially surprising in our investigation of this typology of purity laws was that the laws prohibiting the use of certain animals as food stood apart from the laws of ritual impurity. The latter regulated and provided means for purifying unavoidable and/or temporary states of bodily impurity due to the normal cycle of birth, sex, illness, and death. In contrast, with the dire label of "abomination" and with the total prohibition of ever voluntarily eating the prohibited animals, the food laws seemed in some ways closer to the laws prohibiting the grave sins that caused moral impurity (murder, incest, and idolatry). This separate status of the food laws, marking them off from laws of ritual impurity, is already clear in the Pentateuch. Hence, the Mishna simply carries forward, clarifies, and confirms the pentateuchal distinction by placing the treatment of ritual purity rules—handwashing in particular—within the sixth Order (Seder) of the Mishna, namely, *Toharot* ("Purities"), while placing the laws of forbidden foods with the fifth Order, namely, *Qodašin* ("Holy Things").[186] Granted this continuity (stretching from the Pentateuch to the Mishna) in distinguishing ritual impurity from the food laws, is it likely that the historical Jesus would have answered a pointed question about the ritual impurity of

hands with a reply that dealt instead with the quite different topic of forbidden foods? Was Jesus that ignorant of basic distinctions contained in the
Pentateuch, distinctions that were carried forward in Palestinian Judaism
and finally enshrined in the Mishna? A more plausible explanation is that
we have in Mark 7:1–23 a collection of various Christian traditions that
Mark has welded together with an eye more to literary connections and
Christian theology than to halakic consistency.[187]

Taken individually, these problems inherent in vv 1–5 would not necessarily prove that the situation depicted in this dispute story could not go back
to the time and place of the historical Jesus. The real importance of these
problems is rather that they are consistent with and serve to confirm the
decision that we have already made on other grounds: granted that the bulk
of vv 6–23 is inauthentic, then the scene (vv 1–5) that introduces vv 6–23
and poses the question that these verses supposedly answer must likewise be
judged inauthentic.

III. OTHER POSSIBLE REFERENCES TO RITUAL
PURITY IN THE GOSPELS

The decision that Mark 7:1–23 tells us nothing about the historical Jesus'
views on ritual purity leaves us in a difficult position. Apart from this Marcan pericope, one can find in the Four Gospels only passing references—at
best—to Jesus' stance on ritual purity. The few possibly relevant passages
have often been interpreted in the brighter light of Jesus' statements in Mark
7:1–23. Once 7:1–23 drops out of consideration, the scattered Gospel fragments or allusions lack a larger interpretive context. Thus, what these fragments may or may not say about Jesus and ritual purity becomes even more
debatable now that they have to be read in isolation. This point becomes
painfully clear when we survey the remaining topics of ritual purity on
which the Jesus of the Gospels may indicate an opinion.[188]

(1) *Corpse impurity* was the most virulent of all forms of ritual impurity;
hence its title in later rabbinic literature: "the father of the fathers of impurities." [189] According to the Jewish Scriptures, anyone who touched a corpse,
was in the same enclosed space as a corpse, or simply walked through a
burial field was impure for seven days. The purification process was more
elaborate than most: the unclean person had to be sprinkled by a clean person on the third and seventh day with spring water mixed with the ashes of
a red cow sacrificed for the purpose of this ritual—in addition to the usual
washing of garments, bathing one's body, and waiting till evening (on the

seventh day). Almost inevitably in a society with high rates of infant mortality and female death in childbirth, in addition to short life expectancies compared to those of Western society today, most observant Jews would have regularly contracted corpse impurity. Granted the complicated purification ritual, ordinary Palestinian Jews, who did not belong to any stringent sectarian movement, might well have waited until their next pilgrimage to Jerusalem to be cleansed of corpse impurity.[190] If this is so, then many ordinary Jews might have been in a state of ritual impurity for months at a time.

As for Jesus, the Gospels never explicitly raise the question of his contracting corpse impurity or of his being purified from it. As an itinerant prophet traveling away from his hometown and family for most of his ministry, Jesus may not have had much occasion to touch a corpse or to be in the same room with it. However, as we saw in Volume Two of *A Marginal Jew*, multiple attestation of sources and forms indicates that the historical Jesus claimed to have raised the dead and that his followers believed this claim.[191] At the same time, as we learned from the detailed exegesis of the three narratives describing Jesus raising the dead, these stories have gone through a lengthy process of Christian elaboration. Hence, it would be unwise to press the details of any one story. To be sure, Jesus is presented as touching the daughter of Jairus (Mark 5:41), coming to the grave of Lazarus (John 11:38), and touching the bier of the son of the widow of Nain (Luke 7:14). At least the first two acts would have involved Jesus in corpse impurity.[192] The Gospel texts, though, do not advert to this fact. Indeed, the problem does not seem to be on the mental radar screens of the evangelists. We are never told whether Jesus cared about contracting corpse impurity and what, if anything, he did about it during his journeys through Galilee.

An imaginative interpreter might see a glimmer of awareness of corpse impurity in John's Gospel. John 11:55 mentions that Jews from the countryside went up to Jerusalem before Passover to purify themselves (cf. *J.W.* 1.11.6 §229), while John 12:1 states that Jesus came to Bethany "six days before Passover." [193] Putting these two texts together, one might deduce that 11:55 refers to the seven-day ritual of corpse purification, that Jesus happened to be in Bethany (just outside Jerusalem) *six days* before Passover because he was participating in this purification process, and that therefore he had not bothered about purification from corpse impurity while traveling in Galilee. But this is to deduce a great deal from two passing references that are not directly connected by John.[194]

Allied thematically with the question of Jesus' contracting corpse impurity is a woe-saying found in both Matthew and Luke:

Matt 23:27–28	Luke 11:44
v 27	
Woe to you, scribes and Pharisees, hypocrites,	Woe to you
because you are like decorated tombs,[195] which on	because you are like unseen
the outside appear beautiful, but within are full of	graves,
dead men's bones and every kind of uncleanness.	
v 28	
So too, you outwardly appear righteous to	and people walking on them
people, but inside you are full of hypocrisy and	do not know [that the graves
iniquity.	are there].

Scholars argue over whether these two sayings represent a single Q saying, redacted heavily by Matthew, or whether we are dealing with two different sayings that share the woe-form, the image of graves or tombs, and some sort of contrast between appearance and reality.[196] Since the only Greek words shared by the Matthean and Lucan forms are *ouai hymin* ("woe to you") and *hoti* ("because"), the argument for a common Q saying is tenuous indeed. More likely we have here distinct M and L sayings that may ultimately go back to a single saying of Jesus. In that case, the sayings have developed in separate streams of the oral tradition and have been redacted quite differently by the two evangelists. The positive side of this judgment is that we therefore have multiple attestation for some original saying that lies behind the two present forms. The negative side is that the original form cannot be reconstructed word for word but only vaguely described: in a woe-saying, a form frequently used by Israel's prophets when excoriating their fellow Israelites, Jesus satirizes his opponents by comparing them to tombs and/or the contents of tombs. The satire plays with the contrast between outward appearance (benign) and inner reality (defiling).

In the Matthean form, the opponents have an attractive appearance, like decorated or freshly whitened tombs, but within they are full of defiling moral impurity—just as the tombs are sources of ritual impurity. While the Lucan metaphor is different and simpler—unmarked graves ritually contaminate the people who unwittingly walk over them—the same contrast between what people see and what really exists within forms the basis of Jesus' mocking jab at his opponents. If the opponents were in fact the Pharisees—a detail, however, that may have been added by Matthean and Lucan redaction[197]—Jesus might be attacking the Pharisees for having a great concern for the details of ritual purity while at the same time having a morally defiling effect on their fellow Jews. The problem is that, even if some form of this saying does come from the historical Jesus, it tells us nothing specific about his own views on and observance of corpse impurity. The saying simply reflects the common Jewish belief, based on the laws in Numbers 19 and clearly maintained around the turn of the era,[198] that corpses and graves conveyed ritual impurity. To what extent Jesus himself accepted, rejected, or modified this belief is not indicated.

As long as we are looking at purity material common to Matthew and Luke, we should make a short detour and glance at Matt 23:25–26 ‖ Luke 11:39–41. This saying is akin to Matt 23:27–28 par. in that it has generated debates over its precise source(s), it evinces a metaphorical character, and it may throw light on Jesus' view of purity rules.

Matt 23:25–26	Luke 11:39–41
v 25	v 39
Woe to you, scribes and Pharisees, hypocrites	Now you Pharisees
for you clean the outside of the cup	clean the outside of the cup
and the bowl	and the plate,
but inside you are full of	but the inside of you is full of
greed and licentiousness.	greed and evil.
v 26	v 40
Blind Pharisee,	Senseless ones,
first clean the inside of the cup	did not the maker of the outside
that the outside of it may become clean.	also make the inside?
	v 41
	But, as regards the inside, give
	alms and, behold, all things are
	clean for you.

That the two forms of the saying go back to some common source seems clear. (1) There is common structure: (a) a two-part antithetical structure that opposes the cleaning of the outside of a cup to an inner state of greed; (b) brusque direct address to the person(s) being criticized for lack of moral perception; (c) a comment reestablishing the proper preeminence of inside over outside. (2) There is also common vocabulary, notably in the first part of the saying: the pronoun "you" (*hymeis* or *hymin*), the noun "Pharisee" (*Pharisaios*), the verb "clean" (*katharizō*), the verb "be full of" (*gemō*), the adverbs "outside" (*exōthen*) and "inside" (*esōthen*, also *entos* and *enonta*), the noun "cup" (*potērion*), the noun "greed" (*harpagē*), and the adjective "clean" (*katharos*). At the same time, there are many minor disagreements, some of which can be assigned to the redactional tendencies of each evan-

gelist (e.g., Matthew's fondness for the polemical tag "scribes and Pharisees," especially in his list of seven woes; Luke's concern for the poor and
his praise of almsgiving). The upshot of this brief analysis is that the logion
standing behind Matt 23:25 ‖ Luke 11:39 has a good chance of coming from
Q.[199] Behind Matt 23:26 ‖ Luke 11:40 probably lay a continuation of the Q
saying that emphasized the priority of inner cleanness over outer cleanness;
it would be perilous, though, to conjecture the original wording.[200] Finally,
Luke 11:41, whether L tradition or Lucan redaction, appears to be a secondary addition to the logion.[201]

The decision that the Matthean and Lucan versions stem from the same
Q saying deprives us of an argument from multiple attestation. In any event,
the core saying in Matt 23:25 ‖ Luke 11:39, even if it came from the historical Jesus, would tell us little about Jesus' views of purity laws. This logion,
just like the one on corpse impurity that we have just examined, uses the
issue of ritual purity on a metaphorical level to inculcate the importance of
inner, moral purity.[202]

(2) The story of the woman with a *flow of blood* (Mark 5:25–34), though
often cited as a case of Jesus being defiled by ritual purity, may actually
have no bearing on our study. In the vocabulary of rabbinic purity rules,
the woman described in Mark 5:25–26 would qualify not as a woman who
is menstruating (*niddâ*) but rather as a woman suffering from an abnormal
and chronic flow of bodily fluids from her genital area (*zābâ*), in this case,
blood.[203] The purity laws of the Pentateuch (Lev 15: 25–30) do not state
explicitly that a *zābâ* communicates ritual impurity simply by touching
someone—or, in the case of Jesus, someone's clothing (Mark 5:27–28).[204]
Unless we suppose that ordinary Galilean peasants knew and observed the
more rigorous rules of the Essenes or anticipated the *hălākâ* of the later rabbis, there is no reason to suppose that either the woman or Jesus in Mark
5:25–34 thought that impurity was being communicated by her touching
his garment. Perhaps more to the point, as with the stories of Jesus raising
the dead, the issue of contracting ritual impurity does not seem to be on the
mental horizon of the evangelists as they tell the story of the woman with
the flow of blood. It is later commentators, starting with the Fathers of the
Church, who read the problem into the text.[205]

(3) Akin to the purity rules governing a *zābâ*, and too often confused with
them, are the laws governing *menstruating women* (Lev 15:19–24). Though
these laws do not loom especially large in the Pentateuch, Jewish literature
around the turn of the era reflects increased interest in and disputes about
menstrual impurity.[206] This was, in a sense, prophetic. Actual implementation of the rules governing menstrual impurity—unlike most of the ritual

purity laws—survived the destruction of the temple in A.D. 70 because the rules of menstrual impurity could be and continued to be observed without any recourse to temple ritual. Indeed, with the destruction of the temple, and with it much of the OT purity system, the laws of menstrual impurity grew in importance, becoming enshrined in a whole tractate of the Mishna, *Niddah*.[207] Of all the tractates in the Order of Purities (*Ṭoharot*), only *Niddah* receives a full Gemara in the Babylonian Talmud.[208]

This increased importance of the observance of the rules of menstrual impurity, as opposed to many other purity rules that necessarily fell into obsolescence, is all the more striking when one notices the total absence of any discussion of menstrual impurity in the teaching of Jesus. The complete absence of any sayings or actions of Jesus in regard to menstrual impurity might be attributed simply to Jesus' status as a lifelong celibate.[209] Still, even if we grant that such was Jesus' status, the total silence is remarkable. Jesus' celibacy did not prevent him from delivering a new and startling teaching on divorce. Still more, as we saw in Volume Three of *A Marginal Jew*, Jesus traveled in the company of devoted and apparently affluent women who ministered to the needs of this Nazarene charismatic celibate and his disciples. The picture of a celibate Jewish prophet, teacher, and healer traveling around the Galilean countryside with both male disciples (some of whom had left wives back home) and female supporters (some of whom had left husbands back home) may well have been more than a little disturbing for devout Jews. When we add to this mix the further problem that (a) the women would presumably be menstruating at various times in any given month and that (b) living in close contact on a journey with a group of males, these women would have almost unavoidably exposed the males to impurity on a regular basis, Jesus' total silence on the question of menstrual impurity is remarkable, if not astounding.[210]

In addition, if we may presume that Jesus' male followers were abstaining from sexual activity while traveling with him, both Jesus and his male disciples would regularly have experienced *seminal emission* during sleep. According to Lev 15:16–17, this would have created a state of ritual impurity that had to be removed by bathing one's whole body, washing all the clothes touched by the semen, and waiting until sunset. How Jesus and his disciples dealt with this purity issue as they traveled around rural Galilee in the company of women is never broached by the Gospels. Once again, silence there and nothing more. When we put these silences together with Jesus' apparent silence about corpse impurity, it would seem that Jesus was simply not interested in the purity rules that attracted great attention and debate from many quarters of intertestamental Judaism. It is not that Jesus rejects, argues against, criticizes, or modifies these rules. Unlike such issues as divorce, oaths, and sabbath, which he does address, for Jesus the whole system of purity does not seem to exist—at least as an object of reflection and teaching.

While one might argue that this silence is due to the omission or suppression of historical material by early Christians, this hardly seems an adequate explanation. Certainly, up until A.D. 70 and perhaps beyond, a significant segment of the nascent Christian movement consisted of Christian Jews. Moreover, Mark 7:1–23 witnesses to the ability of first-generation Christians to develop stories and sayings about impurity when it suited their purposes. Hence, the most likely conclusion from the data available to us is that Jesus never made any significant pronouncements on purity rules and that, given the interest in this material at his time, his silence is best interpreted as lack of concern or studied indifference. What, if anything, he did about purity rules while traveling in mixed company around rural Galilee is simply unknowable today.

(4) As far as purity rules are concerned, the Gospel stories about Jesus healing *skin diseases* (commonly but inaccurately translated as "leprosy")[211] are somewhat similar to those dealing with the raising of the dead. Once again, multiple attestation of sources and forms argues that Jesus claimed to heal lepers and that this claim was believed by his followers.[212] However, not every passage dealing with Jesus and leprosy depicts Jesus as having physical contact with lepers. The healing story in Mark 1:40–45 parr. does state that Jesus touched the leper as he healed him; but in the story of the ten lepers in Luke 17:11–19, Jesus heals the lepers at a distance. Whether the narrative detail of touch in the Marcan story can be claimed to be historical must remain doubtful, since we have no multiple attestation for that particular story and a fortiori for that one detail.[213] Perhaps more relevant is the observation that, just as in the stories of raising the dead, the Gospel narratives give no indication of seeing a problem in Jesus' touching the leper. The issue is not on the evangelists's mental horizon.

In fact, the whole question of the historicity of Jesus' touching the leper may be beside the point. While Lev 13:45–46 commands that the leper cry out "Unclean! unclean!" and live apart, "outside the camp," the laws governing leprosy in Leviticus 13–14 do not, strictly speaking, forbid a leper to touch a person and—more important for our purposes—do not explicitly state that a person who touches a leper is rendered unclean.[214] One might argue that this rule is taken for granted, but this presumption runs into practical difficulties. If it is presumed that touching a leper renders one unclean, then one would have to know how long the person touching the leper is in a state of impurity and what the rituals are that render him clean—all the more so since the leper himself may be in a state of impurity indefinitely. The silence of the Law on these key points makes the presumption that a person touching a leper is rendered unclean highly suspect.

Granted, later rabbinic law decreed that touching a leper renders one unclean, and one can find this opinion as early as Josephus' apologetic work, *Against Apion*.[215] However, in the relevant passage in *Against Apion* (1.31 §281), Josephus is engaged in a fiery polemic against the Egyptian historian Manetho over the latter's claim that Moses was expelled from the Egyptian city of Heliopolis because he was a leper. To rebut this charge, Josephus points to Moses' rigorous laws ostracizing lepers in Leviticus. Josephus argues that Moses would never have imposed such stringent regulations on lepers if he himself had been a leper. In the heat of the debate, Josephus claims that Moses specifies in the Law that any person who touches lepers or dwells under the same roof with them is rendered unclean. This specification is patently not in the Mosaic Law, and it may be telling that Josephus does not make this claim about a defiling touch when he treats the subject in his slightly earlier work, *The Jewish Antiquities*.[216] Hence one is left wondering what exactly Josephus is doing in *Ag. Ap.* 1.31 §281. Is he exaggerating in order to strengthen his apologetic argument?[217] Or is he accurately reflecting pre-70 Jewish practice in Palestine, despite the fact that he is writing in Rome at the end of the 1st or the beginning of the 2d century A.D.? Or is he giving us the first glimmering of a new halakic development that will become enshrined in the Mishna? There is no sure way of knowing.

Unfortunately, Josephus is the earliest firm attestation we have in Judaism of this idea that touching a leper is defiling. By contrast, the material from the Dead Sea Scrolls contains no clear affirmation on the subject. Most of the passages treating leprosy do not raise the issue of touch. The only possibly relevant text, 4Q274, is both fragmentary and ambiguous.[218] In any event, the stringent purity rules of Qumran or of the Essenes in general were hardly those of the Galilean equivalent of "the man in the street." Perhaps more to the point, the fragments of the *Damascus Document* from Cave 4 at Qumran demand that a priest inspect the body, beard, and hair of a leper in the most rigorous fashion imaginable—counting, for example, dead hairs and living hairs on the leper's body. That the priest could possibly do this without touching the leper is almost inconceivable, and yet there is not the glimmer of an idea that the priest is in danger of contracting impurity by his inspection.[219] One must therefore remain doubtful as to whether the later rabbinic view about touching a leper was shared by ordinary Palestinian Jews—or even stringent sectarians—at the time of Jesus. We have no positive evidence that it was; the rigorous inspection of a leper by a priest demanded by the fragments of the *Damascus Document* seems to argue in the opposite direction.

Finally, much is often made of Jesus' command in both the Marcan and Lucan stories that the lepers immediately present themselves before a priest to obtain an official declaration that they are clean and to offer the prescribed sacrifice. To be sure, Jesus is following the prescriptions of the Mosaic Law by giving this command, but one cannot deduce much from this detail as regards Jesus' own stance vis-à-vis the Mosaic Law. (a) From the practical point of view, the ostracized lepers could not return to and be reintegrated into ordinary social and religious life without a "clean bill of health" from a priest.[220] (b) From a form-critical point of view, going to a priest for a declaration of being cleansed acts as the confirmation or demonstration of the miracle, a regular part of any miracle story of healing.[221] In sum, the few references in the Gospels to Jesus' healing lepers tell us nothing about Jesus' teaching on or observance of the purity laws.

IV. CONCLUSIONS ON JESUS AND RITUAL PURITY

The readers who have patiently journeyed through this long chapter may feel disappointed as they come to the end of the road. Most of the material we have investigated has proved to be either inauthentic or silent on the question of Jesus' attitude toward ritual purity. Tremendous effort seems to have been expended to no purpose. I beg to differ with such a conclusion. As we have observed elsewhere in our quest, though results from specific probes of the Jesus tradition may at first seem completely negative, they often yield important insights.[222] Such, I would maintain, is the case here.

(1) Our judgment that, apart from the logion on *qorbān*, the controversy and teaching in Mark 7:1–23 do not come from the historical Jesus makes a significant contribution to the quest. From Rudolf Bultmann through Ernst Käsemann to Roger Booth and Jonathan Klawans, various parts of this lengthy pericope have been used by eminent scholars to establish the attitude of Jesus toward Jewish purity laws. It is with a certain sense of liberation and relief that we have come to the inverse insight that this whole approach is wrongheaded. With the possible exception of the tradition behind Mark 7:10–12 (the *qorbān* saying), the multilayered units that make up 7:1–23 represent various stages of Jewish-Christian tradition and Marcan redaction. With the exception, then, of 7:10–12, nothing goes back to the historical Jesus. As far as the material preserved in the Gospels allows us to

judge, the historical Jesus never made any programmatic pronouncements on issues like handwashing before meals or the distinction between clean and unclean foods.

(2) This silence, which in isolation might lack any great impact on the quest, takes on weightier significance when put in the broader context of other Jesus traditions (already judged authentic) that might reasonably be expected to bring up questions of ritual purity. For instance, stories about Jesus coming into contact with dead bodies and sayings about tombs might be expected to raise the question of the most virulent form of ritual impurity, corpse impurity. Women who experience either normal or abnormal flows of blood and who come into contact with Jesus might be expected to raise the question of touching a *niddâ* or a *zābâ*. A group of men traveling together for some length of time while abstaining from sexual activity might be expected to raise questions about regularly recurring impurity from seminal emissions during sleep. In the view of many scholars, stories of Jesus dealing with lepers might be expected to raise questions about contracting impurity from a leper. Yet, in every case, no matter what the specific issue involved, the authentic Jesus tradition is completely silent on the topic of ritual purity—sometimes in stark contrast to debates in the early church.

Yet can anything be concluded from the mere fact of Jesus' silence? Logically, silence means something or nothing, depending on the larger context in which it occurs. Granted the broader context of concern about and debates over purity laws both in 1st-century Judaism and 1st-century Christianity, the silence of Jesus, particularly when he is involved in situations that would naturally raise the issue of purity, inevitably takes on significance. Compared to his Jewish contemporaries and compared to the Christian Jews who emerge from his movement, Jesus stands out like a sore theological thumb (thus supplying an argument from discontinuity). Apparently, for Jesus ritual purity is not only not a burning issue, it is not an issue at all. But why should that be?

(3) Whatever the reason, it cannot be that the historical Jesus was indifferent to questions of Jewish Law in general or, even more, rejected the Mosaic Law in toto like some extreme Marcionite or Gnostic. We have already seen that Jesus tackled and made specific pronouncements about disputed questions like divorce, oaths, and sabbath observance. Whatever his position on the Mosaic Law, it was neither total rejection nor blithe ignoring of the Law as a whole. Rather, as our treatment of divorce, oaths, and sabbath already intimated, and as our treatment of purity laws now makes even more likely, it is a basic mistake to try to find one coherent line of thought or systematic approach to the Mosaic Law on the part of Jesus. Christian theologians in

particular are often driven by a desire to find some "principle" (love is the perennially favorite candidate) from which Jesus' various teachings on the Law can be derived or deduced. But there is no such principle. To hark back to all that we have learned in the first three volumes of *A Marginal Jew*, Jesus saw himself as an eschatological prophet and miracle worker along the lines of Elijah. He was not a systematic teacher, scribe, or rabbi; he was a religious charismatic. Now it is of the nature of a religious charismatic to derive his or her teaching not from the traditional channels of authority (e.g., Scripture, law, custom, liturgical or political office) or from detailed logical argumentation. The religious charismatic, implicitly or explicitly, claims to know directly and intuitively what God's will is in a particular situation or on a particular question. There is thus no appeal from or reasoning to a specific teaching of a charismatic like Jesus. He knows what he knows because he has, as it were, a direct pipeline to God's will. The characteristic "Amen I say to you," with which Jesus prefaces some of his pronouncements, is his particular way of emphasizing this point: the words I speak to you are true because I speak them, and that is the end of the matter. As the Elijah-like prophet of the end time who seeks to regather all Israel and prepare it for God's kingdom (imminent and yet somehow present), he and he alone can tell Israel how to interpret and practice God's Law as befits members of the kingdom. Nothing more and nothing less explains what seems to us to be a patchwork approach to the Law on Jesus' part. In short, Jesus' studied indifference to ritual impurity must be seen within this larger framework of his claim to be the charismatic prophet of the end time.

NOTES TO CHAPTER 35

[1] The bibliography on Jewish purity laws, purity issues in the New Testament (especially Mark 7:1–23), and allied topics is vast. I provide here a basic bibliography of books and articles (ordered chronologically) that in turn will offer the interested reader still more resources: Adolf Büchler, *Der Galiläische 'Am-ha'Ares des zweiten Jahrhunderts. Beitrage zur inneren Geschichte des palästinischens Judentums in dem ersten zwei Jahrhunderten* (Vienna: Alfred Hölder, 1906); idem, *Studies in Sin and Atonement in the Rabbinic Literature of the First Century* (London: Oxford University, 1928); idem, "The Law of Purification in Mark vii. 1–23," *Exp Tim* 21 (1909–1910) 34–40; J. H. A. Hart, "Corban," *JQR* 19 (1907) 615–50; Wilhelm Brandt, *Die jüdische Reinheitslehre und ihre Beschreibung in den Evangelien* (BZAW 19; Giessen: Töpelmann, 1910); Solomon Zeitlin, "The Halaka in the Gospels and its Relation to the Jewish Law at the Time of Jesus," *HUCA* 1 (1924) 357–73; C. H. Turner, "Parenthetical Clauses in Mark," *JTS* 26 (1925) 145–56; Abraham I. Schechter, *Lectures on Jewish Liturgy* (Philadelphia: Jewish Publication Society,

1933); David Daube, "Public Pronouncement and Private Explanation in the Gospels," *ExpTim* 57 (1945–46) 175–77; H. Idris Bell, "The Gospel Fragments P. Egerton 2," *HTR* 42 (1949) 53–63; S. Stein, "The Dietary Laws in Rabbinic and Patristic Literature," *Studia Patristica. Volume Two. Papers Presented to the Second International Conference on Patristic Studies Held at Christ Church, Oxford, 1955* (ed. K. Aland and F. L. Cross; Berlin: Akademie, 1957) 141–54; Jacob Neusner, "The Fellowship in the Second Jewish Commonwealth," *HTR* 53 (1960) 125–42; S. Safrai, "Teachings of Pietists in Mishnaic Literature," *JJS* 16 (1965) 15–33; Mary Douglas, *Purity and Danger. An Analysis of the Concepts of Pollution and Taboo* (London/ New York: Routledge, 1966, 2002 [with new preface]); Stephen M. Reynolds, "ΠΥΓΜΗΙ (Mark 7:3) as 'Cupped Hand,' " *JBL* 85 (1966) 87–88; Joseph M. Baumgarten, "The Essene Avoidance of Oil and the Laws of Purity," *RevQ* 6 (1967) 183–92; Helmut Merkel, "Markus 7.15: das Jesuswort über die innere Verunreinigung," *ZRGG* 20 (1968) 340–63; Charles Carlston, "The Things that Defile (Mark VII.15) and the Law in Matthew and Mark," *NTS* 15 (1968–69) 75–96; Martin Hengel, "Mc 7:3 *pygmē*: Die Geschichte einer exegetischen Aporie und der Versuch ihrer Lösung," *ZNW* 60 (1969) 182–98; Wilfried Paschen, *Rein und Unrein* (STANT 24; München: Kösel, 1970); M. Simon, "The Apostolic Decree and Its Setting in the Ancient Church," *BJRL* 52 (1970) 437–600; Thomas L. Budesheim, "Jesus and the Disciples in Conflict with Judaism," *ZNW* 62 (1971) 190–209; Jacob Milgrom, "Prolegomenon to Leviticus 17:11," *JBL* 90 (1971) 149–56; idem, "Sin-Offering or Purification-Offering?" *VT* 21 (1971) 237–39; Klaus Berger, *Die Gesetzesauslegung Jesu. Ihr historischer Hintergrund im Judentum und im Alten Testament. Teil I: Markus und Parallelen* (WMANT 40; Neukrichen-Vluyn: Neukirchener, 1972); Neil J. McEleney, "Authenticating Criteria and Mark 7:1–23," *CBQ* 34 (1972) 431–60; John Bowker, *Jesus and the Pharisees* (Cambridge: Cambridge University, 1973); Jacob Neusner, *The Idea of Purity in Ancient Judaism. The Haskell Lectures 1972–1973* (SJLA 1; Leiden: Brill, 1973); Baruch Levine, *In the Presence of the Lord. A Study of Cult and Some Cultic Terms in Ancient Israel* (SJLA 5; Leiden: Brill, 1974); Jacob Neusner, *A History of the Mishnaic Law of Purities* (SJLA 6; 22 vols.; Leiden: Brill, 1974–77); Robert J. Banks, *Jesus and the Law in the Synoptic Tradition* (SNTSMS 28; Cambridge: Cambridge University, 1975); Benjamin Mazar, *The Mountain of the Lord* (Garden City, NY: Doubleday, 1975); W. D. McHardy, "Mark 7:3. A Reference to the Old Testament?" *ExpTim* 87 (1975–76) 119; J. M. Ross, "With the Fist," *ExpTim* 87 (1975–76) 374–75; Lawrence H. Schiffman, *The Halakhah at Qumran* (SJLA 16; Leiden: Brill, 1975); Hans Hübner, "Mark vii.1–23 und das 'Judisch-Hellenistische' Gesetzesverständnis," *NTS* 22 (1976) 319–45; Jacob Neusner, " 'First Cleanse the Inside.' The 'Halakhic' Background of a Controversy-Saying," *NTS* 22 (1976) 486–95; Graydon F. Snyder, "The *Tobspruch* in the New Testament," *NTS* 23 (1976–1977) 117–20; Gedalyahu Alon, *Jews, Judaism and the Classical World. Studies in Jewish History in the Times of the Second Temple and Talmud* (Jerusalem: Magnes, 1977); Joseph M. Baumgarten, *Studies in Qumran Law* (SJLA 24; Leiden: Brill, 1977); Emanuel Feldman, *Biblical and Post-Biblical Defilement and Mourning. Law as Theology* (Library of Jewish Law and Ethics; New York: Yeshiva University, 1977); Jan Lambrecht, "Jesus and the Law: An Investigation of Mark 7:1–23," *ETL* 53 (1977) 24–82; reprinted in *Jésus aux origines de la christologie* (BETL 40; ed. J. Dupont; 2d ed.; Leuven: Leuven University/Peeters, 1989) 358–413 with addenda on pp. 413–15 and 428–29; Aharon Oppenheimer, *The 'Am ha-Aretz. A Study in the Social History of the Jewish People in the Hellenistic-Roman Period* (ALGHJ 8; Leiden: Brill, 1977); K. Romaniuk, "Le problème des Paulinismes dans l'Evangile de Marc," *NTS* 23 (1976–1977) 266–74; K. Tagawa, " 'Galilée et Jérusalem.' L'attention portée par l'Evangéliste Marc à l'histoire de son temps," *RHPR* 57 (1977) 439–70; Robert C. Tannehill, "The Disciples in Mark. The Function of Narrative Role," *JR* 57 (1977) 386–405; Michael J. Cook, *Mark's Treatment of the Jewish Leaders* (NovTSup 51; Leiden: Brill, 1978); Ellis Rivkin, *A Hidden Revolution. The Pharisees' Search for a Kingdom Within* (Nashville: Abingdon, 1978); Stephen Westerholm, *Jesus and Scribal Authority* (ConBNT 10; Lund: Gleerup, 1978); Arland Hultgren, *Jesus and His Adversaries* (Minneapolis: Augsburg, 1979); Barbara Thiering, "Inner and Outer Cleansing at Qumran as a Background to New Testament Baptism," *NTS* 26 (1979–80) 266–77; Joseph M. Baumgarten, "The Pharisaic-Sadducean Controversies about Purity and the Qumran Texts," *JJS* 31 (1980) 157–70; Joanna Dewey, *Markan Public Debate. Literary Technique, Concentric Structure, and Theology in Mark 2:1–3:6* (SBLDS 48; Chico, CA: Scholars, 1980); N. R. Petersen, "The Composition of Mark 4:1–8:26," *HTR* 73 (1980) 194–217; John K. Riches, *Jesus and the Transformation of Judaism* (London: Darton, Longman & Todd, 1980); Jacob Milgrom, "The Paradox of the Red Cow (Num. xix)," *VT* 31 (1981) 62–72; Yochanan Ronen, "Mark 7:1–23: 'Tradition of the Elders,' " *Immanuel* 12 (1981) 44–54; Mary Douglas, *Natural Symbols. Explorations in Cosmology* (New York: Pantheon, 1982, originally 1970); Isidor Grunfeld, *The Jewish Dietary Laws* (2 vols.; 3d ed.; London/Jerusalem/New York: Soncino, 1982); Hyam Maccoby, "The Washing of Cups," *JSNT* 14 (1982) 3–15; Elizabeth S. Malbon, "Galilee and Jerusalem. History and Literature in Marcan Interpretation," *CBQ* 44 (1982) 242–55; Ehud Netzer, "Ancient Ritual Baths (*Miqvaot*) in Jericho," *The Jerusalem Cathedra. Studies in the History, Archaeology, Geography and Ethnography of the Land of Israel. Volume Two* (ed. L. I. Levine; Jerusalem/Detroit, MI: Yad Izhak Ben-Zvi Institute/Wayne State University, 1982) 106–19; Jacob Neusner, "Two Pictures of the Pharisees. Philosophical Circle or Eating Club," *ATR* 64 (1982) 525–38; Heikki Räisänen, "Jesus and the Food Laws: Reflections on Mark 7:15," *JSNT* 16 (1982) 79–100; idem, "Zur Herkunft von Markus 7.15," *Logia. Les Paroles de Jésus. Mémorial Joseph Coppens* (BETL 59; ed. J. Delobel et al.; Leuven: Peeters, 1982) 477–84; Phillip Sigal, "Matthean Priority in Light of Mark 7," *Proceedings. Eastern Great Lakes Biblical Society. Volume 2* (Grand Rapids, MI: Eastern Great Lakes Biblical Society, 1982) 76–95; Jacob Milgrom, *Studies in Cultic Terminology* (SJLA 36; Leiden: Brill, 1983); Robert Parker, *Miasma. Pollution and Purification in Early Greek Religion* (Oxford: Clarendon, 1983); G. Wenham, "Why Does Sexual Intercourse Defile?" *ZAW* 95 (1983) 432–34; Nahman Avigad, *Discovering Jerusalem* (Oxford: Blackwell, 1984; originally 1980); T. Frymer-Kensky, "Pollution, Purification, and Purgation in Biblical Israel," *The Word of the Lord Shall Go Forth. Essays in Honor of David Noel Freedman in Celebration of his Sixtieth*

Birthday (ed. C. L. Meyers and M. O'Connor; Winona Lake, IN: Eisenbrauns, 1983) 399–414; B. Van Iersel, "Locality, Structure, and Meaning in Mark," *LB* 53 (1983) 45–54; Ronny Reich, "A *Miqweh* at 'Isawiya near Jerusalem," *IEJ* 34 (1984) 220–23 + pl. 28; Marla J. Selvidge, "Mark 5:25–34 and Leviticus 15:19–20. A Reaction to Restrictive Purity Regulations," *JBL* 103 (1984) 619–23; D. Wendebourg, "Die alttestamentlichen Reinheitsgesetze in der frühen Kirche," *ZNW* 95 (1984) 149–70; James D. G. Dunn, "Jesus and Ritual Purity," *A cause de l'évangile* (Jacques Dupont Festschrift; LD 123; Paris: Cerf, 1985) 251–76; Martin Hengel, *Studies in the Gospel of Mark* (London: SCM, 1985); M. Kichelmacher and I. Magli, "A Brief Anthropological Analysis of Connections Between 'Impurity,' 'Zaraʿat' and Slander in Jewish Culture," *Koroth* 9 (1985) 136–43; Michael Newton, *The Concept of Purity at Qumran and in the Letters of Paul* (SNTSMS 53; Cambridge: Cambridge University, 1985) 10–51; Robert A. Wild, "The Encounter between Pharisaic and Christian Judaism. Some Early Gospel Evidence," *NovT* 27 (1985) 105–24; David F. Wright, "Papyrus Egerton 2 (the *Unknown Gospel*)—Part of the *Gospel of Peter*?" *Second Century* 5 (1985–86) 129–50; David P. Wright, "Purification from Corpse-Contamination in Numbers XXXI 19–24," *VT* 35 (1985) 213–23; Roger P. Booth, *Jesus and the Laws of Purity. Tradition History and Legal History in Mark 7* (JSNTSup 13; Sheffield: JSOT, 1986); Daniel Boyarin, "Voices in the Text. Midrash and the Inner Tension of Biblical Narrative," *RB* 93 (1986) 581–97; Gerhard Dautzenberg, "Gesetzeskritik und Gesetzesgehorsam in der Jesustradition," *Das Gesetz im Neuen Testament* (QD 108; ed. K. Kertelge; Freiburg: Herder, 1986) 46–70; Richard K. Fenn, "Sources of Social Credit in 1st Century Palestine. Immanence and Authority in the Jesus Movement," *Ex Auditu* 2 (1986) 19–33; Hans Hübner, *Das Gesetz in der synoptischen Tradition: Studien zur These einer progressiven Qumranisierung und Judaisierung innerhalb der synoptischen Tradition* (2d ed.; Göttingen: Vandenhoeck & Ruprecht, 1986, originally 1973); Marius Young-Heon Lee, *Jesus und die jüdische Autorität. Eine exegetische Untersuchung zu Mk 11,27–12,12* (FB 56; Würzburg: Echter, 1986); Elizabeth S. Malbon, *Narrative Space and Mythic Meaning in Mark* (San Francisco: Harper & Row, 1986); Jerome H. Neyrey, "The Idea of Purity in Mark's Gospel," *Social-Scientific Criticism of the New Testament and Its Social World* (Semeia 35; Decatur, GA: Scholars, 1986) 91–128; Heikki Räisänen, *The Torah and Christ. Essays in German and English on the Problem of the Law in Early Christianity* (Publications of the Finnish Exegetical Society 45; Helsinki: Finnish Exegetical Society, 1986); Daniel R. Schwartz, "Viewing the Holy Utensils (P. Ox. V, 840)," *NTS* 32 (1986) 153–59; M. Slusser, "The Corban Passages in Patristic Exegesis," *Diakonia. Studies in Honor of Robert T. Meyer* (ed. T. Halton and J. P. Williman; Washington: Catholic University of America, 1986) 101–7; Michael Fitzpatrick, "From Ritual Observance to Ethics: The Argument of Mark 7:1–23," *AusBR* 35 (1987) 22–27; N. Kiuchi, *The Purification Offering in the Priestly Literature. Its Meaning and Function* (JSOTSup 56; Sheffield: JSOT, 1987); Ronny Reich, "Synagogue and Ritual Bath during the Second Temple and the Period of the Mishna and Talmud," *Synagogues in Antiquity* (ed. A. Kasher et al.; Jerusalem: Yad Yitzḥak Ben-Tsevi, 1987) 205–12; David P. Wright, *The Disposal of Impurity. Elimination Rites in the Bible and in*

Hittite and Mesopotamian Literature (SBLDS 101; Atlanta: Scholars, 1987); Klaus Berger, "Jesus als Pharisäer und frühe Christen als Pharisäer," *NovT* 30 (1988) 231–62; Barnabas Lindars, "All Foods Clean: Thoughts on Jesus and the Law," *Law and Religion: Essays on the Place of the Law in Israel and Early Christianity* (ed. Barnabas Lindars; Cambridge: James Clarke, 1988) 62–71; Bruce J. Malina, "A Conflict Approach to Mark 7," *Forum* 4 (1988) 3–30; Jerome H. Neyrey, "A Symbolic Approach to Mark 7," *Forum* 4 (1988) 63–91; John J. Pilch, "A Structural Functional Analysis of Mark 7," *Forum* 4 (1988) 31–62; Ronny Reich, "The Hot Bath-House (balneum), the Miqweh and the Jewish Community in the Second Temple Period," *JJS* 39 (1988) 102–7; Joshua Schwartz, "On Priests and Jericho in the Second Temple Period," *JQR* 79 (1988) 23–48; Peter J. Tomson, "Zavim 5:12— Reflections on Dating Mishnaic Halakhah," *History and Form. Dutch Studies in the Mishnah. Papers Read at the Workshop "Mishnah"* (Publications of the Juda Palache Institute 4; ed. A. Kuyt and N. A. Van Uchelen; Amsterdam: University of Amsterdam, 1988) 53–69; Noam Zohar, "Repentance and Purification. The Significance and Semantics of $ht't$ in the Pentateuch," *JBL* 107 (1988) 609–18; Iain Ruai Mac Mhanainn Bóid, *Principles of Samaritan Halachah* (SJLA 38; Leiden: Brill, 1989); Elizabeth S. Malbon, "The Jewish Leaders in the Gospel of Mark. A Literary Study of Marcan Characterization," *JBL* 108 (1989) 259–81; Jacob Milgrom, "Rationale for Cultic Law: The Case of Impurity," *Thinking Biblical Law* (*Semeia* 45; Atlanta: Scholars, 1989) 103–9; R. J. Miller, "The Inside Is (Not) the Outside. Q 11:39–41 and Thomas 89," *Forum* 5 (1989) 92–105; Frans Neirynck, "The Apocryphal Gospels and the Gospel of Mark. 5: Papyrus Egerton 2," *The New Testament in Early Christianity. La réception des écrits néotestamentaires dans le christianisme primitive* (BETL 86; ed. J. M. Sevrin; Leuven: Leuven University, 1989) 161–67; Lawrence H. Schiffman, "The Temple Scroll and the Systems of Jewish Law of the Second Temple Period," *Temple Scroll Studies* (Journal for the Study of the Pseudepigrapha Supplement Series 7; ed. G. J. Brooke; Sheffield: JSOT, 1989) 239–55; S. H. Smith, "The Role of Jesus' Opponents in the Markan Drama," *NTS* 35 (1989) 161–82; Joseph M. Baumgarten, "The 4Q Zadokite Fragments on Skin Disease," *JJS* 41 (1990) 153–65; Roger P. Booth, *Contrasts. Gospel Evidence and Christian Beliefs* (W. Sussex: Paget, 1990); James D. G. Dunn, *Jesus, Paul and the Law. Studies in Mark and Galatians* (London: SPCK, 1990); Martin Goodman, "Kosher Olive Oil in Antiquity," *A Tribute to Geza Vermes. Essays on Jewish and Christian Literature and History* (JSOTSup 100; ed. P. R. Davies and R. T. White; Sheffield: Sheffield Academic Press, 1990) 227–45; idem, "Sacred Scripture and 'Defiling the Hands,' " *JTS* 41 (1990) 99–107; Jack D. Kingsbury, "The Religious Authorities in the Gospel of Mark," *NTS* 36 (1990) 42–65; Jacob Milgrom, "The Scriptural Foundations and Deviations in the Laws of Purity of the *Temple Scroll*," *Archaeology and History in the Dead Sea Scrolls. The New York University Conference in Memory of Yigael Yadin* (Journal for the Study of the Pseudepigrapha Supplement Series 8; JSOT/ASOR Monographs 2; ed. L. H. Schiffman; Sheffield: JSOT, 1990) 83–99; Lawrence H. Schiffman, "The Impurity of the Dead in the *Temple Scroll*," ibid., 135–56; Kevin Reinhart, "Impurity/No Danger," *History of Religions* 30 (1990) 1–24; E. P. Sanders, "The Synoptic Jesus and the Law," *Jewish*

Law from Jesus to the Mishnah. Five Studies (London: SCM, 1990) 1–96, esp. 23–42; Heikki Sariola, *Markus und das Gesetz. Eine redaktionskritische Untersuchung* (Annales Academiae scientiarum fennicae; Dissertationes Humanarum Litterarum 56; Helsinki: Suomalainen Tiedeakatemia, 1990); T. C. Skeat, "A Note on *pygmē* in Mark 7:3," *JTS* 41 (1990) 525–27; Peter J. Tomson, *Paul and the Jewish Law. Halakha in the Letters of the Apostle to the Gentiles* (CRINT 3/1; Assen/Maastricht/Minneapolis: Van Gorcum/Fortress, 1990); Jacob Milgrom, *Leviticus* (AB 3, 3A, and 3B; New York: Doubleday, 1991, 2000, 2001); Albert I. Baumgarten, "Rivkin and Neusner on the Pharisees," *Law in Religious Communities in the Roman Period. The Debate over* Torah *and* Nomos *in Post-Biblical Judaism and Early Christianity* (Studies in Christianity and Judaism 4; ed. P. Richardson and S. Westerholm; Waterloo, Ontario: Wilfrid Laurier University, 1991) 109–25; Joseph M. Baumgarten, "Recent Qumran Discoveries and Halakhah," *Jewish Civilization in the Hellenistic-Roman Period* (ed. S. Talmon; Philadelphia: Trinity, 1991) 147–58; Shaye J. D. Cohen, "Menstruants and the Sacred in Judaism and Christianity," *Women's History and Ancient History* (ed. S. B. Pomeroy; Chapel Hill: University of North Carolina, 1991) 273–99; James D. G. Dunn, *The Partings of the Ways between Christianity and Judaism and Their Significance for the Character of Christianity* (London: SCM, 1991); Jacob Milgrom, "The Composition of Leviticus, Chapter 11," *Priesthood and Cult in Ancient Israel* (JSOTSup 125; ed. Gary A. Anderson and Saul M. Olyan; Sheffield: Sheffield Academic Press, 1991) 182–91; idem, "Deviations from Scripture in the Purity Laws of the *Temple Scroll*," *Jewish Civilization in the Hellenistic-Roman Period* (ed. S. Talmon; Philadelphia: Trinity, 1991) 159–67; David P. Wright, "The Spectrum of Priestly Impurity," *Priesthood and Cult in Ancient Israel* (JSOTSup 125; ed. Gary A. Anderson and Saul M. Olyan; Sheffield: Sheffield Academic Press, 1991) 150–81; John Christopher Thomas, "The Fourth Gospel and Rabbinic Judaism," *ZNW* 82 (1991) 159–82; Gary A. Anderson, "The Interpretation of the Purification Offering in the *Temple Scroll* (11QTemple) and Rabbinic Literature," *JBL* 111 (1992) 17–35; Joseph M. Baumgarten, "The Purification Rituals in *DJD* 7," *The Dead Sea Scrolls. Forty Years of Research* (STDJ 10; ed. D. Dimant and U. Rappaport; Leiden: Brill, 1992) 199–209; Bruce Chilton, "The Purity of the Kingdom as Conveyed in Jesus' Meals," (SBLASP 31; ed. Eugene H. Lovering; Atlanta: Scholars, 1992) 473–88; idem, *The Temple of Jesus. His Sacrificial Program within a Cultural History of Sacrifice* (University Park: Pennsylvania State University, 1992); Shaye J. D. Cohen, "Purity and Piety. The Separation of Menstruants from the Sancta," *Daughters of the King. Women and the Synagogue* (ed. Susan Grossman and Rivka Haut; Philadelphia: Jewish Publication Society, 1992) 103–15; James D. G. Dunn, "Jesus, Table-Fellowship, and Qumran," *Jesus and the Dead Sea Scrolls* (ed. James H. Charlesworth; New York: Doubleday, 1992) 254–72; Sean Freyne, "Locality and Doctrine. Mark and John Revisited," *The Four Gospels 1992. Festschrift Frans Neirynck. Volume III* (ed. F. van Segbroeck et al; Leuven: Leuven University, 1992) 1889–1900; Philip Jenson, *Graded Holiness. A Key to the Priestly Conception of the World* (JSOTSup 106; Sheffield: JSOT, 1992); Menahem Kister, "Some Aspects of Qumran Halakhah," *The Madrid Qumran Congress. Proceedings of the International Congress*

on the Dead Sea Scrolls, Madrid, 18–21 March, 1991. Volume Two (STDJ 11; ed.
J. T. Barrera and L. V. Montaner; Leiden: Brill, 1992) 571–88; E. P. Sanders, Juda-
ism. Practice and Belief. 63 BCE–66 CE (London: SCM; Philadelphia: Trinity, 1992);
Lawrence H. Schiffman, "Was There a Galilean Halakhah?" The Galilee in Late
Antiquity (ed. Lee I. Levine; New York: The Jewish Theological Seminary/Harvard
University, 1992) 143–56; Daniel R. Schwartz, " 'Kingdom of Priests'—A Pharisaic
Slogan?" Studies in the Jewish Background of Christianity (WUNT 60; Tübingen:
Mohr [Siebeck], 1992) 44–56; Terrance Callan, "The Background of the Apostolic
Decree (Acts 15:20,29; 21:25)," CBQ 55 (1993) 284–97; Roland Deines, Jüdische
Steingefässe und pharisäische Frömmigkeit. Ein archäologisch-historischer Beitrag
zum Verständis von Joh 2,6 und der jüdischen Reinheitshalacha zur Zeit Jesu
(WUNT 2/52; Tübingen: Mohr [Siebeck], 1993); Mary Douglas, In the Wilderness.
The Doctrine of Defilement in the Book of Numbers (JSOTSup 158; Sheffield:
JSOT, 1993); S. Friedman, "The Holy Scriptures Defile the Hands. The Transfor-
mation of a Biblical Concept in Rabbinic Theology," Minḥah le-Naḥum. Biblical
and Other Studies Presented to Nahum M. Sarna in Honour of his 70th Birthday
(JSOTSup 154; ed. Marc Brettler and Michael Fishbane; Sheffield: JSOT, 1993)
117–32; Hannah K. Harrington, The Impurity Systems of Qumran and the Rabbis.
Biblical Foundations (SBLDS 143; Atlanta: Scholars, 1993); Walter Houston, Purity and Monotheism. Clean and Unclean Animals in Biblical Law (JSOTSup 140;
Sheffield: JSOT, 1993); Jacob Milgrom, "On the Purification Offering in the Temple
Scroll," RevQ 16 (1993) 99–101; idem, "The Concept of Impurity in Jubilees and
the Temple Scroll," RevQ 16 (1993) 277–84; idem, "The Rationale for Biblical Impurity," JANESCU 22 (1993) 107–11; Jacob Neusner, Judaic Law from Jesus to the
Mishnah. A Systematic Reply to Professor E. P. Sanders (South Florida Studies in
the History of Judaism 84; Atlanta: Scholars, 1993); Ronny Reich, "The Great
Mikveh Debate," BARev 19 (1993) 52–53; Joseph M. Baumgarten, "Liquids and
Susceptibility to Defilement in New 4Q Texts," JQR 85 (1994) 91–101; idem, "Pu-
rification after Childbirth and the Sacred Garden in 4Q and Jubilees," New Qum-
ran Texts and Studies. Proceedings of the First Meeting of the International
Organization of Qumran Studies, Paris, 1992 (ed. G. J. Brooke with F. García
Martínez; Leiden: Brill, 1994) 3–10; idem, "Zab Impurity in Qumran and Rabbinic
Law," JJS 45 (1994) 273–77; Ilana Be'er, "Blood Discharge: On Female Im/purity in
the Priestly Code and in Biblical Literature," A Feminist Companion to Exodus to
Deuteronomy (ed. Athalya Brenner; Sheffield: Sheffield Academic Press, 1994)
152–64; Daniel Boyarin, Intertextuality and the Reading of Midrash (Bloomington/
Indianapolis: Indiana University, 1994, originally 1990); Shaye J. D. Cohen, "Juda-
ism at the Time of Jesus," Jews and Christians Speak of Jesus (ed. A. E. Zannoni;
Minneapolis: Fortress, 1994) 3–12; Anthony Saldarini, "Pluralism of Practice and
Belief in First-Century Judaism," ibid., 13–34; G. Feeley-Harnik, The Lord's Table.
The Meaning of Food in Early Judaism and Christianity (Washington/London:
Smithsonian Institution, 1994); Bernard S. Jackson, "The Prophet and the Law in
Early Judaism and the New Testament," Jewish Law Association Studies VII. The
Paris Conference Volume (ed. S. M. Passamaneck and M. Finley; Atlanta: Scholars,
1994) 67–112; Peter S. Zaas, "Paul and the Halakhah: Dietary Laws for Gentiles in

I Corinthians 8–10," ibid., 233–45; Yitzḥak Magen, "Jerusalem as a Center of the Stone Vessel Industry during the Second Temple Period," *Ancient Jerusalem Revealed* (ed. H. Geva; Jerusalem: Israel Exploration Society, 1994); 244–57; Jacob Milgrom, "Confusing the Sacred and the Impure. A Rejoinder," *VT* 44 (1994) 554–59; Jacob Neusner, *Purity in Rabbinic Judaism. A Systematic Account* (South Florida Studies in the History of Judaism 95; Atlanta: Scholars, 1994); Zeev Safrai, *The Economy of Roman Palestine* (London/New York: Routledge, 1994); Gregory Salyer, "Rhetoric, Purity, and Play: Aspects of Mark 7:1–23," *The Rhetoric of Pronouncement* (Semeia 64; Atlanta: Scholars, 1994) 139–69; Lawrence H. Schiffman, "Pharisaic and Sadducean Halakhah in Light of the Dead Sea Scrolls. The Case of Tevul Yom," *Dead Sea Discoveries* 1 (1994) 285–99; Sorour Souroudi, "The Concept of Jewish Impurity and Its Reflection in Persian and Judeo-Persian Traditions," *Irano-Judaica III. Studies Relating to Jewish Contacts with Persian Culture Throughout the Ages* (ed. Shaul Shaked and Amnon Netzer; Jerusalem: Ben Zvi Institute, 1994) 142–65; Michael D. Swartz, " 'Like Ministering Angels.' Ritual Purity in Early Jewish Mysticism and Magic," *AJS Review* 19 (1994) 135–67; Joseph M. Baumgarten, "The Laws about Fluxes in 4QTohoraª (4Q274)," *Time to Prepare the Way in the Wilderness* (STDJ 16; ed. D. Dimant and L. Schiffman; Leiden: Brill, 1995) 1–8; Jacob Milgrom, "4QTohoraª: An Unpublished Qumran Text on Purities," ibid., 59–68; Joseph M. Baumgarten, "The Red Cow Purification Rites in Qumran Texts," *JJS* 46 (1995) 112–19; Craig A. Evans, *Jesus and His Contemporaries. Comparative Studies* (AGJU 25; Leiden: Brill, 1995); Paula Fredriksen, "Did Jesus Oppose the Purity Laws?" *Bible Review* 11 (1995) 18–25, 42–47; Florentino García Martínez, "The Problem of Purity. The Qumran Solution," *The People of the Dead Sea Scrolls. Their Writings, Beliefs and Practices* (ed. F. G. Martínez and J. T. Barrera; Leiden: Brill, 1995); Hannah K. Harrington, "Did the Pharisees Eat Ordinary Food in a State of Ritual Purity?" *JSJ* 26 (1995) 42–54; Martin Hengel and Roland Deines, "E. P. Sanders' 'Common Judaism,' Jesus, and the Pharisees," *JTS* 46 (1995) 1–70; René Kieffer, "Traditions juives selon Mc 7,1–23," *Texts and Contexts. Biblical Texts in Their Textual and Situational Contexts. Essays in Honor of Lars Hartman* (ed. T. Fornberg and D. Hellholm; Oslo: Scandinavian University, 1995) 675–88; Jonathan Klawans, "Notions of Gentile Impurity in Ancient Judaism," *AJS Review* 20 (1995) 285–312; Israel Knohl, *The Sanctuary of Silence. The Priestly Torah and the Holiness School* (Minneapolis: Fortress, 1995); Tan Giok Lie, "Analysis of Jesus' Teaching Episode within the Framework of the Seven Components of Teaching: Conflict over the Tradition of Ceremonial Defilement (Matt 15:1–20; Mark 7:1–23)," *STJ* 3 (1995) 83–94; Ronny Reich, "The Synagogue and the *Miqweh* in Eretz-Israel in the Second-Temple, Mishnaic, and Talmudic Periods," *Ancient Synagogues. Historical Analysis and Archaeological Discovery.* (SPB 47; 2 vols.; ed. Dan Urman and Paul V. M. Flesher; Leiden/New York/Cologne: Brill, 1995) 1. 289–97; Lester Grabbe, "Synagogues in Pre-70 Palestine: A Re-Assessment," ibid., 1. 17–26; Paul Virgil McCracken Flesher, "Palestinian Synagogues before 70 C.E.: A Review of the Evidence," ibid., 1. 27–39; Rolf Rendtorff, "Another Prolegomenon to Leviticus 17:11," *Pomegranates and Golden Bells. Studies in Biblical, Jewish, and Near Eastern Ritual, Law, and Literature in*

Honor of Jacob Milgrom (ed. David P. Wright, David Noel Freedman, and Avi Hurvitz; Winona Lake, IN: Eisenbrauns, 1995) 23–28; Albert Baumgarten, "The Temple Scroll, Toilet Practices, and the Essenes," *Jewish History* 10 (1996) 11–13; Edward M. Cook, "A Ritual Purification Center," *BAR* 22 (1996) 39, 48–51, 73–75; Kurt Erlemann, "Papyrus Egerton 2. 'Missing Link' zwischen synoptischer und johanneischer Tradition," *NTS* 42 (1996) 12–34; J. Joosten, *People and Land in the Holiness Code. An Exegetical Study of the Ideational Framework of the Law in Leviticus 17–26* (VTSup 67; Leiden: Brill, 1996); James Kugel, "The Holiness of Israel and the Land in Second Temple Time," *Text, Temple and Tradition. A Tribute to Menahem Haran* (ed. M. V. Fox et al.; Winona Lake, IN: Eisenbrauns, 1996); William R. G. Loader, "Challenged at the Boundaries. A Conservative Jesus in Mark's Tradition," *JSNT* 63 (1996) 45–61; J. Magonet, " 'But If It Is a Girl She is Unclean for Twice Seven Days . . .' The Riddle of Leviticus 12.5," *Reading Leviticus. A Conversation with Mary Douglas* (JSOTSup 227; ed. J. F. A. Sawyer; Sheffield: Sheffield Academic Press, 1996) 144–52; Daniela Piattelli and Bernard S. Jackson, "Jewish Law during the Second Temple Period," *An Introduction to the History and Sources of Jewish Law* (Oxford: Clarendon, 1996) 19–56; John C. Poirier, "Why Did the Pharisees Wash Their Hands?" *JJS* 47 (1996) 217–33; Eyal Regev, "Ritual Baths of Groups and Sects in Israel in the Days of the Second Temple," *Cathedra* 79 (1996) 3–21; Frank Matera, *New Testament Ethics* (Louisville: Westminster/John Knox, 1996) 25–30; Peter S. Zaas, "What Comes Out of a Person Is What Makes a Person Impure. Jesus as Sadducee," *Jewish Law Association Studies VIII. The Jerusalem 1994 Conference Volume* (ed. E. A. Goldman; Atlanta: Scholars, 1996) 217–26; Hans Dieter Betz, "Jesus and the Purity of the Temple (Mark 11:15–18). A Comparative Approach," *JBL* 116 (1997) 455–72; Bruce Chilton and Craig A. Evans, *Jesus in Context. Temple, Purity, and Restoration* (AGJU 39; Leiden: Brill, 1997); Roland Deines, *Die Pharisäer. Ihr Verständnis im Spiegel der christlichen und jüdischen Forschung seit Wellhausen und Graetz* (WUNT 101; Tübingen: Mohr [Siebeck], 1997); Esther Eshel, "4Q414 Fragment 2. Purification of a Corpse-Contaminated Person," *Legal Texts and Legal Issues. Proceedings of the Second Meeting of the International Organization for Qumran Studies, Cambridge, 1995. Published in Honour of Joseph M. Baumgarten* (STDJ 23; ed. Moshe Bernstein et al.; Leiden: Brill, 1997) 3–10; Lester L. Grabbe, "4QMMT and Second Temple Jewish Society," ibid., 89–108; Hannah K. Harrington, "Holiness in the Laws of 4QMMT," ibid., 109–28; Hanan Eshel, "A Note on 'Miqvaot' at Sepphoris," *Archaeology and the Galilee. Texts and Contexts in the Graeco-Roman and Byzantine Periods* (South Florida Studies in the History of Judaism 143; ed. D. R. Edwards and C. T. McCollough; Atlanta: Scholars, 1997) 131–33; Jonathan Klawans, "The Impurity of Immorality in Ancient Judaism," *JJS* 48 (1997) 1–16; R. A. Kugler, "Holiness, Purity, the Body and Society," *JSOT* 76 (1997) 3–27; Joel Marcus, "Scripture and Tradition in Mark 7," *The Scriptures in the Gospels* (BETL 81; ed. C. M. Tuckett; Leuven: Leuven University/Peeters, 1997) 177–95; Gerard Mussies, "Jesus and 'Sidon' in Matthew 15/Mark 7," *Bijdr* 58 (1997) 264–78; Eyal Regev, "The Use of Stone Vessels at the End of the Second Temple Period," *Judea and Samaria Research Studies. Proceeding of the 6th An-*

nual Meeting—1996 (ed. Ya'acov Eshel; Kedumim-Ariel: Research Institute, College of Judea and Samaria, 1997); N. A. van Uchelen, "Halakha at Qumran?" *RevQ* 70 (1997) 243–53; Jürgen Wehnert, *Die Reinheit des "christlichen Gottesvolkes" aus Juden und Heiden. Studien zum historischen und theologischen Hintergrund des sogenannten Aposteldekrets* (FRLANT 173; Göttingen: Vandenhoeck & Ruprecht, 1997); Benjamin G. Wright III, "Jewish Ritual Baths. Interpreting the Digs and the Texts. Some Issues in the Social History of Second Temple Judaism," *The Archaeology of Israel. Constructing the Past, Interpreting the Present* (JSOTSup 237; ed. N. A. Silberman and D. Small; Sheffield: Sheffield Academic Press, 1997) 190–214; Marcus Borg, *Conflict, Holiness and Politics in the Teachings of Jesus* (Harrisburg, PA: Trinity, 1998, originally 1984); Jonathan Klawans, "Idolatry, Incest, and Impurity. Moral Defilement in Ancient Judaism," *JSJ* 29 (1998) 391–415; Rebecca Macy Lesses, *Ritual Practices to Gain Power. Angels, Incantations, and Revelation in Early Jewish Mysticism* (HTS 44; Harrisburg, PA: Trinity, 1998); William Loader, "Mark 7:1–23 and the Historical Jesus," *Colloquium* 30/2 (1998) 123–51; Risto Uro, "Thomas and Oral Gospel Tradition," *Thomas at the Crossroads. Essays on the Sayings Gospel Q* (Studies of the New Testament and Its World; ed. R. Uro; Edinburgh: Clark, 1998) 8–32; Joseph M. Baumgarten, "The Purification Liturgies," *The Dead Sea Scrolls after Fifty Years. A Comprehensive Assessment. Volume Two* (ed. Peter W. Flint and James C. VanderKam; Leiden: Brill, 1999) 200–212; Philip R. Davies, "Food, Drink and Sects: The Question of Ingestion in the Qumran Texts," *Food and Drink in the Biblical Worlds* (Semeia 86; Atlanta: SBL, 1999) 151–63; Peter J. Tomson, "Jewish Food Laws in Early Christian Discourse," ibid., 193–211; Christine Hayes, "Intermarriage and Impurity in Ancient Jewish Sources," *HTR* 92 (1999) 3–36; Martha Himmelfarb, "Sexual Relations and Purity in the Temple Scroll and the Book of Jubilees," *Dead Sea Discoveries* 6 (1999) 11–36; Hyam Maccoby, *Ritual and Morality. The Ritual Purity System and Its Place in Judaism* (Cambridge: Cambridge University, 1999); Scot McKnight, "A Parting within the Way. Jesus and James on Israel and Purity," *James the Just and Christian Origins* (NovTSup 98; ed. Bruce Chilton and Craig A. Evans; Leiden: Brill, 1999) 83–129; Fritz Stoltz, "Dimensions and Transformations of Purification Ideas," *Transformations of the Inner Self in Ancient Religions* (Studies in the History of Religions [*Numen* Book Series] 83; Leiden: Brill, 1999) 211–29; Mary Douglas, *Leviticus as Literature* (Oxford: Oxford University, 1999); idem, "A Bird, a Mouse, a Frog, and Some Fish: A New Reading of Leviticus 11," *Literary Imagination, Ancient and Modern* (David Grene Festschrift; Chicago/London: University of Chicago, 1999) 110–26; Markus Bockmuehl, *Jewish Law in Gentile Churches. Halakhah and the Beginning of Christian Public Ethics* (Edinburgh: Clark, 2000); François Bovon, "Fragment Oxyrhynchus 840. Fragment of a Lost Gospel. Witness of an Early Christian Controversy over Purity," *JBL* 119 (2000) 705–28; Jonathan Klawans, *Impurity and Sin in Ancient Judaism* (Oxford: Oxford University, 2000); idem, "Ritual Purity, Moral Purity, and Sacrifice in Jacob Milgrom's *Leviticus*," *RelSRev* 29 (2003) 19–28; idem, *Purity, Sacrifice, and the Temple* (Oxford: Oxford University, 2006); Bart J. Koet, "Purity and Impurity of the Body in Luke-Acts," *Purity and Holiness. The Heritage of Leviticus* (Jewish and Christian Perspectives 2; ed. Marcel J. H. M. Poorthuis and Joshua Schwartz; Leiden: Brill, 2000) 93–106; Chaim Milikowsky, "Reflections on Hand-Washing, Hand-Purity, and Holy Scripture in Rabbinical Literature," ibid., 149–62; Jacob Milgrom, "The Dynamics of Purity in the Priestly System," ibid., 29–32; Eric Ottenheijm, "Impurity between Intention and Deed: Purity Disputes in First Century Judaism and in the New Testament," ibid., 129–47; Eyal Regev, "Non-Priestly Purity and Its Religious Aspects according to Historical Sources and Archaeological Findings," ibid., 223–44; idem, "Pure Individualism. The Idea of Non-Priestly Purity in Ancient Judaism," *JSJ* 31 (2000) 176–202; Baruch J. Schwartz, "Israel's Holiness: The Torah Traditions," *Purity and Holiness. The Heritage of Leviticus* (Jewish and Christian Perspectives Series 2; ed. Marcel J. H. M. Poorthuis and Joshua Schwartz; Leiden: Brill, 2000) 47–59; Joshua Schwartz, "On Birds, Rabbis and Skin Disease," ibid., 207–22; Peter J. Tomson, "Jewish Purity Laws as Viewed by the Church Fathers and by the Early Followers of Jesus," ibid., 73–91; Cana Werman, "The Concept of Holiness and the Requirements of Purity in Second Temple and Tannaic Literature," ibid., 163–79; Aharon Shemesh, "The Holiness According to the *Temple Scroll*," *RevQ* 19 (2000) 369–82; Jesper Svartvik, *Mark and Mission. Mk 7:1–23 in Its Narrative and Historical Contexts* (ConBNT 32; Stockholm: Almqvist & Wiksell, 2000); Risto Uro, " 'Washing the Outside of the Cup.' *Gos. Thom.* 89 and Synoptic Parallels," *From Quest to Q. Festschrift for James M. Robinson* (BETL 146; ed. J. Ma. Asgeirsson, K. De Troyer, and M. W. Meyer; Leuven: Leuven University, 2000) 303–22; Charlotte Fonrobert, *Menstrual Purity* (Stanford, CA: Stanford University, 2000); Martha Himmelfarb, "Impurity and Sin in 4QD, 1QS, and 4Q512," *Dead Sea Discoveries* 8 (2001) 9–37; Tom Holmén, *Jesus and Jewish Covenant Thinking* (Biblical Interpretation Series 55; Leiden: Brill, 2001); Menahem Kister, "Law, Morality, and Rhetoric in Some Sayings of Jesus," *Studies in Ancient Midrash* (ed. J. L. Kugel; Cambridge, MA: Harvard University Center for Jewish Studies, 2001); Anders Runesson, "Water and Worship. Ostia and the Ritual Bath in the Diaspora Synagogue," *The Synagogue of Ancient Ostia and the Jews of Rome. Interdisciplinary Stuides* (Skrifter Utgivna av Svenska Institutet I Rom 4/57; ed. Birger Olsson, Dieter Mitternacht, and Olof Brandt; Stockholm: Paul Åströms, 2001) 115–29; Peter J. Tomson, *"If This Be from Heaven. . . ." Jesus and the New Testament Authors in their Relationship to Judaism* (Biblical Seminar 76; Sheffield: Sheffield Academic Press, 2001); Hannah K. Harrington, *Holiness. Rabbinic Judaism and the Graeco-Roman World* (London/ New York: Routledge, 2001); Lawrence H. Schiffman, "Jewish Law at Qumran," *Judaism in Late Antiquity. Part Five. The Judaism of Qumran: A Systemic Reading of the Dead Sea Scrolls* (Boston/Leiden: Brill, 2001) 75–90; Johann Maier, "Purity at Qumran: Cultic and Domestic," ibid., 91–124; Justin Taylor, "The Jerusalem Decrees (Acts 15.20, 29 and 21.25 and the Incident at Antioch (Gal 2.11–14)," *NTS* 46 (2001) 372–80; Bruce Chilton, Craig A. Evans, and Jacob Neusner, *The Missing Jesus. Rabbinic Judaism and the New Testament* (Boston/Leiden: Brill, 2002); James D. G. Dunn, "Jesus and Purity. An Ongoing Debate," *NTS* 48 (2002) 449–67; idem, *Jesus Remembered* (Grand Rapids, MI: Eerdmans, 2002); Thomas R. Hatina, *In Search of a Context. The Function of Scripture in Mark's Narrative*

(JSNTSup 232; Studies in Scripture in Early Judaism and Christianity 8; London/ New York: Sheffield Academic Press, 2002); William R. G. Loader, *Jesus' Attitude towards the Law. A Study of the Gospels* (Grand Rapids, MI/Cambridge: Eerdmans, 2002, originally 1997); David J. Rudolph, "Jesus and the Food Laws. A Reassessment of Mark 7:19b," *EvQ* 74 (2002) 291–311; Thomas Kazen, *Jesus and Purity Halakhah. Was Jesus Indifferent to Impurity?* (ConBNT 38; Stockholm: Almqvist & Wiksell, 2002); Halvor Moxnes, "Jesus the Jew. Dilemmas of Interpretation," *Fair Play. Diversity and Conflicts in Early Christianity. Essays in Honor of Heikki Räisänen* (ed. I. Dunderberg, C. Tuckett, and K. Syreeni; Leiden: Brill, 2002) 83–103; Jacob Neusner, *The Halakhah. Historical and Religious Perspectives* (Brill Reference Library of Ancient Judaism 8; Leiden: Brill, 2002); idem, *Judaism When Christianity Began. A Survey of Belief and Practice* (Louisville: Westminster/John Knox, 2002); Liora Ravid, "Purity and Impurity in the Book of *Jubilees*," *Journal for the Study of the Pseudepigrapha* 13 (2002) 61–86; Ronny Reich, "They *Are* Ritual Baths," *BARev* 28/2 (2002) 50–55; Franz Georg Untergassmair, "Jesus und die jüdische Gesetzestradition im Lichte urchristlicher Interpretation (Mk 7,1–13)," *Forschungen zum Neuen Testament und seiner Umwelt* (Albert Fuchs Festschrift; Linzer Philosophisch-Theologische Beiträge 7; ed. Christoph Niemand; Frankfurt: Lang, 2002) 175–90; Christine E. Hayes, *Gentile Impurities and Jewish Identities* (Oxford: Oxford University, 2002); James G. Crossley, "Halakah and Mark 7.4. '. . . and beds,' " *JSNT* 25 (2003) 433–47; John C. Poirier, "Purity beyond the Temple in the Second Temple Era," *JBL* 122 (2003) 247–65; Eyal Regev, "Abominated Temple and a Holy Community: The Formation of the Notions of Purity and Impurity in Qumran," *Dead Sea Discoveries* 10 (2003) 243–78; Michael J. Kruger, *The Gospel of the Savior. An Analysis of P.Oxy 840 and Its Place in the Gospel Traditions of Early Christianity* (Texts and Editions for New Testament Study 1; Leiden/Boston: Brill, 2005); Jay Sklar, *Sin, Impurity, Sacrifice, Atonement: The Priestly Conceptions* (Hebrew Bible Monographs 2; Sheffield: Sheffield Phoenix Press, 2005); Hannah K. Harrington, "Purity and the Dead Sea Scrolls—Current Issues," *Currents in Biblical Research* 4 (2006) 397–428; Jonathan D. Lawrence, *Washing in Water. Trajectories of Ritual Bathing in the Hebrew Bible and Second Temple Literature* (SBL Academia Biblica 23; Atlanta: SBL; Leiden: Brill, 2006); Eyal Regev, *Sectarianism in Qumran. A Cross-Cultural Perspective* (Religion and Society 45; Berlin/New York: de Gruyter, 2007), esp. 95–32. For a brief history of views on purity in 20th-century literature, see Harrington, *The Impurity Systems*, 2–28; Klawans, *Impurity and Sin*, 3–20.

[2] The classic case is that of Mary Douglas, who notably shifted her anthropological interpretation of the food laws in Leviticus from her earlier *Purity and Danger* (1966) to her later *Leviticus as Literature* (1999); see her prefatory remarks in the latter work, pp. v–viii as well as pp. 134–75; and her programmatic essay, "A Bird, a Mouse, a Frog, and Some Fish," *Literary Imagination, Ancient and Modern*, 110–26. Klawans (*Impurity*, 18) cannot refrain from smiling at the fact that, by changing her position, Douglas "has pulled the carpet out from under those" who used her earlier *Purity and Danger* to interpret ritual impurity in terms of "an overly hier-

archical picture of biblical priests or ancient Pharisees." See also the comments on Douglas's earlier work by Neusner, *The Idea of Purity*, 119–29; Harrington, *Holiness*, 171. Social-science exegesis is fine—but whose social science is one using?

[3] As I indicated in Volume One of *A Marginal Jew* (pp. 112–14), I do not think that, in general, the scattered *agrapha* (supposed sayings and deeds of Jesus usually preserved in fragmentary form in documents dating from the early Christian centuries) give any reliable information about the historical Jesus. In my opinion, this holds true of a Greek papyrus fragment called Oxyrhynchus Papyrus 840 (P.Oxy. 840), which purports to narrate a vitriolic debate on purity between Jesus and a Pharisaic chief priest in the Jerusalem temple. A full examination of the text and the many questions surrounding it is presented in Kruger, *The Gospel of the Savior*. His conclusions are that the papyrus fragment dates from ca. A.D. 300–350 and that its content was originally composed ca. A.D. 125–150, shows indirect dependence on the canonical Gospels, is the product of a Jewish-Christian sect of Nazarenes that was debating rabbinic Judaism on questions of purity, and is an original composition of the author, who did not use earlier sources apart from memories of the canonical Gospels (see, e.g., pp. 45, 203–4, 238, 244, 265). These conclusions make it virtually certain that the fragment gives us no reliable data about the historical Jesus. For a different view of P.Oxy. 840, namely, that the fragment reflects controversies about baptism in the early church, see Bovon, "Fragment Oxyrhynchus 840," 705–28.

[4] For basic philological information on *ṭāhôr* (or the *defective scriptum* form *ṭāhōr*) and *ṭāmē'* and allied words, see H. Ringgren, "*ṭāhar*, etc.," *TDOT* 5 (1986) 287–96; G. André and H. Ringgren, "*ṭāmē'*, etc.," *TDOT* 5 (1986) 330–42; see also Friedrich Hauck, "*koinos*, etc.," *TDNT* 3 (1965) 789–809. The most frequent use of *ṭāhôr* ("clean") and *ṭāmē'* ("unclean") in the Jewish Scriptures is in the context of cult; less frequent is the use in moral/ethical contexts. Indeed, as Houston (*Purity and Monotheism*, 42) notes, the adjective *ṭāmē'* occurs almost exclusively in a ritual context, while the verb form has a wider range. The adjective *ṭāhôr* is also used of gold and objects made of gold. The usual translations of the two adjectives *ṭāhôr* and *ṭāmē'* in the LXX are *katharos* and *akathartos* respectively. The adjective *koinos* (literally, "common," "shared") is not used of forbidden foods or other matters of ritual impurity in the protocanonical books of the LXX (contrast Mark 7:2,5; Acts 10:14; 11:8; more vaguely, Rom 14:14). It is found a few times in reference to forbidden foods in the deuterocanonical/apocryphal books (see 1 Macc 1:47,62). Building on the work of Paschen (*Rein und Unrein*, 165–67), Brooks (*Jesus and the Laws of Purity*, 120–21) suggests that forbidden animals came to be called *koina* in 1 Maccabees because their edibility was "common" to the surrounding Gentile nations while such foods were unclean to the Jews. (Paschen [ibid., 167] also points out that this development may have been helped by the fact that, even in ordinary Greek, *koinos* could at times carry a pejorative meaning: "common" in the sense of vulgar as opposed to "refined.") Brooks theorizes that the new Jewish meaning of *koinos* as "unclean" was then transferred by analogy from forbidden

foods to the types of ritual uncleanness that are contagious (e.g., unclean vessels and liquids). The factitive verb *koinoō*, when it has the special meaning "to make ritually unclean," "to defile ritually," is clearly a secondary formation from the adjective *koinos* in its special Jewish sense of "ritually unclean"; see 4 Macc 7:6. For more detailed consideration of these and other terms for purity and impurity, see Paschen, *Rein und Unrein*, 19–81; and, more schematically, David P. Wright, "Unclean and Clean (Old Testament)," *AYBD*, 6. 729–41; Hans Hübner, "Unclean and Clean (New Testament)," ibid., 741–45. In the NT, one of the most surprising divergences from the usage of the LXX is the fact that the adjective *akathartos* ("unclean," the usual LXX translation of the Hebrew adjective *ṭāmēʾ*) is never used for ritual uncleanness in the Four Gospels. In Mark, *akathartos* occurs eleven times, always of an "unclean" spirit in the context of an exorcism; remarkably, it does not occur in the dispute over purity rules in Mark 7:1–23. Curiously, Matthew uses *akathartos* only twice, both times in an exorcism context. The same phenomenon is found in Luke's Gospel, where the six occurrences all refer to an unclean spirit or demon in a context of exorcism. John's Gospel does not use *akathartos*, a fact perhaps connected with the absence of exorcisms in the Fourth Gospel. The picture changes somewhat as we move outside the Four Gospels. The Acts of the Apostles has five occurrences of *akathartos*. Acts 5:16 and 8:7 use *akathartos* in the Gospel-like context of exorcisms, while Acts 10:14,28; 11:8, all dealing with Peter's vision and the conversion of Cornelius, use the intriguing combination of *koinon ē [or: kai] akatharton* (anything "common or [or: and] unclean"). One might conjecture from this combination that early on Christian Jews adopted the late LXX terminology of *koinos* ("common") for ritually unclean objects (including forbidden foods) and that the Gentile Luke felt a need to make this special usage intelligible to a wider Gentile audience by adding the explanatory *akathartos* ("unclean"). Outside of the Gospels and Acts, the most frequent use of *akathartos* is found in a notably Jewish-Christian work, the Revelation of John; the adjective is used five times of unclean spirits, birds, beasts, or in general of unclean (i.e., sinful) acts. In the Pauline corpus, *akathartos* occurs only three times: 1 Cor 7:14, where we have a puzzling mixture of moral and ritual connotations in regard to the children of mixed marriages; 2 Cor 6:17, a quotation of LXX Isa 52:11a, in a context warning against contact with unbelievers; and Eph 5:5, referring to an immoral person. Complicating the picture even more is that the antonym, *katharos* ("clean," "pure"), is never used in Mark and occurs sparingly in the other three Gospels (Matthew 3x, Luke 1x, and John 4x). The physical image of cleanliness, still clearly present in passages like John 13:10, is most frequently used in the NT as a metaphor for moral purity, though the ritual sense is sometimes present, often mixed in with a moral connotation (e.g., Matt 23:26). The ritual sense is still clear in Rom 14:20, while ritual and moral senses are combined in Titus 1:15. Physical and ritual cleanness may be combined in passages like Matt 27:59 and Heb 10:22. The upshot of this brief survey is that one must be extremely careful when dealing with the question of moral and/or ritual purity and impurity in the NT, since the academic categories and distinctions that we legitimately employ may not correspond to the Greek words that occur in a given context. One must always attend to the presence or absence of key terms and to their specific meaning as determined by a specific context.

⁵ On this, see Neusner, *The Idea of Purity*, 1.

⁶ If one wants to speak of the metaphorical use of impurity language, terms like "metaphorical" or "figurative" are perhaps best applied to general statements about sin in the Psalms and the Prophets (often in poetical texts), where sinfulness in general is likened to a stain that must be washed away (e.g., Ps 51:4–5,9; Isa 1:15–17). In such passages, the procedures for removing ritual impurity (most notably, washing) are used metaphorically for God's forgiveness of sin in response to human repentance and reform. What marks off this truly metaphorical use is that the precise rules of ritual purity (e.g., waiting until sunset after immersion, the number of days one must wait before entering the temple after severe impurity) play no role; at the same time, the effects of grave moral impurity (defiling the land, being cut off from the people) do not hold in these general statements about sinfulness. Perhaps part of the problem in debating when the use of impurity language is truly metaphorical or figurative (see Klawans's discussion in *Impurity and Sin*, 32–36; cf. Neusner, *The Idea of Purity*, 9) is that, in a broader sense, all religious language is metaphorical. In the end, Kazen (*Jesus and Purity* Halakhah, 204–7) is probably right in suggesting that we would do best not to introduce categories like "literal" and "metaphorical" into our discussion of OT purity rules.

⁷ It needs to be emphasized that, in this initial exposition, ritual impurity and moral impurity are considered as they are presented in the legal corpora of Leviticus and Deuteronomy. As will be seen, the relationship between these two types of purity changes as we move from the original sense of the Torah texts to their reinterpretation in the Dead Sea Scrolls and later on in the rabbinic literature.

⁸ For the distinction between ritual and moral purity, see Klawans, *Impurity*, 21–42; for the idea of genealogical impurity, see Hayes, *Gentile Impurities*, 3–44. For a different approach that perhaps strives too much to establish continuity from the biblical through the intertestamental to the rabbinic period, see Maccoby, *Ritual Purity and Morality*, esp. 193–208. In what follows, for the sake of pedagogical clarity I use the categories developed and defended by Klawans; a similar tack is taken by Svartvik, *Mark and Mission*, 354–73; and by Kazen in his *Jesus and Purity* Halakhah (see, e.g., 3–4), though with various caveats and modifications. This is not to canonize one approach among many, but to adopt a useful expository tool for readers who may not be familiar with this confusing field. Similar to but not the same as Klawans's categories are those of Wright, "Unclean and Clean (Old Testament)," 729–41. Wright distinguishes between "permitted" impurities (which are natural and necessary, roughly the equivalent of Klawans's "cultic" impurities) and prohibited impurities (which are controllable by humans and therefore not natural and necessary, roughly the equivalent of Klawans's "moral" impurities). As both authors admit, there are certain instances of impurity that defy any neat systemati-

zation; the various laws about touching, carrying, and eating various animals are a clear example.

⁹ Granted the connection of ritual impurities with the grand life cycle of birth, sex, disease, and death, it is hardly surprising that in both the OT and the Mishna the three great sources of ritual impurity are corpses (and those contaminated by them), normal and abnormal genital discharges, and "leprosy." On this, see Kazen, *Jesus and Purity* Halakhah, 4–7. Only certain types of diseases come under the rubric of ritual impurity, namely, those diseases that demand some process of ritual purification when the disease ceases: various abnormal genital discharges and various skin diseases labeled *ṣāraʿat* (usually but incorrectly translated as "leprosy"; the term also covers various fungal growths in houses and fabrics). On the meaning of "leprosy" as a human skin disease in the Bible, see *A Marginal Jew*, 2. 699–700. Another curious type of impurity, one that fittingly comes under the rubric of "ritual" or "cultic" impurity, is the impurity that certain cult personnel or objects incur during the performance of particular rites of purification (e.g., the scapegoat rite on Yom Kippur).

¹⁰ Klawans (*Impurity and Sin*, 23) lists three distinctive characteristics of ritual impurity: (1) ritual impurity is generally natural and more or less unavoidable; (2) it is not sinful to contract ritual impurity; (3) ritual impurity conveys an impermanent contagion. One might add that pathological conditions such as unusual genital discharges and certain types of skin disease (usually translated arbitrarily as "leprosy") constitute special cases, since they occur in the lives of only some people and are not always temporary conditions. Moreover, in the Bible some passages connect "leprosy" with moral failures, but that is not the prevailing view in the Scriptures.

¹¹ In his treatment of purity rules, Paschen (*Rein und Unrein*, 61–64) emphasizes the idea of the destructive sphere of death. I prefer to approach the purity rules from the more complicated viewpoint of the whole ebb and flow of the powers of life and death. In this, I stand closer to Maccoby (*Ritual and Morality*, 207), who objects to Jacob Milgrom's emphasis on the power of death alone. Still, I readily admit that my approach is only a simplified pedagogical entrée into the very complex reality of purity rules. It is by no means meant to be a complete explanation of a phenomenon that probably defies any one neat and unified explanation. Again, I agree with Maccoby that behind all the rules of ritual purity there may have originally stood various reasons rather than a single rationale and that we must allow for an element of arbitrariness (ibid., 205).

¹² On this, see Harrington, *Holiness*, 11–12; cf. Houston, *Purity and Monotheism*, 54. Although Harrington is speaking primarily of the concept of holiness in rabbinic Judaism, her basic definition of God's holiness holds true for the biblical period as well. In the view of Jenson (*Graded Holiness*, 48 n. 14), separateness is not the basic meaning of holiness but rather its necessary consequence. In Houston's opinion (*Purity and Monotheism*, 55), "theologically, separation exists for the sake

of holiness. Holiness is the prior demand, certainly in the Holiness Code." For the view that one should distinguish between two distinct Semitic roots that are both spelled *qdš*, the first meaning "separated" and the second meaning "clean," "purified," see Schwartz, "Israel's Holiness," 47–48.

[13] While it is true that ritual purity was important in the biblical period because it was a necessary precondition for entering the temple, one should not make the mistake of reducing the significance of ritual purity solely to the question of access to the temple (for the opposite view, see Maccoby, *Ritual Purity and Morality*, 206). To this extent—though Poirier may push his point too far—I agree with the basic claim of Poirier ("Purity beyond the Temple," 265; see also his "Why Did the Pharisees Wash Their Hands?" 217–33) that it is a mistake to accept "the notion that the ritual purity laws of Second Temple Judaism existed *solely* for the sake of the temple" (emphasis mine). Even in the biblical period, observant Jews avoided unclean foods and Jewish women purified themselves after their menstrual period, even though such day-to-day observances of the purity laws had no direct connection with entering the temple—all the more so in the case of Diaspora Jews who lived at great distances from the temple and could not hope to enter it on a regular basis; on this point, see Paschen, *Rein und Unrein*, 60–61. Or, to take another example, those afflicted with "leprosy" were excluded from Jewish towns and villages as well as from the temple. To be sure, in the Jewish Scriptures, the vocabulary of "clean–unclean" occurs primarily in reference to cultic acts. But as Neusner (*The Idea of Purity*, 1, 26, 30, 32, 38, 118) and other scholars emphasize, one must remember the built-in bias of our sources: the treatment of clean and unclean is transmitted to us largely through the priestly stream of OT traditions (chiefly Leviticus and Numbers), a stream that naturally focuses on the relation of purity/impurity to the temple cult. According to Neusner (p. 26), the Hebrew root *ṭmʾ* ("unclean") occurs approximately 283 times and the root *ṭhr* ("clean") occurs approximately 212 times; the majority of instances occurs either in the priestly sources or in references to the cult.

[14] Not surprisingly, the main corpus of purity laws in the OT come from the priestly tradition (broadly understood, e.g., the whole Book of Leviticus and Numbers 19); see Paschen, *Rein und Unrein*, 42. Nevertheless, collections of purity rules are also found outside the priestly tradition, e.g., the list of prohibited foods in Deut 14:3–21.

[15] The various degrees of separation create a system of gradation in holiness and correspondingly in purity; see Wright, "Unclean and Clean (Old Testament)," 738–39; and at much greater length, Jenson, *Graded Holiness*, 15–39. This first chapter of Jenson's monograph presents his basic explanation of the "Holiness Spectrum" (as seen in the priestly writings) in its spatial, personal, ritual, and temporal dimensions; the spectrum is then explained in detail in the subsequent chapters. Within this Holiness Spectrum, Jenson (p. 37) distinguishes the five gradations of very holy, holy, clean, unclean, and very unclean. These five gradations correspond to the five

spatial dimensions of the holy of holies, the holy place, the court of the temple, the camp (as understood in the priestly writings), and the place outside the camp. The five gradations likewise correspond to the *personal* dimensions of the high priest, priests, levites and clean Israelites, Israelites with minor impurities, and Israelites with major impurities (plus the dead). The five gradations correspond to the *ritual* dimensions of sacrifices that are not eaten, sacrifices eaten by priests only, sacrifices eaten by nonpriests, purification lasting one day, and purification lasting seven days. Only the first three gradations have corresponding *temporal* dimensions: Yom Kippur, festivals and sabbaths, and common days. Jenson candidly admits that he is presenting an "ideal representation." One might indeed argue about various aspects of this ideal representation, but it does illustrate well the spatial and ritual degrees of holiness in ancient Israelite thought. Clearly, the holy and the pure were closely related, but they were not simply identified; cf. Neusner, *The Idea of Purity*, 18.

[16] As Jenson (*Graded Holiness*, 49) observes, this process of moving into a state of holiness is necessary for human beings, who do not remain permanently in a holy state. In this they differ from certain objects (e.g., the ark of the covenant) that, once consecrated, are permanently holy. The pivotal intersection of the pure and the holy in human life is that becoming ritually pure is a necessary precondition for approaching holy space (the temple) and holy objects (sacrificial food).

[17] Harrington (*Holiness*, 39), following Milgrom, points out that both holiness and ritual impurity are highly contagious; they are forces that act upon persons and things that exist in the middle, neutral, or "inactive" states of the "pure" (as opposed to "impure") and the "profane" (or "common," as opposed to "holy"). Hence, as Paschen (*Rein und Unrein*, 64) points out, purity, in contrast to impurity and holiness, is not transferable. There are thus four stages of being, ranging from the holy (*qādôš*), through the pure (*ṭāhôr*) and the profane (*ḥōl*), to the impure (*ṭāmē'*). The two extreme—and extremely contagious—poles (or "antonyms") of the holy and the impure must not be allowed to meet head-on. As Harrington states (p. 39), "contact between these two categories brings disaster." Notice, this is not necessarily true of the mere opposites, pure and impure (as Jenson [*Graded Holiness*, 43] notes, holy and profane, clean and unclean are opposite pairs). For example, a pure Israelite is obliged to contract ritual impurity in order to bury a deceased parent; this good and pious act certainly does not bring about disaster. Jenson (pp. 47–48) claims that the holy-and-profane pair expresses reality primarily from the divine sphere, while the clean-and-unclean pair expresses reality primarily from the human sphere. Since, however, the holy God and his holy temple dwell in the midst of Israel, the two spheres overlap in a complex way.

[18] On this, see Neusner, *The Idea of Purity*, 1; Harrington, *Holiness*, 174; Maccoby, *Ritual and Morality*, 154; cf. Ronny Reich, "They *Are* Ritual Baths," *BARev* 28/2 (2002) 50–55, esp. 53. Harrington notes that the adjective *ṭāhôr* ("clean") "rarely refers to physical cleanliness."

¹⁹ The difference between ritual and moral impurity is expressed not only in terms of cause and effect but also in the vocabulary used to describe moral impurity. While both types of impurity are described as *ṭāmēʾ* ("unclean," "impure"), only moral impurity is described as an "abomination" (so, e.g., *tôʿēbōt* in Lev 18:30) and as something that "pollutes"(*ḥānap* in Hiphil in Num 35:33).

²⁰ That grossly immoral acts render the sinner (morally) impure is affirmed by such texts as Lev 18:20,23 (*lĕtomʾâ*) and 18:24 (*tiṭṭammēʾû*).

²¹ Notice how the verb *ṭāmēʾ* ("to become unclean") is used of the sinner and then of the land in successive verses (Lev 18:24–25).

²² Perhaps the most striking proof that moral impurity does not create ritual impurity is that the perpetrator of grave sin does not defile the temple by his or her presence. For example, when a wife is suspected of adultery, she is compelled to undergo an ordeal within the sacred precincts (Num 5:11–31); there is no indication of any fear on the part of the priest that the adulteress's presence would defile the sacred place. Similarly, accused killers might seek refuge in the sanctuary (Exod 21:13–14). As Klawans points outs (*Impurity and Sin*, 29), in the Mosaic Law moral impurity does have an affect on the sanctuary, but not because the sinner enters the sanctuary. Rather, the sinner's moral impurity affects the sanctuary even from afar.

²³ See Klawans ("Ritual Purity, Moral Purity, and Sacrifice," 21) on Jacob Milgrom's view that a "sin offering" is actually a "purification offering"; it does not effect atonement for the individual sinner but rather purges the temple of the defilement caused by the sinner's immoral behavior. Klawans (pp. 23–26) observes that, like many other scholars, Milgrom treats the laws of ritual purity sympathetically while denigrating animal sacrifice as a fossilized vestige from a dim past. Wright ("Clean and Unclean [Old Testament]," 733–34) is of the opinion that deliberate sins could be dealt with by way of confession and sacrificial expiation (the normal means for dealing with inadvertent sins) if the sinner repented.

²⁴ Svartvik (*Mark and Mission*, 348–49, 373–75), while basically following the line of argument of Klawans, develops it by claiming that ritual impurity is a matter of *hălākâ* while moral impurity is a matter of *ʾaggādâ*. He then proceeds to use this distinction to help interpret Mark 7:1–23. The problem with using this distinction to explain Mark (or the supposed setting in the ministry of the historical Jesus) is that the Hebrew nouns *hălākâ* and *ʾaggādâ* may not have existed in the pre-70 period; or, if they did exist, there is no indication of the technical sense of the nouns found in the later rabbinic literature; cf. John P. Meier, "Is There *Hălākâ* (The Noun) at Qumran?" *JBL* 122 (2003) 150–55. I do not doubt that the two realities designated by the two nouns existed, but, without these two terms available as categorical tools, the creation of the theoretical distinction seen in the rabbinic literature would be difficult to formulate, articulate, or apply.

[25] Hayes (*Gentile Impurities*, 5–7) basically accepts Klawans's distinction between ritual and moral impurity, but emphasizes that around the time of Ezra and Nehemiah the more stringent group among those who had returned from the Babylonian exile created an innovation within the Israelite view of purity, i.e., genealogical purity. Concern about defiling "holy seed"—a concern that in the Pentateuch is restricted to the high priest and in a looser way to priests in general—is "democratized" in the Book of Ezra to the extent that it now holds true of all Israelites (pp. 19–44).

[26] See Hayes, *Gentile Impurities*, 58–59. For "mainstream" Jewish views of converts to Judaism in the late Second Temple period, see Josephus, *Ag. Ap.* 2.28 §209–10; Philo, *De virtutibus* 20 §102–4. For developments in the later rabbinic period, which lies beyond our focus, see *Gentile Impurities*, 107–92.

[27] While there are important distinctions in vocabulary and content between the purity laws of Leviticus and those of Deuteronomy (e.g., in regard to the use of terms like *šeqeṣ*, *ṭāmēʾ*, and *tôʿēbâ*; see Houston, *Purity and Monotheism*, 60–61; cf. Douglas, "A Bird," 114), 1st-century Jews would naturally have read the various purity laws as one corpus coming from God through Moses. Hence, I do not treat in detail what was no doubt a complicated history of composition and tradition in both Leviticus 11 and Deuteronomy 14; see Paschen, *Rein und Unrein*, 43. I also do not treat in detail the distinction between animals that could never be eaten in any circumstance (e.g., pigs) and animals that could not be eaten because of the precise nature of their death: i.e., animals that had died naturally without being properly slaughtered (*nĕbēlâ*) and animals that had been torn by wild beasts (*ṭĕrēpâ*). In the latter two cases, an easy means of purification is provided: washing one's garments, bathing one's body, and remaining unclean until evening (Lev 17:15); in these cases there is none of the sense of irremediable abomination that attaches to eating pork. While these are important distinctions within the legal corpora of the Pentateuch, these distinctions do not play a role in the dispute in the NT over whether Christians can eat "unclean" foods.

[28] Yet a certain relationship with ritual purity laws cannot be denied. The redactor of Leviticus apparently saw a connection, since the laws governing clean and unclean food (Lev 11:1–23) are followed in Leviticus by laws of ritual purity (Leviticus 12–15: e.g., childbirth, "leprosy," and bodily discharges). A clear link is created in Lev 11:24, where the thought passes from animals that may never be eaten to the temporary ritual impurity that arises from touching the carcass of any unclean land animal. Klawans (*Impurity and Sin*, 31–32) notes how modern scholars differ on whether the law of prohibited foods should be treated under ritual or moral purity (or the equivalent categories proposed by various authors). One later indication that the dietary laws do not, strictly speaking, belong with the laws of ritual purity is the fact that the tannaitic rabbis, in creating the structure of the Mishna, placed the treatment of dietary rules not in the Order of Purities (Seder Ṭohorot) but in the Order of Holy Things (Seder Qodashim). On this, see Svartvik, *Mark and Mission*, 372–73.

[29] Notice that it is not the animal itself, created by God and therefore presumably good, that is the abomination, but rather the eating of the forbidden animal that is abominable.

[30] On this, see Houston, *Purity and Monotheism*, 28, 53–54; Sanders, "The Synoptic Jesus," 24. Perhaps it is taken for granted that the freely chosen act of eating forbidden food signifies that the perpetrator has willfully and permanently departed from the covenant people of Israel. In the face of such total abandonment of the chosen people, there is no point in providing means for restoring one's ritual purity or in specifying punishment to be meted out within the covenant community. In regard to 1st-century Jewish Palestine, Sanders (ibid., 27–28) suggests that, except in the partially Gentile cities, non-kosher food would be difficult to obtain and so non-observance of the basic food laws would be almost impossible simply from a practical point of view. (But what of shellfish along the Palestinian coast?)

[31] For a list of the main explanations proffered and major authors who champion them, see Wright, "Unclean and Clean (Old Testament)," 729–41, esp. 739–40; Jenson, *Graded Holiness*, 75–80; Houston, *Purity and Monotheism*, 68–123; cf. Neusner, *The Idea of Purity*, 12; Kazen, *Jesus and Purity Halakhah*, 2–3.

[32] See, e.g., the comments of Klawans ("Ritual Purity, Moral Purity, and Sacrifice," 20–21) on the dubious enterprise of explaining all rules of ritual purity in terms of warding off the forces of death; cf. Harrington, *Holiness*, 170–71. Paschen (*Rein und Unrein*, 61–64) is a prime example of scholars who champion the view that the impurity of death is at the root of all impurity. By contrast, Klawans suggests that there may be no single common denominator underlying all the purity rules. Hence, instead of speaking of a single purity system, Klawans (*Impurity and Sin*, 36–38) prefers to speak of two purity systems, one ritual and one moral, with the dietary laws lying in between.

[33] Hence the term "Holiness Code," applied to this part (chaps. 17–26) of the Book of Leviticus.

[34] For example, *Jubilees* emphasizes moral purity while not spending much time on ritual purity. The *Temple Scroll* (whose composition probably preceded the founding of the Qumran community) expands the ritual impurity rules of the Pentateuch and introduces bribery as a new moral impurity defiling the temple. The situation in the *Damascus Document* is more difficult to judge (e.g., the precise import of CD 4:12–5:11 is debated among scholars), probably because of its complex history of composition; but the general distinction between ritual and moral impurity seems to hold, though the *Damascus Document* broadens the category of sexual sin. The concern about sexual sin defiling the sanctuary seems to be a common concern among a number of intertestamental works, including *1 Enoch* 1–36, the possible Jewish substratum of the *Testaments of the Twelve Patriarchs*, and the *Psalms of Solomon*. For all these works, see Klawans, *Impurity and Sin*, 43–62.

Even if one disagrees with Klawans on some individual points of interpretation, his general thesis seems to be substantiated: in many writings of the late Second Temple period (excluding the works proper to Qumran), the distinction between ritual and moral impurity is maintained. For a study of the notion of purity in 4QMMT and CD in particular, see Regev, "Abominated Temple," 243–78.

[35] See *De specialibus legibus* 1.48 §257–61; 1.50 §269–71. Klawans (*Impurity and Sin*, 64–65) notes two additions that Philo makes to the view of impurity in Leviticus and Deuteronomy: (1) all kinds of sins, and not just idolatry, incest, and murder, defile the soul; (2) there is an explicit analogy between ritual and moral impurity, the first reminding us of the second.

[36] Klawans (*Impurity and Sin*, 90–91; cf. Neusner, *The Idea of Purity*, 54–55) emphasizes that this holds true only of the documents that, in his opinion, originated in the Qumran sect: e.g., the *Rule of the Community*, the *War Scroll*, the *Pesher on Habakkuk*, and the *Hodayot* hymns. In contrast, the *Temple Scroll* and the so-called *Halakic Letter*, which he judges to be "protosectarian," do not evince this integration of the two types of impurity. For a more extensive treatment of purity rules at Qumran, see Harrington, *The Impurity Systems*, 47–67; cf. Newton, *The Concept of Purity*, 10–51. Klawans (*Impurity and Sin*, 12) criticizes Harrington for not recognizing that sin was a source of impurity at Qumran and therefore for not detecting important differences between the Qumranites and the tannaitic rabbis on the (ritually) defiling power of sin. In a similar way, by emphasizing that various documents found at Qumran may precede the foundation of the community, Maier ("Purity at Qumran," 91–124) avoids Harrington's tendency to homogenize the different views expressed in the Qumran material. Maier also contends that the purity rules of the Qumran texts should not be seen primarily as products of biblical exegesis (pp. 96–97), a position at odds with Harrington's claim (*The Impurity Systems*, 59) that the Qumran sectarians saw their purity rules as arising from the interpretation of Scripture. For a detailed study of purity rules in key sections of the *Rule of the Community*, see Paschen, *Rein und Unrein*, 85–152.

[37] Klawans, *Impurity and Sin*, 95.

[38] Klawans suggests that the compartmentalization seen in the Mishna may have existed already in the Pharisaic *ḥăbûrâ* ("fellowship" or "association"). Kazen (*Jesus and Purity Halakhah*, 216–17) disagrees, suggesting that compartmentalization would more likely have been the approach of the Sadducees, while the Pharisees may have approached closer to the view of Qumran in that they saw links between bodily impurity and sin. All this is highly speculative, all the more so because there is no firm proof for the existence of a "Pharisaic *ḥăbûrâ*" in the pre-70 period. On this, see *A Marginal Jew*, 3. 385 n. 161. In his *Jüdische Steingefässe*, Deines supplies archaeological support (especially in regard to stone vessels that did not communicate impurity) for widespread concern about purity on the part of the Palestinian Jews at the turn of the era. Whether his further claim that this widespread concern

can be traced chiefly or solely to the Pharisees' teaching and practice is debatable. The "library" from Qumran, in addition to other intertestamental Jewish writings, argues for the existence of various sects and parties in Palestinian Judaism of the time, all with their own concerns about and interpretations of the purity laws. Moreover, the fact that, on a given legal point, the practice of most 1st-century Palestinian Jews coincided with that of the Pharisees does not automatically prove that the Pharisees had convinced ordinary Jews to adopt their specifically Pharisaic practice. It is also possible that in various observances the Pharisees simply agreed with the ordinary practice of most Palestinian Jews. Poirier ("Purity beyond the Temple," 258), who argues that during Second Temple Judaism there was a widespread practice of purity that was not necessarily temple-oriented, holds that this pervasive concern with purity cannot be reduced to the influence of the Pharisees; "the impulse to non-priestly purity was much more widespread."

[39] On the "expansionist" tendency in Second Temple Judaism, see Kazen, *Jesus and Purity* Halakhah, 72–78.

[40] This seems to be the case in the curious incidents recounted in *Ant.* 20.8.9 §181 and 20.9.2 §206–7: wicked chief priests have their slaves seize the tithes due ordinary priests while the tithes are still on the threshing floor; as a result, some of the poorer priests starve to death. It is difficult to believe that the relatives or colleagues of these priests—or simply pious Jews in general—would allow these priests to die simply from want of food. The implication seems to be that these particular priests believed that they could not eat ordinary (profane) food. Sanders ("The Synoptic Jesus," 24–25) suggests that, in the 1st century, some priests might have read the rules about offerings due priests in Deut 18:1–4 to mean that the priests could eat *only* sacrificial offerings and dues. There is a faint echo of this incident in an anecdote Josephus tells (*J.W.* 2.8.8 §143–44) about Essenes who, though expelled from their community for serious transgressions, nevertheless refuse to eat food that does not meet the special Essene requirements of purity; consequently, such ex-Essenes often starve to death. The common element underlying these two quite different cases may be the traditional zeal and rigor that devout priests brought to the purity rules of the temple. In another case recounted by Josephus, priests held captive in Rome refuse to eat anything except figs and nuts (*Life* 3 §14)—a radical way of ensuring that they never accidentally taste non-kosher food or eat from cooking vessels previously used for non-kosher foods. For the various problems of interpretation that this brief reference entails, see Steve Mason, *Flavius Josephus. Translation and Commentary. Volume 9. Life of Josephus* (Leiden/Boston/Cologne: Brill, 2001) 23–24. In still another case, Josephus apparently (the text is somewhat obscure in *Ant.* 3.15.3 §320–21) recounts how, during a celebration of the Feast of Unleavened Bread that took place in the midst of a severe famine, the priests refused to touch the only bread available because it was leavened (this, at least, is the likely sense of the text). Interestingly, Josephus does not make the same claim about the Jewish laity during this crisis, although they would have been faced by the same dilemma. On this passage, see Louis H. Feldman, *Flavius Josephus. Translation and*

Commentary. Volume 3. Judean Antiquities 1–4 (Leiden/Boston/Cologne: Brill, 2000) 328–29.

[41] For example, we are told (*m. ʿEd.* 5:2; *Ḥul.* 8:1) that the House of Shammai maintained that fowl could be served on the same table with cheese as long as the two were not eaten together, while the House of Hillel maintained that fowl and cheese simply could not be served together at the same table. There is no indication that such differences resulted in the Shammaites and the Hillelites refusing to share table fellowship with one another.

[42] For the sake of uniform terminology, in what follows "the pericope" will refer to the whole of Mark 7:1–23; various subdivisions will be referred to as "units" or "subunits." More specifically—as we shall see from the results of the literary analysis to follow—Mark 7:1–13 will be referred to as "the first half of the pericope," while 7:17–23 will be referred to as "the second half of the pericope." Mark 7:14–15 will be called "the transitional verses" "the pivotal transition," or simply "the pivot."

[43] One of the problems of the fine work of Svartvik (*Mark and Mission*) is that, while he casts his net very widely over such disparate topics as the present state of Marcan studies and the patristic interpretation of Mark 7:15, the whole text of Mark 7:1–23 is never exegeted in great detail. He does, however, provide a good overview of the larger context of Mark 7:1–23 within the "bread section" of Mark's Gospel; see pp. 295–305; cf. *A Marginal Jew*, 2. 905–6. Svartvik argues well that a dominant theme of the bread section is the relation between Jews and Gentiles, with Mark 7:15 in effect granting a carte blanche for the Gentile mission of Mark's day.

[44] On all this, see the standard Marcan commentaries, e.g., Pesch, *Das Markusevangelium*, 1. 367–84 (with the customary labels of *Streitgespräch* and *Lehrgespräch*); so also Sariola, *Markus und das Gesetz*, 23; similarly, Guelich, *Mark 1–8:26*, 360–62, 371–73. While I distinguish vv 14–15 from the two main parts of the pericope (a position that is close to that of Marcus, *Mark 1–8*, 447–48), many others (e.g., Pesch), make v 14 the beginning of the second part. Unlike many commentators, Francis J. Moloney (*The Gospel of Mark* [Peabody, MA: Hendrickson, 2002] 137) prefers a three-part division: (1) introduction, vv 1–5; (2) Jesus' defense of his disciples, vv 6–13; (3) Jesus' new law of purity stated (a) to the people, vv 14–15, and then (b) to the disciples, vv 17–23. Kazen (*Jesus and Purity Halakha*, 60–61) counts six parts to 7:1–23 without concerning himself with the fine points of literary structure. The attentive reader will notice that nothing is said about v 16 ("if anyone has an ear to hear, let him hear"—or, as in some manuscripts, "let him who has an ear to hear, hear"). The reason for the omission of any treatment of v 16 is the near unanimous view of critics that v 16 is a gloss inserted into the text of Mark 7 by a later scribe, who took the sentence from Mark 4:23 (or 4:9). Although present in the majority of later Greek texts, Mark 7:16 is absent from early and important

manuscripts like Vaticanus and Sinaiticus. On this, see Metzger, *TCGNT* (2d ed., 1994) 81.

[45] Mark 2:16 speaks (in the most likely reading of the text, as seen, e.g., in the Codex Vaticanus) of "the scribes of the Pharisees," but 7:1 is the first occasion in Mark where we hear of the two distinct groups (Pharisees and scribes) acting side by side. The highly unusual nature of the phrase "the scribes of the Pharisees" is probably what led many later Christians scribes (e.g., in the codices Alexandrinus, Ephraemi Rescriptus, and Bezae) to change the wording to the more customary "the scribes and the Pharisees."

[46] As Marcus notes (*Mark 1–8*, 444), in ancient Jewish polemics, "hypocrite" is often used to mean "a person whose interpretation of the Law differs from one's own." A prime example is the polemic found in the some of the Dead Sea Scrolls. According to Marcus, the "seekers after smooth things" (CD 1:18; 1QpNah 1:2)—be they Pharisees or other sectarian opponents—are accused of being "hypocrites" (a plausible translation of *naʿălāmîm* in 1QH 4:13) because they practice an exegesis rooted in the "stubbornness of their heart" (*šĕrîrût libbām* in 1QH 4:15)—which, apparently for the Qumranites, means an interpretation of Torah obligations that is too lenient. In contrast, early Christian polemics often fault the Pharisees for being too stringent or severe.

[47] On *qorbān*, see *A Marginal Jew*, 3. 582–84. Marcus (*Mark 1–8*, 450) makes an intriguing suggestion about the polemic of the Marcan Jesus in 7:6–13. Could the Marcan Jesus be turning around a charge that Jews made against Christian teaching on the abolition of food laws? After all, at least in the Marcan understanding of 7:15, Jesus puts his own teaching on the purity of all foods above the food laws enshrined in Leviticus.

[48] On the crowd(s) in the Gospels, see *A Marginal Jew*, 3. 21–30.

[49] I translate the Greek noun *parabolē* in Mark 7:17 as "aphorism" to capture the nature of Mark 7:15 as a striking and memorable yet also terse, dense, and puzzling saying that is ultimately subversive of the traditional order. (Other commentators prefer to translate *parabolē* as "maxim" or "epigrammatic saying.") Mark's somewhat surprising use of *parabolē* at this point (the word has not appeared since 4:34) serves to connect the whole pericope of 7:1–23 with the parable discourse in chap. 4, with which it has a number of structural similarities. Yet the precise sense of *parabolē* in 7:17 shifts from the meaning of the word in chap. 4 (so rightly Marcus, *Mark 1–8*, 455); Mark 7:15 does not present us with an illustrative story or comparison as in chap. 4. Still, the basic Hebrew meaning of *māšāl* (the Hebrew word often translated by *parabolē*) is not entirely left behind. Mark 7:15 is a terse, memorable saying that teases the mind into active thought; its riddle-like nature demands interpretation; see Gundry, *Mark*, 354; cf. Svartvik (*Mark and Mission*, 220) on the various meanings of *parabolē* in Mark. Here, for Mark, is the true connector among

the various uses of *parabolē* in his Gospel: a "parable" become intelligible to human beings only when Jesus supplies the correct interpretation.

[50] As most commentators note, Jesus' withdrawal from public to private space, the approach of the disciples asking him to explain in private the mysterious teaching he proposed in public, Jesus' rebuke of the disciples because of their lack of understanding, and then his acceding to their request for a further explanation are all typical techniques of Mark's redactional composition. The clearest example is the parable discourse in Mark 4, notably 4:10–13; other partial examples can be found in 9:28–29; 10:10–12; 13:3–4. Along with other indications of Marcan redaction throughout this pericope, this sign of Mark's hand will prove important later on in our analysis.

[51] On the delimitation of Mark 7:1–23 as a single pericope, see Moloney, *Mark*, 136–37.

[52] I purposely say "the person of Jesus" and not "the word 'Jesus' " because, in a style typical of Mark, the proper noun "Jesus" never occurs in the whole of the pericope. Jesus is always referred to either by a personal pronoun (the opponents gather around "him" in v 1 and ask "him" a question in v 5 about "your" disciples, just as the disciples ask "him" in v 17) or by the understood but unstated subject in a main verb ("and [he] said to them," v 9; "[he] said to them," v 14; "and [he] says to them," v 18; "but [he] said," v 20). Indeed, the word "Jesus" never appears in the whole of chap. 7; interestingly, the only other chapter in Mark of which this is true is chap. 4, which contains the parable discourse. Typically, Matthew redacts Mark 7:1–23 by identifying the main character in the opening words of his parallel pericope (Matt 15:1): "Then Pharisees and scribes come *to Jesus*."

[53] Since, in the structured translation that follows, I translate the Greek very literally in order to point out all the connecting elements, I keep the wooden translation "man" and the corresponding pronoun "him" (the Greek constantly uses the masculine singular form *auton*). From the sweeping scope of the pronouncements, however, it is clear that the application of the sayings is universal, applying to men and women equally.

[54] McEleney ("Authenticating Criteria," 459) suggests that, in the Marcan text as we have it, the phase "this people" in the citation of Isa 29:13 (Mark 7:6) is understood to stand in opposition to Christians. Granted the redactional observation about "all the Jews" in 7:3, this is quite probable. On "all the Jews," see Kazen, *Jesus and Purity* Halakha, 64; Svartvik, *Mark and Mission*, 297–98. Svartvik points out how unusual the usage of *Ioudaios* in 7:3 is. Apart from this one text, *Ioudaios* in Mark is entirely restricted to the Passion Narrative of Mark 15 (vv 2,9,12,18,26) and to the question of Jesus being "King of the Jews." By contrast, the usage in 7:3 is much closer to the polemical usage found in John's Gospel.

[55] For a consideration of the literary components of vv 1–13, see Untergassmair, "Jesus und die jüdische Gesetzestradition," 177–80. Some of Untergassmair's conclusions about historicity, tradition, and redaction suffer from the limitation of his focus to vv 1–13 instead of taking in the whole of vv 1–23.

[56] Also reinforcing the literary connections are the various verbs connected with the vocabulary of "tradition": *krateō* ("hold on to" in vv 3,8), *paralambanō* ("receive [as tradition]" in v 4), *histēmi* ("establish"), and *paradidōmi* ("hand on [as tradition]" in v 13).

[57] Some commentators (e.g., R. T. France *The Gospel of Mark* [New International Greek Testament Commentary; Grand Rapids, MI/Cambridge, UK: Eerdmans/Paternoster, 2002] 285–88) see a careful escalation in Jesus' accusation: the opponents *neglect* [*aphentes*] the commandment of God in 8 (end of first reply), *render void* [*atheteite*] the commandment of God in v 9 (beginning of second reply), and *nullify* [*akyrountes*, a technical legal term in the Greek papyri] the word of God in v 13 (end of second reply). While this is possible, the escalation demands that we not give *aphentes* in v 8 the strong sense of "abandon" and that we make a distinction between *atheteite* and *akyrountes*, both of which can carry the sense of "declare or make null and void." Moreover, all three verbs occur at times in legal contexts.

[58] While I think that the balance of irony and satire is the preferable way of explaining the double use of *kalōs*, it is possible to take v 9 as a question: "Do you do well to render void . . . ?" In favor of taking v 9 as a question are Donahue and Harrington, *Mark*, 222.

[59] See, e.g., the different opinions and reconstructions of the tradition history suggested by Lambrecht, "Jesus and the Law," 400–405; Booth, *Jesus and the Laws of Purity*, 55–114, with a schematic outline on pp. 51–53; Marcus, *Mark 1–8*, 447–48. Kazen (*Jesus and Purity* Halakha, 62) pronounces himself skeptical about redaction-critical studies that disentangle tradition from redaction in Mark 7:1–23; cf. McEleney, "Authenticating Criteria," 459.

[60] Representative positions on tradition and redaction are listed by Lambrecht, "Jesus and the Law," 362–72. The great proponent of Mark as a conservative redactor is Pesch, *Das Markusevangelium*, 1. 368, 378. Pesch thinks that the *Streitgespräch* over the tradition of the elders (7:1–13) may have been taken over by Mark in its present form; he allows for some slight Marcan redactional intervention in 7:14–23.

[61] This is similar to the approach taken by Lambrecht, "Jesus and the Law," 374.

[62] Such "imitative" redaction can be seen in the way Matthew takes over and imitates both Mark and Q (and presumably his "M" tradition as well).

[63] On discerning typically Marcan redaction, see Lambrecht, "Jesus and the Law," 374–77, 404–5.

[64] On the many parenthetical explanations and generalizing statements in vv 1–13, see Untergassmair, "Jesus und die jüdische Gesetzestradition," 177–80.

[65] France (*Mark*, 279) disputes the common view that Mark 7:2–5 contains an anacoluthon (i.e., v 5 is the awkward continuation of the sentence that was interrupted at the end of v 2 by the parenthetical remarks in vv 3–4). France prefers the view that vv 1–2 form a complete sentence (instead of v 1 being a complete sentence by itself), with *kai idontes* in v 2 being a further participial clause coordinated with *elthontes apo Hierosolymōn* (v 1) and governed by *synagontai* as its main verb. While possible, this theory suffers from a serious difficulty. Within the narrative, *elthontes* (v 1) represents an action that is over and done with as the encounter begins, while *idontes* (v 2) describes an action that is happening or has just happened as the Pharisees voice their objection to Jesus in v 5. It is therefore difficult to read *kai idontes* as being coordinated with *elthones* in the one and the same sentence of which *synagontai* is the sole main verb. Moreover, Gundry (*Mark*, 357) claims that, if one does not read v 1 as a separate sentence, the explanatory statement beginning in v 3 ("for the Pharisees and all the Jews . . .") would have to be taken as the explanation of why the Pharisees and scribes gathered around Jesus. All in all, I think that seeing an awkward anacoluthon in vv 2–5 is the better interpretation of the syntax. Pesch (*Das Markusevangelium*, 1. 368), who champions the idea of Mark as a conservative redactor, thinks that the explanations in vv 2–4 need not have been introduced by Mark himself but could instead represent oral tradition. Since my concern is solely the question of what if anything comes from the historical Jesus, I do not bother to distinguish different levels of Christian redaction.

[66] Paschen (*Rein und Unrein*, 200) takes the unlikely view that *katharizōn panta ta brōmata* ("making all foods clean") in Mark 7:19 was already present in Mark's tradition and that Mark took it over out of fidelity to his tradition.

[67] See *A Marginal Jew*, 3. 306–8, 320–21.

[68] Commentators often point out that the *Letter of Aristeas* §305 likewise engages in factually incorrect universalization when it ascribes the ritual of handwashing (in connection with prayer as a preparation for reading and translating the Scriptures) to all Jews (*hōs de ethos esti pasi tois Ioudaiois, aponipsamenoi tē thalassē tas cheiras . . .*). For the Greek text and a French translation, see André Pelletier (ed.), *Lettre d'Aristée à Philocrate* (SC 89; Paris: Cerf, 1962) 232–33. Two points should be noted: (1) Comparing the *Letter of Aristeas* §305 with Mark 7:3, we see that the same basic universalization can be used for either positive (apologetic) or negative (polemical) purposes by different religious groups. (2) The fact that the *Letter of Aristeas* engages in factually incorrect universalization for a positive purpose does not make the universalization any less false from the perspective

of historical fact. Hence, one wonders what Moloney (*Mark*, 138) means when he states that, although the reference to "all the Jews" is "not precise, it can hardly be called 'incorrect.' "

[69] See *A Marginal Jew*, 3. 413.

[70] The classic study on the subject is Frans Neirynck, *Duality in Mark* (BETL 31; Leuven: Leuven University, 1972).

[71] In his *Duality in Mark*, Neirynck (pp. 139–91) presents the entire Greek text of Mark with all possible examples of duality underlined. It is instructive to see how large a part of the text of Mark 7:1–23 winds up being underlined (pp. 158–59).

[72] In Lambrecht's judgment ("Jesus and the Law," 377), fourteen out of twenty-two verses in 7:1–23 show signs of redactional activity. Beyond the major indicators that we have seen in our survey, one could descend to the question of individual words that are typically Marcan: e.g., the verb *synagomai* ("gather together"), which Mark uses to introduce new situations (e.g., 2:2; 4:1; 5:21; 6:30; 7:1, usually in the sense of some group gathering around Jesus, often with the preposition *pros* or *epi*); the verb *eperōtaō* ("ask"), which in both absolute and relative numbers is much more frequent in Mark than in the other Gospels and Acts (Matt 8x, Mark 25x, Luke 17x, John 2x, Acts 2x).

[73] For this common form of prophetic speech (usually predicting an imminent catastrophe) and the different labels used to designate it, see John J. Schmitt, "Pre-exilic Hebrew Prophecy," *AYBD*, 5. 482–89, esp. 484. For "reproach," words like "invective," "reason," "indictment," and "accusation" are also used; for "threat," words like "judgment," "sentence," and "verdict" also appear.

[74] For the exegesis of the MT in context, see Joseph Blenkinsopp, *Isaiah 1–39* (AYB 19; New York: Doubleday, 2000; reprint New Haven: Yale University Press) 402–6.

[75] My translation seeks to represent exactly the move back and forth between the singular and the plural in the Hebrew wording of the MT; this results in a certain harshness in the English translation.

[76] Some commentators on Isaiah suggest that the concrete object of Isaiah's indictment is the foreign policy of King Hezekiah of Judah around 703–701 B.C., when Judah sought help from Egypt against Assyria; so Otto Kaiser, *Isaiah 13–39* (OTL; Philadelphia: Westminster, 1974) 274.

[77] For notes on the Hebrew text, see Blenkinsopp, *Isaiah 1–39*, 403. For photographic plates of the Great Isaiah Scroll from Qumran (1QIsaᵃ), made by John C. Trever, see Frank Moore Cross et al. (eds.), *Scrolls from Qumrân Cave I* (Jerusa-

lem: Albright Institute of Archaeological Research/The Shrine of the Book, 1972) 16–123. Isa 29:13–14 is found on p. 61 (plate XXIII), lines 22–25. For scribal indications of large and small units in the text of 1QIsa³, see Odil Hannes Steck, *Die erste Jesajarolle von Qumran (1QIsa³)* (SBS 173; 2 vols.; Stuttgart: KBW, 1998). For an English translation of Isa 29:13–14 from1QIsa³ with notes collating the text with the MT and the LXX, see Martin Abegg, Jr., Peter Flint, and Eugene Ulrich, *The Dead Sea Scrolls Bible* (San Francisco: Harper, 1999) 131. Among the few differences (beyond mere spelling differences) in 1QIsa³ at 29:13 that critics highlight are the phrases "fear of me" rather than "their fear of me"(so the MT) and "like commandments of men" rather than "a commandment of men" (so the MT). Paulson Pulikottil (*Transmission of Biblical Texts in Qumran. The Case of the Large Isaiah Scroll 1QIsa³* [Journal for the Study of the Pseudepigrapha, Supplement Series 34; Sheffield: Sheffield Academic Press, 2001] 139) thinks that the change to "like commandments of men," which creates a comparison rather than an identity with the fear of God, is an example of the theological exegesis seen in 1QIsa³. At the same time, one should note that the comparative particle *kě* ("like," "as") is also found at this point in the text in the Aramaic *Targum of Isaiah*. Unfortunately, the Isaiah fragments from Cave 4 of Qumran do not include Isa 29:13, though 4QIsa^k contains partial lines from Isa 28:26–29:9. See Eugene Ulrich, Frank Moore Cross, et al. (eds.), *Qumran Cave 4. X. The Prophets* (DJD 15; Oxford: Clarendon, 1997) 125–27. For critical comparisons of the text forms in the MT, the LXX, Mark/Matthew, and the *Targum of Isaiah*, see Krister Stendahl, *The School of St. Matthew and Its Use of the Old Testament* (ASNU 20; 2d ed.; Lund: Gleerup, 1954, 1968) 56–58; Robert Horton Gundry, *The Use of the Old Testament in St. Matthew's Gospel* (Leiden: Brill, 1975) 14–16. For the Aramaic text (with English translation) of Isa 29:13–14 in the *Targum of Isaiah*, see J. F. Stenning, *The Targum of Isaiah* (Oxford: Clarendon, 1949) 92–95; and the critical edition of Alexander Sperber, *The Bible in Aramaic. Volume III. The Latter Prophets According to Targum Jonathan* (Leiden: Brill, 1962) 57. An English translation with critical notes is available in Bruce D. Chilton, *The Isaiah Targum* (The Aramaic Bible 11; Wilmington, DE: Glazier, 1987) 58. In dealing with the *Targum of Isaiah*, it is wise to remember the blunt evaluation of Sperber (*The Bible in Aramaic. Volume III*, xi): "The text of the Targum to the Latter Prophets has come down to us in a most deplorable state of corruption."

[78] For an analysis of the differences between the MT and the LXX and between the LXX and Mark 7:6–7, see Lambrecht, "Jesus and the Law," 384–86.

[79] It is possible that Mark, for all his abbreviation of the first part of Isa 29:13, keeps the verb *tima* ("honors") in Mark 7:6 because he wishes to create a cross-reference to the first quotation in Jesus' second reply (7:10): "Honor [*tima*] your father and your mother." On this, see Gundry, *Mark*, 350. In any event, Mark substitutes the 3d person singular form of the verb *tima* ("honors") for the plural found in the LXX (*timōsin*, "they honor"), apparently preferring a grammatically correct agreement of the singular noun (*laos*, "people") with the singular verb to the LXX's

constructio ad sensum, which uses the plural verb because of the plural sense inherent in "people" (in the Hebrew text, the singular noun *'ām*). The Codices Bezae and Freerianus read "loves" instead of "honors" in Mark 7:6, but this is rightly considered by most commentators to be a secondary alteration of Mark's text; see, however, the hesitation of Stendahl, *The School of St. Matthew*, 57. Bezae has a number of erratic readings in Mark 7:6–8. Some commentators (e.g., Donahue and Harrington, *Mark*, 226; cf. Marcus, *Mark 1–8*, 450) suggest that the reference to "lips" in Isa 29:13, as cited in Mark 7:6, may intend to create an ironic connection with the Pharisees' concern about what passes the lips, i.e., food. But the word "lips" is never taken up in the surrounding argument. Moreover, if Mark had wanted to create such a connection, it would have made more sense for him to have used the longer form of LXX Isa 29:13, which includes the phrase "with its mouth."

[80] Many commentators on Isaiah maintain that the Greek word *matēn* ("in vain") in Isa 29:13 comes from a misreading of the Hebrew word *wthy*, which the MT vocalizes as the verb *wattĕhî*, i.e., the verb "to be" in the 3d person feminine singular imperfect with the *wāw conversivum*, with the simple meaning in this context of "is." Supposedly, the LXX translator mistook *wthy* as the noun *wĕtōhû*, meaning "and the emptiness," with the clause meaning "and their fear of me [their cultic worship] is emptiness"; on this, see, e.g., France, *Mark*, 284; cf. Loader, "Mark 7:1–23," 130. Indeed, Kaiser (*Isaiah 13–39*) claims that this was the original meaning of the Hebrew text, which the LXX has rightly understood and which the MT has misunderstood. However, along with Blenkinsopp (*Isaiah 1–39*), I think that the MT is the correct reading of the Hebrew. Indeed, I would go a step further and question whether the LXX's *matēn* is to be explained as a misreading of the Hebrew consonants *wthy* as *wĕtōhû*. Two considerations make this theory of a misreading less certain than some think: (1) The Hebrew verb "to be" (*hāyâ*) is so omnipresent in the Jewish Scriptures, while the Hebrew noun "emptiness" (*tōhû*) is so rare by comparison (twenty occurrences in the whole of the Jewish Scriptures), that it is difficult to understand why the LXX translator read the very common verb "to be" as the relatively rare noun "emptiness." However, to be fair, its should be noted that *tōhû* occurs more often in the Book of Isaiah than in any other Hebrew book in the Jewish canon. (2) More to the point, the Greek adverb *matēn* is used in the LXX to translate five different Hebrew words. By far the most common Hebrew word represented by *matēn* is the Hebrew adverb *ḥinnām* ("in vain"); the Hebrew words that are less frequently translated by *matēn* include *'awen*, *hebel*, *šāw'*, and *šeqer*. Except for the hypothetical case of Isa 29:13, the Hebrew noun *tōhû* is never translated in the LXX by *matēn*; rather, it is translated by *abatos*, *adikos*, *aoratos*, *apollyein*, *dipsos*, *erēmos*, *eis kenon*, *mataios*, *ta mēden onta*, and *oudeis*. In short, therefore, I tend to think that *matēn*, like the rest of the last clause in LXX Isa 29:13, represents not a mistaken reading of the Hebrew text but rather a creative, interpretative translation thereof. Admittedly, though, certainty on this point is impossible.

[81] In regard to the introduction of an active participle "teaching" (*didaskontes*) in the LXX, there is an intriguing parallel with the text of the later Aramaic *Tar-*

gum of Isaiah. The final clause in *Tg. Isa.* 29:13 reads, "and their fear of me is like a commandment of men who teach [*malĕpîn*]." Since the *Targum of Isaiah* was written centuries after the LXX translation of Isaiah, and since the active participle "teaching" is witnessed in neither the Great Isaiah Scroll from Qumran nor the MT, I tend to think that the *Targum of Isaiah* may have been influenced at this point by the LXX tradition.

[82] See Blenkinsopp, *Isaiah 1–39*, 77. Especially in LXX Isaiah, one must hold open the possibility that a variant reading is the result not of a mistake or a different Hebrew source-text but rather a desire to interpret and actualize the prophetic text. On this, see Arie van der Kooij, "The Old Greek of Isaiah in Relation to the Qumran Texts of Isaiah: Some General Comments," *Septuagint, Scrolls, and Cognate Writings* (SBLSCS 33; Atlanta: Scholars, 1992) 195–213. See also Isaac Leo Seeligmann, *The Septuagint Version of Isaiah. A Discussion of Its Problems* (Leiden: Brill, 1948).

[83] Strangely, Moloney (*Mark*, 139) claims that in 7:6–13, the Marcan Jesus charges "this people" with "changing the divine doctrines of Torah into human precepts." Rather, Jesus accuses his opponents of transforming mere human commandments into divine doctrines while they neglect or annul the true commandment of God.

[84] Donahue and Harrington (*Mark*, 222) suggest that the syntax of 7:8 (with the participle *aphentes* ["neglecting"] dependent on the main verb *krateite* ["hold to"]) emphasizes the causal connection between the observance of human tradition and the neglect of the divine command.

[85] The noun *entolē* ("commandment") occurs only six times in Mark (7:8,9; 10:5,19; 12:28,31), and each time it cites one or more commandments of God in the Pentateuch. On this, see Donahue and Harrington, *Mark*, 222. Outside of the NT passages that echo Isa 29:13 (Mark 7:7; Matt 15:9; Col 2:22), the unusual plural *didaskalias* ("teachings") occurs in the NT only at 1 Tim 4:1, once again in a negative, polemical sense. At least in the NT passages dependent on Isa 29:13, the plural form of *didaskalias* may be intended to create an implicit contrast between the one, unitary will of God expressed in Scripture as opposed to the many commandments and teachings invented by human beings. On this, see Untergassmair, "Jesus und die jüdische Gesetzestradition," 185.

[86] On this, see Booth, *Jesus and the Laws of Purity*, 90–94; cf. McEleney, "Authenticating Criteria," 459; Lambrecht, "Jesus and the Law," 389. While Booth briefly entertains the possibility that Jesus cited the Aramaic *Targum of Isaiah* from the *Targum Jonathan to the Prophets* (the existence of which cannot be proven for the 1st century A.D. and the redaction of which occurred in Babylon centuries later), he wisely concludes that Mark 7:6–8 is a creation of Christian polemics. Equally wise is his decision not to call upon the parallel material in *Egerton Papyrus 2*, which he considers secondary. On the secondary nature of the material in *Egerton*

Papyrus 2, see *A Marginal Jew*, 1. 118–20; cf. Gundry, *Mark*, 362; Joachim Jeremias and Wilhelm Schneemelcher, "Papyrus Egerton 2,"*New Testament Apocrypha. I. Gospels and Related Writings* (2d ed.; ed. Wilhelm Schneemelcher; Tübingen: Mohr [Siebeck]; Cambridge, UK: James Clarke; Louisville: Westminster/John Knox, 1991) 96–97.

[87] The scholarly debate over what is the problem that the author of Colossians is trying to address has a long history; for earlier treatments see the collection of essays in Fred O. Francis and Wayne A. Meeks (eds.), *Conflict at Colossae* (SBLSBS 4; rev. ed.; Missoula, MT: Scholars, 1975). For more recent treatments, see Richard E. DeMaris, *The Colossian Controversy. Wisdom in Dispute at Colossae* (JSNTSup 96; Sheffield, UK: JSOT, 1994); Clinton E. Arnold, *The Colossian Syncretism. The Interface between Christianity and Folk Belief at Colossae* (WUNT 2/77; Tübingen [Mohr], 1995); Troy W. Martin, *By Philosophy and Empty Deceit*. Colossians *As Response to a Cynic Critique* (JSNTSup 118; Sheffield, UK: Sheffield Academic Press, 1996).

[88] For the high christology of Colossians, see George H. van Kooten, *Cosmic Christology in Paul and the Pauline School. Colossians and Ephesians in the Context of Graeco-Roman Cosmology* (WUNT 2/171; Tübingen: Mohr [Siebeck], 2003); Frank J. Matera, *New Testament Christology* (Louisville: Westminster/John Knox, 1999) 135–46; Ralph P. Martin and Brian J. Dodd (eds.), *Where Christology Began. Essays on Philippians 2* (Louisville: Westminster/John Knox, 1998); Ralph P. Martin, *Carmen Christi* (rev. ed.; Grand Rapids, MI: Eerdmans, 1983).

[89] Cf. Kazen, *Jesus and Purity* Halakha, 64. That we are dealing both in Mark and in Colossians with a type of early Christian polemic that circulated in different local churches is made all the more likely by the fact that earlier on, in chap. 2, the author of Colossians warns the Christians of Colossae against the empty deceit of a philosophy that simply reflects "the tradition of men" (*tēn paradosin tōn anthrōpōn*), the same phrase that occurs in Mark 7:8. Although this phrase is not directly connected with the allusion to Isa 29:13 in Col 2:22, the general proximity of the two phrases adds to the likelihood that we are dealing with a set *topos* of early Christian polemic. There may even be an echo of this theme in the polemical remark of Tit 1:14: "instead of paying attention to Jewish myths and *commandments of men*." Stendahl (*The School of St. Matthew*, 57) points out that the use of Isa 29:13 in Christian polemics continues into the patristic literature: e.g., *1 Clement* 15:2 (most of the MSS agree almost exactly with Mark 7:6); Justin Martyr in *Dialogue with Trypho* 78. 11 (citing the whole of Isa 29:13–14 and conforming almost exactly to the shorter LXX version of the text); and *Papyrus Egerton 2* (though its fragmentary nature makes any judgment difficult, it seems to follow for the most part the shorter LXX version). One might add the citation of Isaiah in *2 Clement* 3:5, which, except for two minor variations, agrees with Mark's abbreviated citation of Isa 29:13 in 7:6. The many textual variations suggest an interaction of written and oral sources in the patristic period.

[90] Stendahl (*The School of St. Matthew*, 58) states bluntly, "the LXX form is a *sine qua non* for the narratives of Mark and Matthew." At least on the strictly textual question, Gundry's judgment is similar (*The Use of the Old Testament*, 15–16): despite "minor stylistic departures from the LXX," Mark's citation remains Septuagintal throughout, "particularly in *porrō apechei*, *matēn*, *didaskontes*, the unusual plural *didaskalias*, and the double use of the root *didask-* for one Hebrew word—all, except the first, against the MT." See also Sariola, *Markus und das Gesetz*, 32–33.

[91] Other verses from the larger context of Isaiah 29 also appear in polemical passages within the NT. For example, Isa 29:16 is cited by Paul in Rom 9:20 in his lengthy scriptural argument concerning the unbelief of Israel; he also seems to allude to Isa 29:10 in his mixed citation in Rom 11:8.

[92] See, e.g., Pesch, *Das Markusevangelium*, 1. 373; Guelich, *Mark 1–8:26*, 367–68; France, *Mark*, 284.

[93] Loader ("Mark 7:1–23 and the Historical Jesus," 130) considers it possible that Mark's citation of Isa 29:13 reflects a variant Hebrew text, but in the end he opts for the view that Mark 7:6–13 is a secondary expansion of the earliest form of the anecdote that lies behind 7:1–23. Gundry (*Mark*, 351) tries to cover his bets by suggesting that either Jesus cited the LXX or that he knew a Hebrew text tradition closer to the LXX.

[94] On the languages used in 1st-century Palestine and Jesus' knowledge of them, see *A Marginal Jew*, 1. 255–68.

[95] Indeed, it may well be that the Christian scribe responsible for the rewording and placement of Isa 29:13 is Mark himself. As Donahue and Harrington note (*Mark*, 221), in his citations of and allusions to the OT, Mark shows a fondness for Isaiah; see 1:2–3; 2:7; 3:21; 9:12; 10:34,45; 11:17; 12:32,40; 13:8,31; 14:49,61; 15:27. When quoting the OT, Mark does not often name the author of the OT book being cited. For relatively rare examples of naming the author who is about to be quoted, see the references to "Moses" in 7:10; 10:4; 12:19,26; and "David" in 12:36–37. Much more common are anonymous citations and allusions, as in 4:11–12,32; 8:18;10:6–8,19; 11:9–10,17; 12:10–11,29–33; 13:14,24–26; 14:27,62; 15:24,34. Hence it is not without significance that, apart from 7:6, the only time the name of Isaiah appears in the Gospel of Mark is in the introduction to another explicit OT citation, namely, 1:2. The choice and placement of the (mixed) citation at the very beginning of the Gospel are obviously Mark's own doing; and it is Mark, speaking in his own voice, who states flatly (ignoring the fact that the first part of the quotation is from Exod 23:20 conflated with Mal 3:1), "As it stands written in *Isaiah the prophet*." Moreover, the Isaiah quotation in Mark 1:3, like the Isaiah quotation in Mark 7:6–7, follows the LXX rather than the MT. In sum, then, in Mark 7 Jesus sounds very much like Mark himself when Jesus introduces the Isaiah

quotation in v 6 with "Well did *Isaiah prophesy* . . . as it stands written. . . ." As elsewhere in Mark 7:1–23, the voice of Jesus and the voice of Mark seem to blend into one.

[96] The wording of the Decalogue commandment in Mark 7:10, "honor your father and *your* mother" (with the possessive pronoun "your" [*sou*] repeated with "mother"), has its exact parallel in Deut 5:16; most LXX manuscripts of Exod 20:12 lack the second "your."

[97] Mark 7:10 shows slight and insignificant variations in wording from LXX Exod 21:16: (1) Mark 7:10 omits the personal pronoun *autou* ("his") after both "father" and "mother"; the possessive pronoun follows both nouns in both LXX Exod 21:16 and LXX Lev 20:9. The omission is probably just Mark's abbreviation of the LXX text in view of the use of a personal pronoun after both "father" and "mother" in the immediately preceding quotation from the Decalogue. The abbreviation is simply stylistic, to avoid unnecessary repetition. Other possible explanations include the influence of oral catechesis and the fact that various Greek manuscripts and versions take different approaches to translating or not translating the Hebrew pronominal suffixes; on this, see Stendahl, *The School of St. Matthew*, 54–55. (2) The wording of the prohibition of speaking ill of parents in Mark 7:10 is *ho kakologōn patera ē matera thanatē teleutatō* (literally, "he who speaks ill of father or mother is to meet his end by death"). The redundant phrasing, which means "he will surely die," represents the Hebrew construction of the absolute infinitive of a verb plus the finite form of the same verb to express certainty or rhetorical emphasis. Mark 7:10 keeps the Semitic construction, although the finite verb (*teleutatō*) does not come from the same root as the noun in the dative (*thanatō*, representing the Hebrew absolute infinitive). The wording of Mark 7:10 is basically the same as LXX Exod 21:16 in B (Codex Vaticanus), with two minor changes: (a) in LXX Exod 21:16, the dative noun (*thanatō*) occurs at the end of the command, after the verb, not before the verb, as in Mark; (b) in LXX Exod 21:16, the verb is 3d person singular future indicative active (*teleutēsei*, "he shall meet his end"), while in Mark 7:10 the verb is the 3d person singular present imperative active (*teleutatō*, "he is to [or: must] meet his end"). These two minor stylistic differences may be explained in a number of different ways: (a) Mark 7:10 may have been influenced by the constructions in the surrounding verses of LXX Exod 21:16. Verse 15 uses the construction *thanatē thanatousthō* ("he is to be put to death by death," where the verb is the 3d person singular imperative passive), while v 17 reads *thanatō teleutatō*. (b) Mark 7:10 may have been influenced by the parallel command in LXX Lev 20:9, which (i) places the dative noun (*thanatō*) before the verb, as in Mark, and which (ii) has the main verb in the 3d person singular imperative, as in Mark (though the verb in LXX Lev 20:9 is *thanatousthō* ["he is to be put to death"], which is the imperative passive). In any case, none of these variations changes the sense of the command. As for the MT of Exod 21:17, the only significant difference from LXX Exod 21:16 is that the Hebrew participle that serves as the subject of the sentence is *mĕqallēl*, literally, "he who curses." The LXX's *ho kakologōn* carries the more general meaning "he who

speaks evil to [or: of]," "he who reviles," or "he who insults." The strict equivalent of the Hebrew verb *qillēl* ("to curse") is the Greek verb *araomai* or *kataraomai*. Yet *kakologeō* is used to translate the Piel form *qillēl* in Exod 22:27; 1 Kgs 3:13; Prov 20:20 (= LXX Prov 20:9a); and the Hiphil form *hēqallu* in Ezek 22:7. In any case, Mark's version of the command is clearly Septuagintal. (Other possible explanations of some of the variant readings of Mark 7:10, which take into account the variant readings in the LXX Codex A [Alexandrinus] and other Greek OT manuscripts, can be found in Gundry, *The Use of the Old Testament in St. Matthew's Gospel*, 12–13; and Stendahl, *The School of St. Matthew*, 54–56.) In any event, the basic thrust of the commandment remains the same in the MT, the LXX, and Mark 7:10. In this, the second reply of Jesus in Mark 7:9–13 differs from his first reply in 7:6–8: the cogency of Jesus' argument in the second reply does not depend on the wording of the LXX as opposed to that of the MT, as is the case in his first reply.

[98] On this see Pesch, *Das Markusevangelium*, 1. 374. Pesch notes that the Marcan Jesus enunciates an "antithesis" in 7:10–11, reminiscent of the Matthean antitheses in Matt 5:21–48. The difference, though, is clear. In Mark 7:10–11, the antithesis is between what Moses said in Exodus and what the Pharisees say in their tradition. Thus, the opposition Mark sets up in vv 10–11 is not between Torah commandment (honoring parents in Exodus 20:12) and Torah commandment (the binding force of vows in Numbers 30) but between Torah commandment and Pharisaic tradition (so Guelich, *Mark 1–8:26*, 370). In Matt 5:21–48, the antithesis is between "what was said" (implicitly by God in the Mosaic Law) and what "*I* say"—the christological claim in Matthew being much more emphatic.

[99] In 7:9, it is difficult to decide whether the verb in the purpose clause should be read as *stēsēte* ("establish," "uphold") or *tērēsēte* ("keep," "observe"). While some weighty manuscripts (Sinaiticus, Alexandrinus) read *tērēsēte* (with Vaticanus reading the present tense, *tērēte*), it seems more likely to me that the unusual locution "you establish your tradition" invited the scribal change to the more usual "you observe your tradition." The fierce accusation that the opponents render void the commandment of God *precisely in order to establish* their tradition fits in better with the escalation of the polemical rhetoric.

[100] Sariola (*Markus und das Gesetz*, 33) refers to this structure as a "ring composition," but it comes down to the same insight: v 9 and v 13 are basically parallel. Granted the escalation in the polemical rhetoric, it is possible that "the word of God" (*ton logon tou theou*, a phrase that occurs only here in Mark's Gospel) in 7:13 means the whole of God's revelation to Israel or the whole of the Scriptures. Jesus would then be making the astounding accusation that the Pharisees, by their tradition, nullify the whole of God's revelation. Since such a charge seems extreme even in this polemical context (*contra* Sariola, *Markus und das Gesetz*, 55), it is more likely that, in light of the *inclusio* between 7:9 and 7:13, that "the word of God" refers to the particular commandments under discussion; on this, see France, *Mark*, 288.

[101] Here I differ with Sariola (*Markus und das Gesetz*, 35–36), who claims that Jesus' second reply was the original answer to the Pharisees' question in v 5; in a similar vein, Untergassmair, "Jesus und die jüdische Gesetzestradition," 177–84. To make this position feasible, Sariola has to grant (1) that there must have been some formula of introduction for this answer; and (2) that vv 9b–13 is not really a direct answer to the question in v 5. In the end, Sariola never adequately treats the objection that vv 9–13 present an obscure example of *hălākâ* (namely, a dispute over the proper practice of *qorbān*) that makes sense only as a concrete illustration of the general principle and accusation announced in vv 6–8. Verses 9–13 do not fit directly after v 5; if vv 6–8 are taken away, then some other hypothetical transition must be created by the critic to connect v 5 with vv 9–13. In short, Sariola (pp. 32–33) is right about the redactional nature of vv 6b–8; he is wrong about the conclusion he draws concerning vv 9b–13. A similar criticism may be made against the position of Untergassmair, who does not appreciate sufficiently the secondary nature of the redactional framework of v 9b + v 13a. Without this redactional *inclusio*, Jesus' second reply cannot be the immediate answer to the opponents' question in v 5.

[102] On this, see Lambrecht, "Jesus and the Law," 389.

[103] See *A Marginal Jew*, 3. 511–12 and the accompanying notes. The reader will pardon me for repeating the substance of that treatment here. I cannot reasonably expect every reader of Volume Four to have Volume Three within easy reach, and the data about *qorbān* are essential to my discussion here.

[104] The problem of conflicting rights and obligations in the matter of oaths and vows was not a new topic invented around the turn of the era. One can see the roots of the problem in the treatment of the validity and annulment of vows in Numbers 30. Interestingly, from this early formulation of the problem, one sees that we are dealing with an androcentric universe. The question of a man's vow is covered in a single verse (v 3), with a flat statement of the man's obligation to fulfill his vow to the letter. The rest of the chapter treats the question of under what circumstances a father can annul his daughter's vow and a husband can annul his wife's vow.

[105] See 1QS 1:16–2:18 for the ceremony of entrance and 2:19–3:12 for the annual ceremony of the renewal of the covenant. While the exact relationship of the community at Qumran to the larger Essene movement is still debated (and hence the relationship of the *Rule of the Community* to the *Damascus Document*), I incline to the opinion that Qumran served as a sort of "mother house" or spiritual center for the Essenes living in conventicles dispersed around Palestine.

[106] As often with the use of Scripture at Qumran (and in the NT), the original meaning of the OT text is "bent" to serve the purpose of the latter-day interpreter. The original meaning of Mic 7:2 is quite general. It is part of a lament over the apparently universal triumph of evil in society. Mic 7:2 as a whole reads in the MT:

"The pious man has perished from the land; and there is no one upright among men. All of them lie in ambush to shed blood; one man hunts his brother [i.e., his fellow Israelite] with a net [*ḥērem*]." The Essene interpreter "bends" and particularizes the meaning of the second half of v 2 by understanding the noun *ḥērem* ("net") in its other possible meaning: "something dedicated to God and so withdrawn from any profane use." The verb *ṣûd* ("hunt") then naturally takes on its other possible meaning: "catch," "capture," or "entrap." Thus, a very general condemnation of injustice in society is narrowed down to the very special case of using the dedication of one's goods to God to avoid sharing them with one's neighbor in need. Remarkably, the Essene interpreter achieves this practical application of the text not by changing the wording of the text (except for the substitution of "one's fellow" for "one's brother") but by choosing alternate meanings for two key words.

[107] In the case alleged by Jesus in Mark 7:10–12, it is unclear whether (a) the son is really dedicating some possession to the Jerusalem temple or whether (b) with a rash oath, the son declares, "This money is *qorbān* as far as you are concerned"—and then later regrets his rashness and seeks to have the vow annulled. On the two possibilities, see Moloney, *Mark*, 140–41; Guelich, *Mark 1–8:26*, 369. It is also unclear whether, in the alleged case, the son would retain use of the dedicated property at least for a certain time. Retention of the item declared *qorbān* for one's own use, even though it is withdrawn from another's use, seems to be presupposed by some of the cases discussed by the rabbis in *m. Nedarim*; this is France's interpretation (*Mark*, 287) of the anecdote in *m. Ned.* 5:6.

[108] For a reference to support of elderly parents, see J. J. Stamm with M. E. Andrew, *The Ten Commandments in Recent Research* (SBT 2/2; Naperville, IL: Allenson, 1967) 95–96; Theodor Herr, *Die Zehn Gebote* (Würzburg: Naumann, 1992) 75–77; France, *Mark*, 286. That Jews around the time of Jesus understood "honoring" one's parents to include the support of elderly parents is shown by Philo's treatment in *De decalogo* 23 §111–20.

[109] On this inscription and on *qorbān* in general, see Joseph A. Fitzmyer, "The Aramaic *Qorbān* Inscription from Jebel Hallet eṭ-Ṭûri and Mk 7:11/Mt 15:5," *Essays on the Semitic Background of the New Testament* (SBLSBS 5; Missoula, MT: Scholars, 1974) 93–100; Karl H. Rengstorf, "*korban, korbanas*," *TDNT* 3 (1965) 860–66; A. I. Baumgarten, "*Korban* and the Pharisaic *Paradosis*," *Journal of the Ancient Near Eastern Society* 16–17 (1984–85) 5–17; Sanders, *Jewish Law*, 51–57; Max Wilcox, "Corban," *AYBD*, 1. 1134.

[110] Since the first syllable of *qrbn* is closed and lacks the accent, the word can be vocalized as either *qorbān* (short o) or *qurbān* (short u). Both vocalizations are found in the scholarly literature.

[111] Here I side with Fitzmyer's translation of the Aramaic inscription, as opposed to the translation originally offered by Jozef T. Milik; see Fitzmyer, "The Aramaic

Qorbān Inscription," 94–96. For a different view on the ossuary inscription, see Baumgarten, "*Korban*," 7; Sanders, *Jewish Law*, 55. If the inscription refers only to the bones contained in the ossuary, one is tempted to take the Aramaic to mean that the bones are to be treated with reverence, *as though* they were an offering to God—something that, strictly speaking, they could never be since bones are ritually unclean. If, however, the ossuary contained something else of value, the statement could be taken literally: this object *is* dedicated to God and hence withdrawn from all other use.

[112] As Sariola observes (*Markus und das Gesetz*, 35), *ho estin* ("that is") is an explanatory formula that is typically Marcan. The natural surmise is that we are dealing with a tradition that reaches back to a Semitic stratum (where *qorbān* was a word whose meaning was obvious) that Mark must not only translate but also explain with philological notes.

[113] In this phrase, the genitive *theou* is objective: a gift given to God. In the shift in meaning from vow to oath that is apparent in Josephus' usage, one can see a similarity to CD 16, where the vocabulary of oath (*šĕbûʿâ*) easily slides into the vocabulary of vow (*neder*). As we have seen in Chapter 33, Section II.A., the precise distinctions between oaths and vows created by later rabbis and Christian theologians may not have been all that clear to most Jews at the turn of the era. Indeed, Baumgarten ("*Korban*," 8 n. 21) notes that "Philo does not seem to have known the distinction between vows and oaths." We may well ask: if Philo, the greatest Jewish genius produced by the ancient Jewish Diaspora, did not know this distinction, how many ordinary Jews inside or outside Palestine knew it? Hence the later rabbinic material dealing with oaths and vows should be used with caution for Jewish texts around the turn of the era. In translating the Hebrew word *qorbān* into Greek as *dōron* ("gift"), Josephus is following the constant usage of the LXX, where *qorbān* (as distinct from the word *qurbān*, "supply," "procurement") is almost always rendered by *dōron*.

[114] On the story, see Baumgarten, "*Korban*," 10–12.

[115] See Pesch, *Das Markusevangelium*, 1. 375. It must be remembered that we identify the "you" of Mark 7:11–12 with the Pharisees because of the first unit of the Marcan composition, 7:1–5. By itself, 7:11–12 does not indicate who the interlocutors are.

[116] For an earlier and less critical consideration of possible explanations of the *qorbān* passage, see Joseph Klausner, *Jesus of Nazareth* (New York: Macmillan, 1925) 289–90.

[117] This is the view of many commentators; see, e.g., Guelich, *Mark 1–8:26*, 368; cf. Booth, *Jesus and the Laws of Purity*, 95; Kazen, *Jesus and Purity* Halakha, 64; cf. Tomson, "Jewish Purity Laws," 85. Lambrecht ("Jesus and the Law," 389–90) is

more hesitant; he thinks that it is extremely difficult to isolate any preexisting unit within Mark 7:6–13, though there may be some traditional elements that Mark uses.

[118] Now and then the suggestion is made that the historical Jesus debated the *qorbān* question with some priests, who would have been especially interested in the inviolable nature of a vow dedicating money or property to the Jerusalem temple. While it is impossible to disprove such a hypothesis, one must acknowledge its gratuitous nature. As the Jewish literature around the turn of the era shows, interest in the dedication of goods to God and/or the temple was hardly restricted to the priests who actually ministered in the temple.

[119] This Marcan pattern of public pronouncement and private explanation has often been compared to a similar pattern found in rabbinic literature; see, e.g., Daube, "Public Pronouncement," 175–77. Yet differences should be underlined in the special case of Mark 7:1–23: (1) The puzzling public pronouncement in 7:15 is addressed by Jesus not to the opponents who raised the initial objection in v 5 (i.e., "the Pharisees and some of the scribes" of v 1, who by v 15 have strangely disappeared from the stage) but rather to the newly summoned "crowd" of v 14. (2) The private explanation in vv 18–23 does not offer a strikingly different line of reasoning from the puzzling public teaching in v 15; rather, it simply "unpacks" the teaching by clarifying its rationale and ramifications. Hence, the structure of the argument in Mark 7:1–23 is notably different from an anecdote (often cited in relation to Mark 7:1–23) concerning Joḥanan ben Zakkai's explanation of the ritual of purification from corpse impurity, a ritual that uses the ashes of a red cow mixed with water. Joḥanan first gives one explanation, an ad hominem retort, to a Gentile in public: you Gentiles use water in your magic rituals, especially your exorcisms. He then gives a different explanation in private to his unsatisfied disciples: neither the corpse nor the ritual of purification has any intrinsic power; it is all a matter of obeying God's commandments in acknowledgment of his sovereignty. It is telling that this anecdote appears only late in the midrashic literature of the rabbinic period (*Tanḥuma Ḥuqat, Pesiqta de Rab Kahana, Numbers Rabba*); in the view of Neusner (*The Idea of Purity*, 105–6), it cannot be assigned with complete confidence to talmudic times at all.

[120] See, e.g., Taylor, *The Gospel According to St. Mark*, 343; Guelich, *Mark 1–8:26*, 374; Marcus, *Mark 1–8*, 453; Paschen, *Rein und Unrein*, 156–58; Sariola, *Markus und das Gesetz*, 50 (who remarks on the unrealistic situation: the crowd suddenly appears on stage, while the Pharisees and scribes suddenly disappear); Carlston, "The Things That Defile," 91–93.

[121] In comparing statistics, one must remember how much shorter Mark is than the other three Gospels. According to the count of Robert Morgenthaler (*Statistik des neutestamentlichen Worschatzes* [Zurich/Frankfurt: Gotthelf, 1958] 164), Luke contains 19,404 words (plus Acts with 18,374 words), Matthew contains

18,278 words, and John contains 15,420 words, compared with Mark's mere 11,229 words.

¹²² See Donahue and Harrington, *The Gospel of Mark*, 223–24.

¹²³ The only notable exception would be the extreme allegorists mentioned by Philo of Alexandria; see his *De migratione Abrahami*, 16 §89–93. That the first half of Mark 7:15 does indeed refer to ritual purity and not, in a metaphorical way, to moral purity, is indicated both by the use of the verb *koinoō* and by the consideration that Jesus would hardly deny that the evil speech and habits of bad companions, by "entering into" a person, could defile that person in a moral sense.

¹²⁴ See Bultmann, *Geschichte*, 110 (Carlston ["The Things That Defile," 94] remarks that Bultmann's acceptance of the logion's authenticity has settled the matter for many critics); Ernst Käsemann, "The Problem of the Historical Jesus," *Essays on New Testament Themes* (SBT 41; London: SCM, 1964; original German article, 1954) 15–47, esp. 39; Norman Perrin, *Rediscovering the Teaching of Jesus* (NTL; London: SCM, 1967) 149–50. For other authors who have supported the authenticity of some form of Mark 7:15, see Lambrecht, "Jesus and the Law," 362–64 and notes. Svartvik (*Mark and Mission*, 4) considers the view that Mark 7:15 belongs to the *ipsissima verba Jesu* to be "mainstream interpretation"; Svartvik, however, considers this view untenable.

¹²⁵ So, e.g., Sanders, *Jewish Law from Jesus to the Mishnah*, 28.

¹²⁶ On the Semitic speech pattern of dialectical negation, see Arnulf Kuschke, "Das Idiom der 'relativen Negation' im NT," *ZNW* 43 (1950–51) 263; and Heinz Kruse, "Die 'dialektische Negation' als semitisches Idiom," *VT* 4 (1954) 385–400. See also Räisänen, "Jesus and the Food Laws," 82. In favor of understanding Mark 7:15 in the mouth of the historical Jesus as an example of dialectical negation is Marcus (*Mark 1–8*, 453), who points to Philo's affirming that true defilement is injustice and impiety, while at the same time maintaining the importance of observing the laws of ritual impurity (*De specialibus legibus* 3 §208–9). For other upholders of the view that the historical Jesus meant Mark 7:15 in the sense of dialectical negation, see Houston, *Purity and Monotheism*, 275; Klawans, *Impurity and Sin*, 146–49. Carlston ("The Things That Defile," 95) basically adopts this approach without a formal discussion of "dialectical negation."

¹²⁷ As I noted in Chapter 31, this is the usual interpretation of Hos 6:6; see, e.g., Frank I. Andersen and David Noel Freedman, *Hosea* (AYB 24; Garden City, NY: Doubleday, 1980; reprint New Haven: Yale University Press) 430.

¹²⁸ See Loader ("Mark 7:1–23," 145–46), who also points to Mark 13:11, ". . . it is not you who are speaking [at your trial] but the Holy Spirit." Oddly, Loader does not mention the cases in which Mark does express an exclusive antithesis.

[129] Joachim Jeremias, *New Testament Theology. Part One. The Proclamation of Jesus* (London: SCM, 1971) 18. Jeremias claims that in the long list of antithetical logia of Jesus compiled in the notes on pp. 15–16, the stress is almost always on the second half of the saying. That the *māšāl* in Mark 7:15 should be interpreted according to the rule of end stress is affirmed by Paschen, *Rein und Unrein*, 181.

[130] Examples could be easily multiplied; see, e.g., Mark 8:35: "For whoever wishes to save his life will lose it; but whoever loses his life for my sake and that of the gospel will save it"; Mark 10:27: "With men it is impossible, but not with God; for all things are possible with God"; see also 10:43; 12:25.

[131] Since the three arguments I am treating here usually deal with the logia in Mark, Matthew, and *Gospel of Thomas* in their present forms, and not in some hypothetical original Aramaic form, I frame my argument according to the present Greek text of Mark 7:15. It is worth noting that critics who discuss a hypothetical original Aramaic form of Mark 7:15 do not agree on the wording of the original saying; see, e.g., Räisänen's critique ("Jesus and the Food Laws," 83) of the Aramaic retroversion offered by Paschen (*Rein und Unrein*, 177). Gundry (*Mark*, 365) agrees with Räisänen that the forceful rhetoric of *ouden* and *dynatai* stands in the way of interpreting Mark 7:15 in a relative sense; similarly, Sariola, *Markus und das Gesetz*, 54. Hence, I disagree with McEleney's claim ("Authenticating Criteria," 449–50) that *dynatai* represents the weak use of the verb in an auxiliary sense and that therefore "can defile" hardly means more than "does defile."

[132] Svartvik (*Mark and Mission*, 375–409) takes the unusual approach of employing the theory of end stress (i.e., the emphasis lies on the second half of the *māšāl*) to suggest that Jesus' original intent was to rebuke his opponents for engaging in *lāšôn hārāʿ* ("evil speech," such as slander or malicious gossip). To accomplish this, Svartvik combines patristic exegesis of Mark 7:15 with growing rabbinic concern about *lāšôn hārāʿ*. As with his appeal to rabbinic literature in general, this process involves some questionable use of much later material to explain the NT.

[133] In the discussion that follows, I take for granted that "those things that come out of a man" referred from the start to sinful thoughts, words, and actions and not to physical excretions (human feces and/or urine). On the possibility of interpreting the saying as referring to excrement, see France, *Mark*, 289; cf. Gundry, *Mark*, 355. The reasons why I do not think that a reference to human excrement is possible in Mark 7:15 are as follows: (1) The purity laws of the Leviticus, Numbers, and Deuteronomy never list feces or urine among the sources of ritual impurity. The law in Deut 23:13–15 that commands defecation outside the camp refers to the special situation of a military camp engaged in "holy" war, and even in this special situation the feces are not said to cause ritual defilement (contrast the man in vv 11–12, who does become unclean because of his nocturnal emission). The need to defecate *outside* the camp is traced rather to the special holiness of a military camp; excrement within the camp is designated as "something indecent [ʿerwat dābār]," not as some-

thing "impure" (v 15). Hence, I think Paschen's claim (*Rein und Unrein*, 178) that excrement is ritually impure misinterprets Deut 23:13–15. (2) If both urine and feces ("those things that come out of a man") caused ritual impurity simply by contact, the whole purity system would be unworkable in practice, for all Jews would be almost constantly in a state of impurity. (3) The special cases sometimes cited by commentators (Ezek 4:12–15 and *J.W.* 2.8.9 §147–49) do not represent the pentateuchal laws of ritual impurity as they were accepted by and incumbent on the vast majority of Jews around the turn of the era. Ezek 4:12–15 depicts the extraordinary case of the (notably strange) priest-prophet being ordered by God to cook his food over human excrement as a prophetic symbol of the ghastly suffering and deprivation that the siege of Jerusalem and the exile of its population would involve. Walther Eichrodt (*Ezekiel* [OTL; Philadelphia: Westminster, 1970] 86) claims that the food that Ezekiel is supposed to eat would itself be impure according to the laws of Lev 19:19 and Deut 22:9 (i.e., because the bread would be made from mixed grains—though how Eichrodt extracts this meaning from Ezek 4:12–15 is not clear). For other critical views, see G. A. Cooke, *The Book of Ezekiel* (ICC: Edinburgh: Clark, 1936) 55; Walther Zimmerli, *Ezechiel* (BKAT 13; 2 vols.; Neurkirchen-Vlyun: Neukirchener Verlag, 1969) 1. 126–28. None of the commentators addresses the precise question of why the food cooked over human excrement would be ritually impure when such a case is never envisioned in the pentateuchal laws. In any event, impurity in Ezekiel 4:12–15 seems to arise from cooking food over human excrement, not simply from a person's physical contact with the excrement. As for Josephus' description of the Essenes, the special, punctilious observance of the Essenes in regard to human feces is a prime example of a practice that marked them off as a sectarian group (note Josephus' editorial remark at the end of §149).

[134] Loader ("Mark 7:1–23," 148 n. 64) tries to answer this argument by pointing to the dialectical negations contained in Mark 9:39 and 13:11, but neither of these two texts contains the emphatic rhetoric of *ouden estin . . . ho dynatai*. Sariola (*Markus und das Gesetz*, 54) rightly sees that the formulation of Mark 7:15 is too strong for a relative interpretation.

[135] To be sure, the words *ouden . . . alla* and *dynamai* are frequent in Mark; but these words are so common in Greek that one cannot automatically delete them from the saying as Marcan redaction. In Räisänen's view ("Jesus and the Food Laws," 81), even if these words were omitted as Marcan redaction, the basic meaning of the logion would remain unchanged. Indeed, Räisänen thinks that even the wording of Matt 15:11 does not essentially alter the meaning of the affirmation found in Mark 7:15. Even the conservative France (*Mark*, 279, 290) remarks that any attempt to see Matt 15:11 as totally innocuous in regard to the continued validity of the food laws is naive.

[136] This is a recurring problem in the otherwise fine work of James D. G. Dunn, *Jesus Remembered* (Christianity in the Making 1; Grand Rapids, MI/Cambridge, UK: Eerdmans, 2003). See, e.g., his treatment of the Synoptic pericope of the stilling

of the storm (pp. 217–18), where the obvious Matthean redactional interventions in both style and theology are brushed aside in favor of a common oral tradition. It is not surprising, then, that common oral tradition is called upon to solve the relationship between Mark 7:14–23 and Matt 15:10–20, with no great probing of the clear signs of the usual way Matthew redacts Mark (pp. 573–77).

[137] See Gerhard Barth, "Das Gesetzesverständnis des Evangelisten Matthäus," Günther Bornkamm, Gerhard Barth, and Heinz Joachim Held, *Überlierferung und Auslegung im Matthäusevangelium* (WMANT 1; 5th ed.; Neukirchen-Vluyn: Neukirchener Verlag, 1968) 54–154, esp. 80–83. I should note as an aside that I do not entirely agree with Barth's evaluation of Matthew's redactional theology, but Barth clearly demonstrates Matthew's editorial hand rewriting Mark. The same is true of the treatment by Carlston, "The Things That Defile," 75–96. Although they consider the possibility that Matt 15:1–20 might represent a more primitive tradition, Davies and Allison (*Matthew*, 2. 516–17) come down in the end on the side of Matthew reworking Mark. This judgment includes Matt 15:11 vis-à-vis Mark 7:15 (pp. 526–31). In the same vein, see Donald A. Hagner, *Matthew* (Word Biblical Commentary 33A and 33B; 2 vols.; Dallas: Word, 1993, 1995) 2. 427–37.

[138] The noun *stoma* ("mouth") never occurs in Mark and occurs only once in John. Matthew has eleven occurrences (the vast majority of which are either M tradition or Matthean redaction), while the longer Gospel of Luke has nine.

[139] In favor of the secondary nature of the last part of G. *Thom.* 14 and its dependence on Matt 15:11 is Michael Fieger, *Das Thomasevangelium* (NTAbh 22; Münster: Aschendorff, 1991) 74–76; cf. Booth, *Jesus and the Purity Laws*, 98; Loader, "Mark 7:1–23," 138–45. In my opinion, the change of "man" to "you" and "your" in G. *Thom.* 14 is occasioned by the larger context in logion 14, where Jesus is issuing a number of commands to his disciples (actually, a pastiche of sayings, often with a typically gnostic inversion of meaning, that are taken from, e.g., Matt 6:1–8 and Luke 10:8–9). On this point and on the general question of Matthew's redaction of Mark 7:15, see Gundry, *Mark*, 363–64. It is curious that Svartvik (*Mark and Mission*, 154) rightly observes that the last part of G. *Thom.* 14 is closest to Matthew in vocabulary and form, to Mark in content, and to Luke in application, and yet does not draw the most likely conclusion that the saying results from the meshing of elements from Matthew and Luke (and perhaps Mark as well); for his analysis of G. *Thom.* 14, see pp. 139–56. This point is not sufficiently appreciated by Kazen (*Jesus and Purity* Halakhah, 86), who thinks that Mark 7:15, "albeit in an earlier form, closer to Mt 15:11 or Gos. *Thom.* 14, taken in a relative sense, could represent Jesus' answer to a question about hand washing." Kazen's monograph, while displaying an admirable command of Second Temple Judaism, secondary literature, and various contemporary methods, suffers from the fact that it never undertakes a verse-by-verse exegesis of the key pericope, Mark 7:1–23.

[140] For other glaring examples of the dependence of the *Gospel of Thomas* on the Synoptic Gospels, see Charles L. Quarles, "The Use of the *Gospel of Thomas* in

the Research on the Historical Jesus of John Dominic Crossan," *CBQ* 69 (2007) 517–36.

141 The reader is reminded that, because of the detailed examination of the Greek text that this study demands, I purposely use the wooden, literalistic translation of *anthrōpos* as "man," since it is accompanied by the masculine pronoun *auton* ("him"). Both the use of *anthrōpos* instead of *anēr* ("male") and the sweeping, universal thrust of the Marcan saying make clear that the Marcan Jesus is speaking of every human being (or at least every Jew), not just males.

142 On this, see Räisänen, "Jesus and the Food Laws," 83. In Räisänen's view, Matt 23:25 cannot be counted as independent attestation of the saying in Mark 7:15, since Matt 23:25 is not critical of food laws per se. Luke 11:41 might be so construed, but this verse (according to Räisänen) is secondary to Matt 23:25. Moreover, in the opinion of Räisänen, Luke 10:8 reflects the later Gentile mission; its authenticity would render the later hesitancy of Peter in Acts and the whole subsequent debate unintelligible.

143 On the likelihood that Jesus was not married, see *A Marginal Jew*, 1. 332–45. On the married status of Peter and of "the other apostles and the brothers of the Lord," see Mark 1:30; 1 Cor 9:5; cf. *A Marginal Jew*, 3. 222.

144 See *A Marginal Jew*, 2. 439–50.

145 On this, see Svartvik, *Mark and Mission*, 305, 346.

146 The lack of any discernible *Wirkungsgeschichte* (i.e., the impact or effect that a saying of Jesus had or should have had on subsequent Christian history) of Mark 7:15 in the first Christian generation is for Räisänen ("Jesus and the Food Laws," 79–100, esp. 86–90) a major reason for denying that the saying goes back to the historical Jesus; likewise, Svartvik, *Mark and Mission*, 109–204 (which provides an intriguing survey of the logion's *Wirkungsgeschichte* in the patristic church); Carlston, "The Things That Defile," 95 (for the form of the saying found in Mark 7:15); Klawans, *Impurity and Sin*, 145, 147.

147 I add "all the food laws" as a qualifier in Luke's case because of the pragmatic concession to Jewish sensibilities expressed in the so-called Apostolic Letter or Apostolic Decree (Acts 15:29), following the advice of James (15:20). For detailed treatments of the narratives of Peter's conversion of Cornelius (Acts 10:1–11:18) and the so-called Council of Jerusalem (Acts 15:1–35), see C. K. Barrett, *The Acts of the Apostles* (ICC; 2 vols.; Edinburgh: Clark, 1994, 1998) 1. 488–543; 2. 695–746; Joseph A. Fitzmyer, *The Acts of the Apostles* (AYB 31; New York: Doubleday, 1998; reprint New Haven: Yale University Press) 446–73, 538–69. Barrett's commentary is especially useful for questions of text criticism and Greek vocabulary and syntax; his judgments on the larger sense of the text within Luke's theology are sometimes questionable.

[148] Indeed, if, as some think, Mark 7:15 (or some more primitive form thereof) was open to the "mild" interpretation that inner moral purity was more important than external ritual purity, the logion could have been quoted and argued in that sense by Paul's opponents.

[149] On this question, see *A Marginal Jew*, 1. 45–47, and the literature cited in nn. 24–25.

[150] Granted the cluster of sayings of Jesus cited or paraphrased in 1 Corinthians 7, 9, and 11, it is all the more remarkable that Mark 7:15 or some paraphrase thereof is not cited by Paul in his discussion of meat sacrificed to idols in 1 Corinthians 8 and 10. For instance, Mark 7:15 would fit quite neatly after the citation of LXX Ps 23:1 in 1 Cor 10:26.

[151] In contrast, oath-taking was never a focal point of debate between Paul and his Jewish-Christian adversaries or—as far as we know—among any other groups in first-generation Christianity. Indeed, as we have seen in Chapter 33, Jesus' prohibition of oaths was probably not widely known in first-generation Christianity, either inside or outside Pauline circles. This is at least partly explained by the fact that the prohibition was preserved and handed down only in the narrow and isolated conduits of the M tradition (Matt 5:34–37) and Jas 5:12.

[152] Commentators debate the exact nature of the food problem treated by Paul in Romans 14, along with the relevance of the similar (though not the same) problem of food sacrificed to idols in 1 Corinthians 8–10. For a survey of all the major opinions that have been proposed, see C. E. B. Cranfield (*The Epistle to the Romans* [ICC; 2 vols.; Edinburgh: Clark, 1975,1979] 2. 690–98), who rightly, in my view, opts for the position that the problem at Rome concerns those Christian Jews who still felt an obligation to observe the ritual food laws of the OT. However, as Cranfield notes, the practice of abstaining from wine (Rom 14:21) does not fit this profile, and so perhaps we must allow that, in the Jewish Diaspora, syncretistic tendencies from pagan religious-philosophical movements had become entangled with Jewish purity laws. In any event, (1) the presence of the vocabulary of *koinon* and *katharos* (vv 14, 20), applied to food whose permissibility is disputed, (2) the absence of vocabulary pointing in another direction (e.g., *eidōlothyta*, "meat sacrificed to idols"; for authors who see a possible connection between Mark 7:15 and the question of food sacrificed to idols, see Loader, "Mark 7:1–23," 128 with n.13), and (3) the mild, sympathetic approach of Paul to the "weak," who feel obliged to abstain from meat and wine, all point to a pastoral problem (rather than a matter of principle, on which Paul would be much more adamant) involving some Christian Jews who still feel constrained by purity rules. On the larger question of the place of Romans 14 within the overarching argument of the Epistle to the Romans, see the various essays in Karl P. Donfried (ed.), *The Romans Debate* (rev. ed.; Peabody, MA: Hendrickson, 1991); especially to be noted are Robert J. Karris, "Romans 14:1–15:13 and the Occasion of Romans," 65–84; Karl P. Donfried, "False Presup-

positions in the Study of Romans," 102–25; Robert J. Karris, "The Occasion of Romans: A Response to Professor Donfried," 125–27; F. F. Bruce, "The Romans Debate—Continued," 175–94; Francis Watson, "The Two Roman Congregations: Romans 14:1–15:13," 203–15.

[153] The adjective *koinon* ("common") is the same word used for the unwashed hands of the disciples in Mark 7:2, with the allied verb *koinoō* used in Mark 7:15; the meaning of *koinon* in Rom 14:14 is clearly "ritually unclean."

[154] Cranfield, (*The Epistle to the Romans*, 2. 712–13) considers it "high likely" (n. 2 on p. 713) that the slogans of the "strong" (alluded to in vv 14 + 20) appealed to Jesus' teaching and that Paul agreed that these slogans were true to the teaching of Jesus. Michael Thompson (*Clothed with Christ* [JSNTSup 59; Sheffield: JSOT, 1991] 199) considers an echo of Jesus' saying "virtually certain." James D. G. Dunn (*Romans* [Word Biblical Commentary 38A and 38B; 2 vols.; Dallas: Word, 1988] 2. 818–20) thinks that behind Paul's statements here in Romans lies an ambiguous logion of the historical Jesus (a "weaker" version closer to Matt 15:11 and *G. Thom.* 14); hence what we find here in Paul is not an exact quotation of a particular saying of Jesus but a "reexperienced tradition of Jesus still heard as the word of the Lord," a good example of the "penumatic character of Paul's use of the Jesus and kerygmatic traditions." See also Otto Michel, *Der Brief an die Römer* (MeyerK 4; 4th ed.; Göttingen:Vandenhoeck & Ruprecht, 1966) 343 n. 5. Ernst Käsemann (*An die Römer* [HNT 8a; Tübingen: Mohr (Siebeck), 1973] 359) considers the whole debate over whether Paul in Rom 14:14 is appealing to a word of Jesus an idle question.

[155] On this point, see Loader, "Mark 7:1–23," 144; cf. Svartvik, *Mark and Mission*, 115–16. While Cranfield (*The Epistle to the Romans*, 2. 712) leans toward an allusion to the teaching of the historical Jesus, he allows for the possibility that by the phrase "in the Lord Jesus" Paul was simply stating that his emphatic teaching on the subject was an insight that flowed from his union with the risen Jesus, or that it was "consonant with God's self-revelation in Jesus Christ as a whole," or that his certainty of the truth of his position rested on the authority of the risen Lord. Interestingly, Joseph A. Fitzmyer (*Romans* [AYB 33; New York: Doubleday, 1992; reprint New Haven: Yale University Press] 694–95) translates *en kyriō Iēsou* thus: "As one who is in the Lord Jesus, I know and am convinced. . . ." Still, Fitzmyer (p. 969) allows that v 14 "may also echo Jesus' saying." By contrast, Hans Lietzmann (*An die Römer* [HNT 8; 5th ed.; Tübingen: Mohr (Siebeck), 1971] 117) rejects the idea that Paul is thinking of a traditional saying of Jesus. In my opinion, Paul's usage elsewhere cautions against seeing a phrase like "in the Lord Jesus" as appealing to the teaching of the earthly Jesus. Paul uses other kinds of phrases when he appeals to Jesus' teaching during the public ministry; see, e.g., 1 Cor 7:10–11, "I command, not I, but the Lord"; 9:14, "likewise, the Lord commanded . . ."; 11:23, "for I received from the Lord what I also handed on to you, that the Lord Jesus. . . ." The use of phrases like "in the Lord" or the use of the personal name "Jesus" elsewhere in Paul does not necessarily point to a saying of Jesus during his public ministry;

see, e.g., Gal 5:10; Phil 2:24; 1 Thess 4:1; 2 Thess 3:4. Hence, I am not convinced by Thompson's arguments (*Clothed in Christ*, 185–99) in favor of an echo of Jesus' saying.

[156] See Räisänen, "Jesus and the Food Laws," 88.

[157] See Svartvik, *Mark and Mission*, 128. Indeed, if Luke already had in mind the events and controversies of Acts 10–15 as he was writing his Gospel, he had no choice but to omit Mark 7:15 and the surrounding material. To have presented Jesus affirming Mark 7:15 during the public ministry would have made the stories in Acts 10–15 unintelligible; Schürmann (*Das Lukasevangelium*, 1. 526) seems to miss this point. Implicitly, then, Luke indicates by his omission that Mark 7:15 cannot be a saying of the earthly Jesus if anything like the events recorded in Acts 10–15 ever occurred in the early church. On the larger question of the Great Omission (or the "Big Omission"), i.e., Luke's omission of the material in Mark 6:45–8:26, see Schürmann, *Das Lukasevangelium*, 1. 525–27; Fitzmyer, *The Gospel According to Luke*, 1. 770–71; Marshall, *Luke*, 364. Even if one thinks that Luke has omitted a good deal of this Marcan material because it contains repetitions or because it brings Jesus outside of Galilee proper, such reasoning does not explain the omission of the unparalleled Mark 7:15, which demands a Jewish setting.

[158] James' provisos are not contradictory to Peter's basic insight about the Gentiles' being exempt from circumcision and the Mosaic Law; rather, as Fitzmyer (*Acts*, 554, 557) puts it, "Luke presents James as a church official who seeks a reasonable compromise in the interest of the church at large. . . . James's regulations seek only a *modus vivendi* of Gentiles among Jewish Christians and imply no salvific purpose in them." Fitzmyer's judgment on this point seems preferable to that of Barrett (*Acts*, 2. 745), who thinks that the requirements of the Apostolic Decree are seen by Luke "presumably as a condition of salvation." This would result in a very strange decision by the apostles and elders in Jerusalem: circumcision (the initial problem raised in Acts 15:1–5) is not declared necessary for salvation, but the observance of certain kosher food laws is.

[159] For the text-critical problems as well as the problems of source criticism and interpretation connected with these four prohibitions, see Barrett, *Acts*, 2. 730–37, 745–46; Fitzmyer, *Acts*, 556–58, 561–66. Barrett's hesitation (*Acts*, 2. 732–33) about the meaning of the some of the items forbidden by the Apostolic Decree (e.g., does *haima* mean consuming an animal's blood—the usual interpretation—or shedding human blood?) results in a less than clear interpretation of the Apostolic Decree within the overall historical and theological perspectives of Luke.

[160] For the many problems connected with interpreting the clash at Antioch recounted in Gal 2:11–14, see Heinrich Schlier, *Der Brief an die Galater* (MeyerK 7; 4th ed.; Göttingen: Vandenhoeck & Ruprecht, 1965) 81–117; Hans Dieter Betz, *Galatians* (Hermeneia; Philadelphia: Fortress, 1979) 103–12; Frank J. Matera, *Ga-*

latians (Sacra Pagina 9; Collegeville, MN: Liturgical Press, 1992) 84–91; James D. G. Dunn, *The Epistle to the Galatians* (Black's NT Commentary 9; Peabody, MA: Hendrickson, 1993) 115–31. Commentators argue over the extent to which Peter and other Jewish Christians had abandoned Jewish purity laws when eating with Gentiles (and also to what extent the Lord's Supper was involved). In any event, the people from James considered the breach of Jewish observance to be serious enough to pressure Peter and the others to separate themselves from table fellowship with the Gentile Christians, despite the conflict such action was likely to produce. See also Raymond E. Brown and John P. Meier, *Antioch and Rome* (New York/ Ramsey, NJ: Paulist, 1983) 36–44.

[161] On this, see Räisänen, "Jesus and the Food Laws," 89. Gundry's attempt (*Mark* 370–71) to explain away the ignorance of first-generation Christianity in regard to Mark 7:15 is a prime example of unconvincing apologetics; see also the more nuanced (but still unconvincing) approach of Guelich, *Mark 1–8:26*, 376. As Loader ("Mark 7:1–23," 147 n. 58) points out, "Gundry's belief that Peter stands behind Mark makes the ambiguity theory [i.e., that Jesus's pronouncement on food laws was ambiguous from the start] doubly difficult."

[162] Some commentators (e.g., Moloney, *Mark*, 138, 142, 144) suggest that Mark's statement in 7:2 that "some" of the disciples ate with impure hands points to a division and conflict within the Christian community over purity laws; see the options laid out by Marcus, *Mark 1–8*, 440. This may be a case of over-interpreting the text. The basic conflict in 7:1–23 lies between Jesus on the one hand and the Pharisees and "some" of the scribes on the other. (Are we to think that Mark portrays the scribes as divided on the issue of purity laws because he refers to them as "some of the scribes"?) More to the point, when Jesus enters the house in v 17, "his disciples" ask him to explain his aphorism, and he directs his explanation "to them," saying apparently to all the disciples without differentiation, "Are *you* [emphatic in the Greek] also without understanding?" Thus, Mark's presentation gives no indication that the disciples are divided over the issue; the division is read into the text by commentators who know the history of first-generation Christianity from other NT books. Here I agree with Sariola (*Markus und das Gesetz*, 57–60), who holds that the purity laws are no longer a problem for Mark and his addressees.

[163] On this, see Booth, *Jesus and the Laws of Purity*, 74; cf. Sariola, *Markus und das Gesetz*, 40.

[164] See Sariola, *Markus und das Gesetz*, 36 (along with n. 92), 38. For a summary of Marcan stylistic traits, see Paschen, *Rein und Unrein*, 159.

[165] For the label "rationalistic," see Guelich, *Mark 1–8:26*, 377; Sariola (*Markus und das Gesetz*, 46) considers the tone of vv 18d–19b,20b to be sarcastic, with no understanding of the Jewish ritual purity. Some commentators refer to the explanation in v 19 as crude or vulgar, but such an evaluation may reflect modern Western

rather than ancient Semitic sensitivities. As France (*Mark*, 291) points out, in some contexts *koilia* can at times be used to mean one's inner being, in a sense not all that different from *kardia* ("heart"; so LXX Ps 39:9; Prov 20:27; Hab 3:16). But the context here, as in some other NT passages, indicates that the word refers to a person's stomach, digestive system, or worldly appetites, taken in a negative sense; see, e.g., Rom 16:18; 1 Cor 6:13; Phil 3:19. As many commentators point out (e.g., Guelich, *Mark 1–8:26*, 378), the use of "heart" in Mark 7:19 echoes its appearance in the Isaiah citation in 7:6. However, the link is purely verbal; the use of the heart imagery in the two contexts is quite different.

[166] In itself, the verb *katharizō* could mean either "declare clean" or "make clean," depending on the context. As Marcus points out (*Mark 1–8*, 455), both senses can be found in the LXX (e.g., Lev 13:6,23; Exod 29:36–37). Insofar as Jesus in 7:15 is enunciating a startling new teaching, he is obviously "declaring" something. Yet since, in Mark's theology, the Jesus who makes this declaration is the Son of God, Son of Man, and Messiah who teaches and acts with authority (*exousia*), the declaration is thought of as "performative,", i.e., effecting what it says. By declaring all foods pure, Jesus now makes them so—something they were not before; cf. Acts 10:15: "What God has made clean [*ekatharisen*], you are not to call common [*koinou*]." Marcus (p. 457) suggests that Mark may have added his awkward editorial comment at the end of v 19 because he was aware that the reasoning in v 19 would not convince a "Torah-observant Jew." For the opposite view, that the Marcan Jesus is declaring that the food laws never had validity and that *katharizōn* therefore means "declare clean," not "make clean," see Loader, "Mark 7:1–23," 125–26. On the question of the awkward syntax of *katharizōn*, see Guelich, *Mark 1–8:26*, 378.

[167] On the catalogues of virtues and vices in the NT, see Siegfried Wibbing, *Die Tugend- und Lasterkataloge im Neuen Testament* (BZNW 25; Berlin: Töpelmann, 1959) 77–127, esp. 78–87. In contrast to the Pastoral Epistles, which employ many words not found in other NT catalogues, the catalogue of vices in Mark 7:21–22 is quite similar in vocabulary to the catalogues found in the NT epistles apart from the Pastorals. If cognate words are counted, only two phrases in Mark 7:21–22 (*hoi dialogismoi*, "evil thoughts," and *ophthalmos ponēros*, "an evil eye") do not occur in similar lists in the NT (e.g., Rom 1:29–31; 13:13; 1 Cor 5:10–11; 6:9–10; 2 Cor 12:20–21; Gal 5:19–21; Eph 4:31; 5:3–5; Col 3:5,8; Pet 2:1; 4:3,15; see also Rev 9:21; 21:8; 22:15; Paschen [*Rein und Unrein*, 187–94] also sees a connection between Mark 7:21–22 and the numerical proverb in Prov 6:16–19). When one joins these observations to the fact that the vice list of Mark 7:21–22 has no parallel (outside of Matt 15:19) in the whole of the Four Gospels, the natural conclusion is that Mark's list is a product of early Christian preaching, not the preaching of the historical Jesus. Hence, while a study of the precise words used in the list as well as the numerical pattern of plural and singular nouns that Mark creates would be interesting (see Gundry, *Mark*, 355–56; France, *Mark*, 291–92; Lambrecht, "Jesus and the Law," 398–99), it would not serve the purpose of our quest. It is worth not-

ing, though, that the final vice *aphrosynē* ("lack of understanding," "foolishness") in 7:22 is probably a redactional *inclusio* created by Mark to link up with the initial rebuke to the disciples in v 18 (*asynetoi*, "lacking in understanding," "foolish").

168 For example, Booth (*Jesus and the Laws of Purity*, 23–53) identifies less Marcan redaction than does Lambrecht ("Jesus and the Law," 358–413, with addendum to literature on pp. 413–15 and 428–29).

169 *Contra* Poirier, "Why Did the Pharisees Wash Their Hands?" 217–33, esp. 225–26. That Poirier can claim that Mark 7:1–23 is essentially a unity (with the exception of vv 9–13) stems directly from his failure to do a detailed study of the Marcan redaction of 7:1–23, of the various stages of the tradition history of the Greek text, and of the unique suitability of the LXX form of Isa 29:13 for the argument of the Marcan Jesus within the larger context of 7:1–23. Poirier then compounds the problem by conflating the multiple questions in Mark 7:1–23 with the different question of the purity of the inside and outside of cups and plates in the Q tradition preserved in Matt 23:25–26 ‖ Luke 11:39–40 (on which see below). His subsequent appeal to obscure passages in the Tosepta and the Babylonian Talmud only makes the muddle worse.

170 Because I conclude that vv 1–5 do not go back to the ministry of the historical Jesus, I do not spend any time discussing the numerous individual problems of text criticism and interpretation contained in these verses. For standard treatments, see, e.g., Guelich, *Mark 1–8:26*, 363–66; Marcus, *Mark 1–8*, 440–43. For the convenience of the curious reader, I list here briefly my views on a number of debated points: (1) "The Pharisees and some of the scribes coming from Jerusalem" (7:1) echoes and develops Mark's earlier mention of some sort of investigative commission composed of "the scribes who had come down from Jerusalem" (3:22). The idea that a group of Pharisees and scribes would come from Jerusalem to investigate whether Jesus' disciples ate bread with unwashed hands in itself strains credulity; see Sariola, *Markus und das Gesetz*, 29. (2) As I have already indicated, in my opinion, the phrase "some of his disciples" in 7:2 does not reflect a dispute or split in Mark's community over observance of food laws. When the second half of the pericope finally takes up the question of the foods laws, it is "his disciples" in general in v 17 who raise the question. In reply, the Marcan Jesus issues his typically stern and undifferentiated rebuke to the disciples in general (v 18); apparently all of them fail to understand that nothing entering a man can defile him. Granted this lack of differentiation among the disciples, the phrase "some of his disciples" in v 2 may simply be an example of Marcan duality, with "some of his disciples" balancing "some of the scribes" in v 1. (3) The problem of the parenthetical explanations and generalizing statements was treated above, in section II. C. (4) Short of discovering new sources, I doubt that scholars will ever agree on the meaning of the puzzling Greek noun *pygmē* in v 3. In my structured translation in II.B., I rendered it as "with a fistful of water," but it might well mean instead "with a cupped hand," "up to the wrist," or "up to the elbow"; on this, see Hengel, "Mc 7:3 *pygmē*," 182–98; Skeat,

"A Note," 525–27. A few manuscripts simply omit the word (no doubt because the scribe thought the noun unintelligible in the context), while others substitute a more intelligible word (e.g., *pykna*, "often"). (5) At the beginning of v 4, I rendered the elliptical *ap' agoras*, "from the marketplace," as "[when they come in] from the marketplace, unless they immerse themselves, they do not eat." Indeed, a few manuscripts supply the phrase "when they come" to clarify the sense of the phrase. Another possible translation is "[anything they bring] from the marketplace they do not eat unless they sprinkle it," reading the verb *rantisōntai* instead of *baptisōntai*. On the various possibilities, see Lambrecht, "Jesus and the Law," 377 with n. 58. (6) Some manuscripts include "and beds" at the end of the list of things washed in v 4. External and internal arguments for and against the reading tend to cancel one another out. It may well be that a learned scribe supplied "and beds" under the influence of Leviticus 15 (which mentions unclean beds, while not specifying if and how they are to be rendered clean), though it is possible instead that Mark included the phrase as part of his sarcastic and generalizing attack.

[171] On "all the Jews" being "hyperbole," exaggeration, or an inaccuracy, see Gundry, *Mark*, 349; Harrington, *The Impurity Systems*, 280; Paschen, *Rein und Unrein*, 172. France (*Mark*, 281–82) states that "all the Jews" is more impressionistic than historically accurate and that, even among the Pharisees, the practice may have been less rigorous or uniform than Mark claims. Svartvik (*Mark and Mission*, 297) is refreshingly blunt in saying that "all the Jews" is probably historically untrue. See also Booth (*Jesus and the Laws of Purity*, 153), who accepts Alon's view: claiming that all Israel practiced handwashing in Jesus' time is an "exaggerated generalization." Maccoby (*Ritual and Morality*, 155–61) readily admits that ritual handwashing was not required for laypeople by Pharisees in the pre-70 period. He proceeds to save the historicity of the Marcan dispute by claiming that Jesus was rejecting a type of handwashing that was simply a matter of good manners and hygiene. He even suggests the possibility that Jesus was a member of a Hasidic group of Pharisees who rejected hygienic concerns as showing lack of faith in God's protection. All this unsubstantiated speculation takes us from Mark's text; more to the point, it never engages the key question of whether the Marcan dispute of 7:1–23 goes back to the historical Jesus.

[172] On this, see Booth, *Jesus and the Laws of Purity*, 156–58. Booth observes that the only pentateuchal law that involves the washing of hands by laypeople (apart from any other part of the body) is Lev 15:11, which commands that if a *zāb* (a man with an abnormal sexual discharge) touches another person without having rinsed his hands in water, the other person shall wash his clothes, bathe in water, and be unclean until evening. As Booth affirms (p. 174), in the Pentateuch, as a general rule, ordinary food is not susceptible to ritual impurity. A prime example of this rule is Deut 12:15,20–21, which permits nonsacrificial meat to be slaughtered away from the sanctuary; vv 15 and 22 pointedly state that the unclean and the clean may eat it. The great exception to this general rule is found in Lev 11:33–34,37–38, which affirms that ordinary food in a vessel is rendered unclean if (a) it is moistened by a

drinkable liquid and then (b) the dead body of one of the unclean creatures "that swarm on the ground" (v 29) falls upon it. Likewise, seed outside a vessel becomes unclean if these two conditions are verified. For some of the exegetical problems involved in this passage, see Booth, ibid., 174–75.

173 Both the prophets and the Psalms use the metaphor of washed or clean hands to signify moral purity; the origin of the metaphor probably lies in the ritual hand-washing practiced by priests during temple liturgies (so, e.g., Ps 26:6). The obligation of *priests* to wash their hands and their feet before entering "the meeting tent" or approaching the altar to offer sacrifice is prescribed in Exod 30:19–21; cf. 40:31–32. As for the deuterocanonical/apocryphal books of the OT, the extraordinary and highly fictional situation of the heroine Judith, who, upon leaving the camp of Holofernes each night, bathes in a spring before praying around dawn (Jdt 12:7–8), can hardly be used as an argument for handwashing as a common practice among Jewish laypeople before meals in the 2d or 1st century B.C. (The book of Judith probably dates from the middle of the 2d century B.C. in Palestine.) Even in the Judith story, Judith does not eat a meal until the following evening (12:9); the bathing (*ebaptizeto*, immersion, not mere handwashing) is clearly connected with prayer, not eating, and may be conditioned by the unusual situation of Judith's temporary stay in the tent of a Gentile enemy of Israel.

174 The *Damascus Document*, in particular, seems concerned that purification by water involve enough water to cover the whole body of the person being purified; see CD 10:10–11 (= fragmentary texts in 4Q266, fragment 8, col. 3, lines 9–10; 4Q270, fragment 6, col. 4, line 20). The *Rule of the Community* specifies that evil men who do not belong to the community are not allowed to "go into the water" in preparation for the communal meal (1QS 5:13–14). This picture of the Essenes (or Qumranites) bathing their bodies before partaking of the holy meal of the community is confirmed by Josephus (*J.W.* 2.8.5 §129). Thus, at least for the Essenes, the constant rule was full bathing, not handwashing, before meals. Sanders ("The Synoptic Jesus and the Law," 31) states categorically that "there is no evidence from rabbinic literature that Pharisees washed hands before eating ordinary meals." In Sanders's view, the Pharisees practiced ritual handwashing in three contexts: (1) before handling food that would go to the priesthood, (2) before the Pharisees' own sabbath and festive meals, and (3) after handling the Scriptures. As for Diaspora Judaism, a key passage in the *Sibylline Oracles* (3. 591–93) is unfortunately plagued with a text-critical problem. The worshipers referred to in the text are said to raise their holy arms heavenward, rising early from their beds and ever cleansing their *flesh* [or alternately: *hands*] with water. Somewhat more clearly, *Sib. Or.* 4. 165–66 speaks of people washing their bodies in rivers and raising hands to heaven to ask for forgiveness. In any case, the context in the two *Sibylline Oracles* passages, as in Judith, is one of prayer, not meals. Such also is the case in the *Letter of Aristeas* §305–6, where the Jewish translators of the Hebrew Scriptures into Greek wash their hands in the sea in the morning and pray to God before undertaking their task of translation. Sanders (ibid., 30) comments that ritual handwashing is thus

attested in Diaspora Judaism earlier than in Palestine. In any case, it would not have been a practice proper to the Pharisees alone (ibid., 41). On all this, see Runesson ("Water and Worship," 115–29), who notes that ritual washing in connection with cultic activities such as prayer is well attested in Greco-Roman religions, from which it may have spread to Diaspora Judaism. One might even hypothesize that ritual handwashing before meals spread from temple-less Diaspora Judaism to a temple-less Palestinian Judaism after A.D. 70. The attempt by Poirier ("Why Did the Pharisees Wash Their Hands?" 217–33) to use the ritual handwashing of Diaspora Jews to substantiate the practice of handwashing before ordinary meals among pre-70 Pharisees in Palestine lacks any solid historical evidence.

[175] The Hebrew text in *m. 'Ed.* 5:6 that describes Eleazar's position is *piqpēq bĕtohŏrat yādayim*. For the problem of whether the original form of the name was Eleazar ben Ha-Ner or Eleazar ben Enoch, see Milikowsky, "Reflections," 151 n. 9. Milikowsky wishes to make a distinction between "washing of hands" and "purity of hands"; but that distinction is not found before the Babylonian Talmud, and even there manuscripts vary in terminology (see ibid., 151 n. 10).

[176] In *t. Ber.* 5:13, we are told that washing one's hands with water before the meal is optional, washing one's hands with water after the meal is obligatory; literally, the Hebrew text reads: "First water [is] option, second water [is] obligation" (*mym r'šwnym ršwt 'ḥrwnym ḥwbh*). Yet the larger context in *t. Ber.* 4–6 shows a wide range of differing opinions on the order and obligatory nature of various ritual acts during a meal (especially a communal or solemn meal). For example, *t. Ber.* 5:26 includes, under the rubric of an alternate interpretation, the statement that handwashing must always precede a meal. For the corresponding text in the Jerusalem Talmud, see Tzvee Zahary, *The Talmud of the Land of Israel. Volume 1. Berakhot* (Chicago/London: University of Chicago, 1989) 285–86. In Zahary's translation, the text reads in *y. Ber.* 8:2: "It was taught [that washing one's hands with] water before the meal is optional. [Washing one's hands with] water after the meal is compulsory." A fuller explanation of this teaching is found in *Bemidbar Rabba* 20:21 (on Numbers 24:3). For an English translation, see Judah J. Slotki, *Midrash Rabba. Numbers in Two Volumes* (2 vols.; London: Soncino, 1939) 2. 816: "Halacha: If a man has eaten without previously washing his hands, does he incur a penalty? Our Rabbis have taught: Washing the hands before a meal is optional; after a meal it is obligatory." It should be noted, though, that the discussion that follows upon the statement of the basic rule urges the importance of washing one's hands before meals.

[177] The manuscript text of *t. Ber.* 5:27 reads *'ên nĕṭîlat yādayim lĕḥûllîn* ("there is no washing of hands for profane foods"). However, the printed editions include the addition *min hattôrâ* ("from the Torah"), thus restricting the sweeping statement to the question of what is or is not contained in the Law of Moses; on this, see Milikowsky, "Reflections," 149 n. 3. The Hebrew text of the statement of the House of Hillel in *b. Ber.* 52b reads *'ên nĕṭîlat yādayim lĕḥûllîn min hattôrâ* (literally, "there is no washing of hands for profane foods from the Torah").

[178] On this, see Sanders, "The Synoptic Jesus and the Law," 40.

[179] On this, see Milikowsky, "Reflections," 151.

[180] The claim that ritual handwashing before ordinary meals, as prescribed in the Mishna and later rabbinic documents, was widely practiced by many Jewish laypeople in pre-70 Palestine is argued at length by Deines in his monograph *Jüdische Steingefässe*. Deines argues that the large number of stone vessels that appear in and around Jerusalem starting in the 1st century B.C. and continuing up to the destruction of Jerusalem in A.D. 70 demonstrates that many ordinary Jews had adopted the ritual handwashing practice of the Pharisees, which is mirrored in the later rabbinic literature. The reason there was such a large production of stone vessels was that, according to Pharisaic and rabbinic purity rules, stone vessels were not susceptible to impurity. Hence, they were greatly in demand once a large number of the common people accepted and practiced the rule of the Pharisees that hands must be washed before ordinary meals. Deines's presentation is ingenious and displays great knowledge of both the archaeological material and the rabbinic texts. However, a number of problems arise when his argument is examined in detail: (1) There are the significant presuppositions that Deines brings to his task. (a) As is made clear in his later work, *Die Pharisäer* (WUNT 101; Tübingen: Mohr [Siebeck], 1997), Deines seeks to rehabilitate the view that the pre-70 Pharisees were recognized by ordinary Palestinian Jews as embodying "normative Judaism" and as the leaders of the relatively new institution of the synagogue (on the questionable nature of the presupposition that the pre-70 Palestinian synagogue was a particularly Pharisaic institution, see Grabbe, "Synagogues," 17–26, esp. 23). According to Deines, though ordinary Jews accepted the authority of the Pharisees and sought to imitate their example, they did not do so with complete consistency; on all this, see my review essay, "The Quest for the Historical Pharisee," *CBQ* 61 (1999) 713–22. (b) To know what the pre-70 Pharisees taught and practiced, one may use with confidence large amounts of later rabbinic works, ranging from the Mishna to the Talmuds; here Deines shows the influence of his mentor Martin Hengel. Those who do not accept these presuppositions about "normative Judaism" and the near-identification of the Pharisees with the later rabbis (and I do not) will not be convinced by Deines's arguments; for my view of the Pharisees, see *A Marginal Jew*, 3. 289–388. (2) As Deines himself shows, most of the large archaeological finds of pre-70 stone vessels are located in and around Jerusalem in Judea. By contrast, relatively little has been found in Galilee, especially in the small towns and the countryside where Jesus was especially active. Curiously, there are no significant finds around Cana of Galilee, a location that is a major focus of Deines's investigation because of the mention of the "six stone jars for Jewish purification" in John 2:6. (3) Since I have already shown on other grounds (*A Marginal Jew*, 2. 934–50) that the story of Jesus' changing water into wine at the wedding feast of Cana is most likely a creation of the Fourth Evangelist, with no "core event" going back to the historical Jesus, Deines's appeal to John 2:6 to confirm his argument fails to convince. (4) The material found at Qumran also creates difficulty for Deines's argument. (a) Although many stone

vessels are found at Qumran, no texts from the Dead Sea Scrolls enjoin ritual hand-washing before meals as obligatory, just as no text insists on the use of stone vessels because they are immune from contracting impurity. To be sure, many of the Qum-ran documents were originally composed prior to the great surge in the stoneware industry around Jerusalem. But not all the texts found at Qumran need be dated so early, and some of the texts may reflect groups outside the closed Qumran commu-nity. Moreover, we can see from the multiple copies of certain texts that texts were subject to revision as they were copied down through the decades; yet neither the obligation of ritual handwashing nor the immunity of stone vessels from impurity was ever introduced into any text. (b) Deines makes a great deal of his argument de-pend on the immunity of stone vessels to impurity, a teaching found in the Mishna (*Kelim* 10:1; *Ohol.* 5:5; 6:1; *Para* 5:5; *Yad.* 1:2) and presumed to be in force in the pre-70 period. Yet such a halakic view does not seem to have held sway at Qumran. While the text of CD 12:15–17 is obscure and different emendations of individual words are offered by scholars (see, e.g., Joseph M. Baumgarten, "The Essene Avoid-ance of Oil and the Laws of Purity," *RevQ* 6 [1967] 183–92; Hanan Eshel, "CD 12:15–17 and the Stone Vessels Found at Qumran," *The Damascus Document. A Centennial of Discovery* [Studies on the Text of the Desert of Judah 34; ed. Joseph M. Baumgarten, Esther G. Chazon, and Avital Pinnick; Leiden/Boston/Cologne: Brill, 2000] 45–52 [with further views and bibliography]; cf. Martin Goodman, "Kosher Olive Oil in Antiquity," *A Tribute to Geza Vermes* [ed. Philip R. Davies and Richard T. White; Sheffield: JSOT, 1990] 227–45), the text indicates that stone vessels can convey impurity (possibly by way of oil stains, according to one reading of the text; cf. *J.W.* 2.8.3 §123). Hence the presence and use of many stone vessels at Qumran cannot be connected with and cannot prove the existence of a belief that stone vessels could not transmit impurity. (See also the reference to [stone] mortars needing cleansing from corpse impurity in 11QTemple 49:14.) At this point, the whole thrust of Deines's argument—that the widespread presence of stone vessels around the turn of the era evinces an expanded view of purity and the common ac-ceptance of the obligation of ritual handwashing before meals—becomes dubious.

[181] Booth (*Jesus and the Laws of Purity*, 189) honestly admits that, besides the Pharisees, there is "no evidence of other sects practicing handwashing before ordi-nary food prior to Jesus' time." Since Booth also honestly admits that handwashing before meals cannot be attributed indiscriminately to all pre-70 Pharisees, his need to find some group to which he can attribute the practice leads him to the nebulous ḥăbērîm. This strategy, however—as I point out in the main text—leads to a greater problem. We can prove that a group called the Pharisees existed in pre-70 Jewish Palestine. We cannot say the same thing of the ḥăbērîm, nor can we be sure that they were, as Booth's explanation demands that they be, a subset of the pre-70 Phari-sees. Along the way, of course, Mark's "some of the scribes" in 7:1 must be quietly dropped.

[182] For Booth's identification of "the Pharisees" in Mark 7:3 with ḥăbērîm in par-ticular, see his *Jesus and the Laws of Purity*, 190–98, 201–2; cf. Svartvik, *Mark and Mission*, 371–72; Klawans, *Impurity and Sin*, 108–9, 150.

[183] On this, see *A Marginal Jew*, 3. 385 n. 161. I stress that I speak here of the technical, sectarian sense of the noun *ḥābēr*. In its nontechnical sense of "companion," "fellow," "associate," it is attested in the OT, especially in exilic and postexilic literature, including passages in Ben Sira. Interestingly, the usage in Ben Sira lacks a specifically religious tone. By contrast, in Isaiah, when the word is used of a religious group, it refers to pagans worshiping an idol (so the MT of Isa 44:11). There seem to be three occurrences of *ḥābēr* in the Dead Sea manuscripts; however, all three attestations occur in fragmentary material and so remain less than certain; see Martin G. Abegg et al. (eds.), *The Dead Sea Scrolls Concordance. Volume One. The Non-Biblical Texts from Qumran [Part One]* (Leiden/Boston: Brill, 2003) 250. As for the abstract noun *ḥăbûrâ* ("fellowship"), there is no clear attestation before the Mishna; it is lacking both in Abegg, ibid., 249–50, and in David J. A. Clines (ed.), *The Dictionary of Classical Hebrew. Volume III* (Sheffield: Sheffield Academic Press, 1996) 148–56. There are, however, rare occurrences of the nouns *ḥibbûr* ("company," "community," found once in CD 12:8) and the biblical *ḥebrâ* ("company," "community") at Ps 122:3 (if emended) and Job 34:8. For the questionable view that the Pharisees and the *ḥăbērîm* were nearly identical, see Poirier, "Why Did the Pharisees," 217–33, esp. 217 n. 4.

[184] Constrained by the logic of his argument, Booth (*Jesus and the Laws of Purity*, 217) strikes the phrase "tradition of the elders" from the primitive (and, in his view, historical) form of the tradition since he restricts the group that practices handwashing to a subset of the Pharisees, the *ḥăbērîm*. One might observe that this destroys one of the key links between the incident recounted in vv 1–4 and the question asked in v 5.

[185] So Booth (*Jesus and the Laws of Purity*, 205–6, 214), who naturally interprets Mark 7:15 in a relative rather than absolute sense. Loader ("Mark 7:1–23," 132) thinks that at the origin of Mark 7:1–23 lies a *chreia* (i.e., apophthegm, a short anecdote with a punch line by a famous teacher) reflected in 7:(2),5,15.

[186] The tractate within the Order of Purities that treats handwashing is *Yadayim* ("Hands"), while the tractate within the Order of Holy Things that treats forbidden foods is *Ḥullin* ("Profane Food").

[187] Like many other commentators, Sariola (*Markus und das Gesetz*, 49) reaches the conclusion on the basis of form, tradition, and redaction criticism that behind Mark 7:1–23 lies two different traditions: a *Streitgespräch* about eating with unwashed hands (i.e., vv 5–6a,9b–11c,11e) and a *Lehrrede* (a doctrinal dictum) concerning true impurity (i.e., v 15); a pre-Marcan editor joined the two traditions and supplied parenthetical explanations. What is intriguing here is that a distinction made on the basis of modern methods of Gospel criticism coincides with Jewish distinctions between different types of purity laws that wound up in different Orders of the Mishna.

[188] Our focus on the teaching or behavior of the historical Jesus during his public ministry means that certain texts will not be considered: (1) possible references to

purity in the Infancy Narratives (e.g., Luke 2:22, a garbled reference in any case; cf. *A Marginal Jew*, 1. 210); (2) possible references after Jesus' death (e.g., Matt 27:59–60); (3) possible references in narratives and sayings that have already been judged not to go back to the historical Jesus (e.g., John 2:1–11; cf. *A Marginal Jew*, 2. 934–50).

[189] The rabbinic phrase "father of the fathers of impurity" reflects the fact that persons or vessels rendered impure by a corpse became sources of impurity for other persons or vessels, more or less on a level with lepers and those experiencing genital discharges. For corpse impurity in Scripture, Jewish literature, and the Jesus tradition, see Kazen, *Jesus and Purity* Halakhah, 164–96. The relevant texts include Num 19:11,14,16. The purification ritual was taken most seriously; anyone who did not submit to it was to be "cut off" from the people of Israel.

[190] See the comment of Philo in *De specialibus legibus* 1.48 §261, with the description and allegorical interpretation of the sacrifice of the red cow and the mixing of its ashes with the water of purification in 1.49–50.

[191] *A Marginal Jew*, 2. 773–873.

[192] Kazen (*Jesus and Purity* Halakhah, 176–77) notes that touching the bier would have involved seven-day impurity in the rabbinic system; he thinks this would have been true of the time of Jesus as well; cf. Marshall, *Luke*, 286. In the case of the raising of Jairus' daughter, Guelich (*Mark 1–8:26*, 302) reasons, not without a little casuistry of his own, that the miracle itself "makes the issue [of corpse impurity] moot by removing the cause of the defilement." For a different view, see Donahue and Harrington, *Mark*, 177–78; cf. France, *Mark*, 235. Interestingly, many major commentaries on the Gospel of John never raise the question of corpse impurity in the case of Lazarus; in this, they share the mental horizon of the Fourth Evangelist.

[193] On John 11:55, see Brown, *The Gospel According to John*, 1. 444. Many commentators on John do not raise the question of a possible connection between 11:55 and 12:1 in regard to the laws of corpse impurity.

[194] Some commentators draw into this discussion of Jesus and corpse impurity the passing reference to the traveler left "half-dead" (*hēmithanē*) in the Lucan parable of the Good Samaritan (Luke 10:30); see Kazen, *Jesus and Purity* Halakhah, 189–93. I do not deal with the question here because (1) the reference lies within the story-world of a parable for which we lack multiple attestation, a parable that at least in its present form may well be the product of Luke's special L tradition and Luke's redactional activity; (2) the precise motivation (purity concerns about touching a possible corpse?) of the priest and Levite in passing by the half-dead man "on the opposite side" is not made clear in the parable; (3) in any case, the parable does not supply us with any reliable knowledge about Jesus' views on corpse impurity.

[195] The precise meaning of the participle *kekoniamenois* is disputed. The traditional translation is "whitewashed," referring perhaps to the custom of applying whitewash to tombs before the feast of Passover to warn passers-by who were unfamiliar with the area against contaminating themselves ritually; see *m. Šeqal.* 1:1; *m. Moʿed Qat.* 1:2. One might object, though, that such whitewashing could hardly be called "beautiful" and would not supply the necessary contrast between outward appearance and inner reality, since the whole purpose of the whitewash was to proclaim to the unsuspecting person the defiling reality within. Hence other translations have been suggested, including "plastered" or "decorated" (especially if Matthew's *taphois* is taken in the sense of "monuments" or even "ossuaries" instead of just "tombs" or "graves"). On the different possibilities, see Davies–Allison, *The Gospel According to Saint Matthew*, 3. 300–301.

[196] For a discussion of the various views on sources, see Davies–Allison, *The Gospel According to Saint Matthew*, 3. 300; John S. Kloppenborg, *Q Parallels*, 112; Fitzmyer, *The Gospel According to Luke*, 2. 942–44; Catchpole, *The Quest for Q*, 268. The double brackets, single brackets, and parentheses in the attempted reconstruction of the primitive Q form by Robinson, Hoffmann, and Kloppenborg (*The Critical Edition of Q*, 276–77) speak volumes. If from *ouai hymin . . . hoti* a credible Q logion can be reconstructed, then any reconstruction of any logion is possible. Hence, methodologically, I find the idea of M and L sayings more tenable.

[197] Matt 23:27 has the clearly Matthean tag "scribes and Pharisees" inserted after the introductory "woe to you"; it is a Matthean refrain that ties together six of the seven "woes" that Matthew has redacted in chap. 23. Luke 11:44 does not specify who the "you" are; only the wider Lucan context (11:37–39) indicates that they are Pharisees. Matthew and Luke's basic agreement on the opponents being Pharisees (if we overlook the fact that Matthew writes "scribes and Pharisees") might argue for the designation being original; but is this anything more than a chance agreement in selecting the most likely stock opponents as the object of the barb?

[198] See, e.g., 4Q274, fragment 1, col. 1, line 9; 4Q396, col. 4, lines 1–2 (4QMMT^c); 4Q397, fragments 6–13, line 11 (4QMMT^d); Josephus, *Ag. Ap.* 2.26 §205; *m. Kelim* 1:4; *m. Ohol.* 17–18.

[199] On this point, see Fitzmyer, *The Gospel According to Luke*, 2. 943.

[200] The difficulty involved in conjecturing an original Q form can be seen in the valiant but inevitably vague attempt of Robinson, Hoffmann, and Kloppenborg, *The Critical Edition of Q*, 268–73.

[201] Fitzmyer (*The Gospel According to Luke*, 2. 943) points to the absence of any parallel in the Matthean version, Luke's typical concern with almsgiving and the poor, and his use of a favorite adversative conjunction *plēn* ("except," "but").

[202] On the Matthean form of the saying and its metaphorical character, see Hagner, *Matthew*, 2. 671; on the Lucan form, see Marshall (*Luke*, 494–96), who thinks that Luke's formulation is probably secondary. Conjectures about (mis)translations of various Aramaic words are too hypothetical to be of help here; hence, I disagree with Davies and Allison (*Matthew*, 3. 299), who appeal to hypothetical differences in Aramaic versions of the saying. On this point, see Fitzmyer, *The Gospel According to Luke*, 2. 947. However, I do think that Davies and Allison are right on the basic point (p. 296): Matt 23:25–26 is not about the literal purity of vessels, nor is v 25 to be understood literally while v 26 is understood figuratively. From start to finish, the two verses speak of the scribes and Pharisees in metaphorical terms. Davies and Allison also point out (p. 297) why *G. Thom.* 89 is best understood as a secondary abbreviation of the Synoptic (specifically, the Lucan) tradition; so too Fitzmyer, *The Gospel According to Luke*, 2. 944.

[203] Some commentators speak of the poor woman being in a constant state of ritual impurity, never being able to enter the temple or to share in the Passover meal. Strictly speaking—if we are supposing a historical event—this goes beyond what is said and what is credible. While the woman's problem may have been chronic, it would be quite impossible for the woman to be suffering constantly from a flow of blood for twelve years; she would have died long before the twelve years were up. One must think in terms of some chronic but not constant problem.

[204] On this, see Kazen, *Jesus and Purity* Halakhah, 138–44. Part of the exegetical problem arises from an apparent inconsistency in Leviticus 15. Lev 15:11–12 states that a *zāb* (i.e., a male with an abnormal flow of bodily fluids from his genital area) defiles other persons as well as vessels by touching them, unless he has washed his hands first. Yet nothing is stated about a "female discharger" (a *zābâ*) defiling another person by touching him or her. Some commentators argue that it is logical to infer that the female discharger contaminates in the same way as the male, while others deny the inference. It is curious that the Masoretic text of Lev 15:27 specifies that a person who touches the bedding of a *zābâ* or anything on which she has sat becomes unclean, but says nothing about the touch of a *zābâ* defiling another person or of another person touching a *zābâ* and thus becoming unclean (contrast the *zāb* in 15:7 + 11). Complicating this observation is the fact that some Hebrew manuscripts and the Septuagint translation of Lev 15:27 state that anyone touching a *zābâ* is defiled; nevertheless, even this alternate reading does not claim that a *zābâ* defiles another by touching him or her. Complicating the debate still further is the fact that Leviticus 15 does not make clear whether the male discharger contaminates another person if he merely touches the other person's clothes rather than his or her body. Despite the lack of a clear law on the matter in Leviticus 15, Kazen thinks that the woman with the flow of blood in Mark 5 would have conveyed impurity to Jesus by touching his clothing, but Kazen's highly speculative reconstruction relies on a complicated interplay of Qumranic and rabbinic texts (see, e.g., 4Q274, fragment 1, and 4Q277, fragment 1). To be sure, *m. Zabim* 5:1 broadens the law of Leviticus 15: in the Mishna, the *zâb* (and presumably the *zābâ*) communicates impurity *either*

by touching another *or* by being touched by another. This goes beyond the laws of Leviticus 15 and may be an attempt to introduce symmetry into the somewhat asymmetrical laws. In any case, it should be noted that neither in the Pentateuch nor in the rabbinic literature is such touching considered a moral transgression; all that is required after such a touch is the usual process of ritual cleansing. On this, see Fonrobert, *Menstrual Purity*, 193–95. In short, one should avoid the sweeping and all-too-assured generalizations found in many commentaries on Mark; see, e.g., Guelich, *Mark 1–8:26*: "This woman was not only defiled, she defiled anything and everyone she touched. Her illness had left her personally, socially and spiritually cut off"; cf. Pesch, *Markusevangelium*, 1. 301–2; France, *Mark*, 236; Donahue and Harrington, *Mark*, 173–74.

[205] See Fonrobert's discussion (*Menstrual Purity*, 186–98) of the treatment of the question in the *Didascalia Apostolorum* and Dionysius of Alexandria.

[206] See, e.g., the accusation in *Ps. Sol.* 8:12 that the Hasmonean priests offer sacrifice "with menstrual blood"; the author of this psalm could be a priest of the old Zadokite line, an Essene, or a Pharisee. Interestingly, women who follow Sadducean rules of menstrual purity are equated with female Samaritans in *m. Nid.* 4:2. Menstrual impurity is also treated in the Dead Sea Scrolls: e.g., CD 5:6–7; possibly 4Q270, fragment 7, col. 1, lines 12–13; 4Q274, fragment 1, col. 1, lines 6–9; 4Q284, fragment 3; 11QTemple 48:15–17.

[207] The various meanings of *niddâ* should be distinguished. In the OT, the word refers to menstruation or to the ritual impurity caused by menstrual blood. The special phrase *mê niddâ* ("water of purification") refers to the ritual water used to purify people of corpse impurity (Num 19:9–13,20–21). In rabbinic literature, especially the Mishna, the word primarily refers to the woman experiencing menstruation; see Fonrobert, *Menstrual Purity*, 18. Fonrobert disagrees with the traditional view that menstrual purity rules received so much attention in the rabbinic literature because they, unlike so many purity laws, could still be observed after the destruction of the temple. In keeping with her feminist hermeneutic of rabbinic texts, she prefers to see the mishnaic tractate *Niddah* as a theoretical, halakic text "which discusses Jewish law as an abstract construct" (ibid., 23).

[208] The Gemara in the Palestinian Talmud covers only the first three chapters of the Mishna.

[209] On this question, see *A Marginal Jew*, 1. 332–45.

[210] Even if we do not suppose that the more detailed rules of the mishnaic tractate *Niddah* were in force at the time of Jesus (or were observed by Jesus' disciples), the simple rules of Lev 15:19–24 would have created enough practical problems for a traveling group composed of both male and female Jews. For instance, according to Leviticus, the menstruating woman was in a state of ritual impurity for seven days;

anyone touching her during that time was unclean until evening; anything on which she lay or sat was unclean; anyone who touched where she had slept had to wash his garments, bathe himself in water, and remain unclean until evening; anyone who touched anything on which she had sat had to go through the same routine.

[211] On the question of the nature and vocabulary of "leprosy" in the Bible, see *A Marginal Jew*, 2. 699–700. For the sake of convenience (especially brevity of phrasing), I use the traditional words "leper" and "leprosy" in the main text, but the reader should imagine these words with quotation marks around them.

[212] The argument is laid out and the relevant texts are analyzed in *A Marginal Jew*, 2. 698–706.

[213] Kazen (*Jesus and Purity* Halakhah, 104–7) points out that stretching out one's hand toward and/or touching the person to be healed is not as common an element of Hellenistic miracle stories as has been claimed. Nevertheless, it is not entirely absent in such stories, especially when the one doing the touching is a god; hence, an argument from dissimilarity or uniqueness would not be cogent.

[214] Loader (*Jesus' Attitude towards the Law*, 23) is led astray by relying on earlier Marcan commentators when he claims without reservation that "touching a leper would have rendered Jesus unclean until the evening."

[215] See *m. Zabim* 5:6; Josephus, *Ag. Ap.*, 1.31 §281.

[216] See *Ant.* 3.11.3–4 §261, §264–68; on this passage, see the commentary by Feldman, *Flavius Josephus. Volume 3. Judean Antiquities 1–4*, 308–10.

[217] In his commentary on the passage, John M. G. Barclay (*Flavius Josephus. Translation and Commentary. Volume 10. Against Apion* [Leiden/Boston: Brill, 2007] 151 n. 955) observes that "the ban against living under the same roof is a development well beyond the biblical laws." He rightly recognizes the rhetorical thrust of Josephus' claim: "Josephus has an interest in stressing the social isolation required by the laws, to underline the mismatch with Manetho's story."

[218] The problems connected with 4Q274 fragment 1, col. 1, are many. The text itself is fragmentary and suffers from many internal lacunae. Then, too, the exact nature of the group or groups being discussed in this list of purity rules is not entirely clear. The text seems to deal with the interaction among various people who have different types of impurity; the concern is that they not compound the problem of impurity by touching (or, possibly, having sexual intercourse with) one another. Hence, it remains uncertain whether the "everyone who touches" in the rule enunciated in lines 8–9 ("and everyone who touches anyone of these impure persons during the seven days of his purification shall not eat") refers to someone in this group suffering from various impurities or to anyone at all. Dependent on this choice in turn

is the decision as to whom "*his* purification" refers—the one touching or the one touched? The problem is complicated still more by the fact that part of the phrase "of his purification" is conjectural. More to the point, though, Joseph Baumgarten, the editor of the text in DJD, thinks that 4Q274 fragment 1, col. 1, does not speak of a leper at all; he suggests that the first three lines of the text, which include the cry "Unclean! unclean!," refer to a *zāb* (a man with an irregular and chronic flow of fluid from his genital area), not to a leper, though he notes that Jacob Milgrom understands these lines instead as referring to a leper. For his presentation of the text, a translation, and a commentary, see Joseph Baumgarten et al. (eds.), *Qumran Cave 4. XXV. Halakhic Texts* (DJD 35; Oxford: Clarendon, 1999) 99–103. Thus, whether the text is relevant at all to our purpose remains debatable. As for the major documents found at Qumran, in the Temple Scroll (11Q19), 46:16–18 sets aside special places for lepers as well as those suffering from various bodily discharges; 48:14–17 also specifies separate places for lepers "lest they enter your cities and defile them." Here the point is that the whole city would be defiled by the mere presence of a leper within it; this is not the same thing as an individual contracting impurity by touching a leper. As for the so-called Halakic Letter (4QMMT), 4Q396, col. 3, lines 3–11 treat the stringent rules isolating lepers from any place enjoying holy purity and from holy food; again, the precise question of an individual touching a leper is not raised.

[219] For a composite text of these Cave 4 fragments of the Damascus Document—4Q^{a,d,g,h}, i.e., 4Q266, 269, 272, and 273—see Charlesworth (ed.), *The Dead Sea Scrolls. Volume 2*, 64–75 (cf. CD 13:3–7, which makes just a passing reference to inspection by a priest). Although Kazen (*Jesus and Purity* Halakha, 109–16), by reading together the relevant texts of Qumran, Josephus, and the rabbis, comes to the conclusion that touching a leper would have rendered a person unclean in 1st-century Judaism, I do not think that the evidence previously examined proves his point for early 1st-century Palestine.

[220] So, e.g., France, *Mark*, 119–20.

[221] See, e.g., Guelich, *Mark 1–8:26*, 72.

[222] See, e.g., the sayings of Jesus that set a time limit for the coming of the kingdom (*A Marginal Jew*, 2. 339–48), the so-called nature miracles (2. 874–1038), or Jesus' supposed connection with the Essenes (3. 488–549).

CHAPTER 36

WIDENING THE FOCUS: THE LOVE
COMMANDMENTS OF JESUS

I. INTRODUCTION: THE VARIOUS
COMMANDMENTS OF LOVE

At the end of Chapter 31, which treated the general problem of Jesus and the Law, I explained the reason for the order of topics in this volume. Put simply, the nature of the Gospel material does not allow us to suppose a priori that Jesus' teaching on Torah flows in a smooth, logical progression from one grand principle to various moral conclusions. As we saw, Matt 5:17 ("Do not think that I have come to destroy the Law or the prophets; I have come not to destroy but to fulfill"), so often cited as the clearest summary of Jesus' view of the Law, is most likely a Christian creation. Moreover, contrary to the common tendency of Christians extracting moral theology from the Gospels, one cannot presume, prior to a detailed examination of the data, that love or any other lofty moral value provides a single principle that neatly organizes Jesus' scattered pronouncements into a coherent system. Lacking the presumption of any such principle or system, I decided that the only approach that did justice to the variegated teachings in the Gospel sources was to probe discrete halakic pronouncements on individual points of the Law. Preference was given to those questions that enjoyed multiple attestation or some other indicator suggesting that the tradition went back to Jesus himself.

Accordingly, Volume Four of *A Marginal Jew* has treated Jesus' commandments or pronouncements on such different topics as divorce, oaths, sabbath, and purity rules—major social institutions and/or religious practices of concern to 1st-century Jews. The very variety and concreteness of these questions reinforce our picture of Jesus as a 1st-century Jewish teacher deeply engaged in the halakic debates of his day. Yet the fact that Jesus discussed a wide range of legal topics and issued some startling pronounce-

478

ments makes all the more pressing the question of whether—and, if so, how—Jesus related to the Mosaic Law as a whole. Only if we can discern Jesus' stance vis-à-vis the Torah as a whole do we have the right to speak of an overarching "moral teaching" or "moral vision" that Jesus inculcated. Even then, we must remember that Jesus spoke in terms of Torah, commandments, and doing God's will, and not in terms of an abstract "morality" or "moral system."

I suggest in this chapter that, putting aside Christian creations ancient (Matt 5:17) and modern (moral theology), we probably find our best opportunity for discerning Jesus' general approach to the Law in his strikingly different way(s) of articulating the basic command to love.[1] Here I refer not to anything and everything Jesus ever said about love, mercy, giving, and forgiving. Not only would that bring us too far afield and involve us in many logia whose authenticity is difficult to assess, but, more to the point, such a broad sweep would also lose the focus of this whole volume: individual *commands* or *prohibitions* of Jesus that relate directly to the Mosaic Law. Let us therefore simply stipulate for the record and grant what no serious critic denies: Jesus was in favor of love, mercy, and forgiveness. What Jewish teacher of the time wasn't?[2] The question we pursue in this chapter is the more focused one of Jesus' *command* that x must (or "shall") love y. Indeed, in one case we shall examine, Jesus' command consciously employs the very wording of commands found in the Jewish Scriptures. Our approach thus places the otherwise amorphous and sprawling topic of love in the limited and structured context of the Law, *hălākâ*, and the other commands of Jesus already studied in this volume.

Paradoxically, when it comes to Jesus' commandment(s) of love, we both possess and lack multiple attestation. We possess multiple attestation in the sense that three major sources—Mark, Q, and John—depict Jesus enjoining some sort of commandment of love. (1) In Mark 12:28–34 parr., Jesus, citing Deut 6:4–5, inculcates total love of God as the *first* commandment of all, while pointedly adding to it love of neighbor (Lev 19:18b) as the *second* commandment. (2) In the Q tradition (Matt 5:44 ‖ Luke 6:27), Jesus commands his disciples to love their enemies, this time without citing the Torah. (3) In John 13:34, during the Last Supper, Jesus gives his disciples "a new commandment": "As I have loved you, you also—love one another" (repeated in John 15:12,17).

Some might wish to add to this list the so-called Golden Rule (Matt 7:12 ‖ Luke 6:31): "Do to others what you want them to do to you." However, in the NT—as well as in the ancient Mediterranean world in general—the Golden Rule does not employ the vocabulary of love; hence, strictly speaking, it is not a *love* commandment. Then, too, the absence of the vocabulary of love may not be purely accidental: a cold, critical eye could see in the Golden Rule nothing more than enlightened self-interest. For the sake of completeness, though, I will discuss the Golden Rule briefly after the love commands proper to Mark and Q, but I do not count it among the *love* commands of Jesus.

In sum, in light of the triple attestation of Mark, Q, and John, one might be justified in asserting, by way of a vague generalization, that the historical Jesus issued some sort of commandment or commandments enjoining love. But my guarded phrasing—"some sort of commandment"—points up the problem of this multiple attestation. As the attentive reader notes immediately, these three commands of love are quite distinct in their extent and rationale. They are not to be simplistically conflated or harmonized. For instance, Q's love of enemies both omits love for God and goes beyond Mark's love of neighbor. Then, too, Q's rejection of an ethic of reciprocity among equals (Luke 6:32–35 ‖ Matt 5:46–47) stands in tension with John's emphasis on reciprocal love within the community ("one another"). For that matter, it stands in tension with Q's own Golden Rule, which Q (at least if Luke preserves the more original order of the sayings) positions right in the middle of its exposition of love of enemies (Luke 6:31 within 6:27–35).

Hence the paradox: despite the multiple attestation of Jesus' command to love (in some formulation or other), no single form of his various love commands enjoys multiple attestation. The "double command of love" (God and neighbor) is found only in the Marcan tradition.[3] The command to love one's enemies is found only in Q. To be sure, similar traditions that speak of blessing persecutors are found in the Christian parenesis of the NT epistles (e.g., Rom 12:14), but the direct and laconic command "love your enemies" is strikingly absent. Finally, *Jesus'* command to love "one another" is found only in the Johannine tradition.[4] We must therefore examine each form of the love command separately both to grasp its specific content and to decide whether it comes from the historical Jesus. Such a compartmentalized approach will keep us from unconsciously meshing one form of the love command with another.

In addition, this "segmented" approach helps highlight an important truth that is easily obscured by the unexamined consensus of almost all Christians. Most believers take for granted that what lies at the heart of Jesus' message and what is repeated incessantly throughout his preaching is love, both love of neighbor and love of enemies. This is the received "gospel" of generations who have grown up believing that all you need is love. However, if we restrict ourselves for the moment to the Synoptic Gospels, one would not get such an impression from the sayings of Jesus.[5] "Love" as a verb or a noun occurs relatively rarely on the lips of Jesus. When it does occur, Jesus is often citing a text from the Jewish Scriptures or commenting on it.

To take a prime example: in Mark's Gospel, apart from the teaching on the love of God and neighbor, in which Jesus simply cites two commandments from the Torah (Mark 12:29–31), the word "love" never occurs on the lips of Jesus. The Q tradition taken over by Matthew and Luke, with its command to love one's enemies, supplies a few more examples. In addition, Matthew inserts the OT command to love one's neighbor twice into his Marcan and Q traditions. All in all, granted the huge amount of sayings material we have in the three Synoptic Gospels, the times Jesus uses the word "love" in a command or exhortation are surprisingly few.[6] And at this point we are not even probing the question of whether most of these sayings come from the historical Jesus. When we add to the relative paucity of sayings on love the relative paucity of times that Jesus speaks of one's "neighbor" or one's "enemy,"[7] we begin to feel uneasy about blithe homiletic generalizations proclaiming love to be the center of Jesus' message.

One might indeed argue that love is present not so much in Jesus' words as in his actions: his healings, his concern for the poor, and the welcome he extends to toll collectors, sinners, and the other marginalized of society. This is all well and good, but the question raised by Volume Four of *A Marginal Jew* is Jesus' relation to and teaching about the Mosaic Law. Granted this focus, the question of "Jesus and love" must address Jesus' *statements* about love, which in turn involve his various *commandments* of love—commandments that are few and far between. What and whence are the different types of love commandments attributed to him, what does each one mean, and does any of them really come from the historical Jesus? These are the questions this chapter must face.[8]

II. THE DOUBLE COMMAND OF LOVE IN THE GOSPEL OF MARK

A. THE PLACE OF THE DOUBLE COMMAND OF LOVE (MARK 12:28–34)

As we saw in the story of the Sadducees' question about the resurrection (Mark 12:18–27),[9] the pericope in which Jesus teaches the double commandment of love (12:28–34) stands within a series of verbal attacks on Jesus by the Jerusalem authorities and Jesus' counterattacks on them, all set in the temple during the last days of Jesus' public ministry. This cycle of Jerusalem dispute stories and questions (11:27–12:40), placed by Mark at the end of the ministry, corresponds to a Galilean cycle of dispute stories and questions set in the beginning of the ministry (2:1–3:6).[10] Although sometimes referred to simply as the Jerusalem dispute stories (*Streitgespräche*) in Mark, this collection of pericopes has both a looser structure and more variegated content than the corresponding Galilean cycle. Actually, Mark 11:27–12:40 contains three stories of dispute or conflict, a polemical parable, one friendly academic conversation, a christological question posed and left hanging by Jesus, and a final vitriolic attack by Jesus on the scribes. Let us quickly reconnoiter this sprawling swath of text before we focus on Mark 12:28–34.

The *first* pericope of the cycle (11:27–33), which is preceded by the triumphal entry into Jerusalem, the "cleansing" of the temple, and the withering of the cursed fig tree, serves as the grand opening of the cycle. It does this by raising the basic question of Jesus' authority, the point at issue throughout the cycle. Fittingly, the adversaries launching the attack are the chief priests, the scribes, and the elders, the three groups that will condemn Jesus to death in the coming Passion Narrative (chaps. 14–15). By way of *inclusio*, the object of Jesus' counterattack at the end of the cycle is one of these three groups, the scribes (12:35 + 38).[11] In the *second* pericope (12:1–12), the parable of the evil tenants of the vineyard, Jesus turns the tables by indicting in veiled language the attackers named in the first pericope. They are the ones who will compass the death of the beloved son.[12] The *third* pericope (12:13–17) is the hypocritical question about paying taxes to Caesar. Tellingly, it is posed by the unlikely partnership of Pharisees and Herodians (v 13). This odd alliance appears again in Mark only at the end of the Galilean cycle of dispute stories (3:6), where these same groups plan to destroy Jesus.[13] This cross-reference not only binds the two cycles and thus the beginning and the end of the public ministry together; it also keeps up the ominous drumbeat of the deadly hostility of Jesus' opponents, a hostility that will soon have its way. Yet, in the teeth of this enmity, the Marcan Jesus shows himself to be the victor in each case, for he possesses authority (*exousia*; see 11:28), unlike the Jerusalem authorities who will put him to death.

Contrasting with and yet complementing the underlying theme of death is the explicit question about the resurrection of the dead, posed by the Sadducees in the *fourth* pericope (12:18–27), their only appearance in the Gospel. Mark clearly wishes to array every Jewish party or group he can think of to present a united front of Jewish authorities against Jesus. Once again, Jesus defeats his opponents, vindicating not only his authority to interpret the Scriptures correctly but also the doctrine of the resurrection of the dead, which, in Mark's story, Jesus will soon embody in his own person. The reader is increasingly led to understand that one of the underlying themes that tie together all the disparate material in this cycle is death and resurrection, the mystery soon to be enacted in the Passion Narrative.

This gloomy backdrop, set up by stark, dark, laconic Mark, is suddenly and strangely pierced by a ray of light in the *fifth* pericope (12:28–34), the last in the cycle that actually involves an interchange of question and answer between two parties. In contrast to the hostile tone before and after, this pericope on the double commandment presents a single scribe who sincerely asks Jesus about the first commandment. When Jesus responds by citing in order and yet binding together Deut 6:4–5 and Lev 19:18b, the scribe proclaims that Jesus has answered well. Almost like a good catechism student, the scribe then dutifully repeats the gist of Jesus' reply, modified by his own emphases. Jesus, in turn "seeing that he [the scribe] had answered with insight [*nounechōs*]," responds with praise that, in Mark's mind, is also an invitation to go further by accepting Jesus fully: "You are not far from the kingdom of God." This public acknowledgment of Jesus' correct interpretation of Scripture (continuing a theme from the previous pericope on the resurrection), an acknowledgment made by the only Jewish authority proclaimed by the Marcan Jesus to be sincere and intelligent, has the effect of silencing all opposition (12:34).

At this point, for the second time in the cycle, Jesus goes on the attack (in the *sixth* pericope, 12:35–37), posing a question to the crowds about the proper interpretation of Ps 110:1: "The Lord said to my lord, 'Sit at my right hand'. . . ." In Mark's view, this text is a christological prophecy of Jesus' exaltation after his death, his definitive vindication over his enemies. The crowd listening to Jesus' rhetorical question apparently enjoys not only Jesus' teaching but also his implicit assault on the scribes, who—Mark implies—do not know how to interpret Ps 110:1 correctly. This implied attack on the scribes becomes explicit in the *seventh* and final pericope of the cycle (12:38–40), in which Jesus warns against the scribes' ostentatious display of their status and piety, even as they oppress the poor (12:40: "devouring the houses of widows"). The word "widows" acts as a catchword introducing the following pericope of the widow's mite (12:41–44), itself something of a bridge to the eschatological discourse (chap. 13, delivered opposite the doomed temple) and the climactic Passion Narrative (chaps. 14–15). In giving "all that she had, her whole life [= livelihood]," the widow exemplifies both Jesus' critique of the exploitative religious authorities in the previous pericope and Jesus' own total gift of his life in the subsequent Passion Narrative.

It is within the grand sweep of this Jerusalem cycle of disputes and questions, attacks and counterattacks, that one can appreciate fully how out of place and what an "odd duck" the pericope on the double commandment of love is. Instead of *groups* of hostile authorities trying to trap or discredit Jesus with trick questions, or instead of Jesus attacking his opponents with trick counterquestions, an accusatory parable, hardly veiled mockery, and finally outright denunciation, we have in 12:28–34 a *single* scribe who is moved to ask Jesus a question precisely because he sees that Jesus has answered his adversaries "well" (*kalōs*). This scribe emphasizes his agreement with Jesus by repeating Jesus' answer in digest form and is finally evaluated by Jesus as having answered with insight (*nounechōs*).[14] We are in a different world from the rest of the Jerusalem cycle of disputes. Even this early on, before we have done a verse-by-verse analysis of the pericope, we begin to sense that this story of the double commandment, which simply does not fit the tone of the rest of the Jerusalem cycle, originally had a life of its own apart from the present Marcan composition. This impression is reinforced by the fact that, except for this pericope, Mark's portrayal of the scribes is unrelievedly negative, as we shall see below. In short, to anticipate for a moment what we shall observe in greater detail in the next section, the pericope of the double commandment does not fit neatly into either its redactional Marcan context or Mark's redactional portrait of the scribes. Whatever the ultimate judgment regarding historicity is, we are most likely dealing with a pre-Marcan unit that circulated independently in the early oral tradition. To confirm that preliminary judgment, we now move to an analysis of the structure and content of Mark 12:28–34.

B. THE STRUCTURE AND CONTENT OF MARK 12:28–34

Although, as we have just seen, there are reasons for supposing that the Marcan story of the double commandment goes back to a pre-Marcan oral tradition, the pericope as it stands is a Marcan composition. Hence, before we can deal at length with the question of sources and possible origin in the historical Jesus, we must come to grips with the text that Mark has given us.

1. *The Structure of Mark 12:28–34*

The structure of Mark 12:28–34 is both straightforward and complex at the same time.[15] More important, it provides some initial clues for the question of tradition and redaction.

A. Introduction (setting the scene): vv 28abc

    v 28a And one of the scribes, having approached,

    v 28b having heard them arguing,

    v 28c **having seen that he [Jesus] <u>answered</u> them [the Sadducees] <u>well</u>**

B. Scribe's first address to Jesus (question): vv 28de

    v 28d <u>asked</u> him:

    v 28e "Which is [the] first *commandment* of all?" [16]

C. Jesus' first reply to the scribe (answer): vv 29–31

    v 29a Jesus <u>answered</u>:

    v 29b "[The] first is

    v 29c 'Hear, O Israel, the Lord our God is one Lord,[17]

    v 30a and you shall love the Lord your God

    v 30b from your whole heart and from your whole soul
          and from your whole mind and from your whole strength.'

    v 31a [The] second [is] this:

    v 31b 'You shall love your neighbor as yourself.'

    v 31c Greater than these [two] is no other *commandment*."

B'. Scribe's second address to Jesus (approval): vv 32–33

    v 32a And the scribe *said to him*:

    v 32b "<u>Well</u> [spoken], teacher;

    v 32c in truth have you said that he is one

    v 32d and there is no other except him;

    v 33a and to love him from [one's] whole heart
          and from [one's] whole understanding and from [one's] whole
            strength

    v 33b and to love [one's] neighbor as oneself

    v 33c is greater than all holocausts and sacrifices.

C'. Jesus' second reply to the scribe (approval and conclusion
of dialogue): v 34abc

    v 34a And Jesus, **having seen that he <u>answered</u> intelligently,**

    v 34b *said to him*:

    v 34c "You are not far from the kingdom of God."

A'. Conclusion to the Jerusalem dialogues: v 34d

    v 34d And no one dared to <u>ask</u> him [anything] further.

The basic structure of the pericope is clear enough, yet it contains some intriguing complications and divergences from the usual pattern of a Gospel dialogue story, hostile or friendly. The narrative opening (in the voice of the evangelist in 28abc) corresponds to the narrative conclusion (in the voice of the evangelist in v 34c). Thus, we have the outer, encasing structure of A–A'.[18] In a sense, though, this pericope has two conclusions. The narrative conclusion in v 34d closes off not so much this individual pericope as the whole series of conversations, almost all of them hostile, that began with the initial challenge to Jesus' authority in Mark 11:27–33. Verse 34c, while serving as Jesus' second reply to the scribe, also concludes the dialogue proper and thus maintains the unspoken rule that Jesus must always have the last and decisive word in any theological dialogue.

Within this framework of introduction and conclusion(s), the heart of the pericope consists of the simple pattern of the scribe's address to Jesus and Jesus' reply to the scribe. However, in this case—and uniquely among Synoptic dispute stories and scholastic dialogues—the pattern is doubled.[19] Hence we have the unusual pattern of B–C *plus* B'–C'. The first exchange is the usual one of the interlocutor's question and Jesus' answer, with the question being quite brief (five words in Greek) and the answer quite long (fifty-four words). This first exchange is held together by an *inclusio*, namely, the word "commandment" (*entolē*) in the scribe's question (v 28e) and at the end of Jesus' answer (v 31c).

This pattern of brevity and length is reversed in the second round of dialogue, an exchange of approbations tied together by "and [he] said to him" (*kai eipen autō*, v 32a + 34b). The scribe's admiring reaction (v 32b–33c), which repeats Jesus' reply but also abridges and expands various parts of it to overlay the scribe's own interpretation, consists of forty-six words—thus gracefully restricting the scribe's glossed repetition to fewer words than the master's original teaching. In contrast, Jesus' concluding approbation (v 34c) is a mere eight words, three more than the scribe's initial question. Hence Jesus' two statements in the pericope (vv 29b–31c + v 34c) are both longer than the corresponding sentences spoken by the scribe (v 28e + vv 32b–33c). In this way, along with the parallel structure of the scribe's first address to Jesus *and* Jesus' first reply to the scribe, the scribe's second address to Jesus *and* Jesus' second reply (the B–C, B'–C' pattern), there is also a chiastic structure of short speech—long speech—long speech—short speech.[20]

The pericope is held together literarily not only by these major components of the overall structure but also by a number of deft cross-references and repetitions of individual words. The scribe twice gives a positive evaluation to Jesus' teaching with the adverb *kalōs* ("well"), first in the scribe's unspoken thoughts ("having seen that he answered them well," v 28c) and then in his voiced acclamation ("well [spoken], teacher," v 32b).[21] Both times *kalōs* is emphasized by being placed first in its clause. The scribe's insightful evaluation of Jesus in the introduction ("having seen that he answered them well," v 28c) corresponds to the (naturally) insightful evaluation of the scribe by Jesus in the first conclusion of the pericope ("having seen that he answered intelligently," v 34a). Indeed, the precise parallel in the Greek words of v 28c and v 34a (*idōn hoti . . . apekrithē*, "having seen that he answered") serves a couple of ends. First, it makes clear the mutual nature of the approbation that is only in the scribe's thoughts in v 28c but is expressed verbally by Jesus in v 34. While the scribe sees Jesus in an approving light but does not say so at the beginning of the story, Jesus sees the scribe in an approving light and says so at the end. Second, the rare adverb *nounechōs* ("intelligently," "wisely," "insightfully") resumes the previous two uses of *kalōs* ("well") and lifts them to a crescendo at the end of the story. To answer well is above all to answer with understanding and insight.

One might observe here as an aside that this structural analysis already casts doubt upon the minority view that Mark 12:28–34 is actually a hostile dispute story, with the scribe portrayed as a clever adversary outwitted by a still more clever Jesus. The repeated approval of Jesus by the scribe (first in his mind and then in his speech), the mutual statements of approval by the scribe and by Jesus, and the escalation of the approving evaluation of the scribe's "well" to Jesus' "intelligently" in the second reply all make a negative evaluation of the scribe as a hostile character unlikely from the start.

A further insight underscored by our survey of the macro- and microstructures of this pericope is that this double dialogue within a narrative frame is not a pure Marcan creation. As we have already seen, this positive dialogue stands out like a theological sore thumb amid the series of hostile exchanges and statements both before and after it, just as the lone sympathetic scribe stands out amid the unrelentingly negative portrayal of "the scribes" (always in the plural) in Mark's Gospel. If Mark had created 12:28–34 out of whole cloth, it only seems reasonable that he would have made the pericope cohere much better with the polemical tone of the whole of chaps. 11–12. One sees why some critics strain to turn 12:28–34 into a hostile dispute story; they do what they think Mark should have done—and what Matthew actually does. What Mark in fact does is to tie this stray pericope to what precedes by a reference to Jesus' defeat of the hostile Sadducees, an event that encourages the scribe to engage in positive dialogue—though we are not told *why* the Sadducees' defeat motivates the scribe. At the end of 12:28–34, Mark proceeds to tie this positive exchange with a scribe to Jesus' negative monologue aimed at "the scribes" in 12:28–34. Mark indicates in v 34d that Jesus' wise answer discouraged his enemies from attempting any more trick questions. Thus, faced with a recalcitrant pericope that is starkly opposite in tone from the rest of the material in the Jerusalem exchanges, Mark does the best he can. But the awkwardness of the connections he forges remains apparent; the seams still show.[22] In short, we are confirmed in our view that we are dealing in Mark 12:28–34 with an isolated pre-Marcan tradition that Mark has taken into his Jerusalem cycle of exchanges. Probably the fact that this pericope can serve Mark's over-arching purposes in chaps. 11–12—the public display and vindication of Jesus' teaching authority, his superiority to all Jewish parties and teachers, and the foreshadowing of the temple's doom—outweighs in Mark's eyes the inconvenience of shoehorning 12:28–34 into its present position.

2. Exegesis of Mark 12:28–34

What follows is not a thorough exegesis of the pericope in all its dimensions, but rather a brief verse-by-verse interpretation of the literary unit both to ascertain the overall meaning of 12:28–34 and to highlight certain points that are relevant to our quest. The viewpoint used as we move through the verses will be primarily that of Mark's redactional theology.

The initial phrase of v 28, "and *one of the scribes*, having approached . . . ," signals that, in the midst of the fierce Jerusalem conflicts Mark has been narrating, something unusual is about to happen. As a stock character in Mark's narrative, "the scribes" span the whole of the Gospel from 1:22 (unlike the scribes, Jesus has authority to teach) to 15:31 (the scribes join the chief priests and the elders in mocking Jesus on the cross). As these two examples show, the intensity of the negative or hostile tone used to describe "the scribes" may vary in Mark, but the scribes are never depicted in a posi-tive light—except in Mark 12:28–34. The difference is announced to the attentive reader by the opening words, "*one* of the scribes." Elsewhere Mark always speaks of the scribes in the plural; they are a monochromatic collec-tivity arrayed as a foil to or opponent of Jesus.[23] From 8:31 (the first passion prediction) onward, Jesus prophesies that the scribes will join the elders and the chief priests in rejecting him. The scribe's deadly role is repeated in Jesus' third and longest passion prediction (10:33), which begins to be ful-filled as soon as he enters Jerusalem and "cleanses" the temple (11:18). The next day, the scribes join the high priests and elders in attacking Jesus ver-bally. By way of *inclusio*, Jesus returns the compliment by attacking them indirectly in 12:35–37 (right after our pericope) and directly in vv 38–40. Jesus' passion predictions are then fulfilled to the letter in the Passion Narrative of chaps. 14–15, where the scribes are present from the hatching of the plot (14:1) to the final mockery at the cross (15:31).[24]

This explains why Mark, when faced with a contrary tradition (12:28–34) that presented a Jewish scribe in a positive light agreeing with Jesus' teaching, pointedly begins his narrative with "*one* of the scribes" (*heis tōn grammateōn*). Dissenting from the view of many commentators, I do not think that the numeral "one" (*heis*) in v 28 is simply the equivalent of the indefinite article "a" (a weak *tis* in Hellenistic Greek).[25] Rather, Mark stresses that out of the *massa damnata* of the scribes, there comes forth one—and only one—scribe who recognizes Jesus as an impressive teacher, asks a sincere question, and receives Jesus' answer with enthusiastic approbation. In Mark's eyes, then, this one scribe can act both as a foil to all his insincere and malign colleagues and as an all-the-more credible witness to Jesus, the superior teacher who "teaches the way of God in truth" (cf. 12:14). It is not by accident, then, that the word "scribe" (*grammateus*) occurs in the singular in Mark's Gospel only in our pericope (12:32). This scribe is indeed singular in more than one sense; he is the exception that proves the rule.

Unlike Matthew, Mark does not say that the scribe is a Pharisee. Hence, strictly speaking, Mark does not tell us why the scribe approves of Jesus' answer that the resurrection of the dead is taught in Scripture. However, unlike Matthew, Mark makes clear that denial of the resurrection is what defines the Sadducees as a special party.[26] Accordingly, Mark may well suppose that Jews in general—and so this scribe in particular—accept the resurrection. Thus, when the scribe sees his own position on the resurrection vindicated by Jesus' argument, which is taken from the Torah (Exod 3:6,15–16) and which resolves a problem created by a commandment of the Torah (Deut 25:5–6), the scribe feels encouraged to pose his question about the commandments contained in the Torah.

Translated with wooden literalness, the scribe's question (v 28e) is difficult to understand: "Of what sort is [the] first commandment of all [things]?" However, the interrogative pronoun *poia*, while strictly meaning "what sort of?", can have in Hellenistic Greek the blander sense of "which?" or "what?" That seems to be the meaning here. Likewise, *pantōn* ("of all things") is strictly speaking the genitive plural *neuter*, while *entolē* ("commandment") is *feminine*. Nevertheless, in Hellenistic Greek, the neuter plural (*pantōn*) can stand for the feminine plural of "all" (*pasōn*) in a construction of this type.[27] Hence I think that the standard translation is probably the correct one: "What is [the] first commandment of all [the commandments]?"

One reason why I am especially careful about the correct translation here is that it is vital to stick as closely as possible to Mark's wording. All too many commentators read into the scribe's terse question more than it says by importing ideas from Matthew or Luke's version of this scene. In Mark, "first" seems to mean "first in importance and/or rank." Nothing in the Marcan form of the question or the answer affirms that this first commandment is a summary of the whole Law, or that the whole Law depends on this first commandment, or that all other commandments can be derived from or reduced to this one commandment.[28] Such ideas come from reading Matthew's version of the story (especially 22:40, rightly or wrongly understood) into Mark's pericope.

In v 29, Jesus responds that the first commandment is contained in the *Shemaʿ*, the well-known profession of faith in and love of Yahweh, taken from Deut 6:4–5. Actually, by the later rabbinic period, the prayer called the *Shemaʿ* had come to be defined as containing three texts joined together: Deut 6:4–9; 11:13–21; Num 15:37–41. At the time of Jesus, though, the text seems to have varied in length and content.[29] Jesus focuses on the fundamental point proclaimed at the beginning of the *Shemaʿ*: belief in the one true God of Israel (Deut 6:4) and its necessary consequence, a love of God that is complete and undivided (Deut 6:5).[30] Mark's listing of four different human faculties—heart, soul, mind, strength—underscores the totality of the Israelite's commitment to Yahweh in both worship and daily life.[31] Strictly speaking, Jesus' citation encompasses an initial command ("Hear, O Israel!"), which introduces a profession of faith ("the Lord [= Yahweh] our God"), which then issues in the command of total love ("and you shall love . . ."). The Marcan Jesus, however, understands the whole text he cites as constituting a single commandment (v 29ab): "Jesus answered: '[The] first [commandment] is. . . .'"

At this point, modern Americans need to pause for a moment to remind themselves that "love" in this text does not mean first of all strong emotions, which, of their nature, ebb and flow. In OT references to love for God, loving is above all a matter of willing and then doing, though emotion is hardly excluded from the total experience.[32] This emphasis on willing and doing rather than emoting becomes abundantly clear if we take into account an important background to the idea of covenant in Deuteronomy, namely, the treaties (covenants) of the ancient Near East.[33] In some of these treaties, the vassal, perhaps after being defeated in battle, promises to "love" his suzerain. What is being stipulated by the treaty is scarcely a required amount of gushing feelings but rather the fulfillment of the obligations that the suzerain imposes on the vassal in the treaty, above all the obligation of maintaining an exclusive relationship with the suzerain. Fittingly, Deut 6:4–5 is positioned in the opening section of Deuteronomy, with its rehearsal of the past history of God's dealings with Israel and of the resulting exclusive covenant between Yahweh and his chosen people. Only after that foundation is laid are the individual commandments of the Torah spelled out at length (chaps. 12–26). Hence, Jesus is quite literally correct: the *Shemaʿ* of Deuteronomy comes first, before all the detailed commandments covering particular aspects of Israelite life-in-the-covenant.[34] What comes first, what is basic and most important, what makes sense of all the rest is the faith and love (obedience) proclaimed in the *Shemaʿ*.[35]

The entire Marcan pericope dealing with the scribe's question could have ended right here. The scribe asked about the first commandment, and Jesus has given an impressive, memorable answer. But, unbidden by the scribe's question, and hence asserting his own initiative, authority, and insight into the Law,[36] Jesus proceeds to add a second command, which he places alongside the first (v 31ab): "[The] second [commandment] is this: 'You shall love your neighbor as yourself.' " Jesus suddenly and deftly jumps from Deuteronomy to Leviticus. At first glance, Leviticus might seem an odd choice after the *Shemaʿ* of Deuteronomy, since Leviticus is largely a collection of laws governing the priests, the Levites, ritual purity, and liturgical ceremonies. Bypassing all of these laws, Jesus instead gravitates toward a list of obligations to one's fellow human beings (Lev 19:11–18).[37] The list divides into four subunits, each ending with the solemn theological basis of the social obligations: "I am the Lord" (*ʾănî yahweh* in vv 12,14,16,18). The final small bundle of social obligations (Lev 19:17–18), which forbids hatred, revenge, or grudges nurtured against fellow Israelites, reaches its positive culmination in Lev 19:18b: "You shall love your neighbor as yourself."[38] As in Deuteronomy so here in Leviticus, the word "love" carries the concrete sense of willing and doing good, not feeling good. Now, however, the object of this love is not God but a particular human being. This human being is designated as *rēaʿ* in the Hebrew, as *plēsion* in the Greek of the Septuagint, and traditionally—though somewhat misleadingly—as "neighbor" in English.

The Hebrew noun *rēaʿ* allows of a wide range of meanings. From the broad and bland "another person" or "the other," it can carry the sense of the other human being(s) whom one meets and deals with on a regular basis, a fellow member of one's ethnic or religious community, a friend, a companion, a confidant, a beloved, or what we would call a neighbor.[39] For the precise meaning in any given case, we must look to the specific context. If we broaden our focus to Lev 19:16–18, verses that all contain similar social laws, the nouns that refer to the same or similar type of person as *rēaʿ* include "your kinsman," "your brother," "a member of your people," and "the sons of your people."[40] Hence, the most likely meaning of *rēaʿ* in Lev 19:18b is "a fellow member of the cultic community of Israel," "a fellow adult male who is a full 'citizen' of the Israelite people."[41] This "neighbor" in v 18b is implicitly distinguished in Leviticus 19 from the "resident alien" (*gēr* in v 34), a person who has certain rights in a community of which the individual is not a full member.[42] The very fact that the redactor of Leviticus 19 thinks it necessary to include a separate command to love the resident alien ("you shall love him as yourself") indicates that the resident alien is not included in Lev 19:18b under the category of "neighbor"(*rēaʿ*).[43]

To love this "neighbor" (i.e., *rēaʿ*) means to will good and do good to him, even if one feels some personal enmity toward him.[44] More specifically, in the immediate context, loving one's fellow Israelite means promoting, protecting, and, if need be, restoring that person's rights, honor, and status in the community. Thus, to love one's neighbor is to demonstrate and maintain solidarity among the full members of God's people, a pressing need during and after the Babylonian exile, when Leviticus probably received its final form.[45] This context helps us to understand the concluding phrase "as yourself [*kāmôkā*]." The point of this phrase is not the modern psychological insight (however true) that one cannot love another person unless one first loves oneself.[46] Nor is "as yourself" an abbreviated way of giving a reason or motivation for loving one's neighbor (e.g., the neighbor "who is like you" or "since he is like you"). Rather, "like you" modifies the verb "love" and states the measure or standard of the love to be given the neighbor. Since the neighbor is a full fellow-member of the cultic community of Israel—a full "citizen" just as much as the "you" who is addressed in the command—the neighbor must be accorded all the rights, privileges, support, and honor that the person addressed in the command expects and receives from the community.[47]

Interestingly, as is its wont in its treatment of the Pentateuch,[48] the Septuagint translates *rēaʿ* in Lev 19:18b as *plēsion*, literally, "one who is near," thus occasioning the common English translation of "neighbor."[49] Indeed, the Greek translation is taken by some commentators to mean that the Septuagint version of Lev 19:18b is commanding universal love of the human race. However, the immediate context of Lev 19:18b, even in the Greek translation (which speaks of "your brother" and "the sons of your people"), indicates that the point of reference remains a fellow member of the people of Israel, and not, as is sometimes claimed, human beings in general.[50]

A point that is at times missed by commentators on Mark 12:31 is that nothing in this text suggests that the Marcan (or the historical) Jesus is shifting the meaning of the Greek *plēsion* or the Hebrew *rēaʿ* so that it signifies something different from its original meaning in Lev 19:18b. All too often we automatically read into Mark 12:31 the different context and message of Luke 10:25–37. There the double command of love—and specifically the command to love one's neighbor—acts as a springboard for Luke's parable of the Good Samaritan. The parable itself ingeniously transforms the meaning of "neighbor" to signify both anyone in need (no matter what the person's race or religion) and then (in a clever twist at the end of the parable) anyone who shows active, practical compassion to the person in need. Nothing in the Marcan text intimates that the broadened Lucan meaning is present in Mark 12:28–34. Rather, in the context of a Jewish Jesus citing the Jewish Scriptures of Deuteronomy and Leviticus to a learned Jewish scribe within the precincts of the Jerusalem temple, the original meaning of *rēaʿ* (*plēsion*) in Lev 19:18b as "a fellow Israelite" is the natural one.[51] Only our knowledge of Luke's parable and our unconscious tendency to conflate different-though-similar Synoptic traditions (e.g., the command to love one's enemies and the Golden Rule) cause us to expand the sense of "neighbor" in Mark 12:31. This is an illegitimate move if our task is simply to exegete Mark 12:28–34 in order to grasp the message of Mark (and possibly that of the historical Jesus).[52]

The indisputably Jewish horizon of Jesus' citation of Deut 6:4–5 and Lev 19:18b is underlined by the exegetical technique that Jesus is apparently employing. In joining together two disparate commandments from two different books of the Pentateuch, Jesus is using a Jewish method of interpretation that the rabbis would later name *gĕzērâ šāwâ*.[53] This hermeneutical technique allowed a rabbi to bring together two different Scripture texts for mutual interpretation if both contained the same key word or phrase. To be sure, the formal term *gĕzērâ šāwâ*, as well as the rules governing its use and its combination with other hermeneutical rules, is found only later on in the rabbinic literature, starting with the Tosepta.[54] Still, apparently some form of the method was already in use in Jesus' day, as can be seen both from Jewish literature and from the NT, where Paul and the author of the Epistle to the Hebrews employ it in their writings.[55]

Thus, employing this technique of the *gĕzērâ šāwâ*, Jesus connects two disparate commandments from two different books of the Pentateuch on the grounds that both texts contain the phrase "and you shall love [someone]." Indeed, in coupling these two commandments, widely separated in space in successive books of the Pentateuch, Jesus shows a remarkable knowledge of the Hebrew text of the Mosaic Torah. For, in the entire corpus of the Jewish Scriptures, there are only four texts that contain the precise verb form *wěʾāhabtā* ("and you shall love . . .") + direct object of the person loved.[56] The two key texts are precisely the two that Jesus quotes: Deut 6:5 ("and you shall love the Lord . . .") and Lev 19:18b ("and you shall love your neighbor . . ."). The two other texts with this grammatical construction are simply echoes of the two major ones. Deut 11:1 ("and you shall love the Lord your God and keep his charge . . .") is merely a brief reprise of 6:5. Similarly, in Lev 19:34 ("and you shall love him [the resident alien] like yourself"), the redactor of Leviticus is consciously extending the law of love of neighbor in Lev 19:18b to cover the resident alien as well. Beyond these four texts, then, the verb form *wĕʾāhabtā* ("and you shall love . . .") + direct object of the person never occurs again in the entire corpus of the Jewish Scriptures. Seizing on this fact, Jesus uses the technique later known as the *gĕzērâ šāwâ* to exalt the two key commandments of love that share this extremely rare grammatical form. At the same time, Jesus reverses their order of appearance in the Pentateuch to make love of God the *first* commandment and love of neighbor the *second*, contrary to the order of the books of Leviticus and Deuteronomy. This may help explain Jesus' punctiliousness in pointedly announcing the numerical order of the two commandments.[57]

Yet this is not the whole story of Jesus' deceptively simple yet subtle teaching on the two commandments of love. That Jesus, despite his insistence on the order of "first" and "second," is nevertheless consciously binding the two different commandments together is emphasized by the conclusion of his reply to the scribe: "There is no other commandment greater than these two." Jesus thus creates an intriguing dialectic. Unlike a good deal of American theology toward the end of the last century, he avoids reducing love of God to the level of love of neighbor or even, worse still, collapsing love of God into love of neighbor. The two loves remain distinct and ordered: God first, neighbor second.[58] At the same time, Jesus joins these two loves closely together and sets them above every other commandment in the Torah. These two commandments, and presumably these two alone, are superior to and more important than any other Mosaic commandment.[59] To combine the two love commands as a unit superior to all other commands and yet, within this combination, to distinguish love of God as first and therefore as superior to love of neighbor, displays a remarkable and subtle balance on Jesus' part. But let us not get ahead of ourselves. To return to the perspective of the redactor of the Gospel: Mark's purpose, to extol Jesus as *the* authoritative teacher, is masterfully achieved.[60]

In Mark's presentation, Jesus' mastery is not lost on the scribe. As the second half of the pericope begins, the scribe enthusiastically acclaims Jesus as a teacher who has once again spoken well (*kalōs* in v 32),[61] an accolade that (the reader knows) repeats the approbation that the scribe silently gave to Jesus' reply to the Sadducees back in v 28. Mark may have even held back the respectful vocative "teacher" (*didaskale*, addressed by the scribe to Jesus) until this second round of conversation in order to indicate that the scribe, having had his own question skillfully answered, now publicly recognizes Jesus as *the* authoritative teacher. The scribe now becomes like an excited student who wants to show his teacher not only that he has understood the lesson but also that he can give it back in his own words and with his own insights added. At this point, the pericope becomes a true dialogue between scholars, the scribe modifying and thus applying Jesus' answer to the specific theological locus in which the two find themselves: the Jerusalem temple.[62]

The scribe's important modifications of Jesus' answer are threefold. First, in v 32, instead of simply parroting the first part of the *Shemaʿ*, known word for word by every pious Jew, the scribe underlines the all-too-relevant message contained in the *Shemaʿ*: monotheism. Using phrases and themes that occur in the surrounding context of Deuteronomy (e.g., Deut 4:35,39; 5:6–9; 6:14–15) as well as elsewhere in the Jewish Scriptures (Exod 8:6; 2 Sam 7:22; 1 Kgs 8:60; 2 Kgs 19:19; 2 Chr 33:13; Isa 37:20; 43:10; 44:6; 45:21), the scribe stresses the oneness of the true God; there is simply no other god in addition to him. While this may seem a case of exegeting the obvious, one should remember the theological locus of the dialogue: the Jerusalem temple. Whatever Mark may or may not know about Roman control of the temple from the fortress Antonia, his Passion Narrative shows that at least he knows that Jerusalem and therefore the temple were ultimately controlled by the pagan Romans. Whether one thinks of the Palestinian Jews of Jesus' day or the Gentile Christians of Mark's day, principled monotheists were a pitifully small group in a sea of polytheists, who dominated the politics, culture, and religion of the Mediterranean world. One need only think of the pagan temples in Caesarea Maritima, the Roman capital of Judea. The emphasis on monotheism, far from irrelevant or merely a later Christian catechetical device, is thus well situated geographically and theologically.[63]

The second modification of Jesus' teaching by the scribe (in v 33ab) involves abbreviating the command to love God ("the Lord our God" becomes "him" and the human faculties are reduced to three) and directly joining this command to the command to love one's neighbor. The two commandments are reduced in turn to two parallel infinitives ("and to love . . . and to love"), which are made coequally the subjects of the verb "is." What Jesus had indicated in his concluding statement in v 31c ("there is no other commandment greater than these [two]") is thus spelled out by the scribe. In other words, this second modification emphasizes the unity of the two commandments

of love. Their proper order ("first" . . . "second") is only tacitly intimated by
the order in which they are mentioned.

In the third and final modification, the scribe's midrash on Jesus' concluding statement (v 31c) specifies which commandments in particular are inferior to the two great commandments of love: the commandments governing
the sacrificial cult in the temple.[64] Once again, the scribe's interpretation is
locally as well as theologically conditioned. Some Marcan commentators
speak of a denigration or even rejection of temple sacrifice in 12:33c. On the
level of a possibly historical event ca. A.D. 30 or even on the level of 12:28–
34 as an independent oral tradition, "rejection" is too strong a word. From
the OT prophets to the polemics at Qumran, reform-minded Jews excori-
ated abuses in the sacrificial system of the temple for various reasons without rejecting sacrifices as such.[65] Nevertheless, the idea of the total rejection
and cessation of temple sacrifices may be intimated on the level of Mark's
redactional composition and theology. In the order of Mark's narrative, not
all that long after the scribe extols the double command of love above all
sacrifices (12:33), Jesus himself predicts the destruction of the temple and
hence the cessation of sacrifices in 13:1–2, a destruction that may be fore-
shadowed by the rending of the temple veil at Jesus' death (15:38).[66]

Far from being put out by the scribe's midrashic modifications, Jesus, paralleling the scribe's initial approbation of Jesus, expresses his own approbation of the scribe. Jesus judges that the scribe has interpreted and developed
Jesus' teaching in an intelligent, insightful way (nounechōs). Among all the
Streitgespräche (dispute stories) and Schulgespräche (scholastic dialogues)
of the Synoptics, this pericope alone is a true positive dialogue, a creative
give-and-take among two teachers of Torah.[67]

And yet . . . agreement with Jesus' teaching on the Mosaic Law, however
laudable and welcome amid all the attacks on Jesus in the temple, is not
enough—certainly not enough for Mark. From chap. 1 onward, Mark has
presented Jesus as the secret Messiah and Son of God who both proclaims
the imminent coming of God's kingdom and already begins to effect God's
kingly rule in word and deed. In agreeing with Jesus' teaching on the Law
but in going no further, the scribe has shown that he is "not far from the
kingdom of God."[68] This startling litotes is unparalleled in the NT. No
other person and no other thing in the NT are ever said to be "not far from
the kingdom of God" (ou makran ei apo tēs basileias tou theou).[69] The
point for Mark is that, for all his splendid qualities, the scribe, not unlike
the all-too-eager rich man portrayed in Mark 10:17–22, still lacks the one
essential thing (cf. Mark 10:21).[70] In the case of the scribe, the one essential thing would mean accepting into his own life Jesus' full message of the

kingdom coming yet present—which, for Mark, means in the end accepting Jesus himself as Messiah and Son of God. Ultimately, for Mark, monotheistic confession is true but incomplete without christological confession.

With that, the pericope proper comes to an ambiguous end in v 34c. This is, after all, the Gospel of stark, dark, laconic Mark. All that remains is for Mark to draw another "finish line," indicating that this spectacular positive demonstration of Jesus' teaching authority, publicly acknowledged by *one* Jewish scribe, has put an end to verbal attacks on Jesus by his opponents.[71] From now on (12:35–40), the Marcan Jesus goes on the attack against "the scribes"—notably in the plural.

In sum, our survey has brought into relief the tug-of-war between Mark's redactional theology and the tradition lying behind 12:28–34:[72]

(1) On the one hand, despite the recalcitrant nature of the tradition he has received, Mark skillfully adapts the material to his redactional purposes.

(a) Paradoxically, while Mark 12:28–34 is not itself a dispute story, it becomes the climax and conclusion of all the dispute stories in the entire Gospel as well as of the Jerusalem dispute stories in particular. From Mark 2:1 onward (the scribes being the opponents in 2:6), Jesus has been assailed by various hostile groups, all challenging his God-given authority to teach, forgive, or heal. Now, at the end of Jesus' public ministry and of all these individual conflicts—and now, on the threshold of the final conflict in the Passion Narrative—Jesus' teaching authority is not simply vindicated; it is positively extolled by none other than a Jewish scribe. This triumph may include an implicit apologetic vis-à-vis well-disposed Jews: Jesus' authoritative teaching is not some new, heterodox doctrine but rather the summation of all that is best in Israel's own tradition.[73]

(b) Not by accident, Jesus' triumph over the Jerusalem authorities is attested by a Jerusalem scholar in the temple precincts, along with an ominous reference to the love commandments' superiority to the temple's sacrificial cult, soon to be terminated.

(c) When one looks at Jesus' two responses to the scribe (vv 29–31 + v 34), one sees that in both cases Mark is at pains to show that Jesus is the superior, Jesus is the one in control. When the scribe asks what is the first commandment, Jesus decides to teach him the first *and* the second commandments. When the scribe paraphrases Jesus' answer intelligently, Jesus commends him in guarded fashion for not being far from the kingdom. While Mark 12:28–34 may be a friendly scholastic dialogue, it is not a dialogue among equals. Only one party enjoys the initiative and the upper hand.

(d) Indeed, despite the scribe's sincere agreement with and praise of Jesus, theologically he is still not where he should be. At the end of the pericope

(12:34c), Mark intimates that acceptance of Jesus' teaching on the Law is not enough to be actually *in* the kingdom of God. Accepting the proclamation of the kingdom involves in the end accepting the proclaimer himself as Messiah and Son of God.

(2) On the other hand, for all Mark's deft redaction, this pericope gives signs of not being Mark's creation out of whole cloth.

(a) As we have seen, this is the only time a single scribe, as opposed to the faceless group of "the scribes," takes the stage and finds a unique voice. This lone scribe is singular in more than the numerical sense, since his positive approach and still more positive reaction to Jesus are the exact opposite of the unrelievedly negative portrait of the scribes that Mark inculcates throughout his Gospel.

(b) That this lone scribe is indeed sincere in his intention and words has already been shown in the analysis of the pericope's cross-references (v 28c + 32b + 34a) and content. In the larger context of all the dispute stories in Mark, here silence *does* speak and absence *is* proof. For, consistently throughout the Marcan dispute stories, the hostility, malice, or hypocrisy of the opponents is highlighted in no uncertain terms either in Mark's narrative comments or in the words of the interlocutors themselves.[74] In this larger framework, the complete absence of any reference to the scribe's malicious intentions, his hypocrisy, his plan to trap Jesus, or his plotting to destroy Jesus says as much as the scribe's explicit praise of Jesus. We have here the very rare case of an early Christian tradition willing to portray positively a Jewish teacher who agrees with and praises Jesus, but who does not follow Jesus as a disciple (at least within the story).[75] We are not surprised to notice that, given the increasing polemics between Jews and Christians in the latter part of the 1st century, such a figure quickly disappears from the Synoptic tradition.

(c) Tied in with the unique nature of Jesus' interlocutor is the unique nature of the literary unit we have inspected. Insofar as it is a friendly exchange, Mark 12:28–34 is usually designated a *Schulgespräch*, that is, a "scholastic dialogue," an irenic conversation among teachers and/or students of the Law. Yet the specific scholastic dialogue found in Mark 12:28–34 has a quirky structure witnessed nowhere else in the Synoptic tradition of disputes or scholastic dialogues. Alongside the usual exchange between a Jewish authority asking Jesus a question and Jesus responding, we have a whole "second round" of dialogue. In this second round, the Jewish authority repeats Jesus' teaching approvingly even as he glosses it with his own interpretation, an interpretation that Jesus in turn basically approves, but with a final caveat. Nowhere else in any Synoptic conversation about the Law, whether hostile or friendly, do we have this back-and-forth *plus* back-and-forth movement, which truly mirrors what occurs in a friendly discussion among scholars (such events do actually happen). Thus, not only does Mark 12:28–34 stand over against some general tendencies of Mark's redactional theology; it also stands over against the literary form of dispute story and scholastic dialogue as seen in the rest of the Synoptic tradition.

(d) A final indication that Mark 12:28–34 is not simply Mark's own creation is that it focuses on the fundamental question of the proper place and interpretation of the Mosaic Law as a whole and in its parts. This is a question that does not absorb Mark in the way it absorbs Matthew and Luke–Acts—witness the total absence in Mark of the word "law" (*nomos*), along with the absence of the noun's various Greek derivatives.[76] To be sure, the answers Matthew and Luke–Acts give to the question of the theoretical place and practical observance of the Mosaic Law in the Christian church are quite different. But both Matthew and Luke–Acts appreciate the enormity of the question in principle and struggle at length to articulate a coherent solution.[77] No such concern or struggle is evinced by Mark, who has other theological fish to fry.

In conclusion, there is more than sufficient reason for holding that Mark 12:28–34, for all its Marcan redaction, contains pre-Marcan tradition. Since in tone, content, and intention it does not really fit with the conflict stories that precede it or with Jesus' attack on the scribes that follows it, the core of Mark 12:28–34 probably circulated originally as an isolated oral tradition. Considering the almost unique appearance of a positive portrait of a Jewish scribe agreeing with Jesus on legal questions and indeed praising him on his position, I think that the tradition is quite early—which pushes us toward the beginning of the first Christian generation (A.D. 30–70). This conclusion brings us to the further question: Does the tradition contained in Mark 12:28–34 come from the historical Jesus, or is it a creation stemming from the very early days of the Jewish-Christian church?

C. The Argument for the Historicity of Mark 12:28–34

1. *A Brief Articulation of the Argument*

In such a complicated question as whether the historical Jesus actually taught the double commandment of love, it is perhaps best to start with a brief enunciation of my argument in favor of historicity. Then I will fill in the details.[78]

In a nutshell, my argument is from discontinuity. In Mark 12:28–34, Jesus' teaching on the double commandment of love does four noteworthy things: (i) Jesus cites both Deut 6:4–5 and Lev 19:18b word for word (and not just a paraphrase, summary, or allusion). Remarkably, neither Deut 6:4–5 nor Lev 19:18b is ever cited word for word as a commandment of the Torah in either the rest of the OT or the Jewish intertestamental literature, including Philo, Josephus, and Qumran (apart from fragmentary manuscripts of Deuteronomy found in the caves). (ii) Jesus cites not just one of these pentateuchal texts but both of them, placed back to back. (iii) Even as he juxtaposes these two texts, Jesus explicitly orders them numerically, insisting that Deut 6:4–5 is the *first* commandment of all and that Lev 19:18b is the *second*. (iv) Jesus concludes this dialectic of combination yet numerical differentiation with an affirmation of the superiority of these two commandments over all other commandments: no other commandment is greater than these two.

As the logic of this argument makes evident, if no Jewish text before or during the time of Jesus does even the first of these four noteworthy things (i.e., cites either Deut 6:4–5 or Lev 19:18b word for word), then obviously no Jewish text of this period does the second, third, or fourth thing either. Thus, both the precise wording and the overall configuration of this teaching on the double commandment of love are unique to Jesus within the larger context of Jewish literature before or during his ministry. To be sure, one can find at times intimations or foreshadowings of Jesus' peculiar dialectic of love in pre-70 Jewish literature, but never the full fourfold form.

Even more startling is the discontinuity of Jesus' double commandment vis-à-vis the rest of the NT. Many Christians, if asked, would naturally suppose that this "signature" teaching of Jesus is repeated elsewhere in the NT. If by "this teaching of Jesus" we mean the teaching characterized by the four points previously listed, then the answer to the question of whether this teaching is repeated anywhere else in the NT is definitely no. On the one hand, Deut 6:4–5 is never cited word for word in the rest of the NT. Indeed, explicit references to human love for God are relatively rare in the NT outside the Gospels. The proper human relationship to God is more often expressed by such verbs as "believe," "know," and "obey." [79] On the other hand, Lev 19:18b is cited a few times, notably by Paul (Rom 13:9; Gal 5:14) and by the Epistle of James (2:8). But nowhere in the NT outside of Mark 12:28–34 parr. is Lev 19:18b directly joined to the deuteronomic command to love God, to say nothing of establishing a numerical order between the two commandments and putting them together above all other commandments.

Remarkably, Jesus' double command of love is likewise missing in action in a great deal of early Christian literature outside the NT.[80] The first

Christian echo of Jesus' joining of the two commandments is found in the *Didache*, and even there (*Did.* 1:2) we do not have the full citation of the two OT texts. As in Luke 10:27, the two commands in the *Didache* are contracted by using the verb "to love" only once; "the Lord your God" becomes "the God who made you"; and, finally, a negative form of the Golden Rule is appended for good measure. This is a prime example of the type of conflation and digest of Jesus' teachings produced by diligent Christian catechists. In his *Dialogue with Trypho* (*Dial.* 93.2), Justin Martyr likewise gives us a catechetical summary of what he explicitly identifies as a saying of "our Lord and Savior Jesus Christ." After alluding to Matthew's version of the Gospel story with terminology befitting Philo or Josephus ("in two commandments all justice and piety [*dikaiosynēn kai eusebeian*] are fulfilled"), Justin cites an abbreviated form of the two love commandments, with the telltale Lucan trait of a single use of the verb "to love."[81] In sum, there is a clear discontinuity between Jesus' double command of love (as presented in Mark 12:28–34 parr.) on the one hand and both Jewish and NT literature at the turn of the era on the other. Let us now flesh out this basic argument from discontinuity—in a sense, an argument from absence—by examining its various parts in detail.[82]

2. Discontinuity: The Old Testament

Especially for Christians who are so used to hearing Deut 6:4–5 and Lev 19:18b cited together in liturgy and homilies, it comes as a shock to realize that neither of these two texts—to say nothing of their combination—is ever cited again in the OT. Granted, one can speak of echoes or fragments of these two commands elsewhere in the OT, but the full text of either Deut 6:4–5 or Lev 19:18b must wait for Mark 12:28–34 to enjoy a complete literary reprise.

In Deuteronomy itself, which is one of the richest OT books in the theological use of the word "love," Deut 6:4–5 reverberates in a number of other passages, but is never repeated in full. Deut 10:12–13 comes closest when it commands Israel "to fear Yahweh your God, to walk in his ways, and to love him and to serve Yahweh your God with your whole heart and with your whole soul, to keep the commandments of Yahweh and his statutes." One notes immediately the equivalence for the Deuteronomist of loving, fearing, and serving Yahweh, which means in practice keeping his commandments. One sees also how a partial reprise of the totality formula ("with all your . . .") can easily be affixed to some other verb besides "love." In fact, sometimes it is this totality formula rather than the vocabulary of love that provides the reference back to Deut 6:4–5.

A prime example of this is the praise that the deuteronomistic historian heaps on the pious King Josiah when he claims that "there never was before him [i.e., Josiah] a king like him, who turned to Yahweh with all his heart, with all his soul, and with all his strength according to the whole Torah of Moses; and after him none arose like him" (2 Kgs 23:25). The triple form of the totality formula (heart, soul, and strength) is exactly that of Deut 6:5, though both the verb "to love" and the literary form of a commandment are lacking. Yet the addition in 2 Kgs 23:25 of "according to the whole Torah of Moses" is clearly a reference back to Deuteronomy—a fortiori in the case of King Josiah, who, just prior to this encomium, promulgates a rediscovered Torah scroll that many modern scholars identify as a primitive form of Deuteronomy (Deut 22:3–23:24). Other occurrences of this totality formula are scattered about the OT, but often the allusion to Deut 6:4–5 is vague at best.[83]

Similarly, the love command in Lev 19:18b is never repeated word for word in the rest of the OT. As already noted, the closest parallel is the extension of the love commandment to the resident alien (Lev 19:34). But nowhere in the OT outside of Lev 19:18b is anyone commanded by God to love his neighbor. In all this, one must remember the narrow focus of our inquiry. The OT has a great deal to say about love both human and divine. The love relationship between God and Israel is treated at length in the prophets, notably Hosea and Jeremiah, and is celebrated in the Psalms. Our precise question, though, is whether the commandments to love God and neighbor *in the wording* of Deut 6:4–5 and Lev 19:18b ever occur again in the OT. To that question the answer must be no.

This absence holds true of the deuterocanonical books of the OT (i.e., the Apocrypha) as well as of the protocanonical books (i.e., the Jewish Scriptures). We find some vague allusions to Lev 19:18b in Ben Sira, but neither the literary form nor the thought is that of the love command. Contrary to the leveling tendency of Lev 19:18b, Sir 13:1–23 reflects on how impossible it is to sustain an authentic friendship between the rich and people of lesser means. Hence, says Ben Sira, one should associate with one's socioeconomic equals. It is in the spirit of this sapiential pragmatism that Ben Sira remarks (13:14–15 in the Hebrew text): "All flesh loves its own kind, and every man the one who is like himself. All flesh stays close to its own kind, with his own kind a man associates." [84] For all his guardedness about Hellenistic culture, Ben Sira reflects here the typical Greek ethos of reciprocity among friends who are social equals.[85]

This ethic of friendship is seen in Ben Sira's delightful essay on table etiquette (31:12–32:13). Admonishing his students not to be greedy and grasping at a banquet, Ben Sira directs in 31:15a: "Realize that your companion [at table] feels as you do." The Hebrew at this point has a slight echo of Lev 19:18b in that it reads literally: "Know your neighbor [r^ck] as your own soul [$npšk$]."[86] The second half of the verse (31:15b) then strikes a note reminiscent of the reciprocity ethic found in the Golden Rule: ". . . and bear in mind what you yourself hate." A similar message of equality and reciprocity among friends of the same social level is given to the person presiding at a banquet (32:1): with the guests "be to them as one of themselves."

A better chance for espying a reference to the command to love one's neighbor may be found in Sir 17:12–14 (or: vv 10–12), where Ben Sira clearly refers to the giving of the covenant and the commandments at Sinai. In v 14b, Ben Sira sums up God's commands to the Israelites by saying: "he [the Lord] gave commandments to them, each concerning his neighbor." While a reference to Lev 19:18b in particular is possible, the general reference to giving commandments about one's neighbor may point instead to the second table of the Law, that is, the social commandments of the Decalogue.[87] Indeed, some would see in the two halves of v 14 ("and he said to them, 'Take care to avoid every kind of injustice,' and he gave commandments to them, each concerning [his] neighbor") an allusion to the two tables of the Decalogue, but that is perhaps stretching a good point one table too far.

The final echo of the love command in Ben Sira is intriguing in that it concerns not a social equal but a slave (7:21): "Cherish an understanding slave as life itself; and do not deny him his freedom."[88] In this case, the reason for cherishing or loving a person as life itself (or as oneself) resides in the master's esteem for a wise slave, whom the master makes (in a minimal sense) a social equal by granting him his freedom. In sum, then: with his meshing of Hebrew wisdom and Hellenistic ethics, Ben Sira tends to focus love or concern for another on specific groups or individuals in society. While his ethical vision can encompass within one essay the various duties that a person owes the different strata of society, there is no single sweeping command of love à la Lev 19:18b.

Thus, we find no citations of Deut 6:4–5 and Lev 19:18b in the later books in the OT—to say nothing of the commandments' juxtaposition and enumeration as first and second. However, we do find at times in the OT a general tendency to summarize the obligations of the Law in a short list.[89] Instances include Hos 2:19–20 (2:21–22 in the MT); 12:6 (12:7 in the MT); Mic 6:8; Ps 15:2–5; and Zech 7:9–10. These lists vary in content, though justice, mercy, and honesty in dealing with one's neighbor occur frequently. Interestingly, especially in the prophets and the psalms, these lists appear in a context of temple cult or ritual actions. The point is often made, in one way or another, that what God primarily seeks from Israel is sincere worship of and obedience to him, which expresses itself especially in justice and mercy toward one's neighbor. With the hindsight of Jesus' teaching on the double commandment of love, we might, with a little imagination, intuit the outlines of his approach to the Law in these OT texts. However, this is to do theology through a rearview mirror. What one can say is that the teaching of Jesus the Jew on the double commandment does not come out of nowhere. It has been nurtured by tendencies already at work in the OT. We will now see how some of these tendencies develop in various streams of Judaism around the turn of the era, foreshadowing but never clearly articulating Jesus' yoking of Deut 6:4–5 and Lev 19:18b as the first and second commandments of the Law.

3. Discontinuity: Absence in the Dead Sea Scrolls

When we turn from the urban and urbane Ben Sira to the Essene sectarians, we notice an intriguing difference. Exhortations to love, care, and concern abound, but are limited to the "brothers," the true Israelites who are members of the sect. At first sight, it seems promising that various commands from the bundle of social obligations in Lev 19:17–18 are at times cited. Quite curious, therefore, is the fact that, while other commands from Lev 19:17–18 are repeated almost word for word, we never find an exact word-for-word citation of Lev 19:18b. Instead, Lev 19:18b appears only in allusions or in adaptations of the text to the sect's perspective. A prime example of this strange phenomenon is CD 9:2, which cites the first part of Lev 19:18 (i.e., v 18a) word for word: "You shall not take vengeance on and you shall not hold a grudge against the sons of your people." At that point, the author of the *Damascus Document* breaks off without completing the verse with v 18b: "and you shall love your neighbor as yourself." There almost seems to be a perverse determination to cite the surrounding text while omitting the love commandment. Just a little further on (CD 9:7–8), Lev 19:17b is cited: "You shall firmly rebuke your neighbor [rēʿêkā] and shall not incur sin because of him." [90] Yet, despite the appearance of the vocabulary of rēaʿ (which is not in MT Lev 19:17b), Lev 19:18b is not taken up. The closest the *Damascus Document* comes to a direct citation is within a lengthy list of community obligations in CD 6:14–7:2. Sandwiched in between the obligations "to set apart the holy things" and "to strengthen the hand of the oppressed, the poor, and the resident alien" is the command (CD 6:20–21) that "each man is to love his brother as himself." That is, each member of the Essene community is to love his fellow Essenes as himself. [91]

Indeed, although every chapter of Leviticus is referenced in the nonbiblical documents at Qumran, Lev 19:18b is absent from all these texts. This absence of Lev 19:18b in the nonbiblical writings is compounded by an odd accident. Although sixteen manuscripts of Leviticus itself are preserved among the Dead Sea finds, not one fragment contains Lev 19:18b.[92] No one doubts that the manuscripts of Leviticus originally contained our sought-for text. Decay simply caused by accident a strange symmetry between citations of Leviticus in the documents created by the sect and the biblical scrolls preserved by the sect.

The same strange phenomenon of absence holds true of Deut 6:4–5 in Qumran's nonbiblical scrolls as well. Even though the *Rule of the Community* from Cave 1 (1QS) contains a detailed ritual of a renewal of the covenant, complete with blessings and curses à la Deuteronomy, the *Shemaʿ* of Deut 6:4–5 is never cited. The same absence is attested in the other sectarian documents. However, we are more fortunate when it comes to the thirty-three Deuteronomy scrolls numbered among the Dead Sea finds.[93] Here the text of Deut 6:4–5 is present, though, as fate would have it, in fragmentary form. No one manuscript of Deuteronomy from Qumran contains the whole of Deut 6:4–5 without some lacuna.[94]

With no direct citation of Deut 6:4–5 or Lev 19:18b in any of the nonbiblical scrolls, it follows logically that we cannot find at Qumran a direct parallel to Jesus' juxtaposition of the two great love commands. Yet one could argue that the *Rule of the Community* (*serek hayyaḥad*) is not without some hint or foreshadowing of Jesus' double command.[95] To espy this foreshadowing, though, we must broaden the focus of our hermeneutical lens to take in the larger flow of thought in column 1 of the *Rule*. The opening words of the *Rule* (preserved in fragmentary form) speak of the community's obligation "to seek God with all one's heart and with all one's soul . . . and to love everything that he has chosen . . . and to love all the sons of light" (1QS 1:1–2,3–4,9). Granted, these obligations are scattered in a much longer list of duties, including the command to hate all the sons of darkness (1QS 1:10). Still, in the opening declaration of the basic obligations of the members of the "new covenant" at Qumran, we find at the very beginning of the *Rule* an obligation to seek God, enunciated with an echo of Deut 6:5 ("with all one's heart and with all one's soul"). Moreover, while all sorts of obligations separate this primordial duty to seek God in lines 1–2 from the obligation to love all the sons of light in line 9, this reference to loving the sons of light is the first time that the verb "to love" is used with persons as the direct object in the *Rule*.[96] However shadowy it may be, one may perceive a certain intimation of Jesus' double command in the basic commands given to "the sons of light"—the obligation of love being restricted, naturally, to the members of the Qumran community

To be sure, these "sightings" of the double command of love are intimations at best, intuited by us because we know Jesus' teaching in Mark 12:29–31. The fact remains that Jesus' dense, laconic articulation of the double command of love, with Deut 6:4–5 and Lev 19:18b cited word for word, is found nowhere at Qumran.

4. *Discontinuity: Absence in the Old Testament Pseudepigrapha*

Foreshadowings and intimations of Jesus' double command can also be found in the collection of nonbiblical Jewish material from the turn of the era that scholars vaguely label "OT Pseudepigrapha," although direct citations of Deut 6:4–5 and Lev 19:18b are again lacking.[97] A prime candidate for such foreshadowing is the *Book of Jubilees*, which did not originate at Qumran, though multiple copies of the work have been found there.[98] In *Jubilees*, when Abraham delivers his farewell address (in the typical genre of a testament) to his various sons and grandchildren, he starts by listing a number of basic commands. This rambling list begins (20:2): "that they should guard the way of the Lord so that they might do righteousness and each might love his neighbor."[99] This list then goes on at great length, enjoining circumcision and emphasizing in particular the avoidance of fornication, pollution, impurity, and idolatry. Despite the long and meandering nature of this catalogue, one cannot help being struck by the prominence at the beginning of the list of the one basic obligation to adhere to the Lord, which is followed almost immediately by a clear echo of Lev 19:18b, though the key phrase "as yourself" is lacking. Likewise lacking at the beginning of the list is an allusion to Deut 6:4–5; there is no mention of loving the Lord with all one's heart. It is only later on in the list, amid a number of other exhortations, that Abraham commands his offspring "to love the God of heaven." This late reference to loving God, sandwiched in between warnings against impurity and idolatry, is followed immediately by the blanket injunction "to be joined to all he [God] commands." There is therefore no sense in this catalogue that the commandments placed at the beginning of the list are essentially greater than those mentioned later.

A similar, though shorter, list of obligations is found in *Jub.* 7:20, where Noah gives his grandsons various commandments, including that "each one love his neighbor." Again, "like himself" is lacking, and there is no mention in the immediate context of loving God. Finally, a farewell address of Isaac to Esau and Jacob begins with a generic exhortation to righteousness and uprightness. But its main focus is the command to love one's brother (36:4). Within this context appears a brief enunciation of the command to fear and worship God (36:7), but this is quickly followed by a repetition of the command to love one's brother (36:8).[100]

Thus, in both the Dead Sea Scrolls and *Jubilees*, what we find is a certain "seedbed" or intimation of what will come in Jesus' double command, but nothing more. Another type of foreshadowing that we see in these texts is the growing tendency to summarize the commandments of the Law in certain key obligations, with obedience to God and/or love for fellow members of the community (however narrowly defined) placed early on in the lists.[101] Hence, while Jesus' double command is new in its formulation, conciseness, and insistence on the superiority of the two commandments of love to all other commandments, it is not entirely bereft of precursors within Palestinian Judaism at the turn of the era.

At this point in the argument, many commentators would insist on spending a great deal of time on another literary corpus usually placed under the rubric of OT Pseudepigrapha, namely, the *Testaments of the Twelve Patriarchs*.[102] This collection of pseudepigraphic deathbed exhortations of the twelve sons of Jacob (= the twelve patriarchs) has been championed by some scholars as the prime example of a genuine Jewish parallel to the double command in Mark 12:28–34.[103] For a number of reasons, I consider this claim wrongheaded.

First of all, the date and provenance of the *Testaments* are highly debatable. The Greek manuscripts on which most of our knowledge of these works must depend all date from the medieval or modern period.[104] Second, and more important, the *Testaments* display clear evidence of Christian authorship of or influence on the final form of the text. The extent of this Christian authorship or influence is debated among scholars; positions range from maximalist to minimalist. Third, the problem of just how much Christian intervention there is in the *Testaments* is compounded by the fact that a good deal of the moral exhortations permeating the *Testaments* is of a generic Stoic type. Such brand-X Stoic moralism would be at home in either Jewish or Christian writings of Late Antiquity. Hence, while one can argue that a large amount of the material in the *Testaments* is not specifically Christian, that argument cuts both ways: a large amount of the material is not specifically Jewish either. From the NT through the Fathers of the Church down to present-day homilies, a good deal of general Christian moral exhortation could just as easily be labeled Jewish (or humanistic) as Christian. On this point, I am inclined to agree with the great scholar of the *Testaments*, Marinus de Jonge, who insists that the generic Stoic moralism of the *Testaments* does not automatically favor Jewish rather than Christian composition.[105]

In sum, granted the late date of our manuscripts, the obvious Christian interpolations, and the generic nature of the parenesis, one must treat the *Testaments* as they stand today as Christian compositions.[106] To be sure, Jewish traditions and in some cases Jewish documents lie behind the *Testaments* as we have them. That a "testaments of the patriarchs" tradition existed in Judaism around the turn of the era is made likely by the Aramaic fragments of a Levi document (plus one fragment of a Naphtali document) found at Qumran.[107] This *Aramaic Levi* is not the *Testament of Levi* as we know it in its present form; indeed, it is not even labeled a testament. Still, *Aramaic Levi,* as well as other similar fragments found at Qumran, makes it probable that there was a "testament tradition" in late Second Temple Judaism that may have served as the ultimate matrix for our present *Testaments of the Twelve Patriarchs.*[108] However, short of new manuscript discoveries, we cannot know the precise nature and extent of the Jewish traditions underlying our *Testaments.* Once we catalogue the *Testaments of the Twelve Patriarchs* as primarily Christian documents, using them as a source of or parallel to Jesus' teaching on the double commandment of love from the Second Temple period is untenable.

Nevertheless, to be on the safe side, let us for a moment play the devil's advocate. Let us suppose, for the sake of argument, that scholars like Jürgen Becker are correct and that we can discover the layers of Jewish material underlying our present *Testaments*—a feat de Jonge considers impossible.[109] Let us further suppose that the moral exhortations that show no clear Christian content are Jewish traditions from around the turn of the era. Can we then, at least, find exact parallels to or sources of Jesus' teaching?

The answer is no. Nowhere in the *Testaments* do we find any teaching that possesses the constellation of the four distinguishing characteristics that we have isolated in Mark 12:28–34.[110] To begin with, nowhere in the *Testaments* is either Deut 6:4–5 or Lev 19:18b cited fully and explicitly. To be sure, general exhortations to love God and one's neighbor (or, more frequently, to love one's brother or one another) are at times found back to back.[111] But these two obligations usually appear in long lists of various commandments and are sometimes separated from each other.[112] Moreover, in keeping with the testamentary genre, these exhortations or commands are always the directives issued by one of the patriarchs to his children, never a command spoken directly by God to all Israel.[113] More to the point, love of God and love of neighbor are never presented as the *first* and *second* commandments of the Law, as the two commandments superior to all other commandments, or as some sort of summary of the whole Law (as Matthew will make them). Thus, even if we were to grant that the moral exhortations in the *Testaments* go back to the time of Jesus, we still would not have a true source of or parallel to the four-part configuration that makes Jesus' teaching unique. We would rather have, as at Qumran and in *Jubilees*, a foreshadowing or intimation of what was to come. Personally, though, when it comes to the *Testaments*, I doubt that we have even that.

5. Discontinuity: Absence in Philo and Josephus

We have glimpsed some foreshadowings and intimations of Jesus' double command in the corpus of the Dead Sea Scrolls and *Jubilees*. Yet, for a sustained attempt to summarize the Law in two basic duties, one to God and one to our fellow humans, we must turn to the philosophical mind-set of Greek culture.[114] In the Western Diaspora, we find a number of Greek-speaking Jewish intellectuals who take over and adapt Greek philosophical and rhetorical traditions in order to present Israelite teaching on the Law in a manner intelligible and attractive to Hellenistic minds. Already in the classical Greek writings of Aristophanes and Demosthenes as well as of the philosophers, there was a tendency to sum up human obligations toward the gods and toward one's fellow humans as *eusebeia* ("reverence," "piety") on the one hand and *dikaiosynē* ("justice," "righteousness") on the other.[115] One can trace this long-lived tradition down to the Stoic Epictetus and beyond. Granted, this philosophical model was not always presented in the same way or with the same precise vocabulary. For instance, Aristotle and some other philosophers subordinated *eusebeia* to *dikaiosynē* as the grand virtue.

Not surprisingly, Greek-speaking Jewish writers preferred the two-part pattern. That Diaspora Jews were summarizing the commandments of the Law under the two categories of *eusebeia* and *dikaiosynē* as early as the 2d century B.C. is clear from the *Letter of Aristeas*.[116] For example, in *Ep Arist.* §131, "our lawgiver" (Moses) is said to have given the Jews commandments regarding *eusebeia* and *dikaosynē*. So intent is the author on bringing all the pentateuchal laws under this twofold rubric that even the kosher food laws are interpreted as an expression of *dikaiosynē* (*Ep. Arist.* §168–71). Clearly, for the sake of presenting the Jewish Law as an ordered, philosophical system, a Greek intellectual grid is being imposed on the variegated commandments of the Torah.[117]

Within Hellenistic Judaism, Philo may have been especially attracted to this sort of bipartite summation of obligations because he was the first major Jewish thinker to reflect at length on the Decalogue, devoting a whole treatise to the subject. In *De decalogo* (*On the Decalogue*), Philo tries, as a pedagogical technique, to subordinate various individual commandments to one specific commandment of the Decalogue, thus creating a coherent system of Jewish legal/moral teaching in the Greek mode. The natural division of the Decalogue into two tables—the prior commandments dealing with duties to God, the latter dealing with duties to one's fellow Israelites—provided a perfect opening for Philo to cap his Jewish-Greek synthesis with the traditional Greek pair of virtues, reverence and justice.[118] However, while Philo regularly uses *eusebeia* (sometimes in tandem with *hosiotēs* ["holiness"]) for duties to God, he often substitutes *philanthrōpia* ("love of humanity") for *dikaiosynē* for duties to humans, though the two nouns can occur together.

Perhaps the best known text in which Philo summarizes all moral obligations under two headings is *De specialibus legibus* (*On the Special Laws*) 215 §63. There we are told that above all the individual virtues studied in the Jewish Law stand the two highest "summaries," "principles," or "chief points" (*kephalaia*, literally, "little heads").[119] It is noteworthy that, precisely in this key statement, Philo says that the first summary heading is "reverence and holiness" (*eusebeias kai hosiotētos*) and the second is "love of humanity and justice" (*philanthrōpias kai dikaiosynēs*). Thus, despite his emphasis on the two-part structure of the Law, Philo feels no need to reduce everything to two unchangeable words or formulas. In fact, Philo varies his language from passage to passage, though *eusebeia* and *philanthrōpia* remain his favorite nouns to summarize humanity's twofold obligation. Clearly, in such passages as the one in *On the Special Laws* §63, Philo's usual two-part summary of the Law is not, strictly speaking, a summary in terms of two types of *love*, but rather of reverence and philanthropy.

There are, however, a few rare passages in which Philo does summarize these two key Greek virtues as two types of love.[120] As one might expect, these passages are found in the larger context of his discussion of the Decalogue. Curiously, it is precisely as Philo berates those who pay attention to only one table of the Decalogue, either duties to God or duties to humans (*On the Decalogue* 22 §109–10), that he uses two compound adjectives to describe both sets of duties in terms of two types of love—a combination that is unusual for him. People who devote all their time to serving God and who thus ignore their fellow humans are *philotheoi* ("loving God"), while those who make the opposite mistake are *philanthrōpoi* ("loving humans"). Tellingly, Philo speaks of those who have just one of these attributes as having reached the goal of "virtue" (*aretē*) only halfway; one must strive to attain the goal with both virtues. Clearly, Philo's focus here is on a combination of two virtues that encompass all human obligations as contained in the Decalogue, not on a combination of the two particular commandments of Deut 6:4–5 and Lev 19:18b, neither of which stands in the Decalogue.

The other passage in Philo that comes close to the double commandment of *love* in Mark 12:28–34 likewise uses two compound adjectives. But here Philo speaks not of humanity's obligations in general but rather of the sterling character of one specific individual, Moses. In his *De vita Mosis* (*The Life of Moses*) 2.31 §163, Philo depicts Moses on Mt. Sinai, conversing with God as the riotous sounds of idolatry in the Israelite camp below reach his ears. Philo tells us that Moses was unsure whether to leave God's presence to restore order to the camp; he felt torn because he was both *theophilēs* ("one who loves God") and *philanthrōpos* ("one who loves humanity"). God's command to descend resolves the issue. Once again, the context for the two adjectives summarizing two basic obligations is the Decalogue, not the two commandments that Jesus cites and that lie outside the Decalogue. Perhaps more significant, though, one begins to notice a particular characteristic of Jesus' teaching on the double commandment that ties him more closely to Qumran and *Jubilees* than to *Aristeas* or Philo. Drawing upon Stoic moral philosophy, *Aristeas* and Philo naturally employ abstract nouns and adjectives to speak of one's obligations toward God or humans. Jesus stands squarely in the Jewish-Palestinian tradition that echoes the various commandments of the Pentateuch by speaking of obligations in terms of verbs, whether they are future, imperative, or infinitive in form.[121]

It is also telling that Philo, for all his commentaries on individual laws of the Pentateuch, including some laws in Leviticus 19, never explicitly cites or comments on Lev 19:18b. One is left wondering why. One possible explanation is that, within Philo's larger vision, which owes much to middle Platonism and Stoicism, love of one's fellow human beings is relativized by the mystic's desire for union with the divine.[122] The ultimate goal of Philo's religious-philosophical program is the mystical ascent of the individual soul to God. The union that the mystic strives for is understood in terms not of *agapē* but of *erōs*, the word Philo uses to express a passionate spiritual love of the transcendent. In this context, concern for one's neighbor and for the larger community is an obligation that certainly must be met. But neighbors and human communities belong to the world below with its distracting needs and desires, impeding the vision of God. Fellow humans may be useful in the preliminary stage of one's ascent to God, but ultimately they must be left behind.

In addition, while *philanthrōpia* ("love of humans") demands our concern and care for those around us, it is carefully restricted to those who are worthy of our love. There can be no love of sinners, for the wise man must not be endangered by contact with the enemies of virtue. Indeed, the wise man should keep himself at a distance from the common herd of people, with their tendency toward evil. Strange to say, while Philo puts firm restrictions on the wise man's involvement with other people, he extends *philanthrōpia* to animals and plants as members of the natural order that God created. One begins to sense the limitations of *philanthrōpia* in Philo's system. In fact, when *philanthrōpia* comes into conflict with *dikaiosynē* ("justice"), *philanthrōpia* must give way, lest the order of justice in society be subverted. In the end, Philo's yoking of reverence and philanthropy looks less like the double command of love than a first glance would suggest.

Not surprisingly, when it comes to summarizing obligations under the headings of "reverence" and "justice," Josephus continues down the road trodden by Philo. Naturally, the historian Josephus does not engage in the lengthy philosophical disquisitions about the Decalogue and the whole Law that we find in Philo. Nevertheless, Josephus reflects the tendency of Hellenistic Judaism to subsume all human duties under two headings. Unlike Philo, though, he holds fast to the traditional Greek nomenclature of reverence (*eusebeia*) and justice (*dikaiosynē*). In this, he may be rejecting, at least implicitly, Aristotle's subordination of *eusebeia* to *dikaiosynē*. Still, as with Philo so with Josephus, scholars search—in my opinion, fruitlessly—for some passage that will parallel Jesus' double commandment. A few texts at first seem promising, but ultimately disappoint. For instance, in his discussion of the Essenes, Josephus' description of Essene ritual appears for an instant to come close to Jesus' enumeration of the two main obligations of the Law.[123] However, when we read the whole text, our hopes are dashed. Josephus tells us (*J.W.* 2.8.7 §139–40) that, at the time of an Essene's entrance into the community, the candidate swears with fearful oaths *first* [*prōton*] to reverence [*eusebēsein*] the divinity, *then* [*epeita*] to observe justice in his dealings with humans. Unfortunately for parallel-hunters, Josephus does not stop here. He continues his second point ("then") with further obligations, which include "always to hate the unjust and to fight together with the just." This is not exactly Jesus' second command of love. More to the point, neither of Josephus' two main obligations employs the vocabulary of love. In the end, what remains especially remarkable in all this philosophical systematizing of the Law is that neither Philo nor Josephus ever quotes Deut 6:4–5 or Lev 19:18 word for word.[124]

What is the relevance of all this to Jesus' double commandment of love? In recent decades, a good number of scholars have followed the approach taken by Klaus Berger: one should see in Diaspora Judaism's summation of the Law in terms of *eusebeia* and *dikaiosynē* (or *philanthrōpia*) the true historical source of the tradition of the double commandment found in Mark 12:28–34.[125] In the light of our survey of relevant parallels, I think that this approach is misguided. Whether they are the documents composed at Qumran and *Jubilees* or the works of Philo and Josephus, a major difference between all these supposed parallels and Mark 12:28–34 holds firm. None of these writings, from Palestine or from the Diaspora, contains the four distinguishing characteristics of Jesus' double command. None of them (i) explicitly cites Deut 6:4–5 and Lev 19:18b word for word, (ii) joins these two texts back to back, (iii) puts them in numerical order as first and second, and (iv) states that no other commandment is greater than these two. If even one of these four characteristics of Jesus teaching was absent from the supposed Jewish parallels, we might point out a certain amount of discontinuity. When instead we find that the entire constellation of these four characteristics, the entire *Gestalt*, of Jesus' teaching on the double commandment is lacking in any and all of these Jewish parallels, then the argument from discontinuity becomes practically irrefutable.

6. *Discontinuity: Absence in the Early Rabbis*

What if we broaden our search for Jewish parallels to the time after Jesus—to the time, strictly speaking, after Second Temple Judaism, which ends in A.D. 70? Even in the early rabbinic literature—the first example of which is the Mishna, redacted ca. A.D. 200—we find at best scattered citations of Deut 6:4–5 or Lev 19:18b. Nowhere are they cited together, to say nothing of the other distinguishing characteristics of Jesus' teaching in Mark 12:29–31.

Sometimes, in search of some structural parallel to Mark 12:28–34, modern scholars will point to the Jewish tendency, seen already in different ways in Palestinian and Diaspora Judaism of the pre-70 period, to summarize commandments under some general principle or rubric. In rabbinic Judaism, such an overarching principle, topic, rule, or norm for many commandments is called a *kĕlāl*.[126] However, none of the rabbinic examples cited by scholars really parallels what Jesus does in Mark 12:28–34. The early rabbis speak of "a" *kĕlāl* or "a great" *kĕlāl*, under which a certain number of similar commandments are subsumed.[127] They do not speak of "the" one *kĕlāl* that summarizes all other commandments in the Law or serves as a grand principle from which all other commandments of the Law can be derived. Rather, under a general principle (*kĕlāl*), a number of related commandments can be listed, but there are different principles for different areas of the Torah. No one *kĕlāl* can cover or summarize everything in the Law.

This point is often forgotten when modern scholars highlight the first and probably best-known example of a citation-with-comment of Lev 19:18b to be found in early rabbinic literature, namely, the commentary on Leviticus called *Sipra*. Reflecting on Lev 19:18b, Rabbi Aqiba is presented as declaring: "This is a great general rule [*kĕlāl*] in the Torah." [128] In evaluating this text as a supposed parallel to Mark 12:28–34 parr., a number of considerations are important, yet often neglected. First, *Sipra* as it stands has undergone a number of stages of tradition and redaction; the basic core of the work seems to go back to the second half of the third century A.D. [129] We have no Jewish commentary on Lev 19:18b before that period—and certainly none from the time of Jesus. [130] Second, the Hebrew of Aqiba's widely quoted pronouncement (*zeh kĕlāl gādôl battôrâ*) is properly translated: "This is *a* great [or: important] general rule in the Law." All too often modern commentators supply a definite article that is not in the Hebrew text (reading *hakkĕlāl* instead of *kĕlāl*), so that the quotation becomes: "This is *the* general rule in the Law." Inserting the definite article introduces a NT slant into a rabbinic text that does not seek *the* one grand principle from which the whole Law derives or on which it depends. [131] Third, prima facie evidence that Aqiba's statement about Lev 19:18b is not meant to be the one grand principle of the Torah is the fact that his declaration is immediately followed in *Sipra* by the contradictory opinion of Rabbi Ben Azzai. Ben Azzai holds that a greater general rule can be found in Gen 5:1: "This is the book of generations of man ['*ādām*, i.e., humanity] on the day God created man; in the image of God he created him." [132] Remarkably, this disagreement between Aqiba and Ben Azzai is allowed to pass without comment, and *Sipra* proceeds immediately to treat Lev 19:19. In fact, Aqiba's view of Lev 19:18b is never taken up again and discussed anywhere else in early rabbinic literature. It hardly seems likely, then, that Aqiba was understood to be declaring that a half-verse of Leviticus was *the* one grand principle on which the whole Law depended, from which the whole Law could be deduced, or by which the whole Law could be summarized. The upshot of all this is that, even apart from the fact that *Sipra* was written centuries later than Mark's Gospel, Aqiba's comment on Lev 19:18b is entirely different in range and purpose from Jesus' double commandment of love in Mark 12:28–34.

It may well be that this misinterpretation of Aqiba's statement stems from a Christian reading of his words—a Christian reading that derives not from Mark 12:28–34 but rather from Matthew's reworking of Mark in Matt 22:34–40. It is Matthew and Matthew alone, perhaps echoing early rabbinic discussions, who adds at the end of his version of the story (22:40): "on these two commandments hang the whole Law and the prophets." The question of whether "hang on" means "derivable from," "reducible to," or "summarized by" is irrelevant to our purpose.[133] The rabbinic-sounding conclusion in Matt 22:40 is a redactional addition by Matthew; it tells us nothing about the teaching of the historical Jesus.

In the end, though, even if one inserted the definite article into Aqiba's declaration, it would make little difference for our overall quest. In *Sipra* in particular and in the early rabbinic literature in general, we never find most of the distinguishing characteristics of Jesus' teaching: placing Deut 6:4–5 and Lev 19:18b back to back, enumerating them as first and second, and claiming that no other commandment is greater than these two. In NT exegesis, finding parallels is important. Noticing differences is just as important.

7. *Discontinuity: Absence in the Rest of the New Testament*

It is surprising enough to most people that the double command of love is found nowhere in the OT, intertestamental literature, or in early rabbinic writings. What is more surprising, perhaps astounding, to Christians is that Jesus' double command (as found in Mark 12: 28–34 parr.) is paralleled in no other text in the NT. In a strange "parallel" to the Jewish material of the pre-70 period, the rest of the NT fails to meet almost all of the four distinguishing characteristics of Jesus' teaching. I say "almost all" because, in a few cases in the NT, the first characteristic (i.e., word-for-word citation of the text of Deut 6:4–5 and Lev 19:18b) is partially paralleled. This complicated statement—reflecting a complicated situation—needs some explanation.

On the one hand, Deut 6:4–5 is never explicitly cited again in the NT. There are allusions to the text, but, curiously, the most significant allusion is an early Christian attempt to develop high christology by "splitting the atom" of the *Shemaʿ*.[134] In 1 Cor 8:6, Paul (or the tradition he has learned) divides up the three key words in the *Shemaʿ*: "Lord [in Greek, *kyrios*]," "God [in Greek, *theos*]," and "one [in Greek, *heis*]." Paul distinguishes and yet unites these various terms to express the relationship of "God" (the Father, designated as *theos*) and the "Lord" (Jesus Christ, designated as *kyrios*) to the events of both creation ("all things") and salvation ("we" Christians):

"But for us [Christians] there is

[i]	[ii]
one God the Father,	*one Lord* Jesus Christ,
from whom all things [exist] and	*through* whom all things [exist] and
for whom we [Christians exist], and	*through* whom we [Christians exist]"

This is an intriguing Christian midrash on the *Shemaʿ*, to be sure, but hardly a direct citation. One can find other echoes of the "one God" or "one Lord" terminology elsewhere in the NT (e.g., Eph 4:6 + 4:5), but nothing comes close to an explicit citation.

On the other hand, Lev 19:18b, unlike Deut 6:4–5, is explicitly cited a few times in the NT.

(1) Apart from Mark 12:28–34 parr., Matthew inserts Lev 19:18b into two traditions he has received, one from Q and one from Mark:

(i) As a preface to the Q tradition commanding love of enemies (Matt 5:44b ‖ Luke 6:27b), Matthew adds by way of contrast Lev 19:18b (Matt 5:43b): "You shall love your neighbor." [135] Matthew drops the final words "as yourself" from this command so as to make room for an antithetical statement within v 43: ". . . and you shall hate your enemy." One can easily see Matthew's reason for dropping "as yourself": it would make no sense to say "you shall hate your enemy as yourself." Perfect balance between the two parts of v 43 demands that "as yourself" be omitted.[136] Being a lover of antitheses and contrast, Matthew then uses v 43 as the first half of the last of his six antitheses (5:21–48) at the beginning of the Sermon on the Mount. The result is that vv 43–44 serve as the climactic member of Matthew's antithetical series: "You have heard that it was said, 'You shall love our neighbor' and you shall hate your enemy; but I say to you, love your enemies."

(ii) The second of Matthew's redactional insertions of Lev 19:18b in found in his reworking of Mark's story of the rich man's question to Jesus about obtaining eternal life (Mark 10:17–22 ‖ Matt 19:16–22).[137] At the end of an eclectic list of the social commandments of the Decalogue, cited by the Marcan Jesus (Mark 10:19), Matthew tacks on Lev 19:18b (Matt 19:19), this time with "as yourself" included. Once again, the Matthean redactional hand is recognizable. The insertion fits in perfectly with Matthew's reworking of the Marcan version of the double command of love. For Matthew, love is the hermeneutical key for interpreting and doing the Law.

(2) Paul also cites Lev 19:18b twice, once in Galatians and once in Romans. Both Pauline passages make the same basic affirmation, but serve different purposes in their respective contexts. In his fiery and polemical letter to the Galatians, Paul spends most of the epistle battling those Christian Jews who wish to impose circumcision, kosher food laws, and other boundary-defining "works of the Law" on Paul's Gentile converts. Having argued fiercely that the Gentile Christians in Galatia have been freed from the Law (at least in the sense of these legal observances), Paul the pastor pivots in chap 5. He starts warning the Galatians that their freedom from the Mosaic Law must not serve as an excuse for selfish immorality, but rather

as a call to serve one another in love. It is in this context that Paul states (Gal 5:14): "The whole Law has been brought to fulfillment in one sentence, namely, 'You shall love your neighbor as yourself.' "[138]

In the more irenic Romans, which is not written in the heat of battle against Christian-Jewish "circumcisers," Paul exhorts the various Christian groups in Rome to accept and bear with one another despite their differences. In Rom 13:8–10, he urges the payment of the debt of mutual love, "for he who loves the other person has fulfilled the Law" (13:8).[139] Indeed, Paul continues in v 9, the social commandments of the Decalogue and any other commandment as well "are summed up in this one commandment, 'You shall love your neighbor as yourself.' " Thus, whether in a polemical or in an irenic context, Paul balances his message of freedom from the Law with an insistence that the love commandment in Lev 19:18b must be fulfilled by the Christian. In the larger context of Paul's insistence that in Christ there is neither Jew nor Greek, "your neighbor" (*ton plēsion sou*) has been broadened out from its original meaning of "fellow Israelite." Yet, granted the immediate context of mutual love within the community, Paul probably understands "your neighbor" in Gal 5:14 and Rom 13:9 as a fellow Christian, whether Jew or Greek, slave or free, male or female (Gal 3:28). In other passages (e.g., 1 Thess 5:15; Gal 6:10), Paul speaks of the Christian's obligation to do good to all people, but in both Gal 5:14 and Rom 13:9 the immediate concern is overcoming strained relations within the Christian community.[140]

(3) The Epistle of James is a less focused, more general piece of Jewish-Christian parenesis than Galatians or Romans. Yet it, too, invokes Lev 19:18b to address the problem of relations within the Christian community, specifically, the problem of showing favoritism to the well-off in the Christian assembly. It is to oppose this socioeconomic partiality that the author states firmly (Jas 2:8): "But if you fulfill the royal law according to the Scripture passage, 'You shall love your neighbor as yourself,' you do well." In a way reminiscent of Rom 13:8–10, the author proceeds to quote some of the social commandments of the Decalogue, while making a different point than Paul does. James stresses that a failure to keep just one commandment of the Law means that one has sinned against the whole Law—though "Law" seems here to refer to the basic moral obligations expressed in the Decalogue and Lev 19:18b rather than "the works of the Law" that are the center of attention in Galatians. Indeed, James never brings up "the works of the Law" in the sense of circumcision and the food laws.

Luke Timothy Johnson makes the intriguing observation that in Jas 2:5, just a few verses before the citation of Lev 19:18b in Jas 2:8, James speaks of God choosing the poor in the world "as heirs of the kingdom that he promised *to those who love him* [*tois agapōsin auton*]." Thus, within a few verses, we have a reference both to love of God and love of neighbor.[141] But are we to imagine that James knew that Jesus taught the double command and echoes it here? Granted that James shows elsewhere a knowledge of the sayings of Jesus (e.g., the prohibition of oaths in Jas 5:12, as we saw in Chapter 33), the allusion to the double commandment in Jas 2:5 + 8 is possible. One must admit, though, that one has to look hard to see the two parts of the double command, since "to those who love him" is part of James' own speech in 2:5 and not a formal citation of a commandment of the Pentateuch, as is the case with Lev 19:18b in Jas 2:8.[142] Moreover, the phrase "to those who love him" in 2:5 supplies something of an *inclusio* with James' opening words in 2:5: "Listen, my beloved [*agapētoi*] brothers. . . ." [143] Still, calling Lev 19:18b "the royal [*basilikon*] law" in 2:8 may be an attempt to link love of neighbor to 2:5, where James speaks of the poor as "heirs of the kingdom [*basileias*] which he promised to those who love him." All in all, an allusion to the double command is a possibility, but still a far cry from formally citing both Scripture texts and placing them back to back as the first and second commandments.

What, then, can be said of the use of Lev 19:18b in Paul and James? Their independent use of the text, a text never explicitly cited word for word elsewhere in Second Temple Judaism (outside the Christian cases of Mark 12:28–34 parr.; Matt 5:43; and Matt 19:19), argues for a 1st-century Christian catechetical tradition that employed Lev 19:18b as a hermeneutical key for understanding Christian moral obligation in individual cases.[144] Neither in Paul nor in James is Lev 19:18b invoked to declare all individual moral commandments (specifically, those of the Decalogue) null and void. Rather, Lev 19:18b is used to guide the Christian along the proper path of fulfilling individual moral obligations.

Intriguingly, what was true of Jesus' prohibition of oaths in Jas 5:12 may also be true of the use of Lev 19:18b in both the Pauline and Jamesian traditions. In both cases we may have an example of the teaching of the historical Jesus being handed down anonymously in epistolary parenesis, as distinct from its use-with-attribution in the Gospels.[145] That may well be the case, although we should note by way of proviso that our final judgment about the historicity of Mark 12:28–34 has not yet been rendered. In any event, though, what should strike us is the difference between the use of Lev 19:18b in epistolary parenesis and its function in Mark 12:28–34. In the epistolary tradition, Lev 19:18b stands alone as the text interpreting, fulfilling, or summing up the Law. A direct citation of Deut 6:4–5 is conspicuous by its absence.[146] Then, too, clearly in Paul and to some extent in James, Lev 19:18b acts as the summation, quintessence, or representative of the whole Law. The whole Law "has reached *fulfillment*" in love of neighbor (Gal 5:14). "He who loves the other person *has fulfilled* the Law" (Rom 13:8). All the commandments of the Decalogue "are *summed up*" in love of neighbor (Rom 13:9). Therefore "love is the *fulfillment* of the Law" (Rom 13:10). The command to love one's neighbor is the *royal* law (Jas 2:8).[147]

But this is not the claim Jesus makes in Mark 12:28–34. Rather, Jesus states that, in the Mosaic Law, love of God and love of neighbor rank first and second in importance; no other commandment is greater than these two. The Marcan Jesus says nothing about these two commandments—let alone simply love of neighbor—being the summation or the fulfillment of the whole Law. As we have seen, it is Matthew who first moves in that direction by adding to Mark's story the famous concluding principle (Matt 22:40): "on these two commandments the whole Law and the prophets depend [literally, 'hang']." From the viewpoint of tradition history, what we see in Paul and James is a further step in the adaptation of the tradition for catechetical purposes. Lev 19:18b, extracted from the larger tradition about Jesus' teaching of the double commandment, becomes the all-sufficient instrument for instructing converts on the proper way to interpret the Law and apply it to individual situations.

To sum up: in relation to Mark 12:28–34 parr., the rest of the NT differs from the literature of Second Temple Judaism in one and only one characteristic. While, apart from Mark 12:28–34 parr., the NT never cites Deut 6:4–5 word for word, it does contain explicit citations of Lev 19:18b, twice in Matthew's Gospel and three times in the epistolary literature. Beyond this partial correspondence to the first characteristic of Mark 12:28–34 parr., the rest of the NT fails to match the four characteristics just as much as the Jewish intertestamental literature prior to A.D. 70. Since the rest of the NT (i) never explicitly cites Deut 6:4–5, obviously (ii) it never juxtaposes that text to Lev 19:18b; (iii) it never enumerates the two love commandments as first and second; and (iv) it never declares that no other commandment is greater than these two. Thus, apart from the two citations of Lev 19:18b in Matthew and the three citations in Paul and James, Jesus' teaching on the double commandment of love is just as discontinuous with the rest of the NT as it is with the writings of Second Temple Judaism. Our conclusion is clear: the criterion of discontinuity argues strongly that the historical Jesus taught the double commandment of love by binding together and yet ranking Deut 6:4–5 and Lev 19:18b and that this core teaching is reliably preserved in Mark 12:29–31.

The attentive reader will notice that, in the last sentence, I carefully restricted my judgment in favor of historicity to Jesus' words about the two commandments of love in vv 29–31 of Mark 12. Strictly speaking, the argument from discontinuity that I have laid out affects only Jesus' unique way of citing and commenting on Deut 6:4–5 and Lev 19:18b in Mark 12:29–31.[148] Many form critics hold that most if not all of the dispute stories and scholastic dialogues in the Synoptic Gospels were created by the early church to enshrine and explain core sayings of Jesus that originally circulated without a narrative context. I readily admit this possibility in at least some cases. As we have seen in Chapter 32, it is possible, though not certain, that the stray saying(s) of Jesus prohibiting divorce may have generated the dispute story on divorce in Mark 10:2–12.

Nevertheless, creation of a narrative by the early church to frame a saying of Jesus is not an equally valid explanation in every instance. As we saw in Volume Three of *A Marginal Jew*, Jesus' dispute with the Sadducees about the resurrection (Mark 12:18–27) probably preserves the memory of an actual debate between Jesus and some members of the Sadducean party in Jerusalem, and not just an isolated saying of Jesus.[149] Indeed, in the debate over the resurrection of the dead as preserved in 12:18–27, it is nigh impossible to extract a saying of Jesus that would make complete sense apart from the sustained argument of which it is a part. This is not to say that we have in 12:18–27 a word-for-word transcript of the original event. It is simply to say that, in the case of the debate over the resurrection, the primitive tradition already contained the sayings of Jesus within a narrative context and that this primitive unit most likely reflects an actual event in the ministry of Jesus.

Is the same true of Mark 12:28–34? On the one hand, it is theoretically possible that Jesus' teaching on the double command of love originally circulated simply as an isolated saying. On the other hand, the very wording of Jesus' saying as we have it in Mark 12:29–31 seems to demand some sort of introduction or setup. A saying that begins out of nowhere with "The first is 'Hear, O Israel . . .' " is at best unclear in purpose and function, and perhaps even in precise content. If we do not accept an occasion like the one depicted in Mark 12:28 (i.e., the question of the scribe in the temple), we are left manufacturing a purely hypothetical occasion via our imagination.

Moreover, I think that there are some considerations that argue in favor of the basic historicity of the incident recounted in Mark 12:28–34. Apart from 12:28–34, not only Mark but almost the entire Synoptic tradition run counter to the idea of a sympathetic Jewish scribe who engages Jesus in a legal discussion resulting in agreement and mutual approbation.[150] Hence, the figure of "the good scribe" may go back to an actual incident during Jesus' ministry. Then, too, that Jesus should begin his answer by quoting the beginning of the *Shema*ʿ (starting at Deut 6:4) would make perfect sense in the setting of the Jerusalem temple—a fortiori, if we may trust the Mishna (*Tamid* 5:1) that the recitation of the *Shema*ʿ was part of the temple's daily liturgy.

As already noted, Jesus' mention of monotheism and the scribe's emphatic repetition of that key doctrine are historically quite plausible if we think of the Roman soldiers in the Fortress Antonia peering down into the temple courtyard where Jesus and the scribe are speaking.[151] In addition, Jesus' presence in the temple suggests that the time frame of the exchange is one of the great pilgrimage feasts, when the prefect Pontius Pilate would come up to Jerusalem with his troops from the Roman capital of Caesarea Maritima, a city adorned with pagan temples. Hence, the emphasis on monotheism by Jesus and the scribe is perfectly intelligible in the original Jewish context and need not be a later creation of Jewish-Christian catechesis intended for Gentile converts.

Likewise, the scribe's exaltation of the two commandments of love above all temple sacrifices has not only its solid basis in the teaching of the OT prophets but also its natural setting in the temple precincts. That Jesus goes out of his way at the end of the encounter to praise the scribe (however guardedly) is again unparalleled in the Synoptic tradition and may in fact have been how the original exchange ended. In all of this, I am not claiming that we have the equivalent of a tape recording of the original event in Jesus' ministry. As I indicated at the beginning of our survey of Mark 12:28–34, the redactional hand and concerns of Mark are clear. Still, nothing argues against the basic historicity of the narrative frame, which makes perfect sense in context. If we reject Mark's narrative while accepting the authenticity of Jesus' core teaching on the double commandment of love, then we must invent our own setting to take the place of Mark's. I am not sure that that would be an improvement.

A final objection to taking Mark's narrative frame as historical is that it is unthinkable that a Jewish scribe would pose a question like "Which is the first commandment of all?" Many scholars point to rabbinic teachings holding that all 613 commandments of the Torah are of equal weight.[152] Rabbis spoke of "light" and "heavy" commandments, but by that they meant, among other things, the relative difficulty or expense involved in obeying individual commandments.[153] In principle, since no one could know the exact reward or punishment for keeping or breaking a particular commandment, all commandments were to be observed with equal care. Hence, say many critics, it is unthinkable that a Jewish scribe would ever raise the question of which commandment was the first.[154]

While this description of the rabbis' approach to the Law is correct, a basic point is often missed by scholars who use the rabbinic material to deny the historical likelihood of the scribe's question to Jesus in Mark 12:28. The portrait of a monolithic Torah composed of 613 equally important commandments is a rabbinic construct. There is no proof that such a doctrine was generally accepted in pre-70 Judaism.[155] Indeed, the ease with which Philo summarizes all the obligations of the Law under the two "heads" (*kephalaia*) of *eusebeia* and *philanthrōpia* suggests a different approach, at least in Diaspora Judaism. Even in Palestinian Judaism, some pre-70 writings show a tendency to enunciate basic obligations that act as overarching principles of Jewish life. One need think only of the beginning of Qumran's *Rule of the Community* or *Jubilees*'s emphasis on lists of key obligations, which at times include obedience to the Lord and love of one's neighbor.

Admittedly, none of these tendencies in either Diaspora or Palestinian Judaism prepares us sufficiently for the startling exchange in Mark 12:28–34. My argument in favor of historicity is, after all, an argument from *discontinuity*. Philo was an original Jewish genius, but so was Jesus—though in a very different way. Still, both Philo in the Diaspora and *Jubilees*-plus-Qumran in Palestine show that seeking summaries and chief principles of the Law was "in the air." That both the scribe and Jesus could have been influenced by such intellectual currents in Jerusalem, the crossroads of the Jewish world, is quite possible. The excesses of portraying Jesus as a Cynic philosopher should not make us allergic to admitting that Jesus was influenced by the wider Greco-Roman culture. In sum, Mark 12:28–34 narrates an impossible event only if all Palestinian Jews ca. A.D. 30 thought exactly like Amoraic rabbis.[156] That is hardly the case. Hence, in my view, the overall Marcan narrative frame, as well as the key sayings of Jesus in 12:29–31, may well be historical.

8. An Argument from Multiple Attestation?

Some scholars would argue that, instead of or in addition to the argument from discontinuity, an argument for historicity can be mounted from multiple attestation of sources.[157] These scholars emphasize that Matthew and Luke's versions of the dialogue in Mark 12:28–34 are strikingly different from Mark's and at the same time have many elements in common. They therefore conclude that some other source besides Mark must be contributing to at least one and possibly both of the parallel stories in Matthew and Luke. The critics, however, divide on how this other source should be imagined. A Q tradition shared by Matthew and Luke? A special M tradition? A special L tradition? In the end, many commentators allow for a mix of the Marcan tradition (perhaps in an earlier form), some other oral or written tradition, and the redactional tendencies of each evangelist.[158]

In a sense, I should welcome this suggestion of another source, since it would provide a second argument for historicity, namely, the criterion of multiple attestation of sources. If I judged the suggestion of a second source valid, I would readily mount the argument. However, I think that this suggestion is a prime example of how the insights of redaction criticism tend to be forgotten in recent Gospel research in favor of a multiplication of other sources, especially oral traditions.[159] In my opinion, careful examination of the redactional context, style, and theology of Matthew and Luke makes it more likely that their versions of Mark 12:28–34 are simply the results of their own creative activity, recasting the Marcan text for their own purposes. To argue this position at length would take a whole monograph. As a matter of fact, that is precisely what Jarmo Kiilunen has produced in a volume that analyzes in great detail Matthew and Luke's redactional appropriation of Mark 12:28–34.[160] For the full argument in favor of Mark as the sole source of the parallels in Matthew and Luke, I refer the interested reader to Kiilunen's work; it would be redundant to reproduce the whole debate here. What I will do is summarize ever so briefly some of Kiilunen's arguments showing that the "minor agreements" of Matthew and Luke against Mark do not necessitate a second source for their versions of the Marcan story.

It is important to begin any consideration of the minor agreements with some general considerations of method. According to the two-source hypothesis, which I follow, both Matthew and Luke, a few decades after Mark's composition of his Gospel, decided independently of each other to write an expanded Gospel, with Mark as the basic narrative source. However, both Matthew and Luke were better Greek stylists who accordingly rewrote Mark to improve his Greek as well as to rework his theology according to their own insights. Granted this scenario of two educated Christians rewriting Mark for smoother Greek and smoother theology a decade or two after Mark composed his work, one should not be surprised that, at times, Matthew and Luke independently choose the same "improvements."[161] One would be surprised if they didn't. The changes to Mark that are common to Matthew and Luke must be weighed against all the times that the two evangelists change Mark in different ways. If one keeps this overall scenario in mind, many of the "minor agreements" are not all that startling and do not demand a second hypothetical source. Moreover, whenever a "minor agreement" is claimed, one should carefully check to see whether the change common to Matthew and Luke actually occurs in the same place in their narratives, means the same thing, and functions theologically in the same way. In a number of cases, surface agreements, on closer inspection, turn out to be modifications of Mark that function quite differently in Matthew and Luke. When Matthew and Luke depart from Mark, each often goes his separate way both in narrative setting and in theological message, despite an appearance of sameness.

A prime example of Matthew and Luke going their separate ways as they redact Mark is the general context in which their versions of Mark 12:28–34 are situated in their Gospels. Matthew's parallel (Matt 22:34–40) retains the narrative context of Mark, that is, the final disputes in the last days of Jesus' ministry in Jerusalem. As in Mark, so in Matthew, the scholastic dialogue about the double commandment of love is preceded by the Sadducees' question about the resurrection of the dead and is followed by Jesus' question about the Messiah being the son of David. In striking contrast, Luke places the tradition about the double commandment much earlier in his Gospel (Luke 10:25–28), in the first part of the Great Journey Narrative of Jesus up to Jerusalem (chaps. 9–19). Such a retrojection of a Marcan narrative is nothing new for Luke. For instance, Luke takes Mark's story of Jesus' rejection at Nazareth (Mark 6:1–6) and, with much rewriting and expansion, uses it as the inaugural event of Jesus' ministry. (Luke 4:16–30).[162] The same sort of retrojection occurs when Luke takes Mark 12:28–34 and places it, with much reworking, near the beginning of Jesus' journey to Jerusalem. Indeed, the gap created by Luke's transposition of the double commandment tradition still shows in the flow of Luke's narrative of Jesus' last days in Jerusalem. In particular, the transition (Luke 20:39–40) from Luke's version of the dispute over the resurrection of the dead (20:27–38) to Jesus' question about David's son (20:41–44) is somewhat awkward, as it has to skip over the missing pericope of the double commandment.[163]

Let us now move from the general to the particular by examining two prominent and related "minor agreements" in the pericope of the double commandment, using them as two test cases in the complicated argument over sources.[164]

(i) Both Matthew and Luke apparently describe the interlocutor as a lawyer (*nomikos*) instead of a scribe (*grammateus*), as in Mark. I say "apparently," since the presence of *nomikos* in Matt 22:35 is not absolutely certain. Some Greek manuscripts lack it, and some critical editions of the Greek NT put the word in brackets in Matt 22:35.[165] But, for the sake of argument, let us grant its presence in Matthew, the only time the word would occur in that Gospel.

That Luke should substitute "lawyer" (*nomikos*) for Mark's "scribe" (*grammateus*) is hardly surprising, since Luke's Gospel uses *nomikos* more than all other NT books combined.[166] Moreover, Luke's own redactional conclusion (11:53) to Jesus' woes against the Pharisees and the lawyers (11:42–53) shows that Luke tends to equate scribes and lawyers. In addition, Luke never uses "scribe" (*grammateus*) in the singular to designate a Jewish scribe/lawyer. In contrast, he uses *nomikos* in both the singular and the plural; hence its occurrence in his version of the Marcan dialogue, where the singular form is required by the story. If Matthew does in fact use *nomikos* in Matt 22:35, this unique appearance of the word in Matthew's Gospel may be explained fairly easily by Matthew's redactional techniques in rewriting Mark. Matthew, like Luke—though at a different place in the narrative and for a different reason—has introduced the vocabulary of Law (*nomos*) into a Marcan pericope that is bereft of it. Matthew's love of *inclusio* and key words, used to tie a pericope together, is evident here. The lawyer (*nomikos*) in 22:35 naturally asks a question in v 36 about the "great commandment *in the Law* [*en tǭ nomǭ*]." The Matthean Jesus obligingly ends the pericope in v 40 with a grand programmatic statement about the whole Law (*nomos*) and the prophets, which conveniently supplies the *inclusio* with "lawyer" and "Law" at the beginning of the pericope.

(ii) But what about the fact that the phrase "in the Law" occurs in both Matthew's and Luke's version yet is absent in Mark's? In Luke, the phrase appears in a different place and with a different function, as compared with Matthew's Gospel.[167] Unlike Matthew's lawyer (Matt 22:36), the Lucan lawyer does not mention Law or commandments in his opening question to Jesus (Luke 10:25). Rather, the lawyer, like Luke his ventriloquist, is interested in the larger, universal question of how one inherits eternal life. It is Jesus, skillfully playing a ping-pong battle of wits with the lawyer from v 25 down to v 37, who introduces the topic of the Law in his counterquestion in v 26: "In the Law—what is written?" The phrase "in the Law" is purposely thrown forward in the question to make the sly point: "You're a *lawyer*. You, not I, are the expert who should know that the answer to your question is to be found *in the Law* and where *in the Law* you can find it—all without asking a non-expert like me!"

Notice, then, the difference between Matthew's use of "in the Law" and Luke's use.[168] In Matthew, who is passionately concerned about the question of the Mosaic Law throughout his Gospel, the key phrases "lawyer," "in the Law," and "the whole Law" are used to frame his pericope because he wants the entire unit to fit into his grand program of the proper understanding and doing of the Law. In contrast, after the Lucan Jesus uses his question about the Law as a rhetorical counterthrust and pedagogical incentive to move the lawyer forward in his train of thought, the word as well as the literary leitmotif and theological problem of the Law disappear entirely from Luke's version of the pericope. Indeed, even the abbreviated twofold command of love (expressed with a single verb in Luke 10:27) serves only as a springboard to the question of the true meaning of neighbor in the attached parable of the Good Samaritan, the true focal point of Luke 10:25–37. In the end, Luke's redaction-plus-expansion of the Marcan pericope of the double command has nothing to do with theoretical questions about the Mosaic Law that so occupy Matthew. It has everything to do with mercy and practical aid shown to a person in need, regardless of race and religion.[169]

I have gone into these two examples of "lawyer" and "in the Law" to show how striking minor agreements of Matthew and Luke against Mark might, at first glance, argue strongly for a second source and yet, on closer examination, turn out to be hardly probative. Instead of a second source, the stylistic tendencies and theological concerns of Matthew and Luke, when studied both in this pericope and throughout their respective Gospels, yield an adequate explanation of their changes—at times, coincidentally the same—to Mark's text.[170] These two examples illustrate in miniature what Kiilunen demonstrates at length in his monograph. There is no need to drag the patient reader through every other example; Kiilunen's book may be consulted at leisure for further details.

There is, however, another reason why I can afford to waive further argumentation, a strategic reason at that. My ultimate purpose in this section of Chapter 36 has been to argue for the historicity of the tradition enshrined in Mark 12:28–34. I consider the argument from discontinuity to be both strong and sufficient in this case; but, after all, discontinuity is only one criterion. Those critics who maintain that Matthew and/or Luke have a second source beside Mark only strengthen my ultimate claim of historicity. They kindly supply a second argument, from multiple attestation of sources. Hence, far from being fiercely polemical in my rejection of their view, I am quite willing to tolerate it, even though I think it wrong, since it only bolsters my own case.

Thus, whether solely on the ground of discontinuity, or also on the ground of multiple attestation, I think that the evidence favors the historicity of at least the core teaching of Jesus on the double command of love in Mark 12:29–31. I am also inclined to accept the surrounding story of Jesus' friendly dialogue with a scribe as basically historical, but this position is not necessary to my claim. The historical Jesus stands apart from both the Judaism of his day and the earliest Christian authors (with the exception, obviously, of Mark 12:28–34 parr.) by selecting Deut 6:4–5 and Lev 19:18b from the whole corpus of the Mosaic Law, quoting these two texts word for word, putting them back to back as the first and second commandments in importance, and declaring that no other commandment is greater than these two.

Perhaps at this point—though only as a confirmation of a position already established—one might also invoke the criterion of coherence. The vast majority of portraits of the historical Jesus maintain that, in his action as well as in his teaching, Jesus made mercy, forgiveness, healing, and outreach to sinners hallmarks of his prophetic ministry to Israel in "the last days." I would add that not only does the double command of love fit in with this overall picture of Jesus' mission; it fits in more specifically with his self-conception as the eschatological prophet called to begin the regathering of a scattered Israel in the end time. Why, out of the whole Torah, does Jesus select precisely Deut 6:4–5 and Lev 19:18b? In the *Shema*, Yahweh summons his whole people to the obedience of love, the basic obligation that ties all members of Israel to God and to one another in the covenant. The varied divisions within 1st-century Judaism were straining this unity of the people of God, sometimes to the breaking point. Hence, true obedience in love to the one God who created Israel and is now regathering it in the last days necessarily involves a full implementation of the obligation to love one's "neighbor," taken in the original sense of Lev 19:18b: one's fellow member of the cultic community of the one Israel established by the one true God. Seen in this prophetic, eschatological context of the regathering of Israel, the first commandment naturally "begets" the second.[171] Far from being opposed to or disconnected with his mission as eschatological prophet, Jesus' double command of love coheres perfectly with it.

Once again, the historical Jesus proves to be the halakic Jesus, the Jesus who thinks long and hard about the Mosaic Law and who comes up with some startling and at times unprecedented pronouncements about it. Indeed, in Mark 12:29–31, he comes up with his pronouncement by using the hermeneutical technique later called the *gĕzērâ šāwâ*—thus proving himself a "rabbi" before the rabbis.[172] The upshot of his interpretation of the two commandments is that the command to love enjoys primacy in the Law. But this primatial love is also a carefully ordered love: God first, neighbor second. Moreover, as the whole teaching of Jesus throughout the Gospels shows, it is a truly biblical, Jewish love. While certainly not divorced from emotions, it is first of all a matter of willing and doing good, not feeling good.

We return, then, to our theme song of the historical Jesus being the halakic Jesus. A "historical" Jesus who is not involved in the lively halakic debates of his fellow Jews in 1st-century Palestine, who does not reason about the Law in typically Jewish fashion, and who does not display his charismatic authority as the eschatological prophet by issuing some startling legal pronouncements, is not the historical Jesus. He is instead a modern and largely American construct, favored by some Christians because he is appealing to the marketplace of popular religion in the United States today—a religion that is highly emotional, mostly self-centered, predictably uninterested in stringent commandments, and woefully ignorant of history. This American "historical" Jesus could never have interacted with 1st-century Palestinian Jews, a community centered on the Law and a community that, unlike many present-day Americans, understood perfectly what its God meant when he *commanded* love.

III. THE COMMAND TO LOVE ENEMIES IN THE Q TRADITION

A. CLARIFYING THE QUESTION

We now move from the Marcan tradition of the double commandment of love (for God and neighbor) to the Q tradition of the command to love one's enemies. Let us begin by clarifying the exact question addressed in this section of Chapter 36. As I emphasized at the beginning of this chapter, my concern is not everything Jesus ever said or did about love, forgiveness, or compassion, but simply and solely the sayings in which Jesus *commands love*. Granted this objective, our attention narrows very quickly as we come to the all-important block of Q material found in Luke 6:27–36 par.[173] Within this heterogeneous collection of exhortations to nonviolence, nonretaliation, generosity, and mercy, our sole focus is the arrestingly laconic command in Matt 5:44b ‖ Luke 6:27b: "Love your enemies" (*agapate tous echthrous hymōn*). The simple reason for this benign neglect of the rest of the Q material in this pericope is that nowhere else in this meandering composition do we have a new, distinct articulation of the love commandment.[174]

Before we begin our investigation of the connection of "love your enemies" to the historical Jesus, it would be helpful to make a few preliminary observations about this counterintuitive command.

(1) In comparison with the relatively lengthy double command of love (forty-four Greek words in Mark 12:29–31), the command to love one's enemies is almost disconcertingly brief and blunt. In Greek it is only four

words, which could be reduced to two or three words in Hebrew or Aramaic.[175]

(2) One reason for this brevity is that Jesus is not citing Scripture texts, as in the double command. Rather, he is speaking simply on his own authority and in his own words. (In fact, both Matthew and Luke, in different formulations, have Jesus introduce the command with "I say.") The brevity may serve a rhetorical purpose in that it adds to the forcefulness—not to say shock value—of this contrary-to-commonsense command. Here form, function, and content coalesce.

(3) One of the few things that the command to love enemies has in common with the double command of love is that each is witnessed in only one source, in this case, Q. Hence, like the double command, the command to love enemies can find no support from the criterion of multiple attestation.[176]

(4) This lack of support results in another similarity to the double command: the only likely candidate among arguments for the historicity of the command to love enemies is the criterion of discontinuity. But does the criterion work in this case? As we shall see, the answer is a qualified yes. I should explain this fudge factor, "qualified." The argument from discontinuity cannot be used to support the historicity of a good deal of the material that follows upon and supposedly explains the love-of-enemies command in Luke 6:27–36 par.[177] Discontinuity applies only to the precise laconic command we find in Luke 6:27b par., namely, the exact words "love your enemies." Exhortations to practice nonretaliation as well as positive benevolence abound in the various cultures of the ancient Near East. What is different from and unparalleled in all such examples from these cultures is the brutally brief direct command, "love your enemies."[178]

(5) The presence of ancient parallels to most of the Q sayings in Luke 6:27c–36 par. is not the only thing that separates this block of Q material from its famous introduction, "love your enemies" (Luke 6:27b par.). Remarkably, many of the sayings that follow the command to love enemies have no essential connection with this command.[179] The reason why modern readers sometimes miss this point is that all too often phrases like "non-violence," "nonretaliation," and "love of enemies" are thrown together as though they all meant more or less the same thing and covered the same actions. Such homiletic great-heartedness only produces a terminological and conceptual muddle. Nonviolence, nonretaliation, and love of enemies do not necessarily mean the same thing.[180]

For example, in polite society, retaliation for a verbal slight or even a physical punch might well be nonviolent but still quite brutal, whether it is fiery public denunciation or ice-cold social ostracism. On the other hand, love of enemies might at times demand violent action—for instance, if I were to defend a personal enemy being threatened by a masked robber in a dark alley. Let us suppose that, witnessing the crime from a distance, I snuck up behind the robber and hit him over the head, rendering him unconscious. Strictly speaking, the violence I inflicted on the robber would not be retaliation on my part, since I was not the one being threatened or robbed. My action vis-à-vis the robber would not be a response to or "pay back" for the robber's (nonexistent) action vis-à-vis myself. We would have a case of violence toward an aggressor that would not be retaliation but would be an expression of love for my enemy. Or imagine another scenario: I lavish huge gifts of money on an enemy and social competitor in the firm hope that his deep-rooted tendencies toward prodigal spending, excessive drinking, and unbridled promiscuity—all facilitated by my monetary largess—will lead him to public disgrace and financial ruin. In this case, *doing* good (in the sense of giving generously to another without demanding repayment) does not flow from *willing* good; it is not love.

(6) These bizarre examples serve to remind us of the biblical meaning of the *command* to love: to will good and so to do good to another. Thus, in Luke 6:27b par., Jesus is brusquely commanding his disciples to will good and to do good to their enemies, not to have warm, loving feelings toward their enemies.[181] Apart from the near impossibility of commanding people to feel specific emotions (especially loving emotions directed toward one's enemy), one would have to ask how the purported enemies would still be perceived as enemies in the eyes of the disciples if the disciple felt nothing but the warmest of loving emotions toward these "enemies." But all this is beside the point, since Jesus is not so foolish as to command emotions. He is rather commanding his disciples to will good and to do good to their enemies, no matter how the disciples may feel about them, and *no matter whether the enemies remain enemies despite the goodness shown them.* This last point needs to be stressed. Too many homiletic commentaries on the varied exhortations in Luke 6:27–36 par. introduce the idea that the astounding actions Jesus urges (e.g., turning the other cheek) are aimed at bringing about a change of heart in the other person. The truth is that not a word about such a hope of conversion is ever expressed in this pericope— even though hope of conversion or reconciliation is voiced in many ancient wisdom traditions.[182]

(7) In sum, all these observations on religious love in the Scriptures are meant to highlight a fact often missed by exegetes: most of the sayings in Luke 6:27–36 par. have nothing to do with the command to love one's en-

emies. The only logia that provide concrete examples of the command to love one's enemies are the ones that immediately follow: "Do good to those who hate you, bless those who curse you, pray for those who abuse you" (Luke 6:27cde), or, alternately, "Pray for those who persecute you" (Matt 5:44c).[183] The other commands that follow are examples of nonviolence, nonresistance, strategies for survival in instances of injustice or violence that one cannot control, or simply unlimited generosity toward those who make demands on us.[184] Apart from the repetition of the initial love command (Luke 6:27b) in Luke 6:35a, nothing is explicitly said in any of these logia about loving one's enemies. I suspect that, if a person ignorant of the Gospels read most of the sayings from Luke 6:28–36 par. detached from their present context, such a person would not spontaneously identify the sayings as a commands to love enemies. We see here the power of authorial composition. The composer(s) of the Q document, by gathering these disparate logia together under the initial startling demand, "love your enemies," could imbue the whole collection of sayings with the aura of being examples of the love of enemies—something that these sayings definitely are not when taken in isolation. And that is what these sayings originally were: isolated logia circulating in the oral tradition.[185] Hence we have no basis on which to claim that the historical Jesus considered them examples of his command to love enemies—presuming that these sayings were ever spoken by Jesus. To return to our main point: our task and the nature of the material demand that, forsaking all others, we cling to "love your enemies" as the sole focus of our quest.[186]

With the other sayings put aside, I believe that an argument from discontinuity can be made for the saying that is our sole concern. My claim is that the laconic and disturbing command "love your enemies" finds no exact word-for-word iteration anywhere in the OT, the intertestamental literature prior to A.D. 70, the rest of the NT, or even the literature that is especially relevant to this topic, namely, pagan philosophical works that are roughly contemporary with the NT. I should make one point clear from the start: by "exact iteration" I mean that no parallel, however close in thought or spirit, uses the terse, stark juxtaposition of the ever-popular direct imperative "love" with the impossible object "enemies." As with the double command of love, so with the command to love enemies, the argument from discontinuity demands a speedy tour through the various bodies of ancient literature that might supply the Holy Grail of "exact iteration."

B. "Love Your Enemies": Is There an Exact Parallel?

The wisdom tradition of the ancient Near East was well acquainted with the advice not to pay back evil with evil. At times, simple passive nonretaliation is counseled; at other times, positive benevolence is suggested, especially if there is a hope of winning over (or publicly shaming) the offending party. Different approaches to the problem often reflect different socioeconomic locations in society. Passive nonretaliation was the usual course of action for subordinates and the marginalized, particularly clients, slaves, and tiny sectarian movements. Astounding beneficence was a possible path for patrons, rich people, or rulers who wanted to display their superior virtue or sovereign power in public.[187] Indeed, disdain for the rabble with its debased moral sensibility is the smug stance of some wise men and philosophers who reject retaliation.[188]

Ancient examples of renouncing retaliation are found in both Egyptian and Babylonian wisdom literature. The Egyptian *Instruction of Amen-em-Ope* warns: "Do not say, 'I have found a strong superior, for a man in your city has injured me.' Do not say, 'I have found a patron, for one who hates me has injured me.' For surely you do not know the plans of god, lest you be ashamed on the morrow. Sit down at the hands of the god, and your silence will cast them down."[189] The Babylonian *Counsel of Wisdom* advises: "Unto your opponent do no evil; your evildoer recompense with good; unto your enemy let justice [be done] . . . let not your heart be induced to do evil."[190] Often, as one would expect with wisdom, there is some pragmatic motive or goal involved in renouncing retaliation. More generally, the students of wisdom are reminded that they cannot know or control the future, which lies in the hands of the god(s).[191]

1. "Love Your Enemies": Absence in the Old Testament

It is within this matrix and milieu that we should read the sapiential and even some of the legal texts of ancient Israel. Understandably, when it comes to nonretaliation or even positive benevolence toward enemies, we find the idea more widely attested in Israel's wisdom tradition than in its law codes. Within a collection entitled "Other Sayings of the Wise," Prov 24:29 supplies a classic example: "Do not say, 'Just as he did to me, so I shall do to him; I shall repay the man according to his deed.' "[192] Similar is the warning in Prov 20:22, but now supplied with a theological basis: "Do not say, 'I shall requite evil'; hope in [or 'wait for'] Yahweh, and he will help you." Here there is a consoling hint that Yahweh will take care of the desired requiting.[193] This counsel that one should leave revenge to God (or the gods) is, as already indicated, standard fare in the wisdom of the ancient Near East. This not-entirely-edifying hope is openly expressed in Prov 24:17–18: "When your enemies [or: 'your enemy'] fall, do not make merry; and when he stumbles, let not your heart leap for joy—lest Yahweh see, be displeased, and turn away his anger from him."

The paradoxical attitude of these verses stems from the basically practical and sometimes downright cynical worldview of wisdom. The wise person naturally wants an enemy who has caused him injury to be punished. But, just as one does not presume to preempt God's action by taking vengeance, so one keeps a sober demeanor when God chooses to act and requite. In the wisdom literature, God is sometimes seen as an absolute and distant sovereign whose will (one is tempted to say whims and moods) is difficult to discern. Hence, even while privately enjoying the discomfort of one's enemy, the wise person, like a discreet courtier, avoids unseemly visible Schaden-freude. The hubris of the innocent servant who is enjoying his vindication all too publicly may displease God, who definitely wants his human retainers to know their place and stay in it. Thus, precisely because the wise person passionately wants his enemy to be punished, he never shows the outward glee that could spoil the inner joy.[194] As often in sapiential literature, we are dealing with how-to-get-along-in-the-world (and with God) wisdom, not with sublime summits of human morality.

These various prohibitions against retaliation in Proverbs are balanced at one point by a positive command to aid one's enemy—a positive admonition that nevertheless is not without a hint of ultimate revenge at God's hands. Prov 25:21–22 advises: "[v 21] If the one who hates you is hungry, give him bread to eat; and if he is thirsty, give him water to drink. [v 22] For you will heap burning coals upon his head, and Yahweh will repay you."[195] Taken by itself, v 21 seems to supply us with a specific instance of love of enemies, that is, willing good and doing good to someone who hates the just person. But is the giver of bread and water really *willing good* to his enemy? Verse 22 gives an ambiguous reason for what looks like magnanimous charity in v 21. Commentators argue endlessly over the precise meaning of the meta-phor of "heaping burning coals" upon the head. Explanations of the meta-phor range from ancient Near Eastern methods of punishment to a ritual of penance or from instilling a sense of shame to the removal of punishment.[196] Some exegetes see here a grim expectation that the just man's kindness will only increase the final punishment of his enemy at God's hands (taking v 22b to mean "and Yahweh will *avenge* you"). Others detect a hope that the enemy will be moved to a change of heart or at least to a sense of shame at his actions (taking v 22b to mean "and Yahweh will *reward* you," i.e., for seeking the conversion of your enemy). Without a larger context it is impossible to be sure of the original meaning. I incline to the darker view that we have here an aggravated version of the ancient advice to leave punishment to God. This would fit in with the general sapiential idea that (i) not preempting God's avenging deed and (ii) not displaying joy when it comes guarantee that God will act in his own good time. A fortiori, adds v 22b, being kind to an (unrepentant) enemy in the meantime only ensures that the divine punishment will be all the more severe.

Ben Sira continues the key sapiential theme of leaving punishment of the wicked to God, but he embeds the theme in a more explicitly theological and moral context, assimilating international wisdom to the faith of Israel. In an essay on anger, revenge, and forgiveness (Sir 27:22–28:11), Ben Sira warns that those who practice vengeance will experience the vengeance of the Lord, who keeps a careful record of their sins (28:1).[197] Knowing full well that he is not God, the wise person realizes that he must forgive the injustice done him by his neighbor (tō plēsion sou) if he himself is to have his sins forgiven when he prays (28:2). Ben Sira urges awareness of one's own sinfulness, frailty, and mortality as grounds for being ever ready to forgive others and avoid conflict (28:3–7). Our author may be thinking in particular of the command to love one's neighbor (Lev 19:18b) when he, in effect, inculcates its negative form (28:7): "Keep in mind the commandments, and do not hate your neighbor [tō plēsion]." [198] All this reminds us that, while Sir 28:2–11 breathes an air of generous human forgiveness inspired by God's forgiveness, the context is focused on one's neighbor (however quarrelsome) rather than one's long-term enemy. In 12:1–7, Ben Sira carefully distinguishes worthy and unworthy recipients of one's beneficence. He commends doing good to a pious man, for such a deed brings reward either from the recipient or from God (v 2). But one should give no comfort or help to the wicked and sinful, for they will turn generous aid into a weapon against the giver (vv 3–6). Opposing sinners is simply a matter of imitating God since "even the Most High hates sinners, and on the impious he takes revenge" (v 7). There is no room here for love of enemies.[199]

When we turn from the sapiential texts of Second Temple Judaism to the laws of the Pentateuch, we may feel that we have entered a world closer in tone to the stern Ben Sira than to the magnanimous exhortations scattered in the Book of Proverbs. Within the Mosaic Torah, strict retaliation is enjoined as an obligation in various law codes, notably at Exod 21:23–25; Lev 24:19–20; and Deut 19:21. The usually humane Deuteronomy is unsparing on this subject: "Your eye shall not pity [the offender]: life for life, eye for eye, tooth for tooth, hand for hand, foot for foot." At first glance, this much-repeated law of retaliation ("talion") seems hopelessly contradictory to the wisdom sayings we have just examined. However, one must bear in mind the very different "settings in life" (*Sitze im Leben*) of these two types of literature. Proverbs and Ben Sira are addressing students in school on how to succeed in life and how to conduct one's professional as well as personal relationships to gain honor and happiness. The law codes are instructing judges (and society in general) how justice is to be meted out in the court held at the city gate—a strict justice that aims at preventing an endless spiral of vengeance among feuding families or clans.

Yet even in the law codes themselves, we find laws that mitigate the spirit of strict retribution. The best-known example of this countertendency in the legal texts occurs in the so-called Covenant Code (or Book of the Covenant) found in Exod 20:22–23:19, which contains many civil, criminal, and ritual laws similar to those in other law codes of the ancient Near East. More specifically, the verses that concern us are located in what some scholars refer to as the "Code of Justice" in Exod 23:1–8(9).[200] Sandwiched between rules demanding fair legal procedures (Exod 23:1–3 + 6–9) are two surprising commands that have nothing to do with the juridical process as such and that probably could not be enforced legally.[201] Exod 23:4–5 reads: "If you come upon an ox of your enemy or his donkey wandering off, you shall immediately return it to him. If you see the donkey of a person who hates you lying underneath its burden, you shall by no means abandon him. You shall immediately help him with it."[202] These two casuistic laws (with the "if . . . then" pattern) stick out like legal sore thumbs from the surrounding context (23:1–3 + 6–9), which is formulated in apodictic style (with the absolute "you shall not . . ."). The laws before and after vv 4–5 deal with public social space, especially that of the court. Verses 4–5 deal instead with a one-on-one situation, with no one else on the scene to witness the event or to demand observance of the law. Despite the juridical trappings, therefore, 23:4–5 moves in the direction of wise counsel and moral exhortation.[203]

The place of these two verses in the *Covenant* Code is nevertheless fitting, since the two laws aim at maintaining the solidarity necessary for the survival of the covenant community of Israel, despite the personal antagonisms that inevitably arise in a close-knit society. In substance, though not in vocabulary, we have in vv 4–5 two commands to love one's enemy. At the same time, one notices clear differences from the command in Luke 6:27b par. The form of the commands in Exod 23:4–5 is casuistic, that of Luke 6:27b par. apodictic. In this instance, form truly corresponds to content. Within a law code, Exod 23:4–5 seeks to legislate (or perhaps issue an exhortation) for certain precise cases,[204] with the enemy being a personal enemy known from daily exchanges in the local community.[205] Quite different in form and thrust is the terse "love your enemies," with no indication of a limitation of the obligation to certain circumstances or to personal enemies. More significant still is the unmediated collision of the positive verb "love" with the negative noun "enemy," expressed in Aramaic in a two-word theological hand grenade. Still, even when we grant all these differences, Exod 23:4–5 stands out in the Jewish Scriptures as the grand example (in effect, though not in vocabulary) of a command to love enemies—at least some enemies in some circumstances.

At the same time, one must admit that some parts of the Pentateuch in particular and the OT in general either permit or actually command the hatred and/or destruction of enemies. In the Pentateuch and in Joshua, Yahweh orders Israel to destroy the indigenous nations of Canaan, both to punish them for their sins and to prevent Israel from adopting their idolatrous practices. Israel is to doom the pagan nations in the promised land to obliteration and show them no mercy (Deut 7:1–5,24–26). Likewise, Israel is to wipe out hostile nations in the territories adjoining the promised land, for example, the Amalekites, the Ammonites, and the Moabites (Exod 17:8–16; Deut 26:17–19). The Book of Joshua narrates the partial extermination of the native populations of Canaan, including the slaughter of nearly all the inhabitants of cities like Jericho and Ai (Josh 6:16–17,21; 8:24–25). The campaign continues in 1 Sam 15:1–35, where Yahweh orders King Saul to exterminate the Amalekites. In fact, Yahweh decides to depose Saul from the kingship because Saul does not slaughter everyone. While relations with neighboring populations were not always so bloody in actual fact, the basic enmity lived on. In the 2d century B.C., Ben Sira states openly (50:25–26): "My soul loathes two nations, and the third is not even a people: those who dwell in Seir [= Edom] and Philistia, and the foolish nation that lives in Shechem [= the Samaritans]."[206] One could multiply examples from Israel's history, but the basic point is clear. In some Scripture texts, hatred and/or destruction of the national enemies of Israel are obligations imposed by Yahweh, the divine warrior, on his holy people, who must engage in holy war. The doomed nations are first of all enemies of God and therefore enemies of the people of God, for whom they pose a fatal temptation to apostasy.

In the Psalms, we find alongside this theme of Yahweh dooming the nations to destruction a more personal obligation imposed on the righteous: to hate those individual Israelites whose evil deeds make them enemies of God and therefore of the pious psalmist. The parade example is Ps 139:21–22, where the just man cries out to God in protestation: "Do I not hate those who hate you, Yahweh? . . . With a perfect hatred I hate them; they are enemies unto me." One should note the theological order in the psalmist's thought, an order that is similar to the case of hating national enemies. The psalmist does not ask Yahweh to count the psalmist's enemies as his enemies too. The order is the opposite. The psalmist affirms his solidarity with Yahweh: he counts as his own enemies those who are already Yahweh's enemies because of their evil deeds. It is in such a light that we should read the various curses that lace some of the psalms as well as the warnings of the prophets. Psalm 109, for example, is made up largely of bloodcurdling curses traded back and forth by the psalmist and his enemies. Close behind in its venom ranks Psalm 35.

In defense of the psalmist and other pious cursers like Jeremiah (e.g., Jer 15:11,15;18:18–23; 20:11–12), we should remember that the righteous tell how they at first treated their opponents with kindness, forgiveness, and prayer, only to be met with hatred and plots. At this point, talion kicks in on the individual as well as on the national level. In the mind of the individual just man as well as the nation, all this is simply a matter of asking the ultimate arbiter and guardian of right and wrong to ensure that justice will triumph in a world where it is too often defeated. Then as now, the Near East and Middle East were often nasty, brutal, murderous places where the law of the wild was kill or be killed. Perhaps we should be startled not so much at the curses demanding vengeance as at the OT passages speaking of moderation, nonretaliation, and forgiveness. The library of books that Christians call the OT encompasses the lives of nations and individuals over more than a millennium. We should not be surprised that it is a mixed bag containing some very mixed-up people. Such is the human condition, even when claiming the approbation of God. Other major religions of the world, notably Christianity, can supply similar examples.

2. *"Love Your Enemies": Absence at Qumran*

The stark dualism that marks Essene thought finds its classic expression in the rule of life that governed the community at Qumran.[207] The famous opening of the *Rule of the Community* (*serek hayyaḥad*) is chilling in its clear-eyed, absolute distinction between good and evil human beings. Right at the beginning of the *Rule*, we are told that "to seek God with all one's heart and with all one's soul" (1QS 1:1–2) means, on the abstract level, "to love everything that he [God] has chosen and to hate everything that he has rejected" (1QS 1:3–4). Concretely, this requires members of the community "to love all the sons of light"—that is, all the fellow members of the conventicle—and "to hate all the sons of darkness"—all other human beings, Jews and Gentiles alike (1QS 1:9–10).[208] Soon after this give-no-quarter opening, we hear the blessings and curses that were pronounced during the annual ceremony of covenant renewal (cf. 1QS 2:19). The curses deny the wicked any mercy and consign them to the gloom of eternal fire (1QS 2:7–8). Indeed, in an ironic reversal of the priestly blessing in the Book of Numbers (Num 6:24–26), the Qumranites pray: "May God *not* be merciful when you cry out [to him] and may he *not* grant pardon and atonement for your iniquities. May he raise up the countenance of his anger to wreak vengeance on you and may there be no peace for you" (1QS 2:8–9).

After such a fiery affirmation of the vengeance to be inflicted on the wicked (i.e., anyone not a member of the Qumran community), one might expect the *Rule* to continue with detailed regulations about how the Qumranites are to harm outsiders. We are therefore startled to read in 1QS 10:11–18 a renunciation of any personal retaliation aimed at the unrighteous. Rather, with a sense of his own frailty and limitations, the Qumranite avers: "I know that in his [= God's] hand [is] the judgment of every living thing and that all his deeds are trustworthy. . . . I shall not pay back to anyone the recompense due [his] evil; [rather,] with goodness shall I pursue a man. For with God [lies] the judgment of every living being, and he [i.e., God] will pay back to each man the recompense due him." We are reminded here of the wise counsel of Proverbs: leave vengeance to God. However, at Qumran wisdom has meshed with prophecy to form apocalyptic. Accordingly, a final act of vengeance awaits the wicked in the end-time, and the Qumranites look forward to sharing in the revenge. The same Qumranite who disavows vengeance in the present moment (1QS 10:16–18) adds an all-important proviso in 10:19–21: "I shall not contend with the men of the pit [i.e., those doomed to final destruction] until the day of vengeance. But I shall not turn away my anger from the men of iniquity, and I shall not be pleased until he [God] has carried out [his] judgment . . . and I shall show no mercy to all those who turn aside from the path [of righteousness]." [209]

Hence, the Qumranite's refusal to exact vengeance on the wicked in the present moment is simply an expression of eschatological patience. The Qumranite trusts that God will pass a merciless judgment on evildoers at the end of the present state of the world. [210] The darker aspect of wisdom's renunciation of retaliation is here projected onto an apocalyptic screen. In fact, the script for the feature film to be played on that screen is found in the *War Scroll* (1QM, 4QM), in which the infantry and cavalry of the sons of light fight for forty years against the Kittim (originally the Seleucids, but later the Romans), who represent all the sons of darkness. The result is carnage and the total destruction of the evil empire. The immutable decree of God, fixing the "lots" of the good and the wicked, thus reaches its climax and conclusion. In such a scenario, the command "love your enemies" makes no sense. One must hate one's enemies (i.e., all the sons of darkness), for only in that way can one align oneself with God, who likewise hates them and dooms them to eternal destruction.

3. *"Love Your Enemies": Absence in the Old Testament Pseudepigrapha*

As we saw in our treatment of the double commandment of love, *Jubilees* contains a number of references to love of one's brother or neighbor. But it never enjoins love of enemies. This is quite understandable, given *Jubilee*'s abiding concern that Israelites, both in marriage and more generally in social relationships, carefully keep themselves separate from non-Israelites. This separation from Gentiles extends not only to eating with them but also to any sort of association (see, e.g., *Jub.* 22:16). In contrast, careful social interaction rather than total separation is the program of the *Letter of Aristeas*, whose ethics reflect the widespread influence of Stoicism on Hellenistic culture, including that of Diaspora Jews. Magnanimity and generosity toward all are urged on the king of Egypt, the fictitious interlocutor at the great banquet (culinary and intellectual) that lies at the heart of *Aristeas* (§187–294). What might be considered a vague negative form of the Golden Rule is given universal range as well as a theological basis by one of the Jewish guests advising the king (§207): "Insofar as you do not wish evils to come upon you, but to partake of every blessing, [it would be wisdom] if you put this [principle] into practice with your subjects, *including the wrongdoers*, and if you admonished the good and upright also mercifully. For God guides all men in mercy."[211] An intriguing glance into the mind of popular Hellenistic philosophy is then given by the king's query (§225), "How can one despise his enemies?" The question presupposes that one does not need to love one's enemies but rather to demonstrate to them and others one's own moral superiority and detachment from base emotions like anger and anxiety. (We will see this concern return in Seneca and Epictetus.) The reply that one of the Jewish guests gives the king follows the king's own line of thought: "By practicing good will to all men and by forming friendships, *you will owe no obligation to anyone.*"

Thus, the reason for universal beneficence is a desire to show one's emotional independence of and moral aloofness from the common run of men. Such philosophical detachment does not, however, exclude seeking the betterment of opponents. When the king asks (§227), "To whom must one be generous?" a Jewish guest replies by making a careful distinction that extends magnanimity even to opponents (though the ultimate intention of the magnanimous person remains somewhat ambiguous in the Greek): "[We should be generous] toward those who are amicably disposed to us. This is the general opinion. My belief is that we must (also) show liberal charity to our opponents so that in this manner we may convert them to what is proper and fitting to them [or possibly: 'to ourselves']."[212] A major concern of the Stoic—namely, to be free from negative feelings that would disturb one's peace of mind—is one reason for such beneficence to all. When the king asks how to be free from sorrow (§232),[213] a Jew answers: "By pursuing righteousness, doing no harm to anyone, and helping everyone. The fruits of righteousness make for freedom from sorrow [alypian]." Thus, in effect and in a roundabout way, Aristeas teaches love of enemies, but hardly with the brief and blunt command, "love your enemies"—and not without a pragmatic touch of self-interest.

The impact of Stoic philosophy, with its emphasis on the need for reason to control all emotions, is even clearer in the Fourth Book of Maccabees, which exalts pious reason's ability to conquer even the torments of martyrdom.[214] This philosophical stance, when wedded to the Jewish Law, results in something of a mixed picture when it comes to love of enemies. On the positive side, in a remarkable synthesis of Stoicism and the commands we have examined in Exod 23:4–5 (plus a touch of Deut 20:19), 4 Maccabees insists (2:14): "Do not think it a paradox when reason, on account of the Law, can control even enmities, not cutting down the cultivated trees planted by one's enemies in war, saving the possessions of one's adversaries from those who would destroy them, and helping to raise up [animals] that have fallen [under their burdens]."[215] In effect though not in formulation, we have here love of enemies, at least certain enemies in certain circumstances. This kindness even toward enemies is based—as one might expect from a type of Diaspora Judaism deeply imbued with Stoic morality—on the sovereign rule of serene reason over turbulent emotions. Such total mastery of emotions by reason is shown concretely by both the aged priest Eleazar and the seven young brothers, all of whom, along with the brothers' mother, suffer terrible torture and death for their loyalty to the Torah (13:1–9). We will meet this kind of philosopher-saint again (though in pagan garb and mindset) in Epictetus' portrait of the Cynic.[216]

However, there is the other side of the coin in 4 Maccabees. In contrast to the general affirmation of kindness toward enemies proclaimed in 4 Macc 2:14, the scenes of martyrdom do not contain any expression of love or any articulation of a prayer for the martyrs' persecutor, Antiochus IV Epiphanes, the villain of the piece. On the contrary, the seven brothers whom Antiochus condemns to torture and death revile him with the promise of his eternal damnation. The first brother, for instance, prays that divine providence will "punish the accursed tyrant" (9:24). By way of *inclusio*, the seventh brother returns to the promise that God "will punish you [i.e., Antiochus] both in this life and after your death" (12:18). Tellingly, at the conclusion of the seventh brother's speech, the narrator resumes his story with "and having spoken these curses."[217] While the reactions of the martyrs to their persecutor are perfectly understandable from a human point of view, they lie at the antipodes from the words of Jesus in Luke 6:27–28: "Love your enemies, do good to those who hate you, bless those who curse you, pray for those who abuse you." Love of enemies apparently comes in different shapes and sizes.

Closely allied with love of enemies—though not to be simply identified with it—is the principle of nonretaliation, which receives striking articulation in the Jewish-Hellenistic novel called *Joseph and Aseneth*. Unfortunately, not unlike the *Testaments of the Twelve Patriarchs*, both the date and the provenance of *Joseph and Aseneth* are debated. Suggestions for a date of composition range from the 2d century B.C. to ca. A.D. 200, though a date in the early years of the 2d century A.D. seems likely.[218] There appear to be some Christian interpolations, though their extent is unclear. For the sake of argument, though, let us grant, as many do, that the core of the work is a Jewish-Hellenistic romance (novel) written somewhere around the turn of the era. Granted this hypothesis, we are understandably struck by a remarkable parallel to the way Paul enjoins nonretaliation in his epistles. In *Joseph and Aseneth*, both Levi, Joseph's brother, and Aseneth, Joseph's wife, twice affirm the basic prohibition of retaliation. In 23:9, as he restrains his brother Simeon from killing the son of Pharaoh, who has threatened to kill them, Levi asserts: "It is not fitting for a God-fearing man *to render evil for evil [apodounai kakon anti kakou]* to his neighbor." Levi repeats this admonition with the same key words in 29:3: "It is not fitting for a God-fearing man to render evil for evil [*apodounai kakon anti kakou*]." Aseneth affirms the same attitude of "not rendering evil for evil [*mē apodidontes kakon anti kakou*]" (28:4). When Simeon objects to such mercy, Aseneth insists (28:14): "By no means, brother, shall you render evil for evil to your neighbor [*mēdamōs . . . apodōseis kakon anti kakou*]."

The formulation of the principle in 28:4 is especially striking, since, although it is never found in this precise wording in the OT,[219] it matches almost exactly the words that Paul uses to inculcate nonretaliation in 1 Thessalonians and Romans. In 1 Thess 5:15a, Paul orders: "See to it that no one renders evil for evil to anyone [*horate mē tis kakon anti kakou tini apodō*]." Similarly, amid a string of exhortations in Romans 12, Paul in 12:17a uses the participial form that is quite close to *Joseph and Aseneth* 28:4: "rendering evil for evil to no one [*mēdeni kakon anti kakou apodidontes*]." This is hardly a case of Paul reading and quoting *Joseph and Aseneth*, especially since the latter was probably written in the late 1st or early 2d century A.D. Rather, we are dealing here with a widespread and long-lived principle from the wisdom tradition, as we have already seen from parallels reaching as far back as the Babylonian *Counsel of Wisdom*. Indeed, that this international axiom was known to more than one NT author can be seen from the exact parallel to Paul's dictum found in 1 Pet 3:9: "not rendering evil for evil [*mē apopdidontes kakon anti kakou*]." [220]

Thus, when it comes to this particular axiom of nonretaliation, the NT is inventing nothing. It is rather taking over a common wisdom tradition found in the ancient Near East, in religions of the ancient Mediterranean world, and in popular Hellenistic philosophy, especially Stoicism. To be sure, the axiom "do not render evil for evil" is not, strictly speaking, a command to love one's enemies. In fact, some of the texts of *Joseph and Aseneth* speak explicitly of one's "neighbor." Nonetheless, for all practical purposes, the prohibition of retaliation inculcates love of enemies in the specific context of *Joseph and Aseneth*,[221] where angry brothers are told not to kill those who have tried to kill them.[222]

An intriguing side point in all this is that, while this axiom is shared by more than one NT author, it is not shared—as far as we know—by Jesus. To be sure, in the Q tradition, Jesus issues the laconic command, "love your enemies," and then proceeds to emphasize passive resistance as well as superabundant generosity toward opponents. Yet, unlike Paul, 1 Peter, and *Joseph and Aseneth*, Jesus never utters the popular axiom, "do not render evil for evil" anywhere in the Four Gospels.[223] Paradoxically, therefore, Jesus stands out from his intellectual environment both for what he does say ("love your enemies") and for what he doesn't say ("do not render evil for evil"). We are reminded once again that nonretaliation and love of enemies are not precisely the same thing; one principle can be formally enunciated without formally enunciating the other.

As I conclude this section on the OT pseudepigrapha, I should note that some commentators include in their surveys *2 Enoch*, alias *Slavonic Enoch*.[224] However, in our treatment of Jesus' prohibition of oaths in Chapter 33, we saw that *2 Enoch* is a late work (certainly after A.D. 70), with a number of Christian interpolations, if not a thoroughgoing Christian redaction. Hence, it is a highly questionable source for "background" or "parallels" to Jesus' command to love one's enemies. For the sake of completeness, though, let me state for the record that *2 Enoch* contains the standard ancient prohibition of retaliation with the standard reason: the Lord will be the avenger of the righteous on the day of judgment (2 *Enoch* 50:3–4). Just as a person asks good things from God, so let that person give good things to every human being (61:1–2). One should never bear malice in the heart toward anyone; rather, charitable aid should be offered to all, especially the needy (44:4). As in the *Testaments of the Twelve Patriarchs*, this general kind of parenesis could be either Jewish or Christian. Be that as it may, nowhere in 2 *Enoch* do we find the direct, laconic command "love your enemies." [225]

4. "Love Your Enemies": Absence in Philo and Josephus

As we have seen in our discussion of the double commandment of love, Philo is deeply influenced by Stoic morality. It is fascinating to observe how, in his typical synthesis of disparate traditions, he meshes Stoicism with OT laws. A prime example is his explanation of the commandments in Exod 23:4–5 to help raise up an enemy's animal when it falls under its burden and to bring back an enemy's straying animal.[226] Not surprisingly, he treats observance of these laws as matters of virtue in his treatise *On the Virtues* (*De virtutibus*), specifically under the grand virtue of *philanthrōpia*, "love of human beings" or, more generally, "humaneness." The command to raise up an enemy's animal, says Philo (*On the Virtues* 23 §116–18), teaches us not to take pleasure in the misfortune that befalls those who have been hostile to us. Such pleasure is an indecent passion. Similarly, the benevolence shown in restoring a wandering animal to one's enemy profits the generous person more than his enemy, for the generous person thus gains the nobility of genuine goodness. Moreover, this gracious act will put an end to the hostility. Philo thus provides two philosophical underpinnings to the OT laws: growth in personal virtue (generosity toward one's enemy redounds to the virtue of the magnanimous person) and practical diplomacy (the act puts an end to the enmity). But nowhere in Philo do we hear the blunt command "love your enemies."

As with Philo, *philanthrōpia* is a watchword for Josephus, especially when he has to fend off the scurrilous anti-Jewish propaganda that accused Jews of hating the whole human race. Josephus' quintessential apologetic work rebutting such accusations is his treatise *Against Apion*, composed somewhere around A.D. 100. While Josephus addresses a number of anti-Jewish writers in the two books that make up this work, the initial part of book two is aimed at Apion, a grammarian from Alexandria.[227] One of Apion's calumnies is that the Jews swear by God the Creator not to show benevolence to any non-Jew, especially Greeks (*Ag. Ap.* 2.10 §121). Josephus' response takes first a negative and then a positive tack. First, he insists that Jews are neither hostile to nor envious of Greeks. Then, on the positive side, he adduces as evidence of Jewish benevolence the fact that many Greeks have become proselytes to Judaism, embracing "our laws" (2.10 §123).[228] Josephus concludes by joining the two arguments: even those proselytes who later reverted to paganism have never claimed that they heard any Jew swearing such an oath of enmity (2.10 §124). At the same time, Josephus honestly admits that Gentiles with only a tangential relationship to the Jewish community are not admitted to the inner life of Judaism (2.28 §209–10).

Josephus returns to this argument toward the end of *Against Apion* (2.36 §261), stressing that Jewish openness to converts is evidence of Jews' love of humanity (*philanthrōpia*) and magnanimity (*megalopsychia*). Perhaps to counter the often-misunderstood exclusivity of Jews, Josephus goes out of his way to emphasize that Jews feel obligated to do good to foreigners. In enumerating the various ways Jews assist non-Jews, Josephus includes being kind and moderate (*epieikeis*) even toward those engaged in armed conflict with Jews (the allusion to Deut 20:19, already heard in 4 Macc 2:14, resonates here). So deeply are gentleness (*hēmerotēs*) and humane feeling (*philanthrōpia*) inculcated in Jews by their training that these virtuous attitudes are extended even to brute beasts (2.29 §211–13). One sees how *philanthōpia* in this context (where it is extended even to animals) can have, as elsewhere in Philo and Josephus, the general sense of "humane feeling" and not specifically "love for human beings." In fact, Josephus never uses either the verb *agapaō* or the verb *phileō* (both meaning "to love") with "enemies" as the direct object. Despite his emphasis on the humane rules that Jews observe when battling their enemies, Josephus—especially in the wake of the First Jewish War (A.D. 66–70)—would probably have thought a command like "love your enemies" wildly unrealistic and humanly impossible.

5. "Love Your Enemies": Greco-Roman Philosophers

When we studied Jesus' prohibition of oaths in Chapter 33, we were confronted with a surprising phenomenon. The closest parallels to Jesus' total prohibition that we could find were not in the OT, intertestamental literature, or the early rabbis, but rather in some of the Greek philosophers and those Jewish writers heavily influenced by them, notably Philo. We run into a somewhat similar case when it comes to Jesus' command to love enemies.[229] It is not that we find some 1st-century pagan philosopher issuing the laconic, apodictic command "love your enemies." What we do find in the late Stoicism of the Roman empire is a number of statements and exhortations from Stoic philosophers, stretching from Musonius Rufus to Marcus Aurelius, that provide us with fairly close parallels to Jesus' command. Space does not allow us to go on a grand tour of various schools of Greek and Roman philosophy or even of the whole history of Stoicism.[230] For convenience' sake, I will restrict the following treatment to the two great Stoic philosophers closest to the time of Jesus, Seneca (ca. 4 B.C.–A.D. 65) and Epictetus (ca. A.D. 55–135).

Significant statements about the proper ethical treatment of enemies are found in four works of Seneca: *De otio* ("On Leisure"), *De beneficiis* ("On Benefits"), *De ira* ("On Anger"), and *De constantia* ("On Steadfastness"). In *De otio* 1 §4, Seneca gives a brief summation of his view: those politicians and philosophers who are involved in public life must constantly work for the common good in order to help one and all, "even our enemies with our aged hand." When we are met with ingratitude on the part of those we have aided, says Seneca, we should imitate the gods. They shower their gifts both on those ignorant of them and on those who have proven ungrateful. So we should give freely to all, even to those who have been ungrateful for our beneficial actions. For if we drive such a person away, we turn a dubious friend into a sure enemy, who will spread malicious gossip about us (*De beneficiis* 7.30 §2).

Apparently even Seneca sensed that such sweeping philosophical magnanimity was simply impossible for any philosopher-politician who wanted to survive long-term in the Roman empire. Hence, Seneca makes a careful distinction between two types of ingrates. In doing so, he happens to provide us with a startling parallel to Jesus' thought—and very words—in Matthew's version of the command to love one's enemies (Matt 5:44–45). In *De beneficiis* 4.26 §1–3 (cf. 7.31 §2–5), Seneca first proposes the general rule of *imitatio dei*: imitate the gods in their giving of gifts even to the ungrateful, "for the sun also rises on evil men, and the seas lie open to pirates." While Seneca accepts this basic principle of imitating the gods, he hastens to add that Stoics distinguish between two types of ingrates. On the one hand, some people are ungrateful simply because they are fools. On the other hand, certain people are ungrateful because they are naturally inclined to this vice. Seneca holds that a good man should do good to the first type, but not to the second, on whom any benefit would be wasted. In a sense, Seneca is just doing here what any moral philosopher has to do. First comes the grand, guiding principle; then come the distinctions necessary to apply the principle to the vicissitudes of daily living. One sees immediately the difference in mind-set between the philosopher-politician from Rome and the eschatological prophet from Nazareth.

On the allied topic of retaliation, Seneca echoes the common wisdom of the ancient world by reprobating the desire to repay injury with injury.

Revenge, says Seneca, is inhuman (*De ira* 2.32–34). As one would expect in the ancient Mediterranean world, Seneca understands retaliation in terms of honor and shame. Contrary to popular opinion, Seneca maintains that revenge is a shameful act because it drags the injured person down to the level of the one who injured him. A virtuous Roman is conscious of his superiority to the offender. Here Seneca proposes a paradox: the best way to humiliate the offending party—and so to take a refined type of revenge—is to treat the offender as unworthy of the time and effort needed to take revenge. A noble Roman is like the king of beasts; he does not even pay attention to the barking of puppies around him.

Thus, the proper response to those who cannot control their passions is disdain on the part of the noble man, who maintains his peace of mind far above the rabble. In this way, the true Stoic controls his emotions and walls himself off from all the threats and rewards that could disturb his inner equilibrium. Scorn for our inferiors keeps us from even noticing the injuries they inflict (*De constantia* 4 §1; *De ira* 3.5 §8). In addition, by refusing to retaliate, the wise man may both win over those enemies who are his inferiors and ward off further injuries from those enemies who are his superiors. In short, brushing aside insults from enemies is one important way in which we are to strive to lead a peaceful life. For, in the end, says Seneca, anger and revenge seem foolish and futile when we contemplate the brevity of life. Death will soon make equals of us all (*De ira* 3.42 §3–4; 3.43 §1–2). Nevertheless, Seneca the politician thinks that at times it may be the obligation of the wise man to punish evildoers, sometimes severely. The sage does so not because he is emotionally upset by the injury done him but because the offenders need correction and perhaps may be induced to cease doing evil (*De constantia* 12 §3; 13 §1–2).

In sum, we see that, for Seneca, the treatment of enemies is mostly a question about retaliation. The main answer to the question of retaliation lies not in a commandment spoken by a god, and certainly not in an eschatological ethic proclaimed by a prophet, but rather in the inner self of the wise man, who rules his passions by reason and so manufactures his own happiness. The theme of the imitation of the gods makes some brief appearances, especially in relation to ungrateful people, who can be tolerated when they are simply silly and not wicked. In the end, though, when it comes to the question of retaliation against enemies, the basis or measure of moral actions is oneself—provided the self is great, noble, and philosophical. Communing with this self, Seneca apparently does not hear the apodictic command "love your enemies" as a law of nature. While this unperturbed philosopher managed to put up with Nero for quite a while, one cannot imagine Seneca loving the emperor or blessing his persecutor as he sat in his hot tub after slitting his veins.

The same desire to control one's feelings completely is the foundation of Epictetus' insistence on not responding to someone who insults him. No doubt this approach served Epictetus well during the years when he was a slave in Rome. The ultimate Stoic, Epictetus chooses as his ideal a stone, since a stone is impervious to all insults and pain (*Discourses* 1.25 §29; cf. 3.13 §11–13). Consequently, Epictetus' refusal to retaliate is based not so much on concern for his enemy as concern for himself. His goal is to maintain his own inner calm and dignity. As he states with admirable candor if not charity, "no one is dearer to me than myself" (3.4 §9). Hence, it is absurd to allow oneself to be upset and overcome by the abuse inflicted by someone else. Such abuse can even be a positive advantage if the philosopher uses it to train himself in "dispassionateness [*to aorgēton*]" (3.20 §9).

Granted this basic philosophical stance, it is at first surprising to read Epictetus' description of his philosophical hero, the Cynic, who for Epictetus is something of a "super-Stoic." The subversive lifestyle of the Cynic, who challenged the conventional norms of society, often met opposition. If he is beaten in punishment for his offensive public demonstrations of contempt for society, the Cynic, with the help of God, "must love [*philein*] the men who beat him, as he is the father, the brother of them all" (3.22 §54).[231] The Cynic, Epictetus tells us, abstains from marriage because he considers the whole human race his children (3.22 §81–82). In that spirit, "he approaches all of them and cares for all of them . . . he does this as a father, as a brother, as a servant of the common father, Zeus." At first glance, one is hard pressed to square this positive presentation of love of enemies with Epictetus' overall Stoic view of life.

Perhaps two factors help explain this presentation of love for all human beings, even to the point of suffering for them with a father's love. First, Epictetus is not speaking here of the ethical obligations of human beings in general, or even of those of the ordinary student of Stoicism. He is focusing on an ideal type, the Cynic, who by definition is outside the norms and the normal. The Cynic is the celibate "apostle" of the gods, sent as their herald to all humanity. Second, the Cynic's sacrificing love for all humans receives an explicit theological basis that we do not find in Epictetus' teachings that extol the self or the stone. With the Cynic, we touch upon that strange current of personal, emotional religion in Epictetus that seems somewhat at odds with the Stoic philosophy he inherited, which is based on pantheistic monism. That is, in Epictetus' cosmology, everything is made up of the same "stuff," the same ultimate matter. Stoicism is thoroughgoing materialism.

The human soul or the gods are simply more refined, ethereal types of this "stuff," a sort of fiery breath. Ultimately, nature and the gods—or the god or Zeus (the terms are used interchangeably)—are one and the same. It is in this sense that the divine reason or spirit pervades and orders nature and is reflected in the reason of the individual, which is a fragment of the reason of Zeus. Moreover, since all human beings are composed of the same "stuff" and share the same divine reason, they are all related to one another as brothers, just as they are related to Zeus as their common father.[232] How the affective and deeply personal religious note struck in the portrait of the Cynic's love for all humans—as well as elsewhere in Epictetus—fits in with the pantheistic monism of Stoicism is difficult to say. Perhaps it doesn't.

In any event, we have in Epictetus' depiction of the Cynic a rare case of a Stoic philosopher extolling self-sacrificing love for all, including one's enemies. At the same time, we must admit that we are dealing with an abstract philosophical ideal. Epictetus does not turn to all his students and/or readers and command them: "Love your enemies." The idea of love of enemies is indeed present in a few passages of the *Discourses*. The laconic, abrupt, and blunt four-word command—in other words, the "exact iteration"—is absent.[233]

6. "Love Your Enemies": Absence in the Rest of the New Testament

If I have stressed that the exact wording, the "exact iteration," of the capsule-like command "love your enemies" is lacking in all Jewish and pagan authors before and around the time of Jesus, one reason for this emphasis is that it helps highlight the strangest absence of all: the absence of this precise command anywhere in the NT outside of the Q tradition enshrined in Matt 5:45b and Luke 6:27b. "Love your enemies" is absent from Mark, the rest of Q, the special material of Matthew and Luke, and is especially foreign to the Gospel, Epistles, and Revelation of John. Curiously, it is especially in the Pauline epistles that we find echoes of some of the other commands present in Luke 6:27–36 par. But entirely missing in the parenesis of the epistles is "love your enemies," the command that, as it were, unleashes all the other commands in Luke 6:27–36 par. Perhaps the closest extended parallel to our Q pericope in the epistles is Rom 12:9–21, which begins with an exhortation to sincere love (v 9a) and ends with a command expressing the principle of nonretaliation (v 21): "Do not be overcome by evil, but overcome evil with good."[234] Thus, the general tone, topic, and flow of thought resemble Luke 6:27–36 par., though the concrete metaphors and examples found in the Q tradition are lacking in Romans 12.

The initial exhortation to sincere love in Rom 12:9a is followed by a flood of various commands, expressed by participles, adjectives, imperatives, and infinitives. Early on in the almost stream-of-consciousness flow of participles, Paul urges the Romans to show tender affection toward one another with brotherly love (v 10a). After the varied exhortations expressed by participles come to an end in v 13, v 14 begins with verbs in the imperative: "*Bless those who persecute you, bless* and do not *curse*." The words I emphasize in Rom 12:14 echo the sayings in the Q tradition that follow immediately upon the initial command "love your enemies"—though the exact wording of these sayings differs in Matthew and Luke. Right after "love your enemies" (Matt 5:44b), Matthew continues in 5:44c with "pray *for those who persecute you*." In Luke, instead, "love your enemies" (Luke 6:27b) is followed by "do good to those who hate you" (6:27c), "*bless* those who *curse* you" (6:28a), "pray for those who abuse you" (6:28b). The themes of "praying for" or "blessing" "those who persecute you" or "curse you" thus seem to go back to a shared tradition, perhaps a collection of the words of Jesus either in the Q document or still in purely oral form.[235] The striking point here is that, for all the close parallels to Jesus' commands in Luke 6:27–28 and Matt 5:44, the one command that is completely absent is the especially-memorable-because-brutally-direct "love your enemies."[236]

Returning to Paul: Romans 12 continues in vv 15–16 with exhortations to empathy, humility, and unity. In v 17, Paul turns explicitly to the theme of nonretaliation, using the formula that we have seen numerous times in the parallels from the ancient Near East and Mediterranean world. As we have already noted, in v 17a Paul echoes almost exactly the rejection of retaliation that we have encountered in *Joseph and Aseneth*: "rendering to no one evil for evil [*mēdeni kakon anti kakou apodidontes*]." Quite fittingly—in light of all we have seen—Paul does not attempt to ground this widely attested formula of nonretaliation in the words of Jesus, since the formula is totally absent from the logia of Jesus, as far as we know them. Instead, Paul appeals to the Jewish Scriptures, especially the wisdom tradition that inculcates nonretaliation: Deut 32:35 and Prov 25:21–22. Placed back to back in Rom 12:19–20, these two texts proclaim the common wisdom of the ancient Near East: do not retaliate; instead, do good to your enemy and let God exact retribution. Perhaps to conclude the thought on a more positive note, Paul rephrases the principle of nonretaliation at the end of his treatment without a reference to retribution, divine or human (v 21): "Do not be overcome by evil, but overcome evil with good."

I have traced Paul's thought as it weaves through Rom 12: 9–21 to underline two points: (1) Paul's teaching on nonretribution is the common one we have found in the many non-Christian sources we have investigated.

(2) To them he joins specifically Christian commands to bless one's persecutors instead of cursing them. Despite this weaving together of non-Christian and Christian strands of teaching on nonretaliation, and despite the close connection in thought between "bless your persecutors" (Rom 12:14a) and "love your enemy," the latter blunt command stands out by its absence—not only here in Rom 12:9–21, where the parallels would make us expect it, but also anywhere else in the NT.

Our basic argument, therefore, is clearly one of discontinuity. Sayings urging nonretaliation are common property throughout the ancient Near East, the OT, Judaism, and pagan Greco-Roman culture. The reasons for nonretribution vary greatly, from the pragmatic-humanistic to the spiritual-theological. At times, one even finds exhortations to do good to one's opponents. In a few cases (e.g., Epictetus), the verb "love" appears in the context, though in Epictetus the overarching point is love for all human beings on the part of a philosopher who is in perfect control of his emotions. Nowhere, though, in the huge amount of material that ancient parallels provide us do we find the terse, direct, disturbing command "love your enemies." [237]

Our argument that this command goes back to Jesus thus rests on discontinuity. Granted, the argument from discontinuity in the case of "love your enemies" may not seem as strong as in the case of the double commandment of love. After all, the double commandment enjoys a fourfold configuration that makes Mark 12:29–31 stand out starkly over against all supposed parallels. Still, at the core of Mark 12:29–31 we have simply two quotations from the Mosaic Torah. The uniqueness of Jesus' teaching on the double commandment is rooted not in the unheard-of wording of his saying but rather in the creative union he forges between Deut 6:4–5 and Lev 19:18b. In contrast, the discontinuity of "love your enemies" lies in the terse words themselves. The troubling content is embodied in a troubling formulation, all the more forceful for its brevity and originality.

As a distinguished Jewish scholar once pointed out to me, there is a remarkable "in-your-face" quality about some of Jesus' sayings that make them especially disconcerting, shocking, and therefore memorable. In a sense, this observation about the confrontational quality of logia like "love your enemies" is simply another way of expressing the criterion of coherence as well as discontinuity. The historical Jesus seems to have gone out of his way to make some of his most disturbing or challenging teachings all the more disturbing by expressing them in brief, blunt formulations. [238] We have already awarded the palm of authenticity to sayings like "swear not at all," "come, follow me," "let the dead bury their dead," "whoever loses his life will save it," "you cannot serve God and Mammon" and "what God has

joined let no one separate." In due time, Jesus' last short and shocking statement, "this is my body," will be added to the list. Thus, "love your enemies"
fits the peremptory style of this puzzling prophet perfectly. To the argument
from discontinuity we may add—granted, as an afterthought—the argument from coherence.

IV. THE GOLDEN RULE IN THE Q TRADITION

Some readers may question why, after lengthy considerations of the double
command of love and the command to love enemies, I give relatively short
shrift to the beloved maxim of so many Sunday school lessons and sermons,
the Golden Rule. In this section, I will briefly lay out my reasons.

To begin at the beginning: What is the Golden Rule? The label "Golden
Rule" cannot be dated earlier than the 16th century, though the reality is
ancient.[239] Christians automatically identify the Golden Rule with a maxim
attributed to Jesus and present in Matthew and Luke, though not in Mark.
The natural inference is that the Golden Rule stood in Q, despite the slightly
different formulations offered by Matthew and Luke. Matt 7:12 reads: "All
whatsoever you wish that humans do to you, so you also do [imperative
mood] to them." Luke 6:31 has instead: "And just as you wish that humans
do to you, do to them likewise." Whatever the precise wording in Q,[240] the
basic sense is clear and identical in both versions. From this one formulation
of the saying, we can already intuit the basic traits that make a saying "the
Golden Rule": (i) The Golden Rule is a succinct maxim; (ii) it gives general
direction about moral behavior among humans; (iii) at least implicitly, it
presupposes or hopes for reciprocity in social interaction; (iv) in such reciprocal relationships, one uses one's own desires as a measuring rod to tailor
one's behavior toward others; (v) the rule does not include the word "love";
(vi) the rule does not refer directly to God.[241]

As one can see from this description, the primary reason that I do not give
the saying detailed consideration among the love commandments of Jesus
is that it is not, strictly speaking, a love commandment. In neither Matthew
nor Luke, nor in any of the formulations of the Golden Rule in the early
church, does the verb "love" occur in the commandment. Moreover, one
might argue that the Golden Rule is not a "commandment" in the theological sense of the word used in the rest of this chapter. The authority of the
Golden Rule rests neither on God giving a command nor on any religious
figure announcing God's command. Rather, the Golden Rule presupposes
human autonomy in moral matters. In following the Golden Rule, an indi-

vidual decides how he or she wishes to be treated and then makes that the standard for treating others. It is therefore not by accident that there is no reference to God, explicit or implicit, in the Golden Rule. The rule makes as much sense to an atheist as to a Jew or a Christian, and is equally practicable. Hence, unless the designation "love commandment" loses its plain meaning (which it unfortunately does in many commentaries), the Golden Rule does not belong in this category.[242] A second reason for giving the Golden Rule scant attention is that, unlike the double command of love and the command to love enemies, there are no solid grounds for affirming that the Golden Rule was ever uttered by the historical Jesus.

Perhaps some Christians will be shocked by such a claim. Not only do they take for granted that the Golden Rule *originated* with Jesus, they also view it as the *summit*, sum, and substance of Jesus' ethical teaching. The latter impression, however, comes largely from Matthew's redaction of the logion. Lifting it from the position it probably had in the Q material preserved in Luke 6:27–36, Matthew places the Golden Rule at the end of a block of scattered sayings (7:12, concluding 7:1–11) as he moves toward the finale of the Sermon on the Mount.[243] Having taken 7:12ab, the Golden Rule proper, from Q, Matthew then appends his own solemn yet startling statement in 7:12c: "For this is *the Law and the prophets*." Matthew thus creates an *inclusio* with his grand programmatic pronouncement back in 5:17: "Do not think that I have come to destroy *the Law or the prophets*; I have come not to destroy but to fulfill." One cannot help wondering whether, in this case, Matthew has not been carried away by his passion for structure and *inclusio*. It is far from clear how a widely known maxim of pagan Greco-Roman ethics could be equivalent to or the summary of the Law and the prophets. At least when Matthew repeats this tag in 22:40 ("For on these two commandments hang *the whole Law and the prophets*"), he is referring to two great commandments of the Torah (Deut 6:4–5 and Lev 19:18b) welded together by Jesus. A saying that has as its ultimate origin a popular pagan proverb—however hallowed by being enshrined in Q—hardly carries the same weight. In short, it is Matthew, and Matthew alone, who creates the impression that a common saying of popular pagan ethics sums up, in Jesus' eyes, the Jewish Scriptures.[244] As we shall now see, there is good reason for doubting that Jesus held such a strange view.

(1) The Golden Rule certainly did not originate with Jesus. One or another form of the maxim circulated far and wide in ancient Greek culture, long before it was taken up by Jewish and then Christian literature.[245] The roots of the Golden Rule ultimately lie in the advice to refrain from retaliation that we have already seen in the wisdom traditions of the ancient Near

East. Over time, ancient Greek culture developed various ways of mitigating or hemming in strict retaliation. One tool of humane mitigation was what we call the Golden Rule, which probably arose in the folk ethic of ordinary people. This moral guideline marked a notable development in the ethics of Western culture inasmuch as the Golden Rule moves away from a demand for strict retaliation and toward an ethic of reciprocity: treating others as one wants to be treated. In most cases, the person following the Golden Rule hopes and may even expect that his or her ethically measured behavior will call forth similar behavior in the other person—the very presupposition of an ethic of reciprocity. Indeed, such an expectation as the basis of an ethic of reciprocity is expounded at length by Greco-Roman philosophers, though the maxim itself does not necessarily make such an expectation explicit.

The first formulations of the Golden Rule that we can find in Greek literature come from the historian Herodotus on the one hand and from the sophists on the other.[246] In his *Histories* (3.142), Herodotus (5th century B.C.) supplies a primitive, negative form of the rule when he recounts how Maeandrius, the ruler of Samos, addressed the Samians in his inaugural speech: "What I disapprove of in the actions of my neighbor, that—as best I can—I will not do."[247]

Herodotus' use of the Golden Rule may owe something to the influence of the Greek sophists, who were especially interested in first analyzing the basic principles implicit in popular morality and then formulating them in pithy maxims. The sophist and rhetorician Isocrates (436–338 B.C.) was an influential figure in the dissemination of the Golden Rule. Indeed, within the same work, he gives voice to the rule in both positive and negative forms (*Nicocles or the Cyprians*, 49 and 61). In the positive formulation in 49, Nicocles is represented as addressing his people on the mutual obligations of ruler and subjects. Reflecting the fact that the Golden Rule admits of many versions and paraphrases, Nicocles articulates an interesting three-sided version of the Golden Rule: "It is necessary for you to act in your relations to others as you expect me to act in my relations to you." In 61, he states the principle in its common negative form: "Do not do to others the things that anger you when you experience them from others." Like many other authors, Isocrates applied the general rule to specific relationships among specific groups. For example, in his *To Demonicus*, 14, he writes: "In your relations with your parents, be the kind of person you pray that your own children will be in their relations with you." Gradually, the Golden Rule expands from being wise counsel for certain groups in certain situations to being a general principle for all human beings in all their social actions.

From the 4th century B.C. onward, the Golden Rule becomes such common currency among Greek (and later Roman) writers that a comprehensive treatment of authors and their quotations would fill a whole chapter of this book. Suffice it to say that we find various forms of the rule cited by collectors of maxims (e.g., the *Sentences of Sextus*), orators like Demosthenes, popular writers like Xenophon, historians like Cassius Dio, biographers like Diogenes Laertius, and poets like Ovid. At times, the same work employs both the positive and the negative form of the rule, even back to back, as in the *Sentences of Sextus* (saying 89 [positive] and saying 90 [negative]).[248] The ancients apparently sensed no great difference between the two forms.[249]

Interestingly, this ultimate expression of popular ethics was not extolled in the great philosophical systems of Plato and Aristotle, and it is lacking in the fragmentary sayings of the oldest Stoics.[250] Only around the turn of the era, as philosophy becomes increasingly, even primarily, concerned with ethics, did the Golden Rule achieve prominence in the writings of major philosophers. Seneca, for instance, holds that the Golden Rule belongs to those maxims that must be immediately clear to anyone, without any further grounding in philosophical reason. With classical succinctness, he sums up the rule in a positive formulation: "Let us give [benefits] as we would wish to receive [them]."[251] When discussing the question of the proper treatment of slaves, he articulates a conclusion that is another example of the Golden Rule applied to particular social relationships: "This, however, is my precept put in a nutshell: as you would want your superior [in the social order] to live with you, so should you live with your inferior."[252]

It is probably through the popular Stoic philosophy of the Hellenistic period that the Golden Rule entered Jewish thought in both the Diaspora and Palestine. The perfect testimony for this embrace at home and abroad is the presence of the rule both in the *Letter of Aristeas* (written in Greek, most likely in Alexandria) and in the deuterocanonical/apocryphal books of Tobit and Ben Sira (both written in Palestine in Hebrew, or more likely in Aramaic in the case of Tobit).[253] The form of the Golden Rule found in *Ep. Aris.* §207, which we encountered when considering the background for love of enemies, is still somewhat inchoate and rambling, a mixture of positive and negative ideas: "Insofar as you [i.e., the king] do not wish evils to come upon you, but to partake of every blessing, [it would be wisdom] if you put this [principle] into practice with your subjects, including the wrongdoers."[254] It is curious that this Greek-Diaspora formulation in *Aristeas* lacks the sharp pithiness that we find in Tobit, at home in Palestine (4:15): "What you hate, do to no one [*ho miseis mēdeni poiēsēs*]."[255] As we have already seen, Ben Sira applies the Golden Rule or a reasonable facsimile thereof to the specific case of table etiquette (Sir 31:12–32:13). He reminds the guest at a banquet (31:15): "Know your neighbor as your own soul [i.e., realize that your neighbor feels as you do], and bear in mind what you yourself hate."[256]

Granted the popularity of the Golden Rule in Judaism around the turn of the era, it is not surprising that it was taken over by the rabbis. The most famous example of rabbinic assimilation of the rule to specifically Jewish concerns is the anecdote about Shammai and Hillel recounted in the Babylonian Talmud (*b. Šabb.* 31a). According to the story, one day a Gentile man comes to the shop of the famous but severe rabbinic scholar Shammai. The Gentile tells Shammai that he will become a Jew if Shammai can teach him the whole Torah [*kōl hattôrâ*] in the time during which the Gentile can remain standing on one foot. The impatient Shammai drives the Gentile away with his measuring rod. The Gentile then goes to the equally famous but much more patient and gentle rabbi, Hillel. Faced with the same challenge, Hillel replies: "What is hateful to you, do not do to your fellow. That is the whole Torah in its entirety; the rest is commentary on it. Go and learn."

While this anecdote is widely celebrated in scholarly circles, it is often not read critically. For a critical interpretation, four points need to be borne in mind: (i) We know very little about "the Hillel of history," who lived at the end of the 1st century B.C. Many texts reflect "the talmudic Hillel" of rabbinic tradition.[257] (ii) This most famous of all stories about Hillel does not appear in rabbinic literature before the Babylonian Talmud (5th–6th century A.D.); it does not occur in the corresponding place in the Palestinian (Jerusalem) Talmud. (iii) This story reflects the growing tendency of the rabbinic tradition to portray Shammai as harsh and forbidding, while Hillel is increasingly "canonized" as the patient, gentle proponent of a humane, reasonable approach to interpreting Torah. (iv) In this specific anecdote, one must attend to what Hillel does and does not say. He does not tell the Gentile that all the latter need do in order to become a Jew is to observe the (negatively formulated) Golden Rule. Rather, in keeping with the story's implicit lesson on how to attract Gentiles instead of driving them away, Hillel starts with the Golden Rule, a popular ethical principle that the Gentile probably already knew. That is where Hillel *begins*, but that is not where he or the anecdote *ends*. In a manner not unlike that of a Greco-Roman "pronouncement story" (or *chreia*), Hillel saves his "punch line" and therefore his most weighty directive to the end. After citing the Golden Rule, Hillel pointedly adds that the Gentile must go and learn "the rest." In Hillel's view, the Golden Rule does not shunt aside the corpus of Jewish laws as otiose or optional. The "commentary" on the whole Torah must be studied and implemented by the Gentile if he is to become a Jew. But Hillel, the perfect pedagogue, entices the Gentile into the new, fascinating, but bewildering world of Torah by inviting him to view it through the pragmatic prism of the Golden Rule. Thus, *b. Šabb.* 31a is a fine example of the assimilation of a universal (and, for ancient Mediterranean culture, a preeminently Greco-Roman) maxim of popular ethics into the halakic world of rabbinic Judaism.[258]

The upshot of our quick tour of the widespread use of the Golden Rule in the ancient world is that, unlike the cases of the double command of love and the command to love enemies, the criterion of discontinuity or dissimilarity does not apply here.[259] The Golden Rule most certainly did not originate with Jesus. When one remembers that the Golden Rule also lacks multiple attestation (it occurs only in Q), it is easy to see why one might begin to question whether the historical Jesus ever taught the Golden Rule. No criterion argues strongly in its favor.

(2) One might even argue that the Golden Rule is not consistent with Jesus' legal/ethical/moral demands. In other words, it cannot even meet the criterion of coherence. A number of sayings attributed to Jesus—notably in the Q block mirrored in Luke 6:27–36—indicate that Jesus criticized the ethic of reciprocity ("hand washes hand") common in the Greco-Roman world. But the Golden Rule is one expression, however refined and elegantly formulated, of precisely such an ethic of reciprocity.[260] The jarring juxtaposition of Jesus' critique of reciprocity and the Golden Rule's extolling of reciprocity in Luke 6:31–36 (and probably in Q) is clear to anyone who reads these verses aloud and in sequence. No sooner does Jesus trumpet the Golden Rule in v 31 than he continues: "And if you love those who love you, what credit do you gain? For even the sinners love those who love them. And if you do good to those who do good to you, what credit do you gain? Even the sinners do the same. And if you give loans to those from whom you hope to receive repayment, what credit do you gain? Even sinners lend to sinners in hope of getting back the same amount. Instead, love your enemies and do good and lend, expecting nothing in return." One readily sees why Matthew, with his love for orderly development, moved the Golden Rule out of this Q block of material (Matt 5:38–48), where it does not fit, and repositioned it later on in his Sermon on the Mount (7:12). The clash between the Golden Rule and Jesus' withering blast against a morality of "I'll scratch your back and you'll scratch mine" is as astounding as it is little noted by most Christians.[261] One is reminded that Q is something of a grab bag of various sayings on a general topic rather than a carefully thought-out theological system.

The problem of whether the Golden Rule satisfies the criterion of coherence, however, is not limited to Q or Luke 6:27–36. One could raise the broader question of whether the cautiously calculating desire for reciprocal benefits embodied in the Golden Rule coheres with the fierce, all-encompassing demands expressed in Jesus' double command of love and his command to love one's enemies. Putting the question still more broadly, one could ask whether the Golden Rule, while a useful (and hence popular) guide to daily living, fits in at all with the often radical demands of the eschatological prophet that we have examined throughout this volume. To be sure, it is always possible that Jesus simply was not consistent in his teaching. He was, after all, not only an eschatological prophet but also a teacher of wisdom. It may also be that, at various times, he adapted himself and his message to a not-too-bright and not-too-heroic audience. Still, since the Golden Rule can meet neither the criterion of discontinuity nor the criterion of multiple attestation, and since even the criterion of coherence does not argue clearly in its favor, I incline to the view that the Golden Rule was not taught by the historical Jesus.[262] It is more likely a prime example of a popular maxim of Greco-Roman ethics, already assimilated into Judaism, that was secondarily placed on the lips of Jesus by Christian Jews who revered him, among other things, as their ethical master. Being equally intelligible and acceptable to Jews and Gentiles, it could serve as a handy catechetical tool (note its presence in the *Did.* 1:2) for Christian missionaries of any stripe.[263]

I readily admit, though, that the case against the claim that the Golden Rule was taught by the historical Jesus is not airtight. After all, in most instances, it is nigh impossible to prove a negative in ancient history. Hence, I am willing to live with the position of those who prefer a judgment of *non liquet* (not clear either way).[264] In the end, whether or not the patient reader agrees with me on excluding the Golden Rule from the teaching of the historical Jesus, our brief examination of this princely principle of pragmatism is not for naught. If nothing else, our long pilgrimage through the last three sections of this chapter has taught us not to lump the Golden Rule together with Jesus' double command of love and/or his command to love enemies— as so many do. To this extent, we have learned to be more discerning than many modern scholars, to say nothing of Q and the *Didache*, both of which display the weakness of an eclectic approach to Jesus in particular and morality in general.

Having exhausted the Synoptic material on real or supposed love commandments, let us turn now to the Johannine tradition, which, whatever else may be said of it, at least has a genuine love command.

V. THE LOVE COMMAND IN THE JOHANNINE TRADITION

A. The Theological Context of the Love Command within John's Gospel

Within the NT, Jesus' command, "as I have loved you, you also—love one another," is found only in John's Gospel, and in John's Gospel only in two statements made during the Last Supper (John 13:34; 15:12 + 17).[265] Hence, it is important to read this specifically Johannine command in the context of the theology of the Fourth Gospel, which is quite different from that of the Synoptics.[266] Put in a nutshell, what distinguishes the theology of John's Gospel is the combination of (1) high christology in a densely concentrated form, (2) a strongly realized eschatology, and (3) a stark dualism. Let us examine each of these characteristics in turn.[267]

1. High Christology

Other passages of the NT mention Christ's preexistence (e.g., Phil 2:6–11; Col 1:15–20; Heb 1:1–4), but John's Gospel is the only book of the NT that bases its whole understanding of Christ's person and work on a theology of preexistence and incarnation.[268] In this respect, the Prologue (John 1:1–18) is indeed a programmatic announcement of the whole Gospel's point of view. The Fourth Gospel is unique within the NT because it *thematizes* preexistence and incarnation, that is, it makes them the foundation and direct object of theological reflection throughout the work.[269] Undergirding whatever narrative or speech is being presented at the moment is John's archetypal story: God the Father sends his only Son (= the Son of God, the Word) into the hostile world to save, not condemn it.[270] The Word becomes flesh so that the saving divine word may be spoken in human words, allowing the light of revelation to shine in the darkness of this fallen world and so provoke belief or unbelief. Having obediently completed his mission, the Son returns (or ascends) back to the Father by way of the cross, which is his definitive glorification. Expressed in an alternate pattern: the preexistent, heavenly Son of Man descends from the "above world" of light into the "below world" of darkness to shed the light of his truth, thus offering the possibility of either salvation or damnation, depending on the individual's reaction to the light. The Son of Man then reverses course, ascending back to the "above world" by being exalted on the throne of the cross, the definitive act of revelation, which brings salvation or judgment to onlookers, depending on how they see.[271]

   In this high christology of preexistence and incarnation, all religious symbols and systems collapse into the person of the Word made flesh.[272] This dense christological concentration, this christological "implosion," allows Jesus to say with solemn simplicity: "I am." Indeed, "I am"—whatever. Fill in the blank with anything good and saving, and I am it, and no one else is. Any and every symbol of revelation and salvation is absorbed into Jesus. As a result, the Johannine spotlight is focused intensely and exclusively on Jesus. That is one reason why, in John's Gospel, there is no developed theology of church, no stories of the disciples performing miracles or being sent out on a short mission during Jesus' public ministry, and no extensive body of ethical directions à la the Sermon on the Mount. Christology not only takes center stage; it takes up the whole stage. One must understand the Johannine love command in this intensely christological context. Christ alone is the basis and standard of everything else.

2. Strongly Realized Eschatology

Precisely because the event that early Christians expected at the parousia—the descent of the glorious Son of Man from heaven to earth to bring final judgment—has already happened in the incarnation, the events of the end time are already present in Jesus' ministry. By bringing the saving light of revelation down from heaven to earth, the Son of Man, the eschatological judge, precipitates judgment right now by forcing humans to line up for or against him, by forcing them to believe or reject his revelation right now. As they accept or reject it, so they are saved or condemned now—in the present moment of belief or unbelief. *Now* is the judgment (John 3:18–21; 12:31), *now* is the resurrection of the dead (5:24–26).

3. Stark Dualism

This brief sketch of John's christology and eschatology inevitably involves a narrative employing sharp contrasts between hostile forces. In John's cosmic drama, the sin of the world, humanity's basic rebellion against God and his claims on it, has aggravated and transformed the natural distance between heaven and earth, God and the world, into fierce alienation. The descent and ascent of the Son of Man are meant to bridge the chasm caused by sin, restoring the proper bonds between the loving Creator and his rebellious creation. But some humans willfully shut their eyes to the light the Son brings and is. They thus create and inhabit the darkness that defines "the world" in John's negative sense: all those humans who reject Jesus by refusing to believe his message.

Actually, John's story of salvation implicitly involves more than one type of dualism.[273] While the "cosmological dualism" of heaven and earth, Creator and creature, can be bridged by the incarnation, cross, and resurrection of the Son, the "dualism of decision," the dualism of belief and unbelief that splits humanity into two warring camps of human existence, cannot be bridged or eliminated. In cosmological dualism, God can love the world, the Word can become flesh, the heavenly can descend to earth to open up the way to heaven for all who believe. But, in the dualism of decision, light (= revelation of the truth) cannot become darkness (= willful rejection of the truth), no more than darkness can become light. Individuals may pass over from one camp to the other (think of the oscillation of Simon Peter or Nicodemus), but the camps as such remain unalterably opposed.

By the time the Last Supper has arrived, the disciples of Jesus (Judas excepted) dwell in the camp of light, while those who reject Jesus (= the world in the negative sense of the word) abide in the camp of darkness. With typical Johannine symbolism, Judas is depicted as leaving the lit supper room, where the Light of the World now speaks only to his own, those he has separated from the world. Fulfilling Jesus' sad prophecy, Judas chooses instead to plunge into the darkness of those who hate the light. John ends the scene with three mournful monosyllables (John 13:30): "It was night." Only then, after the one person who never really belonged to the community of believers has departed, can Jesus proceed to reveal his "new," eschatological commandment of love to those who have taken their stand on the right side of the dualism of decision: "As I have loved *you* [the small, purified group of faithful disciples gathered around Jesus], so you too—love *one another* [the fellow members of the faithful group]." [274]

It is therefore in this triple context of high christology, realized eschatology, and stark dualism that we must hear and understand the love command of the Johannine Jesus. It is his last will and testament to the community of believers as he takes his leave of them in the farewell discourses of the Last Supper. Perhaps the best way to deepen our understanding of this unique command is to compare it in venue, audience, and content to the love commands of the Synoptics.

B. THE LOVE COMMANDS: JOHN AND THE SYNOPTICS COMPARED

When we compare John with the Synoptics on any topic, we are often struck by the sharply different, sometimes polar-opposite way in which the same narrative or saying is presented in John. Whether we examine the Baptist's prophecy of "the coming one," Peter's confession of faith in Jesus, the anointing of Jesus by a woman, or the overall Passion Narrative, the same event or saying winds up in John with different wording, different theological content, and often a different setting. In this respect, the Johannine command of love does not disappoint.

When we focus on the various forms of love commandments in the Gospels, we notice—even apart from the key question of content—two significant points of contrast: different settings and different audiences.[275] In the Synoptics, the love commands are spoken in public, and the audience is not restricted to the disciples—if, indeed, the disciples are present at all. In Mark's version of the double command of love (Mark 12:28–34 parr.), the sole direct recipient of Jesus' teaching is a Jewish scribe who is well-disposed toward Jesus but not (yet?) one of his disciples (12:34: "You are not far from the kingdom of God"). The wider audience that is brought on stage at various points in Mark's larger narrative (Jesus is teaching in the Jerusalem temple) is made up of various opponents (chief priests, elders, scribes, Pharisees, Herodians, and Sadducees) as well as the faceless crowd. Jesus' disciples, the people whom one would expect to be the immediate recipients of such an important teaching, are almost completely missing from the chain of dispute stories and discussions that Mark sets in Jerusalem (12:27–44). Only at the very end of the dispute cycle, as Jesus is about to leave the temple, does he "call his disciples over" (v 43: *proskalesamenos tous mathētas autou*) to point out the widow who is contributing her last coins to the temple treasury. Hence, we cannot even be sure that, in Mark's mind, the disciples are present to hear Jesus teach the double command of love. The reader may presume that they are, but Mark has no interest in mentioning their presence on the sidelines.

When we turn to the command to love enemies (Luke 6:27 ‖ Matt 5:44), the venue is still public (with a plain or a mountain as the scenic locale), but now the disciples form the primary audience. Nevertheless, both Matthew and Luke supply a crowd as a secondary audience or outer circle of listeners (Matt 4:25–5:1; 7:28–29; and Luke 6:17–19; 7:1). Thus, for all the differences between the double command of love and the command to love enemies, the setting is some public space, and the audience is never restricted solely to the disciples.

The contrast with John's Gospel could not be starker. During the public ministry, when the Johannine Jesus publicly and repeatedly engages his opponents and the crowds in heated debates and lively exchanges, often followed by a lengthy monologue, Jesus never issues a love commandment to his audience. In fact, the Johannine Jesus never delivers any detailed teaching of ethical directives such as we find in the Sermon on the Mount. (In this respect, one might almost call the Fourth Gospel amoral.) Accordingly, the relatively few occurrences of the verb *agapaō* ("to love") during the public ministry (3:16,19,35; 8:42; 10:17; 11:5; 12:43) are all in the indicative and are usually found in the comments of the evangelist. Most of these seven passages depict God the Father or Jesus loving in a positive sense, while "humans" (*hoi anthrōpoi*) love all the wrong things. However, once the public ministry ends and the Johannine Jesus is sequestered with his chosen disciples at the Last Supper (chaps. 13–17), there is an explosion of "love talk."[276] The verb *agapaō*, having occurred only seven times in the first twelve chapters of the Gospel, now appears twenty-five times in the brief compass of chaps. 13–17, in one time frame and in one place.[277] Except for the three initial occurrences (13:1[*bis*],23), spoken by the narrator in his own voice, all the instances of *agapaō* are on the lips of Jesus as he expounds on the love relationships involving the Father and the Son, the Son and his disciples, and the disciples among themselves.[278]

Thus, one can detect in both the Synoptics and John a certain correspondence between setting-*plus*-audience on the one hand and the type of love command taught by Jesus on the other. In the Synoptics, the double command of love and the command to love enemies, both publicly delivered, are in principle directed to all (or, at least in the Synoptic story-world, all Jews). All are obliged to love God, neighbor, and yes, says Jesus, even enemies. In John, the private setting and narrow audience at the Last Supper correspond to the restricted nature of the love that Jesus commands. The disciples of Jesus are commanded to "love *one another*"—not enemies, not even neighbors in the sense of all fellow Israelites.[279]

Whether or not one wishes to label the Johannine community a "sect"— and the debate usually comes down to what one means by a "sect"[280]—the Fourth Gospel and the Johannine Epistles project the contours of a group of Christians somewhat alienated from the larger world and tending to turn their gaze inward.[281] Traumatized by two schisms in their brief history—first the break with the Jewish synagogue that was their home and matrix and then a breakup within their own ranks—the Johannine Christians are intent on maintaining what bonds of love remain to them in their community. In a curious way, the Johannine form of the love command brings us back to the theme of reciprocal love, but the reciprocity is now quite different from the ethic of reciprocity denounced by the Synoptic Jesus in Luke 6:32–34 par.[282] The Johannine love command does not inculcate the mutual favors that oil the wheels of society and help one get along and get ahead. Rather, the purpose of the Johannine command is the sustenance and solidarity of a small group of Christians who feel besieged by a hostile world. The more these Christians are convinced that the world hates them and wishes to kill them—which is what Jesus tells them in John 15:18; 17:14;16:2—the more they feel the need to pull together in a community of mutual love. According to John's theology, this mutual love participates in the love flowing between the Father and the Son and between the Son and individual believers.

There is, then, in this Johannine type of love—and, specifically, in the Johannine love commandment—both an ontological and an ethical dimension: that is, both a grounding in God's very being and an impulse to human action. First, in the order of being: the mutual love of the Johannine Christians is rooted in, participates in, and is made possible by the eternal love between the Father and the Son (John 17:24; cf. v 5).[283] This eternal love of God entered—yes, invaded—the God-hating world via the incarnation of the Word (John 3:16). Those who believe in the words spoken by the Word made flesh become his disciples—which means that they come to know the Son's love for themselves. Still more, through the Son, they come to know the Father's love both for the Son and for the Son's disciples. Thus, the mutual love commanded by Jesus is first of all based on a new type of existence, a being-drawn-into the community of love that is the eternal life of the Father and the Son. As the Father "abides" (or, alternately, "is") in the Son and the Son in the Father, so too the Son abides in the believers and the believers in the Son (14:10–11,20–23; 15:4–10; 17:20–26).[284] Mutual love is grounded in mutual indwelling.

At the same time, though, this ontologically based love is not a mystical "flight of the alone to the alone," a withdrawal of the individual from social responsibility into a private world of religious ecstasy.[285] Not by accident, John places the first enunciation of Jesus' love command (13:34) after Jesus' "sacramental" washing of his disciples' feet (13:4–17), which is itself prefaced by the evangelist's comment on Jesus' love for his own "to the utmost" (13:1).[286] Jesus' humble service—lowering himself to a task proper to a slave—symbolizes the cleansing power of his coming death (v 10), communicates that power to those who are willing to "have a share" with him in his sacrificial service (v 8), and provides his disciples with a graphic example (*hypodeigma* in v 15) of the kind of servant-love that they are to practice toward one another in imitation of him.

This emphasis on a love that embodies itself in concrete moral actions is colorfully expressed in the second context of the Johannine love command, namely, the discourse on the vine and the branches in John 15:1–8. The branches, that is, the disciples who draw their life from Christ the vine (v 4), must show forth the reality of that ontologically grounded life by "bearing fruit" (v 5), in other words, by visible ethical activity in the community. "Fruit" is a common metaphor in the NT for the moral attitude or action that should mark a follower of Christ (e.g., Gal 5:22; Phil 1:11; Jas 3:18;

Heb 12:11; cf. Matt 3:8; 21:43). The most famous example of this metaphor (though used negatively) is Jesus' rule of discernment in the Sermon on the Mount (Matt 7:20; cf. vv 15–27): "By their fruits you shall know them." The fact that "fruit" has this moral connotation in John 15 is clear from the immediately following context, which speaks of keeping the commandments, specifically the commandment of mutual love (15:9–17).[287]

But to return to the scene of the foot washing in John 13: the one jarring note amid the symbolism of mutual service in the early part of chap. 13 is the presence of Judas Iscariot, first noted in 13:2,10–11, and then focused on in vv 21–30. Fittingly, it is only after Judas leaves the supper room and plunges into the night of evil (v 30) that Jesus draws the ultimate lesson from his sacramental act of washing. In the narrowed circle of true disciples now cleansed of the betrayer—and only in this context in the whole Gospel— Jesus pronounces the Johannine version of the love command (13:34–35): "A new commandment I give you, that you love one another. As I have loved you, you also—love one another." The ontologically grounded love must become embodied in specific humble acts of service toward fellow members of the community.

In sum, the mutual love commanded by the Johannine Jesus is both (i) *ontologically* grounded (i.e., based on the permanent bond of life and love existing between the Father and the Son and then between the Son and his disciples) and (ii) *ethically* articulated (i.e., put into practice by moral deeds of service that reflect Jesus' great deed of service, his death on the cross).[288] Both the ontological and ethical dimensions of this love command are subtly underlined by the all-important subordinate clause in 13:34 and 15:12, introduced by the Greek conjunction *kathōs* ("as," "just as," "to the degree that," but also "inasmuch as," "since"): "Love one another *as* [but also: 'since'] I have loved you." This saving ambiguity of *kathōs* allows it to say two things at once in 13:34:[289]

(i) *Kathōs* can carry the sense of "inasmuch as," "since," "on the basis of the fact that." In this sense, Jesus' love is the foundation and the enabling cause of the disciples' love for one another. The Son's incarnation brings God's love into a loveless world, and the Son's climactic exaltation on the cross reveals God's love to the supreme degree.[290] It is that love on the cross, symbolically breathed out as spirit (John 19:30), symbolically poured out as blood and water (19:34), that creates the community of love at the foot of the cross, the community constituted by the newly formed family of Jesus' mother and her spiritual son, the beloved disciple (19:26–27).[291] The Johannine disciples can fulfill Jesus' command of love only because they have been empowered to do so by the loving service of Jesus unto death. It is not for nothing that the love command voiced in 15:12 is preceded by Jesus' sober and ego-deflating warning: "Without me you can do nothing" (15:5). The *kathōs* ("since") of the Johannine love command thus hammers home the ontological-christological basis that alone makes Christian love possible.

(ii) At the same time, *kathōs* (in the sense of "as," "just as," "to the degree that") bespeaks the standard, the model, the example and exemplar by which something is measured. By his service unto death on the cross, symbolized at the Last Supper, Jesus has not only empowered the disciples to love; he has also given them the perfect paradigm of how broad and deep their love for one another must be. Ontological-christological basis and ethical-christological model: both are summed up by Jesus' profound proviso: "*as* [and 'since'] I have loved you."

Stepping back for a moment from all this detailed exegesis, we can see how the christological implosion that is the hallmark of Johannine theology— the collapsing of all religious categories and symbols into the person and work of Jesus—is perfectly exemplified in this love command, the one specific moral command that Jesus issues to his disciples in the whole of the Fourth Gospel. We need only compare the Johannine love command with the Synoptic love commands to appreciate the difference. The double command of love is simply made up of two OT commandments skillfully combined by Jesus. The implicit christology of the Marcan pericope lies in the way the authority of Jesus is questioned and vindicated in his impressive teaching. However, taken by itself, the double command of love is christological neither in its content nor in its wording.

The same is true of the laconic "love your enemies" of the Q tradition. Once again, whatever christological overtones accrue to the text come from the larger context, in which the authoritative prophet of the end time lays out the manner of life and the obligations incumbent on his disciples. The introductory "but I say to you," supplied secondarily and in different ways by Matthew and Luke, confers some christological coloring on a command totally bereft of any christology at its core. The very fact that the basic substance, though not the exact wording, of Jesus' command to love enemies can be found in pagan philosophers of the period reminds us how lacking in christology are the bare syllables, "love your enemies." In stark contrast, the very wording of the Johannine command of love proclaims Christ as its empowering basis and ethical standard: "As and since I have loved you, you also—love one another." In John's Gospel, even moral teaching—to the extent that it exists in John at all—collapses into christology.[292]

C. THE QUESTION OF HISTORICITY

As the astute reader may suspect, I have spent so much time examining the special theological context of the Johannine love command not simply to savor the intriguing if idiosyncratic theology of the Fourth Gospel. Everything we have seen so far bears on the question of whether John's form of the love command comes from the historical Jesus. Establishing the historicity of this command is already made difficult not only by the lack of multiple attestation of the saying but also by the special type of isolation that characterizes it. The love command of John 13:34 (repeated in 15:12) is isolated not only from the other three Gospels but also from the body of John's Gospel. It is secluded in the segregated setting of the Last Supper, with no echo elsewhere in the Fourth Gospel.[293] When one adds to this isolation within the various Gospel traditions its peculiarly Johannine stamp, reflecting John's special theology of preexistence, incarnation, realized eschatology, and indwelling, it becomes very difficult to maintain that this form of the love command goes back to the historical Jesus. The Johannine character embodied in the command of 13:34 is not just a matter of John's special phraseology or his conscious placement of the command at the Last Supper. The basis and standard of love articulated in the Johannine command are inextricably bound up with the grand theological synthesis that permeates John's Gospel. One cannot peel away the Johannine husk of this commandment to get at an original core reaching back to Jesus. John's christological implosion lies at the very heart of the Johannine love command.

What we have, then, in John 13:34 and 15:12 is a specifically Johannine reworking of some general tradition about a love commandment. At best, one might suggest that the Johannine community retained a memory, however vague, that Jesus commanded love. The community would then have proceeded to express this memory in a formulation that matched its theoretical christology as well as its practical needs as a group of Christians in crisis. One must admit, though, that not even this much of a connection with the historical Jesus is strictly required to explain the Johannine form of the love command. One might suppose instead that the Johannine love command is simply the Johannine rereading of Lev 19:18b ("you shall love your neighbor as yourself") in the light of the community's high christology plus its social tensions. If one abstracts from the christological basis and scope of the command, what one has is simply an exhortation to mutual love within the community. Throughout this chapter, we have seen at length how various Jewish writings around the turn of the era urged mutual love and solidarity. In a number of cases, Lev 19:18b loomed in the background, though it was never explicitly quoted. We might well have a similar scenario in the case of the Johannine love command. This becomes all the more likely when one considers that the breadth of the love commanded is similar in Lev 19:18b and John 13:34 (cf. 15:12). As we have already seen, the "neighbor" (rēaʿ) to be loved in Lev 19:18b is any other Israelite who belongs to the cultic community. Similarly, "one another" (allēlous) in John 13:34 + 15:12 signifies any other member of the Johannine community. All within the community are included in the commandment, but none outside the community.

This insight prompts one to ponder the lack of any command to love one's enemies in the Fourth Gospel. Despite this absence, some commentators argue that love of enemies is implied or at least not excluded by the Fourth Gospel—at least when the whole range of John's theology is taken into account. After all, the great announcement of John's Gospel is that "God so loved the [God-hating, hostile] world that he sent his only Son." Should we not suppose that the disciples of the Son are obliged to love in the same way? This argument, however appealing at first sight, becomes dubious once we examine the specific context of the Johannine love command: not just the segregated, "under-siege" atmosphere of the Last Supper, but more especially the words of Jesus immediately following the love command in 15:12. In 15:13, Jesus proceeds to explain the extent of the love command by implicitly presenting himself as a model of sacrificial love: "Greater love than this no one has, that one lay down his life for his friends." The beneficiaries of this supreme, ideal love inculcated by the Johannine Jesus are one's *friends*. Lest we miss the point, Jesus immediately tells the small circle of disciples, "*You* [emphatic] are my friends." [294] Note: such love for one's *friends* is proclaimed to be the *greatest* love that can exist, period. In other words, no greater love than self-sacrifice for one's friends (in context, the obedient disciples of Jesus) exists on John's theological radar screen. Put more bluntly: love of enemies does not exist on the radar screen.

This emphasis on mutual love, along with an absence of any imperative to love enemies, all within the context of an eschatological community of believers living with a sense of rejection and danger, has led some commentators to compare the Johannine group with Qumran. [295] While there are many points of comparison—from the stark dualism of a community under siege to fiery polemics against the temple authorities in Jerusalem—there is an all-important difference. At Qumran, alongside the obligation to love the other "sons of light" in one's own community, there is the equal and openly expressed command to hate all the "sons of darkness"—that is, everyone not in the Essene community (1QS 1:9–10). The belief that God so loved the God-hating world that he sent his only Son to save it, the hope that the community's mutual love may act as an attractive witness, drawing others to believe, and the final prayer of Jesus that the world might be saved—all these factors keep the Fourth Gospel from inculcating a positive obligation to hate (cf. John 3:16–17; 11:51–52; 12:20–24,32; 17:20–23; 20:21–23).[296]

In the end, though, we must admit that, while the Johannine command of love has a christological depth lacking in the corresponding Synoptic commands, the Synoptic command to love enemies, not to mention its command to pray for persecutors and to bless those who curse Christians, finds no real correlative in John. The extent of the love command in John is, mutatis mutandis, no greater than that of Lev 19:18b: the fellow members of one's own community. Hence, one may wonder whether the Johannine love command stems even indirectly from Jesus or whether it is simply John's Christian appropriation of the love command from Leviticus.[297]

D. THE LOVE COMMAND IN THE JOHANNINE EPISTLES

Our survey of the tradition of a love command in the Johannine writings would not be complete without a side glance at the Johannine Epistles.[298] For all practical purposes, this comes down to examining the First Epistle of John, since 3 John never mentions a love command and 2 John simply repeats from 1 John the command "that we love one another" (v 5), without any real development of it.[299]

The First Epistle of John is a fascinating document.[300] In it, we hear a teacher of the community—probably someone other than the author of the Fourth Gospel—who is steeped in the Johannine tradition, but who is rethinking and reapplying it in a new and different time of crisis. More specifically, the author of the First Epistle is struggling to reinterpret the Gospel of John in the light of a schism that has arisen in the community since the Gospel was written—a schism that the Gospel may have even willy-nilly precipitated. To be sure, the author of the First Epistle basically affirms the message of the Gospel in the face of this new challenge to the community's existence, but he does so with some "clarifications" or revisions. Apparently the "secessionists," those who have left the community, have pushed the Fourth Gospel's emphasis on Christ's divinity to the point of diminishing, if not effacing, the saving significance of Jesus' human life and death here on earth. Moreover, whether from charismatic enthusiasm or from a gnosticizing denigration of the physical realities of this world, the secessionists seem to downplay the importance of Christian moral activity and the real possibility of Christians' falling into sin. In the eyes of our author, the secessionists' denial that the Son of God came "in the flesh" (1 John 4:2–3;

2 John 7) leads logically to a denial of the importance of Christian moral action "in the flesh." In brief, what is at issue is the embodiment of the divine
in the human.[301]

In response to this crisis, the author of the First Epistle "pulls back"
somewhat from the more radical and innovative thrust of the Fourth Gospel
in favor of the decades-old Johannine tradition he has known, a tradition
closer to "mainstream" Christianity.[302] In contrast to the Fourth Gospel,
the First Epistle gives more emphasis to the human, embodied dimension of
Jesus' earthly life, to his death as an atoning sacrifice for sin, to the problem
of ongoing sinfulness in the life of the believer, and to the saving appearance
of Christ on the last day. The impact of this shift in theological emphasis
can be seen in a two-pronged message pervading the First Epistle: (i) genuine
Christian faith is faith in the Son of God who truly became human, assum-
ing a true human body and suffering a true human death for our sins (1 John
1:1–4; 2:1–2,22–25; 3:23; 4:2,9; 5:5–12) and (ii) genuine love for fellow
members of the community must be embodied in practical deeds of charity
(2:9–11; 3:11–18; 4:7–12,20–21). Put simply: an embodied Son of God demands embodied acts of love from his followers.

It is within this context that we should understand the "re-reception" of
the command of mutual love from the Fourth Gospel. That such a rethinking
of the love command is intended by the author of 1 John is suggested by the
explosion of "love" vocabulary in the First Epistle.[303] Although it is only five
chapters long, it employs the verb *agapaō* more often (twenty-eight times in
all) than almost any other book in the NT. Indeed, only the Fourth Gospel
(twenty-one chapters in length) has more occurrences (thirty-seven times).
When it comes to the noun *agapē*, 1 John has eighteen occurrences compared to the Fourth Gospel's mere seven instances. The adjective *agapētos*
("beloved") never appears in the Gospel of John, but it occurs six times in
1 John.[304] Clearly, love is very much on the mind of the author of the First
Epistle.

Yet the precise words of Jesus as found in John 13:34 and 15:12 ("as I
have loved you, you also—love one another") are never cited, nor is any
commandment of love explicitly referred back to Jesus as its source. Rather,
the love command is reworked as the author's own exhortation, expressed in
the author's own words. For example, although 1 John harks back at times
to the Gospel's phraseology of loving "one another" (3:11,23; 4:7,11,12), the
First Epistle regularly prefers to speak of loving "the brother," that is, one's
fellow Christian in the community. (From Paul onward, "brother" is a common NT term for a fellow Christian.)[305] A still more intriguing and significant modification of the Gospel's presentation is that the author of 1 John

feels ambivalent about calling the love command "new [*kainos*]," as the Gospel emphatically does in John 13:34.[306] While granting that it is "new" in the sense of the dawning of a new eschatological period in which Christians now live (1 John 2:8), the author first insists that it is "old" (*palaios*).[307] It is old in the sense that it belongs to the tradition that Johannine Christians have heard "from the beginning" of their existence as believers (1 John 2:7; cf. 1:1 and the constant emphasis on "from the beginning" in this tradition-minded work).[308]

This harking back to traditional formulations that are probably earlier than the composition of the Fourth Gospel may explain why in 1 John, as distinct from the Gospel, we possibly hear echoes of the double command of love. In fact, some critics claim to espy an X-ray outline, as it were, of the double command in the author's insistence on the Christian's obligation to believe in the Son of God and to love one another. The prime text here is the chiastic pronouncement in 1 John 3:23: "And this is his *commandment*, that we believe in the name of his Son Jesus Christ and that we love one another, just as he gave us a *commandment*." In my opinion, though, seeing the double command of love in such a passage—where one obligation is described in terms of faith and the other in terms of love—requires a true stretch of the exegetical imagination.[309]

An echo of the double command of love is more likely in those passages where the love of God and the love of one's brother are clearly linked—though not in the neat "first" and "second" order of Mark 12:29–31 and not with explicit citations of Deut 6:4–5 and Lev 19:18b. Perhaps the most emphatic passage in 1 John yoking love of God and love of brother is found in 4:20–21, where the author rebukes those whose supposed love for God is not embodied in love for one's brother: "If anyone says, 'I love God,' and hates his brother, he is a liar. For the person who does not love his brother whom he has seen cannot love the God whom he has not seen. And this is the commandment we have from him, that the person who loves God must love his brother as well."[310] This passage is reminiscent of Jesus' double command of love (Mark 12:29–31) in that (i) it combines love of God and love of a human being as two loves that necessarily belong together; (ii) the obligation to love is qualified as a "commandment" (*entolē*, the same terminology as in Mark);[311] and (iii) the commandment is ultimately traced back one way or another to God himself.

At the same time, we must admit some weighty differences. (i) To be sure, the two OT commandments that Jesus cites in Mark 12:29–31 obviously come from God, since they are direct citations of commandments in the written Mosaic Torah. But the innovative act of selecting Deut 6:4–5 and

Lev 19:18b from all the laws of the OT and of binding them together as "first" and "second" comes solely from Jesus. If we are speaking not of two disparate commandments from the OT but rather of *the* double command of love, then we must confess that this double command is a creation of Jesus and Jesus alone. A sense of the origin of the double command in Jesus is totally lacking in 1 John 4:20–21, where "the commandment" is simply said to come "from him," namely, from God the Father, the only person mentioned in the immediately preceding context.[312] (ii) Not only does 1 John 4:20–21 not cite Deut 6:4–5 and Lev 19:18b word for word, the only two words in common with Mark 12:29–31 are "love" and "God." One is hard-pressed to find an allusion to Deut 6:4–5 and Lev 19:18b, let alone a citation. (iii) 1 John 4:20–21 rightly speaks of "this commandment" in the singular because the only imperatival statement in these verses is "a person must love his brother." Love of God is taken for granted as the given, not as something explicitly commanded. It is the agreed-upon basis from which the author argues to the necessity of loving one's brother if one wants to make a valid claim to love God. In fact, nowhere in 1 John is the love of God (i.e., a human's love for God) ever expressed as an obligation or commandment. It is difficult to speak of a double command of love in 1 John if love of God is never formulated as a command.[313]

Thus, while it is tempting to see in passages like 1 John 4:20–21 an echo of Jesus' double command of love, the echo is too faint to be probative.[314] Our earlier judgment that the Marcan account of Jesus' teaching on the double command (Mark 12:29–31) lacks independent multiple attestation anywhere else in the NT must stand.[315] Still, it is intriguing to compare the possible background of the love command in the Gospel of John with that of the First Epistle. The Gospel's command to love one another can be understood simply as the "re-reception" of the command to love one's neighbor (Lev 19:18b), with John's high Christology ("as I have loved you") substituting for "as yourself" as the measuring rod of love.[316] In contrast, the First Epistle of John, with its emphasis on appealing to "what was from the beginning [of the Johannine tradition about Jesus]" may be reaching back to a part of the Jesus tradition preserved in the Johannine community but not taken up in the Fourth Gospel. The inextricable bond between loving God and loving one's brother that 1 John 4:20–21 affirms could possibly be a "re-reception" (or simply a distant echo?) of Jesus' double command of love by the Johannine community. This is an intriguing conjecture, but only a conjecture.

In the end, unlike Mark's double command of love and Q's command to love one's enemies—both of which we have judged authentic—the love command in the Fourth Gospel should probably be honored simply as a great contribution of the evangelist (and/or the final redactor), reflecting creatively on the core Christian message in the light of both the OT and his community's tradition. In all likelihood, it does not go back to the historical Jesus.

VI. CONCLUDING REFLECTIONS ON THE LOVE COMMANDMENTS

At the beginning of this chapter, I inculcated the need to differentiate the various love commands in the Gospels according to source and content. At the end of this long trek through the Synoptics, the Fourth Gospel, and the Johannine Epistles, the necessity of distinguishing the "whence" and "what" of each type of love command is abundantly clear. Clear also is the reason why one would accept one form of the love command as coming from Jesus, while another form has to be judged a creation of the early church.

Contrary to what I myself expected going into this project, I have found that the double command of love (love for God and for one's neighbor) has the best likelihood of coming from the historical Jesus. In the case of this Marcan tradition, the argument from discontinuity is quite strong. Absolutely no Jewish writing before (or even soon after) the time of Jesus presents us with a double command of love that possesses the four striking (and dialectical) characteristics of the Marcan pericope: (i) The texts of Deut 6:4–5 and Lev 19:18b are quoted word for word. (ii) The two texts are welded together by being cited back to back. (iii) Despite this stark juxtaposition, the two texts are nevertheless carefully distinguished: the order of their importance is emphasized by labeling Deut 6:4–5 as the *first* commandment and Lev 19:18b as the *second*. (iv) Despite this distinction, these two commandments are then bundled together as superior to all other commandments.

In sharp contrast to all this dazzling dialectic of combination yet distinction of two commandments contained in the written Torah is the brutally terse command "love your enemies," contained nowhere (in those precise words) in the OT and only in the Q tradition within the Gospels. We have in the command to love enemies no citation or allusion to OT texts (with an implicit appeal to the authority of Scripture), no relating or ordering of commandments to the Mosaic Law, and no narrative setting like Mark 12:28–34 to supply a larger context of meaning. The blunt, laconic "love your enemies" stands alone and isolated even in Q, the surrounding material wandering off to scatter-shot exhortations. For a modern reader, the only similarity to the double command of love, apart from the verb "love," is that the argument for historicity rests solely on discontinuity. Once again, there is no multiple attestation of independent sources. The argument from discontinuity proves more tricky in the case of love of enemies than it did in the case of the double command. The basic substance of a command or exhortation to love enemies can be found in Jewish, pagan, and early Christian sources. The one thing that cannot be found anywhere in the ancient Mediterranean world prior to Jesus is the terribly terse, totally unexplained, in-your-face demand "love your enemies." Consequently, while the argument from discontinuity is more tenuous in this case, I am inclined to allow that the Q command to love enemies, as well as the Marcan tradition of the double command, goes back to the historical Jesus.

Not so the Johannine command "as I have loved you, you also—love one another." One might object that we have here the same situation that we find in the Q command to love enemies. A lack of multiple attestation, one might argue, is countered by a lack of parallels before the time of Jesus. Should not the argument from discontinuity apply to John's version as well? The problem is that, when one examines the Johannine love command in detail, one discovers that the lack of parallels in Jewish or pagan literature—not to mention the rest of the NT—is to be explained by the thoroughly Johannine character of this love command. As our overview of John's thought-world has shown, the Johannine love command is rooted in and indeed grows straight out of the fertile but idiosyncratic soil of John's theology. In John's Gospel, every religious institution, structure, symbol, category, or title collapses into the person of the Johannine Jesus. The same is true of the sole specific moral command in the whole of the Gospel. In John, the measure and ground of love become the divine love made human in the Incarnate Word ("as *I* have loved you"). Accordingly, the object of love—every Israelite (the "neighbor") in Mark and every foe (one's "enemies") in Q—is narrowed down to the members of the Johannine community, those who have accepted this divine love and who share it with others who do the same ("love *one another*").

We are left, then, with the Marcan and Q forms of the love command as the two commands that probably come from the historical Jesus. What larger ramifications does such a judgment hold?

First, the two types of commands confirm a portrait of the historical Jesus that has slowly emerged in our investigation. The historical Jesus is both deeply steeped in the Jewish Scriptures—as well as the legal debates about them—and at the same time open to the cultural influences of the larger Greco-Roman world. On the one hand, the double command of love shows us a Jesus who is able to hold his own in a conversation with a learned Jewish scribe, a Jesus who knows and can cite specific texts of the written Torah, a Jesus who can range nimbly across the vast number of commandments in the Torah to pluck out and combine two commandments on love, and, most startlingly, a Jesus who knows how to use the hermeneutical technique of the *gĕzērâ šāwâ* to construct his argument. On the other hand, as we have seen at length, the clearest contemporary parallels to Jesus' teaching on love of enemies are found in pagan Stoic philosophers. Seneca even uses the same Hemingwayesque argument that "the sun also rises." The fact that sober questers for the historical Jesus rightly reject a "relevant" Jesus dressed as a Jewish-hippie-iconoclastic-Cynic philosopher dabbling in academic postmodernism does not mean that we should engage in a rearguard apologetic that rejects all Hellenistic influence on this 1st-century Palestinian Jew. From the creation of a circle of disciples following him on his itinerant ministry to his radical critique of all oath-taking, Jesus may indeed have imbibed aspects of Hellenistic culture, a culture to which Palestinian Judaism had been exposed from the late 4th century B.C. onward.

At the same time, everything we have seen in these four volumes of *A Marginal Jew* has hammered home the basic truth that Jesus was first, last, and always a product of the Judaism native to the land of Israel. This fourth volume in particular has stressed that "Jesus the Jew" becomes more than a fashionable academic slogan only when this Jew is embedded in the various halakic discussions and debates roiling Palestinian Judaism around the turn of the era. This is true even of the double command of love. One cannot entirely exclude possible influence from a Hellenistic Judaism that exalted the two virtues of reverence for God (*eusebeia*) and justice toward one's fellow humans (*dikaiosynē*). Yet, tellingly, Jesus not only conducts his discussion of the double command within the precincts of the Jerusalem temple in the presence of learned scribe but also, and more significant, articulates his teaching not in terms of philosophical virtues but in terms of concrete commandments cited from the Mosaic Torah—the obligations being expressed not by abstract nouns but rather by verbs with imperative force. This is the manner of discussing and distilling commandments of the Law that one sees increasingly in Palestinian Judaism in the centuries preceding Jesus. Still more significant, as already mentioned, Jesus uses the hermeneutical tool later canonized by the rabbis as the *gĕzērâ šāwâ* to reach his conclusion about the first and second commandments of the Law. While one can find some partial examples of this hermeneutical technique at Qumran, Jesus may have been the first Jew named in written sources to formulate a legal argument from the *gĕzērâ šāwâ* so explicitly. The historical Jesus is indeed the halakic Jesus. No "historical Jesus" lacking such legal engagement and halakic expertise need apply.

This remarkable case of Jesus explicitly employing the *gĕzērâ šāwâ*—perhaps the first Jew we can name who did so—invites further reflection. In Volume One of *A Marginal Jew*, I had to struggle mightily with round-about arguments to establish that Jesus was not illiterate. The best indirect argument I could muster was that all the Gospels agree that Jesus not only taught the common people but also engaged in scriptural debates with Jewish scholars in both Galilee and Jerusalem. The mere fact that Jesus could participate actively in such debates without totally discrediting himself in the eyes of ordinary Jews argues not only for his basic literacy but also for a fair knowledge of the written Torah of Moses. The specific case of the double command of love, with its elegant and explicit use of the *gĕzērâ šāwâ*, makes the general argument sketched in Volume One much more detailed and convincing as we reach the end of Volume Four.

Still, such a conclusion makes all the more pressing the question raised in Volume One and not answered there. To what extent was Jesus formally educated, and where could a boy from a hole-in-the-wall town like Nazareth receive such an education? Since theories about Jesus being exposed to Buddhism in Tibet or magic in Egypt have already had their day (no doubt they will be resuscitated on cable TV), perhaps some American novelist might regale us with a scenario of Jesus outshining every other Jewish boy in Gamaliel's Torah school in Jerusalem, while a young know-it-all from Tarsus throws a fit for being outdone. If we prefer not to embrace such made-for-the-movies hypotheses, then, failing some spectacular archaeological discovery, we will probably never know how a woodworker from Nazareth wound up with such a remarkable degree of competence in the Torah.[317] Anyone can declare himself a charismatic prophet. Getting the *gĕzērâ šāwâ* right requires study.

All these ruminations bring us back full circle to the question with which this chapter began. Beyond all the individual legal pronouncements Jesus issued during his public ministry, did he ever give an indication of his stance vis-à-vis the Law as a whole? The answer this chapter gives is a qualified yes. I say "qualified" because the answer is not the full, programmatic type of answer that we get—and would prefer—from Matt 5:17–20 or from Matthew's reworking of Mark's pericope on the double commandment. But at least the bare-bones tradition behind Mark 12:28–34 shows us that the historical Jesus did not simply issue ad-hoc halakic pronouncements on scattered topics like divorce, oaths, or the sabbath. He did reflect on the totality of Torah and did extract from that totality the love of God and the love of neighbor as the *first* and *second* commandments of the Torah, superior to all others. Love—of God first and of our neighbor second, in that pointed order—is supreme in the Law. Other statutes—while by no means rejected or denigrated—are of lesser importance.

That much the historical Jesus says. But that is all he says. Once we move on to claiming that Jesus made love the hermeneutical key for interpreting the whole Law or the supreme principle from which all other commandments can be deduced or by which they can be judged, we have shifted from the historical Jesus to the Matthean Jesus—the original sin of most Christian exegetes expounding on the historical Jesus and the Law. It is Matthew, and Matthew alone, who both draws the two love commandments closer together and, more significant, states that the *whole Law* "hangs upon" (depends on? is deducible from? is to be interpreted by?) these two commandments taken together. With Matthew we have the first great (Jewish-) Christian exercise in making the *hălākâ* of the Jewish Jesus serviceable to an embryonic Christian system of morality. It is an important step in Christian thought, but one that is not to be attributed to the historical Jew named Jesus.

Like a good pagan Stoic, let us be satisfied with what we have. By using the *gĕzērâ šāwâ*, the historical Jesus extracts and orders Deut 6:4–5 and Lev 19:18b as the first and second commandments of the Torah, above all other statutes of the Law. This is startling and innovative enough. This is sufficient proof that Jesus the Jew reflected not only on individual halakic questions alive in Judaism at his time but also—in a truly creative fashion—on Torah as a whole in relation to its parts. And, in the end, his reflection led to love—specifically, to love of God and love of neighbor as supreme. All you need is love? Hardly. For Jesus, you need the Torah as a whole. Nothing could be more foreign to this Palestinian Jew than a facile antithesis between Law and love. But love, as commanded by the Law, comes first—and second.

NOTES TO CHAPTER 36

[1] The reader can well imagine that a complete bibliography on the topic of Jesus' teaching on love would fill volumes. All one can hope to do here is to offer a representative sample of books and articles reflecting different points of view on different aspects of the topic. For basic philological information on the Hebrew and Greek vocabulary of love, see Jan Bergman, A. O. Haldar, and Gerhard Wallis, " '*āhabh, 'ahᵃbhāh, 'ahabh, 'ōhabh*," *TDOT* 1 (1974) 99–118; Gottfried Quell and Ethelbert Stauffer, "*agapaō*, etc.," *TDNT* 1 (1964) 21–55; Gustav Stählin, "*phileō*, etc.,"

TDNT 9 (1974) 113–71; Ceslas Spicq, Agapè *dans le Nouveau Testament* (3 vols.; Paris: Gabalda, 1958, 1959, 1959) [an English translation with most of the footnotes of the French original omitted and the material apportioned differently can be found in *Agape in the New Testament* (St. Louis/London: Herder, 1963)]; Robert Joly, *Le vocabulaire chrétien de l'amour est-il original?* Philein *et* agapan *dans le grec antique* (Brussels: Presses universitaires de Bruxelles, 1968). Since Jesus' love commandments in the NT use only the vocabulary of *agapaō*, I focus on that word-field. For a fuller investigation of love and allied concepts in both OT and NT, one would have to expand the philological investigation to include such Hebrew words as *ḥesed* ("loyalty," "loving kindness") and *raḥămîm* ("mercy") as well as Greek words like *eleos* ("mercy") and *splagchnizomai* ("to feel compassion").

Works that can offer a general introduction to and further bibliography on love include Katherine Doob Sakenfeld, "Love, Old Testament," *AYBD*, 4. 375–81; William Klassen, "Love, NT and Early Jewish Literature," *AYBD*, 4. 381–96; Wilhelm Lütgert, *Die Liebe im Neuen Testament* (Giessen/Basel: Brunnen, 1986; originally 1905); James Moffatt, *Love in the New Testament* (New York: Smith, 1930); Anders Nygren, *Agape and Eros* (Philadelphia: Westminster, 1953; Swedish original 1930–36); Viktor Warnach, *Agape. Die Liebe als Grundmotiv der neutestamentlichen Theologie* (Düsseldorf: Patmos, 1951); Victor Paul Furnish, *The Love Command in the New Testament* (Nashville/New York: Abingdon, 1972); Jürgen Becker, "Feindesliebe–Nächstenliebe–Bruderliebe. Exegetische Beobachtungen als Anfrage an ein ethisches Problemfeld," *Zeitschrift für evangelische Ethik* 25 (1981) 5–18; Hubert Meisinger, *Liebesgebot und Atruismusforschung. Ein exegetischer Beitrag zum Dialog zwischen Theologie und Naturwissenschaft* (Novum Testamentum et Orbis Antiquus 33; Freiburg: Universitätsverlag; Göttingen: Vandenhoeck & Ruprecht, 1996).

For a sampling of further literature, see Rudolf Bultmann, "Aimer son prochain, commandement de Dieu," *RHPR* 10 (1930) 222–41; Günther Bornkamm, "Das Doppelgebot der Liebe," *Neutestamentliche Studien für Rudolf Bultmann* (2d ed.; ed. Walther Eltester; Berlin: Töpelmann, 1957) 85–93; Albrecht Dihle, *Die Goldene Regel* (Studienhefte zur Altertumswissenschaft 7; Göttingen: Vandenhoeck & Ruprecht, 1962); Olof Linton, "St. Matthew 5,43," *ST* 18 (1964) 66–79; Jerome Rausch, "The Principal [*sic*] of Nonresistance and Love of Enemy in Mt 5:38–48," *CBQ* 28 (1966) 31–41; W. C. van Unnik, "Die Motivierung der Feindesliebe in Lukas VI 32–35," *NovT* 8 (1966) 284–300; Franz Mussner, "Der Begriff des 'Nächsten' in der Verkündigung Jesu. Dargelegt am Gleichnis vom barmherzigen Samariter," *Praesentia Salutis* (Kommentare und Beiträge zum Alten und Neuen Testament; Düsseldorf: Patmos, 1967) 125–32; Gerhard Barth, "Das Gesetzesverständnis des Evangelisten Matthäus," in Günther Bornkamm, Gerhard Barth, and Heinz Joachim Held, *Überlieferung und Auslegung im Matthäusevangelium* (WMANT 1; 5th ed.; Neuchirchen-Vluyn: Neukirchener Verlag, 1968) 54–154, esp. 70–73 [= "Matthew's Understanding of the Law," *Tradition and Interpretation in Matthew* (Philadelphia: Westminster, 1963) 58–164, esp. 75–80] ; Jay B. Stern, "Jesus' Citation of Dt 6,5 and Lv 19,18 in the Light of Jewish Tradition," *CBQ* 28 (1966) 312–16; Walter Bauer, "Das Gebot der Feindesliebe und die alten Christen," *Auf-*

sätze und Kleine Schriften (ed. Georg Strecker; Tübingen: Mohr [Siebeck], 1967) 235–52; O. J. F. Seitz, "Love Your Enemies," *NTS* 16 (1969–70) 39–54; Charles Talbert, "Tradition and Redaction in Romans XII. 9–21," *NTS* 16 (1969–70) 83–94; Christoph Burchard, "Das doppelte Liebesgebot in der frühen christlichen Überlieferung," *Der Ruf Jesu und die Antwort der Gemeinde* (Joachim Jeremias Festschrift; ed. Eduard Lohse, Christoph Burchard, and Berndt Schaller; Göttingen: Vandenhoeck & Ruprecht, 1970) 39–62; Klaus Berger, *Die Gesetzesauslegung Jesu. Teil I: Markus und Parallelen* (WMANT 40; Neukirchen-Vluyn: Neukirchener Verlag, 1972) 56–257; Dieter Lührmann, "Liebet eure Feinde (Lk 6,27–36/ Mt 5,39–48)," *ZTK* 69 (1972) 412–38; Leonard Goppelt, "Jesus und die 'Haustafel'-Tradition," *Orientierung an Jesus* (Josef Schmid Festschrift; Freiburg/Basel/ Vienna: Herder, 1973) 93–106; Andreas Nissen, *Gott und der Nächste im antiken Judentum. Untersuchungen zum Doppelgebot der Liebe* (WUNT 15; Tübingen: Mohr [Siebeck], 1974); Alexander Sand, *Das Gesetz und die Propheten* (Biblische Untersuchungen 11; Regensburg: Pustet, 1974) 41–51; Arland J. Hultgren, "The Double Command of Love in Mt 22:34–40," *CBQ* 36 (1974) 373–78; idem, *Jesus and His Adversaries* (Minneapolis: Augsburg, 1979) 47–50; Robert Banks, *Jesus and the Law in the Synoptic Tradition* (SNTSMS 28; Cambridge: Cambridge University, 1975) 164–70; Michael Lattke, *Einheit im Wort* (SANT 41; Munich: Kösel, 1975); Oswald Bayer, "Sprachbewegung und Weltveränderung. Ein systematischer Verusch als Auslegung von Mt 5,43–48," *EvT* 35 (1975) 309–21; Paul Hoffmann and Volker Eid, *Jesus von Nazareth und eine christliche Moral* (QD 66; Freiburg/ Basel/Vienna: Herder, 1975) 147–85; Ingo Broer, "Die Antithesen und der Evangelist Mattäus," *BZ* 19 (1975) 50–63; Kenneth J. Thomas, "Liturgical Citations in the Synoptics," *NTS* 22 (1975–76) 205–14; idem, "Torah Citations in the Synoptics," *NTS* 24 (1977–78) 85–96; Robert A. Guelich, "The Antitheses of Matthew V. 21–48: Traditional and/or Redactional?" *NTS* 22 (1976) 444–57; Rolf Eulenstein, " 'Und wer is mein Nächster?' Lk. 10,25–37 in der Sicht eines klassischen Philologen," *TGl* 67 (1977) 127–45; Luise Schottroff, "Non-Violence and the Love of One's Enemies," *Essays on the Love Commandment* (Philadelphia: Fortress, 1978) 9–39; Reginald H. Fuller, "The Double Commandment of Love: A Test Case for the Criteria of Authenticity," ibid., 41–56; Walter Diezinger, "Zum Liebesgebot Mk xii, 28–34 und Parr," *NovT* 20 (1978) 81–83; Gerd Theissen, "Gewaltverzicht und Feindesliebe (Mt 5,38–48/Lk 6,27–38) und deren sozialgeschichtlicher Hintergrund," *Studien zur Soziologie des Urchristentums* (WUNT 19; Tübingen: Mohr [Siebeck], 1979) 160–97; John Piper, *'Love your enemies.' Jesus' Love Command in the Synoptic Gospels and in early Christian Paraenesis* (SNTSMS 38; Cambridge/ London/New York: Cambridge University, 1979); Rudolf Laufen, *Die Doppelüberlieferungen der Logienquelle und des Markusevangeliums* (BBB 54; Bonn: Hanstein, 1980); Pheme Perkins, *Love Commands in the New Testament* (New York/Ramsey, NJ: Paulist, 1982); S. G. Wilson, *Luke and the Law* (SNTSMS 50; Cambridge: Cambridge University, 1983) 14–15; Philip Kanjuparambil, "Imperatival Participles in Rom 12:9–21," *JBL* 102 (1983) 285–88; George M. Soares-Prabhu, "The Synoptic Love-Commandment: The Dimensions of Love in the Teaching of Jesus," *Jeevadhara* fascicle 74, vol. 13 (March–April, 1983) 85–103;

Hans-Werner Bartsch, "Traditionsgeschichtliches zur 'goldenen Regel' und zum Aposteldekret," *ZNW* 75 (1984) 128–32; Jean-Gaspard Mudiso Mbâ Mundla, *Jesus und die Führer Israels* (NTAbh 17; Münster: Aschendorff, 1984) 110–233; William Klassen, *Love of Enemies* (Philadelphia: Fortress, 1984) 72–109; H. W. Hollander and M. de Jonge, *The Testaments of the Twelve Patriarchs. A Commentary* (Studia in Veteris Testamenti Pseudepigrapha 8; Leiden: Brill, 1985) 82–85; Jürgen Sauer, "Traditionsgeschichtliche Erwägungen zu den synoptischen und paulinischen Aussagen über Feindesliebe und Wiedervergeltungsverzicht," *ZNW* 76 (1985) 1–28; Oda Wischmeyer, "Das Gebot der Nächstenliebe bei Paulus," *BZ* 30 (1986) 161–87; Hans-Peter Mathys, *Liebe deinen Nächsten wie dich selbst* (OBO 71; Freiburg: Universitätsverlag; Göttingen: Vandenhoeck & Ruprecht, 1986); Hans Hübner, *Das Gesetz in der synoptischen Tradition* (2d ed.; Göttingen: Vandenhoeck & Ruprecht, 1986) 81–112; Marinus de Jonge, "Die Paränese in den Schriften des Neuen Testaments und in den Testamenten der Zwölf Patriarchen. Einige Überlegungen," *Neues Testament und Ethik* (Rudolf Schnackenburg Festschrift; ed. Helmut Merklein; Freiburg/Basel/Vienna: Herder, 1989) 538–50; Rudolf Pesch, "Jesus und das Hauptgebot," ibid., 99–109; Heinz-Wolfgang Kuhn, "Das Liebesgebot Jesu als Tora and als Evangelium," *Vom Urchristentum zu Jesus* (Joachim Gnilka Festschrift; ed. Hubert Frankemölle and Karl Kertelge; Freiburg/Basel/Vienna: Herder, 1989) 194–230; Jacob Kremer, "Mahnungen zum inner-kirchlichen Befolgen des Liebesgebotes," ibid., 231–45; Jarmo Kiilunen, *Das Doppelgebot der Liebe in synoptischer Sicht. Ein redaktionskritischer Versuch über Mk 12,28–34 und die Parallelen* (Annales Academicae Scientiarum Fennicae B/250; Helsinki: Suomalainen Tiedeakatemia, 1989); Martin Evang, *"ek kardias allēlous agapēsate ektenōs*. Zum Verständnis der Aufforderung und ihrer Begründungen in 1 Petr 1,22f.," *ZNW* 80 (1989) 111–23; Simon Légasse, *"Et qui est mon prochain?"* (LD 136; Paris: Cerf, 1989); Kari Syreeni, "Matthew, Luke, and the Law. A Study in Hermeneutical Exegesis," *The Law in the Bible and in Its Environment* (ed. Timo Veijola; Helsinki: Finnish Exegetical Society; Göttingen: Vandenhoeck & Ruprecht, 1990) 126–55; Raphael Jospe, "Hillel's Rule," *JQR* 81 (1990–91) 45–57; Heinz Kremers, "Gerechtigkeit und Liebe im Judentum und Christentum," *Liebe und Gerechtigkeit* (Neukirchen-Vluyn: Neukirchener Verlag, 1990) 47–56; Gianni Barbiero, *L'asino del nemico* (AnBib 128; Rome: Biblical Institute, 1991); Albert Fuchs, "Die Last der Vergangenheit. Bemerkungen zu J. Kiilunen, Das Doppelgebot der Liebe in synoptischer Sicht," *Studien zum Neuen Testament und seiner Umwelt* 16 (1991) 151–68; Raymond F. Collins, "Golden Rule," *AYBD*, 2. 1070–71; William Klassen, " 'Love Your Enemies': Some Reflections on the Current Status of Research," *The Love of Enemy and Nonretaliation in the New Testament* (ed. William M. Swartley; Louisville: Westminster/John Knox, 1992) 1–31; Dorothy Jean Weaver, "Transforming Nonresistance: From Lex Talionis to 'Do Not Resist the Evil One,' " ibid., 32–71; Richard A. Horsley, "Ethics and Exegesis: 'Love Your Enemies' and the Doctrine of Nonviolence," ibid., 72–101; Walter Wink, "Neither Passivity nor Violence: Jesus' Third Way (Matt. 5:38–42 par.)," ibid., 102–25 [responses of Horsley and Wink to each other's essays are found on pp. 126–32 and 133–36 respectively]; Pheme Perkins, "Apocalyptic Sectarianism and Love

Commands: The Johannine Epistles and Revelation," ibid., 287–96; David Rensberger, "Love for One Another and Love for Enemies in the Gospel of John," ibid., 297–313; Michael Ebersohn, *Das Nächstenliebegebot in der synoptischen Tradition* (Marburger Theologische Studien 37; Marburg: Elwert, 1993); Jörg Augenstein, *Das Liebesgebot im Johannesevangelium und in den Johannesbriefen* (BWANT 7/14; Stuttgart/Berlin/Cologne: Kohlhammer, 1993); Karl Kertelge, "Das Doppelgebot der Liebe im Markusevangelium," *TTZ* 103 (1994) 38–55; Joel Marcus, "Authority to Forgive Sins upon the Earth: The *Shema* in the Gospel of Mark," *The Gospels and the Scriptures of Israel* (JSNTSup 104; ed. Craig A. Evans and W. Richard Stegner; Sheffield: Academic Press, 1994) 196–211; Dale C. Allison, Jr., "Mark 12. 28–31 and the Decalogue," ibid., 271–78; Hans Dieter Betz, *The Sermon on the Mount* (Hermeneia; Minneapolis: Fortress, 1995) 274–328, 591–614; James McIlhone, "Not Far from the Kingdom: A Scribe in Mark," *Chicago Studies* 34/1 (1995) 53–62; Robert H. Gundry, "A Rejoinder on Matthean Foreign Bodies in Luke 10,25–28," *ETL* 71 (1995) 139–50; Frans Neirynck, "The Minor Agreements and Lk 10,25–28," ibid., 151–65; John J. Kilgallen, "The Plan of the 'Nomikos' (Luke 10.25–37)," *NTS* 42 (1996) 615–19; Oscar S. Brooks, "The Function of the Double Love Command in Matthew 22:34–40," *AUSS* 36 (1998) 7–22; David H. Edgar, "The Use of the Love-Command and the *Shemaʿ* in the Epistle of James," *Proceedings of the Irish Biblical Association* 23 (2000) 9–22; Jean-François Baudoz, "Ethique et mystique dans le Quatrième Evangile, 'Je vous donne un commandement nouveau,' Jn 13,34," *Révue d'éthique et de théologie morale "Le Supplément"* 214 (September, 2000) 35–44; Serge Ruzer, "The Double Love Precept in the New Testament and in the Rule of the Congregation," *Tarbiz* 71 nos. 3–4 (2002) 353–70 (in modern Hebrew; English abstract on pp. V–VI); Paul Foster, "Why Did Matthew Get the *Shema* Wrong? A Study of Matthew 22:37," *JBL* 122 (2003) 309–33; George Keerankeri, *The Love Commandment in Mark* (AnBib 150; Rome: Biblical Institute, 2003); Jordi Latorre I Castillo, "Levi sacerdote en los Testamentos de los Doce patriarcas," *EstBib* 62 (2004) 59–75; Xavier Léon-Dufour, *To Act According to the Gospel* (Peabody, MA: Hendrickson, 2005) 139–48; Enno E. Popkes, *Die Theologie der Liebe Gottes in den johanneischen Schriften* (WUNT 2/197; Tübingen: Mohr [Siebeck], 2005).

[2] One might point to the reported severity of the Sadducees and some of the hate-filled polemics of Essene literature, but, even in these cases, there are countervailing indicators. For cases when the Sadducean *hălākâ* was at times more severe than that of the Pharisees (or "the sages") but at other times more lenient or merciful, see Meier, *A Marginal Jew*, 3. 399–406. While the Essene literature contains fierce statements about the obligation to hate the sons of darkness or other enemies (see, e.g., 1QS 1:9–11; 2:4–3:6), other texts speak at times of renouncing vengeance against one's enemies, at least in the present (see, e.g., 1QS 10:17–18). We shall examine some of these passages below.

[3] As we shall see, I do not think that there are separate Q, M, or L traditions behind the Matthean or Lucan version of the double command of love. Matthew

and Luke have simply reworked the Marcan pericope for their own redactional purposes.

[4] Other exhortations to mutual love, forgiveness, or acceptance can be found elsewhere in the NT, but they are not presented as the words of Jesus. See, e.g., 1 Thess 4:9; Rom 13:8; Eph 5:2; 1 Pet 1:22; 2:17.

[5] On the relatively few occurrences of "love," "neighbor," and "enemy" in the sayings of Jesus, especially in those that could with fair probability be attributed to the historical Jesus, see Becker, "Feindesliebe," 6.

[6] In Mark the verb *agapaō* ("love") occurs on Jesus' lips only in his citation of Deut 6:5 and Lev 19:18b in Mark 12:30–31. The scribe repeats the two commands in v 33. Mark 10:21 narrates that Jesus loved the rich man who comes to him. Besides repeating Jesus' double command in 22:37,39, Matthew uses the verb in the Q tradition of love of enemies in Matt 5:43–44,46 (twice). He has Jesus cite Lev 19:18b in Matt 19:19; finally, there is the Q saying on loving or hating a master in Matt 6:24. Luke's use of the verb "love" in his version of the Q tradition of love of enemies is found in 6:27,32 (three times), 35; the parallel to Matt 6:24 is in Luke 16:13. The double command of love is found in Luke 10:27. Other scattered references are 7:42,47 (twice); 11:43. Luke 7:5 is spoken by the Jewish elders. Quite startling are the statistics on the noun *agapē* ("love"). It never occurs in Mark, and it occurs once each in Matthew (24:12) and Luke (11:42). The adjective *agapētos* ("beloved") occurs three times in Mark, twice in the voice of God from heaven (1:11; 9:7) and once in the parable of the evil tenants of the vineyard (12:6). Matthew replicates the two cases of the voice of God, deletes the occurrence in the parable of the evil tenants, and adds one occurrence in an aside of his own (12:18, a modified form of Isa 42:1). Apart from the voice of God in 3:22, Luke's only occurrence is in the parable of the evil tenants (20:13). The verb *phileō* ("love") is used only once in Mark 14:44, and there in the sense of "to kiss" (a common meaning of this verb in Hellenistic Greek). The parallels to this passage are Matt 26:48 and Luke 22:47. Luke has only one other occurrence of the verb (20:46). Matthew has four other cases (6:5; 10:37 [twice]); 23:6). The noun *philēma* ("kiss") occurs only in Luke 7:45 and 22:48. The noun *philos* ("friend") occurs nowhere in Mark and once in Matthew, when Jesus reports the slur spoken by his opponents (11:19), "a friend of toll collectors and sinners." With his notable adaptation to Greco-Roman culture and to its ethos of friendship, Luke (who uses *phileō* only twice) diverges sharply from the other Synoptics in using *philos* fifteen times, by far the largest number of occurrences in any book in the NT. The abstract noun *philia* ("friendship") occurs only once in the NT, in Jas 4:4. The verb *eraō* and the noun *erōs*, often associated with passionate or sexual love, never occur in the NT. All in all, in my opinion, the Synoptic sayings containing "love" vocabulary that have a strong claim to historicity are the Marcan tradition of the double commandment of love, the Q tradition of the command to love one's enemies, and the Q tradition on hating one master and loving another (on the last, see *A Marginal Jew*, 3. 517–18).

[7] Mark uses *plēsion* ("neighbor") twice, both cases being citations of Lev 19:18b in the pericope of the double command of love (12:31,33). Jesus speaks the citation the first time, the scribe the second time. Luke has three occurrences, all in the lengthy pericope on the double command of love followed by the parable of the Good Samaritan. Here the lawyer uses the noun twice and Jesus once (Luke 10:27,29,36). Besides taking over Mark's story of the double command, in which Matthew reduces the use of *plēsion* to a single occurrence, Matthew inserts Lev 19:18b into the Q tradition of love of enemies (Matt 5:43) and into the Marcan story of the rich man (Matt 19:19). John never uses *plēsion* as a noun designating a person (see John 4:5). As for the noun *echthros* ("enemy"), it occurs only once in Mark, when Jesus cites Ps 110:1 (Mark 12:36). Apart from the repetition of this citation in Matthew and Luke, Matthew uses *echthros* twice in Jesus' command to love enemies (5:43–44), three times in his explanation of the parable of the weeds and the wheat (13:25,28,39), and in a citation of Mic 7:6 in Matt 10:36 ("the enemies of a man will be those of his own household"). Apart from the three cases he takes over from Mark and Q (Luke 6:27,35; 20:43), Luke has two occurrences of *echthros* in the canticle of Zechariah in his Infancy Narrative (1:71,74), and three occurrences in his special material (10:19; 19:27,43). In my opinion, apart from the command to love one's enemies, few of these "enemy" passages have a strong claim to historicity.

[8] One therefore needs to understand from the beginning the narrow focus of this chapter. Its particular scope explains why only passages dealing with the verb *agapaō* in an imperative sense are considered. This is not to reduce Jesus' total message or even his message about love to a study of the words *agapaō* and *agapē*. On the danger of such reductionism, see Furnish, *The Love Command*, 20.

[9] See my comments in *A Marginal Jew*, 3. 414–15.

[10] Various commentators end the Jerusalem cycle at 12:37, 12:40, or even 12:44. Since 12:38–40 continues in a more direct fashion Jesus' assault on the scribes, which has begun indirectly in 12:35–37, I prefer to see vv 38–40 as the conclusion of the cycle. While the story of the widow's mite (vv 41–44) prolongs *sotto voce* Jesus' attack on the authorities, he is no longer addressing his adversaries or the crowd about his adversaries. Rather, he now calls to himself his disciples, who do not speak, react, or argue, but simply hear Jesus' private teaching. Hence, given both its structure and its audience, vv 41–44 cannot count as a dispute story or a scholastic dialogue. It functions more as a transition or bridge to Jesus' private teaching to four disciples in the eschatological discourse (chap. 13). For a full treatment of the Jerusalem cycle of dispute stories, see Mudiso Mbâ Mundla, *Jesus und die Führer*; for the Galilean cycle, see Joanna Dewey, *Markan Public Debate* (SBLDS 48; Chico, CA: Scholars, 1980).

[11] The *inclusio* is strengthened by the fact that both at the beginning and at the end of the cycle Jesus turns the tables and goes on the attack.

[12] While the audience of the parable of the evil tenants of the vineyard (12:1–12) is not explicitly named, the statement in 12:1 that Jesus "began to speak to them [*autois*] in parables" necessarily, in the narrative context, goes back to the last-named group, which is "the chief priests and the scribes and the elders" of 11:27. They are likewise designated as *autois* ("and Jesus said to *them*") in 11:29. They are also the unnamed subjects of the 3d person plural verbs in 11:31,32, and 33. More important, they are the obvious audience in v 33b, "and Jesus said to them [*autois*]," which in turn is picked up immediately by the *autois* in 12:1. They are therefore the hostile group reacting negatively to the parable in 12:12: "And they were seeking to lay hold of him, and [= but] they feared the crowd, for they knew that he had spoken the parable against them."

[13] On this pericope and on the Herodians in general, see *A Marginal Jew*, 3. 560–65.

[14] The adverb *nounechōs* (v 34a) occurs nowhere else in either the LXX or the NT—perhaps another indication that we are not dealing in 12:28–34 with a purely redactional creation of Mark. Similarly, the word order of *kai + eipen* + indirect object in the dative + subject in v 32a ("and the scribe said to him") is a clear example of non-Marcan Greek style; see Pesch, *Markusevangelium*, 2. 242.

[15] The basic outline of Mark 12:28–34 presented in the main text is widely accepted by commentators; see, e.g., Craig A. Evans, *Mark 8:27–16:20* (Word Biblical Commentary 34B; Nashville: Nelson, 2001) 261. I must take responsibility for the particular details of the structure I propose.

[16] In the Greek, the adjectives "first" and "second" (in vv 28–31) lack the definite article, which I supply in my translation simply for the sake of smooth English. Some commentators suggest that the lack of definite articles emphasizes the quality of being first and the quality of being second in importance (so Gundry, *Mark*, 710–11; Keerankeri, *The Love Commandment*, 81). When one considers the multiple cases of asyndeton (no connecting conjunction) in the pericope, another possibility is that the lack of definite articles simply fits the tight, compressed style of the unit.

[17] On the various possible translations, depending on whether one supplies an implicit copulative verb between the first *kyrios* ("Lord") and *ho theos hēmōn* ("our God") in 12:29 and whether one translates *heis* as "one" or "alone," see Keerankeri, *The Love Commandment*, 27–31; Gundry, *Mark*, 715. The original Hebrew of Deut 6:4 (*yahweh 'ĕlōhênû yahweh 'eḥād* = "Yahweh our God Yahweh one [or: 'alone'])") is ambiguous since it is a typical Hebrew nominal clause lacking the copulative verb "is," which could be understood in more than one place. Possible translations of the Hebrew include "Yahweh is our God, Yahweh is one," "Yahweh is our God, Yahweh alone," "Yahweh our God is one Yahweh," "Yahweh our God, Yahweh is one." The LXX tries to resolve the ambiguity by adding the verb *estin* ("is") at the end of the nominal clause: *kyrios ho theos hēmōn kyrios heis estin*.

The most likely interpretation of the resulting Greek sentence is "the Lord our God is one Lord," and this seems to be the meaning in Mark 12:29c, which follows the LXX exactly.

[18] As Fuller ("The Double Commandment," 46) notes, v 28 is a painfully over-loaded introduction and thus an indicator of redactional activity. Mark uses v 28 to tie 12:28–34 to the preceding context; similarly, Mudiso Mbâ Mundla, *Jesus und die Führer*, 126–27; Francis J. Moloney, *The Gospel of Mark* (Peabody, MA: Hendrickson, 2002) 240.

[19] Technically, it is not correct to say that the pattern of question and answer is doubled, since the second address of the scribe to Jesus (vv 32–33) is not a question but a repetition (with comment) of Jesus' reply to the scribe's question. Indeed, in his second reply, Jesus sees "that he [the scribe] had *answered* intelligently"; hence Mark does not consider the scribe's second intervention in vv 32–33 to be some sort of further question.

[20] The structural analysis of Keerankeri (*The Love Commandment*, 70–71) takes a slightly different route, but the conclusions are basically the same.

[21] As France (*The Gospel of Mark*, 479) correctly observes, *kalōs* in 12:28 does not simply mean "cleverly," in the sense that Jesus has escaped a trap; similarly, Evans, *Mark 8:27–16:20*, 262–63. Rather, the scribe sees that Jesus' answer is "good, wholesome, satisfying," thus moving the scribe to seek Jesus' opinion about a much more fundamental matter. This is a more likely interpretation than that of Gundry (*Mark*, 710), who suggests that the scribe, witnessing Jesus best the Sadducees, may desire "to do a better job than they of dragging Jesus into a theological quagmire."

[22] Apart from content, one stylistic sign that Mark 12:28 + 34 constitute Mark's own redactional framework is the *inclusio* created by the verb *eperōtaō* ("to ask," a favorite verb of Mark), placed at the end of the narrative section of v 28 and again at the end of the narration in v 34.

[23] See Mark 1:22; 2:6,16; 3:22; 7:1; 8:31; 9:11,14; 10:33; 11:18,27; 12:35,38; 14:1,43,53; 15:1,31. On Mark's view that Jesus has authority and the scribes do not, see Richard J. Dillon, " 'As One Having Authority' (Mark 1:22): The Controversial Distinction of Jesus' Teaching," *CBQ* 57 (1995) 92–113; see also Scaria Kuthirak-kattel, *The Beginning of Jesus' Ministry According to Mark's Gospel (1,14–3,6)* (AnBib 123; Rome: Biblical Institute, 1990) 128–32.

[24] It cannot be stressed enough that we are dealing here with Mark's redactional theology and not with the events of Jesus' trial and death as best they can be reconstructed by historical research. On what can be said historically of Jewish scribes at the time of Jesus, see Meier, *A Marginal Jew*, 3. 549–60; on scribes in Mark, see esp. pp. 554–55.

[25] I do not dispute the fact that Mark uses *heis* at times in the sense of *tis*, either with the meaning of "someone," "a certain person," or with the "weak" meaning of "a"; see, e.g., 5:22; 10:17; 12:42. Sometimes, however, the sense is not entirely clear; e.g., does *mia tōn paidiskōn* in 14:66 mean "one of the maidservants"(so the *RSV*, the *NRSV*, and the revised NT of the *NAB*) or "a maidservant"? In any case, Mark also uses *heis* in the "strong" sense of "one" with the partitive genitive, as in v 28 (*tōn grammateōn*); see, e.g., 9:42; 14:10,20,43. In favor of taking *heis* in the sense of *tis* (hence, "a scribe") are Max Zerwick and Mary Grosvenor, *A Grammatical Analysis of the Greek New Testament* (5th ed.; Rome: Biblical Institute, 1996) 148; Pesch, *Markusevangelium*, 2. 237 (though cf. p. 248); Mudiso Mbâ Mundla, *Jesus und die Führer*, 127; Gundry, *Mark*, 710. In contrast, France (*The Gospel of Mark*, 476) emphasizes *heis* as an indicator that this scribe "stands alone."

[26] Contrast Mark's *Saddoukaioi . . . hoitines legousin* ("Sadducees, i.e., those who say . . ." in 12:18) with Matthew's *Saddoukaioi legontes* ("Sadducees, saying" in 22:23). The former construction defines the Sadducees as the group that denies the resurrection; the latter construction does not necessarily have that meaning. Note the attempts of later Christian scribes to make Matthew say what Mark says by changing Matt 22:23 to read *Saddoukaioi hoi legontes* (third correcting hand of Sinaiticus) or *hoi Saddoukaioi hoi legontes* (family 13). On this point, see Meier, *Law and History*, 18–19.

[27] For the data on both *poia* and *pantōn*, see Bauer, *Wörterbuch*, s.v.; France, *The Gospel of Mark*, 479; Keerankeri, *The Love Commandment*, 78. Those who reject Berger's insistence (*Gesetzesauslegung*, 188) that *poia* has a qualitative sense here ("what kind of?") include Gundry, *Mark*, 714; on the other hand, Pesch (*Markusevangelium*, 2. 238) stresses the note of quality in *poia*. As Gundry rightly observes, "Jesus answers by identifying a commandment, not by describing one." Gundry also correctly notes that we have examples of *pantōn* referring to feminine plural nouns as far back as Thucydides; so too, Mudiso Mbâ Mundla, *Jesus und die Führer*, 129. Interestingly, later Christian scribes (e.g., Alexandrinus, family 13, most later Greek manuscripts) substituted *prōtē pantōn tōn entolōn* ("first of all the commandments," with *pantōn*, the masculine or neuter form of the adjective modifying *entolōn*, the plural feminine noun) for the simple *prōtē* ("first") in Mark 12:29. This shows how readily *pantōn* could be used for feminine plural nouns in the Greek of Late Antiquity. Hence there is no need to adopt the view of Ebersohn (*Das Nächstenliebegebot*, 170–71) that *pantōn* is a true neuter plural with the sense of "which is the first commandment over all or in general, i.e., among all things."

[28] This point is often missed by commentators, who all too easily drift back and forth between the Marcan and the Matthean formulations. The Marcan Jesus says *only* that love of God and love of neighbor are the first and second commandments respectively. Nothing is said about their being the summary, principle, or basis of the whole Law. For an example of commentators' confusion on this point, see Berger, *Gesetzesauslegung*, 64.

²⁹ This is a likely conclusion drawn from the variety of texts found in the Nash Papyrus (a 2d-century B.C. papyrus sheet from Egypt, containing the Decalogue and the *Shema'*), as well as in the tefillin (the phylacteries worn by Jewish men at prayer) and the mezuzahs (containers holding texts from Deuteronomy affixed to doorposts of Jewish houses) found among the Dead Sea documents. On this, see Marcus, "Authority," 196; Stefan C. Reif, *Judaism and Hebrew Prayer. New Perspectives on Jewish Liturgical History* (Cambridge, UK/New York: Cambridge University, 1993) 82–84; Foster, "Why Did Matthew Get the Shema Wrong?" 327–30. Whether we can say, as Marcus does, that the *Shema'* "probably already had a pivotal place in the worship of the Second Temple" is debatable. That the *Shema'* was recited daily in the Jerusalem temple after the recitation of the Decalogue is affirmed in *m. Tamid* 5:1, but we lack such clear attestation from a pre-70 document. Indeed, Foster (pp. 325–26) suggests that the statement in *m. Tamid* 5:1 may be an attempt to legitimize rabbinic prayer practice by retrojecting it into a Second Temple setting. Foster (pp. 321–22) thinks that, in the pre-70 period, neither the precise wording of the *Shema'* nor the Jewish communal liturgy in general was as fixed as the later rabbinic sources portray them. In this regard, Josephus is often cited in order to defend the claim that the *Shema'* was recited twice daily in pre-70 Palestinian Judaism; see *Ant.* 4.8.13 §212–13; cf. Mudiso Mbâ Mundla, *Jesus und die Führer*, 177. But what Josephus tells us in this passage is that Jews give thanks to God twice a day, at dawn and before going to sleep. Nothing is said about the text used in this prayer; in fact, Josephus does not say that a single set text is used by all. However, the immediately added reference to writing on one's door the greatest of God's beneficent works and displaying them on one's arms (i.e., the mezuzah and the tefillin) makes it likely that the twice-daily prayer is indeed the *Shema'*. Two things, though, should be noted: (1) The precise extent of the text recited or written is not stated by Josephus. (2) Josephus is not speaking in this passage about the liturgy in the Jerusalem temple; what is in view is the pious practice of the individual Jew (note the *hekaston* ["each individual"] in §213).

³⁰ On this, see Gundry (*Mark*, 715), who thinks that the paratactic "and" before "you shall love" in Mark 12:30a means "therefore."

³¹ On the different connotations of "heart," "soul," "mind," and "strength," see Berger, *Gesetzesauslegung*, 71–72; Mudiso Mbâ Mundla, *Jesus und die Führer*, 161–68; Gundry, *Mark*, 715; Keerankeri, *The Love Commandment*, 37–39. Later rabbinic and Christian commentators read all sorts of fine distinctions into the different human faculties, but originally the rhetorical emphasis was on the total, undivided nature of the Israelite's love for Yahweh. Insofar as distinctions can be drawn in the holistic anthropology of ancient Hebrew thought, "heart" (*lēb* or *lēbāb* in Hebrew, *kardia* in Greek) was the psychological core of the person, the center from which thought, choice, and emotions proceeded. The Hebrew *lēb* had a stronger intellectual tone than "heart" does for us today. Hence, it is represented in some Greek translations, alongside *kardia*, by such words as *dianoia* ("mind," "capacity to think," "act of thinking") and *synesis* ("understanding," "insight"). The

word often translated as "soul" (*nepeš* in Hebrew, *psychē* in Greek) refers first of all to the throat, then to the breath of life or the life force that animates the body, and then more specifically to a person's feelings; originally, the Hebrew word had no connotation of immortality. The Hebrew word translated as "strength" or "might" is *mě'ōd*, which, with two exceptions, always appears in the Jewish Scriptures as an adverb meaning "very." The only two passages in the Jewish Scriptures in which it occurs as a noun meaning "strength" are Deut 6:5 (our text) and an "echo" of Deut 6:5, i.e., 2 Kgs 23:25, which praises King Josiah (the parallel statement to 2 Kgs 23:25 found in LXX 2 Chr 35:19 does not exist in the corresponding place in the MT). In later commentaries, "strength" was often taken to refer to all of one's personal resources, including property and money.

There is a wide and bewildering range of variations in the lists of the human faculties (as well as the prepositions used before them) in the MT, the LXX, and the three Synoptic Gospels. The variations are often used in arguments about the literary dependence of one text on another. To summarize these differences: the special formulation of the four human faculties in Mark 12:30 (heart, soul, mind, and strength [*kardia*, *psychē*, *dianoia*, and *ischys*], all governed by the proposition "from" [*ex* in the Greek]) is unique within the full range of textual forms found in the MT, the LXX, and the NT. The MT and the LXX texts of Deut 6:5, Matt 22:37, and even the scribe's paraphrase in Mark 12:33 all list only three faculties. The MT lists heart, soul, and strength, each governed by the Hebrew preposition *bě* ("in," "with," "by"). The LXX has the same three faculties, with the Greek *kardia* translating the Hebrew *lēbāb*, *psychē* translating *nepeš*, and *dynamis* translating *mě'ōd*. Instead of a wooden, literal translation of the Hebrew preposition *bě* by the Greek *en* (literally, "in," but understood in context as having the instrumental sense of "with" or "by"), the LXX employs the preposition *ex* ("from") with all three nouns, thus following standard Greek usage; see Berger, *Gesetzesauslegung*, 68. Mark follows the LXX when it comes to the prepositions. His substitution of *ischys* for the LXX's *dynamis* to denote "strength" may be influenced by LXX 4 Kgdms 23:25 and LXX 2 Chr 35:19, both of which echo LXX Deut 6:5 but use *ischys* instead of *dynamis*. Matthew, while dependent on Mark as his literary source for the story of the double commandment of love, changes Mark's four faculties back to three faculties, as in the MT and the LXX. Curiously, though, he keeps Mark's *dianoia* ("mind") as his third faculty, dropping all mention of "strength"; in this, he is unique among all these versions of Deut 6:5. At the same time, Matthew departs from Mark's use of the preposition *ex* (which follows the LXX); here Matthew follows the MT in using the Greek preposition *en* (reflecting the Hebrew *bě*) before all three faculties. The scribe's paraphrase in Mark 12:33, while also listing only three faculties, has the unique list of *kardia* ("heart"), *synesis* ("understanding"), and *ischys* ("strength"). The introduction of *synesis* (perhaps conflating *psychē* and *dianoia*?) may be Mark's redactional attempt to underscore the note of the intellectual grasp of the Torah's meaning, an idea befitting a learned Jewish scribe in a legal discussion. The scribe's list in 12:33 continues Mark's imitation of the LXX's preposition *ex* for all the faculties. In some ways, the version in Luke 10:27 presents us with the most "blended" or conflated text of all. Spoken only by the lawyer (*nomikos*) in dialogue with Jesus, the citation of Deut 6:5 has the four faculties listed by Jesus in Mark 12:30, but with *dianoia* ("mind") moved to the end of the list. Luke follows Mark in using the preposition *ex* for the first faculty, but then seems to follow the MT in using *en* for the other three faculties (thus agreeing with Matthew).

However confusing this brief survey may seem, a full inventory of all variations would be more confusing still. For the sake of brevity and clarity, I have omitted the textual variants of the LXX (not to mention other Greek recensions) and of the Synoptics found in some manuscripts; on this point, see Thomas, "Liturgical Citations," 205–14; Foster, "Why Did Matthew Get the *Shema* Wrong?" 319–21. For the most part, these variants are the results of later Christian scribes trying to bring some uniformity into the different readings. For instance, I tend to think that this is the case with the appearance of *dianoia* for *kardia* in a scribal correction of Deut 6:5 in Vaticanus. One must remember that the LXX codices we have are the products of Christian scribes, who at times would alter the OT text to make it conform to a NT citation of that text. Still, it is true that at times in the LXX (e.g., Jos 22:5) *dianoia* ("mind") is used to translate *lēb* ("heart"); but, in this case, Alexandrinus reads *kardia* instead. All things considered, it is at least possible that Mark (or his source) consciously decided to use both Greek translation variants (*kardia* and *dianoia*) in Mark 12:30 to render *lēbāb* in Deut 6:5.

In the end, whatever the use of these variants for making decisions about literary relationships among the Synoptics, I do not think that they are of much use when it comes to questing for the historical Jesus. (1) As the Qumran discoveries have shown, the texts of the Jewish Scriptures, in both Hebrew and Greek forms, were still in a fair amount of flux in Palestine around the turn of the era; we are not to think in terms of one fixed text in either Hebrew or Greek. (2) In the oral culture of the ancient Near East, most Jews would have known the sacred texts from hearing them read, discussed, and preached upon in the synagogues, not from possessing personal copies that they could read whenever they wished. In such a situation, variants in oral repetition of the same text would not be unusual. (3) The oral tradition played a special and intensified role when it came to Deut 6:4–5, the first part of the *Shemaʿ*; we must allow for variations in liturgical and catechetical use beyond the mere repetition or memorizing of any given Scripture text read in the synagogue; on this, see Foster, "Why Did Matthew Get the *Shema* Wrong?" 309–33. (4) If we judge the event narrated in Mark 12:28–34 to be basically historical, then the question arises whether Jesus, while normally conversing in Aramaic, would have cited Deut 6:4–5 in Hebrew, since he was quoting a sacred text in a legal discussion with a learned scribe. I think this more likely, though one cannot exclude the possibility of Jesus citing Deut 6:4–5 in Aramaic, especially if he was concerned about a large audience around him understanding the whole discussion. Hence, despite all the controversy surrounding the question of the various forms of Deut 6:5 in Synoptic studies, I do not think that this question contributes anything to our quest for the historical Jesus; accordingly, I will not pursue the point further.

[32] Keerankeri (*The Love Commandment*, 31) puts the matter in a somewhat abstract, philosophical way when he states that in Deuteronomy, love for God is "the

inner holistic orientation of the human person to God based on his/her deliberate decision." But Keerankeri goes on to stress that this love finds concrete expression in the observance of God's commandments. In Deuteronomy, loving God often stands parallel to fearing God, walking in his ways, obeying him, serving him, and most especially keeping his commandments; see Berger, *Gesetzesauslegung*, 63. On the concentration of the theme of love (in the theological sense) in the deuteronomic tradition and on love as behavior as well as emotion, see Bergman, Haldar, and Wallis, " 'āhabh, etc.," 114–15; cf. Meisinger, *Liebesgebot*, 10. Needless to say, the emotional and even erotic element of love (in Hebrew, the noun 'ăhābâ) is clearly present in many OT passages referring to human love, most notably in the Song of Songs.

[33] On this, see Sakenfeld, "Love (OT)," 376. It should be noted that, while some scholars of ancient Near Eastern covenants distinguish between the "stipulations" of the covenant and laws, the scribe and Jesus in Mark 12:28–34 both speak simply of the "commandment(s)." On the problem of the form, content, and terminology of ancient Near Eastern covenants, see George E. Mendenhall and Gary A. Herion, "Covenant," *AYBD*, 1. 1179–1202.

[34] This is not to deny that some important individual commandments occur before the *Shema*ʿ in the early chapters of Deuteronomy, notably those of the Decalogue (Deut 5:6–21). But the vast majority of individual commandments, especially those focused on particular cases, occur in chaps. 12–26.

[35] On this, see Berger, *Gesetzesauslegung*, 64.

[36] While this scholastic dialogue is indeed irenic, one cannot miss the atmosphere of an "agonistic" Mediterranean culture in which males had to defend and promote their prowess (physical, intellectual, or spiritual) in the public arena. Both Jesus and the scribe engage in a bit of one-upmanship in adding to or commenting on the insightful statement of the other party. In v 31, Jesus is implicitly pointing out something that the scribe may not have realized: if there is a first commandment, almost necessarily there is a second. Jesus draws that conclusion of his own accord and proceeds to address the question that the conclusion involves: if there is a second commandment, what is it and how does it relate to the first and to the other commandments?

[37] For a detailed study of Lev 19:18b that seeks to point up its theological connection with the love for one's enemy shown in Exod 23:4–5, see Barbiero, *L'asino*, 205–96.

[38] For a detailed analysis of the structure of Lev 19:17–18, see Keerankeri, *The Love Commandment*, 45–47. Relying on the work of Barbiero (*L'asino*, 265–70), Keerankeri points out that, given the immediately preceding prohibitions against hating or seeking revenge on one's fellow Israelite, the positive command to love one's neighbor is in effect a command not to hate one's enemy—though, in this con-

text, the category of enemy is restricted to a personal enemy among the members of one's own people, and the state of enmity seems occasional and passing rather than systemic and permanent.

[39] See D. Kellermann, "*rēaʿ*, etc.," *TDOT* 13 (2004) 522–32, esp. 525–27.

[40] In Lev 19:16, we have a parallel between "your kinsmen [or: 'a member of your people']" (*ʿammêkā*) and "your fellow man" (*rēʿekā*). In v 17 the parallel is between "your brother" (*ʾāḥîkā*) and "a member of your community" (*ʿamîtekā*). In v 18 the parallel is between "the brothers of your people" (*běnê ʿammekā*) and "your fellow man" (*rēʿăkā*).

[41] Ebersohn (*Das Nächstenliebegebot*, 39–42) stresses that the "your neighbor"(*rēʿăkā*) is a person of the same legal, social, and religious status (at least in principle) as the "you" addressed in the command: a full member of the Israelite community; similarly, Kellermann, "*rēaʿ*," 527; Mathys, *Liebe*, 39. One should note Ebersohn's proviso of "in principle"; in Berger's view (*Gesetzesauslegung*, 88–89), the redactor of Leviticus sees *rēaʿ* as including poor Israelites, who are also full members of the community.

[42] See D. Kellermann, "*gûr*, etc.," *TDOT* 2 (1977) 439–49, esp. 443: "In the OT, the *ger* occupies an intermediate position between a native (*ʾezrach*) and a foreigner (*nokhrî*)."

[43] See Nissen, *Gott*, 286.

[44] Kellermann ("*rēaʿ*," 527) observes that "the notion that one should love one's neighbor appears in the OT only in Lev. 19:18b."

[45] On this social context, see Keerankeri, *The Love Commandment*, 51–52; likewise, Ebersohn (*Das Nächstenliebegebot*, 54–55), who stresses the call for mutual solidarity in the command; cf. Meisinger, *Liebesgebot*, 10. Mathys (*Liebe*, 5) points out that in Lev 19:18b, the sign that *rēʿăkā* ("your neighbor") is the object of the verb is the preposition *lě*, which is an Aramaism (only one of a number of Aramaisms in Leviticus 19). Mathys thinks that we have here an indication that Lev 19:18 was written in exilic times.

[46] See Nissen, *Gott*, 283–84.

[47] The classic example of this love in the OT, according to Keerankeri (*The Love Commandment*, 54), is the case of David and Jonathan in 1 Samuel (especially chaps. 18–20), where Jonathan is said to love David "as his own life" or "as his own self" (*kěnapšô* in 18:1; "life" [*nepeš*] is used here, as often in Hebrew, as a reflexive pronoun). The community dimension of this love is expressed not only by the use of the word *běrît* ("covenant") for their relationship but also by the fact that Jonathan,

in effect, waives his rights to the royal succession in favor of David and for the good of the people Israel. While the relationship is deeply emotional, Jonathan's love is expressed above all in his self-sacrificing deeds.

[48] In the whole of the LXX, *plēsion* is employed 112 times to translate *rēaʿ*. For statistics on other Greek words used to translate *rēaʿ*, see Kellermann, "*rēaʿ*," 531.

[49] The adjective *plēsios* occurs in this sense as early as Homer, but even in classical Greek, from Xenophon onward, the adverb *plēsion* (from the singular neuter form of the adjective) is used with the definite article as a noun in the sense of "neighbor," "one who is close by," "one's fellow man"; see Berger, *Gesetzesauslegung*, 100–101. The vast majority of passages with *ho plēsion* are found in the LXX and NT. The Greek *plēsion* is used exclusively to translate the Hebrew *rēaʿ* in the Holiness Code of Leviticus; this is also the predominant usage throughout the LXX Pentateuch. The claim is often made (e.g., by Berger, *Gesetzesauslegung*, 103–4; Kellermann, "*rēaʿ*," 531; Mudiso Mbâ Mundla, *Jesus und die Führer*, 191) that the use of *plēsion* in Lev 19:18b shows a widening of the category of persons covered by this law, potentially to all human beings. Ebersohn (*Das Nächstenliebegebot*, 50–51) rightly rejects this view (as does Nissen [*Gott*, 285 n. 854]) in the case of Lev. 19:18b. Even in the LXX translation of Lev 19:16–18, the presence of phrases like "in your people" (*en tō ethnei sou*), "your brother" (*ton adelphon sou*), "the sons of your people" (*tois huiois tou laou sou*) guarantees that the phrase "your neighbor" (*ton plēsion sou*) in v 18b will be taken in the sense of a fellow member of the Israelite community. In fact, a narrowing of sense (and therefore of rights) can be seen in the parallel law of Lev 19:34. While the MT commands that "you shall love him (i.e., the resident alien [*gēr*]) as yourself," the LXX Lev 19:34 translates *gēr* as *prosēlytos*, which Hellenistic Jews took to mean a Gentile who fully converted to Judaism. On all this, see Meisinger, *Liebesgebot*, 14.

[50] The Vulgate of Lev 19:18 is even less open to an interpretation in terms of universal love. Lev 18:19a speaks of *civium tuorum* ("your fellow citizens"), while 18:19b uses *amicum tuum* ("your friend") for *rēʿăkā*.

[51] On this point, see France, *The Gospel of Mark*, 480–81; Ebersohn, *Nächstenliebegebot*, 177.

[52] Note, e.g., how Pesch (*Markusevangelium*, 2. 241) seeks to expand the meaning of "neighbor" in Mark 12:31 by introducing a consideration of the Golden Rule (a Q tradition that never appears in Mark). Keerankeri (*The Love Commandmenet*, 138) rightly points out that Mark, who, in his whole Gospel, uses *plēsion* only in 12:31 + 33, gives no indication that he is changing the meaning of "neighbor"as found in Lev 19:18b. On this, see also Ebersohn, *Das Nächstenliebegebot*, 177.

[53] On the *gĕzērâ šāwâ*, see H. L. Strack and Günter Stemberger, *Introduction to Talmud and Midrash* (2d ed.; Minneapolis: Fortress, 1996) 18–19; Saul Lieber-

man, "Rabbinic Interpretation of Scripture," *Hellenism in Jewish Palestine* (Texts and Studies of the Jewish Theological Seminary in America 18; 2d ed.; New York: Jewish Theological Seminary, 1962) 47–82, esp. 57–62; Moshe J. Bernstein and Shlomo A. Koyfman, "The Interpretation of Biblical Law in the Dead Sea Scrolls: Forms and Methods," *Biblical Interpretation at Qumran* (ed. Matthias Henze; Grand Rapids, MI/Cambridge, UK: Eerdmans, 2005) 61–87; cf. Furnish, *The Love Command*, 28; Berger, *Gesetzesauslegung*, 170 n. 1. This phrase (perhaps meaning "equal ordinance" or "equal statute," though the precise etymology is debated) appears as a hermeneutical category for the first time in the list of the seven *middôt* (hermeneutical rules) of Hillel in the Tosepta (see *t. Sanh.* 7:11; cf. *t. Pesaḥ.* 4:13); the *gĕzērâ šāwâ* is the second of the seven rules. It is roughly equivalent to the interpretative rule of Alexandrian grammarians called *kata to ison sygkrisis* (or *sygkrisis pros ison*), "comparison with the equal." It is perhaps not by accident that the technical terminology and analysis of this *sygkrisis* arise in the Alexandrian schools in the 2d century A.D., and the *gĕzērâ šāwâ* appears in the *Tosepta* in Palestine in the 3d century A.D. One should not imagine, though, that the influence of hermeneutical analysis flowed in only one direction, from Greek rhetoricians to Jewish rabbis. In any event, in both Greek rhetoric and Jewish hermeneutics, individual hermeneutical practices no doubt preceded formal reflection on theoretical method and technical terminology. That seems to be the case with Qumran, Jesus, and the NT authors.

[54] On this point, see Bernstein and Koyfman, "The Interpretation of Biblical Law," 79. As the authors point out, many of the rabbinic rules of interpretation are one or another form of analogical reasoning. Hence, it is not surprising that modern commentators will differ among themselves when identifying the inchoate methods of interpretation at Qumran and in the NT with specific rabbinic rules. On the wider problem of scriptural interpretation at Qumran and in Second Temple Judaism in general, see Moshe J. Bernstein, "The Contribution of the Qumran Discoveries to the History of Early Biblical Interpretation," *The Idea of Biblical Interpretation* (James L. Kugel Festschrift; ed. Hindy Najman and Judith H. Newman; Supplements to the Journal for the Study of Judaism 83; Leiden/Boston: Brill, 2004) 215–38; Gabriel Barzilai, "Incidental Biblical Exegesis in the Qumran Scrolls and Its Importance for the Study of the Second Temple Period," *Dead Sea Discoveries* 14/1 (2007) 1–24.

[55] See Joachim Jeremias, "Zur Gedankenführung in den paulinischen Briefen," *Abba* (Göttingen: Vandenhoeck & Ruprecht, 1966) 269–76, esp. 271–72. Jeremias points to the use of the *gĕzērâ šāwâ* by the anonymous author of the Epistle to the Hebrews in Heb 7:1–3 and by Paul in Rom 4:1–12. One could easily add other NT examples, e.g., Heb 4:3–6. On the use of linguistic analogy (an early form of what the rabbis will call the *gĕzērâ šāwâ*) in interpreting legal material in the Dead Sea Scrolls, see Bernstein and Koyfman, "The Interpretation of Biblical Law," 84–86; cf. Moshe J. Bernstein, "Interpretation of Scriptures," *Encyclopedia of the Dead Sea Scrolls* (2 vols.; Oxford: Oxford University, 2000) 1. 376–83.

As one example of the hermeneutical technique of linguistic analogy similar to the *gĕzērâ šāwâ*, Bernstein and Koyfman ("The Interpretation of Biblical Law," 84) point to 11QTemple 51:11–18, which treats the problem of a bribed judge (conflating Deut 1:16–17 with 16:18–20). In order to draw the legal conclusion that the death penalty is warranted in the case of the bribed judge (the original text of Deuteronomy states no penalty), the author of 11QTemple implicitly calls upon the case of the false prophet in Deut 18:20–22, which specifies the death penalty for the false prophet. Without explicitly citing Deut 18:20–22, the author of 11QTemple uses it to interpret Deuteronomy's discussion of the bribed judge. 11QTemple declares that the bribed judge should be put to death, apparently on the hermeneutical grounds that the only two pentateuchal passages that contain the phrase *lō' tāgûr(û)* ("you shall not be afraid") are Deut 1:17 and Deut 18:22. Similar implicit uses of analogy to interpret a text of the Pentateuch are found in Philo; see, e.g., *Quis rerum divinarum heres (Who Is the Heir of Divine Things?)* 56 §275–83. One must observe, though, that the argument from analogy is somewhat underdeveloped in these examples when compared to the explicit citations of two OT texts to illuminate each other that we find in the Gospels, Paul, and the Epistle to the Hebrews. In the NT we have what I would call the *gĕzērâ šāwâ* "in the strong sense."

Even the NT examples, however, should be differentiated. In Rom 4:1–12; Heb 4:3–6; and Heb 7:1–3, we have in each case the exact same type of combination: a narrative text of Genesis is brought into hermeneutical combination with a psalm text, always to make a doctrinal point (justification by faith, the eschatological sabbath rest for the people of God, and the eternal priesthood of Christ). In contrast, in Mark 12:29–31, Jesus combines two legal texts from the Pentateuch to issue a legal decision; perhaps this difference in the use of the *gĕzērâ šāwâ* is another indication that the core tradition of Mark 12:28–34 comes from Jesus himself and not the early church.

⁵⁶ On this, see Diezinger, "Zum Liebesgebot," 82. The technical grammatical form of the verb *wĕ'āhabtā* is the perfect with *waw conversivum*. Berger (*Gesetzesauslegung*, 96) points out the extreme rarity of the verb "to love" (*'āhab*) in the Holiness Code and the Priestly Code of Leviticus and in the Book of the Covenant in Exodus. In contrast, the verb occurs much more frequently in Deuteronomy, with both God and human beings as the object.

⁵⁷ France (*The Gospel of Mark*, 480) suggests that the two commandments refer to the two "tables" or parts of the Decalogue; cf. Allison, "Mark 12. 28–31," 271–78; Evans, *Mark 8:27–16:20*, 265. While this is possible, the Marcan Jesus (unlike Philo and Josephus) nowhere directly speaks of the Decalogue (or "The Ten Words") as such. The closest we come to such a reference is in Mark 10:19, when Jesus replies to the question of the rich man by citing most of the "social commandments" from the second table of the Decalogue. But, even here, not all the commandments of the second table are listed ("thou shalt not covet . . ." is missing), while a commandment not belonging to the Decalogue ("thou shalt not defraud") is included.

⁵⁸ One can only read with bewilderment Furnish's comment (*The Love Command*, 27–28) on Jesus' clear ordering of the two commandments in Mark 12:29–31: "In effect, then, the scribe is being told that no *one* commandment can be marked as 'first,' but that these two together (love of the one God and love of one's neighbor) constitute the essence of the law. . . . The 'second' commandment is not of 'second importance.' It is, simply, the second of the two mentioned." One sees the danger of confusing historical-critical exegesis with theologizing on a Gospel text to make it satisfy some contemporary *Zeitgeist*. Often one ends up blatantly contradicting what the text clearly says. See Gundry's justified criticism (*Mark*, 716) of Furnish's reductionism. Banks (*Jesus and the Law*, 167) likewise insists on the hierarchy created by "first" and "second." On the dialectic of the two commandments that are united in a hierarchical order above all other commandments, see Keerankeri, *The Love Commandment*, 136–37. Berger (*Gesetzesauslegung*, 174, 190–91) also notes the hierarchy implicit in the Marcan distinction of "first" and "second," though he considers this differentiation a secondary development in the Marcan form of the tradition (contrast Matthew and Luke). On the contrary, if, as I maintain, Mark is the sole source of the Matthean and Lucan versions of the double commandment, then we must draw the intriguing conclusion that Matthew's "similar to" (*homoia* in Matt 22:39) and Luke's connection of the two commands by only one verb ("you shall love" for both objects) and a simple "and" (*kai*) in 10:27 must be seen as secondary attempts to bind the two commands more closely together. Mark's insistence on "first" and "second" firmly resists any attempt to put the two commands on the same level or to reduce one to the other. On this, see Mudiso Mbâ Mundla, *Jesus und die Führer*, 195.

⁵⁹ Some commentators point out that, from a purely logical point of view, to state that no other commandment is greater than the two love commandments (Mark 12:31c) does not necessarily mean that other commandments are less important than these two. At least in theory, one could conclude that all other commandments are just as important as the two love commandments; on this, see Ebersohn, *Das Nächstenliebegebot*, 171. I would reply that such a conclusion might be tenable if all we had were Mark 12:31c. But if Jesus states in answer to the scribe's question that love of God is the *first* commandment, if he then goes out of his way to add (unbidden) that love of neighbor is the *second* commandment, and if he then concludes this ordering by observing that no other commandment is greater than these two, it seems to follow logically that other commandments would necessarily rank at least as third (and presumably fourth, fifth, etc.).

⁶⁰ To grasp the full ingenuity of Jesus' combination, one must remember that Deut 6:4–5 is not one commandment among many, contained within a lengthy list of various commandments. As we have seen, it is the fundamental obligation of the covenant, on which all individual commandments are based. In contrast, Lev 19:18b is simply one commandment, however noble, within a string of social commandments in Leviticus 19. To pluck Lev 19:18b out of this list and put it alongside the basic obligation of the covenant is daring halakic interpretation. On this, see Berger, *Ge-*

setzesauslegung, 136. Berger refuses to allow that, in this unheard-of combination of Deut 6:4–5 and Lev 19:18b, Jesus of Nazareth might actually have demonstrated a remarkable creativity in reinterpreting Torah that had no precise antecedent in Palestinian Judaism. Instead, Berger constructs a contorted explanation of how the core teaching of the double commandment in Mark 12:28–34 arose in Hellenistic Judaism, was developed by Philo, was expressed in the catechesis of Diaspora Judaism and then of early Hellenistic-Jewish Christianity, and was finally placed on the lips of the Marcan Jesus—oddly, to leave no trace anywhere else in the NT.

[61] Mudiso Mbâ Mundla (*Jesus und die Führer,* 138) is probably correct that *kalōs* in v 32 stands as an independent exclamation of agreement and not as a part of the following clause with *eipes*; see the parallel usage in Rom 11:20.

[62] Thomas ("Liturgical Citations," 209) fails to appreciate the full import of the scribe's modifications, calling them "stylistic" changes "to avoid exact repetition of Jesus' words." That is true, but hardly the full explanation.

[63] So Gundry, *Mark,* 714.

[64] The *pantōn* ("all") in "is greater than *all* holocausts and sacrifices" (v 33c) probably picks up and interprets the *pantōn* ("first commandment of *all*") in v 28e; see Pesch, *Markusevangelium,* 2. 242.

[65] On this point, see the whole argument in Jonathan Klawans, *Purity, Sacrifice, and the Temple* (Oxford: Oxford University, 2006), esp. 75–100 and 145–74; cf. Mudiso Mbâ Mundla, *Jesus und die Führer,* 201–3; Banks, *Jesus and the Law,* 168. Perhaps the best known OT text on this subject is Hosea 6:6: "I desire mercy and not sacrifice, the knowledge of God rather than holocausts." The conjunction of "mercy" and "knowledge of God" is especially suggestive, since one could see in (or read into?) these two phrases summaries (granted, in reverse order) of the two commandments of love. Other texts extolling obedience toward God, justice toward one's neighbors, or some other value over sacrifice and ritual include 1 Sam 15:22; Isa 1:11–17; Jer 6:20; 7:22–23; Amos 5:21–25; Mic 6:6–8; Ps 40:6–8; Ps 51:16–17; Prov 21:3. Hence, there is no need to see the emphasis on the superiority of love over sacrifice ("critique of cult") in Mark 12:28–34 as an indication that the story is stamped by the ideology of "Hellenistic [i.e., Diaspora] Judaism." For a different view, see Pesch, *Markusevangelium,* 2. 243–44.

[66] On this, see Keerankeri, *The Love Commandment,* 169 n. 384.

[67] In favor of the category of *Schulgespräch* for Mark 12:28–34 is Pesch (*Markusevangelium,* 2. 237), who notes the unusual structure of this dialogue; similarly, Bornkamm, "Doppelgebot," 85; Berger, *Gesetzesauslegung,* 183–84; Mudiso Mbâ Mundla, *Jesus und die Führer,* 143. Keerankeri (*The Love Commandment,* 71–74) is so impressed by the different structure of this pericope that he claims that

the category of *Schulgespräch* does not quite fit. Keerankeri prefers to use the label of *Dialoggespräch* ("dialogue conversation"), which, in his definition, includes the elements of (a) well-intentioned question; (b) Jesus' answer; (c) appreciation with paraphrase, repetition, and creatively developed commentary on the answer; (d) appreciative comment and recognition from Jesus. I leave it to the reader to decide whether *Dialoggespräch*, contrasted with *Schulgespräch*, is a distinction without a difference or perhaps a tautology.

[68] Keerankeri (*The Love Commandment*, 173) suggests that Jesus is affirming a simultaneous closeness and distance vis-à-vis the kingdom in the case of the scribe.

[69] I readily admit that "far" and "not far" are used theologically in other types of statements in the NT: e.g., Acts 17:27 (God is "not far" from any one of us). In addition, phrases like "those who are far off" or "you who were once far off" are used in various contexts to describe either Diaspora Jews or Gentile converts to Christianity; see, e.g., Acts 2:39; 22:21; Eph 2:13,17. The unusual phrasing, "not far from the kingdom of God," does not justify the judgment of those commentators (e.g., Pesch [*Markusevangelium*, 2. 244], agreeing with Bornkamm ["Doppelgebot," 90–91]) who claim that the kingdom in Mark 12:34 is thought of not as an eschatological reality but as an ecclesiological one. The very first statement Jesus makes in Mark's Gospel about the kingdom uses a spatial metaphor: "The kingdom of God has drawn near [*ēggiken*]" (Mark 1:15). Throughout Mark's Gospel, various spatial metaphors are used to express relationship, positive or negative, to the kingdom: the kingdom of David is coming (11:10); one accepts, enters, or does not enter into the kingdom (10:15,23–25); Jesus will drink wine anew in the kingdom of God (14:25). While the spatial metaphor in 12:34 is different and indeed unique, that alone does not support the idea that the kingdom in 12:34 is not eschatological. One might also dispute the supposed opposition between "eschatological" and "ecclesiological," but that is another matter.

[70] Once again, Furnish (*The Love Command*, 28 n. 12 [continuing on p. 29]) tries to unsay what Mark says by insisting that Jesus' litotes is "unqualifiedly affirmative: the scribe is said to belong to the Kingdom." While Bornkamm ("Doppelgebot," 85, 90–91) claims that there is full agreement between Jesus and the scribe and that Mark makes the scribe his own spokesman (a questionable position), he does admit that the scribe remains on the "threshold" of the kingdom. A similar view is taken by Burchard ("Das doppelte Liebesgebot," 57), who remarks that the litotes is positively meant but that it also means "not yet in"; so too, McIlhone, "Not Far," 61.

[71] Gundry (*Mark*, 712) suggests that the combination of *ouketi* ("no longer," "no further") plus the imperfect verb *etolma* ("was daring") makes Jesus' victory in 12:28–34 "both permanent and inclusive of his earlier answers too."

[72] In keeping with his theory of Mark as a conservative redactor and of an extensive pre-Marcan Passion Narrative (reaching all the way back to Peter's con-

fession of faith near Caesarea Philippi), Pesch (*Markusevangelium*, 2. 236) thinks that Mark has not inserted redactional changes within the pericope proper. In effect, though, all this does is move the question of tradition and redaction back to what the pre-Marcan redactor(s) of the tradition did. In his judgment, though, Pesch is not far from the mainstream opinion of NT exegetes exemplified by, e.g., Bornkamm ("Doppelgebot," 92), Burchard ("Das doppelte Liebesgebot," 43–44, 46), and Furnish (*The Love Command*, 30): except for Mark's redactional hand in the introduction (v 28a) and the conclusion (v 34b), neither the content nor the style of this passage exhibits particularly Marcan elements. Indeed, the amount of vocabulary and stylistic traits not witnessed elsewhere in Mark definitely points to pre-Marcan tradition.

[73] This is pointed out by Evans, *Mark 8:27–16:20*, 267; Keerankeri, *The Love Commandment*, 171–72. On Mark's strong christological claim (Jesus is the only teacher, and all teaching must be referred back to Jesus) in this pericope, see Berger, *Gesetzesauslegung*, 187. While Ebersohn (*Das Nächstenliebegebot*, 179–81) recognizes in Mark 12:28–34 the apologetic theme that Christianity flows from Judaism, he also insists that Mark emphasizes a sharp contradiction between Christianity and the Judaism of Mark's own day. Ebersohn detects this polemical note because he interprets the scribe (wrongly, in my view) as an antagonist who tries to trap Jesus but who himself (ironically) gets trapped by Jesus.

[74] See, e.g., Mark 2:6,16; 3:2,5–6,22; 7:7–13; 8:11–15; 9:14; 10:2; 11:18,27–33; 12:12,13–15,24,27.

[75] The arguments from both structure and content are missed by commentators who claim that the scribe is just as antagonistic (at least initially) as the Pharisees and Sadducees in the previous dispute stories; so, e.g., Gundry, *Mark*, 710; Ebersohn, *Das Nächstenliebegebot*, 169–70. Representing the common view that the scribe is positively portrayed from the beginning are France, *The Gospel of Mark*, 476; Pesch, *Markusevangelium*, 2. 237, 243. Perhaps the only significant parallel to such a figure is the sympathetic-but-not-totally-committed Nicodemus in John's Gospel; see John 3:1–15; 7:50. His reappearance at the burial of Jesus (19:39) is ambiguous and has been interpreted in different ways by different commentators. One might even argue from this multiple attestation of sources (sympathetic scribe in Mark and sympathetic Nicodemus, "the teacher of Israel," in John 3:10) that, in actual fact, some Jewish scholars of the Law in Jerusalem were sympathetic to Jesus' teaching during the public ministry, but did not join his group.

[76] Contrast the total absence of *nomos* in Mark with the eight occurrences in Matthew, the nine occurrences in Luke, and the seventeen occurrences in Acts. Mark also lacks derivative words like *nomikos* and *nomodidaskalos*. In the relatively few cases when Mark treats legal questions directly and at length, he prefers the word *entolē* ("commandment"; see 7:8–9; 10:5,19; 12:28,31). In all these cases,

the context contains a citation of one or more commandments in the written Law of Moses.

[77] For an introduction to the approaches of Matthew and Luke to the problem of the Mosaic Law and for further bibliography, see W. D. Davies, *The Setting of the Sermon on the Mount* (Cambridge: Cambridge University, 1966); Barth, "Das Gesetzesverständnis," 54–154; Banks, *Jesus and the Law*; Meier, *Law and History*; Wilson, *Luke and the Law*; Hübner, *Das Gesetz in der synoptischen Tradition*; Syreeni, "Matthew, Luke, and the Law," 126–55.

[78] Curiously, a number of commentators seem to presume the historicity of at least Mark 12:29–31 without supplying a detailed argument in favor of historicity. This is the case, e.g., of Bornkamm ("Doppelgebot," 85–93), who makes at best only glancing references to an argument from discontinuity (p. 86) and possibly multiple attestation (pp. 92–93).

[79] On this, see Furnish, *The Love Command*, 28.

[80] Becker ("Feindesliebe," 14) emphasizes this lack of resonance outside the NT. Becker cites the *Letter of Polycarp* 3:3 as an example of such resonance, but the text ("love of God and of Christ and of [one's] neighbor goes before" faith) seems to me a very distant allusion at best. Becker (p. 16) seems correct that in the earliest days of Christianity the double command of love did not enjoy the high evaluation and position of esteem that it was accorded later on. Burchard ("Das doppelte Liebesgebot," 45–46) thinks that both Justin Martyr and the *Letter of Poycarp* betray knowledge of the Synoptic Gospels. In the case of *Did.* 1:2, Burchard (p. 50) hesitates, saying that it is secondary vis-à-vis the Synoptics but leaving open the precise nature of dependence; cf. Légasse, *"Et qui est mon proachain?"* 63.

[81] In a paraphrase of the first (or "great") commandment to love God in his *First Apology* (*Apol.* 1.16.6) Justin employs the exact same catechetical addition found in *Did.* 1:2: "the God who made you [*ton theon ton poiēsanta se*]." The second love commandment shows the influence of Christian catechetical exuberance in that sometimes loving one's neighbor as oneself is no longer enough. *Did.* 2:7 and *Epistle of Barnabas* 19:5 insist that "you shall love your neighbor [or some equivalent thereof] more than [literally: 'above'] your own soul [*psychēn*, which could also be translated 'life' or 'self']." The conflating tendency of Christian catechesis and homiletics can also be seen in the first half of logion 25 in the *Coptic Gospel of Thomas*: "Jesus said, 'Love your brother like your soul [the Greek word *psychē* is used here].' " Loving one's *brother* reflects the Johannine version of Jesus' love command (e.g., 1 John 2:10; 4:21), while the use of *psychē* reflects the Christian catechetical tradition seen in the *Didache* and the *Epistle of Barnabas*.

[82] For a succinct argument for the historicity of the core of Mark 12:28–34, see Mudiso Mbâ Mundla, *Jesus und die Führer*, 222–26.

[83] Elsewhere in the OT (including the deuterocanonical books), the totality (or intensification) formula can be found, e.g., in Tob 13:6 ("if you turn to him [God] with your whole heart and with your whole soul"); Sir 6:26 ("with all your soul come to her [Wisdom], and with all your might keep to her ways").

[84] In some enumerations of the verses, vv 14–15 are counted as vv 15–16. I base my translation on the critical text reconstructed by Jeremy Corley, *Ben Sira's Teaching on Friendship* (Brown Judaic Studies 316; Providence, RI: Brown University, 2002) 118. The phrase "the one who is like himself" is rendered in the Greek as *ton plēsion autou* ("his neighbor"). As Patrick W. Skehan and Alexander A. Di Lella (*The Wisdom of Ben Sira* [AYB 39; New York: Doubleday, 1987; reprint New Haven: Yale University Press] 254) point out, 13:14–15 (or vv 15–16) recycle well-known proverbs common to the sapiential tradition of the ancient Mediterranean world.

[85] On friendship in Ben Sira, see Corley, *Ben Sira's Teaching*, passim. On p. 213, Corley observes that Egyptian sapiential literature as well as Greek thought on friendship (especially that of Theognis) is combined by Ben Sira with the traditional wisdom of Israel to forge a new synthesis that speaks to "an increasingly hellenized society."

[86] Note that *rēaʿ* here is a fellow diner at a banquet, not any and every fellow Israelite.

[87] The Greek text of 17:14b reads literally "and he commanded them, each concerning the neighbor" (*kai eneteilato autois hekastō peri tou plēsion*). On the meaning of this verse, see Ebersohn, *Das Nächstenliebegebot*, 98. Skehan and Di Lella (*The Wisdom of Ben Sira*, 282–83) push the idea of a reference to the second table of the Decalogue further. Claiming that the first half of v 14 ("take care to avoid every kind of injustice") refers to the negative commands of the first table of the Decalogue, Skehan and Di Lella then conclude that v 14 is alluding not only to the two tables of the Decalogue but also, in consequence, to the commandment to love God (Deut 6:5) and the commandment to love one's neighbor (Lev 19:18b). This is something of a logical leap. If one is focused on the wording of the Decalogue (as this hypothesis demands), one must admit that the sabbath command is positive in its wording, not negative ("remember the sabbath day to keep it holy" in Exod 20:8), although this command certainly involves avoiding various actions that are perfectly good in themselves. One must also ignore the fact that Philo, the first Jewish writer to reflect at length on the Decalogue, also counts "honor your father and your mother," another positive commandment, as belonging to the first table of the Decalogue. Indeed, one wonders whether anyone would think of Sir 17:14 as alluding to Deut 6:4–5 and Lev 19:18b if we did not already know Jesus' teaching on the double command of love. In my view, it is more likely that Sir 17:14 is a case of antithetical parallelism, especially since v 14a speaks of *pantos adikou*, "every kind of injustice." While quite broad in its range of meaning, *adikos* ("unjust,"

"crooked," "contrary to what is right") more easily refers to contravention of our duties to our fellow human beings, as shown from the widespread Greek philosophical distinction between *eusebeia* ("reverence" toward God) and *dikaiosynē* ("justice" toward other human beings)—a distinction taken up, as we shall see, by Philo and Josephus.

[88] Choosing the right translation for Sir 7:21 is difficult, since the Hebrew manuscripts differ in their readings, while the LXX inverts the wording with "let your soul love an understanding servant." Hebrew manuscript A reads the rare verb *ḥbb* ("love"), while manuscript C reads the usual verb for love (*ʾhwb*). I indicate my choice of *ḥbb* by translating it as "cherish." The command that one not refuse the slave his freedom may indicate that the slave is a fellow Hebrew, since Hebrew slaves had the legal right of manumission after six years of service; on this, see Skehan and Di Lella, *The Wisdom of Ben Sira*, 205. The point of comparison in the Hebrew text is simply *knpš*, "as life" or "as self," with no personal pronoun added; it is supplied in the free Greek translation.

[89] On this, see Mathys, *Liebe*, 167–71.

[90] CD 9:8 reads *rēʿêkā* ("your neighbor," i.e., your fellow Israelite in the Essene community), while the MT has *ʿămîtekā* ("fellow member of your people").

[91] See Meisinger, *Liebesgebot*, 18. That an allusion to Lev 19:18b is intended is made all the more likely by an allusion in CD 7:2 to Lev 19:17–18a, again with "his brother" substituted for "a fellow member of your people" and "the sons of your people." For the use of *rēaʿ* ("neighbor") and *ʾāḥ* ("brother") in Qumran's citations of or allusions to verses in Leviticus 19, see Berger, *Gesetzesauslegung*, 117–20.

[92] See Martin Abegg, Jr., Peter Flint, and Eugene Ulrich, *The Dead Sea Scrolls Bible* (San Francisco: Harper, 1999) 77–78, 97; see also David L. Washburn, *A Catalog of Biblical Passages in the Dead Sea Scrolls* (Text Critical Studies 2; Atlanta: SBL, 2002) 43.

[93] Deuteronomy is second only to the Book of Psalms (which is represented by no less that forty) in the number of manuscripts found in the Judean Wilderness. On the texts of Deuteronomy in the Dead Sea Scrolls, see Florentino García Martínez, "Les manuscrits du désert de Juda et le Deutéronome," *Studies in Deuteronomy* (C. J. Labuschagne Festschrift; VTSup 53; ed. Florentino García Martínez; Leiden/Cologne/New York: Brill, 1994) 65–82. Interestingly, so fluid is the tradition to which phylactery texts belong that some of the phylacteries from Qumran lack the *Shemaʿ*; on this, see J. T. Milik, "Tefillin, Mezuzot, Targums," in R. de Vaux and J. T. Milik (eds.), *Qumrân Grotte 4. II* (DJD 6; Oxford: Clarendon, 1977) esp. pp. 38–39, 49–57, 62, 72, 80–85. It is at Murabbaʿat that we get one of the best preserved texts of Deut 6:4–5, contained in a phylactery; see P. Benoit, J. T. Milik, and R. de Vaux (eds.), *Les Grottes de Murabbaʿat* (DJD 2; Oxford: Clarendon, 1961) 85.

[94] The totality (or intensification) formula reminiscent of Deut 6:5 is found in a fair number of passages in the Dead Sea Scrolls: e.g., CD 15:9,12; 1QS 5:8–9; 1QS 1:1–2 (with restorations). There is a partial echo of Deut 6:5 in an unfortunately fragmentary text in 1QH 6:26 (= Sukenik's 14:26): "I love [or: 'will love'] you willingly and with my whole heart . . . [possibly: 'I will bless you']."

[95] On this, see Ebersohn, *Nächstenliebegebot*, 106–7; cf. Ruzer, "The Double Love Precept," V–VI.

[96] If one could take the phrase in lines 3–4, "to love everything he has chosen," in a personal sense, i.e., "to love everyone he has chosen," the parallel to the double command would be much closer. However, the immediate context seems to be speaking of things, not persons.

[97] See Steve Delamarter, *A Scripture Index to Charlesworth's* The Old Testament Pseudepigrapha (London/New York: Sheffield, 2002) 16–17, 67, 69. In the entire huge corpus of writings gathered under the title of *The Old Testament Pseudepigrapha* in the two volumes published by James H. Charlesworth (Garden City, NY: Doubleday, 1983, 1985)—a corpus that includes a fair amount of Christian material—there is not one direct citation of the love commandments, i.e., Lev 19:18b and/or Deut 6:5. In a few scattered works, almost all of which were composed after the life of Jesus, there are allusions to the opening words of the *Shema* (Deut 6:4).

[98] On *Jubilees*, see *A Marginal Jew*, 3. 348–49 n. 14.

[99] The translation is taken from O. S. Wintermute, "Jubilees," *OTP*, 2. 93.

[100] An echo of Deut 6:5 might be detected in some uses of the totality formula in *Jub.* 1:15–16; 16:25; 22:28; 29:20; 35:12. However, while the formula occurs at times with the verb "to love," a number of passages refer to the love of one human for another.

[101] The tendency to summarize legal and moral obligations can be seen early on in the wisdom tradition. Israelite wisdom seeks to find the *rʾōš* ("beginning," "principle," "sum," "epitome") of wisdom in the fear of the Lord, which in turn translates into keeping his precepts (see, e.g., Prov 1:7; 9:10; Ps 111:10; Sir 1:14; 24:1,23). Strictly speaking, though, the tendency toward summarizing receives its Gospel expression more in Matthew's redacted form of the Marcan tradition.

[102] See especially the treatment in Ebersohn, *Nächstenliebegebot*, 57–96; cf. Nissen, *Gott*, 230–44; Berger, *Gesetzesauslegung*, 160–62. The reason Ebersohn spends so much time on the *Testaments* is that, in his view (p. 252), the tradition of the double command that he sees in the *Testaments* and in Philo invalidates the argument for historicity from the criterion of discontinuity; the double command of love does not come from the historical Jesus.

[103] See, e.g., the claim by Allison ("Mark 12. 28–31," 270) that Jesus' double command cannot be considered unprecedented because there are a number of "near parallels" (the qualification is telling), among which passages from the *Testaments* and Philo are prominent.

[104] For a description of the Greek manuscripts, see Marinus de Jonge et al., *The Testaments of the Twelve Patriarchs. A Critical Edition of the Greek Text* (PVTG 1/2; Leiden: Brill, 1978) xi–xxv. De Jonge notes (p. xxx): "There are only few certain references to and no explicit quotations from the *Testaments* in Christian sources dating from the period before the oldest manuscripts." My translations of various passages of the *Testaments* are based on this critical edition.

[105] Among his various writings that deal with this point, see Marinus de Jonge, "Die Paränese," 538–50; idem, "The *Testaments of the Twelve Patriarchs* and the 'Two Ways,' " *Biblical Traditions in Transmission* (Michael A. Knibb Festschrift; ed. Charolotte Hempel and Judith M. Lieu; Supplements to the Journal for the Study of Judaism 111; Leiden/Boston: Brill, 2006) 179–94; see in particular pp. 179–81, 194. In H. W. Hollander and M. de Jonge, *The Testaments of the Twelve Patriarchs. A Commentary*, the authors point out (pp. 47, 84–85) that a great deal of what one could call Hellenistic-Jewish parenesis can be found in Justin's *Dialogue with Trypho* and Irenaeus' *Adversus Haereses*.

[106] See Marinus de Jonge, *The Testaments of the Twelve Patriarchs. A Study of Their Text, Composition and Origin* (Van Gorcum's Theologische Biblioteek 25; 2d ed.; Assen/Amsterdam, 1975); note in particular de Jonge's revision of his views in the preface to the 2d edition, pp. 5–7 (unnumbered). Yet he states (p. 7) that "he remains unconvinced of the results of further scissors-and-paste procedures carried out in recent years, and prefers to emphasize the importance of a study of the Testaments in their present state—a document in which the capacity of the early Church to assimilate Jewish (particularly Hellenistic Jewish) material comes to the fore in a very interesting way." See also the more recent statement of his position in M. de Jonge, *Pseudepigrapha of the Old Testament as Part of Christian Literature* (SVTP 18; Leiden/Boston: Brill 2003) 71–177, esp. 84–106. Basically agreeing with de Jonge's approach, though without examining the *Testaments* in detail, is James R. Davila, *The Provenance of the Pseudepigrapha: Jewish, Christian, or Other?* (Supplements to the Journal for the Study of Judaism 105; Leiden/Boston: Brill, 2005) 232–33.

[107] For an attempt at a reconstitution of the *Aramaic Levi Document* by meshing the Qumran fragments with the medieval fragments from the Cairo Geniza, see Jonas C. Greenfield, Michael E. Stone, and Esther Eshel, *The Aramaic Levi Document. Edition, Translation, Commentary* (SVTP 19; Leiden/Boston: Brill, 2004). Reflecting the views of Stone, this volume (p. 19) espouses a date of composition for the original *Aramaic Levi Document* in "the third century or very early second century BCE." Taking issue with this opinion, James Kugel ("How Old Is the

Aramic Levi Document?" Dead Sea Discoveries 17 [2007] 291–312) argues that the *Aramaic Levi Document* was "put into its final form late in the second century" (p. 312).

[108] On this question, see de Jonge, "The *Testaments of the Twelve Patriarchs* and Related Qumran Fragments," and "Levi in the Aramaic Levi Document and in the *Testament of Levi*," *Pseudepigrapha of the Old Testament as Part of Christian Literature*, 107–23 and 124–40 respectively. De Jonge lists all the fragments that might be related in some way to the *Testaments* in "The *Testaments of the Twelve Patriarchs* and Related Qumran Fragments," 107, and goes on to summarize his basic position on *Aramaic Levi* on pp. 108–9: "It may be regarded as certain that *T. Levi* is directly or indirectly dependent on a written source identical or very similar to the Aramaic Levi Document (hereafter ALD). This also explains why *T. Levi* differs so much from the other eleven testaments, in structure as well as in content [similarly Kugel, "How Old Is the *Aramaic Levi Document*?" 291]. At the same time, comparing *T. Levi* with ALD brings out interesting Christian elements in the testament, which are structural rather than incidental and can, therefore, not be eliminated as later interpolations." In contrast, Ebersohn (*Nächstenliebegebot*, 62) thinks that the Aramaic fragments from Qumran show no link of literary dependence but rather the existence of a common oral tradition. He observes that the *Testaments* display none of the sectarian particularism of the Essenes.

[109] For his major statement on the tradition history of the *Testaments*, see Jürgen Becker, *Untersuchungen zur Entstehungsgeschichte der Testamente der zwölf Patriarchen* (AGJU 8; Leiden: Brill, 1970). He distinguishes three stages of development: (1) a basic document composed by a Hellenistic-Jewish author; (2) additions made within a Hellenistic-Jewish milieu; (3) Christian redaction; on this, see pp. 373–77. In agreement with Becker's basic approach are Ebersohn, *Nächstenliebegebot*, 59; Reinhard Weber, *Das Gezetz im hellenistichen Judentum* (Arbeiten zur Religion und Geschichte des Urchristentums 10; Frankfurt: Lang, 2000) 154–79. Ebersohn (p. 62) correctly observes that the Hebrew *Testament of Naphtali* is a late work that does not aid our understanding of the tradition history of the *Testaments*.

[110] On this, see Légasse, *"Et qui est mon prochain?"* 62–63.

[111] The prime example of the double command is in the *Testament of Issachar* (*T. Iss.* 5:1–3, translation and emphasis mine): "Keep therefore the Law of God, my children, and acquire simplicity; and walk in innocence, not interfering with the commandments of the Lord and the affairs of [your] neighbor. But *love the Lord and [your] neighbor*; show mercy to poverty and sickness. Bow your back in submission to farming . . . offering gifts to the Lord with thanksgiving." One notices immediately that, far from being the two greatest commandments of the Law, love of the Lord and of one's neighbor are simply two commandments listed among many others, including being a hardworking farmer. The compression of the two

love commands into one ("love the Lord and [your] neighbor") may reflect the compressed redaction of Mark 12:30–31 by Luke in 10:27, where "the Lord your God" and "your neighbor" become the dual object of the once-mentioned verb *agapēseis* ("you shall love"). The compression in *T. Iss.* 5:2 has gone one step further than Luke in that the formula of totality ("from your whole heart") has been omitted after "love the Lord."

Sometimes in the *Testaments* it is fear of God that is directly joined to love of neighbor, while love of God is mentioned in the wider context; so, e.g., *T. Benj.* 3:1,3,4b: "And you, therefore, my children, love the Lord, the God of heaven, and keep his commandments. . . . Fear the Lord and love [your] neighbor. . . . He who fears God and loves his neighbor cannot be wounded by the Beliar's spirit of the air." See also *T. Dan* 5:2–3: "Speak truth, each to his neighbor. . . . Love the Lord your whole life long and one another with a sincere heart." Love of God and of all humanity is mentioned in narrative form in *T. Iss.* 7:6: "I loved the Lord with all my strength; similarly I also loved every human being like my children." A looser connection of the two obligations is found in *T. Gad* 4:1–2: "Therefore keep yourselves, my children, from hatred, for it commits iniquity against the Lord himself. For it does not wish to listen to [the] words of his commandments concerning love of [one's] neighbor, and it sins against God." Here nothing is said about love of God or, indeed, about two distinct obligations; rather, hatred of one's neighbor is seen as a sin against God. In fact, some texts of the *Testaments* that are cited by scholars in regard to Jesus' double command speak explicitly either of love of neighbor or love of God, but not of both together. Loving one's brothers or one another is mentioned in *T. Sim.* 4:7; *T. Zeb.* 8:5; *T. Jos.* 17:1–3. In *T. Jos.* 11:1 we have the unusual combination of "fear God and honor your brothers." *T. Reu.* 6:9 seems to distinguish between neighbor and brother: "I adjure you by God . . . do truth, each to his neighbor, and [practice] love, each to his brother"; *T. Benj.* 10:3 reads: "Do truth and justice, each with his neighbor . . . and keep the Law of the Lord and his commandments." *T. Gad* 6:1–3 repeatedly insists: "Each of you, love your brother . . . loving one another . . . therefore, love one another from [the] heart"; similarly, 7:7: "Love one another in uprightness of heart." As some of these examples indicate, the *Testaments* speak more frequently of fearing (*phobeomai*) God and/or keeping (*phylassō*) the Law or the commandments than of loving him; on this, see Ebersohn, *Nächstenliebegebot*, 94. Even from this quick survey, one sees that speaking globally of the double command of love in the *Testaments* is a gross oversimplification. In the end, even if we were to grant that all these texts were the product of pre-70 Judaism—something I doubt—the fourfold configuration of Jesus' teaching in Mark 12:29–31 finds no real parallel.

[112] On this, see Mudiso Mbâ Mundla, *Jesus und die Führer*, 215.

[113] See Ebersohn, *Nächstenliebegebot*, 141.

[114] In regard to the double command, Berger treats Philo on pp. 156–60 and Josephus on pp.152–54 of his *Gesetzesauslegung*; Nissen dedicates the whole final section of his book (*Gott*, 417–502) to Philo. See also Reinhard Weber, *Das "Ge-*

setz" bei Philon von Alexandrien und Flavius Josephus (Arbeiten zur Religion und Geschichte des Urchristentums 11; Frankfurt: Lang, 2001).

[115] While *eusebeia* and *dikaiosynē* are favorites in this type of discourse, other abstract words are used along with or instead of them; e.g., *hosiotēs* ("holiness") along with *eusebeia* and *philanthrōpia* ("love of humanity") along with *dikaiosynē*. Other substitutes and combinations are found at times; on this, see Berger, *Gesetzesauslegung*, 144 n. 1, as well as his entire treatment of the pagan classical and Hellenistic Greek tradition on pp.143–51.

[116] For an introduction to the *Letter of Aristeas*, see R. J. H Shutt, "Letter of Aristeas," in Charlesworth's *OTP*, 2. 7–11. While noting that various critics have dated *Aristeas* from 250 B.C. to A.D. 100, Shutt states that the majority view favors 150–100 B.C.; he himself suggests 170 B.C. as a likely date.

[117] While the basic grid consists of *eusebeia* and *dikaiosynē*, Berger (*Gesetzesauslegung*, 155–56) points out that, at various points in *Aristeas*, *eusebeia* is connected with *agapē* ("love"); *dikaiosynē* is likewise related at times to *eleos* ("mercy") and *philanthrōpia* ("love of humanity"). We are thus reminded that the philosophical terminology used by Hellenistic Jews in their attempt to provide a systematic approach to the Law was somewhat fluid.

[118] One must remember here that Philo is following a traditional Jewish numbering of the commandments, so that the command to honor father and mother counts as the fifth commandment (so too in most Protestant enumerations). In *De decalogo* 22 §106–7, Philo must strain to explain how this commandment belongs with the first table, which deals with obligations to God. While Philo admits that this commandment sits on the border between the two tables, sharing something of both, he argues that parenthood makes human beings like God, who "begets" all things. Hence, honoring father and mother can be assigned to the first table of the Decalogue. One sees here the fierce desire to impose a neat, balanced system on recalcitrant data.

[119] The Greek word *kephalaion* serves in the LXX to translate the Hebrew *r'ōš* ("head") and *rē'šît* ("beginning," "principle," "epitome"); likewise, the Aramaic *r'ēš* ("head") in Dan 7:1.

[120] The passage in *De decalogo* 22 §109–10 is emphasized by Allison, "Mark 12. 28–31," 272–73. However, while this passage is perhaps the closest one can find to Mark 12:28–34 in the corpus of pre-70 Jewish literature, it hardly matches the four distinguishing characteristics of Jesus' teaching that I have previously listed.

[121] On this, see Fuller, "Double Commandment," 50.

[122] For the following remarks on *philanthrōpia* and its limits in Philo, I am dependent on Nissen, *Gott*, 478–502; references to individual passages in Philo may

be found there. Nissen (p. 502) concludes his survey of Philo with the comment: "A double command of love in its Jewish sense, in its breadth as well as its boundaries, is therefore impossible in Philo."

123 On this text, see Légasse, *"Et qui est mon prochain?,"* 63.

124 Berger (*Gesetzesauslegung*, 77) sees a strong allusion to Deut 6:4–5 in Philo's *De decalogo* 14 §64. In my view, apart from a variation on the totality formula ("with mind and speech and every power"), there is no clear reference to Deut 6:4–5 here; Philo's text is a fairly straightforward application of the first commandment of the Decalogue to the pagan practice of worshiping heavenly bodies. In contrast to Deut 6:4–5, Berger (p. 115 n. 1) readily admits that there is neither a citation of nor even an allusion to Lev 19:18b in Philo and Josephus. This is all the more striking since Philo does comment at length on Lev 19:14 in *De specialibus legibus* 4.38 §197–202, only to move immediately to Lev 19:19 in 4.39 §203.

125 One should distinguish among the various views of those who accept the Hellenistic-Jewish schema of *eusebeia* and *dikaiosynē* as a way of explaining the present form of Mark 12:28–34. For example, on the one hand, Berger uses this Hellenistic-Jewish tradition to deny that Mark 12:28–34 comes from the historical Jesus (*Gesetzesauslegung*, 176); in a similar vein, Burchard, "Das doppelte Liebesgebot," 51–62. On the other hand, Pesch (*Markusevangelium*, 2. 244) thinks that the core of the Marcan tradition ultimately goes back to Jesus, but that the present formulation of the pericope is influenced by Hellenistic-Jewish tradition, as taken over by Hellenistic-Jewish Christians; similarly, Bornkamm, "Doppelgebot," 86.

126 In the Jewish Scriptures, the Hebrew noun *kĕlāl* occurs only once, as the proper name "Chelal" in Ezra 10:30. The word occurs as a common noun in the Dead Sea Scrolls in 4Q 169, fragment 3–4, column 2, line 6, in the sense of "totality"; a second occurrence of the noun in the scrolls is possible, but uncertain. The use of *kĕlāl* to mean "rule," "norm," or "principle" thus seems to be a rabbinic innovation. As Strack and Stemberger note (*Introduction to the Talmud and Midrash*, 19), the fifth of the seven *middôt* ("rules of interpretation") of Hillel in the Tosepta is called the *kelal u-ferat u-ferat u-kelal*, i.e., the argument that qualifies the general by the particular and the particular by the general.

127 See, e.g., the phrase *kĕlāl gādôl* (literally, "a great principle") in *m. Šabb.* 7:1; Jacob Neusner (*The Mishnah* [New Haven/London: Yale University, 1988] 187) translates it as "a general rule." On commandments of the Torah that act as general principles without being thought to contain everything in the Torah, see Nissen, *Gott*, 241.

128 Aqiba's statement is found in *Sipra*, Parashat Qedoshim, Pereq 4. On this text and parallels to it, see Kuhn, "Das Liebesgebot," 207–8.

[129] See Strack and Stemberger, *Introduction*, 263.

[130] Some of the sayings in *m. 'Abot* (e.g., 2:10,12) echo or apply the love command of Lev 19:18b, but none of them cites the biblical text or directly comments on it. Such sayings should not be seen as examples of the Golden Rule; on this, see Nissen, *Gott*, 398.

[131] On this, see Nissen, *Gott*, 289, especially n. 870; cf. Bornkamm, "Doppelgebot," 86. An example of the mistranslation can be found in Irving Mandelbaum's rendering of the text in Jacob Neusner et al., *Sifra. An Analytical Translation* (Brown Judaic Studies 138, 139, and 140; Atlanta: Scholars, 1988) 3. 109: "This is the [*sic*] encompassing principle of the Torah." An examination of various editions of the Hebrew text of *Sipra* shows that there is no definite article before *kĕlāl*; see, e.g., *Sifra. Venice Edition 1545* (Jerusalem: Makor, no date); *Sifra* (New York: Om, 1946).

[132] Commentators argue over whether Ben Azzai intends to extend the commandment of love to all humanity (if, indeed this is the meaning of *'ādām* here) by declaring that Gen 5:1 is a general principle that is greater than Lev 19:18b; see, e.g., Berger, *Gesetzesauslegung*, 131. The question is not relevant to the point I am making in the main text.

[133] For various interpretations, see Banks, *Jesus and the Law*, 169.

[134] On an allusion to the *Shemaʿ* in 1 Cor 8:6, see Hans Lietzmann, *An die Korinther I/II* (HNT 9; 5th ed.; supplemented by Werner Georg Kümmel; Tübingen: Mohr [Siebeck], 1969) 37.

[135] On the use of Lev 19:18b in Matt 5:43, see Robert A. Guelich, *The Sermon on the Mount* (Waco, TX: Word, 1982) 225; Strecker, *Bergpredigt*, 90; Ulrich Luz, *Matthew 1–7* (Minneapolis: Augsburg, 1989) 339, 343–44; Davies and Allison, *The Gospel According to Saint Matthew*, 1. 548–50; Hagner, *Matthew*, 1. 133–34.

[136] Note that Matthew retains "as yourself" in his other redactional insertion of Lev 19:18b, i.e., at Matt 19:19. "As yourself" is dropped in 5:43 simply because the rhetorical balance of the verse requires it; on this, see Furnish, *The Love Comand*, 50–51.

[137] On this, see Davies and Allison, *The Gospel According to Saint Matthew*, 3. 44; Ulrich Luz, *Matthew 8–20* (Hermeneia; Minneapolis: Fortress, 2001) 512.

[138] On Gal 5:14, see Heinrich Schlier, *Der Brief an die Galater* (MeyerK 7; 4th ed.; Göttingen: Vandenhoeck & Ruprecht, 1965) 244–47; Franz Mussner, *Der Galaterbrief* (HTKNT 9; Freiburg/Basel/Vienna: Herder, 1974) 369–73; Hans Dieter Betz, *Galatians* (Hermeneia; Philadelphia: Fortress, 1979) 274–76; Frank J. Matera, *Ga-*

latians (Sacra Pagina 9; Collegeville, MN: Liturgical Press, 1992) 197–98; James D. G. Dunn, *The Epistle to the Galatians* (Black's NT Commentary 9; London: Black, 1993) 288–92.

[139] On Rom 13:8–10, see Otto Michel, *Der Brief an die Römer* (MeyerK 4; 4th ed.; Göttingen: Vandenhoeck & Ruprecht, 1966) 323–27; Ernst Käsemann, *An die Römer* (HNT 8a; Tübingen: Mohr [Siebeck], 1973) 344–48; Dunn, *Romans*, 2. 774–83; Fitzmyer, *Romans*, 676–80; Wischmeyer, "Das Gebot," 161–87, esp. 179–80.

[140] On this, see Augenstein, *Das Liebesgebot*, 173–74. Note also that in Gal 6:10, even as Paul exhorts the Galatians to do good to all, he adds the specification "especially to those who belong to the household of faith."

[141] Johnson, *The Letter of James*, 235; similarly, Edgar, "The Use of the Love-Command," 15.

[142] Part of the difficulty of interpretation here arises from the disagreement among commentators as to how much of a shift in theme we should see in Jas 2:8, which begins with *ei mentoi*. Should these words be translated "if, though . . . ," "if, actually . . . ," or "if, indeed . . ."? As often in James, the logical connection between sections is less than pellucid.

[143] Then, too, as Dibelius (*Der Brief des Jakobus*, 120, 172) points out, "those who love him [i.e., God or the Lord]" is a common traditional formula used to designate pious Jews, as the many passages that Dibelius cites from the LXX and the intertestamental literature show. This observation somewhat weakens the claim that "those who love him" must be an allusion to Deut 6:5 via the double command of Jesus. With fitting modesty, Edgar ("The Use of the Love-Command," 15) states that "it [Jas 2:5] is by no means a clear allusion to the language of Deut 6:5, but it is at least a possibility." Edgar proceeds to argue for allusions to the *Shemaʿ* elsewhere in James, but sometimes the supposed allusion rests simply on the appearance of the numeral *heis* ("one") used in reference to God. Perhaps his strongest candidate is Jas 4:12, where the *heis*-formula ("one is the lawgiver") occurs in the same sentence as the word *plēsion* ("neighbor"); yet even here the lack of the vocabulary of love and the very different point being made in the verse make an allusion to the *Shemaʿ* highly debatable.

[144] See Perkins, *Love Commands*, 85–86. Matthew's Gospel might be seen as an example of how this catechetical tradition was received and reworked in the second Christian generation.

[145] On this, see Allison, "Mark 12. 28–31," 274.

[146] See Légasse, *"Et qui est mon prochain?"* 62.

[147] Contrary to Johnson's view (*The Letter of James*, 230), I think that both "royal law" and "according to the Scripture" in Jas 2:8 refer to the citation to Lev 19:18b that follows immediately; cf. Lütgert, *Die Liebe*, 248; Edgar, "The Use of the Love-Command," 12. Indeed, Leviticus 19 in general seems to be quite important for James; it is alluded to a number of times in the Epistle, as Johnson points out (p. 31).

[148] See Légasse, *"Et qui est mon prochain?"* 145.

[149] See *A Marginal Jew*, 3. 411–44.

[150] Matthew (through the mouth of Jesus) speaks of scribes who, from the context, are Christian teachers (13:52; 23:34). In 8:19, Matthew depicts a Jewish scribe who offers to follow Jesus wherever he goes. Jesus' off-putting reaction as well as the general context makes it unclear whether the scribe is meant to be seen in a positive or negative light. Luke, on the whole, follows the Marcan presentation of the Jewish scribes, although their portrait becomes somewhat vaguer in Luke. On this, see *A Marginal Jew*, 3. 549–60.

[151] Here I differ notably with Bornkamm ("Doppelgebot," 87) and many others who claim that the inclusion of a reference to the oneness of Israel's God in Mark 12:29 makes sense only in the Greek-speaking Jewish Diaspora and Hellenistic-Jewish Christianity, the true matrices (they would claim) of the Marcan form of the pericope.

[152] See, e.g., Ebersohn, *Nächstenliebegebot*, 170.

[153] The terminology of "light" and "heavy" commandments could mean different things in different contexts; see Meier, *Law and History*, 90–91; Nissen, *Gott*, 338–39. Among the various meanings found in rabbinic literature, one can distinguish the following: (1) Commandments were light or heavy depending on the expenditure of energy or money involved in keeping them (even up to the point of risking one's own life). (2) Light and heavy were distinguished according to the different degrees of ritual impurity or holiness involved. (3) The violation of light commandments could be atoned for by repentance (and, in various cases, monetary compensation and temple sacrifices); violation of heavy commandments could require the death penalty. (4) Light commandments were those to which many people, practically speaking, did not pay much attention. I do not treat these distinctions in detail here because they are much more relevant to material in Matthew's Gospel (e.g., Matt 5:17–20) than to Mark 12:28–34. On the question of the inviolability of the Law as a whole and hence the equal importance of all the commandments that make up the Law, see Nissen, *Gott*, 335–42.

[154] This is one of the objections against historicity raised by Burchard, "Das doppelte Liebesgebot," 52–54; as with many treatments of this question, the later rab-

binic sources are simply presumed to be describing the uniform or at least dominant view among 1st-century Palestinian Jews.

155 The exact enumeration of the commandments in the Law seems to have been in flux during the tannaitic period. For instance, in the rabbinic commentary on Deuteronomy called *Sipre* (redacted in the late 3d century A.D.), Parashat Reeh, Piska §76, Rabbi Shimeon ben Azzai comments on Deut 12:23, a text that seems to put unique emphasis on the command not to drink blood. Ben Azzai asks rhetorically whether there are not 300 commandments in the Torah that are positive. This number contradicts the opinion that later became universal, namely, that there are 613 commandments in the Torah, made up of 248 positive commandments and 365 prohibitions. Hans Bietenhard (*Sifre Deuteronomium* [Judaica et Christiana 8; Bern: Peter Lang, 1984] 245 n. 4) thinks that Ben Azzai means 300 to be taken as a round number rather than an exact count. Reuven Hammer (*Sifre. A Tannaitic Commentary on the Book of Deuteornomy* [New Haven/London: Yale University, 1986] 426 n. 2) agrees, adding, on the authority of Louis Finkelstein, that "a specific figure [of commandments in the Torah] did not exist during Tannaitic times." By the time of the Babylonian Talmud, the number 613 (divided into 248 and 365) seems to have gained "canonical" status; see, e.g., *b. Mak.* 23b–24a. For the Hebrew text of *Sipre*, see Louis Finkelstein, *Siphre ad Deuteronomium* (Berlin: Jüdischer Kulturbund, 1939); the saying of Ben Azzai is found on p. 141, line 5. For an English translation of Ben Azzai's opinion, see Jacob Neusner, *Sifre to Deuteronomy* (Brown Judaic Studies 98 and 101; Atlanta: Scholars, 1987) 1. 218. For an English translation of *b. Mak.* 23b–24a, see H. M. Lazarus, *The Babylonian Talmud. Seder Nezikin. Makkoth* (London: Soncino, 1935) 169.

156 Contrary to treatments of the double commandment by many NT critics, I do not include at this point a consideration of the famous reply of Hillel to a would-be Gentile convert to Judaism, as reported in *b. Šabb.* 31a: "What is hateful to you, do not do to your fellow. That is the whole Torah in its entirety; the rest is commentary on it. Go and learn." Despite frequent references to this saying as one example of "the love commandment," the word "love" does not occur in the saying. This teaching of Hillel is rather an example of the so-called Golden Rule, well known among the ancient Greeks and taken over in due time by both Jews and Christians. (The highly questionable identification of the Golden Rule spoken by Hillel with the love commandment of Lev 19:18b is made by H. Freedman, *Shabbath* [2 vols.; London: Soncino, 1938] 1. 140 n. 6.) Another reason for not bringing up Hillel's saying at this point is that is not does appear in rabbinic literature as a supposed pronouncement of Hillel before the Babylonian Talmud (5th–6th century A.D.); using it as a "source" or "parallel" to Jesus' teaching is therefore questionable. The same is true of citing Aqiba on Lev 19:18b as a grand principle of the Law (*contra* Bornkamm, "Doppelgebot," 86). I will treat the Golden Rule and the talmudic anecdote about Hillel in Section IV.

157 A glancing reference to such an argument is made by Fuller, "The Double Commandment," 47; cf. Perkins, *Love Commands*, 25.

158 For every conceivable theory of sources that has been applied to this pericope, see Kiilunen, *Doppelgebot*, 13–18; similarly, Mudiso Mbâ Mundla, *Jesus und die Führer*, 113–19; Hultgren, *Jesus and His Adversaries*, 48. Major examples of theories put forward include: all three Synoptics represent versions independent of one another (see, e.g., Ernst Lohmeyer, *Das Evangelium des Matthäus* [ed. Werner Schmauch; 4th ed.; Göttingen: Vandenhoeck & Ruprecht, 1967] 327); both Matthew and Luke had access to an alternate form of the Marcan text (a type of "primitive Mark" hypothesis); Luke had his own special tradition; Matthew and Luke's versions are simply the result of their reworking of Mark; Matthew and Luke both combined Marcan and Q versions of the story; Luke knew Matthew as well as Mark; Matthew and Luke both knew a revised version of Mark (the "deutero-Mark" hypothesis); Mark represents a conflated or harmonized version of Matthew and Luke (the "two-Gospel" hypothesis); Matthew had his own special tradition, which he reworked under the influence of Mark and Q, while Luke made no use of Mark at all, using his own special tradition instead. Some explain the special Lucan form as probably reflecting a different incident in Jesus' ministry; see, e.g., Evans, *Mark 8:27–16:20*, 262 (echoing T. W. Manson). Berger (*Gesetzesauslegung*, 203) suggests that, alongside Mark, Matthew and Luke had access to a common tradition that was parallel to an early stage of the present Marcan composition. Fuller ("Double Commandment," 41) favors the classical two-source theory: both Mark and Q had versions of Jesus' teaching of the double commandment; Luke, in particular, conflates Q with Mark. Other scholars who incline toward some sort of a two-source solution, with Q the most common candidate for being the second source alongside Mark, include Bornkamm, "Doppelgebot," 92 (though he holds open the possibility that Luke 10:25–28 may preserve the oldest form of the tradition, which in turn may coincide with the primitive source of Mark); Kertelge, "Doppelgebot," 38–55. Burchard ("Das doppelte Liebesgebot," 41–44) remains somewhat hesitant about whether the common source Matthew and Luke used besides Mark was Q or some stray tradition.

159 This is a weakness in the otherwise sound methodology that James D. G. Dunn lays out in his important work, *Jesus Remembered* (Christianity in the Making 1; Grand Rapids, MI/Cambridge, UK: Eerdmans, 2003) 173–254; see also pp. 584–86.

160 Since the divergences from Mark are much more notable in Luke's version than in Matthew's, Kiilunen devotes more space (pp. 51–77) to Luke's story of the lawyer challenging Jesus, which acts as a springboard to the parable of the Good Samaritan. Kiilunen points out in particular how Luke rewrites Mark 12:28–34 with an eye to another Marcan pericope, the story of the rich man in Mark 10:17–22. On this last point, see also Fuller, "Double Commandment," 42–43. Also in favor of the view that Matthew and Luke depend solely on Mark for the tradition of the double commandment are Ebersohn, *Nächstenliebegebot*, 155; Mudiso Mbâ Mundla, *Jesus und die Führer*, 119; Meisinger, *Liebesgebot*, 29.

161 On this, see Kiilunen, *Doppelgebot*, 19–21.

¹⁶² See Kiilunen, *Doppelgebot*, 27; Burchard ("Das doppelte Liebesgebot," 42) misunderstands Luke's redactional activity here.

¹⁶³ On this, see Kiilunen, *Doppelgebot*, 29. Burchard ("Das doppelte Liebesgebot," 42) speaks of the "splinters" from Mark 12:28a,32a,34c that are strung together to form a conclusion for the disputes with the Sadducees in Luke 20:39–40.

¹⁶⁴ Kiilunen (*Doppelgebot* 18–19) lists all the significant "minor agreements" of Matthew and Luke against Mark 12:28–34. They include: (1) *nomikos* ("lawyer") in place of Mark's *grammateus* ("scribe"); (2) the questioner "tests" Jesus (*peirazōn* in Matthew, *ekpeirazōn* in Luke); (3) the questioner prefaces his opening question with *didaskale* ("teacher"); Mark's scribe addresses Jesus as *didaskale* only in the "second round" of the conversation (Mark 12:32); (4) Matthew and Luke both have the phrase *en tō nomō* ("in the Law"), which is absent in Mark; (5) Matthew and Luke introduce Jesus' reply with "but he said to him" (*ho de ephē autō* in Matt 22:37; *ho de eipen pros auton* in Luke 10:26), while Mark 12:29 reads "Jesus answered." (6) Matthew and Luke lack Jesus' citation of Deut 6:4, present in Mark; (7) Matthew and Luke are closer together in the wording of the citation of Deut 6:5, though Luke partially agrees with Mark; (8) the scribe's lengthy repetition of and commentary on Jesus' citation of the two commandments (Mark 12:32–33) are absent in Matthew and Luke. For a briefer list, see Fuller, "Double Commandment," 41. In the main text, I take up the first and fourth minor agreements to provide examples of how they are explainable simply as redactional changes that Matthew and Luke would naturally have been moved to make in the Marcan text without any impulse from another source. For a number of the other minor agreements, I think that the reader can easily see how, since Matthew and Luke both abbreviate Mark's text (as they often do), a number of changes would spontaneously occur in both of their Gospels (e.g., the omission of the scribe's lengthy repetition of Jesus' answer).

¹⁶⁵ The vast majority of Greek witnesses (e.g., Sinaiticus, Vaticanus, Codex Bezae, etc.) as well as most ancient translations have *nomikos* at Matt 22:35; hence, I grant its presence for the sake of argument. However, an important cluster of Greek minuscule texts known as family 1 (often categorized as "Caesarean witnesses"), as well as a small number of ancient translations and (at times) Origen, omits the word. The uncertainty of text critics is reflected in the fact that various editions of the *UBSGNT* put *nomikos* at Matt 22:35 in brackets and give it a "C" rating (considerable degree of doubt). Interestingly, even though Kiilunen notes (*Doppelgebot*, 37 n. 9) that a large number of distinguished exegetes (e.g., Schmid, Lagrange, Lohmeyer, Kilpatrick, Knox, Creed, Beare, Sand, and Gnilka) consider *nomikos* secondary in Matt 22:35, Kiilunen himself accepts it as part of the original text.

¹⁶⁶ Luke's Gospel has seven out of the ten occurrences in the NT; on Luke's use of *nomikos*, see *A Marginal Jew*, 3. 557–58.

[167] On this, see Kiilunen, *Doppelgebot*, 58–59; cf. Fuller, "Double Commandment," 42–44.

[168] On this, see Berger, *Gesetzesauslegung*, 232–35, 254–55; cf. Banks, *Jesus and the Law*, 170; Sand, *Gesetz*, 41 n. 72.

[169] So, correctly, Wilson, *Luke and the Law*, 14–15; Perkins, *Love Commands*, 22–23.

[170] I am not denying that there are "Mark–Q overlaps" in Matthew and Luke that are signaled at least in part by their minor agreements. Indeed, the presence of overlaps is fairly clear in such material as the missionary discourses and the accusation that Jesus performs exorcisms by Beelzebul. The argument for Mark–Q overlaps in these and other cases is laid out convincingly by Laufen's work, *Doppelüberlieferungen*. I am simply claiming that the minor agreements are not sufficiently probative in Mark 12:28–34 to argue for a Mark–Q overlap in this pericope. In this I agree with Laufen (p. 87).

[171] On this, see Pesch, "Jesus und das Hauptgebot," 107.

[172] Here I play on the ambiguous meaning of the term "rabbi." As we can see not only in the case of Jesus (e.g., Mark 9:5; Matt 26:49; John 1:38,49; 3:2) but also in that of John the Baptist (John 3:26), "rabbi" in the early part of the 1st century A.D. was a title of respect given to religious leaders and teachers who attracted a following, whether or not the individual had any formal training and official authorization to teach. In the post-70 period, the title gradually became restricted to those who had spent a good deal of time studying with a respected teacher of Torah and who were then "ordained," i.e., authorized to teach Torah themselves by the "laying on of hands."

[173] To "clear the ground," I should state briefly my view about the origin of Matthew's Sermon on the Mount (chaps. 5–7) and Luke's Sermon on the Plain (6:20–49). At the root of these two redactional compositions, in my opinion, lies a primitive collection of Jesus' sayings, already ordered in blocks of related material. This primitive "sermon" was taken up into the Q tradition, though Matthew and Luke may have known it in slightly different versions of Q. Luke basically preserves the Q form of the sermon, though not without some redactional reordering, rewording, and insertions of material from his own L tradition (on this, see Bultmann, *Geschichte*, 100; Fitzmyer, *The Gospel According to Luke*, 1. 627–28). Hence, in this section, I tend to cite verse numbers according to Luke's Gospel. In contrast, Matthew undertakes a massive expansion of the primitive sermon, meshing the Q material with blocks of his M tradition along with some traces of Mark's Gospel. Especially in the first half of his Sermon on the Mount (5:3–6:18), Matthew uses numerical patterns (notably the number three and multiples thereof) to structure his heterogeneous material in order to give it a sense of coherence and homogeneity

that it does not really have. This is true in particular of the six antitheses (5:21–48). I follow Lührmann ("Liebet eure Feinde," 412–16) and many other commentators (e.g., Furnish, *The Love Command*, 45–46; Sauer, "Traditionsgeschichtliche Erwägungen," 6–7; Kuhn, "Das Liebesgebot," 204–5; Schürmann, *Das Lukasevangelium*, 1.345; Guelich, "The Antitheses," 449–50) in holding that Matthew has constructed two separate antitheses (the fifth on nonretaliation [5:38–42] and the sixth on love of enemies [5:43–48]) by reordering the material present in Q, adding material from his M tradition, and encompassing the whole within his redactional framework of six antitheses. Hence, the antithesis in Matt 5:43–44 ("You have heard that it was said, 'You shall love your neighbor and hate your enemy'; but I say to you, 'Love your enemies' ") goes back to Matthew, not to the historical Jesus. The apparent parallel in Luke to Matthew's antithetical formula (Luke 6:27a: "But I say to you who are listening . . .") serves not to introduce an antithesis to a previously stated command but rather to supply a transition from the dark woes that have preceded (6:24–26, the woes being an apostrophe to people not actually present in Luke's scene). If we judge the woes to be a Lucan insertion into the Q sermon, then most likely the transitional 6:27a is Lucan redaction as well. Siegfried Schulz (*Q. Die Spruchquelle der Evangelisten* [Zurich: Theologischer Verlag, 1972] 127), however, thinks that behind both Matthew and Luke's formulations lies a simple "I say to you" (*legō hymin*) in Q. In any event, Luke 6:27a is not the remnant of a primitive antithetical formula retained by Matthew; on this, see Furnish, ibid., 55.

Quite different is the approach of Betz in his monumental *The Sermon on the Mount*. In Betz's view, the Sermon on the Mount and the Sermon on the Plain are two independent compositions created by the early Jesus movement, the former for the instruction of Jewish converts, the latter for the instruction of Gentile converts. The two Sermons were composed prior to or concurrent with Paul's letters, thus, somewhere around A.D. 50. Betz's theory has not attracted a large following, and for good reasons. One glaring reason is that the Sermon on the Mount, in its final form, is a prime example of Matthew's own vocabulary, style, structuring techniques, and theology. Only someone who programmatically ignores the redactional realities of Matthew's Gospel could constantly avert his eyes from Matthew's editorial hand pervading the Sermon on the Mount and connecting it with the rest of his Gospel. Hence, while Betz's work is a mine of discrete packets of information (which I have consulted with gratitude), his overarching theory of sources diminishes the usefulness of the volume as a whole.

Nevertheless, even if one accepts the commonly held view of sources that I have adopted above, a serious problem remains: the exact wording and order of the Q material enshrined in Luke 6:27–36 par. is by no means certain; on this point, see Schottroff, "Non-Violence," 22; Schulz, *Q*, 127–31. The redactional hands of both Matthew and Luke are present, though not always distinguishable in a particular verse. It is telling that in *The Critical Edition of Q* (ed. James M. Robinson, Paul Hoffmann, and John S. Kloppenborg; Leuven: Peeters, 2000), the attempt to present the original Q wording of Luke 6:27–36 par. results in a column that is a string of empty spaces, question marks, and single and double brackets. Consequently, I do not attempt to isolate an "original" text in what follows; for various hypothetical reconstructions, see Lührmann, ibid., 412–38; Furnish, ibid., 45–59; Piper, 'Love Your Enemies,' 49–65; Becker, "Feindesliebe," 6–14; Sauer, ibid., 5–14. Fortunately, such a restoration would be beside the point for our purpose. Our sole focus is the *command* to love enemies, not the subsequent logia that are not essentially connected with this command. This disconnect is mirrored in the fact that the love command proper enjoys exactly the same wording in both Matthew and Luke: *agapate tous echthrous hymōn*. None of the subsequent sayings in Luke 6:27–36 par. possesses the same word-for-word agreement in Matthew and Luke and hence the same confident restoration in *The Critical Edition of Q* (see pp. 56–73). Accordingly, Lührmann (ibid., 427) thinks that the oldest stratum of the tradition contained only a one-part command, "love your enemies." As Hoffmann and Eid point out (*Jesus von Nazareth*, 153), since the Q block reflected in Luke 6:27–36 par. is a secondary composition, the command, "love your enemies," must be interpreted on its own when one takes up the question of the historical Jesus.

[174] Luke repeats the command to love enemies (from 6:27b) in 6:35a. Commentators debate whether Luke himself is responsible for this repetition, which supplies a certain structural element to a largely unstructured unit, or whether the repetition already existed in Q and Matthew omitted it when he reordered the material to create the fifth and sixth antitheses (Matt 5:38–48). The other instances of the verb *agapaō* ("love") in this Q pericope are all in the indicative or the participial form, e.g., "and if you love those who love you" (*kai ei agapate tous agapōntas hymas*) in Luke 6:32a par.

[175] The Hebrew version of the command would be three words if we supposed that the Hebrew indicator of the direct object (*'ēt*) were used as a separate word: *'ehĕbû 'ēt 'ōyĕbêkem*. However, the use of *'ēt* in this construction, while normal, is not absolutely necessary. The situation would be different if the Aramaism found in Lev 19:18b (i.e., the preposition *lĕ* used as the indicator of the direct object) were employed, since the preposition *lĕ* would be attached directly to the object, giving us only two words. The same would be true if the saying were retroverted into Aramaic.

[176] I agree with Lührmann ("Liebet eure Feinde," 416–17) that the command "love your enemies" occurs nowhere else in early Christian literature independently of Matthew and/or Luke—or a catechetical conflation thereof. The occurrences that we find in the patristic literature of the second century regularly display the tendency of Christian catechists to soften, conflate, or explain NT texts; such is the case, e.g., in the *Did.* 1:3 (conflation of Matthew and Luke with pragmatic rationalization); *2 Clem.* 13:4 (with a strong Lucan tone); and Justin Martyr, *1 Apology* 15:9–10 (conflation of Matthew and Luke, with probable dependence on some written collection of sayings of Jesus for catechetical purposes). For a discussion of this point in reference to "love your enemies," see Kuhn, "Das Liebesgebot," 196–97. As Kuhn notes (p. 198), it is around the middle of the 2d century A.D., with the rise of the Apologists, that the command to love enemies becomes very popular

with Christian writers as a way of refuting pagan charges that Christians hate the human race. For a detailed study of the early Christian reception of the command to love enemies, see Bauer, "Das Gebot," 235–52, esp. 241–42. In favor of explaining the form of the commands in the *Didache* and Justin Martyr in terms of oral tradition is François Bovon, *Luke 1* (Hermeneia; Minneapolis: Fortress, 2002) 232. One difficult problem in this debate is that the canonical Gospels, once they were written, circulated, taught, and preached upon, became the source of further oral traditions.

[177] Klassen (*Love of Enemies*, 76) observes that many of the concrete examples Matthew gives in 5:38–48 come from the Jewish wisdom tradition and offer no new content; it is the fact that they stand under the rubric of loving one's enemies that gives them new meaning.

[178] Lührmann ("Liebet eure Feinde," 427–28) misses this vital point and hence dismisses the criterion of discontinuity in this case. Consequently, it is only by a convoluted argument that he can finally arrive at the conclusion that the historical Jesus radicalized the OT command to love one's neighbor with the command to love one's enemy (p. 436).

[179] See, e.g., Furnish, *The Love Command*, 56; Sauer, "Traditionsgeschichtliche Erwägungen," 14–15.

[180] On this, see Horsley, "Ethics and Exegesis," 81–83. The fine work of Barbiero (*L'asino del nemico*) may not distinguish sufficiently enough among these various terms and ideas.

[181] Cf. Luz, *Matthew 1–7*, 341; Guelich, *The Sermon on the Mount*, 228; Johnson, *The Gospel of Luke*, 27; Marshall, *The Gospel of Luke*, 259; Seitz, "Love Your Enemies," 44.

[182] It is remarkable how often the theme of turning one's enemy into a friend is used by commentators to explain (soften?) the fierce demands of Luke 6:27–36 par. See, e.g., Schottroff, (Non-Violence," 14, 23), who insists that love of an enemy seeks to transform the enemy (on the redactional level of the Gospels, by converting them to Christianity); cf. Becker, "Feindesliebe," 9; Theissen, "Gewaltverzicht," 195. I do not dispute the ultimate truth of Schottroff's statement, which is echoed in various ways by ancient Near Eastern wisdom, Greco-Roman philosophers, and some passages in the NT. I simply point out that such a rationale is not articulated in Luke 6:27–36 par. Klassen (*Love of Enemies*, 85) is therefore quite correct when he observes: "All utilitarian support for the commandment is undercut. It may indeed be that by loving your enemies you will change them into friends, but there is no hint of this in the statement"; cf. Davies and Allison, *The Gospel According to Saint Matthew*, 1. 552; Luz, *Matthew 1–7*, 342. Equally true is Klassen's remark (p. 91) that nothing in Luke 6:27–36 commands us to *forgive* our *enemies*: "To offer for-

giveness to those who are not interested in it is always to cheapen forgiveness." To be sure, one can find many other Gospel passages where Jesus commends or commands forgiveness, but we are not justified in reading such texts into the present Q pericope, where the command to forgive is noticeably absent.

[183] It is nigh impossible to decide whether Matthew or Luke represents the more original tradition in these expansions of the basic love commandment. As Perkins (*Love Commands*, 38) observes, we may be dealing with different oral or written traditions taken over by the two evangelists (or possibly their different versions of Q). Whether these expansions on the love command go back to the historical Jesus is also difficult to determine, since we hear similar statements about nonretaliation in Paul's description of his behavior as a Christian apostle in 1 Cor 4:12–13: "when reviled, we bless; when persecuted, we put up with it; when slandered, we entreat." Taking into account Matthean and Lucan redactional tendencies, Perkins (p. 39) suggests that a primitive form of the early Christian commandment to love enemies may have run as follows: "Love your enemies; do good to those who do evil to you; pray for those who curse you, that you may be sons of the Most High [or: the Father]." Whether this version can be traced back to the historical Jesus is hard to say. The theme of imitating the god(s) as a motive for nonretaliation or doing good toward enemies can be found in the Greco-Roman philosophers (e.g., Seneca) as well as Jewish authors.

[184] As Hoffmann and Eid point out (*Jesus von Nazareth*, 159), many of the concrete examples that follow the command to love enemies in Luke 6:27–36 par. are not, strictly speaking, models of nonresistance or nonretaliation. Simple nonresistance, understood as passively acceding to a person's (perhaps unreasonable or unjust) action or demand, would be expressed by commands like "accept the slap on your cheek," "give him the tunic he demands," "go the mile with him"—i.e., without resistance, complaint, or any further response. Instead, the logia of Luke 6:29 and Matt 5:39bc–41 demand surprising, positive actions that go far beyond what is demanded. On this, see Theissen, "Gewaltverzicht," 177–78.

[185] See, e.g., Bultmann's suggestion (*Geschichte*, 92) that Matt 5:46–47 may be secondary in relation to vv 44–45.

[186] Once we treat "love your enemies" in isolation, we must face an unpleasant truth that many commentators try to avoid: we have no context to tell us who the "enemies" in this command are. The Romans, the Herodians, the priestly aristocracy, government bureaucrats, the rich, those who harassed Jesus' followers even during his public ministry, and personal enemies in small village societies have all been proposed. But the proposals inevitably attach other sayings or parables of Jesus to the command to love one's enemies in order to arrive at the desired "target" of love. If we accept that, in the earliest attainable tradition, "love your enemies" circulated on its own as an isolated logion, then the definition of "enemies" remains open-ended. For all we know, that may have been what Jesus, the great spinner of riddles

and parables, intended. Against any attempt to limit the scope of "enemies" (as, e.g., Horsley ["Ethics and Exegesis," 91–92] does) is Kuhn, "Das Liebesgebot," 229.

[187] The difference between renunciation of retaliation by the "underdog" and its renunciation by the powerful is highlighted by Schottroff, "Non-Violence," 17–20; cf. Perkins, Love Commands, 34–35. Shottroff's tendency to mesh the themes of nonretaliation, nonviolence, and love of enemies does not help the clarity of her argument. Theissen ("Gewaltverzicht,"163) pushes the point even further: contrary to Nietzsche, love of enemies in the ancient world is not the reaction of the oppressed but the behavior of the superior person; it represents the generalizing of a royal attitude that even the oppressed can assume.

[188] On the major ancient Near Eastern texts that are relevant to the study of OT wisdom, especially the Book of Proverbs, see William McKane, Proverbs (OTL; Philadelphia: Westminster, 1970) 51–208. On the different socioeconomic statuses reflected in different approaches to the problem of violence and retaliation (notably in the different arenas of law and wisdom teaching), see Barbiero, L'asino, 5–6 (reflecting the views of Luise Schottroff).

[189] ANET (3d. ed., 1969), 424 (with slight alterations). The text is taken from the twenty-first chapter, col. 22, lines 1–8, of an ancient Egyptian papyrus whose precise date is uncertain (perhaps 7th–6th century B.C.). The Instruction of Amenem-Ope has a close relation to some of the material in the OT Book of Proverbs, esp. Prov 22:17–24:22; see also 20:22; 27:1.

[190] ANET, 426; it is uncertain how long before 700 B.C. this text was written.

[191] Granted the international and "ecumenical" nature of wisdom, one is not surprised to find similar traditions in many other parts of the world, e.g., southern and eastern Asia, but the point here is the immediate historical milieu of the OT wisdom tradition.

[192] Many of the older commentators see in this text and similar proverbs one part of a trajectory moving from the old spirit of retaliation toward "the advance of moral and refined feeling," culminating in the Sermon on the Mount; see, e.g., C. H. Toy, The Book of Proverbs (ICC; Edinburgh: Clark, 1899) 454–55; cf. more recently Hans F. Fuhs, Das Buch der Sprichwörter (FB 95; Würzburg: Echter, 2001) 338. McKane (Proverbs, 575) notes that 24:29 is concerned not with the theological basis of its advice (i.e., leave punishment to God) but rather with what is "socially desirable and beneficial." For a consideration of these wisdom texts in the light of Exod 23:4–5, see Barbiero, L'asino, 92–104.

[193] With his great concern for seeing "advancing moral feeling" in these proverbs, Toy (The Book of Proverbs, 392) insists that there is no reference to revenge in this verse; God is represented "not as avenging but as saving." R. N. Whybray (Proverbs

[NCB; Grand Rapids, MI: Eerdmans, 1994] 300) is perhaps more clear-eyed when he admits that v 22 affirms that punishment will be inflicted by Yahweh, "who will also right the wrongs . . . from which the victims have suffered." This is also the view of McKane, *Proverbs*, 548.

[194] As usual, Toy (*The Book of Proverbs*, 448) tries to avoid the note of vengeance in Prov 24:18. Whybray (*Proverbs*, 350–51) again proves more candid: Prov 24:18 finds it acceptable for the just man "to hope that his enemy will meet with a bad end" and that "Yahweh will not be deflected from destroying him." "Refraining from gloating over his [the enemy's] discomfiture, therefore, is not inspired by sympathy for him, but, on the contrary, is intended to ensure that Yahweh does" exact vengeance. "In other words, the spirit of revenge appears to be approved rather than disapproved." Even more emphatic is McKane (*Proverbs*, 404): "The absence of every trace of human feeling for the enemy . . . is uncanny and unpleasant. The attitude . . . is measured with an eery, impersonal coldness." The point of v 18 "is not that mercy should be shown to a defeated enemy, but that one should refrain from gloating over him so that Yahweh's anger may not relent and his ruin may be final."

[195] The nouns "bread" and "water," present in the MT, are absent in some of the ancient versions (e.g., the LXX); hence, some modern translations omit them.

[196] Not surprisingly, Toy (*The Book of Proverbs*, 468) sees in the metaphor of fiery coals a representation of the pangs of contrition: "the enemy will be converted into a friend." Fuhs (*Sprichwörter*, 300) mentions a possible reference to an Egyptian penitential ritual, but he notes that there is no evidence of such a ritual in Palestine. Whybray (*Proverbs*, 367–68) points out that, while fire can act as a purgative force, the metaphor is not applied in this way in the OT to a person's head. Elsewhere in the OT (Ps 18:8,12 [= 2 Sam 22:9,13]; Ps 140:10 [MT v 11]), "the raining down of live coals signifies punishment or destruction." In the end, though, Whybray thinks that this inexplicable metaphor suggests, in context, contrition and reconciliation. McKane (*Proverbs*, 591) is less sanguine: "To show kindness and magnanimity to an enemy . . . is to deal with him in a salutary way and to bring on a punishment which is self-inflicted."

[197] We do not have the Hebrew for this passage; hence, I rely on the Greek version.

[198] Skehan and Di Lella (*The Wisdom of Ben Sira*, 364) seem certain about the reference to Lev 19:18b here.

[199] Migaku Sato (*Q und Prophetie* [WUNT 2/29; Tübingen: Mohr [Siebeck] 1988] 222–23) affirms that Jesus' command to love enemies is not found with this radical formulation anywhere in Jewish wisdom literature. Hence, Sato thinks that the command most likely comes from the historical Jesus.

[200] On this pericope, see Barbiero, *L'asino*, 17–71.

[201] The difference in content is mirrored in the different legal formulations that are employed. The laws before and after Exod 23:4–5 are apodictic; vv 4–5 are casuistic. On the question of whether we actually have a "mixed form" here, see Barbiero, *L'asino*, 72.

[202] Verse 5 seems corrupt in the MT; what I offer is a commonly employed hypothetical restoration of the original text. I use the adverb "immediately" in my translation of vv 4–5 to express the emphatic force of the Hebrew absolute infinitive. "You shall by no means abandon him" is literally "you shall refrain from abandoning him." The LXX deals with the difficult v 5 by paraphrasing: "you shall not pass it by but you shall lift it up with him." For a full treatment of Exod 23:4–5 and allied material, see Barbiero, *L'asino*, 72–130; on translation problems, see esp. 74–92.

[203] On this, see Barbiero, *L'asino*, 72–73. Barbiero notes the absence of any specific legal penalty for not observing the "laws" in Exod 23:4–5.

[204] Perhaps the two laws are intended as examples for similar action in other emergency situations involving an enemy, but this is not said or even intimated in the text.

[205] This seems to be presupposed by the context. In this, the Hebrew 'ōyēb ("enemy") diverges from the common use of this noun in the Pentateuch, where it usually means the national enemies of the people Israel; on this, see Piper, *'Love Your Enemies,'* 28.

[206] On this text, see *A Marginal Jew*, 3. 539.

[207] The question of the hatred of enemies at Qumran has already been discussed in *A Marginal Jew*, 3. 529–30. I do not repeat all the observations made there.

[208] Josephus (*J.W.* 2.8.7 §139) says that a person entering the Essene community must swear "to hate forever the unjust" (*misēsein d'aei tous adikous*).

[209] On this text, see Perkins, *Love Commands*, 28–30. Once again, we are reminded by these texts that nonretaliation or nonviolence is not the same thing as love of enemies. The Qumranite renounces retaliation or violence against his enemies in the present moment, but hardly out of love for them.

[210] On this point, see Hübner, *Das Gesetz*, 99–104.

[211] Translations of *Aristeas* are taken from R. J. H. Shutt, *Letter of Aristeas*, in Charlesworth's *OTP*, 2. 26 (with slight alterations and emphasis added). On the not-very-tight expression of the Golden Rule, see André Pelletier, *Lettre d'Aristée a Philocrate* (SC 89; Paris: Cerf, 1962) 196 n. 1.

212 The last words of the Greek text are ambiguous because *heautois* (the 3d person plural of the reflexive pronoun), while usually meaning "to themselves" (therefore, in context, to the opponents), can in Koine Greek also mean "to ourselves." The former interpretation is found in the translations of Shutt, of Francesca Calabi (*Lettera di Aristea a Filocrate* [Milan: Rizzoli, 2002] 137), and of H. St. J. Thackeray (*The Letter of Aristeas* [London: SPCK; New York: Macmillan, 1917] 68). Piper ('*Love Your Enemies*,' 36), however, favors the latter interpretation: "that by this means we may win them over to the right and to what is advantageous to ourselves"; so too, Pelletier, *Lettre d'Aristée a Philocrate*, 205; Perkins, *Love Commands*, 32.

213 As Moses Hadas (*Aristeas to Philocrates* [New York: Harper & Brothers, 1951] 190) notes in his commentary on the text, sorrow or grief (*lypē*) was "the chief 'perturbation' against which Hellenistic philosophers sought to arm their adherents."

214 On the use of Hellenistic philosophy by the author of 4 Maccabees to show that the Hellenistic tyrant is actually the uncivilized barbarian and that the Jews who cling to the Torah embody the ideals of Greek philosophy, see David A. deSilva, "Using the Master's Tools to Shore Up Another's House: A Postcolonial Analysis of 4 Maccabees," *JBL* 126 (2007) 99–127, esp. 103–4. On the problems involved in dating and placing the composition of 4 Maccabees, see p. 101 nn. 8 and 10 (continued on p. 102); cf. David A. deSilva, *4 Maccabees* (Sheffield: Academic Press, 1998) 12–25

215 As David A. deSilva points out (*4 Maccabees. Introduction and Commentary on the Greek Text in Codex Sinaiticus* [Septuagint Commentary Series; Leiden/Boston: Brill, 2006] 99–100), OT texts like Exod 23:4–5 and Deut 20:19–20 were used by various Jewish apologists to counter pagan claims that Jews hated the human race. As we shall see below, both Philo (using Exod 23:4–5) and Josephus (using Deut 20:19–20) echo the point made by 4 Macc 2:14. See also the comments by Moses Hadas, *The Third and Fourth Books of Maccabees* (New York: Harper & Brothers, 1953) 154–55.

216 On the seven brothers as exemplars of philosophers who are free from slavery to the passions, see deSilva, *4 Maccabees. Introduction and Commentary*, 203–4.

217 DeSilva (*4 Maccabees. Introduction and Commentary*, 202) observes that, in the theology of 4 Maccabees, "the death of the martyrs is connected causally" both to the punishment of the tyrant by God's justice and to the deliverance of Israel by God's mercy.

218 On the question of dating, see Sabrina Inowlocki, *Des idoles mortes et muettes au Dieu vivant* (Turnhout, Belgium: Brepols, 2002) 24–26. The first years of the 2d century A.D. are favored by Marc Philonenko, who has edited the critical edition, *Joseph et Aséneth* (SPB 13; Leiden: Brill, 1968) 109.

[219] The LXX form of Prov 17:13 provides some verbal similarity, though the thrust is different: *hos apodidōsin kaka anti agathōn, ou kinēthēsetai kaka ek tou oikou autou* ("he who renders evil for good—evil shall not be removed from his house").

[220] On the use of this axiom in Paul and 1 Peter, see Perkins, *Love Commands*, 90–91; on 1 Peter in particular, see Piper, *'Love Your Enemies,'* 119–28.

[221] When one considers that, at least in *The Letter of Aristeas* and *Joseph and Aseneth*, we have in substance, though not in exact formulation, a type of command to love enemies, one must question the sweeping judgment of Nissen (*Gott*, 316): "Therefore in Judaism there is no love for one's enemy, even when the enmity is based on purely personal and not religious-moral grounds. Such a love is not only not verified in the sources preserved for us; it is from the start excluded and must be excluded."

[222] It should be noted, though, that, while the axiom of nonretaliation is clearly articulated in *Joseph and Aseneth*, it is expressed with different nuances in different passages. On the one hand, it is formulated in terms of "one's neighbor" in 23:9 and 28:14. On the other hand, in 28:4, Aseneth forbids rendering evil for evil "to any human being"; in 29:3, Levi mentions "the enemy" later on in his statement. For an English translation of the work, see C. Burchard, *Joseph and Aseneth*, in Charlesworth's *OTP*, 2. 177–247. I employ my own translations of the relevant Greek passages in the main text.

[223] Piper (*'Love Your Enemies,'* 53) suggests that the command of the Matthean Jesus (Matt 5:39) "not to resist the evil one" (or, alternately, "not to resist evil"), placed as it is in the fifth antithesis in opposition to the law of talion (5:38: "an eye for an eye and a tooth for a tooth"), acted as "the incentive and criterion" for the early church's frequent use of the Jewish formulation of the principle, "not rendering evil for evil." As elsewhere in his book, Piper presumes what is to be proved, namely, that the historical Jesus actually spoke the fifth antithesis. I incline to the view that the fifth antithesis proper (Matt 5:38–39) is the creation of Matthew or possibly of his special tradition; cf. Guelich, *The Sermon on the Mount*, 251. If, as I think (see my *Law and History in Matthew's Gospel*, 157 n. 77), 5:39 refers to voluntarily abstaining from judicial proceedings against an unjust legal adversary, the *Sitz im Leben* of the prohibition is civil suits in law courts (as, indeed, is the case in 5:38,40, and probably 39bc). Such a *Sitz im Leben* is attested in the first Christian generation by 1 Cor 6:1–8, where Paul excoriates the Corinthians for suing one another in pagan courts. He tells his litigious converts that they should rather suffer the injustice done them than go to court. Such a pastoral problem in the early church seems a much more likely matrix for the teaching of Matt 5:38–39 than a group of disciples traveling around Galilee with Jesus. In any event, nowhere in the Gospels is Jesus presented as uttering the terse formula found in both *Joseph and Aseneth* and Paul: "not rendering evil for evil" (*mē apodidontes kakon anti kakou*).

[224] So, e.g., Piper, *'Love Your Enemies,'* 36–37. For an English translation, see F. I. Andersen, *2 (Slavonic Apocalypse) of Enoch*, in Charlesworth's *OTP*, 1. 91–221.

[225] As I have already indicated in this chapter (II.C.4.), the date and provenance of the *Testaments of the Twelve Patriarchs* are too problematic to allow them to be used for "background" illustrating Jesus' love commands. In any event, the precise command, "love your enemies," is not found anywhere in the *Testaments*, though various exhortations to have mercy on all, even sinners, do occur. See, e.g., *T. Benj.* 4:2–3 (with perhaps an echo of Rom 12:21 and with the action of *agapaō* pointedly restricted to the righteous); *T. Jos.* 18:1–2.

[226] In his commentary, Philo reverses the order of the commandments as found in the MT, the LXX, and the Vulgate of Exod 23:4–5.

[227] Thus, the title of the whole treatise, *Against Apion* (a title not given the work by Josephus), is something of a misnomer, since the two books range widely over a number of anti-Jewish authors.

[228] On this argument, see Perkins, *Love Commands*, 33; she notes that conversion as a motive for nonretaliation is much more frequent in Jewish sources than in Stoic ones.

[229] On this, see Kuhn, "Das Liebesgebot," 224. Kuhn, however, thinks that, while the statements of pagan popular philosophy offer the closest parallels to Jesus' command *in formulation*, they are farther away *in substance* than the corresponding Jewish texts.

[230] For a treasure trove of parallels from Greek and Roman philosophers, as well as from later rabbis and patristic writers, see Betz, *The Sermon on the Mount*, 274–328 (for Matt 5:38–48) and 591–614 (for Luke 6:27–36); cf. Schottroff, "Non-Violence," 9–39, esp. 17–22; Perkins, *Love Commands*, 31.

[231] Commenting on this text from Epictetus, Furnish (*The Love Command*, 49–50) makes a trenchant point against Spicq's views on the meanings of the two key Greek verbs for love found in the NT, *agapaō* and *phileō*. On the one hand, in the depiction of the Cynic loving those who beat him as though he were their father or brother, *phileō* signifies not only love of enemies but also a love that is familial. On the other hand, *agapaō* in Luke 6:32 par. refers to the reciprocal, tit-for-tat love practiced even by "sinners" and "tax collectors" among themselves. Hence, neat, clear-cut distinctions between *agapaō* and *phileō* are not to be presupposed for Greek literature around the time of the NT. The meanings of the verbs must be judged by their immediate contexts. This is all the more the case since, as Joly has pointed out (*Le vocabulaire chrétien*, passim), by the early Christian era, *agapaō* was gradually replacing *phileō* as the common verb for love. For an overview of NT words for love, see Furnish, ibid., 219–31.

[232] Theissen ("Gewaltverzicht," 172–73) highlights two basic reasons for nonretaliation in Stoic thought, especially that of Epictetus: (1) the desire of the Stoic to be independent and unperturbed vis-à-vis all external suffering; (2) the fact that all human beings are related to one another.

[233] The exact iteration of "love your enemies" is likewise absent in the early rabbinic literature. To be sure, the rabbinic literature is replete with exhortations to love, mercy, reconciliation, charity toward those in need, and a peaceable spirit. In addition, the wisdom tradition of nonretaliation and avoidance of glee over an enemy's discomfort is developed by the rabbis. Indeed, the commands to help one's personal enemy that are found in Exod 23:4–5 are extended by some rabbis to non-Israelites. If I do not lead the patient reader through another survey of rabbinic literature, the reason is simple: scholars are in agreement that the laconic, direct command, "love your enemies," is not present in early rabbinic literature. On this, see Luz, *Matthew 1–7*, 340–41.

[234] On the Pauline "parallels" to the command to love one's enemies, see Furnish, *The Love Command*, 61–62, 106; Sauer, "Traditionsgeschichtliche Erwägungen," 17–23; Piper, '*Love Your Enemies*,' 101–19; Kuhn, "Das Liebesgebot," 198–202. Sauer (pp. 19–21) seeks to isolate the precise wording of various pre-Pauline traditions in Rom 12:9–21, but I remain diffident about such an attempt, all the more so since Sauer uses passages from the *Testaments of the Twelve Patriarchs* to argue his case. On the question of the sources and style of Rom 12:9–21, see Talbert, "Tradition," 83–94; Kanjuparambil, "Imperatival Participles," 285–88.

[235] I speak of "themes" here because some of the individual words function differently in the Q and Pauline traditions. For example, the verb "curse" (*kataraomai*) refers to the action of the persecutors in Q; in Paul, it refers to an action forbidden to Christians. However, the ultimate point is the same. In Romans, Christians are exhorted in particular not to curse their persecutors presumably because that is what the persecutors are doing to the Christians.

[236] Here is where Sauer's attempt to deny that "love your enemies" goes back to the historical Jesus falls apart. He is able to find parallels to most of the material in Luke 6:27–28 in Paul's epistles, especially Rom 12:9–21. But his claim ("Traditionsgeschichtliche Erwägungen," 25) that "love your enemies" has as its parallel Paul's citation of Prov 25:21–22 in Rom 12:20 is an act of desperation to save a faulty thesis. Whatever the exact meaning of Prov 25:21–22 (see earlier for its ambiguous nature), it is not an "exact iteration" of "love your enemies." Nowhere in the Pauline epistles do we find this brief and blunt command. Contrary to Sauer's thesis (p. 37) that "love your enemies" is a secondary addition to the primitive parenesis witnessed in both Rom 12:9–21 and the primitive Q form of Luke 6:27–36, the criterion of discontinuity points in the direction of "love your enemies" being a matrix of the abundant Christian parenesis found in both the epistles and the Gospels. On the relation of the epistles and the Gospels in handing on the parenetic material of the Jesus tradition, see Goppelt, "Jesus," 93–106.

237 Here I agree with Betz (*The Sermon on the Mount*, 301 n. 798) against Sauer ("Traditionsgeschichtliche Erwägungen," 1–28). While rightly admitting that the historical Jesus was influenced by ancient wisdom traditions, Betz (ibid., with emphasis in the original) observes: "What remains decisive is that the command [of Jesus] to *love* the enemy is not attested in the wisdom texts." Shottroff ("Non-Violence," 32 n. 39) admits: "I know of no instance where agape is directed to the enemy in the non-Christian world," though she acknowledges that Seneca and Epictetus come close. For other authors favoring the authenticity of "love your enemies," see Bauer, "Das Gebot," 235; Kuhn, "Das Liebesgebot," 200–201, 224; Piper, '*Love Your Enemies*,' 56. Meisinger (*Liebesgebot*, 43) thinks that, of all the "love material" in the sayings of Jesus, the command to love enemies has the greatest probability of coming from Jesus himself. Indeed, even such classical skeptics as Rudolf Bultmann and Herbert Braun affirm the origin of the command in the historical Jesus. Furnish (*The Love Command*, 66) sums up the matter well: "It is Jesus' command to *love* the enemy which most of all sets his ethic of love apart from other 'love ethics' of antiquity, and which best shows what kind of love is commanded by him." Furnish then adds intriguingly: "It is significant that the Synoptics present Jesus as one who 'commands' love and not as one who 'inspires' it."

238 For a study of the rhetoric of Jesus as expressed in gnomic language, including his legal pronouncements, see Ian H. Henderson, *Jesus, Rhetoric and Law* (Biblical Interpretation Series 20; Leiden/New York/Cologne: Brill, 1996). The results are somewhat weakened by the absence of a rigorous and systematic approach to deciding which particular sayings come from the historical Jesus.

239 The classic work on the subject, Dihle's *Regel*, states that the designation "the Golden Rule" cannot be traced back earlier than the 16th century (p. 8 n. 1). I am largely dependent on Dihle for my treatment of the Golden Rule, although I do not necessarily accept his philosophical and theological interpretations of certain texts, notably Jesus' teachings in the Gospels. Dihle tends to read Jesus through the bifocals of Paul; whether he understands Paul correctly is another question. Some authors use the term "Silver Rule" to refer to the negative form of the Golden Rule; so Carey A. Moore, *Tobit* (AYB 40A; New York: Doubleday, 1996; reprint New Haven: Yale University Press) 171. I do not employ the term myself.

240 In Robinson et al., *The Critical Edition of Q*, 66–67, the hypothetical Q form that is reconstructed is basically the Lucan form, slightly emended by the Matthean form: *kai kathōs thelete hina poiōsin hymin hoi anthrōpoi, houtōs poieite autois* ("And as you wish that humans do to you, so do to them").

241 This definition, however flexible, serves to delimit the Golden Rule from general sapiential warnings against retaliation as well as from the double command of love, the command to love one's neighbor, and the command to love one's enemy. The ethic of the Golden Rule implies (i) a certain imaginative leap into the other person's shoes or psyche—the other person is thus taken seriously as another human being interacting morally with oneself—as well as (ii) a readiness to seize the

initiative and act first (at least in the positive form of the Golden Rule). The idea of being obliged to seize the initiative may be the one valid difference that would make the positive form of the Golden Rule ethically superior to the negative form; cf. Luz, *Matthew 1–7*, 427; in a slightly different vein, Nissen, *Gott*, 395. Hagner (*Matthew*, 1. 176) formulates this ethical superiority from a logical point of view: "The positive form must include the negative form but not vice versa." Yet, as we can see from the appearance of the two forms of the rule in the same work (e.g., *The Sentences of Sextus*, sayings 89 and 90), this difference was not generally noted or commented on in the ancient world. On various opinions about whether there is a difference between the positive and negative forms, see Betz, *The Sermon on the Mount*, 510.

[242] On this, see Nissen, *Gott*, 396. Simply as a matter of fact, the vast majority of ancient Greco-Roman, early Jewish, and early Christian texts articulating the Golden Rule do not employ the word "love."

[243] On this, see Luz, *Matthew 1–7*, 425; also Marshall, *The Gospel of Luke*, 261; Schürmann, *Das Lukasevangelium*, 1. 350–51.

[244] On the question of the *inclusio* with Matt 5:17 and of 7:12's supposed function as "not only the quintessence of the law and the prophets but also the quintessence of the sermon on the mount and thus the quintessence of Jesus' teaching in general," see Davies and Allison, *The Gospel According to Saint Matthew*, 1. 685–86. For a different point of view, see Luz, *Matthew 1–7*, 427 n. 11. Whatever the redactional intention of Matthew (and all the redactional theology in the world cannot change what the wording of the Golden Rule itself says), the Golden Rule, viewed with the cold eye of historical criticism, sums up neither all the material in Matthew's Sermon on the Mount nor, a fortiori, all the material that the Matthean Jesus teaches throughout the Gospel. Davies and Allison proceed to mesh (and blur) the Golden Rule, the double command of love (22:34–40), the command to the rich man in Matt 19:16–22, esp. v 19b), and the command to love one's enemies in Matt 5:44. One is not surprised to see Davies and Allison conclude that "the golden rule is really just another way of delivering that demand [i.e., the demand to love one's neighbor]." This is a confusion of categories and content, occasioned by Matthew's love of *inclusio*, literary structure, and thematic cross-references. As a general though not golden rule, commentators on Matthew tend to suffer from a redactional blindness when it comes to the Golden Rule (Hans Dieter Betz is a prime example; Ulrich Luz is a notable exception); many commentators on Luke tend to be more clear-eyed.

[245] As Dihle notes (*Regel*, 10 n. 2), the Golden Rule is such a universal insight of practical wisdom that various formulations of the maxim can be found in ancient and modern cultures around the world, notably Buddhism and Confucianism; on this, see Moore, *Tobit*, 179; Betz, *The Sermon on the Mount*, 509. Since our concern in this chapter is only with the milieu and matrix of the moral teachings of Jesus and his early followers, our treatment is restricted to Greco-Roman and Jewish backgrounds.

246 Bovon (*Luke 1*, 241 n. 68) points back even further to a passage in Homer's *Odyssey* (Od. 5.188–91), where Calypso speaks to Odysseus: "But I am thinking and planning for you just as I would do it for my own self, if such needs as yours were to come upon me; for the mind in me is reasonable, and I have no spirit of iron inside my heart. Rather, it is compassionate." (The translation used by Bovon is that of Richmond Lattimore.) It should be noted, though, that we are dealing in this Homeric text with a mythological sea nymph taking an oath not to harm the hero of the epic in a particular dramatic situation: Odysseus suspects that Calypso will do him harm once he sets sail on his raft and so entreats her to take an oath that she will not do so. This is hardly the same thing as a historical religious leader or teacher of wisdom laying down a precept to be observed by human beings in general. Another text often claimed to contain a still earlier formulation of the Golden Rule is the combination of narrative and wise sayings entitled *Ahiqar*. The separate traditions of story and sayings probably reach as far back as the 7th century B.C. However, the earliest manuscript we have is an incomplete Aramaic papyrus from the Jewish colony at Elephantine; the manuscript is dated to the late 5th century B.C. For an introduction to as well as a translation of the text, see J. M. Lindenberger, *Ahiqar*, in Charlesworth's *OTP*, 2. 479–507. The narrative section tells the story of a high-ranking Assyrian official, Ahiqar, who is falsely accused of treason and condemned by the king to death. In columns 3–4, §40–54, the king's officer, Nabusumiskun, who has been ordered to kill Ahiqar, finds him and tells him what has happened. Ahiqar then reminds Nabusumiskun that long ago he (Ahiqar) had rescued Nabusumiskun from an undeserved death at the hand of the present king's father. During that time of peril, Ahiqar hid Nabusumiskun in his home and treated him as a brother. Ahiqar now demands repayment in kind (§ 51–52): "Now it is your turn to treat me as I treated you. Do not kill me (but) take me to your house until the times change." While all this is reminiscent of the Golden Rule, no actual rule or proverb is cited. Rather, in a specific case in a narrative, one person requests that another person who received some benefit from him in the past now repay the favor with exactly the same benefit. To be sure, we have here the idea of tit-for-tat reciprocity that underlies the Golden Rule, but the idea is embodied in an ad hoc request in a specific dramatic narrative. It is perhaps telling that only in the later Armenian recension, copied by Christian scribes, do we have the Golden Rule articulated as a principle: "Son, that which seems evil unto thee, do not to thy companion" (Armenian *Ahiqar*, 8.88). While Lindenberger favors the view that *Ahiqar* was the source of the negative Golden Rule in Tob 4:15, he admits that "this is by no means certain" (p. 490 n. 67).

247 Dihle (*Regel*, 96–97) thinks that, even by the time of Herodotus, the sentiment voiced by Maeandrius was a traditional saying, since almost the same statement is found later on in Herodotus' work (7.136) in the mouth of the Persian king Xerxes. While Dihle's basic point may be correct, one should note that, in the latter context, Xerxes' words are basically an example of the noble royal figure refusing to take vengeance on Spartan emissaries, even though the Spartans had earlier killed Persian heralds. This is the sense of Xerxes' affirmation that "he himself would not do what he disapproved of in them."

[248] For the Greek text and an English translation of the *Sentences of Sextus*, see Richard A. Edwards and Robert A. Wild, *The Sentences of Sextus* (Chico, CA: Scholars, 1981) 26–27. Saying 89 reads: "As you wish your neighbors to treat you, so treat them," which saying 90 supplements with the negative formulation: "What you censure, do not do." *The Sentences of Sextus* is a collection of general, pithy, epigrammatic sayings that grew over the span of centuries. It probably began as a pagan collection, but its final form reflects Christian redaction and the influence of the NT. Hence, one must be careful about citing sayings 89 and 90 as pagan rather than Christian examples. Fragments of a Coptic version of the *Sentences* have been found in Codex XII at Nag Hammadi; unfortunately, sayings 89 and 90 are not among the fragments preserved. For a translation, see Frederik Wisse, "The Sentences of Sextus," *The Nag Hammadi Library in English* (3d ed.; San Francisco: Harper & Row, 1988) 503–8.

[249] Fitzmyer (*The Gospel According to Luke*, 1. 639–40) holds that the Golden Rule should not be seen as superior to the Silver (i.e., the negative formulation of the rule). Indeed, what either rule suggests or requires depends very much on the context of the given situation. Moore (*Tobit*, 180) humorously points out the difficulty of moving from abstract principle to concrete application: "For example, how should the Golden Rule be morally applied by a generous cannibal or a considerate polygamist to his male houseguest?" On this, see Betz, *The Sermon on the Mount*, 509 n. 654.

[250] See Betz, *The Sermon on the Mount*, 510.

[251] *Sic demus quomodo vellemus accipere* (*De beneficiis*, 2.1 §1).

[252] *Haec tamen praecepti mei summa est: sic cum inferiore vivas quemadmodum tecum superiorem velis vivere* (*Moral Epistles to Lucilius*, 47.11).

[253] The original language, date, and place of composition of Tobit continue to be debated among scholars. For brief considerations of the various solutions, see Moore, *Tobit*, 33–39; Helen Schüngel-Straumann, *Tobit* (Herders theologischer Kommentar zum Alten Testament 36; Freiburg/Basel/Vienna: Herder, 2000) 39–41; Benedikt Otzen, *Tobit and Judith* (London: Sheffield Academic Press, 2002) 57–59; Joseph A. Fitzmyer, *Tobit* (Commentaries on Early Jewish Literature; Berlin/New York: de Gruyter, 2003) 18–28, 50–54. It may well be that Tobit went through a number of stages of tradition and redaction both outside and inside Palestine. My own view is that the final redaction of the book took place in Palestine somewhere between 300 and 170 B.C. Fitzmyer (p. 52) prefers a narrower range of 225–175 B.C., though earlier stages of the book may have been written in either the Eastern Diaspora or Egypt. Cave 4 of Qumran has given us one Hebrew fragment and four Aramaic fragments of Tobit. More likely than not, Tobit was written in Aramaic and then translated into Hebrew; on this, see Joseph A. Fitzmyer, "The Aramaic and Hebrew Fragments from Qumran Cave 4," *CBQ* 57 (1995) 655–75, esp. 670; idem, *Tobit*, 3–27.

254 This example from *Aristeas* is at best inchoate, since it lacks both succinctness and a clear expression of the idea of reciprocity. The Diaspora tradition of the Golden Rule continues and reaches clearer expression in Philo; see, e.g., the citation of his *Hypothetica* in Eusebius, *Praeparatio Evangelica*, 8.7 §6: "What someone hates to suffer [or: 'experience'], let him not do [*ha tis pathein echthairei mē poiein auton*]." For a critical edition of the text, see Karl Mras (ed.), *Eusebius Werke. Achter Band. Die Praeparatio Evangelica. Erster Teil* (GCS 8/1; Berlin: Akademie, 1954) 430.

255 The text is exactly the same in the two main textual traditions of Greek Tobit, G^{I} (the shorter text) and G^{II} (the longer text). The fragmentary mixed text labeled G^{III} does not contain 4:15a. While the Vetus Latina (the Old Latin version) reflects the succinct phrasing of the Greek tradition, Jerome supplies a more verbose form in his translation, which is numbered 4:16 in the Vulgate; see Vincent T. M. Skemp, *The Vulgate of Tobit Compared with Other Ancient Witnesses* (SBLDS 180; Atlanta: SBL, 2000) 144–45. On the various textual traditions, see Christian J. Wagner, *Polyglotte Tobit-Synopse* (Abhandlungen der Akademie der Wissenschaften in Göttingen, Philologisch-Historische Klasse, 3d series, vol. 258; Mitteilungen des Septuaginta-Unternehmens 28; Göttingen: Vandenhoeck & Ruprecht, 2003) 44–45. For a study of the character and original form of G^{I}, see Robert Hanhart, *Text und Textgeschichte des Buches Tobit* (Abhandlungen der Akademie der Wissenschaften in Göttingen, Philologisch-Historische Klasse, 3d series, vol. 139; Mitteilungen des Septuaginta-Unternehmens 28; Göttingen: Vandenhoeck & Ruprecht, 1984). On the Golden Rule in Judaism, see Merten Rabenau, *Studien zum Buch Tobit* (BZAW 220; Berlin/New York: de Gruyter, 1994) 55–56; Moore, *Tobit*, 171, 178–80.

256 Rabenau (*Studien*, 56) thinks that the Greek translation of Sir 31:15 moves Ben Sira's counsel closer to the Golden Rule. As I have indicated when treating the double command of love (II.C.2), I think rather that the Hebrew of v 15a (literally, "know your neighbor as your own soul [or: 'self']") echoes the command to love one's neighbor (Lev 19:18b), while the Hebrew of v 15b (literally, "and bear in mind what you hate") moves closer to the Golden Rule. Still, one must remember that the context of Sir 31:15 is table manners at a banquet; the "neighbor" or "fellow" is one's fellow guest and the admonition warns against grabbing greedily at the food that another guest might want.

257 In his *The Rabbinic Traditions about the Pharisees before 70* (South Florida Studies in the History of Judaism 202, 203, and 204; 3 vols.; Atlanta: Scholars, 1999; reprint of Leiden: Brill, 1971) 3. 359–60, Jacob Neusner takes Reginald H. Fuller to task for not considering Hillel's famous dictum when he discusses the Pharisees' traditions around the time of Jesus. Then Neusner adds almost as an afterthought: "To be sure, Hillel may never have said any such thing." But if one is dealing with the "background" or "milieu" of Jesus' teaching or that of the pre-70 Pharisees, that historical question is of the essence. On the question of what we can hope to know about individual Pharisees in the pre-70 period, see Joseph Siev-

ers, "Who Were the Pharisees?" *Hillel and Jesus* (ed. James H. Charlesworth and Loren L. Johns; Minneapolis: Fortress, 1997) 137–55. Jospe ("Hillel's Rule," 45–57) makes the intriguing (though highly speculative) suggestion that there is a multiple play on words (in both Hebrew and Latin) in the anecdote; if so, we have another reminder that we are dealing with a learned and artificial scholastic composition, not a videotape replay of an event in the life of the "historical Hillel."

[258] On all this and specifically on Hillel's reply as a *captatio benevolentiae* rather than a complete answer, see Nissen, *Gott*, 390–97. Nissen also points to a similar anecdote, told of Rabbi Aqiba, in *'Abot R. Nat.*, version B, chap. 26; for a critical translation with notes, see Anthony J. Saldarini, *The Fathers According to Rabbi Nathan* (SJLA 11; Leiden: Brill, 1975) 155 (and compare chap. 29 on p. 171, containing concrete applications of the Golden Rule from Rabbi Eliezer). In *'Abot R. Nat.*, version B, chap. 26, Aqiba relativizes the Golden Rule (i) by emphasizing how impossible it is to learn the whole Law at one time and (ii) by referring to the Golden Rule as "a [not *the*] general rule." Another relatively late occurrence of the negative form of the Golden Rule in rabbinic Judaism occurs in the *Targum Pseudo-Jonathan to the Pentateuch*, which in its present form is the most expansive of the targums on the Pentateuch. The text of the targum adds to Lev 19:18 a formulation of the Golden Rule similar to the one attributed to Hillel: "That which is hateful to you, do not do to him [i.e., a fellow member of the Jewish community]." For translation and commentary, see Martin McNamara, Robert Hayward, and Michael Maher, *Targum Neofiti 1: Leviticus. Targum Pseudo-Jonathan: Leviticus* (The Aramaic Bible 3; Collegeville, MN: Liturgical Press, 1994) 177; the Golden Rule is also inserted into v 34 (p. 180). In contrast, the Golden Rule is notably absent from the form of Lev 19:18 found in the Targum *Neofiti*; see ibid., 73. Beverly P. Mortensen (*The Priesthood in Targum Pseudo-Jonathan* [Studies in the Aramaic Interpretation of Scripture 4; 2 vols.; Leiden/Boston: Brill, 2006] 2. 649) notes that the addition of the Golden Rule to Lev 19:18 is unique to *Pseudo-Jonathan* among the classical targums on the Pentateuch.

[259] One might try to construct an "attenuated" argument from discontinuity insofar as almost all the early Jewish and Christian examples of the Golden Rule outside of the Gospels have the negative form, while the Q saying attributed to Jesus by Matthew and Luke has the positive form. However, the inchoate and rambling form of the Golden Rule in the *Ep. Aris.* §207 is at least partially positive. Moreover, a number of the pagan Greco-Roman versions, reaching from Isocrates to Seneca, are cast in the positive form. Hence, if the Golden Rule was placed on the lips of Jesus by the early Christians, there is no reason why they might not have adopted the positive form, especially since a large majority of the commands in the surrounding Q context (roughly mirrored in Luke 6:31–36) are positive rather than negative.

[260] On this, see Luz, *Matthew 1–7*, 426–47.

[261] Dihle (*Regel*, 113–14) tries valiantly but unconvincingly to remove this contradiction in Luke (and ultimately Q) by the desperate expedient of taking *poieite*

in Luke 6:31 not as an imperative ("do!") but a descriptive indicative ("you are do-ing"). In this way, 6:31 is read not as a command articulating the Golden Rule but rather as a description of what the audience (made up of disciples?) actually does. Verse 31 would thus be a rebuke that continues in the subsequent verses. The basic problem with this approach is simple: the expectations of the ancient reader. In the face of the countless examples of the Golden Rule in ancient pagan, Jewish, and Christian documents—most with an imperative mood and/or meaning—Dihle has to suppose that the reader of Luke could somehow intuit that *poieite* should be read as indicative rather than imperative. If Luke had wanted to express the indicative with absolute clarity, all he would have had to do was write the verb in the singu-lar, which would remove any ambiguity. While Betz (*The Sermon on the Mount*, 599–600) rejects Dihle's approach, he struggles in his own (and, in my view, equally unconvincing) way to avoid a clash between the Golden Rule and the immediately following critique of an ethic of reciprocity (Luke 6:31–34). One should note that rejection of an ethic of mere reciprocity is not restricted to Christianity; Epictetus, for example, mocks an ethic of mutual back-scratching when he depicts philosophy students trading compliments over their essays (*Discourses*, 2.17 §34–36).

262 So, among other critics, Collins, "Golden Rule," 1070.

263 As we have seen, *Did.* 1.2 is a mélange of the double command of love (ex-pressed with Lucan-like compression) and a negative form of the Golden Rule. In-deed, the *Didache*'s formulation of the Golden Rule ("But all whatsoever you wish not to be done to you, you also do not do to another"), taken by itself, is an intrigu-ing study in conflation. This negative form of the rule is the more common one in Judaism (from Tobit to Hillel) and is also witnessed in various early Christian documents. For example, the 3d-century *Oxyrhyncus Papyrus* 654, lines 36–37 (with restorations), reads in part: "and that which is hateful, do not do [*kai hoti miseitai mē poieite*]." The saying in this papyrus, which apparently comes from a Greek manuscript containing some form of the *Gospel of Thomas*, is repeated in saying 6 of the *Coptic Gospel of Thomas*: "and that which you hate, do not do [*petet^emmoste ^emmof ^emp^eraaf*]." On these Greek and Coptic texts, see Harold W. Attridge and Bentley Layton, *Nag Hammadi Codex II,2–7* (NHS 20 and 21; ed. Bentley Layton; 2 vols.; Leiden: Brill, 1989) 1. 116 and 54 respectively. In addition, the Greek of Codex Bezae (5th century A.D.) inserts a negative form of the Golden Rule into the text of the Apostolic Letter at Acts 15:20,29.

But to return to the *Didache*: despite the fact that the *Didache* follows the com-mon Jewish-Christian negative form of the rule, the first four Greek words of the *Didache*'s version (*panta de hosa ean* ["but all whatsoever"]) parrot almost exactly the first four Greek words of the Matthean positive version of the rule (*panta oun hosa ean*). As many commentators on Matthew note, the phrase *panta oun hosa ean* reflects typically Matthean style and vocabulary and, with its notable differ-ence from the version in Luke 6:31, almost certainly comes from Matthew's re-dactional hand; so, e.g., Davies and Allison, *The Gospel According to Matthew*, 1. 686 (continued on 687) n. 31. In sum, the *Didache*'s version of the Golden Rule shows a knowledge both of Matthew's Gospel (with its redactional positive form of the rule) and of the negative form of the rule common in the Jewish (and early Christian) tradition. One might also make a further point against claiming *Did.* 1.2 as an independent witness (criterion of multiple attestation) to the saying's origin in the historical Jesus. Many critics hold that the title(s) or *incipit* of the *Didache*—the Bryennois manuscript has a short title, "Teaching of the twelve apostles," followed by a long title, "Teaching of the Lord through the twelve apostles to the nations"—is secondary. For example, Kurt Niederwimmer (*The Didache* [Hermeneia; Minneapolis: Fortress, 1998; German original 1993] 56–57) states: "It is probable . . . that neither title is original. . . . The two titles . . . both come from a later time and are irrelevant for the interpretation of the document"; cf. Koester, *Ancient Christian Gospels*, 32. Moreover, the earliest form of the title when it was attached may well have been simply "Teaching of the apostles." If these judgments are basically correct, then the commands in 1.2 were not explicitly attributed to Jesus in the earliest form of the *Didache*. When it comes to arguments from multiple attestation of the Golden Rule in early Christian texts, some of the supposed "parallels" adduced by critics are not examples of the Golden Rule at all. For example, Betz's appeal (*The Sermon on the Mount*, 516 n. 695) to 1 *Clem.* 13.2 is, in my view, mistaken, since the sayings cited in 1 *Clem.* 13.2 are parallels not to the Golden Rule but to other logia in the Sermon on the Mount/Sermon on the Plain. These logia employ the "divine passive" and refer therefore to recompense from God on the last day, not from a fellow human being in this life. In general, I think that the early Christian writings that Betz cites in n. 695 as independent witnesses are in fact dependent on Matthew and/or Luke—or possibly on an early Gospel harmony or catechism derived from them. On the larger question of the use of Gospel harmonies in Christian literature of the 2d century, see M.-E. Boismard (with A. Lamouille), *Le Diatessaron: de Tatien à Justin* (EBib n.s. 15; Paris: Gabalda, 1992).

²⁶⁴ Going beyond a mere *non liquet*, Betz (*The Sermon on the Mount*, 513) affirms that the historical Jesus did teach the Golden Rule. His position rests partly on his idiosyncratic view of sources and partly on his claim that the Golden Rule does not clash with the surrounding material in Q. As can be seen from my argument throughout this section, I disagree on both counts.

²⁶⁵ In the articulations of the love command in John 13:34 and 15:12 + 17, the evangelist supplies both a shorter form ("love one another") and a longer form ("as I have loved you, so you—love one another"). Clearly, the shorter form is simply an abbreviated or summary version of the longer form for which it stands. Hence, in the main text I focus on the longer form. As for the grammar of these commands, it should be noted that the command proper ("love one another") is expressed by the conjunction *hina* with the subjunctive. In 13:34ab ("a new commandment I give you, that [*hina*] you love one another") the *hina* clause could be understood as a substantive clause in apposition to and explaining the noun *entolēn* ("commandment"), as a *hina* clause serving as the equivalent of a complementary (or possibly a final) infinitive, or as an independent clause with imperatival *hina* introducing the subjunctive; on the question of the grammar of the sentence, see Brown, *The Gospel*

According to John, 2. 607; Rudolf Schnackenburg, *Das Johannesevangelium. III. Teil* (HTKNT 4/3; Freiburg/Basel/Vienna: Herder, 1975) 60. Whatever the precise grammatical explanation preferred, the subjunctive *agapate* stands for the imperative; the present tense suggests ongoing action. The same can be said of the grammar of John 15:12; in John 15:17, perhaps the *hina* clause is best understood as a substantive clause in apposition to the demonstrative pronoun *tauta*, though a final sense ("in order that you may love one another") cannot be entirely excluded; see Brown, ibid., 2. 665. As we shall see below, there are echoes of these love commands in the First Epistle of John (including similar grammatical constructions in 1 John 3:23; 4:21); but in 1 John the command to love is never directly quoted as coming from Jesus.

[266] There is neither need nor space at this point to lay out in great detail my views on the tradition and redaction of the Fourth Gospel. Suffice it to say that, in the four volumes of *A Marginal Jew*, all that we have seen while treating the sayings and deeds of Jesus recounted in John as well as in the Synoptics tends to confirm the following positions: (1) The Fourth Gospel draws upon a pool of oral tradition similar to but not the same as that of the Synoptics; in other words, John's Gospel is literarily independent of the Synoptics. (2) The material in the Fourth Gospel went through a number of stages of oral and written versions before it reached the basic written form we have today. I remain uncertain as to whether we can speak of a single written Sign Source or Revelation Discourse Source prior to the composition of the Gospel. The existence of a primitive Johannine Passion Narrative in written form seems likely. (3) After the evangelist whom we call John finished his work, a final redactor added chap. 21, chaps. 15–17, and other scattered material (e.g., 4:2). These additions were made to an already fixed written text; the final redactor did not undertake a massive rewriting of the whole Gospel. (4) As for the three Johannine Epistles, I think that they were composed by one author (neither the evangelist nor the final redactor of the Fourth Gospel), writing after the composition of the Fourth Gospel and with a knowledge of it. In these positions, I basically follow the mature work of Raymond E. Brown in his *The Community of the Beloved Disciple* (New York: Paulist, 1979) and his *The Epistles of John* (AYB 30; Garden City, NY: Doubleday, 1982; reprint New Haven: Yale University Press). One reason I do not argue all these positions in detail is that a contrary position (e.g., that the Johannine epistles were written before the Gospel and possibly by the evangelist) would not make a great difference in my final conclusions. As for the stratum or strata of the Johannine tradition to which the two expressions of the Gospel's love command (John 13:34; 15:12) belong, opinions differ. As Rensberger ("Love for One Another," 298–302) points out in his survey, both Fernando Segovia and Urban von Wahlde reach the conclusion that the love-commandment passages in 13:34–35 and 15:9–17 are secondary additions to the Gospel and have theological connections to 1 John. Rensberger himself holds open the possibility that both passages are at home in the theological and social context of the original Gospel, though 15:9–17 may be a redactional expansion on 13:34–35 when the persecution suffered by the Johannine community increased. My own view is that 13:34 more likely comes

from the hand of the Fourth Evangelist, while 15:12, like chap. 15 in general, comes from the final redactor. Nevertheless, the overall conclusions I draw in the main text do not depend on choosing one of these detailed theories.

[267] This brief sketch of Johannine theology simply sums up the common opinion among many exegetes. It is anything but original, borrowing heavily from major authors of Johannine commentaries and studies. Among the most influential are Rudolf Schnackenburg, *The Gospel According to St John. Volume One* (London: Burns & Oates; New York: Herder and Herder, 1968) 153–72; Raymond E. Brown, *The Gospel According to John* (AYB 29 and 29A; 2 vols.; Garden City, NY: Doubleday, 1966, 1970; reprint New Haven: Yale University Press) 1. cv–cxxviii; idem, *The Epistles of John*, 47–115; idem, *An Introduction to the New Testament* (AYBRL; New York: Doubleday, 1997; reprint New Haven: Yale University Press) 333–94; idem (with Francis J. Moloney), *An Introduction to the Gospel of John* (AYBRL; New York: Doubleday, 2003; reprint New Haven: Yale University Press) 220–77. Also worthy of note are C. H. Dodd, *The Interpretation of the Fourth Gospel* (Cambridge: Cambridge University, 1965) 133–285; Ernst Käsemann, *Jesu letzter Wille nach Johannes 17* (2d ed.; Tübingen: Mohr [Siebeck], 1967); Wilhelm Thüsing, *Die Erhöhung und Verherrlichung Jesu im Johannesevangelium* (NTAbh 21; 3d ed.; Münster: Aschendorff, 1979); D. Bruce Woll, *Johannine Christianity in Conflict* (SBLDS 60; Chico, CA: Scholars, 1981); Rodney A. Whitacre, *Johannine Polemic* (SBLDS 67; Chico, CA: Scholars, 1982); C. K. Barrett, *Essays on John* (Philadelphia: Westminster, 1982); Fernando F. Segovia, *Love Relationships in the Johannine Tradition* (SBLDS 58; Chico, CA: Scholars, 1982); idem, *The Farewell of the Word* (Minneapolis: Fortress, 1991); Godfrey C. Nicholson, *Death as Departure. The Johannine Descent–Ascent Schema* (SBLDS 63; Chico, CA: Scholars, 1983); Robert Kysar, *John* (Minneapolis: Augsburg, 1986); Marianne Meye Thompson, *The Humanity of Jesus in the Fourth Gospel* (Philadelphia: Fortress, 1988); eadem, *The God of the Gospel of John* (Grand Rapids: Eerdmans, 2001); Jerome H. Neyrey, *An Ideology of Revolt. John's Christology in Social-Science Perspective* (Philadelphia: Fortress, 1988); William Loader, *The Christology of the Fourth Gospel. Structure and Issues* (BBET 23; Frankfurt: Lang, 1989); Urban von Wahlde, *The Johannine Commandments. 1 John and the Struggle for the Johannine Tradition* (Theological Inquiries; New York/Mahwah: Paulist, 1990); John Painter, *The Quest for the Messiah. The History, Literature and Theology of the Johannine Community* (Edinburgh: Clark, 1991); G. R. Beasley-Murray, *Gospel of Life. Theology in the Fourth Gospel* (Peabody, MA: Hendrickson, 1991); John Ashton, *Understanding the Fourth Gospel* (Oxford: Clarendon, 1991); idem, *Studying John. Approaches to the Fourth Gospel* (Oxford: Oxford University, 1995); Udo Schnelle, *Antidocetic Christology in the Gospel of John* (Minneapolis: Fortress, 1992; German original 1987); Martin Scott, *Sophia and the Johannine Jesus* (JSNTSup 71; Sheffield: JSOT, 1992); D. Moody Smith, *The Theology of the Gospel of John* (Cambridge: Cambridge University, 1995); Christina Hoegen-Rohls, *Der nachösterliche Johannes. Die Abschiedsreden als hermeneutischer Schlüssel zum vierten Evangelium* (WUNT 2/84; Tübingen: Mohr [Siebeck], 1996); Rob-

ert T. Fortna and Tom Thatcher (eds.), *Jesus in Johannine Tradition* (Louisville: Westminster/John Knox, 2001); J. Louis Martyn, *History and Theology in the Fourth Gospel* (3d ed.; Louisville: Westminster/John Knox, 2003); Amy-Jill Levine (ed.), *A Feminist Companion to John* (2 vols.; London/New York: Sheffield Academic Press, 2003); Wendy E. Sproston North, "John for Readers of Mark?" *JSNT* 25 (2003) 449–68; Jürgen Becker, *Johanneisches Christentum* (Tübingen: Mohr [Siebeck], 2004); Ian D. Mackay, *John's Relationship with Mark* (WUNT 2/182; Tübingen: Mohr [Siebeck], 2004); Robert Kysar, *Voyages with John. Charting the Fourth Gospel* (Waco, TX: Baylor University, 2005); Cornelis Bennema, "The Sword of the Messiah and the Concept of Liberation in the Fourth Gospel," *Bib* 86 (2005) 35–58; Paul N. Anderson, *The Fourth Gospel and the Quest for Jesus* (Library of NT Studies 321; London/New York: Clark, 2006); John C. Stube, *A Graeco-Roman Rhetorical Reading of the Farewell Discourses* (Library of NT Studies 309; London/New York: Clark, 2006); Peter M. Phillips, *The Prologue of the Fourth Gospel. A Sequential Reading* (Library of NT Studies 294; London/New York: Continuum, 2006); Warren Carter, *John. Storyteller, Interpreter, Evangelist* (Peabody, MA: Hendrickson, 2006); John A. Dennis, *Jesus' Death and the Gathering of True Israel* (WUNT 2/217; Tübingen: Mohr [Siebeck], 2006); Philip F. Esler and Ronald Piper, *Lazarus, Mary and Martha. Social-Scientific Approaches to the Gospel of John* (Minneapolis: Fortress, 2006); Michael Martin, "A Note on the Two Endings of John," *Bib* 87 (2006) 523–25; Jerome H. Neyrey, "Worship in the Fourth Gospel: A Cultural Interpretation of John 14–17," *BTB* 36 (2006) 107–17, 155–63; idem, " 'I Am the Door' (John 10:7,9): Jesus the Broker in the Fourth Gospel," *CBQ* 69 (2007) 271–91; Paul N. Anderson, Felix Just, and Tom Thatcher (eds.), *John, Jesus, and History. Volume 1* (Symposium Series 44; Atlanta: SBL, 2007); Mary L. Coloe, *Dwelling in the Household of God. Johannine Ecclesiology and Spirituality* (Collegeville, MN: Liturgical Press, 2007); Michael A. Daise, *Feasts in John* (WUNT 2/229; Tübingen: Mohr [Siebeck], 2007); Edward W. Klink III, *The Sheep of the Fold. The Audience and Origin of the Gospel of John* (Cambridge, UK/New York: Cambridge University, 2007); Robert Kysar, *John, the Maverick Joseph* (3d ed.; Louisville: Westminster/John Knox, 2007). While I disagree with some of his interpretations, it is impossible to ignore the classic works of Rudolf Bultmann: *Das Evangelium des Johannes* (MeyerK 2; 19th ed.; Göttingen: Vandenhoeck & Ruprecht, 1968); *Theology of the New Testament* (2 vols.; London: SCM, 1965) 2. 3–92.

[268] I presuppose here the majority view of NT exegetes on the subject of preexistence in the NT; some scholars, however, question the presence of the idea of preexistence in such passages as Phil 2:6–11; Col 1:15–20; or Heb1:1–4. For a fair treatment of the question within the larger context of NT Christology, see Raymond E. Brown, *An Introduction to New Testament Christology* (New York/Mahwah, NJ: Paulist, 1994).

[269] Most NT scholars hold that the Synoptic Gospels contain no theology of preexistence and incarnation; for a balanced summary of views, see Brown, *An*

Introduction to New Testament Christology, 105–52, 196–213. However, some maintain that preexistence and incarnation are at least implicitly present in the Synoptics, though these two doctrines are never thematized. On this, see, e.g., Simon J. Gathercole, *The Preexistent Son* (Grand Rapids, MI/Cambridge, UK: Eerdmans, 2006) 293–97.

[270] On sending and sonship in the Fourth Gospel, see Juan P. Miranda, *Der Vater, der mich gesandt hat* (Europäische Hochschulschriften 23/7; Frankfurt: Lang, 1972); idem, *Die Sendung Jesu im vierten Evangelium* (SBS 87; Stuttgart: KBW, 1977).

[271] On Son of Man christology in John, see Francis J. Moloney, *The Johannine Son of Man* (Rome: LAS, 1976); Delbert Burkett, *The Son of the Man in the Gospel of John* (JSNTSup 56; Sheffield: JSOT, 1991).

[272] On this, see Schnackenburg, *The Gospel According to St John. Volume One*, 154–64; also Perkins (*Love Commands*, 104–5), who rightly sees the connection between this christological concentration and the special Johannine approach to the tradition of love commandments.

[273] The fact that there are different types of dualism intersecting in John's theology is often overlooked in favor of global statements about "Johannine dualism." On the variety of dualisms in John, see Jürgen Becker, "Beobachtungen zum Dualismus im Johannesevangelium," *ZNW* 65 (1974) 71–87. I take over only some of Becker's observations in my brief summary.

[274] The complex Johannine reworking of the tradition of Jesus' love command(s)— a reworking that welds together ontological basis and ethical thrust within the larger context of John's high christology, realized eschatology, and stark dualism— may explain why the command is qualified as "new" (*kainos* in 13:34, an adjective that otherwise appears in John only at 19:41, where it describes the tomb in which Jesus is laid). We shall examine these components of the Johannine love command in what follows. Despite the fact that this "new commandment" is delivered at the Last Supper, I doubt that there is any connection with the theme of "new covenant," since the Fourth Gospel and the Johannine Epistles never use the word "covenant" (*diathēkē*) and since the eucharist (which is connected with the phrase "new covenant" only in Luke 22:20 and 1 Cor 11:25) is never mentioned in the Johannine version of the Last Supper. On this point, I differ with Brown, who sees allusions to the new covenant and even to the eucharist in various places in John 13–17; see, e.g., his comments in *The Gospel According to John*, 2. 612–14, 672–73; cf. Popkes, *Die Theologie der Liebe*, 271. I incline instead toward the view of Schnackenburg (*Das Johannesevangelium. III. Teil*, 59–60; similarly his *Die Johannesbriefe* [HTKNT 13/3; 4th ed.; Freiburg/Basel/Vienna: Herder, 1970] 111– 12), who locates the newness of the command in the very person and work of Jesus: Jesus' loving service (demonstrated in the foot washing) and his self-sacrifice unto death give his command of love a unique, eschatological character. For a similar

view, see Rensberger, "Love for One Another," 304; Furnish, *The Love Command*, 138–39; Lütgert, *Die Liebe*, 137–67. For a discussion of the "newness" of the commandment that never quite reaches a clear conclusion, see Lattke, *Einheit*, 214–17.

275 On differences between the Synoptic and the Johannine love commands, see Popkes, *Die Theologie der Liebe*, 259–63.

276 Along with many other scholars commenting on the farewell discourses in John's Gospel (e.g., Brown, *The Gospel According to John*, 2. 597–601; Berger, *Gesetzesauslegung*, 121), Perkins (*Love Commands*, 104–5) points to the background of "testamentary literature" in the Second Temple Judaism. In such testamentary literature, a patriarch or some other venerable figure, prior to his death, delivers his spiritual last will and testament to his sons or disciples. These testaments usually include a review of the hero's past life in light of his imminent death, predictions about his descendants' future, and an earnest exhortation to unity and mutual love (along with instruction about other more specific virtues and vices). One finds all three elements (minus detailed moral instruction on individual virtues) in the farewell discourses of the Johannine Last Supper. The *Testaments of the Twelve Patriarchs* represent the full flowering of the genre; however, in my opinion, the final form of the *Testaments* reflects Christian cultivation of the genre.

277 A similar picture results from examining the use of the noun *agapē* ("love"), which occurs outside the Last Supper in John only at 5:42, while appearing during the Last Supper at 13:35; 15:9,10 [*bis*],13; 17:26. The verb *phileō* is much less important in John. Apart from chap. 21 (most probably added by the final redactor), *phileō* occurs eight times in the Gospel, three times at the Last Supper. John never uses the abstract noun *philia* for "love," and even the six occurrences of *philos* ("friend")—three in the Last Supper context—pale in comparison with its fifteen occurrences in Luke. More to the point, only *agapaō* is used to articulate the love command; *phileō* occurs neither in the love command nor in the explanatory sentences that follow upon it. The reason for this relative absence of *phileō* has nothing to do with a supposed difference in meaning between the two verbs. The verbs *agapaō* and *phileō* are, for all practical purposes, synonymous in John. Any difference in meaning arises from the immediate context in which the verbs are used. The limited use of *phileō* in John reflects not some special Christian theology of love but rather the verb's slow decline vis-à-vis *agapaō* in Hellenistic Greek; on this, see Joly, *Le vocabulaire*, 48–49, 54–56. On the love vocabulary in the Johannine corpus, see Stählin, "*phileō*, etc.," 129–36; 163–67; Meisinger, *Liebesgebot*, 150.

278 Brown (*The Gospel According to John*, 2. 682) speaks of "the chain of love" found in such passages as John 15:9,12; cf. Meisinger, *Liebesgebot*, 180; D. Moody Smith, *John* (Abingdon NT Commentaries; Nashville: Abingdon, 1999) 284.

279 On this, see Schnackenburg, *Das Johannesevangelium. III. Teil*, 61, 124; cf. Bultmann, *Das Evangelium des Johannes*, 405–6, 417 with n. 4. J. H. Bernard (*Gospel According to St John* [ICC; 2 vols.; Edinburgh: Clark, 1928] 2. 486) makes

an intriguing remark on the love command in John 15:12–13 as compared with the all-embracing love of Christ for sinners that is hailed in Rom 5:7–8: "But here [in John 15:12–13] something less is commended to the imitation of the Christian disciple, for the 'new commandment' does not speak of universal brotherhood, but only of the obligations of Christian brethren to each other." Ernst Haenchen (*John 2* [Hermeneia; Philadelphia: Fortress, 1984; German original 1980] 117–18) interprets the love command in an even more restrictive manner: "In this passage [the love command in John 13:34], John does not have in view the worldwide church, but the small band of disciples for whom this Gospel was written."

[280] See my comments in *A Marginal Jew*, 2. 448–50. Against labeling the Johannine community a sect is Popkes, *Die Theologie der Liebe*, 40–41, 267; in favor of the label is Perkins, "Apocalyptic Sectarianism," 290. A classic essay on the subject is Wayne Meeks, "The Man from Heaven in Johannine Sectarianism," *JBL* 91 (1972) 44–72; useful monographs include Marinus de Jonge, *Jesus Stranger from Heaven and Son of God* (SBLSBS 11; Missoula, MT: Scholars, 1977); Wolfgang Langbrandtner, *Weltferner Gott oder Gott der Liebe* (Beihefte zur biblischen Exegese und Theologie 6; Frankfurt: Lang, 1977); Neyrey, *An Ideology of Revolt*.

[281] I do not deny that the Gospel contains references to the disciples' mission to the larger world (e.g., John 4:31–38,42; 17:20–23; 20:21–23; 21:1–14), but this theme is not a major focus of the Gospel. One almost gets the sense that John understands mission in terms of the community of disciples living a life of such great love for one another that nonbelievers will be attracted to the group. In other words, the community acts as a magnet by its witness (cf. John 12:20–26,32). On the question of mission in John, see Miguel R. Ruiz, *Der Missionsgedanke des Johannesevangeliums* (FB 55; Würzburg: Echter, 1986); Teresa Okure, *The Johannine Approach to Mission* (WUNT 2/31; Tübingen: Mohr [Siebeck], 1988); cf. Perkins, *Love Commands*, 120.

[282] On the theme of reciprocity in "the new commandment" of John's Gospel, see Lattke, *Einheit*, 212.

[283] So, rightly, Furnish, *The Love Command*, 133.

[284] Significantly, the mutual indwelling extolled in John's Gospel is expressed both by the verb *menō* ("to dwell," "to abide," "to remain") and *eimi* ("to be"). The union between the Father and the Son, the union between the Son and the believer, and the union among believers are permanent because they are all ultimately grounded in the very being of the Father and the Son, in which the believers share.

[285] On the question of mysticism in John, see Jey J. Kanagaraj, *'Mysticism' in the Gospel of John* (JSNTSup 158; Sheffield: JSOT, 1998).

[286] On the foot washing in John 13, see Georg Richter, *Die Fusswaschung im Johannesevangelium* (Biblische Untersuchung 1; Regensburg: Pustet, 1967); Sandra Schneiders, "The Foot Washing (John 13:1–20): An Experiment in Hermeneutics," *CBQ* 43 (1981) 76–92; Francis J. Moloney, "A Sacramental Reading of John 13:1–38," *CBQ* 53 (1991) 237–56; John C. Thomas, *Footwashing in John 13 and the Johannine Community* (JSNTSup 61; Sheffield: JSOT, 1991); Larry P. Jones, *The Symbol of Water in the Gospel of John* (JSNTSup 145; Sheffield: JSOT, 1997).

[287] Hence, contrary to the opinion of Perkins (*Love Commands*, 106–7), I do not think it likely that the fruit metaphor in John 15:1–8 symbolizes missionary endeavor and evangelization, a meaning that the metaphor has in some NT contexts (e.g., Rom 1:13). Meisinger (*Liebesgebot*, 158–59) does not entirely reject a missionary reference, but thinks that it is present only indirectly: reciprocal love and unity (the main meaning of the metaphor of fruit) can have a witnessing function that draws the world to faith.

[288] On this, see Brown, *The Gospel According to John*, 2. 680–81. In his essay, "Joh 15,13. Eine Studie zum Traditionsproblem des Johannes-Evangeliums," *Botschaft und Geschichte* (2 vols.; Tübingen: Mohr [Siebeck], 1953, 1956) 1. 204–20, Martin Dibelius rightly emphasizes the "metaphysical" nature of love relationships in the Last Supper discourses in John 13–17; love involves the communication and sharing of divine revelation, which in turn communicates a sharing in the divine nature (pp. 208–14). In this light, it is understandable why the Johannine type of love extends only to the believer and not to the unbelieving world. However, Dibelius is so insistent that there is no emotional or ethical component in Johannine love that he claims that John 15:13 ("greater love than this no one has, that one lay down his life for his friends") must come to the evangelist from his tradition, since the verse clearly speaks of the emotion of heroic love (p. 216), an ethical idea that is contrary to the evangelist's own metaphysical conception of love. In my opinion, Dibelius is guilty of the all-too-familiar Teutonic either-or approach to NT texts. He fails to appreciate the dialectical mind of the evangelist, who delights in playing with polar opposites, only to bring them at last into a paradoxical union. Whatever his sources, the evangelist (as well as the final redactor) quite consciously combines metaphysical/ontological and ethical/moral elements in his conception of love. On this, see Meisinger, *Liebesgebot*, 152–58, 180–81.

[289] On the double meaning of *kathōs* ("just as" and "since"), see Schnackenburg, *Das Johannesevangelium. III. Teil*, 60; Bultmann, *Das Evangelium des Johannes*, 403; Popkes, *Die Theologie der Liebe*, 258.

[290] The aorist *ēgapēsa* ("I have loved" or simply "I loved") in John 13:34 and 15:12 points to the past saving events of Christ's incarnation, life, and (anticipated) death and resurrection; Brown (*The Gospel According to John*, 2. 664) sees in particular a reference to Jesus' death, mentioned in 15:13. At the same time, a present sense ("I love you") cannot be completely excluded, especially if one sees behind

the Greek aorist a Hebrew or Aramaic perfect verb with a stative sense; on this, see Zerwick and Grosvenor, *A Grammatical Analysis*, 332–33.

[291] See the treatment of these symbolic scenes in Schnackenburg, *Das Johannesevangelium. III. Teil*, 319–28, 333–45.

[292] This christological concentration can be seen as well by comparing John's use of the Greek noun *entolē* ("command" or "commandment") with that of the Synoptics and Paul. As Furnish (*The Love Command*, 137–38) points out, Paul and the Synoptics consistently use the noun "commandment(s)" to refer to the ordinances of the OT (a rare exception being Luke 15:29). The noun *entolē* is never used in this way by the Fourth Evangelist. With the exception of John 11:57 ("the chief priests and the Pharisees had given commands . . ."), John always employs *entolē* either of the command of God that directs Jesus' entire mission in the world (e.g., John 10:18; 12:49–50; 15:10) or the command(s) given by Jesus to his disciples (e.g., 13:34; 14:15,21; 15:10,12,17). One notices immediately that, just as with the vocabulary of love, so with the vocabulary of commands, the majority of occurrences is located in the context of the Last Supper in John. In Furnish's opinion, John's alteration between "commandment" and "commandments" is purely stylistic, and should not be pressed into meaning that the many commandments of the old law are summed up in the one commandment of love. For a different view, see Stephen S. Smalley, *1,2,3 John* (Word Biblical Commentary 51; Waco, TX: Word, 1984) 206–7.

[293] According to Furnish, *The Love Command*, 134–36.

[294] While we may see in this use of *philoi* ("friends") in John 15:13–15 an echo of the Hellenistic ethic of friendship, we must remember that its application in the farewell discourses is limited by the fact that Jesus, even in his self-sacrifice for his own, remains the *kyrios* ("lord," "master"; so, e.g., 13:13–16). On this, see Stählin, "*phileō*, etc.," 165; cf. Marie-Joseph Lagrange, *Saint Jean* (EBib; 5th ed.; Paris: Gabalda, 1936) 407.

[295] See, e.g., the seminal essays in James H. Charlesworth (ed.), *John and the Dead Sea Scrolls* (New York: Crossroad, 1990).

[296] On love of fellow members of the community at Qumran and in John's Gospel, see Brown, *The Gospel According to John*, 2. 613. As Rensberger ("Love for One Another," 304–9) observes, Bultmann is probably correct that the Johannine community is open to those who are of the world if they finally choose to enter the community of faith (e.g., the Samaritans who acknowledge Jesus as "the Savior of the world," in 4:42); in a similar vein, Furnish, *The Love Command*, 141–48. But, as Rensberger emphasizes, until those who belong to the world enter the community of faith (and so cease to belong to the "world" in the negative sense), they are not included in the "one another" to whom the Johannine love command is restricted. True, John's Gospel does not explicitly command hatred of outsiders in

the manner of Qumran's *Rule of the Community* (1QS). Still, the statements made about "the Jews" in the Fourth Gospel, especially the Johannine Jesus' branding of those Jews who believe in him as children of the devil (John 8:31–47), come perilously close to hatred, if indeed they have not crossed the line into hatred. Hence, Rensberger (p. 307) wonders how effective the witness of the unified Johannine community could have been when the outside world saw the witness accompanied by such hostility to the community's opponents. More positive in his approach is Meisinger (*Liebesgebot*, 161–71), who reads Jesus' love command in the Fourth Gospel through the lens of John 3:16 ("for God so loved the world . . ."). Meisinger reasons that, since part of the evil of the world is that it loves only its own (John 15:18–19), the Johannine community necessarily rejects such narrow love. Hence, while the community is not explicitly commanded by Jesus to love the world, such love can be assumed. I cannot help feeling that there is an apologetic slant to this interpretation.

[297] On this, see Rensberger, "Love for One Another," 304.

[298] The reader will notice that I do not include a treatment of the Revelation of John. The fiery, imminent, apocalyptic hope of the Book of Revelation (which, in any event, many exegetes would not include in the Johannine corpus) has no room for a command to love enemies. Indeed, the somewhat unseemly thirst for vengeance on persecutors and the unmitigated glee at their grisly punishment—however metaphorical and mythological the setting—seem to stand in opposition to the Q command to love enemies. Once we become acquainted with the tone of the Book of Revelation, we are not surprised that the risen Christ praises the church at Ephesus because "you hate the works of the Nicolaitans [a Christian group obviously at odds with the author of Revelation], which I also hate" (Rev 2:6). Thus, we are left not only with a church that hates but a Christ that hates. This may not be the same as Qumran's hatred for all the sons of darkness, but it is not far from it. On love and hatred in the Book of Revelation, see Perkins, "Apocalyptic Sectarianism," 290–91.

[299] For a consideration of 2 John and 3 John on their own terms, see Judith Lieu, *The Second and Third Epistles of John: History and Background* (Edinburgh: Clark, 1986).

[300] The position that I summarize here is basically that of Brown in his *The Epistles of John*, 69–115.

[301] For a fuller explanation and justification of this brief sketch, see Brown, *The Epistles of John*, 50–55, 73–86.

[302] Some scholars might object to the very idea of a "mainstream" Christianity at the end of the 1st century A.D., given the many different and competing Christian groups at the time. Yet I would maintain that, if we look at the Synoptic Gospels

plus the Pauline Epistles (authentic and pseudonymous) taken together, there are certain common positions that undergird what can be called—to be sure, with suitable vagueness—mainstream Christianity. Such common positions would include the pivotal and irreplaceable work and person of Jesus Christ, the necessary and saving nature of his death (viewed, at least at times, as a sacrifice for sins), the triumph of Christ's resurrection from the dead, the obligation of Christians to undertake a worldwide mission to spread the message of Christ, the necessity of God's grace (or justification or forgiveness or love) if humans are to be saved, the need for people accepting the Christian message to make a clear break with a past life of sin and to begin a new life of moral endeavor (sometimes associated with the rite of baptism), the danger of Christians' falling back into sin after conversion, the need to belong to a group of disciples (or Christian community or a church) engaged in shared life and worship, and the hope that Christ will come in glory to save his own and bring this present age to its conclusion. Some might object that many of these positions are not shared by works like the *Coptic Gospel of Thomas*, to say nothing of other, more specifically gnostic, writings from Nag Hammadi. As I indicated in *A Marginal Jew*, 1. 112–41, I think a sober examination of these works (as opposed to increasingly sensationalistic and irresponsible treatments in the American media—and, sadly, in some segments of American academia) argues convincingly for their composition around the middle of the 2d century A.D., if not later.

[303] On "love of the brethren" in the Johannine Epistles (treated especially in 1 John 2:9–11; 3:11–18,23; 4:7,11–12,20–21; 5:1–2), see Brown, *The Epistles of John*, 83–86; Schnackenburg, *Die Johannesbriefe*, 117–21. On the use of "brother" (*adelphos*) to designate *solely* a fellow member of the Johannine community—and pointedly not other Christians who, like the secessionists, reject the christology of the author of the Epistles—see Brown, ibid., 269–73. I find this position more likely than that of Schnackenburg, who claims (ibid., 120–21) that, in his use of *adelphos*, the author of 1 John oscillates between the sense of true-believing Christian (e.g., 3:13) and the sense of human beings in general (e.g., 3:14). I think the sudden change of meaning within two verses is highly unlikely. Actually, love of the "brothers" (no doubt understood by the author to include the female members of the community) in the Johannine Epistles is quite narrow. It is compatible not only with not loving the world and those things that are of the world (1 John 2:15) but also with shunning the secessionists, granting them no hospitality, and not even greeting them (2 John 10–11). True, the author of the Johannine Epistles does not command hatred of the secessionists, but one wonders whether branding former fellow members of the community as deceivers and antichrists (1 John 2:18–19; 2 John 7) falls all that short of religious hatred. Perhaps one reason why our epistolary author does not directly command hatred of his opponents is that "hating the brothers" is one of the weighty accusations that he hurls against both the secessionists and the world (1 John 2:9–11; 3:10–15); hence, he can hardly urge it himself. On the narrowness of love of the brothers in the Johannine Epistles, see Perkins, "Apocalyptic Sectarianism," 289–90; eadem, *Love Commands*, 105–6. In contrast, Popkes (*Die Theologie der Liebe*, 131) seeks to soften the hard edges of the Johannine command to

love the brothers. Going still farther, Augenstein (*Das Liebesgebot*, 181–82) claims that the Johannine love command not only does not exclude love of enemies but actually includes it. Augenstein seems so focused on the background of the Johannine love command in Lev 19:18b that he misses the foreground of the polemics in the Johannine Epistles.

304 I include the statistics on *agapētos* for the sake of completeness, though the presence of the adjective may not be all that significant, since all the occurrences are in the vocative and hence are occasioned by the literary genre employed. On *agapētos* in the Johannine Epistles, see Brown, *The Epistles of John*, 263–64, cf. 254.

305 A representative sample, mostly from the epistolary literature, includes 1 Thess 1:4; 2:1; 2 Thess 1:3; 1 Cor 5:11; 2 Cor 1:1,8; Gal 1:2,11; Rom 1:13; 8:29; Phil 1:12; Phlm 1:7; Col 1:1–2; Eph 6:23; 1 Tim 6:2; Heb 3:1; Jas 1:2; 1 Pet 5:12; 2 Pet 1:10; Acts 6:3; 9:30; 10:23; Rev 1:9; 12:10. Berger (*Gesetzesauslegung*, 121) observes that, in the later books of the NT, love of neighbor tends to be replaced by love of brothers.

306 On the difficult line of thought in 1 John 2:7–8, see Brown, *The Epistles of John*, 263–69. Perhaps the best explanation is that of Schnackenburg, *Die Johannesbriefe*, 110–11 (similarly Furnish, *The Love Command*, 151–52): the author of 1 John is wary of any "innovation" or "new" content in teaching because he sees the secessionists as "progressives" (cf. 2 John 9) who are introducing new—and false—teaching. Hence, in 1 John 2:7, the author, thinking of the secessionists, at first denies that the commandment that he is inculcating is "new" in the negative sense of a false innovation; rather, it belongs to the traditional teaching of the Johannine community that was "from the beginning." Then, remembering that the commandment is called "new" in the Fourth Gospel, the author corrects himself in v 8, explaining that the commandment is new in the sense that it has become an eschatological reality in Christ and is becoming an eschatological reality in the Johannine community. Interestingly, while alluding to the Fourth Gospel and the commandment's realization in Christ, the author never explicitly says that the commandment was taught by Christ as new.

307 In fact, the author resolves his ambiguity in 2 John 5 by insisting more radically that the love command is not new but "from [the] beginning"—thus (at least verbally) breaking with the claim of the evangelist. Perhaps since 2 John is apparently a real letter, while 1 John is more of a tractate commenting on main themes of the Gospel, the author of the Johannine Epistles feels freer to express his own unvarnished view in 2 John. Perhaps, as well, the struggle with the "innovative" and "progressive" secessionists has become even fiercer by the time 2 John is written. Taking a somewhat different tack, Brown (*The Epistles of John*, 664) explains 2 John 5 thus: "The implication is that his [the author's] request involves a basic Christian commandment, not something new asked in his own name." But would the author of 2 John, who presumably both wrote 1 John and knew the Fourth

Gospel, use the phrase "a new commandment" in reference to the love command in this pedestrian way?

308 When the author of 1 John says in 2:7 that the new/old command of love is the command "that you had from the beginning . . . the word that you heard," I take this to refer to the time when his audience first heard and accepted the Christian message in its Johannine form. The repeated motif of "from the beginning" is the Johannine version of "give me that good old-time religion." Thus, I do not take "that you had from the beginning" as referring specifically to Jesus' teaching of the commandment. Here I differ from Brown's interpretation (*The Epistles of John*, 265), which, while allowing for the interpretation I prefer, also introduces a reference to Jesus' self-revelation to his disciples during his ministry. On the different possible meanings of "from the beginning" in the Johannine Epistles, see Brown, ibid., 155–58. Strange to say, Brown seems to go against his own position when, in a comment on 1 John 3:23, he states (p. 464) that "even though Jesus gave the commandment to love one another (John 13:34; 15:10 [*sic*],17), we have seen that regularly I John attributes commandments to God . . . and II John 4–5 uses a *kathōs* clause (as here) to refer to a commandment to love one another that we have received 'from the Father.' "

309 See Brown's comment in *The Epistles of John*, 290; cf. Furnish, *The Love Command*, 150. As Popkes (*Die Theologie der Liebe*, 125–26) observes, what we have in 1 John 3:23 is a double command of faith and love, not a double command of love. It should be noted that the verses immediately preceding 1 John 3:23 (i.e., vv 17–22) focus on the believers' relationship to God (the Father), not the Son; more specifically, v 22 affirms that "we keep his [God the Father's] commandments." In 3:17–23, Christ is mentioned only in v 23b as the object of the act of faith that believers are commanded (by God the Father) to make. Hence, in light of the general context and especially of the affirmation in v 22 that believers keep the commandments of God the Father, the last clause in v 23 ("just as he gave a commandment to us") almost necessarily understands God the Father as the subject of the verb "gave." Here I differ with Schnackenburg (*Die Johannesbriefe*, 208), who takes "Jesus Christ" as the understood subject of the verb "gave." Rather, on this point, I agree with Georg Strecker, *The Johannine Letters* (Hermeneia; Minneapolis: Fortress, 1996; German original 1989) 127; also Smalley, *1,2,3 John*, 209.

310 A more roundabout connection of love of God with love of one's brother is found in 1 John 5:1–2.

311 A curious similarity of Mark to 1 John (but not John's Gospel) is that both Mark and 1 John use *entolē*, but neither uses *nomos*.

312 Commenting on 1 John 4:21, Brown (*The Epistles of John*, 534) argues strongly that the source of the command is God the Father, not Christ, noting that "the epistolary author consistently attributes the commandment to God." Contrary to his

interpretation of 1 John 3:23, Schnackenburg (*Die Johannesbriefe*, 250 n. 2) admits that in 4:21 the source of the command is God the Father. Smalley (*1,2,3 John*, 265) tries to have it both ways by arguing that, while the love command stems ultimately from God the Father, it was eventually articulated by Jesus. J. L. Houlden (*The Johannine Epistles* [Harper's NT Commentaries; New York: Harper & Row, 1973] 120 n. 2) wavers, but prefers taking Christ as the source of the command; likewise in favor of Christ as the source is F. F. Bruce, *The Epistles of John* (Grand Rapids, MI: Eerdmans, 1970) 100. In this regard, it should be noted that, unlike the Fourth Gospel, the First Epistle of John restricts the use of *theos* ("God") to God the Father. The one possible exception to this rule is 1 John 5:20, where the affirmation "this is the true God [*houtos estin ho alēthinos theos*]" probably but not certainly refers back to "his Son, Jesus Christ" earlier in the verse (so Brown, *The Epistles of John*, 625–26, along with Bultmann, Schnackenburg, and many others).

[313] It is telling that in 1 John 4:11 the prior love of God for the believer results in the obligation of the believer to love fellow believers, not God: "Beloved, if God so loved us, we in turn ought to love one another." While God might be the understood object of the statement "we love" in 1 John 4:19, one's brother might also be understood as the object; on this, see Brown, *The Epistles of John*, 532. Indeed, Schnackenburg (*Die Johannesbriefe*, 249) argues strongly for "the brother" as the understood object of the verb "we love" in 4:19 (though Schnackenburg takes the verb as cohortative ["let us love"] rather than as indicative ["we love"], the interpretation Brown prefers).

[314] Here I disagree with Furnish (*The Love Command*, 151), who says of 1 John 4:20–21 + 5:1–2, "This is the only New Testament passage outside the Synoptic Gospels where we can be fairly sure of a direct reference to the Great Commandment [i.e., the double command of love of God and love of neighbor] with equal stress on each of its parts." Similarly, I disagree with Schnackenburg (*Die Johannesbriefe*, 121), who maintains that in 1 John 4:21, "the author refers clearly enough to the double command of love of God and love of neighbor" (while on p. 251 he adds that what 1 John is really doing is harmonizing the Synoptic account of the double command of love with the Johannine "new command" of love). Strecker (*The Johannine Letters*, 173) basically agrees with Schnackenburg, though with some caveats. From this supposed reference to the double command of love, Schnackenburg draws the even more unlikely conclusion that "brother" in v 21 refers to human beings in general (similarly Furnish, *The Love Command*, 152–53). As a result, Schnackenburg must contend that the author suddenly shifts his thought back to true-believing Christians in 5:1–2. In my view, there are too many oscillations of focus in Schnackenburg's reading of 1 John's teaching on the commandment of love. Like Schnackenburg, Popkes (*Die Theologie der Liebe*, 145–46, 294–96) sees in 1 John 4:21 a reference to the Synoptic double command of love, which Popkes thinks the author has consciously integrated into his own argument, which focuses on mutual love within the community. Hence, Popkes, unlike Schnackenburg, does not see a reference to human beings in general in 1 John 4:21. More cau-

tious than either Schnackenburg or Popkes is Augenstein (*Das Liebesgebot*, 180), who ends his consideration of 1 John 4:21 with the suggestion that, in the Johannine corpus, a knowledge of the Synoptic double command is love is not to be excluded. See also Perkins (*Love Commands*, 118–20), who sees in 1 John 4:21 not only a Johannine type of double command of love but also a wider sense of "brother," i.e., one's neighbor, anyone with whom one has dealings; cf. Meisinger, *Liebesgebot*, 173–74.

[315] On this, see Burchard, "Das doppelte Liebesgebot," 44 n. 19.

[316] Hence, far from seeing the Johannine love command as the antithesis of the command to love one's neighbor (Lev 19:18b)—a position rightly rejected by Schnackenburg (*Das Johannesevangelium. III. Teil*, 59), among others—I understand the Johannine love command to be a Christian re-reception of the OT command. More emphatic on this point is Augenstein (*Das Liebesgebot*, 177–79), who thinks that the love command in John's Gospel depends on Lev 19:17–18 either directly or through the mediation of other writings. Augenstein hesitates on whether the *Testaments of the Twelve Patriarchs* played a part in this mediation. Taking a valid insight farther than I would, Popkes (*Die Theologie der Liebe*, 294–96) argues that, since in John's Gospel, God the Father and Jesus are one, love for the Father and love for Jesus coincide. Hence, the theme of love for Jesus in the Fourth Gospel can be seen as the Johannine transformation of the command in Deut 6:4–5 to love God. At this point, one begins to sense that we are moving from grasping John's own theology to theologizing on the basis of John. A similar idea is proposed by Perkins (*Love Commands*, 116): if we look at the whole of the Fourth Gospel, the double command of love in the Johannine tradition appears to have been, "love Jesus and the brethren."

[317] For the problem of Jesus' education and his status as a *tektōn* ("woodworker" for want of a better translation), see *A Marginal Jew*, 1. 268–85.

CONCLUSION TO
VOLUME FOUR

As I come to write the conclusion to this volume, the temptation is to take the easy way out. All I need do is gather together and repeat my opinions about each of the legal questions that we have explored chapter by chapter. If it is to be simply a laundry list of findings, the conclusion writes itself. The problem is that such an approach would be of no great help to the readers of this volume. They are more than capable of going back and reading the summary statement at the end of each chapter for themselves. Such a conclusion would add nothing new to this book except pages.

Much more useful to the reader who has been immersed in a sea of halakic detail is to step back, get a sense of the whole, and ask some "big questions." As we end our trek down the road of Jesus' statements on law and morality, perhaps the biggest question is simply: What has been grasped beyond a myriad of minutiae? In brief, both insight and enigma. As I explained in the introduction, this volume is dedicated to exploring the first of the four final enigmas: Jesus and Torah, Jesus' parables, Jesus' self-designations, and Jesus' death. As we have seen and will see, each enigma, upon probing, yields some insights and yet retains some mystery. The insights themselves have their shadow side, suggesting that we speak of both positive and negative (or inverse) insights. That is certainly the case with Jesus and the Law. Let us begin by pondering the positive insights we have gained.

I. POSITIVE INSIGHTS

1. On the positive side, the greatest single gain is that we have rescued the hallowed phrase "Jesus the Jew" from its status as a hollow academic slogan. From the 1970s onward, scholars such as Geza Vermes, James H. Charlesworth, E. P. Sanders, and Jacob Neusner have hammered home the

vital importance of seeing Jesus within and as part of the living and lively world of 1st-century Palestinian Judaism.

Unfortunately, the response of all too many American academics has been lip service. One need only page through the many Jesus books that enshrine the word "Jew" in their titles or trumpet it in their prefaces to grasp the gap between rhetoric and reality. To be sure, many American books on the historical Jesus now avoid the denigrating parodies of Torah or the Pharisees ensconced in older German tomes. In place of parodies, one finds a politically correct shift away from portraying a Jesus who attacks the Law, at least in its Pharisaic interpretation, to a Jesus who attacks hierarchy, priesthood, and temple—the latter suspects being assigned the role of villain in our more enlightened age.

Nevertheless, the result of this politically correct realignment is not a detailed consideration either of the nature and role of the Torah in 1st-century Palestine or of Jesus' complicated stance toward it. Instead, whether from ignorance or laziness, the tangled topic of Torah is dismissed with a few jejune comments about Jesus being a Law-observant Jew. His individual pronouncements on the Law and their relation to the views of contemporary Jewish groups may be given a polite nod, but nothing more. One would hardly guess from these books that the discoveries at Qumran and the reinvigorated study of OT Pseudepigrapha have forced scholars to rethink the legal world of Judaism at the turn of the era. It is telling, for instance, that the rich hoard of halakic material from Cave 4 at Qumran is rarely mentioned and never probed in depth.

Whatever the errors of Volume Four of *A Marginal Jew*, and no doubt they are many, this volume at least rejects a major academic failure of Jesus research: mouthing respect for Jesus' Jewishness while avoiding like the plague the beating heart of that Jewishness: the Torah in all its complexity. However bewildering the positions Jesus sometimes takes, he emerges from this volume as a Palestinian Jew engaged in the legal discussions and debates proper to his time and place. It is Torah and Torah alone that puts flesh and bones on the spectral figure of "Jesus the Jew." No halakic Jesus, no historical Jesus. This is the reason why many American books on the historical Jesus may be dismissed out of hand: their presentation of 1st-century Judaism and especially of Jewish Law is either missing in action or so hopelessly skewed that it renders any portrait of Jesus the Jew distorted from the start. It is odd that it has taken American scholarship so long to absorb this basic insight: either one takes Jewish Law seriously and "gets it right" or one should abandon the quest for the historical Jesus entirely. One need not pore over Qumran scrolls day and night to grasp this point. It simply stands to reason that any Jew who chose to mount the public stage in early 1st-century Palestine and present himself as a religious teacher ("rabbi" in the loose sense of the word) would have to discuss and debate the Torah both as a whole and in its parts. Strange to say, the more American books on Jesus strive to be "relevant," "cutting-edge" tomes that create "a new paradigm," the more they tend to lose sight of this obvious point. The patient reader of Volume Four of *A Marginal Jew* may at this juncture be sick unto death of the mantra, "the historical Jesus is the halakic Jesus." But at least such readers have been inoculated for life against the virus that induces legal amnesia in most Americans writing on Jesus. The halakic dimension of the historical Jesus is never exciting but always essential. It is, thankfully, one of the main reasons why the historical Jesus is not and never will be the American Jesus. If Volume Four has done nothing else than inculcate this insight, it has done enough.

2. This basic gain, namely, the appreciation of the importance of the Jewish Law to the Jewish Jesus, naturally leads to a second gain. Any investigator of the historical Jesus—whether Christian, Jewish, Muslim, or agnostic—is inevitably confronted with the personal, existential question: What, finally, do you think of the various moral teachings of Jesus that result from his engagement with Torah? No doubt the answers given by the different participants in my mythical "unpapal conclave" would be quite varied. A Jew might applaud Jesus' moderate, commonsense approach to sabbath observance, while finding his total prohibition of divorce and oath-taking both alien and unworkable. The Christian might accept Jesus' prohibition of divorce in theory, while unearthing all sorts of reasons why a Christian need not hold to the prohibition in practice (Law versus Gospel, the ideal versus the real, the unparalleled pressures of modern life, my best friend is divorced, etc.). Except for a few radical Protestant groups, almost all Christians would explain away Jesus' total prohibition of oaths. How exactly it would be explained away would be of no great concern. The only necessary thing would be to explain it away at all costs. The agnostic would certainly join the Jew, Christian, and Muslim in praising Jesus' emphasis on love, though love of God as the supreme value would be quietly collapsed into love of neighbor. Love of enemies might be extolled as a noble ideal or rejected as a neurosis-inducing impossibility. In any case, it would be widely ignored in practice.

The important point here is that wrestling with the question of Jesus and the Law should be more than a purely theoretical topic for experts. Unlike some other more abstruse areas of Jesus research (e.g., Jesus' exact relationship to John the Baptist or the precise type of eschatology Jesus proclaimed), the specific legal teachings of the historical Jesus invite or perhaps even force serious questers to ask themselves what they really think about Jesus' specific commands. Raising this question of existential meaning is not a covert way of transforming a strictly historical investigation into a theological disquisition, a way of sneaking the Christ of faith in the backdoor of research on the historical Jesus and the Law. Any historian investigating in depth the life, thought, and impact of Immanuel Kant, Karl Marx, Sigmund Freud, Bertrand Russell, or Andy Warhol must struggle to understand and evaluate the values the person espoused and the values the person lived by (the two are not always the same). A historian need not share the subject's philosophical or religious worldview in order to understand it intellectually and grapple with it existentially. Hence, to sidestep the question of human truth and values in the case of the historical Jesus simply because he is a pivotal religious figure betokens a curious conception of what history is and what it can contribute to the project of being fully human.

What the response of each investigator to Jesus' Torah-teaching might or should be is not for me to say. Rather, what I am saying is that anyone doing research into Jesus' teaching on the Law, by the sheer nature of the material treated, is inevitably faced with questions of value and meaning on both a personal and a societal level. It strikes me as odd that some authors who trumpet the supposed relevance of Jesus as social critic or political force ignore the question of relevance and truth when it comes to some of the best-attested items in the inventory of Jesus' moral directives. Dodging such items is the opposite of being relevant. I would argue instead that it is precisely because Jesus' legal/moral teachings often strike us as off-putting, alien, or utopian that they are so relevant. For the moral person, believer or agnostic, nothing can be more relevant or useful to the examined life than a challenge posed by a moral vision diametrically opposed to one's own. Indeed, if we find Jesus' total rejection of divorce or oaths bizarre or unworkable, we might at least take comfort in the thought that most of his contemporaries probably felt the same way. In offending most moral people now as then, Jesus (whether one believes in him or not) remains relevant by simply saying no—no to values and actions that most moderns take for granted and would defend as moral and necessary. There is a value simply in being forced to rethink what we have always taken for granted. Besides, if we feel put off by the quirky, contrarian teachings of Jesus on the Law, at least that response serves as a fair guarantee that we are not merely projecting our moral agenda onto a blank screen called Jesus.

3. This leads to a third insight, one that cuts through a great deal of inherited rhetoric about the historical Jesus. From the time of Enlightenment thinkers in general and Thomas Jefferson in particular up to various forms of liberal theology in the 20th century, a common approach to Jesus has been to extol the pure moral voice of the historical figure while lamenting

the supposed dogmatic distortions introduced into his portrait as early as the Four Gospels. In the parade example of this approach, Jefferson quite literally adopted the scissors-and-paste method, cutting up the pages of a New Testament, excising the miracle stories, and pasting together the mostly ethical passages that he deemed to be the genuine teaching of Jesus.[1] As in certain other matters, Jefferson was wrong on more than one count. Apart from the fact that, as we have seen in Volume Two of *A Marginal Jew*, the claim and belief that Jesus worked miracles goes back to Jesus himself (whatever one makes of that claim),[2] the moral teachings in the Gospels that most likely come from the historical Jesus are not necessarily the ones that enlightened people today would care to hail and adopt. One need only think of Jesus' total prohibition of divorce and all oaths. Worse still, the positive form of the Golden Rule, to which many Enlightenment types would naturally gravitate because of its pagan origin and a-theistic content, was probably never taught by the historical Jesus.

Even seeking refuge in the double command of love raises problems for the enlightened—if one insists on appealing to the historical Jesus. As we have seen, there is no reason to think that, when Jesus cited Lev 19:18b, "you shall love your neighbor as yourself," he meant anything other than what the Hebrew text means by *rēaʿ*, namely, a fellow Israelite who belongs to the social and cultic community that worships Yahweh alone as the one true God (as proclaimed in Deut 6:4–5). Judged from the standpoint of today's openness to world religions and to a globalized community of inherently equal human beings, the historical Jesus who teaches the double command of love may appear distressingly provincial. The Jesus of the Four Gospels, whose double command of love is naturally interpreted in light of Luke's parable of the Good Samaritan (Luke 10:25–37) and Matthew's scene of a final judgment based on good works done to the marginalized (Matt 25:31–46), suddenly seems more palatable. In the end, a rigorous quest for the Torah-teaching of the historical Jesus renders the Enlightenment program of surgically extracting Jesus the ethicist from the redactional overlay of the Gospels untenable. Some might think this a negative insight. I consider it a positive gain. If we wish to extol the moral teaching of Jesus, we should at least have a clear-eyed vision of what it is.

II. NEGATIVE (OR INVERSE) INSIGHTS

The positive insights previously listed are not the sole upshot of our trek through Volume Four. We must be honest: after a lengthy struggle with the halakic material in the Gospels, and despite the positive insights we

VOLUME FOUR: LAW AND LOVE

have gained, we are still left with a certain sense of frustration. The enigma remains. The question of Jesus and the Law refuses to be answered by one neat solution with no loose ends. Trying to understand why this is so may yield, in a backhanded sort of way, some insights as well.

1. When I reflect on why the quest for the halakic Jesus remains difficult and elusive, I am reminded of the title of a book by John Dominic Crossan, *In Fragments*.[3] In a nutshell, the fragmentary nature of our knowledge about Jesus' legal positions creates a special problem for Jesus research. Compared with the information we have about Jesus' basic proclamation of the kingdom of God, his healing activity, or his teaching on discipleship, the legal material that can be reasonably traced back to the historical Jesus is distressingly sparse and scattered. Personally, I cannot help thinking that, during his two-to-three-year ministry, Jesus engaged in many more halakic discussions with companions or competitors. We must allow for the possibility that a fair amount of Jesus' *hălākôt* have been lost to history. One reason for this loss may be summed up in the watchword of traditional German form criticism: *Sitz im Leben* (setting in life). The early Christian movement naturally selected and passed on those teachings of Jesus that it found particularly useful in spreading its message and winning converts. Especially as it moved out into the larger Gentile world, some of Jesus' inner-Jewish debates may have struck audiences as irrelevant or even unintelligible.

Indeed, in place of Jesus' own Torah-teachings, the problem of a Jewish movement reaching out to a Gentile constituency created a need for new halakic decisions never covered by Jesus' instructions. It is to the exigencies of this different legal situation, with its crying need for moral catechesis suited to uncircumcised Gentile Christians, that we probably owe such legal/moral sayings as the revocation of food laws in Mark 7:15 (secondarily attributed to Jesus) as well as the positive form of the Golden Rule (which was widespread in popular pagan philosophy). Thus, it may be—I am engaging here in conjecture—that some of the concrete halakic pronouncements of the historical Jesus may have fallen by the wayside, making room for directives more relevant to Gentiles who had joined a largely Jewish movement and who needed a Gentile-Christian moral compass. In a sense, the Four Gospels present us with four different attempts at this hermeneutical rethinking of Jesus' *hălākâ* in the late 1st century. Perhaps, granted the partial transformation of a Galilean rabbi into a Gentile guru, we should be grateful that a fair amount of fragments of *hălākâ* from the historical Jesus were preserved. The mainstream Christian movement was thus kept from the full-blown Marcionite or Gnostic option, with its denigration and rejection of Christianity's Jewish heritage. Even apart from any faith commitment, historians must be grateful for this turn of events. Without the preservation of that Jewish heritage, any reconstruction of the historical Jesus would be nigh impossible.

2. The fragmentary nature of the legal teachings of the historical Jesus that have come down to us suggest a further important but negative insight. In Jesus' *hǎlākâ* (as far as we can know it), one cannot discern any moral or legal "system" containing some organizing principle or center that makes sense of the whole. Some scholars might object that the double command of love does function in effect as a sort of principle, center, or basis for Jesus' moral teachings. But that is to fall into the trap of reading Mark through the lens of Matthew. It is Matthew, not Mark, who binds the first and second commandments closer together (the second is "like" the first) and declares that "the whole Law and the prophets hang on [depend on, can be deduced from, or are summed up in] these two commandments" (Matt 22:39–40).

Even in Matthew, though, the drive to systematize morality, clear as it is in some passages (e.g., the six antitheses in Matt 5:20–48), never really arrives at any coherent moral "system." A Matthew who can state in 7:12 that the Golden Rule (an originally pagan precept that has no theistic content or basis) is the Law and the prophets and then state in 22:40 that the whole Law and the prophets depend on love of God (Deut 6:4–5) and love of neighbor (Lev 19:18b), a Matthew who can speak of Jesus fulfilling the Law and the prophets (5:17) and in the next breath can present Jesus announcing the prohibition of both divorce and all oath-taking, a Matthew who can make love of enemies the high point of the Sermon on the Mount (5:48) and then construct seven vitriolic woes that caricature and denounce "the scribes and the Pharisees" as hypocrites and murderers (23:13–36) is a Matthew who is reaching toward but has not succeeded in forging a coherent system of Christian morality. We may give him credit for being the first Christian theologian to attempt such a synthesis. What we may not do is project his attempt on to the historical Jesus, who in his legal pronouncements shows no such concern for system-building. We should always remember that in Mark 12:29–31, as opposed to Matthew's reworked version, Jesus simply states that love of God is the first commandment, that love of neighbor is the second, and that no other commandment is greater than these. That is all. Presumably, the fact that there is a first and a second commandment implies that there is a third, fourth, fifth, and so on. Jesus, however, shows no interest in spelling out any such "hierarchy of values."

3. Indeed, if we turn from Jesus' double command of love to the other halakic teachings that we have analyzed in this volume, we are hard pressed

to discern any precise logical link between these individual *hălākôt* and the double command of love. To take a few examples:

(a) Even Jesus' other love command, that is, "love your enemies," has no discernible link to the double command. Jesus certainly makes no such connection, and in itself "love your enemies" has no theistic basis or content. Pagan philosophers urge equivalent forms of the command, and one could imagine an agnostic ethicist espousing the command on pragmatic or humanistic grounds.

(b) As for the prohibition of oaths, Jesus does give his reason for the prohibition, but the reason is not love. Rather, the reason (as distilled from Matt 5:34–37 ‖ Jas 5:12) is the majestic transcendence of the all-truthful God, who is not to be dragged into court as a witness to the sometimes truthful statements of mere humans.

(c) When it comes to divorce, the casuistic form of the prohibition (e.g., Luke 16:18) gives no specific reason for the prohibition beyond Jesus' blunt affirmation that divorce and remarriage constitute adultery. The apodictic command (Mark 10:9) gives a directly theistic basis to the prohibition (God has joined the two together), but does not spell out any detailed rationale for the prohibition. If we were to suppose that the reasoning recounted in Mark 10:2–8 derives from the historical Jesus, then the reason for his prohibition is not love but apocalyptic eschatology (or, as some would prefer to call it, restoration eschatology). The Marcan Jesus argues in vv 2–8 that the good, wholesome order of marriage ordained by God at the creation (Genesis 1–2) and then attenuated by divorce (Deut 24:1–4) in view of men's "hardness of heart" is now being restored in the end-time.

Interestingly, theologians sometimes invoke Jesus' love commands to explain the prohibition of divorce, arguing that Jesus' radical demand for unrestricted love, love not only for neighbors but even for enemies, requires a total and permanent love between husband and wife that necessarily precludes divorce. Others instead would see in Jesus' prohibition of divorce his concern for the relative powerlessness of ordinary Palestinian-Jewish women in the face of their husbands' almost unlimited power to compel or refuse a divorce. To be sure, I do not deny the importance of these considerations when constructing a Christian moral theology. The seeds of these ideas may well be present in the Gospels. But nothing in the material that can be attributed to the historical Jesus speaks of such concerns. His prohibition of divorce shows no connection with any of his love commands.

(d) The same must be said of Jesus' various sayings on the sabbath. While there is a "humanistic" ring to Jesus' dictum, "the sabbath was made for human beings and not human beings for the sabbath" (Mark 2:27), the implicit argument, as we have seen, is again based on the creation story in

Genesis. When it comes to Jesus' statements on the permissibility of aiding (specifically, healing) humans on the sabbath, the underlying argument is a type of "a fortiori" or "a minori ad maius" logic. That is, it is the sort of reasoning from the lesser case to the greater case (or vice versa) that the later rabbis would call *qal wāḥômer* ("light and heavy").[4] By this logic, if one is allowed to perform such-and-such a work on the sabbath, then all the more should one be allowed to perform another, more pressing work. From our hermeneutical vantage point, we may indeed discern a loving concern for humans in need underlying Jesus' teaching on sabbath observance, but Jesus himself makes no such appeal to a love command to justify his views.

In sum, the historical Jesus never directly connects his individual halakic pronouncements to some basic or organizing principle of love. Surprisingly, this lack of an explicit rationale for his positions extends even to the citation of Scripture. The historical Jesus rarely, if ever, directly quotes Scripture passages as the basis or rationale of his moral teaching. In the double command of love, Deut 6:4–5 and Lev 19:18b constitute the very content of the command, not the basis or rationale on which the command rests or from which it flows. Elsewhere, Jesus alludes at times to Scripture passages, but does not usually quote them explicitly in his halakic argumentation.[5]

4. In the end, we are forced back to an insight that is naturally unwelcome to the Christian desire to systematize, namely, the ad hoc and unexplained quality of Jesus' various pronouncements on legal/moral questions. Throughout this volume, we have noticed the implicit tone of "it's so because I say it's so."[6] As we have often seen in the four volumes of *A Marginal Jew*, Jesus was, if nothing else, a charismatic religious leader, specifically a charismatic prophet. If we use the term "charismatic" in its proper sociological sense—as opposed to the popular American sense of a flashy but hollow entertainer who is simply the creation of publicists and the media—it is the very nature of a charismatic religious leader to claim to derive his or her authority not from traditional channels (e.g., law, custom, ordination, election, hereditary succession, seniority, lengthy study and experience) but rather directly from God.[7] The religious charismatic intuitively knows God's will both in general and in particular, and that is sufficient reason for the charismatic's pronouncements and commands. The striking—indeed at his time unparalleled—formula that Jesus used to introduce various pronouncements, "Amen I say to you," sums up this claim of the charismatic leader and (more specifically in Jesus' case) the eschatological prophet.[8] Obviously, such a claim would not endear the charismatic to the acknowledged religious authorities, whether priestly or scribal.[9]

It may be, then, that the only explanation for Jesus' varied statements on the Law is the very general one of the charismatic authority that he attributed to himself as the prophet sent to Israel in the end-time.[10] Perhaps we might push this insight a step further: Jesus' self-presentation to Israel as the *Elijah-like* prophet of the end-time may help elucidate why he dares to appropriate to himself the authority to make startling decisions about the Law, with no priestly status or formal scribal training on which to base his authority. If we glance forward to the Mishna and Tosepta, we see an increasing expectation in Judaism that, when Elijah returned, he would explain obscure passages in the Torah, settle legal disputes among the rabbis, and/or resolve questions of legal ownership (see, e.g., *m. ʿEd.* 8:7 [cf. *t. ʿEd.* 3:4] ; *m. B. Meṣ.* 1:8; 2:8; 3:4–5; *m. Šeqal.* 2:5; *m. Soṭah* 9:15).[11]

Intriguingly, an earlier form of this hope that a future prophet would resolve halakic problems is reflected in 1 Maccabees. In 1 Macc 4:46, Judas Maccabeus and his colleagues decide to dismantle the stones of the altar of holocaust that had been defiled by the Gentiles and to build a new altar with fresh, uncut stones. Since they lacked any legal directive or precedent as to how they should treat the defiled stones, "they stored the stones on the temple mount in a proper place until a prophet should come to deliver a [divine] response [to the question of what to do] with the stones." [12] Similarly, in 1 Macc 14:41, when the newly liberated Judeans and their priests had to face the question of how they were to be ruled in their semiautonomous state (under the suzerainty of the Syrian King Demetrius), they agreed to accept the Hasmonean general Simon as "[political and military] leader and high priest in perpetuity until there should arise a trustworthy prophet." [13]

Thus, in 1 Maccabees, unresolved legal questions ranging from cultic purity and temple apparatus to the proper governance of the people by a civil ruler who is also the high priest are expected to be settled by some future prophet whose coming is awaited by the faithful. By the time of the Mishna, this vague hope of a future prophet who would resolve halakic issues had received more precise contours in the figure of the eschatological Elijah. If such a hope already existed in the early 1st century A.D., it could help explain how Jesus' pronouncements on the Torah fit into his larger understanding of himself as the Elijah-like prophet of the end-time. Admittedly, though, this suggestion must remain a conjecture, since we lack hard evidence for the idea of Elijah-as-Torah-interpreter in pre-70 Judaism. The Dead Sea Scrolls do not supply the "missing link." [14]

Still, even without such evidence, the resounding conclusion of the OT collection of the minor prophets (the Scroll of the Twelve) may have provided a sufficient catalyst for Jesus' combination of his role as eschatological Elijah with his role as interpreter of Torah. While this suggestion must remain very tentative, the famous prophecy of Malachi (Mal 3:22–24 in the MT, Mal 4:4–6 in some English translations) about Elijah's coming—a prophecy that already puts back to back Moses as mediator of Law and Elijah as end-time prophetic preacher of conversion to Israel—may have supplied Jesus with the spiritual impulse to combine the two roles.[15] In this key prophetic text, after speaking of "the day when I act" (i.e., the day of judgment against the wicked), Yahweh delivers his final admonition: "Remember the Torah of Moses my servant, which I commanded him at Horeb, statutes and ordinances for all Israel" (Mal 3:22 in the MT).[16] Then follows the famous prophecy of v 23: "Behold I am sending you Elijah the prophet before the day of Yahweh, the great and terrible [day]." Verse 24 then ends this admonition-plus-prophecy—as well as the whole Book of Malachi and the larger Scroll of the Twelve—with a description of Elijah's eschatological function: "to turn the hearts of fathers toward [their] sons and the hearts of sons toward their fathers, lest I come and strike the land with total destruction."[17]

The concatenation of themes in this passage is striking: (i) the prophet issues a call to remember and obey the Torah of Moses; (ii) this call is issued in view of the coming of the prophet Elijah; (iii) Elijah is to return to Israel prior to the yôm yahweh, the day of the Lord, that is, Yahweh's final appearance to judge and save; (iv) Elijah will come precisely to ensure that a reconciled and united Israel will experience this yôm yahweh as a day of restoration and not of doom. Even without the explicit rabbinic teaching on Elijah as interpreter of Torah, this admonition-plus-prophecy, perched as it is at the end of Malachi and thus at the end of the whole collection of the twelve minor prophets, probably serves as a sufficient seedbed for Jesus' fusing of the functions of eschatological prophet and teacher of Torah in his own person.[18] This is all conjecture, to be sure; but it is a conjecture that fits well with the overall picture of the Jewish prophet-plus-teacher that has emerged from these four volumes of A Marginal Jew.

5. Granted this fusion of Law and eschatology in Jesus' message, one might refer, in a very vague and general sense, to Jesus' teaching on Torah as "eschatological morality" or "kingdom ethics," that is, the life that conforms to the coming of God's kingdom in the end time. However, while such terminology is popular among scholars, two caveats are in order: (i) Jesus does not explicitly ground any of his legal pronouncements in the presence or the coming of the kingdom of God. In the halakic commands of Jesus that we have judged authentic, the terminology of "kingdom" is noticeably absent. (ii) Even if we speak (though Jesus does not) of "kingdom ethics," we should remember that this is not the same thing as Albert Schweitzer's famous idea of the "interim ethic" supposedly taught by Jesus. Portraying Jesus as an apocalyptic fanatic, Schweitzer explained Jesus' radically stringent moral demands in terms of his apocalyptic expectation that only a very short time remained before the kingdom of God fully arrived.[19]

In my opinion, Schweitzer's conception of an interim ethic does not do justice to the already/not-yet structure of Jesus' preaching and ministry. Granted Jesus' paradoxical proclamation of a kingdom both present and yet coming fully in the future, the disciples are not being told simply to screw up their courage, clench their teeth and fists, and observe an extreme ethic for a brief period while they await the kingdom's complete arrival in the very near future (as Schweitzer would have it). Rather, in Jesus' view of things, the halakic life he demands of his disciples is one that already is made possible by and responds to the power of God's rule, present in the Jesus' preaching and actions. Thus, Jesus' legal commands express the proper eschatological implementation of God's will as expressed in Torah—an eschatological implementation that is meant not just for a short, sui generis interval but for the whole future of Israel as God's people, restored in the end time. All this, I readily admit, is my own way of putting together the pieces of the puzzle. But it is the most satisfying explanation I can find of how Jesus the eschatological prophet-like-Elijah meshes with Jesus the demanding teacher of Torah. The enigma is illuminated and yet remains.

Having wrestled with and gained some insight into the enigma of Jesus' teaching on Torah, we must turn out attention in the next volume of *A Marginal Jew* to the three outstanding enigmas: the riddle-speech of Jesus' parables, the riddle-speech of his self-designations, and the final riddle of his death. Like the first, these three enigmas will yield some insights while retaining something of their mystery.

NOTES TO CONCLUSION

[1] On Jefferson's project, see *A Marginal Jew*, 2. 632 n. 2. One is not surprised that the titles of his two attempts at presenting an Enlightenment Jesus are entitled *The Philosophy of Jesus* and *The Life and Morals of Jesus of Nazareth*.

[2] See *A Marginal Jew*, 2. 617–45.

[3] John Dominic Crossan, *In Fragments. The Aphorisms of Jesus* (San Francisco: Harper & Row, 1983).

[4] On the terminology and the concept of *qal wāḥômer*, see Strack and Stemberger, *Introduction to the Talmud and Midrash*, 18.

[5] One might point to Mark 10:2–8 as an exception. But here (a) it is debatable whether the scriptural argument comes in fact from the historical Jesus, and (b) the Pharisees are the ones who initiate the legal question of divorce, thus implicitly pro-

posing Deut 24:1–4 for discussion. In the "dogmatic" rather than "moral" question of the general resurrection of the dead (Mark 12:18–27 parr.), Jesus indeed argues from a pentateuchal text (Exod 3:6,15), but only after the Sadducees cite another pentateuchal text (Deut 25:5–6) as a reason for denying the resurrection of the dead. When I state that the historical Jesus did not regularly quote Scripture in his halakic arguments, I omit from consideration those Gospel sayings or narratives that I judge not to have come from the historical Jesus: e.g., the dispute about plucking grain on the sabbath in Mark 2:23–26 (which in any case does not contain a direct citation of Scripture) and Matthew's redactional insertion of Hos 6:6 into the plucking-of-the-grain dispute (Matt 12:7).

[6] On the implicit claim to authority contained in Jesus' gnomic sayings about legal issues, see Henderson, *Jesus, Rhetoric and Law*, 401–6.

[7] Here I echo a basic insight of Max Weber, expressed in a number of his writings but conveniently summarized in his *The Theory of Social and Economic Organization* (New York: Oxford University, 1947). Weber famously distinguishes three types of legitimate authority according to each one's basis or origin: rational, traditional, and charismatic. (In the main text, I conflate the first two, for the sake of economy, into "traditional channels.") Weber defines charismatic authority as follows (pp. 358–59): "The term 'charisma' will be applied to a certain quality of an individual personality by virtue of which he is set apart from ordinary men and treated as endowed with supernatural, superhuman, or at least specifically exceptional powers or qualities. These are such as are not accessible to the ordinary person, but are regarded as of divine origin or as exemplary, and on the basis of them the individual concerned is treated as a leader. . . . What is alone important is how the individual is actually regarded by those subject to charismatic authority, by his 'followers' or 'disciples.' . . . It is recognition on the part of those subject to authority which is decisive for the validity of charisma." (For the German original, see *Wirtschaft und Gesellschaft. Grundriss der verstehenden Soziologie* [5th ed.; Tübingen: Mohr (Siebeck), 1972; 1st ed., 1921] 124, 140. It should be noted that the English translation used here is only part one of the German work.) Weber's analysis of the charismatic has been both widely disputed and extensively developed in subsequent research. For example, in the United States, where business, politics, and religion often intersect, social scientists have applied the category of the charismatic to successful business leaders. Of the vast literature in the field, one specimen may serve: Jay A. Conger, *The Charismatic Leader. Behind the Mystique of Exceptional Leadership* (San Francisco/London: Jossey-Bass, 1989). Conger helpfully notes that, by definition, the charismatic leader is a person out of the ordinary, someone who does not fit regular categories. Here lies the reason why even sociologists have difficulty offering an exact definition of what constitutes a charismatic person. While Conger intentionally focuses on secular leaders in the American business community, some of the traits he isolates find intriguing analogies in charismatic religious leaders like Jesus. For instance, according to Conger, the charismatic leader is dissatisfied with the status quo, sees the need for speedy and significant changes, formulates a vision

of a different and better future as well as the way to achieve that future, and uses powerful rhetorical skills (especially metaphors, analogies, and stories) to communicate his vision and win over followers. The charismatic leader knows how to use different kinds of language for different audiences; the audiences in turn come to trust the leader as someone who knows more than they do. His followers become personally committed to him, feeling that they share his vision and will share in his success when his vision is realized. Conger rightly stresses an important sociological insight: charisma is a social reality presupposing a dynamic relationship between a leader and the group who accepts his leadership. To put the point in religious terms, there can be no charismatic hermit, if the hermit strictly avoids all communication with other humans. The hermit may be an extremely holy person, perhaps a miracle worker, but, without social interaction with followers, he cannot be a charismatic leader. Naturally, one key element missing in Conger's secular model is empowerment or inspiration coming directly from God apart from rational or legal channels; that is the insight Weber in particular has emphasized. Sociological presentations similar to Conger's can be found in any number of recent works. See, e.g., Michael D. Mumford et al., *Pathways to Outstanding Leadership* (Mahwah, NJ/London: Erlbaum, 2006). Mumford (p. 6) highlights those personal attributes of the charismatic leader that help magnify the impact of the vision that the leader articulates: apparent self-sacrifice, manifest confidence, interpersonal attractiveness, and communication skills. The leader draws followers to himself because the followers receive from him a sense of personal meaning and group identity as well as shared emotional experiences and a shared future evoked by the leader's powerful use of images. My purpose in mentioning these sociological studies is not to adopt a particular school of sociological thought or to defend one detailed definition of the charismatic leader, but simply to indicate that my remarks on Jesus as charismatic leader in the main text draw on widely held views among sociologists. For a classic example of the application of the category of the charismatic leader to Jesus, see Martin Hengel, *The Charismatic Leader and His Followers* (New York: Crossroad, 1981); the German original is *Nachfolge und Charisma* (BZNW 34; Berlin: Töpelmann, 1968).

[8] On "Amen," see *A Marginal Jew*, 2. 306, 367 n. 62, and 370 n. 67.

[9] Needless to say, in this clash of the religious charismatic with traditional religious authority, Jesus is hardly unique in human history. To take just two examples from the Catholic tradition, both Francis of Assisi and Girolamo Savonarola were prominent charismatic leaders of the medieval period who ran into difficulty with established authorities. As their two cases show, tensions between charism and traditional authority may be resolved in different ways at different times.

[10] One point cannot be stressed too much in this suggestion: I am asking about the immediate source or locus of Jesus' personal authority as he presumes to interpret the Torah. In no way does the claimed source of his special charismatic authority negate for him the authority of the Mosaic Law as coming from God. The very fact that Jesus undertakes to use his charismatic authority to interpret the Torah indi-

cates that he does not understand his charisma as simply denying or obliterating the traditional authority of the Torah.

[11] See Joshua Gutmann et al., "Elijah," *Encyclopaedia Judaica* (22 vols.; Detroit/ New York: Thomson Gale, 2007) 6. 331–37; Karin Hedner-Zetterholm, "Elijah and the Messiah as Spokesmen of Rabbinic Ideology," *The Messiah in Early Judaism and Christianity* (ed. Magnus Zetterholm; Minneapolis: Fortress, 2007) 57–78. One should note that already in *m. 'Ed.* 8:7 the precise nature of the halakic role of Elijah in the end time is debated, with different rabbis having different conceptions of that role.

[12] On this passage, see Jonathan A. Goldstein, *I Maccabees* (AYB 41; Garden City, NY: Doubleday, 1976; reprint New Haven: Yale University Press) 285. Goldstein offers a rationale for Judas' decision that reflects later rabbinic argumentation, but any such reasoning is notably absent from the text of 1 Macc 4:44–46.

[13] On this text, see Goldstein, *I Maccabees*, 507–8. As Goldstein notes, "in perpetuity" signifies that Simon's heirs are to inherit the double office after him.

[14] Some scholars might object that we can in fact find the missing link between OT texts that mention a future prophet and rabbinic statements about Elijah as the eschatological interpreter of the Law. The missing link, they would contend, is supplied by the references to an eschatological prophet in the Dead Sea Scrolls. However, texts in the scrolls that speak explicitly of such a prophet are both rare and vague. The most famous one is found in 1QS 9:11 (the *Rule of the Community*), which speaks of the community's careful teaching and observance of the Torah "until there come a prophet and the anointed ones [or: 'messiahs'] of Aaron and Israel." Even this text, which is the clearest reference to the coming of a prophet in messianic times, is problematic, since the fragmentary text E of the *Rule of the Community* from Cave 4 (4Q259, column 3) lacks these words, either because a later editor deleted the three eschatological figures or because an earlier form of the *Rule of the Community* lacked the reference. On this problem, see James H. Charlesworth et al. (eds.), *The Dead Sea Scrolls. Volume 1. Rule of the Community and Related Documents* (Tübingen: Mohr [Siebeck]; Louisville: Westminster/John Knox, 1994) 41 n. 227 and 89 n. 26. Our next best hope is the *Testimonia* from Cave 4 (4Q175), which is made up of a catena of Scripture texts without any explanation of their meaning or relationship. Included in this *Testimonia* are three texts that follow one another in this order: Deut 18:18–19 (Moses' prophecy that God will raise up for the people a prophet like Moses and that the people are to obey the prophet's words), Num 24:15–17 (Balaam's prophecy about a star from Jacob and a scepter from Israel), and Deut 33:8–11 (Moses' blessing of the faithful priest Levi). Some commentators see here the scriptural basis for the three figures mentioned in 1QS 9:11, though not all agree. In any case, we must admit that neither in the *Rule of the Community* nor in the *Testimonia* is the (or an) eschatological prophet identified as the (or an) interpreter of the Law in the end-time, much less as Elijah. Some have

tried to make this identification more cogent by appealing to CD 6:10–11, which speaks of the eschatological time "when there arises one who teaches righteousness at the end of the days." Whether this person is the original founder of the Qumran community (the Teacher of Righteousness) come back from the dead or an eschatological teacher in the likeness of the original Teacher of Righteousness is unclear. In any case, the text does not explicitly identify him either with the figure of the eschatological prophet mentioned in 1 QS 9:11 or specifically with the prophet Elijah, although various commentators have made the identification. While Adam S. van der Woude (*Die messianischen Vorstellungen der Gemeinde von Qumrân* [Studia semitica neerlandica 3; Assen: van Gorcum, 1957] 55) supports this identification and John J. Collins (*The Scepter and the Star* [AYBRL; New York: Doubleday, 1995; reprint New Haven: Yale University Press] 113–14) thinks it attractive though not certain, I remain doubtful. The case would be strengthened if the future person who teaches righteousness could be identified with the "interpreter of Torah" mentioned in CD 7:18–19, who is seen as the "star from Jacob." The interpreter of the Law is also mentioned in the scriptural collection called *4Q Florilegium* (4Q174, fragment 1, column 1, line 11), in connection with another figure, the "branch of David." In these two texts, the interpreter of the Law may be the priestly Messiah of Aaron. Such an identification is by no means certain, but it is more likely than an identification with the eschatological prophet. All in all, I do not see anywhere in the Dead Sea Scrolls a clear reference to an eschatological prophet (or, more specifically, Elijah) who will have as one of his major functions the interpretation of the Law in the last days. In the end, even apart from the function of eschatological interpretation of the Law, one must agree with Collins (ibid., 75) that "the eschatological prophet is an elusive figure in the Qumran scrolls." Very rare, likewise, is any explicit reference (outside the biblical scrolls) to the prophet Elijah. One clear attestation is found in a very fragmentary Aramaic text, 4Q558, line 4: "therefore I shall send you Elijah before. . . ." This sentence may be nothing more than a citation of Mal 3:23 in Aramaic; in any event, contrary to some scholarly claims, nothing in this fragment indicates that Elijah will be the precursor of the Messiah. On the problem of the eschatological prophet and Elijah at Qumran, see also Geza Vermes, *The Complete Dead Sea Scrolls in English* (New York: Penguin, 1997) 86–87; Julio Trebolle Barrera, "Elijah," *Encyclopedia of the Dead Sea Scrolls* (ed. Lawrence H. Schiffman and James C. VanderKam; 2 vols.; Oxford/New York: Oxford University, 2000) 246; Joseph A. Fitzmyer, *The One Who Is to Come* (Grand Rapids, MI/Cambridge, UK: Eerdmans, 2007) 8–115; Al Wolters, "The Messiah in the Qumran Documents," *The Messiah in the Old and New Testaments* (ed. Stanley E. Porter; Grand Rapids, MI/Cambridge, UK: Eerdmans, 2007) 75–89. I touch only lightly here on this vast problem because the question of whether various "messianic" titles and/or functions were attributed to the historical Jesus will be taken up in a later volume.

[15] It may be that two different editorial hands added v 22 and vv 23–24 respectively. In any case, Jews at the time of Jesus would have read the text of Malachi as a whole, without our modern concern for tradition and redaction. For a sample of different opinions on critical questions concerning vv 22–24, see David L. Petersen,

Zechariah 9–14 and Malachi (Louisville: Westminster/John Knox, 1995) 227–33; Andrew E. Hill, *Malachi* (AYB 25D; New York: Doubleday, 1998; reprint New Haven: Yale University Press) 363–90, esp. 363–66. Petersen (p. 227) calls 3:22–24 an "Epilogue," while Hill (p. 365) refers to two appendixes. On later attempts to re-order the text in ancient manuscripts and translations, see Hill, ibid., 366. That the original Hebrew text of Mal 3:22–24 is faithfully preserved in our MT is confirmed by the fragments of Malachi found in Cave 4 at Qumran. For the text of column 4 of manuscript 4QXII[a], which contains (with lacunae) Mal 3:14–24, see Eugene Ulrich et al. (eds.), *Qumran Cave 4. X. The Prophets* (DJD 15; Oxford: Clarendon, 1997) 228–29. In the Qumran text of Mal 3:22–24 preserved in column 4, the only deviation from the MT (as far as we can tell, given the lacunae) is the use of the more common Hebrew spelling of the name Elijah, *'ēliyyāhû*, instead of the rarer form *'ēliyyâ*, which seems to be the original form used in Mal 3:23. Column 4 confirms the MT order of vv 22–24, without the inversion of verses found in the LXX (where v 22 of the MT is transposed to the end of the book) and without the later repetition of v 23 after v 24, an addition enjoined by the rabbis in public recitation in order to avoid having the Book of Malachi and the whole collection of the twelve minor prophets end with the negative, threatening tone of v 24.

[16] Hill (*Malachi*, 370) thinks that "the Law of Moses" is best understood here as a reference to the whole of the Pentateuch. On the problem of the meaning of *tôrâ* in Malachi, see Alwin Renker, *Die Tora bei Maleachi* (Freiburger Theologische Studien; Freiburg/Basel/Vienna: Herder, 1979); see esp. 98–101. In any event, it seems likely that a Jew in Jesus' day would naturally take "the Law of Moses" in Mal 3:22 to refer to the Pentateuch.

[17] Commentators differ on whether "fathers" and "sons" refers to faithful ancestors versus their unfaithful descendants in Malachi's day (so Hill, *Malachi*, 387–88) or to the parents and children of Malachi's day (so Beth Glazier-McDonald, *Malachi the Divine Messenger* [SBLDS 98; Atlanta: Scholars, 1987] 254–55). In either case, the overall reference is to a restored, reconciled Israel.

[18] Hill (*Malachi*, 365) thinks that the final editor of the Book of Malachi purposely draws together the two "ideal figures" of Moses and Elijah as the personifications of the Hebrew legal and prophetic traditions, linking the two basic theological building blocks of the Jewish Scriptures. I do not go into Ben Sira's reference in Sir 48:10 to the Elijah-prophecy of Mal 3:23–24 because it adds nothing new for our purposes. Indeed, the reference to the Torah of Moses in Mal 3:22 is absent, though the Moses-like theophany at Horeb/Sinai is mentioned (Sir 48:7).

[19] Albert Schweitzer, *Geschichte der Leben–Jesu–Forschung* (2 vols.; Munich/Hamburg: Siebenstern Taschenbuch, 1966; 1st ed., 1906) 2. 204–50. For a brief description of Schweitzer's idea, see "Interim Ethic," *The Westminster Dictionary of Christian Ethics* (ed. James F. Childress and John Macquarrie; Philadelphia: Westminster, 1986) 307.

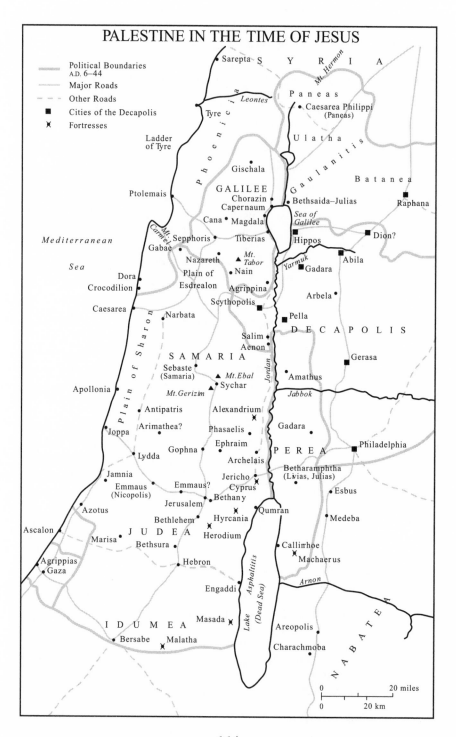

PALESTINE IN THE TIME OF JESUS

Political Boundaries
A.D. 6–44

Major Roads

Other Roads

■ Cities of the Decapolis

✗ Fortresses

Sarepta

S Y R I A

Mt. Hermon

Leontes

P h o e n i c i a

Paneas

Caesarea Philippi
(Paneas)

Tyre

Ladder
of Tyre

U l a t h a

Gischala

G a u l a n i t i s

B a t a n e a

GALILEE

Ptolemais

Chorazin
Capernaum

Bethsaida–Julias

Raphana

Cana

Magdala

Sea of
Galilee

Mediterranean

Mt. Carmel

Sepphoris

Tiberias

Hippos

Dion?

Gabae

Nazareth

Mt.
Tabor

Abila

Dora

Crocodilion

Plain of
Esdrealon

Nain

Sea

Agrippina

Gadara

Caesarea

Narbata

Scythopolis

Arbela

Pella

D E C A P O L I S

P l a i n   o f   S h a r o n

Salim
Aenon

S A M A R I A

Sebaste
(Samaria)

Mt. Ebal

Sychar

Amathus

Gerasa

Apollonia

Mt. Gerizim

Jabbok

J o r d a n

Antipatris

Alexandrium

Joppa

Arimathea?

Phasaelis

Gadara

Lydda

Gophna

Ephraim

P E R E A

Philadelphia

Archelais

Jamnia

Emmaus?

Betharamphtha
(Livias, Julias)

Emmaus
(Nicopolis)

Jericho
Cyprus

Esbus

Azotus

Bethany

Jerusalem

Qumran

Medeba

Ascalon

Bethlehem

Hyrcania

Marisa

J U D E A

Herodium

Callirhoe

Agrippias
Gaza

Bethsura

Hebron

Machaerus

Engaddi

Lake
Asphaltitis
(Dead Sea)

Arnon

I D U M E A

Masada

Areopolis

N A B A T E A

Bersabe

Malatha

Charachmoba

0   20 miles

0   20 km

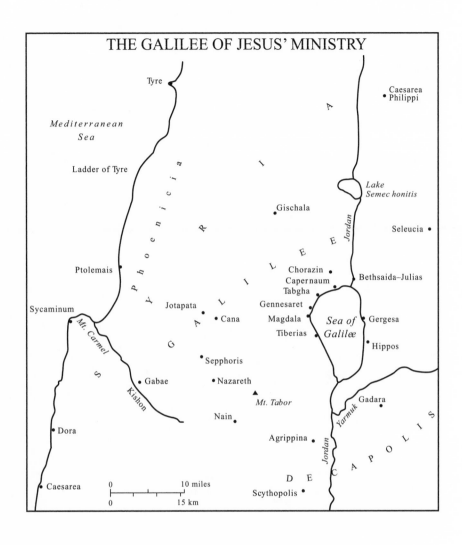

THE GALILEE OF JESUS' MINISTRY

Mediterranean Sea

Tyre

Caesarea Philippi

Ladder of Tyre

Lake *Semechonitis*

Gischala

Seleucia

Ptolemais

Chorazin
Capernaum
Tabgha
Gennesaret

Bethsaida–Julias

Sycaminum

Jotapata

Cana

Magdala

Tiberias

Gergesa

Sea of Galilee

Hippos

Sepphoris

Gabae

Nazareth

Mt. Tabor

Nain

Dora

Agrippina

Gadara

Caesarea

0   10 miles

0   15 km

Scythopolis

Phoenicia

Galilee

Mt. Carmel

Kishon

Jordan

Yarmuk

Jordan

DECAPOLIS

665

THE FAMILY OF HEROD THE GREAT

Herod the Great had ten wives. Only the wives and descendants of direct interest to students of the NT are listed here.

b. = born
d. = died
r. = reigned
m. = married
K. = King
E. = Ethnarch
T. = Tetrarch

King Herod the Great
b. ca. 73 B.C.
d. 4 B.C.

m.

MARIAMME I (Hasmonean) d. 29 B.C.
Aristobulus IV d. 7 B.C.; m. Bernice I

- Herod (of Chalcis)
  m. Bernice II
  r. Chalcis A.D. 41–48 (K.)
  d. A.D. 48

- Herod Agrippa I
  r. tetrarchies of Philip and Lysanias as K.
  from A.D. 37—tetrarchy of Antipas
  added A.D. 40—Judea and Samaria added
  A.D. 41–44
  d. A.D. 44

- Herodias
  m. (1) Herod (misnamed Philip)*
  (2) Herod Antipas

MARIAMME II
Herod (misnamed Philip)
m. Herodias
Salome III
m. Philip

MALTHACE (Samaritan)
- Archelaus
  r. 4 B.C.–A.D. 6 (E.)

- Herod Antipas
  m. (1) Daughter of Aretas IV (Nabatean K.)
  (2) Herodias
  r. 4 B.C.–A.D. 39 (T.)

CLEOPATRA (of Jerusalem)
Philip
m. Salome III
r. 4 B.C.–A.D. 34 (T.)
d. A.D. 34

*Mark's Gospel confuses Herod, the son of Mariamme II, with Philip; this has led some NT scholars to speak (wrongly) of "Herod Philip" as Herodias' first husband.

THE REGNAL YEARS OF THE ROMAN *PRINCIPES* (EMPERORS)
Compared with the dates of the Prefects/Procurators of Judea, Samaria, and Idumea

OCTAVIAN (AUGUSTUS)	[Prefects]	
31 B.C. (battle of Actium)	Coponius A.D.	6–9
27 B.C. (assumes title of Augustus)	M. Ambivius	9–12 (?)
A.D. 14 (dies)	Annius Rufus	12–15 (?)
TIBERIUS		
14–37	Valerius Gratus	15–26
	Pontius Pilate	26–36
	Marcellus	36–37
GAIUS (CALIGULA)		
37–41	Marullus	37–41 (?)
CLAUDIUS	[Reign of Agrippa I over the restored	
41–54	kingdom of the Jews, 41–44]	
	[Procurators]	
	C. Cuspius Fadus	44–46
	Tiberius Julius Alexander	46–48
	Ventidius Cumanus	48–52
NERO		
54–68	M. Antonius Felix	52–60 (?)
	Porcius Festus	60–62 (?)
	Lucceius Albinus	62–64
	Gessius Florus	64–66
GALBA, OTHO, VITELLIUS		
(all in 69)		
VESPASIAN	Jewish Revolt	66–70
69–79		

List of Abbreviations

Mart. Isa. Martyrdom of Isaiah
Odes Sol. Odes of Solomon
Pss. Sol. Psalms of Solomon
Sib. Or. Sibylline Oracles
T. 12 Patr. Testaments of the Twelve Patriarchs
T. Levi Testament of Levi
T. Benj. Testament of Benjamin, etc.
Acts Pil. Acts of Pilate
Apoc. Pet. Apocalypse of Peter
Gos. Eb. Gospel of the Ebionites
Gos. Eg. Gospel of the Egyptians
Gos. Heb. Gospel of the Hebrews
Gos. Naass. Gospel of the Naassenes
Gos. Pet. Gospel of Peter
Gos. Thom. Gospel of Thomas
Prot. Jas. Protevangelium of James
Barn. Barnabas
1-2 Clem. 1-2 Clement
Did. Didache
Diogn. Diognetus
Herm. Hermas,
    Man. Mandate
    Sim. Similitude
    Vis. Vision
Ign. *Eph.* Ignatius, Letter to the Ephesians
    Magn. Ignatius, Letter to the Magnesians
    Phld. Ignatius, Letter to the Philadelphians
    Pol. Ignatius, Letter to Polycarp
    Rom. Ignatius, Letter to the Romans
    Smyrn. Ignatius, Letter to the Smyrneans
    Trall. Ignatius, Letter to the Trallians
Mart. Pol. Martyrdom of Polycarp
Pol. *Phil.* Polycarp to the Philippians
Bib. Ant. Ps.-Philo, Biblical Antiquities

3. Abbreviations of Names of Dead Sea Scrolls and Related Texts

CD   Cairo (Genizah text of the) Damascus (Document)
Hev   Nahal Hever texts
Mas   Masada texts
Mird   Khirbet Mird texts
Mur   Wadi Murabbaʿat texts
p   Pesher (commentary)
Q   Qumran

1Q, 2Q, 3Q, etc.   Numbered caves of Qumran, yielding written material; followed
         by abbreviation of biblical or apocryphal book
QL   Qumran literature
1QapGen   *Genesis Apocryphon* of Qumran Cave 1
1QH   *Hôdāyôt (Thanksgiving Hymns)* from Qumran Cave 1
1QIsa[a, b]   First or second copy of Isaiah from Qumran Cave 1
1QpHab   *Pesher on Habakkuk* from Qumran Cave 1
1QM   *Milḥāmāh (War Scroll)*
1QS   *Serek hayyaḥad (Rule of the Community, Manual of Discipline)*
1QSa   Appendix A *(Rule of the Congregation)* to 1QS
1QSb   Appendix B *(Blessings)* to 1QS
3Q15   *Copper Scroll* from Qumran Cave 3
4QEn   fragments of *1 Enoch*
4QFlor   *Florilegium* (or *Eschatological Midrashim*) from Qumran Cave 4
4QMess ar   Aramaic "Messianic" text from Qumran Cave 4
4QMMT   fragments of the so-called Halakic Letter
4QpNah   *Pesher on Nahum* from Qumran Cave 4
4QpPs   fragments of a Pesher on various Psalms
4QPrNab   *Prayer of Nabonidus* from Qumran Cave 4
4QTestim   *Testimonia* text from Qumran Cave 4
4QTLev ar[a]   fragments of the so-called Aramaic *Testament of Levi*
4QPhyl   Phylacteries from Qumran Cave 4
11QMelch   *Melchizedek* text from Qumran Cave 11
4QVisSam   *The Vision of Samuel*
4Q246   *Aramaic Apocalypse*
4Q521   *Messianic Apocalpyse*
11QTemple   *The Temple Scroll*
11QtgJob   *Targum of Job* from Qumran Cave 11

4. Targums

Tg. Onq.   *Targum Onqelos*
Tg. Neb.   *Targum of the Prophets*
Tg. Ket.   *Targum of the Writings*
Frg. Tg.   *Fragmentary Targum*
Sam. Tg.   *Samaritan Targum*
Tg. Isa.   *Targum of Isaiah*
Pal. Tgs.   *Palestinian Targums*
Tg. Neof.   *Targum Neofiti*
Tg. Ps.-J.   *Targum Pseudo-Jonathan*
Tg. Yer. I   *Targum Yerušalmi I**
Tg. Yer. II   *Targum Yerušalmi II**
Yem. Tg.   *Yemenite Targum*
Tg. Esth. I, II   *First or Second Targum of Esther*

* optional title

5. ABBREVIATIONS OF ORDERS AND TRACTATES IN MISHNAIC AND RELATED LITERATURE

To distinguish the same-named tractates in the Mishna, Tosepta, Babylonian Talmud, and Jerusalem Talmud, I use italicized *m.*, *t.*, *b.*, or *y.* before the title of the tractate. Thus *m. Pe'a* 8:2; *b. Šabb.* 31a; *y. Mak.* 2.31d; *t. Pe'a* 1.4 (Zuck. 18 [= page number of Zuckermandel's edition of the Tosepta]).

'Abot   'Abot
'Arak.   'Arakin
'Abod. Zar.   'Aboda Zara
B. Bat.   Baba Batra
Bek.   Bekorot
Ber.   Berakot
Beṣa   Beṣa (= Yom Ṭob)
Bik.   Bikkurim
B. Meṣ.   Baba Meṣi'a
B. Qam.   Baba Qamma
Dem.   Demai
'Erub.   'Erubin
'Ed.   'Eduyyot
Giṭ.   Giṭṭin
Ḥag.   Ḥagiga
Ḥal.   Ḥalla
Hor.   Horayot
Ḥul.   Ḥullin
Kelim   Kelim
Ker.   Keritot
Ketub.   Ketubot
Kil.   Kil'ayim
Ma'aś.   Ma'aśerot
Mak.   Makkot
Makš.   Makširin (= Mašqin)
Meg.   Megilla
Me'il.   Me'ila
Menaḥ.   Menaḥot
Mid.   Middot
Miqw.   Miqwa'ot
Mo'ed   Mo'ed
Mo'ed Qat.   Mo'ed Qaṭan
Ma'aś. Š.   Ma'aśer Šeni
Našim   Našim
Nazir   Nazir
Ned.   Nedarim
Neg.   Nega'im
Nez.   Neziqin

Nid.   *Niddah*
Ohol.   *Oholot*
ʿOr.   *ʿOrla*
Para   *Para*
Peʾa   *Peʾa*
Pesaḥ.   *Pesaḥim*
Qinnim   *Qinnim*
Qidd.   *Qiddušin*
Qod.   *Qodašin*
Roš. Haš.   *Roš Haššana*
Sanh.   *Sanhedrin*
Šabb.   *Šabbat*
Šeb.   *Šebiʿit*
Šebu.   *Šebuʿot*
Šeqal.   *Šeqalim*
Soṭa   *Soṭa*
Sukk.   *Sukka*
Taʿan.   *Taʿanit*
Tamid   *Tamid*
Tem.   *Temura*
Ter.   *Terumot*
Ṭohar.   *Ṭoharot*
Ṭ. Yom   *Ṭebul Yom*
ʿUq.   *ʿUqṣin*
Yad.   *Yadayim*
Yebam.   *Yebamot*
Yoma   *Yoma (= Kippurim)*
Zabim   *Zabim*
Zebaḥ   *Zebaḥim*
Zer.   *Zeraʿim*

6. ABBREVIATIONS OF OTHER RABBINIC WORKS

ʾAbot R. Nat.   *ʾAbot de Rabbi Nathan*
ʾAg. Ber.   *ʾAggadat Berešit*
Bab.   *Babylonian*
Bar.   *Baraita*
Der. Er. Rab.   *Derek Ereṣ Rabba*
Der. Er. Zuṭ.   *Derek Ereṣ Zuṭa*
Gem.   *Gemara*
Kalla   *Kalla*
Mek.   *Mekilta*
Midr.   *Midraš*; cited with usual abbreviation for biblical book; but *Midr. Qoh.* = *Midraš Qohelet*

Pal.   Palestinian
Pesiq. R.   Pesiqta Rabbati
Pesiq. Rab. Kah.   Pesiqta de Rab Kahana
Pirqe R. El.   Pirqe Rabbi Eliezer
Rab.   Rabbah (following abbreviation for biblical book: *Gen. Rab.* [with periods]
              = *Genesis Rabbah*)
Ṣem.   Ṣemaḥot
Sipra   Sipra
Sipre   Sipre
Sop.   Soperim
S. ʿOlam Rab.   Seder ʿOlam Rabbah
Talm.   Talmud
Yal.   Yalquṭ

7. Abbreviations of Nag Hammadi Tractates

Acts Pet. 12 Apost.   Acts of Peter and the Twelve Apostles
Allogenes   Allogenes
Ap. Jas.   Apocryphon of James
Ap. John   Apocryphon of John
Apoc. Adam   Apocalypse of Adam
1 Apoc. Jas.   First Apocalypse of James
2 Apoc. Jas.   Second Apocalypse of James
Apoc. Paul   Apocalypse of Paul
Apoc. Pet.   Apocalypse of Peter
Asclepius   Asclepius 21–29
Auth. Teach.   Authoritative Teaching
Dial. Sav.   Dialogue of the Savior
Disc. 8–9   Discourse on the Eighth and Ninth
Ep. Pet. Phil.   Letter of Peter to Philip
Eugnostos   Eugnostos the Blessed
Exeg. Soul   Exegesis on the Soul
Gos. Eg.   Gospel of the Egyptians
Gos. Phil.   Gospel of Philip
Gos. Thom.   Gospel of Thomas
Gos. Truth   Gospel of Truth
Great Pow.   Concept of our Great Power
Hyp. Arch.   Hypostasis of the Archons
Hypsiph.   Hypsiphrone
Interp. Know.   Interpretation of Knowledge
Marsanes   Marsanes
Melch.   Melchizedek
Norea   Thought of Norea
On Bap. A   On Baptism A
On Bap. B   On Baptism B

On Bap. C   *On Baptism C*
On Euch. A   *On the Eucharist A*
On Euch. B   *On the Eucharist B*
Orig. World   *On the Origin of the World*
Paraph. Shem   *Paraphrase of Shem*
Pr. Paul   *Prayer of the Apostle Paul*
Pr. Thanks.   *Prayer of Thanksgiving*
Sent. Sextus   *Sentences of Sextus*
Soph. Jes. Chr.   *Sophia of Jesus Christ*
Steles Seth   *Three Steles of Seth*
Teach. Silv.   *Teachings of Silvanus*
Testim. Truth   *Testimony of Truth*
Thom. Cont.   *Book of Thomas the Contender*
Thund.   *Thunder, Perfect Mind*
Treat. Res.   *Treatise on Resurrection*
Treat. Seth   *Second Treatise of the Great Seth*
Tri. Trac.   *Tripartite Tractate*
Trim. Prot.   *Trimorphic Protennoia*
Val. Exp.   *A Valentinian Exposition*
Zost.   *Zostrianos*

8. Works of Josephus

Ag. Ap.   *Against Apion*
Ant.   *Jewish Antiquities*
J.W.   *The Jewish War*

9. Abbreviations of Commonly Used Periodicals, Reference Works, and Serials

(Titles not found in this list are written out in full. Titles of periodicals and books are italicized, but titles of series are set in roman characters, as are acronyms of authors' names when they are used as sigla.) Short, one-word titles not on this list are not abbreviated.

AAS   *Acta apostolicae sedis*
AASOR   Annual of the American Schools of Oriental Research
AcOr   *Acta orientalia*
ACW   Ancient Christian Writers
AfO   *Archiv für Orientforschung*
AGJU   Arbeiten zur Geschichte des antiken Judentums und des Urchistentums
AH   F. Rosenthal, *An Aramaic Handbook*
AJA   *American Journal of Archaeology*
AJBA   *Australian Journal of Biblical Archaeology*
AJP   *American Journal of Philology*
AJSL   *American Journal of Semitic Languages and Literature*

AJT   American Journal of Theology
ALBO   Analecta lovaniensia biblica et orientalia
ALGHJ   Arbeiten zur Literatur und Geschichte des hellenistischen Judentums
AnBib   Analecta biblica
ANEP   J. B. Pritchard (ed.), *Ancient Near East in Pictures*
ANESTP   J. B. Pritchard (ed.), *Ancient Near East Supplementary Texts and Pictures*
ANET   J. B. Pritchard (ed.), *Ancient Near Eastern Texts*
Ang   Angelicum
AnOr   Analecta orientalia
ANQ   Andover Newton Quarterly
ANTF   Arbeiten zur neutestamentlichen Textforschung
ANRW   Aufstieg und Niedergang der römischen Welt
AOAT   Alter Orient und Altes Testament
AOS   American Oriental Series
AP   J. Marouzeau (ed.), *L'Année philologique*
APOT   R. H. Charles (ed.), *Apocrypha and Pseudepigrapha of the Old Testament*
Arch   Archaeology
ARW   Archiv für Religionswissenschaft
ASNU   Acta seminarii neotestamentici upsaliensis
ASOR   American Schools of Oriental Research
ASS   Acta sanctae sedis
AsSeign   Assemblées du Seigneur
ASSR   Archives des sciences sociales des religions
ASTI   Annual of the Swedish Theological Institute
ATAbh   Alttestamentliche Abhandlungen
ATANT   Abhandlungen zur Theologie des Alten und Neuen Testaments
AtBib   H. Grollenberg, *Atlas of the Bible*
ATD   Das Alte Testament Deutsch
ATR   Anglican Theological Review
Aug   Augustinianum
AusBR   Australian Biblical Review
AUSS   Andrews University Seminary Studies
AYB   Anchor Yale Bible
AYBD   Anchor Yale Bible Dictionary
AYBRL   Anchor Yale Bible Reference Library
BA   Biblical Archaeologist
BAC   Biblioteca de autores cristianos
BAGD   W. Bauer, W. F. Arndt, F. W. Gingrich, and F. W. Danker, *Greek-English Lexicon of the NT*
BAR   Biblical Archaelogist Reader
BARev   Biblical Archaeology Review
BASOR   Bulletin of the American Schools of Oriental Research
BBB   Bonner biblische Beiträge
BBET   Beiträge zur biblischen Exegese und Theologie

BCSR *Bulletin of the Council on the Study of Religion*

BDB F. Brown, S. R. Driver, and C. A. Briggs, *Hebrew and English Lexicon of the Old Testament*

BDF F. Blass, A. Debrunner, and R. W. Funk, *A Greek Grammar of the NT*

BDR F. Blass, A. Debrunner, and F. Rehkopf, *Grammatik des neutestamentlichen Griechisch*

BeO Bibbia e oriente

BETL Bibliotheca ephemeridum theologicarum lovaniensium

BEvT Beiträge zur evangelischen Theologie

BFCT Beiträge zur Förderung christlicher Theologie

BGBE Beiträge zur Geschichte der biblischen Exegese

BHEAT Bulletin d'histoire et d'exégèse de l'Ancien Testament

BHH B. Reicke and L. Rost (eds.), *Biblisch-Historisches Handwörterbuch*

BHK R. Kittel, *Biblia hebraica*

BHS Biblia hebraica stuttgartensia

BHT Beiträge zur historischen Theologie

Bib Biblica

BibB Biblische Beiträge

BibBh Bible bhashyam

BibLeb Bibel und Leben

BibOr Biblica et orientalia

BibS(F) Biblische Studien (Freiburg, 1895–)

BibS(N) Biblische Studien (Neukirchen, 1951–)

BIES Bulletin of the Israel Exploratory Society (= Yediot)

BIFAO Bulletin de l'institut français d'archéologie orientale

Bijdr Bijdragen

BIOSCS Bulletin of the International Organization for Septuagint and Cognate Studies

BJPES Bulletin of the Jewish Palestine Exploration Society

BJRL Bulletin of the John Rylands University Library of Manchester

BK Bibel und Kirche

BKAT Biblischer Kommentar: Altes Testament

BLit Bibel und Liturgie

BN Biblische Notizen

BO Bibliotheca orientalis

BR Biblical Research

BSac Bibliotheca Sacra

BSOAS Bulletin of the School of Oriental (and African) Studies

BT The Bible Translator

BTB Biblical Theology Bulletin

BTS Bible et terre sainte

BurH Buried History

BVC Bible et vie chrétienne

BWANT Beiträge zur Wissenschaft vom Alten und Neuen Testament

ByF Biblia y Fe

BZ Biblische Zeitschrift

BZAW   Beihefte zur *ZAW*
BZNW   Beihefte zur *ZNW*
BZRGG   Beihefte zur *ZRGG*
CAH   Cambridge Ancient History
CahEv   Cahiers évangile
CahRB   Cahiers de la Revue biblique
Cah Théol   Cahiers théologiques
CAT   Commentaire de l'Ancien Testament
CB   Cultura bíblica
CBQ   Catholic Biblical Quarterly
CBQMS   Catholic Biblical Quarterly—Monograph Series
CC   Corpus christianorum
CCath   Corpus catholicorum
CH   Church History
CHR   Catholic Historical Review
CIG   Corpus inscriptionum graecarum
CII   Corpus inscriptionum iudaicarum
CIL   Corpus inscriptionum latinarum
CIS   Corpus inscriptionum semiticarum
CJ   Classical Journal
CJT   Canadian Journal of Theology
CNT   Commentaire du Nouveau Testament
ConB   Coniectanea biblica
ConBNT   Coniectanea biblica, New Testament
ConBOT   Coniectanea biblica, Old Testament
ConNT   Coniectanea neotestamentica
CP   Classical Philology
CQ   Church Quarterly
CQR   Church Quarterly Review
CRAIBL   Comptes rendus de l'académie des inscriptions et belles-lettres
CRINT   Compendia rerum iudaicarum ad Novum Testamentum
CSCO   Corpus scriptorum christianorum
CSEL   Corpus scriptorum ecclesiasticorum latinorum
CTJ   Calvin Theological Journal
CTM   Concordia Theological Monthly (or CTM)
CTQ   Concordia Theological Quarterly
CurTM   Currents in Theology and Mission
DACL   Dictionnaire d'archéologie chrétienne et de liturgie
DBSup   Dictionnaire de la Bible, Supplément
DJD   Discoveries in the Judaean Desert
DRev   Downside Review
DS   Denzinger-Schönmetzer, *Enchiridion symbolorum*
DTC   Dictionnaire de théologie catholique
EBib   Études bibliques
EDB   L. F. Hartman (ed.), *Encyclopedic Dictionary of the Bible*
EHAT   Exegetisches Handbuch zum Alten Testament

EKKNT   Evangelisch-katholischer Kommentar zum Neuen Testament
EKL   Evangelisches Kirchenlexikon
EncJud   Encyclopedia Judaica (1971)
EnchBib   Enchiridion biblicum
ErIsr   Eretz Israel
ErJb   Eranos Jahrbuch
EstBib   Estudios bíblicos
EstEcl   Estudios eclesiásticos
EstTeol   Estudios teológicos
ETL   Ephemerides theologicae lovanienses
ETR   Études théologiques et religieuses
EvK   Evangelische Kommentare
EvQ   Evangelical Quarterly
EvT   Evangelische Theologie
EWNT   H. Balz and G. Schneider (eds.), *Exegetisches Wörterbuch zum Neuen Testament*
ExpTim   Expository Times
FB   Forschung zur Bibel
FBBS   Facet Books, Biblical Series
FC   Fathers of the Church
FRLANT   Forschungen zur Religion und Literatur des Alten und Neuen Testaments
GAT   Grundrisse zum Alten Testament
GCS   Griechische christliche Schriftsteller
GKB   Gesenius-Kautzsch-Bergsträsser, *Hebräische Grammatik*
GKC   *Gesenius' Hebrew Grammar*, ed. E. Kautzsch, tr. A. E. Cowley
GNT   Grundrisse zum Neuen Testament
GRBS   Greek, Roman, and Byzantine Studies
Greg   Gregorianum
GTA   Göttinger theologische Arbeiten
GTJ   Grace Theological Journal
HALAT   W. Baumgartner et al., *Hebräisches und aramäisches Lexikon zum Alten Testament*
HAT   Handbuch zum Alten Testament
HDR   Harvard Dissertations in Religion
HeyJ   Heythrop Journal
HibJ   Hibbert Journal
HKAT   Handkommentar zum Alten Testament
HKNT   Handkommentar zum Neuen Testament
HNT   Handbuch zum Neuen Testament
HNTC   Harper's NT Commentaries
HR   History of Religions
HSM   Harvard Semitic Monographs
HSS   Harvard Semitic Studies
HTKNT   Herders theologischer Kommentar zum Neuen Testament

HTR   Harvard Theological Review
HTS   Harvard Theological Studies
HUCA   Hebrew Union College Annual
HUT   Hermeneutische Untersuchungen zur Theologie
IB   Interpreter's Bible
IBS   Irish Biblical Studies
ICC   International Critical Commentary
IDB   G. A. Buttrick (ed.), *Interpreter's Dictionary of the Bible*
IDBSup   Supplementary volume to *IDB*
IEJ   Israel Exploration Journal
Int   Interpretation
IOS   Israel Oriental Studies
ITQ   Irish Theological Quarterly
JA   Journal asiatique
JAAR   Journal of the American Academy of Religion
JAC   Jahrbuch für Antike und Christentum
JAL   Jewish Apocryphal Literature
JANESCU   Journal of the Ancient Near Eastern Society of Columbia University
JAOS   Journal of the American Oriental Society
JAS   Journal of Asian Studies
JB   A. Jones (ed.), *Jerusalem Bible*
JBC   R. E. Brown et al. (eds.), *The Jerome Biblical Commentary*
JBL   Journal of Biblical Literature
JBR   Journal of Bible and Religion
JDS   Judean Desert Studies
JEH   Journal of Ecclesiastical History
JEOL   Jaarbericht . . . ex oriente lux
JES   Journal of Ecumenical Studies
JETS   Journal of the Evangelical Theological Society
JHNES   Johns Hopkins Near Eastern Studies
JHS   Journal of Hellenic Studies
JJS   Journal of Jewish Studies
JMES   Journal of Middle Eastern Studies
JNES   Journal of Near Eastern Studies
JPOS   Journal of the Palestine Oriental Society
JPSV   Jewish Publication Society Version
JQR   Jewish Quarterly Review
JQRMS   Jewish Quarterly Review Monograph Series
JR   Journal of Religion
JRelS   Journal of Religious Studies
JRH   Journal of Religious History
JRS   Journal of Roman Studies
JRT   Journal of Religious Thought
JSHRZ   Jüdische Schriften aus hellenistisch-römischer Zeit
JSJ   Journal for the Study of Judaism in the Persian, Hellenistic and Roman Periods

JSNT   *Journal for the Study of the New Testament*
JSNTSup   Journal for the Study of the New Testament—Supplement Series
JSOT   *Journal for the Study of the Old Testament*
JSOTSup   Journal for the Study of the Old Testament—Supplement Series
JSS   *Journal of Semitic Studies*
JSSR   *Journal for the Scientific Study of Religion*
JTC   *Journal for Theology and the Church*
JTS   *Journal of Theological Studies*
Judaica   *Judaica: Beiträge zum Verständnis . . .*
KAT   E. Sellin (ed.), Kommentar zum A. T.
KB   L. Koehler and W. Baumgartner, *Lexicon in Veteris Testamenti libros*
KD   *Kerygma und Dogma*
KJV   *King James Version*
KlT   Kleine Texte
LB   *Linguistica biblica*
LCC   Library of Christian Classics
LCL   Loeb Classical Library
LCQ   *Lutheran Church Quarterly*
LD   Lectio divina
LLAVT   E. Vogt, *Lexicon linguae aramaicae Veteris Testamenti*
LPGL   G. W. H. Lampe, *Patristic Greek Lexicon*
LQ   *Lutheran Quarterly*
LR   *Lutherische Rundschau*
LS   *Louvain Studies*
LSJ   Liddell-Scott-Jones, *Greek-English Lexicon*
LTK   *Lexikon für Theologie und Kirche*
LTP   *Laval théologique et philosophique*
LumVie   *Lumière et vie*
LW   *Lutheran World*
McCQ   *McCormick Quarterly*
MDB   *Le monde de la Bible*
MDOG   Mitteilungen der deutschen Orient-Gesellschaft
MeyerK   H. A. W. Meyer, Kritisch-exegetischer Kommentar über das Neue
          Testament
MGWJ   *Monatsschrift für Geschichte und Wissenschaft des Judentums*
MM   J. H. Moulton and G. Milligan, *The Vocabulary of the Greek Testament*
MNTC   Moffatt NT Commentary
MPAIBL   Mémoires présentés à l'académie des inscriptions et belles-lettres
MScRel   *Mélanges de science religieuse*
MTZ   *Münchener theologische Zeitschrift*
Mus   *Muséon*
MUSJ   *Mélanges de l'université Saint-Joseph*
NAB   *New American Bible*
NCB   New Century Bible
NCCHS   R. D. Fuller et al. (eds.), *New Catholic Commentary on Holy Scripture*

NCE M. R. P. McGuire et al. (eds.), *New Catholic Encyclopedia*
NEB *New English Bible*
Neot *Neotestamentica*
NFT New Frontiers in Theology
NHS Nag Hammadi Studies
NICNT New International Commentary on the New Testament
NICOT New International Commentary on the Old Testament
NIV *New International Version*
NJBC *New Jerome Biblical Commentary*
NJV *New Jewish Version*
NKZ *Neue kirchliche Zeitschrift*
NovT *Novum Testamentum*
NovTSup Novum Testamentum, Supplements
NRT *La nouvelle revue théologique*
NTA *New Testament Abstracts*
NTAbh Neutestamentliche Abhandlungen
NTD Das Neue Testament Deutsch
NTF Neutestamentliche Forschungen
NTS *New Testament Studies*
NTTS New Testament Tools and Studies
Numen *Numen: International Review for the History of Religions*
OBO Orbis biblicus et orientalis
OIP Oriental Institute Publications
OLP *Orientalia lovaniensia periodica*
OLZ *Orientalistische Literaturzeitung*
Or *Orientalia* (Rome)
OrAnt *Oriens antiquus*
OrChr *Oriens christianus*
OrSyr *L'Orient syrien*
OTA *Old Testament Abstracts*
OTL Old Testament Library
OTP J. Charlesworth, *The Old Testament Pseudepigrapha*
PAAJR *Proceedings of the American Academy for Jewish Research*
PCB M. Black and H. H. Rowley (eds.), *Peake's Commentary on the Bible*
PEFQS *Palestine Exploration Fund, Quarterly Statement*
PEQ *Palestine Exploration Quarterly*
PG J. Migne, Patrologia graeca
PGM K. Preisendanz (ed.), *Papyri graecae magicae*
Phil *Philologus*
PJ *Palästina-Jahrbuch*
PL J. Migne, Patrologia latina
PO Patrologia orientalis
PSB *Princeton Seminary Bulletin*
PSTJ *Perkins School of Theology Journal*
PTMS Pittsburgh Theological Monograph Series

PVTG   Pseudepigrapha Veteris Testamenti graece
PW   Pauly-Wissowa, *Real-Encyclopädie der klassichen Altertumswissenschaft*
PWSup   Supplements to PW
QD   Quaestiones disputatae
QDAP   *Quarterly of the Department of Antiquities in Palestine*
RAC   *Reallexikon für Antike und Christentum*
RANE   Records of the Ancient Near East
RArch   *Revue archéologique*
RB   *Revue biblique*
RCB   *Revista de cultura bíblica*
RE   *Realencyclopädie für protestantische Theologie und Kirche*
REA   *Revue des études anciennes*
RechBib   Recherches bibliques
REJ   *Revue des études juives*
RelS   *Religious Studies*
RelSoc   *Religion and Society*
RelSRev   *Religious Studies Review*
RES   *Répertoire d'épigraphie sémitique*
ResQ   *Restoration Quarterly*
RevExp   *Review and Expositor*
RevistB   *Revista bíblica*
RevQ   *Revue de Qumran*
RevScRel   *Revue des sciences religieuses*
RevSem   *Revue sémitique*
RGG   *Religion in Geschichte und Gegenwart*
RHE   *Revue d'histoire ecclésiastique*
RHPR   *Revue d'historie et de philosophie religieuses*
RHR   *Revue de l'histoire des religions*
RIDA   *Revue internationale des droits de l'antiquité*
RivB   *Rivista biblica*
RNT   Regensburger Neues Testament
RQ   Römische Quartalschrift für christliche Altertumskunde und Kirchenge-
       schichte
RR   *Review of Religion*
RRef   *La revue reformée*
RSO   *Rivista degli studi orientali*
RSPT   *Revue des sciences philosophiques et théologiques*
RSR   *Recherches de science religieuse*
RSV   *Revised Standard Version*
RTL   *Revue théologique de Louvain*
RTP   *Revue de théologie et de philosophie*
RUO   *Revue de l'université d'Ottawa*
RV   *Revised Version*
SacEr   *Sacris erudiri*
SANT   Studien zum Alten und Neuen Testament

SB   Sources bibliques
SBA   Studies in Biblical Archaeology
SBAW   Sitzungsberichte der bayerischen Akademie der Wissenschaften
SBB   Stuttgarter biblische Beiträge
SBFLA   Studii biblici franciscani liber annuus
SBJ   La sainte bible de Jérusalem
SBLASP   Society of Biblical Literature Abstracts and Seminar Papers
SBLDS   SBL Dissertation Series
SBLMasS   SBL Masoretic Studies
SBLMS   SBL Monograph Series
SBLSBS   SBL Sources for Biblical Study
SBLSCS   SBL Septuagint and Cognate Studies
SBLTT   SBL Texts and Translations
SBM   Stuttgarter biblische Monographien
SBS   Stuttgarter Bibelstudien
SBT   Studies in Biblical Theology
SC   Sources chrétiennes
ScEccl   Sciences ecclésiastiques
ScEs   Science et esprit
SCHNT   Studia ad corpus hellenisticum Novi Testamenti
SCR   Studies in Comparative Religion
Scr   Scripture
ScrB   Scripture Bulletin
ScrHier   Scripta hierosolymitana
SD   Studies and Documents
SE   Studia Evangelica I, II, III, etc. (= TU 73 [1959], 87 [1964], 88 [1964], 102 [1968], 103 [1968], 112 [1973])
Sem   Semitica
SHT   Studies in Historical Theology
SJ   Studia judaica
SJLA   Studies in Judaism in Late Antiquity
SJT   Scottish Journal of Theology
SMSR   Studi e materiali di storia delle religioni
SNT   Studien zum Neuen Testament
SNTSMS   Society for New Testament Studies Monograph Series
SO   Symbolae osloenses
SOTSMS   Society for Old Testament Study Monograph Series
SP   J. Coppens et al. (eds.), Sacra pagina
SPap   Studia papyrologica
SPAW   Sitzungsberichte der preussischen Akademie der Wissenschaften
SPB   Studia postbiblica
SPC   Studiorum paulinorum congressus internationalis catholicus 1961 (2 vols.)
SR   Studies in Religion/Sciences religieuses
SSS   Semitic Study Series
ST   Studia theologica

STANT Studien zum Alten und Neuen Testament
STDJ Studies on the Texts of the Desert of Judah
Str-B [H. Strack and] P. Billerbeck, *Kommentar zum Neuen Testament*
StudNeot Studia neotestamentica
StudOr Studia orientalia
SUNT Studien zur Umwelt des Neuen Testaments
SVTP Studia in Veteris Testamenti pseudepigrapha
SymBU Symbolae biblicae upsalienses
TAPA Transactions of the American Philological Association
TBei Theologische Beiträge
TBl Theologische Blätter
TBü Theologische Bücherei
TBT The Bible Today
TCGNT B. M. Metzger, *A Textual Commentary on the Greek New Testament*
TD Theology Digest
TDNT G. Kittel and G. Friedrich (eds.), *Theological Dictionary of the New Testament*
TDOT G. J. Botterweck and H. Ringgren (eds.), *Theological Dictionary of the Old Testament*
TextsS Texts and Studies
TF Theologische Forschung
TGl Theologie und Glaube
THKNT Theologischer Handkommentar zum Neuen Testament
ThStud Theologische Studien
TLZ Theologische Literaturzeitung
TP Theologie und Philosophie
TPQ Theologisch-Praktische Quartalschrift
TQ Theologische Quartalschrift
TRE Theologische Realenzyklopädie
TRev Theologische Revue
TRu Theologische Rundschau
TS Theological Studies
TSK Theologische Studien und Kritiken
TToday Theology Today
TTZ Trierer theologische Zeitschrift
TU Texte und Untersuchungen
TWAT G. J. Botterweck and H. Ringgren (eds.), *Theologisches Wörterbuch zum Alten Testament*
TWNT G. Kittel and G. Friedrich (eds.), *Theologisches Wörterbuch zum Neuen Testament*
TynBul Tyndale Bulletin
TZ Theologische Zeitschrift
UBSGNT United Bible Societies *Greek New Testament*
UNT Untersuchungen zum Neuen Testament
USQR Union Seminary Quarterly Review
VC Vigiliae christianae

VCaro Verbum caro

VD Verbum domini

VE Vox evangelica

VF Verkündigung und Forschung

VKGNT K. Aland (ed.), *Vollständige Konkordanz zum griechischen Neuen Testament*

VP Vivre et penser (= *RB* 1941–44)

VS Verbum salutis

VSpir Vie spirituelle

VT Vetus Testamentum

VTSup Vetus Testamentum, Supplements

WDB Westminster Dictionary of the Bible

WHAB Westminster Historical Atlas of the Bible

WHJP World History of the Jewish People

WMANT Wissenschaftliche Monographien zum Alten und Neuen Testament

WO Die Welt des Orients

WTJ Westminster Theological Journal

WUNT Wissenschaftliche Untersuchungen zum Neuen Testament

WVDOG Wissenschaftliche Veröffentlichungen der deutschen Orientgesellschaft

WZKM Wiener Zeitschrift für die Kunde des Morgenlandes

WZKSO Wiener Zeitschrift für die Kunde Süd- und Ostasiens

ZAW Zeitschrift für die alttestamentliche Wissenschaft

ZDMG Zeitschrift der deutschen morgenländischen Gesellschaft

ZDPV Zeitschrift des deutschen Palästina-Vereins

ZHT Zeitschrift für historische Theologie

ZKG Zeitschrift für Kirchengeschichte

ZKT Zeitschrift für katholische Theologie

ZMR Zeitschrift für Missionskunde und Religionswissenschaft

ZNW Zeitschrift für die neutestamentliche Wissenschaft

ZRGG Zeitschrift für Religions- und Geistesgeschichte

ZTK Zeitschrift für Theologie und Kirche

ZWT Zeitschrift für wissenschaftliche Theologie

10. MISCELLANEOUS ABBREVIATIONS

ET English Translation

LXX The Septuagint

MT Masoretic Text

NT New Testament

OT Old Testament

par(r). parallel(s) in the Gospels

Vg The Vulgate

VL Vetus Latina (Old Latin)

‖ two pericopes (often in the Q document) that are basically parallel, though possibly with some differences in wording

Scripture and Other Ancient Writings Index

Author Index

Subject Index